THE COOK'S COUNTRY COOKBOOK

THE Cook's Country COOKBOOK

REDISCOVERING AMERICAN HOME COOKING
with 500 Classic, Regional, and Heirloom Recipes

FROM THE EDITORS AT AMERICA'S TEST KITCHEN

COLOR PHOTOGRAPHY Keller + Keller
BLACK AND WHITE PHOTOGRAPHY Daniel J. van Ackere
ILLUSTRATION Greg Stevenson

America's
TEST KITCHEN

BROOKLINE, MASSACHUSETTS

America's Test Kitchen
17 Station Street
Brookline, MA 02445

ISBN-13: 978-1-933615-34-9
ISBN-10: 1-933615-34-6
Library of Congress Cataloging-in-Publication Data
The Editors at America's Test Kitchen

The Cook's Country Cookbook
Rediscovering American Home Cooking,
with 500 Classic, Regional, and Heirloom Recipes

1st Edition
ISBN-13: 978-1-933615-34-9
ISBN-10: 1-933615-34-6
(hardcover): U.S. $34.95; Can. $37.95
I. Cooking. I. Title
2008

Manufactured in the United States of America

10 9 8 7 6 5 4 3 2 1

Distributed by America's Test Kitchen,
17 Station Street, Brookline, MA 02445

Senior Editor: Lori Galvin
Editorial Assistant: Elizabeth Pohm
Design Director: Amy Klee
Art Director: Greg Galvan
Designer: Tiffani Beckwith
Photography: Keller + Keller, Daniel J. van Ackere
Food Styling: Mary Jane Sawyer
Front Cover Cast Photograph: Christopher Churchill
Illustration: © Greg Stevenson/www.i2iart.com
Production Director: Guy Rochford
Senior Production Manager: Jessica Lindheimer Quirk
Traffic and Project Manager: Alice Cummiskey
Imaging and Color Specialist: Andrew Mannone
Production and Imaging Specialist: Lauren Pettapiece
Copyeditor: Barbara Wood
Proofreader: Christine Corcoran Cox
Indexer: Elizabeth Parson

The Staff of *Cook's Country* Magazine:

Editorial Director: Jack Bishop
Deputy Editor: Bridget Lancaster
Senior Editors: Scott Kathan, Jeremy Sauer
Associate Editors: Cali Rich, Diane Unger
Assistant Editor: Meredith Butcher
Test Cooks: Kelley Baker, Kris Widican
Assistant Test Cooks: Lynn Clark, Meghan Erwin
Contributing Editor: Eva Katz

America's
TEST KITCHEN

CONTENTS

This book has been tested, written, and edited by the folks at America's Test Kitchen, a very real 2,500-square-foot kitchen located just outside of Boston. It is the home of *Cook's Country* magazine and *Cook's Illustrated* magazine and is the Monday-through-Friday destination for more than three dozen test cooks, editors, food scientists, tasters, and cookware specialists. Our mission is to test recipes over and over again until we understand how and why they work and until we arrive at the "best" version.

We start the process of testing a recipe with a complete lack of conviction, which means that we accept no claim, no theory, no technique, and no recipe at face value. We simply assemble as many variations as possible, test a half dozen of the most promising, and taste the results blind. We then construct our own hybrid recipe and continue to test it, varying ingredients, techniques, and cooking times until we reach a consensus. The result, we hope, is the best version of a particular recipe, but we realize that only you can be the final judge of our success (or failure). As we like to say in the test kitchen,

"We make the mistakes, so you don't have to."

All of this would not be possible without a belief that good cooking, much like good music, is indeed based on a foundation of objective technique. Some people like spicy foods and others don't, but there is a right way to sauté, there is a best way to cook a pot roast, and there are measurable scientific principles involved in producing perfectly beaten, stable egg whites. This is our ultimate goal: to investigate the fundamental principles of cooking so that you become a better cook. It is as simple as that.

You can watch us work (in our actual test kitchen) by tuning in to *Cook's Country from America's Test Kitchen* (www.cookscountrytv.com) or *America's Test Kitchen* (www.americastestkitchen.com) on public television, or by subscribing to *Cook's Country* magazine (www.cookscountry.com) or *Cook's Illustrated* magazine (www.cooksillustrated.com). We welcome you into our kitchen, where you can stand by our side as we test our way to the "best" recipes in America.

When I was a kid growing up in Vermont, I used to spend a lot of time in the summers at the Bartlett Lot. You got there by walking up an old logging road, past Charlie Bentley's sugarhouse, and up through the gravel pit. I still remember coming out of the dark woods into the sun-drenched lot, a high steep pasture with a view right down to the Battenkill. In the middle of the lot was an old barn, a place where my sister and I used to spend busy afternoons looking for treasure. For the most part, this turned out to be nothing more than hand-forged nails, but she and I hoarded them like panned gold. We were rarely interrupted in our treasure hunts, but on one unforgettable afternoon we stopped to watch Colonel Vaughn's barn throw up columns of thick smoke from down in the valley as it slowly burned to the ground.

Since then, I have spent a lot of time in old barns and with old cookbooks, and my interest transcends the merely historical. There are plenty of country antiques that still make sense today: the White Mountain ice cream freezer, the hand-cranked seeder, the wall-mounted ice crusher, the jar-lifter used in canning, and the man-powered harrow with the large metal wheel. And I have fond memories of our party line phone from the 1950s, anything pulled by a horse including a corn binder and a sickle bar mower, and the small bells attached to domesticated turkeys.

In the kitchen, my appetite for old or regional American recipes is no less keen. But separating the wheat from the chaff is heavy lifting. I can look at an old silage chopper and realize that one is likely to lose an arm using it, but when it comes to a recipe for Tres Leches Cake, 24-Hour Picnic Salad, or Creole Fried Chicken, how is one to know if it is a keeper without actually making it? There's the rub. The American culinary repertoire is replete with lost, regional, family, heirloom, and classic recipes and so many of them are richly appealing. But one has to ask, "Do they work?" And I don't just mean do they turn out okay. I mean, "Do they make sense in a modern kitchen in the early part of the twenty-first century?"

This is a huge project, one that *Cook's Country* magazine (and now our sister public television show, *Cook's Country from America's Test Kitchen*, as well) has taken on as its mission. Seek out the rare and the common, the regional and the national, the personal and the classic and then select those that add up to a collection of recipes that truly expresses the genius, fun, and enthusiasm of the American table. The next step is as important. Put these recipes through an extensive test kitchen process to make sure they really work, the first time and every time.

I am reminded of the old joke about the horse of many names. A flatlander drives off the road and his car gets stuck in a ditch. Along comes a farmer with a workhorse and he is asked for help. He hitches the horse up to the car and yells, "Pull, Tiffany!" The horse doesn't move an inch. Then he yells, "Pull, Montana!" The horse barely stirs. Then he yells, "Pull, Dixie!" The horse stands at attention. Then the farmer yells out, "Pull, Morgan!" and the horse steps right up in the harness and pulls the car easily out of the ditch. The flatlander looks in amazement and asks, "Couldn't you remember the name of your own horse?" The farmer smiles and says, "Well, that's not how it is. He's blind and I didn't want him to think that he would have to do all that pullin' on his own!"

Like a good country story, you never know how it is going to end. That's the mark of a good storyteller, but it's not the mark of a good recipe. You want a cookbook that is full of surprises—recipes that are fresh, appealing, and intriguing—but you want to be sure of a tasty and enjoyable outcome.

So here is a volume that looks over the vast history of American cooking, makes some fascinating as well as everyday choices—Strawberry Poke Cake, Firecracker Chicken, Loaded Baked Potato Soup, Jucy Lucy Burgers, Tennessee Whiskey Pork Chops, and Chocolate Blackout Cake to name just a few—and then makes them foolproof. That's a good story (and a good cookbook) by any stretch of the imagination.

Christopher Kimball
Founder and Editor,
Cook's Country and *Cook's Illustrated*
Host, *Cook's Country from America's Test Kitchen*
and *America's Test Kitchen*

CHAPTER ONE

Starters and Snacks

STARTERS AND SNACKS

Spiced Nuts

Although spiced nuts can be enjoyed any time of the year, they are especially nice around the holidays when a freshly made batch perfumes the house with their heady aroma. Besides finding the right mix of spices, the key to this recipe is figuring out how to attach them to the nuts. No one wants to put a hand into a bowl of sticky and/or greasy nuts.

We found that first tossing the nuts with melted butter yielded a spotty coating—and yes, they were oily, too. Simmering the nuts in a spiced corn syrup glaze made the coating too candy-like and chewy. We had the best results when we mixed the nuts with egg whites, let the excess liquid drain away, and then tossed the nuts with the spice and sugar mixture. This technique created a cohesive, delicate shell around each nut. And toasting the nuts on a baking sheet in a relatively cool oven allowed plenty of time for the nuts and their coating to crisp up. Our recipes yield a generous amount of 10 cups. These nuts make a great holiday gift packed into a decorative tin lined with waxed or parchment paper.

SPICED NUTS

MAKES ABOUT 10 CUPS
Salted nuts will be too salty in this recipe. The recipe can easily be halved.

2	large egg whites
2	tablespoons water
2	teaspoons salt
2	pounds unsalted raw pecans, cashews, walnuts, or whole unblanched almonds
1⅓	cups sugar
4	teaspoons ground cinnamon
2	teaspoons ground ginger
2	teaspoons ground coriander

1. Adjust the oven racks to the upper-middle and lower-middle positions and heat the oven to 300 degrees. Line 2 baking sheets with parchment paper. Whisk the egg whites, water, and salt in a large bowl. Add the nuts and toss to coat. Drain in a colander for 5 minutes.

2. Mix the sugar, cinnamon, ginger, and coriander in a large bowl. Add the drained nuts and toss to coat. Spread the nuts evenly on the prepared baking sheets and bake until dry and crisp, 40 to 45 minutes, rotating and switching the positions of the baking sheets halfway through baking. Cool the nuts completely. Break the nuts apart and serve. (The nuts can be stored at room temperature in an airtight container for up to 3 weeks.)

Variations
BARBECUED SPICED NUTS
Add ¼ cup ketchup to the egg white mixture in step 1 and replace the cinnamon, ginger, and coriander with 2 teaspoons chili powder, 2 teaspoons paprika, 1 teaspoon ground cumin, ¼ teaspoon cayenne pepper, and ⅛ teaspoon ground cloves.

CURRIED SPICED NUTS
Replace the cinnamon, ginger, and coriander with 2 teaspoons each curry powder, paprika, and ground cumin.

Party Snack Mixes

Crunchy, salty, and borderline addictive, homemade party snack mix is guaranteed to disappear quickly at any gathering. But after making a back-of-the-box recipe recently, we felt there was room for improvement. The cereal and other snacks (which included pretzels, Melba toast, and nuts) were tossed with melted margarine and a splash of Worcestershire before being sprinkled with seasoned salt. It's not that we're complaining—we had more than a few handfuls—but we knew it could be so much better.

In head-to-head tests, the nutty sweetness of melted butter was preferred to margarine and olive oil, both of which left a greasy finish. Though Worcestershire sauce certainly added flavor to the mix, some tasters found it too dominant. Substitutes such as soy sauce, hot sauce, and barbecue sauce were more successful, lending inspired flavors without steamrolling the other ingredients.

As for the seasonings, a few carefully chosen dried spices gave well-rounded flavors without the staleness of seasoned salt. Bold seasonings such as chili powder, garlic powder, cayenne pepper, and ground ginger held their flavor through baking (unlike more subtle spices such as paprika and onion

powder, whose flavor faded). When it came to the baking, the original recipe was pretty much spot-on: 45 minutes in a 250-degree oven was sufficient to bloom the spices and crisp the snacks.

We found that no one combination of snacks was best. Along with the usual Chex cereal, Melba toast, and nuts, we punctuated the mixes with unexpected ingredients such as oyster crackers, smoked almonds, and wasabi peas.

ASIAN FIRECRACKER PARTY MIX

MAKES ABOUT 10 CUPS
Wasabi peas can be found in the international aisle of most grocery stores.

5	cups Rice Chex cereal
2	cups sesame sticks
1	cup wasabi peas
1	cup chow mein noodles
1	cup honey-roasted peanuts
6	tablespoons unsalted butter, melted
2	tablespoons soy sauce
1	teaspoon ground ginger
¾	teaspoon garlic powder
¼	teaspoon cayenne pepper

1. Adjust an oven rack to the middle position and heat the oven to 250 degrees. Combine the cereal, sesame sticks, wasabi peas, chow mein noodles, and peanuts in a large bowl. Whisk the butter and soy sauce in a small bowl, then drizzle over the cereal mixture. Sprinkle evenly with the ginger, garlic powder, and cayenne and toss until well combined.

2. Spread the mixture over a rimmed baking sheet and bake, stirring every 15 minutes, until golden and crisp, about 45 minutes. Cool to room temperature. Serve. (The mix can be stored in an airtight container at room temperature for up to 1 week.)

THE AMERICAN TABLE
THE HISTORY OF BREAKFAST CEREAL
- -

Breakfast cereal is a relatively new addition to the American culinary landscape. About 100 years ago, a number of health-conscious entrepreneurs, most notably Will Keith (W. K.) Kellogg, began to market grain-based cereals as a healthful, filling, and affordable alternative to the traditional meat-and-eggs breakfast. While these first cereals were little more than primitive granola—some even needed to be soaked in water overnight to make them edible—consumers slowly began to warm to them. The breakfast cereal industry truly boomed in the 1920s, when milk pasteurization made fresh milk more readily available.

BBQ PARTY MIX

MAKES ABOUT 10 CUPS

Fritos corn chips work well in this recipe.

- 5 cups Corn Chex cereal
- 2 cups corn chips
- 1 cup Melba toast rounds, lightly crushed
- 1 cup pretzel sticks
- 1 cup smoked almonds
- 6 tablespoons unsalted butter, melted
- ¼ cup barbecue sauce
- 1 teaspoon chili powder
- ½ teaspoon dried oregano
- ¼ teaspoon cayenne pepper

1. Adjust an oven rack to the middle position and heat the oven to 250 degrees. Combine the cereal, corn chips, Melba toast, pretzels, and almonds in a large bowl. Whisk the butter and barbecue sauce in a small bowl, then drizzle over the cereal mixture. Sprinkle evenly with the chili powder, oregano, and cayenne and toss until well combined.

2. Spread the mixture over a rimmed baking sheet and bake, stirring every 15 minutes, until golden and crisp, about 45 minutes. Cool to room temperature. Serve. (The mix can be stored in an airtight container at room temperature for up to 1 week.)

FISHERMAN'S FRIEND PARTY MIX

MAKES ABOUT 10 CUPS

The test kitchen prefers Frank's Red Hot Sauce. If using a spicier brand, you may not need as much.

- 5 cups Corn Chex or Rice Chex cereal
- 2 cups oyster crackers
- 1 cup Pepperidge Farm Cheddar Goldfish
- 1 cup Pepperidge Farm Pretzel Goldfish
- 1 cup Melba toast rounds, lightly crushed
- 6 tablespoons unsalted butter, melted
- 2 tablespoons hot sauce (see note above)
- 1 tablespoon fresh lemon juice
- 1 tablespoon Old Bay seasoning

1. Adjust an oven rack to the middle position and heat the oven to 250 degrees. Combine the cereal, oyster crackers, Goldfish, and Melba toast in a large bowl. Whisk the butter, hot sauce, and lemon juice in a small bowl, then drizzle over the cereal mixture. Sprinkle evenly with the Old Bay and toss until well combined.

2. Spread the mixture over a rimmed baking sheet and bake, stirring every 15 minutes, until golden and crisp, about 45 minutes. Cool to room temperature. Serve. (The mix can be stored in an airtight container at room temperature for up to 1 week.)

Holiday Cheese Balls

Stacked high in the refrigerator section of the supermarket, cheese balls promise to be the perfect holiday hors d'oeuvre. But promises are made to be broken. With their unnatural orange hue and a flavor that's more Cheetos than cheddar, supermarket cheese balls make you wonder if there's any real cheese in them at all.

By using real cheese, we figured we were already well on our way to creating a superior recipe. For the optimal consistency—firm, yet spreadable—we used equal parts semisoft cheese (such as cheddar) and cream cheese. For a silky texture, we added a few tablespoons of mayonnaise and tossed everything into the food processor. We found that small amounts of assertive ingredients like Worcestershire, cayenne pepper, and garlic enhanced the cheese flavor without compromising texture.

After a few hours in the fridge to firm up, our cheese balls were almost ready to go, needing only a roll in toasted nuts, fresh herbs, or crushed tortilla chips before serving.

CLASSIC CHEDDAR CHEESE BALL

SERVES 15 TO 20

Serve with your favorite crackers.

- 2 **cups shredded extra-sharp cheddar cheese**
- 1 **(8 ounce) package cream cheese, softened**
- 2 **tablespoons mayonnaise**
- 1 **tablespoon Worcestershire sauce**
- 1 **garlic clove, minced**
- ¼ **teaspoon cayenne pepper**
- ½ **cup sliced almonds, toasted**

1. Process all of the ingredients (except the almonds) in a food processor until smooth, scraping down the sides as necessary, about 1 minute. Transfer the cheese mixture to the center of a large sheet of plastic wrap.

2. Seal the cheese in the wrap and shape into a rough ball (the mixture will be somewhat loose). Refrigerate until firm, about 3 hours. (The cheese ball can be refrigerated for up to 2 days.) Once the cheese ball is firm, reshape it as necessary into a smooth sphere. Unwrap the cheese ball and roll it in the almonds. Let it sit at room temperature for 15 minutes before serving.

ZESTY SMOKED SALMON CHEESE BALL

SERVES 15 TO 20

Bagel chips are especially good with this cheese ball.

- 2 **cups shredded dill Havarti cheese**
- 1 **(8 ounce) package cream cheese, softened**
- 2 **tablespoons mayonnaise**
- 4 **ounces smoked salmon, chopped**
- 1 **shallot, minced**
- 1 **teaspoon grated fresh lemon zest and**
  1 tablespoon fresh lemon juice
- ½ **cup minced fresh chives**

1. Process all of the ingredients (except the chives) in a food processor until smooth, scraping down the sides as necessary, about 1 minute. Transfer the cheese mixture to the center of a large sheet of plastic wrap.

2. Seal the cheese in the wrap and shape into a rough ball (the mixture will be somewhat loose). Refrigerate until firm, about 3 hours. (The cheese ball can be refrigerated for up to 2 days.) Once the cheese ball is firm, reshape it as necessary into a smooth sphere. Unwrap the cheese ball and roll it in the chives. Let it sit at room temperature for 15 minutes before serving.

PORT WINE–BLUE CHEESE BALL

SERVES 15 TO 20

Your favorite crackers or toasted slices of crusty bread are good with this cheese ball.

- 1 **cup crumbled blue cheese**
- 1 **cup shredded mozzarella cheese**
- 1 **(8 ounce) package cream cheese, softened**
- 2 **tablespoons mayonnaise**
- 1 **tablespoon port wine**
- 1 **garlic clove, minced**
- ½ **cup pecans, toasted and chopped fine**

1. Process all of the ingredients (except the pecans) in a food processor until smooth, scraping down the sides as necessary, about 1 minute. Transfer the cheese mixture to the center of a large sheet of plastic wrap.

2. Seal the cheese in the wrap and shape into a rough ball (the mixture will be somewhat loose). Refrigerate until firm, about 3 hours. (The cheese ball can be refrigerated for up to 2 days.) Once the cheese

ball is firm, reshape it as necessary into a smooth sphere. Unwrap the cheese ball and roll it in the pecans. Let it sit at room temperature for 15 minutes before serving.

MEXICALI CHEESE BALL

SERVES 15 TO 20

If you can't find blue tortilla chips, regular tortilla chips work just fine.

2	cups shredded pepper Jack cheese
1	(8 ounce) package cream cheese, softened
3	tablespoons prepared salsa
2	tablespoons chopped fresh cilantro
1	garlic clove, minced
½	cup blue corn tortilla chips, crushed (see note above)

1. Process all of the ingredients (except the crushed chips) in a food processor until smooth, scraping down the sides as necessary, about 1 minute. Transfer the cheese mixture to the center of a large sheet of plastic wrap.

SHAPING A CHEESE BALL

1. Place the processed cheese mixture in the center of a large sheet of plastic wrap.

2. Twist the cheese to seal it in the wrap and shape the cheese into a rough ball.

---

2. Seal the cheese in the wrap and shape into a rough ball (the mixture will be somewhat loose). Refrigerate until firm, about 3 hours. (The cheese ball can be refrigerated for up to 2 days.) Once the cheese ball is firm, reshape it as necessary into a smooth sphere. Unwrap the cheese ball and roll it in the crushed chips. Let it sit at room temperature for 15 minutes before serving.

Cheese Rounds

Homemade cheddar cheese rounds are as easy as hors d'oeuvres get. Just mix shredded cheddar cheese, flour, and softened butter to form the dough; refrigerate until firm; slice; and bake. But while the best versions are flaky-crisp and pleasantly sandy—like tiny rounds of savory shortbread— many that we tried were tough and floury, with little cheddar flavor.

Some recipes called for three times as much flour as cheese (these baked up too crackery), and others used half as much flour as cheese (and were greasy and chewy). Tasters preferred a middle ground of 1½ cups of flour and 2 cups of cheese mixed with a stick of softened butter. Sharp cheddar (rather than mild) and cayenne pepper bumped up the flavor. Still, the rounds were plagued by a slight raw-flour taste.

Could nuts mask the floury taste? We discovered that by finely grinding pecans in the food processor, we could use them in place of some of the flour. The moisture from the pecans made the rounds slightly softer, so we added a tablespoon of cornstarch to the dough, which left the rounds with a crisp, pleasantly shortbread-like texture to go along with their nutty, cheddary flavor.

CHEDDAR CHEESE ROUNDS

MAKES ABOUT 5 DOZEN CHEESE ROUNDS

Orange-colored sharp cheddar will give the rounds a deep golden hue. To make this dough with a hand-held mixer, chop the nuts finely and then mix all the ingredients until combined, about 3 minutes.

¼	cup pecans
1¼	cups all-purpose flour
1	tablespoon cornstarch
2	cups shredded sharp cheddar cheese (see note above)
8	tablespoons (1 stick) unsalted butter, cut into pieces and softened
¼	teaspoon cayenne pepper
½	teaspoon salt

1. Process the pecans, flour, and cornstarch in a food processor until finely ground. Add the remaining ingredients and pulse until a dough forms. Turn the dough out onto a lightly floured surface and roll into two 8-inch logs. Wrap tightly with plastic wrap and refrigerate until firm, at least 1 hour or up to 3 days. (The logs can also be wrapped in plastic, then foil, and frozen for up to 1 month. Defrost in the refrigerator before proceeding with step 2.)

2. Adjust the oven racks to the upper-middle and lower-middle positions and heat the oven to 400 degrees. Line 2 baking sheets with parchment paper. Unwrap and slice the logs into ¼-inch rounds and place the rounds ¾ inch apart on the prepared baking sheets. Bake until golden, about 15 minutes, switching and rotating the baking sheets halfway through baking. Let cool 3 minutes on the sheets, then transfer to a wire rack and cool completely. Serve. (The rounds can be kept in an airtight container at room temperature for up to 3 days.)

Creamy Dips

One big difference between cookbooks from the sixties and seventies and cookbooks from today is the dip recipes. The former have lots of creamy party dips based on sour cream and mayonnaise, while newer cookbooks have recipes for more eclectic sorts of dips made with pureed beans, roasted vegetables, and exotic ingredients such as pomegranate molasses and tahini. Yet there is something very satisfying about dipping a crisp carrot stick or salty potato chip into a cool, savory, creamy dip, and, in fact, these old standbys can be just as delicious as their modern competitors. However, the richness of both sour cream and mayonnaise can easily dominate a dip that is seasoned too timidly. These dips need to be seasoned with gusto. That means mostly fresh ingredients—and plenty of them.

After much trial and error with these dips, we found the combination of mayonnaise and sour cream to be the ideal medium for carrying fresh and vibrant flavors. This combination also has the perfect consistency for dipping and scooping. As for the ratio, we found equal portions to be ideal. The mayonnaise adds body and richness, while the sour cream brings a bright freshness to the dip. We also found that light mayonnaise and sour cream fare pretty well in these dips. They tend to taste a bit flatter and result in a dip that is slightly less creamy and silky, but they are certainly worth trying if you're looking to trim some fat and calories.

GREEN GODDESS DIP

MAKES ABOUT 1¾ CUPS

Prepare this dip at least 1 hour ahead of time or even a day in advance to allow the flavors to blend. You can use either light or regular sour cream and mayonnaise.

¾	cup sour cream (see note above)
¾	cup mayonnaise (see note above)

2 garlic cloves, chopped
¼ cup chopped fresh parsley
2 teaspoons chopped fresh tarragon
1 tablespoon fresh lemon juice
2 anchovy fillets
¼ cup minced fresh chives
Salt and pepper

In a food processor, process the sour cream, mayonnaise, garlic, parsley, tarragon, lemon juice, and anchovy fillets until smooth and creamy, scraping down the sides of the bowl once or twice. Transfer the mixture to a medium bowl; stir in the chives. Season with salt and pepper to taste. Chill until the flavors meld, about 1 hour. (The dip can be covered and refrigerated for up to 2 days.) Serve cool or at room temperature.

CLAM DIP WITH BACON AND SCALLIONS

MAKES ABOUT 2 CUPS

Prepare this dip at least 1 hour ahead of time or even a day in advance to allow the flavors to blend. You can use either light or regular sour cream and mayonnaise.

4 slices bacon, cut into ¼-inch pieces
¾ cup sour cream (see note above)
¾ cup mayonnaise (see note above)
1 teaspoon fresh lemon juice
1 teaspoon Worcestershire sauce
2 (6½-ounce) cans minced clams, drained
2 medium scallions, sliced thin
Salt and pepper
Cayenne pepper

1. Fry the bacon in a small skillet over medium heat until crisp, 6 to 8 minutes. Transfer the bacon with a slotted spoon to a paper towel–lined plate and let cool.

2. Whisk together the sour cream, mayonnaise, lemon juice, and Worcestershire sauce in a medium bowl. Stir in the minced clams, scallions, and reserved bacon. Season to taste with salt, pepper, and cayenne. Chill until the flavors meld, about 1 hour. (The dip can be covered and refrigerated for up to 2 days.)

Chunky Guacamole

For great guacamole, it goes without saying that ripe avocados are a must, but so is a light hand. In many recipes the guacamole is ruined because the avocados are mashed to death, leaving a puree that's better served with a baby spoon than a crispy chip. To provide a little textural contrast, we found that mashing two-thirds of the avocado and roughly chopping the rest were the keys to a silky-yet-chunky dip.

As for the flavor, almost all basic guacamole recipes rely on the same ingredients: garlic and onion for bite, jalapeño for kick, cilantro for a refreshing herbal element, and a splash of lime juice to brighten it all up. Our tasters were happy with everything except the raw onion, which they felt was harsh and overpowered the avocados. In an attempt to temper the onions, we experimented with yellow, red, and white varieties and even shallots, but a mere tablespoon still proved to be too much for tasters. Scallions worked better, adding a nice depth to the guacamole, but even they were slightly harsh.

To mellow the scallions' flavor, we steeped the more assertive white parts, along with the garlic and jalapeño, in lime juice for a few minutes before combining them with the avocados. The acidity of the juice mellowed the onion flavor. With a pinch or two of salt (don't use too much if you are serving the guacamole with salty tortilla chips), we had a recipe that wouldn't disappoint.

CHUNKY GUACAMOLE

MAKES ABOUT 3 CUPS

Preparing guacamole ahead of time helps the flavors marry, but it should not be prepared more than 1 day in advance. To prevent the dip from turning brown, press a sheet of plastic wrap directly onto the surface and refrigerate until ready to use. We prefer pebbly-skinned Hass avocados to the smoother Fuerte variety.

- 2 scallions, sliced thin, green and white parts separated
- 1 jalapeño chile, seeded and minced
- 1 garlic clove, minced
- ¼ teaspoon grated fresh lime zest and 2 tablespoons fresh lime juice
- 3 avocados, pitted, skinned, and chopped
- 3 tablespoons chopped fresh cilantro
  Salt

1. Combine the white parts of the scallions, the jalapeño, garlic, and lime juice in a large bowl. Let sit for 30 minutes.

2. Add two-thirds of the avocado to the bowl with the jalapeño mixture and mash with a potato masher until smooth. Gently fold in the remaining chopped avocado. Gently stir in the lime zest, green parts of the scallions, and cilantro. Season with salt to taste. Serve.

TEST KITCHEN SHORTCUT

Mincing Jalapeños: Jalapeños and other chiles add welcome heat to many dishes, but that heat can sting unprotected hands. If you don't have a glove handy to protect your hand, grab a small plastic sandwich bag, turn it inside out, and hold the pepper with your hand wrapped in the bag. The leftover chile can be pulled right into the bag and reserved for a later use.

SHOPPING WITH THE TEST KITCHEN

Avocados: Our Chunky Guacamole starts with perfectly ripe Hass avocados, but finding them at the ideal level of ripeness can be difficult. When these avocados are at their creamy best, they are purple-black (not green) and yield slightly when gently squeezed. Avoid avocados that are overly mushy or bruised or flat in spots or whose skin seems loose—these are well past their prime. If you can't find perfectly ripe avocados, buy the fruit while it's still hard and be patient. Even though we tried all the tricks—from burying the avocados in rice to enclosing them in a paper bag (with or without another piece of fruit)—we found that nothing sped the ripening process except time. Left on the countertop, even the hardest of avocados will ripen to perfection in 2 to 5 days.

One-Minute Salsa

A jarred salsa might be quick, but it's never very good—that is, unless you like watery, bland salsa. We wanted to create a fresh salsa with not much more effort.

Instead of coring, seeding, and dicing fresh tomatoes, we found that canned diced tomatoes work great in salsa, as long as you drain them first. Canned pickled jalapeños add heat and a vinegary kick—and we didn't have to wear rubber gloves (as we do when working with fresh jalapeños) when we opened the can.

To boost the flavor and color of this salsa, we augmented these canned products with fresh red onion (for color, sweetness, and bite), cilantro, lime juice, and garlic. To save on chopping, we turned to the food processor. A final quick drain of the finished salsa got rid of excess moisture.

ONE-MINUTE SALSA

Make sure to drain both the tomatoes and the jalapeños before processing.

- ½   **small red onion**
- ¼   **cup fresh cilantro**
- 1   **tablespoon fresh lime juice**
- 1   **garlic clove, peeled**
- 2   **tablespoons canned pickled jalapeños, drained**
- ¼   **teaspoon salt**
- 1   **(14.5-ounce) can diced tomatoes, drained**

Pulse the onion, cilantro, lime juice, garlic, jalapeños, and salt in a food processor until roughly chopped, about five 1-second pulses. Add the tomatoes and pulse until chopped, about two 1-second pulses. Transfer the mixture to a fine-mesh strainer and drain briefly. Serve. (The salsa can be covered and refrigerated for up to 2 days. Reseason to taste before serving.)

Hot Spinach and Artichoke Dip

Hot spinach and artichoke dip is a chain restaurant staple. Served bubbling hot from the broiler, this creamy, cheesy dip is studded with chunks of artichokes and earthy spinach. Most of the recipes we found called for folding frozen spinach, artichokes, and seasonings into a mixture of softened cream cheese (thinned with mayonnaise or sour cream) and cheddar. But these recipes came out of the oven greasy, pasty, and bland. We found a few recipes that replaced the cream cheese and mayonnaise or sour cream with a flour-thickened cream sauce. The flour stabilized the dip, so the cheese didn't separate

and make things greasy. Tasters preferred the assertive nuttiness of Parmesan to the more traditional cheddar or Monterey Jack. And because the cream sauce was much thinner than cream cheese, the dip was creamy, not pasty or stiff.

As for the headliners, sautéed fresh spinach had an unappealing, slimy texture. Frozen chopped spinach was a better (and easier) option, provided it was squeezed dry to prevent a watery dip. Since fresh artichokes would take too much work, we tested canned, bottled, and frozen artichoke hearts. Tasters dismissed the "tinny" taste of canned artichokes and the greasy, briny flavor of bottled artichokes, but the frozen ones showed promise. To help develop their flavor, we browned them in butter (along with some onion and garlic) before building the sauce. After a quick bake in the oven, we had a fresh-tasting, creamy dip better than any we could order in a restaurant.

HOT SPINACH AND ARTICHOKE DIP

Be sure to squeeze as much liquid as possible from the spinach and artichoke hearts. (For an alternative way to remove water from spinach, see page 19.) Serve with crackers, Melba toast, or tortilla chips.

- 4   **tablespoons unsalted butter**
- 1   **onion, minced**
- 2   **(9-ounce) boxes frozen artichoke hearts, thawed, squeezed dry, and chopped**
- 2   **garlic cloves, minced**
- ¼   **cup all-purpose flour**
- 2   **cups half-and-half**
- 1½   **cups grated Parmesan cheese**
- 1   **tablespoon fresh lemon juice**
- 1   **tablespoon hot sauce**
- 1   **teaspoon salt**
- 1   **(10-ounce) box frozen chopped spinach, thawed and squeezed dry**

1. Adjust an oven rack to the middle position and heat the oven to 450 degrees. Melt 2 tablespoons of the butter in a large saucepan over medium-high heat. Cook the onion until softened, about 5 minutes. Add the artichokes and cook until lightly browned, about 5 minutes. Stir in the garlic and cook until fragrant, about 30 seconds. Transfer the artichoke mixture to a plate and set aside.

2. Melt the remaining 2 tablespoons butter in the now-empty pan. Stir in the flour and cook until just golden, about 1 minute. Slowly stir in the half-and-half, 1¼ cups of the Parmesan, lemon juice, hot sauce, and salt. Reduce the heat to medium-low and simmer until thickened, about 3 minutes. Off the heat, stir in the spinach and reserved artichoke mixture. (At this point, the dip can be refrigerated in an airtight container for up to 24 hours.)

3. Transfer the dip to a 1-quart soufflé or baking dish and sprinkle with the remaining ¼ cup cheese. Bake until golden brown and bubbling, about 15 minutes. Cool for 5 minutes. Serve. (If the dip has been refrigerated, let it sit at room temperature for 1 hour before sprinkling with the cheese. Bake, covered with foil, in a 450-degree oven for 10 minutes. Remove the foil and bake until golden brown and heated through, about 15 minutes longer.)

Seven-Layer Dip

With its bold Tex-Mex flavors and contrasting textures, seven-layer dip sounds like a hit. The ingredient list—refried beans, sour cream, shredded cheese, guacamole, diced tomatoes, scallions, and black olives—is certainly appealing. But most versions of this party classic seem to assume that guests won't notice that the layers are messy and the flavors are tired.

We figured fixing the messy layers would be pretty easy. We'd start with the heavier layers first and try to "stiffen" each for neater spreading. Getting each layer to taste good seemed more challenging, especially after we prepared a number of published recipes. Most of these relied entirely on canned or processed ingredients—and they tasted like it. Even salty chips and cold beers failed to get our tasters excited about these dips.

We began our overhaul of this recipe at the bottom, with the beans. Straight from the can, refried beans tasted stale, and their pasty consistency shattered chips on contact. Knowing that making our own refried beans would take more time than we wanted, we wondered if we could use canned black beans instead of refried. To approximate the texture of refried beans, we mashed the drained black beans (breaking with test kitchen protocol by not rinsing them, which left them silkier and more dip-able) and seasoned them with fresh garlic, chili powder, and lime juice. Five minutes of extra work yielded a big improvement in flavor. One layer down, six to go.

Sour cream is a must for its cool flavor, but it can turn into a runny mess; we needed a way to give it more structure. Since we were going to layer cheese over it anyway, we tried pulsing the cheese (our tasters preferred the creamy kick of pepper Jack) and sour cream together in the food processor to make one unified layer. This worked great, especially when we doubled up on the cheese by adding it again as its own distinct layer.

We tried using store-bought guacamole, but every brand we tested was stale and some were rancid-tasting. Fresh guacamole (see our recipe on page 10) is a must here. Next up was the tomato layer. Our tasters gave an emphatic thumbs down to both canned tomatoes and jarred salsa, complaining that they just didn't taste fresh. But when we tried diced fresh tomatoes, our tasters thought they lacked punch. We found our solution in the form of a homemade pico de gallo, a chunky, dry salsa that we made by combining chopped fresh tomatoes, jalapeños, cilantro, and scallions with lime juice and salt and then letting the mixture drain before adding it to the dip.

A layer of sliced scallions added bite and color. We were almost in the end zone, but we couldn't figure out the final layer of canned sliced black olives. Rinsing helped mitigate the metallic flavor, but the olives were still bland. After several frustrating rounds of testing, we decided to eliminate the olives. Yes, our recipe has just six layers, but each is so distinct and fresh-tasting that no one will complain.

ULTIMATE SEVEN-LAYER DIP

SERVES 8 TO 10

This recipe is usually served in a clear dish so you can see the layers. For a crowd, double the recipe and serve in a 13 by 9-inch glass baking dish. To make pico de gallo in the food processor, start by pulsing the jalapeños with the cilantro until finely chopped. Then add the quartered, cored, and seeded tomatoes and pulse in 1-second bursts until evenly chopped. Add the minced scallions and lime juice and drain as instructed. If you don't have time to make fresh guacamole as called for, simply mash 3 avocados with 3 tablespoons fresh lime juice and ½ teaspoon salt.

- 4   large tomatoes, cored, seeded, and chopped fine
- 2   jalapeño chiles, seeded and minced
- 3   tablespoons chopped fresh cilantro
- 6   scallions, 2 minced and 4 with green parts sliced thin (white parts discarded)
- 2   tablespoons plus 2 teaspoons fresh lime juice
      Salt
- 1   (15.5-ounce) can black beans, drained but not rinsed
- 2   garlic cloves, minced
- ¾   teaspoon chili powder
- 1½ cups sour cream
- 4   cups shredded pepper Jack cheese
- 3   cups Chunky Guacamole (page 10)
      Tortilla chips for serving

1. Combine the tomatoes, jalapeños, cilantro, minced scallions, and 2 tablespoons of the lime juice in a medium bowl. Stir in ⅛ teaspoon salt and let stand until the tomatoes begin to soften, about 30 minutes. Strain the mixture into a clean bowl and discard liquid.

2. Pulse the black beans, garlic, remaining 2 teaspoons lime juice, chili powder, and ⅛ teaspoon salt in a food processor until the mixture resembles a chunky paste. Transfer to a bowl and wipe out the food processor. Pulse the sour cream and 2½ cups of the cheese until smooth. Transfer to a separate bowl.

3. Spread the bean mixture evenly over the bottom of an 8-inch square glass baking dish or 1-quart glass bowl. Spread the sour cream mixture evenly over the bean layer and sprinkle evenly with the remaining 1½ cups cheese. Spread the guacamole over the cheese and top with the tomato mixture. Sprinkle with the sliced scallions and serve with the tortilla chips. (The dip can be refrigerated for up to 24 hours. Let stand at room temperature for 1 hour before serving.)

Variation
ULTIMATE SMOKY SEVEN-LAYER DIP
Pulse 1 to 3 teaspoons minced canned chipotle chiles in adobo with the black beans in step 2. Along with the sliced scallions, garnish the dip with 4 slices cooked and crumbled bacon.

Spicy Beef Nachos

Most of the "ultimate nachos" we've ordered in restaurants come to the table loaded down with bland, greasy beef, dry beans, and cold strings of unmelted cheese smothering tough, soggy chips. They might be an "ultimate" kitchen disaster but are otherwise unremarkable. That's a shame, because great nachos shouldn't be that hard to prepare. Our ideal nachos would be hot, crisp chips covered with spicy beef, creamy refried beans, gooey melted cheese, and plenty of jalapeños.

To season the beef boldly, we tested a slew of spices before settling on a smoky mixture of chili powder, cumin, and oregano. Tomato paste, brown sugar, and canned chipotle chiles added a sweet richness and touch of heat, while fresh lime juice brightened it all up. To take care of the grease problem, we used 90-percent lean ground beef and drained the cooked meat on paper towels, pressing with more towels to blot up excess fat.

Our tasters preferred refried beans to plain beans, but when used straight out of the can, the beans had a stodgy flavor and chalky texture that were a turn-off. Processing the beans with pickled jalapeños and cheese produced a lively, spreadable puree. As for the cheese, it turns out that cheddar (the choice in many recipes) doesn't melt nearly as well as Monterey Jack. Our tasters preferred the kick of pepper Jack, but plain Jack is fine, too.

Early in our testing, we had been dumping a bag of tortilla chips on a platter, piling them with the toppings, and baking them until the cheese melted. After much trial and error, we learned two tricks about assembly that make for better nachos. First, the order of ingredients is important. After the chips, the beans should be added first, so you can spread them evenly; the beef comes next, so it can adhere to the beans and not roll off the chips; then the cheese goes on, to blanket everything. Second, to prevent all the toppings from being eaten with the top layer of chips, we found it necessary to make two layers of chips and toppings.

A quick addition of sliced fresh jalapeños turned up the heat and brought the pepper count to five: chili powder, chipotle chile, pepper Jack cheese, pickled jalapeños, and fresh jalapeños.

ULTIMATE SPICY BEEF NACHOS

SERVES 8

Top with our One-Minute Salsa (page 11), sour cream, chopped cilantro, and diced avocado.

REFRIED BEANS
- ½ cup canned refried beans
- 3 tablespoons shredded pepper Jack cheese
- 1 tablespoon chopped canned pickled jalapeños

SPICY BEEF
- 2 teaspoons vegetable oil
- 1 small onion, minced
- 3 garlic cloves, minced
- 1 tablespoon chili powder
- 1 teaspoon ground cumin
- ½ teaspoon dried oregano
- 1 teaspoon salt
- 1 pound 90-percent lean ground beef
- 2 tablespoons tomato paste
- 1 teaspoon brown sugar
- 1 medium canned chipotle chile, chopped, plus 1 teaspoon adobo sauce
- ½ cup water
- 2 teaspoons fresh lime juice

ASSEMBLY
- 1 (9½-ounce) bag tortilla chips
- 4 cups shredded pepper Jack cheese
- 2 jalapeño chiles, sliced into thin rings

1. Adjust an oven rack to the middle position and heat the oven to 400 degrees.

2. FOR THE BEANS: Pulse all of the ingredients in a food processor until smooth. Transfer to a bowl and cover with plastic wrap.

3. FOR THE BEEF: Heat the oil in a large skillet over medium heat until shimmering. Cook the onion until softened, about 4 minutes. Add the garlic, chili powder, cumin, oregano, and salt and cook until fragrant, about 1 minute. Add the beef and cook, breaking the meat into small bits with a wooden spoon and scraping the pan bottom to prevent scorching, until no longer pink, about 5 minutes. Add the tomato paste, sugar, chile, and adobo sauce and cook until paste begins to darken, about 1 minute. Add the water, bring to a simmer, and cook over medium-low heat until the mixture is nearly dry, 5 to 7 minutes. Stir in the lime juice and transfer the mixture to a plate lined with several layers of paper towels. Use more paper towels to blot up excess grease.

4. TO ASSEMBLE: Spread half of the chips on a large serving platter or 13 by 9-inch baking dish. Dollop half of the bean mixture over the chips, then spread evenly. Scatter half of the beef mixture over the beans, top with 2 cups of the cheese and half of the jalapeños. Repeat with the remaining chips, beans, beef, 2 cups cheese, and jalapeños. Bake until the cheese is melted and just beginning to brown, 12 to 14 minutes. Serve with salsa and other desired garnishes.

TEST KITCHEN SHORTCUT

Safe Grating: To prevent scraping your knuckles on the teeth of a sharp box grater, try wearing a dishwashing glove. The sturdy glove not only protects your hands; it will also help you keep a sure grip on blocks of cheese.

REMOVING THE GREASE

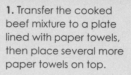

1. Transfer the cooked beef mixture to a plate lined with paper towels, then place several more paper towels on top.

2. Using your hands, press the paper towels in order to extract as much extra grease as possible from the beef.

SHOPPING WITH THE TEST KITCHEN

Tortilla Chips: A sturdy chip is a must when making our Ultimate Spicy Beef Nachos. Tostitos was the top-rated brand in a kitchen taste test, but not all varieties are suitable for nachos. We liked Tostitos Natural Chips—they're hearty and will support plenty of toppings.

Deviled Eggs

Sometimes the simplest recipes are the trickiest to execute, and we've made more than our fair share of deviled eggs with greenish yolks and bland fillings. We wanted to bulletproof this recipe, and we figured we would start with the most difficult task: hard-cooking the eggs.

There's no way to watch the egg cook under its shell, and the test kitchen's fail-safe tool for checking doneness—the instant-read thermometer—isn't an option. Most recipes have you simmer the eggs for a specified period, but they tend to turn out greenish eggs that look like something out of Dr. Seuss. After some research, we learned that the green color appears when the iron in the yolk reacts with the sulfur in the white to produce ferrous sulfide. Prolonged heating is the culprit.

This led us to wonder if all those not-so-foolproof recipes were falling down over the definition of "simmer." We found that eggs cooked for 15 minutes at a hard simmer (might as well call it a boil) overcook, while those cooked for 15 minutes at a gentle simmer don't. To remove the guesswork, in the test kitchen we start the eggs in cold water, bring the water to a boil, then turn off the heat and put the cover on the pan. The residual heat cooks the eggs, which are done in exactly 10 minutes. Plunging the eggs into ice water stops the cooking process and prevents the green ring from forming.

At this point in testing we noticed a lot of inconsistency in the location of the yolks. Sometimes they were in the center, sometimes so close to the edge that the whites ripped as soon as we tried to extract the yolk. We surfed the Web for ideas on how to center the yolks and found dozens of bizarre tips, everything from spinning eggs like a top on the counter (definitely messy, as one or two eggs will topple onto the floor) to spinning eggs with a spoon as they cook (decidedly dangerous, as splashes of boiling water are inevitable). The best idea involved placing the carton of eggs on its side in the refrigerator the day before the eggs were to be cooked. Evidently, this moves the yolk away from the large end of the egg—which is where the yolk generally settles after packaging—to the center.

With the eggs cooked, it was time to mash the yolks and season them with the usual suspects: mayonnaise, vinegar, and mustard. Plain mayonnaise is too bland, but Miracle Whip (called for in many recipes) has an odd sweet-tart flavor that tasters did not love. Instead, mixing a little sour cream with plain mayonnaise added that much-needed punch.

As for mustard, plain yellow was too bland, but Dijon was too potent; spicy brown mustard (like Gulden's) was a good compromise. Fancier recipes use cider vinegar or even balsamic vinegar, but we found that plain old distilled white vinegar produced quite enough pucker without adding any distracting flavors. Now our deviled eggs were truly foolproof.

FOOLPROOF DEVILED EGGS

MAKES 1 DOZEN FILLED HALVES
To center the yolks, turn the carton of eggs on its side in the refrigerator the day before you plan to cook the eggs.

HARD-BOILED EGGS
  6 large eggs

FILLING
  2 tablespoons mayonnaise
  1 tablespoon sour cream
  ½ teaspoon distilled white vinegar
  ½ teaspoon spicy brown mustard (such as Gulden's)
  ¼ teaspoon sugar
  ⅛ teaspoon salt
  ⅛ teaspoon pepper

PEELING HARD-BOILED EGGS

1. Once the eggs have finished cooking, pour out the boiling water and shake the pan back and forth to crack the shells.

2. Transfer the eggs to a bowl of ice water. The cracks will allow more air and water to get in between the white and the shell, making it easier to peel the eggs.

FILLING DEVILED EGGS

Squeeze the filling from the plastic bag into the egg whites, mounding the filling slightly. Filling the eggs this way, rather than with a spoon, is fast and tidy.

1. FOR THE EGGS: Place the eggs in a medium saucepan, add water to cover by 1 inch, and bring to a boil over high heat. Remove the pan from the heat, cover, and let stand 10 minutes. Meanwhile, fill a medium bowl with 1 quart water and 1 dozen ice cubes. Pour off the water from the saucepan and gently shake the pan back and forth to crack the shells. Transfer the eggs to the ice water with a slotted spoon and let cool 5 minutes. Peel the eggs and slice in half lengthwise; transfer the yolks to a fine-mesh sieve.

2. FOR THE FILLING: Use a spatula to press the egg yolks through the sieve and into a bowl. Add the remaining ingredients, mashing the mixture against the sides of the bowl until smooth.

3. Arrange the whites on a serving platter. Add the egg yolk mixture to one corner of a large plastic storage bag and twist the bag to keep the filling in the corner. Snip off about ½ inch of the corner of the bag and squeeze the filling into the egg whites, mounding the filling just above the whites. Serve immediately. (The deviled eggs can be made up to 2 days ahead. Wrap the peeled egg-white halves tightly with a double layer of plastic wrap and place the filling in a zipper-lock plastic bag, squeezing out all the air. Refrigerate until ready to fill and serve.)

Variations
ITALIAN DEVILED EGGS

Top the eggs with ⅛ teaspoon red pepper flakes, 1 tablespoon capers, and 2 teaspoons minced fresh parsley.

FIESTA DEVILED EGGS

Stir 1 teaspoon adobo sauce from canned chipotle chiles into the yolk mixture. Sprinkle the eggs with 1 slice cooked and crumbled bacon, and 1 scallion, chopped fine.

Stuffed Mushrooms

Warm, earthy mushroom caps stuffed with creamy cheese are pretty high up on our list of favorite party snacks. But really good stuffed mushrooms are elusive, and when it's our party, we wish they were easier to make. We set out to develop a recipe for great stuffed mushrooms that we could make ahead and quickly reheat when our guests arrived.

One of the biggest problems with stuffed mushrooms is sogginess. The only way to get water-laden button mushroom caps to shed their liquid is to roast them prior to stuffing. Using a common technique, we seasoned the mushrooms with olive oil, lemon juice, salt, and pepper before roasting them (gill side down, so the excess moisture could drain away) in a hot oven. These mushrooms were indeed dry, but the bottoms were so tough they were difficult to bite through.

Thinking the hot baking sheet was to blame for the toughness, we roasted the caps on a wire rack so that air could circulate around them. This solved the problem of the leathery bottoms, but our tasters commented that there didn't seem to be a lot of mushroom flavor. Maybe we couldn't afford to waste the flavorful liquid the mushrooms were shedding. To keep that liquid, we roasted the mushrooms gill side up. Now the liquid pooled in the caps, infusing the mushrooms—not the pan—with flavor. A flip to gill side down for the final 10 minutes ensured that the caps shed any excess moisture.

Now we had firm-but-tender, flavorful mushroom caps; it was time to tackle the stuffing. We created three cheesy no-cook fillings, filled the mushrooms, and heated them for another 10 minutes. Our recipe was very good, but tasters wanted something crunchy to contrast with the smooth filling. Dusting the stuffed mushrooms with fresh bread crumbs did the trick. The crumbs toasted in the hot oven, becoming golden and crunchy.

BEST STUFFED MUSHROOMS

MAKES 24 STUFFED MUSHROOMS

Mushrooms shrink significantly as they cook, so choose large "stuffer mushrooms." We use a plastic storage bag to hold the filling as we stuff the mushrooms; the technique is identical to how we fill deviled eggs (see page 17).

TOPPING

1	slice hearty white sandwich bread, quartered
1	tablespoon chopped fresh parsley
2	garlic cloves, minced
2	tablespoons olive oil

MUSHROOMS

24	large white mushrooms, stems removed
¼	cup olive oil
1	teaspoon fresh lemon juice
¼	teaspoon salt
⅛	teaspoon pepper
1	recipe stuffing (page 19)

1. FOR THE TOPPING: Pulse the bread in a food processor to coarse crumbs. Mix the parsley, garlic, and oil in a bowl. Stir the crumbs into the oil mixture to coat. Set aside.

STEMMING MUSHROOMS

Grasp the stem where it joins the cap and gently wiggle the stem back and forth until it pops off in one solid piece.

2. FOR THE MUSHROOMS: Adjust an oven rack to the middle position and heat the oven to 450 degrees. Line a rimmed baking sheet with foil and set a wire rack inside the baking sheet. Toss the mushrooms with the oil, lemon juice, salt, and pepper in a bowl. Arrange the mushrooms gill side up on the rack and roast until the juices are released, about 20 minutes. Turn the caps over and roast until the mushrooms are well browned, about 10 minutes.

3. Remove the baking sheet from the oven. Flip the roasted mushrooms gill side up and cool slightly. Fill a zipper-lock plastic bag with the stuffing and snip off one corner, then fill the mushrooms. Press each cap (stuffing side down) into the bread-crumb topping to coat, and arrange the caps (topping side up) on the rack. Bake until the filling is hot and the topping is golden brown, about 10 minutes. Cool about 5 minutes before serving. (The unbaked stuffed mushrooms can be stored, stuffing side up, on a paper towel–lined plate covered tightly with plastic wrap, and refrigerated for up to 3 days. The bread-crumb topping can be refrigerated separately for up to 3 days. Add the crumb topping just before baking.)

CHESAPEAKE SHRIMP STUFFING

For information about buying shrimp, see the note on page 22. If you prefer, substitute ½ cup lump crab meat for the shrimp.

¼	pound cooked, peeled shrimp
½	cup shredded cheddar cheese
2	ounces cream cheese, softened
2	tablespoons drained jarred roasted red peppers, chopped
3	scallions, sliced thin
1	garlic clove, minced
1	tablespoon fresh lemon juice
½	teaspoon Old Bay seasoning
¼	teaspoon salt
⅛	teaspoon pepper

Process all of the ingredients in a food processor until smooth. Transfer the mixture to a zipper-lock plastic bag until ready to use.

TEST KITCHEN SHORTCUT

Ridding Spinach of Water: Rather than spending time—and energy—wringing defrosted frozen spinach dry in a kitchen towel, try this trick. Place the defrosted spinach in a colander set over a bowl, press a layer of plastic wrap on top of the spinach, set a heavy can on top of the plastic, and let stand for about 10 minutes, pressing firmly on the can once or twice. The weight of the can will press out any liquid, freeing you up for other kitchen tasks.

GOAT CHEESE AND HERB STUFFING

The herbs can be varied to include parsley, chives, or oregano.

4	ounces goat cheese, softened
2	ounces cream cheese, softened
1	tablespoon olive oil
1	garlic clove, minced
1	tablespoon chopped fresh basil
1	tablespoon chopped fresh tarragon
2	teaspoons minced fresh thyme
¼	teaspoon salt
⅛	teaspoon pepper

Process all of the ingredients in a food processor until smooth. Transfer the mixture to a zipper-lock plastic bag until ready to use.

SPINACH AND LEMON STUFFING

½	cup frozen spinach, defrosted and squeezed dry
½	cup shredded cheddar cheese
2	ounces cream cheese, softened
2	tablespoons olive oil
1	garlic clove, minced
2	tablespoons fresh lemon juice
3	scallions, sliced thin
½	teaspoon salt
⅛	teaspoon pepper

Process all of the ingredients in a food processor until smooth. Transfer the mixture to a zipper-lock plastic bag until ready to use.

Buffalo Wings

First conceived of at the Anchor Bar in Buffalo, New York, in the 1960s, Buffalo wings are now found throughout the country at any bar or Super Bowl party worth its salt. The combination of chicken wings slathered with hot sauce and dunked in blue cheese dressing may seem odd, but it is actually a harmonious union. The sauce's bright heat is tamed by the soothing, creamy dip.

For Buffalo wings, the raw chicken wing itself is almost always cut into two segments, and the relatively meatless wing tip is removed. The wings come packaged as whole wings or already cut into pieces affectionately referred to as drumettes. We found that precut wings were often poorly cut and unevenly sized, so we chose to buy whole wings and butcher them ourselves, which was easy and economical. With kitchen shears or a sharp chef's knife, the wing is halved at the main joint and the skinny tip of the wing is lopped off and discarded (or saved for stock).

While the wings were easy to butcher, cooking them proved a little trickier because of their high fat content. At the Anchor Bar, Buffalo wings are deep-fried, which renders the fat and leaves the skin crisp and golden. But deep-frying can be a daunting project in a home kitchen, with hot fat splattering about, coating the stovetop and stinging uncovered arms. We found that if we used a deep Dutch oven and kept the oil at a constant 360 degrees, splattering oil was minimal (and much safer) and cleanup easy.

We tossed the wings with salt, pepper, and cayenne pepper and then fried them for about 12 minutes, or until golden. While these wings were juicy and crisp, most tasters wanted an even crispier exterior. We did not want to resort to a batter, so we tried dredging the wings, testing one batch dredged in flour and another in cornstarch. The cornstarch provided a thin and brittle coating, not unlike tempura, that was the tasters' favorite. We found that thoroughly drying the chicken with paper towels prior to tossing it with the cornstarch and seasonings ensured crisp skin and no gumminess.

Now we were ready to tackle the sauce. Most recipes we found agreed that authentic Buffalo wing sauce, as made at the Anchor Bar, is nothing but Frank's Red Hot Sauce and butter or margarine, blended in a 2-to-1 ratio. Most recipes also suggest intensifying the sauce's heat with a bit of Tabasco or

CUTTING UP CHICKEN WINGS

1. With a chef's knife, cut into the skin between the larger sections of the wing until you hit the joint.

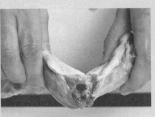

2. Bend back the two sections to pop and break the joint.

3. Cut through the skin and flesh to separate the two meaty portions completely.

4. Hack off the wing tip and discard (or save for making stock).

other hot pepper sauce because, on its own, Frank's is not quite spicy enough. While we liked this simple sauce, most tasters wanted something a little more dynamic. We included brown sugar to round out the flavors. A little cider vinegar balanced out the sugar and added a pleasing sharpness.

Creamy blue cheese dressing and carrot and celery sticks are the classic accompaniments to Buffalo wings. For our dressing, we picked a mild blue cheese and combined it with buttermilk and sour cream for tang and richness and with mayonnaise for body. A little white wine vinegar brightened the flavors, a pinch of sugar added just the right touch of sweetness, and garlic powder, which we normally shy away from, added a subtle background note rather than the assertive bite that comes with fresh garlic.

Our final Buffalo wings buck tradition just a bit, but only in the service of delivering a close-to-foolproof and tasty recipe for a crowd-pleasing favorite.

BUFFALO WINGS

SERVES 6 TO 8

Frank's Red Hot Sauce is not terribly spicy. We like to combine it with a more potent hot sauce, such as Tabasco, to bring up the heat.

SAUCE

4	tablespoons unsalted butter
½	cup Frank's Red Hot Sauce
2	tablespoons hot pepper sauce, plus more to taste (see note above)
1	tablespoon dark brown sugar
2	teaspoons cider vinegar

WINGS

1–2	quarts peanut oil for frying
1	teaspoon cayenne pepper
1	teaspoon pepper
1	teaspoon salt
3	tablespoons cornstarch
18	chicken wings (about 3 pounds), wing tips removed and remaining wings separated into 2 parts at joint

VEGETABLES AND DRESSING

4	medium celery ribs, cut into thin sticks
2	medium carrots, peeled and cut into thin sticks
1	recipe Blue Cheese Dressing (page 30)

1. FOR THE SAUCE: Melt the butter in a small saucepan over low heat. Whisk in the hot sauces, brown sugar, and vinegar until combined. Remove from the heat and set aside.

2. FOR THE WINGS: Heat the oven to 200 degrees. Line a baking sheet with paper towels. Heat 2½ inches of the peanut oil in a large Dutch oven over medium-high heat to 360 degrees. While the oil heats, mix the cayenne, pepper, salt, and cornstarch together in a small bowl. Dry the chicken with paper towels and place the pieces in a large mixing bowl. Sprinkle the spice mixture over the wings and toss with a rubber spatula until evenly coated. Fry half the chicken wings until golden and crisp, 10 to 12 minutes. With a slotted spoon, transfer the fried chicken wings to the baking sheet. Keep the first batch of chicken warm in the oven while frying the remaining wings.

3. TO SERVE: Pour the sauce mixture into a large bowl, add the chicken wings, and toss until the wings are uniformly coated. Serve immediately with the celery and carrot sticks and the Blue Cheese Dressing on the side.

Classic Shrimp Cocktail

Nothing is more basic than shrimp cocktail: boiled shrimp served cold with cocktail sauce, typically a blend of bottled ketchup or chili sauce spiked with horseradish. Can something so simple and good be improved upon? We thought so and set out to do just that.

The easiest way to intensify the flavor of shrimp is to cook them in their shells. But, as we found out, this method has its drawbacks. First of all, it's far easier to peel shrimp when they are raw than when they have been cooked in liquid. More important, however, the full flavor of the shells is not extracted during the relatively short time required for the shrimp to cook through. It takes a good 20 minutes for the shells to impart their flavor to the cooking water, and this is far too long to keep shrimp in a pot. Instead, we decided to make a shrimp stock by simply placing the shells in a pot with water to cover, then simmering them for 20 minutes.

Next, we thought it would be best to see what other ingredients would complement the flavor of the shrimp without overpowering it. After trying about 20 different combinations, we settled on a combination of white wine, lemon juice, and a more-or-less traditional combination of herbs—peppercorns, coriander, bay leaves, parsley, and tarragon.

Although we were pleased at this point with the quality of the shrimp's flavor, we thought it could be still more intense. We decided to try to keep the shrimp in contact with the flavorings for a longer period of time. What worked best, we found, was to bring the cooking liquid to a boil, turn off the heat, and add the shrimp. Depending on their size, we could leave them in the liquid for up to 10 minutes, during which time they would cook through without toughening, all the while taking on near-perfect flavor.

Improving traditional cocktail sauce proved to be a tricky business. Starting with fresh or canned tomatoes, we discovered, just didn't work. The result was often terrific (some might say preferable), but it was not cocktail sauce.

We decided to buy bottled ketchup and season it ourselves. Cocktail sauce benefits from a variety of heat sources, none of which should overpower the other and the sum of which should allow the flavor of the shrimp to come through. Horseradish is a must, and we also liked the addition of chili powder, cayenne, and black pepper, and some lemon juice for an acidic kick.

Finally, we decided to make a sauce variation with lime juice, hot chiles, and brown sugar—a good balance of sweet and spicy. Supplemented with garlic, ginger, and scallions, this sauce was a welcome (and potent) change from classic tomato-based cocktail sauce.

CLASSIC SHRIMP COCKTAIL

SERVES 4

The test kitchen prefers frozen shrimp—they are frozen soon after being caught, which preserves their fresh flavor, while "fresh" shrimp sold in the supermarkets often decline in flavor between the time they're caught and then shipped to market. Shrimp are sold by size as well as by the number needed to make a pound, usually given in a range (a pound of jumbo shrimp, for example, recommended in this recipe, usually consists of 16 to 20 shrimp and is referred to as 16/20 count). Choosing shrimp by the numerical rating is more accurate than choosing by size label—one store's large might be another's extra-large. When using larger or smaller shrimp, increase or decrease the cooking time by 1 to 2 minutes. To devein the shrimp, use a paring knife to make a shallow slit along the back of each shrimp. With the tip of the blade, lift up and loosen the vein and discard.

To thaw frozen shrimp quickly, place the shrimp in a salad spinner (without the top) and fill it with cold tap water. After a few minutes, lift the colander out of the bowl and empty the water. Your shrimp should be perfectly thawed.

1   **pound jumbo shrimp (16 to 20 per pound), peeled and deveined, shells reserved**

1   **teaspoon salt**

1   **cup dry white wine**

4   **whole black peppercorns**

5   **coriander seeds**

½   **bay leaf**

5   **sprigs fresh parsley**

1   **sprig fresh tarragon**

1   **teaspoon fresh lemon juice**

1. Bring the reserved shells, 3 cups water, and the salt to a boil in a medium saucepan over medium-high heat; reduce the heat to low, cover, and simmer until fragrant, about 20 minutes. Strain the stock through a sieve into a bowl, pressing on the shells to extract all the liquid.

2. Bring the stock and remaining ingredients except the shrimp to a boil in a 3- or 4-quart saucepan over high heat; boil 2 minutes. Turn off the heat and stir in the shrimp; cover and let stand until the shrimp are firm and pink, 8 to 10 minutes. Drain the shrimp, reserving the stock for another use. Plunge the shrimp into ice water to stop the cooking, then drain again. Serve the shrimp chilled with cocktail sauce (recipes follow).

CLASSIC COCKTAIL SAUCE

MAKES ABOUT 1 CUP,
ENOUGH FOR 1 POUND JUMBO SHRIMP

For maximum flavor, use horseradish from a newly bought jar and mild chili powder.

1   **cup ketchup**

2½   **teaspoons prepared horseradish**

¼   **teaspoon salt**

¼   **teaspoon pepper**

1   **teaspoon ancho or other mild chili powder**
      Pinch cayenne pepper

1   **tablespoon fresh lemon juice**

Stir all of the ingredients together in a small serving bowl; adjust the seasonings as desired.

SPICY CARIBBEAN-STYLE COCKTAIL SAUCE

MAKES ABOUT ½ CUP,
ENOUGH FOR 1 POUND JUMBO SHRIMP

This cocktail sauce is a sweet and spicy alternative to our classic version. Because this sauce is potent, less is needed to accompany the same amount of shrimp.

1   **garlic clove, minced to a paste with**
      ⅛ teaspoon salt

1½   **tablespoons minced fresh ginger**

2   **medium scallions, minced**

1   **large jalapeño chile, seeded and minced**

¼   **cup fresh lime juice (2 limes)**

¼   **cup packed light brown sugar**

Stir all of the ingredients together in a small serving bowl; adjust the seasonings as desired.

Bacon-Wrapped Shrimp

Bacon-wrapped shrimp are one of those cocktail party standbys that rarely make an appearance in today's trendy food magazines. And that's a shame, because it's such a simple (dare we say, elegant) dish and, most of all, downright tasty. The smoky flavor of the bacon is a rich complement to the briny flavor of the shellfish. Too often, though, this dish is marred by soggy, chewy bacon and rubbery, overcooked shrimp. We set out to find a never-fail recipe for this cocktail party classic.

In our testing, we learned that you don't want shrimp so small that the bacon acts as a blanket and completely overwhelms the flavor of the shrimp. We like extra-large shrimp for this dish. (Our variation substitutes large sea scallops for the shrimp.)

As for the bacon, we found that a whole slice was too much for one shrimp. Not only was the smoky flavor overwhelming, but it also turned the appetizer greasy. We found that cutting the bacon slices into smaller strips worked much better.

As for broiling, we found the shrimp cooked through before the bacon had time to brown and crisp. To jumpstart the bacon, we turned to the microwave. We simply placed the bacon pieces over four layers of paper towels on a microwave-safe plate, then covered them with two more layers of paper towels. After a few tries, we found that one to two minutes on high worked well. From there, it was a cinch to wrap the bacon around the shrimp and pop the whole ensemble under the broiler. One final, finishing touch was minced fresh chives, sprinkled on just before serving.

BROILED BACON-WRAPPED SHRIMP

MAKES 21 TO 25 PIECES

- 4   slices bacon
- 1   pound extra-large (21 to 25 per pound) shrimp, peeled and deveined
- ¼   teaspoon salt
- ⅛   teaspoon pepper
      Pinch cayenne pepper
- 2   tablespoons minced fresh chives

1. Adjust an oven rack 6 inches from the broiler element and heat the broiler. Line a broiler-pan bottom with foil and top with the slotted broiler-pan top.

2. Slice each piece of bacon lengthwise into two long, thin strips, then cut each strip into three short pieces (you should have a total of 24 bacon pieces). Spread the bacon pieces out over 4 layers of paper towels on a microwave-safe plate, then cover with 2 more layers of paper towels. Microwave on high until the bacon fat begins to melt but the bacon is still pliable, 1 to 2 minutes.

3. Meanwhile, place the shrimp in a medium bowl. Sprinkle the salt, pepper, and cayenne over the shrimp and toss to coat.

4. Wrap a piece of the microwaved bacon around the center of each shrimp, and place on the broiler-pan top, pinning the bacon ends underneath the shrimp. Broil until the shrimp are pink and the edges of the bacon are brown, rotating the broiler pan halfway through cooking, 3 to 4 minutes. Skewer the shrimp and bacon with toothpicks, transfer to a serving platter, and sprinkle with the chives. Serve immediately.

Variation
BROILED BACON-WRAPPED SEA SCALLOPS

When buying scallops, be sure to buy large sea scallops rather than the small bay scallops. Also make sure to remove and discard the crescent-shaped side muscle attached to each scallop before using; this tendon toughens when cooked. To remove it, simply peel it away.

Substitute 24 large sea scallops (about 1 pound) for the shrimp.

CHAPTER TWO

Salads and Dressings

SALADS AND DRESSINGS

Herb Vinaigrettes

Homemade vinaigrettes are simple to make, good to have on hand, and a darn sight better than bottled salad dressings. The problem with most herb vinaigrettes is that the subtle herb flavor can get lost behind strong vinegars, pungent mustards, and assertive olive oils. We set out to create herb-packed dressings that would be great on delicate greens yet also flavorful enough to spoon onto roasted meat or steamed fish for an added boost.

We began by making basic herb vinaigrettes with vegetable, canola, olive, and extra-virgin olive oils. Tasters much preferred the dressing made with regular olive oil; it added some flavor (more than the canola or vegetable oil did) without overpowering the herb character (like the extra-virgin olive oil did).

As for the mixing method, we tried whisking the oil and vinegar together in a bowl, shaking them in a jar, and emulsifying them in a blender. Tasters preferred the bolder herb flavor of the dressing made in the blender, as the pulverizing extracted more flavor from the fresh herbs. Looking for even more flavor, we tried bumping up the amount of herbs and adding them at different times during the blending—all to no avail.

Then a colleague suggested making homemade herb oil. At first this sounded like a tiresome project. But we found that gently heating some olive oil with a fresh herb created an infused oil that was loaded with flavor—and it took just 2 to 3 minutes. We turned off the heat, let the herbs steep for 5 minutes longer, and then proceeded to use this herb oil to make dressing. Tasters liked the addition of shallot, garlic, mustard, and more fresh herbs to create dressings with plenty of personality.

OREGANO–BLACK OLIVE VINAIGRETTE

MAKES 1 CUP

Don't add the olives to the blender; they will turn the dressing black.

- ¾   cup olive oil
- 2   tablespoons minced fresh oregano
- 1   shallot, peeled
- 1   garlic clove, peeled
- ¼   cup red wine vinegar
- ½   teaspoon salt
- ¼   teaspoon pepper
- 1   tablespoon Dijon mustard
- ¼   cup pitted kalamata olives, minced

1. Heat ¼ cup of the oil with 1 tablespoon of the oregano in a medium saucepan over medium heat until the oregano turns bright green and small bubbles appear, 2 to 3 minutes. Turn off the heat and steep 5 minutes.

2. Process the shallot, garlic, vinegar, salt, pepper, mustard, and remaining 1 tablespoon oregano in a blender until the garlic and shallot are finely chopped, about 15 seconds. With the blender running, slowly add the remaining ½ cup oil and steeped oregano oil and continue to process until the dressing is smooth and emulsified, about 15 seconds. Transfer to a bowl and stir in the olives. (The dressing can be refrigerated in an airtight container for up to 3 days.)

THYME-MUSTARD VINAIGRETTE

MAKES 1 CUP

Whole-grain mustard adds texture to this dressing, but you can use any mustard in its place.

- ¾   cup olive oil
- 2   tablespoons minced fresh thyme
- 1   shallot, peeled
- 1   garlic clove, peeled

¼ cup cider vinegar

½ teaspoon salt

¼ teaspoon pepper

2 tablespoons whole-grain mustard
   (see note above)

1. Heat ¼ cup of the oil with 1 tablespoon of the thyme in a medium saucepan over medium heat until the thyme turns bright green and small bubbles appear, 2 to 3 minutes. Turn off the heat and steep 5 minutes.

2. Process the shallot, garlic, vinegar, salt, pepper, mustard, and remaining 1 tablespoon thyme in a blender until the garlic and shallot are finely chopped, about 15 seconds. With the blender running, slowly add the remaining ½ cup oil and steeped thyme oil and continue to process until the dressing is smooth and emulsified, about 15 seconds. (The dressing can be refrigerated in an airtight container for up to 3 days.)

FRESH BASIL VINAIGRETTE

MAKES 1 CUP

Basil is not as potent as other herbs, so you need to use an entire bunch.

¾ cup olive oil

2 cups chopped fresh basil

1 shallot, peeled

1 garlic clove, peeled

¼ cup red wine vinegar

¼ cup water

½ teaspoon salt

¼ teaspoon pepper

2 teaspoons Dijon mustard

1. Heat ¼ cup of the oil with 1 cup of the basil in a medium saucepan over medium heat until the basil turns bright green and small bubbles appear, 2 to 3 minutes. Turn off the heat and steep 5 minutes.

SECRETS TO BIG HERB FLAVOR

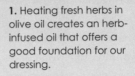

1. Heating fresh herbs in olive oil creates an herb-infused oil that offers a good foundation for our dressing.

2. Making the dressing in a blender (and adding more fresh herbs) extracts every bit of flavor from the herbs.

2. Process the shallot, garlic, vinegar, water, salt, pepper, and mustard in a blender until the garlic and shallot are finely chopped, about 15 seconds. With the blender running, slowly add the remaining ½ cup oil and steeped basil oil and continue to process until the dressing is smooth and emulsified, about 15 seconds. Pack the remaining 1 cup basil into the blender and process until the dressing is smooth, about 15 seconds. (The dressing can be refrigerated in an airtight container for up to 3 days.)

Italian Dressing Mix

There is something to be said for the convenience of shelf-stable dried salad dressing mixes: just add oil, vinegar, and water; shake; and serve. But most mixes are sugary sweet and taste stale. We wanted to create a dressing mix that had fresher herb flavor, and enough thickness to cling to a salad.

We found several recipes that attempted to re-create supermarket dressing mixes using similar ingredients: sugar, dehydrated onion and garlic, and myriad dried herbs. After assembling our own variations on this theme, we quickly realized that we didn't have to empty the spice rack to achieve big flavor. In addition to the onion and garlic, all we needed were a little dried oregano and dried basil, plus red pepper flakes for heat and color. Rehydrating the onion, garlic, and herbs in water and vinegar in the microwave bloomed their flavors and also enhanced the vinegar, which made for a richer dressing.

Lemon juice added sparkle to the dressing, and a bit of sugar balanced the acidity. But we don't always have a fresh lemon on hand. A colleague suggested replacing the sugar and lemon with powdered lemonade mix—and to our surprise, it added just the right amount of sweetness and acidity.

The last problem was textural: we wanted the dressing to be thick and emulsified. Common emulsifiers like mustard powder and cornstarch didn't work, but pectin (a fruit-based thickener commonly used in jams and jellies) bulked the dressing up perfectly. We finally had a convenient salad dressing mix with a lively herb flavor that was ready at a moment's notice.

ITALIAN DRESSING MIX

MAKES 1 CUP OF MIX, ENOUGH FOR
ABOUT 10 BATCHES OF DRESSING

Each batch of dressing makes about ½ cup, enough to dress 4 quarts of salad greens and serve 6 to 8 people. Leftover dressing can be refrigerated for up to 3 days.

¼	cup powdered lemonade mix
3	tablespoons dehydrated minced onion
3	tablespoons dehydrated minced garlic
3	tablespoons pectin (Sure-Jell)
1	tablespoon dried oregano
2	teaspoons dried basil
1	teaspoon red pepper flakes
1	tablespoon salt

1. TO MAKE THE MIX: Whisk all of the ingredients in a bowl until well combined. Store in an airtight container for up to 3 months.

2. TO MAKE THE DRESSING: Whisk 1½ tablespoons of the mix, 2 tablespoons red wine vinegar, and 1 tablespoon water in a bowl. Cover with plastic wrap and microwave until the garlic and onion are just softened, about 15 seconds. Cool to room temperature, then slowly whisk in 6 tablespoons olive oil.

Ranch Dressing

Ranch dressing was made famous in the 1950s at the Hidden Valley Guest Ranch in Santa Barbara, California. The recipe was so popular that it was bought and marketed by a large corporation, which proceeded to introduce the herbed buttermilk dressing to the rest of the country in both powdered and bottled form. Although the stuff made from a powdered mix or picked up in a bottle at the supermarket is still what many of us think of as ranch dressing, it doesn't compare with freshly made.

Most recipes call for buttermilk, thickened with either mayonnaise or sour cream, along with an array of herbs and seasonings. We tried to follow a strictly buttermilk-mayonnaise or buttermilk–sour cream path but found that neither sufficed. Mayonnaise gave the dressing a nice, round sweetness, but sour cream was a good thickener and also added tartness to the buttermilk—too much tartness when used alone with the buttermilk. By using all three ingredients, however, we gave the dressing a nice balance of flavors and a pleasing consistency.

To season this buttermilk base, we tried a number of ingredients called for in other recipes, including Worcestershire sauce, Dijon mustard, lime juice, red wine vinegar, celery seed, and a host of dried herbs. In the end, we found that fresh herbs and seasonings were the keys to a bright, authentic flavor. Fresh parsley and cilantro accented by scallion, shallot, and garlic were the Southern California flavors we were looking for. We found it best to mash the garlic into a paste, allowing the garlic flavor to blend quickly and smoothly with the other ingredients. We added minced red pepper for crunch and color and lemon juice to brighten all the flavors.

We found that this dressing worked best over sturdy greens such as romaine, iceberg, and green leaf lettuce or spinach. Softer lettuces, such as Boston or Bibb, wilted quickly under the weight of this creamy mixture. Several tasters liked the way the tartness of the buttermilk accented the bitterness of greens such as arugula and radicchio.

RANCH DRESSING

MAKES ABOUT ¾ CUP

Sturdy greens such as romaine and iceberg lettuce are ideal partners with this thick dressing.

½	garlic clove, peeled
¼	teaspoon salt
¼	small red bell pepper, minced
1	medium scallion, minced
1	small shallot, minced
1½	teaspoons minced fresh parsley
½	teaspoon minced fresh cilantro
½	teaspoon fresh lemon juice
	Pinch pepper
¼	cup buttermilk
¼	cup mayonnaise
2	tablespoons sour cream

1. Roughly chop the garlic, then sprinkle it with the salt. With a chef's knife, mash the mixture to a smooth paste.

2. Mix the garlic paste, bell pepper, scallion, shallot, parsley, cilantro, lemon juice, and pepper together in a medium bowl. Add the buttermilk, mayonnaise, and sour cream and whisk until smooth. (The dressing can be refrigerated in an airtight container for up to 4 days.)

Blue Cheese Dressing

Blue cheese dressing is not only excellent tossed with greens; it is a classic accompaniment (with carrot and celery sticks) to Buffalo Wings (page 21). But some blue cheese dressings can be overpowering—either from the blue cheese itself or from a seasoning, such as garlic. We aimed to develop a cool and creamy blue cheese dressing with balanced flavors.

We tested a variety of blue cheeses, from the stinkiest French-style varieties to those found domestically. Tasters gave their thumbs up to mild blue cheeses—several domestic cheeses fit that bill.

We combined the crumbled cheese with buttermilk and sour cream for tang and richness and with mayonnaise for creaminess. A little white wine vinegar brightened the flavors and a pinch of sugar brought everything together. We were almost there, but we got stopped in our tracks with the garlic. It overpowered the other flavors and tasted harsh. Although we normally stay away from garlic powder, here it blended well with the other ingredients and added a subtle background note rather than the assertive bite that we were getting with the fresh garlic.

BLUE CHEESE DRESSING

MAKES ABOUT 1½ CUPS

Use a mild blue cheese such as Danish blue or Stella blue cheese from Wisconsin. Both of these cheeses are widely available in supermarkets.

1	cup crumbled blue cheese
6	tablespoons buttermilk
6	tablespoons sour cream
4	tablespoons mayonnaise
4	teaspoons white wine vinegar
½	teaspoon sugar
¼	teaspoon garlic powder
	Salt and pepper

Mash the blue cheese and buttermilk in a small bowl with a fork until the mixture resembles cottage cheese with small curds. Stir in the sour cream, mayonnaise, vinegar, sugar, and garlic powder. Adjust seasoning with salt and pepper to taste. (The dressing can be refrigerated in an airtight container for up to 1 week.)

Green Goddess Dressing

Green goddess is a thick, creamy salad dressing made with mayonnaise and fresh herbs. Drizzled over a wedge of crisp lettuce, it offers a potent first taste of spring. This recipe first appeared in 1923 on the menu of San Francisco's Palace Hotel, created by the hotel chef in honor of British actor George Arliss, who was staying at the hotel while starring in a play titled *Green Goddess*.

Contemporary versions of this recipe are thick, more like mayonnaise than salad dressing. Tasters rejected them as well as versions made with avocado, an ingredient not found in the original recipe but now common. The avocado bullied the other flavors and turned the dressing into a dip.

Some recipes include a dairy ingredient to thin out the stiff mayonnaise. Milk and cream made the dressing too runny. Buttermilk reminded tasters of ranch dressing, and yogurt was much too tart. In the end, sour cream gave the dressing the proper texture and added a subtle tang.

As the name implies, "green goddess" contains multiple herbs, tarragon being the most prominent. To our amazement, the milder, mellower flavor of dried tarragon was preferable to the strong, grassy flavor of fresh. To help wake up the flavor of the dried tarragon, we found it best to soak it for 15 minutes; otherwise it was too tame. Tasters also liked fresh parsley and chives, a bit of lemon juice, garlic, and anchovies, which gave the dressing some kick.

Our dressing tasted great, but it wasn't really "green." We solved the problem by breaking with tradition. Rather than stirring the ingredients by hand, we used a blender, which broke down the herbs more thoroughly than a knife and turned the dressing bright green. After an hour in the refrigerator, where the flavors could meld, our version of this California classic was ready to pour over lettuce and become a smash hit.

GREEN GODDESS DRESSING

MAKES ABOUT 1¼ CUPS

To appreciate the full flavor of this rich dressing, drizzle it over chilled wedges of mild iceberg lettuce or leaves of romaine lettuce. A blender yields a brighter, slightly more flavorful dressing, but a food processor will work, too.

2	teaspoons dried tarragon
1	tablespoon fresh lemon juice
1	tablespoon water
¾	cup mayonnaise
¼	cup sour cream
¼	cup roughly chopped fresh parsley
1	medium garlic clove, chopped
1	anchovy fillet, rinsed and dried
¼	cup minced fresh chives
	Salt and pepper

1. Combine the tarragon, lemon juice, and water in a small bowl and let sit for 15 minutes.

2. Blend the tarragon mixture, mayonnaise, sour cream, parsley, garlic, and anchovy in a blender until smooth, scraping down sides as necessary. Transfer to a medium bowl, stir in the chives, and season with salt and pepper to taste. Chill until the flavors meld, about 1 hour. (The dressing can be refrigerated in an airtight container for up to 1 day.)

French Dressing

Before Julia Child taught us about real French cooking, generations of Americans grew up on a sweet-and-sour red dressing made with ketchup and oil. Despite its name, this French dressing has its roots in America. We did some sleuthing in old cookbooks, and the earliest recipe we could find dated back to 1930 and appeared in the *Heinz Book of Salads.* (Even then, food companies were developing recipes so consumers would use their products.) Hundreds of French dressing recipes filled cookbooks in the ensuing decades.

At their core, these recipes share a base of tomato (usually ketchup), vegetable oil, vinegar, and sugar. Most of the ones that we tried were too sweet and too bland. We decided to examine each ingredient to improve the overall flavor of this simple salad dressing.

We found recipes calling for everything from chili sauce to tomato paste. The version made with chili sauce tasted, not surprisingly, like chili sauce, and neither tomato juice (not tomato-y enough) nor tomato paste (too tomato-y) tasted right. Ketchup it was.

Ketchup is already sweet, so adding more sugar can be problematic. Many recipes have you add sugar by the cupful. We found that 2 tablespoons was plenty. The typical recipe also calls for distilled white vinegar, but we sought something more flavorful. Lemon juice made the dressing taste like a Bloody Mary—not bad served in a frosty glass, but less than ideal when tossed with greens. A batch made with cider vinegar had a distinctive apple flavor that tasters either loved or hated. White wine vinegar, which provided fruitiness with a kick, was the favorite.

We wanted to keep prep work to a minimum, but grated onion, an ingredient in several older recipes we found, added a sweet, sharp depth. A little Tabasco Sauce perked up the other flavors. Although these changes are fairly simple, they yield a dressing with more personality than anything you can buy.

ALL-AMERICAN FRENCH DRESSING
MAKES 1 CUP

Odds are that you have everything you need in the pantry to make this quick and easy salad dressing. Use the large holes of a box grater to grate the onion, and remember that a little bit of grated onion goes a long way. This dressing is traditionally served with iceberg or other mild lettuces such as green leaf, red leaf, romaine, Boston, or Bibb. We think its sweet-and-sour punch also works well with bitter greens, such as Belgian endive, radicchio, and watercress.

½	cup ketchup
½	cup vegetable or canola oil
¼	cup white wine vinegar or distilled white vinegar
2	tablespoons sugar
1	teaspoon grated onion
¼	teaspoon hot sauce (or more to taste)

Add all of the ingredients to a lidded container and shake vigorously until combined. (The dressing can be refrigerated in an airtight container for up to 1 week.)

Variation
CREAMY FRENCH DRESSING
MAKES ABOUT 1¼ CUPS

Mayonnaise tones down the kick of the vinegar and makes this creamy orange dressing more kid friendly.

1	cup All-American French Dressing
¼	cup mayonnaise

Whisk the dressing and mayonnaise together in a bowl until smooth. (The dressing can be refrigerated in an airtight container for up to 1 week.)

Washing Greens 101: Simply rinsing greens under running water doesn't always remove the dirt that collects in crevices and folds. That's why we use a salad spinner for both washing and drying salad greens. Place the greens in a salad spinner, with the basket in its bowl. Fill the bowl with water, swirl the greens, and then lift the basket out of the bowl, leaving the sediment behind. If your greens are especially dirty, do this several times. Be sure to rinse the bowl before returning the basket to spin the greens dry. After spinning, we like to blot the greens dry with paper towels because we have found that even the best salad spinners don't dry greens completely. If you don't plan on using the greens immediately, you can refrigerate them in the spinner bowl with the lid firmly in place for several days.

Waldorf Salad

Waldorf salad was created by Oscar Tschirky, maître d'hôtel at the Waldorf-Astoria Hotel in New York. Although the original salad (which dates back to 1896) contained only tart apples and crisp celery bound with a little mayonnaise, walnuts and raisins were added to the mix in subsequent years. In recent decades, recipe writers have tried to "update" Waldorf salad by adding everything from oranges and marshmallows to Cajun spices and whipped cream. After making several of these concoctions, tasters unanimously preferred this crisp, clean salad in its original form, with only walnuts and raisins added to the apples and celery.

Because this simple salad calls for only a few ingredients, it is important that each be fresh and thoughtfully prepared. To start, we found the apples tasted better when they were peeled. Granny Smiths are traditional in this salad, and we liked the crispness and tartness they brought to the dish. Instead of mincing the celery into tiny bits, as if it were a

garnish, we sliced it into substantially sized, attractive half-moon shapes, which made the salad taste more balanced.

Toasting the walnuts is also essential for best flavor. Tossing the apples, celery, walnuts, and raisins with mayonnaise yielded a slightly one-dimensional, flat-tasting salad. We found that seasoning the salad ingredients with salt, pepper, and lemon juice before adding the mayonnaise made everything taste brighter. The only liberty we took in updating this recipe was to add a little tarragon, which gave a pleasant herbal, anise flavor to this simple salad.

WALDORF SALAD

SERVES 4

This salad can be served over a bed of greens as a light main course for lunch or in place of coleslaw as a side dish to sandwiches and grilled foods.

¼	cup walnuts
2	medium Granny Smith apples, peeled, cored, and cut into ½-inch dice (about 2½ cups)
4	celery ribs, peeled and cut crosswise into ¼-inch pieces (about 2½ cups)
⅓	cup raisins
1	tablespoon fresh lemon juice
1	teaspoon chopped fresh tarragon
¼	teaspoon salt
	Pinch pepper
⅓	cup mayonnaise

1. Toast the walnuts in a dry skillet over medium heat, stirring frequently, until fragrant, 4 to 5 minutes. Cool the walnuts and then roughly chop them into ⅓-inch pieces.

2. Toss the chopped walnuts, apples, celery, and raisins together in a medium bowl. Season with the lemon juice, tarragon, salt, and pepper and toss again. Stir in the mayonnaise and serve immediately.

Caesar Salad

Dumping a potent mixture of anchovies, garlic, and Worcestershire sauce over romaine lettuce doesn't sound appealing, but those ingredients (along with raw egg, olive oil, lemon juice, mustard, croutons, and Parmesan cheese) are the foundation of Caesar salad. In most Caesar recipes the forceful flavors run out of control, resulting in a dressing that tastes fishy, too garlicky, or just plain sour. Good Caesar dressing demands a delicate balance of these strongly flavored ingredients.

Traditional Caesars are thickened with an emulsion of raw egg and oil; for food safety reasons, we wanted to find a replacement for the egg. Mayonnaise, which is made from eggs and oil and comes already emulsified, was the obvious choice, and it worked perfectly when thinned with olive oil. Extra-virgin olive oil was too strong; tasters preferred the milder flavor of regular olive oil.

To keep the flavors in balance, we decreased the lemon juice from the ¼ cup called for in most recipes to 1 tablespoon. When fortified with 1 tablespoon each of white wine vinegar, Worcestershire sauce, and Dijon mustard, the dressing had the right balance of acidity and pungency. A mere two anchovies (some recipes use up to five) provided a welcome depth and complexity. And mixing everything together in a blender ensured a stable dressing that didn't separate.

We had one last ingredient to deal with: garlic. Most Caesar recipes go way overboard. We used just one raw garlic clove in the dressing to keep its sharpness at bay, but we added another layer of mellow garlic flavor by tossing cubes of fresh bread with garlic oil and baking them to make croutons. Parmesan cheese in both the dressing and the finished salad provided a classic touch. Tasters agreed that this was a Caesar truly worth hailing.

CAESAR SALAD

SERVES 6 TO 8

Two 10-ounce bags of chopped romaine lettuce can be substituted for the hearts. The croutons and dressing can be made up to 2 days in advance. Store the croutons at room temperature and refrigerate the dressing.

- ½   cup olive oil
- 2   garlic cloves, minced
- 1   (12-inch) piece French baguette, cut into ½-inch cubes (about 4 cups)
    Salt and pepper
- ½   cup mayonnaise
- ¼   cup finely grated Parmesan cheese, plus 1 cup shredded
- 2   anchovy fillets, rinsed and patted dry
- 1   tablespoon fresh lemon juice
- 1   tablespoon white wine vinegar
- 1   tablespoon Worcestershire sauce
- 1   tablespoon Dijon mustard
- 3   romaine lettuce hearts, torn into bite-sized pieces (about 12 cups; see note above)

1. Adjust an oven rack to the middle position and heat the oven to 350 degrees. Whisk the oil and garlic in a large bowl. Reserve half of the oil mixture. Toss the bread cubes with the remaining oil mixture and season with salt and pepper. Bake the croutons on a rimmed baking sheet until golden, about 20 minutes. Cool completely.

2. Process the mayonnaise, grated Parmesan, anchovies, lemon juice, vinegar, Worcestershire, mustard, ½ teaspoon salt, and ½ teaspoon pepper in a blender until smooth. With the blender running, slowly add the reserved oil mixture until incorporated.

3. Toss the romaine, shredded Parmesan, and dressing in a large bowl. Toss in the croutons and serve.

Spinach Salad with Hot Bacon Dressing

In the salad world, not much satisfies like a wilted spinach salad—a hearty mix of earthy spinach, warm, bacon-enriched dressing, and creamy hard-boiled eggs—but most recipes turn out salads that are not only lifeless and limp but overdressed and greasy as well.

The theory behind a wilted spinach salad is simple: the hot bacon dressing wilts the tough spinach leaves to an even tenderness. In practice, however, pouring hot dressing over spinach reduces some of the leaves to overcooked mush, while others remain raw. This is particularly true when using delicate baby spinach (as most modern recipes do), which wilts if you look at it crossly. The classic version of this salad relies on hearty, mature spinach (the kind with the curly leaves), which is much more forgiving. In fact, these leaves stand their ground to a fault—when doused with the hot vinaigrette, they wilt a bit, but not enough to become completely tender.

To help mature curly spinach wilt, most recipes take the low road and just increase the amount of dressing, which results in a sloppy pile of spinach swimming in a puddle of vinegar and bacon fat. We wondered if adding a bit of heft to the dressing (rather than increasing the volume) might weigh the spinach down and help it wilt.

Tasters liked a dressing with equal parts bacon drippings and cider vinegar. (We were surprised how much vinegar was needed to counter the richness of the bacon and eggs.) To add some heft, we sautéed red onion in the bacon drippings and added a dollop of Dijon mustard for heat and pungency. But even with the weight of additional ingredients, the spinach was still slightly underwilted. To achieve the ideal texture, a colleague suggested partially cooking the spinach before tossing it with the hot dressing.

The microwave proved utterly disastrous, leaving us with rubbery, soggy spinach even before the dressing entered the equation. The sauté method was hard to manage and really clumsy. (Try fitting a whole bag of spinach in a 12-inch skillet.) Ultimately, steaming proved to be the ticket.

Trading our skillet for a Dutch oven, we rendered the bacon, added the remaining dressing ingredients, took the pan off the heat, topped it all with the spinach, and put the lid on the pot. After only 15 seconds, we turned out the salad, dressing and all, into a mixing bowl for a quick toss. The steamy heat in the easy-to-handle Dutch oven had produced a perfect, evenly wilted salad. And with just a few wedges of hard-boiled egg, we finally had a wilted spinach salad that was worthy of its reputation.

SPINACH SALAD WITH HOT BACON DRESSING

SERVES 4 TO 6

Although most bagged spinach is supposedly washed before bagging, we have often found that some leaves remain gritty. Give the leaves a quick rinse and then dry them in a salad spinner before preparing the recipe. See page 16 for instructions on how to hard-boil eggs.

8	slices thick-cut bacon, halved lengthwise and cut crosswise into ½-inch pieces
1	(10-ounce) bag curly-leaf spinach, stemmed and torn into bite-sized pieces
½	red onion, sliced thin
2	garlic cloves, minced
½	teaspoon salt
½	teaspoon pepper
2	teaspoons sugar
¼	cup cider vinegar
1	tablespoon Dijon mustard
3	hard-boiled eggs, peeled and quartered (optional; see note above)

1. Fry the bacon in a Dutch oven over medium-high heat until crisp, about 7 minutes. Using a slotted spoon, transfer the bacon to a paper towel–lined plate and pour off all but ¼ cup of the bacon fat. Place the spinach in a large bowl next to the stove.

2. Return the pot to medium-high heat and cook the onion, garlic, salt, pepper, and sugar until the onion is softened, about 3 minutes. Working quickly, add the vinegar and mustard and scrape the bottom of the pot with a wooden spoon to loosen the browned bits. Remove the pot from the heat, add the spinach, and cover, allowing the spinach to steam until just beginning to wilt, about 15 seconds.

3. Transfer the steamed spinach and hot dressing to an empty bowl and toss lightly with tongs. Divide the salad among individual plates and garnish with the reserved bacon and eggs (if using). Serve.

Chopped Salad

This classic ladies' lunch dish, which had its heyday during the 1950s, was designed to be easy to eat using only a fork while balancing the plate on top of your knees. All the components of the salad are chopped into bite-sized pieces and lightly dressed with oil and vinegar.

There's still much to love about this recipe. When correctly made, this salad combines lettuces and vegetables in a pleasing fashion and offers a range of textures, colors, and flavors. Many recipes for chopped salad call for numerous and lavish vegetable garnishes, but we found that simpler, more modern salads made with only a few fresh vegetables—cucumber, bell pepper, and radish, as well as tomato—and mild greens tasted best. Although these salads may be simple, we found that a couple of key points distinguish mediocre versions from truly stellar ones.

First, we found that the vegetables should be cut into pieces of similar size. Small pieces (cherry tomatoes cut in half, cucumber and bell pepper cut into

¼-inch dice) are just right. Although this entails slightly more work and attention than rough chopping, the results are worth the extra effort. As for the greens, we found that romaine, Boston, Bibb, green leaf, and red leaf lettuces were easy to cut into forkable bites and paired well with the vegetables. Tasters did not like spicy greens in this salad. Better to let the tomatoes, cucumbers, and other additions contribute contrasting flavors; our tasters liked mild greens in the background. Finally, it's imperative to use a light hand with the dressing. In too many recipes the lettuces and vegetables are doused in dressing, and the resulting salad is limp and heavy.

As for the dressing, we found a light lemon vinaigrette with some fresh herbs set off the fresh vegetables and lettuces best. Heavier dressings made with sour cream or mayonnaise physically swamped the small pieces of vegetable, and more potent vinaigrettes, made with balsamic or red wine vinegar, were overpowering. We also discovered that a little sugar in the vinaigrette helped boost the flavors of the vegetables, making the overall salad much livelier.

When serving the chopped salad, we preferred to use the lettuce as a base for the chopped vegetables. Wanting all the components to be properly dressed, we used half of the vinaigrette to dress the greens and the other half to dress the collective garnishes. This two-step dressing process ensures that everything is properly coated and also allows the salad to be plated in the most attractive fashion.

CHOPPED SALAD

SERVES 4 TO 6

This basic recipe can be altered depending on the vegetables you have on hand. See the variations for some ideas.

LEMON-HERB VINAIGRETTE

¼	cup olive oil
1	tablespoon fresh lemon juice
2	teaspoons Dijon mustard
½	shallot, minced

1	teaspoon minced fresh parsley
1	teaspoon minced fresh chives
1	teaspoon minced fresh thyme
¼	teaspoon salt
⅛	teaspoon pepper
⅛	teaspoon sugar

SALAD

8	cups mild salad greens (such as romaine, Boston, Bibb, green leaf, or red leaf lettuce), cut into 1-inch pieces
½	pint cherry tomatoes, halved
1	small cucumber, peeled, seeded, and cut into ¼-inch dice
1	small yellow bell pepper, seeded and cut into ¼-inch dice
5	medium radishes, stems trimmed, cut in half lengthwise, then sliced thin into half-moons

1. FOR THE DRESSING: Whisk all of the ingredients together in a small bowl and set aside.

2. FOR THE SALAD: Toss the salad greens with half the dressing in a medium bowl. Mix the tomatoes, cucumber, bell pepper, and radishes together in another medium bowl and toss with the remaining dressing.

3. Arrange the salad greens on a serving platter or on individual plates. Spoon the chopped vegetables over the greens and serve immediately.

Variations

CHOPPED SALAD WITH FENNEL, GREEN APPLE, AND RADISHES

Omit the mustard and thyme from the dressing. For the salad, replace the tomatoes, cucumber, and bell pepper with 2 medium Granny Smith apples, peeled, cored, and cut into ¼-inch dice, and 1 small fennel bulb, tops trimmed, cored, and cut into ¼-inch dice.

PREPARING FENNEL

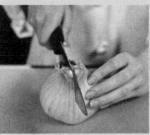 

1. Trim the feathery fronds and stems. Trim a thin slice from the base and remove any blemished outer layers. Cut the bulb in half lengthwise through the base.

2. Cut out the pyramid-shaped core from each half. Lay the cored fennel on a work surface and cut in half crosswise. Cut the fennel into ¼-inch strips and then into ¼-inch dice.

CHOPPED SALAD WITH AVOCADO, JICAMA, AND CUCUMBER

Replace the lemon juice in the dressing with lime juice, omitting the mustard and replacing the parsley, chives, and thyme with 1 tablespoon minced fresh cilantro. For the salad, replace the tomatoes, bell pepper, and radishes with ½ medium jicama, peeled and cut into ¼-inch dice, and 1 medium avocado, pitted, skinned, and cut into ¼-inch dice.

Cobb Salad

This salad originated in Hollywood in 1926 at the Brown Derby, a local restaurant where the stars of the day were known to dine. As the story goes, Bob Cobb, owner of the Brown Derby, made this salad late one night from a bunch of leftovers in the refrigerator and some freshly crisped bacon swiped from a busy chef. The classic version of this main-course salad features chicken, avocado, tomatoes, blue cheese, bacon, and plenty of salad greens.

Since its invention many years ago, Cobb salad

has been reproduced and replicated all over the country, with many versions straying far from the original recipe. After tracking down and testing the original version, we found little to change except a few measurements.

The original recipe calls for several types of salad greens. We decided to group the greens into mild and spicy categories, leaving the exact mixture (and shopping list) up to you. In case you don't have leftover chicken in your refrigerator, we found it easiest to broil boneless, skinless chicken breasts. Although other cuts of chicken tasted fine, the boneless breasts were easy to cut into attractive slices without having to maneuver around any bones. The fact that they were boneless also allowed them to cook more quickly under the broiler. By brining the chicken (soaking it in a salty, slightly sweet solution) for about 30 minutes, we were able to ensure that the chicken would remain moist, tender, and flavorful even when chilled.

As for the dressing, the original Cobb salad called for oil, Worcestershire sauce, red wine vinegar, lemon juice, and Dijon mustard. This combination of ingredients may sound odd, but tasters really liked its unique flavor. Not needing to change this authentic dressing too much, we simply altered the ratio of oil to vinegar to 4 to 1, which gave it a more balanced flavor. We found it best to dress the individual components in this composed salad separately, before arranging them on a single platter or individual plates. This method ensured that every element in the salad was seasoned properly and allowed us to assemble the salad in a most attractive fashion. The wedges of hard-boiled egg are the exception to this rule; they are likely to break apart when tossed with vinaigrette. We found it best to arrange the egg wedges (as well as the slices of chicken) over the salad greens and then drizzle some dressing right over them.

COBB SALAD

SERVES 6

If you have 4 cups of leftover chicken on hand, you can omit steps 1 through 3. See page 16 for instructions on how to hard-boil eggs.

CHICKEN
- 2 tablespoons salt
- ½ cup sugar
- 3 boneless, skinless chicken breast halves (about 1 pound), trimmed, tenderloins removed and reserved for another purpose
  Vegetable oil spray

DRESSING
- ½ teaspoon Dijon mustard
- 1 teaspoon fresh lemon juice
- ½ teaspoon Worcestershire sauce
- 1 small garlic clove, minced to a paste
- 2 tablespoons red wine vinegar
- ½ cup olive oil
- ¼ teaspoon sugar
- ¼ teaspoon salt
  Pinch pepper

SALAD
- 8 cups mild salad greens (romaine, Boston, Bibb, and/or iceberg lettuce)
- 4 cups spicy salad greens (curly endive, watercress, and/or arugula)
- 2 hard-boiled eggs (see note above), each sliced into eight ⅓-inch wedges
- 2 avocados, pitted, skinned, and cut into ⅓-inch slices
- 2 medium tomatoes, cored and cut into ¼-inch wedges
- 6 slices bacon, fried until crisp and crumbled
- 1 tablespoon minced fresh chives
- ½ cup crumbled Roquefort cheese

1. FOR THE CHICKEN: Dissolve the salt and sugar in 1 quart of cool water in a gallon-sized zipper-lock plastic bag or plastic container. Submerge the chicken in the salt solution and refrigerate for 30 minutes.

2. Adjust an oven rack so it is 6 inches away from the broiler element. Remove the chicken from the brine and dry thoroughly with paper towels. Coat the broiler-pan top with the vegetable oil spray and lay the chicken breasts on top. Place the broiler-pan top over the broiler-pan bottom and place under the broiler. Broil the chicken until lightly browned, 3½ to 4 minutes. Flip the chicken over and broil until cooked fully, 3½ to 4 minutes longer.

3. Place the chicken on a clean plate and cover with plastic wrap. Poke a few vent holes in the plastic wrap and refrigerate the chicken while preparing the other salad ingredients.

4. FOR THE DRESSING: Whisk all of the ingredients together in a small bowl and set aside.

5. TO ASSEMBLE THE SALAD: Slice the chicken on the bias into ¼-inch pieces. Toss the mild and spicy salad greens with ⅓ cup of the dressing in a large bowl. Arrange the dressed salad greens on a large serving platter or on individual plates. Arrange the chicken slices and wedges of hard-boiled egg over the salad greens and drizzle with 2 tablespoons of the dressing. Toss the avocados and tomatoes with the remaining dressing in a medium bowl. Arrange the pieces of avocado and tomato over the salad. Sprinkle the bacon, chives, and cheese over the salad and serve immediately.

Shrimp Salad

Maybe it's a good thing that most shrimp salads are drowning in a sea of gloppy mayonnaise. The dressing might be bland, but at least it helps camouflage the sorry state of the rubbery, flavorless boiled shrimp. We wanted to find a cooking technique that would deliver perfectly cooked shrimp without the extra work of grilling, roasting, or sautéing. And was it too much to ask that the shrimp have some flavor of their own?

To begin, we rounded up some creamy-style shrimp salad recipes. Most call for boiling a flavorful liquid of white wine, lemon juice, herbs, spices, and water (called a court-bouillon by the French). After the shrimp are submerged into this hot liquid, the pot is removed from the heat and covered for about 10 minutes. Many of the recipes call for quickly shocking the shrimp in an ice bath to prevent overcooking. Although they looked perfect, shrimp prepared this way were in fact flavorless and tough. Reducing the time the shrimp spent in the liquid did make them more tender, but it did nothing to improve their flavor.

But we had a trick up our sleeves: a technique practiced in the 1970s by the French chef Michel Guérard. He poached proteins by starting them in cold liquid. The cold proteins and broth heat simultaneously, unlike the traditional poaching technique in which the shrimp proteins immediately turn opaque (and rubbery) upon submersion in hot water. In this way the shrimp would better absorb flavors from the poaching liquid—a kind of turbo-charged flavor injection.

In the test kitchen we took the court-bouillon ingredients—leaving out the white wine, which tasters found overwhelming—and added the shrimp. We then heated the liquid to various temperatures: too low and the shrimp were mushy; too high and they turned tough. Eventually, we discovered that heating the liquid to a near simmer (165 degrees) was ideal. The shrimp were actually flavorful, and their texture was so firm and crisp that several tasters compared them to lobster.

All we needed now was the perfect deli-style dressing. Mayonnaise provides creamy cohesiveness, but we didn't want it to mask the shrimp's flavor or drown out the other ingredients. After testing several amounts, tasters felt a perfect coating was ¼ cup per 1 pound of shrimp. Minced celery, minced shallot, chopped herbs, and fresh lemon juice added unifying aromatic and herbal notes and a pleasant vegetal crunch and acidity. With less mayonnaise, we found we could also add variety to the salads with bolder flavors like chipotle chile, orange, and roasted red pepper.

SHRIMP SALAD

SERVES 4

This recipe can also be prepared with large shrimp (31 to 40 per pound); the cooking time will be 1 to 2 minutes less. The shrimp can be cooked up to 24 hours in advance, but hold off on dressing the salad until ready to serve. The recipe can be easily doubled; cook the shrimp in a 7-quart Dutch oven and increase the cooking time to 12 to 14 minutes. Serve the salad on a bed of greens or on a buttered and grilled bun.

1	pound extra-large shrimp (21 to 25 per pound), peeled and deveined (see note above)
¼	cup plus 1 tablespoon fresh lemon juice (2 to 3 lemons), spent halves reserved
5	sprigs plus 1 teaspoon minced fresh parsley
3	sprigs plus 1 teaspoon minced fresh tarragon
1	teaspoon whole black peppercorns plus pepper
1	tablespoon sugar Salt
¼	cup mayonnaise
1	shallot, minced
1	small celery rib, minced

1. Combine the shrimp, ¼ cup of the lemon juice, the reserved lemon halves, parsley sprigs, tarragon sprigs, whole peppercorns, sugar, and 1 teaspoon salt with 2 cups cold water in a medium saucepan. Place the saucepan over medium heat and cook the shrimp, stirring several times, until pink, firm to the touch, and the centers are no longer translucent, 8 to 10 minutes (the water should be just bubbling around the edge of the pan and register 165 degrees on an instant-read thermometer). Remove the pan from the heat, cover, and let the shrimp sit in the broth for 2 minutes.

2. Meanwhile, fill a medium bowl with ice water. Drain the shrimp into a colander, and discard the lemon halves, herbs, and spices. Immediately transfer the shrimp to the ice water to stop cooking and chill thoroughly, about 3 minutes. Remove the shrimp from the ice water and pat dry with paper towels.

3. Whisk together the mayonnaise, shallot, celery, remaining 1 tablespoon lemon juice, minced parsley, and minced tarragon in a medium bowl. Cut the shrimp in half lengthwise and then each half into thirds; add the shrimp to the mayonnaise mixture and toss to combine. Adjust the seasoning with salt and pepper to taste and serve.

Variations

SHRIMP SALAD WITH ROASTED RED PEPPER AND BASIL

This Italian-style variation is especially good served over bitter greens.

Omit the tarragon sprigs from the cooking liquid. Replace the minced parsley, minced tarragon, and celery with ⅓ cup thinly sliced jarred roasted red peppers, 2 teaspoons rinsed capers, and 3 tablespoons chopped fresh basil leaves.

SHRIMP SALAD WITH AVOCADO AND ORANGE

Avocado and orange are a refreshing addition to this salad.

Omit the tarragon sprigs from the cooking liquid. Replace the minced parsley, minced tarragon, and celery with 4 halved and thinly sliced radishes; 1 large orange, peeled and cut into ½-inch pieces; ½ ripe avocado, cut into ½-inch pieces; and 2 teaspoons minced fresh mint leaves.

SPICY SHRIMP SALAD WITH CORN AND CHIPOTLE

Chipotle gives this salad a spicy kick; use less if you prefer milder heat.

Substitute the juice from 3 to 4 limes for the lemon juice (use the spent halves in the cooking liquid) and omit the tarragon sprigs from the cooking liquid. Replace the minced parsley, minced tarragon, and celery with ½ cup cooked corn kernels, 2 minced canned chipotle chiles in adobo (about 2 tablespoons), and 1 tablespoon minced fresh cilantro leaves.

Marinated Tomato Salad

A great summer tomato is best modestly dressed —salt, pepper, a good quality olive oil, and nothing more. But most tomatoes, even in summer, need some help to become an inspired salad. Rather than mask the tomatoes' flavor by piling on the ingredients, we wanted to improve it.

Marinating sliced tomatoes in a lively vinaigrette sounds like a great idea—until the salt in the dressing coaxes liquid out of the tomatoes and waters down the salad. We wanted to create flavorful tomato salads with dressings that would enhance—not drown out—the tomatoes.

The logical first step was to try to rid the tomatoes of some of their excess moisture before adding the dressing. We sliced the tomatoes into wedges and, following test kitchen protocol, salted them and placed them on paper towels to drain. After 15 minutes, the tomatoes had purged some of their liquid and were ready to absorb a bold dressing of olive oil, vinegar, garlic, and black pepper. After letting the tomatoes sit in the vinaigrette for another 15 minutes, they were bursting with flavor, and the texture of the salad was uncompromised by excess moisture.

To complement the tomatoes, we added small amounts of potent ingredients such as arugula, fennel, jalapeño, and olives. Soft cheeses, white beans, and avocado added creamy counterpoints. Fresh herbs completed the transformation of the tomatoes from ho-hum to first-rate.

MARINATED TOMATO SALAD WITH ARUGULA AND GOAT CHEESE

SERVES 4

To make crumbling the goat cheese less messy, first let the cheese firm up in the freezer for 15 minutes.

1½	pounds ripe tomatoes, cored and sliced into ½-inch wedges
½	teaspoon salt
2	cups baby arugula
2	tablespoons extra-virgin olive oil
1	tablespoon red wine vinegar
1	garlic clove, minced
½	teaspoon pepper
¼	cup chopped fresh basil
¼	cup crumbled goat cheese (see note above)

1. Toss the tomatoes and salt in a large bowl, then transfer them to a paper towel–lined baking sheet; let drain for 15 minutes.

2. Return the drained tomatoes to the bowl and toss with the arugula, oil, vinegar, garlic, pepper, and basil. Let marinate for 15 minutes. Sprinkle the cheese over the salad. Serve.

MARINATED TOMATO SALAD WITH FENNEL AND BLUE CHEESE

SERVES 4

We prefer mildly flavored, crumbly blue cheeses in this recipe. Stella brand blue cheese is the test kitchen's favorite supermarket blue cheese.

1½	pounds ripe tomatoes, cored and sliced into ½-inch wedges
½	fennel bulb, cored and sliced thin
½	teaspoon salt
2	tablespoons extra-virgin olive oil
1	tablespoon white wine vinegar
1	garlic clove, minced
½	teaspoon pepper
¼	cup chopped fresh tarragon
¼	cup crumbled blue cheese (see note above)

1. Toss the tomatoes, fennel, and salt in a large bowl, then transfer to a paper towel–lined baking sheet; let drain for 15 minutes.

2. Return the drained tomatoes and fennel to the bowl and toss with the oil, vinegar, garlic, pepper, and tarragon. Let marinate for 15 minutes. Sprinkle the cheese over the salad. Serve.

MARINATED TOMATO SALAD WITH OLIVES AND WHITE BEANS

SERVES 4

Cannellini beans are white Italian kidney beans. If you can't find them, great Northern beans or navy beans can be substituted. Toast the pine nuts in a dry skillet over medium heat, shaking often, until golden brown, about 5 minutes.

1½	pounds ripe tomatoes, cored and sliced into ½-inch wedges
½	teaspoon salt
1	(16-ounce) can cannellini beans, drained and rinsed (see note above)
2	tablespoons extra-virgin olive oil
1	tablespoon balsamic vinegar
1	garlic clove, minced
½	teaspoon pepper
2	teaspoons minced fresh rosemary
¼	cup pitted kalamata olives, finely chopped
¼	cup toasted pine nuts (see note above)

1. Toss the tomatoes and salt in a large bowl, then transfer to a paper towel–lined baking sheet; let drain for 15 minutes.

2. Return the drained tomatoes to the bowl and toss with the beans, oil, vinegar, garlic, pepper, rosemary, and olives. Let marinate for 15 minutes. Sprinkle the pine nuts over the salad. Serve.

MARINATED TOMATO SALAD WITH JALAPEÑO AND QUESO BLANCO

SERVES 4

Queso blanco, also called queso fresco, is a crumbly, slightly salty cheese commonly used in Mexican recipes. If your supermarket doesn't carry it, substitute a mild feta or farmer's cheese.

1½	pounds ripe tomatoes, cored and sliced into ½-inch wedges
½	teaspoon salt
2	tablespoons extra-virgin olive oil
1	tablespoon fresh lime juice
1	garlic clove, minced
1	jalapeño chile, seeded and chopped fine
1	ripe avocado, pitted, skinned, and chopped
½	teaspoon pepper
¼	cup chopped fresh cilantro
¼	cup crumbled queso blanco (see note above)

1. Toss the tomatoes and salt in a large bowl, then transfer to a paper towel–lined baking sheet; let drain for 15 minutes.

2. Return the drained tomatoes to the bowl and toss with the oil, lime juice, garlic, jalapeño, avocado, pepper, and cilantro. Let marinate for 15 minutes. Sprinkle the cheese over the salad. Serve.

Three-Bean Salad

If your mother made three-bean salad (and she probably did), it likely featured a sweet, vinegary dressing mixed with canned green, yellow, and kidney beans and a bite of red onion. This salad was good but never great. We wondered if this classic American recipe could be improved with modern ingredients and techniques.

When we began researching the origins of this picnic standby, we discovered that most of the recipes for it have remained essentially unchanged since the 1950s. Given the evolution of the ingredients and cooking techniques used over the past fifty years, we knew this salad could benefit from some updating.

Our goal was a fresh taste (something other than canned beans came to mind) and a light, sweet, and tangy dressing that would unite the subtle flavors of the beans without overpowering them. To that end, we divided our testing into three categories: improving the flavor and the texture of the beans; determining the right mix of vinegar and oils for the marinade; and addressing the question of sweetness, which was handled differently in almost every recipe we looked at. (Although we did find a few recipes that did not include a sweetener, sugar in one form or another seemed to differentiate three-bean salad from a simple oil and vinegar vegetable salad.)

We decided to first test boiling, blanching, and steaming the green and yellow beans. Not surprisingly, the less time the beans were cooked, the better they stood up in the dressing. Our 10- and 20-minute boiled beans were soft and flavorless, but those blanched for 1 and 2 minutes each weren't cooked enough. We eventually settled on boiling the beans for 5 minutes. This was long enough to remove their waxy exterior and thereby allow the marinade to penetrate, but not long enough to break down their cell structure and make them mushy. After draining the beans, we plunged them into cold water to stop the cooking. Steamed beans held up fairly well, but they didn't have the crunch of the boiled and shocked beans.

Next we moved on to the kidney beans. None of the recipes recommended cooking dried beans—they all called for canned. Just to be sure, we cooked up two batches of beans, then marinated them overnight. Not only were the canned beans a lot easier to use, but they tasted just as good.

With the beans ready for dressing, we moved on to the marinade. Many of the recipes we found were vague: they didn't say what type of vinegar to use, or what type of oil. After testing eight oil varieties and seven types of vinegar, we found that we preferred canola oil for its mild flavor and red wine vinegar for its tang.

We were ready to test types of sugar. We also wanted to test an idea we had run across in several recipes—cooking the sugar, vinegar, and oil together. We quickly realized that this dramatically improved the flavor of the dressing. We tried cooking vinegar mixed with brown sugar, with honey, and with white sugar over medium heat. The white sugar version won hands down; the cooking process created a syrup with its own unique flavor—sweet and tangy at the same time. It turns out that both heat and the type of sugar used make all the difference between a so-so marinade and a tasty one.

THREE-BEAN SALAD

SERVES 8 TO 10

This recipe is the all-American classic—the varia-tion gives the salad a Southwestern spin. Prepare this salad at least 1 day before you plan on serving it. The beans taste better after marinating in the dressing.

1   cup red wine vinegar
¾   cup sugar
½   cup canola oil
2   garlic cloves, minced
     Salt and pepper
½   pound green beans, trimmed and cut
     into 1-inch pieces
½   pound yellow wax beans, trimmed
     and cut into 1-inch pieces
1   (15.5-ounce) can red kidney beans,
     drained and rinsed
½   medium red onion, chopped
¼   cup minced fresh parsley

1. Heat the vinegar, sugar, oil, garlic, 1 teaspoon salt, and pepper to taste in a small nonreactive sauce-pan over medium heat, stirring occasionally, until the sugar dissolves, about 5 minutes. Transfer to a large nonreactive bowl and cool to room temperature.

2. Bring 3 quarts water to a boil in a large sauce-pan over high heat. Add 1 tablespoon salt and the green and yellow beans and cook until the beans are crisp-tender, about 5 minutes. Meanwhile, fill a medium bowl with ice water. When the beans are done, drain and immediately plunge them into the ice water to stop the cooking process; let sit until chilled, about 2 minutes. Drain well.

3. Add the green and yellow beans, kidney beans, onion, and parsley to the vinegar mixture and toss well to coat. Cover and refrigerate overnight to let flavors meld. Let stand at room temperature 30 min-utes before serving. (The salad can be covered and refrigerated for up to 4 days.)

Variation

THREE-BEAN SALAD WITH CUMIN, CILANTRO, AND ORANGES

Separate 2 medium oranges into segments, remove the membrane from the sides of each segment, then cut each segment in half lengthwise. Set aside. Substi-tute ¼ cup fresh lime juice for ¼ cup of the red wine vinegar, and heat 1 teaspoon ground cumin with the vinegar mixture. Substitute minced fresh cilantro for the parsley and add the halved orange segments to the vinegar mixture along with the beans.

SEGMENTING AN ORANGE

1. Start by slicing a ½-inch piece from the top and bottom of the orange. With the fruit resting flat against a work surface, use a very sharp paring knife to slice off the rind, including all of the bitter white pith. Try to follow the contours of the fruit as closely as possible.

2. Working over a bowl to catch the juices, slip the knife blade between a membrane and one section of fruit and slice to the center. Turn the blade so that it is facing out and slide the blade from the center out along the membrane to completely free the section.

Succotash Salad

Succotash sounds stuffy and old-fashioned—something your grandmother might have prepared. But at its simplest, this summer side dish is nothing more than lima beans and corn cooked with butter and sometimes cream. Sounds delicious (and it can be), but even good succotash is awfully rich. Could we rethink this recipe and make it lighter? A room-temperature salad sounded appealing and modern.

We quickly determined that frozen lima beans were completely acceptable. Fresh lima beans were hard to find and not worth the 40 minutes it took to shell and cook them. When it came to the corn, however, frozen was fine, but tasters really liked fresh. For more crunch, we added green beans, a common ingredient in succotash recipes. We found it easy to cook all the vegetables in one pot. The green beans needed a head start, but otherwise the timing was simple. Rinsing the cooked vegetables under cool running water set their color and kept them from softening further.

As for the dressing, we chose a simple mixture of olive oil and lemon juice. A little honey brought sweetness to the salad—much as the sweet cream does in the original recipe. For a splash of color and flavor, we finished the salad with minced red onion and chopped fresh basil. This cool, light salad now seems in sync with modern tastes, or warm nights. It's perfect with fish, chicken, or almost anything from the grill.

SUMMER SUCCOTASH SALAD

SERVES 4

This salad can be kept covered and refrigerated for up to 1 day. If making the salad in advance, add the basil just before serving.

- 3 tablespoons olive oil
- 1½ tablespoons fresh lemon juice
- 1 teaspoon honey
- ½ small red onion, minced
  Salt and pepper
- ¾ pound green beans, trimmed and cut in half crosswise
- 2 ears corn, kernels removed from cobs
- ½ pound frozen lima beans
- 2 tablespoons chopped fresh basil

1. Stir the oil, lemon juice, honey, red onion, and salt and pepper to taste together in a small bowl.

2. Bring 2½ quarts water to a boil in a large saucepan. Add 1 teaspoon salt and the green beans and cook for 1 minute. Add the corn and lima beans and cook until tender, about 5 minutes. Drain the vegetables into a colander and rinse them under cold running water until cool. Drain the vegetables well and transfer to a serving bowl.

3. Toss the vegetables with the dressing to coat evenly. Stir in the basil and season with salt and pepper to taste. Serve.

24-Hour Picnic Salad

What could be better than a make-ahead picnic salad? We'd heard about one version that features layers of iceberg lettuce, peas, hard-boiled egg, shredded cheddar cheese, and bacon, all neatly arranged in a huge glass bowl. On top, the layer of iceberg is coated with a thick dressing, spread to the edges, like frosting on a cake. Called 24-Hour Picnic Salad because it's made a day in advance, the salad gets tossed together just before serving. The lettuce and vegetables remain crisp and the creamy dressing brings all the flavors together. What a great idea, we thought, so we decided to create our own version.

We found a handful of recipes online and prepared them in the test kitchen. All shared the concept of layering the ingredients, but most of these salads were overdressed with thick, bland, and sweet dressings (mostly just sugar and mayo) that didn't properly coat the salad. We had a lot of work to do.

We tried using other lettuces, but iceberg retained the most crunch after sitting with the dressing for a day. We found that soft ingredients like mushrooms, spinach, and scallions wilted into mush, while crunchy ones like celery, bell pepper, cucumber, and red onion stayed crisp. Tasters preferred assertive blue cheese over the mild flavor of cheddar, especially when we layered the dressing and blue cheese together, which allowed the flavors to mingle overnight.

For the dressing, our first step was to cut back on the sugar and add tart cider vinegar and hot sauce for brightness and depth. The flavor was great, but the dressing was still too thick to blend into the salad. Thinning it out caused the dressing to run down through the ingredients overnight, resulting in soggy vegetables.

Then we remembered one recipe we had found (and quickly dismissed) that called for salting the layers of lettuce. We dutifully prepared the recipe and the next day found a pool of water sitting in the bottom of the bowl. We were sure we had made a mistake, but we tossed the salad together anyway and were pleasantly surprised that the thick dressing combined with the water to coat the salad beautifully. We had the perfect make-ahead salad.

24-HOUR PICNIC SALAD

SERVES 12

Frank's Red Hot Sauce is our favorite brand of hot sauce. If using a hotter brand, such as Tabasco, reduce the amount to 1 tablespoon. See page 16 for instructions on how to hard-boil eggs.

SALAD

1	medium head iceberg lettuce, cored and chopped rough (about 6 cups)
	Salt
½	medium red onion, sliced thin

6	hard-boiled eggs (see note above), peeled and chopped
1½	cups frozen peas
4	celery ribs, sliced thin
1	red bell pepper, seeded and chopped
1	medium cucumber, halved lengthwise, seeded, and sliced thin
1	pound bacon, cooked and crumbled
1½	cups crumbled blue cheese

DRESSING

1½	cups mayonnaise
3	tablespoons cider vinegar
2	tablespoons hot sauce (see note above)
2	teaspoons sugar
1½	teaspoons pepper

1. FOR THE SALAD: Place half of the lettuce in a large serving bowl and sprinkle with ½ teaspoon salt. Rinse the sliced onion under cold water; pat dry with paper towels. Layer the onion, eggs, peas, celery, bell pepper, and cucumber over the lettuce. Add the remaining lettuce to the bowl, sprinkle with ½ teaspoon salt, and top with the bacon and cheese.

2. FOR THE DRESSING: Combine all of the ingredients and spread the dressing evenly over the top of the salad. Cover with plastic wrap and refrigerate for at least 8 hours or up to 24 hours. Remove the plastic wrap and toss until the salad is evenly coated with the dressing. Serve.

TEST KITCHEN SHORTCUT

Salad Bowl Improvisation: To show off the multiple layers of the 24-Hour Picnic Salad, we like to serve it in a clear bowl. If you don't have a big glass bowl, you might have a suitable substitute on hand. The bowl from our top-rated OXO Good Grips salad spinner works perfectly for this recipe.

Creamy Buttermilk Coleslaw

Whether served on the side or piled high right on top of a pulled pork sandwich, it's hard to imagine eating barbecue without cool, creamy coleslaw. We especially like tangy buttermilk coleslaw with barbecue, but not when the slaw makes a watery pool on the plate. Part of the problem is the buttermilk, which tastes great but makes a thin dressing. The other part of the problem is the cabbage, which sheds liquid as the slaw sits and turns the already thin dressing downright watery. Many recipes tackle this problem by having you salt the shredded cabbage to remove excess water before dressing it. The salting worked like a charm, as the salted cabbage shed nearly $\frac{1}{3}$ cup of liquid after just one hour.

But this method doesn't address the bigger problem: the thin buttermilk. To thicken the dressing, we wanted to add a creamier ingredient. Mayonnaise had the right body, but dulled the buttermilk flavor too much. Sour cream had great tang, but it left the dressing thin. The solution was to use both mayonnaise (to thicken the dressing) and sour cream (to restore some tang). To bring the dressing's flavors into balance, we found that 2 tablespoons of sugar gave the dressing a nice hit of sweetness and that Dijon mustard added a subtle sharpness. Tasters also liked a hefty amount of chopped scallions—not only for their oniony flavor but also for the flecks of color that they lent our creamy slaw.

CREAMY BUTTERMILK COLESLAW

SERVES 8 TO 10

Make this slaw up to 1 hour before serving.

- 1 medium head green cabbage, cored and chopped fine
- 2 large carrots, peeled and shredded on box grater
- Salt
- ⅔ cup buttermilk
- ½ cup mayonnaise
- ¼ cup sour cream
- 8 scallions, chopped fine
- 2 tablespoons sugar
- 1 teaspoon Dijon mustard
- ¼ teaspoon pepper

1. Toss the cabbage and carrots with 1 teaspoon salt in a colander set over a medium bowl. Let stand until wilted, about 1 hour. Rinse the cabbage and carrots under cold water, drain, dry well with paper towels, and transfer to a large bowl.

2. Stir in the remaining ingredients plus salt to taste. Refrigerate until chilled, about 15 minutes. Adjust seasonings and serve.

Memphis Chopped Coleslaw

Memphis chopped coleslaw is studded with celery seed and crunchy green bell pepper and tossed with an unapologetically sugary mustard dressing that's balanced by a bracing hit of vinegar. With its bold, brash flavors, this bright yellow slaw is a perfect match for even the spiciest and smokiest barbecue.

We started with the cabbage. Because of its high water content, raw cabbage exudes liquid when tossed with a dressing, making the slaw loose and watery. In the test kitchen we remedy this by salting the chopped cabbage before dressing it; the salt wilts and tenderizes the cabbage, drawing out excess moisture along the way. Prepared in this manner, the cabbage is the base for a sturdy coleslaw that can hold in the fridge for a day without becoming soggy.

When we started researching recipes, we were intrigued that many called for a combination of refrigerator staples (yellow mustard, mayonnaise, sour cream, and ketchup) to give the dressing complex flavor. Tasters told us the complexity was there, but some felt the dressing lacked punch. Switching from ketchup to garlicky chili sauce helped, as did adding shredded onion. Using spicy jalapeño (instead of green bell pepper) and brown sugar (instead of white) gave just the right mix of savory and sweet.

But even though the dressing had the bold tastes we wanted, the flavors still seemed somehow divergent. In one recipe we found, the sauce was simmered before being poured over the cabbage to help the flavors meld. This sounded promising, but we feared the heat of the sauce might cook the cabbage and make it soft and soggy. We couldn't have been more wrong. Although the cabbage did absorb some of the hot dressing, it remained crunchy and was seasoned from the inside out. Finally, we had a bold, crisp slaw that was packed with flavor and not waterlogged.

MEMPHIS CHOPPED COLESLAW

SERVES 8 TO 10

In step 1, the salted, rinsed, and dried cabbage mixture can be refrigerated in a zipper-lock plastic bag for up to 24 hours.

1	medium head green cabbage, cored and chopped fine
1	jalapeño chile, seeded and minced
1	carrot, peeled and shredded on box grater
1	small onion, peeled and shredded on box grater
2	teaspoons salt
¼	cup yellow mustard
¼	cup chili sauce
¼	cup mayonnaise
¼	cup sour cream
¼	cup cider vinegar
1	teaspoon celery seed
⅔	cup packed light brown sugar

1. Toss the cabbage, jalapeño, carrot, onion, and salt in a colander set over a medium bowl. Let stand until wilted, about 1 hour. Rinse the cabbage mixture under cold water, drain, dry well with paper towels, and transfer to a large bowl.

2. Bring the mustard, chili sauce, mayonnaise, sour cream, vinegar, celery seed, and sugar to a boil in a saucepan over medium heat. Pour over the cabbage mixture and toss to coat. Cover with plastic wrap and refrigerate for 1 hour or up to 1 day. Serve.

HOW TO CHOP CABBAGE

1. Cut the cabbage into quarters, then trim and discard the hard core.

2. Separate the cabbage into small stacks of leaves that flatten when pressed.

3. Cut each stack of cabbage leaves into ¼-inch strips.

4. Cut the cabbage strips into ¼-inch pieces.

All-American Potato Salad

American potato salad contains mayonnaise, mustard, vinegar, pickles, celery, onion, and sometimes hard-boiled eggs. Although this recipe is easy to execute, we have eaten enough sloppy, boring potato salads to know that there's room for improvement.

Our first recipe tests focused on the potato variety. We found that firm Red Bliss potatoes made the neatest salad. Unfortunately, tasters also thought they made the blandest salad. Russet potatoes tasted great but were extremely mushy. Yukon golds offered the best balance of sturdiness and flavor. The skins on Red Bliss potatoes are quite palatable, but no one liked the papery skins on the Yukon golds, so we peeled the potatoes before cubing and cooking them.

With the potatoes chosen, it was time to focus on the dressing. Mayonnaise is the base ingredient, but frankly, it can smother other flavors. We wondered if some other creamy ingredient could perk up our salad. Tasters thought yogurt and buttermilk were too tart but raved when we tried sour cream.

Sweet yellow mustard was the tasters' favorite, beating out Dijon (too spicy) and brown (too ugly). For crunch, we added celery, red onion, and dill pickles. We found a few recipes that supplemented the celery flavor with celery seed, and everyone in the test kitchen approved of this addition.

To further brighten this creamy salad, we tried adding various vinegars and lemon juice, but they tended to overwhelm the other flavors. It wasn't until we added some pickle juice—yes, the liquid in the pickle jar—that our dressing really came together. Why did pickle juice work so well? Dill pickles are packed in a brine made with vinegar that has been diluted with water (so it's not harsh), tempered with sugar, and then flavored with spices and garlic. Pickle juice is also convenient we already had the jar open.

Although the dressing now had great flavor, it was merely coating the potatoes, not getting inside. Could we get that flavor deep inside the potatoes? The solution was as close as a recipe for French potato salad, in which a simple vinaigrette is drizzled over drained potatoes when they're still hot and is absorbed as they cool. Pouring a mayonnaise-based dressing over hot potatoes would result in a runny mess, but singling out a couple of intensely flavored ingredients—in this case, the mustard and pickle juice—worked perfectly.

ALL-AMERICAN POTATO SALAD

SERVES 4 TO 6

Make sure not to overcook the potatoes or the salad will be quite sloppy. Keep the water at a gentle simmer and use the tip of a paring knife to judge the doneness of the potatoes. If the knife inserts easily into the potato pieces, they are done. See page 16 for instructions on how to hard-boil eggs.

2	pounds Yukon gold potatoes, peeled and cut into ¾-inch cubes
	Salt
3	tablespoons dill pickle juice, plus ¼ cup finely chopped dill pickles
1	tablespoon yellow mustard
¼	teaspoon pepper
½	teaspoon celery seed
½	cup mayonnaise
¼	cup sour cream
½	small red onion, minced
1	celery rib, chopped fine
2	hard-boiled eggs, peeled and cut into ¼-inch dice (optional; see note above)

1. Place the potatoes in a large saucepan with cold water to cover by 1 inch. Bring to a boil over high heat, add 1 teaspoon salt, reduce the heat to medium-low, and simmer until the potatoes are tender, 10 to 15 minutes.

2. Drain the potatoes thoroughly, then spread them out on a rimmed baking sheet. Mix 2 tablespoons of the pickle juice and the mustard together in a small bowl, drizzle the pickle juice mixture over the potatoes, and toss until evenly coated. Refrigerate until cooled, about 30 minutes.

3. Mix the remaining 1 tablespoon pickle juice, the chopped pickles, ½ teaspoon salt, pepper, celery seed, mayonnaise, sour cream, red onion, and celery in a large bowl. Toss in the cooled potatoes, cover, and refrigerate until well chilled, about 30 minutes. (The salad can be refrigerated in an airtight container for up to 2 days.) Gently stir in the eggs, if using, just before serving.

Ranch Potato Salad

With its tangy, creamy base and big hits of garlic, dill, and cilantro, it's easy to see why cooks employ ranch dressing for dishes other than green salad. Perhaps the most popular of these dishes is ranch potato salad, in which a bottle of the creamy dressing is poured over boiled potatoes.

We weren't surprised that tasters rejected recipes calling for just these two ingredients—bottled salad dressing and boiled potatoes. Bottled ranch dressing is too sweet and bland. To make this recipe worthwhile, we'd have to whip up a quick ranch dressing. Potatoes generally require a heavy hand with seasonings, and this dish was no exception. Our homemade dressing would have to pack a real wallop.

Starting with the potatoes, we found that tasters preferred the firmness of the red potatoes. We also found that peeling the potatoes allowed them to absorb more dressing.

Most recipes for homemade ranch dressing start with a base of buttermilk and mayonnaise, and that's where we began. We doubled the amount of cilantro used in most recipes and found that fresh garlic and

scallions added welcome bite. The dill proved to be a little trickier—too little fresh dill and tasters didn't know it was there, but too much made the dressing taste overpoweringly grassy. The solution was to use just ⅛ teaspoon dried dill. Dijon mustard and vinegar provided acidity and flavor, and for a sweet counterpoint we added chopped roasted red peppers.

This dressing tasted great on the spoon, but tossing it with hot boiled potatoes cooked the buttermilk and mayo into a decidedly unappealing slimy texture. Tossing the dressing with cooled potatoes resulted in a salad that still tasted a little flat because the dressing wasn't permeating the spuds. To better season the potatoes, we pulled the Dijon and some of the vinegar out of the dressing and tossed them with the hot potatoes. After the seasoned potatoes cooled, we mixed them with the flavorful dressing. Even tasters who claimed not to like ranch dressing came back for seconds of our Ranch Potato Salad.

THE AMERICAN TABLE
HIDDEN VALLEY RANCH DRESSING

The original ranch dressing first became popular at the Hidden Valley Guest Ranch near Santa Barbara, California, in the late 1950s. It began as a dried herb mixture that Steve Henson, the ranch's owner, combined with mayonnaise and buttermilk to make a creamy, tangy dressing for the ranch's house salad. It was so well received that guests clamored for bottles of the dressing to take home with them. Recognizing the potential of his concoction, Henson began marketing the mix in small packets, and the rest is culinary history. The little packets are still around, but the dressing really took off in 1983 when manufacturers figured out how to bottle this creamy dressing in a shelf-stable format.

RANCH POTATO SALAD

SERVES 6 TO 8

We prefer the flavor of white wine vinegar here, but distilled white vinegar is an acceptable substitute.

- 3 pounds red potatoes, peeled and cut into ¾-inch chunks
  Salt
- ¾ cup mayonnaise
- ½ cup buttermilk
- ¼ cup white wine vinegar (see note above)
- ¼ cup drained jarred roasted red peppers, chopped fine
- 3 tablespoons finely chopped fresh cilantro
- 3 scallions, chopped fine
- 1 garlic clove, minced
- ⅛ teaspoon dried dill
- 2 teaspoons pepper
- 2 tablespoons Dijon mustard

1. Bring the potatoes, 1 tablespoon salt, and enough water to cover by 1 inch to a boil in a large pot over high heat. Reduce the heat to medium and simmer until the potatoes are just tender, about 10 minutes. While the potatoes simmer, whisk the mayonnaise, buttermilk, 2 tablespoons of the vinegar, the red peppers, cilantro, scallions, garlic, dill, 1 teaspoon salt, and 2 teaspoons pepper in a large bowl.

2. Drain the potatoes, then spread them in an even layer on a rimmed baking sheet. Whisk the mustard and the remaining 2 tablespoons vinegar in a small bowl. Drizzle the mustard mixture over the hot potatoes and toss until evenly coated. Refrigerate the potatoes until cooled, about 30 minutes.

3. Transfer the cooled potatoes to a bowl with the mayonnaise mixture and toss to combine. Cover and refrigerate until well chilled, about 30 minutes. Serve. (The salad can be refrigerated in an airtight container for up to 2 days.)

Barbecued Macaroni Salad

As an accompaniment to a char-grilled burger or smoke-ringed rack of ribs, plain old macaroni salad can seem awfully boring. Mayonnaise and pasta aren't exactly the most exciting (or flavorful) ingredients. When a colleague told us about macaroni salad with barbecue flavors, we thought we had the perfect way to shake up this often dull recipe.

Unfortunately, in most of the recipes we found the pasta was simply drowned in ketchup-y barbecue sauce that was much too sweet and sticky. In the end, we found that a combination of barbecue sauce and mayonnaise proved more effective; the assertive tang of the barbecue sauce was nicely balanced by the neutral creaminess of the mayonnaise.

To punch up the barbecue flavor, we added chili powder, garlic powder, cider vinegar, and hot sauce. For freshness and texture, bell pepper, celery, and scallions introduced just the right vegetal bite. This spicy summertime side dish is built to stand up to the heartiest grilled foods.

BBQ MACARONI SALAD

SERVES 8 TO 10

We like the sweet, smoky flavor of Bull's-Eye barbecue sauce, but feel free to substitute your favorite. As the salad sits, it can become dry; just before serving, stir in a few tablespoons of warm water to bring back its creamy texture.

- Salt
- 1 pound elbow macaroni
- 1 red bell pepper, seeded and chopped fine
- 1 celery rib, chopped fine
- 4 scallions, sliced thin
- 2 tablespoons cider vinegar

1 teaspoon hot sauce

1 teaspoon chili powder

⅛ teaspoon garlic powder

Pinch cayenne pepper

1 cup mayonnaise

½ cup barbecue sauce (see note above)

Pepper

1. Bring 4 quarts water to a boil in a large pot. Add 1 tablespoon salt and the macaroni and cook until nearly tender, about 5 minutes. Drain in a colander and rinse with cold water until cool, then drain once more, briefly, so that the pasta is still moist; transfer to a large bowl.

2. Stir in the bell pepper, celery, scallions, vinegar, hot sauce, chili powder, garlic powder, and cayenne and let sit until the flavors are absorbed, about 2 minutes. Stir in the mayonnaise and barbecue sauce and let sit until the salad is no longer watery, about 5 minutes. Season with salt and pepper to taste and serve. (The salad can be covered and refrigerated for up to 2 days. Check seasonings before serving.)

Variation
MEATY BBQ MACARONI SALAD
Our BBQ Macaroni Salad tastes great alongside any grilled fare, but for a heartier salad you can add browned sausage, kielbasa, or deli ham.

Heat 1 teaspoon vegetable oil in a nonstick skillet over medium-high heat until shimmering. Add 8 ounces smoked sausage, kielbasa, or deli ham, cut into ½-inch chunks, and cook until browned, about 5 minutes. Transfer the meat to a paper towel–lined plate and proceed with the recipe, adding the browned meat with the vegetables in step 2.

Antipasto Pasta Salad

An antipasto platter includes a variety of cured meats, cheeses, and pickled vegetables. As a whole, it's full-flavored and hearty—perfect attributes for a main-course pasta salad. But the recipes we tried for this type of salad were greasy and heavy, with lackluster dressing and not enough flavor in the pasta itself.

We started with the deli meats and tried a variety of meats from our supermarket deli. We were surprised to find that prosciutto fared poorly. Its flavor was just too delicate for this salad. We did like pepperoni and sopressata (a spicy, cured Italian sausage), and salami worked well, too. From previous testing, we learned that microwaving the meat, wrapped in paper towels, helped remove excess grease. When ordering your meat at the deli counter, be sure to have it sliced thick—thinly sliced meat gets lost in this salad.

Next we moved on to the cheese. Tasters dismissed mild-flavored cheeses like mozzarella and regular provolone, but aged provolone, with its sharp flavor, won everyone over.

For vegetables, we didn't want to stray too far from the items you'd find on an antipasto platter—olives, roasted red peppers, pepperoncini, marinated mushrooms, artichoke hearts, and sliced fennel were just some of the vegetables we chose for our tests. In the end, tasters preferred roasted red peppers for sweetness, pepperoncini for heat, and mushrooms for earthy flavor. (Kalamata olives and jarred artichoke hearts were close runners-up, so they're good options if you have them on hand.) Although we used jarred roasted red peppers and pepperoncini, we felt we needed to go the homemade route with the marinated mushrooms—jarred versions we tried were not worth the expense. After a little testing we found an easy way to infuse our mushrooms with flavor in just a few minutes: by sautéing them in a portion of the vinaigrette.

Pasta salads typically use a 2-to-1 ratio of oil to

vinegar, but since the meats and cheese were so rich, we found that we had to nearly reverse this ratio. Some vinegary brine from the pepperoncini further sharpened the dressing. We felt that we were almost there, but the dressing seemed too thin. We needed some sort of thickening agent to emulsify it. First, we tried mustard, but its flavor overshadowed the dressing. In our next test we added a few tablespoons of mayonnaise. This was perfect—it added body to help the dressing cling to the pasta, and its mild flavor didn't mute or detract from the dressing's other seasonings.

For the pasta, we liked short, curly pasta shapes best—their curves catch the dressing and cradle the meats, cheese, and vegetables far better than short, straight pasta shapes like ziti or rigatoni. Most pasta salad recipes call for rinsing the cooked noodles, but this method left us with bloated pasta that didn't absorb any flavor from the dressing. Tossing the hot pasta with the dressing and extra vinegar made the pasta an equal partner in this bold Italian-style salad supper.

ANTIPASTO PASTA SALAD

SERVES 6 TO 8

If you like, add 1 cup chopped, pitted kalamata olives or 1 cup jarred artichokes, drained and quartered, to this salad.

- 8   ounces sliced pepperoni, cut into ¼-inch strips
- 8   ounces thick-sliced sopressata or salami, halved and cut into ¼-inch strips
- ½   cup plus 2 tablespoons red wine vinegar
- 6   tablespoons extra-virgin olive oil
- 3   tablespoons mayonnaise
- 1   (12-ounce) jar pepperoncini, drained (2 tablespoons juice reserved), stemmed, and chopped coarse
- 4   garlic cloves, minced
- ¼   teaspoon red pepper flakes
- Salt and pepper
- 1   pound short, curly pasta, such as fusilli or campanelle
- 1   pound white mushrooms, quartered
- 1   cup grated aged provolone cheese
- 1   (12-ounce) jar roasted red peppers, drained and chopped coarse
- 1   cup chopped fresh basil

1. Bring 4 quarts water to a boil in a large pot for the pasta. Meanwhile, place the pepperoni on a large paper towel–lined plate. Cover with another paper towel and place the sopressata on top. Cover with another paper towel and microwave on high for 1 minute. Discard the paper towels and set the pepperoni and sopressata aside.

2. Whisk 5 tablespoons of the vinegar, the olive oil, mayonnaise, pepperoncini juice, garlic, red pepper flakes, ½ teaspoon salt, and ½ teaspoon pepper together in a medium bowl.

3. Add 1 tablespoon salt and the pasta to the boiling water. Cook, stirring often, until the pasta is just past al dente. Drain the pasta and return it to the pot. Pour ½ cup of the dressing and the remaining 5 tablespoons vinegar over the pasta and toss to combine. Season with salt and pepper to taste. Spread the pasta on a rimmed baking sheet and cool to room temperature, about 30 minutes.

4. Meanwhile, bring the remaining dressing to a simmer in a large skillet over medium-high heat. Add the mushrooms and cook until lightly browned, about 8 minutes. Transfer to a large bowl and cool to room temperature.

5. Add the meat, provolone, roasted red peppers, basil, and cooled pasta to the mushrooms and toss to combine. Season with salt and pepper to taste before serving.

Gelatin Molds

Gelatin molds, or Jell-O molds, might elicit groans from certain corners, but we're willing to bet that even the most highbrow have fond memories of digging into a colorful, wobbly gelatin salad at at least one family celebration. We aimed to develop a gelatin mold that would taste as good as it looked. In their heyday, especially during the Great Depression, gelatin molds were more a repository for leftovers (i.e., limp lettuce or yesterday's vegetables), than a colorful treat. Thus, we skipped ingredients best left lingering in the refrigerator drawer. Tasters gave a thumbs up to fruit—especially canned mandarin oranges and maraschino cherries. Cottage cheese, a popular addition to gelatin molds, was eschewed in favor of sour cream. Sherbet worked well, too. And coconut milk was another worthy addition—it gave one of our molds a rich, tropical flavor. Because it's been decades since the tinned mold was a fixture in kitchens across America, our gelatin mold also works in a nonstick Bundt pan. Just remember to spray the inside with vegetable oil spray to get a clean release.

APRICOT-ORANGE GELATIN MOLD

SERVES 8 TO 10

Orange-flavored gelatin can be substituted for apricot.

    4   (3-ounce) boxes apricot-flavored gelatin
    2   cups boiling water
    2   cups apricot nectar, chilled
    2   cups orange sherbet, softened
    1   cup sour cream
    2   (15-ounce) cans mandarin oranges,
        drained and halved

1. Dissolve the gelatin in the boiling water in a large bowl. Stir in the chilled nectar. Refrigerate, uncovered, until slightly set (the mixture should have the consistency of egg whites), about 45 minutes.

2. Lightly coat a 12-cup mold or nonstick Bundt pan with vegetable oil spray. With an electric mixer at medium-high speed, whip the slightly set gelatin until foamy and well blended, about 1 minute. In a separate bowl, whip the sherbet and sour cream at medium-high speed until smooth. Combine the sherbet mixture with the gelatin and whip on medium-low speed until completely combined and free of streaks. Fold in the oranges. Pour into the prepared mold and refrigerate, uncovered, until set, about 4 hours. (The mold can be refrigerated for up to 2 days.) When ready to serve, invert onto a large plate.

AMBROSIA GELATIN MOLD

SERVES 8 TO 10

Shake the can of coconut milk before opening—the fat tends to separate.

    4   (3-ounce) boxes pineapple-flavored gelatin
    2   cups boiling water
    2   (13.5-ounce) cans coconut milk
  1½   cups mini-marshmallows
    1   (15-ounce) can mandarin oranges,
        drained and halved
    1   (10-ounce) jar maraschino cherries,
        drained and halved

1. Dissolve the gelatin in the boiling water in a large bowl. Stir in ½ cup cold water and the coconut milk. Refrigerate, uncovered, until slightly set (the mixture should have the consistency of egg whites), about 1 hour.

2. Lightly coat a 12-cup mold or nonstick Bundt pan with vegetable oil spray. Whisk the slightly set gelatin until well blended, then fold in the marshmallows, oranges, and cherries. Pour into the prepared mold and refrigerate, uncovered, until set, about 4 hours. (The mold can be refrigerated for up to 2 days.) When ready to serve, invert onto a large plate.

CHAPTER THREE

Soups, Stews, and Chilis

SOUPS, STEWS, AND CHILIS

Chicken Noodle Soup

Few kitchen failures are more disappointing than bad homemade chicken noodle soup. Since making soup from scratch takes a lot more effort than opening a can of Campbell's, it's awfully deflating when the chicken turns out tough and dry and the broth is only one step up from dishwater.

First, some basic chicken facts. The breast meat doesn't add much flavor to the broth, and it cooks in a flash. Most of the flavor comes from the dark meat and bones—and it takes time for them to give up their essence to the broth (and in that time the white meat overcooks).

During early tests, we found that most tasters didn't care for dark meat in the finished soup; they wanted tender chunks of white meat. With this in mind, we decided to try making the broth with dark meat, removing it, and then quickly poaching the white meat in the broth to finish the soup. Our job was made that much easier when we realized we didn't have to cut up a whole chicken ourselves but could simply buy chicken parts.

Our first thought was to brown the dark meat so that it would release its flavor more quickly. Instead of simply poaching the meat in water (which takes 2 to 3 hours), we browned the chicken, poured off the excess grease, then added water, salt, and bay leaves. After 45 minutes of simmering, our broth was plenty strong, and the dark meat had held up to the cooking—it was still moist and tender enough to use in chicken salad or even soup, if you're a fan of dark meat.

We conducted a side-by-side tasting of broths made with just wings, just drumsticks, and just thighs. The broth made with the thighs had the cleanest, most intense chicken flavor, although, like the other two, it was too greasy. This was easily remedied by removing the skin after browning the thighs and quickly degreasing the broth with paper towels.

Next we began to tinker with the addition of white meat. We found that raw boneless, skinless breasts could be poached in the simmering broth during the last 15 minutes of cooking. They could then be removed from the broth, cooled, shredded, and added back to the soup during the last minutes of cooking to reheat.

With the main components of the soup—the broth and the meat—taken care of, all we had to do was put the supporting elements together. Because we'd gone to a fair amount of trouble to create a great broth and tender meat, we did not want to overwhelm them with too many other ingredients. Tasters liked onion, carrot, and celery, and we found that sautéing the vegetables in a thin film of oil (rather than just poaching them in the broth) intensified their flavor. We let the vegetables finish cooking in the broth, along with some minced fresh thyme, to meld all the flavors.

We found that the noodles were best cooked right in the broth, where they soaked up chicken flavor. Once the noodles are cooked, however, the soup must be served immediately. When we tried refrigerating leftovers, the noodles became bloated and mushy.

Taking up the suggestion of several fellow cooks, we finished our soup with a handful of fresh parsley and then watched with satisfaction as tasters emptied their bowls. No truly homemade soup is quick, but this recipe is pretty easy to follow, and the results are much better than anything that comes out of a can.

CHICKEN NOODLE SOUP

SERVES 8 TO 10

The thighs are used to flavor the broth; once the broth is strained, shred the thigh meat and reserve it for another use. If you prefer dark meat in your soup, you can omit the chicken breasts and add the shredded thigh meat to the soup instead.

BROTH

12	bone-in, skin-on chicken thighs (about 4 pounds)
	Salt and pepper
1	tablespoon vegetable oil
1	onion, chopped
3	quarts water
2	bay leaves
2	large boneless, skinless chicken breasts (about 1 pound)

SOUP

1	tablespoon vegetable oil
1	onion, minced
1	carrot, sliced thin
1	celery rib, halved lengthwise, then sliced thin
2	teaspoons minced fresh thyme
6	ounces wide egg noodles
¼	cup minced fresh parsley
	Salt and pepper

1. FOR THE BROTH: Pat the thighs dry with paper towels and season with salt and pepper. Heat the oil in a large Dutch oven over medium-high heat until smoking. Cook half of the thighs skin side down until deep golden brown, about 6 minutes. Turn the thighs and lightly brown the second side, about 2 minutes. Transfer to a strainer-lined large bowl. Repeat with the remaining thighs and transfer to the strainer. Remove and discard the skin from the thighs; discard the fat in the bowl. Pour off the fat from the pot, add the onion, and cook over medium heat until just softened, about 3 minutes. Add the

DEGREASING CHICKEN BROTH

1. Place a paper towel on top of the slightly cooled broth. Gather the corners of the towel and lift it out of the broth.

2. Allow the excess broth to drip back into the bowl and repeat with fresh towels, as necessary.

thighs, water, bay leaves, and 1 tablespoon salt to the pot. Cover and simmer for 30 minutes. Add the chicken breasts and continue simmering until the broth is rich and flavorful, about 15 minutes.

2. Strain the broth into a large container, let stand at least 10 minutes, then remove the fat from the surface. Meanwhile, transfer the chicken to a cutting board to cool. Once cooled, remove the thigh meat from the bones, shred, and reserve for another use. (The thigh meat can be refrigerated for up to 2 days or frozen for up to 1 month.) Shred the breast meat and reserve for the soup.

3. FOR THE SOUP: Heat the oil in the now-empty Dutch oven over medium-high heat until shimmering. Add the onion, carrot, and celery and cook until the onion has softened, 3 to 4 minutes. Stir in the thyme and broth and simmer until the vegetables are tender, about 15 minutes. Add the noodles and shredded breast meat and simmer until the noodles are just tender, about 5 minutes. Off the heat, stir in the parsley and season with salt and pepper to taste. Serve. (The broth and shredded breast meat can be refrigerated for up to 2 days or frozen for up to 1 month before being used to make soup. To avoid soggy noodles and vegetables, continue the recipe with step 3 just before you plan on serving it.)

Hearty Beef and Vegetable Soup

Using homemade beef stock is a guaranteed method for producing great beef and vegetable soup, but most of us buy broth in a can and then try to doctor it up. Unfortunately, most of these quick fixes are ultimately unsatisfying. Could we start with canned broth and create a really good soup with tender, flavorful chunks of beef, a meaty broth, and perfectly cooked vegetables?

After some disappointing tests with meaty bones and canned broth, we realized this approach would take hours to yield good results. A restaurant might have all day to coax flavor from inexpensive bones, but we wanted something faster. We needed meat—and lots of it. Because we didn't want the soup to cost a fortune, we focused on reasonably priced cuts that could serve a dual purpose, first as a broth enhancer and later as a soup ingredient. Our plan was as follows: brown the meat to build flavor, pour off any rendered fat, add the canned broth, simmer until the meat was tender and the broth flavorful, and, finally, shred the beef and add it back to the pot with some vegetables to make soup.

Lean cuts from the round yielded tasteless broth and chewy bits of overcooked beef. Cuts from the chuck tasted better but were too greasy. Boneless blade steaks, which are very beefy but not terribly

CUSTOMIZE YOUR SOUP

It may be impossible to please all of the people all of the time, but that doesn't mean you can't try. Our Hearty Beef and Vegetable Soup is easily customized, letting you use vegetables you like and/or have on hand. Feel free to mix and match, but don't add more than 2 cups total vegetables, pasta, noodles, or rice. The vegetables can cook right in the soup pot, but pasta, noodles, and rice should be precooked separately so they don't make the broth too thick.

	SOUP ADDITIONS	PREPARATION	AMOUNT	WHEN TO ADD
LONG-COOKING	Red potatoes	Scrubbed, then diced	Up to 2 cups	With broth in step 4
	Parsnips	Peeled, then diced	Up to ½ cup	With broth in step 4
	Sweet potatoes	Peeled, then diced	Up to 2 cups	With broth in step 4
	Turnips	Peeled, then diced	Up to ½ cup	With broth in step 4
LAST-MINUTE	Frozen lima beans	None	Up to ½ cup	5 minutes before soup is done
	Frozen peas	None	Up to 1 cup	2 minutes before soup is done
	Baby spinach	None	Up to 2 cups	1 minute before soup is done
	Pasta, egg noodles, or rice	Cooked and drained	Up to 2 cups	Just before serving

fatty, were just the thing. Three pounds' worth made a good broth and provided enough meat for a hearty soup.

Our broth was now meaty, but there was no disguising the faint tinny taste of the canned beef broth. Cutting the beef broth with a little water helped, as did a spoonful of tomato paste, but the best solution was to add several cups of chicken broth. Doctoring beef broth with chicken broth might seem strange, but it works.

As for the other soup ingredients, we added onion and carrots (along with some drained canned tomatoes) once the broth was finished cooking so that the broth would taste like meat, not sweet vegetables. Herbs and garlic fared better when added to the broth as it cooked. Our tasters liked a combination of bay leaves and thyme, along with a whole head of garlic. Although this sounds like a lot of garlic, it became surprisingly mellow when simmered for so long.

We found that other vegetables—everything from potatoes and parsnips to peas and spinach—could be added directly to the finished broth. You just need to time the addition of each vegetable correctly. We created a handy chart (on page 59) that will help you customize our soup with the vegetables you like best.

HEARTY BEEF AND VEGETABLE SOUP

SERVES 6 TO 8

Follow the chart on page 59 to add other ingredients to this soup.

BROTH

- 3 pounds beef blade steaks (about 8 steaks)
   Salt and pepper
- 2 tablespoons vegetable oil
- 1 tablespoon tomato paste
- 4 cups low-sodium chicken broth
- 4 cups low-sodium beef broth
- 2 cups water

- 1 garlic head, top third cut off and discarded, loose outer papery skin removed
- 2 bay leaves
- ½ teaspoon dried thyme

SOUP

- 1 tablespoon unsalted butter
- 1 medium onion, minced
- 2 medium carrots, peeled, halved lengthwise, and cut into ¼-inch half-moons
- 1 (14.5-ounce) can diced tomatoes, drained
   Salt and pepper
   Minced fresh parsley

1. FOR THE BROTH: Season the blade steaks with salt and pepper. Heat 1 tablespoon of the oil in a Dutch oven over medium-high heat until shimmering. Add half of the steaks and cook until well browned on both sides, about 8 minutes. Set the steaks aside on a plate. Repeat with the remaining 1 tablespoon oil and steaks.

2. Pour off the fat from the Dutch oven and return to medium-high heat. Add the tomato paste and cook, mashing the paste with a wooden spoon, for 30 seconds. Add the chicken broth, beef broth, and water, and scrape any browned bits from the bottom of the pot with the wooden spoon. Return the steaks and any accumulated juices to the pot. Add the garlic head, bay leaves, and thyme and bring to a simmer, using a wide, shallow spoon to skim off foam or fat that rises to the surface. Reduce the heat to medium-low and simmer gently (do not boil) until the meat is tender, about 2 hours (do not cover the pot.)

3. Transfer the steaks and garlic head to a rimmed plate to cool. Once cool enough to handle, shred the meat into bite-sized pieces, discarding any fat. Using tongs, squeeze the garlic cloves into a small bowl. Mash with a fork until a paste forms. Pour the broth through a fine-mesh strainer. Return the shredded beef and garlic paste to the broth. (The broth can be refrigerated for up to 3 days or frozen for up to 2 months.)

4. FOR THE SOUP: Melt the butter in a clean Dutch oven over medium heat. Add the onion and carrots and cook until the onion is softened but not browned, about 5 minutes. Add the tomatoes and broth. Bring to a simmer, reduce the heat to medium-low, and cook until the carrots are tender, about 20 minutes.

5. To serve, season with salt and pepper to taste and sprinkle with the parsley.

Pittsburgh Wedding Soup

Pittsburgh wedding soup (also called Italian wedding soup) has an interesting history that actually has nothing to do with matrimony. The recipe is based on a centuries-old southern Italian meat and vegetable soup called minestra maritata; the "marriage" (maritata) is of flavors and ingredients—in this case, meatballs and greens. Lovers of this Italian soup are passionate about it, but nowhere is it more popular than in Pittsburgh, where it appears on menus at high-end and fast-food restaurants alike. You can even order wedding soup at the local McDonald's. And of course it's a staple at wedding receptions in the Pittsburgh area.

Wedding soup is traditionally made with a slow-simmered homemade chicken broth. To streamline this recipe, our goal was to start with decent store-bought broth and make it taste better. Cooking garlic and red pepper flakes in olive oil before adding the broth was an obvious first step to building better flavor. The meat varies from only ground beef to a combination of pork and beef. We tried them both, but what our tasters really loved was meat loaf mix (a mixture of ground beef, pork, and veal). Some recipes suggest cooking the meatballs separately and then adding them to the soup. However, we found that poaching the raw meatballs directly in the broth not only saved time but also added more flavor to the broth.

The greens proved to be a challenge. Most recipes call for stirring chopped spinach or escarole into the soup just before serving. But our tasters found these greens too bland and too delicate (they dissolved into the soup). After testing several different types of hearty greens, we settled on chopped kale. It added great flavor and texture and was hearty enough to withstand the hot broth.

Our pasta choices were small—literally. Most recipes call for tiny ditalini, tubetti, or orzo. Of these, tasters preferred the slender pieces of orzo, which easily fit on the spoon. A final garnish of grated Parmesan and a splash of fruity olive oil just before serving lent extra depth of flavor.

PITTSBURGH WEDDING SOUP

SERVES 6 TO 8

If meat loaf mix isn't available, substitute 1 pound of 85-percent lean ground beef. Serve this soup with extra Parmesan cheese and a drizzle of extra-virgin olive oil.

MEATBALLS

2	slices hearty white sandwich bread, torn into pieces
½	cup whole or low-fat milk
1	large egg yolk
½	cup grated Parmesan cheese
3	tablespoons minced fresh parsley
3	garlic cloves, minced
¾	teaspoon salt
½	teaspoon pepper
½	teaspoon dried oregano
1	pound meat loaf mix

SOUP

1	tablespoon extra-virgin olive oil
2	garlic cloves, minced
¼	teaspoon red pepper flakes
3	quarts low-sodium chicken broth
1	large head kale or Swiss chard, stemmed, leaves chopped
1	cup orzo
3	tablespoons minced fresh parsley
	Salt and pepper

1. FOR THE MEATBALLS: Using a potato masher, mash the bread and milk in a large bowl until smooth. Add the remaining ingredients, except the meat loaf mix, and mash to combine. Add the meat loaf mix and knead by hand until well combined. Form the mixture into 1-inch meatballs (you should have about 55 meatballs) and arrange them on a rimmed baking sheet. Cover with plastic wrap and refrigerate until firm, at least 30 minutes. (The meatballs can be made up to 24 hours in advance.)

2. FOR THE SOUP: Heat the oil in a Dutch oven over medium-high heat until shimmering. Cook the garlic and red pepper flakes until fragrant, about 30 seconds. Add the broth and bring to a boil. Stir in the kale or Swiss chard and simmer until softened, 10 to 15 minutes. Stir in the meatballs and orzo, reduce the heat to medium, and simmer until the meatballs are cooked through and the orzo is tender, about 10 minutes. Stir in the parsley and season with salt and pepper to taste. Serve. (Leftover soup can be refrigerated for up to 3 days.)

TEST KITCHEN SHORTCUT
- -

Easy Mini Meatballs: We found that the large end of a melon baller guarantees uniform meatballs that will cook evenly. The melon baller also greatly speeds up the shaping process.

Hearty Beef Stew

Beef stew should be rich and satisfying. Our goal in developing a recipe for it was to keep the cooking process simple without compromising the stew's deep, complex flavor. We focused on these issues: What cuts of beef respond best to stewing? How much and what kind of liquid should you use? When and with what do you thicken the stew?

Experts tout different cuts as being ideal for stewing. Our advice is to buy a steak or roast from the chuck and cube it yourself. Precut stewing beef often includes irregularly shaped end pieces from different muscles that cannot be sold as steaks or roasts because of their uneven appearance. Because of the differences in origin, precut stewing cubes in the same package may not be consistent in the way they cook or taste. If you cut your own cubes from a piece of chuck, you can be sure that all the cubes will cook in the same way and have the flavor and richness of chuck.

Having settled on our cut of beef, we started to explore how and when to thicken the stew. Dredging meat cubes in flour is a roundabout way of thickening stew. The floured beef is browned, then stewed. During the stewing process, some of the flour from the beef dissolves into the liquid, causing it to thicken. Although the stew we cooked this way thickened up nicely, the beef cubes had a "smothered steak" look.

We then tried thickening the stew with flour after sautéing onions and garlic, right before adding the liquid. This method tasted as good as the stew made with flour-tossed beef, but it didn't mar the texture of the meat.

We next focused on stewing liquids. We tried water, wine, store-bought beef broth, store-bought chicken broth, combinations of these liquids, and beef stock. Stews made with water were bland and greasy. Stews made entirely with wine were too strong. The stew made from beef stock was delicious, but we decided that beef stew, which has many hearty ingredients contributing to its flavor profile, did not absolutely need beef stock, which is quite time-consuming to make. When we turned to store-bought broths, the chicken outscored the beef broth. The stew made entirely with chicken stock was good, but we missed the acidity and flavor provided by the wine. In the end, we preferred a combination of chicken stock and red wine.

We tested various amounts of liquid and found that we preferred stews with a minimum of liquid, which helps to preserve a strong meat flavor. With too little liquid, however, the stew may not cook evenly, and there may not be enough "sauce" to spoon over starchy accompaniments. A cup of liquid per pound of meat gave us sufficient sauce to moisten a mound of mashed potatoes or polenta without drowning them. We tested various kinds of wine and found that fairly inexpensive fruity, full-bodied young wines, such as Chianti or Zinfandel, were best.

To determine when to add the vegetables, we made three different stews, adding carrots, potatoes, and onions to one stew at the beginning of cooking and to another stew halfway through the cooking process. For our third stew, we cooked the onions with the meat but added steamed carrots and potatoes when the stew was fully cooked.

The stew with vegetables added at the beginning was thin and watery. The vegetables had fallen apart and given up their flavor and liquid to the stew. The beef stew with the cooked vegetables added at the last minute was delicious, and the vegetables were the freshest and most intensely flavored. However, it was more work to steam the vegetables separately. Also, the flavor of vegetables cooked separately from the stew didn't really meld all that well with the other flavors and ingredients. We preferred to add the vegetables partway through the cooking

process. They didn't fall apart this way, and they had enough time to meld with the other ingredients. There is one exception to this rule. Peas were added just before serving the stew to preserve their color and texture.

HEARTY BEEF STEW

SERVES 6 TO 8

Make this stew in an ovenproof Dutch oven, preferably with a capacity of 8 quarts but nothing less than 6 quarts. Choose one with a wide bottom; this will allow you to brown the meat in just two batches.

3	pounds beef chuck roast, trimmed and cut into 1½-inch cubes
	Salt and pepper
3	tablespoons vegetable oil
2	onions, chopped
3	garlic cloves, minced
3	tablespoons all-purpose flour
1	cup full-bodied red wine
2	cups low-sodium chicken broth
2	bay leaves
1	teaspoon dried thyme
4	medium red potatoes (about 1½ pounds), peeled and cut into 1-inch cubes
4	large carrots (about 1 pound), peeled and cut into ¼-inch slices
1	cup frozen peas (about 6 ounces), thawed
¼	cup minced fresh parsley

1. Adjust an oven rack to the lower-middle position and heat the oven to 300 degrees. Dry the beef thoroughly on paper towels, then season it generously with salt and pepper. Heat 1 tablespoon of the oil in a large ovenproof Dutch oven over medium-high heat until shimmering, about 2 minutes. Add half of the meat to the pot so that the individual pieces are close together but not touching. Cook, not moving the pieces until the sides touching the pot are well browned, 2 to 3 minutes. Using tongs, turn each piece and continue cooking until most sides are well browned, about 5 minutes longer. Transfer the beef to a medium bowl, add 1 tablespoon more oil to the pot, and swirl to coat the pan bottom. Brown the remaining beef; transfer the meat to the bowl and set aside.

2. Reduce the heat to medium, add the remaining 1 tablespoon oil to the empty Dutch oven, and swirl to coat the pan bottom. Add the onions and ¼ teaspoon salt. Cook, stirring frequently and vigorously, scraping the bottom of the pot with a wooden spoon to loosen browned bits, until the onions have softened, 4 to 5 minutes. Add the garlic and continue to cook for 30 seconds. Stir in the flour and cook until lightly colored, 1 to 2 minutes. Add the wine, scraping up the remaining browned bits from the bottom and edges of the pot and stirring until the liquid is thick. Gradually add the broth, stirring constantly and scraping the pan edges to dissolve the flour. Add the bay leaves and thyme and bring to a simmer. Add the meat and return to a simmer. Cover and place the pot in the oven. Cook for 1 hour.

3. Remove the pot from the oven and add the potatoes and carrots. Cover and return the pot to the oven. Cook just until the meat is tender, about 1 hour. Remove the pot from the oven. (The stew can be covered and refrigerated for up to 3 days. Bring to a simmer over medium-low heat before continuing.)

4. Add the peas, cover, and allow to stand for 5 minutes. Stir in the parsley, discard the bay leaves, adjust the seasonings, and serve immediately.

SHOPPING WITH THE TEST KITCHEN

Red Wine for Stew: When making a dish that uses red wine, our tendency is to grab whichever inexpensive dry red is on hand. But we began to wonder what difference particular wines would make in the final dish and decided to investigate.

We called on the advice of several local wine experts, who gave us some parameters to work with when selecting red wines to use in a braise such as beef stew or cacciatore. When choosing a red wine for a basic stew, look for one that is dry (to avoid a sweet sauce) and with good acidity (to aid in breaking down the fibers of the meat). Keep in mind that any characteristic found in the uncooked wine will be concentrated when cooked.

We found that softer, fruity wines such as Merlot were too sweet for beef stew or cacciatore. We also learned that it's best to avoid wines that have been "oaked," usually older wines; the oak flavor tends to become harsh and bitter as the wine is cooked.

SHOPPING WITH THE TEST KITCHEN

Inexpensive Dutch Ovens: We use our trusty Dutch oven for cooking up many dishes from chilis and soups to stews and braises. What do we look for in a Dutch oven? We like one with a minimum capacity of 6 quarts. The bottom should be thick, so that it maintains moderate heat, and the lid should fit tightly. Our test kitchen is stocked with many of our two favorites made by All-Clad and Le Creuset, but some of us are reluctant to shell out over $200 to buy one. So we tested Dutch ovens in the under $100 range and came up with a less expensive alternative. The Tramontina 6.5-Quart Cast Iron Dutch Oven is comparable in size to the All-Clad and Le Creuset ovens and performs nearly as well. And, at $40, it costs a fraction of the price of either.

Hearty Vegetable Soup

A brothy soup with bits of vegetables is fine most of the year, but in the dead of winter we want a soup thick enough to stick to our spoon and our ribs. Long simmering of starchy root vegetables (especially potatoes) or dried beans is the most common way to create a really hearty soup. But is it the only way?

Some recipes allow you to speed up the process by pureeing part of the soup once the vegetables are tender. We found this technique added more body to the soup and helped infuse the broth with more vegetable flavor, but the soup was still not hearty enough. A selection of winter vegetables (our tasters liked carrots, parsnips, and onions) and the starchiest potatoes (russets instead of waxy red potatoes) helped, too, but the soup still wasn't ready for main-course status.

Maybe pureeing a starchy ingredient with part of the soup would make it thicker. Our first thought was canned beans, but our tasters were unimpressed, calling the soup "mealy," with an easily identifiable "grainy bean texture." Tasters also rejected cooked rice, which gave the soup an overwhelming rice flavor and unappealing viscous texture.

The surprise solution was plain old sandwich bread, lightly toasted to remove moisture and to help the slices dissolve in the blender. The bread gave the soup an almost creamy consistency (several tasters insisted we had sneaked in some heavy cream) and did not interfere with the vegetable flavor.

We now had a rich, hearty vegetable soup that cooked in less than 30 minutes, but it needed some color and variety in texture. A little fresh spinach and either frozen lima beans or peas helped, as did herbs such as thyme and rosemary. To keep the flavor of the rosemary from overpowering the other ingredients, we simmered a whole sprig and then removed it before serving. Cannellini beans (not pureed this time) were also a nice addition. Tasters wanted a little acidity to finish the soup, and they preferred slightly sweet balsamic vinegar to other vinegars or lemon juice. In the end, we had a vegetable soup with a hearty, slow-cooked texture but without the slow cooking—and it was as easy as sliced bread.

HEARTY VEGETABLE SOUP

SERVES 6 TO 8

This soup won't freeze very well, but leftovers can be refrigerated for up to 3 days.

2	tablespoons vegetable oil
3	large carrots, peeled and cut into ¾-inch pieces
2	large parsnips, peeled and cut into ¾-inch pieces
2	small onions, peeled and cut into ½-inch pieces
6	garlic cloves, minced
8	cups low-sodium chicken broth
2	medium russet potatoes, peeled and cut into 1-inch pieces
2	teaspoons minced fresh thyme
1	sprig fresh rosemary
2	bay leaves
2	slices hearty white sandwich bread, lightly toasted
2	cups curly-leaf spinach, stemmed and chopped
1	(14.5-ounce) can cannellini beans, drained and rinsed
1	(10-ounce) package frozen baby lima beans or peas
	Balsamic vinegar
	Salt and pepper

1. Heat the oil in a large heavy-bottomed pot over medium-high heat until shimmering. Add the carrots, parsnips, and onions and cook until lightly browned and softened, 5 to 7 minutes. Add the garlic and cook until fragrant, about 30 seconds. Add the broth, potatoes, thyme, rosemary, and bay

leaves and bring to a boil. Reduce the heat to low, cover, and simmer until the vegetables are soft, about 15 minutes.

2. Remove and discard the rosemary and bay leaves. Transfer 3 cups of the solids, 1 cup of the broth, and the bread to a blender and puree until smooth. Stir the puree back into the pot, add the spinach, cannellini beans, and lima beans or peas and cook over medium heat until the spinach is tender and the beans are heated through, about 8 minutes. Stir in 1 tablespoon balsamic vinegar and season with salt and pepper to taste. Serve, passing extra vinegar at the table.

Butternut Squash Soup

Butternut squash soup is essentially a simple soup. With squash, a cooking liquid, some aromatic ingredients, and a blender, the soup can be made without much commotion. But many squash soups hardly live up to their potential. Rather than being lustrous, slightly creamy, and intensely "squash-y" in flavor, they are vegetal or porridge-like, and they sometimes taste more like a squash pie than a squash soup.

Knowing that our basic method would be to cook the squash and then puree it with a liquid, our first test focused on how to cook the squash for the soup. We tried roasting, as we hoped to avoid the chore of peeling the squash's tough outer skin. All we had to do was slice the squash in half, scoop out the seeds, and roast it on a rimmed baking sheet—but it produced a caramel-flavored soup with a gritty texture. Roasting also took at least an hour—too long for what should be a quick, no-nonsense soup.

In an effort to save time without sacrificing the quick preparation we liked from the roasting test, we decided to try steaming the squash. In a large Dutch oven, we sautéed shallots in butter (we tried garlic

and onion but found them too overpowering), then added water and brought the mixture to a simmer. We seeded and quartered the squash and placed it in a collapsible steaming insert, then added the squash and insert to the Dutch oven. We covered the pan and let the squash steam for 30 minutes until it was tender enough to show no resistance to a fork. This method proved to be successful. We liked it because all of the cooking took place in just one pot, and, as a bonus, we ended up with a squash-infused cooking liquid that we could use as a base for the soup.

But there was a downside. Essentially, steaming had the opposite effect of roasting: whereas roasting concentrated the sugars and eliminated the liquid in the squash (which is what made the roasted squash soup gritty), steaming added liquid and diluted the squash's flavor. As we were preparing squash one morning, it occurred to us that we were throwing away the answer to more squash flavor—the seeds and fibers. Instead of trashing the scooped-out remnants, we added them to the sautéed shallots and butter. In minutes the room became fragrant with an earthy, sweet squash aroma, and the butter in our Dutch oven turned a brilliant shade of saffron. We added the water to the pan and proceeded with the steaming preparation. After the squash was cooked through, we strained the liquid of seeds, fibers, and spent shallot, then blended the soup.

To intensify the sweetness of the squash (but not make the soup sweet), we added a teaspoon of dark brown sugar just before serving. Not only was this batch of squash soup brighter in flavor, but it was more intense in color as well. To round out the flavor and introduce some richness we added ½ cup of heavy cream. Now the soup was thick, rich, and suffused with pure squash flavor. After pureeing the soup, we heated it briefly over a low flame and stirred in a little freshly grated nutmeg. In under 1 hour and with only one pot, we made a squash soup that sacrificed no flavor and offered autumn in a bowl.

BUTTERNUT SQUASH SOUP

SERVES 4 TO 6

If you don't own a collapsible metal steaming basket, the removable insert from a pasta pot works well, too. Some nice accompaniments to this soup are lightly toasted pumpkin seeds, a drizzle of aged balsamic vinegar, or a sprinkle of paprika.

4	tablespoons unsalted butter
1	large shallot, minced
3	pounds butternut squash (about 1 large squash), cut in half lengthwise, each half cut in half crosswise, seeds and strings scraped out and reserved (about ¼ cup)
6	cups water
	Salt
½	cup heavy cream
1	teaspoon dark brown sugar
	Pinch freshly grated nutmeg

1. Melt the butter in a large Dutch oven over medium-low heat until foaming. Add the shallot and cook, stirring frequently, until translucent, about 3 minutes. Add the squash seeds and strings, and cook, stirring occasionally, until the butter turns saffron-colored, about 4 minutes.

2. Add the water and 1 teaspoon salt to the pot and bring to a boil over high heat. Reduce the heat to medium-low, place the squash cut side down in a steamer basket, and lower the basket into the pot. Cover and steam until the squash is completely tender, about 30 minutes. Take the pot off the heat, and use tongs to transfer the squash to a rimmed baking sheet. When cool enough to handle, use a large spoon to scrape the flesh from the skin. Reserve the squash flesh in a bowl and discard the skin.

3. Strain the steaming liquid through a fine-mesh strainer into a second bowl; discard the solids in the strainer. (You should have 2½ to 3 cups of liquid.) Rinse and dry the pot.

4. Puree the squash in batches in a blender, pulsing on low and adding enough reserved steaming liquid to obtain a smooth consistency. Transfer the puree to the pot and stir in the remaining steaming liquid, cream, and brown sugar. Warm the soup over medium-low heat until hot, about 3 minutes. Stir in the nutmeg and adjust the seasonings, adding salt to taste. Serve immediately. (The soup can be refrigerated in an airtight container for several days. Warm over low heat until hot; do not boil.)

CUTTING BUTTERNUT SQUASH

1. Set the squash on a damp kitchen towel to hold it in place. Position the cleaver on the skin of the squash.

2. Strike the back of the cleaver with a mallet to drive the cleaver into the squash. Continue to hit the cleaver until the cleaver cuts through the squash and opens it up.

TEST KITCHEN SHORTCUT

Drip-Free Ladling: There's an easy way to keep drips and spills to a minimum when ladling soups or stews. Before lifting the filled ladle up and out of the pot, dip the bottom back in the pot, so that the liquid comes about halfway up the ladle. The tension on the surface of the soup grabs any drips and pulls them back into the pot.

Fresh Tomato Soup with Basil

You think you know tomato soup. It's velvety smooth and creamy—perfect for a cold winter day. But there's another tomato soup—one made without cream, so you can really taste the tomatoes. It's usually flavored with onions, garlic, and basil and is the perfect way to use a surplus of ripe summer tomatoes.

We quickly discovered that soups made with just tomatoes and seasonings were best. Added liquids, such as chicken broth or even tomato juice, diluted the tomato flavor. But even without adding any liquid, we found this soup could be watery. To concentrate the tomato flavor and evaporate excess moisture, we switched from the stovetop to the oven—through roasting. We tossed the tomatoes with onion, garlic, and olive oil and slid them into the oven. Roasting caramelizes the sugars in the tomatoes and really brings out their flavor. Once they were roasted, we pureed the tomatoes in a blender. This soup was good, but the 90 minutes of roasting had taken its toll on the tomatoes at the expense of freshness.

So, for our next test, we decided to finish the soup with chopped fresh tomatoes. Everyone in the test kitchen gave a thumbs up to the fresh flavor they added but complained about the firm chunks of tomatoes floating in the smooth soup. We then remembered how we treat tomatoes for salsa: we salt the tomatoes to soften their structure and break them down. So we tossed the reserved tomatoes with a bit of salt and let them sit for 30 minutes. We added the salted tomatoes to a pot with the pureed roasted tomatoes and let everything cook for just 5 minutes. At last our tomato soup boasted complex flavor heightened by tiny bursts of fresh tomato.

FRESH TOMATO SOUP WITH BASIL
SERVES 4 TO 6

Depending on the juiciness of your tomatoes, you may need to thin the soup with a little water.

- **5** pounds ripe beefsteak or plum tomatoes, cored and quartered, plus 1 pound tomatoes, cored and diced medium
- **2** onions, chopped
- **8** garlic cloves, peeled and left whole, plus 1 clove, minced
- **3** tablespoons extra-virgin olive oil
  Salt
  Sugar
- **1** cup chopped fresh basil

1. Adjust an oven rack to the upper-middle position and heat the oven to 450 degrees. Combine the quartered tomatoes, onions, whole garlic cloves, oil, ½ teaspoon salt, and ¼ teaspoon sugar in a large roasting pan. Roast, stirring once or twice, until the tomatoes are brown in spots, about 1½ hours. Let cool 5 minutes. Working in two batches, process the roasted tomato mixture in a food processor until smooth. (The pureed mixture can be refrigerated for up to 1 day.)

2. When ready to serve, combine the diced tomatoes, minced garlic, basil, and ¼ teaspoon salt in a bowl and marinate for 30 minutes. Transfer to a large saucepan, add the pureed tomato mixture, and simmer over medium heat until the diced tomatoes are slightly softened, about 5 minutes. Season with salt and sugar to taste. Serve.

Loaded Baked Potato Soup

Take a baked potato and pile it high with all of the fixin's: cheese, bacon, scallions, and sour cream. Now take that same loaded baked potato, buzz it in the blender with a little broth, and heat it on the stove—presto, loaded baked potato soup! That's exactly what we tasted when we ordered the "Loaded Baked Potato Soup" during a recent trip to a restaurant.

Most recipes for this type of soup start with baking the potatoes in the oven, which ensures that the soup tastes "baked" and more deeply flavored than potato soups that are boiled. But it takes over an hour to bake a potato, and that meant that from start to finish our soup was closing in on 2 hours to make. That seemed too long for a simple soup.

A few recipes offered the microwave as a shortcut to cooking the potatoes. Sure, the 10 minutes or so in the microwave was a big time-saver, but the potatoes felt mealy and tasted stale. Boiling russet potatoes gave us our best results yet, at least in terms of texture. The potatoes were tender and moist, but because we had been peeling them (the skins were soggy when cooked in the soup), the baked flavor was gone. We hoped the other fixin' ingredients would help.

Starting by frying up bacon was mandatory. When the rendered fat was used to cook the other ingredients, the bacon flavor permeated the soup, and the crisped bacon pieces were ready to be used as a garnish. Scallions were another story; when they were added to the soup at the onset, their delicate flavor and bright color were exhausted by the end of the cooking time. Instead, we cooked some chopped onion in the bacon fat and saved the scallions for garnish.

For more "loaded" flavor we whisked in some sour cream right before serving (being careful not to boil the soup to avoid curdling the sour cream), and this soup was bordering on just right.

The soup tasted like all the best parts of a loaded baked potato—plenty of smoky bacon, cheese, and sour cream—but one thing was missing; without the flavor from the potato skin, our soup didn't taste "baked." Luckily, a colleague happened to spy the discarded potato peelings in the trash and wondered if they could be fried in the bacon fat (like a fried potato skin) and used as a flavorful garnish. We gave the next batch a try, and the cooked skins added the exact "baked" flavor that had been lacking.

In half the time it takes to actually bake a potato, we had all the flavor of a loaded one—and we could eat it with a spoon.

LOADED BAKED POTATO SOUP

SERVES 8

If you prefer, replace the thyme sprig with ¼ teaspoon dried thyme (no need to remove it in step 3). Reserving some of the potatoes in step 3 results in a chunkier soup. For a smooth soup, puree all the potatoes.

- 8 slices bacon, chopped
- 3 pounds russet potatoes, scrubbed
- 1 large onion, chopped
- 2 garlic cloves, minced
- 2 tablespoons all-purpose flour
- 4 cups low-sodium chicken broth
- 1 cup heavy cream
- 1 sprig fresh thyme
- 4 cups shredded sharp cheddar cheese, plus additional for garnish
- 1 cup sour cream, plus additional for garnish
  Pepper
- 3 scallions, sliced thin

1. Cook the bacon in a Dutch oven over medium heat until crisp, about 8 minutes. While the bacon is cooking, use a vegetable peeler to remove wide strips of peel from the potatoes; reserve the peels.

Cut the peeled potatoes into ¾-inch pieces. Using a slotted spoon, transfer the bacon to a plate lined with paper towels. Add the reserved potato skins to the bacon fat in the pot and cook until crisp, about 8 minutes. Using a slotted spoon, transfer the potato skins to the plate with the bacon.

2. Add the onion to the fat remaining in the pot and cook over medium heat until golden, about 6 minutes. Stir in the garlic and flour and cook until fragrant, about 1 minute. Gradually whisk in the broth and cream, stir in the thyme and potatoes, and bring to a boil over high heat. Reduce the heat to medium-low, cover the pot, and cook until the potatoes are tender, about 7 minutes.

3. Discard the thyme and transfer 2 cups of the cooked potatoes to a bowl. Puree the remaining soup in batches in a blender until smooth. Return the soup to the pot and warm over medium-high heat. Off the heat, stir in the cheese until melted, then whisk in the sour cream. Return the reserved potatoes to the pot and season the soup with pepper. Ladle the soup into bowls, and garnish with the bacon, fried potato skins, scallions, cheese, and sour cream.

Creamy Broccoli and Cheddar Soup

Broccoli-cheddar soup is old-fashioned comfort food. But for something so simple (basically broccoli, chicken broth, cream, and cheese), a lot can go wrong. Many recipes yield either a gloppy, glorified cheese sauce or a mealy mess of bland, gray vegetables. We wanted a creamy soup that tasted like fresh, bright green broccoli.

Since this soup is almost always pureed, we wondered if we could include the fibrous stalks for flavor. (The outside of the stalks is always the most fibrous part, so it's important to peel broccoli stalks with a vegetable peeler before cooking.) We made what amounted to a broccoli stock by sautéing broccoli stalks with onion and garlic and then adding chicken broth and cooking the stock until the stalks were soft. It was only then that we added the broccoli florets and cream; this ensured that the florets didn't overcook and retained their bright color and fresh flavor.

We kept increasing the amount of broccoli until we were using 1½ pounds (twice as much as in many recipes) for just six bowls of soup. The soup was so thick from the broccoli and cheddar (added at the end to keep it from separating and clumping) that we didn't need to thicken the soup with flour or cornstarch.

CREAMY BROCCOLI AND CHEDDAR SOUP

SERVES 6

Taste the soup before adding any salt; both the cheese and the chicken broth can be quite salty.

3	tablespoons unsalted butter
1	large onion, chopped
2	garlic cloves, chopped
1½	pounds broccoli, stalks peeled and cut into ½-inch slices, florets chopped into ½-inch pieces
4	cups low-sodium chicken broth
1	cup heavy cream
¼	teaspoon ground nutmeg
3	cups shredded mild cheddar cheese, plus extra for garnish
	Salt
	Cayenne pepper

1. Melt the butter in a large pot over medium heat. Add the onion and cook until soft, about 5 minutes. Add the garlic and cook until fragrant, about 30 seconds. Add the broccoli stalks and cook until bright green and just beginning to soften, about 5 minutes. Stir in the broth, increase the heat to medium-high, and simmer until the stalks are tender, about 5 minutes. Add the florets, cream, and nutmeg and simmer until the florets are tender, about 5 minutes.

2. Puree the soup in two batches in a blender until smooth, return to the pot, and bring to a simmer over medium heat. Stir in the cheese until melted and season with salt and cayenne. Serve, garnished with extra cheese. (The soup can be refrigerated for up to 3 days. Reheat over medium heat until hot, but do not boil or the cheese will separate.)

Split-Pea Soup

Old-fashioned recipes for ham and split-pea soup start with the bone from a large roast ham that has been nearly picked clean. The bone and some split peas are thrown in a pot with some water and cooked until the meat falls off the bone. By that time, the fat has discreetly melted into the liquid, and the peas have become creamy enough to thicken the soup.

We love split-pea soup made this way, but times have changed. Except for the occasional holiday, most cooks rarely buy a bone-in ham, opting more often for the thin-sliced deli stuff. We wondered if we could duplicate this wonderful soup without buying a huge ham.

The answer, we found, is a ham steak. They are often sold precooked and offer plenty of meat to eat along with the split peas. Mincing the steak fine and then sautéing it along with the aromatics—onion, garlic, and carrots—evenly distributes its salty, smoky flavor throughout the broth in short order. As for seasoning, we found bay leaves to be a subtle but necessary flavor booster. Other typical split-pea soup ingredients—like potatoes, salt pork, celery, leeks, thyme, and red pepper flakes—were unnecessary, masking the flavor of the ham and split peas rather than enhancing them. Cooking the vegetables in butter also added richness to the soup, and a pinch of sugar balanced the saltiness of the ham. It turns out that for great ham and split-pea soup, less is more.

EASY SPLIT-PEA SOUP WITH HAM
SERVES 6 TO 8
If you have any leftover roast ham in your refrigerator, feel free to use it in place of the ham steak (though you may need to adjust the seasonings).

3	tablespoons unsalted butter
1	medium onion, chopped
2	carrots, peeled and chopped
3	garlic cloves, minced
1	pound ham steak, chopped fine
	Pinch sugar
1	pound dried split peas, picked over and rinsed
6	cups low-sodium chicken broth
2	cups water
2	bay leaves
	Pepper

1. Melt the butter in a large stockpot over medium heat. Add the onion, carrots, garlic, ham, and sugar; cover and cook until the vegetables are soft, 8 to 10 minutes.

2. Add the peas, broth, water, and bay leaves; increase the heat to high and bring to a boil. Reduce the heat to medium-low and simmer until the peas are soft, about 40 minutes. Discard the bay leaves and add pepper to taste. Serve. (The soup can be refrigerated for several days or frozen for up to 1 month. Because split peas continue to soak up liquid over time, the soup may be dense when reheated. If the soup is too thick, stir in water ¼ cup at a time until the consistency is to your liking. Simmer over medium-low heat until the soup is hot.)

New England Clam Chowder

We love homemade clam chowder almost as much as we love good chicken soup. But we must confess that many cooks (including some who work in our test kitchen) don't make their own chowder. Although they might never buy chicken soup, they seem willing to make this compromise. We wondered why.

Time certainly isn't the reason. You can actually prepare clam chowder much more quickly than you can a pot of good chicken soup. The reason why many cooks don't bother making their own clam chowder is the clams. First of all, clams can be expensive. Second, clams are not terribly forgiving—you must cook them soon after their purchase, and then the soup itself must be quickly consumed. Last, chowders are more fragile (and thus more fickle) than other soups. Unless the chowder is stabilized in some way, it curdles, especially if the soup is brought to a boil.

Our goals for this soup, then, were multiple but quite clear. We wanted to develop a delicious, traditional chowder that was economical, would not curdle, and could be prepared quickly. We started with the clams.

Cherrystones offered good value and flavor. (Quahogs, pronounced *KO-hogs*, are often used for chowder, but seemed too large to us and turned out tough and stringy.) The chowder made from cherrystones was distinctly clam-flavored, without an inky aftertaste. Because there are no industry sizing standards for each clam variety, you may find some small quahogs labeled as cherrystones or large cherrystones labeled as quahogs. Regardless of designation, clams much over 4 inches in diameter will deliver a distinctly metallic, inky-flavored chowder.

Some recipes suggest shucking raw clams and then adding the raw clam bellies to the soup pot. In other recipes the clams are steamed open. We found that steaming clams open is far easier than shucking them. After 7 to 9 minutes over simmering water, the clams open as naturally as budding flowers.

Although many chowder recipes instruct the cook to soak the clams in saltwater spiked with cornmeal or baking powder to remove grit, we found the extra step of purging or filtering hard-shell clams to be unnecessary. All of the hard-shells we tested were relatively clean, and what little sediment there was sank to the bottom of the steaming liquid. Getting rid of the grit was as simple as leaving the last few tablespoons of broth in the pan when pouring it from the pot. If you find that your clam broth is gritty, strain it through a coffee filter.

At this point we turned our attention to texture. We wanted a chowder that was thick but still a soup rather than a stew. Older recipes call for thickening clam chowder with crumbled biscuits; bread crumbs and crackers are modern stand-ins, but these never fully dissolved. We discovered fairly quickly that flour was necessary, not only as a thickener but also as a stabilizer, because unthickened chowders separate and curdle. Of the two flour methods, we opted to thicken at the beginning of cooking rather than at the end. Because our final recipe was finished with cream, we felt the chowder didn't need the extra butter that would be required if we added the flour in a paste to the finished soup.

For potatoes, we found that waxy red boiling potatoes are best for creamy-style chowders. They have a firm but tender texture, and their red skins look appealing.

We now had two final questions to answer about New England clam chowder. First, should it include salt pork or bacon? Second, should the chowder be enriched with milk or cream?

Salt pork is the more traditional choice in chowder recipes, although bacon has become popular in recent decades. We made clam chowder with both salt pork and bacon, and tasters liked both versions.

Frankly, we ended up using such small amounts of pork in our final recipe that either salt pork or bacon is fine. Bacon is more readily available and, once bought, easier to use up.

As for the cream versus milk issue, we found that so much milk was required to make the chowder look and taste creamy that it began to lose its clam flavor and became more like a mild bisque or the clam equivalent of oyster stew. Making the chowder with almost all clam broth (5 cups of the cooking liquid from steaming the clams), then finishing the stew with a cup of cream, gave us what we were looking for—a rich, creamy chowder that tasted distinctly of clams.

NEW ENGLAND CLAM CHOWDER

SERVES 6

If desired, replace the bacon with 4 ounces of finely chopped salt pork. Note that the chowder is best served at once. Reheating will make the clams tough and chewy.

7	pounds medium hard-shell clams, such as cherrystones, washed and scrubbed clean
4	slices thick-cut bacon, cut into ¼-inch pieces (see note above)
1	large Spanish onion, chopped
2	tablespoons all-purpose flour
1½	pounds red potatoes (about 3 medium), scrubbed and cut into ½-inch dice
2	bay leaves
1	teaspoon minced fresh thyme or ¼ teaspoon dried
1	cup heavy cream
2	tablespoons minced fresh parsley Salt and pepper

1. Bring 3 cups water to a boil in a large stockpot or Dutch oven. Add the clams and cover with a tight-fitting lid. Cook for 5 minutes, uncover, and stir with a wooden spoon. Quickly cover the pot and steam until the clams just open, 2 to 4 minutes. Transfer the clams to a large bowl; cool slightly. Open the clams with a paring knife, holding the clams over a bowl to catch any juices. With the knife, sever the muscle that attaches the clam to the shell and transfer the meat to a cutting board. Discard the shells. Mince the clams; set aside. Pour the clam broth into a 2-quart Pyrex measuring cup, holding back the last few tablespoons of broth in case there is sediment; set the clam broth aside. (You should have about 5 cups. If not, add bottled clam juice or water to make this amount.) Rinse and dry the stockpot or Dutch oven, then return the pot to the burner.

2. Fry the bacon in the empty pot over medium-low heat until the fat is rendered and the bacon is crisp, 5 to 7 minutes. Add the onion and cook, stirring occasionally, until softened, about 5 minutes. Add the flour and stir until lightly colored, about 1 minute. Gradually whisk in the reserved clam broth. Add the potatoes, bay leaves, and thyme and simmer until the potatoes are tender, about 10 minutes. Add the reserved minced clams, the cream, parsley, and salt (if necessary) and pepper to taste; bring to a simmer, but do not boil. Remove the pan from the heat, discard the bay leaves, and serve immediately.

Variation

QUICK PANTRY NEW ENGLAND CLAM CHOWDER

From late summer through winter, when clams are plentiful, you'll probably want to make fresh clam chowder. But if you're short on time or find that clams are scarce and expensive, the right canned clams and bottled clam juice deliver a chowder that's at least three notches above canned chowder in quality. We tested seven brands of minced and small whole canned clams and preferred Doxsee minced clams teamed with Doxsee clam juice, as well as Snow's minced clams and Snow's clam juice.

Follow the recipe for New England Clam Chowder, substituting 4 (6.5-ounce) cans minced clams, juice drained and reserved, for the fresh clams with 1 cup water and 2 (8-ounce) bottles clam juice. Add the clam juice mixture and clam meat at the same points in step 2 that the fresh clam broth and meat are added.

SHOPPING WITH THE TEST KITCHEN

Buying Clams by Weight or Number: Judging by most recipes, there is no consistent or accurate method of designating the amount of clams needed for a given chowder. Some recipes call for some amount of shucked clams, giving the cook no idea how many whole clams to buy. Other recipes call for X number of "hard-shell clams," apparently not taking into account the size differences between a quahog and a littleneck. Likewise, there are no industry sizing standards for each clam variety. Clam size and name vary from source to source, so that one company's cherrystone clam might be another company's quahog.

We wondered if calling for X pounds of clams, regardless of size, would yield similar quantities of meat and liquid. Working with 1-pound quantities, we shucked quahogs, cherrystones, and littlenecks. The number of clams per pound varied greatly (two of our quahogs equaled 1 pound, but it took 2 dozen littlenecks to equal the same weight). So, even though clams are usually sold by the piece at the fish market, we find it more accurate to measure them by weight rather than quantity. Just ask your fish market to weigh the clams as they count them. Regardless of clam size, you'll need 7 to 8 pounds to make our clam chowder recipe.

Creole-Style Shrimp and Sausage Gumbo

Gumbo, like all great folk recipes, is open to plenty of individual interpretation. Generally speaking, though, this Creole-style stew usually includes some combination of seafood, poultry, or small game along with sausage or some other highly seasoned, cured smoked pork, plus onion, bell pepper, and celery. Quite often, gumbos are thickened with okra or ground dried sassafras leaves, known as filé (pronounced *fee-LAY*) powder. Last, but very important, most gumbos are flavored with a dark brown roux, and it is roux that is the heart of a good gumbo.

A roux is nothing more than flour cooked in fat to form a paste that is used to thicken sauces. But unlike a white, blond, or beige roux, the dark brown roux is cooked much longer over low heat for up to 60 minutes. This breaks down the starches in the flour to the point where the roux offers relatively little thickening power, but instead, imbues gumbo with a complex, toasty, smoky flavor and a deep, rich brown color that define the dish. We wondered if there was a way to shorten this time for a more practical recipe.

For our testing, we began with the widely used 1-to-1 ratio of all-purpose flour to vegetable oil, using ½ cup of each. We preheated the oil over medium-high heat for only about 2 minutes before adding the flour, then lowering the heat to medium to cook the roux. At 20 minutes, the roux had cooked to a deep reddish brown. It yielded absolutely acceptable results, but we began to have trouble incorporating the simmering stock into the roux. Switching the all-purpose flour from a high-protein, unbleached brand to a slightly lower-protein, bleached national brand did improve the texture of the gumbo slightly, but the separation of the flour and oil upon the addition of simmering liquid continued to perplex us. Eventually, we found some recipes in our research that said either the roux or the stock should be cooled before combining them. Sure enough, cooling the stock (which took less time than cooling the roux) did the trick.

As for seasoning our gumbo, we settled on 6 garlic cloves, along with dried thyme and bay leaves. For spicy heat, tasters preferred ½ teaspoon of cayenne pepper to the vinegary taste of bottled hot sauce. Last, we considered whether to thicken the gumbo with okra or filé powder. We think both are probably acquired tastes. Thus far, everyone had been satisfied without either, and because both added distinct—and, to some, unwelcome—flavors, we decided to reserve them for the variations on the master recipe.

CREOLE-STYLE SHRIMP AND SAUSAGE GUMBO

SERVES 6 TO 8

Making a dark roux can be dangerous. The mixture reaches temperatures in excess of 400 degrees. Therefore, use a deep pot for cooking the roux and long-handled utensils for stirring it, and be careful not to splash it on yourself. One secret to smooth gumbo is adding shrimp stock that is neither too hot nor too cold to the roux. For a stock that is at the right temperature when the roux is done, start preparing it before you tend to the vegetables and other ingredients, strain it, and then give it a head start on cooling by immediately adding ice water and clam juice. So that your constant stirring of the roux will not be interrupted, start the roux only after you've made the stock. Alternatively, you can make the stock well ahead of time and bring it back to room temperature before using it. Spicy andouille sausage is a Louisiana specialty that may not be available everywhere; kielbasa or any fully cooked smoked sausage makes a fine substitute. Gumbo is traditionally served over white rice.

1½	pounds small shrimp (51 to 60 per pound), shells removed and reserved
1	cup bottled clam juice
3½	cups ice water

½	cup vegetable oil
½	cup all-purpose flour, preferably bleached
2	onions, chopped fine
1	red bell pepper, seeded and chopped fine
1	celery rib, chopped fine
6	garlic cloves, minced
1	teaspoon dried thyme
1	teaspoon salt
¼	teaspoon cayenne pepper
2	bay leaves
1	pound smoked sausage, such as andouille or kielbasa, cut into ¼-inch slices
½	cup minced fresh parsley
4	scallions, sliced thin
	Pepper

1. Bring the reserved shrimp shells and 4½ cups water to a boil in a stockpot or large saucepan over medium-high heat. Reduce the heat to medium-low and simmer for 20 minutes. Strain the stock and add the clam juice and ice water (you should have about 2 quarts of tepid stock, 100 to 110 degrees); discard the shells. Set the stock aside.

2. Heat the oil in a Dutch oven or large heavy-bottomed saucepan over medium-high heat until it registers 200 degrees on an instant-read thermometer, 1½ to 2 minutes. Reduce the heat to medium and gradually stir in the flour with a wooden spatula or spoon, working out any lumps that form. Continue stirring constantly, reaching into the edges of the pan, until the mixture has a toasty aroma and is deep reddish brown, about the color of an old copper penny or between the colors of milk chocolate and dark chocolate, about 20 minutes. (The roux will become thinner as it cooks; if it begins to smoke, remove the pan from the heat and stir the roux constantly to cool slightly.)

3. Add the onions, bell pepper, celery, garlic, thyme, salt, and cayenne to the roux and cook, stirring frequently, until the vegetables soften, 8 to 10 minutes.

Add 1 quart reserved stock in a slow, steady stream while stirring vigorously. Stir in the remaining stock. Increase the heat to high and bring to a boil. Reduce the heat to medium-low, skim the foam off the surface, add the bay leaves, and simmer, uncovered, skimming any foam that rises to the surface, about 30 minutes. (The mixture can be covered and set aside for several hours. Reheat when ready to proceed.)

4. Stir in the sausage and continue simmering to blend flavors, about 30 minutes. Stir in the shrimp and simmer until cooked through, about 5 minutes. Off the heat, stir in the parsley and scallions and adjust the seasonings with salt, pepper, and cayenne to taste. Remove the bay leaves and serve immediately.

Variations

SHRIMP AND SAUSAGE GUMBO WITH OKRA

Fresh okra can be used in place of frozen, though it tends to be more slippery, a quality that diminishes with increased cooking. Substitute an equal amount of fresh okra for frozen; trim the caps, cut the pods into ¼-inch slices, and increase the sautéing time with the onion, bell pepper, and celery to 10 to 15 minutes.

Add 10 ounces thawed frozen cut okra to the roux along with the onion, bell pepper, and celery. Proceed as directed.

SHRIMP AND SAUSAGE GUMBO WITH FILÉ

Add 1½ teaspoons filé powder along with the parsley and scallions after the gumbo has been removed from the heat. Let rest until slightly thickened, about 5 minutes. Adjust the seasonings and serve.

CHICKEN AND SAUSAGE GUMBO

If you like, add okra or filé to this recipe by following the directions in the two above variations for Creole-Style Shrimp and Sausage Gumbo. Make sure the stock is tepid (100 to 110 degrees) before adding it to the roux.

10	bone-in chicken thighs (about 3½ pounds), trimmed of excess skin and fat
	Salt and pepper
¼	cup plus 1 tablespoon vegetable oil, or more as needed
½	cup all-purpose flour
2	onions, chopped fine
1	red bell pepper, seeded and chopped fine
1	celery rib, chopped fine
6	garlic cloves, minced
1	teaspoon dried thyme
	Cayenne pepper
6	cups low-sodium chicken broth, warmed slightly
2	bay leaves
1	pound smoked sausage, such as andouille or kielbasa, cut into ¼-inch slices
½	cup minced fresh parsley
4	scallions, sliced thin

1. Season the chicken liberally with salt and pepper. Heat 1 tablespoon oil in a large Dutch oven over medium-high heat until shimmering but not smoking, about 2 minutes. Add five chicken thighs, skin side down, and cook, not moving them until the skin is crisp and well-browned, about 5 minutes. Using tongs, flip the chicken and brown on the second side, about 5 minutes longer. Transfer the browned chicken to a large plate. Brown the remaining 5 chicken thighs, transfer them to the plate, and set aside. Drain the fat from the pan and strain it through a fine-mesh strainer lined with cheesecloth and into a measuring cup. The remaining oil should be entirely free of any particles. Add enough vegetable oil (about ¼ cup) to yield ½ cup total fat.

2. Heat the chicken fat–vegetable oil mixture in a clean Dutch oven over medium-high heat until it registers 200 degrees on an instant-read thermometer, about 1½ to 2 minutes. Reduce the heat to medium and gradually stir in the flour with a wooden spoon or spatula, working out any lumps that form. Continue stirring constantly, reaching into the edges of the pan, until the mixture has a toasty aroma and is a deep reddish brown, about the color of an old copper penny or between the colors of milk chocolate and dark chocolate, about 20 minutes. (The roux will become thinner as it cooks; if it begins to smoke, remove the pan from the heat and stir the roux constantly to cool slightly.)

3. Add the onions, bell pepper, celery, garlic, thyme, 1 teaspoon salt, and ¼ teaspoon cayenne to the roux and cook, stirring frequently, until the vegetables soften, 8 to 10 minutes. Add the chicken broth in a slow, steady stream while vigorously stirring. Stir in 2 cups water and the bay leaves and place the browned chicken thighs in a single layer in the pot. Increase the heat to high and bring to a boil. Reduce the heat to medium-low and skim off any foam that rises to the surface. Simmer for 30 minutes.

4. Stir in the sausage and continue simmering to blend the flavors, about 30 minutes longer. Off the heat, stir in the parsley and scallions and adjust the seasonings with salt, pepper, and cayenne to taste. Serve immediately.

All-American Beef Chili

The flavors of ground beef chili should be rich and balanced, the texture thick. Unfortunately, many basic recipes yield a pot of underspiced, underflavored chili reminiscent of Sloppy Joes. Our goal was to develop a no-fuss chili that tasted far better than the sum of its common parts.

Most of the recipes for this plainspoken chili begin with sautéing onions and garlic. Tasters liked red bell peppers added to these aromatics. After this

first step, things became less clear. The most pressing concerns were the spices and the meat. There were also the cooking liquid and the proportions of tomatoes and beans to consider.

Our first experiments with these ingredients followed a formula we had seen in lots of recipes: 2 pounds ground beef, 3 tablespoons chili powder, 2 teaspoons ground cumin, and 1 teaspoon each red pepper flakes and dried oregano. In many recipes the spices are added after the beef has been browned, but we knew from work done in the test kitchen on curry that ground spices taste better when they have direct contact with hot cooking oil.

To see if these results would apply to chili, we set up a test with three pots of chili—one with the ground spices added before the beef, one with the spices added after the beef, and a third in which we toasted the spices in a separate skillet and added them to the pot after the beef. The batch made with untoasted spices added after the beef tasted weak. The batch made with spices toasted in a separate pan was better, but the clear favorite was the batch made with spices added directly to the pot before the meat. In fact, subsequent testing revealed that the spices should be added at the outset—along with the aromatics—to develop their flavors fully.

Although we didn't want a chili with killer heat, we did want real warmth and depth of flavor. To boost flavor, we increased the amount of chili powder from 3 tablespoons to 4, added more cumin and oregano, along with coriander, and tossed in some cayenne pepper for heat.

It was now time to consider the meat. The quantity (2 pounds) seemed ideal when paired with two 15-ounce cans of beans (tasters preferred dark red kidney beans or black beans, which hold their shape during cooking). We found that chili made with 85-percent lean ground beef was full-flavored—using a greater fat percentage made a greasy chili, and leaner meat made a dry chili.

As for cooking liquid, we tried batches made with water, chicken broth, beef broth, wine, beer, and no liquid at all except for that in the tomatoes (the last option was beefy-tasting and by far the best). Tomatoes were definitely going into the pot, but we had yet to decide on the type and amount. We first tried two 28-ounce cans of diced tomatoes, pureeing the contents of one can in the blender to thicken the sauce. These tomatoes made for a watery sauce. Next we paired one can of tomato puree with one can of diced tomatoes and, without exception, tasters preferred the thicker consistency. The test kitchen generally doesn't like the slightly cooked flavor of tomato puree, but this recipe needed the body it provided. In any case, after the long simmering time, any such flavor was hard to detect.

Almost there, we found that lime wedges, passed separately at the table, both brightened the flavor of the chili and accentuated the heat of the spices. Thick, rich, with just enough spice and full flavor, this all-American chili is tough to beat.

ALL-AMERICAN BEEF CHILI WITH KIDNEY BEANS

SERVES 8 TO 10

Good choices for condiments include diced fresh tomatoes, diced avocado, sliced scallions, chopped red onion, chopped cilantro leaves, sour cream, and shredded Monterey Jack or cheddar cheese. The flavor of the chili improves with age; if possible, make it a day or two in advance and reheat before serving. Leftovers can be frozen for up to a month.

2	tablespoons vegetable oil
2	onions, minced
1	red bell pepper, seeded and chopped
6	garlic cloves, minced
¼	cup chili powder
1	tablespoon ground cumin
2	teaspoons ground coriander
1	teaspoon red pepper flakes
1	teaspoon dried oregano
½	teaspoon cayenne pepper
2	pounds 85-percent lean ground beef
2	(16-ounce) cans dark red kidney beans, drained and rinsed
1	(28-ounce) can diced tomatoes
1	(28-ounce) can tomato puree
	Salt
2	limes, cut into wedges

1. Heat the oil in a large Dutch oven over medium heat until shimmering but not smoking. Add the onions, bell pepper, garlic, chili powder, cumin, coriander, red pepper flakes, oregano, and cayenne and cook, stirring occasionally, until the vegetables are softened and beginning to brown, about 10 minutes. Increase the heat to medium-high and add half the beef. Cook, breaking up the chunks with a wooden spoon, until no longer pink and just beginning to brown, 3 to 4 minutes. Add the remaining beef and cook, breaking up the chunks with the wooden spoon, until no longer pink, 3 to 4 minutes.

2. Add the beans, tomatoes, tomato puree, and ½ teaspoon salt. Bring to a boil, then reduce the heat to low and simmer, covered, stirring occasionally, for 1 hour. Remove the cover and continue to simmer 1 hour longer, stirring occasionally (if the chili begins to stick to the bottom of the pot, stir in ½ cup water and continue to simmer), until the beef is tender and the chili is dark, rich, and slightly thickened. Adjust the seasonings with additional salt to taste. Serve with the lime wedges and condiments (see note above), if desired.

Variation

BEEF CHILI WITH BACON AND BLACK BEANS

Cut 8 slices bacon into ½-inch pieces. Fry the bacon in a large Dutch oven over medium heat, stirring frequently, until browned, about 8 minutes. Pour off all but 2 tablespoons of the fat, leaving the bacon in the pot. Follow the recipe for All-American Beef Chili with Kidney Beans, substituting the bacon fat in the Dutch oven for the vegetable oil and an equal amount of canned black beans, drained and rinsed, for the dark red kidney beans.

TEST KITCHEN SHORTCUT

Quick Chilling: Soups and stews often taste best the day after they are made, but they should be cooled to room temperature before being refrigerated. Here's a quick way to bring down the temperature of a hot pot of soup or stew. Fill a large plastic beverage bottle almost to the top with water, seal it, and freeze it. Use the frozen bottle to stir the soup or stew in the pot; the ice inside the bottle will cool down the soup or stew rapidly without diluting it.

Cincinnati Chili

We had traveled to Cincinnati for the sole purpose of tasting the city's famous chili, but we were still surprised when it was placed on our tray. It was brown, thin, and served over a mound of spaghetti—it was nothing like the thick, red stew we've called "chili" our entire lives. We quickly learned that this chili is almost never served by itself; it is either spooned atop hot dogs (called Coneys) or ladled over spaghetti. What's more, Cincinnati residents top their chili with beans, onions, oyster crackers, and a high pile of shredded cheese. As for the flavor, Cincinnati chili is packed with warm spices, such as cinnamon, allspice, and cloves, that taste more like Morocco than Tex-Mex. Although it looked a bit odd, we were immediately impressed by this strange concoction.

On our first day back in the test kitchen, we pulled together every recipe we could find in hopes of re-creating that chili. Unfortunately, what we discovered was a list of ingredients that read like a veritable census of spices. In addition to the warm spices we had detected on our trip, many recipes included nutmeg, mace, ginger, mustard, thyme, and even chocolate to round out the flavor. Through several tests, we cut the ingredients down to a manageable list. Cinnamon, allspice, chili powder, and oregano made the cut. Chocolate (despite whisperings that it's a secret ingredient in some of the city's chili

---

THE AMERICAN TABLE
CINCINNATI CHILI

Where do the citizens of Cincinnati go for their chili? There are hundreds of choices, from mega-chains like Skyline and Gold Star to small independents like Camp Washington and U.S. Chili. After visiting a half dozen chili parlors in one day (yes, we ate a lot of chili), we favored Empress Chili, the birthplace of Cincinnati chili.

Empress Chili was opened by two Greek immigrants, Tom and John Kiradjieff, in 1922. What was originally a hot dog cart set up outside a burlesque club has become a chain with ten franchises. We ate at the Vine Street location, where the ambiance is Greek diner meets high school cafeteria. The food is served on thick white plates and cafeteria-style trays that you slide down the counter to the cashier. Each tiny table is stocked with hot sauce, paper napkins, and oyster crackers to crumble over the chili.

On our first visit the franchise owner, Edie, called out from behind the counter to check on us before turning to her next customer. And if we weren't charmed enough by the friendly midwestern atmosphere, as we sat down to eat we watched a police officer walk behind the counter to pour himself a root beer before heading out on patrol.

parlors) didn't—whether we used cocoa powder or bar chocolate, our tasters didn't like it. With a bit of tomato paste for color and richness, and dark brown sugar to add a molasses tang, we had authentic Cincinnati flavor with a minimum of spice jars.

But Cincinnati chili isn't defined by spices alone—another hallmark is the saucy, ultra-tender texture of the ground beef. From our time in Cincinnati, we knew that most chili parlors boil the raw meat in water, drain it, and then add it to the spiced liquid. Boiling helps keep the beef extremely tender during the cooking process, which takes just minutes, not hours as in most chili recipes. Instead of boiling the beef in a separate pot (a procedure that makes sense in a big restaurant kitchen but not at home), we hoped to simmer the raw meat directly in the spices and liquid; this way, we could get the correct texture while also infusing the meat with flavor (and saving on dishes).

For our simmering medium, we sautéed some onion and garlic with the dry spices and then added chicken broth (beef broth deadened the flavors) and tomato sauce (for its smooth texture). After simmering the ground beef for about 15 minutes, the chili was flavorful and the meat very tender. We boiled up some spaghetti, spooned our chili on top, and added cheese, onion, beans, and oyster crackers. After just one bite, we felt like we were back in Cincinnati.

SHREDDING CHEESE FOR CINCINNATI CHILI

To get the longest, thinnest strands of cheese possible—a hallmark of Cincinnati Chili, run the cheese down the length of the box grater in a slight arcing motion; this way the shreds will run the entire length of the block of cheese.

CINCINNATI CHILI

SERVES 6 TO 8

Use canned tomato sauce for this recipe—do not use jarred spaghetti sauce. Shredded cheddar cheese and chopped onion are traditional garnishes to this dish. Sprinkle over the chili just before serving.

1	tablespoon vegetable oil
2	onions, minced
1	garlic clove, minced
2	tablespoons tomato paste
2	tablespoons chili powder
1	tablespoon dried oregano
1½	teaspoons cinnamon
	Salt
¾	teaspoon pepper
¼	teaspoon allspice
2	cups low-sodium chicken broth
2	cups canned tomato sauce
2	tablespoons cider vinegar
2	teaspoons dark brown sugar
1½	pounds 85-percent lean ground beef

1. Heat the oil in a Dutch oven over medium-high heat until shimmering. Cook the onions until soft and browned around the edges, about 8 minutes. Add the garlic, tomato paste, chili powder, oregano, cinnamon, 1 teaspoon salt, pepper, and allspice and cook until fragrant, about 1 minute. Stir in the chicken broth, tomato sauce, vinegar, and sugar.

2. Add the beef and stir to break up the meat. Bring to a boil, reduce the heat to medium-low, and simmer until the chili is deep brown and slightly thickened, 15 to 20 minutes. Season with salt to taste and serve. (The chili can be refrigerated in an airtight container for up to 3 days or frozen for up to 2 months.)

Ranch Chili

When it comes to making a great chili (with pork, beef, or any other meat), it's easy to take a wrong turn before you even know it. You need to purchase the right cut of meat, one with enough fat in it to cook up nice and tender. For pork chili, many recipes call for pork tenderloin, a lean, dry, and somewhat flavorless cut. Another bad choice—one found in many recipes—is pork loin, which turns out dry, tough cubes of meat. We had much better luck with a cut from the shoulder (also a less expensive cut). A shoulder chop has big flavor and is nicely marbled with fat, but most supermarkets sell only thinly cut shoulder chops, which are too small for chili. A better choice is a pork shoulder roast (often referred to as a Boston butt). It was easy to get 1-inch cubes out of this substantial cut.

Even with the right cut, lots of folks make tough chili (we've done it ourselves plenty of times) because they simply do not cook the meat long enough. A minimum of 2 hours on the stove makes this tough piece of meat fork-tender. In fact, cooking it even longer makes the meat even silkier and softer.

When it came to adding beans to the chili, we toyed around with the idea of starting out with dried beans, but the extra steps and time involved made us rethink this option (and the allure of ready-to-go, no-work-involved canned beans was just too attractive to ignore). But don't even think about adding canned beans to the chili at the outset. We tried it and got blown-out, mushy beans and an unappetizing chili. It's a much better idea to add these already tender beans toward the end of the cooking time. Just 30 minutes before serving the chili, gently stir in the beans and they'll soak up flavor and keep their shape.

As for what kind of beans to use, tasters preferred creamy red kidney beans (both light and dark) to starchier pinto beans—the most common choice in this rustic chili. But, honestly, either kind will work.

Now it was finally time to bring in the distinctly sweet, spicy, and smoky flavors that set ranch chili apart from better-known chili dishes. We had to chuckle when we read other recipes that called for cups (yep, cups) of ketchup, barbecue sauce, and even liquid smoke. We found heat in fresh jalapeños and regular off-the-supermarket-shelf chili powder; when mixed with a little cumin and dried oregano, this made for a great chili blend. Instead of achingly sweet ketchup or barbecue sauce, we used canned tomatoes and a bit of brown sugar to sweeten the chili and balance the spiciness. No liquid smoke was necessary; we got all of the

TRIMMING THE MEAT

1. With your hands, pull the roast apart at the fatty seams and then separate the muscles with a knife.

2. Trim the thick pieces of fat from each piece of meat.

3. Using an upward sawing motion, remove the smaller pieces of fat and the translucent membrane called silver skin.

4. Cut the trimmed meat into rough 1-inch cubes. You should have about 2½ pounds of trimmed meat.

good smokiness and rich flavor we wanted from browned-to-a-crisp bacon.

We serve this chili with sliced scallions and shredded Monterey Jack cheese. And nothing works better than cornbread for mopping up the bottom of the chili bowl.

RANCH CHILI

SERVES 4 TO 6

For spicier chili, boost the heat with a pinch of cayenne pepper or a dash of hot sauce. This chili tastes even better when made a day in advance. If you plan to serve it the next day, don't add the beans until you have reheated the chili—this will keep them nice and firm. Good choices for condiments include diced fresh tomatoes, lime wedges, diced avocado, sliced scallions, chopped red onion, chopped cilantro leaves, sour cream, and shredded Monterey Jack or cheddar cheese.

3½	pounds boneless Boston butt pork roast, trimmed of excess fat and cut into 1-inch cubes
	Salt and pepper
8	slices bacon, chopped fine
1	onion, minced
3	jalapeño chiles (each about 2½ inches long), seeded and minced
3	tablespoons chili powder
1	tablespoon ground cumin
1½	teaspoons dried oregano
5	garlic cloves, minced
1	tablespoon brown sugar
1	(28-ounce) can diced tomatoes
3	cups water
2	(16-ounce) cans red kidney beans, drained and rinsed

1. Toss the pork cubes with salt and pepper; set aside. Fry the bacon in a large, heavy soup kettle or Dutch oven over medium heat until the fat renders and the bacon crisps, about 10 minutes. Remove the bacon with a slotted spoon to a plate lined with paper towels; pour all but 2 teaspoons of fat from the pot into a small bowl; set aside.

2. Increase the heat to medium-high, add half of the meat to the now-empty pot, and cook until well browned on all sides, about 5 minutes. Transfer the browned meat to a bowl. Brown the remaining meat, adding another 2 teaspoons bacon fat to the pot if necessary. Transfer the second batch of meat to the bowl.

3. Reduce the heat to medium-low and add 3 tablespoons bacon fat to the now-empty pot. Add the onion, jalapeños, chili powder, cumin, and oregano; cook, stirring occasionally, until the vegetables are beginning to brown, 4 to 5 minutes. Add the garlic and brown sugar; cook until just fragrant, about 15 seconds. Add the diced tomatoes and scrape the pot bottom to loosen any browned bits. Add the reserved bacon, browned pork, and water; bring to a simmer. Continue to cook, uncovered, at a slow simmer until the meat is tender and the juices are dark and starting to thicken, about 2 hours.

4. Add the beans, reduce the heat to low, and simmer, uncovered, stirring occasionally, for 30 minutes. Adjust the seasoning with additional salt if necessary and serve with the condiments (see note above).

Variation
RANCH CHILI FOR A CROWD

Our recipe can be doubled, but if you try to brown four batches of the meat in the same pan, the drippings will burn. We recommend that you brown the extra meat (in two batches) in a separate skillet. You can pick up the recipe from step 3, cooking twice as many vegetables in the large pot. Don't let the browned bits in the extra skillet go to waste. Use 1 cup of the water to deglaze the empty skillet, then add this liquid to the stew.

CHAPTER FOUR

On the Side

ON THE SIDE

Green Bean Casserole

Often referred to as the Classic Green Bean Bake, this casserole was developed by Campbell's in 1955 using frozen green beans, canned cream of mushroom soup, and a topping of canned fried onions. Touted by the company as "delicious and easy to make, easy to remember, and leaves room for creativity," the original recipe used only convenient, prepackaged ingredients. We wanted to resurrect this dinosaur and transform it with fresh instead of prepared ingredients to make it taste better—much better.

Although the original recipe used frozen beans, we found they tasted watery and mushy in this dish. Fresh beans not only offered more flavor, but we were able to cook them to the appropriate doneness and leave a little bit of crunch. We tried sautéing and steaming the green beans but ended up liking the bright green color and seasoned flavor obtained when they were blanched (submerged briefly in boiling water). We found the beans tasted best when blanched in 4 quarts of water heavily seasoned with 2 tablespoons of salt for 4 to 5 minutes. We then plunged the beans into ice water (a process called shocking) to stop them from further cooking. Blanching, then shocking, allowed us to maximize control over the cooking process, which meant that the beans were perfectly cooked every time.

Our next concern was the cream-based mushroom sauce. We did not want the thick and pasty texture of condensed soup. What we did want was a smooth, velvety sauce filled with true mushroom flavor. We began by testing two popular methods for making a cream sauce: reducing the cream to the proper consistency, and thickening the cream with flour and butter (also known as a roux).

Sauces made by simply reducing cream were too heavy and took too much time for our holiday-sized casserole, and sauces thickened with flour tasted pasty and lacked depth of flavor. By combining the methods—using a little flour and reducing the sauce a bit—we got a svelte, flavorful sauce that was neither too rich nor too floury. Briefly testing half-and-half and whole milk, we found neither up to sharing the title ring with the lush, luxurious heft of heavy cream. We tried adding cheese but found the extra flavor to be overpowering and unnecessary.

We had been using white button mushrooms but were disappointed with their lack of flavor. By replacing half of the button mushrooms with cremini and using some dried porcini, we were able to give the sauce a full, earthy, and complex mushroom flavor. Although we liked the flavor of portobellos, we found their meaty texture required a different cooking time and made them more difficult to incorporate into our otherwise streamlined recipe.

Onion, garlic, and fresh thyme were great companion flavors for the mushrooms, while chicken stock helped to pull all the flavors in the sauce together. Although we tried adding bacon, white wine, Madeira, and shallots to the sauce, we found their flavors unwelcome and discordant.

With the green beans and mushroom sauce nailed down, all that was left was the fried onion topping. Deep-frying our own onions was out of the question because of the time it takes, but we found the canned fried onions simply tasted too commercial to use on their own. By mixing the canned fried onions with some fresh seasoned bread crumbs, we were able to remove the "from the can" taste of the traditional topping.

GREEN BEAN CASSEROLE

SERVES 8 TO 10

All the components of this dish can be cooked ahead of time. The assembled casserole needs only 15 minutes in a 375-degree oven to warm through and brown.

TOPPING

4	slices hearty white sandwich bread, torn into large pieces
2	tablespoons unsalted butter, softened
¼	teaspoon salt
⅛	teaspoon pepper
3	cups canned fried onions

BEANS

	Salt
2	pounds green beans, ends trimmed, cut on the diagonal into 2-inch pieces
½	ounce dried porcini mushrooms, rinsed well
6	tablespoons unsalted butter
1	onion, minced
12	ounces white button mushrooms, cut into ¼-inch slices
12	ounces cremini mushrooms, cut into ¼-inch slices
2	tablespoons minced fresh thyme
¼	teaspoon pepper
3	garlic cloves, minced
2	tablespoons all-purpose flour
1	cup low-sodium chicken broth
2	cups heavy cream

1. FOR THE TOPPING: Pulse the bread, butter, salt, and pepper in a food processor until the mixture resembles coarse crumbs, about ten 1-second pulses. Transfer to a large bowl and toss with the onions; set aside.

2. FOR THE BEANS: Adjust an oven rack to the middle position and heat the oven to 375 degrees. Bring 4 quarts water to a boil in a large pot. Add

2 tablespoons salt and the beans. Cook until bright green and slightly crunchy, 4 to 5 minutes. Drain the beans and plunge immediately into a large bowl filled with ice water to stop cooking. Spread the beans out on a paper towel–lined baking sheet to drain.

3. Meanwhile, cover the dried porcini mushrooms with ½ cup hot tap water in a small microwave-safe bowl; cover with plastic wrap, cut several steam vents with a paring knife, and microwave on high power for 30 seconds. Let stand until the mushrooms soften, about 5 minutes. Lift the mushrooms from the liquid with a fork and mince using a chef's knife (you should have about 2 tablespoons). Pour the liquid through a paper towel–lined sieve and reserve.

4. Melt the butter in a large nonstick skillet over medium-high heat until the foaming subsides, about 1 minute. Add the onion, button mushrooms, and cremini mushrooms and cook until the mushrooms release their moisture, about 2 minutes. Add the porcini mushrooms along with their strained soaking liquid, thyme, 1 teaspoon salt, and pepper and cook until all the mushrooms are tender and the liquid has reduced to 2 tablespoons, about 5 minutes. Add the garlic and sauté until aromatic, about 30 seconds. Add the flour and cook for about 1 minute. Stir in the broth and reduce the heat to medium. Stir in the cream and simmer gently until the sauce has the consistency of a dense soup, about 15 minutes.

5. Arrange the beans in a 3-quart gratin dish. Pour the mushroom mixture over the beans and mix to coat the beans evenly. Sprinkle with the bread-crumb mixture and bake until the top is golden brown and the sauce is bubbling around the edges, about 15 minutes. Serve immediately.

ULTIMATE SPICY BEEF NACHOS (page 14)

TOP: **ULTIMATE SEVEN-LAYER DIP** (page 13), **ALL-AMERICAN POTATO SALAD** (page 49); BOTTOM: **ZESTY SMOKED SALMON CHEESE BALL** (page 6), **BEST STUFFED MUSHROOMS WITH GOAT CHEESE AND HERB STUFFING** (page 19)

MARINATED TOMATO SALAD WITH ARUGULA AND GOAT CHEESE (page 41)

TOP: **SUPER-STUFFED BAKED POTATOES** (page 114), **GRILLED CORN ON THE COB WITH BASIL PESTO BUTTER** (page 100)
BOTTOM: **SUGAR-GLAZED ROASTED CARROTS** (page 98), **CAESAR SALAD** (page 34)

CRUNCHY POTATO WEDGES (page 118)

TOP: **PITTSBURGH WEDDING SOUP** (page 61), **COBB CHICKEN SALAD** (page 137)
BOTTOM: **MONTE CRISTO SANDWICH** (page 133), **HEARTY VEGETABLE SOUP** (page 65)

RANCH CHILI (page 82)

CHICAGO-STYLE PEPPERONI PAN PIZZA (page 147)

Green Beans Amandine

When French cuisine first became popular in this country in the early 1960s, green beans amandine (also called "almondine") was one of the signature recipes. A simple dish of tender green beans tossed with crisp, toasted almonds and a light lemon-butter sauce, it was refined yet not intimidating. Unfortunately, the recipes we tried yielded limp beans swimming in pools of numbingly acidic sauce, with soft, pale almonds thrown on as an afterthought.

To build our own version of this iconic recipe, we saw no reason to deviate from the test kitchen's method for steaming the green beans with a little water in a covered skillet: beans cooked this way were consistently crisp-tender. Most recipes tell you to pour 4 tablespoons of melted butter over 2 pounds of beans, but we had better results—and nuttier flavor—using just 3 tablespoons of butter cooked until it was light brown. We tried toasting the almonds in the rich browned butter to enhance their flavor, but the butter burned by the time the almonds were toasted. Instead, we dry-toasted the almonds in the skillet before browning the butter. This produced a flavorful mixture of golden brown nuts and browned butter, which we could pour into a bowl while the beans cooked in the same skillet.

When we added the butter and almond mixture and 2 teaspoons of lemon juice to the cooked beans, the sharp lemon flavor overwhelmed the entire dish. Instead of simply reducing the amount of juice (we really weren't using all that much), we wondered if we could temper its bite. We tried adding the lemon juice to the hot butter and almond mixture while the beans cooked, and sure enough, the heat took the edge off the lemon juice, leaving behind a more subtle, balanced flavor.

GREEN BEANS AMANDINE

SERVES 8

Use a light-colored traditional skillet instead of a darker nonstick skillet for this recipe to easily monitor the butter's browning.

- ⅓ cup sliced almonds
- 3 tablespoons unsalted butter, cut into pieces
- 2 teaspoons fresh lemon juice
- 2 pounds green beans, ends trimmed
- ½ cup water
- Salt

1. Toast the almonds in a large skillet over medium-low heat, stirring often, until just golden, about 6 minutes. Add the butter and cook, stirring constantly, until the butter is golden brown and has a nutty aroma, about 3 minutes. Transfer the almond mixture to a bowl and stir in the lemon juice.

2. Add the beans, water, and ½ teaspoon salt to the empty skillet. Cover and cook, stirring occasionally, until the beans are nearly tender, 8 to 10 minutes. Remove the lid and cook over medium-high heat until the liquid evaporates, 3 to 5 minutes. Off the heat, add the reserved almond mixture to the skillet and toss to combine. Season with salt to taste. Serve.

SHOPPING WITH THE TEST KITCHEN

Almonds: Almonds are sold in an array of varieties. Which almonds do we prefer? It depends on the recipe. For decorating cookies, we usually prefer the clean presentation of whole skinless blanched almonds. For other baked goods, leafy salads, and light side dishes like our Green Beans Amandine, we find that thinly sliced raw almonds deliver a nice, light flavor and texture. And we love the substantial crunch of thick-cut slivered almonds in stir-fries and rice pilafs. Like all nuts, almonds are highly perishable and best stored in the freezer to prevent spoilage.

Broccoli and Cheese Casserole

It's our strong belief in the test kitchen that smothering broccoli with cheese sauce is more than just a sneaky way to get kids to eat their vegetables. Adults love it, too. Shamefully, and all too often, this classic dish comes to the table with overcooked and washed-out-looking broccoli swimming in a gloppy, greasy, broken cheese sauce. We wanted to create an attractive broccoli and cheese casserole with character and dimension—one you could serve to company and that would entice even the pickiest eaters. Our challenge, then, was to construct a casserole with bright green broccoli—tender, not mushy—an elegant cheese sauce, and a golden bread-crumb topping.

In our initial tests we tried a variety of methods to cook the broccoli. Sautéing the broccoli before assembling the casserole resulted in unevenly colored broccoli, with alternating splotches of olive drab and bright emerald green. Thinking we could save some time and effort, we tried throwing the broccoli into the casserole raw. The results were abysmal: by the time the broccoli was tender, it was army green, the sauce was curdled and broken, and the bread crumbs were overly browned.

The tests confirmed what we already knew to be true—namely, that broccoli requires a moist-heat cooking method to keep the florets tender and to make sure the tough stalks cook through. Ordinarily, our test-kitchen recommendation is to steam broccoli, as it tends to absorb too much moisture when boiled. For this casserole, however, we didn't mind the extra moisture and thought boiling would be quick and easy. In addition, partially cooking, or blanching, the broccoli in salted boiling water would ensure that the broccoli would be fully seasoned to its core. Most important, we favored blanching as a fast way to set that fresh green color.

With the broccoli cooked, we could now focus on the cheese sauce. Recipes we found included a variety of styles, though most of them were implausibly rich. Yolks and cream seemed too heavy; this was a vegetable dish, after all. We looked to some classic French recipes for inspiration and saw flour-thickened, milk-based sauces (béchamels) ladled over a variety of blanched vegetables. The lighter consistency and flavor of the béchamel better allowed the taste of the vegetables to come through. What's more, this flour-bound sauce didn't separate into a curdled mess while in the oven, as some of the richer sauces had.

But the béchamel alone didn't give this dish enough punch, so we added sharp cheddar cheese—the customary accompaniment to broccoli—to our working béchamel. Now closer to a Mornay sauce, our sauce tasted good, but it seemed somewhat heavy and cloying to most of the tasters. Cutting the milk with a portion of chicken broth lightened the sauce and gave it a rounder, more savory edge that tasters enjoyed.

But the sauce still required some help. Sharp cheddar imparted a grainy texture to the otherwise supple sauce. We experimented with other styles of cheddar and found that cutting the sharp cheese with mild-tasting, creamy Colby cheese yielded the best-textured sauce. For a little nuance, we added a pinch of cayenne pepper, minced garlic, and dried mustard, flavorings we borrowed from our favorite macaroni and cheese sauce. Also borrowed from our macaroni and cheese was the crispy golden topping, made with a simple combination of white sandwich bread and butter. Far from its French roots, perhaps, this casserole with its creamy "Mornay" sauce is good enough to attract even the most finicky of eaters.

BROCCOLI AND CHEESE CASSEROLE

SERVES 6 TO 8

If you cannot find Colby cheese, longhorn will work just as well.

TOPPING

2	slices hearty white sandwich bread, torn into large pieces
1	tablespoon unsalted butter, melted

FILLING

	Salt
2	pounds broccoli (about 1 large bunch), florets trimmed to 1-inch pieces, stalks peeled and chopped into ½-inch pieces
3	tablespoons unsalted butter
1	medium garlic clove, minced
½	teaspoon dry mustard
	Pinch cayenne pepper
3	tablespoons all-purpose flour
1½	cups whole milk
1	cup low-sodium chicken broth
2	cups shredded Colby cheese
1	cup shredded sharp cheddar cheese
	Pepper

1. FOR THE TOPPING: Process the bread and butter in a food processor until coarsely ground, about six 1-second pulses; set aside.

2. FOR THE FILLING: Adjust an oven rack to the middle position and heat the oven to 400 degrees. Bring 4 quarts water to a boil in a large pot. Add 1 tablespoon salt and the broccoli to the boiling water; cover and cook until bright green and crisp-tender, about 3 minutes. Drain the broccoli and leave it in the colander; set aside.

3. Meanwhile, melt the butter in a medium saucepan over medium heat. Stir in the garlic, mustard,

and cayenne; cook until fragrant, about 30 seconds. Add the flour and cook, stirring constantly, until the flour turns golden, about 1 minute. Slowly whisk in the milk and broth; bring to a simmer and cook, whisking often, until large bubbles erupt at the surface and the mixture is slightly thickened, about 5 minutes. Off the heat, whisk in the Colby and cheddar. Season to taste with salt and pepper.

4. Spread the broccoli in a 13 by 9-inch baking dish (or shallow casserole dish of similar size). Whisk the cheese sauce again briefly and pour over the broccoli. Sprinkle with the bread-crumb topping. Bake until golden brown and bubbling around the edges, about 15 minutes. Cool for 5 minutes before serving.

Variation

BROCCOLI AND CHEESE CASSEROLE WITH ROASTED RED PEPPERS

Add a 13-ounce jar of roasted red peppers, drained, rinsed, patted dry, and chopped medium, to the seasoned sauce in step 3.

CUTTING UP BROCCOLI

1. Hold the broccoli upside down on a cutting board. Trim the florets from the stalk, separating the larger florets into 1-inch pieces, if necessary.

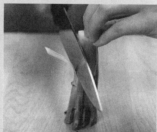

2. Trim the top and bottom from the stalk. Cut away ⅛ inch of the tough outer peel and cut the stalk in half lengthwise and then into ½-inch pieces.

Glazed Roasted Carrots

Let's face it. Carrots are not the sexiest vegetable in the produce aisle, but they are reliable most any time of year. When roasted, they can make an excellent side dish. The perfect roast carrots are tender and sweet, with a caramelized crust. High heat and sugar are the usual means of coaxing this kind of browning out of carrots, but it's a high-wire act. Carrots can go from crunchy and pale to mealy and charred in a matter of minutes.

Our first decision took place in the produce aisle. Although baby carrots require no preparation (just open the bag and dump them into a pan), the results we got with them were disappointing. After 10 minutes in the oven, they were shriveled and soggy. Maybe the pool of water in most bags of baby carrots was the culprit. In any case, these carrots are often bland and woody. It was worth taking an extra 10 minutes to peel and cut grown-up-size carrots ourselves.

When we tested roasting times and temperatures, we found that shorter and hotter were better. When cooked for a long time in a moderate oven, the carrots ended up soggy and overcooked before any real caramelization could occur. We had the best results in a very hot oven set to 475 degrees. Heating the baking sheet before adding the carrots jump-started the browning process. In less than 20 minutes the carrots were perfectly cooked.

Carrots tossed in butter browned a bit better than those tossed in oil, but the addition of sugar—just 1 tablespoon for 1½ pounds of carrots—made a big difference. Granulated sugar was up to the job, but we got really dramatic results when we tried dark brown sugar.

After peeling our weight in carrots, we had finally developed a reliable recipe. Best of all, it was quick and easily adapted to flavor variations, so no one would be bored at the table.

SUGAR-GLAZED ROASTED CARROTS
SERVES 4 TO 6

If the carrots have very narrow tips, trim the thin ends; they scorch easily.

- 1½ pounds medium carrots, peeled and cut into 2 by ½-inch pieces
- 2 tablespoons unsalted butter, melted
- 1 tablespoon dark brown sugar
- ½ teaspoon salt
- ½ teaspoon pepper

1. Adjust an oven rack to the middle position and heat the oven to 475 degrees. Heat a rimmed baking sheet in the oven for 10 minutes.

2. Toss the carrots, melted butter, sugar, salt, and pepper in a medium bowl until thoroughly combined. Remove the pan from the oven and place the carrots in a single layer on the hot baking sheet. Roast until the carrots are beginning to brown on the bottom, about 15 minutes.

3. Remove the pan from the oven, toss the carrots, and continue to roast until they are tender and deep amber in color, about 3 minutes. Serve.

CUTTING CARROTS

1. Cut a peeled carrot into thirds, with each piece measuring roughly 2 inches long.

2. Cut each piece in half or quarters lengthwise to yield pieces that are ½ inch thick.

MAPLE-NUT CARROTS

Combine 2 tablespoons maple syrup, ½ teaspoon vanilla extract, ¼ teaspoon chili powder, and ½ cup toasted and chopped walnuts in a bowl. Add the maple mixture when the carrots are tossed in step 3.

HERB-GARDEN CARROTS

Add 1 teaspoon chopped fresh tarragon and 1 teaspoon chopped fresh parsley when the carrots are tossed in step 3.

Grilled Corn on the Cob

Grilling corn sounds like a simple proposition, so we were amazed at how many techniques our research turned up. We found recipes that suggested grilling the corn husk on (soaked in water or dry), husk off, and partially husked; over a hot fire or a medium fire; and even parboiled.

After trying all of these methods, we learned that our tasters wanted corn with a distinctly grilled taste and lightly charred kernels; unfortunately, no single technique was perfect. Although grilling the corn husk on or partially husked helped keep the kernels moist, tasters felt that the husk imparted an unwelcome grassy flavor to the corn. For the best caramelized, smoky flavor, we were going to have to grill the corn shucked.

The husked corn picked up a nice smoky taste from the grill, but the kernels quickly turned tough and dry. Lowering the heat meant longer cooking and mealy, starchy corn—high heat (and fast cooking) was the way to go. We tried basting the corn with oil, butter, and even bacon fat, but all three left the corn greasy. A suggestion from a colleague had

us basting the corn with sugar water, and although that corn burned, it got us thinking. A few recipes we tried in earlier tests had called for soaking the corn (still in the husk) in water before grilling. The corn stayed very tender, but it tasted grassy and steamed and lacked grilled flavor. Soaking husked corn might be worth a shot.

For our next test, we soaked the shucked cobs in cold water before they went on the grill. Although they sputtered and steamed at first, in the end the corn was nicely browned and clearly more tender than it had been in other tests. In the test kitchen we often presoak lean meats such as chicken and pork in salt water (a process called brining) to add flavor and moisture during cooking. We figured if it works for meat, why not for corn? We whisked some salt into a bowl of water and soaked the corn for an hour; after just a few minutes on the grill, it was apparent we were on the right track. The slightly charred kernels had plumped visibly, and the corn was tender and seasoned throughout from the salt-water soak.

Ultimately, we found that a 30-minute brine protected corn from drying out on the grill. Brushed with softened butter and sprinkled with salt (or spread with one of our flavored butters), this was grilled corn that finally lived up to the hype.

GRILLED CORN ON THE COB WITH BARBECUE-SCALLION BUTTER

SERVES 4 TO 6

If your corn isn't as sweet as you'd like, stir ½ cup sugar into the water along with the salt. Avoid soaking the corn for more than 8 hours, or it will become overly salty. Skip using a flavored butter and simply use plain butter, if you like.

    Salt and pepper
 8 ears corn, husks and silk removed

8   tablespoons (1 stick) unsalted butter, softened

2   tablespoons barbecue sauce

1   scallion, minced

1. In a large pot, stir ½ cup salt into 4 quarts cold water until dissolved. Add the corn and let soak for at least 30 minutes or up to 8 hours.

2. Meanwhile, use a fork to stir together the butter, barbecue sauce, and scallion. Set aside.

3. Grill the corn over a hot fire, turning every 2 to 3 minutes, until the kernels are lightly charred all over, 10 to 14 minutes. Remove the corn from the grill, brush with the butter, and season with salt and pepper to taste. Serve.

Variations

GRILLED CORN ON THE COB WITH LATIN-SPICED BUTTER

Replace the barbecue sauce and scallion with 1 minced garlic clove, 1 teaspoon chili powder, ½ teaspoon ground cumin, and ½ teaspoon grated fresh lime zest. (Sprinkle the cobs with ½ cup grated Parmesan, if desired.)

GRILLED CORN ON THE COB WITH BASIL PESTO BUTTER

Replace the barbecue sauce and scallion with 1 tablespoon basil pesto and 1 teaspoon fresh lemon juice.

GRILLED CORN ON THE COB WITH CHESAPEAKE BAY BUTTER

Replace the barbecue sauce and scallion with 1 tablespoon hot sauce, 1 teaspoon Old Bay seasoning, and 1 minced garlic clove.

Creamed Corn

Although creamed corn is available any time of year out of the can, it doesn't compare with the clean, sweet flavor of late-summer corn gently simmered with fresh cream. But if you don't handle the fresh corn and cream correctly, you wind up with that overcooked, just-out-of-the-can flavor you were trying to avoid.

Many recipes start with boiling the corn on the cob, then cutting the kernels off the cob and mixing them with a cream sauce. With this technique, however, the corn loses much of its sweet, delicate flavor to the cooking water. We quickly rejected this method in favor of recipes in which the corn kernels (which are first cut free from the cobs) are simmered directly in the cream. This technique releases their sugary, summery flavor into the sauce, which is where you want it to be.

Simply simmering fresh corn kernels in cream, however, wasn't enough. It produced a thin, lumpy mixture that lacked the thickened, spoonable texture we desired. Scraping the pulp out of the spent cobs helped a bit, but we wanted the sauce a bit thicker. Flour and cornstarch just made the sauce gummy and overwhelmed the flavor of the corn. We then tried grating a few of the ears, which broke down some of the kernels into smaller pieces. This did the trick. By grating some of the raw kernels off the cob, we were able to release more of the corn's natural thickener. We found that grating about half of the corn in our recipe thickened the sauce sufficiently.

After making a few batches of this recipe with different types of corn, we realized that the cooking times can differ, depending on the corn's variety and age. Some batches cooked perfectly in only 10 minutes; others needed 5 minutes longer. We also found that as the corn and cream cook and thicken, the heat needs to be adjusted to keep the mixture at a simmer to prevent the bottom from burning.

As for other ingredients, we tried using half-and-half instead of heavy cream, but tasters missed the luxurious flavor and heft provided by the latter. A little shallot, garlic, and fresh thyme complemented the delicate flavor of the corn, while a pinch of cayenne pepper added a little kick.

CREAMED CORN

SERVES 6 TO 8

For the best texture and flavor, we like a combination of grated corn, whole kernels (cut away from the cobs with a knife), and corn milk (scraped from all ears with the back of a knife). See the photos below for tips on cutting the kernels off some ears of corn and grating (milking) the rest of the corn.

5	medium ears fresh corn, husks and silk removed
2	tablespoons unsalted butter
1	shallot, minced
1	garlic clove, minced
1½	cups heavy cream
½	teaspoon minced fresh thyme
	Pinch cayenne pepper
	Salt and pepper

PREPARING THE CORN

1. Cut whole kernels from some of the corn. Use the back of a knife to firmly scrape the pulp from these cobs.

2. Grate the kernels from the remaining ears and scrape the pulp from these cobs using the back of a butter knife.

1. Using a chef's knife, cut the kernels from 3 ears of the corn and place in a medium bowl. Firmly scrape the cobs with the back of a knife to collect the pulp and milk in the same bowl. Grate the remaining 2 ears of corn on the coarse side of a box grater set in the bowl with the cut kernels. Firmly scrape these cobs with the back of a knife to collect the pulp and milk in the same bowl.

2. Melt the butter in a medium saucepan over medium-high heat. When the foaming subsides, add the shallot and cook until softened but not browned, 1 to 2 minutes. Add the garlic and cook until aromatic, about 30 seconds. Stir in the corn kernels and pulp as well as the cream, thyme, cayenne, ¼ teaspoon salt, and ⅛ teaspoon pepper. Bring the mixture to a simmer and cook, adjusting the heat as necessary and stirring occasionally, until the corn is tender and the mixture has thickened, 10 to 15 minutes. Remove the pan from the heat, and season with salt and pepper to taste. Serve.

Variation

CREAMED CORN WITH BACON AND BLUE CHEESE

Use your favorite kind of blue cheese for this variation. Because of the saltiness of the bacon and blue cheese, it may not be necessary to add salt.

5	medium ears fresh corn, husks and silk removed
4	slices bacon, cut into ½-inch pieces
1	shallot, minced
1	garlic clove, minced
1½	cups heavy cream
½	teaspoon minced fresh thyme
	Pinch cayenne pepper
½	cup crumbled blue cheese
	Salt and pepper

1. Cut the kernels from 3 ears of the corn and transfer them to a medium bowl. Firmly scrape the cobs with the back of a butter knife to collect the pulp and milk in the same bowl. Grate the remaining 2 ears of corn on the coarse side of a box grater set in the bowl with the cut kernels. Firmly scrape these cobs with the back of a butter knife to collect the pulp and milk in the same bowl.

2. Cook the bacon in a large nonstick skillet over medium-high heat until crisp and brown, about 5 minutes. Transfer the bacon to a paper towel–lined plate to drain; set aside.

3. Remove and discard all but 2 tablespoons rendered bacon fat from the pan. Add the shallot and cook until softened but not browned, 1 to 2 minutes. Add the garlic and cook until aromatic, about 30 seconds. Stir in the corn kernels and pulp as well as the cream, thyme, and cayenne. Bring the mixture to a simmer and cook, adjusting the heat as necessary and stirring occasionally, until the corn is tender and the mixture has thickened, 10 to 15 minutes. Remove the pan from the heat and stir in the cheese. Season with salt and pepper to taste. Serve.

Corn Fritters

Nothing quite beats ears of fresh summer corn that are simply boiled and buttered. At least that holds true for the first half of corn season. But after weeks of eating boiled corn as the vegetable side dish for dinner, most people want a change of pace. Corn fritters are a surprisingly simple way to turn fresh ears of corn into something truly memorable.

Fritters are sometimes thought of as heavy, but the opposite is true. Good fritters are actually quite light—ideally, little corn pancakes that are creamy in the middle and crisp on the outside. After spending a week making stacks (and stacks) of hot fritters, we

found that the amount of flour in the batter has the greatest effect on texture. Many recipes use 1 cup of flour or more, but our batter has just 3 tablespoons, so these fritters are especially light.

There's just no such thing as too much corn in a corn fritter. Because we wanted to see the corn as well as taste it, we cut some kernels whole off the cob with a knife and grated the rest of the corn on a box grater. And to make sure that we extracted every last bit of flavor from every cob, we used a knife to scrape out any remaining corn pulp. We packed in still more corn flavor by adding a little cornmeal to the batter.

These fritters taste like a hot, buttered ear of corn, but they are sturdy enough to dip into salsa, sour cream, or maple syrup—our personal favorite.

FARM STAND CORN FRITTERS

MAKES 12 FRITTERS
Serve these crisp corn fritters with almost anything from the grill. The batter can be covered and refrigerated for up to 4 hours. Refer to the photos on page 101 when preparing the corn in step 1.

1½	pounds fresh corn (2 large or 3 to 4 medium ears), husks and silk removed
1	large egg, beaten lightly
3	tablespoons all-purpose flour
3	tablespoons cornmeal
2	tablespoons heavy cream
1	small shallot, minced
½	teaspoon salt
	Pinch cayenne pepper
½	cup corn oil or vegetable oil, or more as needed

1. Using a chef's knife, cut the kernels from 1 to 2 ears of the corn and place in a bowl (you should have about 1 cup whole kernels). Grate the kernels from the remaining 1 to 2 ears of corn on the large holes of a box grater (you should have a generous

½ cup grated kernels) into the bowl with the cut kernels. Using the back of a knife, firmly scrape any pulp remaining on all the cobs into the bowl. Stir in the egg, flour, cornmeal, cream, shallot, salt, and cayenne.

2. Heat the oil in a large, heavy-bottomed nonstick skillet over medium-high heat until shimmering. Drop 6 heaping tablespoonfuls of the batter into the pan, spacing them evenly apart. Fry until golden brown, about 1 minute per side. Transfer the fritters to a plate lined with paper towels. If necessary, add more oil to the skillet and heat until shimmering; fry the remaining batter. Serve the fritters immediately.

Southern-Style Greens

Uttering the words *collard greens* can bring out the Southern drawl in almost anyone. Along with turnip and mustard greens and kale, these tough, leafy greens are the cornerstone of true Southern cooking. Although many old-fashioned recipes tell you to cook greens for hours to make them tender, we found that they are actually easy to overcook. Yet when undercooked, they are tough and chewy with a tannic bite. We wanted authentic, perfectly cooked Southern greens, with lots of flavor and a healthy chew.

More tender greens (such as spinach) can simply be wilted in a hot pan, but tough greens don't have enough moisture to withstand this cooking technique; they scorch before they wilt. Authentic Southern recipes call for boiling collards (as well as kale and turnip or mustard greens) in water for hours, usually with pork. When the greens and pork are done boiling, the remaining cooking liquid is called pot likker and is often served as an accompaniment to the greens or as a gravy. We found that this time-consuming traditional method results in greens that are overdone, with a bland, lackluster flavor. The boiling did, however, rid the greens of

their harsh tannic flavor. We then tested boiling the greens for shorter amounts of time and found that 7 or 8 minutes were enough for the greens to become tender. This short boiling time also mellowed their flavor without causing them to lose too much of their signature bite.

With a quick wring to rid them of extra water, all these greens needed now was some Southern seasoning. In the South greens are typically cooked and served with pork, and we liked the smoky, potent flavor of bacon in our greens. We used the rendered fat from the bacon to sauté some aromatics. We found that red onion, garlic, and brown sugar rounded out the flavor of the greens, while a little chicken stock helped the greens soak up all these new flavors. Finally, we found that a little cider vinegar drizzled over the top added a nice, bright punch.

SOUTHERN-STYLE GREENS

SERVES 4

To prepare kale, collards, and mustard greens, hold each leaf at the base of the stem over a bowl filled with water and use a sharp knife to slash the leafy portion from either side of the thick stem. Turnip greens are most easily stemmed by grasping the base of the stem between your thumb and index finger and stripping off the leaf with your other hand.

	Salt
2	pounds tough, assertive greens, such as collards, kale, mustard, or turnip, stemmed, washed in several changes of cold water, and coarsely chopped
4	slices bacon, chopped fine
2	teaspoons unsalted butter
1	red onion, minced
2	garlic cloves, minced
1	teaspoon brown sugar
½–¾	cup low-sodium chicken broth
1½	teaspoons cider vinegar
	Pepper

1. Bring 2 quarts water to a boil in a soup kettle or other saucepan. Add 1½ teaspoons salt and the greens and stir until wilted. Cover and cook until the greens are just tender, 7 to 8 minutes. Drain in a colander. Rinse the kettle with cold water to cool, then refill with cold water. Pour the greens into the cold water to stop the cooking process. Lift a handful of greens out of the water, and squeeze until only droplets fall from them. Repeat with the remaining greens.

2. Cook the bacon in a large sauté pan over medium heat until lightly browned but not too crisp, 7 to 8 minutes. Transfer the bacon with a slotted spoon to a paper towel–lined plate.

3. Add the butter to the hot bacon fat and heat over medium heat until it has melted and the foaming has subsided, about 1 minute. Add the onion and sauté until softened and browned, about 10 minutes. Add the garlic, brown sugar, cooked greens, and cooked bacon and toss. Add ½ cup broth and cook over medium-high heat, adding more broth if necessary, until the greens are tender and juicy and most of the broth has been absorbed, about 5 minutes. Add the vinegar and season with salt and pepper to taste. Serve immediately.

Variations

SOUTHERN-STYLE GREENS WITH ANDOUILLE SAUSAGE AND RED PEPPER
Replace the bacon in step 2 with 10 ounces andouille sausage, cut in half lengthwise and then sliced crosswise into ¼-inch pieces. Cook the andouille over medium heat until cooked through, about 5 minutes. Transfer the cooked sausage to a paper towel–lined plate. In step 3, add 4 tablespoons butter to the pan and add ½ large red bell pepper, cut into ½-inch dice, along with the onion. Proceed as directed, adding the cooked sausage back to the pan along with the greens.

SOUTHERN-STYLE BEANS AND GREENS
Add 2 (15.5-ounce) cans white beans, drained and rinsed, and 1 tablespoon minced fresh savory along with the cooked greens in step 3.

Oven-Fried Onion Rings

Oven-fried onion ring recipes promise to eliminate the mess associated with deep-frying, but they don't really work—at least none of the recipes we've tried. With the oven, we have gotten dehydrated onion rings, tough onion rings, and soggy onion rings but have never come close to the deep-fried crunch and flavor of the real thing.

Deep-fried onion rings start with sliced onions that are dunked in a thick batter, usually made with flour, egg, and liquid. When fried, the batter forms a crisp shell that helps the onions steam and become tender. When we tried it in the oven, however, the batter slid off the rings and stuck to the baking sheet instead.

Dredging the onion rings in flour first helped—the batter now had something to cling to. As for what went into the batter, we dismissed milk and mayonnaise before hitting on the right combination of buttermilk, egg, and flour. This batter was pretty good, but we wanted more crunch and thought an additional crumb coating might help.

Tossing our batter-dipped onion rings with bread crumbs was a step in the right direction, but our tasters wanted even more crunch. At the local supermarket we bought anything that looked as if it might make a good crumb coating, including cornmeal, cornflakes, Melba toast, Weetabix cereal, Ritz crackers, and saltines. Back in the test kitchen, only the saltines were met with even a lukewarm reception; their salty kick was well liked, but the crumbs were too powdery.

We headed back to the market and searched for less obvious options. If we wanted deep-fried flavor, then what about mixing the saltines with potato chips? This worked far better than we expected. The crushed saltines added a nice salty kick and absorbed excess grease from the potato chips. It was almost impossible to tell that these super-crunchy onion rings had come out of the oven.

For 4 to 6 servings of rings made from 2 large onions, 6 tablespoons of vegetable oil was just right, giving the rings a good sear without making them too oily. Admittedly, these onion rings, like many other oven-fried recipes, are not low in fat, but that was not our goal. We wanted deep-fried flavor without the mess or the smell—and this recipe delivers on both counts.

OVEN-FRIED ONION RINGS

MAKES 24 RINGS, SERVING 4 TO 6
Slice the onions into ½-inch-thick rounds, separate the rings, and discard any rings smaller than 2 inches in diameter.

½	cup all-purpose flour
1	large egg, room temperature
½	cup buttermilk, room temperature
¼	teaspoon cayenne pepper
	Salt and pepper
30	saltines
4	cups kettle-cooked potato chips
2	large yellow onions, cut into 24 large rings (see note above)
6	tablespoons vegetable oil

1. Adjust the oven racks to the lower-middle and upper-middle positions and heat the oven to 450 degrees. Place ¼ cup of the flour in a shallow baking dish. Beat the egg and buttermilk in a bowl. Whisk the remaining ¼ cup flour, cayenne, ½ teaspoon salt, and ¼ teaspoon pepper into the buttermilk mixture. Pulse the saltines and chips together in a food processor until finely ground; place in a separate shallow baking dish.

2. Working one at a time, dredge each onion ring in the flour, shaking off excess. Dip in the buttermilk mixture, allowing the excess to drip back into the bowl, then drop into the crumb coating, turning each ring to coat evenly. Transfer to a large plate.

3. Pour 3 tablespoons of the oil onto each of two rimmed baking sheets. Place in the oven and heat until just smoking, about 8 minutes. Carefully tilt the heated sheets to coat evenly with the oil, then arrange the onion rings on the sheets. Bake, flipping the onion rings over and switching and rotating the baking sheets halfway through baking, until golden brown on both sides, about 15 minutes. Briefly drain the onion rings on paper towels. Serve immediately. (The onion rings can be breaded in advance and refrigerated for up to 1 hour. Let them sit at room temperature for 30 minutes before baking; if baked straight from the fridge, the onions will not soften properly and will remain crunchy.)

Easy Peas

Although we think most vegetables are better fresh than frozen, peas are an exception. Their natural sugars turn to starch within hours after being picked, which means that fresh peas are mealy unless cooked the same day they are harvested. Frozen peas are harvested, cooked, and frozen within hours of being picked, which locks in their sweet flavor.

What's the best way to bring frozen peas back to life at home? Most cooks dump the peas into a pot of salted water or microwave them. Once tender, the peas are drained and tossed with butter and seasonings. This simple method isn't bad, but could we do better?

Our first thought was to cook the peas in something more flavorful than salted water; we hoped the cooking liquid could also work as a sauce. So we piled ingredients into a saucepan and brought the liquid to a boil. Unfortunately, by the time the liquid reduced to a saucy consistency, the peas had turned army green. We had better luck when we added the peas (still frozen) to an almost finished sauce. By the time the peas were tender, they had soaked up plenty of flavor, and the sauce was the perfect consistency.

You can use almost any liquid (orange juice, cream, or chicken broth) and add spices, herbs, toasted nuts, or ham to jazz things up.

CREAMY PEAS WITH HAM AND ONION

SERVES 4 TO 6

Because the cream is reduced to the proper consistency before the peas are added to the pan, the peas should be cooked with the cover on.

2	tablespoons unsalted butter
6	ounces ham steak, cut into ½-inch pieces
1	red onion, halved and sliced thin
⅔	cup heavy cream
1	tablespoon chopped fresh tarragon or parsley
	Salt and pepper
1	pound frozen peas, not thawed

1. Melt the butter in a large skillet over medium-high heat. Add the ham and cook until browned, about 5 minutes. Add the onion and cook until soft and beginning to brown, about 5 minutes.

2. Add the cream, tarragon or parsley, and salt and pepper to taste. Bring to a simmer and cook until the cream just begins to thicken, about 3 minutes. Stir in the peas, cover, and cook until tender, about 5 minutes. Season with salt and pepper to taste. Serve.

Variations
SMASHED MINTY PEAS

Be careful not to overprocess the peas.

½	cup low-sodium chicken broth
1	pound frozen peas, not thawed
2	cups chopped Boston or Bibb lettuce
2	tablespoons chopped fresh mint
4	tablespoons unsalted butter
	Salt and pepper

1. Bring the broth, peas, lettuce, mint, butter, and salt and pepper to taste to a simmer in a medium saucepan over medium-high heat. Cover and cook until the peas are tender, 8 to 10 minutes.

2. Transfer to a food processor and pulse until coarsely mashed, about ten 1-second pulses. Season with salt and pepper to taste. Serve.

DILLY PEAS AND CARROTS

Because carrots require more cooking time than peas, they get a head start in this recipe.

2	cups baby carrots, cut crosswise into thirds
½	cup fresh orange juice and 1 tablespoon fresh grated orange zest (2 oranges)
	Salt
1	pound frozen peas, not thawed
2	tablespoons unsalted butter
1	tablespoon minced fresh dill

Bring the carrots, orange juice, and ½ teaspoon salt to a simmer in a medium saucepan over medium-high heat. Cover and cook until the carrots are crisp-tender, about 4 minutes. Add the peas, orange zest, butter, and dill, increase the heat to high, and cook, uncovered, until the peas are tender and the liquid is syrupy, about 5 minutes. Season with salt to taste. Serve.

Frozen Peas: Yes, frozen peas really do taste better than the "fresh" peas you can buy at the supermarket. Those fresh peas probably started out tasting great, but within hours of harvest the natural sugars in peas turn to starches. By the time you get "fresh" supermarket peas home, they are mealy and bland. In fact, in a blind taste test against three leading brands of frozen peas (Birds Eye, Green Giant, and Cascadian Farm), fresh peas came in last. All three brands of frozen peas were sweet and tasty—no doubt because they were cooked and frozen the day they were harvested, which locked in their sweetness and held off their quick march to starchy and bland.

Creamy Mashed Sweet Potatoes

We're no stranger to candied sweet potatoes or even sweet potato pie, but we wanted to create a savory mash, rich with the earthy flavor of sweet potatoes—and save the marshmallows for dessert.

Baking, steaming, microwaving, and boiling are all methods used to cook sweet potatoes for mashing, but each has its problems. Baking whole sweet potatoes yields a full-flavored mash, but the lengthy baking time and the need to peel scalding-hot potatoes make this method a hassle. Steaming the potatoes leaves them tasteless, and cooking them in the microwave ruins their texture. Boiling the sweet potatoes, the most common method, produces the worst results: a waterlogged mush with washed-out flavor.

We found that the secret to getting silky and full-flavored mashed sweet potatoes was to thinly slice the potatoes and cook them covered, on the stovetop, over low heat in a small amount of liquid and sugar. When the sweet potatoes are fall-apart tender, they can be mashed right in the pot—no draining, no straining, no fuss.

This method works because the low heat allows the moisture-rich sweet potatoes to shed their liquid, which in turn produces steam that cooks them. By the time the sweet potatoes are tender, they have reabsorbed their natural juices, thus retaining all of their flavor. Although the sweet potatoes do shed a good amount of moisture during cooking, a small amount of starter liquid—our tasters preferred a combination of butter and cream—is needed to begin the process.

Our basic mash recipe is rich in sweet potato flavor, but if you're looking for something a little more creative for the holidays or a special occasion, try one of the variations; they're quick and easy, and they won't leave you with a toothache.

CREAMY MASHED SWEET POTATOES
SERVES 4 TO 6

This recipe can be doubled and prepared in a Dutch oven, but the cooking time will need to be doubled as well.

- 4 tablespoons unsalted butter, cut into 4 pieces
- 3 tablespoons heavy cream
   Salt and pepper
- 1 teaspoon sugar
- 2 pounds sweet potatoes (2 large or 3 medium), peeled, quartered lengthwise, and cut into ¼-inch slices (see page 108)

1. Combine the butter, 2 tablespoons of the cream, ½ teaspoon salt, ¼ teaspoon pepper, sugar, and sweet potatoes in a large saucepan. Cook, covered, over low heat until the potatoes are fall-apart tender, 35 to 40 minutes.

2. Off the heat, add the remaining 1 tablespoon cream and mash the sweet potatoes with a potato masher. Serve. (The potatoes can be prepared up to 2 days in advance. Mash the potatoes as directed in step 2, but hold off on adding the last tablespoon of cream. When you want to serve the potatoes, cover them with plastic wrap, microwave until hot, and then stir in the remaining cream and any last-minute flavorings, such as scallions, bacon, or herbs.)

Variations

SMOKEHOUSE MASHED SWEET POTATOES

Add ⅛ teaspoon cayenne pepper to the saucepan in step 1. In step 2, mash ½ cup shredded smoked Gouda cheese with the sweet potatoes and cover with the lid until the cheese melts, about 1 minute. Sprinkle with 6 ounces chopped and cooked bacon and 1 thinly sliced scallion.

HERBED MASHED SWEET POTATOES WITH CARAMELIZED ONION

If you prefer, substitute ¼ teaspoon dried thyme for the thyme sprig (but do not remove in step 2).

Add 1 sprig fresh thyme to the saucepan in step 1. While the sweet potatoes are cooking, melt 1 tablespoon butter in a small nonstick skillet and add 1 small minced onion, ¼ teaspoon sugar, and ¼ teaspoon salt. Cook over low heat until the onion is caramelized, about 15 minutes. Discard the thyme and mash the potatoes as directed in step 2. Stir in the onion and 1 tablespoon sour cream.

SLICING SWEET POTATOES

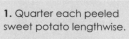

1. Quarter each peeled sweet potato lengthwise.

2. Cut each quarter crosswise into ¼-inch slices.

Mashers: There are two classic styles of potato masher: the wire-looped masher with a zigzag presser and the disk masher with a perforated round or oval plate. We tested eight mashers to see which would have the most comfortable grip and the most effective mashing mechanism. In general, the disk mashers outperformed the wire-looped models, and the WMF Profi Plus Stainless Steel Potato Masher ($15.99) was our favorite. With its small holes, this oval-based masher turned out soft and silky spuds with little effort. Its rounded edges snuggled right into the curves of the saucepan, enhancing its efficacy, and its round handle was easy to grip.

Savory Sweet Potato Casserole

It took us a long time to realize that sweet potatoes don't have to be candied. Our epiphany came when we were served a decidedly savory sweet potato casserole that resembled jazzed-up scalloped potatoes. This casserole featured creamy, cheesy sweet potatoes accented with smoky bacon and a subtly spicy bite, all under a coating of crunchy bread crumbs. We had to re-create this dish for ourselves.

Baking a casserole of raw sweet potatoes created an unevenly cooked disaster, so we turned to pre-cooking the sweet potatoes and then baking them. We tried boiling, baking, and microwaving, but we found that gently simmering the sweet potatoes in a combination of heavy cream and buttermilk (similar to the method we use in the test kitchen for traditional scalloped potatoes) was the most successful option. The sweet potatoes were soft (not mealy) and absorbed the flavors of the dairy mixture. Unlike regular potatoes, sweet potatoes don't soak up moisture, so they required only half as much dairy as regular potatoes.

Now that the sweet potato mixture was pre-cooked, it was easy to assemble our casserole. We mixed in bacon for salt and smoke, cayenne pepper for kick, cheddar cheese for richness, and chopped scallions for a fresh bite. We topped the seasoned sweet potatoes with coarse bread crumbs, melted butter, and more cheddar, then popped the casserole into the oven. After just 15 minutes, it emerged golden and bubbly, with rich, savory flavor that was even better than we remembered.

SPICY SWEET POTATO AND BACON CASSEROLE

SERVES 10

For a milder heat, reduce the cayenne pepper to ¼ teaspoon.

4	slices hearty white sandwich bread, torn into large pieces
2	tablespoons unsalted butter, melted
2½	cups shredded sharp cheddar cheese
8	slices bacon, chopped
1	onion, minced
4	garlic cloves, minced
½	teaspoon cayenne pepper (see note above)
5	pounds sweet potatoes (about 8 medium), peeled, halved lengthwise, and sliced thin
¾	cup heavy cream
¾	cup buttermilk
2½	teaspoons salt
5	scallions, sliced thin

1. Adjust an oven rack to the middle position and heat the oven to 425 degrees. Pulse the bread, butter, and ½ cup of the cheese in a food processor until coarsely ground.

2. Cook the bacon in a Dutch oven over medium heat until crisp, about 8 minutes. Transfer the bacon to a paper towel–lined plate and pour off all but 1 tablespoon of the fat. Cook the onion until softened, about 5 minutes. Add the garlic and cayenne and cook until fragrant, about 30 seconds. Stir in the sweet potatoes, cream, buttermilk, and salt. Reduce the heat to medium-low and cook, covered, until the potatoes are just tender, about 30 minutes. Off the heat, stir in the remaining 2 cups cheese, cooked bacon, and 4 of the scallions.

3. Transfer the mixture to a 13 by 9-inch baking dish and top with the bread crumbs. Bake until the crumbs are golden brown, about 15 minutes. Cool 10 minutes, then sprinkle with the remaining scallion. Serve. (The casserole can be prepared through step 2 and refrigerated for up to 1 day. The bread-crumb mixture should be refrigerated separately and will keep for up to 2 days. When ready to bake, cover the casserole with foil and bake until hot and bubbly, about 40 minutes. Uncover, sprinkle with the bread crumbs, and bake until the topping is golden brown, about 15 minutes.)

Creamy Mashed Potatoes

During the holiday season, we shelve our tried-and-true recipe for mashed potatoes in favor of a much more luxurious mash, one that is silky smooth and loaded with cream and butter. But there's a fine line between creamy and gluey. Sometimes our potatoes are as good as any you might get in the finest restaurant. Other times they closely resemble paste or Spackle. Why is this simple recipe (with just potatoes, cream, butter, and salt) so fickle?

The problem is the starch. When the cooked potatoes are mashed, some starch is released, which helps to make the potatoes incredibly smooth and creamy. But if you've ever mashed potatoes with an electric mixer, you've seen what happens when you get too much of a good thing: the mixer releases too much starch from the potatoes and turns them into a gluey mess.

Finding the right type of potato was our first challenge. Russets yielded a fluffy, relatively light mash. We wanted something a bit creamier and more substantial. Red potatoes were too dense and gluey. Yukon golds were the perfect compromise—creamier than russets but not sticky and heavy like the red potatoes.

Preparing potatoes for mashing is pretty straightforward. The potatoes are peeled, cut into chunks, boiled, drained, and mashed. Could we improve upon this method? We found a few recipes that suggested microwaving or baking the potatoes, but the results were grainy. We finally hit upon a simple refinement borrowed from classic french-fry recipes, which call for rinsing the cut potatoes to wash away excess starch. What if we adapted this idea for mashed potatoes? Cutting the potatoes into round slices (rather than the usual chunks) would expose more surface area, so we ran a test with rinsed versus unrinsed rounds of potatoes. The difference was significant. The rinsed potatoes were much creamier (and not at all gluey) when mashed.

To remove any water still clinging to the potatoes, we returned them to the empty pot and set it over low heat (excess water reduces the amount of butter and cream the potatoes can hold).

As for the butter and cream, it is very important not to add these ingredients cold to hot potatoes. Melting the butter and heating the cream ensure that the potatoes will arrive at the table hot.

Creamy potatoes demand a fair amount of butter and cream, but too much will turn them soupy.

After testing various amounts of each, our tasters decided that 1½ sticks of butter and 1½ cups of cream gave 4 pounds of potatoes the best flavor and texture.

These rich potatoes are an indulgence, and we would never douse them with gravy (use a leaner recipe if that's your goal). Eat these mashed potatoes just as they are, so you can appreciate every drop of cream.

SUPER-CREAMY MASHED POTATOES

SERVES 8 TO 10

This recipe can be cut in half, if desired.

4	pounds Yukon gold potatoes, peeled
12	tablespoons (1½ sticks) unsalted butter, cut into 6 pieces
1½	cups heavy cream
2	teaspoons salt

MAKING CREAMY MASHED POTATOES

1. Cut the potatoes into ¾-inch rounds and toss the potatoes in a colander under running water to rinse away as much starch as possible.

2. When the potatoes are tender, drain and then dry them thoroughly in an empty pot over low heat.

1. Cut the potatoes into ¾-inch slices. Place the potatoes in a colander and rinse under running water, tossing with your hands, for 30 seconds. Transfer the potatoes to a Dutch oven, add water to cover by 1 inch, and bring to a boil over high heat. Reduce the heat to medium and boil until the potatoes are tender, 20 to 25 minutes.

2. Meanwhile, heat the butter and cream in a small saucepan over medium heat until the butter is melted, about 5 minutes. Keep warm.

3. Drain the potatoes and return them to the Dutch oven. Stir over low heat until the potatoes are thoroughly dried, 1 to 2 minutes. Set a ricer or food mill over a large bowl and press or mill the potatoes into the bowl. Gently fold in the warm cream mixture and salt with a rubber spatula until the cream is absorbed and the potatoes are thick and creamy. Serve.

SHOPPING WITH THE TEST KITCHEN

Ricers: For silky-smooth mashed potatoes, the best tool is a potato ricer—a device that resembles an oversized garlic press. Cooked spuds are loaded into a hopper and squeezed (or "riced") through a sieve-like disk: brilliant, but not complicated. We pressed our way through seven ricers and found most models riced potatoes acceptably. Look for a ricer with a large hopper as well as interchangeable fine and coarse disks; sturdy, ergonomic handles that don't require brute force to squeeze; and a pot extension grip to hold the ricer steady. Our favorite was the R.S.V.P. International Classic Kitchen Basics Potato Ricer ($11.99). Its hopper holds 1¼ cups of sliced potatoes. It has a clamp to hold the ricer disk in place and a masher plate that opened nearly 180 degrees to more easily fill the hopper.

Mashed Potato Casserole

The appeal of mashed potato casserole is considerable, with the promise of fluffy, buttery, creamy potatoes nestled under a savory golden crust. And with all the mashing and mixing done beforehand, it's the perfect convenience dish when you have company—you can prepare this casserole a day in advance and just pop it into the oven before mealtime. But upon making several existing recipes, we found that most simply have you throw mashed potatoes into a casserole dish and bake them in the oven. The results were bland, gluey, dense potatoes that were definitely not worth the convenience.

To fix this recipe, we focused first on the choice of potato. We prepared casseroles with russet, Yukon gold, and all-purpose potatoes and determined that russets were the least heavy of the lot. Heavy cream was much too rich for this dish, but whole milk tasted too lean. We split the difference with half-and-half, which helped to lighten the dish, but tasters weren't happy until we cut the half-and-half with chicken broth, which kept the potatoes moist and provided an even lighter texture.

Taking a cue from shepherd's pie (another recipe in which mashed potatoes are baked), we tried beating eggs into the potato mixture. An egg or two helped a little, but it wasn't until we added four that we achieved the fluffy, airy texture we wanted. And since the potatoes were rising in the dish, the top crust was browning even better than before.

We usually like to mash potatoes with a potato ricer, but since we had broken out our hand-held mixer to beat the eggs into the potatoes, we wondered if we could simplify things by using it to mash the potatoes. In the past, the test kitchen has found that hand-held mixers make mashed potatoes gluey, but that wasn't an issue here, because the eggs gave the casserole an airy lift.

In some recipes the mashed potatoes are seasoned with ingredients such as dried mustard and thyme, but we preferred the sharpness of Dijon mustard and fresh garlic. Not only was this dish easy to make ahead of time, but our tasters agreed that these potatoes—with their creamy, light interior and crisp, brown crust—were now the star of the table.

MASHED POTATO CASSEROLE

SERVES 6 TO 8

The casserole may also be baked in a 13 by 9-inch pan.

4	pounds russet potatoes, peeled and cut into 1-inch chunks
½	cup half-and-half
½	cup low-sodium chicken broth
12	tablespoons (1½ sticks) unsalted butter, cut into pieces
1	garlic clove, minced
2	teaspoons Dijon mustard
2	teaspoons salt
4	large eggs
¼	cup finely minced fresh chives

1. Adjust an oven rack to the upper-middle position and heat the oven to 375 degrees. Bring the potatoes and water to cover by 1 inch to a boil in a large pot over high heat. Reduce the heat to medium and simmer until the potatoes are tender, about 20 minutes.

2. Heat the half-and-half, broth, butter, garlic, mustard, and salt in a saucepan over medium-low heat until smooth, about 5 minutes. Keep warm.

3. Drain the potatoes and transfer to a large bowl. With an electric mixer on medium-low speed, beat the potatoes, slowly adding the half-and-half mixture, until smooth and creamy, about 1 minute. Scrape down the bowl; beat in the eggs one at a time until incorporated, about 1 minute. Fold in the chives.

4. Transfer the potato mixture to a greased 2-quart baking dish and use a fork to make a peaked design on top of the casserole. Bake until the potatoes rise and begin to brown, about 35 minutes. Let cool for 10 minutes. Serve. (The baking dish with the potatoes can be covered with plastic wrap and refrigerated for up to 24 hours. When ready to bake, let the casserole sit at room temperature for 1 hour. Increase the baking time by 10 minutes.)

Scalloped Potato Casserole

Most every cook knows the basic recipe for scalloped potatoes: layer thinly sliced potatoes and cheese in a shallow casserole dish, cover with liquid, and bake. In the best of all worlds, the potatoes form dense layers, the liquid reduces to a creamy, flavorful sauce, and the cheesy crust is golden and crisp. But scalloped potatoes are often heavy and bland.

Using just cream makes the dish too rich and greasy. But leaner dairy choices can curdle in the oven. Our solution was to cut the heavy cream with a little chicken broth. Simmering fresh thyme and garlic with the cream and broth made the sauce taste better. As for the cheese, we decided to pair Gruyère or Swiss (for both their meltability and their flavor) with Parmesan (for its browning ability and its flavor).

ENSURING A BROWNED, CRUSTY TOP

For better browning and an impressive presentation, use a fork to make a peaked design on top of the potato casserole.

Russet, all-purpose, and Yukon gold potatoes all worked well, although the russets, with their tender bite and earthy flavor, were our favorite. More important than the type of potato used is the way the potatoes are sliced—very thin, if they are to cook evenly. Unless you have excellent knife skills, a mandoline is recommended.

A top layer of golden, bubbly cheese was nice, but we wanted a topping worth fighting for. We remembered a savory bread pudding with crisp bread cubes poking out of the custard. Unconventional as it might seem, a bread topping looked great on our scalloped potatoes, and its tasty crunch kept everyone in the kitchen coming back for more.

SCALLOPED POTATO CASSEROLE

SERVES 8 TO 10

This casserole can be assembled—leave off the bread—and refrigerated for up to 24 hours before baking. When ready to bake, add the bread topping and bake according to the recipe. If you're cooking for a crowd, double the ingredients and use two baking dishes of similar size.

4	garlic cloves, 1 clove cut in half lengthwise, remaining cloves minced
1	tablespoon unsalted butter, softened
1	cup shredded Gruyère or Swiss cheese
1	cup coarsely grated Parmesan cheese
1½	cups heavy cream
1½	cups low-sodium chicken broth
2	teaspoons minced fresh thyme
⅛	teaspoon ground nutmeg
¾	teaspoon salt
⅛	teaspoon pepper
2½	pounds russet potatoes (4 to 5 medium), peeled and sliced ⅛ inch thick
4–5	slices hearty white sandwich bread, crusts removed, torn into pieces (about 4 cups)

MAKING A CRISP TOPPING

For an extra-crisp crust, press roughly torn pieces of sandwich bread into the casserole right before it goes into the oven.

1. Adjust an oven rack to the middle position and heat the oven to 350 degrees. Use the cut side of the halved garlic to rub the sides and bottom of a 2-quart shallow baking or gratin dish. Allow the garlic in the dish to dry briefly, about 2 minutes, then coat the dish with the softened butter. Combine the cheeses in a small bowl.

2. Bring the minced garlic, cream, broth, thyme, nutmeg, salt, and pepper to a boil in a large saucepan over medium-high heat. Reduce the heat to medium-low and simmer until the liquid is reduced to 2½ cups, about 5 minutes. Remove from the heat and gently stir in the potatoes.

3. Spoon half of the potato mixture into the prepared dish. Sprinkle with half of the cheese, add the remaining potato mixture, and press with a spatula to compact. Press the bread pieces into the casserole. Bake for 40 minutes. Sprinkle the remaining cheese on top and continue baking until golden and bubbling, 25 to 30 minutes. Remove from the oven and let rest for 20 minutes before serving.

Mandolines: If you don't own a food processor, a mandoline can quickly slice potatoes for Scalloped Potato Casserole (page 113) and other dishes where thinly sliced vegetables are required. In testing mandolines, we found two that took top honors. OXO's V-Blade Mandoline Slicer ($49.99) has a V-shaped blade that is ideal for both firm and delicate produce. It felt safe and comfortable and came with a rimmed, long-pronged hand guard. A close second is a handheld, no-frills model—a simple slicer from Kyocera ($27), which is a real bargain.

Super-Stuffed Baked Potatoes

Who doesn't like a big stuffed baked potato—one with a crisp, crunchy shell, filled with creamy well-seasoned potato? Some recipes for stuffed baked potatoes yield a dry and bland filling in a soggy skin. We wanted to tackle those issues and more in developing a truly great stuffed baked potato.

We started by precooking the potatoes in the microwave. The flesh wasn't as fluffy as when we baked the potatoes in the oven, but the microwave shaved an hour off the cooking time and the differences disappeared once we added the cheese and butter. Most recipes for stuffed baked potatoes call for cutting the potatoes in half, but the end results looked like floppy potato skins. We prefer to lop off just the top quarter of the potato and then hollow it out. Once dried in the oven, these crispy shells hold more filling. We tried fillings based on cream cheese, sour cream, heavy cream, and evaporated milk, but our tasters preferred Boursin cheese. This creamy cheese gave our filling garlic and herb flavor and a smooth texture. We boosted the flavor even more by cooking minced garlic in butter and adding that to the cheese mixture.

After hollowing out the potatoes, there was enough filling for each, but not enough to mound on top. More cheese just weighed down the potato. A simple solution was to cook an extra potato just for its flesh (discarding the shell). We now had enough filling to mound into each potato shell. We sprinkled more cheese over the top for a final burst of flavor.

SUPER-STUFFED BAKED POTATOES

SERVES 6

This recipe calls for 7 potatoes, but only 6 of them make it to the table. The remaining potato is used for its flesh; you should have 5 cups of scooped potato flesh in step 2.

7	large russet potatoes (about 12 ounces each), scrubbed
6	tablespoons unsalted butter, 3 tablespoons melted
	Salt
1	(5.2-ounce) package Boursin cheese, crumbled
½	cup half-and-half
2	garlic cloves, minced
¼	cup minced fresh chives
1	teaspoon pepper

1. Adjust an oven rack to the middle position and heat the oven to 475 degrees. Set a wire rack inside a rimmed baking sheet. Prick the potatoes all over with a fork, place on a paper towel, and microwave on high until tender, 20 to 25 minutes, turning the potatoes over after 10 minutes.

2. Slice and remove the top quarter of each potato, let cool for 5 minutes, then scoop out the flesh, leaving a ¼-inch layer of potato on the inside.

Discard 1 potato shell. Brush the remaining shells inside and out with the melted butter and sprinkle the interiors with ¼ teaspoon salt. Transfer the potatoes, scooped side up, to the baking sheet fitted with the wire rack and bake until the skins begin to crisp, about 15 minutes.

3. Meanwhile, mix half of the Boursin and the half-and-half in a bowl until blended. Cook the remaining 3 tablespoons butter with the garlic in a saucepan over medium-low heat until the garlic is straw-colored, 3 to 5 minutes. Stir in the Boursin mixture until combined.

4. Set a ricer or food mill over a medium bowl and press or mill the potatoes into the bowl. Gently fold in the warm Boursin mixture, 3 tablespoons of the chives, ½ teaspoon salt, and pepper until well incorporated. Remove the potato shells from the oven and fill with the potato-cheese mixture. Top with the remaining crumbled Boursin and bake until the tops of the potatoes are golden brown, about 15 minutes. Sprinkle with the remaining chives. Serve.

MAKING STUFFED POTATOES

1. Slice the top quarter off the potato before scooping out its interior.

2. Use a spoon to scoop out the interior of the potato, being careful to leave a ¼-inch layer of potato in the shell.

Boursin Cheese: Boursin is a soft, spreadable cheese that comes in several varieties available in every supermarket. The Garlic and Fine Herbs flavor was a key ingredient in our Super-Stuffed Baked Potatoes (page 114), as it added creamy texture, cheese flavor, and a big hit of aromatic garlic and herbs. This versatile cheese works well as a sandwich spread (try it with roast beef), as a stuffing for chicken breasts, spread on steaks, in mashed potatoes, on crackers, in dips, or as part of a cheese plate.

Baked Potato Fans

Baked potato fans were popularized as Hasselback potatoes, the namesake dish of the restaurant at the Hasselbacken Hotel in Stockholm, Sweden. American recipes stay true to the original concept by combining the fluffy interior of a baked potato with the crisp, golden exterior of an oven fry—all with that distinctive, fanned-out presentation.

The fanning is accomplished by slicing almost all the way through a whole potato crosswise along its length at ¼-inch intervals, leaving the bottom of the potato intact and allowing the slices to gently fan open like an accordion as the potato bakes. The skin crisps while the fans create openings into which seasonings, cheese, and bread crumbs can be sprinkled before a final pass in the oven. This dish sounded fit for company, but we were glad we tried out a few recipes first; these potatoes were harder to manipulate than we expected.

Most recipes would have you believe that baked potato fans can be made with any type of potato. We learned that was definitely not the case after trying waxy red potatoes, which dried out in the oven, and Yukon golds, which were better but still too dry. The russet, or Idaho, potato was the right choice here, as its starchy flesh translated into a fluffy texture when baked.

Working with the russets, we cut ¼-inch cross-wise slices down the length of each potato, trying to leave the bottom intact to hold the slices together. This was hard to do if the bottom of the potato wasn't almost perfectly flat. Following the lead of one astute recipe, we sliced the bottom from each potato, which gave us a flat surface to work with, and placed a chopstick on either side to prevent the knife from slicing all the way through. We brushed the potatoes with oil and baked them. But after all that work, they barely fanned out. The slices were stuck together. The skin had also developed a leathery texture by the time the inside was cooked through.

We tackled the sticky fans first. Excess starch exposed to the oven heat was creating a tacky seal and causing the fans to stick together. We found that taking the time to rinse the potatoes of that surface starch after they were sliced prevented them from sticking together. Even better, taking a slice off each end of the potato gave the remaining slices more room to fan out as they baked, allowing even more heat to penetrate and crisp their surfaces.

We were pleased that our potatoes now looked like little accordions; it was time to fix the tough, overcooked exteriors. Rather than relying entirely on the dry and sometimes punishing heat of the oven, we precooked the potatoes in the microwave and then moved them to the oven to finish cooking through and crisp up their skins. Brushing the potatoes with oil before baking helped crisp their skins further.

In most recipes the potatoes are sprinkled with a topping of grated cheese, bread crumbs, and seasonings during the last few minutes of baking. Cheddar cheese was too greasy, but a combination of Parmesan (for nutty flavor) and Monterey Jack (because it melts well) was perfect. Store-bought bread crumbs were too sandy, but homemade crumbs stayed moist in the oven, especially with a little melted butter added. Fresh garlic didn't have enough time to cook and mellow, but garlic powder (mixed with some sweet paprika) worked nicely. As a final step, we broiled the potatoes to make the topping irresistibly crunchy.

CRISPY BAKED POTATO FANS

SERVES 4

To ensure that the potatoes fan out evenly, look for uniformly shaped potatoes.

BREAD-CRUMB TOPPING

1	slice hearty white sandwich bread, torn into pieces
4	tablespoons unsalted butter, melted
½	cup shredded Monterey Jack cheese
¼	cup grated Parmesan cheese
1	teaspoon paprika
½	teaspoon garlic powder
	Salt and pepper

POTATO FANS

4	russet potatoes, scrubbed
2	tablespoons extra-virgin olive oil
	Salt and pepper

PREPARING BAKED POTATO FANS

1. Use chopsticks as a foolproof guide for slicing the potato petals without cutting all the way through the potato.

2. Gently flex the fans open while rinsing them under cold running water; this rids the potatoes of excess starch that can impede fanning.

1. FOR THE BREAD-CRUMB TOPPING: Adjust an oven rack to the middle position and heat the oven to 200 degrees. Pulse the bread in a food processor until coarsely ground. Bake the bread crumbs on a rimmed baking sheet until dry, about 20 minutes. Let cool for 5 minutes, then combine the crumbs, butter, cheeses, paprika, garlic powder, ¼ teaspoon salt, and ¼ teaspoon pepper in a large bowl. (The bread-crumb topping can be refrigerated in a zipper-lock plastic bag for up to 2 days.)

2. FOR THE POTATO FANS: Heat the oven to 450 degrees. Cut ¼ inch from the bottom and ends of the potatoes, then slice the potatoes crosswise at ¼-inch intervals, leaving ¼ inch of each potato intact. Gently rinse the potatoes under running water, let drain, and transfer, sliced side down, to a plate. Microwave until slightly soft to the touch, 6 to 12 minutes, flipping the potatoes halfway through cooking.

3. Arrange the potatoes, sliced side up, on a foil-lined baking sheet. Brush the potatoes all over with oil and season with salt and pepper. Bake until the skin is crisp and the potatoes are beginning to brown, 25 to 30 minutes. Remove the potatoes from the oven and heat the broiler.

4. Carefully top the potatoes with the bread-crumb topping, pressing gently to adhere. Broil until the bread crumbs are deep golden brown, about 3 minutes. Serve.

Variation

BLUE CHEESE AND BACON BAKED POTATO FANS

In step 1, substitute ⅓ cup crumbled blue cheese for the Monterey Jack. In step 4, sprinkle 4 slices bacon, cooked until crisp and then crumbled, over the potatoes just prior to serving.

Crunchy Potato Wedges

The fried chicken at KFC is pretty good, but what we really find addictive are their fried potato wedges. The spicy, light, and crunchy coating contrasts perfectly with the fluffy interior. These potatoes taste so much like their fried chicken counterpart that we assume they are made using the same coating. We wanted to duplicate these wedges at home, so we could enjoy them somewhere other than the front seat of our car.

To obtain a perfectly cooked interior and a nicely crisped exterior, we knew we'd have to precook our potato wedges before they were fried—otherwise the outside would burn by the time they were cooked through. Taking a cue from the test kitchen's recipe for steak fries, we placed the cut spuds in a bowl with a little vegetable oil, covered them with plastic wrap, and microwaved them until they were just shy of being done. Since the potatoes were tightly covered, they didn't lose any moisture, which made them fry up especially fluffy inside. Now we could concentrate on the crunch and flavor of the coating.

We started with a traditional fried chicken method, dipping our potato wedges in flour, then buttermilk, then back into the flour before frying. The coating was too heavy and tough. Some fried chicken recipes call for adding baking powder or baking soda to either the flour or the buttermilk. After a few tests, we found that mixing baking soda right into the buttermilk did the trick. You could see the soda reacting with the buttermilk, making it foam and bubble. Potatoes coated with this mixture were especially crunchy and deep golden brown. To lighten things even further, we tried replacing some of the flour with cornstarch. Sure enough, this coating was incredibly crisp and light. Even better, the cornstarch kept the wedges from sogging out even after they'd sat around for a few minutes. During one round of tests, we chomped down on a potato wedge that had been sitting on the plate for 30 minutes. Although it was cold, the coating was still crunchy.

Next we moved on to the seasonings. After trying countless combinations of herbs and spices, we settled on just six: salt, pepper, onion powder, garlic powder, cayenne pepper, and oregano. Together these seasonings approximated KFC's secret blend, but just adding our seasoning mixture to the flour left the wedges somehow lacking. We found that tossing the wedges in the seasoning as they came out of the oil worked better, but the centers of the potatoes were still bland.

Since we season potatoes with salt when we boil them, it only seemed right to season our wedges as they precooked in the microwave. Now the spice flavor permeated the potatoes all the way from their fluffy interiors to their crunchy exteriors. From now on we're frying our wedges at home, rather than hitting the drive-through.

CRUNCHY POTATO WEDGES

SERVES 6

If you don't have buttermilk, substitute 1 cup milk mixed with 1 tablespoon fresh lemon juice. Let the mixture sit 15 minutes before using.

4	teaspoons kosher salt
½	teaspoon pepper
2	teaspoons onion powder
1	teaspoon garlic powder
¾	teaspoon cayenne pepper
1	teaspoon dried oregano
3	large russet potatoes (about 1¾ pounds), scrubbed and cut into ¼-inch wedges
¼	cup vegetable or peanut oil, plus 3 quarts for frying
1½	cups all-purpose flour
½	cup cornstarch
1	cup buttermilk (see note above)
½	teaspoon baking soda

1. Combine the salt, pepper, onion and garlic powders, cayenne, and oregano in a small bowl.

2. Toss the potato wedges with 4 teaspoons of the spice mixture and ¼ cup of the oil in a large microwave-safe bowl; cover tightly with plastic wrap. Microwave on high until the potatoes are tender but not falling apart, 7 to 9 minutes, shaking the bowl (without removing the plastic) to redistribute the potatoes halfway through cooking. Slowly remove the plastic wrap from the bowl (be careful of the steam) and drain the potatoes. Arrange the potatoes on a rimmed baking sheet and cool until the potatoes firm up, about 10 minutes. (The potatoes can be held at room temperature for up to 2 hours.)

3. Heat the remaining 3 quarts oil in a large Dutch oven over high heat to 340 degrees. Meanwhile, combine the flour and cornstarch in a medium bowl and whisk the buttermilk and baking soda in a large bowl. Working in 2 batches, dredge the potato wedges in the flour mixture, shaking off the excess. Dip in the buttermilk mixture, allowing the excess to drip back into the bowl, then coat again in the flour mixture. Shake off the excess and place on a wire rack. (The potatoes can be coated up to 30 minutes in advance.)

4. When the oil is ready, add half of the coated wedges and fry until deep golden brown, 4 to 6 minutes. Transfer the wedges to a large bowl and toss with 1 teaspoon of the spice mixture. Drain the wedges on a baking sheet lined with paper towels. Return the oil to 340 degrees and repeat with the second batch of wedges. Serve with extra seasoning on the side.

ITALIAN-STYLE CRUNCHY POTATO WEDGES

Although these potato wedges are flavorful enough on their own, try them dipped into your favorite marinara sauce.

Replace the onion powder, garlic powder, cayenne, and oregano with 1 tablespoon Italian seasoning and 1 tablespoon grated Parmesan.

FROM-THE-FREEZER CRUNCHY POTATO WEDGES

Our Crunchy Potato Wedges freeze very well.

Follow steps 1 through 4, frying each batch of wedges until they are light golden brown, 2 to 3 minutes. Do not toss with the spice mixture, and drain and cool the potatoes completely on a baking sheet lined with paper towels. Freeze the wedges on a baking sheet until completely frozen, about 2 hours, then transfer the potatoes to a zipper-lock plastic bag and freeze for up to 2 months. When ready to eat, heat 3 quarts oil to 340 degrees and cook the potatoes in 2 batches until deep golden brown, about 3 minutes. Toss with the spice mixture, drain, and serve.

Fried Green Tomatoes

With a crisp coating and clean, tart flavor, fried green tomatoes are a classic Southern side dish and snack. Unripe tomatoes are sliced, breaded, and fried to a deep golden brown and served with hot sauce. When cooked right, these tangy tomato treats are heavenly. When cooked badly, however, the coating turns greasy while the bland tomato is either undercooked and rock hard or overcooked and sticky.

Starting with the tomatoes, we noticed they are found in many sizes, measuring anywhere from 2 to 5 inches across. Although there were no readily discernible differences in flavor among the tomatoes, we liked the medium-sized tomatoes, which ranged from 2½ to 3½ inches. These tomatoes sliced into good-sized portions that were easy to bread and fry in only a few batches. We fried tomatoes sliced to a variety of thicknesses and preferred tomatoes cut into ¼-inch-thick slices. Thicker slices refused to cook through, staying tough and crunchy even when the breading was quite brown. Thinner slices overcooked to a sticky, jam-like consistency. When sliced ¼ inch thick, however, the tomatoes cooked perfectly, turning soft and yielding but not mushy.

Turning our attention to the breading, we tried a number of different methods and ingredients. Some recipes call for only flour, but we liked the authentic flavor of cornmeal. Just dipping the tomato in seasoned cornmeal before frying, however, didn't work so well. The coating fell off in places, leaving the tomato underneath naked, and the cornmeal itself was too potent in terms of flavor and texture. We then tried using a cornmeal pancake–like batter but found the crust a bit doughy and cakey. The classic breading procedure—dipping into flour, then egg, then a seasoned cornmeal-flour mixture—worked well, but this array of ingredients turned somewhat dense and heavy when fried. Taking a cue from some fried chicken recipes, we altered this classic breading by adding some buttermilk and leavener to the egg. This new coating worked easily and tasted great. The leavened buttermilk turned the coating light and supercrisp, while adding a tangy flavor.

After a little more testing, we found that the cornmeal-flour mixture tasted best when seasoned heavily with salt and pepper as well as a little cayenne pepper. We also liked how the tomatoes tasted when fried in vegetable oil. After frying several batches, we noted that the tomatoes fried to a beautiful golden brown without tasting too greasy when the oil was heated to 350 degrees. Served with hot sauce or wedges of lemon, these crisp slices will have you dreaming of unripe tomatoes.

FRIED GREEN TOMATOES

SERVES 4 TO 6

Any firm, underripe tomato can be used in this recipe. A well-seasoned cast-iron skillet is ideal for frying the tomato slices. We prefer a fine-textured cornmeal for this recipe; coarser cornmeal will make the coating excessively crunchy.

2½	cups all-purpose flour
1½	cups fine-ground white or yellow cornmeal, such as Quaker
	Salt and pepper
¼	teaspoon cayenne pepper
1	large egg
1	cup buttermilk
1	teaspoon baking powder
½	teaspoon baking soda
2	medium green tomatoes (about 12 ounces each), cored and cut into ¼-inch slices (for a total of 12 to 14 slices)
1½–2	cups vegetable oil

1. Measure 1 cup of the flour into a large shallow dish. Measure the remaining 1½ cups flour, cornmeal, 1 tablespoon salt, 1 teaspoon pepper, and cayenne into a second large shallow dish. Beat the egg, buttermilk, baking powder, and baking soda in a medium bowl (the mixture will bubble and foam).

2. Working with several slices at a time, drop the tomatoes into the flour and shake the dish to coat. Shake the excess flour from each piece. Using tongs, dip the tomatoes into the buttermilk mixture, turning to coat well and allowing the excess to drip off. Coat the tomato slices with the seasoned flour-cornmeal mixture, shaking off any excess. Place the tomatoes on a wire rack set over a rimmed baking sheet. Repeat with the remaining tomato slices.

3. Pour enough oil into a 12-inch skillet to measure ⅓ inch in depth. Heat the oil over high heat until it reaches a temperature of 350 degrees, 3 to 4 minutes. Gently lay a single layer of tomato slices (about 4 or 5 slices) in the oil and turn the heat down to medium. Fry until the tomatoes are a deep golden brown on the first side, 2 to 2½ minutes, adjusting the heat as necessary to maintain the oil at a temperature of 350 degrees. Gently turn the tomato slices over with tongs and fry until the second side is a deep golden brown, 2 to 2½ minutes. Transfer the fried tomatoes to a rimmed baking sheet lined with paper towels and cool for 1 to 2 minutes. Repeat with the remaining slices, adjusting the heat as necessary to maintain the oil at a temperature of 350 degrees. Serve immediately.

Baked Cheese Grits

A staple of the Southern breakfast table, grits are a hearty and satisfying start to the day. They appear in many guises, including simmered and sweetened with maple syrup or molasses; cooked to a thick consistency, cooled, and fried in slices; and, our favorite, enriched with cheese and spices and baked until brown on the top and creamy in the middle. From experience, however, we have found that baked cheese grits are often far from perfect. They are either bland and watery or too weighted down with ham, sausage, and other potent flavorings. For our recipe we wanted a compromise—hearty, robust flavor that did not overwhelm the subtlety of the grits.

We started by cooking the grits. There are two kinds of grits: instant, which cook in 5 minutes; and old-fashioned, which cook in 15 minutes. In a side-by-side tasting, most tasters thought the instant grits were too creamy and tasted overprocessed. The old-fashioned grits were creamy yet retained a slightly coarse texture that tasters liked.

To add richness without relying solely on butter, as many recipes do, we cooked the grits in milk rather than water. The grits tasted good, but more in a hot breakfast cereal way—not the flavor we were hoping for—and the flavor of the grits disappeared behind the milk flavor. Even when we diluted the milk significantly, the grits tasted too heavily of cooked milk. We then tried a small amount of heavy cream and water mixed together. Everyone liked this batch—the grits were rich but without an overwhelming dairy flavor. We were surprised to find that cooked cream does not develop the same strong "cooked" flavor as milk. This is because the extra fat in cream keeps the milk proteins from breaking down when heated. After a few more batches of varying proportions, we found that 1 part cream to 3 parts water provided the best flavor.

To improve things, we tried a few simple additions that would deepen the flavor of the grits without being overpowering. A small minced onion cooked in the saucepan before adding the liquid brought depth and a touch of sweetness. Many tasters liked a little garlic as well, but others thought the garlic overwhelmed the other flavors, so we left it out. Hot sauce added piquancy that cut through the richness.

With the grits cooked, we needed some cheese to fold in before baking. Recipes we found included everything from pasteurized cheese slices to Spanish Manchego. A Spanish cheese seemed too far afield for this dish, but we were ready to try just about anything. Monterey Jack and pepper Jack cheeses made the grits taste sour, although the jalapeños were appreciated and made us increase our amount of hot sauce. Regular cheddar was bland, but the flavor was getting there. Extra-sharp cheddar proved to be the winner. The flavor was assertive and complemented the subtle corn flavor. Everyone in the test kitchen also liked smoked cheddar but thought that it might be a little strong for the breakfast table.

Now it was time to bake our grits. We knew we wanted a dense texture, more akin to baked polenta than custardy spoon bread. We started off by adding two lightly beaten eggs to the grits before baking, and this provided an airy, almost soufflé-like texture that most tasters found unpleasant. We needed more eggs to bind the grits and give the dish the dense texture we desired. Four eggs made the grits too heavy, and the egg flavor predominated. Three eggs, on the other hand, provided just enough structure without making the grits taste too eggy.

Forty-five minutes in a 350-degree oven (with a little more cheese sprinkled on after 30 minutes to help brown the top) finished off our testing. We had attained our ideal baked grits, rich and flavorful, with a clear corn flavor. And they are neutral enough to pair perfectly with eggs and sausage for breakfast or with roast chicken for dinner.

BAKED CHEESE GRITS

SERVES 4 TO 6

Old-fashioned grits are well worth the extra 10 minutes of cooking; instant grits will bake up too smooth and have an overprocessed flavor. Grits are ready when they are creamy and smooth but retain a little fine-textured coarseness. We preferred a very sharp aged cheddar, but feel free to use any extra-sharp cheddar you like. Or, for a heartier flavor more suitable to brunch or a dinner side dish, substitute smoked cheddar or smoked Gouda.

2	tablespoons plus 1 teaspoon unsalted butter
1	onion, minced
1	cup heavy cream
½	teaspoon hot sauce
½	teaspoon salt
1⅛	cups old-fashioned grits
2	cups shredded extra-sharp cheddar cheese
3	large eggs, lightly beaten
	Pepper

1. Adjust an oven rack to the lower-middle position and heat the oven to 350 degrees. Grease a 9 by 9-inch baking dish with 1 teaspoon of the butter.

2. Heat the remaining 2 tablespoons butter in a large saucepan over medium heat until the foam begins to subside. Add the onion and cook until softened but not browned, about 4 minutes.

3. Add 3 cups water, the cream, hot sauce, and salt and bring to a boil. Whisk in the grits and reduce the heat to low. Cook, stirring frequently, until the grits are thick and creamy, about 15 minutes.

4. Off the heat, thoroughly stir in 1½ cups of the cheese, the eggs, and pepper to taste. Pour the mixture into the greased baking dish, smooth the top with a rubber spatula, and place the grits in the oven.

5. Bake for 30 minutes. Remove the dish from the oven, sprinkle the remaining ½ cup cheese evenly over the top, and return to the oven. Continue baking until the top is browned, about 15 minutes. Let rest for 5 minutes and serve.

Spoon Bread

Spoon bread is a Southern specialty made from a cornmeal batter that is poured into a baking dish and placed in a hot oven until set. The texture is somewhere between rich cornbread and a soufflé (because spoon bread is soft—and must be served with a spoon—it's probably closer to a soufflé). Spoon bread is a side dish that can be served in place of rice or potatoes or for breakfast.

To make spoon bread, you first whisk cornmeal into a simmering liquid and let it thicken to a "mush," as if you were cooking oatmeal. To the cooled mush you add eggs, salt, butter, and other ingredients. The mixture is poured into a baking dish and baked for 35 to 45 minutes. The resulting dish should be light as air, with a tender, rich crumb.

As with many traditional dishes, ingredients and cooking techniques for spoon bread vary enormously. We began to develop the recipe for our ideal spoon bread by figuring out the best way to make the cornmeal mush.

The proportion of liquid to solids differed wildly in the recipes we consulted. After trying various ratios, we eventually settled on a medium-thick batter, using 3 cups liquid to 1 cup cornmeal.

The act of stirring cornmeal into simmering milk can be tricky; if you don't do it properly, the meal can separate from the liquid and turn into a bunch of lumps rather than a smooth mush. Plenty of recipes call for the use of a double boiler to prevent lumping, but our suggestion is to focus intently on the job at hand. Start whisking like crazy and don't stop until the mush is thickened, 2 to 4 minutes later. It's not much of a time investment when you consider the alternative: 20 to 30 minutes of gentle stirring in a double boiler. Keep the cooking temperature low rather than high, because you want the cornmeal to soften as it cooks.

Having settled on the mush-making method, we moved on to consider the individual ingredients of the dish. Spoon bread made with water is like cornbread made with water: lean. Half-and-half proved to be our liquid of choice, supplying just the right amount of richness (cream provided too much, and milk not quite enough).

The oldest recipes for spoon bread call for whole eggs, not separated. A later trend called for separating the eggs and beating them to produce a light, high soufflé. Now we are beginning to see inroads into that procedure, with chemical leaveners compensating for the work the eggs would do. After tasting several dozen of these spoon breads, we found those made with baking powder or baking soda to taste plainly of chemicals. Beaten whites are the best leavener.

Finally, we considered the important question of what type of cornmeal to use. Yellow corn is more common in the North, and Southerners choose white for the same reason. We found that both made good spoon bread, the major difference being that the white produced a bread that was slightly milder in flavor.

A more important variation came with grinds. We prefer a fine grind because it produces a considerably smoother texture. Yellow Quaker cornmeal has a texture akin to table salt and is the proper grind. If you can't get fine-ground cornmeal in your local store, it's no problem. You can approximate a fine grind by putting medium-ground cornmeal in the food processor or, even better, the blender. The processing will take several minutes, but eventually you will have little clouds of powder-fine meal in the bottom of the work bowl or blender jar.

SPOON BREAD

SERVES 6 TO 8

A standard 8-inch soufflé dish works beautifully, but any straight-sided, heavy pan will work, even a cast-iron skillet. Because the spoon bread falls fast from its spectacular height, serve it as quickly as possible; even in its deflated state, though, spoon bread still tastes delicious. Serve leftovers with maple syrup.

- 3   cups half-and-half
- 1   teaspoon salt
- 1   cup fine-ground white or yellow cornmeal, such as Quaker
- 2   tablespoons unsalted butter, plus extra for greasing soufflé dish
- 3   large eggs, room temperature, separated

1. Adjust an oven rack to the middle position and heat the oven to 350 degrees. Butter a 1½-quart soufflé dish.

2. Bring the half-and-half and salt to a simmer in a large, heavy saucepan. Reduce the heat to low. Slowly whisk in the cornmeal. Continue whisking until the cornmeal thickens and develops a satin sheen, 2 to 4 minutes. Turn off the heat and stir in the butter; set the mush aside to cool slightly.

3. Whisk the egg yolks and 1 to 2 teaspoons water together in a small bowl until lemon-colored and very frothy. Stir them into the cooled mush, a little at a time to keep the yolks from cooking. Beat the egg whites to stiff but not dry peaks; gently fold them into the mush mixture.

4. Pour the mixture into the buttered soufflé dish. Bake until the spoon bread is golden brown and has risen above the rim of the dish, about 45 minutes. Serve immediately.

Variation

SPOON BREAD WITH CHEDDAR CHEESE
Add ½ cup shredded sharp cheddar cheese along with the butter.

California Barbecued Beans

In Santa Maria, no plate of grilled sirloin is complete without a generous scoop of barbecued pinquito beans, which are native to the Santa Maria Valley. Rather than being sweet and molasses-y, like most versions of barbecued beans, they are draped in a piquant red chili sauce that's flecked with plenty of smoky-sweet pork. These beans are tangy, smoky, and a little spicy and a perfect accompaniment to grilled steak.

Unfortunately, outside of Santa Maria, pinquito beans and red chili sauce (a canned sauce consisting of pureed red chiles) aren't everyday fare. Pink kidney beans proved to be a good stand-in for the pinquitos. Most recipes call for jarred taco sauce (a pureed condiment that tastes like salsa) as a substitute for the red chili sauce, but we found its flavor and texture too thin. We built a substantial base of flavor by frying bacon and ham with onion and garlic, then tried enhancing the taco sauce–pork mixture with canned enchilada sauce and even Heinz chili sauce. Neither worked as well as a simple combination of tomato puree and brown sugar. Upping the dry mustard to a full tablespoon, more than twice the usual amount, helped recapture some of the chili sauce's bite.

With a foundation of savory pork, a spicy-sweet dose of tomato, and a finishing punch of cider vinegar and cilantro, we managed to re-create the clean, fresh flavor of the original in our California Barbecued Beans.

CALIFORNIA BARBECUED BEANS

SERVES 4 TO 6

If you're thinking ahead, you can soak the beans in 6 cups of water overnight (then skip step 1). If you can find them, pinquito beans (a variety grown in the Santa Maria Valley) are traditional in this dish. Bottled taco sauce is available in the international aisle of most grocery stores. Don't add the tomato puree, taco sauce, brown sugar, and salt before the beans have simmered for an hour; they will hinder the proper softening of the beans. These beans are especially good served with California Grilled Tri-Tip (page 325).

1	pound pink kidney beans, rinsed and picked over (see note above)
4	slices bacon, minced
½	pound deli ham, minced
1	onion, minced
4	garlic cloves, minced
6	cups water
1	cup canned tomato puree
½	cup bottled taco sauce

5	tablespoons light brown sugar
1	tablespoon dry mustard
	Salt
¼	cup chopped fresh cilantro
2	tablespoons cider vinegar

1. Place the beans and 6 cups water in a large Dutch oven. Bring to a boil over high heat and cook for 5 minutes. Remove the pot from the heat, cover, and allow the beans to sit for 1 hour. Drain the beans. Clean and dry the pot.

2. Cook the bacon and ham in a Dutch oven over medium heat until the fat renders and the pork is lightly browned, 5 to 7 minutes. Add the onion and cook until softened, about 5 minutes. Stir in the garlic and cook until fragrant, about 30 seconds. Add the drained beans and water and bring to a simmer. Reduce the heat to medium-low, cover, and cook until the beans are just soft, about 1 hour.

3. Stir in the tomato puree, taco sauce, sugar, mustard, and 2 teaspoons salt. Continue to simmer, uncovered, until the beans are completely tender and the sauce is thickened, about 1 hour. (If the mixture becomes too thick, add water.) Stir in the cilantro and vinegar and season with salt to taste. Serve. (The beans can be refrigerated for up to 4 days.)

Cowboy Beans

Cowboy beans seem to be a cattle-country spin on Boston baked beans (see our recipe for Boston Baked Beans, cooked in a slow cooker, on page 424). In Boston baked beans, navy beans are stewed with salt pork, onion, mustard, and molasses; cowboy beans have pinto beans and barbecued beef or pork as well as a laundry list of various seasonings. We found dozens of recipes for cowboy beans, each a little different from the last. Our goal was to

The fabled chuck wagons of Old West fame first hit the trail shortly after the Civil War. Charles Goodnight, a larger-than-life cattle baron of the Texas Panhandle, had a surplus army cart outfitted with reinforced fittings and enough cabinetry to store the requisite dry goods, equipment, and fuel for a crew of cowboys on the trail. A back flap flipped down to serve as the cook's countertop, on which he prepared a never-ending stream of beans, biscuits, steaks, and coffee.

Chuck wagon cooks—always called Cookie by the cowboys—led as hard a life as those they fed. Cooks were up for hours before the sun rose, whipping up breakfast, and stayed up long into the night cleaning dishes. They also had to keep the wagon stocked with food, fuel, and water—easier said than done on the open plains.

To keep on the good side of Cookie, cowboys followed an unwritten code. If riding close to the wagon, they always stayed downwind so the dirt and dust they kicked up wouldn't get into the food. The same rule applied when it came to dismounting their horses. Cowboys never crowded the cooking fires for warmth, and under no circumstances would they ever help themselves to the last serving without an OK from Cookie.

create the robust flavor characteristic of these beans (sweet, spicy, and smoky), but with commonly available ingredients. That meant no barbecued beef or pork, which might be sitting around in a restaurant kitchen but not in a home kitchen.

First things first—we had to decide on the best method for cooking the beans. As much as we like canned beans, they can't survive a lengthy simmer: dried beans were a must. We liked both pinto and navy beans.

Most cowboy bean recipes instruct you to bring the beans and flavorings to a boil on the stovetop and then slide the pot into the oven. Rush this process, and the beans break apart. We found that the beans needed to cook in a 300-degree oven for about 4 hours. Some things are worth the wait, and good beans are one of them.

With a basic cooking method in hand, we tackled flavor. We first cooked a minced onion in oil but then thought better of the oil. Why not cook the onion in something more robust, like rendered bacon? The smoky meat and rich fat might be the perfect replacement for the "odds and ends" of barbecued meat. We browned a few slices of chopped bacon and then added the onion to soften in the fat. While we were at it, we added a few cloves of minced garlic. These beans were beginning to taste pretty good already.

Traditional recipes undoubtedly include home-brewed barbecue sauce, but we went with bottled sauce and had good results. A couple of tablespoons of spicy brown mustard—common to a lot of recipes—added a zip that tasters appreciated.

The beans were now good but still lacked that special something. We scoured more recipes for anything we might have missed and, lo and behold, we found it: a couple of them called for a mugful of coffee. Now that is out there.

We stirred some coffee into the beans before they went into the oven, and what a difference it made! Its roasted, mildly bitter flavor tied all of the other flavors together for a perfect pot of beans.

COWBOY BEANS

SERVES 4 TO 6

If you're thinking ahead, you can soak the beans in 6 cups of water overnight (then skip step 1). A heavy-bottomed Dutch oven prevents the beans from cooking too rapidly or scorching. Adjust the heat, smoke, or salt by stirring in more Tabasco or barbecue sauce at serving time.

1	pound dried pinto or navy beans, rinsed and picked over
4	slices bacon, chopped fine
1	medium onion, minced
4	medium garlic cloves, minced
4½	cups water
1	cup strong black coffee
⅓	cup packed dark brown sugar
2	tablespoons prepared brown mustard (such as Gulden's)
½	cup plus 2 tablespoons barbecue sauce
½	teaspoon hot sauce
	Salt and pepper

1. Place the beans and 6 cups water in a large Dutch oven. Bring to a boil over high heat and cook for 5 minutes. Remove the pot from the heat, cover, and allow the beans to sit for 1 hour. Drain the beans. Clean and dry the pot.

2. Adjust an oven rack to the lower-middle position and heat the oven to 300 degrees. Add the bacon to the pot and cook over medium heat until lightly browned, 6 to 8 minutes. Stir in the onion and cook until beginning to brown, 6 to 8 minutes. Add the garlic and cook until fragrant, about 30 seconds. Add the drained beans, water, and coffee. Bring to a simmer over high heat and cook for 10 minutes. Add the brown sugar, mustard, ½ cup of the barbecue sauce, hot sauce, and 2 teaspoons salt. Return to a boil over high heat, cover the pot, and transfer to the oven.

3. Cook until the beans are just tender, 2 to 2½ hours. Remove the lid and continue to cook, stirring occasionally, until the liquid has thickened to a syrupy consistency, 1 to 1½ hours. Remove from the oven, stir in the remaining barbecue sauce, and season with salt and pepper to taste. (The beans can be refrigerated for up to 4 days.)

Red Beans and Rice

Louisiana is home to two great cuisines, Creole and Cajun. A blend of French, Spanish, and African influences, Creole cooking is fairly refined and relies on many classic French techniques and ingredients. The Cajun people trace their roots back to France, but they spent nearly 150 years in Canada developing a unique culture of their own. Exiled from Acadia (modern-day Nova Scotia), these people found a home in sparsely populated areas along the Louisiana coast. Their cooking style was more rustic and often quite spicy. Because of their close proximity, it was inevitable that these two distinct styles of cooking would influence each other. Red beans and rice is a prime example.

Originally, red beans and rice was a Creole dish served on wash Mondays. The ham bone left over from Sunday night's dinner was slowly simmered with red beans in a pot on the back burner while the women of the house washed and line-dried clothing. The marrow from the cracked bone flavored the beans and the broth, which slowly thickened over hours of simmering. Eventually, andouille, a heavily spiced and smoked Cajun pork sausage, became part of the standard recipe. The combination of pork products created a rich dish that became a meal when served over rice.

In our attempt to replicate red beans and rice in the test kitchen, we ran into a few obstacles. Realizing that most home cooks do not have a leftover ham bone in their refrigerator, we started with a ham hock in its place. Although some tasters enjoyed the flavor, others found it too salty and smoky, masking the essence of the beans. Bacon, which has a similar but milder flavor profile, was an easy compromise everyone could agree on. Traditional recipes use water as the cooking liquid, but without bones our beans and rice were a bit bland. Replacing the water with chicken broth made the beans taste too "chicken-y"; chicken broth cut with water was just right.

Great-tasting andouille can be hard to find in some parts of the country. If you have access to the real stuff, use it; otherwise, smoky kielbasa is a good alternative. Adding the sausage in the last half hour of cooking keeps it from overpowering the beans or becoming too tough. Spooned over hot white rice and seasoned with a couple of splashes of hot sauce, this Louisiana classic is good enough to eat any day of the week.

RED BEANS AND RICE

SERVES 8 TO 10 AS A SIDE DISH
OR 4 TO 6 AS A MAIN COURSE

Andouille is the traditional sausage for this dish, but we also had good results with kielbasa. Unlike the other dried beans in this chapter, these beans do not need to be soaked prior to cooking.

4	slices bacon, chopped medium
1	small onion, minced
1	green bell pepper, minced
1	celery rib, minced
4	garlic cloves, minced
	Pepper
1	teaspoon minced fresh oregano
1	teaspoon minced fresh thyme
½	teaspoon cayenne pepper
4	bay leaves
	Salt
1	pound dried red kidney beans, rinsed and picked over
7	cups low-sodium chicken broth

7	cups water
½	pound andouille sausage or kielbasa, halved lengthwise and cut into ¼-inch half-moons
6	cups cooked long-grain rice (from 3 cups raw rice)
	Hot sauce

1. Cook the bacon in a large Dutch oven over medium heat until lightly browned and the fat has rendered, about 7 minutes. Add the onion, bell pepper, and celery and cook, stirring frequently, until softened, about 8 minutes. Stir in the garlic and cook until fragrant, about 30 seconds. Add 1 teaspoon pepper, oregano, thyme, cayenne, bay leaves, ½ teaspoon salt, beans, broth, and water and bring to a boil over high heat. Reduce the heat to maintain a vigorous simmer (the mixture will be steaming and several bubbles should be breaking the surface) and cook, uncovered, stirring occasionally, until the beans are soft and the liquid thickens, 2 to 2½ hours.

2. Stir in the sausage and cook until the liquid is thick and creamy, about 30 minutes. Remove and discard the bay leaves and season with salt and pepper to taste. Serve over hot cooked rice with hot sauce, if desired. (Leftover beans can be refrigerated in an airtight container for several days.)

Dirty Rice

Like frugal cooks everywhere, Cajun cooks from generations past found plenty of ways to use every part of the animals they raised. Traditionally, chicken "giblets"—the gizzard, heart, kidneys, and liver—were used to flavor rice, at the same time turning it brown and so giving rise to the name "dirty." But most cooks today aren't raising their own animals, and even if they did want to make dirty rice with its traditional ingredients, finding giblets (outside of the cavity of a store-bought chicken) can be tough. Our goal was simple: develop a modernized recipe for dirty rice, one that is meaty and rich and relies on ingredients easily found at the supermarket.

Before we settled on the issue of the meat, we turned to the rice. We may like our rice dirty, but gummy is another story. Some recipes we tried indeed produced gummy rice. We tried rinsing the rice before cooking, because it removes much of the exterior starch, thereby preventing the grains from sticking together. The resulting rice cooked up light and fluffy, making it perfect not just for dirty rice, but for rice pilafs and even cool rice salads.

With our rice down, we turned to building meaty flavor. After trying everything from bacon and sausage to hamburger meat, we found that ground pork came closest to producing the flavor we'd gotten when we made a batch of dirty rice with giblets. But this dish was still a long way from the real thing. Because chicken livers are still widely available, we wondered if this one member of the original foursome would do the trick. Sure enough, our tasters agreed that rice made with both chicken livers and ground pork brought this Cajun classic side dish home.

DIRTY RICE

SERVES 4 TO 6

To rinse rice, place it in a bowl, cover with cold water, and swish to release the starch. Change the water until it remains nearly clear. Alternatively, place the rice in a fine-mesh strainer set over a large bowl. Run water over the rice and use your hands to swish the rice around to release excess starch. Pour off the water and repeat until the water is no longer cloudy. Serve the cooked rice with hot sauce, if desired.

1	tablespoon vegetable oil
8	ounces ground pork
1	onion, minced
1	celery rib, minced
1	red bell pepper, seeded and minced
3	garlic cloves, minced
4	ounces chicken livers, rinsed, trimmed of fat, and chopped fine
¼	teaspoon dried thyme
¼	teaspoon cayenne pepper
	Salt
2¼	cups low-sodium chicken broth
2	bay leaves
1½	cups long-grain white rice, rinsed
3	scallions, sliced thin

1. Heat the oil in a Dutch oven over medium heat until shimmering. Add the pork and cook until browned, about 5 minutes. Stir in the onion, celery, and bell pepper and cook until softened, about 10 minutes. Add the garlic, chicken livers, thyme, cayenne, and 1 teaspoon salt and cook until browned, 3 to 5 minutes. Transfer to a fine-mesh strainer set over a bowl and cover with foil.

2. Increase the heat to high and add the chicken broth, bay leaves, and rice to the empty pot. Scrape the bottom of the pot with a wooden spoon to remove any browned bits. Bring to a boil, reduce the heat to low, cover, and cook until the rice is tender, 15 to 17 minutes. Remove from the heat, discard the bay leaves, and fluff the rice with a fork. Gently stir in the drained meat and vegetable mixture (discarding any accumulated juices) and sprinkle with the scallions. Serve.

CHAPTER FIVE

Lunch Counter
Specials

LUNCH COUNTER SPECIALS

Classic Grilled Cheese Sandwiches

A grilled cheese sandwich—gooey melted cheese between buttery, crisp slices of toast—is about as good as it gets. We wanted to develop the best approach to this great American lunch counter sandwich. So with the image of a crisp, golden crust and a molten cheese center in mind, we started testing.

First we tested the bread. Flimsy white bread made soggy sandwiches. Sturdy sliced bread with a fine, dense crumb (such as Arnold or Pepperidge Farm) was much, much better. To avoid burning the bread, we found that a steady medium-low heat produced consistently golden brown crusts. The slow cooking also ensured an evenly melted interior.

Butter beat out contenders such as oil, mayonnaise, and vegetable oil spray by a landslide because of its flavor. Melting the butter in the skillet and then adding the sandwiches produced poor results. The first side of the sandwiches had a fairly even layer of butter, but the second side was left high and dry. Melted butter brushed onto the outer sides of the bread (before the sandwiches were assembled) made for much more even cooking.

While turning out one grilled cheese after another, we couldn't help but think how much we like sandwiches made in an Italian panini press. Could we create a mock sandwich press using common kitchen equipment? A lightweight cake pan, used to press the sandwiches lightly, fit the bill. The metal pan serves as a heat conductor that helps to keep the top of the sandwich crisp while the bottom forms its own thick, brown crust.

In addition, we found a host of flavor variations to keep us enjoying grilled cheese in new ways.

CLASSIC GRILLED CHEESE SANDWICHES

SERVES 4

In the test kitchen we like the tang of sharp cheddar tempered by the mild, smoothly melting Monterey Jack. Grilled cheese sandwiches are best cooked two at a time. If you want to keep the first batch hot, place a baking sheet in the oven and heat the oven to 250 degrees. When the first batch is done, slide the sandwiches onto the hot baking sheet to keep them crisp and warm.

- 1⅓ cups shredded sharp cheddar cheese
- ⅔ cup shredded Monterey Jack cheese
- 8 slices hearty white sandwich bread
- 4 tablespoons unsalted butter, melted

1. Combine the cheeses in a bowl. Brush the top side of each slice of bread with melted butter. Flip 4 slices over, sprinkle with the cheese, and compact the cheese lightly with your hand. Cover with the remaining bread slices, buttered side up.

2. Heat a large nonstick skillet over medium-low heat for 1 minute. Place 2 sandwiches in the pan and weight with a round cake pan, pressing lightly. Leave

STEPS TO GREAT GRILLED CHEESE

1. Brushing melted butter on the bread guarantees even coverage and better browning for a crisp, flavorful crust.

2. A round metal cake pan performs double duty as a press to compact the filling and as a heat conductor to crisp the crust.

the cake pan on top and cook until the first side is golden brown, 3 to 5 minutes. Flip the sandwiches, press again with the cake pan, and cook until golden brown, about 2 minutes. Repeat with the remaining 2 sandwiches.

Variations

WINDY CITY GRILLED CHEESE SANDWICHES

If you like a Chicago hot dog, you'll love this sandwich. Press the relish with paper towels to remove excess moisture.

Use 2 cups shredded Swiss cheese. Layer ¼ cup cheese, 1 very thin slice red onion (with rings separated), 1 thin slice bologna, 2 teaspoons Dijon mustard, 1 tablespoon dill pickle relish, another slice bologna, ¼ cup prepared sauerkraut (rinsed and drained), and ¼ cup cheese into each sandwich.

LITTLE ITALY GRILLED CHEESE SANDWICHES

The olive spread (sometimes labeled tapenade) is optional but delicious.

Use 1⅓ cups shredded provolone cheese and ⅔ cup shredded mozzarella cheese. Combine 1 cup jarred roasted red peppers, drained and chopped, with ¼ cup jarred pepperoncini, drained and minced. Layer ¼ cup cheese, 2 thin slices salami, one-quarter of the pepper mixture, 2 additional thin slices salami, 2 teaspoons kalamata olive spread, if using, and ¼ cup cheese into each sandwich.

GRILLED PIMIENTO CHEESE SANDWICHES

Press the tomato slices between paper towels to remove moisture.

Mix 1⅓ cups shredded cheddar cheese and ⅔ cup shredded Monterey Jack cheese with 2 tablespoons mayonnaise, 2 tablespoons jarred pimientos, drained and chopped, 2 teaspoons minced yellow onion, ½ teaspoon hot sauce, and ¼ teaspoon pepper. Layer each sandwich with the cheese mixture and 2 thin slices tomato.

MONTEREY MELTS

Turkey, bacon, and avocado flavor this California classic.

Mix 2 cups shredded Monterey Jack cheese with ¼ cup canned pickled jalapeño chiles, drained and minced. Layer ¼ cup of the cheese-chile mixture, 2 slices deli turkey, 3 strips cooked bacon, several avocado slices, and ¼ cup of the cheese-chile mixture into each sandwich.

Monte Cristo Sandwiches

Many of us enjoyed our first taste of a Monte Cristo sandwich at Disneyland (see "The American Table"). The Monte Cristo starts out like any other grilled Swiss cheese, ham, and turkey sandwich before it is dipped in an egg batter and cooked—only one or two at a time—in a skillet. This lunch favorite is then served with jam, sugar, and/or syrup to create a sweet and savory combination that's hard to beat. Getting them all to the table piping hot is another matter entirely. We could keep our Classic Grilled Cheese Sandwiches (page 131) warm in the oven while we cooked the remainder, two at a time, but Monte Cristos tend to get soggy if not served right away.

Determined to produce a full batch of six piping-hot sandwiches, we abandoned the skillet and turned to oven-frying. For each sandwich, we layered a few slices of ham, turkey, and cheese between pieces of hearty sandwich bread (mushy,

It was the 1940s, but was it San Diego, San Francisco, or L.A.? It seems nearly every major city in California has been tagged as the birthplace of the Monte Cristo sandwich. It is widely assumed that it began as a variation of the French classic known as croque monsieur, a grilled ham and cheese sandwich that's sometimes dipped in batter before being cooked. The Monte Cristo achieved national recognition when it was added to the menus of the Blue Bayou and Tahitian Terrace restaurants at Disneyland in 1966. To this day, the Monte Cristo remains one of the most popular lunch items on the Blue Bayou menu.

airy breads weren't sturdy enough), dipped the sandwich in a mixture of egg and cream, and placed it on a hot oiled baking sheet. After searing both sides for several minutes, our six Monte Cristos were only moderately crisp and browned. Still, the ease of this method made it worth pursuing.

Raising the oven temperature from 400 to 450 degrees promoted browning, but the Monte Cristo's defining dunk in the egg mixture continued to impede crisping. Because French toast is often made with staled bread, we thought we'd try leaving the bread out all day to see if that would help. Sure enough, these sandwiches were crisper, though still not quite crisp enough. What if we toasted the bread before assembling and dunking the sandwiches? More progress. A light toasting dried the bread still more—enough that it could stand up to the egg mixture. Toasting also jump-started browning. Acting on the suggestion of one of the test cooks, we

added a few teaspoons of granulated sugar to the egg mixture. Now the bread browned and caramelized perfectly.

Monte Cristos are traditionally served with a sweet accompaniment, typically powdered sugar, chutney, maple syrup, or jam. After tasting Monte Cristos made with each, tasters preferred the flavor of strawberry jam, even though it was a little too sweet on its own. Mixing Dijon mustard into the jam balanced the flavors, creating a sweet and spicy mixture that tasters liked so much they wanted it spread on the bread as well as served on the side (which is traditional).

The perfect marriage of sweet and savory flavors with a no-fuss cooking method for a crowd, these Monte Cristos can be enjoyed without the roller-coaster ride.

MONTE CRISTO SANDWICHES

SERVES 6

Trim the slices of meat and cheese as necessary to fit neatly on the bread.

- 4 large eggs
- ¼ cup heavy cream
- 2 teaspoons sugar
- ½ teaspoon salt
- ½ teaspoon dry mustard
- ⅛ teaspoon cayenne pepper
- 6 tablespoons strawberry or raspberry jam
- 2 tablespoons Dijon mustard
- 12 slices hearty white sandwich bread, lightly toasted
- 18 thin slices deli Swiss or Gruyère cheese
- 12 thin slices deli ham, preferably Black Forest
- 12 thin slices deli turkey
- 3 tablespoons vegetable oil
  Confectioners' sugar

1. Adjust an oven rack to the upper-middle position and heat the oven to 450 degrees. Whisk the eggs, cream, sugar, salt, dry mustard, and cayenne in a shallow dish until combined. Stir the jam and Dijon mustard together in a small bowl.

2. Spread 1 teaspoon of the jam mixture on one side of each slice of toast. Layer the slices of cheese, ham, and turkey on 6 slices of toast. Repeat with a second layer of cheese, ham, and turkey. Add a final layer of cheese and top with the remaining toast, with the jam side facing the cheese. Using your hands, lightly press down on the sandwiches.

3. Pour the oil onto a rimmed baking sheet and heat in the oven until just smoking, about 7 minutes. Meanwhile, using 2 hands, coat each sandwich with the egg mixture and transfer to a large plate. Transfer the sandwiches to the preheated baking sheet and bake until golden brown on both sides, 4 to 5 minutes per side, using a spatula to flip. Sprinkle with confectioners' sugar and serve immediately with the remaining jam mixture.

SECRETS TO CRISP MONTE CRISTOS

1. Toasting the bread and then coating the sandwiches in an egg batter encourages browning and crispness.

2. Preheating the oiled baking sheet makes the sandwiches sizzle when they hit the pan so that they begin to crisp right away.

Tuna Salad

Grade-school lunches, hospital cafeterias, and second-rate delis have given tuna salad a bad name with mixtures that are typically mushy, watery, and bland. But these poor examples should not cause cooks to lose hope for this old standard. We tackled tuna salad in the test kitchen and came up with a few preparation and flavoring tricks that guarantee a tuna salad that is evenly moist, tender, flaky, and well seasoned every time.

A first-rate tuna salad begins with the best tuna. All tasters favored solid white tuna (in a can, not a pouch) over chunk light for its meaty texture and delicate flavor.

Breaking the tuna apart with a fork was another standard procedure we dumped. In salads made with tuna prepared this way, we'd invariably bite into a large, dry, unseasoned chunk that the fork had missed. Instead, we decided to break down the larger chunks with our fingers until the whole amount was fine and even in texture. This gave the finished salad a smooth, even, flaky texture that all of our tasters appreciated.

As for seasoning, salt and pepper were critical in making the most of tuna's delicate flavor. Fresh lemon juice was equally important, adding some much needed brightness to the flavor.

We were unanimous in finding mayonnaise to be the best binder and found other salad ingredients to be largely a matter of taste. We nonetheless agreed that trace amounts of garlic and mustard added dimension to the overall flavor and that a modest amount of minced pickle provided a touch of piquancy, not to mention a link to tradition.

So forget the sopping, mushy salad you ate in your last beleaguered institutional tuna sandwich. The next time the cold cuts run out, or even before, reach for the tuna that graces even the emptiest pantry, take a little extra care with the contents, and find out how satisfying a well-made tuna salad sandwich can be.

CLASSIC TUNA SALAD

**MAKES ABOUT 4 CUPS,
ENOUGH FOR 6 SANDWICHES**

*We prefer canned solid white tuna, but you can sub-
stitute four 7-ounce foil pouches of white tuna. Tuna
salad can be prepared, covered, and refrigerated a
day in advance. Before serving, freshen the salad with
a spoonful of mayonnaise and a squeeze of lemon
juice. Season with salt and pepper to taste. See page
264 for the results from our tuna testing.*

5	(6-ounce) cans solid white tuna, flaked
2	celery ribs, chopped fine
1	cup mayonnaise
¼	cup minced red onion
¼	cup minced dill or sweet pickles
¼	cup minced fresh parsley
3	tablespoons fresh lemon juice
1	garlic clove, minced
½	teaspoon Dijon mustard
	Salt and pepper

Toss all of the ingredients together in a large bowl
and season with salt and pepper to taste.

Variation
TUNA MELTS

SERVES 8

*Any type of good melting cheese, such as Swiss, ched-
dar, or American cheese, can be substituted for the
provolone. We prefer thin slices of provolone cheese
cut to order at the deli counter (packaged slices
are too thick to melt quickly). Also, four split and
toasted English muffins can be used in place of the
sandwich bread.*

8	slices hearty white sandwich bread
1	recipe Classic Tuna Salad
2	tomatoes, cut into ¼-inch slices
8	slices provolone cheese (8 ounces; see note above)

Adjust an oven rack so that it is 6 inches from the
broiler element and heat the broiler. Arrange the
bread on a rimmed baking sheet. Toast the bread
under the broiler until golden brown on both
sides, about 5 minutes. Spread about ½ cup of
the tuna salad over each slice of toast and top with
sliced tomato, then the provolone. Broil until the
cheese has melted and is beginning to brown, 3 to
6 minutes.

SHOPPING WITH THE TEST KITCHEN

Potato Chips: There are endless potato chip
varieties and flavors, but which bag of plain chips
should the purist reach for? We grabbed eight
national brands and headed into the test kitchen
to find out. Potato chips are made with three basic
ingredients—potatoes, oil, and salt. Tasters preferred kettle-style chips, with Lay's Kettle Chips
as the panel's clear favorite. The classic lunchbox
chip, only better (tasters liked the big potato flavor), these crunchy chips were the thickest ones we
sampled and just salty enough to keep tasters coming back for seconds.

Egg Salad

Egg salad is one of those simple, spur-of-the-
moment comfort foods that should be easy to
make. Yet sometimes it turns out pasty, the overall flavor drab, the mayonnaise excessive, or the
onions too biting. We wanted a well-seasoned mixture of tender diced egg whites bound together
with an egg yolk and mayonnaise dressing.

We quickly found that both a fork and a pastry blender mashed the eggs so much that when
blended with mayonnaise, they became unpleasantly pasty. In addition to being reminiscent of
baby food, this egg salad was quick to ooze out
from between the slices of bread in a sandwich.

After experimenting with various options, we found that eggs diced into small cubes (just under half an inch) gave the salad the texture we had been seeking and sat well in a sandwich. As for the other salad components, minced red onion and celery were favored over bell pepper, which tasted out of place. In addition to mayonnaise, seasonings such as Dijon mustard and fresh lemon juice gave the salad brightness and zip.

CLASSIC EGG SALAD

MAKES ABOUT 2½ CUPS,
ENOUGH FOR 4 SANDWICHES

See page 16 for instructions on how to hard-boil eggs. A mozzarella slicer turns a boiled egg into perfect ⅜-inch cubes. Place the egg in the slicer and cut through it lengthwise. Turn the egg a quarter turn and slice it crosswise. Then rotate the egg 90 degrees and slice it widthwise.

6	hard-boiled eggs (see note above)
¼	cup mayonnaise
2	tablespoons minced red onion
1	tablespoon minced fresh parsley
½	medium celery rib, chopped fine
2	teaspoons Dijon mustard
2	teaspoons fresh lemon juice
¼	teaspoon salt
	Pepper

Dice the eggs into small cubes (see note above). Mix the diced eggs with the remaining ingredients in a medium bowl, including pepper to taste. Serve. (The egg salad can be refrigerated in an airtight container for up to 1 day.)

Chicken Salad

To us in the test kitchen, a jar of mayonnaise and some boiled chicken does not a chicken salad make. Sure, some recipes may throw in a rib of celery here or a hard-boiled egg there, but the end result is always the same: a sloppy, stodgy mess of mayo and under-seasoned chicken masquerading as chicken salad. We wanted to bring flavor to this lunchtime classic.

Since bland chicken begets bland chicken salad, we ignored the fact that most recipes call for poached chicken meat. Instead, we decided to start with a whole bird, seasoning it with salt and pepper and roasting it to a crisp, golden finish. Although tasters appreciated the rich flavor of the roasted chicken, they were turned off by the soft texture of the dark meat in the chicken salad, and we were turned off by the bird's lengthy cooking time.

Switching to white meat, we tried roasting whole chicken breasts, but this still took a good bit of time. Quickly cooking boneless, skinless chicken breasts on the stovetop proved to be a better option. Not only did they cook in mere minutes, but sautéed to a golden brown, they were every bit as tasty as the roasted chicken.

Our goal was to create distinctly flavored chicken salads. Mayonnaise was important in all of them for a smooth and creamy texture, but too much mayo makes any chicken salad heavy and dull. We found that we could replace some of the mayo in each of our dressings with a more flavorful and equally creamy ingredient, such as blue cheese dressing or sour cream. To lighten the texture of our dressings, we added a potent liquid, such as hot sauce or lemon juice. Our revamped dressings were tastier than plain mayo and also less thick, so they didn't weigh the chicken down.

With a sprinkling of fresh herbs, crumbled cheese, or chopped vegetables, these creamy, creatively flavored chicken salads are worlds better than their deli case counterparts.

COBB CHICKEN SALAD

MAKES ABOUT 6 CUPS,
ENOUGH FOR 6 SANDWICHES

Serve on toasted white bread or a baguette. If making the salad in advance, refrigerate the bacon separately. See page 16 for instructions on how to hard-boil eggs.

SAUTÉED CHICKEN BREASTS

4	boneless, skinless chicken breasts (about 1½ pounds)
	Salt and pepper
2	tablespoons vegetable oil

SALAD

½	cup mayonnaise
½	cup crumbled blue cheese
2	tablespoons sour cream
2	tablespoons fresh lemon juice
2	hard-boiled eggs, chopped fine (see note above)
1	avocado, pitted, skinned, and diced
	Salt and pepper
4	slices bacon, cooked and crumbled

1. FOR THE CHICKEN: Pat the chicken dry with paper towels and season with salt and pepper. Heat the oil in a large nonstick skillet over medium heat until shimmering. Cook the chicken until golden brown and cooked through, about 6 minutes per side. Transfer to a plate and refrigerate until chilled, about 30 minutes. Cut into ½-inch chunks. (The chicken can be refrigerated for up to 2 days.)

2. FOR THE SALAD: Mix the mayonnaise, cheese, sour cream, and lemon juice in a large bowl until combined. Add the eggs, avocado, and chicken, then toss gently until coated. Season with salt and pepper. Sprinkle with the crumbled bacon. Serve or cover and refrigerate for up to 2 days.

Variations
CAROLINA PIMIENTO CHEESE CHICKEN SALAD

Serve on a croissant or a split buttermilk biscuit.

1	cup shredded cheddar cheese
½	cup mayonnaise
½	cup jarred chopped pimientos, drained
2	tablespoons sour cream
2	tablespoons fresh lemon juice
⅛	teaspoon cayenne pepper
2	scallions, sliced thin
1	garlic clove, minced
1	recipe Sautéed Chicken Breasts (at left)
	Salt and pepper

Combine the cheese, mayonnaise, pimientos, sour cream, lemon juice, cayenne, scallions, and garlic in a large bowl. Add the chicken and toss until coated. Season with salt and pepper. Serve or cover and refrigerate for up to 2 days.

BUFFALO AND BLUE CHEESE CHICKEN SALAD

Serve this spicy chicken salad on soft onion rolls. Use a mild hot sauce (such as Frank's Red Hot Sauce).

½	cup mayonnaise
¼	cup crumbled blue cheese
3	tablespoons hot sauce (see note above)
2	tablespoons bottled blue cheese salad dressing
2	celery ribs, sliced thin
1	carrot, peeled and chopped fine
1	recipe Sautéed Chicken Breasts (at left)
	Salt and pepper

Combine the mayonnaise, cheese, hot sauce, dressing, celery, and carrot in a large bowl. Add the chicken and toss until coated. Season with salt and pepper. Serve or cover and refrigerate for up to 2 days.

Reuben Sandwiches

A Reuben is a New York deli standard. When it is made well, a towering stack of juicy corned beef is built onto good rye bread, accompanied by Swiss cheese and sauerkraut, and dressed with an ample amount of Thousand Island dressing. Cooked on a buttered griddle, the bread toasts to a dark brown color, the cheese melts into the corned beef and sauerkraut, and the thick pile of corned beef gently heats through. This hefty, mouthwatering sandwich is as close to heaven as a sandwich can get.

Our search for the ultimate Reuben began at the supermarket deli counter. Good corned beef should have a dusty pink color and should be juicy. Don't bother with corned beef that looks dry or has a slimy or tacky texture. After finding some good corned beef (we like Boar's Head), we determined that one sandwich needed 6 ounces of thinly sliced meat, which produces a well-stacked sandwich that is manageable for both the cook and the appetite.

We also noted the importance of using good Swiss cheese, such as Emmentaler. Its smooth, complex flavor is necessary to complement the corned beef. We tried using jarred Thousand Island dressing but had better luck when we made our own. We liked the clean flavor of freshly bagged and jarred sauerkraut from the refrigerated deli case. The sauerkraut needs to be squeezed dry, however, or it will turn the rye bread soggy.

As for grilling a Reuben, most recipes instruct you to butter the griddle or pan, but we found it better to butter the bread. By brushing melted butter directly onto the bread and using a nonstick pan, we were able to use less fat and ensure that the sandwich would not turn out greasy. Last, we found that this well-stacked sandwich cooked more evenly when compacted with a little pressure. We used a heavy stockpot as a sandwich press but also found that a skillet, similar in size to the one in which we cooked the sandwiches, worked well when weighted with a heavy can.

REUBEN SANDWICHES

SERVES 4

For a Rachel sandwich, replace the corned beef with thinly sliced turkey. Coleslaw can be substituted for the sauerkraut.

THOUSAND ISLAND DRESSING

1	garlic clove, peeled
¼	teaspoon salt
3–4	green olives with pimientos, minced
¼	cup minced sweet pickle
½	hard-boiled egg (page 16), minced
1	tablespoon minced fresh parsley leaves
1	teaspoon lemon juice
	Pepper
½	cup mayonnaise
2	tablespoons chili sauce

SANDWICHES

8	slices hearty rye bread
8	slices Swiss cheese (8 ounces)
1	pound sauerkraut (1⅓ cups), rinsed, drained, and squeezed to eliminate excess moisture
1½	pounds thinly sliced corned beef
2	tablespoons unsalted butter, melted

1. FOR THE DRESSING: Roughly chop the garlic, then sprinkle it with the salt. With a chef's knife, mash the mixture to a smooth paste.

2. Mix the garlic paste, olives, pickle, egg, parsley, lemon juice, and a pinch of pepper together in a medium bowl. Add the mayonnaise, chili sauce, and 1 tablespoon water and stir until uniform. (The dressing can be refrigerated in an airtight container for up to 3 days.)

3. FOR THE SANDWICHES: Adjust an oven rack to the middle position and heat the oven to 200 degrees. Assemble 4 sandwiches by layering the ingredients as follows between the slices of bread: 1 tablespoon dressing, 1 slice Swiss cheese, ⅓ cup sauerkraut, 1 more tablespoon dressing, 6 ounces corned beef, 1 more slice Swiss cheese, and finally 1 more tablespoon dressing. Press gently on the sandwiches to set.

4. Brush the tops of 2 of the sandwiches with some of the melted butter. Lay them buttered side down in a large nonstick skillet over medium-low heat. Place a large Dutch oven or heavy stockpot on top of the sandwiches and cook until crisp and golden, about 5 minutes.

5. Remove the pot, brush the tops of the sandwiches lightly with some of the remaining butter, and flip them over. Replace the pot on top of the sandwiches and cook until the second side is crisp and golden, about 5 minutes. Transfer the sandwiches to a wire rack set over a baking sheet and keep them warm in the oven while repeating the process with the remaining 2 sandwiches.

Philly Cheesesteaks

The Philly cheesesteak was born in 1930 at Pat's King of Steaks, located in an Italian-American neighborhood in South Philadelphia. Today you can find a cheesesteak joint on almost every corner in Philly—even in Chinatown—and just about every one has a devoted following. Most Philly cheesesteaks contain a heap of juicy, tender sliced rib-eye steak (most places use rib-eye or chopped round), topped with sweet fried onions and Cheez Whiz, on a soft, chewy sub roll. But do you have to go to Philly for a great cheesesteak? We wanted to develop a homemade version that could stand up to the best in Philadelphia.

We started our testing with the meat—authentic cheesesteaks use rib-eye, but we wanted to see

if we could find other options with the same rich, beefy flavor. So in addition to rib-eye, we made cheesesteaks with top sirloin, top round, blade, chuck, flank, and sirloin tips. Some cuts had good flavor but were too tough; some were nice and tender but lacked flavor. Sirloin tips were perfect—tender, with big flavor—and they were half the price of rib-eye, which also worked quite well.

Unless you have the knife skills of a sushi chef, slicing meat paper-thin is impossible. We tried (and rejected) partially freezing the meat before slicing it as well as using the food processor to slice the meat. We had better luck cutting the room-temperature tips into small chunks and then pounding them with a mallet to produce thin, tender sheets of steak.

Aside from the beef, the most important element in a true Philly cheesesteak is the cheese, and tasters had strong opinions on the subject. We fed them sandwiches made not only with the traditional Cheez Whiz but also with two other Philly favorites, provolone and American. In the end, the test kitchen voted for the provolone. But whichever cheese you end up using, don't go overboard—a real Philly cheesesteak is all about the beef.

PHILLY CHEESESTEAKS

SERVES 4

We prefer thin slices of provolone cheese cut to order at the deli counter (packaged slices are too thick to melt quickly), but American cheese works well, too. If using Cheez Whiz, do not add it to the skillet; microwave ¾ cup in a bowl until warmed through, then spoon it over the assembled sandwiches.

6	teaspoons vegetable oil
2	onions, chopped
1½	pounds sirloin tips, pounded until paper-thin
	Salt and pepper
8	thin slices provolone cheese, cut in half (see note above)
4	(6-inch) sub rolls, slit partially open lengthwise

SLICING STEAK FOR A PHILLY CHEESESTEAK

1. Cut each sirloin tip with the grain into 1-inch cubes.

2. Stagger the beef cubes in a single layer 6 inches apart between two sheets of plastic wrap.

3. Using a meat pounder, pound the cubes until paper-thin.

4. When you're done, the slices of meat should be almost transparent.

1. Heat 2 teaspoons of the oil in a large nonstick skillet over medium-high heat until shimmering. Add the onions and cook until softened and golden, about 5 minutes. Transfer to a small bowl.

2. Heat another 2 teaspoons oil in the empty skillet over high heat until smoking. Place half of the steak slices in the skillet (don't worry if they overlap) and season with salt and pepper. Cook until the meat is no longer pink, about 1 minute per side. Remove the pan from the heat, layer 4 half-slices of cheese over some meat, top with more meat, and finally add 4 more half-slices of cheese. Cover the pan with the lid to melt the cheese, about 1 minute. Divide the meat and cheese between 2 rolls, top with half of the onions, and pour the juices accumulated in the skillet over the meat. Wrap each sandwich tightly in foil and set aside while preparing the remaining sandwiches.

3. Wipe the skillet clean with paper towels and repeat step 2 with the remaining 2 teaspoons oil, meat, cheese, and onions. Wrap the sandwiches in foil and let sit for about 1 minute to let the flavors come together. Serve.

Sloppy Joes

Most of us remember Sloppy Joes from our childhood—and we remember enjoying them. But taking a bite of one today might come as a shock—the candy-like sweetness of the Sloppy Joe sauce will most likely be a turnoff. Could we make a Sloppy Joe that had a perfect balance of sweet and tang, one that adults could cozy up to—and one that would still appeal to kids? We headed into the test kitchen to find out.

Since the sauce is so problematic, we started there. Ketchup is a must, but too much made the sauce saccharine. Most recipes also called for excessive amounts of sugar, which just made things worse. In search of an alternative to "meat candy on a bun," we tested just about every tomato product we could get our hands on.

Heinz chili sauce was the right consistency, but it contained flecks of horseradish that turned the sauce bitter. Canned crushed tomatoes needed lengthy cooking, and tomato paste made the sauce dry and stiff. Tomato puree, however, added the strong tomato flavor we were looking for. When mixed with ketchup and just a teaspoon of brown sugar, it produced a sauce that was first and foremost about tomatoes, with a gentle sweetness that everyone (even the naysayers in the test kitchen) liked.

Besides being too sweet, the Sloppy Joes in most published recipes were also too greasy. After much trial and error, we decided that a middle-of-the-road choice—85-percent lean ground beef—was the best way to cut down on the slick factor.

We also discovered that the way we cooked the meat was just as important as its fat content. Most recipes say to brown the meat completely before adding the liquid ingredients. But each time we did so, our Sloppy Joes turned out tough and crumbly. We eventually stumbled on the key to soft, tender meat: cook it until it is just pink (no further), and then add the remaining ingredients.

In the test kitchen we are never content to leave good enough alone. Colleagues liked our recipe so much that they wanted variations. For Sloppy Joes with a south-of-the-border twist, we added more spices, chiles, and black beans and served the concoction in taco shells. For a final variation, we replaced the ketchup with barbecue sauce to create a smoky version of this family classic.

THE AMERICAN TABLE
SLOPPY JOES
- -

Sloppy Joes were likely created during the Depression as another way to turn ground beef into a hearty meal. They are related to loose meat sandwiches, which were first developed in Iowa during the 1920s. Loose meat consists of ground meat cooked with spices and beef broth but no ketchup or other tomato product.

SLOPPY JOES

SERVES 4

Be careful not to cook the meat beyond pink in step 1; if you let it brown at this point it will end up dry and crumbly. The meat will finish cooking once the liquid ingredients are added. Serve, piled high on a bun, with your favorite pickles. For variations on the classic recipe, see page 142.

2	tablespoons vegetable oil
1	onion, minced
½	teaspoon salt
2	garlic cloves, minced
½	teaspoon chili powder
1	pound 85-percent lean ground beef
	Pepper
1	teaspoon brown sugar
1	cup tomato puree
½	cup ketchup
¼	cup water
¼	teaspoon hot sauce
4	hamburger buns

1. Heat the oil in a large skillet over medium-high heat until shimmering. Add the onion and salt and stir until coated with the oil. Reduce the heat to medium, cover, and cook, stirring occasionally, until the onion is soft, about 10 minutes (if the onion begins to burn after 5 minutes, reduce the heat to low). Add the garlic and chili powder and cook, uncovered, stirring constantly, until fragrant, about 30 seconds. Add the beef and cook, breaking up the meat with a wooden spoon, until just pink, about 3 minutes.

2. Add ¼ teaspoon pepper, the brown sugar, tomato puree, ketchup, water, and hot sauce. Simmer until the sauce is slightly thicker than ketchup, 8 to 10 minutes. Adjust the seasonings. Spoon the meat mixture onto hamburger buns and serve.

Variations

SLOPPY JOSÉS

Increase the chili powder to 1 tablespoon and add 2 tablespoons ground cumin and ¼ teaspoon cayenne pepper along with the garlic and chili powder. Add 1 chipotle chile, minced, and 1 (15.5-ounce) can black beans, drained and rinsed, with the other ingredients at the start of step 2. Substitute 4 taco shells for the hamburger buns.

SMOKY JOES

Replace the ketchup with an equal amount of barbecue sauce. Serve on soft deli-style onion rolls instead of hamburger buns.

Crispy Iowa Skinnies

In the Midwest, pork is king. That's because the heartland of America, sometimes called the Hog Belt, produces most of the pork we eat in this country. But Iowa stands out not only for its pork production but also for its preparation.

Iowa is home to the "skinny," a fried pork sandwich that's as good and as simple as it gets. It starts with a chunk of pork tenderloin that is pounded to platter size before being lightly breaded and fried. A skinny is served on a soft bun with lettuce, tomato, and a slather of mayo.

Nearly every recipe agrees on the meat and the method, but there is little consensus regarding the coating. To get the requisite golden brown, crunchy coating, we tried a number of batters and breadings before settling on a basic flour, egg, and bread-crumb approach. Although we found fresh bread crumbs preferable to the sandy store-bought variety, they cooked up bland and boring. Adding crushed saltines (an ingredient we had come across in a few recipes) to the bread crumbs provided a welcome saltiness and even more crispness, but the flavor was still too mild.

Since these sandwiches are served with mayonnaise, we wondered if switching mayo for the egg might add some flavor. It did, but the layer of mayonnaise made the crumbs greasy. A combination of eggs and mayo fared better, adding a nice richness and sweet tang that enhanced the flavor of the pork without weighing down the crust.

Speaking of the pork, we found that one tenderloin was the perfect amount for four sandwiches. Once it was cut into four pieces and pounded to a ¼-inch thickness (any thicker and the coating burned before the pork was cooked through), a quick spin in the skillet was all it took to make an authentic Iowa skinny.

CRISPY IOWA SKINNIES

SERVES 4

1	pork tenderloin (about 1 pound), cut into 4 pieces and pounded to ¼ inch thick
	Salt and pepper
½	cup all-purpose flour
2	large eggs
¼	cup mayonnaise, plus extra for serving
3	slices hearty white sandwich bread, torn into large pieces
16	saltines
1	cup vegetable oil
4	soft hamburger buns
¼	head iceberg lettuce, shredded
1	medium tomato, sliced

1. Adjust an oven rack to the middle position and heat the oven to 200 degrees. Pat the pork cutlets dry with paper towels and season with salt and pepper.

2. Place the flour in a shallow dish. Beat the eggs and ¼ cup mayonnaise in a second shallow dish. Combine the bread and saltines in a food processor and pulse to fine crumbs; transfer to a third shallow dish.

HOW TO MAKE PORK CUTLETS

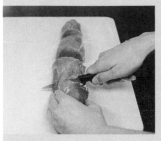 

1. Use a paring knife to remove any silver skin or extraneous fat from the tenderloin. Then cut the tenderloin into 4 equal pieces.

2. Arrange the pieces of tenderloin cut side up on a cutting board. Cover with plastic wrap and pound into ¼-inch-thick cutlets.

3. Coat the cutlets in flour, shaking off the excess. Dip both sides of the cutlets in the egg mixture, then dredge in the crumbs, pressing on the crumbs to adhere. Place the cutlets on a wire rack set over a baking sheet and let dry 5 minutes (or refrigerate for up to 1 hour).

4. Heat ½ cup of the oil in a large nonstick skillet over medium heat until shimmering. Lay 2 cutlets in the skillet and fry until crisp and deep golden, about 2 minutes per side. Transfer to a large paper towel–lined plate and place in the warm oven. Discard the oil, wipe out the skillet, and repeat with the remaining oil and cutlets. Place 1 cutlet on each bun and top with lettuce, tomato, and mayonnaise. Serve.

SHOPPING WITH THE TEST KITCHEN

Mayonnaise: Hellmann's Real Mayonnaise (known as Best Foods west of the Rockies) has been the test kitchen's favorite brand. But Hellmann's now makes a range of products, many with fewer calories and less fat. To find out how they measure up to the original, we tasted four types of Hellmann's plain and in macaroni salad. Here's what we found. (Note that the calorie and fat amounts are per serving.) Hellmann's Real Mayonnaise (90 calories; 10g fat; 1.5g saturated fat) is the gold standard for mayonnaise—"creamy and eggy—just like mayo should be." Tasters also liked Hellmann's Light Mayonnaise (45 calories; 4.5g fat; 0.5g saturated fat) finding it slightly sweeter than the original and praising its thick texture. While some tasters disliked the "tangier" flavor of Hellmann's Canola Cholesterol Free Mayonnaise (45 calories; 4.5g fat; 0g saturated fat), others liked it for its brighter flavor. Hellmann's Reduced Fat Mayonnaise (20 calories; 2g fat; 0g saturated fat) didn't fare as well for having an "off-tasting" flavor. The bottom line? If calories and fat are an issue, Hellmann's Light or Hellmann's Canola Cholesterol Free are good options. Otherwise, stick with the real deal—Hellmann's Real Mayonnaise.

Oyster Po' Boys

The po' boy is a sandwich from New Orleans. Making one calls for hollowing a crisp baguette and filling it with a variety of sandwich meats and seafood. We especially like a po' boy filled with spicy fried oysters "dressed" with mayonnaise, diced pickle, lettuce, and tomato. As you eat this sandwich, the mayonnaise mixes with the juices from the tomatoes, pickles, and spicy oysters to create the unmistakable flavor of an authentic oyster po' boy.

But not all po' boys are created equal. When made with bland, greasy oysters, a cheap, doughy baguette, or "dressed" with aged, lifeless vegetables, this famous New Orleans lunch turns into a bitter disappointment. We decided to find a way to re-create an authentic oyster po' boy at home.

We briefly tested frying the oysters (coated in a cornmeal mixture) at different temperatures and realized that their small size called for a high temperature that would give the cornmeal coating a chance to brown before the oysters became over-cooked and tough. In 375-degree oil, the oysters needed only 2 minutes in the pot to cook perfectly, remaining moist and tender inside and developing a thin, crisp coating outside. We drained the fried oysters on paper towels to rid them of excess oil while the remaining oysters hit the hot oil.

With the fried oysters down, we focused on the remaining components of the sandwich. We decided we should not skimp on the quality of the baguette, the ripeness of the tomato, or the crispness of the lettuce and pickles. Trying to get the mayonnaise to mingle with the juices of the oysters, tomatoes, and pickles made us understand why many recipes recommend pulling out some of the baguette's spongy interior. When a small channel of the interior crumb is removed, there is less bread to soak up these valuable juices. Finally, we noted how fresh the po' boy tasted when fresh lemon juice, salt, and pepper were sprinkled onto the sandwich just before eating.

OYSTER PO' BOYS

SERVES 4

You can shuck your own oysters for this recipe, but we find it much easier to buy them already shucked; they are usually sold in small containers at the fish counter. Baguettes can vary greatly in size; this recipe uses a loaf that is 2 feet long with a 2½-inch diameter. Save the removed bread crumb for other uses, such as making croutons or fresh bread crumbs.

OYSTERS

½	cup fine-ground cornmeal
½	cup all-purpose flour
¾	teaspoon salt
¼	teaspoon pepper
⅛	teaspoon cayenne pepper
½	pound shucked oysters in their liquor (20 to 24 oysters)
6	cups vegetable oil

SANDWICHES

1	long baguette (see note above), split lengthwise and cut into four 6-inch pieces
½	cup mayonnaise
2	teaspoons fresh lemon juice
	Salt and pepper
½	cup minced dill pickles
1	tomato, sliced thin
4	leaves green leaf lettuce

1. FOR THE OYSTERS: Mix the cornmeal, flour, salt, pepper, and cayenne together in a large shallow container. Scoop up about 8 of the oysters with a slotted spoon and allow the excess liquor to drain off briefly. Scatter the drained oysters across the cornmeal mixture and shake the container to coat them evenly. Transfer the breaded oysters to a wire rack set over a large, rimmed baking sheet and repeat with the remaining oysters.

2. Heat the oil in a large Dutch oven over high heat until it reaches 375 degrees (use a candy thermometer attached to the side of the pan or an instant-read thermometer that registers high temperatures). Slip half of the breaded oysters carefully into the hot oil and cook, stirring and prodding them to keep them from sticking together, until they are golden, about 2 minutes. Transfer the fried oysters to a paper towel–lined plate. Return the oil to 375 degrees and fry the remaining breaded oysters.

3. FOR THE SANDWICHES: Hollow out the inside of the baguette pieces by removing some of the interior crumb from both the top and bottom crusts. Spread mayonnaise liberally inside each hollow, sprinkle with the lemon juice, and season with salt and pepper. Spread the pickles and fried oysters on the bottom crusts. Top each sandwich with several slices of tomato, a leaf of lettuce, and finally the upper crust.

Variation

SHRIMP PO' BOYS

Substitute ¾ pound medium (41/50 count) shrimp, peeled and deveined, tossed with 1 large egg, lightly beaten, for the oysters in their liquor.

Stromboli

With their crunchy and golden brown exteriors and flavorful layered meat and cheese fillings, stromboli, a close cousin to calzone, pair well with salad for a welcome change-of-pace dinner. Less doughy than a calzone, stromboli often rely on a sturdy filling of layered deli meats and mozzarella and provolone cheese. Some stromboli, however, can be greasy and/or soggy.

The first step was the dough. Since we desired an easy weeknight dinner, we hoped that store-bought dough would suffice. Readily available in most grocery stores and some pizzerias, store-bought dough was a great time-saving option for our stromboli (although if you have time to prepare your own pizza dough, that's certainly an option). Typically sold in 1-pound balls, store-bought dough gave us the option of making one large stromboli, serving four.

In our recipe search we were constantly reminded that a stromboli is a "rolled sandwich," so it seemed natural to include a variety of deli meats and cheese. And to make this recipe as simple as possible, we wanted to avoid any additional cooking. We settled on a combination of salami, capocollo, and provolone cheese. And to boost the flavor of the meats and cheese, we included jarred roasted red peppers. To avoid any potential problems with these liquid-packed peppers, we thoroughly dried them with paper towels before chopping and adding them to the filling. The results were right on the mark.

We next turned to developing flavor variations. First we tried pesto, but it was too oily; then we tried fresh basil, but the herb turned army green and lifeless. Chopped sun-dried tomatoes were up next, but

their strong flavor overpowered the stromboli's other flavors. It seemed as though the more creative we tried to get with various fillings, the less successful we were, so we decided to stick with simple variations. Tasters gave the thumbs up to a ham and cheddar stromboli and to one with pepperoni and mozzarella.

Switching gears now to the actual baking, we started at 450 degrees. We assumed that a high temperature would be the key to a crispy crust. The crust certainly got crispy, but the inside remained undercooked and doughy. We next decided to cover the stromboli with aluminum foil for the first half of the baking. This gave the interior a sufficient head start, and after 25 minutes we removed the foil to allow for proper browning on the outside. After pulling the stromboli from the oven, we allowed it to cool for at least 5 minutes before slicing. This allowed the cheese enough time to set up and kept it from oozing out when sliced. Tasters could hardly keep their hands off the slices as we served our stromboli in the test kitchen—a good indication of how well this recipe can fit into your repertoire.

STROMBOLI WITH SALAMI, CAPOCOLLO, AND PROVOLONE

SERVES 4

Use 1 pound of your favorite pizza dough recipe, dough from your local pizzeria, supermarket dough, or one 12-ounce or 13.8-ounce pop-open canister of pizza dough (Pillsbury brand).

1	pound pizza dough (see note above)
4	ounces thinly sliced deli salami
4	ounces thinly sliced deli capocollo
4	ounces thinly sliced deli provolone cheese
4	ounces jarred roasted red bell peppers, sliced thin, rinsed, and patted dry (about ½ cup)
½	cup grated Parmesan cheese
1	large egg, lightly beaten
1	teaspoon sesame seeds
	Kosher salt (optional)

1. Adjust an oven rack to the middle position and heat the oven to 400 degrees. Brush a rimmed baking sheet lightly with oil. On a lightly floured work surface, roll the dough into a 12 by 10-inch rectangle, about ¼ inch thick. Place the meat and provolone slices over the dough, leaving a 1-inch border along the edges. Top with the roasted red bell peppers and Parmesan.

2. Brush the edges of the dough with water. Starting from a long side, roll the dough tightly into a long cylinder, pressing the edges to seal. Transfer the stromboli to the prepared baking sheet, seam side down. Brush the egg over the top, and sprinkle with the sesame seeds and kosher salt (if using).

3. Cover the stromboli lightly with aluminum foil that has been sprayed with vegetable oil spray (or use nonstick foil) and bake for 20 minutes. Remove the foil and continue to bake until the crust is golden, about 25 minutes. Transfer the stromboli to a wire rack and let cool for 5 minutes. Transfer to a carving board and slice into 2-inch pieces.

Variations
HAM AND CHEDDAR STROMBOLI
Swiss cheese also works well in this variation.

Omit the roasted red peppers and Parmesan. Substitute 8 ounces thinly sliced deli ham for the salami and capocollo and 4 ounces thinly sliced deli cheddar cheese for the provolone.

PEPPERONI PIZZA STROMBOLI
Omit the roasted red peppers. Substitute 4 ounces thinly sliced pepperoni for the salami and capocollo and 6 ounces mozzarella, shredded (about 1½ cups), for the provolone.

Pepperoni Pan Pizza

Great Chicago-style pan pizza—named for the pan in which the dough rises and is cooked—has an irresistible crust that's crispy on the bottom and soft and chewy in the middle. The generous amount of oil first poured into the pan creates the crisp bottom; the soft interior is harder to figure out. But sometimes the oil goes overboard and the result is a decidedly greasy mess. We wanted to unlock the secret to really great pan pizza—the kind you'd find in the best pizza joints in the Windy City.

Pan pizza isn't something you find in most cookbooks, so we turned to the Internet. After a few clicks, we found a Web site that claimed to reveal the secret behind Pizza Hut's formula. We doubted the recipe was authentic but decided to try it because it included a novel ingredient: powdered milk.

Classic pizza dough contains flour, yeast, water, and olive oil, but never milk. We knew, though, that many tender yeast breads are made with milk. Could powdered milk be the key to soft pizza dough?

This dough was tender, with just the right chew. Because most cooks don't have powdered milk on hand, we wondered if fresh milk would work. It did. In fact, the texture of the crust was even better. Whole milk was fine, but dough made with skim milk rose better and baked up especially soft and light.

All-purpose flour, which yields softer baked goods than bread flour, was the right choice, as was a healthy dose of olive oil (2 tablespoons). Although sugar is not traditional in pizza, tasters thought a little (just 2 teaspoons) made the dough taste better, and we knew that sugar gives yeast a nice jump-start. To deliver our pan pizzas to the table in record time, we used a warm, turned-off oven to help the dough rise faster. Thirty minutes later, we had dough that was ready to shape.

After producing some less than stellar crusts, we discovered it was important not to overwork the dough. Beating the dough into submission with a rolling pin caused it to tear or snap back like a rubber band. In the end we developed the following hybrid method: we used a rolling pin for the first (and easy) part of the process and then stretched the dough over the tops of our knuckles—gently—to finish the job.

With the dough nice and tender, it was time to fine-tune the crispness factor. Three tablespoons of oil in each pan delivered maximum crispness without greasiness. After trying various oven temperatures, we settled on 400 degrees as the best compromise between a crisp bottom and scorched toppings.

Everything was perfect—except for the grease on top of our pies. When just plopped onto the pizza and baked, the pepperoni floated in pools of orange grease. Our first thought was to fry it, just as we'd do with bacon. But this made the pepperoni too crisp and turned it an ugly shade of brown. A colleague suggested the microwave. Layered between paper towels, the pepperoni slices emerged pliable and brightly colored, while the paper towels were soaked with orange fat—the microwave had done its job.

From beginning to end, this pizza can be made in 90 minutes—not as quick as delivery, but less greasy and with the same great crust.

HOW TO MAKE PAN PIZZA

1. Drape a dough round over your knuckles and stretch it to make a 9½-inch circle that is slightly thinner at the center.

2. Place the dough in the oiled pan and gently push it to the edge.

CHICAGO-STYLE PEPPERONI PAN PIZZA

MAKES TWO 9-INCH PIZZAS, SERVING 4 TO 6
Packaged sliced pepperoni and preshredded mozzarella are great time-saving options here.

DOUGH

½	cup olive oil
¾	cup plus 2 tablespoons skim milk, heated to 110 degrees
2	teaspoons sugar
2⅓	cups all-purpose flour, plus extra for the work surface
1	envelope rapid-rise or instant yeast
½	teaspoon salt

TOPPING

1	(3.5-ounce) package sliced pepperoni
1⅓	cups Simple Pizza Sauce (recipe follows)
3	cups shredded part-skim mozzarella cheese

1. TO MAKE THE DOUGH: Adjust an oven rack to the lowest position and heat the oven to 200 degrees. When the oven reaches 200 degrees, turn it off. Lightly grease a large bowl with vegetable oil spray. Coat each of two 9-inch cake pans with 3 tablespoons of the oil.

2. Mix the milk, sugar, and remaining 2 tablespoons oil in a measuring cup.

3. IF USING A STANDING MIXER: Mix the flour, yeast, and salt in a standing mixer fitted with a dough hook. Turn the machine to low and slowly add the milk mixture. After the dough comes together, increase the speed to medium-low and mix until the dough is shiny and smooth, about 5 minutes.

4. IF MIXING BY HAND: Mix the flour, yeast, and salt together in a large bowl. Make a well in the flour, then pour the milk mixture into the well.

Using a wooden spoon, stir until the dough becomes shaggy and difficult to stir. Turn out onto a heavily floured work surface and knead, incorporating any shaggy scraps. Knead until the dough is smooth, about 10 minutes.

5. Turn the dough onto a lightly floured work surface, gently shape into a ball, and place in the greased bowl. Cover with plastic wrap and place in the warm oven until doubled in size, about 30 minutes.

6. TO SHAPE AND TOP THE DOUGH: Transfer the dough to a lightly floured work surface, divide in half, and lightly roll each half into a ball. Following the photos on page 147 and working with 1 dough ball at a time, roll and shape the dough into a 9½-inch round and press into the oiled pan. Cover with plastic wrap and set in a warm spot (not in the oven) until puffy and slightly risen, about 20 minutes. Meanwhile, heat the oven to 400 degrees.

7. While the dough rises, put half of the pepperoni in a single layer on a microwave-safe plate lined with 2 paper towels. Cover with 2 more paper towels and microwave on high for 30 seconds. Discard the towels and set the pepperoni aside; repeat with new paper towels and the remaining pepperoni.

8. Remove the plastic wrap from the dough. Ladle ⅔ cup of the sauce on each round, leaving a ½-inch border around the edges. Sprinkle each with 1½ cups of the cheese and top with the pepperoni. Bake until the cheese is melted and the pepperoni is browning around the edges, about 20 minutes. Remove from the oven; let the pizzas rest in the pans for 1 minute. Using a spatula, transfer the pizzas to a cutting board and cut each into 8 wedges. Serve.

SIMPLE PIZZA SAUCE

MAKES 2⅔ CUPS

This recipe makes enough for four pan pizzas, so you will need only half when making Chicago-Style Pepperoni Pan Pizza. Freeze the remaining sauce for future pizza making.

- 1   **tablespoon olive oil**
- 2   **garlic cloves, minced**
- 1   **(28-ounce) can crushed tomatoes**
     Salt and pepper

Cook the oil and garlic in a medium saucepan over low heat until fragrant, about 2 minutes. Add the tomatoes, increase the heat to medium, and cook until slightly thickened, 10 to 15 minutes. Season with salt and pepper.

Skillet Pizza

A crisp, thin-yet-sturdy crust unburdened by sauce and simply topped with melted cheese and fresh tomatoes is pizza stripped down to its finest. But making thin-crust pizza at home requires a lengthy rise for the dough and plenty of time for a pizza stone (and oven) to get ripping hot. The intense heat makes for a crisp crust, but it also turns the kitchen into a sauna. We challenged ourselves to make the same crisp crust pizza without the hot kitchen.

Making pizza in a skillet is not a new idea. Following the most common method, we made a traditional pizza dough (flour, water, olive oil, salt, sugar, and yeast), let the dough rise for an hour, patted it into a round, and fried it on both sides in a hot oiled skillet. After sprinkling on the toppings and cheese, we covered the pan for a few minutes while the cheese melted. The result definitely wasn't the thin, crisp crust we were striving for (it was more like a thick pan pizza), but the technique did have some promise, as the hot oil gave the crust a golden brown exterior in less than 10 minutes.

An attempt at streamlining the process led us to store-bought pizza dough, but even when rolled paper thin, the yeast in the premade dough produced a crust that was always too thick and chewy. Returning to the homemade dough, we thought that simply omitting the yeast might create a thinner crust. The crust was thin but it was also tough and tasteless. Adding baking powder to the dough was a step in the right direction, as this dough came together quickly, rolled out easily, and would have cooked up light and crisp if there hadn't been a problem with the dough bubbling. To eliminate the bubbles we used a simple tool—a fork—to pop the bubbles as the first side cooked in the skillet (poking before cooking impeded the rise). The bubbling was minimized, and the crust was now evenly browned and incredibly crisp.

But not everything was perfect, as tasters were missing the traditional yeast flavor in the dough. The test kitchen sometimes uses mild American lager to amplify or mimic the flavor of yeast in breads, but after replacing the water in the dough with lager, the yeast flavor was still negligible in the finished pizza. Bolder, darker brown ales, which have a strong yeasty and malty flavor, were a better stand-in for yeast.

To keep the process quick and easy (and to avoid soggy pies), we topped the pizzas with potent no-cook ingredients. Fresh tomatoes (salted and drained to eliminate excess moisture) and basil were the base flavors, and we dressed them up with black olives, roasted red peppers, and prosciutto. Semisoft mozzarella, fontina, and provolone cheeses melted best in the covered skillet, especially when we turned the heat to low after adding the cheeses to allow them to melt without the bottom crust burning. Judging by the constant stream of test cooks asking for another slice of this crisp thin-crust pizza, we'd met our challenge.

SKILLET PIZZA WITH TOMATOES AND MOZZARELLA

MAKES TWO 9-INCH PIZZAS, SERVING 2 TO 4

To save time, combine the cheeses and prepare the dough while the salted tomatoes are draining. When popping the bubbles in the dough in step 3, do so gently to avoid scratching the nonstick pan.

TOPPINGS

4	medium plum tomatoes, cored, seeded, and chopped
½	teaspoon salt
1	cup shredded mozzarella cheese
½	cup grated Parmesan cheese
½	cup finely chopped fresh basil

DOUGH

1	cup all-purpose flour
½	teaspoon baking powder
½	teaspoon sugar
½	teaspoon salt
⅓	cup beer
7	tablespoons olive oil

HOW TO COOK THIN-CRUST SKILLET PIZZA

1. While the first side of the dough cooks, use a fork to gently pop any bubbles that form so that the dough will stay flat and brown evenly. Using tongs, flip the dough over so that the second side can brown in the oil.

2. Sprinkle the dough with toppings and cheese, cover the skillet, and lower the heat. The heat captured in the pan helps to melt the cheese and warm up the other toppings before the bottom crust burns.

1. FOR THE TOPPINGS: Toss the tomatoes and salt in a large bowl, then transfer to a paper towel–lined plate; let drain for 15 minutes. Combine the cheeses and basil in a medium bowl; refrigerate while preparing the dough.

2. FOR THE DOUGH: Combine the flour, baking powder, sugar, and salt in a food processor. With the processor running, slowly add the beer and 1 tablespoon of the oil and process until the dough pulls away from the sides and forms a shaggy ball, about 1 minute. Using floured hands, form the dough into a tight ball and cover loosely with plastic wrap; let rest 10 minutes. (The dough can be wrapped tightly in plastic and frozen for up to 1 week.)

3. Divide the dough in half. On a lightly floured surface, roll each half into a very thin 9-inch round. Heat 3 tablespoons more oil in a large nonstick skillet over medium heat until just smoking. Transfer one dough round to the skillet and cook, poking any bubbles that form with a fork, until the bottom is deep golden brown and crisp, 3 to 4 minutes. Flip the dough and sprinkle with half of the drained tomatoes and half of the cheese mixture. Reduce the heat to low and cook, covered, until the second side is crisp and the cheeses have melted, about 5 minutes. Transfer the pizza to a cutting board. Wipe out the pan and repeat with the remaining 3 tablespoons oil, dough, and toppings. Slice into wedges. Serve.

Variations
SKILLET PIZZA WITH PROVOLONE, OLIVES, AND SPICY PEPPERS

4	medium plum tomatoes, cored, seeded, and chopped
½	teaspoon salt
1	cup shredded provolone cheese
¼	cup drained jarred roasted red peppers, chopped
¼	cup pitted kalamata olives, chopped
2	large jarred pepperoncini, stemmed, seeded, and chopped
½	cup finely chopped fresh basil

Before making the dough, toss the tomatoes and salt in a large bowl, then transfer to a paper towel-lined plate; let drain for 15 minutes. Combine the provolone, roasted peppers, olives, pepperoncini, and basil in a medium bowl; refrigerate until ready to use as directed in step 3.

SKILLET PIZZA WITH FONTINA, GOAT CHEESE, AND PROSCIUTTO

4	medium plum tomatoes, cored, seeded, and chopped
½	teaspoon salt
1	cup shredded fontina cheese
½	cup crumbled goat cheese
2	ounces sliced deli prosciutto, chopped
½	cup finely chopped fresh basil

Before making the dough, toss the tomatoes and salt in a large bowl, then transfer to a paper towel–lined plate; let drain for 15 minutes. Combine the cheeses, prosciutto, and basil in a medium bowl; refrigerate until ready to use as directed in step 3.

SHOPPING WITH THE TEST KITCHEN

Beer for Pizza: Yeast gives traditional pizza dough its complex flavor but requires several hours to work its magic. We found that beer adds a yeasty flavor to our baking powder–leavened pizza dough and rises for just 10 minutes. Although any beer will work here, we prefer full-flavored ales to bitter stouts or mild lagers. Our favorite, Newcastle Brown Ale, won praise for its rich, malty flavor that gave our pizza crust just the right yeast flavor. If you're looking for a non-alcoholic option, our tasters liked O'Douls Amber.

CHAPTER SIX

Hearty Breakfasts

HEARTY BREAKFASTS

Cloudcakes

Recipes for super-fluffy pancakes have lots of nicknames. In addition to Angel Cakes, we have also seen recipes for Cloudcakes (the name we think best describes their texture), Heavenly Hotcakes, and even Zeppelin Pancakes. What do these recipes have in common? Almost all of them rely on separated rather than whole eggs. The yolks are mixed into the batter, and the whites are beaten into a foam that expands during cooking and makes the pancakes rise like a soufflé.

We tried several recipes with beaten egg whites, and they all produced fairly light pancakes. But as for fluffy and tangy pancakes, these recipes didn't come through. Our first thought was to substitute buttermilk for regular milk. Sure enough, the pancakes rose higher and they tasted a bit tangier. Many of the recipes we tried used a lot less flour than liquid, but tasters found that these variations lacked structure and height. We found that a batter made with about the same amount of flour and buttermilk made pancakes with good structure that sat up nicely in the skillet.

So where were we? Well, we had good hearty pancakes that were thick and pretty light, but we were after a griddle cake that really lived up to the name Cloudcake. Our first clue came from a recipe from the Campton Place Hotel in San Francisco, which makes the world's best fluffy pancakes. The hotel chefs use extra whites. We followed their lead, using four whites and two yolks. Now we were getting close to ethereal.

Once in a while, our pancakes just wouldn't rise enough, and we figured that the problem was likely overmixing. Now that we were adding egg whites in a separate step, we were mixing the batter twice. We learned (the hard way) to stop mixing the wet and dry ingredients when they were just barely combined,

with lots of lumps and dry flour visible. The act of folding in the egg whites finished the job.

We had one last concern. Were our pancakes truly tangy? We had seen recipes with sour cream; maybe that would help. We added ¼ cup and held our breath as the batter almost rose out of the pan. Besides giving the pancakes great flavor, the sour cream reacted with the baking soda in the batter to create tremendous lift. Our pancakes finally earned the name Cloudcakes.

CLOUDCAKES

MAKES TWENTY-FIVE 3-INCH PANCAKES,
SERVING 4 TO 6

These very light pancakes are best served with maple syrup. Home stovetops vary, so you may need to adjust the burner setting between medium-low and medium. For maximum rise, allow the eggs and buttermilk to come to room temperature before using them. Low-fat buttermilk works best here; if using fat-free buttermilk, reduce the amount to 1 cup plus 2 tablespoons. Although these pancakes are at their puffiest when served right away, the first few batches can be kept warm in the oven until all the pancakes have been cooked—see page 156 for instruction.

1¼	cups all-purpose flour
1½	tablespoons sugar
1	teaspoon baking soda
¾	teaspoon salt
1¼	cups low-fat buttermilk (see note above)
¼	cup sour cream
2	large eggs, separated, plus 2 extra egg whites
2	tablespoons unsalted butter, melted and cooled
1–2	tablespoons vegetable oil
	Maple syrup for serving

1. Whisk the flour, sugar, baking soda, and salt together in a large bowl. Stir the buttermilk and sour cream together in a medium bowl until combined. Add the egg yolks and butter to the buttermilk mixture and stir well to combine. With an electric mixer or a balloon whisk, beat all 4 egg whites in a large bowl to soft peaks. Pour the buttermilk mixture over the dry ingredients and whisk until just combined. (The batter should be lumpy, with visible streaks of flour.) Using a spatula, carefully fold the whites into the batter until just combined. Do not overmix—a few streaks of egg white should be visible.

2. Heat 2 teaspoons oil in a large nonstick skillet over medium-low heat for 5 minutes. Using a ⅛-cup measure or small ladle, spoon the batter into the pan. Cook until the bottoms are evenly browned, 2 to 3 minutes. Flip the pancakes and cook until golden brown on the second side, 2 to 3 minutes longer. Serve, cooking the remaining batter and using more vegetable oil as needed to grease the pan.

Variations

CINNAMON "TOAST" CLOUDCAKES

Cinnamon and sugar make these pancakes reminiscent of homemade cinnamon toast. They are perfect served with apple butter.

Follow the recipe for Cloudcakes, increasing the sugar to 3 tablespoons and adding 1 teaspoon ground cinnamon to the other dry ingredients in step 1.

PUCKER-UP CLOUDCAKES

Serve these lemon-scented pancakes with blueberry sauce or syrup.

Follow the recipe for Cloudcakes, replacing ¼ cup of the flour with an equal amount of yellow cornmeal and adding 1 teaspoon grated fresh lemon zest to the dry ingredients in step 1.

All-American Pancakes

A big stack of hot flapjacks brings everyone to the breakfast table on time. Unfortunately, most pancakes are either so tough and rubbery that they snap back and smack you in the face or so cottony and tasteless that they must be accompanied by a very tall glass of milk.

After cooking our way through many, many pancake recipes, the test kitchen came to a couple of conclusions: one, we like our pancakes tender and fluffy, but not spongy; two, even though we were after the best pancake, we wanted to avoid any nonsensical techniques or ingredients that would require a jaunt to the grocery store, especially given that we would likely be making these pancakes early in the morning, with only one eye open and one cup of coffee running through our veins.

First up was flour, and because this was to be a no-nonsense recipe we turned to our test-kitchen standard—unbleached flour—pitting it against cake flour and bleached flour, and were happy it came out on top. Sugar was next, and the question was not whether to add it but how much to add. We like pancakes on the sweet side. Two tablespoons turned out to be just right. As for leavener, we were hoping to use just baking powder; but, sure enough, tasters preferred the golden brown color that baking soda provided, so in the end we opted to use both. Two teaspoons of baking powder and ½ teaspoon of baking soda did the job. Finally, a little salt went in to accentuate the whole.

Next we settled on one egg—two eggs made pancakes with an eggy flavor that tasters disliked. What about butter—was it necessary? One quick test later, we found the answer to be an emphatic yes. Without butter the pancakes were more evenly colored (no spots of scorched butter), but they had the cottony interior that we just couldn't stomach. We melted 3 tablespoons of butter and added it to the batter, and everyone was happy.

As for the dairy, we tested milk and buttermilk and also threw half-and-half into the mix to see what would happen. To no one's surprise, buttermilk took first place. This tangy, thick liquid produced a pancake with great flavor and beat-all fluffiness. But to be true to our rule number two, we couldn't pretend that buttermilk would be found on most people's lists of basic pantry ingredients. We needed a substitute.

We added lemon juice to milk to "curdle" it and cooked up a batch of pancakes. Surprisingly, tasters preferred the pancakes made with our mock buttermilk to those made with the real thing. (But if you should happen to have buttermilk on hand when you're feeling in a pancake way, by all means use it.)

The best method for cooking our pancakes was simply to ladle some batter onto a hot nonstick skillet coated with a thin film of vegetable oil. It's important to heat the skillet over medium heat, not high heat; otherwise the pancakes will scorch before they've had time to cook through.

ALL-AMERICAN PANCAKES

MAKES ABOUT SIXTEEN 4-INCH PANCAKES, SERVING 4 TO 6

You can substitute 2 cups buttermilk for the milk and lemon juice mixture. The only way to know when the pan is ready is to make a test pancake about the size of a half-dollar (use 1 tablespoon of batter). If, after 1 minute, the pancake is blond in color, the pan is not hot enough. If, after 1 minute, the pancake is golden brown, the pan is heated correctly. Speeding up the process by heating the pan at a higher temperature will result in a dark, unevenly cooked pancake.

1	tablespoon fresh lemon juice
2	cups milk (see note above)
2	cups all-purpose flour
2	tablespoons sugar
2	teaspoons baking powder
½	teaspoon baking soda
½	teaspoon salt
1	large egg
3	tablespoons unsalted butter, melted and cooled slightly
1–2	teaspoons vegetable oil
	Maple syrup for serving

1. Whisk the lemon juice and milk together in a medium bowl or large measuring cup; set aside to thicken while preparing the other ingredients. Whisk the flour, sugar, baking powder, baking soda, and salt in a medium bowl to combine.

2. Whisk the egg and melted butter into the milk until combined. Make a well in the center of the dry ingredients in the bowl; pour in the milk mixture and whisk very gently until just combined (a few lumps should remain). Do not overmix.

3. Heat a large nonstick skillet over medium heat until hot, 3 to 5 minutes; add 1 teaspoon oil and brush to coat the skillet bottom evenly. Pour ¼ cup batter onto 3 spots on the skillet. Cook the pancakes until large bubbles begin to appear, 1½ to 2 minutes. Using a thin, wide spatula, flip the pancakes and cook until golden brown on the second side, 1 to 1½ minutes longer. Serve immediately. Repeat with the remaining batter, using the remaining vegetable oil only if necessary.

Variation
BLUEBERRY PANCAKES

Rather than following the traditional technique of folding the blueberries into the batter, we like to sprinkle the berries over the pancakes as they begin to set in the pan. This step makes for intact berries and attractive unmottled cakes. When local blueberries are not in season, frozen blueberries are a better alternative. To make sure that frozen berries do not bleed, rinse them under cool water in a mesh strainer until the water runs clear, then spread them on a paper towel–lined plate to dry.

Have ready 1 cup fresh or frozen blueberries, preferably wild, rinsed and dried. Follow the recipe for All-American Pancakes. Sprinkle 1 tablespoon blueberries over each pancake just after pouring the batter into the pan.

TEST KITCHEN SHORTCUT

Keeping Pancakes Warm: A large skillet can turn out only three pancakes at a time, so if you want everyone to eat at the same time, you must keep the first few batches warm. After testing various methods we found in cookbooks (most of which suggest covering the pancakes, which causes them to become steamed and rubbery), we discovered that pancakes will hold for 20 minutes when placed on a greased rack set on a baking sheet in a 200-degree oven. The warm oven keeps the pancakes hot enough to melt a pat of butter, and leaving the pancakes uncovered prevents them from becoming soggy.

German Apple Pancake

Started on the stove and finished in the oven, German apple pancakes (Dutch Babies) bear little resemblance to their American cousin, fluffy flapjacks. Unlike the American version, which owes its cake-like texture to baking powder or baking soda, the German pancake has more in common with a popover, getting its dramatic rise from eggs and a hot oven. The perfect German apple pancake should have crisp, lighter-than-air edges and a custard-like center, with buttery sautéed apples baked right into the batter.

German pancake batter is composed of three main ingredients: flour, eggs, and liquid (usually milk). We began by experimenting with different types of liquid, making pancakes with half-and-half, heavy cream, and a combination of sour cream and milk. The pancake made with heavy cream was leaden and flat, and the sour cream–milk version had a strange, tart flavor. Half-and-half turned out to be the perfect solution. It has just enough butterfat to give the pancake a rich flavor without sacrificing texture. After trying various ratios of half-and-half, eggs, and flour, we found that a combination of 2 eggs, ⅔ cup half-and-half, and ½ cup all-purpose flour made a nicely puffed pancake. The addition of a little sugar, salt, and vanilla gave it just the right balance of flavors.

The next step was to find the perfect oven temperature. Like a popover, this pancake relies on steam (instead of chemical leavening) for its explosive rise. Because the batter is poured into a preheated pan and placed immediately into a hot oven, the surface of the batter sets first. While in the oven the liquid in the batter turns to steam, creating pockets of air that cause the pancake to rise, much like an inflating balloon. After testing a variety of temperatures, we settled on preheating the oven to 500 degrees and lowering it to a more moderate 425 degrees when the pancake went into the oven. The initial high heat gave the batter the quick rise it needed, and the more moderate heat cooked the pancake to perfection.

Our next task was to figure out how to cook the apples. Apples cooked with granulated sugar were sweet but flat-tasting, whereas those cooked with either light or dark brown sugar were fabulous. When the light brown sugar combined with the butter and apples, it made a great sauce that enhanced the apples' clean flavor. Dark brown sugar did the same, producing a slightly smokier caramel with molasses highlights. Adding a little cinnamon and some lemon juice made the apples at once earthy and bright.

Our last task was to figure out which kind of apple to use. We chose ten widely available varieties and made pancakes with each. With their perfect balance of sweetness and tartness, Granny Smith apples were the favorite. Braeburns were also liked; they were more sugary-sweet, with just the slightest hint of lemony brightness.

Inverted onto a serving platter and covered with a snowy dusting of confectioners' sugar (and a generous drizzle of syrup or caramel sauce), this German apple pancake was ideal.

GERMAN APPLE PANCAKE

SERVES 4

A 10-inch ovenproof skillet is necessary for this recipe; we highly recommend using a nonstick skillet for the sake of easy cleanup, but a regular skillet will work as well. You can also use a cast-iron pan; if you do, set the oven temperature to 425 degrees in step 1, and when cooking the apples in step 3, cook them only until just barely golden, about 6 minutes. Cast iron retains heat better than stainless steel, making the higher oven temperature unnecessary. If you prefer tart apples, use Granny Smiths; if you prefer sweet ones, use Braeburns. For serving, dust the apple pancake with confectioners' sugar and pass warm maple syrup or caramel sauce (recipe follows) separately, if desired.

½   cup all-purpose flour
1   tablespoon granulated sugar
½   teaspoon salt

2   large eggs
⅔   cup half-and-half
1   teaspoon vanilla extract
2   tablespoons unsalted butter
1¼ pounds Granny Smith or Braeburn apples (3 to 4 large apples), peeled, quartered, cored, and cut into ½-inch slices
¼   cup packed brown sugar
¼   teaspoon ground cinnamon
1   teaspoon fresh lemon juice
    Confectioners' sugar for dusting

1. Adjust an oven rack to the upper-middle position and heat the oven to 500 degrees.

2. Whisk the flour, granulated sugar, and salt together in a medium bowl. In a second medium bowl, whisk the eggs, half-and-half, and vanilla until combined. Add the liquid ingredients to the dry and whisk until no lumps remain, about 20 seconds; set the batter aside.

3. Heat the butter in a 10-inch ovenproof nonstick skillet over medium-high heat until sizzling. Add the apples, brown sugar, and cinnamon; cook, stirring frequently with a heatproof rubber spatula, until the apples are golden brown, about 10 minutes. Off the heat, stir in the lemon juice.

4. Working quickly, pour the batter around and over the apples. Place the skillet in the oven and immediately reduce the oven temperature to 425 degrees; bake until the pancake edges are brown and puffy and have risen above the edges of the skillet, about 18 minutes.

5. Using oven mitts, remove the hot skillet from the oven and loosen the pancake edges with a heatproof rubber spatula; invert the pancake onto a serving platter. Dust with confectioners' sugar, cut into wedges, and serve.

CARAMEL SAUCE

MAKES ABOUT 1½ CUPS

If you make the caramel sauce ahead, reheat it in the microwave or a small saucepan over low heat until warm and fluid. When the hot cream mixture is added in step 3, the hot sugar syrup will bubble vigorously (and dangerously), so don't use a smaller saucepan.

½	cup water
1	cup sugar
1	cup heavy cream
⅛	teaspoon salt
½	teaspoon vanilla extract
½	teaspoon fresh lemon juice

1. Place the water in a heavy-bottomed 2-quart saucepan; pour the sugar in the center of the pan, taking care not to let the sugar crystals adhere to the sides of the pan. Cover and bring the mixture to a boil over high heat; once boiling, uncover and continue to boil until the syrup is thick and straw-colored (the syrup should register 300 degrees on a candy thermometer), about 7 minutes. Reduce the heat to medium and continue to cook until the syrup is deep amber (the syrup should register 350 degrees on a candy thermometer), about 1 to 2 minutes.

2. Meanwhile, bring the cream and salt to a simmer in a small saucepan over high heat (if the cream boils before the sugar reaches a deep amber color, remove the cream from the heat and cover to keep warm).

3. Remove the sugar syrup from the heat; very carefully pour about one-quarter of the hot cream into it (the mixture will bubble vigorously), and let the bubbling subside. Add the remaining cream, vanilla, and lemon juice; whisk until the sauce is smooth. (The sauce can be cooled and refrigerated in an airtight container for up to 2 weeks.)

Light and Crispy Waffles

Although frozen waffles are little more than vehicles for syrup and butter, they are convenient and they are consistently crisp, unlike some "from scratch" waffles we've eaten. Is it possible to create a homemade waffle that is as crisp as the frozen variety, but with far better flavor? We were determined to find out.

We gathered a slew of recipes, summoned a group of tasters, and fired up the irons. These recipes all included a basic combination of flour, sugar, leavener (baking powder or soda), eggs, fat (butter or oil), and milk or buttermilk. Some recipes included interesting ingredients such as club soda (for light texture) or cooked grits (for toothy bite), but tasters were not impressed. These waffles definitely had more flavor than frozen, but their texture was problematic. A few of the waffles were nice and crisp hot off the iron but then became soggy on the plate.

We noticed that two of the most promising recipes had a common ingredient: beaten egg whites. Although most waffle recipes don't call for separating the eggs, beaten egg whites add lightness to everything from cakes to soufflés, and they worked wonders on waffles, too.

Now our waffles were lighter and fluffier, but they were not nearly crisp enough. We realized that the design of a toaster allows excess moisture to escape, whereas a waffle iron traps steam from the batter and increases the likelihood of a soggy outcome. When we want crispness in other recipes, we usually rely on oil (which is 100 percent fat) rather than butter (which is 80 percent fat and 20 percent water). Would the same trick work with waffles? Though several tasters were partial to the nutty flavor of waffles made with butter, the waffles made with oil were crispier.

Butter was out and oil was in, but our waffles were still a bit soggy. We couldn't get rid of all the moisture—a waffle without milk just isn't possible. Cornstarch is commonly used to combat excess moisture in all kinds of recipes, and we wondered how it would affect our waffles. We replaced some of the flour with cornstarch, working our way up from a scant 2 teaspoons (which made little difference) to a hefty ¾ cup. Our waffles were finally both light and crispy, but could we make them extra-light and extra-crispy?

While discussing our recipe with a colleague, we noticed that another cook had prepared a batch of Rice Krispies Treats. This got us to thinking, and with nothing to lose, we added Rice Krispies to our batter. The cereal added a malty, slightly sweet flavor that tasters loved, and each puffed grain of rice produced a tiny pocket of air in the waffles. Our waffles were seriously crisp, and the Rice Krispies seemed to disappear as the batter cooked, leaving behind only their crunch and lightness. Best of all, our waffles retained their crispy structure, even with a generous topping of butter and syrup.

LIGHT AND CRISPY WAFFLES

MAKES EIGHT 7-INCH ROUND WAFFLES, SERVING 4

Either whole or low-fat milk works here; skim milk, however, is too lean. All waffle irons are not created equal. If your first waffle comes off the iron too pale or too dark, adjust the heat as necessary. Make sure to fill the waffle iron as directed; if you don't use enough batter, the Rice Krispies can scorch. Our waffles are best served right off the waffle iron, but they can be reheated so everyone can eat at once. Transfer the cooked waffles to a wire rack set on a baking sheet in a 400-degree oven and bake until crisp and hot, 3 to 5 minutes.

1¼	cups all-purpose flour
1	cup Rice Krispies
¾	cup cornstarch
¼	cup sugar
1	teaspoon baking powder
½	teaspoon baking soda
¾	teaspoon salt
2	large eggs, separated
1½	cups milk (see note above)
1	teaspoon vanilla extract
½	cup vegetable oil
	Maple syrup, for serving

1. Preheat a traditional waffle iron to medium. Meanwhile, stir the flour, Rice Krispies, cornstarch, sugar, baking powder, baking soda, and salt together in a large bowl. Whisk the egg yolks, milk, vanilla, and oil together in a medium bowl.

2. With an electric mixer or balloon whisk, beat the egg whites in a bowl to soft peaks. Pour the milk mixture over the dry ingredients and whisk until combined. Whisk in the beaten whites until just combined. Do not overmix; a few streaks of egg white should be visible.

3. Pour ⅔ cup batter into the center of the preheated waffle iron and use the back of a dinner spoon to spread the batter toward the outer edges (the batter should reach about ½ inch from the edges of the iron before the lid is closed). Close the lid and cook until deep golden brown, 3 to 4 minutes. Serve immediately, or if you want to freeze the waffles, wrap each cooled waffle in plastic wrap, then freeze in a zipper-lock plastic bag for up to 1 month. To serve, place the waffles on a wire rack set on a baking sheet and bake in a 400-degree oven until crisp and hot, about 5 minutes.

Variation
LIGHT AND CRISPY BELGIAN WAFFLES

Some Belgian waffle makers make one waffle at a time, while others make two.

For single waffle makers, use ⅔ cup batter per waffle. For double waffle makers, use 1⅓ cups batter in total.

Sunday Brunch French Toast

French toast makes a great brunch dish, especially if you own an electric griddle—most models fit about eight slices. But when you don't own a griddle and must make do with a large skillet, you can cook only about two slices at a time. Brunch is no fun when diners must eat in stages as each batch is prepared. The other option—keeping the French toast warm in the oven—isn't much better, since the toast is apt to turn soggy and limp as it warms. Is there a way to make French toast for a group without a griddle? We knew we couldn't use a skillet, which left us pondering whether we could bake our French toast.

We soaked eight slices of hearty white sandwich bread in a mixture of milk and eggs until the bread was wet and heavy, put them on a buttered baking sheet, and popped them into the oven. The results of this first test were discouraging, as the French toast came out of the oven mushy and falling apart. Drying the bread in the oven before the soak gave it enough structure to withstand a long, deep bath in the custard (to ensure a custardy center) without falling apart. To ensure the best possible texture, we found that it was necessary to soak the bread for 30 seconds on each side and then let the slices rest briefly on an elevated rack so that any excess surface custard could drain away, thus preventing a soggy exterior. As we fine-tuned the flavor, tasters let us know they preferred the richness of half-and-half to milk, especially when we added a little lemon juice to mimic the tang of buttermilk—a familiar flavor in many breakfast dishes, such as pancakes and waffles.

The French toast was now custardy and holding together well, but it wasn't browning or getting crisp. In the test kitchen we oven-fry potato wedges by coating a baking sheet with vegetable oil and preheating it in a hot oven. Using this technique, we placed the soaked bread slices on the sizzling oiled sheet and flipped them halfway through cooking. After about 15 minutes, the toast came out crisp and golden on the outside and creamy and custardy inside. Now that we weren't slaving over the stovetop for several skillet batches, we had some time to think about how we could dress up this French toast for guests.

Since we serve French toast with powdered sugar and maple syrup, we wondered if we could incorporate these flavors as a topping in the oven. We made a paste of powdered sugar and maple syrup and brushed it on the toast after we flipped it. Although the powdered sugar became gummy, the maple syrup brought welcome moisture, flavor, and sweetness (and allowed us to eliminate the sugar in the custard). Swapping out the powdered sugar for brown sugar helped the maple topping caramelize into a delectable candied crust that tasters loved. This French toast was so good and so convenient, we think it tops griddle versions.

SUNDAY BRUNCH FRENCH TOAST

SERVES 4

Be sure to use a firm-textured bread such as Arnold Country Classic White or Pepperidge Farm Farmhouse Hearty White.

8	slices hearty white sandwich bread
6	large eggs
¾	cup half-and-half
1	tablespoon vanilla extract
2	teaspoons fresh lemon juice
¼	teaspoon salt
¼	cup vegetable oil
6	tablespoons light brown sugar
1	tablespoon maple syrup
½	teaspoon ground cinnamon

1. Adjust an oven rack to the lower-middle position and heat the oven to 300 degrees. Bake the bread on a rimmed baking sheet until dry, about 8 minutes per side. Let the bread cool 5 minutes. Increase the oven temperature to 475 degrees.

2. Whisk the eggs, half-and-half, vanilla, lemon juice, and salt in a 13 by 9-inch baking dish. Soak 4 slices of the bread in the egg mixture until just saturated, about 30 seconds per side. Transfer to a wire rack and repeat with the remaining bread.

3. Pour the oil onto a rimmed baking sheet, tilting the sheet to coat. Transfer to the oven and heat until just smoking, about 4 minutes. Using a fork, stir the brown sugar, maple syrup, and cinnamon in a small bowl until the mixture resembles wet sand.

4. Arrange the soaked bread on the hot baking sheet and bake until golden brown on the first side, about 10 minutes. Flip the bread and sprinkle evenly with the sugar mixture. Cook until the sugar is deep brown and bubbling, about 6 minutes. Cool the toast on a wire rack for 2 minutes. Serve.

THE SECRET TO OVEN-FRIED FRENCH TOAST

1. Place the custard-soaked bread on a preheated baking sheet coated with oil to create a crisp coating on the exterior of the bread.

2. Sprinkle the toast with a mixture of brown sugar, cinnamon, and maple syrup for a caramelized, golden exterior.

Stuffed French Toast

Good stuffed French toast marries a creamy filling with a really crisp exterior. It's this contrast in textures that makes stuffed French toast different from ordinary French toast. The French toast is "stuffed" by spreading a filling between two slices of regular sandwich bread (the moist filling acts as a seal). The stuffed sandwiches are then dipped in an egg-based batter and cooked in butter, much like regular French toast.

The cookbooks we consulted offered two options for the stuffing: jam or sweetened cream cheese. Tasters overwhelmingly preferred the latter, many likening it to the filling in a cheese Danish. As a bonus, the sweetened cream cheese was better than the jam at holding the bread slices together.

We weren't ready to give up on the jam altogether, however. After more testing, we found that a small amount of jam combined with the cream cheese was a great way to add different flavors. Blueberry jam was a big hit, as was apricot (especially when combined with a bit of almond extract). Apple jelly didn't win much support, though richly flavored apple butter provided a homey apple pie version. Our favorite variation, though unorthodox, was chocolate chip; the chips melted into the cream cheese, making the filling taste just like chocolate cheesecake (you'll probably want to skip the maple syrup on that variation).

We were satisfied with the stuffing, so it was time to focus on the "toast." The typical egg and milk batter used with regular French toast wasn't producing the kind of crisp exterior we envisioned. We found recipes that called for everything from a thick pancake batter to a heavy, cream-based dip, but none yielded a really crisp exterior to contrast with the soft filling.

After yet another failed test, a fellow cook suggested tempura batter. Though we were initially skeptical, the idea made sense. A tempura batter is a thin mixture made with flour, egg, and either sparkling water or beer. Although it traditionally provides a thin, super-crisp coating for seafood and vegetables, why not try it as a dip for French toast?

Beer was certainly not on the menu for breakfast, so we combined sparkling water, flour, and egg. This was perfect; the bread fried up to a crisp golden brown and provided the perfect contrast with the creamy stuffing. We wondered, though, if we really needed the sparkling water. It turns out that it wasn't necessary; the lacy texture that sparkling water provides wasn't crucial to our recipe, and cold tap water served to create the same great crisp texture.

STUFFED FRENCH TOAST

SERVES 4

We like loaves of large-sized sandwich bread for this recipe, with slices about 5 inches by 4 inches. If you use the smaller, standard-sized sandwich bread, you won't need all of the filling.

6	ounces cream cheese, softened
3	tablespoons sugar
¼	teaspoon cinnamon
8	slices hearty white sandwich bread (see note above)
1	large egg
1	cup cold water
½	cup all-purpose flour
1	teaspoon vanilla extract
4	tablespoons unsalted butter
	Maple syrup for serving

1. Combine the cream cheese, sugar, and cinnamon in a medium bowl. Spread on 4 bread slices. Top with the remaining bread slices, pressing down gently, forming 4 sandwiches.

2. Combine the egg, water, flour, and vanilla in a shallow pie plate. Melt 2 tablespoons of the butter in a large nonstick skillet over medium heat. Dip both sides of 2 sandwiches in the batter and place in the skillet. Cook until deep golden brown on both sides, about 3 minutes per side. Repeat with the remaining 2 tablespoons butter and sandwiches.

3. Cut into triangles and serve immediately with maple syrup.

Variations
BLUEBERRY COBBLER FRENCH TOAST
Reduce the amount of cream cheese to 4 ounces and substitute 2 tablespoons blueberry jam for 2 tablespoons of the sugar.

APPLE PIE FRENCH TOAST

Reduce the amount of cream cheese to 4 ounces and substitute 3 tablespoons apple butter for 1½ tablespoons of the sugar.

APRICOT-ALMOND FRENCH TOAST

Reduce the amount of cream cheese to 4 ounces and substitute 2 tablespoons apricot jam for 2 tablespoons of the sugar and ⅛ teaspoon almond extract for the cinnamon.

CHOCOLATE CHIP FRENCH TOAST

Reduce the amount of cream cheese to 4 ounces and substitute ¼ cup semisweet chocolate chips for 1½ tablespoons of the sugar. Omit the cinnamon.

SHOPPING WITH THE TEST KITCHEN

Maple Syrup: Maple syrup is the reduced sap of the sugar maple tree produced in the early spring, most famously in pockets of New England and Canada. Maple syrup is separated by quality into three grades: A, B, and C. Grade A is the purest (and mildest) syrup from the earliest sap of the season. Grade B is slightly darker and possesses a more assertive flavor. Grade C maple syrup is characterized by a harsh, almost molasses-like flavor and is generally available only for commercial use. Although Grade A is the most widely available, we prefer the richer flavor of Grade B syrup, which won praise from our tasters for its subtle vanilla and rum overtones and its potent maple flavor. That said, depending on how you are using it (baking versus drizzling over pancakes), you should rely on your personal preference when deciding whether to use Grade A or Grade B syrup, as both work well in all the recipes in this book. Because of its high moisture level and lack of preservatives, maple syrup is a perishable food product that is susceptible to the growth of yeasts, molds, and bacteria. Refrigeration not only helps maple syrup retain its flavor but it prevents microorganisms from growing as well. Unopened, maple syrup will last several years stored in a cool, dark place. Once opened, it will keep 6 months to a year in the refrigerator.

Flavored Maple Syrups

It's hard to improve upon maple syrup and a pat of butter on top of steaming waffles or pancakes, but if you're looking to spice up your short stack, these variations are sure to please.

BUTTER PECAN MAPLE SYRUP

MAKES ABOUT 2 CUPS

1½	cups maple syrup
2	tablespoons unsalted butter
½	cup pecans, toasted and chopped
¼	teaspoon vanilla extract
	Pinch salt

Simmer all of the ingredients in a small saucepan over medium-low heat until slightly thickened, about 5 minutes.

BLUEBERRY MAPLE SYRUP

MAKES ABOUT 1¾ CUPS

½	cup frozen blueberries
1½	cups maple syrup
¼	teaspoon grated fresh lemon zest
	Pinch salt

Mash the blueberries in a small saucepan over medium heat until the moisture has evaporated, about 5 minutes. Whisk in the remaining ingredients and cook over medium-low heat until slightly thickened, 5 to 7 minutes.

APPLE-CINNAMON MAPLE SYRUP

MAKES ABOUT 1¾ CUPS

1½	cups maple syrup
⅓	cup apple jelly
¼	teaspoon cinnamon
	Pinch salt

Simmer all of the ingredients in a small saucepan over medium-low heat until slightly thickened, 5 to 7 minutes.

Fried Eggs

After cooking dozens of eggs with a variety of techniques, we found that there are three imperatives for making perfect fried eggs. The first is to preheat the pan for 5 minutes over low heat. This ensures a uniformly heated cooking surface (without any hot or cold spots) that will cook the eggs evenly. The second tip, pouring the eggs into the pan from two small bowls rather than cracking them into the pan one by one, assures that the eggs will finish cooking at the same time. It also makes it easier to get the eggs into the pan without breaking the yolks. Finally, by covering the pan, we were able to produce egg yolks with a thick but still runny consistency without overcooking the whites.

POURING EGGS INTO A SKILLET

Crack the eggs into two bowls and slide the eggs into the hot skillet simultaneously, so that all four eggs will be done at the same time.

EASY FRIED EGGS

SERVES 2

If you've just fried bacon or happen to have leftover bacon grease, it can be used in place of the butter. These eggs are best served right out of the skillet. They can, however, be slid onto a plate, covered with foil, and held for up to 5 minutes while you prepare a second batch.

4	large eggs
1	tablespoon unsalted butter (see note above)
	Salt and pepper

Heat a large nonstick skillet over the lowest possible heat for 5 minutes. Meanwhile, crack the eggs into 2 small bowls (2 eggs in each bowl). Add the butter to the hot skillet and melt, swirling to coat the pan. Add the eggs to the pan simultaneously. Sprinkle the eggs with salt and pepper, cover, and cook undisturbed for 2 minutes. Check the eggs and, if necessary, continue to cook, covered, until the eggs have cooked through as desired, up to 3 minutes longer.

Scrambled Eggs

Scrambled eggs may seem straightforward, but we tested a variety of methods for making them and had dramatically different results with each. In the end, we learned that the addition of milk to the eggs makes more flavorful, more tender scrambled eggs. When whisking the eggs and milk together, don't muscle them into a tight froth, which will only result in tough eggs. Instead, for a smooth yellow color and no streaks of white, we whip the eggs with a fork and stop while the bubbles are large. A hot pan and a unique folding method yield the creamiest, softest scrambled eggs. If you push the eggs to and fro with a spatula instead of constantly stirring them (the more conventional method), you will end up with large, airy curds and very fluffy scrambled eggs.

FLUFFY SCRAMBLED EGGS

SERVES 4

If you've just fried bacon or happen to have leftover bacon grease, it can be used in place of the butter. If you are unable to serve the eggs immediately, they can be covered with foil and held for up to 5 minutes. Whole, low-fat, or skim milk can be substituted for the half-and-half, but the eggs will not be as creamy.

8	large eggs
¼	cup half-and-half (see note above)
½	teaspoon salt
⅛	teaspoon pepper
1	tablespoon unsalted butter (see note above)

Whisk together the eggs, half-and-half, salt, and pepper. Melt the butter in a large nonstick skillet over medium-high heat, swirling to coat the pan. Add the eggs and cook while gently pushing, lifting, and folding them from one side of the pan to the other until they are nicely clumped, shiny, and wet, about 2 minutes. Remove the cooked eggs from the pan quickly and serve.

Variations

FLUFFY SCRAMBLED EGGS WITH HAM AND SWISS

Before adding the eggs to the skillet, brown 6 ounces chopped deli ham in 1 tablespoon melted butter, about 2 minutes. Transfer the ham to a small bowl and cover to keep warm. Wipe the skillet clean and proceed with the recipe. Just before removing the cooked eggs from the pan, quickly fold in the ham, ½ cup shredded Swiss cheese, and 2 tablespoons chopped fresh parsley or chives.

FLUFFY SCRAMBLED EGGS WITH ONION AND HERBS

Before adding the eggs to the skillet, sauté 1 minced onion in 1 tablespoon melted butter until golden brown, about 5 minutes. Transfer the onion to a small

FOLDING SCRAMBLED EGGS

As the eggs cook, gently push, lift, and fold them from one side of the pan to the other, using a wooden spoon or heat-proof spatula, until large, airy curds have formed.

bowl and cover to keep warm. Wipe the skillet clean and proceed with the recipe. Just before removing the cooked eggs from the pan, quickly fold in the onion and 2 tablespoons of your favorite minced herbs (we like a combination of fresh parsley and thyme).

Family-Sized Denver Omelet

No one wants to be a short-order cook when hosting a brunch. But a large omelet, one that is large enough to feed four, is tough to pull off. The exterior can turn dry and rubbery while the interior remains wet and raw. We wanted to develop one big omelet with the same lacy, browned exterior and soft, tender center as its individual counterpart. Second, we wanted to pack our omelet with the hearty filling of a Denver-style omelet—ham steak, sautéed peppers and onions, and melted Jack cheese.

Our initial tests were disastrous, with runny eggs on top and burned eggs underneath. Obviously, flipping a behemoth, eight-egg omelet was out of the question. Cooking the omelet over low heat was the key to avoiding scorched eggs on the bottom, but we still had to figure out a way to cook the top of the omelet—and heat through the filling and melt the cheese.

DENVER OMELET

People who live in the West usually call this hearty diner staple a Denver omelet, but in the East it's often called a Western omelet. Whatever you call it, this omelet has a filling that is traditionally mixed in with the eggs, a technique carried over from the dish's origins as a sandwich filling between slices of buttered white bread. If you want to avoid the whole Denver versus Western issue, just order "a cowboy with spurs" the next time you're eating out. If the waitress knows her diner lingo, she'll serve your omelet (Denver or Western) with a side of fries.

Throwing the omelet under the broiler was a decent solution; however, we found it easier just to cover the skillet with a tight-fitting lid, thus trapping the steam and cooking the top layer of eggs. This method also partially melted the cheese. But still, we had trouble heating through our filling. We decided that instead of sprinkling the filling over the set eggs, we'd start the omelet with the filling in the pan (minus the cheese); this way we'd ensure a hot filling from the get-go. After sautéing the ham, onions, and peppers (all finely chopped to distribute well throughout the omelet), we poured in the eggs and proceeded as we had earlier, sprinkling half the cheese over the set omelet and covering the skillet to partially melt the cheese. Shaping this supersized omelet was as simple as sliding it halfway out of the pan and then folding it over onto itself—and the residual heat was also enough to finish melting the cheese perfectly. One final note: we found that spreading some butter over the omelet just before serving added rich flavor and moistness.

FAMILY-SIZED DENVER OMELET

SERVES 4

Make sure to chop the filling ingredients finely; if you don't, the eggs won't set properly and the omelet will fall apart.

- 4 tablespoons unsalted butter
- 4 ounces ham steak, trimmed and chopped fine
- ½ red bell pepper, chopped fine (about ½ cup)
- ½ green bell pepper, chopped fine (about ½ cup)
- 1 onion, minced
- 8 large eggs, well beaten
  Salt and pepper
- 1 cup shredded Monterey Jack cheese
  Hot sauce, for serving

1. Melt 1 tablespoon of the butter in a large non-stick skillet over medium-high heat. Add the ham steak and cook until lightly browned, about 3 minutes. Add the peppers and onion and cook until browned around the edges, 6 to 7 minutes.

2. Reduce the heat to medium and add 2 tablespoons more butter. Once the butter melts, pour in the eggs, and season with salt and pepper. Cook, without stirring, until the edges just begin to set, about 5 seconds; then, with a rubber spatula, stir in a circular motion until slightly thickened, 30 to 60 seconds. Using the spatula, pull the cooked edges toward the center of the pan, tilting the pan to one side so that the uncooked egg runs to the edge of the pan. Repeat until the bottom of the omelet is just set but the top is still very runny, about 1 minute.

3. Cover the skillet with a lid, reduce the heat to low, and cook until the top of the omelet is beginning to set but still moist, 3 to 5 minutes. Remove the pan from the heat and sprinkle the omelet with the cheese. Cover and let the pan sit off the heat until the cheese is partially melted, about 1 minute.

4. Tilt the pan and, using the spatula, push half of the omelet onto a serving platter. Tilt the pan so the omelet flips onto itself and forms a half moon. Spread the remaining 1 tablespoon butter on the omelet and let rest for 1 minute before serving with hot sauce.

HOW TO MAKE AN OVERSIZED OMELET

1. The outside rim of an omelet always cooks quickly. To cook the omelet evenly, pull the cooked edges of egg toward the center of the pan and allow raw egg to run to the edges.

2. When the omelet is set on the bottom but still very runny on the top, it's time to cover the skillet and turn the heat down to low.

3. After the top of the omelet begins to set, sprinkle it with the cheese and let the omelet rest off the heat until the cheese has partially melted.

4. After using a rubber spatula to push half of the omelet onto a platter, tilt the skillet so that the omelet folds over onto itself to make the traditional half-moon shape.

Diner-Style Omelets

A typical omelet can make a fine breakfast or light dinner, but diner-style omelets can satisfy the biggest of appetites. Impossibly tall and fluffy and loaded with cheese and other fillings, these omelets are far from their dainty French cousins. But many recipes for these huge omelets turn out flat and flabby eggs. What do short-order cooks know that we don't?

Most omelet recipes call for the eggs to be quickly beaten with a fork or whisk, but a peek behind the counter at the diner revealed a drastically different mixing method: using a milk-shake blender. Many diners use these blenders (or a similar tool) to incorporate air into the eggs until they've tripled in volume, which results in tall and fluffy cooked omelets. Using five eggs (for a hearty omelet that would serve two), we got the eggs to triple in volume in just a few minutes with a mixer, and the resulting omelet cooked up huge and light—but lacking in richness.

Many omelet recipes instruct you to add milk or cream to the whipped eggs for richness and stability. Tasters liked the flavor of cream, but when we added it to the whipped eggs, the cooked omelet lost its fluffiness and height. Combining the cream and eggs before whipping didn't work, either—the mixture refused to increase in volume, as the fat in the cream was making it impossible to whip air into the eggs. We had much better results when we whipped the cream to soft peaks and then folded it into the whipped eggs. The resulting omelet had rich flavor, creamy texture, and that tall and fluffy diner-style height.

Our final task was to find the perfect cooking technique. Since we were using such a large volume of eggs, the bottom of the omelet was overcooking by the time the top was set. Flipping the big mass of egg was messy and dangerous, so we turned to a method we often use when pan-searing meats: start cooking on the stove and finish in the oven. After letting the bottom of the omelet set on the stovetop, we popped the skillet into a preheated oven, and 6 minutes later the omelet came out puffy, fluffy, and cooked to perfection. All we had to do was fold it in half and we had a diner-style omelet sure to satisfy.

FLUFFY DINER-STYLE CHEESE OMELET

SERVES 2

Although this recipe will work with any electric mixer, a hand-held mixer makes quick work of whipping such a small amount of cream. If using a standing mixer in step 1, transfer the whipped cream to a separate bowl, wipe out the mixing bowl, and then beat the eggs in the clean bowl. To make two omelets, double this recipe and cook the omelets simultaneously in two skillets. If you have only one skillet, prepare a double batch of ingredients and set half aside for the second omelet. Be sure to wipe out the skillet between cooking omelets.

3	tablespoons heavy cream, chilled
5	large eggs, room temperature
¼	teaspoon salt
2	tablespoons unsalted butter
½	cup shredded sharp cheddar cheese

1. Adjust an oven rack to the middle position and heat the oven to 400 degrees. With an electric mixer on medium-high speed, beat the cream to soft peaks, about 2 minutes. Set the whipped cream aside. Beat the eggs and salt in a clean bowl on high speed until frothy and the eggs have tripled in volume, about 2 minutes. Gently fold the whipped cream into the eggs.

2. Melt the butter in a 10-inch oven-safe nonstick skillet over medium-low heat, swirling the pan to completely coat the bottom and sides with melted butter. Add the egg mixture and cook until the edges are nearly set, 2 to 3 minutes. Sprinkle with ¼ cup of the cheese and transfer to the oven. Bake until the eggs are set and the edges are beginning to brown, 6 to 8 minutes.

3. Carefully remove the pan from the oven (the handle will be very hot). Sprinkle with the remaining ¼ cup cheese and let sit, covered, until the cheese begins to melt, about 1 minute. Tilt the pan and, using a rubber spatula, push half of the omelet onto a cutting board. Tilt the skillet so that the omelet folds over onto itself to form a half moon. Cut the omelet in half. Serve.

Variations

SAUSAGE AND PEPPER DINER-STYLE OMELET

Cook 4 ounces bulk sausage in a nonstick skillet over medium heat, breaking up the clumps with a wooden spoon, until browned, about 6 minutes. Transfer to a paper towel–lined plate. Add 1 tablespoon unsalted butter, 1 onion, chopped, and ½ red bell pepper, chopped, to the empty skillet and cook until softened, about 10 minutes. Stir in the sausage and season with salt and pepper. Sprinkle half of the filling over the cheese in step 2 and the remaining filling over the remaining cheese in step 3.

LOADED BAKED POTATO DINER-STYLE OMELET

Microwave 1 large Yukon gold potato, peeled and cut into ½-inch pieces, on high power, covered, in a large bowl until just tender, 2 to 5 minutes. Cook 4 slices of chopped bacon in a nonstick skillet over medium heat until crisp, about 8 minutes. Transfer the bacon to a paper towel–lined plate and pour off all but 1 tablespoon bacon fat. Cook the potatoes in the bacon fat until golden brown, about 6 minutes. Transfer the potatoes to a bowl, add the cooked bacon, and stir in 2 thinly sliced scallions. Season with salt and pepper. Sprinkle half of the filling over the cheese in step 2 and the remaining filling over the remaining cheese in step 3.

Maple Sausage and Waffle Casserole

In its simplest form, a breakfast casserole consists of day-old bread soaked in custard (eggs and cream) and then baked until golden and fluffy. Most recipes also include sausage and cheese. The finished dish is so rich you have to let out your belt before breakfast even begins. This recipe should be lighter and—here's the catch—tastier.

After making several over-the-top recipes, we were convinced that the custard was obliterating the other flavors. We could barely taste the sausage and cheese—they added heaviness but not much else. We knew we needed to lighten the custard. Most recipes use in the range of 4 to 8 eggs and 2 to 3 cups of cream. We couldn't do much about the eggs—we found that 6 was the right number—but could we use less cream or maybe a less rich dairy?

To our surprise, tasters actually preferred a casserole made with whole milk to one made with cream—and just 1½ cups. There was still plenty of fat in our working recipe (from the sausage and cheese), but now we could taste those ingredients instead of just the dairy richness of the custard.

We next tested four types of breakfast sausage (sage, hot, maple, and regular). Tasters liked the touch of sweetness added by the maple sausage. As for the cheese, cheddar and Monterey Jack are the standards, but cheddar is far more flavorful and got the thumbs up in the test kitchen.

Up until this point, we had been using white sandwich bread (as most recipes suggest); we wondered if a change might be in order. We tried French and Italian loaves but they were too chewy. Challah, a slightly sweet, egg-rich Jewish bread, was better but still not perfect. Tasters liked its sweet yeasty flavor but not its dense texture.

After scouring the bread aisle for something sweet but not too heavy, we wandered into the frozen food section and found what we were searching for: frozen waffles. Their airy, fluffy texture made the casserole much lighter than when we used challah or even sandwich bread. And the flavor combination of the waffles and the maple sausage was such a hit with tasters that we decided to replace some of the milk in the custard with maple syrup.

MAPLE SAUSAGE AND WAFFLE CASSEROLE

SERVES 6

Depending on their size and shape, you will need 6 to 8 waffles. Belgian-style frozen waffles are too thick for this recipe. To double the recipe, use a 13 by 9-inch baking dish and increase the baking time by 30 to 40 minutes.

6–8	frozen waffles (½ inch thick; see note above)
12	ounces maple breakfast sausage, crumbled
	Unsalted butter for greasing baking dish
1½	cups shredded cheddar cheese
6	large eggs
1¼	cups whole or low-fat milk
¼	cup maple syrup
¼	teaspoon salt
⅛	teaspoon pepper

1. Adjust an oven rack to the middle position and heat the oven to 375 degrees. Arrange the waffles in a single layer on a baking sheet. Bake until crisp, about 10 minutes per side.

2. Brown the sausage in a nonstick skillet over medium heat, breaking it apart with a spoon, 8 to 10 minutes. Drain on a paper towel–lined plate.

3. Butter an 8-inch square baking dish. Add half of the waffles in a single layer. Add half of the sausage and ½ cup of the cheese. Repeat layering the waffles, sausage, and ½ cup more cheese. Whisk the eggs, milk, maple syrup, salt, and pepper in a medium bowl until combined. Pour the egg mixture evenly over the casserole. Cover the baking dish with plastic wrap and place weights on top. Refrigerate the casserole for at least 1 hour or overnight.

4. Adjust an oven rack to the middle position and heat the oven to 325 degrees. Let the casserole stand at room temperature for 20 minutes. Uncover the casserole and sprinkle the remaining ½ cup cheese over the top. Bake until the edges and center are puffed, 45 to 50 minutes. Cool for 5 minutes. Cut into pieces and serve.

SHOPPING WITH THE TEST KITCHEN

Frozen Waffles: Although we typically make our waffles from scratch, the use of store-bought waffles in our Maple Sausage and Waffle Casserole had us wondering which brand was best. We corralled eight brands of frozen waffles ranging from ordinary (Pillsbury Homestyle) to organic (LifeStream HempPlus) and tasted them topped with maple syrup. Eggo Homestyle was the undisputed winner. Tasters praised these waffles for their buttery, eggy flavor and crisp exterior.

TWO WAYS TO WEIGHT A CASSEROLE

A. Press plastic wrap directly onto the surface of the casserole, top with another 8-inch square baking dish, then weight with heavy canned goods.

B. Press plastic wrap directly onto the surface of the casserole, then place two 1-pound boxes of brown sugar on the plastic wrap and top with a cast-iron pan.

Breakfast Popover Casserole

Impossible Pie was popularized back in the 1970s by the folks at Betty Crocker. The idea is to pour a thinned-out biscuit batter (made with Bisquick, milk, and eggs) on top of the filling ingredients in a pie plate; the batter sinks to the bottom of the dish and "impossibly" forms its own crust when baked. (The pies are also known as Impossibly Easy Pies.) During our research, we found almost every variation imaginable, from coconut cream (reportedly the first Impossible Pie) to asparagus to bacon. We were intrigued enough to try several recipes but found them impossibly heavy and dense. The edges were puffed and crisp, however, reminding everyone in the test kitchen of a super-sized popover and making us wonder if a popover batter would yield lighter results than a biscuit batter.

Popovers also seem to do the impossible, as the heat of the oven transforms their humble ingredients—eggs, milk, flour, salt, and butter—into the culinary equivalent of a hot-air balloon. They are crisp and golden brown on the outside, tender and moist inside. Using the test kitchen's standard popover recipe (2 eggs, 1 cup each of milk and flour, and 1 tablespoon of melted butter), we traded the popover pan for a pie plate and started incorporating some sausage and potatoes.

The sausage was easy; tasters preferred ground bulk sausage over diced links. The potatoes needed a bit more attention. Hoping to save time, we tested frozen hash browns, both shredded and diced. Even when precooked and crisped, the shredded hash browns were lost in the batter and didn't contribute anything. Diced hash browns had better texture, but they also had a stale freezer taste. Switching to freshly diced Yukon gold potatoes was a big improvement. We precooked them in the microwave for 3 minutes before browning them quickly in a skillet. To make sure they didn't lose their crispness, we placed them on top of the popover batter.

Things were tasting good, but they still weren't looking quite right: the popover part of the casserole didn't have the dramatic rise we'd expected. Moreover, it was stubbornly sticking to the glass pie plate, and neither more butter nor more oil was helping. We knew that popovers need intense heat to turn the moisture in the batter to steam, which makes them rise and expand. Preheating the oven and the pan maximizes this process. Preheating an empty glass pie plate is not safe, however, so we switched gears and tried a metal springform pan. The hot pan improved the rise and helped with the sticking issue. As an added bonus, we were able to remove the outer ring of the pan to reveal the visual glory of this puffy creation.

POTATO AND SAUSAGE BREAKFAST POPOVER CASSEROLE

SERVES 6

This recipe requires careful timing. Once the batter is prepared and has been set aside to rest, the potatoes can be microwaved while the sausage is cooking. While the potatoes are being pan-fried, the springform pan (with the cooked sausage) should be preheated in the oven.

2	large eggs
1	cup whole milk
	Salt
1	cup all-purpose flour
1	tablespoon unsalted butter, melted
2	scallions, chopped
¾	pound Yukon gold potatoes (about 2), peeled and cut into ¼-inch dice
1	(12-ounce) package bulk sausage meat
2	tablespoons vegetable oil
½	cup grated Parmesan cheese

ENSURING A CLEAN RELEASE

1. Line the bottom of a springform pan with aluminum foil, attach the sides of the pan, and tuck the foil underneath.

2. Coat the sides and bottom with vegetable oil spray.

1. Adjust an oven rack to the upper-middle position and heat the oven to 425 degrees. Line a 9-inch springform pan with nonstick foil sprayed with vegetable oil spray and set aside on a rimmed baking sheet.

2. Whisk the eggs, milk, and ½ teaspoon salt in a bowl until well combined. Stir in the flour until just incorporated—the mixture will still be a bit lumpy. Whisk in the butter until the batter is smooth. Stir in the scallions and set the batter aside while preparing the filling.

3. Toss the potatoes with 1 tablespoon water in a large microwave-safe bowl. Cover with plastic wrap, cut vent holes in the plastic, and microwave on high power until the potatoes just begin to soften, 3 to 4 minutes. Meanwhile, cook the sausage in a large nonstick skillet over medium heat, breaking up the clumps, until the meat has lost most of its pink color, about 4 minutes. Using a slotted spoon, spread the sausage evenly over the bottom of the prepared springform pan.

4. Heat the oil in the skillet with the sausage fat over medium-high heat until shimmering. Add the potatoes and ¼ teaspoon salt and cook until the potatoes are golden and crisp, 8 to 10 minutes. Drain the potatoes on paper towels.

5. While the potatoes are cooking, place the spring-form pan with the sausage in the oven for 10 minutes. Remove the pan from the oven and, working quickly, sprinkle ¼ cup of the cheese over the sausage and pour the batter evenly over the filling. Scatter the potatoes on the top and sprinkle with the remaining ¼ cup cheese. Bake until puffed and golden, 25 to 30 minutes. Remove the pan from the oven, run a knife around the edges of the pan, and let cool for 5 minutes. Release the outer ring and, using a spatula, transfer the casserole to a serving plate. Serve.

Corned Beef Hash

Corned beef hash is not a breakfast for those who fear fat or like to start the day with yogurt and wheat germ. By its very nature, hash is a hearty, stick-to-your-ribs meal. Legends abound as to the origins of fried meat and potato hash. "Hash house" was a colloquial term in the late nineteenth century for any cheap eating establishment—hash being a fry-up of questionable meat.

Corned beef hash, in particular, can be traced back to New England ingenuity and frugality. What was served as boiled dinner the night before was recycled as hash the next morning. All the leftovers—meat, potatoes, carrots, and sometimes cabbage—would be fried in a skillet and capped with an egg. This being a dish of leftovers, we found traditional recipes to be few and far between, as if corned beef hash were a commonsense dish, unworthy of a recipe. And the recipes we did find produced starchy, one-dimensional hash that was light on flavor. Knowing most people do not have leftovers from a boiled dinner sitting in their refrigerator, we set out to create a flavorful hash with fresh ingredients that was easy to prepare.

Meat and potatoes are the heart and soul of this dish—everything else is just seasoning. Leftover beef from a boiled dinner is ideal, but we found that deli-style corned beef can be just as satisfying. Mincing the beef keeps it tender in the hash.

Potatoes were an easy choice. Texture being foremost, we knew we wanted starchy potatoes that would retain some character but that would soften and crumble about the edges to bind the hash together. Russets were our top choice.

Prior to being combined with the beef, the potatoes must be parboiled. To echo the flavors of the corned beef, we added a couple of bay leaves and a bit of salt to the cooking water and added the diced potatoes. About 4 minutes of cooking after the potatoes had come to a boil yielded perfect potatoes—soft but not falling apart.

As for other vegetables, tasters quickly ruled out anything but onions, which added characteristic body and roundness that supported the meat and potatoes rather than detracting from it. Along with the onions, we chose garlic and thyme to flavor the hash. Garlic sharpened the dish and a minimum of thyme added an earthiness that paired well with the beef.

Although the potatoes loosely bound this mixture, most recipes call for either stock or cream to hold the ingredients more firmly together. We tested both and preferred the richness of the cream. A little hot sauce added with the cream brought some spice to the dish.

Tasters agreed that the eggs served with hash need to be just barely set, so that the yolks break and moisten the potatoes. Although poaching is the easiest technique for preserving a lightly cooked yolk, it can be something of a hassle. We found that we could "poach" the eggs in the same pan as the hash by nestling the eggs into indentations in the hash, covering the pan, and cooking them over low heat. The results were perfect: runny yolks with the eggs conveniently set in the hash and ready to be served.

CORNED BEEF HASH

SERVES 4

A well-seasoned cast-iron skillet is traditional for this recipe, but we prefer a 12-inch nonstick skillet. The nonstick surface leaves little chance of anything sticking and burning. Our favorite tool for flipping the hash is a flat wooden spatula, although a stiff plastic spatula will suffice. We like our hash served with ketchup.

2	pounds russet potatoes, peeled and cut into ½-inch dice
½	teaspoon salt
2	bay leaves
4	slices bacon, diced
1	onion, diced
2	garlic cloves, minced
½	teaspoon minced fresh thyme
1	pound corned beef, minced (pieces should be ¼ inch or smaller)
½	cup heavy cream
¼	teaspoon hot sauce
4	large eggs
	Salt and pepper

1. Bring the potatoes, 5 cups of water, salt, and bay leaves to a boil in a medium saucepan over medium-high heat. Cook the potatoes for 4 minutes, then drain and set the potatoes aside.

2. Place the bacon in a large nonstick skillet over medium-high heat and cook until the fat is partially rendered, about 2 minutes. Add the onion and cook, stirring occasionally, until softened and browned at the edges, about 8 minutes. Add the garlic and thyme and cook until fragrant, 30 seconds. Add the corned beef and stir until thoroughly combined with the onion mixture. Mix in the potatoes and lightly pack the mixture into the pan with a spatula. Reduce the heat to medium and pour the heavy cream and hot sauce evenly over the hash.

Cook undisturbed for 4 minutes, then, with the spatula, invert the hash, a portion at a time, and fold the browned bits back into the hash. Lightly pack the hash into the pan. Repeat the process every minute or two until the potatoes are thoroughly cooked, about 8 minutes longer.

3. Make four equally spaced indentations (each measuring about 2 inches across) on the surface of the hash. Crack one egg into each indentation and sprinkle the egg with salt and pepper. Reduce the heat to medium-low, cover the pan, and cook until the eggs are just set, about 6 minutes. Cut the hash into four wedges, each wedge containing one egg, and serve immediately.

Biscuits and Gravy

Unless you grew up south of the Mason-Dixon Line, a tangy biscuit smothered with a sausage-studded white cream gravy might sound like an odd way to start the day. But after one bite of this Southern specialty, you'll be hooked.

We began researching our ideal version of this hearty breakfast by digging up some biscuit recipes. Identifying the right biscuit for the job was as simple as baking up a batch of each. Flaky breakfast biscuits might be great with butter and jam, but they didn't properly soak up the gravy. Crumbly cream biscuits were too rich and dense for a gravy with similar characteristics. Fluffy buttermilk biscuits, however, provided a substantial tang that complemented the gravy, and they were sturdy enough to absorb some gravy without turning to mush.

We wanted big biscuits—biscuits and gravy is not a dainty meal—so we upped the flour from the standard 2 cups to 3 cups, which allowed us to bake eight big, 3-inch biscuits. To ensure a sturdy, tender texture and buttery flavor, we used a 2-to-1 ratio of butter to shortening—the butter provided the flavor and the shortening made the biscuits tender. We found that briefly kneading the dough yielded biscuits with better structure. We also increased the baking powder and baking soda to provide maximum lift in the oven. Now we had sturdy, tender, and buttery biscuits that were perfect for the meaty gravy.

Traditional Southern cream gravy recipes cook a pound of bulk pork sausage and then sprinkle it with flour, which combines with the sausage fat to form a thickening roux. Dairy is added (tasters much preferred milk to half-and-half and cream, which were too heavy), and the gravy is brought to a simmer. One recurring problem was the quantity of flour: too little flour and the gravy was watery, but too much and it was pasty. We arrived at ¼ cup of flour to 3 cups of milk for a perfect, creamy texture. Bumping up the amount of sausage to 1½ pounds ensured plenty of meat in every bite.

With all these rich ingredients, the gravy was a little bland. We discovered that we could augment the sausage's flavor by adding ground fennel and sage, both seasonings typically found in pork sausage. And a generous dose of pepper gave the gravy some serious heat. Knife and fork in hand, tasters dug in to a new breakfast favorite.

BISCUITS AND SAUSAGE GRAVY

SERVES 8

If you don't have buttermilk on hand, whisk 1 tablespoon fresh lemon juice into 1¼ cups milk and let it stand until slightly thickened, about 10 minutes.

BISCUITS

3	cups all-purpose flour
1	tablespoon sugar
1	tablespoon baking powder
½	teaspoon baking soda
1	teaspoon salt
8	tablespoons (1 stick) unsalted butter, cut into ½-inch pieces and chilled
4	tablespoons vegetable shortening, cut into ½-inch pieces and chilled
1¼	cups buttermilk (see note above)

SAUSAGE GRAVY

¼	cup all-purpose flour
1	teaspoon ground fennel
1	teaspoon ground sage
1½	teaspoons pepper
1½	pounds bulk pork sausage
3	cups whole milk
	Salt

1. FOR THE BISCUITS: Adjust an oven rack to the middle position and heat the oven to 450 degrees. Line a baking sheet with parchment paper. Pulse the flour, sugar, baking powder, baking soda, salt, butter, and shortening in a food processor until the mixture resembles coarse meal. Transfer to a large bowl. Stir in the buttermilk until combined.

2. On a lightly floured surface, knead the dough until smooth, 8 to 10 kneads. Pat the dough into a 9-inch circle, about ¾ inch thick. Using a 3-inch biscuit cutter dipped in flour, cut out rounds of dough and arrange on the prepared baking sheet. Gather the remaining dough, pat into a ¾-inch-thick circle, and cut out the remaining biscuits. (You should have 8 biscuits in total.)

3. Bake until the biscuits begin to rise, about 5 minutes, then rotate the pan and reduce the oven temperature to 400 degrees. Bake until golden brown, 12 to 15 minutes. Transfer to a wire rack and let cool. (The biscuits can be stored in a zipper-lock plastic bag for up to 2 days.)

4. FOR THE SAUSAGE GRAVY: Combine the flour, fennel, sage, and pepper in a small bowl. Cook the sausage in a large nonstick skillet over medium heat, breaking up the meat with a wooden spoon, until no longer pink, about 8 minutes. Sprinkle the flour mixture over the sausage and cook, stirring constantly, until the flour has been absorbed, about 1 minute. Slowly stir in the milk and simmer until the sauce has thickened, about 5 minutes. Season with salt to taste. Serve over split biscuits.

Home Fries

Any decent grill cook can turn a pile of cubed potatoes into perfectly crisp, impeccably seasoned home-fried potatoes—or so it would seem. The well-seasoned flat griddle at the diner certainly helps, but the real secret is precooking the potatoes. Many restaurants use leftover roasted or boiled potatoes to make their home fries. But who has precooked potatoes at home? Skip this step and you'll end up with a greasy mound of crunchy potatoes. So why on earth are they called home fries when they are so impractical to make at home?

Because no one wants to get up at the crack of dawn to boil or roast potatoes, we turned to the quickest cooker in the kitchen: the microwave. In the past we've microwaved diced potatoes with a bit of oil, but in this application we found the flavor of the oil distracting. A touch of butter added a rich, nutty taste to the slightly sweet potatoes, and after just 5 minutes in the microwave the potatoes were partially cooked and ready for the skillet.

We decided to use a nonstick skillet so that we could "home-fry" the potatoes without using excess butter. Unfortunately, the potatoes weren't developing the thick crust we wanted. We tried turning the heat up and down, but neither helped much. To replicate the heavy cast-iron tool used in many diners to press the potatoes flat against the griddle, we slid our heaviest pot (a Dutch oven) on top of the potatoes as they cooked. The weight of the Dutch oven kept the potatoes in constant contact with the hot skillet, producing a thick and even crust—but what a mess.

Setting the Dutch oven aside, we tried packing the potatoes down with a spatula (to approximate the effect of the Dutch oven) and let them cook undisturbed. After 5 minutes the potatoes were beginning to develop a golden brown crust, so we tossed them around, packed them down again, and waited some more. After we repeated this process a few more times, the potatoes were evenly browned and extra-crusty.

The last step was flavoring. Sautéed onion was a must, but when the onions were cooked with the potatoes, their moisture caused the home fries to lose their cherished crust. To keep the potatoes crispy, we browned the onions separately and added them to the pan just before the potatoes were finished. Taking a trick from a local diner, we tried sprinkling the home fries with a bit of garlic salt just before serving. Its deep, savory flavor nicely balanced the sweetness of the onion and potatoes. Finally, we had hassle-free home fries worthy of their name.

SHORT-ORDER HOME FRIES

SERVES 4

Although we prefer the sweetness of Yukon gold potatoes, other medium-starch or waxy potatoes, such as all-purpose or red-skinned potatoes, can be substituted. If you want to spice things up, add a pinch of cayenne pepper.

- 1½ pounds Yukon gold potatoes (4 medium), scrubbed and cut into ¾-inch pieces (see note above)
- 4 tablespoons unsalted butter
- 1 onion, minced
- ½ teaspoon garlic salt
- ½ teaspoon salt
  Pepper

1. Arrange the potatoes in a large microwave-safe bowl, top with 1 tablespoon of the butter, and cover

tightly with plastic wrap. Microwave on high until the edges of the potatoes begin to soften, 5 to 7 minutes, shaking the bowl (without removing the plastic wrap) to redistribute the potatoes halfway through cooking.

2. Meanwhile, melt 1 tablespoon more butter in a large nonstick skillet over medium heat. Add the onion and cook until softened and golden brown, about 8 minutes. Transfer to a small bowl.

3. Melt the remaining 2 tablespoons butter in the now-empty skillet over medium heat. Add the potatoes and pack down with a spatula. Cook, without moving, until the underside of the potatoes is brown, 5 to 7 minutes. Turn the potatoes, pack down again, and continue to cook until well browned and crisp, 5 to 7 minutes. Reduce the heat to medium-low and continue cooking, stirring the potatoes every few minutes, until crusty, 9 to 12 minutes. Stir in the onion, garlic salt, salt, and pepper to taste. Serve.

Variations
GREEK DINER–STYLE HOME FRIES
Add 2 minced garlic cloves, 1 tablespoon fresh lemon juice, and ½ teaspoon dried oregano to the potatoes along with the onion in step 3. Omit the garlic salt.

HOME FRIES WITH FRESH HERBS
In step 3, add 1 teaspoon each chopped fresh basil, parsley, thyme, and tarragon along with the onion.

Oven-Fried Bacon

Many home cooks now use the microwave to cook bacon to cut down on the mess of stovetop frying. In restaurants, many chefs "fry" bacon in the oven, not only to cut down on the mess, but also to cook a large quantity of bacon at once. We decided to try both of these methods to find out which could stand up to the crisp, evenly cooked results of stovetop frying, minus the mess.

The microwave would seem to have the apparent advantage of ease—stick the pieces in and forget about them—but this turned out not to be the case. The bacon was still raw at 90 seconds; at 2 minutes it was medium-well-done in most spots but still uneven; but by 2 minutes and 30 seconds the strips of bacon were hard and flat and definitely overcooked. The finished product didn't warrant the investment of time it would take to figure out the perfect number of seconds. Microwaved bacon is not crisp; it is an unappetizing pinkish gray in color even when well-done, and it lacks flavor.

Moving on to oven-frying, we tried cooking three strips of bacon in a preheated 400-degree oven on a 12 by 9-inch rimmed baking sheet that would contain the grease. The bacon was medium-well-done after 9 to 10 minutes and crispy after 11 to 12 minutes. The texture was more like a seared piece of meat than a brittle cracker, the color was that nice brick red, and all of the flavors were just as bright and clear as when the bacon was pan-fried. And the oven-fried strips of bacon were more consistently cooked throughout, showing no raw spots and requiring no turning or flipping during cooking (which is a must with pan-frying). Because the heat hits the strip from all sides, there is no reason for the bacon strips to curl in one direction or another, and when the strips do curl, the ruffled edges cook as quickly as the flat areas.

Our last test was to try twelve strips of bacon—a pretty full tray—in a preheated oven. This test was also quite successful. The pieces cooked consistently, the only difference being between those in the back and those in the front of the oven; we corrected for this by rotating the tray once from front to back during cooking. That was about the limit of our contact with the hot grease. At last, crisp bacon and easy cleanup.

OVEN-FRIED BACON

SERVES 4 TO 6

Use a large rimmed baking sheet that is shallow enough to promote browning, yet tall enough (at least ¾ inch in height) to contain the rendered bacon fat. If cooking more than one tray of bacon, exchange their oven positions once about halfway through the cooking process.

12 slices bacon, thin- or thick-cut

Adjust an oven rack to the middle position and heat the oven to 400 degrees. Arrange the bacon slices in a large, rimmed baking sheet or other shallow baking pan. Roast until the fat begins to render, 5 to 6 minutes; rotate the pan from front to back. Continue roasting until the bacon is crisp and brown, 5 to 6 minutes longer for thin-sliced bacon, 8 to 10 minutes for thick-cut. Transfer with tongs to a paper towel–lined plate, drain, and serve.

SHOPPING WITH THE TEST KITCHEN

Orange Juice: So-called super-premium orange juices cost nearly twice as much as ordinary not-from-concentrate brands. Are they worth it?

To find out, we tasted six nationally available brands of orange juice alongside freshly squeezed juice made from oranges in our test kitchen. Much to our surprise, the answer is no, with one notable exception—our winner, Natalie's Orchid Island Gourmet Pasteurized Orange Juice ($4.99 for 64-ounce jug). Tasters praised the Natalie's brand for a fresh taste that was just a notch below the true fresh-squeezed juice we included in the lineup. The even bigger surprise? Everyday dairy-section Tropicana Pure Premium 100% Pure and Natural Orange Juice with Some Pulp ($3.99 for 64-ounce carton) came in second, beating out juices twice its price, as well as its own fancier sister brand, Tropicana Pure Valencia. Tropicana got high marks not for tasting particularly fresh, but for its overall good flavor.

Fruit Salads

To us, a bowl of chopped fruit isn't elevated to fruit salad status until it's dressed with a sugar syrup. Sugar syrups, also called simple syrups, can be made in various concentrations, but the most common ratio is 2 parts water to 1 part sugar; the mixture is cooked over low heat to dissolve the sugar, then chilled for use in cocktails, desserts, and, yes, fruit salads. A moderate amount of simple syrup sweetens and moistens cut fruit, but we saw it as something more—a way to add big flavor to an otherwise plain fruit salad.

A classic way to infuse simple syrup with flavor is to add potent seasonings like vanilla, ginger, mint, or even jalapeños as the syrup cooks. Incorporating these ingredients did perk things up a bit, but we wanted even more flavor.

Our cutting board was getting messy with juice and pulp as we chopped our way through pounds of fruit, and we wondered if there was a way to incorporate this juice into our simple syrup. We tried mashing some of the juicier fruits (watermelon, peaches, and cantaloupe) with a splash of citrus in the syrups as they cooked. After straining and cooling the syrups, we poured them over the cut fruit and were amazed at how much flavor they added. These fruit salads are still simple but no longer plain.

PEACH, MANGO, AND BANANA SALAD

SERVES 4 TO 6

Avoid overly ripe bananas; they will break down and make the salad stodgy.

3	ripe peaches, pitted and chopped
2	tablespoons fresh lime juice
2	tablespoons water
2	tablespoons brown sugar
¼	teaspoon vanilla extract
2	mangos, peeled, pitted, and chopped
2	bananas, peeled and sliced into ½-inch rounds

1. Combine ¼ cup of the chopped peaches, lime juice, water, sugar, and vanilla in a saucepan and mash with a potato masher until the peaches break down. Bring to a simmer over medium heat and cook until the sugar dissolves, about 2 minutes. Cool to room temperature and then strain, reserving the juices.

2. Toss the mangos, bananas, remaining peaches, and reserved fruit juice in a large bowl. Let sit for 5 minutes. Serve.

WATERMELON, KIWI, AND STRAWBERRY SALAD

SERVES 4 TO 6

Seedless watermelon works best for this recipe. You will need about a quarter of a large watermelon.

3¼	cups chopped watermelon (see note above)
2	tablespoons water
2	tablespoons honey
1	teaspoon red wine vinegar
1	teaspoon grated fresh ginger
2	ripe kiwis, peeled, halved lengthwise, and sliced thin
1	quart strawberries, hulled and quartered

1. Combine ¼ cup of the chopped watermelon, water, honey, vinegar, and ginger in a saucepan and mash with a potato masher until the watermelon breaks down. Bring to a simmer over medium heat and cook until the honey dissolves, about 2 minutes. Cool to room temperature and then strain, reserving the juices.

2. Toss the kiwis, strawberries, remaining 3 cups watermelon, and reserved fruit juice in a large bowl. Let sit for 5 minutes. Serve.

HONEYDEW, RASPBERRY, AND NECTARINE SALAD

SERVES 4 TO 6

To prevent the raspberries from breaking down, toss the salad gently in step 2.

3¼	cups chopped honeydew melon
2	tablespoons fresh lemon juice
2	tablespoons water
2	tablespoons sugar
4	tablespoons finely chopped fresh mint
2	nectarines, pitted and chopped
1	pint fresh raspberries

1. Combine ¼ cup of the chopped honeydew, lemon juice, water, sugar, and 2 tablespoons of the mint in a saucepan and mash with a potato masher until the honeydew breaks down. Bring to a simmer over medium heat and cook until the sugar dissolves, about 2 minutes. Cool to room temperature and then strain, reserving the juices.

2. Toss the nectarines, raspberries, remaining 3 cups honeydew, remaining 2 tablespoons mint, and reserved fruit juice in a large bowl. Let sit for 5 minutes. Serve.

BOOSTING FRUIT FLAVOR

In many fruit salad recipes the cut fruit is tossed with a simple syrup (water and sugar), infused with spices and herbs. For an extra flavor boost we mashed some of the fruit into the syrup.

CHAPTER SEVEN

Morning and Teatime Treats

MORNING AND TEATIME TREATS

Blueberry Streusel Muffins

You'd think it would be easy to find plenty of great recipes for something as popular as blueberry muffins. But the muffins made from most recipes we've found bake up either dry or spongy, with an ugly blue (or even green!) color and weak blueberry flavor. A streusel topping usually adds to the trouble by being tough, sandy, or so heavy it sinks. We wanted to create a tender, cakey muffin bursting with berries and crowned with chewy nuggets of butter and sugar.

The first step was to create a tender muffin sturdy enough to support the streusel. The test kitchen's blueberry muffin recipe is great, but the use of sour cream makes the muffins too soft and delicate to support streusel. We tried replacing the sour cream with heavy cream, yogurt, milk, and buttermilk and found that buttermilk created muffins with a sturdy-but-light texture.

Our initial testing proved that dealing with the blueberries wasn't as easy as it might seem. Fresh berries are often bland and usually pretty large and juicy, and they made our muffins soggy. Frozen berries are smaller and more flavorful, but they weren't perfect, either. When allowed to thaw—which happened quickly—they stained the batter an unappealing blue. Keeping the berries frozen until the last second helped, and tossing them with flour before adding them to the batter prevented the berries from sinking to the bottom of the muffins.

Although streusel toppings can include oats, nuts, or dried fruit, tasters felt these additions were distracting and preferred a simple mixture of flour, butter, dark brown sugar (for butterscotch flavor), granulated sugar, and cinnamon. Unlike an ultra tender crumb topping, streusel should have a slight chew. Since streusel can be made with cold, room-temperature, or melted butter, we made a batch using each. The streusels made with cold and room-temperature butter baked into dry, powdery crumbs. The streusel made with melted butter was moist enough to clump in the hand, which allowed us to break it into perfect nuggets that provided a nice contrast to the muffins.

BLUEBERRY STREUSEL MUFFINS

MAKES 12 MUFFINS

To prevent a streaky batter, leave the blueberries in the freezer until the last possible moment. Wyman's brand frozen wild blueberries are our first choice, but an equal amount of fresh blueberries may be substituted.

STREUSEL

1¼	cups all-purpose flour
⅓	cup packed dark brown sugar
⅓	cup granulated sugar
½	teaspoon ground cinnamon
	Pinch salt
7	tablespoons unsalted butter, melted

MUFFINS

1	large egg
1	teaspoon vanilla extract
1	cup granulated sugar
1	teaspoon grated fresh lemon zest
4	tablespoons unsalted butter, melted and cooled slightly
½	cup buttermilk
2	cups all-purpose flour
1	tablespoon baking powder
½	teaspoon salt
1½	cups frozen blueberries (see note above)

1. FOR THE STREUSEL: Combine the flour, sugars, cinnamon, and salt in a bowl. Drizzle with the melted butter and toss with a fork until evenly moistened and the mixture forms large chunks with some pea-sized pieces throughout.

2. FOR THE MUFFINS: Adjust an oven rack to the middle position and heat the oven to 375 degrees. Grease and flour a 12-cup muffin tin. Whisk the egg in a medium bowl until pale and evenly combined, about 30 seconds. Add the vanilla, sugar, and zest and whisk vigorously until thick, about 30 seconds. Slowly whisk in the melted butter; add the buttermilk and whisk until combined.

3. Reserve 1 tablespoon of the flour. Whisk together the remaining flour, baking powder, and salt in a large bowl. Using a rubber spatula, gently fold in the egg mixture until just combined. Toss the blueberries with the reserved flour and fold into the batter until just combined.

4. Divide the batter among the muffin cups and top with the streusel. Bake until light golden brown and a toothpick inserted into the center of each muffin comes out with a few crumbs attached, 22 to 28 minutes, rotating the pan halfway through baking. Cool the muffins in the pan for 10 minutes, then carefully transfer the muffins to a wire rack to cool completely. Serve. (The muffins can be stored in an airtight container at room temperature for up to 3 days.)

SHOPPING WITH THE TEST KITCHEN

Kitchen Timers: In the test kitchen, timing is everything. To that end, we tested ten new models designed to handle multitask timing. We were looking for timers with a range of at least 10 hours (for longer braises, brines, and barbecues) that could continue counting after the alarm and could display two times simultaneously. The compact, easy-to-use Polder Dual Timer/Stopwatch ($19.99) impressed us the most (the previous test-kitchen favorite was the Polder Electronic Clock, Timer, and Stopwatch, at $5 less). The Taylor Two Event Big Digit Timer/Clock ($10.99) offers the same functions but isn't so easy to use. At half the price, it's our choice for best buy.

Coffee-Cake Muffins

With a swirl of cinnamon enriching tender cake and a topping of sweet, nutty streusel, a big slice of coffee cake is pretty hard to beat. Compacting all that goodness into muffin form seems like a great idea, but most of the coffee-cake muffins we've tried resemble dry, cottony yellow cupcakes, with little or no cinnamon filling. To hide this misfortune, some recipes simply have you pack mounds of dry, gritty streusel on top, making it seem as if the muffins had been dropped at the beach. We wanted to make a coffee-cake muffin as good as a regular coffee cake, with the option of taking it to go.

Our first objective was to figure out the cake. Most recipes we found were based on cupcake or muffin batters, and the resulting muffins were too fluffy and not as dense and moist as true coffee cake. A few other recipes produced rich coffee-cake batters that were packed with as much as 1½ sticks of butter, 4 eggs, and 1 cup of sour cream. These muffins had good flavor but were too dense and flat. To reduce the density while keeping the richness, we cut back to 2 eggs and 5 tablespoons of butter. But when we tried to cut back on the sour cream, the muffins lost their moist, velvety appeal—the full cup of sour cream would stay.

For the streusel topping, many recipes include a mixture of nuts (pecans were tasters' favorite), sugar, and cinnamon, but this produced the sandy topping we were trying to avoid. Cutting a little butter and flour into the mixture added moisture and allowed the topping to clump and stay put on top of the muffins. Replacing some of the granulated sugar with brown sugar gave the topping deeper flavor.

Hoping that the streusel topping could double as the cinnamon filling, we filled the muffin cups halfway, sprinkled on some of the topping mixture, and added more batter. Unfortunately, the nuts steamed inside the muffins and made everything mushy. This was easily fixed—we pulsed the sugars, cinnamon, butter, and flour (without the nuts) in the food processor and pulled some out to use as the filling. We added pecans to the remaining mixture, pulsed again, and used that as the perfect streusel topping to our sweet, rich coffee-cake muffins.

COFFEE-CAKE MUFFINS

MAKES 12 MUFFINS

Be sure to use muffin-tin liners for this recipe or the cinnamon filling will stick to the pan.

STREUSEL

8	tablespoons granulated sugar
⅓	cup packed light brown sugar
⅓	cup all-purpose flour
1	tablespoon ground cinnamon
4	tablespoons cold unsalted butter, cut into ½-inch pieces
½	cup pecans

MUFFINS

2	large eggs
1	cup sour cream
1½	teaspoons vanilla extract
1¾	cups all-purpose flour
½	cup granulated sugar
1	tablespoon baking powder
¼	teaspoon salt
5	tablespoons unsalted butter, cut into chunks and softened

1. FOR THE STREUSEL: Pulse 5 tablespoons of the granulated sugar, brown sugar, flour, cinnamon, and butter in a food processor until just combined. Reserve ¾ cup of the sugar mixture for the cinnamon filling. Add the pecans and the remaining 3 tablespoons granulated sugar to the food processor with the remaining sugar mixture and pulse until

KEEPING STREUSEL IN PLACE

Place a 2¾-inch cookie cutter over each muffin cup. Sprinkle the streusel topping inside the cookie cutter, lift off the cutter, and then gently pat the streusel into the batter with your fingers.

the nuts are coarsely ground. Transfer to a bowl and set aside for the streusel topping. Do not wash the food processor.

2. FOR THE MUFFINS: Adjust an oven rack to the middle position and heat the oven to 375 degrees. Grease a muffin tin and line it with paper liners. Whisk together the eggs, sour cream, and vanilla in a bowl. Pulse the flour, sugar, baking powder, salt, and butter in the food processor until the mixture resembles wet sand. Transfer to a large bowl. Using a rubber spatula, gradually fold in the egg mixture until just combined. Place 1 tablespoon batter in each muffin cup and top with 1 tablespoon cinnamon filling. Using the back of a spoon, press the cinnamon filling lightly into the batter, then top with the remaining batter. Sprinkle the streusel topping evenly over the batter.

3. Bake until light golden brown and a toothpick inserted into the center of each muffin comes out with a few crumbs attached, 22 to 28 minutes, rotating the pan halfway through baking. Cool the muffins in the pan for 10 minutes, then carefully transfer the muffins to a wire rack to cool completely. Serve. (The muffins can be stored in an airtight container at room temperature for up to 3 days.)

Corn Muffins

Corn muffins, especially those found in coffee-houses, often turn out too coarse, crumbly, and dry. We wanted a mildly sweet muffin with a moist and tender crumb—one that didn't require gulps of coffee or tea to get it down.

Some recipes we came across in our research suggest mixing the cornmeal with a hot liquid before adding it to the batter. This method allows the cornmeal to absorb the liquid while the grain expands and softens. The other wet ingredients are then added to the mush and combined with the dry ingredients. This seemed like a good way to make a moister muffin—or so we thought. Unfortunately, testers found these muffins too dense and strong-tasting, more like cornbread than corn muffins, which should be lighter.

We next made a list of the ingredients that might help produce a moist muffin: butter, milk, buttermilk, sour cream, and yogurt. We tried them all, using different amounts of each. Our initial thought was "butter, butter, butter," with enough milk added to hit the right consistency. When tested, however, these muffins were lacking in moisture. What finally produced a superior muffin was sour cream paired with butter and milk. These muffins were rich, light, moist, and tender—and they beat the coffee-shop variety by a country mile.

CORN MUFFINS

MAKES 12 MUFFINS

Try serving these muffins with butter and honey or jam.

2	cups all-purpose flour
1	cup yellow cornmeal
1½	teaspoons baking powder
1	teaspoon baking soda
½	teaspoon salt
¾	cup sour cream
¾	cup sugar
½	cup whole milk
8	tablespoons (1 stick) unsalted butter, melted and cooled
2	large eggs, lightly beaten

1. Adjust an oven rack to the middle position and heat the oven to 400 degrees. Grease a 12-cup muffin tin.

2. Whisk the flour, cornmeal, baking powder, baking soda, and salt together in a large bowl. In a medium bowl, whisk the sour cream, sugar, milk, melted butter, and eggs together until smooth. Using a rubber spatula, gently fold the sour cream mixture into the flour mixture until just combined.

3. Divide the batter among the muffin cups. Bake until golden brown and a toothpick inserted into the center of each muffin comes out with a few crumbs attached, 15 to 20 minutes, rotating the pan halfway through baking. Cool the muffins in the pan for 10 minutes, then carefully transfer the muffins to a wire rack to cool completely. Serve. (The muffins can be stored in an airtight container at room temperature for up to 3 days.)

TEST KITCHEN SHORTCUT

Applying Vegetable Oil Spray Neatly: Using vegetable oil spray to grease a muffin tin (or other baking pan) is a quick and convenient way to ensure a clean release. But unless you spray very carefully, some of the spray could end up on a counter, a cabinet, or the kitchen floor. To contain the mess, open the dishwasher door, place the muffin tin on the door, and spray away. Any excess or overspray will be cleaned off the door the next time you run the dishwasher.

Bran Muffins

The idea of using bran cereal to make muffins is nothing new. One of the first such recipes appeared on packages of Kellogg's Krumbled Bran in 1916, a time when mass-marketed bran cereals were a novel concept. Today, store shelves are chockablock with bran-based cereals that come in various shapes and sizes, fashioned as twigs, flakes, and granules. Most have accompanying bran muffin recipes.

In the past we have made bran muffins with unprocessed wheat bran from the natural foods store. But these muffins require a special shopping trip. Could a commercial cereal sold at the super-market really deliver good results? If so, which one?

After trying a number of back-of-the-box reci-pes, we admit we found a few muffins with decent bran flavor, but each had issues. The muffins from the recipes we tested using flakes came out flavorless and looked like springy cupcakes instead of the rus-tic muffins we had in mind. The muffins made with granules were also flavorless, and their texture was dense and pasty. The twigs, which were the best of the bunch, provided a deep bran flavor, but getting them to bend to our will was another matter. They weren't fully dissolving into the batter and were even sticking out of the tops of the baked muffins.

Presoaking the twigs in the milk (as recom-mended in most recipes) didn't really work and made the muffins as dense as hockey pucks. The cereal was soaking up all the moisture, which dried out the batter. We decided to switch gears. For our next test we tried grinding the twigs to a powder in a food processor before adding them to the batter. Much better—the muffins had an even crumb, but they were a bit heavy. A compromise was in order. We pulverized half of the cereal and kept the other half whole. When we combined the pulverized and intact bran and added them to the batter, they soft-ened perfectly in only 5 minutes. We finally had the chewy, rustic texture we wanted.

To reinforce the flavor of the bran, we found that mixing some whole-wheat flour with the all-purpose flour worked well, as did replacing the granulated sugar with brown sugar and increasing the amount of molasses. After complaints that the raisins didn't soften enough during baking, we plumped them in the microwave with a little water. We had finally found a way to use a supermarket cereal to create a moist, tender muffin with big bran flavor.

BRAN MUFFINS

MAKES 12 MUFFINS

The test kitchen prefers Kellogg's All-Bran Original cereal in this recipe. Dried cranberries or dried cher-ries may be substituted for the raisins.

1	cup raisins (see note above)
1	teaspoon water
2¼	cups All-Bran Original cereal
⅔	cup packed light brown sugar
3	tablespoons light molasses
1	large egg, lightly beaten
1	large egg yolk
1	teaspoon vanilla extract
6	tablespoons unsalted butter, melted and cooled
1¾	cups plain whole-milk or low-fat yogurt
1¼	cups all-purpose flour
½	cup whole-wheat flour
2	teaspoons baking soda
½	teaspoon salt

1. Adjust an oven rack to the middle position and heat the oven to 400 degrees. Grease a 12-cup muffin tin.

2. Combine the raisins and water in a small microwave-safe bowl and cover tightly with plastic wrap. Poke several small steam vents in the plastic wrap and microwave on high power for 30 seconds. Let stand, covered, until the raisins are softened and plump, about 5 minutes. Transfer the raisins to a paper towel–lined plate; set aside to cool.

3. Process half of the bran cereal in a food processor until finely ground, about 1 minute; set aside. In a medium bowl, whisk together the sugar, molasses, whole egg, egg yolk, and vanilla until the mixture is thick and uniform. Whisk in the melted butter, yogurt, and processed and unprocessed bran cereal to combine. Let the mixture rest until the cereal is evenly moistened (there will still be some small lumps), about 5 minutes.

4. Whisk the flours, baking soda, and salt together in a large bowl. Using a rubber spatula, gently fold the cereal mixture into the flour mixture until just combined. Fold in the cooled raisins.

5. Divide the batter among the muffin cups. Bake the muffins until dark golden and a toothpick inserted into the center of each muffin comes out with a few crumbs attached, 16 to 20 minutes, rotating the pan halfway through baking. Cool the muffins in the pan for 5 minutes, then carefully transfer the muffins to a wire rack to cool completely. Serve. (The muffins can be stored in an airtight container at room temperature for up to 3 days.)

SHOPPING WITH THE TEST KITCHEN

Muffin Tins: With price tags ranging from $5 to a whopping $26, we wondered if there was a good reason for shelling out the big bucks for a simple muffin tin. In our tests, the best tins browned the muffins evenly; the worst tins browned the muffins on top, but left them underbaked on the bottom. Darker coated metals, which absorb heat, do the best job of browning baked goods. The Wilton Ultra-Bake ($7.99) was the clear winner, in part because of its generous 2-inch lip that makes it easy to maneuver this tin in and out of the oven.

Zucchini Bread

When the farmers' market (or your backyard garden) is booming with zucchini, zucchini bread can be the answer. But why are so many zucchini breads low on flavor and downright greasy? The problem with zucchini bread dates back to the health food craze of the 1960s and 1970s, when oil-based vegetable and fruit loaves became popular. Although carrot cake and banana bread are usually pretty good, zucchini bread starts with two big deficits: zucchini, by its nature, is very bland and very watery.

In our experience, some loaves are so tasteless and gummy that they're a waste of otherwise good ingredients. Other recipes are heavy-handed with sugar and spices to cover up the problem, but the resulting loaf is more like zucchini cake. But it doesn't have to be this way. Zucchini bread can be moist, lightly sweetened, and gently spiced.

Part of the appeal of zucchini bread is its simplicity. The technique couldn't be much easier: stir the dry ingredients (flour, leavener, spices, and salt) together in one bowl, stir the wet ingredients and sweetener (oil, eggs, sugar, and often yogurt or sour cream) together in a second bowl, and then fold the dry ingredients into the wet, while adding grated zucchini.

After grating the first batch of zucchini, we noticed an awful lot of water in the bowl. Merely draining off the water had little effect. Loaves without the liquid were still pretty soggy. Other watery vegetables, such as cabbage and eggplant, are sometimes salted before cooking. Taking a cue from this technique, we sprinkled the grated zucchini with a little sugar instead of salt and set it in a colander to drain. This method was evidently too successful—the bread was now much too dry. We needed to try something else.

If zucchini is a water-filled sponge, we figured, then why not treat it that way? We placed grated zucchini in a kitchen towel and wrung out every drop of moisture we could. The texture of the bread made with squeeze-dried zucchini was much better. But everyone still complained about the bland flavor.

Because zucchini bread is supposed to be "healthful," many recipes call for oil rather than butter. It wasn't hard to imagine that melted butter would make a tastier loaf. Sure enough, butter beat oil hands down.

Most zucchini bread recipes also call for either sour cream or yogurt. Tasters liked them both for the tangy flavor they added to the bread (in fact, we decided to add a little lemon juice for even more zip), but they preferred the lighter, cakier texture of the loaf made with yogurt. The sour cream version was dense and heavy by comparison.

Finally, we tackled the spices and sugar, which, in our opinion, are often used too freely. Tasters liked the simple combination of cinnamon and all-spice. As for sugar, we saw recipes that called for anywhere from 1 to 3 cups. Our final recipe ended up near the low end of the scale at just 1½ cups. At last, we had reason to look forward to a bumper crop of zucchini.

ZUCCHINI BREAD

MAKES ONE 8-INCH LOAF

Cut large zucchini in half lengthwise and scoop out the seeds with a spoon before shredding. You can use either whole or low-fat yogurt in this bread, but avoid nonfat, which will make the bread taste dry.

1	**pound zucchini**
2	**cups all-purpose flour**
1	**teaspoon baking soda**
1	**teaspoon baking powder**
1	**teaspoon ground cinnamon**
1	**teaspoon ground allspice**
½	**teaspoon salt**
1½	**cups sugar**
¼	**cup plain yogurt (see note above)**

RIDDING ZUCCHINI OF WATER

1. Using the coarse holes on a box grater, grate the zucchini, peel and all.

2. Place the grated zucchini in a clean dish towel and wring out as much liquid as possible.

2	**large eggs**
1	**tablespoon fresh lemon juice**
6	**tablespoons unsalted butter, melted and cooled**

1. Adjust an oven rack to the middle position and heat the oven to 375 degrees. Generously grease an 8½ by 4½-inch loaf pan.

2. Shred the zucchini and squeeze it dry in a kitchen towel. Whisk together the flour, baking soda, baking powder, cinnamon, allspice, and salt in a large bowl. Whisk together the sugar, yogurt, eggs, lemon juice, and butter in a bowl until combined.

3. Using a spatula, gently fold the yogurt mixture and the zucchini into the flour mixture until just combined. Transfer the batter to the prepared pan.

4. Bake until golden brown and a toothpick inserted in the center comes out with a few crumbs attached, 45 to 55 minutes, rotating the pan halfway through baking. Cool for 10 minutes, then turn out onto a wire rack to cool at least 1 hour before serving. (The bread can be wrapped in plastic wrap and stored at room temperature for up to 3 days.)

FRUITY ZUCCHINI BREAD

Stir ¾ cup golden raisins or chopped dried apricots into the batter along with the zucchini.

NUTTY ZUCCHINI BREAD

Stir ½ cup toasted sliced almonds and ½ cup toasted and chopped pistachios into the batter along with the zucchini.

ZUCCHINI MUFFINS

Grease a 12-cup muffin tin and divide the batter among the muffin cups. Bake on the middle rack of a preheated 375-degree oven until a toothpick inserted into the center of each muffin comes out with a few crumbs attached, 22 to 27 minutes, rotating the pan halfway through baking. These muffins are best served warm.

Cream Cheese Spreads

Our Zucchini Bread (page 187) is good enough to stand on its own, but a slather of cream cheese makes it even better. Try these spreads on bagels, too. These spreads will keep in a covered container in the refrigerator for up to 1 week.

ZESTY APRICOT SPREAD

Using a rubber spatula, combine 8 ounces cream cheese, at room temperature, with ⅓ cup apricot jam, 2 tablespoons confectioners' sugar, and 1 tablespoon grated fresh lemon zest in a bowl until smooth.

MAPLE-CINNAMON SPREAD

Using a rubber spatula, combine 8 ounces cream cheese, at room temperature, with 2 tablespoons maple syrup, 1 tablespoon brown sugar, and ½ teaspoon ground cinnamon in a bowl until smooth.

LEMON-GINGER SPREAD

Using a rubber spatula, combine 8 ounces cream cheese, at room temperature, with ⅓ cup ginger preserves, 1 tablespoon grated fresh lemon zest, and ½ teaspoon ground ginger in a bowl until smooth.

ORANGE SPREAD

Using a rubber spatula, combine 8 ounces cream cheese, at room temperature, with ⅓ cup orange marmalade, 2 tablespoons confectioners' sugar, and 1 tablespoon grated fresh lemon zest in a bowl until smooth.

SWEET PINEAPPLE SPREAD

Using a rubber spatula, combine 8 ounces cream cheese, at room temperature, with 1 (8-ounce) can crushed pineapple, drained, and 2 tablespoons brown sugar in a bowl until smooth.

Cranberry-Nut Bread

We don't make cranberry-nut bread just for ourselves. We make it for the kindergarten teacher, the mail carrier, and anyone else who deserves something homemade. The problem is that this simple bread is often subpar—sunken in the middle, too dense, or so overly sweetened that the contrast between the tart berries and what should be a slightly sweet dough is lost. We wanted to avoid these problems, and we had some other goals in mind as well. We were looking for a crust that was golden brown and evenly thin all the way around and a texture that was somewhere between a dense breakfast bread and a light, airy cake. And, for the sake of convenience, we wanted the batter to fit easily into a standard loaf pan. After we looked at almost sixty recipes, it seemed evident that the mixing method and the leavening were the most important factors in getting the quick bread we were after.

First, we began with the ingredients. We quickly determined that we liked the flavor that butter provided over that of oil, margarine, or shortening. More than one egg made the bread almost too rich and caused the interior to turn somewhat yellow. After testing different amounts and types of sugar, we stuck with 1 cup of granulated sugar, which provided just the right amount of sweetness. Orange zest added not only to the flavor but to the interior appearance as well, thanks to the orange flecks.

We also tinkered with the liquid component. Many recipes called for water or even boiling water, but freshly squeezed orange juice was usually mentioned and offered the best flavor. We compared fresh, home-squeezed orange juice with commercially prepared juices made both from fresh oranges and from concentrate; home-squeezed juice was the winner, hands down.

Not every recipe called for dairy, but we tested everything from heavy cream to sour cream. Both buttermilk and yogurt provided the moistness and tang we were looking for, with buttermilk edging out yogurt by a hairbreadth.

Last, but not least, were the cranberries. The cranberry harvest begins just after Labor Day and continues through early fall, which means that by mid- to late January, no fresh berries are available. Cranberries freeze beautifully, so grab a few extra bags to have on hand and freeze them until you're ready to use them. We found no discernible difference in the finished product between bread made with fresh and bread made with frozen cranberries.

CRANBERRY-ORANGE NUT BREAD

MAKES ONE 8-INCH LOAF

We prefer sweet, mild pecans in this bread, but walnuts can be substituted. Resist the urge to cut into the bread while it is hot out of the oven; the texture improves as it cools, making it easier to slice.

½ cup pecans, chopped (see note above)
1 tablespoon grated fresh orange zest
⅓ cup orange juice
⅔ cup buttermilk
6 tablespoons unsalted butter, melted and cooled
1 large egg, beaten lightly
2 cups all-purpose flour
1 cup sugar
1 teaspoon salt
1 teaspoon baking powder
¼ teaspoon baking soda
1½ cups cranberries, chopped (see note above)

1. Adjust an oven rack to the middle position and heat the oven to 375 degrees. Generously grease an 8½ by 4½-inch loaf pan.

2. Spread the pecans on a baking sheet and toast until fragrant, 5 to 7 minutes. Set aside.

3. Stir together the orange zest, orange juice, buttermilk, melted butter, and egg in a small bowl. Whisk together the flour, sugar, salt, baking powder, and baking soda in a large bowl. Stir the orange-buttermilk mixture into the flour mixture with a rubber spatula until just moistened. Gently stir in the cranberries and pecans. Do not overmix. Scrape the batter into the prepared pan and smooth the surface with a rubber spatula.

4. Bake for 20 minutes, then reduce the heat to 350 degrees; continue to bake until the loaf is golden brown and a toothpick inserted in the center comes out clean, about 45 minutes longer, rotating the pan halfway through baking. Cool in the pan for 10 minutes, then transfer to a wire rack and cool at least 1 hour before serving. (The bread can be wrapped with plastic wrap and stored at room temperature for up to 3 days.)

Tick Tock Orange Sticky Rolls

While the entertainment industry immortalizes its stars in celluloid and cement handprints, Hollywood residents fondly recall another local legend—the Tick Tock Tea Room. From 1930 through 1988, the Tick Tock served up countless platters of meat loaf, roast turkey, and fried chicken to its working-class clientele. The restaurant's defining touch was the complimentary basket of hot sticky rolls that preceded each meal. When the Tick Tock closed its doors over twenty years ago, it also closed the book on those incredible orange rolls.

We found two recipes for these rolls, one from a 1977 *Los Angeles Times* article and one from a 1994 cookbook called *Hollywood du Jour*. The recipes are very similar: dough made from packaged biscuit mix is rolled out, covered with cinnamon sugar and orange zest, and then rolled into a log. Individual pieces are cut, then set in a baking dish (spiral side up, like cinnamon rolls or sticky buns) atop a glaze made with orange juice concentrate, sugar, and butter. When the rolls come out of the oven, they are turned out with the gooey glaze on top. Unfortunately, both recipes produced sloppy, soggy rolls soaked through with glaze.

The fluffy boxed-mix biscuits had soaked up too much liquid. Homemade cream biscuits were sturdier but didn't have much flavor. Biscuits made with buttermilk and melted butter (instead of cream) tasted great and stood up to the glaze better—especially when we defied convention and kneaded the dough before rolling and cutting. After 5 minutes of kneading, the biscuits were still plenty tender, but now they offered some resistance to the glaze.

The candy-sweet original orange glaze started with ¾ cup of orange juice concentrate. We tried fresh and store-bought orange juice, but neither packed enough orange flavor. To temper its sweetness, we reduced the concentrate by ¼ cup and cut the cloying granulated sugar with an equal amount of brown sugar. The glaze was still too thin and easily absorbed into the biscuits, so for our next test, we simmered the ingredients in a saucepan until they formed a thick glaze.

A happy kitchen accident brought this recipe home. We had made the glaze and then gotten distracted before we had a chance to start the dough; by the time the dough was ready, the glaze had hardened in the cake pan. We went ahead and

---

threw the rolls in anyway. Starting with a hardened glaze kept the rolls from soaking up too much liquid, and the rolls now browned much better than when they'd been saturated with the orange syrup. With their orange-cinnamon filling and caramel-y, sticky orange glaze, these Tick Tock Orange Sticky Rolls are simply irresistible.

TICK TOCK ORANGE STICKY ROLLS

SERVES 8

Don't let the rolls sit in the pan for more than 5 minutes after baking. The glaze will begin to harden and the buns will stick.

GLAZE

- ½ **cup frozen orange juice concentrate, thawed**
- ¼ **cup packed light brown sugar**
- ¼ **cup granulated sugar**
- 3 **tablespoons unsalted butter**

FILLING

- ½ **cup packed light brown sugar**
- ¼ **cup granulated sugar**
- 2 **teaspoons ground cinnamon**
- 1 **teaspoon grated fresh orange zest**
- ⅛ **teaspoon ground cloves**
- ⅛ **teaspoon salt**
- 1 **tablespoon unsalted butter, melted**

DOUGH

- 2¾ **cups all-purpose flour**
- 2 **tablespoons granulated sugar**
- 2 **teaspoons baking powder**
- ½ **teaspoon baking soda**
- ½ **teaspoon salt**
- 1¼ **cups buttermilk**
- 6 **tablespoons unsalted butter, melted**

1. FOR THE GLAZE: Grease a 9-inch cake pan. Bring all of the ingredients to a simmer in a small saucepan over medium heat. Cook until the mixture thickens and clings to the back of a spoon, about 5 minutes. Pour the mixture into the prepared pan. Cool until the glaze hardens, at least 20 minutes.

2. FOR THE FILLING: Adjust an oven rack to the lower-middle position and heat the oven to 350 degrees. Combine all of the ingredients except the butter in a bowl. Using a fork, stir in the butter until the mixture resembles wet sand.

3. FOR THE DOUGH: Whisk the flour, sugar, baking powder, baking soda, and salt together in a bowl. Whisk together the buttermilk and butter in a small bowl (the mixture will clump), then stir into the flour mixture until combined. Knead the dough on a lightly floured work surface until smooth, about 5 minutes.

4. Roll the dough into a 12 by 9-inch rectangle. Pat the filling onto the dough, leaving a ½-inch border around the edges. Starting at one long end, roll the dough into a tight cylinder and pinch the seam together. Cut the log into 8 pieces and arrange the pieces, cut side down, on the cooled glaze, placing 1 roll in the center and the remaining rolls around the edge of the pan.

5. Bake until the rolls are golden and the glaze is darkened and bubbling, 18 to 25 minutes, rotating the pan halfway through baking. Cool in the pan for 5 minutes, then turn out onto a platter. Let the rolls sit for 10 minutes before serving.

Monkey Bread

Monkey bread often starts with homemade bread dough that is cut and rolled into small balls. The balls are dipped in butter, rolled in cinnamon sugar, stacked in a tube or Bundt pan, and baked. The pieces of dough appear to melt together, the sugar and butter transformed into a thick, caramel goo that oozes into every nook and cranny. And because the balls of dough are piled one on top of another, the end result is a crowning confection of soft, sweet, sticky, and irresistibly cinnamony bread.

Its origins date back at least a century, and the super-soft Parker House roll is surely a close relation. The name "monkey bread" is enigmatic. Some say it comes from the bread's resemblance to the prickly monkey-puzzle tree. Others think it refers to the way we eat it—that is, using our hands to pull apart the sticky clumps of bread and stuff them in our mouths, just like happy little monkeys. And for those who think monkey bread may be lacking panache, consider that former First Lady Nancy Reagan served monkey bread at the White House.

The oldest monkey bread recipes we found in our research were two-day affairs. The dough was started the night before, refrigerated, and shaped and baked the next day. Contemporary recipes have taken the road of convenience; in most cases they use store-bought biscuit dough. We tried it, but the time saved wasn't worth it. The biscuit dough was too lean, too dry, and too bland.

We looked to the few contemporary recipes that could be made in one day and then made a few adjustments. To provide plenty of lift and yeasty flavor, we used a whole envelope of rapid-rise yeast, which also made this a same-morning operation—no need to plan ahead. Milk and melted butter went in to keep the dough rich and moist, and a little sugar made the bread sweet enough to eat on its own. To compensate for the sweet dough, we changed the granulated sugar normally used to coat the dough balls to the mellower light brown sugar.

Once we piled all the balls into the pan, the monkey bread went into the oven. Once it was out of the oven (after about an hour) and after a few cruel minutes of waiting, we released the bread from its pan, watching the hot caramel drip down the sides. Some recipes call for drizzling a simple confectioners' sugar glaze over the monkey bread, which may seem gratuitous, but we didn't think the glaze made the monkey bread too sweet. In fact, we thought that with the glaze the bread was now just perfect.

MAKING MONKEY BREAD

1. After patting the dough into an 8-inch square, cut the square into quarters.

2. Cut each quarter into 16 pieces.

3. Roll each piece of dough into a rough ball. Then coat the balls with melted butter and sugar.

4. Layer the buttered and sugared dough balls in the buttered Bundt pan.

MONKEY BREAD

SERVES 6 TO 8

The dough should be sticky, but if you find that it's too wet and not coming together in the mixer, add 2 tablespoons more flour and mix until the dough forms a cohesive mass. If you don't have a standing mixer, see our variation, which uses a hand-mixing method. After baking, don't let the bread cool in the pan for more than 5 minutes or it will stick to the pan and come out in pieces. Monkey bread is at its best when served warm.

DOUGH

- 2 tablespoons unsalted butter, softened, plus 2 tablespoons melted
- 1 cup warm milk (110 degrees)
- ⅓ cup warm water (110 degrees)
- ¼ cup granulated sugar
- 1 envelope (2¼ teaspoons) rapid-rise or instant yeast
- 3¼ cups all-purpose flour
- 2 teaspoons salt

COATING

- 1 cup packed light brown sugar
- 2 teaspoons ground cinnamon
- 8 tablespoons (1 stick) unsalted butter, melted

GLAZE

- 1 cup confectioners' sugar
- 2 tablespoons milk

1. FOR THE DOUGH: Adjust an oven rack to the lower-middle position and heat the oven to 200 degrees. When the oven reaches 200 degrees, turn it off. Grease a Bundt pan with 2 tablespoons softened butter. Set aside.

2. In a large liquid measuring cup, mix together the milk, water, melted butter, sugar, and yeast. Mix the flour and salt in a standing mixer fitted with the dough hook. Turn the machine to low and slowly add the milk mixture. After the dough comes together, increase the speed to medium and mix until the dough is shiny and smooth, 6 to 7 minutes. Turn the dough onto a lightly floured work surface and knead briefly to form a smooth, round ball. Grease a large bowl. Place the dough in the bowl and coat the surface of the dough with vegetable oil spray. Cover the bowl with plastic wrap and place in the warm oven until the dough doubles in size, 50 to 60 minutes.

3. FOR THE SUGAR COATING: While the dough is rising, mix the brown sugar and cinnamon together in a bowl. Place the melted butter in a second bowl. Set aside.

4. TO FORM THE BREAD: Gently remove the dough from the bowl and pat into a rough 8-inch square. Using a bench scraper or knife, cut the dough into 64 pieces.

5. Roll each dough piece into a ball. Working with one at a time, dip the balls in the melted butter, allowing the excess butter to drip back into the bowl. Roll in the brown sugar mixture, then layer the balls in the Bundt pan, staggering the seams where the dough balls meet as you build layers.

6. Cover the Bundt pan tightly with plastic wrap and place in the turned-off oven until the dough balls are puffy and have risen 1 to 2 inches from the top of the pan, 50 to 70 minutes.

7. Remove the pan from the oven and heat the oven to 350 degrees. Unwrap the pan and bake until the top is deep brown and the caramel begins to bubble around the edges, 30 to 35 minutes, rotating the pan halfway through baking. Cool in the pan for 5 minutes, then turn out onto a platter and allow to cool slightly, about 10 minutes.

8. FOR THE GLAZE: While the bread cools, whisk the confectioners' sugar and milk together in a small bowl until any lumps are gone. Using a whisk, drizzle the glaze over the warm monkey bread, letting it run over the top and sides. Serve warm.

Variation
MONKEY BREAD WITHOUT A MIXER

In step 2, mix the flour and salt in large bowl. Make a well in the flour, then add the milk mixture to the well. Using a wooden spoon, stir until the dough becomes shaggy and is difficult to stir. Turn out onto a lightly floured work surface and begin to knead, incorporating shaggy scraps back into the dough. Knead until the dough is smooth and satiny, about 10 minutes. Shape into a taut ball and proceed as directed.

Cinnamon Swirl Bread

A sticky cinnamon bun is love at first sight. But with cinnamon swirl bread, the appreciation comes with time. Soft and sturdy, with a neat cinnamon swirl inside, a good loaf will last for days. That means we can stagger out of bed, pop a few slices into the toaster, and fill the kitchen with the aroma of hot cinnamon bread—all before 6:00 A.M.

But making this bread from a handful of recipes tempered some of our initial enthusiasm. The loaves turned out dense and chewy or dry and cottony—not a single one was nice and soft. As for the cinnamon, some loaves offered nothing of the spice while others gushed cinnamon-sugar goo all over the cutting board. But most annoying was that every single loaf of bread came apart at its swirly fault line and spiraled into a cinnamon Slinky. Could we produce a soft, sweet, and structurally sound cinnamon swirl bread that was worth getting out of bed for?

The recipes we uncovered were all based on sweet yeast doughs. Flour, sugar, salt, yeast, and milk were universal. Some loaves included a tablespoon or two of butter, but tasters deemed them too lean and tough, more sandwich bread than morning sweet bread. Loaves with a stick of butter and half a dozen eggs were akin to rich babkas. We chose a middle path, something similar to challah bread. We quickly settled on 3 tablespoons of butter as the right amount for a single loaf, but the eggs proved more difficult to pin down. When we used fewer than two, the bread was too lean, but two or more made the bread bounce. Suspicious that the egg whites were the culprit, we tried using only three yolks and finally achieved a rich but not bouncy crumb.

For the cinnamon-sugar filling, tasters liked a combination of white and light brown sugars, with a hefty 4 teaspoons of cinnamon. One-half cup of the filling gave just the right amount of swirl without the wave of goo. To complement the swirl, tasters liked the bread even more when we added some of the cinnamon sugar directly to the dough and saved a little to sprinkle on top.

The separating spiral was all that stood between us and cinnamon swirl bread perfection. The spiral is formed by patting out the dough, moistening the surface, sprinkling it with the cinnamon-sugar mixture, and then rolling it up into a loaf; the spiral is sandwiched between layers of dough. Milk, corn syrup, beaten egg yolks, and melted butter all worked well to get the cinnamon-sugar mixture to stick to the moist side, but when we rolled the dough up, the mixture wasn't adhering to the dry top layer. We were left with sloppy spirals.

We eventually found salvation in a spray bottle of water. A thin coat of water sprayed on the dough made the cinnamon mixture stick, and then a second light coat sprayed directly onto the mixture created a glue that adhered to the dough when it was rolled. We finally had a filling that stayed intact, in place, and in a perfect swirl. It was time to break out the toaster.

CINNAMON SWIRL BREAD

MAKES ONE 9-INCH LOAF

You will need about 1 tablespoon of melted butter to brush over the loaf before baking. If you don't have a standing mixer, see "Alternative Mixing Methods for Breads and Rolls" on page 237. If you want to start the bread a day ahead, do not let the dough rise in step 4, but refrigerate it overnight or up to 16 hours; let the dough sit at room temperature for 30 minutes, then continue with step 5.

½	cup granulated sugar
¼	cup packed light brown sugar
4	teaspoons ground cinnamon
1¼	cups warm whole milk (110 degrees)
3	tablespoons unsalted butter, melted and cooled, plus extra for brushing (see note above)
2	large egg yolks
4	cups all-purpose flour
1	envelope (2¼ teaspoons) rapid-rise or instant yeast
1½	teaspoons salt

1. Mix the sugars and cinnamon together in a small bowl. Measure out 2 tablespoons and reserve for the topping. Whisk the milk, melted butter, and egg yolks together in a large liquid measuring cup.

2. Combine 3½ cups of the flour, the yeast, salt, and ¼ cup of the sugar mixture in the bowl of a standing mixer fitted with the dough hook. With the mixer on low speed, add the milk mixture and mix until the dough comes together, about 2 minutes.

3. Increase the speed to medium-low and knead until the dough is smooth and elastic, about 8 minutes. (If, after 4 minutes, more flour is needed, add the remaining ½ cup flour, 2 tablespoons at a time, until the dough clears the sides of the bowl but sticks to the bottom.)

4. Turn the dough out onto a lightly floured work surface and knead by hand to form a smooth, round ball. Place the dough in a large, lightly greased bowl and cover with greased plastic wrap. Let rise in a warm place until doubled in size, 1 to 1½ hours.

MAKING CINNAMON SWIRL BREAD

1. Press the dough into a 20 by 8-inch rectangle, with the short side facing you.

2. Spray the dough with water and sprinkle evenly with ½ cup of the cinnamon sugar. Lightly spray the cinnamon sugar–topped dough with water until damp but not wet.

3. Roll up the dough, tucking it under the rolled edge gently with your fingers to keep it tightly rolled. Pinch the seam together to seal.

4. Lay the dough in a greased 9 by 5-inch loaf pan, with the seam facing down.

5. Grease a 9 by 5-inch loaf pan. Turn the dough out onto a lightly floured work surface and press into a 20 by 8-inch rectangle with the short side facing you. Spray the dough lightly with water, then sprinkle evenly with the remaining sugar mixture, leaving a ½-inch border at the far edge. Lightly spray the sugar mixture with water until it is damp but not wet.

6. Loosen the dough from the work surface using a bench scraper or metal spatula, then roll the dough into a tight cylinder and pinch the seam closed. Place the loaf, seam side down, in the prepared pan. Coat the loaf with vegetable oil spray, cover loosely with plastic wrap, and let rise in a warm place until nearly doubled in size and the dough barely springs back when poked with a knuckle, 45 to 75 minutes.

7. Adjust an oven rack to the lower-middle position and heat the oven to 350 degrees. Brush the loaf lightly with butter, sprinkle with the reserved sugar mixture, then spray lightly with water. Bake until golden, 40 to 60 minutes, rotating the loaf halfway through baking. Cool the loaf in the pan for 15 minutes, then turn out onto a wire rack and let cool to room temperature, about 2 hours, before serving.

Variation
CINNAMON-RAISIN SWIRL BREAD
In step 4, after turning the dough out onto the work surface, knead in ½ cup raisins by hand until evenly distributed. Proceed as directed.

Gingerbread

Gingerbread should be tender, moist, and several inches thick. It should be easy enough to assemble just before dinner so squares of warm gingerbread can be enjoyed for dessert. As our early tests proved, these goals are rarely met. Gingerbread has a tendency to be dry and tough, and many recipes are unnecessarily complicated. Yes, you will probably need a lot of ingredients (mostly spices already in your pantry), but the mixing method should be simple. Gingerbread is a quick bread, after all.

To start our kitchen tests, we chose a milk-based gingerbread. Many recipes call for water, but in our initial tests tasters found these breads considerably drier and less rich than those made with milk. Milk fat adds tenderness and flavor; it is a must. With that decision made, we focused next on sweeteners. Most recipes include a dry sweetener—granulated sugar, light brown sugar, or dark brown sugar—as well as a liquid sweetener—molasses most often, but sometimes honey, maple syrup, or corn syrup.

We quickly discovered that molasses is the right liquid sweetener. Honey and corn syrup were judged too bland and boring. Maple syrup had some partisans, but most tasters thought the maple flavor clashed with the spices. We preferred the gentler flavor of light or mild molasses as compared to dark or robust molasses or blackstrap molasses.

Brown sugar is more commonly used in gingerbread recipes than white sugar. We expected to like its heartier, richer flavor. However, tasters preferred samples prepared with granulated sugar. With brown sugar added to the mix, the molasses flavor overwhelmed the spices. Granulated sugar tasted cleaner, allowing the spices to shine through.

As for the spices, tasters liked a combination of ground ginger, cinnamon, cloves, nutmeg, and allspice. We tested and liked both crystallized and grated fresh ginger, but everyone in the test kitchen agreed that regular ground ginger (something most cooks are likely to have in the pantry) delivered excellent results. Finally, we found that a pinch of cocoa, which is sometimes added to gingerbread, added earthiness and complexity.

In kitchen tests butter was the hands-down favorite over vegetable oil and shortening. We found that melting the butter yielded a denser, moister cake. When we creamed the butter and sugar, the result was lighter, fluffier, and more cake-like. As for the eggs, we found that two added too much moisture to the batter, which tended to sink in the middle near the end of the baking time. A single egg ensured sufficient tenderness and proper height.

Although we had been using milk in our recipe, we were intrigued by some old-fashioned recipes that called for sour cream, yogurt, or buttermilk instead. Sour cream and yogurt gave the gingerbread too much tang, and we quickly dropped them from contention. Buttermilk, however, had some nice effects on our recipe. The color was darker and the texture slightly moister. Unfortunately, buttermilk also made the crumb coarser, and the flavor was a bit too strong. By comparison, the gingerbread made with milk had a better rise and finer texture. In the end, we found that a 50-50 ratio of buttermilk and milk offered the best traits of each.

With buttermilk added to the recipe, we found that baking soda was the best leavener. We tested both cake and all-purpose flours and discovered that cake flour was too soft for this recipe—it made gingerbread with an unappealingly doughy texture. All-purpose flour produced the proper structure.

We tested several methods for combining the wet and dry ingredients, including adding the melted fat to the dry ingredients before the liquids as well as beating the butter, sugar, and eggs, then alternately adding wet and dry ingredients. In the end,

the simplest method proved best. We combined all the dry ingredients in one bowl, all the wet ingredients (including the melted butter, egg, and sugar) in another bowl, and then beat the dry ingredients into the wet ingredients, giving ourselves gingerbread that went into the oven in less than 10 minutes and came out tasting great.

GINGERBREAD

SERVES 9

Serve plain or with ice cream or whipped cream.

1¾	cups all-purpose flour
2	teaspoons ground ginger
1	teaspoon Dutch-processed cocoa powder
1	teaspoon ground cinnamon
½	teaspoon ground cloves
½	teaspoon ground nutmeg
½	teaspoon ground allspice
½	teaspoon baking soda
½	teaspoon salt
¾	cup light molasses
¾	cup sugar
8	tablespoons (1 stick) unsalted butter, melted and cooled
1	large egg, room temperature
1	cup buttermilk, room temperature

1. Adjust an oven rack to the middle position and heat the oven to 350 degrees. Following the photos on page 458, line an 8-inch square baking pan with a foil sling and grease the foil. Whisk the flour, ginger, cocoa powder, cinnamon, cloves, nutmeg, allspice, baking soda, and salt together in a medium bowl.

2. In a large bowl, beat the molasses, sugar, and melted butter together with an electric mixer on low speed until combined, 1 to 3 minutes. Beat in

the egg until combined, about 30 seconds. Beat in the buttermilk until combined, about 30 seconds. Beat in the flour mixture until the batter is smooth and thick, 1 to 3 minutes.

3. Scrape the batter into the prepared pan, smooth the top, and gently tap the pan on the work surface to settle the batter. Bake the bread until a toothpick inserted in the center comes out with a few crumbs attached, 35 to 40 minutes, rotating the pan halfway through baking. Let the bread cool completely in the pan, 1 to 2 hours. If desired, remove the bread from the pan, using the foil overhang, before serving.

Variation
GINGERBREAD WITH DRIED FRUIT
Fold ¾ cup raisins, dried cranberries, or chopped prunes into the batter.

Pecan Sour Cream Coffee Cake

Most coffee cakes are nothing more than plain old yellow cake hiding under a crumb topping. They are light and fluffy when they should be moist and rich. And even when the texture is right, often the flavor is not. Why bother with a coffee cake that just whispers (instead of shouts) "nuts"?

A Bundt pan is the traditional choice for coffee cake. Besides producing an attractive, sculptured cake, the pan's shape helps bake the cake from the inside, which is essential when you've got a heavy batter.

Most cake recipes follow the same technique: cream butter and sugar, beat in eggs, and alternate additions of dry ingredients and milk. This method requires 5 to 8 minutes of mixer action and whips a fair amount of air into the batter—perfect for a

TOASTING SPICES, NUTS, AND SEEDS

Toast whole spices, nuts, or seeds in a dry skillet over medium heat, shaking the pan occasionally to prevent scorching. Toast spices until they become fragrant, 1 to 3 minutes. Toast nuts and seeds until they begin to darken slightly, about 3 to 5 minutes.

fluffy yellow cake but all wrong for our idea of coffee cake, which should be rich, moist, and luxurious. We tried a variety of other methods without success until we remembered a little-known cake-mixing method in which softened butter is beaten with some of the liquid ingredients directly into the flour mixture for just 2 minutes. The butter coats the flour, making the cake rich and tender. And without all of the whipping action, the batter is both denser (a good thing) and richer (an even better thing). The cake was still on the dry side, though, and the solution was to replace the milk with sour cream.

Our favorite element in any coffee cake is the streusel layer swirled through the middle. But we could add only so much streusel before it sank to the bottom. To intensify the flavor of the streusel, we toasted the nuts (a step omitted by most recipe writers), but the cake was still lacking in nut flavor.

We tried a variety of techniques, from lining the cake pan with ground nuts to adding whole and roughly chopped nuts to the batter. The winning technique, which made this recipe go from good to great, emerged when we finely ground toasted pecans and added them directly to the flour mixture, making something like a "pecan flour." Now every bite—not just the streusel—was shouting "Nuts!"

PECAN SOUR CREAM COFFEE CAKE

SERVES 12 TO 16

Very soft butter can be incorporated into the cake easily, whereas cold or even cool butter will form unblended nuggets in the batter. You can toast, cool, and grind the nuts for both the streusel and cake together.

STREUSEL

½	cup pecans, toasted, cooled, and ground fine
3	tablespoons dark brown sugar
1	tablespoon all-purpose flour
1	teaspoon ground cinnamon

CAKE

6	large eggs
1¾	cups sour cream
¼	cup maple syrup
1½	tablespoons vanilla extract
3	cups all-purpose flour
½	cup pecans, toasted, cooled, and ground fine
1¼	cups granulated sugar
1½	tablespoons baking powder
1¼	teaspoons baking soda
1	teaspoon salt
16	tablespoons (2 sticks) unsalted butter, cut into ½-inch pieces, room temperature

GLAZE

1	cup confectioners' sugar
2	tablespoons orange juice
1	teaspoon grated fresh orange zest

1. FOR THE STREUSEL: Combine the pecans, brown sugar, flour, and cinnamon in a small bowl and set aside.

2. FOR THE CAKE: Adjust an oven rack to the lowest position and heat the oven to 350 degrees. Grease a 12-cup nonstick Bundt pan. Whisk the eggs, sour cream, maple syrup, and vanilla together in a medium bowl.

3. With an electric mixer, mix the flour, pecans, sugar, baking powder, baking soda, and salt on the lowest setting in a large bowl until combined. Add the butter and half of the egg mixture and beat on the lowest setting, taking care not to splatter the ingredients, until the mixture starts to come together, about 15 seconds. Scrape down the sides of the bowl, add the remaining egg mixture, and beat on medium speed until the batter is light and fluffy, about 2 minutes (scrape down the sides of the bowl again after 1 minute).

4. Add 5 cups batter to the prepared Bundt pan, using a rubber spatula to smooth out the surface. Sprinkle the streusel evenly over the batter and then cover with the remaining batter, spreading it evenly.

5. Bake until a toothpick inserted into the middle of the cake comes out with a few crumbs attached, about 60 minutes, rotating the pan halfway through baking. Cool the cake in the pan on a wire rack for 30 minutes, then invert onto a wire rack to cool completely before glazing, about 1 hour.

6. FOR THE GLAZE: Whisk together the sugar, orange juice, and zest. Using a fork or whisk, drizzle the glaze over the top and sides of the cake. Slice and serve. (The cake can be wrapped in plastic wrap and stored at room temperature for up to 3 days.)

Almond Ring Coffee Cake

Most homemade coffee cakes combine plain yellow cake with brown sugar streusel. Although good, these cakes are pretty plain. When we want something fancier, our thoughts turn to a yeasted coffee cake with buttery layers of rich dough, a sweet almond filling, and a flourish of sliced nuts and white icing. You can buy this kind of coffee cake at the supermarket (think Entenmann's), but most are made with shortening (not butter) and have an artificial flavor. Our goal was to streamline the classic recipe and make it worth doing at home.

The method for making an almond ring coffee cake is pretty standard, and we didn't expect to deviate from the formula. An almond filling is placed on a rectangle of tender yeast dough, and the whole thing is rolled up, formed into a circle, and then cut to create a floral pattern that exposes some of the filling. The ingredients, however, required some testing. Some recipes produced rings that were too dry, and others were too sweet or lacked almond flavor.

We decided to start with the filling. Most recipes use cream cheese enriched with ground almonds and sugar, but we found this combination problematic—the mixture was so soft it leaked out of the dough, and we could barely taste the almonds. We had better luck with almond paste (sold in tubes in the supermarket baking aisle). When mixed with a little cream cheese, it gave us the nutty flavor we were looking for, and it was thick enough to stay put inside the coffee cake.

Most yeasted coffee cakes rely on brioche, a rich dough made with milk, butter, and eggs. Because our almond filling was pretty rich, we found that a lighter dough (made with one stick of butter and not two, as many recipes directed) was better. Three egg yolks gave the dough good structure, and leaving out the whites made the dough easier to handle. (We saved the whites for gluing the garnish of sliced almonds onto the ring.)

After playing around with various amounts of granulated and brown sugar, we made the important discovery of using honey to sweeten the dough. Tasters loved its light caramel flavor; we liked the fact that honey made the dough moister and more tender.

By using a preheated and then turned-off oven as a proofing box, we were able to make our coffee cake in a couple of hours (not all day, as was the case with most recipes we tried). This was a cake we'd be making not just for special occasions, but all year round.

ALMOND RING COFFEE CAKE

MAKES 2 RINGS, EACH SERVING 6

Note that you will need 3 eggs, but that the yolks and whites are used separately. Feel free to bake both cakes at the same time or freeze one for another time. To freeze one cake, let the cakes rise in step 7, then wrap one cake tightly with greased plastic wrap followed by aluminum foil and freeze for up to 1 month. Let the frozen cake thaw in the refrigerator for 12 hours, then return it to room temperature for about 1 hour and bake as directed. This cake also works well with two other fillings—see the variations on page 202.

ALMOND FILLING

1	(7-ounce) tube almond paste
4	ounces cream cheese, softened
½	cup confectioners' sugar

DOUGH

1⅓	cups warm whole milk (110 degrees)
8	tablespoons (1 stick) unsalted butter, melted and cooled

⅓	**cup honey**
3	**large egg yolks, lightly beaten**
2	**teaspoons vanilla extract**
5	**cups all-purpose flour**
1	**envelope (2¼ teaspoons) rapid-rise or instant yeast**
2	**teaspoons salt**

TOPPING

3	**large egg whites, lightly beaten**
½	**cup sliced almonds**
1½	**cups confectioners' sugar**
2	**ounces cream cheese, softened**
2	**tablespoons whole milk**
½	**teaspoon vanilla extract**

1. FOR THE FILLING: Beat the almond paste, cream cheese, and sugar together with an electric mixer on medium speed until smooth. Cover with plastic wrap and refrigerate until ready to use.

2. FOR THE DOUGH: Whisk the milk, melted butter, honey, egg yolks, and vanilla together in a large liquid measuring cup. Combine 4¾ cups of the flour, the yeast, and salt in the bowl of a standing mixer. Using the dough hook, mix on low speed. Add the milk mixture, and mix until the dough comes together, about 2 minutes.

3. Increase the speed to medium and knead until the dough is smooth and shiny, 5 to 7 minutes. (If, after 5 minutes, more flour is needed, add the remaining ¼ cup flour, 1 tablespoon at a time, until the dough clears the sides of the bowl but sticks to the bottom.)

4. Turn the dough out onto a lightly floured work surface and knead by hand to form a smooth, round ball. Place the dough in a large, lightly greased bowl and cover tightly with greased plastic wrap. Let rise in a warm, draft-free place until doubled in size, 1 to 1½ hours.

MAKING A RING-SHAPED COFFEE CAKE

1. Working with one piece of dough at a time, roll the dough into an 18 by 9-inch rectangle. Spread a 1-inch strip of the filling about 1 inch above the bottom edge of the dough.

2. Loosen the dough from the work surface with a bench scraper or metal spatula and carefully roll the dough into an even cylinder. Pinch the seam to seal.

3. Transfer the dough log to a parchment-lined baking sheet, and shape into a ring. Make about 11 cuts around the outside of the ring using a knife or scissors, spacing them 1 to 1½ inches apart.

4. Twist each piece of dough cut side up. Mist the cake with vegetable oil spray, wrap loosely in plastic wrap, and let rise until nearly doubled in size.

5. Line 2 baking sheets with parchment paper. On a lightly floured work surface, divide the dough into 2 equal pieces. Working with one piece of dough at a time, roll the dough into an 18 by 9-inch rectangle. Spread half of the filling in a 1-inch-wide strip about 1 inch above the bottom edge of the dough.

6. Loosen the dough from the work surface using a bench scraper or metal spatula, roll the dough into a tight log, and pinch the seam closed. Transfer the log, seam side down, to one of the prepared baking sheets. Repeat with the remaining dough and filling.

7. Shape each dough log into a ring. Make about 11 cuts around the outside of the ring with scissors or a knife, and twist the pieces upward. Mist both cakes with vegetable oil spray, wrap loosely in plastic wrap, and let rise in a warm place until they have nearly doubled in size and spring back slowly when indented with a finger, 1 to 1½ hours.

8. FOR THE TOPPING: Adjust the oven racks to the upper-middle and lower-middle positions and heat the oven to 375 degrees. Brush the rings with the egg whites and sprinkle with the almonds. Bake the cakes until deep brown, about 25 minutes, switching and rotating the baking sheets halfway through baking.

9. Let the cakes cool for 1 hour. Whisk the sugar, cream cheese, milk, and vanilla together in a small bowl until smooth, then drizzle the mixture over the cakes before serving.

Variations
APRICOT-ORANGE FILLING

MAKES ENOUGH FOR 2 COFFEE-CAKE RINGS

The filling can be refrigerated in an airtight container for up to 3 days.

2	cups dried apricots
1	cup water
3	tablespoons sugar
1	tablespoon grated fresh orange zest
3	tablespoons fresh orange juice
2	tablespoons rum (optional)

1. Bring the apricots, water, and sugar to a boil in a medium saucepan over medium-high heat. Reduce the heat to medium and boil gently, stirring occasionally, until the apricots are soft and the water has nearly evaporated, 16 to 18 minutes.

2. Transfer the warm apricots to a food processor. Add the orange zest, orange juice, and rum (if using), and process until smooth, about 1 minute. Let the mixture cool to room temperature before substituting for the Almond Filling.

BERRY FILLING

MAKES ENOUGH FOR 2 COFFEE-CAKE RINGS

The filling can be refrigerated in an airtight container for up to 3 days.

2½	cups fresh or frozen raspberries, blueberries, or blackberries
3	tablespoons sugar
2	tablespoons fresh lemon juice
2	tablespoons water
1½	tablespoons cornstarch
	Pinch salt

Stir all of the ingredients together in a medium saucepan. Bring to a boil over medium heat, and cook, stirring occasionally, until the mixture is thick and shiny, about 2 minutes. Let the mixture cool to room temperature before substituting for the Almond Filling.

Orange Drop Doughnuts

Cake doughnuts (a relative of batter dropped doughnuts) are an all-American phenomenon that started in the late 1800s, thanks to the availability of baking powder. Many nineteenth-century cookbooks show these quicker doughnuts being rolled and stamped out, just like their yeasted brethren. Eventually, savvy doughnut makers realized that dropping spoonfuls of cake batter into hot oil meant that fresh doughnuts could be on the table in minutes, without the fuss of rolling and stamping.

Drop doughnuts caught on like wildfire, and soon there were flavors of every kind—spiced, chocolate, and orange. In the late 1940s and into the 1950s, the name "orange drop doughnuts" started to appear in Betty Crocker cookbooks and magazines. We tried these recipes, and, truth be told, they were pretty good. With a little more work, we hoped to make a super-orangey doughnut worthy of breakfast in bed.

Some recipes use nearly 3 cups of flour for two dozen doughnuts, but these heavy (yet tasty) lead balloons fell straight to the bottom of our bellies. Two cups of flour—paired with 2 teaspoons of baking powder—worked much better. Two eggs and a little melted butter made these doughnuts properly rich.

As for liquid ingredients, some recipes call for milk as well as orange juice. But diluting the orange flavor just seemed wrong, so we added only juice. For even more orange flavor, we added a whopping tablespoon of grated zest to the batter—far more than the teaspoon or so found in older recipes.

Finally, we took a cue from a few recipes and rolled the hot doughnuts in a batch of homemade orange-flavored sugar. The pleasant aroma of citrus wafted through the test kitchen, and soon our fellow doughnut hounds lined up to enjoy a fresh, hot orange doughnut.

ORANGE DROP DOUGHNUTS

MAKES 24 TO 30 DOUGHNUTS

You'll need 3 oranges for the zest and juice.

COATING

½	cup sugar
1	teaspoon grated fresh orange zest

DOUGHNUTS

	About 2 quarts vegetable oil
2	cups all-purpose flour
2	teaspoons baking powder
¼	teaspoon salt
2	large eggs
½	cup sugar
1	tablespoon grated fresh orange zest
½	cup orange juice
2	tablespoons unsalted butter, melted

1. FOR THE COATING: Pulse the sugar and zest in a food processor until blended, about five pulses. Transfer to a medium bowl. (If making by hand, toss the zest and sugar in a medium bowl using a fork until evenly blended.)

MAKING ORANGE DROP DOUGHNUTS

1. To avoid splashes of oil, use two dinner teaspoons to "drop" the doughnut batter carefully into the oil. Fry until the doughnuts are deep brown and float to the top of the oil.

2. Use a slotted spoon to transfer the doughnuts to a paper towel–lined plate. Then, toss them in the orange sugar.

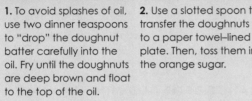

2. FOR THE DOUGHNUTS: Heat 3 inches of vegetable oil in a 4-quart saucepan until the temperature reaches 350 degrees on a candy-thermometer or instant-read thermometer that registers high temperatures. Whisk the flour, baking powder, and salt together in a medium bowl. Whisk together the eggs, sugar, and orange zest in a large bowl. Whisk in the orange juice, then the butter, until well combined. Stir in the flour mixture until evenly moistened.

3. Using two dinner teaspoons, carefully drop heaping spoonfuls of batter into the hot oil. (You should be able to fit about 6 spoonfuls in the pan at one time. Do not overcrowd.) Fry, maintaining the oil temperature between 325 and 350 degrees, until the doughnuts are crisp and deeply browned on all sides, 3 to 6 minutes. Using a slotted spoon, transfer the doughnuts to a paper towel–lined plate. Drain for 5 minutes. Add the doughnuts to the bowl with the orange sugar and toss until well coated. Place on a serving plate and repeat with the remaining batter, regulating the oil temperature as necessary. The doughnuts are best served warm.

Variations

SPICE DROP DOUGHNUTS

Combine ½ cup sugar, 1 tablespoon cinnamon, ¾ teaspoon ground nutmeg, and ½ teaspoon allspice in a medium bowl to make a spice sugar; set aside. Add 1½ teaspoons ground cinnamon and ¼ teaspoon ground allspice to the doughnut batter. Roll the fried, drained doughnuts in the spice sugar before serving.

BANANA DROP DOUGHNUTS

Combine ½ cup sugar and 1 tablespoon ground cinnamon in a medium bowl to make a cinnamon sugar; set aside. Add 1 mashed ripe banana to the batter and add 1 teaspoon ground cinnamon. Roll the fried, drained doughnuts in the cinnamon sugar before serving.

Buttermilk Doughnuts

With no rising required, buttermilk doughnuts are what you want if you're tight on time but crave a tasty, old-fashioned accompaniment to your morning coffee or mug of apple cider. In just 45 minutes you can fry up two dozen robust country doughnuts with great crunch and flavor.

We proceeded to test half a dozen different recipes for non-yeast fried doughnuts, choosing methods that seemed as different as possible so that we could judge a wide range of outcomes. And this is exactly what we got: everything from flat, greasy rounds of dough to high-rise cakey rings. Our final recipe, therefore, needed to give us a doughnut with good crunch and a minimum of grease, a true country doughnut, rather than an airy Dunkin' Donuts confection.

As a starting point, we cobbled together a master recipe using buttermilk, eggs, flour, sugar, baking powder, baking soda, melted butter, salt, and nutmeg. We made up a batch of dough and fried it in generic vegetable oil. The resulting doughnuts were good but needed improvement.

We tried increasing the amount of butter in the recipe, but it did not improve the flavor. We did, however, have some luck when we added one extra egg yolk. This made a moister dough, and the extra fat also created a more tender doughnut. Additionally, we tried boosting the flour by ¼ cup and determined that this drier dough does make a less crispy, but also less greasy, product. It is also a bit firmer and more chewy inside, but the lack of crackle on the outside placed this variation in second place.

With the recipe set, we were ready to begin our most important set of tests, involving frying the doughnuts. In terms of cooking temperature, we found that with the oil at 350 degrees the dough absorbs too much oil, whereas at 385 degrees the outside starts to burn before the inside can cook through. A temperature of 360 degrees seemed the ideal. We discovered, though, that it works best to start out with the oil at 375 degrees because the temperature will fall back to between 360 and 365 degrees as soon as the doughnuts are put in. Also, be sure to bring the oil back up to temperature between batches.

Many recipes call for cooking doughnuts for 1½ minutes per side, a time that we found to be much too long. Once the doughnuts had been placed in the hot oil and flipped, we tested 40 seconds, 50 seconds, 60 seconds, and 70 seconds and found that 50 seconds was ideal. The center was just cooked, and the doughnut did not take on that dry, catch-in-your-throat texture. The big surprise, however, was that doughnuts cooked longer were also greasier. The shorter the frying time, the less chance the oil had to penetrate the dough.

OLD-FASHIONED BUTTERMILK DOUGHNUTS

MAKES 15 TO 17 DOUGHNUTS

You can add ¼ cup of flour to the recipe for a chewier doughnut with a less crisp exterior. Regardless, these doughnuts are best eaten very warm, as soon out of the pot as possible. The dough can be made by hand, using a large bowl with a wooden spoon, or in a mixer as directed.

3½	cups all-purpose flour
1	cup sugar
½	teaspoon baking soda
2	teaspoons baking powder
1	teaspoon salt
1½	teaspoons ground nutmeg
¾	cup buttermilk
4	tablespoons unsalted butter, melted
2	large eggs, plus 1 large egg yolk
	About 1½ quarts vegetable oil

1. Mix 1 cup of the flour, sugar, baking soda, baking powder, salt, and nutmeg in the bowl of a standing mixer fitted with the paddle attachment.

2. Mix the buttermilk, butter, eggs, and egg yolk in a 2-cup liquid measuring cup. Add the buttermilk mixture to the flour mixture; beat on medium speed until smooth, about 30 seconds. Decrease the speed to low, add the remaining 2½ cups flour, and mix until just combined, about 30 seconds. Stir the batter once or twice with a wooden spoon or rubber spatula to ensure that all the liquid is incorporated. (The dough will be moist and tacky, like a cross between cake batter and cookie dough.)

3. Fit a candy thermometer (or instant-read thermometer that registers high temperatures) to the side of a large Dutch oven; gradually heat the oil over medium-high heat to 375 degrees on a candy thermometer or instant-read thermometer that registers high temperatures. Meanwhile, turn the dough onto a heavily floured work surface. Roll with a heavily floured rolling pin to ½-inch thickness. Stamp out the dough rings with a heavily floured doughnut cutter, reflouring between cuts. Transfer the dough rounds to a baking sheet or large wire rack. Gather the scraps and gently press them into a disk; repeat the rolling and stamping process until all the dough is used. (The cut doughnuts can be covered with plastic wrap and stored at room temperature for up to 2 hours.)

4. Carefully drop the dough rings into the hot oil, 4 or 5 at a time, depending on the kettle size. As they rise to the surface, turn the doughnuts with tongs, a Chinese skimmer, or a slotted spoon. Fry the doughnuts until golden brown, about 50 seconds per side. Drain on a paper towel–lined baking sheet or wire rack. Repeat frying, returning the fat to temperature between batches. Serve immediately.

MAKING DOUGHNUTS

1. Roll out the dough on a heavily floured work surface, then stamp out rounds as close together as possible. Gather the scraps, press into a disk, and repeat.

2. Carefully slip the dough rings into the hot oil, a few at a time. As the doughnuts rise to the surface of the hot oil, flip them over with tongs or a slotted spoon.

Variations

POWDERED SUGAR BUTTERMILK DOUGHNUTS

Regular confectioners' sugar breaks down into a gummy glaze on the doughnuts, but Snow White Topping Sugar makes a long-lasting coating. This sugar can be ordered through the Baker's Catalogue (P.O. Box 876, Norwich, Vermont 05055; 800-827-6836; www.kingarthurflour.com).

Toss the doughnuts in nonmelting sugar to coat (about 1 cup) after cooling for 1 minute.

CINNAMON-SUGAR BUTTERMILK DOUGHNUTS

Toss the doughnuts in a mixture of 1 cup granulated sugar and 1 tablespoon ground cinnamon after cooling for 1 minute.

SHOPPING WITH THE TEST KITCHEN

Tongs: Tongs come in handy in a variety of ways in the test kitchen. From safely removing doughnuts from bubbling oil to retrieving an oven thermometer from a hot oven, tongs get the job done. While they are sold in a variety of sizes, for all-purpose kitchen use we like 12-inch tongs—they're long enough to keep your hands a safe distance from the heat, but not so long that they're unwieldy. The OXO Good Grips Locking 12-Inch Tongs ($9.99) are our favorite—they've got slightly concave pincers with gently scalloped edges that are good for grasping hard or irregularly shaped objects.

CHAPTER EIGHT

Bread Basket Favorites

BREAD BASKET FAVORITES

Scoop-and-Bake Dinner Rolls

Homemade dinner rolls are sometimes out of reach for the time-pressed cook. But there is one glimmer of hope: batter-style dinner rolls.

The ingredients for batter-style rolls (flour, yeast, milk, eggs, shortening, salt, and sugar) are simply stirred together into a pancake-batter consistency, briefly risen in the same bowl, and scooped into a muffin tin to bake without ever touching the work surface or your hands. We had never made these rolls before but were intrigued.

The recipes we uncovered promised rich rolls with a soft, moist texture that comes from the large amount of liquid in the batter, which steams in the oven and creates a puffy, popover-like effect.

After testing a handful of recipes, we learned that batter-style rolls really are a snap to put together—we were able to turn them out in minutes, not hours. These rolls have a pungent yeast flavor, however, as the quick rise doesn't give the yeast time to mellow. Just as worrisome, the rolls made from the recipes we tried baked up squat and heavy.

Fixing the flavor was our first challenge. Shortening was the fat of choice in most recipes, but tasters wanted butter, and they weren't happy until the amount stood at 6 tablespoons. The richness of the butter also helped temper the strong yeast flavor, but it made the batter heavier and the rolls flatter. Most recipes call for two eggs, but cutting back to one and switching from milk to water helped to lighten the batter and give the rolls more lift. But it still wasn't enough.

We turned our attention to the mixing method. Standard yeast doughs are kneaded to develop gluten in the flour, which builds structure and height. Kneading the thin batter was out of the question, but what about beating it? A hand-held mixer did the job—and then some, leaving us with rolls that were tall but too tough (from too much gluten). Looking for a gentler approach that would work—but not overwork—the batter, we beat the mixture with a whisk for a few minutes. It worked like a charm, producing the extra lift needed to make these rolls tall but without a trace of toughness.

With their rich flavor, fluffy texture, and quick, easy preparation, homemade rolls never sounded—or tasted—so good.

SCOOP-AND-BAKE DINNER ROLLS

MAKES 12 ROLLS

In step 3, use an ice cream scoop to transfer the sticky batter to the muffin tin. These rolls can easily be made ahead. Here's how: After being covered with greased plastic wrap in step 3, refrigerate the batter in the muffin tin for up to 24 hours. When ready to bake, let the batter sit at room temperature for 30 minutes before proceeding with the recipe.

2¼	cups all-purpose flour
¼	cup sugar
1	teaspoon salt
1	envelope (2¼ teaspoons) rapid-rise or instant yeast
1	cup warm water (110 degrees)
6	tablespoons unsalted butter, softened
1	large egg

1. Adjust an oven rack to the middle position and heat the oven to 200 degrees. Maintain the temperature for 10 minutes, then turn off the oven. Grease a 12-cup muffin tin.

2. Whisk together 1¼ cups of the flour, sugar, salt, and yeast in a large bowl. Whisk in the water, butter, and egg until very smooth, about 2 minutes. Add the remaining 1 cup flour and mix with a rubber spatula until just combined. Cover the bowl with greased plastic wrap and place in the warm oven until the batter has doubled in size, about 30 minutes.

1. Whisk the batter until smooth to develop structure and then stir in the last cup of flour until just combined.

2. Once the batter has risen for 30 minutes, scoop it into a greased muffin tin and let it continue to rise for 15 minutes before baking.

3. Remove the bowl from the oven and heat the oven to 375 degrees. Punch the batter down. Scoop the batter evenly into the muffin cups. Cover with greased plastic wrap and let rise at room temperature until the batter nearly reaches the rims of the muffin cups, about 15 minutes. Remove the plastic wrap and bake the rolls until golden, 14 to 18 minutes. Serve. (The rolls can be stored in an airtight container at room temperature for up to 3 days.)

Parker House Rolls

We have a soft spot for Parker House rolls. The epitome of thin-crusted, fluffy-crumbed American rolls, they're pillowy soft, a little sweet, and packed with butter. They owe their name to Boston's famed Parker House, a hotel that has been a bastion of Brahmin hospitality since the middle of the nineteenth century. Truth be told, the Parker House roll is pretty much a standard dinner roll; it's the shape that matters. It starts off as a round roll that is flattened, buttered, and folded in half. For our version we wanted a simple, rich roll that would be ready in the least time possible.

Almost all of the recipes we gathered had the same ingredients in varying proportions. The rolls made from these recipes were fairly rich, loaded with milk, eggs, butter, and a fair amount of sugar. Each recipe also employed a healthy amount of yeast for a quick rise and big yeast flavor. We tinkered with proportions until we arrived at a roll that was buttery, but not too rich, and very tender-crumbed from the large amount of milk and egg.

With a full envelope of yeast to about 4 cups of flour, we knew a quick rise would not be a problem. After the dough had risen, we divided the dough, and then rounded the individual portions on the work surface until they developed a smooth, tight surface and perfect globe shape. By the time we rounded all twenty-four balls of dough, the first to be rounded had relaxed enough to be shaped. We found that the best way to shape the dough was to lightly flatten it with our palms and then roll it into an oval shape with a small French-style rolling pin or short dowel. We found out the hard way that it is important to keep the edges thicker than the center so that they will adhere to each other when the dough is folded and not puff open during baking.

After folding and spacing the rolls on a baking sheet, we misted them lightly with vegetable oil. They were now ready for their second rise. Traditional recipes suggest dunking the formed rolls in melted butter, but we thought this would be too much of a good thing. Instead, we opted to lightly brush the rolls with melted butter. Once these rolls are baked, give them a 10-minute rest—and then they are ready to serve, preferably with a roast and plenty of gravy.

PARKER HOUSE ROLLS

MAKES 24 ROLLS

You will need about 6 tablespoons of melted butter to brush over the dough during shaping and over the rolls before baking. If you don't have a standing mixer, see "Alternative Mixing Methods for Breads and Rolls" on page 237.

1¼	cups warm whole milk (110 degrees)
8	tablespoons (1 stick) unsalted butter, melted and cooled, plus extra for brushing (see note above)
1	large egg
4–4½	cups all-purpose flour
2	tablespoons sugar
1	envelope (2¼ teaspoons) rapid-rise or instant yeast
1½	teaspoons salt

1. Whisk the milk, melted butter, and egg together in a large liquid measuring cup. Combine 4 cups of the flour, sugar, yeast, and salt in the bowl of a standing mixer fitted with the dough hook. With the mixer on low speed, add the milk mixture and mix until the dough comes together, about 2 minutes.

2. Increase the speed to medium-low and knead until the dough is smooth and elastic, about 8 minutes. (If, after 4 minutes, more flour is needed, add the remaining ½ cup flour, 2 tablespoons at a time, until the dough clears the sides of the bowl but sticks to the bottom.)

3. Turn the dough out onto a lightly floured work surface and knead by hand to form a smooth, round ball. Place the dough in a large, lightly greased bowl and cover with greased plastic wrap. Let rise in a warm place until doubled in size, 1 to 1½ hours.

ROUNDING THE DOUGH FOR ROLLS

1. Gently stretch the dough into one or two even logs according to the recipe. Using a knife, divide the dough into evenly sized pieces.

2. Working with one piece at a time, dimple the top of the dough with your fingertips and then pick up the dough, and gently fold the short ends underneath.

3. Stretch the dough around your thumbs into a smooth, taut ball. This should pull the dough into a roundish shape.

4. Drag the dough in small circles over a clean counter, using a cupped hand, until the dough feels firm and round.

4. Line 2 large baking sheets with parchment paper. Turn the dough out onto a clean work surface, divide it into 2 equal pieces, and, using your hands, stretch each piece into an even 12-inch log. Cut each log of dough into 12 equal pieces and cover with greased plastic wrap. Working with one piece of dough at a time (keep the remaining pieces covered), round the dough into smooth, taut rolls.

1. Use the palm of your hand to flatten each dough round into a ½-inch-thick circle. With a floured rolling pin, gently flatten the dough into an oval with a depressed middle.

2. Lightly brush the dough with melted butter, then fold in half and gently press the dough together at the edges to seal. Just before baking, lightly brush the rolls with more butter.

5. Use your hands and a rolling pin to flatten and roll each piece of dough into an oval with a depressed middle. Brush the oval-shaped pieces of dough with melted butter, then fold into the traditional Parker House shape, pressing lightly on the edges to seal. Lay the rolls on the prepared baking sheets, spaced about 2 inches apart. Mist the rolls with vegetable oil spray, cover loosely with greased plastic wrap, and let rise in a warm place until nearly doubled in size and the dough barely springs back when poked with a knuckle, 45 to 75 minutes.

6. Adjust the oven racks to the upper-middle and lower-middle positions and heat the oven to 350 degrees. Brush the rolls lightly with melted butter, then spray lightly with water. Bake until golden, 20 to 25 minutes, switching and rotating the baking sheets halfway through baking. Let the rolls cool on the baking sheets for 10 minutes, then serve warm.

Fluffy Dinner Rolls

For most of us, a holiday meal wouldn't be complete without a soft dinner roll teetering on the edge of an overflowing plate. In the test kitchen we like rolls that are oversized, slightly sweet, and fluffy enough to take a nap on. But turning out a batch of homemade dinner rolls when holiday stress is running high can be a daunting task. We determined to figure out a way to serve fresh, homemade rolls that would require no more work than store-bought rolls (at least on the big day) but taste much, much better.

Baking the rolls ahead of time and freezing them seemed like a logical option, so we baked up a standard American dinner roll recipe for our first test. These buttery rolls (made with milk, sugar, flour, yeast, and salt) were fine fresh out of the oven, but they turned dry and stale-tasting in the freezer, no matter how carefully we wrapped them or at what stage of the process (unbaked, half-baked, or fully baked) we froze them. Simply put, these rolls were a disaster.

To figure out how to make rolls that would survive the drying environment of the freezer, we began tinkering with the amount of each ingredient. We theorized that the more moisture and fat we could add to the dough, the better our chances for successful freezing. We bumped up the butter from 4 to 7 tablespoons, which did, indeed, turn out a richer roll, but after freezing, it was still too dry. Next, we tried replacing some of the butter with shortening, hoping that the shortening would tenderize the dough and make for a softer crumb after freezing. We substituted 4 tablespoons of shortening for an equal amount of the butter, and our hunch turned out to be right. The rolls baked up higher and much more tender, with the fluffy texture we were looking for. It turns out the shortening coats the gluten strands in the flour more effectively than butter and keeps baked goods from drying out.

We added an egg for extra structure and richness and replaced the sugar with honey, which keeps the rolls moist and tender. Now these rolls withstood even a month in the deep freeze, baking up as soft and fluffy as the day they were made. No one at the table will ever suspect these rolls have been frozen.

FLUFFY DINNER ROLLS

MAKES 15 ROLLS

It is important to keep the pieces of dough covered while rounding them into rolls or they will quickly dry out and develop a "skin." If you don't have a standing mixer, see the Hand-Mixing Method in "Alternative Mixing Methods for Breads and Rolls" on page 237. Don't try to make this bread in a food processor, as the volume of flour and other ingredients makes it difficult to mix the dough properly.

1½	cups whole milk
⅓	cup honey
4	tablespoons vegetable shortening
3	tablespoons unsalted butter
1	large egg, plus 1 egg for the egg wash
5–5½	cups all-purpose flour
1	envelope (2¼ teaspoons) rapid-rise or instant yeast
2	teaspoons salt

1. Microwave the milk, honey, shortening, and butter together in a large liquid measuring cup until the butter and shortening are mostly melted, about 2 minutes. Whisk to melt any remaining pieces of butter or shortening, then set aside to cool until just warm (about 110 degrees). Whisk in the egg.

2. Combine 5 cups of the flour, yeast, and salt in the bowl of a standing mixer fitted with the dough hook. With the mixer on low speed, add the milk mixture and mix until the dough comes together, about 2 minutes.

3. Increase the speed to medium-low and knead until the dough is smooth and elastic, about 8 minutes. (If, after 4 minutes, more flour is needed, add the remaining ½ cup flour, 2 tablespoons at a time, until the dough clears the sides of the bowl but sticks to the bottom.)

4. Turn the dough out onto a lightly floured work surface and knead by hand to form a smooth, round ball. Place the dough in a large, lightly oiled bowl and cover with greased plastic wrap. Let rise in a warm place until doubled in size, 1 to 1½ hours.

5. Following the photos on page 458, line a 13 by 9-inch baking dish with a foil sling and grease the foil. Turn the dough out onto a clean work surface and, using your hands, stretch it into an even 15-inch log. Following the photos on page 211, cut the log into 15 equal pieces and cover with greased plastic wrap. Working with one piece of dough at a time (keep the remaining pieces covered), round the dough into smooth, taut rolls and arrange them in the prepared baking dish.

6. Lightly press on the rolls so they just touch each other. Mist the rolls with vegetable oil spray, cover loosely with plastic wrap, and let rise in a warm place until nearly doubled in size and the dough barely springs back when poked with a knuckle, 45 to 75 minutes.

7. Adjust an oven rack to the lower-middle position and heat the oven to 350 degrees. Beat the remaining egg with 1 tablespoon water and brush the rolls gently with the egg mixture, then spray lightly with water. Bake the rolls until deep golden brown, 25 to 30 minutes, rotating the pan halfway through baking. Let the rolls cool in the pan for 10 minutes, then remove them from the pan using the foil and serve warm.

Popovers

Popovers are impressive because their few humble ingredients—eggs, milk, flour, salt, and butter—are transformed by the heat of the oven into the culinary equivalent of hot-air balloons. We were after the biggest, best-tasting popovers we could make, with huge crowns, lightly crisp, golden brown exteriors, and tender, moist, airy interiors crisscrossed with custardy webs of dough.

The recipes we looked at during our research were remarkably consistent in terms of the ingredients and their proportions. We soon arrived at a list that would stand by us throughout testing: 2 eggs, 1 cup milk, 1 cup flour, ½ teaspoon salt, and 1 tablespoon butter. The variables we needed to test revolved around technique. We started with the choice of baking pan. Could we use a muffin tin, or would a popover pan be necessary?

Our first efforts were baked in a muffin tin, and they failed to impress. Short and squat, with tops that looked something like overstuffed commas, these popovers were far from our ideal. We then tried a popover pan and the shape of the popovers improved—they were taller and puffier—but they still didn't have that beautiful crown we were looking for, and their texture was wrong, more like a dinner roll crossed with a muffin than a popover.

The popovers' resemblance to muffins got us thinking about the way we had been mixing the batter. When mixing muffins, which should be tender, the goal is to develop only enough gluten to hold things together, and this is usually accomplished by gently folding the ingredients. This is what we had been doing with our popover batter, leaving the mixture a little lumpy so as not to overdevelop the gluten. One or two recipes had different advice: whisk the ingredients until smooth. We tried this, and the popovers rose a bit higher and their texture began to improve, becoming slightly airier.

We were now ready to experiment with oven temperature. The rationale for starting with a hot oven (450 degrees in most recipes) and lowering the heat about halfway through baking (to 350 degrees) is to give the popovers the intense heat they need to turn the moisture in the batter to steam. The popovers expand, brown, and set their shape at 450, and the heat is then lowered to let the interior cook through without overcooking the shell. We tried starting the popovers in a cold oven, and we tried baking them at a constant 375 degrees, as recommended in a couple of recipes. The popovers did rise under these conditions, but not as dramatically as when we started at 450 degrees.

Following through on the idea that an initial blast of heat is good for popovers, we also tried preheating the pan (greased with vegetable oil)—and this worked well. Relying on condition and technique, we were able to turn simple ingredients into a morning or dinnertime treat.

POPOVERS

MAKES 6 POPOVERS

Unlike most popover batters, this one is smooth, not lumpy. High heat is crucial to the speedy, high rise of the popovers. When it's time to fill the popover pan with batter, get the pan out of and back into the oven as quickly as possible, and be sure to close the oven door while you pour the batter into the pan. Popovers made in a 12-cup muffin tin won't rise nearly as high as those made in a popover pan, but they can still be quite good. See the variation that follows if you can't locate a popover pan.

2	large eggs
1	cup whole milk
1	cup all-purpose flour
½	teaspoon salt
1	tablespoon unsalted butter, melted
1	tablespoon vegetable oil

1. In a large bowl, whisk the eggs and milk together until well combined, about 20 seconds. Whisk the flour and salt together in a medium bowl and add to the egg mixture; stir with a wooden spoon or spatula just until the flour is incorporated; the mixture will still be lumpy. Add the melted butter. Whisk until the batter is bubbly and smooth, about 30 seconds. Let the batter rest at room temperature for 30 minutes.

2. While the batter is resting, measure ½ teaspoon vegetable oil into each cup of the popover pan. Adjust the oven rack to the lowest position, place the popover pan in the oven, and heat the oven to 450 degrees. After the batter has rested, pour it into a 4-cup liquid measuring cup or another container with a spout (you will have about 2 cups batter). Working quickly, remove the pan from the oven and distribute the batter evenly among the 6 cups in the pan. Return the pan to the oven and bake for 20 minutes, without opening the oven door. Lower the heat to 350 degrees and bake until golden brown all over, 15 to 18 minutes more. Invert the pan onto a wire rack to remove popovers and cool for 2 to 3 minutes. Serve immediately.

Variation
MUFFIN-TIN POPOVERS
MAKES 10 POPOVERS

Proceed as in the preceding recipe, using a 12-cup muffin tin in place of the popover pan and using only the 10 outer cups of the tin. You will need an extra 2 teaspoons of vegetable oil to grease the muffin tin.

Quaker Bonnet Biscuits

Quaker bonnet biscuits, an old-fashioned biscuit shaped like a woman's bonnet viewed from the back, combine the convenience of a biscuit with the soft texture and yeasty flavor of good dinner rolls. Clues to the origin of this recipe proved elusive—that is, until we started searching through old Quaker journals and recipe collections. Our best lead came from a 1915 book titled *Mary at the Farm and Book of Recipes Compiled during Her Visit among the "Pennsylvania Germans,"* by Edith M. Thomas. With a lot of guesswork (Mary's original recipe called for "a quick but not too hot oven"), we prepared this recipe, and it produced a darn good biscuit. But the recipe needed some updating.

We started by cutting the quantity in half to make a more reasonable number of biscuits. Using butter in place of a combination of butter and lard made the rolls taste better, but tasters wanted more butter. In the end, we used the same amount of fat called for in Mary's original recipe but just half the flour. Mary's recipe didn't include salt or sugar, but the rolls tasted better when we added modest amounts of each.

We knew that rapid-rise yeast would speed up the rising time. (It's also more widely available than the cake yeast specified in the original recipe.) After an hour the dough had doubled in size (the usual sign that a yeast dough is ready), so we patted it out and stamped out biscuits. After giving the cut biscuits a second rise, we popped them into the oven, and a few minutes later we had yeasty biscuits that were nice and flaky.

We wanted to shave even more time off this already-shortened recipe. Mary might have had all morning to make them, but we wanted to whip up a batch of these tender biscuits after work for dinner. We were already down from 4 hours to around 2; could we do better?

MAKING QUAKER BONNET BISCUITS

1. Roll the dough into a 12-inch round, ¾ inch thick. Cut out eighteen 2½-inch circles and place them on parchment-lined baking sheets.

2. Reroll the remaining dough to a thickness of ½ inch, then cut out eighteen 1¼-inch rounds.

3. Lightly brush the larger dough rounds with melted butter.

4. Place one smaller round slightly off center on top of each larger round.

During our research we ran across several super-quick Southern yeast biscuit recipes, including Alabama biscuits and angel biscuits, that skipped the initial rising time. As soon as the dough came together, it was rolled out, cut, allowed to rise, and baked. Could a Southern recipe speed up the preparation of these Pennsylvania biscuits?

Judging from the way tasters tore into them, we'd say they approved of these "once-raised" Quaker bonnet biscuits. And if we let the cut biscuits rise in a warm oven, the rising time was just half an hour. We had great biscuits in just an hour—start to finish. That sounds like a recipe that belongs in any modern kitchen.

QUAKER BONNET BISCUITS

MAKES 18 BISCUITS

To make these biscuits without a food processor, freeze the stick of butter until hard and then grate it into the flour mixture using the large holes of a box grater. Toss gently with your hands to evenly distribute the butter, and proceed with the recipe. Note that you will need two sizes of round biscuit cutters for this recipe: a 2½-inch cutter and a 1¼-inch cutter.

- 1   **cup whole milk**
- 1   **large egg**
- 1   **envelope (2¼ teaspoons) rapid-rise or instant yeast**
- 4   **cups all-purpose flour**
- 2   **tablespoons sugar**
- 1½   **teaspoons salt**
- 8   **tablespoons (1 stick) cold unsalted butter, cut into ½-inch pieces, plus 1 tablespoon unsalted butter, melted (for assembling biscuits)**

1. Adjust the oven racks to the upper-middle and lower-middle positions and heat the oven to 200 degrees. Once the oven reaches 200 degrees, maintain the temperature for 10 minutes, then turn off the oven. Line 2 large baking sheets with parchment paper.

2. Stir the milk, egg, and yeast together in a large liquid measuring cup until combined.

3. Process the flour, sugar, and salt in a food processor until combined. Add the chilled butter and pulse until the mixture looks like coarse cornmeal, about fifteen 1-second pulses. Transfer to a large bowl.

4. Stir in the milk mixture until the dough comes together. Turn the dough out onto a lightly floured work surface. Briefly knead to bring the dough together, about 1 minute, adding more flour if necessary to prevent the dough from sticking to the work surface. Following the photos, roll, cut, and assemble the biscuits on the prepared baking sheets. Cover with clean dishtowels and let rise in the warm oven until doubled in size, 25 to 35 minutes.

5. Remove the baking sheets with biscuits from the oven and remove the towel. Heat the oven to 375 degrees. Return the baking sheets to the oven once it is fully preheated. Bake the biscuits until golden brown, about 15 minutes, rotating and switching the baking sheets halfway through the baking time. Serve hot or warm.

Angel Biscuits

A Southern specialty, angel biscuits are modest in height, but remarkably light and fluffy—hence their name. Research revealed the reason for the light, cloud-like texture of these biscuits: they're made with yeast, baking powder, and baking soda, which creates a triple-force lift. The use of three rising agents also explains why these biscuits are sometimes called "bride's biscuits," as even a novice cook (or a new bride) can make light and fluffy biscuits on the first attempt. The rounds of dough are folded in half before baking, causing the ethereally light biscuits to puff into "angel's wings" in the oven.

Digging deeper into the history of angel biscuits, we learned they were conceived as a use for leftover scraps of sour yeasted bread dough. In her 1846 book *Miss Beecher's Domestic Receipt-Book*, Catherine Beecher instructed cooks to "sweeten" (or neutralize) soured yeast-dough scraps with saleratus (a crude chemical leavener similar to today's baking soda), knead in shortening, and cut the "new" dough into biscuits.

But when we baked biscuits from a few modern recipes, not one biscuit was as light and fluffy as we'd hoped. Looking for a bigger and faster rise, we turned to instant yeast. We found that quickly dissolving it in warm buttermilk allowed the yeast to begin working immediately, speeding up the rising time to just 30 minutes and producing the ultra-tender, feathery texture we wanted.

Typically, angel biscuits are made with shortening, rather than butter, to keep the flavor of the fat from competing with the yeast flavor. To minimize oven spread, we reduced the amount of shortening and switched from traditional cake flour to heartier all-purpose flour. Once these hot, feathery biscuits were out of the oven, we could barely wait to slather them with butter.

THE AMERICAN TABLE
GIVING RISE TO CHEMICAL LEAVENERS

Until the early 1800s, bread baking and beer making were linked by one ingredient, yeast, which home bakers would get from their local brewers. But by the 1830s, brewer's yeast came under scrutiny from the temperance movement, which wanted to ban all alcohol. As a result of the anti-alcohol fervor, bakers started to use alternative leaveners. Pearl ash and saleratus had been used for more than a hundred years to leaven thin batters, but they were undependable for breads and biscuits and produced off-flavors. In 1846 Dr. Austin Church helped create sodium bicarbonate (baking soda), which would later be distinguished by its Arm & Hammer logo. Modern baking powder was first mass-produced in 1898, when August Oetker began marketing his stable leavening combination of baking soda and a powdered acid.

ANGEL BISCUITS

MAKES 16 BISCUITS

You will need a 2½-inch round biscuit cutter for this recipe.

1	cup warm buttermilk (110 degrees)
1	envelope (2¼ teaspoons) rapid-rise or instant yeast
2½	cups all-purpose flour
2	teaspoons baking powder
½	teaspoon baking soda
2	tablespoons sugar
1	teaspoon salt
8	tablespoons chilled vegetable shortening, cut into ½-inch pieces
2	tablespoons unsalted butter, melted

1. Adjust the oven racks to the upper-middle and lower-middle positions and heat the oven to 200 degrees. Maintain the temperature for 10 minutes, then turn off the oven. Line two baking sheets with parchment paper.

2. Stir the buttermilk and yeast together until dissolved. In the bowl of a standing mixer fitted with the paddle attachment, mix the flour, baking powder, baking soda, sugar, and salt on low speed until combined. Add the shortening and mix until just incorporated, about 1 minute. Slowly mix in the buttermilk mixture until the dough comes together, about 30 seconds. Fit the mixer with the dough hook and mix on low speed until the dough is shiny and smooth, about 2 minutes.

3. On a lightly floured work surface, knead the dough briefly to form a smooth ball. Roll the dough into a 10-inch circle, about ½ inch thick. Using a 2½-inch biscuit cutter dipped in flour, cut out rounds and transfer to the prepared baking sheets. Gather the remaining dough and pat into a ½-inch-thick circle. Cut the remaining biscuits and transfer to the baking sheets and shape following the photos. Cover the dough with clean kitchen towels and let rise in the warm oven until doubled in size, about 30 minutes.

4. Remove the baking sheets from the oven and heat the oven to 350 degrees. Remove the kitchen towels and bake the biscuits until golden brown, 12 to 14 minutes, switching and rotating the sheets halfway through baking. Remove from the oven and brush the tops with the melted butter. Serve.

Variation
FOOD PROCESSOR ANGEL BISCUITS
In step 2, process the flour, baking powder, baking soda, sugar, and salt until thoroughly mixed. Add the shortening and pulse until only pea-sized pieces of shortening remain, about six 1-second pulses. Add the buttermilk mixture in a steady stream and pulse until the dough comes together, about six more pulses. (The dough will be very sticky.) Turn the dough out onto a floured work surface and knead until shiny and smooth, about 5 minutes, adding more flour as necessary. Continue the recipe with rolling out the dough as directed in step 3.

SHAPING ANGEL BISCUITS

1. Using a ruler, make an indentation through the center of each round. Lightly brush half of the dough with water.

2. Fold each round of dough in half; press lightly to adhere.

Cheese Biscuits

Is there such a thing as a cheese biscuit that's simple to make? Although getting there doesn't take long, good results are far from guaranteed. We think starting with cream biscuits is the best bet for beginners. Simply pouring heavy cream into the dry ingredients replaces the challenging step of cutting cubes of butter into flour. And then if we added cheese, would we be almost there?

After our first attempts, we would have answered no. When tasters used words like "flat," "gummy," and "greasy" to describe our biscuits, we knew we were in trouble. After some head scratching, we realized that excess moisture and fat from the cheese were the culprits. It was pretty easy to solve the moisture issue. We just avoided wet cheeses, such as feta and goat, in favor of cheddar and Parmesan.

With drier cheeses in the mix, our biscuits were no longer flat—but they were still greasy and gummy in the center. After several tests, we found that the dough could handle no more than ½ to ¾ cup of shredded cheese without suffering textural problems (the amount varied based on the fat content of the specific cheese). Unfortunately, this wasn't enough to make really cheesy biscuits.

Our first thought was to top each biscuit with extra cheese prior to baking. Unfortunately, the added weight of the cheese kept the biscuits from rising properly, and the cheese burned before the biscuits were fully cooked. The ultimate (and somewhat unconventional) solution was to sprinkle extra cheese on each biscuit halfway through baking, when we rotated the baking sheet.

EASY CHEDDAR BISCUITS

MAKES 8 BISCUITS

For our tasting of extra-sharp cheddar cheese, see page 220.

2   cups all-purpose flour
2   teaspoons sugar
2   teaspoons baking powder
½   teaspoon salt
¾   cup shredded extra-sharp cheddar cheese
1½   cups heavy cream

1. Adjust an oven rack to the upper-middle position and heat the oven to 425 degrees. Line a baking sheet with parchment paper.

2. Whisk the flour, sugar, baking powder, and salt together in a medium bowl. Stir in ½ cup of the cheese. Add 1¼ cups of the cream and stir with a wooden spoon until a dough forms, about 30 seconds. Transfer the dough from the bowl to a lightly floured work surface, leaving the dry, floury bits in the bowl. In 1-tablespoon increments, add up to ¼ cup more cream to the dry bits in the bowl, mixing with a wooden spoon after each addition, until moistened. Add the moistened bits to the rest of the dough and knead by hand just until smooth, about 30 seconds.

3. Pat the dough into an 8-inch circle, cut into 8 wedges, and place on the prepared baking sheet. Bake until just beginning to brown, 7 to 9 minutes. Remove the baking sheet from the oven, sprinkle the remaining ¼ cup cheese evenly over the biscuits, and return to the oven, rotating the baking sheet from front to back. Bake until golden brown and the cheese topping has melted, 7 to 9 minutes. Serve warm.

Variation
EASY PARMESAN-GARLIC BISCUITS

Replace the cheddar with 1 cup grated Parmesan cheese. Add ¾ cup of the cheese, 2 minced garlic cloves, and ½ teaspoon pepper to the flour mixture. Proceed as directed, sprinkling the remaining ¼ cup cheese over the biscuits halfway through baking.

Extra-Sharp Cheddar Cheese: So what is extra-sharp cheddar? Our research revealed that most extra-sharp cheddars are aged from 9 to 18 months. As cheddar ages, new flavor compounds are created, and the cheese gets firmer in texture and more concentrated in flavor—and it gets sharper.

But is more sharpness desirable? Does it make for better cheddar? To find out which supermarket extra-sharp cheddar cheese our tasters liked best, we purchased nine varieties and headed into the kitchen to sample them. Our tasters generally liked the older cheeses best both for their sharpness and for their denser, more crumbly bite. Our top-rated cheeses—Cabot Private Stock Cheddar Cheese and Cabot Extra Sharp Cheddar Cheese—are both aged for at least 12 months, and tasters rated them among the sharpest. Tasters praised the Cabot Private Stock's considerable but well-rounded sharpness, depth of flavor, and creaminess, while the Cabot Extra Sharp rated a close second overall.

Cheesy Garlic Bread

Based on our experience, garlic bread—with cheese or not—often consists of greasy, soggy bread with a layer of bitter garlic flavor on top and no flavor at all in the middle. Great garlic bread should be light and fluffy on the inside and crunchy on the outside, with the deep perfume of nutty garlic and rich butter throughout.

Our first step was to develop a foolproof garlic bread recipe. We could tackle the cheese component later. We tried raw, roasted, and toasted garlic in combination with butter and olive oil to see which, if any, would yield the right balance of garlic flavor. We mashed the garlic, sliced it, and chopped it. In most cases the flavors were so bitter and pungent our eyes watered. Starting with minced garlic and cold butter in a pan over low heat brought out the nuttiest flavors, but tasters complained about biting into chunks of sharp garlic. Grating the garlic, we found, ensures smooth, evenly distributed bits of garlic and full flavor, and adding a little water to the pan prevents the garlic from drying out and burning. After a few minutes over low heat, the garlic turned into a sticky, golden paste that was perfect for slathering on bread.

Selecting the bread was easy. Supermarket Italian bread was immediately eliminated because of its thin crust and soft, spongy interior. With its crisp crust and chewy interior, a supermarket baguette was a far better choice.

Up to this point we had been slicing the loaf horizontally and baking the halves open-faced until warm and toasty. The garlic-butter mixture was flavoring the top of the bread, but the rest of the loaf was bland. We solved the problem by wrapping the slathered bread in aluminum foil and letting the garlic butter steam for 15 minutes. Unwrapping the bread and opening up the layers for another short stint in the oven made our garlic bread crisp.

As for the cheesy crust, some tasters preferred Parmesan for its potent flavor, while others favored gooey cheeses like mozzarella. Rather than taking the time to grate and shred several cheeses, we picked up a packaged blend of shredded Italian cheeses that satisfied everyone. A quick blast of heat from the broiler melted the cheese and helped crisp the bread even further.

CHEESY GARLIC BREAD

SERVES 6 TO 8

The serrated edges on a bread knife can pull off the cheesy crust. To prevent this, place the finished garlic bread cheese side down on a cutting board. Slicing through the crust (rather than the cheese) first will keep the cheese in place. Shredded Italian cheese blend is sold along with other packaged shredded cheeses in the supermarket.

5	garlic cloves, grated
8	tablespoons (1 stick) unsalted butter, softened
½	teaspoon water
¼	teaspoon salt
¼	teaspoon pepper
1	(18- to 20-inch) baguette, sliced in half horizontally
1½	cups shredded Italian cheese blend

1. Adjust an oven rack to the lower-middle position and heat the oven to 400 degrees. Cook the garlic, 1 tablespoon of the butter, and water in a small nonstick skillet over low heat, stirring occasionally, until straw-colored, 7 to 10 minutes.

2. Mix the hot garlic, remaining 7 tablespoons butter, salt, and pepper in a bowl and spread on the cut sides of the bread. Sandwich the bread back together and wrap the loaf in aluminum foil. Place on a baking sheet and bake for 15 minutes.

3. Carefully unwrap the bread and place the halves, buttered sides up, on the baking sheet. Bake until just beginning to color, about 10 minutes. Remove from the oven and set the oven to broil.

4. Sprinkle the bread with the cheese. Broil until the cheese has melted and the bread is crisp, 1 to 2 minutes. Transfer the bread to a cutting board with the cheese side facing down. Cut into pieces. Serve.

Beer-Batter Cheese Bread

Nothing warms up the house like the smell of baking bread—but making a yeasted loaf from scratch can take half the day. Luckily, there are quick breads, like beer-batter cheese bread, that can be on the table in less than an hour. The basic recipe for this bread is simple: just stir together flour, sugar, cheese, salt, beer, and baking powder; scrape the batter into a loaf pan; pour melted butter on top (to create a rich and craggy crust); and bake. There are no long rises, kneading, or hassle. Best of all, the beer gives this bread a hearty flavor.

Unfortunately, there were a lot of problems with the recipes we found. Many loaves tasted sour, like stale beer, and others had negligible cheese flavor. And some breads were so greasy that we had to pass out extra napkins at each tasting. We wanted a lighter loaf of bread enhanced with the yeasty flavor of beer and a big hit of cheese. And we wanted it to be as easy as advertised.

To test beer flavor, we made two loaves, using an inexpensive American lager in one and a dark ale in the other. The dark ale tasted great in a glass, but its strong flavor turned bitter when baked in the bread. The mild domestic lager (Budweiser and Miller Genuine Draft were our favorites in a later tasting) provided a clean, subtle, grainy flavor without any sourness at all. And although a few recipes specifically called for room-temperature beer, we found no discernible difference between breads baked with warm beer and those baked with cold beer.

Mild cheddar is typically the cheese of choice in this recipe, but no matter how much we used—up to 3 cups for a single loaf—the flavor was, well, mild. We turned to more assertive cheeses like Gruyère, smoked Gouda, and extra-sharp cheddar. The bolder cheeses let us get away with using less (about

1 cup per loaf), so the bread was less greasy. We shredded the cheese to evenly distribute its flavor throughout the loaf.

Although some of the greasiness was gone, the loaves still felt too stodgy and heavy. Increasing the amount of baking powder helped lighten the crumb a little, but we knew that pouring melted butter over the batter before baking—which creates the beautiful crust—was part of the problem. Cutting back the butter from a full stick to half a stick made the loaf considerably lighter while still producing that craggy crust. We finally had a beer-batter cheese bread that was as easy to eat as it was to make.

BEER-BATTER CHEESE BREAD

MAKES ONE 9-INCH LOAF

Brushing butter on top of the loaf before baking makes a super-crisp and flavorful crust. You will need about 1 tablespoon melted butter for brushing the top of the bread.

1	cup shredded Gruyère cheese
2½	cups all-purpose flour
3	tablespoons sugar
4	teaspoons baking powder
1	teaspoon salt
½	teaspoon pepper
1¼	cups light-bodied beer, such as Budweiser
4	tablespoons unsalted butter, melted, plus extra for brushing

1. Adjust an oven rack to the middle position and heat the oven to 375 degrees. Grease an 8½ by 4½-inch loaf pan.

2. Combine the cheese, flour, sugar, baking powder, salt, and pepper in a large bowl. Stir in the beer and melted butter and mix until well combined. Pour into the loaf pan, spreading the batter to the corners, and brush lightly with the extra melted butter.

3. Bake until deep golden brown and a toothpick inserted into the center of the loaf comes out clean, 40 to 45 minutes, rotating the pan halfway through baking. Cool the bread in the pan for 5 minutes, then turn out onto a wire rack. Cool completely and slice as desired. (Although this bread can be kept in an airtight container at room temperature for up to 3 days, after the second day it is best toasted.)

Variations

BEER-BATTER BREAD WITH SMOKED GOUDA AND BACON

Substitute 1 cup shredded smoked Gouda for the Gruyère. Stir 8 slices bacon, cooked until crisp and crumbled, into the bowl with the cheese.

BEER-BATTER BREAD WITH CHEDDAR AND JALAPEÑO

Substitute 1 cup shredded extra-sharp cheddar for the Gruyère. Stir 2 seeded and minced jalapeño chiles into the bowl with the cheese.

SHOPPING WITH THE TEST KITCHEN

Box Graters: Food processors can swiftly shred pounds of cheese or vegetables, but lugging out the appliance for grating a relatively small amount of something, like a pound of carrots for carrot cake, is impractical. That's when we turn to a box grater. But you don't need to risk slicing your knuckles in order to use one. Our favorite is the Oxo Good Grips Box Grater ($14.99). It has a slim body and sharp teeth that require very little effort or pressure when grating. It also comes with a handy clear container marked with cup measurements that snaps on to the bottom for easy storage and cleanup.

BEER-BATTER CHEESE BREAD (page 222)

TOP: **LIGHT AND CRISPY WAFFLES** (page 159), **SUNDAY BRUNCH FRENCH TOAST** (page 160)
BOTTOM: **CINNAMON SWIRL BREAD** (page 195), **POTATO AND SAUSAGE BREAKFAST POPOVER CASSEROLE** (page 171)

CLOUDCAKES (page 153)

TOP: **COFFEE-CAKE MUFFINS** (page 183), **QUAKER BONNET BISCUITS** (page 216)
BOTTOM: **FLUFFY DINNER ROLLS** (page 213), **ALMOND RING COFFEE CAKE** (page 200)

MONKEY BREAD (page 193)

TOP: **CHICKEN, BROCCOLI, AND ZITI CASSEROLE** (page 259), **SCOOP-AND-BAKE DINNER ROLLS** (page 209)
BOTTOM: **SOUTHERN-STYLE SKILLET CORNBREAD** (page 232), **BEEF ENCHILADAS** (page 243)

SKILLET LASAGNA (page 256)

POTLUCK MACARONI AND CHEESE (page 249)

Southern-Style Skillet Cornbread

Unlike sweet and cakey Northern versions that are better suited to the dessert table, Southern cornbread contains neither sugar nor flour, making it savory enough to join the main course. We wanted to make a proper Southern cornbread with hearty corn flavor, a sturdy, moist crumb, and a dark brown crust.

Whereas Northern cornbread is cooked in a baking pan in a moderate oven, Southern skillet cornbread requires a little juggling—but the crisp crust is well worth the effort. The fat (oil, butter, bacon fat, or lard) is preheated in a cast-iron skillet and then combined with a mixture of cornmeal, buttermilk or milk, eggs, baking powder, baking soda, and salt. The batter is poured into the hot greased skillet and cooked in the oven until golden and crusty.

After whipping up a spread of existing recipes, we realized this wasn't going to be easy. One cornbread was flat as a pancake, another was dripping in grease, and most were sorely lacking in flavor. Since corn flavor is absolutely essential to good Southern-style

skillet cornbread, we figured we'd work through flavor issues first and fix the texture later.

We moved forward using the least offensive recipe of the lot, which was made with flavorful whole-grain stone-ground cornmeal. Subsequent testing, however, exposed the stone-ground cornmeal as too gritty, even when we tried grinding it down further in a food processor. We made our next batch with widely available and finely ground Quaker cornmeal. The texture of this cornbread was certainly better, but now the corn flavor was very mild—not really a surprise, since the germ is removed from this cornmeal during processing. Hoping that toasting would intensify its flavor, we spread the finely ground cornmeal on a baking sheet and threw it into the oven. We couldn't believe what a difference a mere 5 minutes of toasting had made: the cornbread now had big corn flavor, with minimal grit.

Increasing the buttermilk, which tasters preferred to milk, added a sharp tang that worked well with the corn. When it came to fat selection, tasters rejected bacon drippings, shortening, and lard, saying that each had a distinct flavor that took away from the corn; a combination of butter (for flavor) and vegetable oil (which can withstand high heat

SECRETS TO SOUTHERN-STYLE SKILLET CORNBREAD

1. Toasting the cornmeal gives the bread richer corn flavor.

2. Combining the hot cornmeal and buttermilk softens the cornmeal, resulting in a tender, sturdy, slightly moist crumb.

3. A greased and thoroughly heated pan creates a crisp crust.

4. Cool the cornbread for 5 minutes. Using good pot holders because the handle is very hot, turn the bread out of the skillet onto a wire rack.

without burning) worked much better. The flavor was now on track, but the texture was too crumbly.

One cornbread recipe we'd seen included instructions for making a cornmeal mush by softening raw cornmeal with boiling water to moisten the bread's texture. Using the same principle, we mixed the hot toasted cornmeal with the buttermilk. The cornmeal softened in just a few minutes; then we mixed the batter and put the skillet into the oven. Now this was the cornbread we remembered—crisp, slightly moist, cohesive and not crumbly, and with bold corn flavor. But would it win over our tasters? We sliced up fat wedges and listened with satisfaction as each taster admitted that when it comes to cornbread, the South just might be onto something.

SOUTHERN-STYLE SKILLET CORNBREAD

SERVES 12

Any 10-inch oven-safe skillet will work here, but our first choice (for both tradition and function) is a cast-iron skillet. Avoid coarsely ground cornmeal, as it will make the cornbread gritty.

2¼	cups cornmeal (see note above)
2	cups buttermilk
¼	cup vegetable oil
4	tablespoons unsalted butter, cut into pieces
1	teaspoon baking powder
1	teaspoon baking soda
¾	teaspoon salt
2	large eggs

1. Adjust the oven racks to the lower-middle and middle positions and heat the oven to 450 degrees. Heat a 10-inch oven-safe skillet on the middle rack for 10 minutes. Bake the cornmeal on a rimmed baking sheet set on the lower-middle rack until fragrant and the color begins to deepen, about 5 minutes. Transfer the hot cornmeal to a large bowl and whisk in the buttermilk; set aside.

2. Add the oil to the hot skillet and continue to bake until the oil is just smoking, about 5 minutes. Remove the skillet from the oven and add the butter, carefully swirling the pan until the butter is melted. Pour all but 1 tablespoon of the oil mixture into the cornmeal mixture, leaving the remaining fat in the pan. Whisk the baking powder, baking soda, salt, and eggs into the cornmeal mixture.

3. Pour the cornmeal mixture into the hot skillet and bake until the top begins to crack and the sides are golden brown, 12 to 16 minutes. Let cool in the pan for 5 minutes, then turn out onto a wire rack. Serve warm.

SHOPPING WITH THE TEST KITCHEN

Cast-Iron Skillets: A cast-iron pan combines the best traits of both nonstick and traditional cookware: You can make eggs and sear steak in the same pan. Its material and weight give it excellent heat retention for high-heat cooking techniques such as frying and searing. You can use it on the stovetop or bake with it in the oven. Preseasoned cast iron comes close to nonstick, especially with repeated use. However, this endorsement comes with two important caveats—you must choose the right pan, and you must be willing to care for it. We ran 8 cast-iron skillets through tests including cooking scrambled eggs, searing steaks, and baking cornbread. In the end, we preferred the classic design—with straight (rather than sloped) sides—and roomy interior of the preseasoned Lodge Logic 12-inch Skillet ($26.95). It performed well in all our cooking tests, its surface gained seasoning during testing, and it will last for generations. If you don't mind a truly heavy pan, the preseasoned Camp Chef 12-inch Skillet is a solid performer for only $17.99. While we often find that you get what you pay for, in the case of cast iron, you don't need to spend more to get more.

All-Purpose Cornbread

Deeply rooted in American culture, cornbread has been around long enough to take on a distinctly different character depending on where it is made. In the South it has become a squat, savory skillet bread. In cooler northern regions, where it has become more cake than bread, it is light, tender, and generously sweetened. Despite these regional variations in texture and appearance, however, cornbread has remained unfortunately constant in one respect: it often lacks convincing corn flavor.

Wanting to avoid a regional food fight, we figured that everyone north and south of the Mason-Dixon Line could agree on one simple notion: cornbread ought to be rich with the flavor of corn. A deeply browned crust also seemed far from controversial, and when it came to texture, we attempted a reasonable regional compromise: moist and somewhat fluffy but neither cakey nor heavy.

Our first tests involved the cornmeal. The different brands ran the gamut from fine and powdery to coarse and uneven, yielding wild variations in texture, from dry and cottony to downright crunchy, but not one produced very much corn flavor. We quickly came to the conclusion that our recipe, like it or not, would have to use a national brand of cornmeal to avoid these huge textural swings. The obvious option was Quaker yellow cornmeal. Reliable though it is, Quaker cornmeal is degerminated—robbed of the germ (the heart of the kernel) during processing. It is thus also robbed of flavor. To boost corn flavor, a few recipes included fresh corn in the batter. While appreciating the sweet corn taste, tasters objected to the tough, chewy kernels. Chopping the corn by hand was time-consuming. Pureeing the corn in the food processor was much quicker and broke down the kernels more efficiently. With pureed corn, our recipe was finally starting to develop a fuller flavor.

The dairy component up until now had been whole milk. To compensate for the extra liquid exuded by the pureed corn, we reduced the amount, but this just made the cornbread bland. We tried substituting a modest amount of buttermilk, which produced both a lighter texture and a tangier flavor. The sweetener also had an effect on texture; honey and maple syrup added nice flavor accents, but they also added moisture. Granulated and light brown sugars made for a better texture, but the light brown sugar did more to accentuate the corn flavor. Two eggs worked well in this bread, offering structure without cakiness. A modest amount of baking powder boosted by a bit of baking soda (to react with the acidic buttermilk) yielded the best rise. For the best flavor and texture, our recipe would also include a lot more butter than many others we found in our research—a whole stick.

For a thick and crunchy crust, we baked the bread in a hot oven—400 degrees, which yielded a crust that was both crunchy and full of buttery, toasted-corn flavor.

ALL-PURPOSE CORNBREAD
SERVES 6

Before preparing the baking dish or any of the other ingredients, measure out the frozen kernels and let them stand at room temperature until needed. When corn is in season, fresh cooked kernels can be substituted for the frozen corn. This recipe was developed with Quaker yellow cornmeal; a stone-ground whole-grain cornmeal will work but will yield a drier and less tender cornbread. We prefer an ovenproof glass baking dish because it yields a nice golden-brown crust, but a metal baking dish (nonstick or traditional) will also work. The cornbread is best served warm; leftovers can be wrapped in aluminum foil and reheated in a 350-degree oven for 10 to 15 minutes.

1½ cups all-purpose flour

1 cup yellow cornmeal (see note above)

2 teaspoons baking powder

¼ teaspoon baking soda

¾ teaspoon salt

¼ cup packed light brown sugar

¾ cup frozen corn kernels, thawed (see note above)

1 cup buttermilk

2 large eggs

8 tablespoons (1 stick) unsalted butter, melted and cooled slightly

1. Adjust an oven rack to the middle position and heat the oven to 400 degrees. Grease an 8-inch square baking dish. Whisk together the flour, cornmeal, baking powder, baking soda, and salt in a medium bowl until combined; set aside.

2. In a food processor or blender, process the brown sugar, thawed corn kernels, and buttermilk until combined, about 5 seconds. Add the eggs and process until well combined (corn lumps will remain), about 5 seconds longer.

3. Using a rubber spatula, make a well in the center of the flour mixture; pour the buttermilk mixture into the well. Begin folding the flour mixture into the buttermilk mixture, using only a few turns to barely combine; add the melted butter and continue folding until the batter is just moistened. Pour the batter into the prepared baking dish; smooth the surface with a rubber spatula. Bake until deep golden brown and a toothpick inserted in the center comes out clean, 25 to 35 minutes. Cool on a wire rack for 10 minutes; invert the cornbread onto a wire rack, then turn right side up and continue to cool until warm, about 10 minutes longer. Cut into pieces and serve.

Variations

SPICY JALAPEÑO-CHEDDAR CORNBREAD

Reduce the salt to ½ teaspoon and the sugar to 2 tablespoons; add ⅜ teaspoon cayenne pepper, 1 medium jalapeño chile, seeded and minced, and ⅔ cup shredded cheddar cheese to the flour mixture in step 1 and toss well to combine. Sprinkle ⅔ cup shredded cheddar cheese over the batter in the baking dish just before baking.

BLUEBERRY BREAKFAST CORNBREAD

Reduce the salt to ½ teaspoon; add 1 cup fresh or frozen blueberries (do not thaw frozen blueberries) to the flour mixture in step 1 and toss well to coat the berries. Reduce the buttermilk to ¾ cup and add ¼ cup maple syrup to the food processor along with the buttermilk. Sprinkle 2 tablespoons granulated sugar over the batter in the baking dish just before baking.

Boston Brown Bread

Rarely eaten more than a hundred miles outside of Boston and almost never served without baked beans, Boston brown bread is a unique loaf. Characteristically steamed in an old coffee can, this chemically leavened bread is robust, dense, and strongly flavored with earthy grains and the bittersweet tang of molasses.

Like Boston baked beans, brown bread is a study in Puritan frugality. Most of the recipes we gathered offered up a simple batter of cornmeal, whole-wheat and rye flours, molasses, raisins or currants, and baking soda for leavening. We appreciated the simple flavors of these uncomplicated recipes, but we found most of them to be unbalanced, tasting predominantly of whole wheat. We wanted a recipe in which all the ingredients were on more equal footing.

We began by changing the flour mixture—lightening the whole-wheat and rye flours with a little unbleached white flour. The addition of the white flour allowed the cornmeal and molasses flavors to come through more clearly.

We also found that the choice of cornmeal makes a real difference in this simple bread. High-quality stone-ground cornmeal was the tasters' favorite for its strong flavor and the pleasing texture it added to the loaf.

We experimented with different kinds of molasses and were most pleased with the darker varieties. Light, or mild, molasses was fine and provided adequate flavor, but dark molasses imparted a heartier flavor that nicely complemented the earthy whole-wheat and rye flours. Blackstrap, the dregs of sugar processing and therefore the strongest-flavored molasses, was too much, giving the loaf a bitter, one-dimensional flavor.

For cooking, there are two schools of thought: steaming and baking. In a side-by-side comparison, tasters favored the steamed loaves over the baked. Most people thought the baked loaves were closer to Irish soda bread in texture and flavor than what they knew as brown bread. While delicious, the baked bread was another species. The steamed loaves were dense, moist, and deeply satisfying.

Traditionally, Boston brown bread is steamed in a large coffee can set in a pan of simmering water on the stovetop. Because many people buy coffee in a bag, we resorted to more readily available containers: loaf pans. Small pans, about 8½ by 4 inches, proved the perfect size for even cooking in about 2 hours. To keep moisture (due to condensation) from seeping into the bread, we sealed a double layer of buttered aluminum foil very tightly around the lip of the pan.

We cooked the loaves in two 8-quart Dutch ovens (one loaf in each pot), with water reaching halfway up the sides of the loaf pans. If you do not have two large Dutch ovens, you can use a deep roasting pan sealed with aluminum foil for one or both of the loaves.

Boston brown bread's robust flavors stand up well to baked beans and pot roasts as well as hearty soups and stews. If you have any leftover bread, try it toasted with butter and jam, especially marmalade. Cream cheese is good, too.

BOSTON BROWN BREAD

MAKES 2 SMALL LOAVES

If you don't have a standing mixer, see the hand-mixing method in "Alternative Mixing Methods for Breads and Rolls" on page 237. Note that the dough is too dense to be mixed in a food processor. Low and steady heat is the key to a tender, moist brown bread. If your burner's flame is too high to allow for a slow, barely bubbling simmer, use a heat diffuser. If you choose to go the classic route and steam the bread in coffee cans, use two 1-pound cans and make sure to liberally butter the insides of the cans. As with the loaf pans, coffee cans should be tightly wrapped with buttered aluminum foil, and the water should reach halfway up the sides of the coffee cans. This bread is best served warm.

2	tablespoons unsalted butter, softened
1	cup cornmeal, preferably stone-ground
1	cup rye flour
½	cup whole-wheat flour
½	cup all-purpose flour
2	teaspoons baking soda
1	teaspoon salt
1	cup raisins
2	cups buttermilk
¾	cup dark molasses

1. Fold two 16 by 12-inch pieces of aluminum foil in half to yield two rectangles, each measuring 12 by 8 inches. With the butter, liberally grease two 8½ by 4½-inch loaf pans as well as the center portion of each piece of foil.

2. In the bowl of a standing mixer fitted with the paddle attachment, combine the cornmeal, flours, baking soda, and salt. Mix on low speed until blended, about 30 seconds. Add the raisins and mix until uniformly dispersed, about 15 seconds longer. With the machine still on low speed, slowly pour in the buttermilk and molasses and mix until fully combined, about 30 seconds. Stir the batter with a rubber spatula for several strokes, scraping the bottom of the bowl to mix in any unincorporated ingredients. Evenly divide the batter between the prepared loaf pans and wrap very tightly with the buttered foil.

3. Set each loaf pan in a large Dutch oven or a roasting pan and fill each vessel with enough water to reach halfway up the sides of each loaf pan. (If your roasting pan is large enough, you may be able to fit both loaves in one pan.) Bring to a simmer over medium-high heat, reduce the heat to low, and cover. (If using a roasting pan, wrap tightly with foil.) Check the water level every 30 minutes to make sure the water still reaches halfway up the sides of the loaf pans. Cook until a skewer inserted in the middle of the loaves comes out clean, about 2 hours. Carefully remove the loaves from the pans and transfer them to a wire rack. Cool for 10 minutes. Slice and serve.

American Sandwich Bread

American loaf breads are quite different from their European cousins, primarily because they contain fat in the form of milk and melted butter, as well as a touch of sweetener. This produces softer, more tender-crumbed loaves that are particularly well suited to sandwiches. These home-style sandwich loaves are baked in metal loaf pans, and their crusts are thin. As we discovered during the testing process, this is not just an exercise in convenience. American sandwich bread is every bit as inspiring as those toothier imports. There is nothing like a fresh-from-the-oven loaf cut into slabs and slathered with butter and honey.

These days, many home cooks might choose to use a bread machine to make this type of bread. In our experience, bread machines produce a crust that is mediocre at best and an interior of unpredictable quality that is all too often cake-like. We set out to develop a good, solid recipe that could be done in a few hours, start to finish, including baking time.

For many home cooks, the other great impediment to making bread at home is the notion of kneading by hand. To find out if this was essential, we used a standard American loaf bread recipe and tested hand-kneaded bread against bread kneaded by machine—in both a standing mixer and a food processor—to find out if hand kneading makes better bread. The results were eye-opening. The hand-kneaded loaf was not as good as the two loaves kneaded by machine. It was denser and did not rise as well, and the flavor lacked the pleasant yeastiness found in the other loaves. After some additional testing and discussion, we hit on a reasonable explanation: when kneading by hand, most home cooks cannot resist adding too much flour, because bread dough is notoriously sticky. In a machine, however, you need no additional flour, and the resulting bread has the correct proportion of liquid to flour.

As we said, one of our objectives in developing this recipe was to produce bread as quickly as possible. Therefore we chose instant yeast. Not only did the instant yeast greatly reduce rising times, but, in a blind tasting, the bread tasted better than loaves made with regular active dry yeast.

AMERICAN SANDWICH BREAD

MAKES ONE 9-INCH LOAF

This recipe calls for a standing electric mixer; if you don't have a standing mixer, see "Alternative Mixing Methods for Breads and Rolls." You can hand-knead the dough, but we found it's easy to add too much flour during this process, resulting in a somewhat tougher loaf. To promote a crisp crust, we found it best to place a loaf pan filled with boiling water in the oven while the bread bakes.

ALTERNATIVE MIXING METHODS FOR BREADS AND ROLLS

We prefer to make breads and rolls with a standing mixer fitted with the dough hook because it's effortless and it produces great bread. For some recipes in this chapter, however, you can use either a food processor or just your hands, following the instructions below.

FOOD PROCESSOR METHOD: Whisk the liquid ingredients together in a liquid measuring cup. Pulse the dry ingredients together in a food processor fitted with the dough blade to combine. With the processor running, pour the liquid mixture through the feed tube and process until a rough ball forms, 30 to 40 seconds. Let the dough rest for 2 minutes and then process for 30 seconds longer. Turn the dough out onto a clean work surface and knead by hand to form a smooth, round ball, about 5 minutes, adding flour as needed to prevent the dough from sticking to the work surface. Transfer to a large, lightly greased bowl, cover with greased plastic wrap, and let rise as directed.

HAND-MIXING METHOD: Whisk the liquid ingredients together in a medium bowl. In a large bowl, whisk the dry ingredients together. Stir the liquid mixture into the dry ingredients with a rubber spatula until the dough comes together and looks shaggy. Turn the dough out onto a clean work surface and knead by hand to form a smooth, round ball, 15 to 25 minutes, adding flour as needed to prevent the dough from sticking to the work surface. Transfer to a large, lightly greased bowl, cover with greased plastic wrap, and let rise as directed.

---

1   cup warm whole milk (110 degrees)
⅓   cup warm water (110 degrees)
3   tablespoons unsalted butter,
     melted and cooled, plus extra
     for brushing
3   tablespoons honey
4   cups bread flour
1   envelope (2¼ teaspoons) rapid-rise
     or instant yeast
2   teaspoons salt

1. Whisk the milk, water, butter, and honey together in a large liquid measuring cup. Combine 3½ cups of the flour, yeast, and salt in the bowl of a standing mixer fitted with the dough hook. With the mixer on low speed, add the milk mixture and mix until the dough comes together, about 2 minutes.

2. Increase the speed to medium-low and knead until the dough is smooth and elastic, about 8 minutes. (If, after 4 minutes, more flour is needed, add the remaining ½ cup flour, 2 tablespoons at a time, until the dough clears the sides of the bowl but sticks to the bottom.)

3. Turn the dough out onto a lightly floured work surface and knead by hand to form a smooth, round ball. Place the dough in a large, lightly greased bowl and cover with greased plastic wrap. Let rise in a warm place until doubled in size, 1 to 1½ hours.

4. Grease a 9 by 5-inch loaf pan. Following the photos on page 240, turn the dough out onto a lightly floured work surface and gently press it into a 9-inch square. Roll the dough into a tight cylinder and pinch the seam closed. Place the loaf, seam side down, in the prepared pan. Mist the loaf with vegetable oil spray, cover loosely with plastic wrap, and let rise in a warm place until nearly doubled in size and the dough barely springs back when poked with a knuckle, 45 to 75 minutes.

5. Adjust an oven rack to the lower-middle position and heat the oven to 350 degrees. Brush the loaf lightly with melted butter, then spray lightly with water. Bake until golden and the center of the bread registers 200 degrees on an instant-read thermometer, 40 to 50 minutes, rotating the loaf halfway through baking. Cool the loaf in the pan for 15 minutes, then turn out onto a wire rack and let cool to room temperature, about 2 hours, before serving.

Variations

BUTTERMILK SANDWICH BREAD

Substitute buttermilk for the milk.

WHEAT SANDWICH BREAD

Toast ¼ cup wheat germ in a dry skillet until fragrant, about 5 minutes, then combine with 2 cups bread flour and 1½ cups whole-wheat flour. Substitute this mixture for the bread flour in the recipe.

OATMEAL SANDWICH BREAD

Bring 1 cup water to a boil in a small saucepan over medium heat. Add 1 cup old-fashioned rolled or quick-cooking oats and cook until softened, about 1 minute. Let cool until just warm. Omit the water in the recipe, reduce the amount of flour in step 1 to 2¾ cups, and add the cooked oat mixture to the dough with the salt.

HONEY-BRAN SANDWICH BREAD WITH SUNFLOWER SEEDS

Substitute ¼ cup wheat bran for ¼ cup of the bread flour and increase the honey to ¼ cup. Add ½ cup unsalted sunflower seeds to the mixer bowl during the final minute of kneading.

Anadama Bread

Anadama is an eccentric name for what amounts to sandwich bread enriched with cornmeal and molasses. Anadama bread has deep roots in rustic New England cookery. As we found, however, this bread can suffer from a variety of ills, including gritty texture, denseness, and saccharine sweetness. We hoped to overcome these problems and make a great loaf, ideal for toasting and sandwiches.

Because anadama is similar to a basic loaf bread, we started off by trying to manipulate our sandwich loaf into anadama bread. We quickly learned that we would have to make some major adjustments. Incorporating the cornmeal into the dough was the first step. Adding raw cornmeal to the dough resulted in gritty bread without much corn flavor. Soaking the cornmeal in the lukewarm milk and water also produced a gritty loaf. We realized that the cornmeal had to be cooked to soften it, but what was the best method? Simmering the cornmeal in milk worked well. After a mere minute of cooking, the cornmeal softened and developed the texture of soft polenta.

We tried various methods to mix the dough. Adding everything together—flour, water, yeast, molasses, and cornmeal mush—yielded unevenly combined dough flecked with lumps of cornmeal mush. The mush had to be combined with the flour prior to adding the other ingredients for the best integration. As little as a minute of mixing adequately blended the cornmeal mush and flour. With the cornmeal mush incorporated, the water, yeast, and molasses were easily added to form a uniform dough.

We found that it was tricky gauging when and if the dough needed more flour during kneading. The molasses made the dough quite sticky, and it looked as if it needed more flour, but when we felt the dough, it rarely needed any flour. Feeling the dough is the best way to tell; if you can touch the dough without it tenaciously sticking to your hands, the dough probably does not need any more flour.

When it did stick, we added flour a tablespoon at a time until the dough reached the right texture. Occasionally scraping the dough off the dough hook and the sides of the work bowl during kneading helped as well. After 10 minutes of machine kneading and a quick turn by hand, the dough was smooth, shiny, and elastic.

Because this dough is sticky, we had trouble kneading it by hand or in a food processor. When we tried to knead it by hand, the dough stuck to our hands and the work surface unless we added more flour, which made the finished loaf tough. As for the food processor, the dough stuck to the blade and could not be properly kneaded. The larger bowl of a standing mixer and the dough hook are the best tools for kneading this dough.

Unfortunately, we found that this dough rose quite a bit more slowly than the dough in our sandwich bread recipe. Even in a warmed oven, it took a full hour and a half to double in bulk. We figured that the heavy cornmeal and molasses weighed down the dough. Adding more yeast made the dough rise faster, but the flavor was adversely affected. After shaping, the dough took another hour and a half to double in bulk—a small inconvenience but well worth it for the flavor.

We baked the risen loaf according to the sandwich bread recipe and, in a slight alteration, we sprinkled a little cornmeal across the loaf after it had been brushed with melted butter to emphasize the nutty corn flavor. The resulting loaf was everything we hoped for: an appealing dark and chewy crust yielding to a moist and dense crumb.

ANADAMA BREAD

MAKES ONE 9-INCH LOAF

You will need about 1 tablespoon of melted butter to brush over the loaf before baking. The dough is very dense and sticky and cannot be kneaded in the food processor or by hand—a standing mixer is necessary.

1	cup whole milk
½	cup water
½	cup yellow cornmeal, plus extra for sprinkling
5	tablespoons light or dark molasses
3	tablespoons unsalted butter, melted and cooled, plus extra for brushing (see note above)
3–3½	cups all-purpose flour
1	envelope (2¼ teaspoons) rapid-rise or instant yeast
2	teaspoons salt

THE AMERICAN TABLE
ANADAMA BREAD

How did a yeasted sandwich bread enriched with cornmeal and molasses get such a funny name? Some sources attribute the unique name to a grumpy nineteenth-century New England farmer or fisherman who cursed his wife, Anna, for the unwavering diet of cornmeal mush she provided for him. A kinder story claims that the husband's comment was made not in anger, but in appreciation for his wife's tasty bread. Most food historians dispute both stories as fiction. The origins of the bread more likely point to Colonial-era settlers, who may have added indigenous ingredients to English-style bread. And frankly, we find the bread's slightly sweet, hearty crumb more intriguing than either its unusual name or its murky beginning. Try making thick slices of toast with anadama, or tear up a slice to dunk into a soup, chowder, or chili. This bread also makes excellent sandwiches—especially grilled ham and cheese or barbecued pork.

SHAPING LOAF BREAD

1. Press the dough into a 9-inch square using your hands.

2. Roll the dough up in a tight cylinder.

3. Pinch the seam together to secure.

4. Fit the dough, seam side down, into a greased 9 by 5-inch loaf pan.

1. Bring the milk and water to a simmer in a small saucepan over medium heat. Whisk in the cornmeal and cook, stirring constantly, for 1 minute. Transfer the mixture to a medium bowl and let stand, stirring occasionally, until just warm (about 110 degrees), about 30 minutes. Stir in the molasses and butter.

2. Combine 3 cups of the flour, yeast, and salt in a standing mixer fitted with the dough hook. With the mixer on low speed, add the cornmeal mixture and mix until the dough comes together, about 2 minutes.

3. Increase the speed to medium-low and knead until the dough is smooth and elastic, about 8 minutes. (If, after 4 minutes, more flour is needed, add the remaining ½ cup flour, 2 tablespoons at a time, until the dough clears the sides of the bowl but sticks to the bottom.)

4. Turn the dough out onto a lightly floured work surface and knead by hand to form a smooth, round ball. Place the dough in a large, lightly greased bowl and cover with greased plastic wrap. Let rise in a warm place until doubled in size, 1 to 1½ hours.

5. Grease a 9 by 5-inch loaf pan. Turn the dough out onto a lightly floured work surface and gently press it into a 9-inch square. Roll the dough into a tight cylinder and pinch the seam closed. Place the loaf, seam side down, in the prepared pan. Mist the loaf with vegetable oil spray, cover loosely with plastic wrap, and let rise in a warm place until nearly doubled in size and the dough barely springs back when poked with a knuckle, 45 to 75 minutes.

6. Adjust an oven rack to the lower-middle position and heat the oven to 350 degrees. Brush the loaf lightly with melted butter, sprinkle with cornmeal, then spray lightly with water. Bake until golden and the center of the bread registers 200 degrees on an instant-read thermometer, 40 to 50 minutes, rotating the loaf halfway through baking. Cool the loaf in the pan for 15 minutes, then turn out onto a wire rack and let cool to room temperature, about 2 hours, before serving.

CHAPTER NINE

Casseroles and Other Potluck Favorites

CASSEROLES AND OTHER POTLUCK FAVORITES

Beef Enchiladas

Traditional beef enchiladas—corn tortillas stuffed with silky, slow-cooked meat and baked under a blanket of hearty chile sauce and cheese—are the ultimate in Mexican comfort food. Too bad they take so long to make. Common shortcuts include using ground beef instead of stew meat and opening canned enchilada sauce instead of making your own from dried chiles and tomato. But the enchiladas we made using these tricks were awful, with none of the richness of the original. Could we shorten the traditional process without shortchanging the flavor?

Starting with the sauce, we hoped that store-bought chili powder would work well as a base. (We didn't want to have to find, toast, and grind our own chiles.) When we tried adding chili powder to pureed tomatoes, however, its flavor was flat. But when we added the chili powder to the sautéing onions and garlic before adding the tomatoes, its flavor opened up and bloomed. The sauce tasted even better when we spiked it with cumin, coriander, and a little sugar for balance.

One benefit of the traditional stewing method is that it tenderizes inexpensive cuts of beef by submerging them in the flavorful sauce over low heat for hours, enriching both the meat and the sauce. Cuts from the chuck (the shoulder) are particularly good here, but large pieces (such as a whole chuck roast) take too long to cook. Cubes of chuck sold as stew meat seemed like a natural choice, but tasters found the flavor to be a little shallow and the texture tender in some bites, chewy in others. We got the soft chew and beefy flavor we were looking for with another cut from the chuck, the inexpensive top blade. While cooking it took 1½ hours, the results were worth it.

Assembling and baking the enchiladas go quickly and smoothly—if you use a few tricks. Authentic recipes call for frying the corn tortillas and then dipping them in sauce to simultaneously soften and season them. This was a lengthy, messy procedure, so we opted instead to microwave the tortillas to soften them before filling them with tender beef, rolling them up, and topping them with sauce and cheese. After they spent just 30 minutes in the oven, we sat down to a plate of spicy beef enchiladas that only tasted as if they took all day to make.

BEEF ENCHILADAS

SERVES 4 TO 6

Cut back on the pickled jalapeños if you like your enchiladas on the mild side. Our flavored sour creams (page 245) are a great finishing touch.

1¼	pounds top blade steaks, trimmed
	Salt
1	tablespoon vegetable oil
2	onions, chopped
3	garlic cloves, minced
3	tablespoons chili powder
2	teaspoons ground coriander
2	teaspoons ground cumin
1	teaspoon sugar
1	(15-ounce) can tomato sauce
½	cup water
2	cups shredded Monterey Jack or mild cheddar cheese
⅓	cup chopped fresh cilantro
¼	cup canned pickled jalapeños, chopped
12	(6-inch) corn tortillas

TRIMMING BLADE STEAKS

The only trick to preparing blade steaks is to cut away the center strip of gristle. To remove the gristle, simply halve each steak lengthwise and then slice it away, as shown here.

1. Pat the meat dry with paper towels and sprinkle with salt. Heat the oil in a Dutch oven over medium-high until shimmering. Cook the meat until browned on both sides, about 6 minutes. Transfer the meat to a plate.

2. Add the onions to the fat left in the pot and cook over medium heat until golden, about 5 minutes. Combine the garlic, chili powder, coriander, cumin, sugar, and 1 teaspoon salt in a small bowl, then stir the mixture into the pot. Cook until fragrant, about 1 minute. Add the tomato sauce and water and bring to a boil. Return the meat and juices to the pot, cover, reduce the heat to low, and gently simmer until the meat is tender and can be broken apart with a wooden spoon, about 1½ hours.

3. Adjust an oven rack to the middle position and heat the oven to 350 degrees. Strain the beef mixture over a medium bowl, breaking the meat into small pieces; reserve the sauce. Transfer the meat to a bowl and mix with 1 cup of the cheese, the cilantro, and jalapeños.

4. Spread ¾ cup sauce in the bottom of a 13 by 9-inch baking dish. Microwave 6 tortillas on a plate on high power until soft, about 1 minute. Spread ⅓ cup beef mixture down the center of a tortilla, roll the tortilla tightly, and set it in the baking dish seam side down. Repeat with the remaining tortillas and beef mixture (you may have to fit 2 or more enchiladas down the sides of the baking dish). Pour the remaining sauce over the enchiladas and spread to coat evenly. Sprinkle the remaining 1 cup cheese evenly over the enchiladas, cover tightly with aluminum foil, and bake until heated through, 20 to 25 minutes. Remove the foil and continue baking until the cheese browns slightly, 5 to 10 minutes. Serve.

Variation
CHICKEN ENCHILADAS

Substitute 1¼ pounds boneless, skinless chicken thighs, trimmed and cut into ¼-inch strips, for the blade steaks. Skip step 1 and heat the oil in the pot over medium heat until shimmering before adding the onions in step 2. Before adding the tomato sauce to the pot, stir in the chicken and coat with the fragrant spices. Increase the amount of water to 1 cup and gently simmer the chicken in the sauce until it is cooked through, 8 to 10 minutes. Strain the sauce, assemble the enchiladas, and bake as directed.

SHOPPING WITH THE TEST KITCHEN

Supermarket Hot Salsas: We don't like jarred salsa. Previous taste tests have been disappointing—almost no jarred salsas have reached "recommended" status, and none have come close to the allure of homemade fresh salsa. But our prior taste tests have focused on mild and medium varieties. Might jarred hot salsas be more interesting than their timid cousins? To find out, we sampled nine national brands and were surprised that most tasters didn't need to quell the burn with cold milk or water as they nibbled. These hot salsas were livelier and better than the mild salsas we've tasted in the past, but even the best were merely good, not great, and didn't approach the quality of fresh salsa. Why? Good salsa relies on the interplay of fresh vegetable flavors and textures. Jarred salsas have the freshness and crispness cooked out of them. Our first-place salsa, Pace Hot Chunky Salsa, came closest to replicating the fresh flavors and colors of homemade salsa, in part because it has a high percentage of tomatoes and vegetables. Most tasters were impressed by this spicy salsa's bright tomato and chile flavors, as well as its chunky texture. Roasted tomatoes in second-place Frontera Hot Habanero Salsa with Roasted Tomatoes and Cilantro produce a smoky, fiery salsa that our tasters appreciated for its complexity.

Flavored Sour Creams

Since a dollop of plain sour cream does wonders for tacos, nachos, and our enchiladas we figured that a doctored dollop might work even better. Here are three southwestern-inspired sour creams that work well as toppings, dips, or simple sauces for grilled fish, chicken, or meats. Each yields about 1 cup and can be refrigerated, covered, for up to 2 days.

CILANTRO-LIME SOUR CREAM

Process 1 cup sour cream, ¼ cup chopped fresh cilantro, 1 teaspoon grated fresh lime zest, ¼ teaspoon pepper, and ⅛ teaspoon salt in a food processor until smooth.

AVOCADO-CHILE SOUR CREAM

Process 1 cup sour cream, ½ avocado, pitted and skinned, 1 jalapeño, seeded and chopped, 1 teaspoon fresh lemon juice, ¼ teaspoon pepper, and ⅛ teaspoon salt in a food processor until smooth.

CHIPOTLE-SCALLION SOUR CREAM

Process 1 cup sour cream, 1 canned chipotle chile in adobo, 1 chopped scallion, ¼ teaspoon pepper, and ⅛ teaspoon salt in a food processor until smooth.

King Ranch Casserole

King Ranch just might be the most famous casserole in Texas. Layers of tender chicken, corn tortillas, and spicy tomatoes are bound together in a rich, cheesy sauce. Favored by home cooks and Junior Leaguers, this subtly spicy casserole dates back to the 1950s. Although owners of the King Ranch, the state's largest cattle operation, deny any hand in its creation, this dish became popular for its mildly spicy southwestern flavors as well as its convenience (most recipes start with one can each of cream of chicken and cream of mushroom soup).

After a disappointing round of tests, we wondered if our Texan friends had been telling us tall tales about this dish. The tortillas were soggy, the chicken was overcooked, and the sauce was made gloppy and bland by the undiluted canned soup. Given the outsized reputation of this dish, we had to do better. We found a few modern recipes that called for a freshly poached chicken and homemade cheese sauce, but their instructions seemed overly fussy for a casserole. Could we find a middle road that lost the canned soup but kept the amount of work reasonable?

Starting with the sauce, we cooked onions and chiles in butter, then added ground cumin and Ro-Tel tomatoes, the Texas brand of spicy canned tomatoes that are the hallmark of this recipe. Instead of draining the tomatoes and discarding the flavorful juice (as most recipes instructed), we reduced the liquid to intensify the tomato flavor. Then we stirred in flour for thickening, cream for richness, and chicken broth for flavor. Twenty minutes of kitchen work yielded a silky, flavorful sauce that put canned soup to shame.

To assemble the casserole, we layered the sauce with corn tortillas and cooked chicken, then topped everything with cheese before baking. After testing various cheeses such as cheddar, Monterey Jack, and Colby, we finally settled on Co-Jack, a blend of the two latter cheeses. This cheese gave our casserole creamy flavor without turning it greasy. Our casserole smelled fantastic coming out of the oven, but the chicken was leathery and the tortillas had disintegrated into corn mush. To solve the chicken problem, we tried layering raw chicken between the tortillas, but it failed to cook through. The solution was to partially poach the chicken in the sauce before assembling the casserole, which guaranteed perfectly cooked, well-seasoned meat.

We tried replacing the soggy tortillas with store bought tortilla chips, but tasters complained about the extra grease in the middle of the casserole.

Crisping the tortillas in the oven (in effect, making homemade chips) kept them from turning to mush in the casserole and cut out the greasiness.

All our casserole needed now was a crisp topping. Having abandoned store-bought tortilla chips inside our casserole, we decided to give them a shot as a crushed-up crunchy topping. The flavor and texture were fine, and after trying different brands to find the perfect fit, we finally hit on one that everyone loved: Fritos corn chips. They crowned this Texas classic with just the right amount of saltiness, corn flavor, and crunch.

KING RANCH CASSEROLE

SERVES 6 TO 8

If you can't find Ro-Tel tomatoes, substitute one 14.5-ounce can diced tomatoes and one 4-ounce can chopped green chiles. Co-Jack is a creamy blend of Colby and Monterey Jack cheeses. Jack cheese can be used in its place.

12	(6-inch) corn tortillas
1	tablespoon unsalted butter
2	onions, minced
2	jalapeño chiles, seeded and minced
2	teaspoons ground cumin
2	(10-ounce) cans Ro-Tel tomatoes (see note above)
5	tablespoons all-purpose flour
1	cup heavy cream
3	cups low-sodium chicken broth
4	boneless, skinless chicken breasts (1½ pounds), halved lengthwise and cut crosswise into ½-inch slices
2	tablespoons chopped fresh cilantro
4	cups shredded Co-Jack cheese (see note above)
	Salt and pepper
2¼	cups Fritos corn chips, crushed

1. Adjust the oven racks to the upper-middle and lower-middle positions and heat the oven to 450 degrees. Lay the tortillas on two baking sheets, lightly coat both sides with vegetable oil spray, and bake until slightly crisp and browned, about 12 minutes. Cool slightly, then break into bite-sized pieces. Using potholders, adjust the top oven rack to the middle position.

2. Heat the butter in a Dutch oven over medium-high heat. Cook the onions, chiles, and cumin until lightly browned, about 8 minutes. Add the tomatoes and cook until most of the liquid has evaporated, about 10 minutes. Stir in the flour and cook for 1 minute. Add the cream and broth, bring to a simmer, and cook until thickened, 2 to 3 minutes. Stir in the chicken and cook until no longer pink, about 4 minutes. Off the heat, add the cilantro and cheese and stir until the cheese is melted. Season with salt and pepper.

3. Scatter half of the tortilla pieces in a 13 by 9-inch baking dish set on a rimmed baking sheet. Spoon half of the filling evenly over the tortillas. Repeat with the remaining tortillas and filling.

4. Bake until the filling is bubbling, about 15 minutes. Sprinkle the Fritos evenly over the top and bake until the Fritos are lightly browned, about 10 minutes. Cool the casserole for 10 minutes. Serve.

SHOPPING WITH THE TEST KITCHEN
- -
Ro-Tel Tomatoes: Carl Roettele opened a small canning plant in Elsa, Texas, in the early 1940s. By the 1950s, his blend of tomatoes, green chiles, and spices had become popular throughout the state and beyond. His spicy tomatoes are used in countless local recipes, including King Ranch casserole and a mixture of Velveeta and Ro-Tel tomatoes known locally as Ro-Tel dip (chili con queso, to the rest of us).

Skillet Macaroni and Cheese

Supermarket macaroni and cheese mixes are certainly convenient and a favorite of kids everywhere, but this meal-in-a-box just doesn't hold the same allure for adults. And many of the "quick" homemade macaroni and cheese recipes are just as lackluster. Typically, a mixture of shredded cheese and condensed cream soup is stirred into hot, buttered macaroni and heated through in the oven—frankly, the flavor is no better than the boxed variety. Using a skillet pasta-cooking method, similar to the method used in Skillet Lasagna (page 256), we knew we could do better.

We brought a mixture of water and evaporated milk (which we preferred over whole milk, which curdled, and heavy cream, which was simply too rich) to a simmer in a large nonstick skillet, stirred in the macaroni, and cooked it until tender. By the time the macaroni was done, there was just enough liquid left in the pan to make a quick sauce. We did so by mixing evaporated milk with cornstarch to thicken it, and for flavor we added dry mustard and hot sauce.

As for the cheese, the star ingredient of this dish, tasters favored a combination of cheddar and Monterey Jack for flavor and meltability. Three cups, gradually stirred in off the heat, provided maximum creaminess and good cheese flavor. A little butter enriched the finished dish, making it smooth and silky. In addition, we came up with a host of flavor variations—one with spicy chipotle chiles, one with ham and peas, another with garlic and broccoli, and a fourth with kielbasa and mustard.

SKILLET MACARONI AND CHEESE

SERVES 4

Small shells can be substituted for the elbows. Pre-shredded cheese works just fine here.

3½	cups water
1	(12-ounce) can evaporated milk
¾	pound elbow macaroni
	Salt
1	teaspoon cornstarch
½	teaspoon dry mustard
¼	teaspoon hot sauce
2	cups shredded cheddar cheese
2	cups shredded Monterey Jack cheese
3	tablespoons unsalted butter
	Pepper

1. Bring the water, 1 cup of the evaporated milk, macaroni, and ½ teaspoon salt to a simmer in a large nonstick skillet over high heat, stirring often, until the macaroni is tender, 8 to 10 minutes.

2. Whisk the remaining ½ cup milk, cornstarch, mustard, and hot sauce together, then stir the mixture into the skillet. Continue to simmer until slightly thickened, about 1 minute.

3. Off the heat, stir in the cheeses, one handful at a time, adding water as needed to adjust the sauce's consistency. Stir in the butter and season with salt and pepper to taste. Serve.

Variations

SPICY SKILLET MACARONI AND CHEESE

Ro-Tel brand tomatoes are diced tomatoes with green chiles and seasonings added.

Add 2 teaspoons minced chipotle chiles in adobo and 1 (10-ounce) can Ro-Tel tomatoes, drained, with the cornstarch mixture in step 2.

SKILLET MACARONI AND CHEESE WITH HAM AND PEAS

Add 4 ounces deli-style baked ham, diced medium, and ½ cup frozen peas with the cornstarch mixture in step 2.

SKILLET MACARONI AND CHEESE WITH BROCCOLI AND GARLIC

Before cooking the macaroni in step 1, cook 1 tablespoon olive oil, 3 minced garlic cloves, and ¼ teaspoon red pepper flakes in the skillet over medium-high heat until fragrant, about 1 minute. Proceed as directed. Stir in 1 (10-ounce) package frozen broccoli florets, thawed and squeezed dry, after the cheese has been incorporated in step 3.

SKILLET MACARONI AND CHEESE WITH KIELBASA AND MUSTARD

Before step 1, heat 1 tablespoon vegetable oil in the skillet over medium-high heat until just smoking. Add ½ pound kielbasa, halved lengthwise and sliced thin, and cook until lightly browned, 3 to 5 minutes. Transfer the kielbasa to a paper towel–lined plate and set aside, then simmer the macaroni as directed in step 1. Add the browned kielbasa and 1 tablespoon whole-grain mustard with the cornstarch mixture in step 2.

Potluck Macaroni and Cheese

Casserole-style macaroni and cheese can be found at every BBQ joint, fish fry, and covered-dish supper all over the South. Why? Because it feeds a crowd and can go straight from the oven to the buffet table. Unlike ultra-creamy stovetop versions that puddle on the plate, this baked mac and cheese absorbs the cheesy sauce as it bubbles away in the oven, evolving into a dense mixture that sets up in hearty scoops, topped with buttery bread crumbs that develop a toasty crunch during baking. We set out to develop the ultimate version of this cheesy treat.

Our research turned up plenty of recipes for baked mac and cheese, but we quickly realized that the majority of them were misnamed—they weren't baked at all. Most of the real cooking (making an egg-based custard or a white sauce) was done on top of the stove, and the casseroles were then finished under the broiler for a few minutes. Impostors!

After making a handful of recipes that actually called for baking the dish, we saw why so many had abandoned the oven. Time after time the custard-based versions came out of the oven broken and curdled. They were failing because they contained eggs, milk, and half-and-half, all ingredients that will separate and clump when baked. Versions based on a white sauce—called béchamel, made by cooking butter, flour, and milk—also separated when baked (even when we increased the amount of flour) but were more promising, because at least they didn't contain eggs.

To avoid the problem of broken béchamel sauce, other casserole recipes call for canned condensed soup to replace the milk, but we weren't about to go that route. We did try another canned product, evaporated milk, which contains stabilizers that prevent it from breaking when heated. When we used evaporated milk in the béchamel, the casserole baked up satiny smooth.

Up until this point we had been adding Monterey Jack, a creamy but very mild cheese. Tasters loved the full flavor of extra-sharp cheddar, but its relatively dry texture meant it didn't melt as well, and it became greasy and separated when baked. A batch made with equal parts cheddar and Monterey Jack was better but still not right.

Since the stabilizers in the condensed milk had helped with the sauce, we wondered if we could rely on a cheese that contained similar stabilizers to fix the separating cheese. We made a batch with

American cheese (for stability), Monterey Jack (for creaminess), and cheddar (for flavor) and had great results. Homemade bread crumbs, enriched with melted butter and Parmesan cheese, created a flavorful, crunchy topping that provided a nice contrast to the soft casserole.

We finally had a baked mac and cheese that was creamy, sturdy, and rich—a potluck supper addition.

POTLUCK MACARONI AND CHEESE

SERVES 8 TO 10

Block American cheese from the deli counter is best for this dish, as prewrapped singles result in a drier mac and cheese.

4	slices hearty white sandwich bread, torn into large pieces
8	tablespoons (1 stick) unsalted butter, (4 tablespoons melted)
¼	cup grated Parmesan cheese
	Salt
1	pound elbow macaroni
5	tablespoons all-purpose flour
3	(12-ounce) cans evaporated milk
2	teaspoons hot sauce
⅛	teaspoon ground nutmeg
1	teaspoon dry mustard
2	cups shredded extra-sharp cheddar cheese
1¼	cups shredded American cheese
¾	cup shredded Monterey Jack cheese

1. Adjust an oven rack to the middle position and heat the oven to 350 degrees. Pulse the bread, 4 tablespoons melted butter, and Parmesan in a food processor until ground to coarse crumbs. Transfer to a bowl.

2. Bring 4 quarts water to a boil in a large pot. Add 1 tablespoon salt and the macaroni to the boiling water and cook until al dente, about 6 minutes. Reserve ½ cup of the macaroni cooking water, then drain and rinse the macaroni in a colander under cold running water. Set aside.

3. Melt the remaining 4 tablespoons butter in the now-empty pot over medium-high heat until foaming. Stir in the flour and cook, stirring constantly, until the mixture turns light brown, about 1 minute. Slowly whisk in the evaporated milk, hot sauce, nutmeg, mustard, and 2 teaspoons salt and cook until the mixture begins to simmer and is slightly thickened, about 4 minutes. Off the heat, whisk in the cheeses and reserved pasta cooking water until the cheese melts. Stir in the macaroni until completely coated.

4. Transfer the mixture to a 13 by 9-inch baking dish and top evenly with the bread-crumb mixture. Bake until the cheese is bubbling around the edges and the top is golden brown, 20 to 25 minutes. Let sit for 5 to 10 minutes before serving.

Chili Mac

Synonymous with simpler times and simpler food, chili mac was once a favorite childhood comfort food whose appeal, for many of us, extends well into adulthood.

Initial testing prompted reminiscing, and the test kitchen was divided about which version of chili mac (Mom's, of course) was best. For some it was a macaroni-and-cheese-like version with a bit of chili stirred in. For others it was predominantly chili with a little macaroni added for heft. Others insisted (after tasting the previous examples) that there could be only one way to make the best chili mac: spicy chili, with elbows stirred in (no other pasta would do) and lots of gooey, melted cheese on top. Our goal was to come up with a recipe that was a combination of the best spicy beef chili and creamy macaroni with cheese.

Our first challenges were finding the correct heat level for the chili and the ideal proportion of chili to macaroni. We focused on the chili first and started with lean ground beef, which we browned, then drained to remove the excess fat. Then we sautéed onion, red bell pepper, and a generous amount of garlic. In lieu of fresh chiles (jalapeños added too much heat), we used chili powder and found that the best way to tame the raw flavor of the powder was to sauté it with the aromatics. Cumin was added along with the chili powder. We then added diced tomatoes, simmered the chili for 20 minutes, and had our first taste. Our chili was spicy enough without being overbearing. The thickness was also ideal: spoonable and thick. Satisfied with our chili, we moved on to the macaroni that needed to be stirred in.

We started by cooking the elbows to the al dente stage. We knew that the macaroni would continue to cook in the oven and would absorb liquid as it baked. What we didn't count on was how much liquid it would soak up. Our macaroni turned dry in the oven. We found that if we reserved some of the pasta cooking water and added tomato puree, our macaroni baked up moist and flavorful.

At this point we needed to put the cheese component into play. We tried casseroles made with cheddar and Monterey Jack cheeses separately, then together. Tasters found the cheddar to be grainy and greasy. The creaminess of the Monterey Jack was just what we were striving for, but the flavor was a bit too mild. We found a hybrid cheese called Co-Jack in our supermarket, a blend of mild Colby and Monterey Jack cheeses. The flavor of the Colby, combined with the creaminess of the Monterey Jack, made these cheeses ideal for topping the chili mac. After just 15 minutes in the oven, the topping turned a bubbly, golden brown.

CHILI MAC

SERVES 6 TO 8

Reserve some of the pasta cooking water so that it can be used to thin out the chili as needed. Ground turkey (1½ pounds) can be substituted for the ground beef. If you can't find Co-Jack cheese, substitute equal amounts of Colby and Monterey Jack cheese.

	Salt
8	ounces elbow macaroni
3	tablespoons vegetable oil
1½	pounds 85-percent lean ground beef
2	onions, chopped
1	red bell pepper, seeded and chopped
6	garlic cloves, minced
2	tablespoons chili powder
1	tablespoon ground cumin
1	(14.5-ounce) can diced tomatoes
1	(28-ounce) can tomato puree
1	tablespoon brown sugar
	Pepper
2	cups shredded Co-Jack cheese (see note above)

1. Adjust an oven rack to the middle position and heat the oven to 400 degrees. Bring 4 quarts water to a boil in a large pot. Add 1 tablespoon salt and the macaroni to the boiling water; cook until al dente, about 5 minutes. Reserve ¾ cup of the pasta cooking water and drain the pasta. Transfer the pasta to a bowl and set aside.

2. Wipe the pot dry. Add 1 tablespoon of the oil and return to medium-high heat until shimmering. Add the beef and cook, breaking up the meat into small pieces with a wooden spoon, until it is no longer pink and beginning to brown, 5 to 8 minutes. Drain the beef in a colander, discarding the drippings, and set it aside.

3. Add the remaining 2 tablespoons oil to the pot and return to medium-high heat until shimmering. Add the onions, bell pepper, garlic, chili powder, and cumin; cook, stirring occasionally, until the vegetables are softened and beginning to brown, about 7 minutes. Add the diced tomatoes, tomato puree, brown sugar, the reserved pasta cooking water, and the drained beef; bring to a simmer and cook, stirring occasionally, until the flavors have melded, about 20 minutes.

4. Stir in the cooked pasta and season with salt and pepper to taste. Pour into a 13 by 9-inch baking dish and sprinkle with the cheese. Bake until the cheese is melted and browned, about 15 minutes. Cool for 5 to 10 minutes before serving.

Easy Meat Lasagna

Most families have homemade lasagna once, maybe twice a year. Lasagna is not enjoyed more frequently because it takes the better part of a day to boil the noodles, slow-cook the sauce, prepare and layer the ingredients, and then finally bake it. Although this traditional method does produce a superior dish, we were interested in an Americanized version, one that could be made in 2 hours or less from start to finish.

We knew from the start that to expedite the lasagna-making process we would have to use no-boil lasagna noodles. After a few initial tests, we discovered that the secret of no-boil noodles is to leave the tomato sauce a little on the watery side. The noodles can then absorb liquid without drying out the dish overall. With this in mind, we got to work on the other components of the lasagna.

We began with our choice of meat for the sauce. Working with a base of sautéed aromatics (onions and garlic), an all-beef sauce turned out to be one-dimensional and dull. But a sauce made with meat loaf mix, a combination of equal parts ground beef, pork, and veal, tasted robust and sweet. The texture wasn't right, though; we wanted something richer, creamier, and more cohesive, so our thoughts turned to Bolognese, the classic 3-hour meat sauce enriched with dairy. Borrowing the notion of combining meat and dairy, we reduced ¼ cup of cream with the meat before adding the tomatoes. The ground meat soaked up the sweet cream, and the final product was rich and decadent. Even better, at this point we had been at the stove for only 12 minutes.

We started building the sauce with two 28-ounce cans of pureed tomatoes, but tasters found that this sauce was too heavy for the lasagna and overwhelmed the other flavors. Two 28-ounce cans of diced tomatoes yielded too thin a sauce. We settled on one 28-ounce can of each. The combination of pureed and diced tomatoes yielded a luxurious sauce, with soft but substantial chunks of tomatoes. We added the tomatoes to the meat mixture, warmed it through (no reduction necessary), and in just 15 minutes on the stove the meat sauce was rich, creamy, ultra-meaty, and ready to go.

Most Americans like their lasagna to be cheesy. It was a given that we would sprinkle each layer with mozzarella cheese—the classic lasagna cheese—and after a test of whole-milk cheese versus part-skim we found that whole-milk mozzarella was better for the job. As for ricotta, we found that it made little difference whether we used whole-milk or part-skim. Both were characteristically creamy and rich. And tasters liked the ricotta even more when mixed with Parmesan cheese. An egg helped to thicken and bind this mixture, and some chopped basil added flavor and freshness. Tucked neatly between the layers of lasagna, this ricotta mixture was just what we wanted.

We found that lasagna made with no-boil noodles takes a little longer in the oven than conventional lasagna. The real time saved is in the preparation. Start to finish, the meat and tomato lasagna took about an hour and a half to make: 40 minutes of prep time, 40 minutes in the oven, and 10 minutes to rest. Not bad for a dish that can typically take all day.

EASY MEAT LASAGNA

SERVES 6 TO 8

If you can't find meat loaf mix for the sauce, substitute ½ pound ground beef and ½ pound sweet Italian sausage, casing removed.

SAUCE

1	tablespoon olive oil
1	onion, minced
6	garlic cloves, minced
1	pound meat loaf mix (see note above)
½	teaspoon salt
½	teaspoon pepper
¼	cup heavy cream
1	(28-ounce) can tomato puree
1	(28-ounce) can diced tomatoes, drained

LAYERS

2	cups whole-milk or part-skim ricotta cheese
1¼	cups grated Parmesan cheese
½	cup chopped fresh basil
1	large egg, lightly beaten
½	teaspoon salt
½	teaspoon pepper
12	no-boil lasagna noodles from one 8- or 9-ounce package
4	cups shredded mozzarella cheese

1. Adjust an oven rack to the middle position and heat the oven to 375 degrees.

2. FOR THE SAUCE: Heat the oil in a Dutch oven over medium heat until shimmering. Add the onion and cook, stirring occasionally, until softened but not browned, about 2 minutes. Add the garlic and cook until fragrant, about 30 seconds. Add the ground meat, salt, and pepper; cook, breaking up the meat into small pieces with a wooden spoon, until it loses its raw color but has not browned, about 4 minutes. Add the cream; bring to a simmer and cook, stirring occasionally, until the liquid evaporates and only the fat remains, about 4 minutes. Add the tomato puree and diced tomatoes; bring to a slow simmer and cook until the flavors are blended, about 3 minutes. Set the sauce aside.

3. FOR THE LAYERS: Mix the ricotta, 1 cup of the Parmesan, basil, egg, salt, and pepper together in a medium bowl until well combined and creamy; set aside.

4. Smear the entire bottom of a 13 by 9-inch baking dish (or a shallow casserole dish of similar size) with ¼ cup of the meat sauce (avoiding large chunks of meat). Place 3 of the noodles in the baking dish to create the first layer. Drop 3 tablespoons of the ricotta mixture down the center of each noodle and level the domed mounds by pressing with the back of the measuring spoon. Sprinkle evenly with 1 cup of the mozzarella. Spoon 1½ cups of the meat sauce evenly over the cheese. Repeat the layering of the noodles, ricotta, mozzarella, and sauce twice more. Place the 3 remaining noodles on top of the sauce, then spread the remaining sauce over the noodles. Sprinkle with the remaining mozzarella and then with the remaining ¼ cup Parmesan.

5. Lightly spray a large sheet of aluminum foil with vegetable oil spray and cover the lasagna. Bake for 15 minutes, then remove the foil. Return the lasagna to the oven and continue to bake until the cheese is spotty brown and the sauce is bubbling, about 25 minutes longer. Cool for 10 minutes before serving.

Vegetable Lasagna

Vegetable lasagna sounds wonderful, but the reality is usually quite disappointing. Too often the dish is bland and watery, nothing like the rich, hearty version made with meat. We knew it was possible to make a great vegetable lasagna, but we wondered if we could make one that was fairly quick.

We knew from past experience that precooking the vegetables not only drives off excess liquid but gives us a chance to boost their flavor, either by caramelizing their natural sugars or by adding ingredients such as olive oil, garlic, red pepper flakes, or herbs. The moisture content of the vegetable determines which cooking technique should be used. For example, mushrooms, because of their high moisture content, are best sautéed or roasted. Almost any vegetable can be cooked and assembled into a lasagna, and we found that the flavor of two vegetables is much more interesting than just one. And to keep prep time to a minimum, it helps if both vegetables are cooked in the same manner.

Basing our master recipe (and the bulk of our testing) on a classic combination of mushrooms and spinach, we noted that 3 cups of cooked vegetables sprinkled between the layers of noodles offered plenty of flavor. We chose our favorite vegetable combinations for the master recipe and a variation; however, this recipe is very versatile and you can easily substitute 3 cups of any cooked vegetables you prefer.

During our testing we discovered that ricotta cheese simply doesn't belong in this lasagna. It turns an unattractive, dirty color as it is spread between the layers with the precooked vegetables, and its wet, creamy texture tastes completely out of place. Rather, tasters preferred vegetable lasagnas that were bound together with lots of shredded mozzarella. To help give the somewhat bland mozzarella some flavor, we found it necessary to also sprinkle a good dose of grated Parmesan between the layers.

Covering the lasagna with aluminum foil is necessary to keep the noodles from drying out; however, it does present a couple of problems. First, the foil tends to stick to the top layer of cheese. Spraying the foil with vegetable oil spray is an easy solution. The other issue is browning the top layer of cheese. When you bake a conventional lasagna uncovered in the oven, the top layer of cheese becomes golden and chewy in spots. We found that by removing the foil during the last 15 minutes of baking, we were able to achieve the color and texture we wanted.

SPINACH AND MUSHROOM LASAGNA WITH TOMATO SAUCE

SERVES 6 TO 8

Cremini mushrooms are particularly good in this dish, but any fresh mushroom is fine. Also, 3½ cups of your favorite prepared tomato sauce can be substituted for the sauce in this recipe (see our tasting of jarred pasta sauces on page 254). Feel free to substitute 3 cups of your favorite cooked vegetables (roasted, steamed, sautéed, grilled, or broiled) for the mushrooms and spinach.

5	tablespoons olive oil
1	(10-ounce) bag curly-leaf spinach, stemmed, and chopped
	Salt and pepper
1	onion, minced
1	pound cremini or white button mushrooms, wiped clean and sliced thin
2	garlic cloves, minced
1	(28-ounce) can crushed tomatoes
2	tablespoons chopped fresh basil
	Water
12	no-boil lasagna noodles from one 8- or 9-ounce package
4	cups shredded mozzarella cheese
1⅓	cups grated Parmesan cheese

1. Heat 1 tablespoon of the oil in a Dutch oven over medium heat until shimmering. Add the spinach in handfuls and cook, stirring, until the spinach is wilted, about 4 minutes. Season with salt and pepper to taste; transfer the spinach to a colander. Gently squeeze any excess liquid from the spinach; set aside (the cooked spinach should measure about 1½ cups).

2. Wipe the pot clean and add 2 more tablespoons oil; return the pot to medium heat until the oil is shimmering. Add the onion and sauté until translucent, about 5 minutes. Add the mushrooms and sauté until they have released their moisture and are golden, 8 to 10 minutes. Season the mushrooms with salt and pepper to taste (the cooked mushrooms should measure about 1½ cups). Transfer to a bowl, add the spinach, and set aside.

3. Add the remaining 2 tablespoons oil and the garlic to the pot; return to medium heat until the garlic is fragrant but not brown, about 30 seconds. Stir in the tomatoes; bring to a simmer and cook until thickened slightly, about 5 minutes. Stir in the basil and season with salt and pepper to taste. Pour the sauce into a large measuring cup and add enough water to make 3½ cups.

4. Spread ½ cup of the sauce evenly over the bottom of a 13 by 9-inch baking dish. Lay 3 of the noodles crosswise over the sauce, making sure they do not touch each other or the sides of the dish. Spread 1 cup of the prepared vegetables evenly over the noodles, ⅔ cup of the sauce evenly over the vegetables, and 1 cup of the mozzarella and ⅓ cup of the Parmesan evenly over the sauce. Repeat this layering of the noodles, vegetables, sauce, and cheeses twice more. For the fourth and final layer, lay the last 3 noodles crosswise over the previous layer and top with the remaining tomato sauce, mozzarella, and Parmesan.

5. Adjust an oven rack to the middle position and heat the oven to 375 degrees. Lightly spray a large sheet of aluminum foil with vegetable oil spray and cover the lasagna. Bake for 25 minutes; remove the foil and continue baking until the top turns golden brown in spots, about 15 minutes. Cool for 10 minutes before serving.

Variation
ROASTED ZUCCHINI AND EGGPLANT LASAGNA
Adjust the oven racks to the upper-middle and lower-middle positions and heat the oven to 400 degrees. Toss 2 medium zucchini and 2 small eggplants, cut into ½-inch dice, with 3 tablespoons olive oil, 4 garlic cloves, minced, and salt and pepper to taste. Spread the vegetables on two greased baking sheets; roast, turning occasionally, until golden brown, about 35 minutes. Set the vegetables aside. Omit steps 1 and 2 and substitute the roasted zucchini and eggplant for the mushrooms and spinach while assembling the lasagna in step 4.

SHOPPING WITH THE TEST KITCHEN

Jarred Pasta Sauces: If you're going to buy pasta sauce, you should know which one tastes best. To find out, we assembled a lineup of nine national brands of marinara (or basic tomato and basil) sauce and called our tasters to the table. Just as important as what our tasters did like—good tomato flavor and a chunky texture—was what they didn't like: overpowering dried herb flavor. Even a sauce with a chunky texture and fresh tomato flavor can be ruined by overseasoning with acrid, stale-tasting dried herbs. Bertolli Tomato and Basil Sauce has a chunky texture and balanced flavor. Because it wasn't overseasoned with dried herbs, tasters thought this sauce compared favorably to homemade sauce.

Skillet Lasagna

Lasagna is a crowd-pleasing dish that never goes out of style. With layers of chewy pasta, hearty sauce, and rich, creamy cheese, it is so good that second helpings are nearly always mandatory. But lasagna is not a dish you throw together at the last minute. Or is it? Lasagna is a casserole traditionally made with fully or partially cooked components that meld together during baking, but we wondered if it was possible to take the same flavors and components of lasagna and cook them on the stovetop in a skillet instead of in the oven. In essence, we wanted to turn an oven-baked casserole into a stovetop skillet casserole.

Our plan was simple. We would first brown the meat and remove it from the pan, then build a thin but flavorful sauce. Then we'd add the pasta (regular lasagna noodles broken into 2-inch lengths), which we figured could be slowly simmered while the pan was covered, giving us some "walk-away" time. We would finish the dish by adding ricotta cheese, Parmesan, and any other flavors we deemed necessary.

Most lasagna sauces require a lengthy simmer, which allows the ingredients to meld and their flavors to develop. But in this skillet version, we aimed to limit the time that it took to simmer the sauce to the time that it took to cook the pasta. Aiming to keep our ingredient list to a minimum, we started with onions and garlic, which gave the sauce its depth. Since this recipe was meant to be a one-dish meal, we felt it necessary to add some protein. Tasters preferred meat loaf mix (a combination of ground beef, pork, and veal sold in one package at most supermarkets). For a flavor variation, tasters liked a combination of Italian sausage and sweet red peppers.

With the aromatics and meat decided, we next turned to the type of tomatoes we would use in the sauce. We started our tests with tomato puree, but found that the sauce was a tad too heavy; also, the pasta tended to sit on top of the sauce, making it cook unevenly. We tried adding a little water to give the pasta a better medium in which to cook, but the resulting lasagna was too bland. Abandoning tomato puree, we switched to a large can of diced tomatoes thinned with a little extra water. This gave the sauce a nicely chunky and substantial texture—and there was just enough liquid to cook the pasta. A small can of tomato sauce fortified the tomato flavor and helped hold the lasagna together. To replicate the cheesiness of a traditional lasagna, we stirred in the ricotta, but this didn't give us the results we were looking for. Once mixed in, the sweet creaminess of the ricotta became lost and succeeded only in making the sauce appear grainy and shockingly pink. Instead we placed dollops of ricotta on top of the lasagna and then re-covered the pan, allowing the added cheese to heat through. This way, the ricotta remained distinct from the other ingredients. The ricotta also created an attractive pattern over the top of the dish, and a sprinkling of freshly chopped basil gave it the flavor of authentic, oven-baked lasagna.

BUILDING SKILLET LASAGNA

1. Sauté the onion, garlic, and meat in the skillet. Scatter the broken noodles over the meat. Then pour the diced tomatoes and tomato sauce over the noodles. Cover and cook.

2. Once the pasta is tender, remove the cover, add the Parmesan and dot with the ricotta. Cover and let the cheese soften off the heat.

SKILLET LASAGNA

SERVES 4 TO 6

A 12-inch nonstick skillet with a tight-fitting lid works best for this recipe.

1	**(28-ounce) can diced tomatoes**
	Water
1	**tablespoon olive oil**
1	**onion, minced**
	Salt
3	**garlic cloves, minced**
⅛	**teaspoon red pepper flakes**
1	**pound meat loaf mix**
10	**curly-edged lasagna noodles, broken into 2-inch lengths**
1	**(8-ounce) can tomato sauce**
½	**cup plus 2 tablespoons grated Parmesan cheese**
	Pepper
1	**cup whole-milk or part-skim ricotta cheese**
3	**tablespoons chopped fresh basil**

1. Empty the can of tomatoes into a 1-quart liquid measuring cup. Add water until the mixture measures 1 quart.

2. Heat the oil in large nonstick skillet over medium heat until shimmering. Add the onion and ½ teaspoon salt and cook until the onion begins to brown, about 5 minutes. Stir in the garlic and red pepper flakes and cook until fragrant, about 30 seconds. Add the ground meat and cook, breaking up the meat into small pieces with a wooden spoon, until it is no longer pink, about 4 minutes.

3. Scatter the pasta over the meat but do not stir. Pour the tomato mixture and tomato sauce over the pasta. Cover and bring to a simmer. Reduce the heat to medium-low and simmer, stirring occasionally, until the pasta is tender, about 20 minutes.

4. Remove the skillet from the heat and stir in ½ cup of the Parmesan. Season with salt and pepper to taste. Dot with heaping tablespoons of the ricotta, cover, and let stand off the heat for 5 minutes. Sprinkle with the basil and the remaining 2 tablespoons Parmesan. Serve.

Variation
SKILLET LASAGNA WITH SAUSAGE AND PEPPERS

Substitute 1 pound Italian sausage, removed from its casing, for the meat loaf mix. Add 1 red bell pepper, seeded and chopped, to the skillet with the onion in step 2.

Eggplant Parmesan

Traditional recipes for eggplant Parmesan instruct you to fry breaded eggplant in copious amounts of oil, which usually results in greasy eggplant with a sodden, unappealing bread-crumb crust. We wanted a fresher, lighter take on this classic Italian dish. Could we eliminate the frying, streamline the dish, and make it taste better than the original?

Most recipes begin with purging (salting) the eggplant to expel bitter juices and prevent the porous flesh from soaking up excess oil. To double-check this theory, we baked some unsalted eggplant. Oil absorption wasn't a problem, but the eggplant did taste bitter, and it had a raw, mealy texture. Thirty minutes of salting remedied the problem. For efficiency's sake, we chose good-sized globe eggplants; we didn't want to multiply the number of slices we'd have to prepare.

We then tested coatings for the eggplant. Flour alone wasn't substantial enough. Eggplant swathed in mayonnaise and then bread crumbs turned slimy. Eggplant coated in a flour-and-egg batter and then bread crumbs was thick and tough. A standard single breading (dipping the eggplant first in egg, then bread crumbs) was too messy—the egg slid right off the eggplant, leaving the crumbs with nothing to which they could adhere.

A double, or bound, breading proved superior. Dipping the eggplant first in seasoned flour, then egg, then bread crumbs (seasoned with Parmesan cheese) created a substantial (but not heavy) and crisp coating that brought the mild flavor and tender, creamy texture of the eggplant to the fore.

After considerable experimentation, we found that the best way to achieve a crisp coating is to bake the breaded slices on two preheated baking sheets, each coated with a modest amount of vegetable oil (olive oil tasted sour), rotating the pans and flipping the slices partway through cooking. At 425 degrees, the slices sizzled during cooking and became fully tender in 30 minutes. Using this technique, we turned out crisp, golden brown disks of eggplant, expending a minimum of effort (and using very little oil). And now, seeing that we weren't busy frying up four batches of eggplant in hot oil, we had time to grate cheese and whip up a quick tomato sauce while the eggplant baked.

We'd already used some Parmesan for breading the eggplant, and a little extra browned nicely on top of the casserole. Mozzarella is another standard addition that gives the casserole its gooey appeal. A quick tomato sauce started off with a few cloves of minced garlic, a sprinkling of red pepper flakes, and some olive oil, followed by three cans of diced tomatoes, just two of them pureed in the food processor to preserve a chunky texture. A handful of fresh basil leaves (we reserved some basil for garnish, too) plus salt and pepper were the final flourishes.

Because breading softens beneath the smothering layers of sauce and cheese, we left most of the top layer of eggplant exposed. This left us with about 1 cup of extra sauce, just enough to pass at the table. Another benefit of this technique was that without excess moisture, the casserole was easy to cut into tidy pieces. With the eggplant fully cooked, the dish needed only a brief stay in a hot oven to melt the cheese.

EGGPLANT PARMESAN

SERVES 6 TO 8

Use kosher salt when salting the eggplant. The coarse grains don't dissolve as readily as the fine grains of regular table salt, so any excess can be easily wiped away. It's necessary to divide the eggplant into two batches when tossing it with the salt. To be efficient, use the 30 to 45 minutes during which the salted eggplant sits to prepare the breading, cheeses, and sauce.

EGGPLANT
- 2 medium globe eggplant (about 2 pounds), cut crosswise into ¼-inch rounds
- 1 tablespoon kosher salt
- 8 slices hearty white sandwich bread, torn into large pieces
- 1 cup grated Parmesan cheese
   Salt and pepper
- 1 cup all-purpose flour
- 4 large eggs
- 6 tablespoons vegetable oil

SAUCE
- 3 (14.5-ounce) cans diced tomatoes
- 2 tablespoons olive oil
- 4 garlic cloves, minced
- ¼ teaspoon red pepper flakes
- ½ cup coarsely chopped fresh basil
   Salt and pepper

LAYERS
- 2 cups shredded whole-milk or part-skim mozzarella cheese
- ½ cup grated Parmesan cheese
- 10 fresh basil leaves, torn, for garnish

1. FOR THE EGGPLANT: Toss half of the eggplant slices and 1½ teaspoons of the kosher salt in a large bowl until combined; transfer the salted eggplant to a large colander set over a bowl. Repeat with the remaining eggplant and kosher salt, placing the second batch on top of the first. Let stand until the eggplant releases about 2 tablespoons liquid, 30 to 45 minutes. Spread the eggplant slices on a triple layer of paper towels; cover with another triple layer of paper towels. Press firmly on each slice to remove as much liquid as possible, then wipe off the excess salt.

2. While the eggplant is draining, adjust the oven racks to the upper-middle and lower-middle positions, place a rimmed baking sheet on each rack, and heat the oven to 425 degrees. Process the bread in a food processor to fine, even crumbs, about fifteen 1-second pulses (you should have about 4 cups). Transfer the crumbs to a pie plate and stir in the Parmesan, ¼ teaspoon salt, and ½ teaspoon pepper; set aside. Wipe out the bowl (do not wash) and set aside.

3. Combine the flour and 1 teaspoon pepper in a large zipper-lock bag; shake to combine. Beat the eggs in a second pie plate. Place 8 to 10 eggplant slices in the bag with the flour; seal the bag and shake to coat the slices. Remove the slices, shaking off the excess flour; dip in the eggs, let the excess egg run off, then coat evenly with the bread-crumb mixture. Lay the breaded slices on a wire rack set over a baking sheet. Repeat with the remaining eggplant.

4. Remove the preheated baking sheets from the oven; add 3 tablespoons oil to each sheet, tilting to coat evenly. Place half of the breaded eggplant slices on each sheet in a single layer. Bake until the eggplant is well browned and crisp, about 30 minutes, rotating and switching the baking sheets after 10 minutes, and flipping the eggplant slices with a wide spatula after 20 minutes. Do not turn off the oven.

5. FOR THE SAUCE: While the eggplant bakes, process 2 cans of the diced tomatoes in the food processor until almost smooth, about 5 seconds. Heat the olive oil, garlic, and red pepper flakes in a large heavy-bottomed saucepan over medium-high heat, stirring occasionally, until fragrant and the garlic is light golden, about 3 minutes; stir in the processed tomatoes and the remaining can of diced tomatoes. Bring the sauce to a boil, then reduce the heat to medium-low and simmer, stirring occasionally, until slightly thickened and reduced, about 15 minutes (you should have about 4 cups). Stir in the basil and season with salt and pepper to taste.

6. TO ASSEMBLE: Spread 1 cup of the tomato sauce in the bottom of a 13 by 9-inch baking dish. Layer in half of the eggplant slices, overlapping them to fit. Distribute another 1 cup sauce over the eggplant; sprinkle with half of the mozzarella. Layer in the remaining eggplant and dot with another 1 cup sauce, leaving the majority of the eggplant exposed so that it will become crisp; sprinkle with the Parmesan and the remaining mozzarella. Bake until the surface is bubbling and the cheese is browned, 13 to 15 minutes. Cool for 10 minutes, scatter the basil over the top, and serve, passing the remaining tomato sauce separately.

Chicken, Broccoli, and Ziti Casserole

Chicken, broccoli, and ziti tossed in a creamy sauce is such a crowd-pleaser that it makes sense to turn it into a crowd-feeding casserole. Adding a blanket of crunchy bread crumbs should make it that much better, but when we tried recipes for this casserole, what came out of the oven was a mess. The pasta was limp, the chicken was dry and tough, and the broccoli was gray and waterlogged. Even worse, the once-silky sauce became stodgy and bland. We wanted our version of this dish to have it all: moist chicken, crisp-tender broccoli, and firm ziti served in a cheesy sauce that stayed creamy even after baking.

We started with the unifying element of the dish: the sauce. Some recipes use a reduced cream sauce, which tasted great but made this casserole so rich that tasters couldn't finish a small portion. Other recipes use a béchamel sauce (made by cooking butter, flour, and milk until thickened), which had a creamy consistency when baked and wasn't too rich. We boosted the flavor by sautéing onion, lots of garlic (six minced cloves), and red pepper flakes in the butter before we added the flour and milk, and by replacing some of the milk with savory chicken broth. Parmesan is the traditional cheese in this dish, but it wasn't adding enough flavor—even in large quantities. Asiago has a sharper, more pungent flavor that stayed strong even when baked.

We quickly found that strips of boneless, skinless chicken breast needed to be precooked before going into the casserole to prevent the other ingredients from overcooking by the time the chicken was done. Browned chicken tasted great, but it became tough and dried out in the oven. Poaching the chicken in the sauce flavored the meat and kept it moist.

Keeping the pasta from overcooking in the oven took more than just draining it when still slightly underdone. We had to undercook the pasta and then rinse it with cold water to completely stop the carryover cooking. The best option for precooking the broccoli turned out to be the microwave. Adding minced garlic and more Asiago to the fresh bread crumbs created a topping that was as flavorful as the casserole itself.

CHICKEN, BROCCOLI, AND ZITI CASSEROLE

SERVES 8

The casserole can be assembled and refrigerated, minus bread crumbs, up to 24 hours. Bring to room temperature before adding the bread crumbs and baking.

4	slices hearty white sandwich bread, torn into large pieces
8	garlic cloves, minced
2½	cups grated Asiago cheese
5	tablespoons unsalted butter, 2 tablespoons melted
	Salt
1	pound ziti
1	onion, minced
¼	teaspoon red pepper flakes
¼	cup all-purpose flour
½	cup white wine
3	cups whole milk
2	cups low-sodium chicken broth
4	boneless, skinless chicken breasts (about 1½ pounds), cut crosswise into ¼-inch slices
¾	pound broccoli florets, cut into 1-inch pieces
	Pepper

1. Pulse the bread, 2 of the minced garlic cloves, ½ cup of the Asiago, and the melted butter in a food processor until ground to coarse crumbs. Set aside.

2. Adjust an oven rack to the middle position and heat the oven to 400 degrees. Bring 4 quarts water to a boil in a large pot. Add 1 tablespoon salt and the ziti to the boiling water and cook until nearly al dente. Drain in a colander and rinse under cold water until cool. Set aside.

3. Wipe the pot dry. Return the pot to medium heat and melt the remaining butter. Cook the onion until softened, about 5 minutes. Add the remaining garlic and red pepper flakes and cook until fragrant, about 30 seconds. Stir in the flour and cook until golden, about 1 minute. Slowly whisk in the wine and cook until the liquid is almost evaporated, about 1 minute. Slowly whisk in the milk and broth and bring to a boil. Add the chicken and simmer until no longer pink, about 5 minutes. Off the heat, stir in the remaining Asiago until melted.

4. Microwave the broccoli, covered, in a large bowl on high power until bright green and nearly tender, 2 to 4 minutes. Stir the cooked broccoli and drained ziti into the pot and season with salt and pepper to taste. Transfer to a 13 by 9-inch baking dish. Sprinkle with the bread-crumb mixture and bake until the sauce is bubbling around the edges and the topping is golden brown, 20 to 25 minutes. Cool for 5 minutes. Serve.

SHOPPING WITH THE TEST KITCHEN

Asiago Cheese: Asiago is a cow's milk cheese made in the mountains of northern Italy. Although Asiago is produced in both fresh and aged forms, it's likely you will find only the aged version in your supermarket's cheese case. Aged Asiago is made with partially skimmed milk and aged for three months to a year. Its nutty, slightly assertive flavor is often described as a cross between cheddar and Parmesan, and its firm texture is perfect for grating on pasta, soups, or salads.

Baked Ziti

Baked ziti sounds simple enough. Take cooked pasta and add tomato sauce, cheese, and maybe some meatballs, sausage, or even eggplant. If this dish is so easy to prepare, then why are most versions so dry, so bland, and so downright unappealing? We knew good baked ziti, which is an Italian American classic (arguably more American than Italian), was possible. We just had to figure out how to do it.

Mozzarella binds the noodles together and makes this baked casserole incredibly rich and gooey. Fresh mozzarella packed in water makes the texture of the finished dish especially moist and creamy and is recommended. Besides adding moisture, we found that fresh mozzarella lent this dish far more flavor than bland, rubbery supermarket mozzarella.

A little less than 3 cups of shredded mozzarella was just right for a pound of pasta. More made this dish too heavy and too rich. In fact, we realized that many American recipes for baked ziti simply include too much cheese, sauce, and other goodies. These ingredients overwhelm the noodles and make the casserole too thick, which extends the cooking time and makes the pasta mushy. We were learning that less is more when it comes to baked ziti.

Even good mozzarella is a bit bland, so we added ½ cup grated Parmesan to perk up the flavor. To ensure that the cheese was evenly distributed throughout the casserole, we layered half the pasta into the baking dish, sprinkled it with half the cheeses, and then added the remaining pasta and cheeses.

The mozzarella is the binder in baked ziti, but it's the tomato sauce that must keep things moist. A smooth sauce made with crushed tomatoes does the job most effectively. Diced tomatoes tasted good but tasters did not like the chunks of tomato, which tended to dry out in the oven. Crushed tomatoes coated the pasta evenly and thoroughly.

Although it seems obvious, the pasta for baked ziti should be slightly undercooked (it's going to soften further in the oven). Too many recipes start with overcooked pasta. By the time the pasta is baked, it's soft and squishy. We also found it helpful to reserve some of the pasta cooking water to help spread the tomato sauce and keep the pasta moist.

Our recipe was coming together. We tested a variety of baking dishes and decided on a relatively shallow 13 by 9-inch dish because it allowed the pasta to heat through quickly. More time in the oven only dries out the noodles or makes them overly soft. With that in mind, we found that a hot 400-degree oven was best. Just 20 minutes in the oven (not the hour called for in many recipes with too much cheese, sauce, and other filling ingredients) yields a casserole with pasta that you still want to eat.

BAKED ZITI WITH TOMATOES AND MOZZARELLA

SERVES 4 TO 6

Melted mozzarella cheese provides the binder for the pasta and the other ingredients in this dish. Use fresh mozzarella if possible—it will provide extra creaminess and moisture.

	Salt
1	pound ziti or other short, tubular pasta
3	tablespoons olive oil
2	garlic cloves, minced
1	(28-ounce) can crushed tomatoes
2	tablespoons coarsely chopped fresh basil
	Pepper
2	cups shredded mozzarella cheese (see note above)
½	cup grated Parmesan cheese

1. Adjust an oven rack to the middle position and heat the oven to 400 degrees. Bring 4 quarts water to a boil in a large pot. Add 1 tablespoon salt and the pasta to the boiling water and cook until al dente. Reserve ¼ cup of the pasta cooking water. Drain the pasta, return it to the pot, and toss with 1 tablespoon of the oil; set aside.

2. Meanwhile, heat the remaining 2 tablespoons oil and the garlic in a medium skillet over medium heat until fragrant but not brown, about 2 minutes. Stir in the tomatoes and simmer until thickened slightly, about 10 minutes. Off the heat, stir in the basil and season with salt and pepper to taste.

3. Add the tomato sauce and reserved pasta cooking water to the pasta; stir to combine. Pour half of the pasta into a 13 by 9-inch baking dish. Sprinkle with half of the mozzarella and half of the Parmesan. Pour the remaining pasta into the dish and sprinkle with the remaining mozzarella and Parmesan. Cover with aluminum foil and bake until the cheese melts, about 15 minutes. Remove the foil and continue to bake until the cheese begins to brown, about 5 minutes. Serve immediately.

Variation

BAKED ZITI WITH CRUMBLED ITALIAN SAUSAGE

SERVES 4 TO 6

Both sweet and hot Italian sausage work fine in this recipe. To remove the sausage from its casing, cut it open at the end and simply squeeze out the ground sausage.

	Salt
1	pound ziti or other short, tubular pasta
2	tablespoons olive oil
1	pound hot or sweet Italian sausage, removed from its casing (see note above)
4	garlic cloves, minced
½	teaspoon red pepper flakes
1	(28-ounce) can crushed tomatoes
2	tablespoons coarsely chopped fresh basil
	Pepper
2	cups shredded mozzarella cheese
½	cup grated Parmesan cheese

1. Adjust an oven rack to the middle position and heat the oven to 400 degrees. Bring 4 quarts water to a boil in a large pot. Add 1 tablespoon salt and the pasta to the boiling water and cook until al dente. Reserve ¼ cup of the pasta cooking water. Drain the pasta, return it to the pot, and toss with 1 tablespoon of the oil; set aside.

2. Meanwhile, heat the remaining 1 tablespoon oil in a large nonstick skillet over high heat until shimmering. Add the sausage and cook, breaking up the meat into small pieces with a wooden spoon, until the sausage loses its raw color, about 5 minutes. Stir in the garlic and red pepper flakes; cook until fragrant, about 30 seconds. Stir in the tomatoes and simmer until thickened slightly, about 10 minutes. Off the heat, stir in the basil and season with salt and pepper to taste.

3. Add the tomato sauce and reserved pasta cooking water to the pasta; stir to combine. Pour half of the pasta into a 13 by 9-inch baking dish. Sprinkle with half of the mozzarella and half of the Parmesan. Pour the remaining pasta into the dish and sprinkle with the remaining mozzarella and Parmesan. Cover with aluminum foil and bake until the cheese melts, about 15 minutes. Remove the foil and continue to bake until the cheese begins to brown, about 5 minutes. Serve immediately.

Turkey Tetrazzini

Are turkey tetrazzini and tuna-noodle casseroles American institutions or national nightmares? In most cases the answer is both, no doubt because most versions of these dishes are so bad. Most often made from a canned-soup base (cream of mushroom, cream of celery, and cream of chicken are the usual choices) mixed with soggy noodles, leftover turkey or canned tuna, and a few stray vegetables from the crisper drawer, these casseroles deliver little in the way of flavor or texture, save for the sometimes crunchy topping of bread crumbs. Ready to give these hard-working classics a well-deserved makeover, we began by shutting the cupboard door to all canned soups and focused on making a sauce from scratch.

Tuna-noodle casserole and turkey tetrazzini are nearly the same dish, and research determined that cream of mushroom soup is the most commonly used sauce base. A mushroom-flavored sauce, therefore, was what we wanted. Testing both a béchamel (flour-thickened milk) and a velouté (flour-thickened broth), we found that neither was perfect. The béchamel sauce tasted too dairy-heavy, and the velouté was simply too light. A sauce made with a combination of milk and broth (thickened with flour) tasted better, but it still lacked some richness. Replacing the milk with half-and-half, we finally landed on the right basic flavor and heft. Four cups of liquid thickened with 4 tablespoons of flour produced enough sauce with the right texture to coat 1 pound of pasta without being either soupy or gummy.

Focusing next on developing the mushroom flavor, we found it necessary to use a whopping 20 ounces of mushrooms. Any less just wouldn't do. Trying both cremini and white button mushrooms in the sauce, we noted that tasters could find no appreciable difference, so we went with the more available and less expensive white button mushrooms. The key to an intense mushroom flavor, we found, is to sauté the mushrooms until they release all their liquid and begin to brown. To round out the flavor of the sauce, onions, garlic, fresh thyme, cayenne, and Parmesan all proved to be absolutely necessary.

Moving on to the vegetables, we noted that many recipes use a lot of celery, which adds crunch but almost no flavor. Interestingly enough, our tasters preferred no celery at all. Bell peppers met a similar fate. Frozen peas were the only vegetable given the thumbs up by the test-kitchen staff, and we found that the peas would not turn soggy if we added them right before baking.

Several recipes we researched call for elbow macaroni; however, we found it too starchy and thick. We preferred fettuccine, linguine, or spaghetti instead, for texture and big structural presence. To make the dish easier to eat, we broke the long pasta into thirds so that there was no need to wind the pasta around a fork.

As for the topping, we decided that store-bought bread crumbs tasted too sandy, and canned fried onions tasted too much like chemicals. Instead, we found it just as easy to grind our own bread crumbs in the food processor with a little butter; they toast nicely in the oven while the casserole bakes.

TURKEY TETRAZZINI

SERVES 6 TO 8

Tetrazzini is also great made with leftover chicken. Don't skimp on the salt and pepper; this dish needs aggressive seasoning. See page 264 for the results from our canned tuna tasting.

TOPPING

- 4 slices hearty white sandwich bread, torn into large pieces
- 2 tablespoons unsalted butter, melted

FILLING

- Salt
- 1 pound fettuccine, linguine, or spaghetti, broken into thirds
- 1 tablespoon olive oil
- 5 tablespoons unsalted butter
- 20 ounces white button mushrooms, wiped clean and cut into ¼-inch slices
- 2 onions, minced
- 4 garlic cloves, minced
- 1 tablespoon minced fresh thyme
- ⅛ teaspoon cayenne pepper
- ¼ cup all-purpose flour
- 2 cups low-sodium chicken broth
- 2 cups half-and-half
- 1 cup grated Parmesan cheese
- Pepper
- 4 cups cooked turkey meat, cut into ½-inch pieces
- 1½ cups frozen peas

1. FOR THE TOPPING: Process the bread and butter in a food processor until coarsely ground, about six 1-second pulses; set aside.

2. FOR THE FILLING: Adjust an oven rack to the middle position and heat the oven to 400 degrees. Bring 4 quarts water to a boil in a large pot. Add 1 tablespoon salt and the pasta to the boiling water and cook until al dente. Drain in a colander and toss with the oil; leave the pasta in the colander and set aside.

3. Wipe the pot dry. Add the butter to the pot and return to medium-high heat until the butter is melted. Add the mushrooms and ½ teaspoon salt; cook the mushrooms until they have released their juices and are brown around the edges, 7 to 10 minutes. Add the onions and cook until softened, about 5 minutes. Stir in the garlic, thyme, and cayenne; cook until fragrant, about 30 seconds. Add the flour and cook, stirring constantly, until golden, about 1 minute. Slowly whisk in the broth and half-and-half; bring to a simmer and cook, whisking often, until lightly thickened, about 1 minute. Off the heat, whisk in the Parmesan. Season with salt and pepper to taste.

4. Add the pasta, turkey, and peas to the sauce; stir to combine. Pour into a 13 by 9-inch baking dish and sprinkle with the bread-crumb topping. Bake until the topping has browned and the sauce is bubbly, 10 to 15 minutes. Serve immediately.

Variation
TUNA-NOODLE CASSEROLE
Follow the recipe for Turkey Tetrazzini, substituting 2 (6-ounce) cans solid white tuna packed in water, drained and flaked into 1-inch pieces with a fork, for the cooked turkey in step 4.

Canned Tuna: Is tuna sold in foil pouches really better than its canned cousin? We sampled eight tunas to find out and were surprised by the results. Tasters found the pouched product too fishy and preferred the milder taste and meatier texture of the canned tunas. Our favorites are Chicken of the Sea Solid White Albacore Tuna in Water, for its moist, chunky texture and mild flavor, and StarKist Solid White Albacore Tuna in Water, for its firm, flaky texture and fresh, mellow flavor.

Shepherd's Pie

Shepherd's pie was originally made from leftover roast lamb mixed with leftover gravy and topped with mashed potatoes. A well-loved staple of the British diet, the dish eventually came to be made with ground lamb rather than the trimmings from a roast so it could be made anytime. On this side of the Atlantic, where most people don't have much taste for lamb, the ground lamb has been traded for ground beef. The result often tastes like boiled hamburger or a bland Sloppy Joe. Putting some meaty flavor back into this retread seemed like a good idea.

After browning onions and carrots, we cooked the ground beef (85-percent lean was the best choice) and added the Worcestershire sauce called for in many recipes. We were sure this was the key to better flavor. Not so. The Worcestershire made the filling taste beefier, but it also added some unpleasant sour notes. We wondered if soy sauce—also known to enhance meat flavor—could pinch-hit. Odd as it may seem, soy sauce worked well, without calling attention to itself.

In the test kitchen we often use tomato paste to add depth to stews and sauces. Just a tablespoon did the trick here. For the liquid ingredient, tasters preferred chicken broth over what they called the "tinny" flavor of beef broth.

Given the popularity of shepherd's pie as pub food, we weren't surprised to find recipes that called for a pint of beer. Guinness, our favorite pub beer, was too bitter. Most mild lagers and ales were fine, but it was an unlikely choice, O'Doul's nonalcoholic amber beer, that tasters deemed their favorite. Its sweet, malty flavor may not be terribly satisfying at a pub, but it worked perfectly in this dish. A splash of cream kept the meat from toughening as it simmered.

The only thing missing was the crown of mashed potatoes. Regular mashed potatoes turned to mush when placed on top of the saucy filling. A stiff mash—with less butter and cream—was needed. Brushing the potatoes with beaten egg helped create a beautiful golden brown crust, as did a quick run under the broiler after the pie had baked for 15 minutes.

SHEPHERD'S PIE

SERVES 6 TO 8

Although just about any mild beer will work in this recipe, we particularly enjoyed the sweet flavor of O'Doul's nonalcoholic amber. Our Shepherd's Pie can be made ahead. Make the filling through step 2, but do not add the peas. Store in an airtight container in the refrigerator for up to 2 days. When ready to proceed, reheat the filling in a large saucepan, stir in the peas, and transfer to a broiler-safe 2-quart casserole. Proceed with the recipe from step 3.

FILLING

- 2 tablespoons unsalted butter
- 1 large onion, minced
- 2 medium carrots, peeled and chopped fine
- 2 pounds 85-percent lean ground beef
  Salt and pepper
- 5 tablespoons all-purpose flour
- 1 tablespoon tomato paste

APPLYING THE POTATO TOPPING

Use a rubber spatula to scrape small piles of potato around the edge of the dish. Dollop more potato into the center and then spread the potato until the filling is covered and is flush with the edge of the dish.

¼	cup heavy cream
1¾	cups low-sodium chicken broth
¾	cup beer (see note above)
2	tablespoons soy sauce
2	teaspoons minced fresh thyme
1	cup frozen peas

TOPPING

2½	pounds russet potatoes, peeled and cut into 2-inch pieces
	Salt
2	tablespoons unsalted butter, melted
⅓	cup heavy cream, warmed
	Pepper
1	large egg, beaten

1. FOR THE FILLING: Heat the butter in a large skillet over medium-high heat until foaming. Add the onion and carrots and cook until soft, about 8 minutes. Add the meat, ½ teaspoon salt, and ½ teaspoon pepper and cook, breaking up the meat into small pieces with a wooden spoon, until browned, about 12 minutes. Add the flour and tomato paste and cook until the paste begins to darken, about 1 minute.

2. Add the cream and cook until it spatters, about 1 minute. Add the broth, beer, soy sauce, and thyme and simmer over medium heat, stirring

frequently, until the mixture is thick but still saucy, 15 to 20 minutes. Remove from the heat, stir in the peas, adjust the seasonings as needed, and transfer to a broiler-safe 2-quart casserole dish.

3. FOR THE TOPPING: Adjust an oven rack to the upper-middle position and heat the oven to 375 degrees. Bring the potatoes, ½ teaspoon salt, and water to cover to a boil in a large saucepan over high heat. Reduce the heat to medium-low and simmer until tender, 15 to 20 minutes. Drain the potatoes, return to the saucepan, and mash the potatoes with the butter and cream until smooth. Season with salt and pepper to taste.

4. Spread the potatoes over the filling, using a spatula to smooth the top. Brush with the egg and drag a fork across the top to make ridges. Bake until the filling is bubbling, about 15 minutes. Turn on the broiler and cook until the top is golden brown, 3 to 5 minutes. Remove from the oven and cool for 10 minutes. Serve.

Tamale Pie

Tamale pie has its roots in southwestern cooking. A mildly spicy ground meat filling is topped with a cornmeal crust and baked. Although time and fashion have altered the recipe from decade to decade, the basic idea remains the same. A good pie contains a juicy, spicy mixture of meat and vegetables encased in or topped with a cornmeal crust that is neither too stiff nor too loose. Bad tamale pies, however, are dry and bland and usually have too much or too little filling.

We did have a number of questions about how to prepare the cornmeal topping. For starters, we tested fine-ground cornmeal (such as Quaker, which is sold in most supermarkets) against coarser meals. As expected, the crust made with fine-ground cornmeal was slightly smoother, but it was also bland in comparison with the toothsome crust made with coarse-ground cornmeal. We made the topping with water and stock as well as with and without butter. Tasters preferred the clean, simple flavor of mush made with just water, salt, and cornmeal. The stock and butter added more flavor and fat to the crust than was necessary. We found that 4 cups water to 1½ cups cornmeal yielded a spoonable texture with enough structure to contain the meat filling.

Authentic and modern recipes use a variety of techniques to make the mush. In some the mush is cooked slowly over low heat to keep it from burning; others use the microwave. We found it difficult to keep an eye on the mush in the microwave, and cooking it low and slow was unnecessary. When we used medium-high heat and a heavy-duty whisk, the mush took only 3 minutes to thicken to the right consistency.

With the cornmeal-mush topping in place, we moved on to the filling. Most recipes use either ground beef or ground pork as the base, but we liked the flavor of both mixed together. An all-beef pie turned out boring and tough, and an all-pork pie was light and mealy. A pie made with equal amounts of beef and pork was flavorful and nicely textured.

Most tamale pie fillings call for tomatoes, corn, and black beans. We found that this simple recipe easily accommodates canned and frozen vegetables with no ill effect on the final flavor. Seasoned with onion, garlic, jalapeño, and a little fresh oregano, the tamale filling tasted fresh and spicy.

Putting together filling and topping was simple. We piled the meat filling into a large baking dish and topped it with cheese and the cornmeal mush, which, as loose as it was, was easy to spread in an even layer to the edges of the dish. A moderately high oven temperature did the best job of setting the crust and heating the filling. The cheese, trapped beneath the cornmeal and above the filling, melted into an appealingly smooth layer.

TAMALE PIE
SERVES 6 TO 8

We like coarse-ground cornmeal (about the texture of kosher salt) for the topping. We had good results with Goya Coarse Yellow Corn Meal. To keep the cornmeal mush at a spreadable consistency, cover it while assembling the pie. If the mush does get too dry, simply loosen it with a little hot water.

FILLING

1	tablespoon vegetable oil
¾	pound 90-percent lean ground beef
¾	pound ground pork
1	large onion, minced
1	jalapeño chile, seeded and minced
2	garlic cloves, minced
1	teaspoon ground cumin
¼	teaspoon cayenne pepper
1	tablespoon chili powder
1	teaspoon salt
1	(14.5-ounce) can diced tomatoes
1	(15.5-ounce) can black beans, drained and rinsed
1	cup fresh or frozen corn
1	tablespoon minced fresh oregano
	Pepper
1	cup shredded Monterey Jack cheese

TOPPING

4	cups water
¾	teaspoon salt
1½	cups coarse cornmeal (see note above)
¼	teaspoon pepper

1. FOR THE FILLING: Grease a 13 by 9-inch baking dish or 6 individual 12-ounce dishes and set aside. Adjust an oven rack to the middle position and heat the oven to 375 degrees.

2. Heat the oil in a large skillet over high heat until shimmering. Add the ground beef and pork and cook, breaking up the meat into small pieces with a wooden spoon, until it is no longer pink and beginning to brown, about 4 minutes. Add the onion and jalapeño and cook until just softened, about 3 minutes. Add the garlic, cumin, cayenne, chili powder, and salt and cook until aromatic, about 30 seconds. Add the tomatoes, black beans, and corn. Simmer until most of the liquid has evaporated, about 3 minutes. Remove the pan from the heat and stir in the oregano and pepper to taste. Set aside.

3. FOR THE TOPPING: Bring the water to a boil in a large heavy-bottomed saucepan over high heat. Add the salt and then slowly pour in the cornmeal while whisking vigorously to prevent lumps from forming. Reduce the heat to medium-high and cook, whisking constantly, until the cornmeal begins to soften and the mixture thickens, about 3 minutes. Remove the pan from the heat and stir in the pepper.

4. Spoon the beef mixture evenly into the prepared dish and sprinkle the cheese evenly over the top of the casserole. Gently spread the cornmeal mixture over the cheese using a flexible rubber spatula, pushing the mixture to the very edges of the baking dish. Cover tightly with aluminum foil and bake for 30 minutes. Remove the foil and continue to bake until the crust is beginning to brown and the filling is bubbly, 15 to 20 minutes. Allow to cool for 10 minutes before serving.

Thanksgiving Turkey Bake

The classic combination of turkey, gravy, stuffing, and cranberry sauce tastes much too good to have only one day a year. Yet it takes about a year to recover from the incredible amount of shopping, prep, and cleanup necessary for such a meal. We wanted to replicate the flavors of this traditional meal, without all the work, in the form of a casserole. What we had in mind was a layered casserole, starting with a layer of sweet and tangy cranberry sauce, covered by well-seasoned bread stuffing, and topped with slices of moist turkey.

Taking a closer look at the slices of turkey, we noted that slicing cutlets from a boneless breast was fairly simple; however, using ready-made turkey cutlets was even easier. Two pounds of cutlets shingled nicely on top of the stuffing in a standard 13 by 9-inch casserole dish served roughly eight people.

Next we moved on to the stuffing. To keep this dish manageable, we relied on packaged stuffing. Following the package instructions (which tell you to rehydrate the stuffing with water and a little butter) didn't work—the stuffing tasted stale and bland. We then tried a few additions to liven up the stuffing, such as sautéed sausage, onions, and celery, as well as some fresh thyme and sage, chicken broth, and eggs. Although the prepackaged flavors were still somewhat evident, the stuffing was much improved. We tried several brands, styles, and flavors of bagged stuffing mix and all worked fine. Tasters did, however, prefer those that were plain or seasoned simply with herbs.

Moving on to the gravy, our goal was to achieve a good flavor despite the fact that we wouldn't have the benefit of any roast turkey drippings. What we did have, luckily, were drippings left from the sautéed sausage used in the stuffing. Using these browned bits, we built a simple gravy by adding some sautéed onions and celery, flour, and broth.

Now we had only a few more details to resolve, beginning with the cranberry sauce. We knew that making cranberry sauce from frozen cranberries is relatively easy, but we decided to give canned whole cranberry sauce a try, thinking that the difference in flavor and texture would be minimal once the dish was baked. The canned variety did the job just fine.

Our final challenge was how to assemble and bake the casserole. The dish requires 30 minutes in the oven to cook the turkey and heat the stuffing; however, the edges and tops of the turkey cutlets turned dry and crisp when not covered with aluminum foil. We found that pouring some of the gravy over the cutlets before cooking added extra flavor and moisture. Although tasty, the casserole was lacking something. Some minced parsley helped matters by providing both color and a fresh flavor, and toasted pecans added a nice texture. This casserole is no replacement for Thanksgiving dinner, but it does satisfy a Thanksgiving craving and can be made in about an hour using only one pot, a large bowl, and a casserole dish.

THANKSGIVING TURKEY BAKE

SERVES 8

We prefer plain dried bread cubes for the stuffing, but if none are available, choose a kind that is minimally flavored.

1	(14-ounce) bag dried bread or cornbread cubes for stuffing (see note above)
3	tablespoons unsalted butter
¾	pound bulk pork sausage (such as Jimmy Dean)
2	onions, minced
3	celery ribs, chopped fine
	Salt
3	garlic cloves, minced
½	teaspoon dried thyme
½	cup all-purpose flour
3	cups low-sodium beef broth
4	cups low-sodium chicken broth
2	bay leaves
	Pepper
2	large eggs, lightly beaten
1	tablespoon minced fresh sage
1	(16-ounce) can whole-berry cranberry sauce
2	pounds turkey cutlets
1	cup pecans, toasted and chopped coarse (see page 198)
¼	cup chopped fresh parsley

1. Adjust an oven rack to the middle position and heat the oven to 400 degrees. Place the bread cubes in a large mixing bowl and set aside. Melt 1 tablespoon of the butter in a Dutch oven over medium-high heat. Add the sausage and cook, breaking up the meat into small pieces with a wooden spoon, until the sausage loses its raw color, about 5 minutes. Transfer to the bowl with the bread cubes.

2. Return the Dutch oven to medium-high heat and melt the remaining 2 tablespoons butter. Add the onions, celery, and ½ teaspoon salt; cook, scraping the browned bits off the bottom of the pot, until dry, sticky, and lightly browned, about 5 minutes. Add the garlic and thyme; cook until fragrant, about 30 seconds. Add the flour and cook, stirring constantly, until golden, about 1 minute. Slowly whisk in the broths; add the bay leaves, bring to a simmer, and cook, whisking often and scraping the browned bits off the bottom of the pot, until the gravy is thickened and you have about 5½ cups, 20 to 25 minutes. Season with salt and pepper to taste.

3. Strain the gravy through a mesh strainer (you should have about 4 cups). Add the strained vegetables (discarding the bay leaves), 1 cup of the gravy, the eggs, and sage to the bowl with the bread cubes; toss to coat evenly.

4. Spread the cranberry sauce evenly over the bottom of a 13 by 9-inch baking dish. Press the stuffing into an even layer on top of the cranberry sauce. Shingle the turkey cutlets over the stuffing, and pour 2 cups strained gravy over the turkey. Cover the dish tightly with aluminum foil and bake until the turkey is fully cooked and the stuffing is hot, 20 to 30 minutes. Cool for 10 minutes. Meanwhile, microwave the remaining gravy on high power until hot, about 2 minutes. Sprinkle the toasted pecans and parsley over the casserole. Serve, passing the extra gravy separately.

Chicken Pot Pie

Most everyone loves a good chicken pot pie, though few seem to have the time or energy to make one. Like a lot of other satisfying dishes, traditional pot pie takes time. Before the pie even makes it to the oven, the cook must poach a chicken, take the meat off the bones and cut it up, strain the stock, prepare and blanch vegetables, make a sauce, and mix and roll out biscuit or pie dough. Given the many time-consuming steps it can take to make a pot pie, our goal was to make the best one we could as quickly as possible. Pot pie, after all, was intended as weeknight supper food.

Our experiences with making pot pie also made us aware of two other difficulties. First, the vegetables tend to overcook. A filling that is chock-full of bright, fresh vegetables going into the oven looks completely different after 40 minutes of high-heat baking under a blanket of dough. Carrots become mushy and pumpkin-colored, and peas and fresh herbs fade from spring green to drab olive. We wanted to preserve the vegetables' color as long as it didn't require any unnatural acts to do so.

We began with the chicken. Many recipes call for poaching bone-in chicken parts, but we wondered if there was a less time-consuming alternative. We turned to quick-cooking boneless, skinless chicken breasts. Parts can take about 40 minutes to cook, whereas boneless breasts take just about 10 minutes. Our only concern with poached boneless, skinless breasts was the quality of the poaching liquid—stock, which is used to build the pie's creamy, flavorful sauce. In previous tests we found that bone-in parts could be poached in store-bought broth (rather than homemade stock) without much sacrifice of flavor. We surmised that the bones and skin improved the flavor of the broth during the long cooking time. But how would boneless, skinless breasts fare in store-bought broth? The answer? Not as bad as we feared. In our comparison of the pies made with boneless breasts poached in homemade stock and store-bought broth, we found little difference in quality. For those who like either dark or a mix of dark and white meat in their pie, boneless, skinless chicken thighs can be used as well.

A good pot pie with fresh vegetables, warm pastry, and a full-flavored sauce tastes satisfying. One with overcooked vegetables tastes stodgy and old-fashioned. So we made pies with sautéed vegetables and parboiled vegetables. After comparing the pies, we found that the vegetables sautéed before baking held their color and flavor best, the parboiled ones less so.

Our final task was to develop a sauce that was flavorful and creamy. The sauce for chicken pot pie is traditionally based on a roux (a mixture of butter and flour sautéed together briefly), which is thinned with chicken broth and often enriched with cream or milk. Because of the dish's inherent richness, tasters preferred milk over cream. To bump up the flavor of the sauce, we tried lemon juice, a flavor heightener we had seen in a number of recipes, but it seemed out place in our pie. Sherry, however, worked perfectly, giving our sauce just the rich finish it needed. At last, we'd turned a Sunday favorite into a weeknight option.

CHICKEN POT PIE

SERVES 6 TO 8

Mushrooms can be sautéed along with the celery and carrots, and blanched pearl onions can stand in for the onion. If you don't want to make your own pie dough, we've found that Pillsbury Just Unroll! Pie Crusts work well. Instead of baking the pie in a 13 by 9-inch baking dish, divide the filling between two 9-inch deep-dish pie plates and bake as directed.

1	recipe Savory Pie-Dough Topping or Fluffy Buttermilk-Biscuit Topping (pages 271 and 272)
1½	pounds boneless, skinless chicken breasts and/or thighs
2	cups low-sodium chicken broth
1½	tablespoons vegetable oil
1	large onion, minced
3	medium carrots, peeled and cut into ¼-inch slices
2	celery ribs, cut into ¼-inch slices
	Salt and pepper
4	tablespoons unsalted butter
½	cup all-purpose flour
1½	cups whole milk
½	teaspoon dried thyme
3	tablespoons dry sherry
1	cup frozen green peas
3	tablespoons chopped fresh parsley

1. Prepare the pie-dough or biscuit topping and refrigerate it until ready to use.

2. Adjust an oven rack to the lower-middle position and heat the oven to 400 degrees. Put the chicken and broth in a small Dutch oven or stockpot over medium heat. Cover and bring to a simmer; cook until the chicken is just done, 8 to 10 minutes. Transfer the chicken to a large bowl, reserving the broth in a glass measuring cup.

3. Increase the heat to medium-high; heat the oil in the now-empty pan. Add the onion, carrots, and celery; sauté until just tender, about 5 minutes. Season with salt and pepper to taste. While the vegetables are sautéing, shred the chicken into bite-sized pieces. Transfer the cooked vegetables to the bowl with the chicken; set aside.

4. Melt the butter over medium heat in the again-empty pan; add the flour and cook until golden, about 1 minute. Whisk in the reserved chicken broth, the milk, any accumulated chicken juices, and thyme. Bring to a simmer, then continue to simmer until the sauce fully thickens, about 1 minute. Season with salt and pepper to taste; stir in the sherry.

5. Pour the sauce over the chicken mixture; stir to combine. Stir in the peas and parsley. Adjust the seasonings as needed. Pour the mixture into a 13 by 9-inch baking dish or six 12-ounce ovenproof dishes. Top with the pie-dough or biscuit topping; bake until the topping is golden brown and the filling is bubbly, 30 minutes for a large pie and 20 to 25 minutes for smaller pies. Allow to cool for 5 to 10 minutes before serving.

Variations
CHICKEN POT PIE WITH SPRING VEGETABLES
Replace the celery with 1 pound thin asparagus stalks, trimmed and cut into 1-inch pieces. Add the asparagus with the peas in step 5.

CHICKEN POT PIE WITH CORN AND BACON
This Southern variation with corn and bacon works especially well with the biscuit topping.

Replace the oil in step 3 with 4 slices bacon, cut crosswise into ½-inch strips. Cook the bacon over medium heat until the fat is rendered and the bacon is crisp, about 6 minutes. Remove the bacon from the pan with a slotted spoon and drain it on paper towels. Cook the vegetables in the bacon fat. Add the drained bacon to the bowl with the chicken and cooked vegetables. Proceed with the recipe, replacing the peas with 2 cups fresh or frozen corn.

Pot Pie Toppings

A pot pie isn't complete or as alluring without a topping—be it flaky pie crust or buttery, tender biscuits. Use either topping with our chicken pot pies on page 270 or beef pot pies on pages 273-274.

SAVORY PIE-DOUGH TOPPING

MAKES ENOUGH FOR 1 POT PIE RECIPE

For a double-crust effect, simply tuck the overhanging dough down into the sides of the pan. This tucked crust will become soft in the oven, like the bottom crust on a pie. You can prepare the dough through step 2 up to 2 days ahead of time and store it, wrapped in plastic wrap, in the refrigerator until ready to use. Let stand at room temperature until malleable.

1½	cups all-purpose flour
½	teaspoon salt
4	tablespoons cold vegetable shortening
8	tablespoons (1 stick) cold unsalted butter, cut into ¼-inch cubes
5	tablespoons ice water

1. Process the flour and salt in a food processor until combined. Add the shortening and process until the mixture has the texture of coarse sand, about 10 seconds. Scatter the butter cubes over the flour mixture; cut the butter into the flour until the mixture is pale yellow and resembles coarse crumbs, with butter bits no larger than small peas, about ten 1-second pulses. Turn the mixture into a medium bowl.

2. Sprinkle 3 tablespoons of the ice water over the mixture. With a rubber spatula, use a folding motion to mix. Press down on the dough with the broad side of the spatula until the dough sticks together, adding the remaining ice water, a little at a time, if necessary. Press the dough into a 5 by 4-inch rectangle and wrap tightly with plastic wrap. Refrigerate until chilled, at least 30 minutes.

3. When the pot pie filling is ready, roll out the dough on a floured surface to a 15 by 11-inch rectangle, about ⅛ inch thick. (If making individual pies, roll the dough ⅛ inch thick and cut 6 dough rounds about 1 inch larger than the dish circumference.) Place the dough over the pot pie filling. Trim the dough to within ½ inch of the pan lip. Tuck the overhanging dough back under itself so the folded edge is flush with the pan lip. Flute the edges all around. Alternatively, don't trim the dough and simply tuck the overhanging dough down into the pan side. Cut at least four 1-inch vent holes in a large pot pie or one 1-inch vent hole in each smaller pie. Proceed with the pot pie recipe.

TOPPING A POT PIE

For pie dough: Roll the dough over a rolling pin and unroll it over the baking dish. Trim the dough to overhang the dish by ½ inch, then fold it under itself, flush with the lip of the dish. Crimp as desired.

For biscuits: Cut the biscuit dough into rounds, then place them evenly over the pot pie filling, spacing them about ¼ inch apart.

FLUFFY BUTTERMILK-BISCUIT TOPPING

MAKES ENOUGH FOR 1 POT PIE RECIPE

Mixing the butter and dry ingredients quickly so the butter remains cold and firm is crucial to producing light, tender biscuits. Make sure that the butter is well chilled before mixing it into the dry ingredients. If your kitchen is exceptionally warm, you may want to chill the flour along with the butter. The cut, unbaked biscuits can be refrigerated on a lightly floured baking sheet, covered with plastic wrap, for up to 2 hours.

- 1 cup all-purpose flour
- 1 cup cake flour
- 2 teaspoons baking powder
- ¼ teaspoon baking soda
- 1 teaspoon sugar
- ½ teaspoon salt
- 8 tablespoons (1 stick) cold unsalted butter, cut into ¼-inch cubes
- ¾ cup cold buttermilk, plus 1 to 2 tablespoons if needed

1. Pulse the flours, baking powder, baking soda, sugar, and salt in a food processor. Add the butter pieces; pulse until the mixture resembles coarse cornmeal with a few slightly larger butter lumps, about ten 1-second pulses.

2. Transfer the mixture to a medium bowl; add the buttermilk and stir with a fork until the dough gathers into moist clumps. If the dough doesn't clump, add the additional buttermilk, one tablespoon at a time, until it comes together. Transfer the dough to a floured work surface and form into a rough ball. Using a rolling pin, gently roll the dough out to ½-inch thickness. Using a 2½- to 3-inch biscuit cutter, stamp out 8 to 12 rounds of dough. Space the biscuits evenly over the filling in the baking dish. If making individual pies, cut the dough into pieces slightly smaller than the circumference of each dish.

Variations

PARMESAN BISCUITS

Decrease the butter to 5 tablespoons. After the butter has been processed into the flour and transferred to the bowl, add 2 cups grated Parmesan cheese; toss lightly, then stir in the buttermilk.

HERB BISCUITS

Add 3 tablespoons minced fresh parsley, or 2 tablespoons minced fresh parsley and 1 tablespoon minced fresh tarragon or dill, after the butter has been processed into the flour.

CORNMEAL BISCUITS

Replace the cake flour with 1 cup fine-ground cornmeal.

Beef Pot Pie

Plainly stated, beef pot pie is beef stew baked under a crusty topping. After hours of slow simmering, the stew is ladled into a baking dish, topped with biscuits or a pastry crust, and cooked even longer. It is an all-day affair, requiring hours of diligent attention. We wanted a simpler, faster alternative. Our goal was to create a richly flavored beef pot pie with all the nuance of a slow-simmered beef stew, in a fraction of the time.

We commenced the testing process with our primary concern: the choice of meat. Beef stew develops its rich flavor through the slow, deliberate simmering of inexpensive yet flavorful cuts of beef. Our favorite cut happens to be chuck roast, a marbled, collagen-rich roast that contains a good deal of flavor, as long as it is cooked slowly over low heat. Cooked quickly and over high heat, it's as tough and bland as a tire. But we wondered if we could hasten its cooking and still turn the tough meat tender by trimming it into smaller cubes—petite ½-inch as opposed to 1½-inch pieces. After browning the meat and simmering it slowly on the stovetop, we found that it was both tender and flavorful within 45 minutes—a far cry from the multihour simmer required for the stew. Now this was in the ballpark for pot pie.

With the meat chosen, we could now work on finessing the pie's flavor. We chose to include traditional onions and carrots, as well as a hint of garlic and a substantial splash of red wine. To extract as much flavor as possible from the vegetables, we diced them small and browned them well. Consequently, the vegetables weren't prime players in the finished dish (as they are in chicken pot pie), but tasters didn't seem to mind; they thought it was all about the meat and sauce.

To further enrich the flavor, we borrowed a trick from Cajun cooking and lightly toasted the flour that is used for a thickener. Subjected to dry heat (with or without oil or butter), flour browns and develops a nutty, malty flavor. We rounded out the filling's flavor with a spoonful of tomato paste—fruity yet densely flavored—and 2 teaspoons of fresh thyme. The flavor was a surprisingly close approximation to slow-cooked stew, ready in just a third of the time.

BEEF POT PIE

SERVES 6 TO 8

For the best flavor, buy a chuck roast and trim and cut it yourself rather than purchasing prepackaged stew meat. Dried thyme (1 teaspoon) can be successfully substituted for fresh. If you don't want to make your own pie dough, we've found that Pillsbury Just Unroll! Pie Crusts work well. Instead of baking the pie in a 13 by 9-inch baking dish, divide the filling between two 9-inch deep-dish pie plates and bake as directed.

1	recipe Savory Pie-Dough Topping or Fluffy Buttermilk-Biscuit Topping (see pages 271 and 272)
3	pounds chuck roast, trimmed and cut into ½-inch cubes
	Salt and pepper
1	tablespoon vegetable oil
1	large onion, minced
2	large carrots, peeled and chopped medium
4	garlic cloves, minced
5	tablespoons all-purpose flour
¾	cup dry red wine
1¾	cups low-sodium chicken broth
1¾	cups low-sodium beef broth
1	tablespoon tomato paste
2	teaspoons minced fresh thyme (see note above)
1	cup frozen peas

1. Prepare the pie-dough or biscuit topping and refrigerate it until ready to use.

2. Dry the beef thoroughly on paper towels, then season it generously with salt and pepper. Heat the oil in a large Dutch oven over medium-high heat until shimmering but not smoking. Sprinkle half of the meat into the pot (the pieces should be close but not touching) and cook, without stirring, until well browned on one side, about 4 minutes. Stir the meat and continue to cook, stirring occasionally, until the meat is completely browned, about 5 minutes longer. Transfer it to a medium bowl. Return the pot to medium-high heat, brown the remaining beef, and transfer it to the bowl.

3. Reduce the heat to medium and add the onion, carrots, and ½ teaspoon salt (add a tablespoon of water if necessary to prevent the browned bits on the pan bottom from burning). Cook, stirring frequently, until the onion has browned lightly and softened, 4 to 6 minutes. Add the garlic and cook until fragrant, about 30 seconds. Add the flour and cook, stirring constantly, until lightly browned, about 1 minute. Gradually whisk in the wine, scraping the browned bits off the bottom of the pan. Whisk in the broths, tomato paste, and thyme. Add the browned meat, including any accumulated juices, and bring to a simmer. Reduce the heat to low, partially cover, and continue to simmer, stirring occasionally, until the meat is tender, about 45 minutes.

4. Meanwhile, adjust an oven rack to the middle position and heat the oven to 400 degrees. When the meat is tender, stir in the peas and transfer the filling to a 13 by 9-inch baking dish or six 12-ounce ovenproof dishes. Top with the pie-dough or biscuit topping; bake until the topping is golden brown and the filling is bubbly, 30 minutes for a large pie and 20 to 25 minutes for smaller pies. Allow to cool for 5 to 10 minutes before serving.

Variations

BEEF POT PIE WITH PORTOBELLO MUSHROOMS, SHERRY, AND ROSEMARY

Add one sprig fresh rosemary to the filling during the final 15 minutes of simmering in step 3. While the filling simmers, melt 2 tablespoons unsalted butter in a large skillet over medium-high heat. Add 1 pound portobello mushroom caps (about 6 medium caps), brushed clean and cut into ½-inch pieces, and ⅛ teaspoon salt; cook, stirring occasionally, until well browned, about 8 minutes. Stir in ⅛ cup dry sherry and scrape the browned bits off the bottom of the skillet, then remove from the heat. Stir the mushroom mixture into the filling with the peas in step 4, and discard the rosemary sprig.

BEEF POT PIE WITH GUINNESS, GLAZED PEARL ONIONS, AND BACON

Replace the chicken broth and red wine with a 12-ounce bottle (1½ cups) of Guinness Extra Stout (or other stout beer) and ½ cup of water. While the filling simmers, cook 6 slices bacon, chopped, in a large nonstick skillet over medium heat, until brown and crisp, 8 to 9 minutes. Remove the bacon from the pan using a slotted spoon and drain on a paper towel–lined plate, leaving the rendered fat in the skillet. Increase the heat to medium-high, add 8 ounces frozen (not thawed) pearl onions and ½ teaspoon sugar, and cook until well browned, 9 to 10 minutes. Transfer the onions to the paper towel–lined plate with the bacon. Stir the bacon and onions into the filling in step 4, omitting the peas.

CHAPTER TEN

Chicken (and Turkey)
Every Way

CHICKEN (AND TURKEY) EVERY WAY

Pecan-Crusted Chicken Cutlets

Adding a pecan crust is a great way to dress up boring chicken cutlets. Too bad this easy-sounding recipe is so problematic. Ground nuts don't readily adhere to the chicken, and when they do, they usually burn long before the chicken is cooked through.

After testing several recipes, we could easily see why everything goes so wrong. Most recipes use only beaten eggs to adhere the nuts to the chicken. We found that eggs alone aren't tacky enough to secure the heavy coating, so the nuts fall off in the pan. We tried the classic breading procedure for cutlets—coating them first in flour, then eggs, and finally the nuts. This method kept the crust in place during frying, but as soon as tasters put fork to chicken, the crust fell away in sheets.

We decided to focus on making the eggs "stickier." After several false starts, we hit upon the solution—Dijon mustard, which turned the eggs thick and gluey. It occurred to us that the egg-mustard mixture was on its way to being a marinade, so we kept going, stirring in minced garlic, salt, pepper, and a little tarragon (to complement the sweetness of the pecans). Not only did the pecan crust stay put in the pan and on the plate, but just 10 minutes in the marinade made the chicken taste much better.

We still had one big problem, though: the nuts were burning. Unlike bread-crumb crusts, which need a fair amount of time in a hot skillet to crisp up, nut crusts brown quickly because of their high oil content. Some recipes solve this burning issue by instructing the cook to bake the coated chicken cutlets, but no one in the test kitchen liked the pallid, soggy results. For a really crisp coating, pan-frying seemed to be our only option.

To keep the nuts from burning, we tried mixing them with some fresh bread crumbs. Their flavor was neutral (other options, such as crushed crackers and cereal, were too distracting), and the crumbs did indeed help to keep the nuts from burning. A few teaspoons of moisture-absorbing cornstarch ensured an ultra-crisp crust, and a pinch each of cinnamon and brown sugar highlighted the subtle sweetness of the pecans.

PECAN-CRUSTED CHICKEN CUTLETS
SERVES 4

Do not process the pecans too finely or their natural oils will be released and you'll end up with pecan paste.

- 2 large eggs
- 4 teaspoons Dijon mustard
- 3 garlic cloves, minced
- 2 teaspoons dried tarragon
  Salt and pepper
- 8 thin-cut boneless, skinless chicken cutlets (about 1½ pounds)
- 2 cups pecans
- 2 slices hearty white sandwich bread, torn into large pieces
- 4 teaspoons cornstarch
- 1 tablespoon dark brown sugar
- ⅛ teaspoon ground cinnamon
- 1 cup vegetable oil

1. Adjust an oven rack to the middle position and heat the oven to 200 degrees. Place a wire rack on a rimmed baking sheet. Whisk the eggs, mustard, garlic, tarragon, ½ teaspoon salt, and ½ teaspoon pepper in a large bowl. Add the chicken, coat well, cover with plastic wrap, and refrigerate while preparing the nut mixture.

2. Pulse the pecans in a food processor until finely chopped, with some pebble-sized pieces. Transfer to a pie plate or a shallow rimmed dish. Pulse the bread in the food processor until finely ground.

Add the bread crumbs to the nuts and stir in the cornstarch, brown sugar, ½ teaspoon pepper, ¼ teaspoon salt, and cinnamon.

3. Working with one at a time, remove the cutlets from the egg mixture, letting the excess drip back into the bowl. Thoroughly coat the chicken with the nut mixture, pressing on the coating to help it adhere, and transfer to a large plate.

4. Heat ½ cup of the oil in a large nonstick skillet over medium-high heat until shimmering. Place 4 cutlets in the skillet and cook until golden brown on both sides, 3 to 4 minutes per side (lower the heat if the crust browns too quickly). Transfer the chicken to the rack on the baking sheet and keep warm in the oven. Discard the oil and solids from the skillet and repeat with the remaining ½ cup oil and cutlets. Season the cutlets with salt and pepper and serve immediately.

Crispy Garlic Chicken Cutlets

Over the years the test kitchen has perfected a method for making crispy chicken cutlets: we coat the cutlets in flour, dip them in an egg wash, then coat them with fresh bread crumbs before pan-frying. But when you add fresh garlic to the mix for more flavor, you also get more problems. Overcooked garlic tastes harsh and bitter, and too much garlic can give you breath that will peel paint. We wanted crispy cutlets with an intensely sweet, sharp—but not overpowering—garlic bite.

Our first test was to try a marinade of minced garlic and oil for the cutlets. Determined to keep the marinating time to under 30 minutes, we kept upping the amount of garlic until we got to four minced cloves, which provided good garlic punch to the breaded and fried chicken (better than when we tried adding fresh garlic to the egg wash). This thick paste of minced garlic, safely tucked under the flour, egg, and bread crumbs, cooked gently and lent a caramelized (rather than burned) garlic flavor.

The whole eggs we were using in the egg wash helped the bread crumbs stick to the chicken, but they made for soggy crumbs when combined with the oil paste. We tried replacing the eggs with mayonnaise and mustard, but both imparted too much flavor. Egg whites, whisked until foamy to increase their sticking power, made the perfect glue, getting the coating to adhere to the chicken without adding competing flavor or grease.

As for the breading, the test kitchen prefers toasted homemade bread crumbs to supermarket crumbs, which can be stale-tasting and gritty. Looking to add another layer of garlic flavor, we tried making crumbs from garlic-flavored croutons and pita chips and supermarket garlic bread. Unfortunately, every product either tasted artificial or made the coating soggy. Returning to white bread, we tried infusing the crumbs with fresh garlic, garlic salt, and garlic powder. The fresh garlic burned on the outside of the cutlets, and the garlic salt didn't provide enough kick; the garlic powder, however, added a welcome and distinct flavor.

Tasters wanted even more garlic flavor, but where else could we add it? The chicken was marinated in garlic, and the bread crumbs were garlic-flavored. The only thing left to flavor was the cooking oil. Throwing whole garlic cloves into hot oil while cooking the chicken brought back the burned flavor. So rather than cooking the garlic with the chicken, we simply added cloves (smashed to release more flavor) to the cold oil and heated them up together. When it was time to add the chicken, we removed the garlic cloves from the hot oil. This batch had it all—mellow, caramelized garlic flavor from the chicken on the inside and a crispy, garlicky crust on the outside.

CRISPY GARLIC CHICKEN CUTLETS

SERVES 3 TO 4

Look for cutlets that are between ¼ inch and ½ inch thick, or make your own by slicing 3 boneless, skinless chicken breasts in half horizontally.

- 1 cup plus 3 tablespoons vegetable oil
- 4 garlic cloves, minced, plus 6 cloves, peeled and smashed
- 6 thin-cut boneless, skinless chicken cutlets (about 1¼ pounds; see note above)
- 3 slices hearty white sandwich bread, torn into large pieces and pulsed in a food processor to coarse crumbs
- 1 cup all-purpose flour
- 3 large egg whites
- 1 tablespoon garlic powder
- 4 teaspoons cornstarch
  Salt and pepper

1. Adjust an oven rack to the middle position and heat the oven to 200 degrees. Combine 3 tablespoons of the oil, the minced garlic, and cutlets in a zipper-lock plastic bag and refrigerate while preparing the remaining ingredients. Bake the bread crumbs on a baking sheet until dry, about 20 minutes.

2. Spread the flour in a shallow dish. In another shallow dish, whisk the egg whites until foamy. Combine the bread crumbs, garlic powder, and cornstarch in a third shallow dish. Remove the cutlets from the bag and season with salt and pepper. One at a time, coat the cutlets lightly with flour, dip in the egg whites, and dredge in the crumbs, pressing to adhere. Place the cutlets on a wire rack set over a baking sheet and let dry for 5 minutes.

3. Heat ½ cup of the oil and 3 smashed garlic cloves in a large nonstick skillet over medium heat until the garlic is lightly browned, about 4 minutes. Discard the garlic and fry 3 cutlets until crisp

and deep golden, about 2 minutes per side. Transfer to a paper towel–lined plate and place in the warm oven. Discard the oil, wipe out the skillet, and repeat with the remaining ½ cup oil, 3 garlic cloves, and cutlets. Serve.

Cheesy Stuffed Chicken Breasts

We have always had a soft spot for chicken breasts stuffed with cheese, but not for all the work they can entail. For a simpler approach to stuffing chicken breasts, we cut a pocket in the thick part of the breast, spoon in a filling, and thread the opening shut with a skewer or toothpick. This way we get a nice little hiding place for the cheesy stuffing—minus the hassle.

For the filling, we've always been partial to mozzarella for its terrifically gooey texture, but which kind is best? Tasters liked the pronounced milky flavor of fresh mozzarella, but it didn't melt as well as block mozzarella. For the best of both worlds, we added a touch of cream to the plain old block mozzarella. It infused the supermarket cheese with a dairy-fresh flavor to go along with its superb meltability. The flavors of basil, garlic, lemon juice, and pepper complemented the cheese nicely.

We wanted a crunchy bread-crumb coating on our cheese-stuffed chicken—as long as the coating stayed put and didn't fall off in the baking dish. To help the bread crumbs adhere, we brushed the chicken with mayonnaise (stickier than the other options we tried, including butter) before sprinkling it with crumbs. After 25 minutes in a 425-degree oven, the chicken was cooked, the cheese had melted, and the bread crumbs were crisped.

Our dish was pretty good, but tasters in the kitchen decided that they wanted tomato sauce, too. We eventually came up with a simpler solution.

We just nestled halved cherry tomatoes around the chicken breasts as they cooked. Once roasted, the sweet-tart tomatoes served as both sauce and vegetable side dish. We now had an easy, flavor-packed chicken dinner ready in less than an hour from start to finish.

CHEESY BASIL-STUFFED CHICKEN BREASTS

SERVES 4

Avoid thin chicken breasts for this recipe; they are difficult to stuff without tearing. Whole-milk block mozzarella will provide the creamiest filling; pre-shredded or part-skim mozzarella will also work, but the filling will be grainy.

1	cup shredded mozzarella cheese (see note above)
¼	cup chopped fresh basil
2	tablespoons heavy cream
1	tablespoon fresh lemon juice
3	garlic cloves, minced
	Salt and pepper
4	boneless, skinless chicken breasts (about 1½ pounds), trimmed
3	tablespoons mayonnaise
2	slices hearty white sandwich bread, torn into large pieces and pulsed in a food processor to coarse crumbs
2	tablespoons extra-virgin olive oil
1	pint cherry tomatoes, halved

1. Adjust an oven rack to the middle position and heat the oven to 425 degrees. Combine the cheese, 2 tablespoons of the basil, the cream, lemon juice, 2 teaspoons of the garlic, ½ teaspoon salt, and pepper to taste in a medium bowl.

STUFFING CHICKEN BREASTS

1. Working carefully, use a sharp paring knife to cut a pocket in the thickest area of the chicken breast. Gently work the knife back and forth until the pocket extends down into most of the breast.

2. Use a small spoon to scoop one-quarter of the filling into each chicken breast. Seal in the filling by threading a toothpick or wooden skewer through the chicken about ¼ inch from the opening.

2. Cut a pocket in each chicken breast, stuff with the cheese mixture, and seal. Transfer the stuffed breasts to a 13 by 9-inch baking dish and spread the tops evenly with the mayonnaise.

3. Combine the bread crumbs, remaining 2 tablespoons basil, remaining 1 teaspoon garlic, and 1 tablespoon of the oil. Sprinkle the crumb mixture over the chicken, pressing lightly to adhere.

4. Toss the tomatoes with the remaining 1 tablespoon oil, ½ teaspoon salt, and pepper to taste. Arrange in the baking dish around the chicken. Bake until the crumbs are golden brown and the thickest part of the chicken registers 160 degrees on an instant-read thermometer, about 25 minutes. Serve.

"Un-Stuffed" Chicken Breasts

We liked our Cheesy Basil-Stuffed Chicken Breasts and wondered how we could streamline the process even further and include heartier stuffings. To do so, we turned to an unlikely method: instead of stuffing the chicken breasts, we decided to top the breasts with the stuffing—an inside-out approach.

We started with boneless, skinless chicken breasts. We lightly browned them in a skillet on one side and turned to the topping. The classic combination of Dijon mustard, thin-sliced ham, and shredded Gruyère cheese came to mind. We first tried slices of Gruyère, but they tended to slide off the chicken; shredded cheese adhered better. To assemble our toppings, we brushed the browned chicken with the mustard, over which we layered the ham and cheese. We then mounded crushed buttery cracker crumbs on top and pressed down to help them stick.

Next, we built a sauce for the chicken by whisking together heavy cream, white wine, and minced fresh dill. We carefully poured the mixture into the skillet around the chicken, being careful not to disturb the crumbs. We then set the skillet over medium-high heat and brought the sauce to a simmer. To finish, we transferred the skillet to the oven to cook the chicken through, heat the topping, and thicken the sauce.

We tested oven temperatures ranging from 400 to 475 degrees and quickly discovered that the higher oven temperature of 475 degrees was best. Initially we were concerned that the chicken would dry out at such a high temperature, but the sauce served to keep it moist and tender, bubbling down to the perfect consistency by the time the chicken had cooked through. For a variation, we incorporated Italian flavors, swapping prosciutto and sharp provolone for the ham and Gruyère and flavoring the sauce with dried porcini mushrooms and fresh sage.

"UN-STUFFED" CHICKEN BREASTS WITH DIJON, HAM, AND GRUYÈRE

SERVES 4

If the sauce becomes too thick, thin it to the desired consistency with hot low-sodium chicken broth or hot water before serving.

- 4 boneless, skinless chicken breasts (about 1½ pounds), trimmed
  Salt and pepper
- 2 teaspoons vegetable oil
- 2 tablespoons Dijon mustard
- 4 slices deli baked ham
- 1 cup shredded Gruyère or Swiss cheese
- 15 Ritz crackers, crushed coarse (¾ cup)
- 1 cup heavy cream
- ½ cup dry white wine
- 1 tablespoon minced fresh dill or parsley

1. Adjust an oven rack to the upper-middle position and heat the oven to 475 degrees.

2. Pat the chicken dry with paper towels and season with salt and pepper. Heat the oil in a large, ovenproof nonstick skillet over medium-high heat until just smoking. Brown the chicken lightly on one side, about 3 minutes.

3. Off the heat, turn the chicken over. Spread 1 teaspoon of the mustard over each breast, then lay 1 slice ham on top. Mound ¼ cup of the cheese over each piece of ham. Sprinkle the cracker crumbs over the cheese and press on the crumbs to adhere.

4. Whisk the cream, wine, and dill or parsley together in a 2-cup liquid measuring cup and pour into the skillet around the chicken, without disturbing the crumbs. Return the skillet to medium-high heat and bring to a simmer. Immediately transfer to the oven. Bake until the thickest part of the chicken breast registers 160 degrees on an instant-read thermometer, 12 to 15 minutes.

5. Transfer the chicken to individual plates. Whisk the remaining mustard into the sauce and season with salt and pepper to taste. Spoon the sauce over the chicken and serve.

Variation

"UN-STUFFED" CHICKEN BREASTS WITH PROSCIUTTO, SAGE, AND PORCINI

There is no need to rehydrate the porcini mushrooms because they will soften in the oven. If the sauce becomes too thick, thin it with hot low-sodium chicken broth or hot water before serving.

Omit the mustard. Replace the ham with prosciutto and the shredded Gruyère cheese with shredded provolone cheese. Replace the dill or parsley with minced fresh sage and add ¼ ounce rinsed and finely chopped dried porcini mushrooms to the cream mixture in step 4.

Chicken Marsala

Chicken Marsala is a well-loved Italian restaurant classic, traditionally made with sautéed chicken cutlets, browned mushrooms, and a rich Marsala pan sauce. But many recipes ruin this preparation with unnecessary ingredients and ill-advised techniques, which can result in chewy, dry, or slimy chicken in a sickeningly sweet sauce.

To make this recipe reliable, we started by cooking thin cutlets in a little oil over varying heat settings. Several sources indicated that thin, lean cutlets are best cooked over gentle heat, but this didn't prove true when we tried it. We found that we needed a hot skillet to achieve good color quickly; when cooked over medium-low heat, the cutlets spent too much time in the pan and dried

out. Some recipes direct the cook to dredge the cutlets in flour before cooking them. This proved to be essential, as the unfloured cutlets turned out tough and stringy.

The first step in building the sauce was browning the mushrooms as well as some aromatic onions and garlic. Next, we deglazed the pan with Marsala and simmered the wine until it thickened slightly. Although either sweet or dry Marsala was acceptable, tasters preferred the sweet variety, cut with a little chicken broth to yield a sauce that was moderately sweet but not saccharine.

Our sauce was nearly perfect, except for the mushrooms. By the time the sauce reduced to the proper thickness, the mushrooms were limp and spongy, and they didn't taste very good—each bite of mushroom was like taking a swig of Marsala. Clearly, the mushrooms were absorbing too much liquid. Removing the browned mushrooms from the pan and simmering just the wine and broth solved the problem.

In some recipes the cutlets are simmered in the sauce as it is being reduced, but tasters thought the resulting cutlets were slimy. Adding the cutlets to the sauce at the last minute (with the mushrooms) gave the chicken enough time to absorb flavors and heat through without becoming slimy.

We now had a foolproof recipe for chicken Marsala—made in less time than it takes to flag down a waiter at a restaurant.

CHICKEN MARSALA

SERVES 4

Look for cutlets that are between ¼ inch and ½ inch thick.

8	thin-cut boneless, skinless chicken cutlets (about 1½ pounds; see note above)
	Salt and pepper
¼	cup all-purpose flour

2   **tablespoons vegetable oil**

3   **tablespoons unsalted butter**

½   **onion, minced**

8   **ounces white mushrooms, trimmed and quartered**

1   **garlic clove, minced**

¾   **cup sweet Marsala**

½   **cup low-sodium chicken broth**

2   **teaspoons fresh lemon juice**

1   **tablespoon chopped fresh parsley**

1. Pat the cutlets dry with paper towels and season with salt and pepper. Dredge the cutlets in the flour to coat and shake to remove the excess. Heat 1 tablespoon of the oil in a large nonstick skillet over high heat until just smoking. Add 4 cutlets and cook until golden brown, 2 to 2½ minutes on each side. Transfer to a large plate and cover with aluminum foil. Repeat with the remaining 1 tablespoon oil and cutlets.

2. Heat 1 tablespoon of the butter in the now-empty skillet over medium-high heat until foaming. Cook the onion and mushrooms until browned, about 5 minutes. Add the garlic and cook until fragrant, about 30 seconds. Transfer the mushroom mixture to a medium bowl and cover with aluminum foil.

3. Add the Marsala and broth to the again-empty skillet, bring to a boil over high heat, and cook until reduced to ½ cup, about 5 minutes. Reduce the heat to medium-low, return the chicken and accumulated juices to the skillet, and turn the chicken to heat through, about 1 minute. Transfer the chicken to a serving platter. Off the heat, whisk in the remaining 2 tablespoons butter, the lemon juice, parsley, and mushroom mixture. Pour the sauce over the chicken. Serve.

Skillet Chicken Parmesan

Most recipes for chicken Parmesan produce casserole-like creations with breaded cutlets buried in a puddle of sauce under a blanket of cheese. The soggy chicken, greasy breading, and bland cheese are rarely appealing. We figured that the only way to keep the breading from becoming soggy was to separate it from the chicken. Unconventional? Yes, but worth a try.

We browned chicken cutlets, added a quick tomato sauce and some cheese, and then sprinkled toasted bread crumbs on the finished dish. The crumbs were crispy and no longer greasy. In fact, they were a bit dry and bland. We remedied this with a little olive oil, fresh basil, and Parmesan. Without breaded cutlets, the dish looked different, but the flavors were the same—maybe better because of the bread crumbs.

Rather than preparing tomato sauce in a separate pan, we wondered if we could just simmer the sauce ingredients with the chicken. Since the cutlets weren't breaded, there was no crisp coating to protect. This worked better than we expected, as the chicken picked up the flavors of garlic, basil, and tomatoes from the sauce. Our recipe now required just one pan and was ready in about 30 minutes.

Tasters still had one complaint: the cheese was bland. Despite its name, chicken Parmesan recipes invariably call for more mozzarella than Parmesan. When we tried the opposite, we found out why: Parmesan cooked up tough and dry. We had better luck when we replaced some of the bland mozzarella with provolone. The cheese was now gooey and flavorful.

SKILLET CHICKEN PARMESAN

SERVES 4

We like the assertive flavor of sharp provolone here, but mild provolone works well, too.

2	slices hearty white sandwich bread, torn into large pieces and pulsed in a food processor to coarse crumbs
3	tablespoons olive oil
1¼	cups grated Parmesan cheese
¼	cup chopped fresh basil
2	garlic cloves, minced
1	(28-ounce) can crushed tomatoes
	Salt and pepper
½	cup all-purpose flour
8	thin-cut boneless, skinless chicken cutlets (about 1½ pounds)
3	tablespoons vegetable oil
¾	cup shredded mozzarella cheese
¾	cup shredded provolone cheese (see note above)

1. Toast the bread crumbs in a large nonstick skillet over medium-high heat until browned, about 5 minutes. Transfer to a bowl. Toss with 1 tablespoon of the olive oil, ¼ cup of the Parmesan, and half of the basil. In a separate bowl, combine the remaining 2 tablespoons olive oil, ¼ cup more Parmesan, the remaining basil, the garlic, tomatoes, and salt and pepper to taste.

2. Place the flour in a dish. Season the chicken with salt and pepper and coat with the flour. Heat 2 tablespoons vegetable oil in the now-empty skillet over medium-high heat until shimmering. Add 4 cutlets and cook until golden brown on both sides, about 5 minutes total. Transfer to a plate and repeat with the remaining cutlets and 1 tablespoon vegetable oil.

3. Reduce the heat to medium-low and add the tomato mixture to the again-empty skillet. Return the cutlets to the pan in an even layer, pressing down to cover with sauce. Sprinkle the mozzarella, provolone, and remaining ¾ cup Parmesan over the chicken. Cover with a lid and cook until the cheese is melted, about 5 minutes. Sprinkle with the bread-crumb mixture and serve.

Glazed Chicken Breasts

Glazing chicken breasts is one way to prevent weeknight chicken from becoming ho-hum. But as we tested a number of different recipes, the problems we encountered centered around dry, flavorless chicken breasts in a glaze that was either overly sweet and gloppy or too thin. And no one likes chicken breasts with soggy skin, a common problem with this recipe. We wanted a browned and moist chicken breast coated with a fresh-flavored glaze just thick enough to cling to the crisp skin.

How do you accomplish these goals? Brown the chicken breasts in a skillet before roasting them, so the skin is crisp, not flabby. We found that a glaze made with preserves worked well; tasters preferred the not-too-sweet flavor of apricot preserves. Orange juice, whose flavor complemented the apricot preserves, helped the glaze stick to the chicken, while preventing it from turning gloppy. Adding chopped dried apricots intensified the glaze's flavor, and adding a healthy dose of lemon juice tempered the glaze's sweetness, giving it a bright and lively character. With a few pantry ingredients we were able to make weeknight chicken that was anything but boring.

PREPARING BONE-IN CHICKEN BREASTS

1. Place the chicken breasts, skin side down, on a cutting board and pull the rib cage taut, away from the meat. Cut in a straight line between the ribs and breast meat to remove the ribs.

2. Turn the chicken breasts skin side up and snip away stray bits of fat and sinew. Chicken fat is butter yellow, in contrast to the skin, which is pinkish white.

APRICOT-GLAZED CHICKEN BREASTS

SERVES 4

To make sure that the chicken cooks evenly, buy large, split chicken breasts that are similar in size—about 12 ounces apiece. Stovetops vary, so check the chicken after about 6 minutes to make sure it isn't browning too quickly.

1	(10- to 12-ounce) jar apricot preserves
½	cup orange juice
3	tablespoons fresh lemon juice
¼	cup dried apricots, quartered
	Salt and pepper
4	bone-in, skin-on split chicken breasts (about 3 pounds), ribs removed (see note above)
2	teaspoons vegetable oil

1. Adjust an oven rack to the middle position and heat the oven to 425 degrees. Whisk the apricot preserves, orange juice, lemon juice, apricots, ⅛ teaspoon salt, and ⅛ teaspoon pepper together in a medium bowl. Season both sides of the chicken breasts with salt and pepper.

2. Heat the oil in a large skillet over medium-high heat until just smoking. Place the chicken breasts, skin side down, in the skillet and cook until well browned and most of the fat has rendered, 8 to 10 minutes. Turn the chicken and lightly brown on the second side, 2 to 3 minutes longer.

3. Transfer the chicken to a medium baking dish and set aside. Discard the fat in the skillet and add the apricot mixture. Simmer vigorously over high heat, stirring constantly, until thick and syrupy, 3 to 4 minutes. Pour the glaze over the chicken and turn the chicken skin side down.

4. Bake, turning the chicken skin side up halfway through cooking, until the thickest part of the breast registers 160 degrees on an instant-read thermometer, 12 to 16 minutes. Transfer the chicken to a platter and let rest for 5 minutes. Meanwhile, transfer the glaze remaining in the baking dish to a small bowl. Serve the chicken, passing the extra glaze separately.

SHOPPING WITH THE TEST KITCHEN

Traditional Skillets: A skillet is the most-used pan in the test kitchen. A slope-sided, flat-bottom skillet is the best choice for sautéing, searing, browning, and pan-frying and just about anything in between. Traditional, stainless steel skillets are best for dishes where browning contributes an essential flavor base, like pan-seared steaks or chicken. To find the best traditional skillet, we tried eight skillets in a number of different applications. The top skillet was the All-Clad Stainless 12-Inch Frypan ($125). All-Clad's flared sides encourage the rapid evaporation of moisture, so pan sauces reduce quickly and foods sear rather than steam.

Classic Barbecued Chicken

Smoky grilled chicken smothered in a thick barbecue sauce is one of America's favorite summer meals. But who hasn't served barbecued chicken that was nearly blackened on the outside yet bloody near the bone? Chicken is hard enough to grill, because the skin races ahead of the meat. Adding barbecue sauce just makes the problem worse. Our goal in developing a foolproof recipe for barbecued chicken was to produce perfectly cooked meat that boasted intense flavor from both the grill and a liberal application of tangy-sweet barbecue sauce.

Most recipes call for searing the chicken quickly over high heat, to render the fat in the skin, and then finishing it over lower heat to gently cook the interior. But we've found that placing raw chicken over a hot (or even medium-hot) fire causes too many flare-ups, resulting in burned skin. The test kitchen has had much better luck starting chicken over lower heat to slowly and completely render the fat without the danger of flare-ups. Following this method, we spread the coals in an even layer on one side of the grill, added the chicken, skin side down, to the other side, and covered the grill. We call this method grill-roasting. Thirty minutes later, we had tender chicken that was almost cooked throughout. But it didn't have much flavor.

We've always been told to never, ever add barbecue sauce to anything until just before it was ready to be pulled off the grill—otherwise the sugar in the sauce will burn. But how could we get deep layers of barbecue flavor without saucing earlier? It occurred to us that if we wanted layers of flavor, we needed to have layers of barbecue sauce.

When the chicken was mostly cooked through over the indirect heat, we moved the pieces to the center of the grill (near the coals, but not over them) and introduced sauce in several applications (and because the chicken wasn't over direct heat, the sauce didn't burn). Constant turning and moderate heat allowed us to continually sauce the chicken for about 20 minutes while it finished cooking. This worked great, because just as one layer of sauce was drying, we were adding another coat on top of it, creating a thick, complex, multilayered "skin" of barbecue flavor.

To finish, we moved the pieces directly over the coals and continued to flip them and slather them with sauce for the final 5 minutes of cooking. We finally had perfectly cooked chicken with intense barbecue flavor.

CLASSIC BARBECUED CHICKEN

SERVES 4 TO 6

You can use a mix of chicken breasts, thighs, and drumsticks, making sure they add up to about 10 pieces. Any more than that and you won't be able to line them up on the grill.

SAUCE

3	cups bottled barbecue sauce
½	cup molasses
½	cup ketchup
¼	cup cider vinegar
3	tablespoons brown mustard
2	teaspoons onion powder
1	teaspoon garlic powder

CHICKEN

1	teaspoon salt
1	teaspoon pepper
¼	teaspoon cayenne pepper
3	pounds bone-in, skin-on chicken pieces (breasts, whole legs, thighs, and/or drumsticks), trimmed and breasts halved

1. FOR THE SAUCE: Whisk together all of the ingredients in a medium saucepan and bring to a boil over medium-high heat. Reduce the heat to medium and cook until the sauce is thick and reduced to 3 cups, about 20 minutes. (The sauce can be refrigerated in an airtight container for up to 1 week.)

2. FOR THE CHICKEN: Mix the salt, pepper, and cayenne in a small bowl. Pat the chicken dry with paper towels and rub the spice mixture all over the chicken pieces.

3. Open the bottom vent of the grill. Light a large chimney starter filled with charcoal briquettes (about 100) and burn until the charcoal is covered with a fine gray ash. Place a 13 by 9-inch disposable aluminum roasting pan on one side of the grill and spread the coals in an even layer over the other side of the grill. Set the cooking grate in place and heat the grill, covered, with the lid vent open completely, for 5 minutes. (For a gas grill, turn all the burners to high, cover the grill, and heat for 15 minutes. Leave the primary burner on high and turn off the other burner[s].) Scrape and oil the cooking grate.

4. Place the chicken, skin side down, on the cooler side of the grill. Cover, with the half-opened lid vent over the chicken, and cook until the chicken begins to brown, 30 to 35 minutes. Move the chicken into a single line close to the coals. (For a gas grill, leave the chicken on the cool side of the grill.) Begin flipping the chicken and brushing with 2 cups of the sauce every 5 minutes until sticky, about 20 minutes. Slide the chicken pieces over the coals and continue to brush them until the sauce on the chicken becomes crusted and the internal temperature of the breast meat registers 165 degrees and the legs, thighs, and drumsticks register 175 degrees on an instant-read thermometer, about 5 minutes. Transfer the chicken to a platter, tent with aluminum foil, and let rest for 10 minutes. Remove the foil and serve, passing the remaining sauce at the table.

Bottled Barbecue Sauces: Homemade barbecue sauce is a project requiring a laundry list of ingredients and a good chunk of time. You don't have to make your own barbecue sauce, but the one you buy should taste—and look—like homemade. We conducted a blind taste test of eight leading national brands to find one we liked. Our favorite is the smoky Bull's-Eye Original BBQ Sauce ($1.79 for 18 ounces). Its thick consistency, dark color, and well-balanced flavor pleased tasters across the board.

Extra-Crunchy Fried Chicken

The best thing about most fast-food fried chicken is the crunchy crust, but the chicken itself often tastes bland and dry. We wanted to make fried chicken in which the chicken and the coating are equal partners—moist, tender chicken coated in an extra-crunchy, well-seasoned crust. And we also wanted fried chicken that was easy enough that we wouldn't be tempted to hit the drive-through.

Our first consideration was the coating. Recipes fall into two camps: the single dip and the double dip. The former involves a dip in buttermilk and a dredge in flour before the chicken hits the hot oil. The latter adds two steps: a dip in egg wash followed by another dredge in flour. The double-dip method was just too messy, so for the sake of the kitchen (and our sanity), the single dip seemed like the way to go.

Just plain flour didn't provide enough crunch, so we looked to crushed Melba toast. The crumbs browned too quickly and did not adhere to the chicken very well, leaving more coating in the oil than on the chicken. We then ran across several recipes that called for coating chicken in store-bought pancake mix. This idea raised several eyebrows, but it seemed worth a shot. Although not perfect, this test was at least partially successful. Because the pancake mix contained baking powder, the coating was light and crisp. The only drawback was that the powder caused the coating to expand slightly, then contract, and eventually flake off. We decided to come up with our own version of pancake mix—one with less baking powder. After testing a number of formulas, we found that a mixture of 3 cups flour and 2 teaspoons baking powder was just enough to lighten the crust, but not to the point where it would fall off the chicken.

During testing, a funny thing happened. We noticed that the coating on the pieces of chicken dredged last was thicker than the coating on those dredged first. What was going on? It seems that each time a piece was dredged, the flour absorbed

some buttermilk from the chicken. By the time we got around to the last couple of pieces, the flour was almost sticky. This resulted in fried chicken with a crunchier, thicker coating. The obvious next test was to add the buttermilk straight to the flour. Instead of a dip in buttermilk and a dredge in flour, we simply dredged the chicken pieces in the combined mixture. Now we had a sturdy, crunchy coating that didn't fall off.

The next problem was dry, overcooked chicken. We often turn to brining (soaking meat or poultry in a saltwater solution) to solve this problem, but because we were using buttermilk anyway, we wondered if buttermilk would be better than water. Starting with 2 cups buttermilk and 2 tablespoons salt, we soaked the chicken pieces before coating them with the buttermilk-flour mixture. This chicken was not only juicy; it was also more flavorful than the chicken brined in saltwater.

To contain the mess of frying, we switched from the traditional skillet to a Dutch oven. The Dutch oven tends to keep the oil in the pot rather than letting it splatter all over the stovetop. So far, so good. We then wondered if covering the pot during some or all of the frying time would help contain the mess. After much testing (and lots of well-fed test cooks), we determined that covering the pot during the first half of the frying time (before flipping the pieces) worked best. The oil recovered heat more quickly, there was less mess, and there was one other unexpected benefit: the cover trapped steam, which made the chicken moister. (We found it interesting that the frying oil never gets completely back up to temperature. It starts at 375 degrees, but most of the frying is done between 300 and 315 degrees.)

Until this point, peanut oil had been our first choice for frying, and it was performing quite well, lending no off-flavors and browning the chicken nicely. But we wanted to test lard and vegetable shortening. Lard, a standby in many Southern kitchens, gave the chicken a deep mahogany color but

SECRETS TO A CRUNCHY COATING

1. Soak the chicken in the buttermilk-salt mixture.

2. Coat the chicken with the buttermilk-moistened flour.

3. Add the chicken to the hot oil and cover the pot to capture the steam.

4. Use tongs to flip the chicken and finish cooking with the cover off.

CHOOSING CHICKEN PARTS

For a mix of light and dark meat, we like to use a whole cut-up bird for fried chicken. Starting with a whole chicken is inexpensive and not terribly difficult. What's more, you get to keep the neck, backbone, and wings for stock. But if you don't want to wrestle with a whole bird, you do have other options. Just make sure the total weight of the parts doesn't exceed 2¾ pounds.

WHOLE LEGS: Buy four legs and separate them into thighs and drumsticks to yield eight pieces. To do so, cut through the line of fat into the joint that separates the thigh and drumstick.

BREASTS: Buy four split breasts and cut each in half crosswise to yield eight pieces.

CUT-UP CHICKEN: Buy one cut-up whole chicken (about 3 pounds), save the wings for stock, and cut each breast in half to yield eight pieces.

---

tinged it with a pork flavor. (We should admit that the supermarket lard in our area is not the best.) Surprisingly, shortening (we used Crisco) was the top performer. Not only did the chicken brown evenly, without even a hint of spottiness, but it tasted like, well, chicken, without a hint of greasiness.

EXTRA-CRUNCHY FRIED CHICKEN

SERVES 4

Keeping the oil at the correct temperature is essential to producing crunchy fried chicken that is neither too brown nor too greasy. Use a candy/deep-fry thermometer to check the temperature of the oil before you add the chicken. If you cannot find a chicken that weighs 3½ pounds or less, or if you don't have a pan that is 11 inches in diameter, you will have to fry the chicken in two batches. Follow the recipe, frying the chicken four pieces at a time and keeping the first batch warm in a 200-degree oven while the second batch is cooking.

2	cups plus 6 tablespoons buttermilk
2	tablespoons salt
1	whole chicken (about 3½ pounds), cut into 8 pieces, giblets discarded
3	cups all-purpose flour
2	teaspoons baking powder
¾	teaspoon dried thyme
½	teaspoon pepper
¼	teaspoon garlic powder
4–5	cups vegetable shortening or peanut oil

1. Whisk together 2 cups of the buttermilk and the salt in a large bowl until the salt is dissolved. Add the chicken pieces to the bowl and stir to coat; cover the bowl with plastic wrap and refrigerate for 1 hour. (Don't let the chicken soak much longer or it will become too salty.)

2. Whisk the flour, baking powder, thyme, pepper, and garlic powder together in a large bowl. Add the remaining 6 tablespoons buttermilk; with your fingers rub the flour and buttermilk together until the buttermilk is evenly incorporated into the flour and the mixture resembles coarse, wet sand.

3. Working in batches of 2, drop the chicken pieces into the flour mixture and turn to thoroughly coat, gently pressing the flour mixture onto the chicken. Shake the excess flour from each piece of chicken and transfer to a wire rack set over a rimmed baking sheet.

4. Heat the shortening or oil (it should measure ¾ inch deep) in a large heavy bottomed Dutch oven with an 11-inch diameter over medium-high heat until it reaches 375 degrees. Place the chicken pieces, skin side down, in the oil, cover, and fry until deep golden brown, 8 to 10 minutes. Remove the lid after 4 minutes and lift the chicken pieces to check for even browning; rearrange if some pieces are browning faster than others. (At this point the oil should be at about 300 degrees. Adjust the burner, if necessary, to regulate the temperature.) Turn the chicken pieces over and continue to fry, uncovered, until they are deep golden brown on the second side, 6 to 8 minutes longer. (At this point, to keep the chicken from browning too quickly, adjust the burner to maintain the oil temperature at about 315 degrees.) Using tongs, transfer the chicken to a plate lined with paper towels; let stand for 5 minutes to drain. Serve.

Variation

EXTRA-SPICY, EXTRA-CRUNCHY FRIED CHICKEN

Add 4 tablespoons hot sauce to the buttermilk-salt mixture in step 1. Replace the dried thyme and garlic powder in step 2 with 1 tablespoon cayenne pepper and 2 teaspoons chili powder.

Oven-Fried Chicken

It's no surprise that oven-fried chicken rarely stacks up in the flavor or crunch department. Many recipes call for dipping boneless, skinless chicken breasts in beaten egg whites or low-fat mayonnaise to help adhere dried bread crumbs or fine-ground cornmeal. But we wanted oven-fried chicken worth eating—not spa food.

No self-respecting fried chicken lover would dream of using anything other than bone-in chicken parts. We settled on bone-in breasts and opted to remove the skin. We knew that removing the skin would cost flavor and moistness, so we borrowed a tried-and-true fried chicken trick and soaked the

parts in robustly seasoned buttermilk.

In search of a tasty coating, we tested some "creative" options offered by writers of oven-fried chicken recipes, including grated Parmesan cheese, dry Cream of Wheat, pulverized shredded wheat, bran flakes, Weetabix cereal, crushed pretzels, packaged stuffing mix, and even ground-up low-fat popcorn. Unfortunately, these ideas solicited little more than amusement from tasters.

Luckily, a mixture of crushed cornflakes and fresh bread crumbs was pretty close to perfect. The bottom of each chicken piece was a bit soggy, but baking the chicken on a wire rack solved this problem and eliminated the need for turning. Because the coating was still a bit dry, we mixed in a modest 2 tablespoons of oil, which gave the baked chicken a genuine "fried" texture.

Our coating now had great crunch, but it needed more flavor. Salt, pepper, and garlic powder picked up on the seasonings we'd added to the buttermilk marinade. We tossed in cayenne pepper for heat and paprika for color. Still not completely satisfied, we added ground poultry seasoning (a humble mixture of ground sage, thyme, and bay leaves), which gave the crust a savory jolt.

The flavorful, craggy, deeply golden brown coating of this batch was a far cry from the lackluster coating found on most "oven-fried" versions. When tasters lined up for seconds, we knew our work was done.

OVEN-FRIED CHICKEN

SERVES 8

To crush the cornflakes, place them inside a plastic bag and use a rolling pin to break them into pieces no smaller than ½ inch.

2	cups buttermilk
2	tablespoons Dijon mustard
	Salt
1½	teaspoons garlic powder

Pepper

1   teaspoon hot sauce

8   bone-in split chicken breasts (10 to
    12 ounces each), skin removed and ribs
    removed (see step 1 on page 285)

1   slice hearty white sandwich bread,
    torn into large pieces and pulsed in a
    food processor to coarse crumbs

2½ cups crushed cornflakes (see note above)

½   teaspoon ground poultry seasoning

½   teaspoon paprika

⅛   teaspoon cayenne pepper

2   tablespoons vegetable oil

1. Whisk the buttermilk, mustard, 2 teaspoons salt, 1 teaspoon of the garlic powder, 1 teaspoon pepper, and the hot sauce together in a large bowl. Add the chicken, turn to coat well, cover, and refrigerate for at least 1 hour, or overnight.

2. Adjust an oven rack to the upper-middle position and heat the oven to 400 degrees. Line a rimmed baking sheet with aluminum foil, set a wire rack on the sheet, and coat the rack with vegetable oil spray.

3. Gently toss the bread crumbs, corn flakes, remaining ½ teaspoon garlic powder, ½ teaspoon pepper, ¼ teaspoon salt, poultry seasoning, paprika, and cayenne in a shallow dish until combined. Drizzle the oil over the crumbs and toss until well coated. Working with one piece at a time, remove the chicken from the marinade and dredge in the crumb mixture, firmly pressing the crumbs onto all sides of the chicken. Place the chicken on the prepared rack, leaving ½ inch between pieces. Bake until the chicken is deep golden brown, the juices run clear, and an instant-read thermometer inserted deep into the breast away from the bone registers 160 degrees, 35 to 45 minutes. Serve.

Variation
FIERY OVEN-FRIED CHICKEN
Follow the recipe for Oven-Fried Chicken, increasing the hot sauce to 1 tablespoon. Replace ¼ teaspoon salt in the crumb mixture with ½ teaspoon chili powder and increase the cayenne to ¼ teaspoon.

Maryland Fried Chicken with Cream Gravy

Whether it's dark meat or light, extra-crispy or original, Americans are very particular when it comes to fried chicken. This is especially true in Maryland, where both raising and frying chickens are ways of life. While other regions of the country rely on a thick buttermilk batter and a deep-fat fryer to deliver a crusty crunch, in Maryland the chicken parts are simply seasoned, floured, and shallow-fried. This old-fashioned cooking method results in crisp, mahogany-colored chicken that, with a gentle tug, sheets off the bone with its deliciously brittle skin still intact. But what really sets Maryland fried chicken apart is the creamy, black pepper–spiked pan gravy that's equally fit for drumstick dunking or mopping up with a biscuit.

To stay true to the Maryland style, we wanted to stick with the flour-dredged, shallow-fried cooking technique. But even though this method produces perfectly browned chicken, our first try resulted in one bland bird. Tasters loved the idea of adding Old Bay seasoning (a ubiquitous blend in the Chesapeake region) to the flour dredge, but it had a scorched flavor coming out of the hot oil. Instead, we added salt, dry mustard, and garlic powder (time-tested fried chicken seasonings) to the flour for a base flavor, then sprinkled the chicken with Old Bay once it came out of the pan. Now the seasoned flour and Old Bay made for a tasty crust, but the chicken itself was barely seasoned.

As it turned out, sprinkling the salt, mustard, and garlic powder directly on the chicken pieces before dredging them in flour was key: it ensured that the seasonings were hitting the meat and not being sloughed off in the excess flour. Resting the seasoned and floured chicken in the fridge for 30 minutes improved it even further, allowing the seasonings and flour to take hold for an extra-tasty, extra-crispy coating.

We next hit a snag when frying our chicken. Batch after batch of the chicken was marred by an odd "fishy" flavor. To find the culprit, we tried adjusting every variable in the recipe, but nothing worked. As a last resort, we switched from vegetable oil (our usual frying medium) to peanut oil (another commonly used frying oil), and the problem was solved. As it turns out, after a total frying time of roughly 30 minutes, the vegetable oil was beginning to break down and impart a spoiled, fishy flavor to the chicken. Peanut oil (which has a higher smoke point) fared better and didn't break down, resulting in no off-flavors in the chicken. We also tried safflower oil, canola oil, and vegetable shortening. The peanut oil was still best, but the vegetable shortening was the runner-up, winning praise for its "clean" flavor.

We now finally turned our attention to the defining element of Maryland fried chicken, the cream gravy. To thicken the gravy, most recipes start with a roux made from pan drippings and flour, and we weren't about to argue with that. As for the liquid base of the gravy, tasters found that milk alone made the gravy too sweet. Cutting it with chicken broth added a savory element but also made the gravy pale and soupy—not the rich and creamy sauce we had imagined. Since adding more flour made the gravy sludgy, we tried keeping the broth but switching the dairy. Half-and-half was a step in the right direction, but cream was a giant leap, providing a silky texture and honest dairy taste. With a good hit of pepper in the gravy, our Maryland fried chicken could stake its claim as a great American recipe.

MARYLAND FRIED CHICKEN WITH CREAM GRAVY

SERVES 4 TO 6

To ensure even cooking, breasts should be halved crosswise and leg quarters separated into thighs and drumsticks.

CHICKEN

4	pounds bone-in, skin-on chicken pieces (see note above)
1	tablespoon dry mustard
1	tablespoon garlic powder
1	teaspoon salt
2	cups all-purpose flour
1	teaspoon baking powder
3	cups peanut oil or vegetable shortening
	Old Bay seasoning

GRAVY

¼	cup pan drippings (from frying chicken)
¼	cup all-purpose flour
2	cups low-sodium chicken broth
1	cup heavy cream
1	teaspoon pepper
	Salt

1. FOR THE CHICKEN: Pat the chicken dry with paper towels. Combine the mustard, garlic powder, and salt in a small bowl and sprinkle evenly over the chicken. Combine the flour and baking powder in a shallow dish and, working with one piece at a time, dredge the chicken parts until well coated, shaking off the excess. Refrigerate on a plate for 30 minutes (or up to 2 hours).

2. Adjust an oven rack to the middle position and heat the oven to 200 degrees. Heat the oil or shortening in a large Dutch oven over medium-high heat to 375 degrees. Arrange half of the chicken in the pot, skin side down, cover, and cook until well browned, about 5 minutes per side. Lower the heat to medium, adjusting the burner as necessary to maintain an oil temperature between 300 and 325 degrees. Cook the chicken, uncovered, turning it as necessary, until cooked through, about 5 minutes. (The internal temperature should register 160 degrees for white meat and 175 degrees for dark meat on an instant-read thermometer.) Transfer the chicken to a wire rack set over a baking sheet, season with Old Bay, and place in the warm oven. Bring the oil back to 375 degrees and repeat with the remaining chicken.

3. FOR THE GRAVY: Pour all but ¼ cup fat from the pot. Stir in the flour and cook until golden, about 2 minutes. Slowly whisk in the broth, cream, and pepper. Simmer until thickened, about 5 minutes. Season with salt and serve with the chicken.

Creole Fried Chicken

Creole fried chicken should be deeply seasoned with the complex, lively heat of black, white, and cayenne pepper. The crust should be crisp and well seasoned, the meat juicy and bursting with flavor.

Most of the recipes for this style of fried chicken are variations on basic Southern fried chicken: the chicken is dipped in buttermilk, dredged in flour, and fried. Creole flavor is introduced by adding store-bought Creole seasoning to the flour. But supermarket Creole seasoning typically tastes of dusty, stale paprika and is far too salty. We made our own Creole seasoning based on its three traditional ground peppers: three parts black, two parts

---

THE AMERICAN TABLE
IS IT CAJUN OR CREOLE?

Both Cajun and Creole cuisines are native to Louisiana, but their origins are very different. Present-day Cajuns are descendants of the Acadians, a group of French settlers who fled British-ruled Nova Scotia to rural Louisiana in 1785. Cajun cooking, based on the hearty country cooking of southern France, is heavily dependent on game and animal fats. Creole cuisine, by contrast, has its roots in the diverse cultures of New Orleans's history: Native American, Caribbean, Spanish, Italian, African, Mexican, and French cuisines are all reflected in sophisticated Creole dishes like gumbo. Both Cajun and Creole cuisines similarly adapted over time to utilize ingredients native to the area, such as bay leaves, filé powder, hot peppers, and rice.

---

cayenne, and one part white. Garlic and onion powders, dried oregano, and celery salt rounded out our homemade mixture, which had more flavor and kick than packaged varieties.

We added our Creole seasoning to the flour and fried up a batch of chicken. Although it was an improvement on the recipes we'd tried, this chicken didn't have enough flavor to earn the Creole tag. We turned to brining, a method in which raw meat is soaked in salted and seasoned water to add flavor and moisture. Most of the flavors in our Creole seasoning didn't carry through in the brine, so we decided to experiment with other ways to flavor it. After some trial and error, we settled on a brine made with water, salt, sugar, garlic powder, Worcestershire sauce (for meaty background flavor), and hot sauce (for heat).

Moving on to the frying, we found that the chicken pieces actually rest on the bottom of the pan (which is hotter than the oil) when shallow-frying. This caused the spices in the flour to burn and turn bitter, necessitating a switch to deep-frying (where the chicken bobs in a deeper pool of oil) for the best-tasting crust. Tasters determined that any sort of egg or dairy—including the buttermilk—in the coating muted the spice flavor, so we simply moved the chicken directly from the brine to the seasoned flour. But the quick dip in seasoned flour wasn't giving us as crisp a crust as we were looking for.

As we stood over a batch of floured chicken, waiting for the oil to heat up, we noticed that after about 10 minutes, the flour coating was becoming wet and doughy. On a lark, we rolled these chicken pieces in the seasoned flour again and carefully lowered them into the oil. The extra coating meant we were rewarded with the crisp, substantial, slightly craggy crust we had hoped for.

One of the hallmarks of Creole cooking is its layering of flavors, and although our chicken was now much better than the batches we'd started with, it was still lacking depth. Instead of using our homemade Creole seasoning just in the flour,

we decided to try sprinkling it on the raw chicken, and then also on the cooked chicken just out of the oil (when the hot crust would most readily absorb flavors). Tasters were pleasantly surprised at how many layers of flavor this simple three-step approach brought to the dish.

CREOLE FRIED CHICKEN

SERVES 4 TO 6

To ensure even cooking, breasts should be halved crosswise and leg quarters separated into thighs and drumsticks. We prefer the big, brash flavor of Tabasco Sauce in this recipe, but any hot sauce will work. In step 1, do not soak the chicken longer than 8 hours, or it will be too salty.

BRINE

1	quart water
¼	cup sugar
3	tablespoons Worcestershire sauce
3	tablespoons hot sauce (see note above)
2	tablespoons salt
1	tablespoon garlic powder
4	pounds bone-in, skin-on chicken pieces (see note above)

SECRETS TO CREOLE FRIED CHICKEN

1. Soaking the chicken in a brine of salt, sugar, Worcestershire, hot sauce, and garlic powder seasons it down to the bone.

2. After brining, a sprinkling of homemade Creole seasoning adds flavor without the dusty saltiness of packaged spice blends.

3. The homemade Creole seasoning lends a potent punch to the chicken's flour coating.

4. For a peppery finish, sprinkle the hot chicken with more of the homemade Creole seasoning when it comes out of the oil.

COATING

- 1 tablespoon pepper
- 1 tablespoon dried oregano
- 1 tablespoon garlic powder
- 2 teaspoons onion powder
- 2 teaspoons cayenne pepper
- 1 teaspoon white pepper
- 1 teaspoon celery salt
- 2 cups all-purpose flour
- 3 quarts peanut oil or vegetable shortening

1. FOR THE BRINE: Whisk the water, sugar, Worcestershire, hot sauce, salt, and garlic powder in a large bowl until the sugar and salt dissolve. Add the chicken and refrigerate, covered, for 1 hour (or up to 8 hours).

2. FOR THE COATING: Combine the pepper, oregano, garlic powder, onion powder, cayenne, white pepper, and celery salt in a large bowl; reserve 4 tablespoons of the spice mixture. Add the flour to the bowl with the remaining spice mixture and stir to combine.

3. Remove the chicken from the refrigerator and pour off the brine. Sprinkle the chicken with 3 tablespoons of the reserved spice mixture and toss to coat. Working in batches of 2, dredge the chicken pieces in the flour mixture. Shake the excess flour from the chicken and transfer to a wire rack. (Do not discard the flour mixture.)

4. Adjust an oven rack to the middle position and heat the oven to 200 degrees. Heat the oil or shortening in a large Dutch oven over medium-high heat to 375 degrees. Return the chicken pieces to the flour mixture and turn to coat. Fry half of the chicken, adjusting the burner as necessary to maintain an oil temperature between 300 and 325 degrees, until deep golden brown

and the internal temperature of the white meat registers 160 degrees (175 degrees for dark meat) on an instant-read thermometer, 10 to 12 minutes. Transfer the chicken to a wire rack set over a baking sheet and place in the warm oven. Bring the oil back to 375 degrees and repeat with the remaining chicken. Sprinkle the crispy chicken with the remaining spice mixture. Serve.

Firecracker Chicken

For those who like their fried chicken spicy, firecracker chicken is the answer. All recipes for firecracker chicken have one thing in common: tongue-tingling heat capable of satisfying any chilehead's cravings for fire. In most recipes boneless chicken breasts are marinated in hot sauce; the chicken is then breaded, pan-fried, and served with more hot sauce. We set out to develop the ultimate recipe for this fiery dish.

Our first question was simple: did we have to make our own hot sauce, or could we just use bottled sauce? Commercial hot sauce turned out not to be bad, but tasters wanted something fresher and more interesting.

The recipes we tested agreed on the chiles, but there was little consensus on the other base ingredients for the spicy marinade/finishing sauce. After testing numerous condiments in the fridge, we settled on an unlikely foundation. Yellow (aka "hot dog") mustard had a bright flavor and color, a welcome pungency, and a consistency that helped it cling nicely to the chicken. As for the spice, tasters liked habanero chiles for their unapologetic burn, but they wanted a more complex heat. We added pickled banana peppers (plus some of their pickling juices) for a nice acidic tang and dry mustard for its sinus-clearing heat.

It was time to move on to the chicken. In classic

SOUTHERN FRIED CHICKEN

Few foods are more closely associated with American cooking, especially Southern cooking, than fried chicken. Some sources suggest that Scottish immigrants to the South brought with them the tradition of frying chicken. As the dish grew in popularity, so did arguments about its proper preparation. Should shortening, bacon drippings, lard, or oil be used as the frying medium? Should a batter or seasoned flour be used to coat the chicken? Should the chicken be deep-fried (that is, submerged in fat as it cooks) or pan-fried (with the fat coming halfway up the sides of each piece)?

The basic fried chicken recipe has spawned countless variations, everything from firecracker (with its spicy sauce) to Maryland fried chicken, which is served with a brown pan gravy.

Perhaps America's most famous fried chicken recipe is Kentucky fried chicken. Harland Sanders created his famous recipe in the 1930s. It relies on a secret blend of eleven herbs and spices and became so popular at his restaurant in Corbin, Kentucky, that the governor awarded Sanders the honorary title of Colonel.

The Colonel's big innovation was the use of a pressure cooker, which cut cooking time from half an hour to just minutes. When his restaurant was forced to close in 1952, the Colonel (already in his sixties) hit the road and began selling his recipe to other restaurants. In 1964 the Colonel had more than 600 franchised outlets and sold his interest for $2 million, not only earning him fame and fortune but guaranteeing that fried chicken would become the most famous recipe from the American South.

fried chicken, the coating adheres to the cut-up chicken parts because the skin is very tacky. But we were using strips of boneless, skinless breasts and encountered problems from the start. To fortify the coating, we used a method the test kitchen developed for our Extra-Crunchy Fried Chicken (page 289) and incorporated some of the liquid (in this case, the mustard sauce) into the flour. The sauce gave the flour the texture of wet sand, so it stuck to the chicken in irregular clumps. When fried, this lumpy texture created thick, crispy pockets of coating that tasters loved. Unfortunately, the coating still wasn't sticking to the chicken.

We eventually figured out the problem. The chicken had soaked up enough of the firecracker marinade that when it hit the hot oil, the extra liquid steamed the coating right off. Two things helped: letting the coated chicken dry out in the refrigerator for 15 minutes, and adding baking powder and cornstarch to the coating (to absorb moisture and encourage browning). The coating was now more clingy but still not quite clingy enough.

The proteins in eggs can "glue" coatings onto countless foods, so we dried the marinated chicken with paper towels, dipped it in beaten eggs, and then rolled it in the moistened flour coating. Sure enough, this chicken fried up beautifully, with a crispy, crunchy coating that adhered to the chicken. But now tasters didn't like the "eggy flavor" this method added!

Using just the egg whites reduced the egg flavor, but the whites were so thin that they didn't hold the coating. We mulled over different ways to thicken the egg whites before it hit us—why not just beat the egg whites? The foamy egg whites held on to a ton of coating. Our firecracker chicken finally packed a crunch—and a kick—that was worthy of its name.

FIRECRACKER CHICKEN

SERVES 6

*If you really like spicy foods, try adding another haba-
nero or two; if you are spice-averse, substitute jalapeños. We like to drizzle the sauce over the chicken strips
just before serving, but the sauce is just as good served
on the side for dipping.*

SAUCE

½	**cup sliced pickled banana peppers, chopped fine, and ¼ cup pickling liquid**
¼	**cup fresh lemon juice**
¼	**cup vegetable oil**
¼	**cup yellow mustard**
3	**tablespoons dry mustard**
2	**tablespoons chili sauce**
2	**tablespoons brown sugar**
3	**garlic cloves, minced**
1	**habanero chile, minced (see note above)**
4	**scallions, sliced thin**

CHICKEN

6	**boneless, skinless chicken breasts (about 2½ pounds), trimmed**
2	**cups all-purpose flour**
½	**cup cornstarch**
1	**tablespoon salt**
1	**teaspoon baking powder**
4	**large egg whites**
1	**cup vegetable oil**

1. FOR THE SAUCE: Whisk all of the ingredients
together in a large bowl.

2. FOR THE CHICKEN: Cover the chicken breasts
with plastic wrap and pound lightly with a meat mallet until about ½ inch thick. Slice the breasts in half
lengthwise and transfer to a large zipper-lock plastic bag. Add ¼ cup of the sauce to the bag, seal,
and gently squeeze the bag to coat the chicken with
sauce. Refrigerate for 30 minutes (or up to 2 hours).

MAKING FIRECRACKER CHICKEN

1. Dip the chicken in the foamy egg whites to anchor the coating. Pat the moistened coating mixture onto the chicken to ensure adhesion.

2. Let the coated chicken strips rest in the refrigerator for 15 minutes and then pan-fry them in oil until very crisp.

3. Meanwhile, in a large bowl, combine the flour,
cornstarch, salt, and baking powder. Add 6 tablespoons of the sauce and, using your hands, combine
until the mixture resembles coarse, wet sand.

4. In another large bowl, whisk the egg whites until
foamy. Remove the chicken from the marinade and
pat dry with paper towels. Working with one strip at
a time, dip the chicken in the egg whites and transfer to the flour mixture, pressing lightly to adhere.
Place the chicken pieces on a wire rack set on a
rimmed baking sheet and refrigerate for 15 minutes
(or up to 4 hours).

5. Adjust an oven rack to the middle position and
heat the oven to 200 degrees. Heat the oil in a large
skillet over medium-high heat until shimmering.
Carefully place half of the chicken strips in the oil
and fry until golden brown and cooked through,
2 to 4 minutes per side. Transfer to a baking sheet
lined with paper towels and place in the warm oven.
Repeat with the remaining chicken strips. Transfer
the chicken to a platter, drizzle with the remaining
sauce, and serve.

Crispy Roast Chicken and Potatoes

At first glance, roasting chicken and potatoes together seems easy enough. Just toss some potatoes into the roasting pan with a whole bird, right? Well, that's exactly what we did, and we ended up with soggy, greasy potatoes. We also ended up with overcooked breast meat, having roasted the chicken breast side up at 400 degrees, the temperature most recipes recommend.

We started by using the test kitchen's method for roasting a whole chicken: breast side down, elevated on a wire rack, at 375 degrees for 35 minutes, then breast side up at 450 degrees for another 30 to 40 minutes. This ensures that the dark meat has more exposure to high heat, promoting even cooking and crispier skin. But we wanted really crisp skin.

We noticed a curious phenomenon during roasting: the rendered fat was literally boiling beneath the skin. We figured that this liquid would keep the skin from getting truly crispy, no matter how high the heat. Maybe poking holes in the skin would release this fat and allow for better crisping. This technique did let the fat seep out from beneath the skin, but it actually left the skin soggy and greasy. Perhaps dredging the chicken in flour, as is done for fried chicken, would help. Nope. The flour simply turned gummy. On our next try we replaced the flour with a sprinkling of cornstarch, a trick used in many Asian stir-fry recipes. By the time we had flipped the chicken breast side up, we knew we were on the right track. The cornstarch was sizzling in the rendering fat and creating an extra-crunchy coating. For one last test, we cranked the oven up to 475 degrees. This super-hot oven made for an even more superior bird, its skin deeply browned and crisp, its meat moist and tender.

To solve the problem of the soggy, greasy potatoes, we tried giving them less oven time. Instead of starting the potatoes along with the chicken, we added them to the roasting pan when we turned the chicken for the third (and last) time. To keep the fat from smoking in this very hot oven, we lined the roasting pan with foil. Then, just before we added the potatoes, we gathered the corners of the foil and discarded the rendered fat (often as much as ¼ cup) that had collected over the first 30 minutes of cooking time. After discarding the fat and foil, we spread the potatoes, cut side down, in the bottom of the hot roasting pan, replaced the V-rack (with the chicken breast side up), and returned the pan to the oven. No more greasy potatoes!

We had two minor problems to solve and we would be done. The first was that fat was pooling around the thighs as the chicken cooled on the V-rack. This problem was easily solved by placing the roasted chicken on an angel-food-cake pan insert for cooling (sitting the bird on an empty soda can also worked). Granted, the chicken looked a bit odd standing upright on the counter, but this was the best way to allow excess fat and juices to drain. The second problem was that a number of folks in the test kitchen thought that the potatoes were lacking in flavor (chicken flavor, that is). To add chicken flavor, we simply poured the juices from the cavity of the chicken (as we were moving it for resting) onto the potatoes and popped them back in the oven to finish cooking. Ten minutes later, they were deep brown and infused with chicken flavor, minus the fat.

Not the simplest roast chicken in the world, perhaps, but by far the best roast chicken and potatoes we've ever tasted.

CRISPY ROAST CHICKEN AND POTATOES

SERVES 4

If you have it, a nonstick roasting pan works best here. If using a chicken larger than 4 pounds, the oven time will need to be lengthened slightly.

- 2 teaspoons cornstarch
  Salt
- 1 (3½- to 4-pound) whole chicken, giblets discarded, skin and inside patted dry with paper towels
- 2 pounds small red potatoes, scrubbed and halved
- 2 teaspoons vegetable oil

1. Line the roasting pan with aluminum foil, letting the foil come up the sides of the pan. Adjust an oven rack to the middle position, place the roasting pan on the rack, and heat the oven to 475 degrees. Coat a V-rack with vegetable oil spray.

2. Combine the cornstarch and 2 teaspoons salt in a small bowl. Use a skewer to poke holes all over the chicken skin. Rub the cornstarch mixture evenly over the chicken.

3. Remove the roasting pan from the oven. Place the chicken, wing side up, on the V-rack, then place the V-rack in the roasting pan. Roast the chicken for 15 minutes. Remove the roasting pan from the oven and, using a wad of paper towels, flip the chicken so that the other wing is facing up. Roast for another 15 minutes.

4. Meanwhile, toss the potatoes, oil, and ½ teaspoon salt in a medium bowl. Remove the roasting pan from the oven and, using potholders, carefully transfer the V-rack with the chicken to a rimmed baking sheet. Gather up the foil by its corners, capturing any fat and juices, and discard. Arrange the potatoes, cut side down, in the roasting pan. Using a wad of paper towels, flip the chicken breast side up on the V-rack. Place the V-rack back in the roasting pan and roast the chicken until an instant-read thermometer inserted into the thickest part of the thigh registers 170 degrees, about 20 minutes.

5. Using a wad of paper towels, remove the chicken from the V-rack and pour the juices from the cavity into the roasting pan with the potatoes. Place the chicken on an angel-food-cake pan insert or an empty soda can to rest upright for 10 to 15 minutes. Meanwhile, toss the potatoes in the chicken juices, return the pan to the oven, and cook until well browned and crisp, 10 to 15 minutes. Carve the chicken and serve with the potatoes.

ROASTING A CRISP CHICKEN

1. Place the chicken, wing side up, on a greased V-rack. Place the V-rack in a preheated roasting pan lined with aluminum foil and roast for 15 minutes. Flip the chicken so that the other wing faces up and roast for another 15 minutes. Remove the rack, discard the foil and grease, and add the potatoes to the pan.

2. Turn the chicken breast side up and return the V-rack to the pan. Roast for another 20 minutes or until done. Remove the rack and chicken, tipping the juices from the cavity back into the pan. Toss the potatoes with the chicken juices and return to the oven to finish cooking.

Garlic Roast Chicken

Flavoring a roast chicken with garlic sounds easy, but while testing existing garlic chicken recipes we learned that the garlic flavor was either nonexistent or so strong the birds were inedible. Some recipes call for sprinkling powdered or granulated garlic over the chicken, but the garlic burned and turned bitter by the time the meat was done. Garlic butter rubbed under the skin tasted steamed and overly pungent. We wanted the sweet, nutty garlic flavor to be strong but not overpowering, with a pan sauce that would enhance the garlic in the chicken.

We started by using the test kitchen's method for roasting a whole chicken: breast side down, elevated on a wire rack, at 375 degrees for 35 minutes, then breast side up at 450 degrees for another 30 to 40 minutes. This ensures that the dark meat has more exposure to high heat, promoting even cooking and crispier skin.

The most promising recipe from our initial tests included instructions for roasted garlic, which was pureed and rubbed over the skin of the chicken during the last 15 minutes of cooking. This chicken exhibited pronounced but not overpowering garlic flavor. Roasted garlic was a good place to start, but roasting whole heads of garlic takes over an hour in the oven. Was there a faster way to roasted garlic flavor?

The test kitchen sometimes cooks garlic in oil to tame its bite and draw out its sweetness. Following this path, we cut garlic cloves in half (to speed their cooking), covered them with olive oil, and cooked them over low heat for just 10 minutes. Then we pureed the softened cloves and olive oil to a smooth paste. We carefully slid the paste under the skin of the breast, thighs, and legs (the paste burned on the exterior of the bird) and rubbed some reserved garlic-infused oil over the outside of the chicken to help crisp the skin. The resulting chicken had moist meat, crisp skin, and a nice garlic punch. We needed 4 tablespoons of garlic puree to spread under the skin. This translated to a whopping 25 cloves!

In the test kitchen we typically add water to the roasting pan to keep the drippings from scorching. We saw this as an opportunity to add more garlic puree and flavorful liquids (tasters liked chicken broth and white wine) that could cook down in the oven and form the foundation of a simple pan sauce. We were now making 8 tablespoons of garlic puree and needed 50 cloves of garlic. For cooks who can't imagine working with so much fresh garlic, we found that prepeeled garlic cloves were just fine in this recipe.

The pan sauce was perfumed with sweet garlic flavor, but the actual bits of garlic were pretty spent; we strained them out. A little cornstarch thickened the sauce, and butter and fresh tarragon added the finishing touches. We finally had a chicken and pan sauce with ultimate garlic flavor.

ROASTING GARLIC CHICKEN

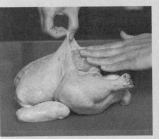 

1. Rub some of the garlic puree under the skin of the chicken. Be sure that the garlic puree coats not only the breast meat but the thigh and leg meat as well. For garlicky, crisp skin, rub the entire exterior of the chicken, front and back, with the reserved garlic oil.

2. Add the remaining garlic puree (along with chicken broth and white wine) to the roasting pan halfway through cooking; the mixture will cook down and serve as the foundation for the pan sauce.

GARLIC ROAST CHICKEN

SERVES 3 TO 4

You will need one 8-ounce jar of peeled garlic cloves or 3 to 4 whole heads of garlic.

50	garlic cloves, peeled and halved (see note above)
¼	cup extra-virgin olive oil
	Salt and pepper
1	(3½- to 4-pound) whole chicken, giblets discarded, skin and inside patted dry with paper towels
1¾	cups low-sodium chicken broth
¾	cup white wine
½	cup plus 1 tablespoon water
1	teaspoon cornstarch
2	tablespoons cold unsalted butter, cut into pieces
2	teaspoons chopped fresh tarragon

1. Adjust an oven rack to the lower-middle position and heat the oven to 375 degrees. Combine the garlic and oil in a small saucepan. Cook, covered, over medium-low heat, stirring occasionally, until the garlic is softened and straw-colored, 10 to 15 minutes. Reserve 1 tablespoon oil and transfer the remaining garlic mixture to a food processor; puree until smooth. Let cool.

2. Combine ¼ cup garlic puree, ¼ teaspoon salt, and ½ teaspoon pepper in a small bowl. Tuck the wings behind the back, then spread the garlic mixture under the skin of the chicken and rub the reserved 1 tablespoon oil over the outside of the chicken. Tie the legs together with kitchen twine. Season the chicken with salt and pepper and arrange, breast side down, on a V-rack set inside a roasting pan. Roast until just golden, about 35 minutes.

3. Remove the pan from the oven and, using a wad of paper towels, flip the chicken breast side up. Raise the oven temperature to 450 degrees. Whisk the broth, wine, ½ cup of the water, and the remaining garlic puree in a measuring cup, then pour into the roasting pan. Return the chicken to the oven and roast until the thigh meat registers 170 to 175 degrees on an instant-read thermometer, 30 to 40 minutes. Transfer the chicken to a cutting board and let rest for 20 minutes.

4. Meanwhile, transfer the pan juices and any accumulated chicken juices to a saucepan; skim the fat. Whisk the remaining water and cornstarch in a small bowl, then add to the saucepan. Simmer until the sauce is slightly thickened, about 2 minutes. Whisk in the butter, then strain into a serving bowl. Stir in the tarragon and season with salt and pepper to taste. Carve the chicken and serve, passing the sauce at the table.

Chicken and Rice with Spring Vegetables

Chicken and rice should be a part of every cook's weeknight repertoire. After all, it's a hot, hearty, one-pot supper that can be on the table in well under an hour. But for all the convenience, most recipes are fraught with problems. All too often the rice is crunchy, the chicken is rubbery, the vegetables are shriveled, and everything is bland.

The key to properly cooked rice lies in the ratio of liquid to rice. We found that 2¼ cups of liquid to 1½ cups of rice produced perfectly plump grains. Since the rice cooks in 30 minutes, we learned it's best to avoid using dark meat (which is better suited to longer cooking). Bone-in, skin-on breasts added a lot of flavor, but their fatty skin left the rice slick and heavy. Boneless, skinless breasts solved the grease problem, but they dried out when cooked with the rice. Ultimately, we found that if we removed the boneless, skinless breasts from the pot (tenting them with aluminum foil to keep them warm) when the rice was halfway done, the chicken was fully cooked and still moist when added back just before serving.

Tasters loved the combination of asparagus and peas. But although the peas were easy—we simply stirred frozen peas into the rice at the end—the asparagus wasn't. Adding asparagus at the outset left it overcooked and bitter, but adding raw spears any later messed up the timing of the rice. We decided to cook the asparagus first. Since blanching and steaming didn't add any flavor, we quickly seared the asparagus before the chicken went into the pan. This way, the perfectly cooked asparagus was nicely caramelized and could be added to the pot along with the peas.

The rice, chicken, and vegetables were properly cooked, but the dish tasted bland. To pump up the flavors, we took a key from rice pilaf and sautéed the rice (along with onion and garlic) before adding the liquid. This added a toasty aroma, but the rice still lacked depth. We tried different types of rice (long-grain was the favorite), bouillon cubes (too assertive and salty), even searing the chicken in butter rather than oil (the butter burned), but nothing worked.

Running out of options, we found our unlikely muse in the supermarket: Rice-A-Roni, which combines pasta with rice to lend a distinct texture and flavor to its boxed dinners. In hopeful desperation, we gave this concept a shot, adding our "roni" in the form of orzo (a rice-shaped pasta). To our surprise, the orzo (with an extra ¼ cup of liquid) cooked at exactly the same rate as the rice and added a welcome texture to the dish. To improve its flavor, we tried toasting the orzo along with the rice, but that didn't do much. Toasting the orzo in a dry pan, however, gave it a deep caramel color and an earthy taste that worked wonders.

For the finishing touch, tasters asked for a few flavorful stir-ins. The addition of fresh basil, raw garlic, and lemon zest transformed this humble dish into something worthy of a special occasion.

CHICKEN AND RICE WITH SPRING VEGETABLES

SERVES 4

The rice will cook unevenly if the pot is uncovered for too long, so work quickly in step 3.

½	cup orzo
4	tablespoons vegetable oil
1	pound asparagus, trimmed and cut into 1-inch pieces
4	boneless, skinless chicken breasts (about 1½ pounds), trimmed
	Salt and pepper
1	cup long-grain white rice
1	onion, minced
4	garlic cloves, minced
2¼	cups low-sodium chicken broth
¼	cup white wine
1	cup frozen peas, thawed
2	tablespoons chopped fresh basil
½	teaspoon grated fresh lemon zest

1. Toast the orzo in a Dutch oven over medium-high heat until deep brown, about 5 minutes. Transfer to a bowl. Heat 1 tablespoon of the oil in the now-empty pot until shimmering. Cook the asparagus until lightly browned and nearly tender, about 3 minutes. Transfer to a plate.

2. Season the chicken with salt and pepper. Heat the remaining 3 tablespoons oil in the again-empty pot until just smoking. Cook the chicken until lightly browned, about 3 minutes per side. Transfer the chicken to a plate, leaving the fat in the pan. Add the rice, onion, and ¾ teaspoon salt to the pot and cook until the rice is sizzling and toasted, about 3 minutes. Add three-quarters of the garlic and cook until fragrant, about 30 seconds. Stir in the toasted orzo, broth, and wine and bring to a simmer. Nestle the chicken into the rice and pour in any juices accumulated on the plate. Cover the pot, reduce the heat to low, and simmer until the chicken is cooked through, about 12 minutes.

3. Working quickly, transfer the chicken to a plate and cover loosely with aluminum foil. Stir the rice, replace the cover, and continue cooking until the rice is tender and the liquid is absorbed, about 12 minutes. Off the heat, gently fold in the peas, basil, zest, remaining garlic, and reserved asparagus. Cover and let sit until heated through, about 2 minutes. Transfer to a serving platter and top with the chicken. Serve.

Modern Chicken Divan

Despite its current reputation as a cheesy, creamy chicken and broccoli casserole you pick up in the frozen-food aisle and reheat in a microwave, chicken Divan has a long and elegant history. The original recipe from New York's famed (and now defunct) Divan Parisien Restaurant dates back almost one hundred years and required a whole poached chicken, boiled broccoli, and a sauce made with béchamel sauce, hollandaise sauce, Parmesan cheese, and whipped cream. The ingredients were combined "à la minute" (just before being plated) and broiled to perfection. Sounds good, but if we're counting right, that's at least five pots, four recipes, and more time than we'd care to spend in the kitchen. No wonder most "modern" recipes rely on canned soup.

To bring chicken Divan into the twenty-first century without compromising the flavors of the original dish, we turned to a trusty skillet. Batch-cooking was in order, and first up was the broccoli. It was easily sautéed and then steamed in a little chicken broth so it emerged flavorful, tender, and emerald green. Boneless, skinless chicken breasts got a similar treatment.

Mimicking the original sauce took some kitchen trickery. Simmering chicken broth with heavy cream (instead of folding in whipped cream at the end) gave the sauce a rich feel, and sherry, Worcestershire, and a full cup of grated Parmesan warmed up the flavors. Our sauce was good, but without the hollandaise (and its decadent egg yolks, butter, and bright lemon juice) it wasn't exactly right. Instead of preparing a separate hollandaise, could we just add these ingredients to our existing sauce? We whisked the yolks and lemon juice together, then tempered the mixture with a little of the hot pan sauce. Once returned to the pan (off the heat so as not to curdle the eggs), along with some butter, the sauce thickened to pure luxury.

We poured the sauce over the waiting chicken and broccoli, topped everything with more Parmesan, and slid the dish under the broiler for a few minutes. We now had chicken Divan that was as opulent as the original but didn't require anywhere near the effort.

MODERN CHICKEN DIVAN

SERVES 4

Use one small onion instead of the shallots, if desired.

3	tablespoons vegetable oil
1½	pounds broccoli, stalks discarded, florets cut into bite-sized pieces
2½	cups low-sodium chicken broth
1½	pounds boneless, skinless chicken breasts, trimmed
	Salt and pepper
¼	cup all-purpose flour
2	medium shallots, minced (see note above)
1	cup heavy cream
½	cup dry sherry
2	teaspoons Worcestershire sauce
1½	cups grated Parmesan cheese
3	large egg yolks
1	tablespoon fresh lemon juice
3	tablespoons unsalted butter

1. Adjust an oven rack to the lower-middle position and heat the broiler. Heat 1 tablespoon of the oil in a large skillet over medium-high heat until just smoking. Add the broccoli and cook until spotty brown, about 1 minute. Add ½ cup of the broth, cover, and steam until just tender, about 1½ minutes. Remove the lid and cook until the liquid has evaporated, about 1 minute. Transfer the broccoli to a plate lined with paper towels; rinse and wipe out the skillet.

2. Heat the remaining 2 tablespoons oil in the now-empty skillet over medium-high heat until smoking. Meanwhile, season the chicken with salt and pepper and dredge in the flour to coat. Cook the chicken until golden brown, 2 to 3 minutes per side. Transfer the chicken to a plate.

3. Off the heat, add the shallots to the skillet, return to medium heat, and cook until just beginning to color, about 1 minute. Add the remaining 2 cups broth and cream and scrape the browned bits from the bottom of the pan. Return the chicken to the skillet and simmer over medium-high heat until cooked through, about 10 minutes. Transfer the chicken to a clean plate and continue to simmer the sauce until reduced to 1 cup, about 10 minutes. Add the sherry and Worcestershire and simmer until reduced again to 1 cup, about 3 minutes.

4. Stir in 1 cup of the Parmesan. Whisk the egg yolks and lemon juice together in a small bowl, then whisk in about ¼ cup of the sauce. Off the heat, whisk the egg yolk mixture into the sauce in the skillet, then whisk in the butter.

5. Cut the chicken into ½-inch-thick slices and arrange on a broiler-safe platter. Scatter the broccoli over the chicken and pour the sauce over the broccoli. Sprinkle with the remaining ½ cup Parmesan and broil until golden brown, 3 to 5 minutes. Serve.

Chicken and Dumplings

Chicken and dumplings may be a cornerstone of American comfort food, but who has time to cut up a chicken, clean and chop the vegetables, make a stock, let the stew simmer, and then finish it off with from-scratch dumplings? We wanted to revamp this old-fashioned recipe by making it quicker and easier.

Our first move was to replace the stock with store-bought broth and the chicken parts with boneless, skinless breasts. The store-bought broth proved a good substitute for homemade, especially after we added all the vegetables and seasonings, but the lean chicken breasts were much trickier. Cooking the breasts from the outset (and later shredding them) made for dry, stringy meat. We eventually had success by poaching the chicken in the broth first and then removing it while we made the stew.

With the basic technique down, we could focus on the vegetables and seasonings. Tasters liked a mix of carrot and onion and welcomed the fresh pop of peas stirred in at the end. Dry sherry, garlic, thyme, and bay leaves added flavor. The best way to give our stew the rich, thick texture it needed was to cook flour in the butter and vegetables early in the process, before adding the broth and cream.

Depending on the recipe origins, dumplings can resemble either noodles or biscuits. Rolled, noodle-style dumplings were too labor-intensive for our streamlined stew. Dropped biscuit-style dumplings (with flour, baking powder, salt, and melted butter and/or dairy) were easier, but we had to get the ingredients right. Milk was too lean and made the dumplings too tough. Melted butter made delicate dumplings that disintegrated into the stew. Cream produced nice, soft dumplings, but they were flat and heavy. Bumping the baking powder up to a full tablespoon (twice as much as in most recipes) gave us perfect—and easy—dumplings that were just as good as Grandma's.

EASIER CHICKEN AND DUMPLINGS

SERVES 6 TO 8

For tender dumplings, the dough should be gently mixed right before the dumplings are dropped onto the stew. This stew can be made ahead. Follow the recipe through step 2, and refrigerate stew and chicken in separate airtight containers for up to 24 hours. When ready to proceed, warm the stew in a Dutch oven and proceed with step 3.

STEW

5	cups low-sodium chicken broth
2	pounds boneless, skinless chicken breasts, trimmed
5	tablespoons unsalted butter
4	carrots, peeled and cut into ¼-inch slices
1	large onion, minced
1	teaspoon salt
3	garlic cloves, minced
6	tablespoons all-purpose flour
¾	cup dry sherry
⅓	cup heavy cream
½	teaspoon dried thyme
2	bay leaves
½	teaspoon pepper
1½	cups frozen peas
4	tablespoons minced fresh parsley

DUMPLINGS

2	cups all-purpose flour
1	tablespoon baking powder
½	teaspoon salt
1⅓	cups heavy cream

1. FOR THE STEW: Bring the broth to a simmer in a Dutch oven over high heat. Add the chicken and return to a simmer. Cover, reduce the heat to medium-low, and simmer until the chicken is just cooked through, about 10 minutes. Transfer the chicken to a plate and tent loosely with aluminum foil. Transfer the broth to a large bowl.

2. Return the empty Dutch oven to medium-high heat and melt the butter. Add the carrots, onion, and salt and cook until softened, about 7 minutes. Stir in the garlic and cook until fragrant, about 30 seconds. Stir in the flour and cook, stirring frequently, for 1 minute. Stir in the sherry, scraping up the browned bits. Stir in the reserved broth, cream, thyme, bay leaves, and pepper and bring to a boil. Cover, reduce the heat to low, and simmer until the stew thickens, about 20 minutes.

3. FOR THE DUMPLINGS: Stir the flour, baking powder, and salt in a large bowl. Stir in the cream until incorporated (the dough will be very thick).

4. TO FINISH: Discard the bay leaves and return the stew to a rapid simmer. Shred the reserved chicken and add it to the stew along with any accumulated juices, the peas, and 3 tablespoons of the parsley. Using 2 large soup spoons or a small ice cream scoop, drop golf ball–sized dumplings onto the stew about ¼ inch apart (you should have 16 to 18 dumplings). Reduce the heat to low, cover, and cook until the dumplings have doubled in size, 15 to 18 minutes. Garnish with the remaining 1 tablespoon parsley. Serve.

MAKING THE DUMPLINGS

1. Use a small ice cream scoop to drop the dumplings onto the stew. Then cook the dumplings in a covered pot over low heat.

2. The dumplings will puff, double in size, and become tender after about 15 minutes in the pot.

Chicken and Mushroom Fricassee

Chicken fricassee is an old-fashioned recipe that deserves a fresh look. Typically, a whole chicken is cut up, browned, braised in wine and broth, and then finished with heavy cream and lemon juice. Some recipes keep it as simple as that, while others include vegetables like pearl onions, carrots, celery, and mushrooms. We've always liked this dish with mushrooms, which lend meatiness and heft to the sauce.

Although chicken fricassee has a solid premise and a long track record, the recipes we tried weren't very good. Cooking white and dark meat together in the same pot is a challenge because they cook at different rates, so the white meat was dried out before the dark meat came up to temperature. The sauces tended toward the thick and stodgy—in fact, in many modern recipes the homemade sauce is replaced with canned cream of mushroom soup. We could see why this dish has fallen off the radar.

Early fricassee recipes relied on a whole bird, but modern supermarkets offer many more choices. After testing various combinations of white and dark meat, we settled on bone-in chicken breasts: the white meat cooked relatively quickly and evenly, and the bones added flavor to the sauce. By the time the chicken was finished cooking in the sauce, however, the skin was flabby and not terribly appealing. We addressed this problem by first browning the chicken, which rendered fat we could use to make the sauce, and then removing the chicken from the pot and discarding the skin— it had served its purpose.

We followed the test kitchen's basic braising method by sautéing onions and garlic with 12 ounces of sliced white mushrooms before adding 2 cups of chicken broth, a cup of white wine, and the browned and skinned chicken pieces. Twenty minutes later, we had perfectly cooked chicken nestled in a bland sauce studded with flavorless mushrooms. How could we get more flavor from the mushrooms?

The simplest fix was to add more. After making batches with several different varieties, we settled on adding an equal amount of meaty portobellos to the white mushrooms. To coax the best flavor and texture out of this big pile of mushrooms, we cooked them, covered, until they were soft and had released their liquid, then we uncovered them and let the liquid reduce and intensify. The sauce now had more mushroom flavor, but it wasn't quite there yet.

Replacing half the chicken broth with beef broth reinforced the meaty quality of the mushrooms. In many recipes the sauce is finished with a cup of heavy cream, but tasters thought all that cream was overwhelming the mushrooms. Cutting back to just ⅓ cup of cream gave the stew all the richness it needed and allowed the mushroom flavor to shine through. Finished with fresh parsley and lemon juice, this simple chicken fricassee is worth adding to any cook's repertoire.

PREPARING PORTOBELLO MUSHROOMS

We use a teaspoon to remove the dark gills on the underside of the portobello mushroom caps for our fricassee. Removing the gills prevents our sauce from turning an unappealing brown color.

CHICKEN AND MUSHROOM FRICASSEE

SERVES 4

Serve this creamy stewed chicken with white rice, egg noodles, biscuits, or crusty bread.

4	bone-in, skin-on split chicken breasts (about 3 pounds), ribs removed (see step 1 on page 285)
	Salt and pepper
2	teaspoons vegetable oil
2	onions, minced
6	garlic cloves, minced
12	ounces white mushrooms, sliced thin
4	large portobello mushroom caps (about 12 ounces), gills removed, halved and sliced thin
1	tablespoon minced fresh thyme
¼	cup all-purpose flour
1	cup low-sodium chicken broth
1	cup low-sodium beef broth
1	cup white wine
⅓	cup heavy cream
4	teaspoons fresh lemon juice
2	tablespoons chopped fresh parsley

1. Pat the chicken dry with paper towels and season with salt and pepper. Heat the oil in a Dutch oven over medium-high heat until just smoking. Cook the chicken, skin side down, until deep golden brown, about 6 minutes. Flip and brown on the second side, about 3 minutes. Transfer the chicken to a plate; remove and discard the skin. Pour off all but 1 tablespoon fat from the pot.

2. Cook the onions in the remaining fat until golden, about 5 minutes. Stir in the garlic and cook until fragrant, about 30 seconds. Add the mushrooms, thyme, and ¼ teaspoon salt. Reduce the heat to medium and cook, covered, stirring occasionally, until the mushrooms have released their juices, about 10 minutes. Uncover and cook until the liquid evaporates and the mushrooms begin to brown, about 7 minutes.

3. Stir in the flour and cook until golden, about 1 minute. Slowly stir in the broths and wine and bring to a boil. Return the chicken and any accumulated juices to the pot. Reduce the heat to low and simmer, covered, until the meat registers 160 degrees on an instant-read thermometer, 20 to 30 minutes. Transfer the chicken to a serving platter and tent with foil.

4. Add the cream to the pot and simmer until the sauce is thickened, about 15 minutes. Stir in the lemon juice and parsley and season with salt and pepper to taste. Pour the sauce over the chicken. Serve.

Chicken Marengo

Many recipes have murky histories, and none more so than chicken Marengo. Legend has it that this stew was invented by Napoleon's chef, a man named Dunand, after a victory over the Austrians near the Italian town of Marengo in 1800. As the story goes, the supply wagons were trailing behind, so Dunand and his minions had to scavenge the countryside for ingredients to cook for their hungry and demanding leader. A stew was supposedly made with chicken (cut up with a saber), tomatoes, brandy from Napoleon's flask, olives, mushrooms, truffles, crayfish, cilantro, bread scraps, and fried eggs. Napoleon loved the dish so much that he demanded it after every ensuing victory.

Food historians take issue with this tale for several reasons. Some claim Dunand wasn't employed by the French army in 1800; others say some ingredients would not have been available in the region.

What is indisputable, however, is that chicken Marengo went on to become a widely popular recipe throughout Europe and America. Recipes for chicken Marengo appeared in American cookbooks as early as 1886 and were featured in the 1887 edition of *Miss Parloa's Kitchen Companion*. (There were actually two recipes; one was fairly plain, and the second included fried eggs and triangles of toast.) By the time the recipe appeared in *The Joy of Cooking*, the truffles, crayfish, and fried eggs were long gone and the focus was on the big flavors in the sauce—tomato, brandy, and olive.

As it was to so many older recipes, the post–World War II era was unkind to chicken Marengo. The sauce was downgraded to canned cream of mushroom soup mixed with canned cream of tomato soup. Chicken Marengo began as a rustic yet noble dish designed to satisfy the hunger of a victorious soldier. We wanted to bring this recipe back to its roots.

In the test kitchen we know that most good stews and braises start with browning the meat to establish a base of flavor. Tasters had a preference for white meat in this recipe, but boneless, skinless breasts didn't brown well and turned rubbery when stewed. Instead, we used skin-on, bone-in breasts; the bones added flavor to the stew, and the skin browned well and contributed flavor of its own.

After browning the chicken, we removed it from the pot to start building the sauce. We sautéed mushrooms, onion, and garlic, then added tomato paste and canned crushed tomatoes. Tasters didn't think the crushed tomatoes were adding enough flavor, so we switched to fresher-tasting canned diced tomatoes, which we quickly buzzed in the food processor to begin the breaking-down process (large chunks were unappealing in this sauce). Tasters wanted a strong hit of brandy; we eventually settled on ½ cup as the right amount for the sauce. We especially liked briny kalamata olives in this dish,

and chopping the olives and adding them at the outset allowed their flavor to permeate the sauce.

Since we weren't removing the chicken skin, we knew we'd have to take measures to prevent it from becoming chewy during the stewing process. First, we made sure to have only enough sauce in the pot to come halfway up the chicken breasts. To keep the skin crisp and the meat moist, we nestled the browned chicken into the sauce skin side up, then placed the pot, uncovered, in a 450-degree oven for about 30 minutes to cook the chicken through and let the sauce reduce and intensify. This gave us a hearty, full-flavored chicken Marengo ready to conquer the modern dinner table.

CHICKEN MARENGO

SERVES 4

Since canned crushed tomatoes are often packed in a stale-tasting tomato sauce, we prefer to use drained diced tomatoes in this recipe. The tomatoes can be roughly chopped by hand or pulsed 3 to 4 times in a food processor.

4	bone-in, skin-on split chicken breasts (about 3 pounds), ribs removed (see step 1 on page 285)
	Salt and pepper
1	tablespoon extra-virgin olive oil
1	onion, minced
4	garlic cloves, minced
10	ounces cremini or white mushrooms, sliced thin
2	teaspoons minced fresh thyme
2	tablespoons tomato paste
1	(28-ounce) can diced tomatoes, drained and roughly chopped (see note above)
¾	cup low-sodium chicken broth
½	cup brandy
¼	cup pitted kalamata olives, chopped fine
¼	teaspoon red pepper flakes
3	tablespoons unsalted butter

1. Adjust an oven rack to the middle position and heat the oven to 450 degrees. Pat the chicken dry with paper towels and season with salt and pepper. Heat the oil in a Dutch oven over medium-high heat until just smoking. Cook the chicken, skin side down, until deep golden brown, about 5 minutes. Flip and brown on the second side, about 2 minutes. Transfer to a plate.

2. Reduce the heat to medium. Add the onion to the fat in the pan and cook until softened, about 5 minutes. Stir in the garlic and cook until fragrant, about 30 seconds. Add the mushrooms, thyme, and ¼ teaspoon salt. Cover and cook, stirring occasionally, until the mushrooms have released their juices, about 10 minutes. Stir in the tomato paste and cook until thickened, about 2 minutes.

3. Stir in the tomatoes, broth, brandy, olives, and red pepper flakes and bring to a boil. Add the chicken pieces, skin side up, along with any accumulated juices. Transfer the pot to the oven and cook, uncovered, until the chicken registers 160 degrees on an instant-read thermometer inserted into the thickest part, about 30 minutes. Transfer the chicken to a serving platter. Stir the butter into the sauce and season with salt and pepper to taste. Pour the sauce around the chicken. Serve.

SHOPPING WITH THE TEST KITCHEN

Kalamata Olives: Although kalamata olives are often packed in olive oil in their native Greece, on American soil we almost always find them swimming in a vinegary brine. We prefer the fresher kalamatas from the refrigerator section of the supermarket, as the jarred, shelf-stable ones are bland and mushy in comparison. If you can't find kalamatas in the refrigerator section of your market, look for them at the salad bar.

Turkey Burgers

A lean, fully cooked turkey burger, seasoned with salt and pepper, is a weak stand-in for an all-beef burger. Simply put, it is dry, tasteless, and colorless. We wanted a turkey burger with beef burger qualities—dark and crusty on the outside and full-flavored and juicy with every bite.

Finding the right meat was crucial to developing the best turkey burger. According to the National Turkey Federation, there are three options: white meat (with 1 to 2 percent fat), dark meat (over 15 percent fat), and a blend of the two (ranging from 7 to 15 percent fat).

At the grocery store we found multiple variations on the white meat/dark meat theme, including higher-fat ground fresh turkey on Styrofoam trays or frozen in tubes like bulk sausage, lower-fat ground turkey breasts, and then there were individual turkey parts we could take home and grind up ourselves. We bought them all, took them back to the test kitchen, and fired up a skillet.

The higher-fat (15-percent) ground turkey turned out to be flavorful and reasonably juicy with a decent, burger-like crust. Frankly, these burgers didn't need too much help. But, given that a great beef burger contains only 20 percent fat, a mere 5 percent fat savings didn't seem worth it.

At the other extreme, with only 1 or 2 percent fat, was ground turkey breast. As we were mixing and forming these patties, we knew we had about as much chance of making them look, taste, and feel like real burgers as we did of making vanilla wafers taste like chocolate chip cookies. They needed a binder to keep them from falling apart. They needed extra fat to keep them from parching and extra fat in the pan to keep them from sticking. And they needed flavor to save them from blandness.

With 7 percent fat, lean ground turkey was the most popular style at all the grocery stores we checked. Burgers made from this mix were dry, rubbery, and mild-flavored. With a little help, however, these leaner patties were meaty enough to have real burger potential.

To improve texture and juiciness, we started with the obvious—milk-soaked bread. For comparison, we also made burgers with buttermilk- and yogurt-soaked bread. All these additions made the burgers feel too much like meat loaf and destroyed whatever meaty flavor there had been, since turkey is mild to start with. The bread and milk lightened the meat's color unpleasantly, and the sugar in both ingredients caused the burgers to burn easily and made it impossible to develop a good thick crust.

We tried other fillers to improve the texture, including cornmeal mush, mashed pinto beans, and minced tempeh, but their flavors were too distinct. Minced, rehydrated dried mushrooms added a moist, chewy texture that the burgers desperately needed. They also offered an earthy, meaty, yet not overly distinct flavor. The real winner, however—for flavor, texture, and easy availability—was ricotta cheese. Moist and chewy, it gave the burgers the texture boost they needed and required very little effort.

Finally, we decided to experiment a bit with added flavorings. We wanted only those that would enhance the burger's taste without drawing attention to themselves. We tried more than twenty-five different flavorings—from fermented black beans to olive paste to teriyaki marinade—and found only two that we liked: Worcestershire sauce and Dijon mustard.

Next we turned to the cooking method. Since turkey burgers must be well-done for safety reasons, cooking them can be a bit tricky—too high a heat and they burn before they're done; too low

and they look pale and steamed. We tried several cooking methods, from broiling to roasting, but nothing compared in quality and ease with our stovetop method. Browning the burgers in a heavy-bottomed skillet over medium heat, then cooking them, partially covered, over low heat gave us a rich-crusted burger that was cooked all the way through.

Although our generous cooking times should ensure a fully cooked burger, as an extra precaution you may want to test for doneness by sticking an instant-read thermometer through the side and into the center of a burger. The burger is done at 160 degrees.

JUICY TURKEY BURGERS

SERVES 4

Ricotta cheese can burn easily, so keep a close watch on the burgers as they cook.

1¼	pounds 93-percent lean ground turkey
½	cup whole-milk ricotta cheese
½	teaspoon salt
½	teaspoon pepper
2	teaspoons Worcestershire sauce
2	teaspoons Dijon mustard
1	tablespoon vegetable or canola oil

1. Combine the ground turkey, cheese, salt, pepper, Worcestershire sauce, and mustard in a medium bowl until blended. Divide the meat into 4 portions. Lightly toss one portion from hand to hand to form a ball, then lightly flatten the ball with your fingertips into a 1-inch-thick patty. Repeat with the remaining portions.

2. Heat the oil in a large heavy skillet (preferably cast iron or stainless steel with an aluminum core) over medium heat until very hot. Swirl the oil in the pan to coat the bottom. Add the burgers and cook over medium heat without moving them until the bottom of each is dark brown and crusted, 3 to 4 minutes. Turn the burgers over; continue to cook until the bottom is light brown but not yet crusted, 3 to 4 minutes longer. Reduce the heat to low, position the cover slightly ajar on the pan to allow steam to escape, and continue to cook for 8 to 10 minutes longer, flipping once if necessary to promote deep browning, or until the center is completely opaque yet still juicy or an instant-read thermometer inserted from the side of the burger into the center registers 160 degrees. Remove from the pan and serve immediately.

Variation
GRILLED TURKEY BURGERS
Grill the burgers over a medium fire until dark spotty brown on the bottom, 7 to 9 minutes. Turn the burgers over; continue grilling 7 to 9 minutes longer or until the bottom is dark spotty brown and the center is completely opaque or an instant-read thermometer inserted from the side of the burger registers 160 degrees. Remove from the grill and serve immediately.

Holiday Stuffed Turkey

Norman Rockwell's image of a giant, bronzed turkey packed with moist stuffing is the Thanksgiving ideal—beautiful to look at and ample enough to provide plenty of meat (both dark and white) for more than one trip to the kids' table and back. But stuffed turkeys, particularly those weighing 20 pounds or more, can be difficult to manage. It's not the huge turkey that gives us pause—it's a great way to feed a crowd—or even the stuffing, which sops up all those tasty turkey drippings; it's the combination of the two. By the time the stuffing reaches 165 degrees (the temperature recommended by the

U.S. Department of Agriculture), the breast meat is pushing 190 degrees (25 degrees higher than ideal), and moist meat is a distant memory that no amount of gravy can recall.

In an attempt to keep the temperature of the stuffing closer to that of the turkey, we tried just about everything we could think of: stuffing a cold turkey with hot stuffing, cooking the stuffed turkey in an oven bag for more even heat, shielding the turkey breast with foil, and on and on. None of these tricks worked; the stuffing just wasn't coming up to temperature as soon as the meat.

PREPARING THE TURKEY

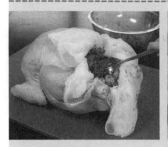

1. Line the empty cavity of the bird with a folded piece of cheesecloth, making sure that the cheesecloth reaches the end of the cavity.

2. Loosely pack the stuffing into the cheesecloth "bag" and tie with kitchen twine. Secure the turkey's legs by tucking the ankles into the pocket of skin at the tail end.

The solution (and a forehead-slapping one at that) came from the mother of one of our test cooks. Just cook the stuffed turkey until the meat is at the appropriate temperature, then remove the stuffing and finish cooking it in the oven while the turkey rests. Finally, we could bring the stuffing up to a safe temperature without overcooking the white meat. A simple solution, indeed, and one with an unexpected benefit: aside from perfectly cooked meat, this technique produced a nice crusty exterior on the stuffing.

With the stuffing's temperature issues resolved, we turned our attention to texture. Most stuffings fail on this front because they bake up wet and spongy inside the turkey—a direct by-product of a heavy hand with the liquid ingredients. After much testing, we found that we needed only 3 cups of liquid (broth was preferred over milk, water, or wine) for almost 20 cups of cubed bread—less than half the liquid called for in some recipes. Tasters preferred the slight chew of a baguette to more delicate breads, especially when it was lightly toasted in a hot oven. A simple combination of vegetables (onion and celery), eggs, and fresh and dried herbs gave the stuffing a balanced flavor, and cooking it in a bag fashioned from cheesecloth made it both tidy and easy to remove from the turkey.

To make sure everyone got a fair share, we prepared almost double the amount of stuffing that would fit in the bird (the turkey's cavity held about 12 cups) and set the excess aside while the turkey roasted. Once the turkey was finished, we combined the reserved stuffing with the stuffing from the bird (along with a liberal saucing of turkey drippings to make up for any lost flavor) and transferred it all to the oven to heat through and crisp up. Finally, with the simplest of solutions, we had found a way to make a giant stuffed turkey that was good eating.

HOLIDAY STUFFED TURKEY

SERVES 15 TO 18

Because large turkeys are prone to drying out in the oven, we highly recommend buying a frozen Butterball. These turkeys are injected with a salt solution that helps them stay moist during cooking. If you choose to roast a fresh bird, brining is the best option (see information on brining on page 311). The stuffing can be prepared a day in advance and refrigerated. When ready to stuff the turkey, transfer 12 cups of stuffing to a microwave-safe bowl, cover with plastic wrap, and microwave on high, stirring once, until warm, about 5 minutes. Proceed as directed in step 3 of the recipe.

  2 **(24-inch) loaves French baguette,
     torn into ¾-inch chunks (about 20 cups)**
 12 **tablespoons (1½ sticks) unsalted butter,
     softened**
  2 **onions, minced**
  4 **celery ribs, chopped fine**
  4 **garlic cloves, minced**

1   teaspoon dried sage

1   teaspoon dried thyme

½   cup chopped fresh parsley
    Salt and pepper

3   cups low-sodium chicken broth

4   large eggs, lightly beaten

1   (36-inch) square cheesecloth, folded into
    quarters, or 1 store-bought stuffing bag

1   (18- to 22-pound) frozen Butterball turkey,
    thawed and patted dry with paper towels
    (neck and giblets reserved for gravy,
    if desired)

1. Adjust the oven racks to the upper-middle and lower-middle positions and heat the oven to 425 degrees. Divide the bread chunks between two rimmed baking sheets and bake, tossing occasionally, until golden brown, about 15 minutes. Transfer to a large bowl. (Do not turn off the oven.)

2. Melt 8 tablespoons of the butter in a large skillet over medium-high heat. Add the onions and celery and cook until softened, about 8 minutes. Stir in the garlic, sage, thyme, parsley, 1½ teaspoons salt, and 1 teaspoon pepper and cook until fragrant, about 1 minute. Off the heat, whisk in 2 cups of the broth, then the eggs. Pour the mixture over the bread and toss until evenly coated.

3. Line the turkey cavity with the cheesecloth or stuffing bag, pack with the warm stuffing, tie the ends of the cheesecloth or bag, and tuck the turkey legs. Transfer the remaining stuffing (8 to 12 cups) to a large microwave-safe bowl. Pour the remaining 1 cup broth over the stuffing, cover with plastic wrap, and refrigerate.

4. Using oven mitts, adjust one oven rack to the lowest position and remove the other rack. Combine the remaining 4 tablespoons softened butter, 1 teaspoon salt, and 1 teaspoon pepper in a small bowl. Rub the mixture all over the turkey and position the turkey, breast side up, on a V-rack set in a large disposable aluminum pan. Set the pan on a rimmed baking sheet and roast for 1 hour. Reduce the oven temperature to 325 degrees and continue to roast until the thickest part of the breast registers 165 degrees and the thickest part of the thigh registers 175 degrees on an instant-read thermometer, 2 to 3 hours longer. Transfer the turkey to a cutting board and let rest 30 minutes, reserving the turkey drippings in the roasting pan.

5. Remove the stuffing bag from the turkey and empty the stuffing into a greased 13 by 9-inch baking dish. Microwave the reserved stuffing on high until hot, 5 to 7 minutes, then add to the stuffing in the baking dish. Pour ½ cup reserved drippings over the stuffing, cover with aluminum foil,

TAKING THE TEMPERATURE OF TURKEY

1. First, insert an instant-read thermometer between the breast and drumstick and into the thickest part of each thigh, staying away from the bone. The temperature should reach 175 degrees.

2. Next, insert the thermometer at the neck end into the breast, holding it parallel to the bird. Confirm the temperature in both sides of the bird. The breast should reach a temperature of 165 degrees.

and bake until the stuffing registers 165 degrees on an instant-read thermometer, about 15 minutes. Remove the foil and bake until the top of the stuffing is browned and crisp, 5 to 10 minutes longer. Transfer the stuffing to a platter and carve the turkey. Serve.

CARVING A TURKEY

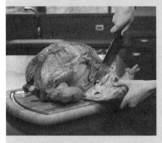

1. Slice through the skin between the breast and leg and, using your hands, pull the leg quarter down until the joint between breast and leg is exposed. Cut between the hip joint and any attached skin. Repeat with the opposite leg.

2. Remove the wings by cutting through the wing joints. Separate the thighs from the drumsticks by cutting between the joint that connects the two. Leave the drumsticks whole and slice the thigh meat off the bone.

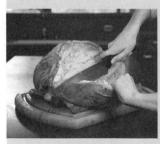

3. Remove the breast meat from the carcass by running the tip of the knife along the breastbone. Use your other hand to hold and pry meat from the bone as you cut.

4. Slice the removed breast meat crosswise into thin slices. Repeat with the other breast.

Stuffed Turkey Breast

We can't imagine Thanksgiving without a 20-pound stuffed turkey, but this recipe gets dusted off only once a year. But boneless, skinless turkey breast, now widely available in supermarkets, weighs just 3 to 4 pounds and is a top contender for a family meal: it's easily stuffed and won't leave behind a week's worth of leftovers. Being without skin, bones, or dark meat, however, this ultra-lean cut often ends up flavorless, overcooked, and utterly dry.

When it comes to flavor, most recipes go wrong by depending on a bland bread stuffing. This type of stuffing is fine for a whole bird, in which the drippings from the turkey carcass help season the stuffing, but for a boneless breast the opposite is true: the stuffing, not the turkey, must provide the flavor.

We took a more aggressive route by substituting potent vegetable- and cheese-based fillings for the plain bread stuffing. Our best attempts relied on relatively moist vegetables—mushrooms and spinach—and assertively flavored ingredients such as garlic, hard cheeses, and fresh herbs. When paired with the turkey, these concentrated stuffings seasoned the typically bland white meat from the inside out.

The stuffings remedied the lack of flavor but not the lack of moisture in the meat. The solution, we hoped, could be found in the cooking method.

Most recipes call for searing the turkey breast in a hot skillet before transferring it to the oven. This method produced a bronzed bird in record time, but searing really dried out the exterior. High-temperature roasting also produced an even brown color, but by the time the turkey was cooked to its core, the outside was, yet again, dry and stringy.

In the end, we found that the only way to guarantee juicy turkey was to keep the oven temperature at 325 degrees. The problem? Tasters were now turned off by the turkey's pallid and flavorless exterior, with some wondering if it had been poached rather than roasted.

Then one test cook suggested coating the turkey with a light sprinkling of sugar, thinking that the sugar would encourage browning. We doubted this would work in such a cool oven, but we were wrong. The sugared turkey displayed a golden exterior, but, even better, it was the tastiest bird yet! Similarly to salt, the sugar had enhanced the natural flavor of the turkey. For yet more flavor, we also sprinkled the roast with salt and a generous amount of freshly ground pepper. Our stuffed turkey breast was now as moist and flavorful as a bone-in bird—and it was a whole lot easier to manage.

STUFFED TURKEY BREAST

SERVES 6 TO 8

Before stuffing the turkey, make sure the stuffing is completely chilled. Some stores only sell boneless turkey breasts with the skin still attached; the skin can be removed easily with a paring knife. This recipe calls for one turkey breast half. Don't buy an entire breast with two lobes of meat—it's too large for this recipe. Once stuffed and tied, the turkey breast can be held in the refrigerator for up to 2 days before roasting. Or just make either stuffing in advance. Both will keep in the refrigerator for up to 3 days.

1	boneless, skinless turkey breast (3 to 4 pounds; see note above)
2	cups stuffing (recipes follow)
2	tablespoons vegetable oil
1	tablespoon sugar
2	teaspoons pepper
1	teaspoon salt

1. Adjust an oven rack to the middle position and heat the oven to 325 degrees. Butterfly the turkey by placing it smooth side down and then slicing through it horizontally to open it up like a book. Cover the turkey with plastic wrap and pound lightly with a meat mallet until about ½ inch thick. Spread the stuffing in an even layer over the turkey. Starting with the short side nearest you, roll up the turkey and tie at 1-inch intervals.

2. Rub the turkey with the oil and sprinkle evenly with the sugar, pepper, and salt. Place on a wire rack set over a rimmed baking sheet and roast, turning every 30 minutes, until the internal temperature reaches 160 degrees on an instant-read thermometer, about 2 hours. Transfer the turkey to a cutting board, cover loosely with aluminum foil, and let rest for 15 minutes. Remove the twine and cut crosswise into ½-inch slices. Serve.

MUSHROOM-MARSALA STUFFING

MAKES ABOUT 2 CUPS

To avoid flare-ups, be sure to remove the pan from the heat before adding the Marsala.

2	tablespoons unsalted butter
1	onion, minced
1	pound white mushrooms, chopped fine
2	garlic cloves, minced
2	teaspoons minced fresh thyme
¼	cup Marsala
1	cup grated Parmesan cheese
2	tablespoons chopped fresh parsley
	Salt and pepper

Melt the butter in a large skillet over medium-high heat until foaming. Add the onion and cook until softened, about 5 minutes. Reduce the heat to medium, add the mushrooms, and cook until the

STUFFING A TURKEY BREAST

   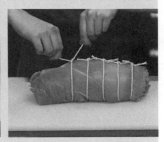

1. With the turkey smooth side down, slice into the thickest part, keeping the knife ½ inch above the cutting board and stopping ½ inch from the edge of the breast.

2. Open the cut breast like a book. Then, place a sheet of plastic wrap over the turkey and pound lightly with a meat mallet until the turkey breast is an even ½ inch in thickness overall.

3. Remove the plastic wrap and spread the stuffing evenly over the turkey, stopping ½ inch from the sides. Starting with the smaller side nearest you, roll the turkey into a tight cylinder.

4. Use butcher's twine to tie the turkey breast at 1-inch intervals. Tuck in the ends of the turkey and loop a piece of twine around the ends to keep the stuffing from falling out.

liquid has evaporated, 10 to 15 minutes. Add the garlic and thyme and cook until fragrant, 30 seconds. Off the heat, stir in the Marsala. Return to the heat and cook until the mushrooms are dry and golden brown, about 5 minutes. Remove from the heat and cool for 10 minutes. Stir in the Parmesan, parsley, and salt and pepper to taste. Refrigerate until ready to use.

LEMONY SPINACH AND FONTINA STUFFING

MAKES ABOUT 2 CUPS

Soggy spinach can make for a watery filling, so wring out excess moisture in a kitchen towel or see our tip on page 19.

2 tablespoons extra-virgin olive oil

1 onion, minced

1 (10-ounce) box frozen spinach, thawed, squeezed dry, and chopped

3 garlic cloves, minced

¼ teaspoon grated fresh lemon zest

2 cups shredded fontina cheese
   Salt and pepper

Heat the oil in a large skillet over medium-high heat until shimmering. Add the onion and cook until softened, about 5 minutes. Stir in the spinach, garlic, and zest and cook until fragrant, 30 seconds. Remove from the heat and cool for 10 minutes. Stir in the fontina and salt and pepper to taste. Refrigerate until ready to use.

CHAPTER ELEVEN

Beef and Pork

BEEF AND PORK

Chicken-Fried Steak

Although this truck-stop favorite often gets a bad rap, chicken-fried steak can be delicious when cooked just right. When cooked wrong, the dry, rubbery steaks snap back with each bite and are coated in a damp, pale breading and topped with a bland, pasty white sauce. When cooked well, however, thin cutlets of beef are breaded and fried until crisp and golden brown. The creamy gravy that accompanies the steaks is well seasoned and not too thick.

The first question we encountered on the road to good chicken-fried steak was what type of steak to use. By design, chicken-frying a steak is a technique used with only the cheapest of cuts. We tested cube, Swiss, top round, bottom round, eye round, chuck, and top sirloin steaks and came up with one winner: the cube steak was our favorite. This steak is lean yet tender; most of the other cuts tested were either fatty or difficult to chew.

What really makes chicken-fried steak great is the coating and subsequent frying. But what kind of coating is best? To find out, we tested straight flour against various contenders, including cornflakes, Melba toast, cornmeal, matzo crumbs, ground saltines, and panko (Japanese bread crumbs). Straight flour was light and clung well to the steak but was simply too delicate for the toothsome meat and cream gravy. Cornflakes and Melba toast both burned and became tough, and the grittiness of cornmeal was simply out of place. Matzo, saltines, and panko all tasted great but quickly grew soggy under the rich cream gravy.

We figured our single-breading technique might be to blame and decided to try double (or bound) breading. With single breading, meat is dipped into egg and then into flour, whereas double breading starts off with an initial dip into flour, then into egg, and again into flour (or into a coating such as those we tried with the steak). In side-by-side tests, we were surprised to discover that single breading was actually messier than double. When initially dipped in flour, the meat becomes dry and talcum-smooth, allowing the egg to cling evenly to the surface. The double breading also offered a more substantial base coat on the meat that didn't become overly thick or tough. Seasoned flour and a double-breading technique yielded a much improved crust.

Although this double breading was far superior to any other breading so far, we were still left wanting a heartier and crunchier crust. We wondered if we could bolster the egg wash with some buttermilk, baking soda, and baking powder, something that we knew worked well with fried chicken. Sure enough, these ingredients turned the egg wash into a thick, foamy concoction. This created a wet yet airy layer into which both layers of flour were able to stick and hydrate. This wet-looking, skin-like coating fried up to an impressive dark mahogany color with a resilient texture that didn't weaken under the gravy.

Equally important to the crust is the cream gravy made from the fried drippings. Not wanting to waste any time while the fried steaks were kept warm in the oven, we found it easy to strain the small amount of hot oil used to fry the steaks right away. Adding the strained bits of deep-fried crumbs back to the Dutch oven, we were ready to make gravy. In most recipes the drippings are simmered with some milk and thickened with flour. To avoid making a floury-tasting sauce, we decided to cook the flour in the fat (that is, make a roux) and then add the milk, along with a splash of chicken broth. We found this technique to be quick and easy, and it produced an authentic-tasting sauce. Onions and cayenne pepper are traditional seasonings for the gravy, but tasters also liked small additions of thyme and garlic (neither of which is authentic). Topped with the light, well-seasoned gravy, this chicken-fried steak is the best any trucker has ever tasted.

CHICKEN-FRIED STEAK

SERVES 6

Getting the initial oil temperature to 375 degrees is key to the success of this recipe. A clip-on candy/deep-fry thermometer is perfect for checking the temperature. If your Dutch oven measures 11 inches across (as ours does), you will need to fry the steaks in two batches.

STEAK

3	cups all-purpose flour
	Salt and pepper
1/8	teaspoon cayenne pepper
1	large egg
1	teaspoon baking powder
1/2	teaspoon baking soda
1	cup buttermilk
6	cube steaks (about 5 ounces each), pounded to 1/3-inch thickness
4–5	cups peanut oil

GRAVY

1	onion, minced
1/8	teaspoon dried thyme
2	garlic cloves, minced
3	tablespoons all-purpose flour
1/2	cup low-sodium chicken broth
2	cups whole milk
3/4	teaspoon salt
1/4	teaspoon pepper
	Pinch cayenne pepper

1. FOR THE STEAK: Combine the flour, 5 teaspoons salt, 1 teaspoon pepper, and the cayenne in a large shallow dish. In a second large shallow dish, beat the egg with the baking powder and baking soda; stir in the buttermilk (the mixture will bubble and foam).

2. Set a wire rack over a rimmed baking sheet. Pat the steaks dry with paper towels and sprinkle each side with salt and pepper. Drop the steaks into the seasoned flour and shake the dish to coat. Shake the excess flour from each steak, then, using tongs, dip the steaks into the egg mixture, turning to coat well and allowing the excess to drip off. Coat the steaks with flour again, shake off the excess, and place them on the wire rack.

3. Adjust an oven rack to the middle position. Set a second wire rack over a second rimmed baking sheet and place on the oven rack; heat the oven to 200 degrees. Line a large plate with a double layer of paper towels. Meanwhile, heat 1 inch of oil in a large Dutch oven over medium-high heat to 375 degrees. Place 3 steaks in the oil and fry, turning once, until deep golden brown on each side, about 5 minutes (the oil temperature will drop to around 335 degrees). Transfer the steaks to the paper towel–lined plate to drain, then transfer them to the wire rack in the oven. Bring the oil back to 375 degrees and repeat the cooking and draining process (use fresh paper towels) with the remaining 3 steaks.

4. FOR THE GRAVY: Carefully pour the hot oil through a fine-mesh strainer into a clean pot. Add the browned bits from the strainer along with 2 tablespoons of the frying oil to the now-empty Dutch oven. Turn the heat to medium, add the onion and thyme, and cook until the onion has softened and begins to brown, 4 to 5 minutes. Add the garlic and cook until aromatic, about 30 seconds. Add the flour to the pan and stir until well combined, about 1 minute. Whisk in the broth, scraping any browned bits off the bottom of the pan. Whisk in the milk, salt, pepper, and cayenne; bring to a simmer over medium-high heat. Cook until thickened (the gravy should have a loose consistency—it will thicken slightly as it cools), about 5 minutes.

5. Transfer the chicken-fried steaks to individual plates. Spoon a generous amount of gravy over each steak. Serve immediately, passing any remaining gravy in a small bowl.

Broiled Steaks

We usually rely on a red-hot skillet or grill for putting a crusty sear on steaks, but we wondered if an oven broiler—which throws out a ton of heat—could do the job just as well. The promise of a perfectly cooked steak without a greasy stovetop or a trip outside to the grill could be very appealing.

We adjusted our oven rack to the top position, preheated the broiler on high, and threw a couple of strip steaks on the broiler pan. The results weren't pretty. Though some of the moisture and fat from the steaks drained through the broiler-pan slits, much of it sat around the steaks, which caused the meat to steam and turn gray, with absolutely no char or crust. And if that wasn't bad enough, the drippings that made their way through the pan burned, filling the test kitchen with smoke.

Getting some color on the steaks was our first order of business. We quickly discovered that the broiler pan—not the broiler itself—was causing most of the problems. Because broiler pans are only about an inch tall, they don't bring steaks close enough to the broiler element to get a proper sear, even on the top oven rack. To remedy this, we brought in a 3-inch-deep disposable aluminum roasting pan, moved the oven rack down a notch, and set the steaks on a wire rack placed over the pan. This brought the meat closer to the heat, where it could acquire a good sear. The wire rack (which is more porous than the broiler-pan rack) also allowed surface moisture to immediately drain away.

Cooking the steaks evenly was another problem. Steaks that went directly from the refrigerator to the broiler had charred exteriors before the centers were done, no matter how many times we flipped them. Letting the steaks sit at room temperature for an hour before cooking helped, but it took too long. Instead, we started the steaks in a moderate oven to take the chill off. We removed them after 6 to 10 minutes, let them rest while the broiler heated, then cooked them as before. This method produced evenly cooked meat every time.

Only one problem remained: the smoke. The fat that was cooking out of the steaks was still burning on the bottom of the pan. To put a stop to the smoke, we tried adding water to the pan, but the steam it produced softened the crust we had worked so hard to create. We tried putting bread in the pan to absorb the grease before it had a chance to burn, but that idea (and the bread) went up in smoke. We had much better results when we covered the bottom of the pan with salt, which soaked up the grease and greatly minimized the smoke. Finally, we had crusty, charred steaks—and a good reason to use our broiler a lot more often.

BROILER PREP

Since oven-rack positioning varies greatly from model to model, we suggest you ensure correct positioning with a dry run before turning on your oven.

1. COLD SETUP: Before preheating your oven and with your oven racks adjusted to the upper-middle and lower-middle positions, place a wire rack on top of a 3-inch-deep disposable aluminum pan and place it on the upper-middle rack. Place the steaks on top of the rack and use a ruler to measure the distance between the top of the steaks and the heating element of the broiler. For optimal searing, there should be ½ to 1 inch of space.

2. MEASURE AND ADJUST: If there is more than 1 inch of space, here are some ways to close the gap. Elevate the aluminum pan by placing it on an inverted rimmed baking sheet; use a deeper-sided disposable aluminum pan; or stack multiple aluminum pans inside one another. If there's less than ½ inch of space, adjust the oven rack or use a shallower pan.

BROILED STEAKS

SERVES 4

To minimize smoking, be sure to trim as much exterior fat and gristle as possible from the steaks before cooking. Try to purchase steaks of a similar size and shape for this recipe. If you like your steaks well-done, continue cooking and flipping as directed in step 3 until the steaks reach the desired internal temperature.

- 4 tablespoons unsalted butter, softened
- 1 teaspoon minced fresh thyme
- 1 teaspoon Dijon mustard
  Salt and pepper
- 4 strip steaks, rib-eye steaks, or tenderloin steaks, 1 to 2 inches thick, trimmed (see note above)

1. Adjust the oven racks to the upper-middle and lower-middle positions and heat the oven to 375 degrees. Beat the butter, thyme, mustard, ¼ teaspoon salt, and ¼ teaspoon pepper in a bowl and refrigerate.

2. Spread 2 cups salt over the bottom of a 3-inch-deep disposable aluminum pan. Pat the steaks dry with paper towels, season with salt and pepper, and transfer to a wire rack. Set the rack over the aluminum pan and transfer to the lower oven rack. Cook for 6 to 10 minutes (see the "Broiling Steaks" chart, "Prebake" column), then remove the pan from the oven. Flip the steaks, pat dry with paper towels, and let rest for 10 minutes.

3. Heat the broiler. Transfer the pan to the upper oven rack and broil the steaks, flipping them every 2 to 4 minutes (see the "Broiling Steaks" chart, "Broil" column), until the meat registers 125 to 130 degrees (for medium-rare) on an instant-read thermometer, 6 to 16 minutes. Transfer the steaks to a platter, top with the reserved butter mixture, and tent with aluminum foil. Let rest for 5 minutes. Serve.

TEST KITCHEN SHORTCUT

Gauging the Temperature of Your Broiler: It's good to know if your broiler runs relatively hot, average, or cold. This information allows you to adjust the cooking time for this recipe (and others) accordingly. To see how your broiler stacks up, heat it on high and place a slice of white sandwich bread directly under the heating element on an oven rack set at the upper-middle position. If the bread toasts to golden brown in 30 seconds or less, your broiler runs very hot, and you will need to reduce the cooking time by a minute or two. If the bread toasts perfectly in 1 minute, your broiler runs about average. If the bread takes 2 minutes or longer to toast, your broiler runs cool and you may need to increase the cooking time by a minute or two.

BROILING STEAKS

The first step to perfectly broiled steaks is knowing exactly how thick your steaks are. Using a ruler, measure each steak and then follow the guidelines below.

STEAK THICKNESS	PREBAKE	BROIL
1 inch	6 minutes	Turn steaks every 2 minutes
1½ inches	8 minutes	Turn steaks every 3 minutes
2 inches	10 minutes	Turn steaks every 4 minutes

Pepper Steak

Some dishes are meant to stay buried deep in our past, but pepper steak is not one of them. Not to be confused with steak au poivre, the bistro classic with the peppercorn coating, pepper steak marries beef with bell peppers, onions, and tomatoes in a savory brown sauce that includes soy sauce. This dish emerged in the early 1960s, just as Americans began to take an interest in Asian cooking. With recognizably American ingredients, it gave many of us our first taste of "Chinese" food. We thought this utterly simple dish was ready for a revival.

Too bad most of the recipes we tried yielded tough meat and bitter peppers. Stir-frying the beef and getting it out of the pan to build the sauce was key; in older recipes the meat is just left in the pan to simmer its way to toughness. Flank steak worked well, but tasters preferred the slightly richer flavor of sirloin steak tips.

Although most vegetables benefit from a quick stir-fry to retain their crunch, tasters rejected the strong bitter flavor of undercooked green peppers. After stir-frying the peppers until lightly browned, we added a little beef broth to the skillet and put the lid on. After 2 minutes, the peppers were tender and their flavor was less harsh and metallic, but they still had a bitter edge. Replacing some of the green peppers with red peppers solved the bitterness problem and improved the appearance of the dish as well.

For the sauce, we used a base of beef broth and sherry thickened with a little cornstarch. This gave the sauce a perfect consistency and sheen. The last step was to warm the final traditional ingredient, diced canned tomatoes, in the sauce.

PEPPER STEAK

SERVES 4

Serve the pepper steak over buttered egg noodles or rice.

2	tablespoons soy sauce
1	pound sirloin steak tips, sliced very thin against the grain
1	cup plus 2 tablespoons low-sodium beef broth
2	tablespoons dry sherry
4	teaspoons cornstarch
2	tablespoons vegetable oil
1	red bell pepper, sliced thin
1	green bell pepper, sliced thin
1	onion, halved and sliced thin
3	garlic cloves, minced
½	cup canned diced tomatoes, drained
	Salt and pepper

1. Toss the soy sauce and steak in a medium bowl. Cover with plastic wrap and refrigerate while preparing the other ingredients. Whisk 1 cup of the beef broth, the sherry, and cornstarch together in a medium bowl.

2. Heat 2 teaspoons of the oil in a large nonstick skillet over medium-high heat until shimmering. Add half of the beef mixture and cook, turning once, until browned at the edges, about 2 minutes. Transfer to a clean plate. Add 2 teaspoons more oil to the pan and repeat with the remaining beef mixture.

3. Add the remaining 2 teaspoons oil to the now-empty pan and heat until shimmering. Add the peppers, onion, and garlic and cook until just beginning to brown, about 4 minutes. Add the remaining 2 tablespoons broth, reduce the heat to low, cover, and cook until the peppers are soft, about 2 minutes.

4. Return the beef to the pan along with the cornstarch mixture. Increase the heat to high and simmer until the sauce is thickened, about 2 minutes. Stir in the tomatoes and season with salt and pepper to taste. Serve immediately, passing extra soy sauce at the table.

SHOPPING WITH THE TEST KITCHEN

Steak Knives: Our experience with steak knives has led us to two conclusions. First, although top dollar may buy top quality, there are reasonably priced knives that perform quite well. Second, we found that serrated edges actually make jagged tears in the beef and are unnecessary if your straight-edged knife is sharp. With that in mind, we tested seven new sets of relatively inexpensive steak knives. Our favorite was the exceptionally sharp and nimble Forschner Rosewood Straight Edge Steak Knife ($79.95 for a set of six). This super-sharp steak knife made quick work of even tough steaks. We also like the sleek and sturdy Cuisinart CA4 Steak Knife ($29.95 for a set of four), which is quite a bargain.

California Barbecued Tri-Tip

In California's Santa Maria Valley they grill tri-tip, a large, boomerang-shaped cut of beef from the bottom sirloin, over red oak embers until it's lightly charred on the outside and rosy on the interior. Unlike most other styles of barbecue, in which the meat is slathered with sauce, Santa Maria tri-tip is seasoned with only salt, pepper, garlic, and the sweet smoke of the grill. It's sliced thin and served with tangy barbecued beans, fresh salsa, and buttered French bread.

Most of the recipes we found for California tri-tip were loaded with problems. Whereas other types of barbecue utilize indirect heat, long cooking

times, and low temperatures, tri-tip recipes call for the meat to be grilled directly over high heat. But grilling a 2-pound, 3-inch-thick cut of meat over a hot fire consistently produced a charred exterior and a very rare center. In addition to the cooking issue, the recipes we tried all left us with overly smoky meat, with nary a hint of garlic flavor.

Tri-tip is usually referred to as a steak, but at this size it needs to be cooked like a roast. Following the test kitchen's method for grilling large cuts, we pushed all the coals to one side of the grill to create a hot cooking zone and a cooler one. This way we could sear the tri-tip over the hot fire and then finish it slowly on the cooler side, leaving it with a flavorful char and a perfectly cooked interior.

For the smoke flavor, we knew from past experience that a handful of soaked wood chips would be plenty; what we didn't anticipate was that searing the tri-tip directly above the smoldering wood chips would leave it tasting like the inside of a chimney. To lessen the impact of the smoke, we held off on the wood chips until after we'd seared the meat and moved it to the cool part of the grill. Doing this allowed the smoke to dissipate slightly before it contacted the meat, perfuming—but not overpowering—the tri-tip with a subtle smoke flavor.

When it comes to seasoning, most recipes rely on garlic salt rather than fresh garlic. But if we added too much garlic salt, it scorched and turned bitter on the grill; if we cut back on the garlic salt, the meat was under-seasoned. We wondered if a marinade with fresh garlic might help infuse the meat with garlic flavor. We made a paste with minced garlic, olive oil, and salt and rubbed it over the tri-tip, leaving it to marinate for just an hour. From here, we wiped off the garlic and oil (the garlic burned if left on the meat), sprinkled the tri-tip with a bit of garlic salt and pepper, and set it on the grill. The double dose of garlic left the exterior of the meat richly seasoned, but the interior of this thick cut of meat was still slightly bland. We solved this problem by pricking the roast with a fork before we applied the marinade; this ensured that the salty garlic paste would penetrate deep into the interior to thoroughly season this hefty cut.

With its beefy, garlicky, and subtly smoky flavor, California barbecued tri-tip is nothing like the barbecue we grew up eating; looks like we've got some catching up to do.

SLICING BOTTOM ROUND

If you can't find tri-tip for our California Barbecued Tri-Tip, substitute bottom round. Because bottom round can be tough, thinly slice the steak on a 45-degree angle, which will dramatically reduce the chewiness.

CALIFORNIA BARBECUED TRI-TIP

SERVES 4 TO 6

If you can't find tri-tip, bottom round is an acceptable alternative (see below for tips on preparing bottom round). The traditional accompaniments to tri-tip are Santa Maria Salsa (page 326) and California Barbecued Beans (page 124).

1	tri-tip roast (about 2 pounds), trimmed (see note above)
6	garlic cloves, minced
2	tablespoons olive oil
¾	teaspoon salt
2	cups wood chips, preferably oak, soaked for 15 minutes in a bowl of water to cover and drained
1	teaspoon pepper
¾	teaspoon garlic salt

1. Pat the roast dry with paper towels. Using a fork, prick the roast about 20 times on each side. Combine the garlic, oil, and salt and rub over the roast. Cover with plastic wrap and refrigerate for 1 hour, or up to 24 hours.

2. Open the bottom vent of the grill. Light a large chimney starter filled with charcoal briquettes (about 100) and burn until the charcoal is covered with a fine gray ash. Spread the coals in an even layer over one half of the grill. Set the cooking grate in place and heat the grill, covered, with the lid vent completely open, for 5 minutes. (For a gas grill, seal the wood chips in a foil packet, cut vent holes in the top [see page 326], and place the packet on the primary burner. Turn all the burners to high, cover the grill, and heat until the wood chips begin to smoke heavily, about 15 minutes.) Scrape and oil the cooking grate.

3. Using paper towels, wipe the garlic paste off the roast. Rub the pepper and garlic salt all over the meat. Grill directly over the coals until well

After spreading the soaked, drained wood chips in the center of a 15 by 12-inch piece of heavy-duty aluminum foil, fold the foil to seal the edges of the packet, then cut 3 or 4 slits to allow smoke to escape.

browned, about 5 minutes per side. (If using a gas grill, place the roast on the side of the grate opposite the primary burner and grill, covered, as directed.) Carefully remove the roast and cooking grate from the grill and scatter the wood chips over the coals. Replace the cooking grate and arrange the roast on the cooler side of the grill. Cover, positioning the lid vent directly over the meat, and cook until the roast registers about 130 degrees (for medium-rare) on an instant-read thermometer, about 20 minutes. (If using a gas grill, leave the primary burner on high and turn off the other burner[s] and grill as directed.) Transfer the meat to a cutting board, tent loosely with aluminum foil, and let rest for 20 minutes. Slice thinly across the grain. Serve.

Santa Maria Salsa

In Santa Maria, the home of California barbecued tri-tip, the preferred barbecued sauce is a simple, chunky salsa made with tomatoes, chiles, celery, dried oregano, and a dash of Worcestershire. At first glance, the ingredients may seem more suited to a Bloody Mary than to barbecue, but the crunchy texture of the celery and the complex, almost meaty flavor of the Worcestershire prove to be a natural match for the tender, smoky tri-tip.

SANTA MARIA SALSA

MAKES ABOUT 4 CUPS

The distinct texture of each ingredient is part of this salsa's identity and appeal, so we don't recommend using a food processor.

- 2 pounds ripe tomatoes, cored and chopped
- 2 teaspoons salt
- 2 jalapeño chiles, chopped fine
- 1 red onion, minced
- 1 celery rib, chopped fine
- 1 garlic clove, minced
- ¼ cup fresh lime juice (2 limes)
- ¼ cup chopped fresh cilantro
- ⅛ teaspoon dried oregano
- ⅛ teaspoon Worcestershire sauce

1. Place the tomatoes in a strainer set over a bowl and sprinkle with the salt; drain for 30 minutes. Discard the liquid. Meanwhile, combine the remaining ingredients in a large bowl.

2. Add the drained tomatoes to the jalapeño mixture and toss to combine. Cover with plastic wrap and let stand at room temperature for 1 hour before serving. (The salsa can be refrigerated for up to 2 days.)

Salisbury Steak

It's hard to imagine that chopped steak could be considered health food, but that's just what Dr. James Henry Salisbury had in mind when he invented his eponymous dish as a "meat cure" for wounded and ill Civil War soldiers (who were instructed to eat it three times a day—with no vegetables allowed). Some sixty years later, during the period of World War I food rations, restaurateurs ground up their lean beef scraps, shaped them into patties, dressed the cooked patties with a rich mushroom cream sauce, and called it Salisbury steak. Most of us knew Salisbury steak only from the cafeteria lunch line and the frozen-food section, but we wanted to make a version worthy of its storied past.

We gathered up several modern recipes and headed to the test kitchen. Most of them featured fatty ground beef drowning in a weak, gray mushroom sauce—tasters felt these versions were more ailment than cure. We decided to use 90-percent lean ground beef. But because Salisbury steak is cooked to well-done, the lean meat needed special handling to keep the patties from becoming dry and tough. The patties are typically sautéed until well-done, removed from the pan while the sauce is made, and then submerged in the simmering sauce to absorb flavor. This technique made the beef tough; quickly browning the patties on both sides (rather than cooking them through) worked much better. We slid the browned patties back into the skillet to gently simmer and finish cooking in the sauce.

Our "steaks" were more tender now, but not tender enough. We tried adding a panade (bread and milk mixed together) to the meat; this did help keep the patties tender, but it also made them taste too much like meat loaf. On a lark, we tried adding the mashed potatoes we had seen in one recipe and were surprised when the spuds gave the meat a silky texture without imparting potato flavor. Wondering if dehydrated potato flakes (instant mashed potatoes) might save a little time (since we couldn't really taste them anyway), we mixed some flakes and milk into the raw meat. These patties were tender and moist, and they held together well.

Most modern recipes call for a bland sauce made of mushrooms, onions, and beef broth, but we wanted to bring richness back to this dish. After sautéing the mushrooms and onions, we added tomato paste for deeper flavor and body. To further enrich the sauce, we tried adding sherry, red wine, white wine, and port. The first three were fine, but port provided the best depth of color and flavor.

Now we had tender and perfectly cooked patties that were infused with great mushroom flavor. With this recipe, you can forget the freezer and enjoy Salisbury steak as it was meant to be.

SALISBURY STEAK

SERVES 4

Tawny port or dry sherry can be substituted for the ruby port.

½	cup whole or low-fat milk
7	tablespoons instant potato flakes (not potato granules)
1	pound 90-percent lean ground beef
	Salt and pepper
4	tablespoons unsalted butter
1	onion, halved and sliced thin
1	pound white mushrooms, sliced thin
1	tablespoon tomato paste
2	tablespoons all-purpose flour
1¾	cups low-sodium beef broth
¼	cup ruby port (see note above)

1. Whisk the milk and potato flakes together in a large bowl. Add the beef, ½ teaspoon salt, and ½ teaspoon pepper and knead until combined. Using wet hands to prevent sticking, shape the mixture into four ½-inch-thick oval patties and transfer them to a parchment-lined plate. Refrigerate for 30 minutes, or up to 4 hours.

2. Melt 1 tablespoon of the butter in a large nonstick skillet over medium-high heat. Cook the patties until well browned, about 5 minutes per side. Transfer to a plate.

3. Add the onion and remaining 3 tablespoons butter to the now-empty empty skillet and cook until the onion is softened, about 5 minutes. Add the mushrooms and ½ teaspoon salt and cook until the liquid has evaporated, 5 to 7 minutes. Stir in the tomato paste and flour and cook until browned, about 2 minutes. Slowly stir in the broth and port and bring to a simmer. Return the patties to the skillet, cover, and simmer over medium-low heat until cooked through, 12 to 15 minutes. Season the sauce with salt and pepper to taste. Serve.

Pot Roast

A good pot roast by definition entails the transformation of a tough (read cheap), nearly unpalatable cut of meat into a tender, rich, flavorful main course by means of a slow, moist cooking process called braising. It should not be sliceable; rather, the tension of a stern gaze should be enough to break it apart. Nor should it be pink or rosy in the middle—save that for prime rib or steak.

The meat for pot roast should be well marbled with fat and connective tissue to provide the dish with the necessary flavor and moisture. Recipes typically call for roasts from the sirloin (or rump), round (leg), or chuck (shoulder). When all was said and done, we found that the chuck cuts cooked up most tender.

Next, it was time to find out what kind of liquid and how much was needed to best cook the roast and supply a good sauce. Using water as the braising medium, we started with a modest ¼ cup, as suggested in a few recipes. This produced a roast that was unacceptably fibrous, even after hours of cooking. After increasing the amount of liquid incrementally, we found that the moistest meat was produced when we added liquid halfway up the sides of the roast (depending on the cut, this amount could be between 2 and 4 cups). The greater amount of liquid also accelerated the cooking process, shaving nearly an hour off the cooking time needed for a roast cooked in just ¼ cup of liquid. Naively assuming that more is always better, we continued to increase the amount of water, but to no better effect. We also found that

it was necessary to cover the Dutch oven with a piece of aluminum foil before placing the lid on top. The added seal of the foil kept the liquid from escaping (in the form of steam) through the loose-fitting lid and eliminated any need to add more liquid to the pot.

Next we tested different liquids, hoping to add flavor to the roast and sauce. Along with our old standby, water, we tested red wine, low-sodium chicken broth, and low-sodium beef broth. Red wine had the most startling effect on the meat, penetrating it with a potent flavor that most tasters agreed was "good, but not traditional pot roast." However, tasters did like the flavor of a little red wine added to the sauce after the pot roast was removed from the pan. Each of the broths on its own failed to win tasters over completely—the chicken broth was rich but gave the dish a characteristic poultry flavor, and the beef broth tasted sour when added solo. In the end, we found that an equal amount of each did the job, the beef broth boosting the depth of flavor and the chicken broth tempering any sourness.

Trying to boost the flavor of the sauce even more, we added the basic vegetables—carrot, celery, onion, and garlic—to the pot as the meat braised. Unfortunately, the addition of raw vegetables made the pot roast taste more like a vegetable stew. We then tried sautéing them until golden brown and found that the caramelized flavor of the vegetables added another layer of flavor to the sauce.

Some recipes specify thickening the sauce with a mixture of equal parts butter and flour (beurre manié); others use a slurry of cornstarch mixed with a little braising liquid. Both techniques made the sauce more gravy-like than we preferred, and we didn't care for the dilution of flavor. We chose to remove the roast from the pot, then reduce the liquid over high heat until the flavors were well concentrated and the texture more substantial.

As for the best cooking method for pot roast, there are two schools of thought: on the stove or in the oven. After a few rounds of stovetop cooking, we felt that it was too difficult to maintain a steady, low temperature, so we began the pot roast in the oven, starting out at 250 degrees. This method required no supervision, just a turn of the meat every 30 to 40 minutes to ensure even cooking. We then tested higher temperatures to reduce the cooking time. Heat levels above 350 degrees boiled the meat to a stringy, dry texture because the exterior of the roast overcooked before the interior was cooked and tender. The magic temperature turned out to be 300 degrees—enough heat to keep the meat at a low simmer, but high enough to shave a few more minutes off the cooking time.

As noted above, pot roast is well-done meat—meat cooked to an internal temperature above 165 degrees. Up to this point, we were bringing the meat to an internal temperature of 200 to 210 degrees, the point at which the fat and connective tissue begin to melt. In a 300-degree oven, the roast came up to that temperature in a neat 2½ hours, certainly by no means a quick meal but still a relatively short time in which to cook a pot roast. But we still had not achieved our goal of fall-apart tenderness.

Then, we stumbled onto an unexpected breakthrough. Some days before, we had forgotten to remove one of the roasts from the oven, allowing it to cook an hour longer than we intended. Racing to the kitchen with our instant-read thermometer, we found the internal temperature of the roast was still 210 degrees, but the meat had a substantially different appearance and texture. The roast was so tender that it was starting to separate along its muscle lines. A fork poked into the meat met with no resistance and nearly disappeared into the flesh. We took the roast out of the pot and "sliced" into it. Nearly all the fat and connective tissue had dissolved into the meat, giving each bite a soft, silky texture and rich, succulent flavor. We "overcooked" several more roasts. Each roast had the same great texture. The conclusion? Not only do you have to cook pot roast until it reaches 210 degrees internally, but the meat has to

remain at that temperature for a full hour. In other words, cook the pot roast until it's done—and then keep on cooking!

SIMPLE POT ROAST

SERVES 6 TO 8

Our favorite cut for pot roast is a chuck-eye roast. Most markets sell this roast with kitchen twine tied around the center; if necessary, do this yourself. Seven-bone and top blade roasts are also good choices for this recipe. Remember to add enough water to come only halfway up the sides of these thinner roasts, and begin checking for doneness after 2 hours. If using a top blade roast, tie it before cooking to keep it from falling apart. Mashed or boiled potatoes are a good accompaniment.

1	boneless chuck-eye roast (about 3½ pounds; see note above), patted dry with paper towels
	Salt and pepper
2	tablespoons vegetable oil
1	onion, chopped
1	carrot, chopped
1	celery rib, chopped
2	garlic cloves, minced
2	teaspoons sugar
1	cup low-sodium chicken broth
1	cup low-sodium beef broth
1	sprig fresh thyme
1–1½	cups water
¼	cup dry red wine

1. Adjust an oven rack to the middle position and heat the oven to 300 degrees. Sprinkle the roast generously with salt and pepper.

2. Heat the oil in a large ovenproof Dutch oven over medium-high heat until shimmering but not smoking. Brown the roast thoroughly on all sides, reducing the heat if the fat begins to smoke, 8 to 10 minutes. Transfer the roast to a large plate; set aside.

3. Reduce the heat to medium; add the onion, carrot, and celery to the pot and cook, stirring occasionally, until beginning to brown, 6 to 8 minutes. Add the garlic and sugar; cook until fragrant, about 30 seconds. Add the broths and thyme, scraping the pan bottom with a wooden spoon to loosen the browned bits. Return the roast and any accumulated juices on the plate to the pot; add enough water to come halfway up the sides of the roast. Cover the pot with a sheet of aluminum foil and then place the lid on top. Bring the liquid to a simmer over medium heat, and transfer the pot to the oven. Cook, turning the roast every 30 minutes, until fully tender and a meat fork or sharp knife slips easily in and out of the meat, 3½ to 4 hours.

4. Transfer the roast to a carving board; tent with aluminum foil to keep warm. Allow the liquid in the pot to settle for about 5 minutes, then use a wide spoon to skim the fat off the surface; discard the thyme sprig. Boil over high heat until reduced to about 1½ cups, about 8 minutes. Add the wine and reduce to 1½ cups, about 2 minutes. Season with salt and pepper to taste.

5. Using a chef's or carving knife, cut the meat into ½-inch slices, or pull it apart into large pieces; transfer the meat to a warmed serving platter and pour about ½ cup of the sauce over the meat. Serve, passing the remaining sauce separately.

Variation
POT ROAST WITH ROOT VEGETABLES
In this variation, carrots, potatoes, and parsnips are added near the end of cooking to make a complete meal.

1. In step 3, when the roast is almost tender (a sharp knife should meet little resistance), transfer the roast to a cutting board. Pour the braising liquid through a mesh strainer and discard the

solids. Return the liquid to the now-empty pot and let it settle for 5 minutes; use a wide spoon to skim the fat off the surface. Return the roast to the liquid and add 1½ pounds (about 8 medium) carrots, peeled and cut into ½-inch slices (about 3 cups), 1½ pounds small red potatoes, halved if larger than 1½ inches in diameter (about 5 cups), and 1 pound (about 5 large) parsnips, peeled and cut into ½-inch slices (about 3 cups), submerging them in the liquid. Return the pot to the oven and continue to cook until the vegetables are almost tender, 20 to 30 minutes.

2. Transfer the roast to a carving board; tent with aluminum foil to keep warm. Add the wine and salt and pepper to taste to the pot; boil over high heat until the vegetables are fully tender, 5 to 10 minutes. With a slotted spoon, transfer the vegetables to a warmed serving bowl or platter. Using a chef's or carving knife, cut the meat into ½-inch slices or pull it apart into large pieces; transfer to the bowl or platter and pour about ½ cup of the sauce over the meat and vegetables. Serve, passing the remaining sauce separately.

Sunday-Best Garlic Roast Beef

Good cooks know that tenderloin and prime rib require very little, other than a nice fat bank account. Preparing a cheaper cut is another matter. These roasts tend to have more gristle, more connective tissue, and flavors that are often sour or liver-y.

For the cut of meat for this recipe, we chose the inexpensive, widely available top sirloin. This hefty cut was an all-around crowd pleaser: tender, juicy, and beefy-tasting.

Our test kitchen has found that large beef roasts cook more evenly at low temperatures. In a hot

1. Insert toasted slivers of garlic into slits cut into the roast. Then combine minced garlic with herbs and salt and rub the mixture over the roast and refrigerate at least 4 hours.

2. Poach halved garlic cloves and herbs in oil. Strain and mash the garlic into a paste, then spread the garlic paste over the browned roast.

oven, the outer portions of the roast tend to overcook by the time the middle is done. However, roasting at a low temperature allows for little flavor development on the exterior of the roast. To ensure a nicely browned exterior, the roast must first be seared.

To simplify matters, we chose not to sear the meat on the stovetop but in a hot oven, turning down the heat once the outside browned. Our first try didn't produce enough browning, though, and we thought it might be the stainless steel pan we were using. Taking a hint from baking—where darker nonstick surfaces produce darker cakes because of better heat absorption—we tried a nonstick roasting pan, and it did a much better job. (You can use a broiler pan in a pinch.)

To punch up the flavor of our roast, we turned to garlic. Tests with slivers of raw garlic inserted into the meat were unsuccessful, as the garlic was harsh-tasting. Toasting unpeeled garlic cloves in a skillet took the nasty bite out of them. For another layer of garlic flavor, we rubbed the meat with a garlic-salt mixture and then refrigerated it. The flavor improved after 4 hours, but we got the best

results when we let the roast rest overnight. To prevent the rub from burning during the high initial heat of searing, we simply wiped it off before searing.

Things were going well, but we still wanted a touch more flavor, and so we applied a cooked garlic paste to the meat after searing it.

In the end, it was the triple garlic whammy that won over the test kitchen. We think this roast can compete with fancy, high-priced prime rib any day of the year.

SUNDAY-BEST GARLIC ROAST BEEF

SERVES 6 TO 8

Look for a top sirloin roast that has a thick, substantial fat cap still attached. The rendered fat will help to keep the roast moist. When making the jus, taste the reduced broth before adding any of the accumulated meat juices from the roast. The meat juices are well seasoned and may make the jus too salty. A heavy-duty roasting pan with a dark or nonstick finish or a broiler pan is a must for this recipe.

BEEF

8	garlic cloves, unpeeled
1	top sirloin roast (4 pounds), with some top fat intact (see note above)

RUB

3	garlic cloves, minced
1	teaspoon dried thyme
½	teaspoon salt

GARLIC PASTE

12	garlic cloves, peeled, cloves cut in half lengthwise
2	sprigs fresh thyme
2	bay leaves
½	teaspoon salt
½	cup olive oil
	Pepper

JUS

1½ cups low-sodium beef broth

1½ cups low-sodium chicken broth

1. FOR THE BEEF: Toast the garlic cloves in a small skillet over medium-high heat, tossing frequently, until spotty brown, about 8 minutes. Set the garlic aside. When cool enough to handle, peel the cloves and cut them into ¼-inch slivers.

2. Using a paring knife, make 1-inch-deep slits all over the roast. Insert the toasted garlic into the slits.

3. FOR THE RUB: Mix the minced garlic, thyme, and salt together in a small bowl. Rub all over the roast. Place the roast on a large plate and refrigerate, uncovered, for at least 4 hours or preferably overnight.

4. FOR THE GARLIC PASTE: Heat the garlic cloves, thyme, bay leaves, salt, and oil in a small saucepan over medium-high heat until bubbles start to rise to the surface. Reduce the heat to low and cook until the garlic is soft, about 30 minutes. Cool completely. Strain, reserving the oil. Discard the herbs and transfer the garlic to a small bowl. Mash the garlic with 1 tablespoon of the garlic oil until a paste forms. Cover and refrigerate the paste until ready to use. Cover and reserve the garlic oil.

5. Adjust an oven rack to the middle position, place a nonstick roasting pan or broiler pan bottom on the rack, and heat the oven to 450 degrees. Using paper towels, wipe the garlic-salt rub off the beef. Rub the beef with 2 tablespoons of the reserved garlic oil and season with pepper. Transfer the meat, fat side down, to the preheated pan and roast, turning as needed until browned on all sides, 10 to 15 minutes.

6. Reduce the oven temperature to 300 degrees. Remove the roasting pan from the oven. Turn the roast fat side up and, using a spatula, coat the top with the garlic paste. Return the meat to the oven and roast until the internal temperature reaches 125 degrees on an instant-read thermometer, 50 to 70 minutes. Transfer the roast to a cutting board, cover loosely with aluminum foil, and let rest for 20 minutes.

7. FOR THE JUS: Drain the excess fat from the roasting pan and place the pan over high heat. Add the broths and bring to a boil, using a wooden spoon to scrape the browned bits from the bottom of the pan. Simmer, stirring occasionally, until reduced to 2 cups, about 5 minutes. Add the accumulated juices from the roast and cook for 1 minute. Pour through a fine-mesh strainer. Cut the roast crosswise, against the grain, into ¼-inch slices. Serve with the jus.

SHOPPING WITH THE TEST KITCHEN

Cheap Beef Roasts: We tested three popular inexpensive roasts and found one champ, one solid pinch hitter, and one roast that you definitely do not want in your lineup. We liked top sirloin roast the best. This cut from the hip area tasted incredibly meaty and had plenty of marbling, which made for a succulent roast. It can also be labeled top butt, top sirloin butt, center-cut roast, or spoon roast. Blade roast came in second place. This roast from the shoulder was beefy and juicy, and its shape made it very easy to slice. A thin line of sinew was the only unpleasant distraction. Bottom round roast was the big loser. This roast from the rump area was tough and lacking in flavor. Even worse was the absence of fat and marbling, which made the meat very dry.

Chicago-Style Italian Roast Beef

In Chicago, spicy Italian roast beef usually starts with an inexpensive rump roast, which is marinated overnight—most often in a blend of Italian spices, garlic, vinegar, and oil (or even bottled Italian dressing)—then oven-braised in beef broth. The roast is sliced thin and served with the spicy jus. The dish originated with street vendors outside the Union Stock Yards and was traditionally served as a sandwich. For home cooks, it makes sense to serve this roast for dinner—and have enough leftovers for sandwiches the next day.

We tested several recipes and immediately identified two problems we wanted to fix—mushy meat with no crusty exterior, and a jus that was too salty but otherwise bland. To start, we had to choose an economical cut of meat. (You'd never use tenderloin or prime rib in this recipe.) Our first test pitted blade and top sirloin roasts against the rump roast. The blade and rump roasts were pretty tough, especially in comparison to the meaty and tender top sirloin roast.

In the past, the test kitchen has found that marinating most cuts of meat can turn them mushy. A spice rub or herb paste provides just as much flavor and works in seconds—not hours—and without the mush. So for our next test, we skipped the overnight marinade and instead rubbed a top sirloin roast with a blend of dried oregano, basil, garlic powder, and red pepper flakes. The spice-rubbed roast tasted better than any roast we had marinated, but it was still too mushy. Roasting the meat in a pan filled with the jus was clearly the problem. Elevating the roast on a rack above the jus was a big improvement.

Our roast still lacked the browned crust we consider the hallmark of a well-cooked roast. We tried browning the spice-coated roast in a skillet, but the smoke was intense and the rub tasted bitter and awful. Browning the meat in the skillet before rubbing it worked great. Once the roast was

MAKING CHICAGO-STYLE ITALIAN ROAST BEEF

1. Brown the meat before roasting to create a flavorful crust on the exterior. Transfer the roast to a V-rack in a roasting pan and begin work on the jus.

2. The browned bits left behind in the pan are the base for the jus. Cook onion, garlic, and seasonings in the skillet, then add the broths and water to help loosen the browned bits.

3. Pour the jus into the roasting pan below the elevated roast so it can catch the flavorful drippings and cook down to the desired consistency while the meat cooks.

4. Apply a flavorful rub, mixed with oil to help it adhere, after browning the roast to prevent the dried herbs from burning.

browned and coated with spices, a low oven temperature of 300 degrees helped it cook evenly and stay juicy inside.

With the roast settled, it was time to address the jus. No one liked the flat flavor of canned beef broth; a mix of chicken and beef broths tasted better. Adding some water to the broths helped tone down the salt (even the low-sodium broths preferred by the test kitchen have quite a bit), but the jus was still bland. Using the browned bits left in the skillet from searing the meat, we added onion and fresh garlic and toasted the dried spices to bring out their flavor. Once the base was established, we added the broths and water and then poured the jus into the roasting pan below the elevated meat so it could catch any drippings exuded during roasting. This way, there was no last-minute fuss; our jus was ready when the roast was done.

Our Chicago-Style Italian Roast Beef has the perfect balance of spice, garlic, and herbs and sports a crusty, browned exterior. Enjoy it for Sunday dinner, but make sure to save leftovers for sandwiches.

CHICAGO-STYLE ITALIAN ROAST BEEF
SERVES 6 TO 8

If your roast is larger than 4 pounds, you may need to increase the cooking time slightly in step 4. Top sirloin roast is also sometimes labeled top butt, top sirloin butt, center-cut roast, or spoon roast. Leftover meat and jus make great sandwiches.

4   teaspoons garlic powder
4   teaspoons dried basil
4   teaspoons dried oregano
1   tablespoon pepper
1   top sirloin roast (4 pounds; see note above), fat trimmed to ¼ inch thick
2   tablespoons vegetable oil
1   onion, minced
3   garlic cloves, minced
1   tablespoon flour
2   cups low-sodium beef broth
2   cups low-sodium chicken broth
1½   cups water
1   teaspoon red pepper flakes
2   teaspoons salt

1. Adjust an oven rack to the lower-middle position and heat the oven to 300 degrees. Combine the garlic powder, basil, oregano, and pepper in a small bowl.

2. Pat the roast dry with paper towels. Heat 1 tablespoon of the oil in a large skillet over medium-high heat until just smoking. Brown the roast all over, about 10 minutes, then transfer to a V-rack set inside a roasting pan.

3. Add the onion to the fat in the skillet and cook over medium heat until softened, about 5 minutes. Stir in the garlic, flour, and 1 teaspoon of the spice mixture and cook until fragrant, about 1 minute. Stir in the broths and water, using a wooden spoon to scrape up the browned bits from the bottom of the skillet. Bring to a boil, then pour into the roasting pan.

4. Stir the remaining 1 tablespoon oil, the red pepper flakes, and salt into the remaining spice mixture. Rub the mixture all over the meat and roast until the meat registers 125 degrees (for medium-rare) on an instant-read thermometer, 75 to 90 minutes. Transfer the roast to a cutting board, tent with aluminum foil, and let rest for 20 minutes.

5. Pour the jus through a fine-mesh strainer and keep warm. Cut the roast crosswise, against the grain, into ¼-inch slices. Serve with the jus.

Herb-Crusted Beef Tenderloin

For a cut of meat that costs about $75, a whole beef tenderloin sure presents a lot of problems for the home cook. Yes, the meat is very tender, but it's not very flavorful. In the test kitchen we think a crusty, browned exterior is a must for this roast.

If a thick seared crust is good, we figured that an additional herb crust would be even better. But this opened up another set of cooking problems: the herbs burn easily or just lose their flavor, and they aren't easily glued to the meat. We had our work cut out for us.

A hot oven can put a decent crust on the meat. We found that 400 degrees offered the best balance of nice browning and even cooking. (At higher temperatures the interior overcooked very easily and the kitchen often filled with smoke.) Tucking the thinner, tapered end of the meat under itself and tying the roast at 1½-inch intervals created a regularly shaped roast and also promoted even cooking. Elevating the roast on a wire rack kept the bottom of the tenderloin from steaming in its own juices.

Our roast was better, but could we make the crust thicker? Knowing that salting raw meat helps to draw out moisture, which results in a drier and crustier exterior, we tried rubbing the meat with salt while it was sitting on the counter to lose its chill. The salting did result in a firmer exterior, but the roast still lacked that deeply browned crust we were looking for. Adding sugar to the salt rub was a key discovery: a mere 2 teaspoons (along with 1 tablespoon of salt) was all that was needed to create a golden brown, perfectly caramelized crust about halfway through the cooking time.

Now we could introduce the herbs. After doing several tests, we found that tasters preferred the combination of parsley and thyme to the aggressive flavors of sage and rosemary. We worked out the right proportions and boosted the herb flavor with minced garlic, but we were having trouble keeping the herb paste on the roast. After some trial and error, we found a flavorful way to glue the herbs to the meat: grated Parmesan cheese.

Our herb crust was flavorful, but could we make it crisper? We tried adding herbed bread crumbs and more Parmesan cheese (a topping that creates a nice crunchy crust on many foods) on top of the herb and cheese paste. This extra crust was perfect, except for one small detail: when we removed the twine prior to carving, the bread crumbs came right off with it. Because we were already removing the half-cooked tenderloin from the oven to smear on the herb paste, we tried removing the twine and adding the bread crumbs at the same juncture. This method worked perfectly, as the shape of the tied meat had been set during the initial cooking. And the bread crumbs turned crisp and golden just as the tenderloin came up to temperature.

The three distinct crusts on this special roast—the oven-seared meat, the herb paste coating, and the herbed bread-crumb crown—make this premium roast something truly special.

TRIMMING A BEEF TENDERLOIN

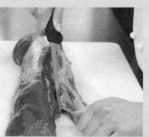 

1. Discard the fatty strip (or chain) that runs along the length of the tenderloin.

2. Remove the sinewy silver skin (and any other large pieces of fat) by inserting the tip of a knife under it and slicing outward at a slight angle.

HERB-CRUSTED BEEF TENDERLOIN

SERVES 12 TO 16

Begin this recipe 2 hours before you plan to put the roast in the oven. The tenderloin can be trimmed, tied, rubbed with the salt mixture, and refrigerated up to 24 hours in advance; bring the roast back to room temperature before putting it into the oven. A warehouse club is a great place to find a good-quality beef tenderloin at a reasonable price, but expect to do some serious trimming at home—you might have to cut 1½ pounds of fat and connective tissue from a 6-pound roast.

1	whole beef tenderloin (5 to 6 pounds), trimmed and patted dry
1	tablespoon kosher salt
1	tablespoon cracked pepper
2	teaspoons sugar
2	slices hearty white sandwich bread, torn into large pieces and pulsed in a food processor to coarse crumbs
½	cup chopped fresh parsley
2	teaspoons plus 2 tablespoons minced fresh thyme
1¼	cups grated Parmesan cheese
6	tablespoons olive oil
4	garlic cloves, minced
1	recipe Horseradish Cream Sauce (recipe follows)

1. Tuck the tail of the tenderloin under and tie the roast. Combine the salt, pepper, and sugar in a small bowl and rub all over the tenderloin. Transfer the tenderloin to a wire rack set on a rimmed baking sheet and let stand at room temperature for 2 hours.

2. Meanwhile, toss the bread crumbs in a medium bowl with 2 tablespoons of the parsley, 2 teaspoons of the thyme, ½ cup of the Parmesan, and 2 tablespoons of the oil until evenly combined. Process the remaining 6 tablespoons parsley, 2 tablespoons thyme, ¾ cup cheese, 4 tablespoons oil, and garlic

in the food processor until a smooth paste forms. Transfer the herb paste to a small bowl.

3. Adjust an oven rack to the upper-middle position and heat the oven to 400 degrees. Roast the tenderloin for 20 minutes and remove from the oven. Using scissors, cut and remove the twine. Coat the tenderloin with the herb paste followed by the bread-crumb topping. Roast until the thickest part of the meat registers about 130 degrees (for medium-rare) and the topping is golden brown, 20 to 25 minutes. (If the topping browns before the meat reaches the preferred internal temperature,

MAKING BEEF TENDERLOIN

1. To ensure even cooking, fold the thin, tapered end under the roast, then tie the entire roast with kitchen twine every 1½ inches.

2. After the meat has cooked for 20 minutes, use scissors to snip the twine; carefully pull it away from the tenderloin.

3. Using a spatula, spread the herb paste evenly over the top and sides of the tenderloin.

4. Press the bread-crumb mixture evenly onto the roast, using your other hand to catch the crumbs and keep them from falling through the rack.

lightly cover with aluminum foil for the balance of the roasting time.) Let the roast rest, uncovered, for 30 minutes on a wire rack. Transfer to a cutting board and carve. Serve.

HORSERADISH CREAM SAUCE

MAKES ABOUT 1 CUP

This sauce can be refrigerated in an airtight container for up to 2 days.

½	cup sour cream
½	cup heavy cream
¼	cup prepared horseradish, drained
2	teaspoons Dijon mustard
1	garlic clove, minced
¼	teaspoon sugar
	Salt and pepper

Mix all of the ingredients, including salt and pepper to taste, in a bowl. Cover and let stand at room temperature for 1 to 1½ hours to thicken.

Port-Braised Short Ribs

In the cooler months, few dishes beat comfort food like beef short ribs braised until tender in a flavorful wine sauce. Short ribs can make for a very special meal, but they take a long time to prepare. First the ribs are browned in batches to build flavor and render exterior fat, then the vegetables are sautéed, and then everything is braised for hours (to break down the tough connective tissue in the meat) in broth flavored with wine and herbs. Unfortunately, when the fat and collagen melt out of the meat, they end up in the sauce. Some recipes go so far as to require refrigerating the cooked ribs in their sauce overnight to make it easier to remove the rendered fat. We wanted to create fork-tender,

silky (but not fatty) short ribs with a bold, clean sauce—and we wanted to serve it on the same day we made it.

Starting with a recipe that employed classic braising technique, we browned a batch of short ribs in a Dutch oven and found about 3 tablespoons of fat left behind in the pot. Not bad, but we knew there was still fat from the ribs' interior to be lost, and we didn't want it to end up in the sauce. Some recipes forgo stovetop browning in favor of roasting the ribs in the oven before braising. We tried this method, and after an hour the ribs had lost plenty of fat—but valuable moisture, too; they looked like beef jerky. For our next test, we covered the ribs with aluminum foil to prevent them from drying out while they roasted. After about 2 hours, we discovered that our nicely browned ribs had rendered a whopping cup of fat. It was time for the sauce.

We built a braising sauce on the stovetop using traditional ingredients: onion, carrot, celery, garlic, tomato paste, red wine, and beef broth. We added the roasted ribs, covered the pot, and transferred it to the oven. Moist, tender meat emerged (the defatted ribs had soaked up the braising liquid), but we wanted bolder flavor. We tried replacing the red wine with port, and tasters loved the rich sweetness it imparted. A little balsamic vinegar added a nice acidity that complemented the meatiness of the ribs, and a sprig of rosemary lent a welcome herbal flavor. This was the bold sauce we sought; the only problem was its thin consistency.

It was tricky to turn the large quantity of liquid required to cover the ribs into a glossy sauce. Simply reducing it left us with an overly sticky sauce (the sweet port reduces to syrup) and not nearly enough for serving—only ½ cup. Instead, we decided to add a thickener to the braising liquid at the outset, hoping that by the time the ribs were done the sauce would have the right consistency. Flour and cornstarch seemed like the logical choices, but they made the braising liquid too thick and gravy-like. We had better luck with instant tapioca, which imparted no flavor of its own and gave the sauce a smoother, more refined consistency. With a quick skimming and straining of the sauce, we now had short ribs that were perfect every time.

PORT-BRAISED SHORT RIBS

SERVES 4 TO 6

Short ribs come in two styles. English-style ribs contain a single rib bone and a thick piece of meat. Flanken-style ribs are cut thinner and have several smaller bones. Either will work here, but we prefer the less expensive and more readily available English-style ribs. These short ribs can be made ahead, so they're great for entertaining. Refrigerate the ribs and sauce, separately, for up to 3 days. When ready to serve, heat the sauce and ribs together over medium heat until the ribs are warmed through.

5	pounds beef short ribs (6 to 8 English-style ribs), trimmed of excess fat (see note above)
	Salt and pepper
1	onion, chopped
1	carrot, peeled and chopped
1	celery rib, chopped
4	garlic cloves, minced
1	tablespoon tomato paste
3	cups low-sodium beef broth
1½	cups ruby port
¼	cup balsamic vinegar
¼	cup Minute tapioca
1	sprig fresh rosemary

1. Adjust an oven rack to the middle position and heat the oven to 375 degrees. Season the ribs with salt and pepper and arrange, bone side up, in a

MAKING BRAISED SHORT RIBS

1. Trim any visible fat from the exterior of the ribs before cooking. If you don't trim the fat, the ribs will be unpalatably greasy. Roast the ribs in an aluminum foil–covered pan to render their fat.

2. Pour off the fat and drippings, reserving just 2 tablespoons for building the sauce. The browned ribs will need about 2 hours of braising in the sauce to become tender.

roasting pan. Cover tightly with aluminum foil and roast until the fat has rendered and the ribs are browned, 1½ to 2 hours. Transfer the ribs to a paper towel–lined plate. Reserve 2 tablespoons of the rendered beef fat and discard the remaining drippings.

2. Reduce the oven temperature to 300 degrees. Heat the reserved fat in a large ovenproof Dutch oven over medium-high heat until shimmering. Cook the onion, carrot, and celery until lightly browned, about 5 minutes. Add the garlic and tomato paste and cook until fragrant, about 1 minute. Add the broth, port, vinegar, tapioca, rosemary, and ribs to the pot and bring to a simmer.

3. Cover the pot and transfer to the oven. Cook until the sauce is slightly thickened and the ribs are completely tender, about 2 hours. Transfer the ribs to a serving platter. Strain and skim the sauce. Serve, passing the sauce at the table.

Oven-Barbecued Beef Brisket

Most Texans will tell you that the secret to blue-ribbon brisket is hours and hours of slow, smoky heat. The low heat (between 200 and 300 degrees) converts collagen (the connective tissue that makes brisket tough) to gelatin, leaving the meat tender. Exposing the meat to smoke for hours creates a distinct barbecue flavor, and it's hard to imagine getting that out of an oven. But we figured it was worth a try. Some of us have tried barbecuing in the snow, and it isn't much fun.

Approximating the temperature of the grill was easy—we just had to set our oven—but capturing the smoky flavor of the grill was another story. Traditional Texas recipes for brisket start with rubbing the meat with spices, and we saw no reason to deviate from this plan. We wrapped the meat in aluminum foil (to keep it from drying out in the oven), and it emerged tender and flavorful—but not smoky.

To add a smoky flavor, some recipes resort to oven-smoking, a technique involving some form of wood product (cedar planks, for instance), but we were looking for something a little less complicated. We tried both marinating the brisket with chipotle chiles (smoked jalapeños) and drizzling it with liquid smoke, but neither worked well.

We were stumped until we thought about the test kitchen's favorite bean recipes, which rely on smoked meats (ham hocks, smoked sausage, or bacon) to add smoky flavor. Bacon seemed like the easiest choice, so we added a few slices to the foil packet with the brisket. We detected a faint whiff of smoke in the meat, so we kept at it. In the end, we found that poking the brisket all over with a fork before wrapping it with a pound (yes, 1 pound) of bacon produced a noticeably sweet-smoky flavor.

In the heat of the oven, the bacon fat rendered and dripped into the holes in the meat, seasoning the brisket throughout.

Because we were cooking the brisket wrapped in bacon and in foil, the exterior was pretty pale. We missed the deeply caramelized, almost crisp crust that graces true barbecued brisket. To remedy this problem, at the end of cooking we removed the bacon, flipped the brisket fat side up, and ran it under the broiler for a couple of minutes. The fat browned nicely, but the meat was still too pale.

Looking at the bacon that we'd removed from the brisket, we got an idea. Using the bacon and the juices from the brisket, we made a quick barbecue sauce and brushed it over the top of the brisket before running it under the broiler again. This time the sauce glazed the top of the brisket, turning it a rich mahogany color that would fool even the most ardent barbecue fan.

THE AMERICAN TABLE
BARBECUE ROOTS

We readily concede that "barbecuing" in the oven is something of a heresy. But our method does have something in common with the earliest barbecue recipes. Many sources say that modern barbecue is a direct descendant of Mexican barbacoa, a traditional cooking technique in which tough cuts of meat are wrapped in leaves from a maguey plant or banana tree and buried in a shallow pit filled with hot coals. Our oven-barbecued brisket trades aluminum foil for leaves and an oven for a hole in the ground, but the concept (tightly wrapped meat cooked slowly in a moderately hot enclosed space) is the same.

OVEN-BARBECUED BEEF BRISKET

SERVES 8 TO 10

Our Smoky Bacon BBQ Sauce is our first choice, but feel free to substitute 3½ cups of store-bought sauce.

BRISKET

1	recipe All-Purpose BBQ Rub (recipe follows)
1	brisket roast (4 to 5 pounds), fat trimmed to ¼ inch thick
1	pound bacon

SAUCE

	Bacon from cooked brisket
1	onion, minced
½	cup cider vinegar
⅓	cup packed dark brown sugar
1–2	cups low-sodium chicken broth
½	cup ketchup
1	canned chipotle chile in adobo, minced

1. FOR THE BRISKET: Adjust an oven rack to the upper-middle position and heat the oven to 275 degrees. Massage the dry rub into the meat and poke all over with a fork. Arrange half of the bacon strips, overlapping slightly, crosswise on the bottom of a broiler-safe 13 by 9-inch baking pan. Place the brisket, fat side down, in the bacon-lined pan and place the remaining bacon strips on top, tucking the ends of the strips underneath the brisket. Cover the pan with aluminum foil and roast until a fork inserted into the brisket can be removed with no resistance, about 4 hours.

2. Remove the pan from the oven and carefully flip the brisket fat side up. Replace the foil and return it to the oven. Turn off the heat and allow the brisket to rest in the warm oven for 1 hour.

3. FOR THE SAUCE: Pour the accumulated juices into a 1-quart liquid measuring cup and set aside. Remove the bacon from the brisket, chop into small pieces, and cook in a medium saucepan over medium heat until the fat has rendered, about 5 minutes. Add the onion and cook until softened, about 5 minutes. Off the heat, add the vinegar and sugar and stir to combine. Return to medium heat and reduce to a syrupy consistency, about 5 minutes.

4. Meanwhile, skim the fat from the reserved juices and discard it. Add enough chicken broth to the juices to make 3 cups. Add the liquid to the saucepan and reduce until the mixture measures 3 cups, about 8 minutes. Off the heat, stir in the ketchup and chipotle. Strain through a fine-mesh strainer, if desired.

5. Turn the oven to broil. Brush the brisket with 1 cup of the sauce and broil until the top is lightly charred and the fat is crisped, 5 to 7 minutes. Transfer the brisket to a cutting board and cut across the grain into ¼-inch slices. Serve with the remaining sauce.

COAXING BBQ FLAVOR FROM YOUR OVEN

1. Massage the dry rub into the meat and poke all over with a fork. Arrange half the bacon crosswise on the bottom of a broiler-safe baking pan.

2. Place the brisket, fat side down, in the bacon-lined pan, and place the remaining bacon on top.

ALL-PURPOSE BBQ RUB

MAKES ABOUT ⅓ CUP

This recipe can be doubled or tripled. Store the extra in an airtight container for up to 1 month.

4	teaspoons brown sugar
4	teaspoons paprika
2	teaspoons dry mustard
2	teaspoons pepper
2	teaspoons salt
1	teaspoon onion powder
1	teaspoon garlic powder
1	teaspoon ground cumin
¼	teaspoon cayenne pepper

Combine all of the ingredients in a bowl, breaking up any lumps of sugar.

SHOPPING WITH THE TEST KITCHEN

Brisket: Because whole beef briskets can weigh well over 10 pounds, they are typically butchered and sold as two separate cuts—"point" and "flat." The flat cut, the most common in grocery stores, is leaner and thinner, with a rectangular shape and an exterior fat cap. The point cut has an irregular shape and contains large interior fat pockets. For our Oven-Barbecued Beef Brisket, we prefer the flat cut, finding that its external fat cap helps to keep the meat moist. Whichever cut you choose, be sure to purchase a brisket of roughly 4 to 5 pounds that still has a good amount of fat attached. Some butchers cut brisket into small 2- to 3-pound roasts. If this is all that you can find, you can substitute two of the smaller cuts; the cooking time may vary slightly.

Meat Loaf

Not all meat loaves resemble Mama's. In fact, some ingredient lists look like the work of a proud child or defiant adolescent. Canned pineapple, cranberry sauce, raisins, prepared taco mix, and even goat cheese have all found their way into published recipes. Rather than feud over flavorings, though, we decided to focus on the meatier issues.

To determine which ground meat or meat mix makes the best loaf, we used a very basic meat loaf recipe and made miniature loaves with the following ground meat proportions: equal parts beef chuck and pork; equal parts beef chuck, pork, and veal; 2 parts beef chuck to 1 part ground pork and 1 part ground veal; 3 parts beef chuck and 1 part ground bacon; all ground beef chuck.

We found out that meat markets haven't been selling meat loaf mix (a mix of beef, pork, and veal) all these years for nothing. As we expected, the best meat loaves were made from the combination of these three meats. The all-beef loaf was coarse-textured, liver-flavored, and tough. Though interesting, the beef-bacon loaves neither looked nor tasted like classic meat loaf. Also, as bacon lovers, we preferred the bacon's smoky flavor and crispy texture surrounding, not in, the loaf.

Although both of the beef-pork-veal mixtures were good, we preferred the mix with a higher proportion of ground chuck. This amount gave the loaf a distinct but not overly strong beef flavor. Mild-tasting pork added another flavor dimension, and the small quantity of veal kept it tender. For those who choose not to special-order this mix or mix it themselves at home, we recommend the standard meat loaf mix of equal parts beef, pork, and veal.

After comparing meat loaves made with and without fillers or binders, we realized that starch in a meat loaf offers more than economy. Loaves made without filler were coarse-textured, dense, and too hamburger-like. Those with binders, on the other hand, had that distinctive meat loaf texture.

But which binder to use? Practically every hot and cold cereal box offers a meat loaf recipe using that particular cereal. We made several meat loaves, each with a different filler. Though there was no clear-cut winner, we narrowed the number from eleven down to three. After tasting all the meat loaves, we realized that a good binder should help with texture but not add distinct flavor. Saltine cracker crumbs fit the bill.

Just as we found that we liked the less distinctly flavored fillers, so we preferred sautéed—not raw—onions and garlic in the meat mix. Because the meat loaf cooks to an internal temperature of just 160 degrees, raw onions never fully cook. Sauté-ing the vegetables is a 5-minute detour well worth the time.

We found our meat loaves in need of some liq-uid to moisten the filler. Without it, the filler robs the meat of its moisture. As with the fillers, we ran across a host of meat loaf moisteners and tried as many as made sense. Tomato sauce made the loaf taste like a meatball with sauce. We liked the flavor of ketchup but ultimately decided that we preferred it baked on top rather than inside. Beer and wine do not make ideal meat moisteners, either. The meat doesn't cook long enough or to a high enough internal temperature to burn off the alcohol, so the meat ends up with a distinctly raw alcohol taste.

As with many other aspects of this home-cooked favorite, we found that there is a good reason why the majority of meat loaf recipes call for some form of dairy for the liquid—it's the best choice. We tried half-and-half, milk, sour cream, yogurt, skim and whole evaporated milk, and even cottage cheese. Whole milk and plain yogurt ended up as our liq-uids of choice, the yogurt offering a complementary subtle tang to the rich beef.

Cooks who don't like a crusty exterior on their meat loaf usually prefer to bake it in a loaf pan.

We found that the high-sided standard loaf pan, however, causes the meat to stew rather than bake. Also, for those who like a glazed top, there is another disadvantage: the enclosed pan allows the meat juices to bubble up from the sides, diluting and destroying the glaze. Similarly, bacon placed on top of the meat loaf curls and doesn't properly attach to the loaf, and if tucked inside the pan, the bacon never crisps.

For all these reasons, we advise against using a standard loaf pan. If you prefer a crustless, soft-sided meat loaf, invest in a meat loaf pan with a perforated bottom and accompanying drip pan. The enclosed pan keeps the meat soft while the perforated bot-tom allows the drippings to flow to the pan below. Although still not ideal for a crispy bacon top, it at least saves the glaze from destruction.

Ultimately, we found that baking a meat loaf free-form on a rimmed baking sheet gave us the results we wanted. The top and sides of the loaf brown nicely, and basting sauces, like the brown sugar and ketchup sauce we developed, glaze the entire loaf, not just the top. Bacon, too, covers the whole loaf. And because its drippings also fall into the pan, the bacon crisps up nicely.

CLASSIC MEAT LOAF WITH BROWN SUGAR–KETCHUP GLAZE

SERVES 6 TO 8

If you like, you can omit the bacon topping from the loaf. In this case, brush on half of the glaze before baking and the other half during the last 15 min-utes of baking. If you can't find meat loaf mix, use 1 pound 85-percent lean ground beef and 1 pound ground pork.

GLAZE

½   **cup ketchup or chili sauce**

¼   **cup packed brown sugar**

4   **teaspoons cider or white vinegar**

MEAT LOAF

2	teaspoons vegetable oil
1	onion, chopped
2	garlic cloves, minced or pressed through a garlic press
2	large eggs
½	teaspoon dried thyme
1	teaspoon salt
½	teaspoon pepper
2	teaspoons Dijon mustard
2	teaspoons Worcestershire sauce
¼	teaspoon hot sauce
½	cup whole milk or plain yogurt
2	pounds meat loaf mix (see note above)
⅔	cup crushed saltine crackers (17 crackers)
⅓	cup chopped fresh parsley
8	slices bacon, or more as needed (amount will vary depending on loaf shape)

1. FOR THE GLAZE: Mix all of the glaze ingredients together in a small saucepan; set aside.

2. FOR THE MEAT LOAF: Adjust an oven rack to the middle position and heat the oven to 350 degrees. Heat the oil in a medium skillet. Add the onion and garlic; sauté until softened, about 5 minutes. Set aside to cool while preparing the remaining ingredients.

3. Mix the eggs, thyme, salt, pepper, mustard, Worcestershire sauce, hot sauce, and milk or yogurt in a medium bowl. Add the egg mixture to the meat in a large bowl along with the crackers, parsley, and cooked onion and garlic; mix with a fork until evenly blended and the meat mixture does not stick to the bowl. (If the mixture sticks, add more milk or yogurt, a couple of tablespoons at a time, until the mixture no longer sticks.)

4. Turn the meat mixture onto a work surface. With wet hands, pat the mixture into a loaf shape

approximately 9 by 5 inches. Place on a foil–lined (for easy cleanup) rimmed baking sheet. Brush with half of the glaze, then arrange the bacon slices crosswise over the loaf, overlapping them slightly, to completely cover the surface. Use a spatula to tuck the bacon ends underneath the loaf.

5. Bake the loaf until the bacon is crisp and the internal temperature of the loaf registers 160 degrees on an instant-read thermometer, about 1 hour. Cool for at least 20 minutes. Simmer the remaining glaze over medium heat until thickened slightly. Slice the meat loaf and serve, passing the remaining glaze separately.

30-Minute Meat Loaf

Most meat loaf recipes call for an hour of baking time in an oven set to 350 or 375 degrees. Add more time to cook some onions and garlic, measure other ingredients, and knead the meat mixture, and you're talking at least 90 minutes to get meat loaf on the table. Not bad considering that most of the time is hands-off, but not good if it's already six o'clock and everyone is hungry.

We decided to streamline the test kitchen's favorite recipe, which calls for meat loaf mix (ground beef, pork, and veal sold in one package at most supermarkets), crushed saltines, a little milk, and eggs. To speed up the process, we found that onion powder and garlic powder were decent substitutes for the real thing and saved 15 minutes of chopping and cooking. Other seasonings—Worcestershire sauce, Dijon mustard, and cayenne pepper—required just a minute or two to assemble and measure.

With the ingredients set, we turned to the cooking method. Based on our research, cranking up the oven temperature to 500 degrees seemed like the best option. The loaf was done in 30 minutes rather

MAKING A BETTER MEATLOAF

1. Sear the tops and bottoms of the tightly packed loaves to develop a crisp and flavorful exterior.

2. Bake the loaves on the top of a preheated broiler pan so excess fat can drip away.

than 60, but it was pale and greasy. (It wasn't in the oven long enough to render all the fat or to brown sufficiently.) Broiling was another common solution offered in "quick" cookbooks, but this method left the top half incinerated and the bottom half soggy and sitting in a puddle of grease. Then we found a recipe that called for dividing the meat loaf mixture into smaller loaves. This was the quickest recipe yet, taking just 25 minutes to bake, but two problems remained: the loaves were swimming in their own grease, and they lacked a browned crust—the hallmark of any respectable meat loaf. Searing the loaves in a skillet on the stovetop and then transferring them to the oven solved the browning issue and cut the total cooking time to just 15 minutes.

Even though much of the fat rendered in the skillet, some excess grease continued to pool around the loaves on the baking sheet. Baking the loaves on a slotted broiler pan solved this problem. Letting the broiler pan preheat in the oven shaved a few more minutes off the cooking time, leaving us with a recipe that could be prepped and cooked in less than 30 minutes.

Their size might be unconventional, but our little loaves are every bit as tasty as any big loaf, with an even better crust.

30-MINUTE MEAT LOAF

SERVES 4 TO 6

If meat loaf mix is not available, substitute ¾ pound each of ground pork and 85-percent lean ground beef. Note that the meat loaves can be made ahead. After forming the loaves, wrap them with plastic wrap and refrigerate overnight. Let the loaves sit at room temperature for 20 minutes before proceeding with step 3.

MEAT LOAVES

- ⅔ cup crushed saltine crackers (17 crackers)
- ¼ cup whole milk
- 3 tablespoons Worcestershire sauce
- ⅓ cup chopped fresh parsley
- 1½ tablespoons Dijon mustard
- 1 large egg
- 1 teaspoon onion powder
- 1 teaspoon garlic powder
- ⅛ teaspoon cayenne pepper
- ½ teaspoon salt
- ½ teaspoon pepper
- 1½ pounds meat loaf mix (see note above)
- 2 teaspoons vegetable oil

GLAZE

- ½ cup ketchup
- ¼ cup packed light brown sugar
- 4 teaspoons cider vinegar

1. FOR THE MEAT LOAVES: Adjust an oven rack to the middle position, place a broiler pan with a slotted top on the oven rack, and heat the oven to 500 degrees.

2. Mix the crackers, milk, Worcestershire sauce, parsley, mustard, egg, onion powder, garlic powder, cayenne, salt, and pepper in a large bowl. Add the meat and mix with your hands until evenly combined. Form into 4 tightly packed loaves, each measuring 4 by 3 inches.

3. Heat the oil in a large nonstick skillet over medium-high heat until just smoking. Cook the loaves until well browned on the top and bottom, 2 to 3 minutes per side.

4. FOR THE GLAZE: While the meat is browning, combine all of the glaze ingredients in a bowl.

5. Carefully transfer the loaves to the slotted broiler-pan top and spoon 1 tablespoon of the glaze over each loaf. Bake until an instant-read thermometer inserted in the middle of a loaf registers 160 degrees, 7 to 9 minutes. Let the loaves rest on the broiler pan for 3 minutes. Serve, passing the remaining glaze at the table.

Meatballs and Marinara

Making big, "Little Italy"–sized meatballs is easy. Making big meatballs that are also tender and moist, with enough structure to hold their shape, is difficult. Most recipes mix equal amounts of ground beef with ground pork and add a panade, a paste made from bread and milk. As soon as we made our first batch of meatballs we could see that we were in trouble. The moment the meatballs went into the pan, they collapsed under their own weight and spread out like soggy hamburger patties.

We rethought our ratios of meat (1-to-1) and switched to 5 parts beef to 1 part pork. We also made a stiffer panade with more bread and less milk. This drier, leaner mixture held its shape well and cooked up easily in the pan, but losing most of the fat meant we were also losing much of the flavor. Adding sautéed onion, garlic, red pepper flakes, dried oregano, and fresh parsley helped. A handful of Parmesan added richness. Our meatballs were getting close, but there was still something missing.

We tried different herbs and cheeses to no avail. Then a colleague suggested substituting raw Italian sausage for the ground pork. Tasters loved the flavor boost the sausage added.

When we started cooking the meatballs, our progress came to a grinding halt. Even in our largest pan, we could fry only five or six meatballs at a time. What's more, the meatballs were so big that they turned crusty and charred on the outside before they were cooked through. Getting frustrated, we turned to the oven. Lower temperatures produced flabby, gray meatballs; we turned up the heat and our luck began to change. At 475 degrees, the meatballs were baking to a nice golden brown. Now, without any babysitting or messy frying, we could focus on the marinara.

To build rich tomato flavor, we fried tomato paste along with the aromatics before adding crushed tomatoes and wine. The resulting sauce had a deep crimson color, a hearty texture, and a flavor that was deep and rich—all in just an hour.

Served over a bowl of steaming-hot spaghetti or eaten with a slice of crusty bread to sop up the sauce, these tender meatballs offer a big taste of Little Italy.

BIG MEATBALLS WITH BIG FLAVOR

1. For a great crust minus the hassle of frying, bake the meatballs in a very hot oven.

2. For the best flavor, let the meatballs sit in the simmering sauce for at least 15 minutes before serving.

MEATBALLS AND MARINARA

SERVES 8 (MAKES ENOUGH TO SERVE WITH
2 POUNDS OF SPAGHETTI)

The meatballs and sauce use the same onion mixture.

ONION MIXTURE

¼	cup olive oil
3	onions, minced
8	garlic cloves, minced
1	tablespoon dried oregano
¾	teaspoon red pepper flakes

MARINARA

1	(6-ounce) can tomato paste
1	cup dry red wine
1	cup water
4	(28-ounce) cans crushed tomatoes
½	cup grated Parmesan cheese
¼	cup chopped fresh basil
	Salt
1–2	teaspoons sugar

MEATBALLS

4	slices hearty white sandwich bread, torn into large pieces
¾	cup whole or low-fat milk
½	pound sweet Italian sausage, casings removed
1	cup grated Parmesan cheese
½	cup chopped fresh parsley
2	large eggs
2	garlic cloves, minced
1½	teaspoons salt
2½	pounds 80-percent lean ground beef

1. FOR THE ONION MIXTURE: Heat the oil in a Dutch oven over medium-high heat until shimmering. Cook the onions until golden, 10 to 15 minutes. Add the garlic, oregano, and red pepper flakes and cook until fragrant, about 30 seconds. Transfer half of the onion mixture to a large bowl and set aside.

2. FOR THE MARINARA: Add the tomato paste to the remaining onion mixture in the pot and cook until fragrant, about 1 minute. Add the wine and cook until slightly thickened, about 2 minutes. Stir in the water and tomatoes and simmer over low heat until the sauce is no longer watery, 45 to 60 minutes. Stir in the cheese and basil and adjust the seasonings with salt and sugar as desired.

3. FOR THE MEATBALLS: While the marinara is simmering, adjust an oven rack to the upper-middle position and heat the oven to 475 degrees. Mash the bread and milk in the bowl with the reserved onion mixture until smooth. Add the remaining ingredients, except the ground beef, to the bowl and mash to combine. Add the beef and knead with your hands until well combined. Form the mixture into 2½-inch meatballs (you should have about 16 meatballs), place on a rimmed baking sheet, and bake until well browned, about 20 minutes.

4. Transfer the meatballs to the pot with the sauce. Simmer for 15 minutes. Serve over pasta. (The meatballs and marinara can be frozen for up to 1 month.)

Jucy Lucy Burgers

Jucy Lucy burgers, popular in pubs and taverns in Minneapolis, contain a pocket of American cheese in the center. Bite into the mildly seasoned ground beef and the melted cheese will ooze right out. It seemed simple—seal a slice of American cheese between two burger patties and throw it in a hot skillet. But our burgers, cooked until well-done to fully melt the cheese, were dry and tough. Worse still, they had suffered a blowout: the cheese melted through the meat, leaving an empty cavern where the cheese had been. Was there a way to keep this Lucy juicy and hold the cheese inside?

Since a thin slice of American cheese simply disappeared during cooking, we tried sandwiching a chunk of cheese between two patties instead. This improved the odds of keeping the cheese inside, but it was still hit or miss. One test cook suggested sealing the cheese inside a small patty and then molding a second patty around the first one. This created a double-sealed pocket that kept the cheesy center in place every time.

High heat scorched the outside of our burgers and left the cheese unmelted. Cooking the burgers over medium heat worked much better, fully cooking the burger and melting the cheese. The burgers were nearly there, but they still weren't as moist as the ones from the tavern. Then we remembered a meatball trick in which a panade—a mixture of bread and milk mashed to a paste—is added to ground beef. This worked, giving us what we had thought was impossible: a tender and juicy well-done burger.

The Jucy Lucys in the Twin Cities are sparsely flavored with salt, pepper, garlic, and Worcestershire sauce. Garlic powder worked better than garlic salt (which was too muted) and minced garlic (too pungent), but we lost the Worcestershire—it made the burgers taste too much like meat loaf. We cooked up a batch of these burgers and let them cool briefly

before diving in. We were rewarded with a warm, melted center of cheese inside an incredible juicy (but not greasy) Lucy—a tasty new way to enjoy an American classic.

JUCY LUCY BURGERS

SERVES 4

Straight from the pan, the cheesy center of the Jucy Lucy will be molten hot. Be sure to let the burgers rest for at least 5 minutes before serving.

2	slices hearty white sandwich bread, torn into large pieces
¼	cup whole or low-fat milk
1	teaspoon garlic powder
¾	teaspoon salt
½	teaspoon pepper
1½	pounds 85-percent lean ground beef
1	slice deli American cheese, ½ inch thick, cut into quarters
2	teaspoons vegetable oil

1. Using a potato masher, mash the bread, milk, garlic powder, salt, and pepper in a large bowl until smooth. Add the beef and gently knead until well combined.

FORMING A JUCY LUCY

1. Using half of each portion of meat, encase the cheese to form a mini burger patty.

2. Mold the remaining portion of meat around the mini patty and seal the edges to form a ball. Flatten the ball to form a ¾-inch-thick patty.

2. Divide the meat mixture into 4 equal portions. Following the photos on page 347, mold each portion of the meat around 1 piece of the cheese. Transfer the patties to a plate and refrigerate for 30 minutes, or up to 24 hours.

3. Heat the oil in a large nonstick skillet over medium heat until just smoking. Add the patties and cook until well browned, about 6 minutes. Flip the burgers, cover the skillet, and continue cooking until well-done, about 6 minutes. Transfer to a plate, tent with aluminum foil, and let rest for 5 minutes. Serve.

Variation
GRILLED JUCY LUCY BURGERS
Prepare Jucy Lucy Burgers through step 2. Scrape and oil the cooking grate. Grill the burgers over a medium fire until well browned and cooked through, 6 to 8 minutes per side. Transfer to a plate, tent with aluminum foil, and let rest for 5 minutes. Serve.

SHOPPING WITH THE TEST KITCHEN

Hot Dogs: Burgers may be popular, but hot dogs aren't far behind. Americans spend over $1.5 billion on store-bought hot dogs each year. To determine which all-beef hot dog is best, we bought nine brands at our local supermarket and headed into the test kitchen to cook and taste them. Not surprisingly, our panel preferred dogs with rich, beefy flavor and a good mixture of seasonings. We were surprised to find that the sugar level tracked with our final rankings; tasters' favorite dogs all contained 0 grams of sugar and were praised for their meaty flavor, whereas the unpopular dogs contained up to 2 grams of sugar. Texture was also important to tasters, who wanted firm dogs that had some snap. Our tasters heralded Nathan's Famous Beef Franks for their meaty, robust flavor and firm texture—qualities that separate them from the overprocessed competition.

SHOPPING WITH THE TEST KITCHEN

Tabletop Grills: We liked the idea of grilling shrimp or beef tableside, just like in restaurants, so we decided to test indoor grills. After dismissing models that required hard-to-find fondue fuel or denatured alcohol, we purchased six brands in two styles: electric and those designed to sit on a stovetop burner. The stovetop models didn't get hot enough and are not recommended. Of the six models tested, only the Sanyo Smokeless Electric Indoor Grill ($39.95) combined a large capacity with easy cleanup and minimal smoke. Our favorite among the electric versions, it most closely mimicked the heat of an outdoor grill and produced the least smoke, due to a basin you must fill with water before cooking.

Smothered Pork Chops

Many of us in the test kitchen have fond memories from our youth of pork chops swimming in a hearty sauce, packed with big onion flavor—smothered pork chops. In our fuzzy nostalgia, we forgot that the chops were probably tough and bland and the sauce gelatinous or floury. No doubt some of our harried mothers relied on canned soup to get dinner to the table quickly. Could we make smothered pork chops without Campbell's prepackaged help?

The most obvious first test was what type of pork chop worked best. We tend to favor thick-cut rib loin chops because they have a higher fat content than other chops, which is important to the chop's flavor. We then cooked chops that were ½ inch to more than an inch thick. Tasters all favored the skinnier chops (½ inch thick), which were more tender than the inch-thick chops.

Because we were using thin chops, we tried shortening the braising time, but with little success. After 15 minutes, they were cooked through, but tough. After 30 minutes, they were more tender and flavorful. Extending the braise for another 15 minutes did little for either texture or flavor, so we left it at half an hour.

We found that adequately browning the chops was essential to developing richness and depth in the meat and the sauce. A thorough drying of the chops with paper towels and a generous coating of salt and pepper prior to browning helped promote a thick crust. The crust is partially washed away during the slow braise, but it enriches the flavor and color of the sauce.

A hefty amount of yellow onions is crucial to the sauce's richness. To add a little sweetness and more color to the sauce, we cooked the onions until they browned a bit and started to soften, about 5 minutes. We knew adding a little salt to the onions while they cooked would help break them down faster, but we were amazed at how efficiently the salt worked. The onions released enough liquid to deglaze (or lift) the fond (the browned bits that adhered to the pan after the chops were browned).

After tasting a variety of liquids for braising, we settled on chicken broth. It provided a supportive background for the onion and pork flavors.

To thicken the sauce, we embraced tradition and used a roux—flour cooked in some type of fat. Roux adequately thickened the sauce, and it added a mildly nutty flavor to the dish. Borrowing a Southern technique, we tried making the roux with rendered bacon fat instead of bland vegetable oil. The sauce tasted fantastic; the smokiness accented the sweet onions and the meatiness reemphasized that of the pork chops. And the crisp bacon bits served well as a crunchy, visually appealing garnish.

Our mothers would be proud. We had an easy, richly flavored dish perfect for a weeknight meal, and there wasn't a can of soup in sight.

SMOTHERED PORK CHOPS

SERVES 4

Make sure the chops are quite dry before browning them to prevent sticking and to promote the best crust. The pork chops pair well with a variety of starches, which you will want to soak up the rich gravy. We liked them best with simple egg noodles, but rice or mashed potatoes also taste great.

4	slices bacon, diced
3	tablespoons all-purpose flour
1¾	cups low-sodium chicken broth
1	tablespoon vegetable oil
4	bone-in rib loin pork chops, ½ to ¾ inch thick
	Salt and pepper
2	onions, halved and sliced thin
2	garlic cloves, minced
1	teaspoon minced fresh thyme
2	bay leaves
1	tablespoon chopped fresh parsley

1. Fry the bacon in a medium saucepan over medium heat until lightly browned and the fat is rendered, 6 to 7 minutes. Remove the browned bacon from the pan with a slotted spoon and set aside on a small plate. Reduce the heat to medium-low and gradually stir in the flour with a wooden spoon, making sure to work out any lumps that may form. Continue stirring constantly, reaching into the edges of the pan, until the mixture is light brown, 4 to 5 minutes. Add the chicken broth in a slow, steady stream while vigorously stirring. Reduce the heat to low and keep the sauce warm.

2. Heat the oil in a large skillet over high heat until shimmering, 2 to 3 minutes. Meanwhile, pat the chops dry with paper towels and season generously with salt and pepper. Place the chops in the pan in a single layer and cook until a deep brown crust forms, about 2 minutes. Turn the chops over and cook for another 2 minutes. Remove the chops from the pan and set aside on a plate.

3. Reduce the heat to medium and add the onions and ½ teaspoon salt to the skillet. Cook, stirring frequently and scraping any browned bits off the bottom of the pan, until the onions soften and begin to brown around the edges, about 5 minutes. Stir in the garlic and thyme and cook until fragrant, about 30 seconds longer. Return the chops to the pan in a single layer and cover each chop with onions. Pour in the warm sauce, add the bay leaves, and cover with a tight-fitting lid. Reduce the heat to low and cook until the meat is tender, about 30 minutes.

4. Transfer the chops to a warmed plate and cover with aluminum foil. Increase the heat to medium-high and cook, stirring frequently, until the sauce thickens to a gravy-like consistency, 4 to 5 minutes. Stir in the parsley and adjust the seasonings as desired. Cover each chop with a portion of the sauce, sprinkle with the reserved bacon, and serve immediately.

Variations

SMOTHERED PORK CHOPS BRAISED IN CIDER WITH APPLES

Replace the chicken broth with an equal amount of apple cider and replace one of the onions with 1 large or 2 small Granny Smith apples, peeled, cored, and cut into ⅓-inch slices. Proceed as directed.

SMOTHERED PORK CHOPS WITH SPICY COLLARD GREENS

Increase the oil to 2 tablespoons, reduce the onions to 1, and increase the garlic to 4 cloves. Once the onion and garlic are cooked, add 4 cups thinly sliced collard greens and ½ teaspoon red pepper flakes to the skillet. Return the browned chops to the pan and proceed as directed.

Tennessee Whiskey Pork Chops

Pairing the earthy, smoky flavor of whiskey with mild pork is a great idea, as evidenced by the many restaurants that now offer Jack Daniel's–style chops. And, apparently, there's more than one way to go about it. We found recipes that use whiskey in sticky glazes, overnight marinades, flaming pan sauces, and more. Which of these approaches, we wondered, would be the best way to create a happy marriage of flavors?

We began testing recipes in which the pork chops were exposed to the whiskey for a long time, via overnight marinades and long, slow simmers. We figured more time would equal more flavor, but these avenues were dead ends. The chops that soaked overnight had a sour, medicinal flavor, and the long-simmered chops were dried out and devoid of any flavor at all, whiskey or otherwise. The notion of marinating the chops for an hour or so was promising (and something we wanted to explore later on), but it was clear that for a real hit of whiskey flavor, we would have to make a sauce.

We chose widely available center-cut chops and used the test kitchen's basic technique for sautéing chops in a hot pan filmed with oil. Our first thought was to add a shot of booze to a finished sauce. This backfired badly—the harsh taste of raw alcohol came through, with none of the deeper, more desirable flavors. Using the whiskey as the base for the sauce, then cooking it down for a few minutes, was much more promising. As the whiskey reduces, the pungent alcohol cooks off and the sugars and other subtler, mellower flavors are concentrated.

Developing a tasty pan sauce was a simple matter of finding the right ingredients to complement the charred, woodsy flavor (and surprising sweetness) of the reduced whiskey. Cider vinegar and cayenne pepper added acidity and heat, and mustard helped to thicken the sauce, as did brown sugar, which also brought a welcome hint of molasses. Cutting the whiskey with an equal amount of apple cider helped to mellow its smokiness. We tried adding a bit of vanilla extract (a common ingredient in dessert sauces made with whiskey) and liked the way it paired with the spicy cayenne pepper in particular.

As much as we liked the pan sauce, we were not ready to abandon the idea of infusing some of that flavor into the meat itself. In earlier tests, a 1-hour marinade had added flavor to the meat, but we didn't want to make a separate marinade and sauce. Could we take a portion of the sauce ingredients and use them as a marinade? Sure enough, the marinade really improved the flavor of the chops, which were now getting that great whiskey flavor from two sources—a marinade and a pan sauce.

It was time to plate these pork chops. But rather than just pour the sauce over them, we decided to reduce it even further until it resembled a thick, syrupy glaze. Then we returned the chops to the pan and let them sit off the heat until the glaze cooled just enough to coat them thoroughly.

TENNESSEE WHISKEY PORK CHOPS

SERVES 4

Refrigerate the marinating chops in a shallow bowl in case the zipper-lock plastic bag leaks. Watch the glaze closely during the last few minutes of cooking—the bubbles become very small as it approaches the right consistency.

- ½ cup Jack Daniel's Tennessee whiskey or bourbon
- ½ cup apple cider
- 2 tablespoons light brown sugar
- 1 tablespoon Dijon mustard
- ⅛ teaspoon cayenne pepper
- ½ teaspoon vanilla extract
- 4 teaspoons cider vinegar
- 4 bone-in center-cut pork chops, about 1 inch thick

- 2 teaspoons vegetable oil
- Salt and pepper
- 1 tablespoon unsalted butter

1. Whisk the whiskey or bourbon, cider, brown sugar, mustard, cayenne, vanilla, and 2 teaspoons of the vinegar together in a medium bowl. Transfer ¼ cup of the whiskey mixture to a gallon-sized zipper-lock plastic bag, add the pork chops, press the air out of the bag, and seal. Turn the bag to coat the chops with the marinade and refrigerate for 1 to 2 hours. Reserve the remaining whiskey mixture.

2. Remove the chops from the bag, pat dry with paper towels, and discard the marinade. Heat the oil in a large skillet over medium-high heat until just beginning to smoke. Season the chops with salt and pepper and cook until well browned on both sides and a peek into the thickest part of a chop using a paring knife reveals still-pink meat ¼ inch from the surface, 3 to 4 minutes per side. Transfer the chops to a plate and cover tightly with aluminum foil.

3. Add the reserved whiskey mixture to the skillet and bring to a boil, scraping up any browned bits with a wooden spoon. Cook until reduced to a thick glaze, 3 to 5 minutes. Reduce the heat to medium-low and, holding on to the chops, tip the plate to add any accumulated juices back to the skillet. Add the remaining 2 teaspoons vinegar, whisk in the butter, and simmer the glaze until thick and sticky, 2 to 3 minutes. Remove the pan from the heat.

4. Return the chops to the skillet and let rest in the pan until the sauce clings to the chops, turning them occasionally to coat both sides, and a peek into the thickest part of a pork chop using a paring knife shows completely cooked meat (145 degrees on an instant-read thermometer), about 5 minutes. Transfer the chops to a platter and spoon the sauce over the meat. Serve.

Smoked Double-Thick Pork Chops

In the heart of grilling season, supermarket butchers tag all sorts of cuts of meat with stickers promising "Always Juicy" and "Great on the Grill!" Recently a package of huge, double-thick pork chops—adorned with a "Great on the Grill!" sticker—caught our eye. They were a good 2 inches thick, with a giant rib bone that could barely be contained by the plastic wrapping. Wanting to see if these mammoths of the meat case would live up to their promise, we bought some and headed to the grill.

These chops were so big that they felt more like mini roasts, so we knew that grilling them over a hot fire, as we do with regular pork chops, was out of the question because the exterior would burn before the inside was done. Brining, a common test-kitchen technique of soaking meat in a saltwater solution to promote even seasoning and cooking, would be redundant because our chops, like most pork sold today, were already "enhanced," or injected with a solution to keep the meat from drying out (hence the "Always Juicy" stickers). Our goal was evenly cooked meat with more flavor than just the salt added during the "enhancement" process.

Tackling the even cooking problem first, we decided to try the authentic barbecue method of "low and slow," whereby meat is cooked, covered and with indirect heat, for a long time on the cooler side of the grill. This technique gives meat plenty of time to cook through evenly at a relatively gentle temperature. We started with a full chimney of coals, hefted our chops onto the grill opposite the coals, and waited patiently for them to cook. When we pulled the lid off an hour later, the good news was that the meat was tender and juicy throughout; the bad news was that it tasted steamed and the exterior was pale.

Normal-sized pork chops are not on the grill long enough to merit smoking. But because these huge chops were spending about an hour on the covered grill, adding wood smoke seemed like a good way to increase the flavor. As it turned out, there's a fine line between subtle flavor and suffocating smoke. After testing wood amounts ranging from ½ cup to 3 cups, we settled on 2 cups of hickory chips. Presoaking the wood chips and wrapping them in a foil packet provided steady smoke throughout the cooking time by slowing the rate at which the wood burned. Our chops were finally moist and tender and had a nice level of smoke flavor, but they were still missing something.

We recalled what we liked most about thinner, quicker-grilling chops: the crisp texture and smoky flavor of a seared crust. To create the most flavorful crust possible, we started by coating the raw chops with a spice rub; after a lot of testing, tasters settled on a combination of brown sugar, fennel, cumin, coriander, paprika, salt, and pepper. When the chops were almost done, we uncovered the grill and moved them to the hot side of the grate. The coals still had enough life left in them to toast the spices on the surface of the meat, giving the chops richer flavor, and the brown sugar in the rub caramelized to a gorgeous mahogany color. With a method that combined elements of barbecue and quick grilling, we'd finally figured out how to make these behemoth chops truly "Great on the Grill!"

SMOKED DOUBLE-THICK PORK CHOPS

SERVES 6 TO 8

We prefer blade chops, which have more fat to prevent drying out on the grill, but leaner loin chops will also work. These chops are huge and are best sliced off the bone before serving.

¼	cup packed dark brown sugar
1	tablespoon ground fennel
1	tablespoon ground cumin
1	tablespoon ground coriander
1	tablespoon paprika

1 **teaspoon salt**

1 **teaspoon pepper**

4 **bone-in blade-cut pork chops (20 to 24 ounces each), about 2 inches thick (see note above)**

2 **cups wood chips soaked for 15 minutes in a bowl of water to cover and drained**

1. Combine the sugar, fennel, cumin, coriander, paprika, salt, and pepper in a small bowl and rub the mixture all over the pork chops. Cover with plastic wrap and refrigerate for at least 1 hour, or up to 24 hours.

2. Seal the wood chips in a foil packet and cut vent holes in the top (see page 326). Open the bottom vent of the grill. Light a large chimney starter filled with charcoal briquettes (about 100) and burn until the charcoal is covered with a fine gray ash. Pour the coals into a pile on one side of the grill and lay the foil packet on the coals. Set the cooking grate in place and heat the grill, covered, with the lid vent open halfway, for 5 minutes. (For a gas grill, seal the wood chips in a foil packet, cut vent holes in the top [see page 326], and place the packet on the primary burner. Turn all the burners to high, cover the grill, and heat until the wood chips begin to smoke heavily, about 15 minutes. Turn the primary burner to medium and turn off the other burner[s], adjusting the temperature of the primary burner as needed to maintain an average temperature of 275 degrees.) Scrape and oil the cooking grate.

3. Arrange the chops, bone side toward the fire, on the cooler side of the grill. Cover (position the lid vent directly over the meat for a charcoal grill) and cook until the chops register 140 to 145 degrees on an instant-read thermometer, 50 to 60 minutes. (If your chops are less than 2 inches thick, start checking their temperature after 30 minutes). Slide the chops directly over the fire and cook, uncovered, until well browned, about 2 minutes per side. Transfer to a platter and let rest for 20 minutes. Serve.

SHOPPING WITH THE TEST KITCHEN

Wood for Smoking: Sprinkling some soaked wood chips (or scattering a few wood chunks) over a pile of hot coals adds a great smoky flavor to grilled foods. While developing our California Barbecued Tri-Tip (page 325) and Smoked Double-Thick Pork Chops (page 352) recipes, we found that the type of wood used can make a huge difference in the finished product. Wood from fruit trees, such as apple, cherry, and peach, produces a slightly sweet smoke with a hint of fruitiness. Hickory and pecan woods both produce a hearty smoke that cuts through even the spiciest rubs. Maple, the traditional choice for ham, produces a mellow, sweet smoke, and oak lends a faint acidic note that many people enjoy. Ultimately, the only wood that left tasters a bit wary was mesquite. Although the heavy, assertive flavor of mesquite smoke was enjoyable in quickly cooked meats, it had a tendency to turn bitter over long periods of cooking.

SHOPPING WITH THE TEST KITCHEN

Cutting Double-Thick Pork Chops: We like juicy blade-end chops that are at least 2 inches thick for our Smoked Double-Thick Pork Chops. If you can't find them prepackaged at your grocery store, just buy a 4½- to 5-pound bone-in blade roast and cut it into 2-inch portions yourself. If you're cutting your own chops, ask your butcher or meat department manager if the chine bone (a part of the backbone) has been removed from the base of the roast; this thick bone can make carving difficult. If the chine bone has not been removed, ask the butcher to cut the chops for you.

Quick and Crunchy Pork Chops

Breaded pork chops are quick and easy, but the shake-in-the-bag-style coatings touted at the supermarket often fall short—tasting off and turning out soggy chops. We wanted two things in breaded pork chops above all else: good flavor and a thick, crunchy crust.

We began by going through a stack of cookbooks and found recipes where the chops were coated with cornflake crumbs, flour, matzo meal, bread crumbs, cornmeal, and more. You name it, we tried it. But these crusts were all too thin and gummy. We realized we needed coarser, sturdier crumbs.

With a heavy-duty plastic freezer bag and a mallet, we found we could turn almost any cracker into crumbs. And we could control their texture. We tried Ritz crackers, saltines, and oyster crackers, but Melba toast was the test-kitchen favorite. Everyone liked its dense, hearty crunch and subtle, toasted flavor. What's more, a 5-ounce box of Melba toast, once crushed, produced the perfect amount of crumbs to coat four chops.

Up until this point, we had been using the Shake 'n Bake method: moisten the chops with water, pile them in the bag with the crumbs, and shake them up. Although mess-free, this method didn't produce the thick, crunchy crust we had envisioned. Too many crumbs fell off. We discovered that getting our hands dirty—by pressing the crumbs into the chops—was more effective. But we still needed something stickier than water to support a super-thick crust.

We tried beaten eggs, buttermilk, heavy cream, sour cream, and milk. All were acceptable in flavor, but none contributed to that elusive crunch. After doing some thinking (and eating yet another pork chop dinner), we realized that everything we had used to adhere the crumbs to the chops was water-based; no wonder the crust was sodden! Plain vegetable oil worked better, but the coating was a bit thin. The winner turned out to be—believe it or not—mayonnaise!

By coating each chop with a tablespoon of mayonnaise (which stuck to the meat like frosting on a cake), we were able to build a thick crust. The Melba mixture stuck to the chop like a champ and staunchly defended its territory. Seasoning the

SECRETS TO BREADED PORK CHOPS

1. Thoroughly coat each chop with 1 tablespoon of mayonnaise.

2. Use your fingers to press the crumbs onto each chop.

3. Bake the breaded chops on a wire rack set over a baking sheet.

4. Insert an instant-read thermometer into the side to determine doneness.

Melba crumbs was easy. Pantry staples such as garlic powder, onion powder, paprika, and dried thyme did the trick.

Now we worked on the cooking method. We started with a 425-degree oven, the temperature recommended on a box of Shake 'n Bake. This part of the recipe was dead on. One part that wasn't, was the advice to cook the chops on a baking sheet; the underside of the chops always turned out soggy. We solved this problem by placing the breaded chops on a wire rack set over a rimmed baking sheet. Finally, we produced truly crunchy pork chops that tasted as great as they looked.

QUICK AND CRUNCHY PORK CHOPS

SERVES 4

For a substantial crust, don't break up the Melba toast too much, and coat the chops well with mayonnaise. Although an instant-read thermometer takes the guesswork out of determining when the meat is done, you can use the "nick-and-peek" method: use a paring knife to make a slit in the top of the pork chop and take a look at the meat's interior. The Melba crumbs can be made weeks in advance and stored in the freezer. Applesauce is a natural served with these chops.

1	(5-ounce) box Melba toast, broken into rough pieces
½	teaspoon salt
½	teaspoon garlic powder
½	teaspoon onion powder
½	teaspoon paprika
½	teaspoon dried thyme
⅛	teaspoon sugar
6	tablespoons mayonnaise
4	boneless center-cut pork chops, about 1 inch thick

1. Adjust an oven rack to the middle position and heat the oven to 425 degrees. Place the Melba toast pieces, salt, garlic powder, onion powder, paprika, thyme, and sugar in a heavy-duty zipper-lock plastic freezer bag. Seal the bag and pound with a heavy blunt object (such as a rolling pin) until the Melba toast is crushed but there are still some crumbs the size of small pebbles. Add 2 tablespoons of the mayonnaise to the bag and work the mayonnaise evenly into the crumb mixture by gently squeezing the outside of the bag. Transfer the Melba-crumb mixture to a large plate.

2. Pat the chops dry with paper towels. Using your fingers, coat 1 chop with 1 tablespoon of the mayonnaise. Transfer to the plate with the Melba crumbs, sprinkle the top of the pork chop with some Melba mixture, and press down firmly on the chop to adhere the crumbs. Flip the chop and repeat, making sure that a thick layer of crumbs coats both sides and edges. Transfer the breaded pork chop to a wire rack set over a rimmed baking sheet. Repeat with the remaining 3 chops, 3 tablespoons mayonnaise, and Melba mixture.

3. Bake the pork chops until the juices run clear and an instant-read thermometer inserted into the center of a chop registers 145 to 150 degrees, 16 to 22 minutes. Remove the chops from the oven and let rest on the rack for 5 to 10 minutes. Serve immediately.

Variations
SESAME PORK CHOPS

Toast ¼ cup sesame seeds in a small skillet over medium-low heat, stirring frequently, until fragrant and golden, 4 to 5 minutes. Substitute sesame-flavored Melba toast for regular Melba toast and add the toasted sesame seeds to the Melba-crumb mixture in step 1.

CORDON BLEU PORK CHOPS
In this variation, ham and cheese top the pork chops before they are breaded.

Place 4 thin slices provolone cheese on top of each pork chop (the pile of cheese should be no more than ¼ inch thick) and tear the cheese to leave a ⅛-inch border on all sides. Top with 1 slice deli ham large enough to cover the cheese completely, and press down on the ham to adhere to the pork chop. Reduce the salt to ¼ teaspoon and increase the cooking time by 1 to 2 minutes.

Chicago-Style Barbecued Ribs

They boast about their barbecue pretty loudly in Chicago, where baby back ribs are slow-smoked to fall-apart tenderness and slathered with a spicy sauce. To understand what makes Chicago ribs the source of so much pride, a few of us from the test kitchen hopped on a plane to eat our way through a half dozen of the Windy City's finest rib joints.

Aside from discovering that we can eat a lot of ribs in two days, we learned that Chicago ribs are typically smoked at about 200 degrees for at least 8 hours (and sometimes for up to a day). This slow-and-low cooking method ensures the moist, tender meat that helps define Chicago ribs.

Back home, we hoped to shorten the cooking time by using a slightly hotter fire, but the resulting ribs were tough and chewy. We had better luck starting the ribs on the grill (so they picked up good color and smoke flavor) and finishing them in a 250-degree oven for another 2 hours or so. Ribs made

this way weren't tough, but they weren't really tender or moist, either.

Some recipes suggested precooking the ribs by poaching them in simmering water, but this made them bloated and bland. Other recipes called for mopping or spraying water on the ribs to ensure moistness. The extra humidity helped, but every time we opened the grill lid to apply water, we also allowed heat to escape. Placing a pan of water in the grill during cooking moistened the ribs without lengthening the cooking time. To create really moist ribs, we took this method one step further and steamed the ribs in the oven as well. After just a few hours, these smoky ribs were so tender that we had trouble picking them up.

We had smuggled several bottles of Chicago barbecue sauce back to the test kitchen; their labels revealed a few unusual ingredients, namely, celery salt and allspice. The other thing that makes this sauce stand out is the heat, which comes from plenty of cayenne pepper. Since Chicago sauce is supposed to be brash and assertive, no simmering was necessary—we just mixed all the ingredients together in a bowl and brushed the sauce on the ribs at the end. These moist, tender, and spicy ribs were just as good as any we had in Chicago.

CHICAGO-STYLE BARBECUED RIBS
SERVES 4 TO 6
The dry spices are used to flavor both the rub and the barbecue sauce. When removing the ribs from the oven, be careful that you do not spill the hot water in the bottom of the baking sheet.

RIBS

1	tablespoon dry mustard
1	tablespoon paprika
1	tablespoon dark brown sugar
1½	teaspoons garlic powder

MAKING CHICAGO-STYLE BARBECUED RIBS

1. Place a disposable pan on the bottom of the grill and fill it with 2 cups of water. The water creates steam that keeps the ribs from drying out.

2. After smoking the ribs, add water to cover the bottom of a rimmed baking sheet. Place a wire rack on the baking sheet, add the ribs, wrap the entire pan in aluminum foil, and bake until tender.

1½	teaspoons onion powder
1½	teaspoons celery salt
1	teaspoon cayenne pepper
½	teaspoon ground allspice
2	racks baby back ribs (about 1½ pounds each), membrane removed
1	cup wood chips (see page 353), soaked for 15 minutes in a bowl of water to cover and drained

SAUCE

1¼	cups ketchup
¼	cup molasses
¼	cup cider vinegar
¼	cup water
⅛	teaspoon liquid smoke

1. FOR THE RIBS: Combine the mustard, paprika, sugar, garlic powder, onion powder, celery salt, cayenne, and allspice in a bowl. Reserve 2 tablespoons of the mixture for the sauce. Pat the ribs dry with paper towels and massage the remaining spice rub into both sides of the ribs. (The ribs can be wrapped in plastic wrap and refrigerated for up to 24 hours.)

2. Open the bottom vent of the grill. Light a large chimney starter filled with charcoal briquettes (100 coals). Arrange a 13 by 9-inch disposable aluminum pan filled with 2 cups water on one side of the bottom of the grill. When the charcoal is covered with a fine gray ash, pour the coals into a pile on the opposite side. Scatter the wood chips over the coals and set the cooking grate in place. (For a gas grill, place the wood chips in a small disposable aluminum pan and place directly on the primary burner. Place another disposable aluminum pan filled with 2 cups water on a secondary burner[s] and set the cooking grate in place. Turn all the burners to high, cover the grill, and heat until the chips are smoking heavily, about 15 minutes. Turn the primary burner to medium and turn off the other burner[s].) Position the ribs over the water-filled pan and cook, covered (open the lid vent halfway on a charcoal grill), rotating and flipping the racks of ribs once, until the ribs are deep red and smoky, about 1½ hours.

3. Adjust an oven rack to the middle position and heat the oven to 250 degrees. Set a wire rack inside a rimmed baking sheet and add just enough water to cover the pan bottom. Arrange the ribs on the wire rack, cover tightly with aluminum foil, and cook until the ribs are completely tender, 1½ to 2 hours. Transfer to a serving platter, tent with foil, and let rest for 10 minutes.

4. FOR THE SAUCE: Meanwhile, whisk the ketchup, molasses, vinegar, water, liquid smoke, and reserved spice rub in a bowl. Brush the ribs with 1 cup of the barbecue sauce. Serve, passing the remaining sauce at the table.

Easy Glazed Pork Roast

A boneless pork roast requires almost no prep. And if you add vegetables to the roasting pan, you've got a complete meal. More often than not, though, pork roasts are dry and poorly browned, and the vegetables are steamed, not roasted. You could brine the pork (that is, soak it in a saltwater solution for an hour) to add moisture, and brown the pork in a skillet to develop a caramelized crust, but these steps take time. How about a quicker, easier solution?

After some testing, we found that coating the pork with a flavorful glaze does the trick on both counts: it adds moisture and gives the pork a deep golden crust as it caramelizes in the oven. Two other easy steps can minimize the problem of dry meat. The first is to remove the pork from the oven once an instant-read thermometer inserted into the very center registers 140 degrees. (This seems like a low temperature, but the residual heat in the roast will cause the temperature to climb to about 150 degrees.) The second is to let the roast rest on a cutting board for 10 minutes before slicing it. This resting time reduces the loss of juices during carving.

And what about those vegetables? For a true roasted flavor, they need more time in the oven than the meat. Once the meat starts to rest on the cutting board, crank up the oven heat, spread out the vegetables, and keep on roasting them.

MARMALADE-GLAZED PORK ROAST WITH PARSNIPS AND ONIONS

SERVES 6

For best results, avoid using enhanced pork (pork injected with a solution of water, salt, and chemicals); it causes the pork to exude excess liquid as it cooks, inhibiting the caramelization of the vegetables.

1   boneless center-cut pork loin roast
    (3 pounds; see note above)
    Salt and pepper
⅓   cup orange marmalade
1   tablespoon chopped fresh rosemary
½   cup orange juice
1   tablespoon olive oil
1   pound parsnips, peeled and cut
    into 3-inch pieces
2   red onions, cut into 1-inch wedges

1. Adjust an oven rack to the middle position and heat the oven to 375 degrees. Place the pork in the center of a large roasting pan and season liberally with salt and pepper.

2. Combine the marmalade and rosemary in a large bowl. Spread half of the marmalade mixture on the pork. Add the orange juice and olive oil to the remaining marmalade mixture. Toss the parsnips and onions with 2 tablespoons of the mixture and season with salt and pepper to taste. Arrange the vegetables around the pork. Roast until an instant-read thermometer inserted in the thickest part of the meat registers 120 degrees, 30 to 45 minutes. Pour the remaining marmalade mixture over the pork, increase the oven temperature to 450 degrees, and roast until an instant-read thermometer registers 140 degrees, 15 to 20 minutes.

3. Transfer the roast to a cutting board and tent with aluminum foil. Toss the vegetables with the pan juices and redistribute evenly over the pan bottom. Roast until the juices thicken and the vegetables caramelize, about 10 minutes. Slice the pork and serve with the roasted vegetables, pouring the pan juice over the meat.

CIDER-GLAZED ROAST PORK LOIN (page 369)

TOP: **PECAN-CRUSTED CHICKEN CUTLETS** (page 277), **CHEESY BASIL-STUFFED CHICKEN BREASTS** (page 280)
BOTTOM: **MEATBALLS AND MARINARA** (page 346), **OVEN-BARBECUED BEEF BRISKET** (page 340)

FIRECRACKER CHICKEN (page 297)

TOP: **PAN-FRIED TROUT** (page 385), **JUCY LUCY BURGERS** (page 347)
BOTTOM: **LEXINGTON-STYLE PULLED PORK** (page 375), **FAMILY-STYLE SHRIMP SCAMPI** (page 392)

CREOLE-STYLE CRAB CAKES (page 397)

TOP: **COUNTRY CAPTAIN CHICKEN** (page 432), **BROILED STEAKS** (page 322)
BOTTOM: **CHICAGO-STYLE BARBECUED RIBS** (page 356), **WEEKNIGHT CHILI** (page 421)

CALIFORNIA BARBECUED TRI-TIP (page 325)

CRISPY ROAST CHICKEN AND POTATOES (page 299)

Old-Fashioned Roast Pork

Pork today is about 30 percent lower in fat than it was twenty years ago. Fat gives meat flavor and keeps it moist during cooking; with so little fat, typical supermarket pork tends to be bland and dry. Although a good sauce can help, today's pork loin will never be as flavorful or succulent as the ones we remember from our childhood.

Because the loin is especially lean, our first thought was to try roasting a fattier cut. The obvious choice was pork shoulder, the classic roast for barbecued pulled pork. The shoulder is nice and fatty, so the meat is especially flavorful and moist. Could we just "barbecue" this cut indoors, without the usual spices or smoke, and make something appropriate for Sunday dinner?

Our first task was to choose a specific roast. A pork shoulder is massive, weighing between 14 and 20 pounds. Because of its size, supermarkets cut the shoulder in half to make it more manageable. The upper portion is sold as either a pork shoulder roast or a Boston butt and weighs 6 to 8 pounds. The lower portion is called the picnic roast and runs about the same size. In side-by-side tests, we preferred the richer flavor and slightly more tender texture of the Boston butt.

Following the lead of barbecue pit masters, we roasted a dozen Boston butts using different combinations of temperature and time. We found that 7 hours (yes, 7 hours) in a 300-degree oven produced meat that was nearly perfect. The connective tissue melted and converted to gelatin, making the meat very tender, and the melting fat kept the meat moist. The results we got when we tried to speed up the process by using a hotter oven simply were not as good. The only problem was that the roast could not be carved into neat slices. What we had were more like shreds and chunks, and it was hard to resist the urge to cover them up with barbecue sauce. We wanted neat slices that we could place on a serving platter.

We tried letting the roast rest longer than the usual 20 or 30 minutes, but even an hour wasn't sufficient. The roast still wouldn't carve neatly and still shed a lot of juice. In frustration, we ended up refrigerating one of our unsliced roasts at the end of a long day in the test kitchen. The next morning, we sliced the cold roast effortlessly into clean slices, poured a bit of liquid over the meat, and warmed the meat in the oven. The roast not only looked better in neat slices but tasted better, too, because the juices had become completely redistributed throughout the meat. This meat was so juicy and succulent it was definitely worth the wait.

GIVING PORK OLD-FASHIONED FLAVOR

1. Trim any excess fat, leaving behind a ⅛-inch layer. Tie the trimmed roast tightly into a uniform shape, with three pieces of kitchen twine running around the width of the roast and one piece running around its length.

2. Rub a mixture of rosemary, sage, fennel seeds, garlic, salt, and pepper over the roast. Roast the pork for 3 hours, add onion wedges, and continue to roast until the meat is extremely tender, 3½ to 4 hours more.

Now that we had our roasting technique, we turned our attention to flavoring the roast. We thought garlic and herbs would be a good match, and tasters agreed, favoring garlic, rosemary, sage, and fennel seeds.

Because we were using liquid to moisten the slices of meat as they reheated, we developed a simple sauce that could be used both to flavor the meat as it reheated and to serve at the table. A classic combination of onions and apples was a nice counterpoint to the rich flavors of the meat. Clearly, the shoulder is the best choice you can make to get old-time flavor out of today's "other white meat."

OLD-FASHIONED ROAST PORK

SERVES 8

Start this recipe a day before serving. A heavy, deep-sided (3-inch) roasting pan is the best choice for this recipe, but a shallow broiler pan also works well.

1	boneless pork shoulder roast (Boston butt, about 6 pounds)
3	garlic cloves, minced
2	teaspoons freshly cracked pepper
1½	teaspoons salt
1	tablespoon chopped fresh rosemary
1	tablespoon chopped fresh sage
1	tablespoon fennel seeds, roughly chopped
2	large red onions, cut into 1-inch wedges
1	tablespoon vegetable oil (if necessary)
1	cup apple cider
¼	cup apple jelly
2	tablespoons cider vinegar

1. Adjust an oven rack to the lower-middle position and heat the oven to 300 degrees. Trim the outer fat from the pork, leaving a ⅛-inch layer. Combine the garlic, pepper, salt, rosemary, sage, and fennel seeds in a small bowl. Following the photos on page 367, tie the pork roast tightly into a uniform shape. Rub with the herb mixture.

2. Transfer to the roasting pan and cook for 3 hours. Scatter the onion wedges around the meat, tossing the onions in the pan drippings to coat. (If the roast has not produced any juices, toss the onions with oil.) Continue roasting until the meat is extremely tender and a skewer inserted into the center meets no resistance, 3½ to 4 hours longer. (Check the pan juices every hour to make sure they have not evaporated. If necessary, add 2 cups water to the pan and stir the browned bits into the water.)

3. Transfer the roast to a large baking dish, place the onions in a medium bowl, and pour the pan drippings into a liquid measuring cup, adding enough water to measure 1½ cups. Allow all to cool for 30 minutes, cover with plastic wrap, and refrigerate overnight.

4. One hour before serving, adjust an oven rack to the middle position and heat the oven to 300 degrees. Cut the cold meat into ¼-inch slices and overlap them in a large baking dish. Spoon the fat layer off the drippings (discard the fat) and transfer the drippings and reserved onions to a medium saucepan. Add the cider, jelly, and vinegar and bring to a boil over medium-high heat, then reduce to a simmer. Spoon ½ cup of the simmering sauce over the pork slices and cover the baking dish with aluminum foil. Place in the oven and heat until very hot, 30 to 40 minutes. Meanwhile, continue reducing the sauce until dark and thickened, 10 to 15 minutes (reheat the mixture just before serving the pork). Serve the pork, spooning the onion mixture over the meat or passing it at the table.

Cider-Glazed Roast Pork Loin

American pigs have had most of the fat bred out of them over the past half century, and as a result, pork loin—a lean cut to begin with—can be pretty dry and bland. A sticky-sweet cider glaze can hide these flaws, but just pouring cider over a roast and shoving it into the oven doesn't work. When we tried this most obvious method, we were shocked to find that the cider made the meat worse: the roast refused to brown as it sat in a watery pool of cider. Glazing a pork roast requires a bit more finesse.

Our first goal was to develop a reliable roasting method without a glaze. To improve browning (and thus add flavor), we tried roasting the meat in a very hot oven. Although most recipes specify 375 or 400 degrees, we discovered that the oven has to be cranked up to at least 450 degrees to brown the exterior. Unfortunately, the meat (especially the outer portion) was chalky and dry by the time the center was done. In the end, we found that browning the pork loin in a skillet and then transferring it to a moderate oven (375 degrees) produced a more evenly cooked, juicier roast.

With our roasting technique under control, it was time to focus on the glaze. To help the glaze cling to the meat, we thought we'd try simmering the cider in the pan we had used to brown the pork. Simmering thickened the cider and punched up the apple flavor, but the glaze still wasn't sticky enough. To make it more syrupy, we tried adding maple syrup, honey, and brown sugar. The maple and honey competed with the apple flavor, and the brown sugar was so sweet it caused our glaze to scorch. Next we tried adding applesauce, apple jelly, and apple butter. The applesauce was too grainy and the jelly too sweet, but the apple butter was just right, contributing substance as well as apple flavor. Shallots and herbs rounded out the flavors of the glaze.

We tested adding the glaze at different stages throughout the cooking process and finally settled on the halfway point. Added earlier, the glaze burned; added later, it didn't reduce enough. We also found it imperative to use a fairly small baking dish. In a shallow broiler pan, the glaze evaporated too quickly. The pork loin fit snugly in a 13 by 9-inch baking dish, where it sat in a deeper pool of glaze.

While our nicely glazed roast pork loin was resting, we noticed that it was "leaking" juices onto the cutting board. Adding those juices to the glaze remaining in the baking dish produced an intensely flavored sauce we could serve with the sliced pork. With a glaze that does double duty as a sauce, our recipe gives pork loin the powerful flavor boost it needs.

CIDER-GLAZED ROAST PORK LOIN

SERVES 6

Make sure to tie the roast at 1½-inch intervals with kitchen twine, if your butcher hasn't already done so.

- 1   boneless center-cut pork loin roast (3 pounds), tied (see note above)
     Salt and pepper
- 2   tablespoons vegetable oil
- 6   shallots, peeled (halved if large)
- 2   cups apple cider
- ½   cup apple butter
- 1   bay leaf
- 1   sprig fresh thyme
- 1   teaspoon cider vinegar

1. Adjust an oven rack to the middle position and heat the oven to 375 degrees. Pat the pork loin dry with paper towels and season with salt and pepper.

2. Heat 1 tablespoon of the oil in a large skillet over medium-high heat until just smoking. Place the pork loin, fat side down, in the skillet and cook, turning it several times, until browned on all sides, 8 to 10 minutes. Transfer the pork, fat side down, to a 13 by 9-inch baking dish and roast until an instant-read thermometer inserted in the thickest part registers 85 degrees, about 25 minutes.

3. While the pork roasts, cook the shallots in the remaining 1 tablespoon oil in the now-empty skillet over medium heat until golden brown, 3 to 5 minutes. Increase the heat to high, add the cider, apple butter, bay leaf, and thyme, and bring to a boil. Cook until thickened, about 8 minutes.

4. After the pork has roasted for 25 minutes, pour the glaze over the pork and, using tongs, roll the pork to coat with glaze. Cook until the internal temperature of the pork registers 145 degrees on an instant-read thermometer, 20 to 30 minutes more, turning once halfway through to recoat with the glaze. Transfer the pork to a cutting board, tent with aluminum foil, and let rest for 20 minutes. Transfer the glaze to a small saucepan, discarding the thyme and bay leaf, and whisk in the vinegar.

5. Before slicing the pork, pour the accumulated juices from the roast into the glaze and warm the glaze over low heat. Cut the roast into ¼-inch slices, transfer to a platter, and spoon ½ cup glaze over the top. Serve, passing the remaining glaze at the table.

Pepper-Crusted Pork Loin

A spicy, savory crust of crushed peppercorns is the perfect adornment for a relatively bland pork loin, but balancing the two elements isn't as easy as it might seem. Pepper-crusted beef works so well because beef has enough richness to offset some of the pepper's sharp heat, but lean pork doesn't have enough flavor to stand up to the same peppery bite. We wanted to find a way to deeply infuse a pork loin with spicy pepper flavor while eliminating the harsh burn.

To get a substantial crust on the entire surface of the pork loin, we started by rubbing 5 tablespoons of cracked peppercorns over the roast. After we browned the pork on the stovetop and finished it in the oven (the test kitchen's technique for most roasts), the jolt of pepper was way too harsh. Cutting back on the amount of peppercorns resulted in a speckled, uneven crust. We hoped the test kitchen's trick of gently heating the peppercorns in oil to bloom their flavor and mellow their heat would work, but the resulting roast still had too much pepper burn.

Since the bite of the cracked pepper was proving to be too strong no matter how we handled it, we wondered if we could temper the pepper's heat, while keeping most of its flavor, by using a finer grind. After testing several grinds from barely cracked to finely ground, tasters settled on a middle ground that allowed for a thinner, milder crust with plenty of pepper flavor. Two tablespoons of coarsely ground pepper gave us the right amount of spice, but it didn't yield enough rub to fully coat the roast.

To stretch the rub, we tried supplementing the pepper with other ingredients; strong spices like mustard, coriander, and cumin overwhelmed the mellow pork, but tasters appreciated the piney tang of fresh rosemary as a complement to the pepper. Adding brown sugar and salt worked to further extend the rub; the sugar tamed the heat even more, and the salt helped carry all the flavors into the meat, especially when we let the rubbed roast sit for an hour. The peppery flavor was definitely still present, but now it brought lively spice and complexity—and no harsh burn—to the mild pork.

There was still one problem: the pepper crust was burning during the initial sear on the stovetop. Simply switching the searing from the stovetop to a hot oven solved the problem. Finishing the roast at a more moderate temperature ensured juicy pork with bold flavor both inside and out. We'd finally made a pepper-crusted pork loin to be proud of.

PEPPER-CRUSTED PORK LOIN

SERVES 6

Serve plain or with fruit chutney, applesauce, or our Cherry-Brandy Sauce (recipe follows).

3	tablespoons light brown sugar
2	tablespoons coarsely ground pepper
2	tablespoons minced fresh rosemary
1½	teaspoons salt
1	boneless center-cut pork loin roast (3 pounds)

1. Combine the sugar, pepper, rosemary, and salt and rub all over the pork. Let the roast stand at room temperature for 1 hour or refrigerate for up to 24 hours.

2. Adjust an oven rack to the upper-middle position and heat the oven to 450 degrees. Arrange the pork on a V-rack set in a roasting pan. Roast for 15 minutes, then lower the oven temperature to 375 degrees and cook until the meat registers

140 degrees on an instant-read thermometer, about 50 minutes longer. Transfer the pork to a cutting board and tent with aluminum foil. Let rest for 20 minutes. Slice the pork and serve.

CHERRY-BRANDY SAUCE

MAKES ABOUT 2 CUPS

If you can't find frozen cherries, substitute one 14.5-ounce can of pitted tart red cherries in water, drained.

4	tablespoons unsalted butter
2	onions, chopped
3	cups low-sodium chicken broth
½	cup brandy
1	(8-ounce) bag frozen pitted sweet cherries, thawed (see note above)
1	cup dried cherries
2	tablespoons balsamic vinegar
	Salt

Melt 2 tablespoons of the butter in a large saucepan over medium heat. Cook the onions until golden, about 8 minutes. Stir in the broth, brandy, and cherries and simmer until thick and syrupy, about 15 minutes. Off the heat, stir in the vinegar and the remaining 2 tablespoons butter. Season with salt to taste. Serve. (The sauce can be refrigerated for up to 2 days.)

SHOPPING WITH THE TEST KITCHEN

Roasting Racks: A roasting rack is as unglamorous as it is essential. It raises poultry and roasts out of the drippings, while giving the oven's heat easy access to the whole surface—a good start toward a well-rendered exterior. We recommend buying a roasting pan that comes with a rack, but if you don't need a new roasting pan you can buy a roasting rack. We like nonadjustable, V-shaped racks because they hold roasts snugly in place and they don't "adjust" when you least expect it. Make sure the rack you buy elevates the roast high enough that the roast doesn't sit in its juices and also leaves enough room for roasting vegetables underneath. The sturdy All-Clad Nonstick Roasting Rack ($24.95) is our favorite. It's large enough to hold two small chickens and has the features we like, including handles on the long sides.

SHOPPING WITH THE TEST KITCHEN

Pepper Mills: Pepper mills come in a range of styles and materials, but performance should be the most important factor in selecting a pepper mill. We rounded up seven pepper mills and put them through their paces to find our favorite. We value output efficiency, but the quality of a pepper mill's grind is just as important. We looked for uniformity in fine-, medium-, and coarse-ground pepper, and we wanted to be able to easily adjust the mill's settings. Our favorite is the Unicorn Magnum Plus ($45), notable for producing an abundance of perfectly ground pepper with minimal effort. With a small, ergonomic crank, the Magnum Plus is the best pepper mill on the market. But if you value fast and easy adjustments between grind settings over extremely high output, the William Bounds ProView Pepper Mill ($39.95) is a very good option. It has adjustable rings for fine, medium, and coarse grinds that testers found intuitive. Although this mill couldn't keep pace with the output of the Magnum Plus, it produced perfectly uniform pepper at all three settings.

Herbed Roast Pork Tenderloin

Recipes abound for herb-flavored pork tenderloin, employing techniques such as crusting, marinating, and stuffing the pork with sundry combinations of herbs. We started testing and off the bat had poor luck with herb crusts—the herbs came close to combusting on the outside of the meat. Marinating the pork in an herb-infused oil took a long time, and the herb payout was minimal. Stuffing was the most promising method.

We butterflied two tenderloins (enough for six people) and rubbed the inside of each with a simple herb paste of parsley and olive oil. We rolled them back up, tied them for even cooking, and roasted them side by side in a 450-degree oven. The herbs stayed bright green but had a dull flavor, and the roasts weren't browning much on the outside; we had a lot of work to do. We decided to start with the stuffing.

After trying several herbs alone and in combination, we discovered that soft herbs like parsley, basil, and tarragon (which have a high moisture content) tasted washed-out, because they were steaming inside the meat. Heartier (and drier) fresh herbs, such as the combination of thyme and sage, won tasters over. Mustard, garlic, and lemon juice and zest added more bold flavors. The final step was replacing the olive oil with rich butter; tasters liked the herb butter so much that we made extra to brush on the finished roasts.

In an attempt to promote browning, we coated the exterior of the roasts with a rub of sugar, salt, and pepper (a little olive oil helped the rub adhere), but these 1½-pound roasts weren't in the oven long enough for the sugar to caramelize. Browning the roasts in a skillet and then transferring them to the oven was the only reliable way to create a good crust without overcooking the meat—but we wanted a good crust with less work.

It was then that we remembered seeing two pork tenderloins tied together into one big roast at the butcher shop. Since this "double wide" tenderloin would take longer to cook, we hoped it would give the sugar-rubbed exterior a chance to brown in the oven. After butterflying and rubbing the roasts, we overlapped them by a couple of inches and folded them up lengthwise into a cylinder. We tied the double roast and cooked it in a 450-degree oven, flipping it once to ensure even cooking. When the super-sized tenderloin came out of the oven, our efforts were rewarded with a nicely browned roast that, when sliced, revealed a juicy spiral of herb-infused meat.

HERBED ROAST PORK TENDERLOIN

SERVES 4 TO 6

Pork tenderloins can vary greatly in weight; try to find 2 large roasts for this recipe. We prefer to cut away the tough silver skin before butterflying.

3 tablespoons unsalted butter, softened
2 tablespoons whole-grain mustard
1 teaspoon grated fresh lemon zest and 1 teaspoon fresh lemon juice (1 lemon)
1 garlic clove, minced
1 tablespoon minced fresh sage
1 tablespoon minced fresh thyme
   Salt and pepper
1 teaspoon sugar
2 pork tenderloins (about 3 pounds total; see note above)
1 tablespoon olive oil

1. Adjust an oven rack to the middle position and heat the oven to 450 degrees. Using a fork, beat the butter, mustard, lemon zest and juice, garlic, sage, thyme, ¼ teaspoon salt, and ¼ teaspoon pepper in a bowl until combined. Reserve 3 tablespoons of the herb-butter mixture. Combine the sugar, ¼ teaspoon salt, and ¼ teaspoon pepper in a small bowl.

2. Pat the tenderloins dry with paper towels and, following the photos, butterfly them. Spread the

---

PREPARING HERBED PORK TENDERLOINS

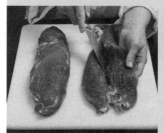   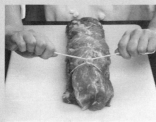

1. Butterfly the tenderloins by laying them flat on a cutting board and slicing down the middle of each. Leave about ¼ inch of meat intact, then open like a book.

2. Spread the interior of each tenderloin with the butter mixture.

3. Arrange the tenderloins so that the thick and thin ends are opposite each other, then overlap the tenderloins halfway. Fold to interlock the cut sides of the tenderloins.

4. Tie the folded tenderloins securely with kitchen twine at 1½-inch intervals.

interior evenly with the herb-butter mixture, interlock the tenderloins, and tie them securely with kitchen twine at 1½-inch intervals. Rub the pork with the oil and sprinkle the sugar mixture evenly over the exterior.

3. Roast the meat on a rimmed baking sheet until the exterior is golden brown and the meat registers 140 to 145 degrees on an instant-read thermometer, about 35 minutes, flipping the pork halfway through cooking. Transfer to a cutting board and brush the top of the pork with the reserved herb-butter mixture. Tent with aluminum foil and let rest for 10 minutes. Remove the kitchen twine. Slice and serve.

Lexington-Style Barbecued Pulled Pork

Lexington-style barbecue (named after Lexington, North Carolina) is unmistakable. Slow-cooked pork shoulder turns out so tender, so sweet, and so smoky that it seems almost unnatural. And the sauce is a revelation—thin and pungent, tart with vinegar and spicy with pepper, its acidity expertly balanced by just a hint of sugar and ketchup. When combined with the succulent, meaty pork shoulder, this barbecue is so good, we were determined to re-create it in the test kitchen.

But making Lexington-style pulled pork at home can be trying, because it calls for hours and hours of diligent grill tending. To see if there was a less labor-intensive way to produce authentic-tasting Lexington barbecued pork, we hit the books. To reduce the cooking time while still maintaining barbecue flavor, some recipes rely on

indoor smokers or even braising the pork shoulder with liquid smoke, but these methods seemed disingenuous. In the test kitchen we often start large pieces of meat on the grill before finishing them in the oven. Theoretically, this allows the meat to take on a smoky, barbecued flavor without having it sit over a live fire all day.

Our first tests using this technique resulted in fork-tender meat in just 4 to 5 hours (2 hours on the grill, the rest in the oven), but the smoke flavor that the grill provided dissipated during the pork's time in the oven, leaving it tasting like it had been simply roasted. To bump up the flavor, we coated the pork with a basic barbecue rub (many recipes include just salt and pepper) before placing it on the grill. To make sure the smoke got down into the meat, we doubled the amount of wood chips called for in most recipes, burning through 4 cups of chips in just 2 hours of grilling. With this treatment, the pork developed a deep red crust (called "bark" in barbecue circles) and a rich, thick smoke ring that stayed with the pork even after a couple of hours in the oven.

Covering the pork and finishing it in a 325-degree oven created moist heat that melted the collagen, turning the tough pork shoulder into a

SETTING UP THE GRILL

Indirect heat is the key to low-and-slow BBQ. Place the roast on the side of the grill opposite the lit coals.

Although North Carolinians agree that pork is the barbecue meat of choice, they're divided when it comes to exactly what cut of pork and what type of sauce should be used. In the eastern part of the state, it's just not barbecue unless it's a whole hog. Known in the Carolinas as a "pig pickin'," this type of barbecue starts with a split hog and ends with succulent meat and crackling-crisp skin. The meat is then literally picked from the bones and lightly seasoned with a thin vinegar and pepper sauce. Western Carolinians eschew the whole hog and go straight for the shoulder—the most marbled and meatiest chunk of the animal. The pork shoulder is cooked just like the whole hog (slow and low over a wood or charcoal fire), but the sauce further stokes the debate. Although still vinegar-based, the barbecue sauce in the western areas is enriched with just enough ketchup and sugar to take the edge off the acidity.

savory, fork-tender piece of meat. It had just the right amount of smoke and seasoning, but now it needed its complement, a splash of that characteristic sweet-and-sour Lexington-style barbecue sauce.

The beauty of this sauce is its simplicity—after all, it's nothing more than vinegar, sugar, pepper, and ketchup. But even with so few ingredients, it still took some testing to get the balance of flavors just right. As a base, cider vinegar was the clear favorite for its fruity taste. But it did have an edge, which was easily curbed by adding an equal amount of water. For a touch of sweetness, we added granulated sugar and just enough ketchup to give the sauce body and a rosy color. Although hot sauce was a common theme in our research, we found the flavor to be distracting. Pepper added a nice earthy bite, and a pinch of red pepper flakes gave the sauce a kick that matched the pungency of the vinegar. Finally, we were ready to put it all together.

After we pulled the pork into shreds, we gave it a little splash of sauce and piled it high onto plates, with sides of coleslaw and pickle chips. At last, we'd found barbecue heaven.

LEXINGTON-STYLE PULLED PORK

SERVES 8 TO 10

Pork butt (often labeled "Boston butt") is usually sold boneless and wrapped in netting but is sometimes available on the bone. If barbecuing a bone-in roast, or if your pork butt weighs more than 5 pounds, plan on an extra 30 to 60 minutes of oven cooking time.

SPICE RUB AND PORK

- 2 tablespoons paprika
- 2 tablespoons pepper
- 2 tablespoons brown sugar
- 1 tablespoon salt
- 1 boneless pork shoulder roast (4 to 5 pounds)
- 4 cups wood chips, soaked for 15 minutes in a bowl of water to cover and drained

SAUCE

- 1 cup water
- 1 cup cider vinegar
- ½ cup ketchup
- 1 tablespoon granulated sugar
- ¾ teaspoon salt
- ½ teaspoon pepper
- ½ teaspoon red pepper flakes

FINISHING THE PORK

1. After taking the pork off the grill, transfer it to a roasting pan, cover the pan with aluminum foil, and finish in a 325-degree oven.

2. Wearing kitchen gloves to protect your hands from the heat, shred (or "pull") the pork into thin strands, adding sauce as you go.

1. FOR THE SPICE RUB AND PORK: Combine the paprika, pepper, sugar, and salt in a small bowl, breaking up any lumps as necessary. Massage the entire pork roast with the spice mixture. (The roast may be wrapped tightly and refrigerated for up to 1 day.)

2. Open the bottom vent of the grill. Light a large chimney starter filled halfway with charcoal briquettes (about 50) and burn until the charcoal is covered with a fine gray ash. Pour the coals into a pile on one side of the grill and scatter the wood chips over the coals. Set the cooking grate in place and heat the grill, covered, for 5 minutes. (For a gas grill, seal the wood chips in a foil packet, cut vent holes in the top (see page 326), and place the foil packet directly on the primary burner. Turn all the burners to high, cover the grill, and heat until the wood chips begin to smoke heavily, about 15 minutes. Turn the primary burner to medium and turn off the other burner[s], adjusting the temperature of the primary burner as needed to maintain an average temperature of 275 degrees.) Scrape and oil the cooking grate.

3. Position the pork on the cooler side of the grill. Cover (position the half-open lid vent directly over the meat on a charcoal grill) and cook until the meat has a dark, rosy crust and the charcoal is spent, about 2 hours.

4. Meanwhile, adjust an oven rack to the lower-middle position and heat the oven to 325 degrees. Transfer the pork to a large roasting pan, wrap the pan and pork tightly in aluminum foil, and roast in the oven until a fork inserted into the pork can be removed with no resistance, 2 to 3 hours. Remove from the oven and let rest, still wrapped in foil, for 30 minutes.

5. FOR THE SAUCE: Whisk together all of the ingredients until the sugar and salt are dissolved. Using your hands, pull the pork into thin shreds, discarding the fat if desired. Toss the pork with ½ cup of the sauce, serving the remaining sauce at the table.

Cider-Baked Ham

A big, smoky ham glazed with sweet apple cider and studded with cloves certainly sounds great. But the reality is that most cider-baked hams are lacking in apple flavor. Could we develop a technique that would infuse ham with big apple flavor?

We quickly discovered that we preferred an uncut cured ham (as opposed to a spiral-cut ham) for this recipe, as uncut ham has a fat layer that can be trimmed and scored to give the glaze something to hang on to. We tried the test kitchen's method for cooking cured ham in an oven bag along with cider and then baked it in a relatively cool oven until the interior reached 100 degrees. We then took off the bag, cranked up the heat, and repeatedly basted the ham until a thick, glossy coating formed. This gave us a nice-looking ham but little apple flavor. Looking for more cider punch, we tried marinating the ham in cider overnight. After several tests, we determined that just 4 hours in the cider was enough time to add significant apple flavor.

But we still needed to work on the glaze. The cider rolled right off the ham and required constant reapplication. Thicker apple jelly and apple butter coated the ham better than the cider, but they didn't provide the same fresh apple flavor. Reducing the cider to a syrupy state on the stovetop proved to be a much better solution; the reduced cider was sticky enough to cling to the ham in just one application, meaning that we didn't have to continually baste our ham, and it provided superior apple flavor. A little mustard added to the glaze provided a spicy contrast to the sweet cider. As a final touch, we concocted a simple brown sugar and pepper mixture to pat on the ham after the glaze was applied; this mixture caramelized into a crunchy, flavorful crust that provided a nice contrast to the tender meat.

Cider-baked hams are traditionally studded with potent cloves. But both powdered and whole cloves proved to be too harsh. Wondering if we could take the edge off of whole cloves by adding them to the cider marinade, we tossed a handful of cloves and a cinnamon stick (which always pairs well with apple) into the mix. This worked great, especially when we first dry-toasted the cloves and cinnamon in a skillet to release their flavor before adding the cider. Now this ham not only looked amazing but had deep cider flavor and a spicy crust.

CIDER-BAKED HAM

SERVES 16 TO 20

We prefer a bone-in, uncut cured ham for this recipe, because the exterior layer of fat can be scored and helps create a nice crust. A spiral-sliced ham can be used instead, but there won't be much exterior fat, so skip the trimming and scoring in step 2. This recipe requires nearly a gallon of cider and a large oven bag. In step 4, be sure to stir the reduced cider mixture frequently to prevent scorching.

1	cinnamon stick, broken into rough pieces
¼	teaspoon whole cloves
13	cups apple cider
8	cups ice cubes
1	bone-in cured half ham (7 to 10 pounds), preferably shank end (see note above)
2	tablespoons Dijon mustard
1	cup packed dark brown sugar
1	teaspoon pepper

SECRETS TO CIDER-BAKED HAM

1. Soaking the ham in spice-infused cider lends a concentrated flavor to the ham.

2. Baking the ham with a cup of cider in the oven bag keeps the meat moist and lends even more cider flavor.

3. Brushing the ham with a sticky cider reduction provides big apple flavor and a base for the crust.

4. Pressing a mixture of brown sugar and pepper onto the ham gives the exterior a spicy-sweet, crackly crust.

1. Toast the cinnamon and cloves in a large saucepan over medium heat until fragrant, about 3 minutes. Add 4 cups of the cider and bring to a boil. Pour the spiced cider into a large stockpot or a clean bucket, add 4 more cups cider and the ice, and stir until the ice is melted.

2. Meanwhile, remove the skin from the exterior of the ham and trim the fat to a ¼-inch thickness. Score the remaining fat at 1-inch intervals in a cross-hatch pattern. Transfer the ham to the container with the chilled cider mixture (the liquid should nearly cover the ham) and refrigerate for at least 4 hours, or up to 12 hours.

3. Discard the cider mixture and transfer the ham to a large oven bag. Add 1 cup fresh cider to the bag, tie securely, and cut 4 slits in the top of the bag. Transfer to a large roasting pan and let stand at room temperature for 1½ hours.

4. Adjust an oven rack to the lowest position and heat the oven to 300 degrees. Bake the ham until the internal temperature registers 100 degrees on an instant-read thermometer, 1½ to 2½ hours. Meanwhile, bring the remaining 4 cups cider and mustard to a boil in a saucepan. Reduce the heat to medium-low and simmer, stirring often, until the mixture is very thick and reduced to ⅓ cup, about 1 hour.

5. Combine the sugar and pepper in a bowl. Remove the ham from the oven and let rest for 5 minutes. Increase the oven temperature to 400 degrees. Roll back the oven bag and brush the ham with the reduced cider mixture. Using your hands, carefully press the sugar mixture onto the exterior of the ham. Return the ham to the oven and bake until dark brown and caramelized, about 20 minutes. Transfer the ham to a cutting board, loosely tent with aluminum foil, and let rest for 15 minutes. Carve and serve.

SHOPPING WITH THE TEST KITCHEN

Inexpensive Saucepans: In the test kitchen, we use our large saucepans for making rice and oatmeal, blanching vegetables, and cooking small amounts of pasta, soup, stew, and all manner of sauces. The test kitchen's favorite large saucepan is the $184 All-Clad 4-Quart Sauce Pan. But can you get away with something less pricey at home? We rounded up 8 large saucepans with traditional finishes and pitted them against the All-Clad in a battery of tests. In the end the All-Clad was the only pan to pass every test with flying colors, but the Berndes Tricion 3.5-Quart Stainless Steel Sauce Pan ($99) performed nearly as well and costs much less. The most important quality for a saucepan is even and slow heating; our testing found the All-Clad and the Berndes, which both feature a full aluminum core, to be the best at this task.

CHAPTER TWELVE

Seafood

SEAFOOD

Salmon Cakes

Fish cakes started out as thrifty New England fare, designed to use up salt-preserved or leftover cooked fish and potatoes. Back in the 1800s, the use of fresh fish would certainly have been regarded as a suspicious extravagance, if not downright odd. But today, raw fish is typically used in salmon cakes (or salmon burgers as they're sometimes called). It was to these burgers that all of the tasters gravitated when we cooked up six different recipes for salmon cakes to kick off our recipe development process. The chunky texture, the moistness, and the direct salmon flavor of the cakes made with fresh fish appealed to all.

We began by trying a couple of methods for breaking down the fish. Predictably, the food processor ground the fish too finely for our tastes, even when we proceeded with the greatest care. As it turned out, chopping the fish by hand was not difficult, and it provided a far smaller margin of error in terms of overprocessing than did the food processor.

As for binders, common choices included eggs, either whole or yolks alone, and mayonnaise. Of the many egg combinations we tried, the yolks alone worked best. But when we tried mayonnaise, everyone preferred it over the egg yolks. Just 2 tablespoons of mayonnaise for the 1¼ pounds of chopped fish we were using added a noticeable creaminess to the cakes' texture and a welcome tang to their flavor. Any more, though, and the cakes began to get a little greasy.

Starchy products—including cooked potato, crushed crackers, dry and fresh bread crumbs, and bread soaked in milk—made up another category of binders worth testing. The cooked potato produced cakes that were rubbery and dry, and both the crushed crackers and dried bread crumbs became leaden and mushy by absorbing too much moisture from the fish, not to mention the fact that they gave the cakes a stale flavor. The milk-soaked bread showed well, but best overall were the fresh bread crumbs we made by simply processing a piece of sturdy white sandwich bread from which we had removed the crusts. The bread crumbs lightened and softened the texture of the cakes, making them smoother and more refined.

With the binding just right, we tried the various flavorings listed in our stack of test recipes. A basic combination of onion, lemon juice, and parsley prevailed, providing simple, bright, fresh flavors. Some tasters objected to the crunch of the minced onion, but we quickly solved that problem by grating it to allow for better integration into the fish mixture.

The next step was to find the crisp, light, golden coating of our dreams. Some recipes left out the coating altogether, but the resulting cakes lacked interest and tasted too fishy. Flour alone soaked right into the fish mixture and became pasty when cooked. Dried bread crumbs alone were okay, but uninspiring. Our stellar coating involves a full breading treatment, which consists of flour, beaten egg, and bread crumbs, applied in sequence. Although this does entail some extra work, the resulting thin, toasty coating is well worth it. A 15-minute stay in the freezer prior to breading, we found, firms the cakes slightly for easier handling and causes some of the surface moisture to evaporate, which helps the coating to adhere.

At last, we were ready to cook our cakes. Pan-frying the cakes in a generous quantity of vegetable oil—it should reach halfway up the sides of the cakes in the pan—for just 2 minutes per side produced a perfect golden crust and moist fish within.

PAN-FRIED FRESH SALMON CAKES

SERVES 4

A big wedge of lemon is the simplest accompaniment to salmon cakes, but any of the dipping sauces on page 401 would be an excellent embellishment. If possible, use super-crisp panko (Japanese bread crumbs) to coat the salmon cakes.

1¼	pounds salmon fillet
1	slice hearty white sandwich bread, crusts removed, torn into large pieces and pulsed in a food processor to fine crumbs
2	tablespoons mayonnaise
¼	cup finely grated onion
2	tablespoons chopped fresh parsley
¾	teaspoon salt
1½	tablespoons fresh lemon juice
½	cup all-purpose flour
2	large eggs, lightly beaten
1½	teaspoons plus ½ cup vegetable oil
1½	teaspoons water
¾	cup plain dried bread crumbs, preferably panko
	Lemon wedges

1. Run your fingers over the surface of the fillet to feel for pinbones, then remove them with tweezers or needle-nose pliers. Using a sharp knife, cut the flesh off the skin, then discard the skin. Chop the salmon flesh into ¼- to ⅓-inch pieces and mix with the fresh bread crumbs, mayonnaise, onion, parsley, salt, and lemon juice in a medium bowl. Scoop a generous ¼-cup portion of the salmon mixture from the bowl and, using your hands, form a patty measuring roughly 2½ inches in diameter and ¾ inch thick; place on a parchment-lined baking sheet and repeat with the remaining salmon mixture until you have 8 patties. Place the patties in the freezer until the surface moisture has evaporated, about 15 minutes.

2. Meanwhile, spread the flour in a pie plate or shallow baking dish. Beat the eggs with 1½ teaspoons of the oil and 1½ teaspoons water in a second pie plate or shallow baking dish. Spread the dried bread crumbs or panko in a third shallow dish. Dip the chilled salmon patties in the flour to cover; shake off excess. Transfer to the beaten egg and, using a slotted spatula, turn to coat; let the excess drip off. Transfer to the bread crumbs; shake the dish to coat the patties completely. Return the breaded patties to the baking sheet.

3. Heat the remaining ½ cup oil in a large heavy-bottomed skillet over medium-high heat until shimmering but not smoking, about 3 minutes; add the salmon patties and cook until medium golden brown, about 2 minutes. Flip the cakes and continue cooking until medium golden brown on the second side, about 2 minutes longer. Transfer the cakes to a plate lined with paper towels to absorb excess oil on the surface, if desired, about 30 seconds, then serve immediately with the lemon wedges or dipping sauce, if desired.

Variations

PAN-FRIED SMOKED SALMON CAKES

Substitute 8 ounces smoked salmon or lox, chopped into ¼- to ⅓-inch pieces, for 8 ounces of the fresh salmon and reduce the amount of salt to ½ teaspoon.

PAN-FRIED FRESH SALMON CAKES WITH CHEESE

Add 2 tablespoons grated Parmesan or Asiago cheese to the salmon mixture and reduce the amount of salt to ½ teaspoon.

Boston Baked Scrod

Named for the old Beantown restaurants that made this dish famous, Boston baked scrod is now a seafood restaurant standard across the country. Every once in a while this simple recipe turns out great, with sweet, tender pieces of cod lightly seasoned with butter and lemon and topped with crisp toasted crumbs. More often than not, however, it's rubbery and bland and topped with a soggy crust. Knowing how good it can be and how awful it usually is, we set out to discover what makes Boston baked scrod worth the effort.

The term scrod, as we quickly found out when shopping, is somewhat controversial and may be used to refer to several types of small fish (weighing less than 2½ pounds or so). It is more accurate to use the term scrod cod when buying fish at the local market to make sure the fish you are getting is really cod. A scrod cod fillet weighs about 1 pound and is enough for two portions. For easy cooking and serving, we found it helpful to cut the strangely shaped fillets in half crosswise. These two pieces, however, are very different in shape and thickness. Knowing that they would not cook at the same rate, we found it necessary to fold the thin tail piece in half to make it as thick as the piece from the head end of the fish.

After fitting four pieces of cod in a glass casserole dish, we baked and broiled up several batches. After testing a variety of oven temperatures and positions, we preferred the 14 minutes it took to cook the fish under the broiler. Positioned 6 inches from the element (ours is electric), the fish cooked through evenly with no ill effect on texture or flavor. Because cod is a relatively wet fish, it stands up well to the broiler's intense heat. We did have decent results in a hot (450-degree) oven, but the baking time was longer than the broiling time, and we still needed to switch on the broiler to brown the crumbs—and so broiling it was.

Although we had now developed a good cooking method, these initial tests drove home how bland the flavor of cod really is. No amount of lemon juice squeezed onto the fish at the table could turn it into a tasty meal. In an effort to zip up the bland cod, we tried broiling the fish with both butter and lemon juice. As the fish broiled, it soaked up some of these flavors and released some of its moisture. The fish not only turned out a bit more seasoned, but a flavorful little sauce was created in the pan. By adding some sautéed shallot, garlic, and fresh parsley to the butter and lemon juice, we brought the cod to a new level, where it tasted both impressive and clean. With a heavy-handed dose of salt and pepper, we had discovered a quick and easy way to make scrod worth eating.

The final component of Boston baked scrod is the toasted fresh bread crumbs that garnish the top of each portion. Made by processing and toasting several slices of hearty white sandwich bread and then seasoning them with salt, pepper, and fresh parsley, these crumbs needed only a minute under the broiler to adhere to the fish and heat through. Topped with crunchy, flavorful crumbs, these well-seasoned fillets of cod and their impromptu sauce are the best representatives of Boston baked scrod we've ever tasted.

BOSTON BAKED SCROD

SERVES 4

Cod fillets average about a pound at most markets. If you cut each fillet in half crosswise, you will have enough for four servings. To keep the thinner pieces from the tail end from overcooking, fold them in half before placing them in the casserole dish.

TOPPING

2 slices hearty sandwich bread, torn into large pieces and pulsed in a food processor to coarse crumbs

1 tablespoon chopped fresh parsley

¼ teaspoon salt

⅛ teaspoon pepper

SCROD

5	tablespoons unsalted butter
1	shallot, minced
1	garlic clove, minced
1½	tablespoons fresh lemon juice
1	tablespoon chopped fresh parsley
	Salt and pepper
2	skinless cod fillets (about 1 pound each), cut in half crosswise

1. FOR THE TOPPING: Adjust one oven rack to the upper-middle position (about 6 inches from the heat source) and another rack to the middle position; heat the oven to 400 degrees.

2. Spread the bread crumbs evenly on a rimmed baking sheet; toast on the lower rack, shaking the pan once or twice, until golden brown and crisp, 4 to 5 minutes. Toss together the bread crumbs, parsley, salt, and pepper in a small bowl; set aside.

3. FOR THE SCROD: Increase the oven setting to broil. Melt the butter in a small skillet over medium-high heat until the foaming has subsided. Reduce the heat to medium, add the shallot and garlic, and sauté until slightly softened, about 1 minute. Remove the pan from the heat, add the lemon juice, parsley, ¼ teaspoon salt, and ⅛ teaspoon pepper, and swirl to incorporate. Set aside.

4. Season the scrod liberally with salt and pepper. Fold the thin tail pieces in half to increase their thickness. Place the fillets in a broiler-safe 13 by 9-inch baking dish and pour the melted butter mixture over the top. Broil until the fish is completely opaque when gently flaked with a paring knife, 14 to 15 minutes. Baste the fish with the pan drippings and top with the bread crumbs. Continue broiling until the crumbs are golden brown, about 1 minute. Using a metal spatula, transfer the fish to individual plates and pour the basting juices around the edges of the fish (not on top, or the bread crumbs will become soggy). Serve immediately.

Pan-Fried Trout

Although this campsite favorite may seem simple and straightforward, pan-frying trout can easily turn ugly. When trout is perfectly cooked, its sweet, delicate flavor is protected by a crisp layer of cornmeal fried until golden brown. When things go wrong, which seems to happen more often than not, the cornmeal remains pale and turns soggy while the trout underneath leaches out sticky white foam, a sure sign it is overdone and dry.

Unless you've been successful on a recent fishing trip, you'll be buying trout at your local supermarket or fish shop. Most markets sell farm-raised trout cut into fillets. Although the varieties of trout taste different, we found only the size of the fillets made a difference when cooking them. Fillets weighing 5 to 7 ounces were the easiest to bread, fry, and serve, each fillet serving as one portion. Although several recipes we found instructed us to remove the skin, we found it necessary to keep the skin intact to prevent the flesh from falling apart, and our tasters considered the crispy fried skin a treat. Trout also has many little pinbones that can be difficult to remove before cooking. In the end, tasters did not mind eating around them or plucking them occasionally from their forks.

We dusted trout with several different types of cornmeal mixtures. Fine-ground cornmeal fried up smooth and crisp, but coarser cornmeal was too chewy and thick to cook through. Coatings made only of cornmeal, however, turned out extremely dense and chewy. By tempering the cornmeal with flour, we were able to make the coating crisp and light without losing any cornmeal flavor. Equal parts cornmeal and flour turned out the most balanced crust, neither too dense nor too floury. Because trout is mildly flavored, it is important to season the coating heavily with salt, pepper, and cayenne pepper.

Simply dusting the trout with the seasoned cornmeal mixture wasn't enough to make great fried trout. What did work was dusting the fish with flour, dipping it in an egg wash, then dusting it with cornmeal (known as a three-stage or bound breading). This produced a crisp, crackling crust that held up long enough for us to serve and eat the fish.

The term pan-frying is defined by the amount of oil in the pan. As opposed to a deep-fry, in which the food is submerged completely in hot oil, pan-fried food is cooked one side at a time in oil that measures partway up the sides of the food. When pan-frying chicken or pork cutlets, it is possible to use a relatively small amount of oil. When we tried to use a modest amount of oil with trout fillets, however, the results were quite poor. The cornmeal crust was undercooked and raw-tasting—we needed more oil and more heat.

We increased the oil to a depth of ½ inch and switched from a skillet to a Dutch oven to minimize splatters. With the oil temperature at 350 degrees, the fillets still fried up pale. Only when we cranked up the temperature of the oil to 400 degrees did the crust turn golden and crisp in a mere 4 minutes. Served with tartar sauce, this picture-perfect, cornmeal-fried trout remains crisp long out of the pan and breaks open to reveal tender, flaky flesh that might be improved only by a lakeside campsite and a good sunset.

PAN-FRIED TROUT
SERVES 4

Although we used an 11-inch sauté pan with sides 2½ inches high during our tests with no problem, we recognize the danger in heating oil to 400 degrees on the stovetop. Just to be safe, we recommend using a Dutch oven with sides at least 5 inches high. The oil will still splatter, however, and should not be left unattended. Use any variety of trout available. We had good luck with red rainbow, white rainbow, and golden trout.

1	cup all-purpose flour
½	cup fine-ground cornmeal
	Salt and pepper
⅛	teaspoon cayenne pepper
2	large eggs
2–3	cups vegetable oil
4	trout fillets (5 to 7 ounces each), skin on
	Lemon wedges or one of the dipping sauces on page 401

1. Set a wire rack over a rimmed baking sheet, place the sheet on an oven rack adjusted to the middle position, and heat the oven to 200 degrees. Place ½ cup of the flour in a shallow dish. In a separate shallow dish mix together the remaining ½ cup flour, the cornmeal, 1 teaspoon salt, ¼ teaspoon pepper, and the cayenne. In a third shallow dish, whisk the eggs with 1 tablespoon of the oil until uniform.

2. Pat the fish fillets dry with paper towels and sprinkle each side with salt and pepper. Drop the fish into the flour and shake the dish to coat. Shake the excess flour from each piece, then, using tongs, dip the fillets into the egg mixture, turning to coat well and allowing the excess to drip off. Coat the fillets with the cornmeal mixture, shake off the excess, and lay the fillets on another wire rack set over a rimmed baking sheet.

3. Heat ½ inch of oil in a large heavy-bottomed Dutch oven over high heat until the oil reaches a temperature of 400 degrees. (The oil should not smoke, but it will come close.) Place 2 trout fillets in the oil and fry, turning once, until golden brown, about 4 minutes. Adjust the heat as necessary to keep the oil between 385 and 390 degrees (use a candy/deep-fry thermometer or an instant-read thermometer that registers high temperatures to gauge the temperature of the oil). Remove the fillets from the oil with a slotted spoon and lay them on a plate lined with several layers of paper towels; blot to help remove any excess oil. Transfer the fried fish to the wire rack in the warm oven. Bring the oil back to 400 degrees and repeat the cooking process with the remaining 2 fish fillets. Serve the fried fish immediately with either the lemon wedges or dipping sauce.

Pan-Fried Catfish

Catfish, thought by many to be a junk fish, never used to be considered the making of a fancy meal. Pan-fried catfish was common in the Low Country (the coastal areas of South Carolina and Georgia), where the fish flourished in local waters. Today, however, catfish is highly sought after and expensive. Although we found pan-frying catfish to be very similar to pan-frying trout, we did stumble across elements of the task that are unique to catfish.

First off, most catfish found at the store is farm-raised in freshwater, although ocean catfish (also known as wolffish) can occasionally be found. The oddly sized fillets of ocean catfish (some are mammoth and others tiny) don't easily lend themselves to pan-frying, but we found the average farm-raised, freshwater fillets usually weigh around ¾ pound. Two fillets of farm-raised catfish will easily serve four people, and we found it best to cut each fillet in half, making it easier both to cook and to serve. We found it best to cut the fillets down the middle

so that each portion has both a thin tail end and a thicker middle. This ensures that each half fillet will cook at the same rate and that each person will have the same ratio of crisp, fried tail to tender, flaky flesh. We also found it necessary to remove the skin and the dark, fatty tissue that lies directly underneath it. Although the skin offended no one, the dark fatty tissue was very fishy-tasting and unappealing.

Like trout, these fillets benefited from being dredged in flour, dipped in an egg wash, and finally coated with a seasoned cornmeal-flour mixture. Also like the trout, they browned beautifully and cooked through in only 4 minutes in ½ inch of 400-degree oil.

PAN-FRIED CATFISH

SERVES 4

To minimize splatters and maximize safety, use a Dutch oven with sides at least 5 inches high (not a regular skillet) when pan-frying the fish.

- 1 cup all-purpose flour
- ½ cup fine-ground cornmeal
  Salt and pepper
- ⅛ teaspoon cayenne pepper
- 2 large eggs
- 2–3 cups vegetable oil
- 2 catfish fillets (about 12 ounces each), skin removed and dark fatty flesh just below the skin trimmed, cut in half lengthwise
  Lemon wedges or one of the dipping sauces on page 401

1. Set a wire rack over a rimmed baking sheet, place the sheet on an oven rack adjusted to the middle position, and heat the oven to 200 degrees. Place ½ cup of the flour in a shallow dish. In a separate shallow dish mix together the remaining ½ cup flour, the cornmeal, 1 teaspoon salt, ¼ teaspoon pepper, and the cayenne. In a third shallow dish, whisk the eggs with 1 tablespoon of the oil until uniform.

2. Pat the fish fillets dry with paper towels and sprinkle each side with salt and pepper. Drop the fish into the flour and shake the dish to coat. Shake the excess flour from each piece, then, using tongs, dip the fillets into the egg mixture, turning to coat well and allowing the excess to drip off. Coat the fillets with the cornmeal mixture, shake off the excess, and lay the fillets on another wire rack set over a rimmed baking sheet.

3. Heat ½ inch of oil in a large heavy-bottomed Dutch oven over high heat until the oil reaches a temperature of 400 degrees. (The oil should not smoke, but it will come close.) Place 2 catfish fillets in the oil and fry, turning once, until golden brown, about 4 minutes. Adjust the heat as necessary to keep the oil between 385 and 390 degrees. (Use a candy/deep-fry thermometer or an instant-read thermometer that registers high temperatures to gauge the temperature of the oil.) Remove the fillets from the oil with a slotted spoon and lay them on a plate lined with several layers of paper towels; blot to help remove any excess oil. Transfer the fried fish to the wire rack in the warm oven. Bring the oil back to 400 degrees and repeat the cooking process with the remaining 2 fish fillets. Serve the fried fish immediately with either the lemon wedges or a dipping sauce.

Oven-Fried Fish

The idea of fried fish fillets coated with cornmeal and cooked to crispy, golden perfection sounds appealing, but we all know that sometimes we don't have time to stand over a skillet of frying fish. That's when oven-frying fits the bill. This easier, relatively mess-free technique seemed well worth a try.

Initial tests using cornmeal couldn't have been farther off the mark. We might as well have dunked our fish into a sandbox: these fillets cooked up bland, dry, and gritty. Even a generously greased baking sheet failed to help.

We wondered if another corn-based product (one with more fat, perhaps) might give the fish the corn crunch we wanted. Taking a "think outside the box" approach, we scoured every section of the supermarket for corn products and came back to the test kitchen with cornflakes, yellow and white tortilla chips, Bugles, Fritos, and cornbread. The cornflakes made a chewy—not crisp—coating on the fish. The coatings made with all varieties of ground corn chips tasted artificial and stale. The cornbread showed the most promise, but it was much too sweet.

Adding some fresh bread crumbs and a savory mix of dry mustard, thyme, garlic powder, cayenne pepper, salt, and pepper tempered the cornbread's sweetness. Even though the cornbread itself has some fat, the coating was still too crumbly and dry. Mixing the crumbs with melted butter gave the coating a crisp "fried" texture.

Next we had to make sure that the seasoned cornbread would adhere to the fish; simply coating the fillets was not enough. Dredging the fish in flour and then dipping it in buttermilk produced a substantial coating with a tangy flavor.

All we needed to do was fine-tune the cooking method. We were certainly on target but found that the bottoms of the fillets were getting a bit soggy. To solve this problem, we preheated an oiled pan. The fish now hit the pan with a sizzle, just as it would a hot skillet. Our oven-fried fish was nicely browned all around and nearly as crispy as pan-fried fish, but it made far less mess and left no lingering fishy odor.

OVEN-FRIED FISH

SERVES 4

Haddock, cod, or even thicker cuts of catfish work well in this recipe. If you have homemade cornbread on hand, use it.

- 2 tablespoons vegetable oil
- 6 ounces store-bought cornbread (one 3½-inch-square piece; see note above)
- 3 slices hearty white sandwich bread, torn into large pieces
- 2 teaspoons dry mustard
- 1 teaspoon dried thyme
- ¼ teaspoon garlic powder
- ¼ teaspoon cayenne pepper
  Salt and pepper
- 3 tablespoons unsalted butter, melted
- ½ cup all-purpose flour
- 1 cup buttermilk
- 4 skinless white fish fillets (6 to 8 ounces each), ¾ to 1 inch thick
  Lemon wedges

1. Adjust an oven rack to the upper-middle position and heat the oven to 450 degrees. Pour the oil onto a rimmed baking sheet and tilt to evenly distribute.

2. Pulse the cornbread in a food processor to coarse crumbs. Transfer the crumbs to a large bowl. Pulse the sandwich bread to fine crumbs. Transfer 1½ cups of the bread crumbs to the bowl with the cornbread; discard the remaining bread crumbs. Toss the crumbs with the mustard, thyme, garlic powder, cayenne, ½ teaspoon salt, and ¼ teaspoon pepper. Drizzle the melted butter over the crumbs and toss until coated.

3. Place the flour in a shallow baking dish and the buttermilk in a second shallow baking dish.

4. Place the oiled baking sheet in the hot oven and heat for 10 minutes while preparing the fish (don't leave it in the oven for more than 10 minutes or the oil will smoke). Pat the fish dry with paper towels and season with salt and pepper. Dip one fillet into the flour, shake off the excess, coat well with the buttermilk, then dredge in the crumb mixture, using your hands to firmly pack the crumbs onto all sides of the fish. Transfer the breaded fillet to a large plate and repeat with the remaining fillets.

5. Place the breaded fish on the preheated baking sheet and bake until the coating is crisp and the fish is cooked through, 12 to 14 minutes. Serve with the lemon wedges.

Stuffed Sole

Thin fillets of sole rolled around a savory stuffing and blanketed with a white sauce are a natural choice for anyone who likes to entertain. Too often, however, this dish tastes like bad banquet fare—overcooked fish, soggy stuffing, and a dull-flavored white sauce. We aimed to create a version of this dish you'd be proud to serve to company: tender, moist fillets, a lively stuffing, and a delicately flavored sauce that pulls the whole dish together. And because the dish has multiple components, we wanted to streamline the prep without compromising this impressive dish.

We started with the filling and dismissed a bread-based stuffing in favor of a Florentine-style filling made with spinach and cheese. Spinach and cheese would pack a lot more flavor than bread crumbs. In lieu of cooking fresh spinach, which would involve multiple steps, we turned to frozen spinach. Using frozen prechopped spinach cut out most of the laborious preparation; all we had to do was make sure it was thawed and thoroughly squeezed dry.

For the white sauce, we developed a rich cream sauce seasoned with garlic, shallot, and thyme. We combined some sauce with the spinach and

Parmesan cheese for a moist, rich filling for the fish and set aside the remainder to pour over the fillets.

Assembling the fish rolls was easy. We lined up the fillets, mounded the filling on each, and folded the end of each fillet over the filling. We then arranged the stuffed fillets, seam side down, in a baking dish and poured the remaining white sauce over them. Sprinkled with Ritz cracker crumbs—tasters liked the crumbs for their buttery flavor and crunchy texture—our dish was ready to bake. After about 15 minutes in a 475-degree oven, the bundles baked up moist and tender with a piping-hot filling and golden, crunchy crumbs—a main course ready to take center stage at any dinner party. And, for an even more upscale version of stuffed sole, we swapped the spinach and cheese for a stuffing containing crab and corn, seasoned with lemon and tarragon.

SOLE FLORENTINE

SERVES 4

Try to buy fish fillets of equal size to ensure even cooking. Be sure to squeeze as much moisture out of the frozen spinach as possible or it will water down the sauce. To check the doneness of the fish, use the tip of a paring knife to gently prod the fish—the flesh should be opaque and flaky, but still juicy. The dish can be assembled (minus the cracker crumbs), wrapped in plastic wrap, and refrigerated for up to 24 hours ahead of baking. Just before baking, sprinkle the fish with the cracker crumbs and increase the baking time to about 20 minutes.

2	tablespoons unsalted butter
1	shallot, minced
2	teaspoons minced fresh thyme
1	garlic clove, minced
2	cups heavy cream
4	teaspoons cornstarch
	Salt and pepper
2	(10-ounce) packages frozen chopped spinach, thawed and squeezed dry
½	cup grated Parmesan cheese
8	boneless, skinless sole fillets (3 to 4 ounces each), ¼ to ½ inch thick
15	Ritz crackers, crushed fine (¾ cup)
	Lemon wedges

1. Adjust an oven rack to the middle position and heat the oven to 475 degrees. Melt 1 tablespoon of the butter in a medium saucepan over medium-high heat. Add the shallot and cook until softened, about 2 minutes. Stir in the thyme and garlic and cook until fragrant, about 30 seconds. Stir in 1¾ cups of the heavy cream and bring to a simmer. Whisk the remaining ¼ cup heavy cream and cornstarch together, then stir into the saucepan. Continue to simmer until the sauce is thickened, about 2 minutes. Season with salt and pepper to taste. Set aside to cool.

2. Combine 1 cup of the sauce, the spinach, and Parmesan in a medium bowl and season with salt and pepper to taste. Pat the fish dry with paper towels and season with salt and pepper. Coat a 13 by 9-inch baking dish with the remaining 1 tablespoon butter.

3. Place the fish on a cutting board, smooth side down. Divide the spinach filling equally among the fish fillets, mounding it in the middle of each fillet. Fold the tapered ends of the fish tightly over the filling and then fold the thicker ends of the fish over the top to make tidy bundles.

4. Arrange the fish bundles in the baking dish, seam side down, leaving space between the rolls. Pour the remaining sauce evenly over the fish.

5. Sprinkle the fish with the Ritz cracker crumbs and bake until all but the very center of the fish turns from translucent to opaque and the filling is hot, 12 to 15 minutes. Serve with the lemon wedges.

Variation

CRAB-STUFFED SOLE

We recommend buying fresh or pasteurized crabmeat (usually sold next to the fresh seafood) rather than the canned crabmeat (packed in tuna fish–like cans) found in the supermarket aisles.

Substitute 12 ounces fresh or pasteurized crabmeat, squeezed dry, for the spinach. Omit the Parmesan and add ½ cup frozen corn kernels, thawed, 2 tablespoons chopped fresh tarragon, 1 tablespoon fresh lemon juice, ½ teaspoon grated fresh lemon zest, and a pinch cayenne pepper.

Baked Stuffed Shrimp

Baked stuffed shrimp certainly sounds like a special-occasion meal. Colossal shrimp are spread open, packed with a buttery stuffing, and baked until the stuffing is crisp and the shrimp are just cooked through. But after preparing several cookbook recipes, we realized that there are two big problems: mushy, bland stuffing and shrimp as chewy as rubber bands. We wanted crisp, flavorful stuffing and perfectly cooked shrimp without heading to a restaurant.

Most stuffing recipes have the cook simply stir melted butter and seasonings into bread or cracker crumbs. After sampling several recipes, tasters preferred the sweeter flavor of fresh bread crumbs. More surprising was that they preferred mayonnaise to butter (which was too greasy) as a binder. Seasoned with mustard, lemon, garlic, cayenne pepper, and a splash of briny clam juice, the stuffing was now very flavorful. Toasting the bread crumbs before baking helped ensure a crispy baked stuffing.

After peeling, deveining, and butterflying the largest shrimp we could find (about 12 shrimp per

PERFECT STUFFED SHRIMP

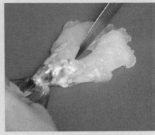

1. Use a sharp paring knife to cut along (but not through) the vein line, then open up the shrimp like a book.

2. Using the tip of the paring knife, cut a 1-inch opening all the way through the center of the shrimp.

3. Flip the shrimp over onto the broiler pan so that they will curl around the stuffing.

4. Divide the stuffing among the shrimp, firmly pressing the stuffing into the opening and to the edges of the shrimp.

pound), we divided the stuffing among the shrimp and popped them into a hot oven. Shrimp shrink and curl as they cook, and as a result the stuffing got forced out like a pilot from an ejector seat. To solve this problem, we turned the shrimp over and pressed the stuffing into them. Instead of pushing the stuffing out, this time the shrimp curled around to cradle it. But when we transferred the shrimp from the baking pan to the serving platter, the stuffing rolled right off. It was only when we accidentally cut clear through a shrimp in the prep stage that we found a way to keep the stuffing in place. Cutting a hole through the center of each butterflied shrimp may seem like a mistake, but as the shrimp contracted in the oven, the stuffing was sealed in place.

The cardinal rule of most shrimp recipes is to cook them quickly; otherwise the shrimp will overcook and become tough. We tried a range of temperatures from 350 to 475 degrees to crisp the stuffing and cook the shrimp; we were able to get the stuffing crisp, but we couldn't seem to avoid tough, rubbery shrimp—even with short cooking times. Thinking of how the test kitchen gently poaches shrimp for shrimp cocktail, we wondered what would happen if we broke the rule and baked the shrimp for a longer time at a lower temperature.

We arranged the shrimp on the pan and gave it a try. Sure enough, after a full 20 minutes at 275 degrees, the shrimp were moist and perfectly cooked—and they actually shrank less in the gentle heat. After a quick flash under the broiler to crisp up the stuffing, we finally had baked stuffed shrimp that were special enough for any occasion.

BAKED STUFFED SHRIMP

SERVES 4 TO 6

If you can't find clam juice, chicken broth will work in a pinch. Any sturdy rimmed baking sheet can be used in place of the broiler-pan bottom.

4	slices hearty white sandwich bread, torn into large pieces and pulsed in a food processor to coarse crumbs
½	cup mayonnaise
¼	cup bottled clam juice (see note above)
¼	cup chopped fresh parsley
4	scallions, chopped fine
2	garlic cloves, minced
2	teaspoons grated fresh lemon zest and 1 tablespoon fresh lemon juice
1	tablespoon Dijon mustard
⅛	teaspoon cayenne pepper
	Salt
1¼	pounds colossal shrimp (about 12 per pound), peeled and deveined

1. Adjust an oven rack to the upper-middle position and heat the oven to 375 degrees. Place the bread crumbs on a broiler-pan bottom and bake until golden and dry, 8 to 10 minutes, stirring halfway through the cooking time. Remove the crumbs from the oven and reduce the oven temperature to 275 degrees.

2. Combine the toasted bread crumbs, mayonnaise, clam juice, parsley, scallions, garlic, lemon zest and juice, mustard, cayenne, and ¼ teaspoon salt in a large bowl.

3. Pat the shrimp dry with paper towels and season with salt. Grease the now-empty broiler-pan bottom. Following the photos, butterfly and cut a hole through the center of each shrimp and arrange, cut side down, on the prepared pan. Divide the bread-crumb mixture among the shrimp, pressing to adhere. Bake until the shrimp are opaque, 20 to 25 minutes.

4. Remove the shrimp from the oven and heat the broiler. Broil the shrimp until the crumbs are deep golden brown and crispy, 1 to 3 minutes. Serve.

Variation

CREOLE BAKED STUFFED SHRIMP WITH SAUSAGE

The smoky, meaty flavor of kielbasa is a nice foil to the sweet shrimp in this variation.

Omit the cayenne and add 1 teaspoon Creole seasoning in step 2. Fold 4 ounces kielbasa sausage, chopped fine, into the filling and proceed as directed.

Family-Style Shrimp Scampi

Shrimp scampi is a straightforward preparation. The shrimp are seared over high heat in garlicky butter, a dash of wine is added to the skillet, and the sauce is finished with lemon juice and parsley.

This formula works in a restaurant when a handful of shrimp are cooked for just one diner, but we quickly found out that it yields rubbery shrimp and a watery sauce when you super-size the recipe to feed a family. We set out to create a big platter of tender shrimp in a rich sauce that would actually cling to the shrimp.

Right away we could see that 2 pounds of shrimp weren't going to fit in our skillet. Turning to the bigger Dutch oven, we started by sautéing four cloves

of garlic in half a stick of butter, adding the shrimp and wine, and covering the pot. As we had hoped, the lid trapped steam in the big pot and helped cook the shrimp gently and evenly. Unfortunately, by the time the sauce was thickened to the proper consistency, the shrimp were very tough.

For our next test, we tried removing the shrimp from the pot when they were partially cooked and simmering the butter and wine (with the lid off) to a saucy consistency. We then added the shrimp back to warm up and finish cooking. This time the shrimp were plump and juicy, but the sauce was still too thin and the reduced wine tasted harsh. Adding bottled clam juice cut the intensity of the wine and created a briny, bright sauce with real depth. Too bad most of the sauce was still resting on the bottom of the platter.

Since many restaurant sauces are thickened with butter added at the end of cooking, we thought we'd give this method a try. We cooked the garlic in just a tablespoon of olive oil before adding the shrimp, wine, and clam juice and covering the pot. Minutes later, we removed the tender shrimp, reduced the sauce to intensify flavors, and began whisking in butter a little at a time. As long as the butter was chilled, it thickened the sauce to a glossy consistency that coated the shrimp nicely. A splash of lemon juice and a generous handful of parsley, and our scampi were perfect.

FAMILY-STYLE SHRIMP SCAMPI

SERVES 4 TO 6

Buy extra-large shrimp (21 to 25 per pound) for this recipe, which makes enough to dress 1 pound of dried pasta (optional).

1	tablespoon olive oil
4	garlic cloves, minced
¼	cup dry white wine
¼	cup bottled clam juice
	Salt and pepper

2 pounds extra-large shrimp (see note above),
   peeled and deveined
4 tablespoons cold unsalted butter,
   cut into 4 pieces
2 tablespoons fresh lemon juice
2 tablespoons chopped fresh parsley
   Lemon wedges

1. Heat the oil in a Dutch oven over medium-high heat until shimmering. Add the garlic and cook until fragrant, about 30 seconds. Add the wine, clam juice, ¼ teaspoon salt, and ⅛ teaspoon pepper; bring to a boil. Add the shrimp, cover, and cook until the shrimp are slightly translucent, about 2 minutes. Reduce the heat to medium, stir, re-cover, and cook until the shrimp are just cooked through, about 2 minutes more.

2. Using a slotted spoon, transfer the shrimp to a medium bowl. Bring the sauce to a boil over medium-high heat and cook until reduced by half, about 1 minute. Whisk the butter, 1 piece at a time, into the sauce; stir in the lemon juice and parsley. Season with salt and pepper to taste and pour the mixture over the shrimp in a serving bowl. Serve with the lemon wedges.

Shrimp Jambalaya

Packed to the gills with shrimp, sausage, rice, and vegetables, jambalaya is the cream of the one-pot crop. But what makes it so attractive—its hodge-podge of textures and flavors—is also what makes it such a challenge to prepare. Whether the rice is too crunchy, the shrimp is too chewy, or everything is just plain overcooked, it can be tough to juggle all these ingredients in just one pot.

After experimenting with various cooking techniques, we found that the ingredients had to be cooked in stages to ensure that each would have

PREVENTING CRUNCHY RICE

Place a sheet of aluminum foil directly on the surface of the rice (and press against the sides of the pot) before the jambalaya goes into the oven. The foil holds in steam, ensuring that the rice cooks perfectly.

optimal flavor and texture. We first rendered the sausage (andouille was the tasters' favorite for its smoky, spicy kick) to release its flavorful fat. With the browned sausage set aside, we added onion, bell pepper, celery, and garlic to the pot. Once they released their aromas and softened, we added rice and then stirred in tomato paste, diced tomatoes, herbs, and chicken broth. Going against the advice in many recipes, we added the shrimp last to keep them from overcooking. So far, so good, except for the flavor of the shrimp. They tasted as bland and boiled as cocktail shrimp, and they contributed no flavor to the dish.

To develop more seafood flavor, we replaced the chicken broth with bottled clam juice. Tasters loved its subtle but sweet brininess. Still, the shrimp themselves remained awfully boring. To pump up their flavor, we tried browning them in the rendered sausage fat. When we added the shrimp to the jambalaya just prior to serving, their flavor was much improved, but they were a little rubbery. After a couple more fruitless tests, a colleague suggested searing the shrimp prior to peeling them. This made sense—restaurant chefs often use flavorful shrimp shells to make stock—and it turned out to be the perfect solution. The shells gave the jambalaya a more complex shrimp flavor, and they kept the flesh of the shrimp from scorching in the pan.

SHRIMP JAMBALAYA

SERVES 4 TO 6

When shopping, look for shrimp that are still in their shells. If you cannot find andouille sausage, substitute an equal amount of chorizo.

2	teaspoons vegetable oil
8	ounces andouille sausage, halved lengthwise, cut into ¼-inch half-moons (see note above)
1	pound large (31 to 40 per pound) shell-on shrimp
1	onion, minced
1	celery rib, chopped fine
1	green bell pepper, chopped fine
5	garlic cloves, minced
1½	cups long-grain white rice
1	tablespoon tomato paste
1	teaspoon salt
½	teaspoon minced fresh thyme
1	(14.5-ounce) can diced tomatoes, drained, ¼ cup juice reserved
2	(8-ounce) bottles clam juice
1	bay leaf
2	scallions, sliced thin

1. Adjust an oven rack to the middle position and heat the oven to 325 degrees.

2. Heat the oil in an ovenproof Dutch oven over medium-high heat until shimmering. Add the sausage and cook until browned, 3 to 5 minutes. Using a slotted spoon, transfer the sausage to a plate lined with a paper towel. Add the shrimp to the pot and cook until the shells are lightly browned on both sides, about 1 minute per side. Transfer the shrimp to a large bowl and refrigerate.

3. Reduce the heat to medium and add the onion, celery, bell pepper, and garlic to the pot. Cook, stirring occasionally, until the vegetables have softened, 5 to 10 minutes. Add the rice, tomato paste, salt, and thyme and cook until the rice is coated with fat, about 1 minute. Stir in the tomatoes, reserved tomato juice, clam juice, bay leaf, and sausage. Place a square of aluminum foil directly on the surface of the rice. Bring to a boil, cover the pot, transfer to the oven, and bake until the rice is almost tender and most of the liquid is absorbed, about 20 minutes.

4. Meanwhile, peel the shrimp (devein if desired) and discard the shells. Remove the pot from the oven, lift off the aluminum foil, and gently stir in the peeled shrimp and any accumulated juices. Replace the foil and lid, return the pot to the oven, and cook until the rice is fully tender and the shrimp are cooked through, about 5 minutes. Remove from the oven, discard the foil and bay leaf, and fold in the scallions. Serve.

Crab Imperial

Crab imperial is a classic Southern seafood dish. It showcases fresh, briny crabmeat lightly bound with a creamy filling, topped with buttered crumbs, and baked until golden and bubbly. Simple and unadorned by definition, a classic crab imperial recipe should showcase the fresh brininess of premium crabmeat. Unfortunately, our research turned up conglomerations of greasy mayonnaise-based dishes, starchy white sauces, and leaden, stuffing-like casseroles. The results hardly did the venerable crab justice. Our goal was for the star of this dish to be the crab, with a minimum of filler. The rest of the filling needed to complement the delicate crab, without being overpowering, and we wanted a topping that was rich, buttery, golden, and crispy.

Although its genesis is unclear, crab imperial is synonymous with the Chesapeake Bay region of Maryland and traditionally features the Atlantic blue crab. Atlantic blue crab is always sold cooked and is available in four grades: lump, backfin, special, and claw. Lump meat is of the highest quality and is nothing but large chunks of meat removed from the body, so consequently it's the priciest of options. Fresh crabmeat is found in plastic containers in the fish department and is often sold pasteurized to prolong its shelf life. If fresh, unpasteurized crabmeat is available, it is well worth the extra money, as its flavor is far superior to the crab that has been subjected to the pasteurization process.

This is a dish that by virtue of its title should be fit for a king, but you shouldn't need the wealth of royalty to prepare it. We knew that to bring the crabmeat to the forefront, we would need at least 1½ pounds of the crustacean. Given the cost of fresh crabmeat, we wondered if we could successfully augment the precious crab with fish that had similar characteristics, without sacrificing the integrity of the dish. We tried shrimp, but found that its assertive flavor and contrasting texture overshadowed the tender sweetness of the crab. We decided that a firm-fleshed white fish might be more appropriate and tested halibut, haddock, and cod. All served admirably as a subtle backdrop to the crab. Their textures were similar, and they neither overshadowed nor detracted from the inimitable crab flavor. We sautéed onion and red bell pepper, then added the white fish and cooked it until it had lost its translucence and was easy to flake and combine with the crab.

To make the filling, we turned to cream cheese thinned with milk. Tasters preferred it to the greasy mayonnaise-based fillings, both because of the consistency it gave the dish and for its richness, which was the perfect foil for the crabmeat. For seasoning we added Worcestershire sauce, Dijon mustard, hot sauce, and Old Bay seasoning. Old Bay is a blend of more than a dozen herbs and spices that is often paired with seafood; in the South it is a must-have when it comes to crabmeat.

We wanted a substantial bread-crumb topping that would add a textural contrast to the tender crab filling. We tested fresh bread-crumb toppings with a multitude of seasonings and in the end decided that the best course of action was to keep it simple. A generous layer of freshly made bread crumbs, mixed with unsalted butter and fresh parsley, was all that was needed to form the golden crust we were seeking, without obscuring the delicate crab flavor.

In this recipe, the crabmeat reigns supreme. Decadently rich and deeply satisfying, a small portion, served with a simple green salad, is a royal feast.

CRAB IMPERIAL

SERVES 6 TO 8

We recommend buying fresh crabmeat for best results—for more information on buying crabmeat, see page 397.

TOPPING

- 4 slices hearty white sandwich bread, torn into large pieces
- 2 tablespoons unsalted butter, melted
- 2 tablespoons chopped fresh parsley

FILLING

- 3 tablespoons unsalted butter
- 2 tablespoons minced onion
- 1 red bell pepper, stemmed, seeded, and chopped fine
- ½ pound firm white fish (such as cod, haddock, or halibut), skinned and cut into ½-inch chunks
- 12 ounces cream cheese
- ¼ cup whole milk
- 3 tablespoons fresh lemon juice
- 1 tablespoon Worcestershire sauce
- 1 tablespoon Dijon mustard
- 2 teaspoons hot sauce
- 1½ teaspoons Old Bay seasoning
- 1 pound lump crabmeat, picked over for bits of shell
  Lemon wedges

1. FOR THE TOPPING: Process the bread and melted butter in a food processor until coarsely ground, about six 1-second pulses. Transfer to a bowl and toss with the parsley; set aside.

2. FOR THE FILLING: Melt 2 tablespoons of the butter in a large nonstick skillet over medium heat. Add the onion and red bell pepper; cook until soft and translucent, 3 to 5 minutes. Add the white fish and cook, stirring occasionally to flake the fish into small pieces, until fully opaque, about 4 minutes. Set aside to cool.

3. Microwave the cream cheese in a large bowl on high power until very soft, 20 to 40 seconds. Whisk in the milk, lemon juice, Worcestershire, mustard, hot sauce, and Old Bay until smooth. Gently fold in the crabmeat and the cooled fish mixture.

4. Adjust an oven rack to the middle position and heat the oven to 400 degrees. Grease the bottom and sides of a 9-inch square baking dish (or a shallow casserole dish of similar size) with the remaining 1 tablespoon butter. Sprinkle 3 tablespoons of the bread-crumb topping evenly over the dish. Spread the crab mixture over the dish and sprinkle with the remaining bread-crumb topping. Bake until browned and bubbling, 20 to 25 minutes. Serve immediately with the lemon wedges and additional hot sauce.

Creole Crab Cakes

Great crab cakes begin with top-quality crabmeat. Simply put, there is no substitute for fresh blue-crab meat, preferably "jumbo lump," which indicates the largest pieces and highest grade. The meat should never be rinsed, but it does need to be picked over to remove any shell or cartilage the processors may have missed.

Choosing a binder for our crab cakes was almost as important as the crabmeat. We tried bread crumbs, crushed potato chips, and crushed saltines. Tasters preferred the saltines; they had no overwhelming flavor, were easy to mix in, and were dry enough that the cakes held together. The trickiest part with the crumbs was knowing when to stop; crab cakes need just enough binder to hold them together but not so much that the filler overwhelms the seafood. We finally settled on 1¼ cups of crushed crackers. Cooks who economize by padding their pricey seafood with more will end up with dough balls, not crab cakes.

The other ingredients we adopted are equally basic. Good, sturdy commercial mayonnaise (we like Hellmann's) keeps the crabmeat moist, and a whole egg helps hold the crab, crumbs, and seasonings together both before and during cooking. Careful mixing is also important when making crab cakes. We found a rubber spatula works best, used in a folding rather than a stirring motion. This is important because you want to end up with a chunky consistency.

We were pleased with our basic recipe on most fronts, but we still had trouble keeping the cakes together as they cooked. Our last breakthrough came when we tried chilling the shaped cakes before cooking. As little as half an hour in the refrigerator made an ocean of difference. The cold firmed up the cakes so that they fried into perfect plump rounds without falling apart.

Now we were ready for the seasoning. We wanted to highlight, not overwhelm, the crab, but we also wanted these cakes to have some zing. We gravitated toward the Creole flavors of Louisiana and included diced green bell pepper, onion, and celery. Tasters also liked the addition of plenty of garlic and some Worcestershire sauce. And dry mustard and cayenne pepper added some real Creole heat.

Pan-fried in vegetable oil, these cakes came out crisp on the outside and moist and flavorful inside.

Served with our quick version of classic rémoulade (a mayonnaise-based sauce) for an additional Creole kick, these crab cakes really do take the cake.

CREOLE-STYLE CRAB CAKES

SERVES 4

You'll need about 30 saltines; crush them until most have turned to dust, with a few larger pieces no bigger than a small pebble. Serve these crab cakes hot with lemon wedges and Quick Rémoulade (recipe follows).

2	teaspoons plus 3 tablespoons vegetable oil
½	onion, minced
½	green bell pepper, seeded and chopped fine
1	celery rib, chopped fine
3	garlic cloves, minced
1½	pounds lump crabmeat, picked over for bits of shell
1¼	cups crushed saltine crackers (see note above)
¼	cup mayonnaise
1	large egg
2	tablespoons heavy cream
1	tablespoon dry mustard
¼	teaspoon cayenne pepper
1	tablespoon Worcestershire sauce

1. Heat 2 teaspoons of the oil in a medium skillet over medium heat. Add the onion, bell pepper, celery, and garlic and cook until soft, about 5 minutes. Transfer to a plate and refrigerate for 5 minutes.

2. Transfer the vegetables to a large bowl. Using a rubber spatula, fold in the crabmeat and ¾ cup of the cracker crumbs, being careful not to break up the large pieces of crab. Whisk the mayonnaise, egg, heavy cream, mustard, cayenne, and Worcestershire together in a small bowl. Fold into the crab mixture. Divide into 8 portions and shape each into a

1¼-inch-thick cake. Transfer to a plate, cover, and refrigerate until well chilled, at least 30 minutes or up to 1 day.

3. Heat the remaining 3 tablespoons oil in a large nonstick skillet over medium-high heat until shimmering. Meanwhile, dredge the crab cakes in the remaining ½ cup cracker crumbs and press to adhere the crumbs to the cakes. Cook 4 crab cakes until well browned on both sides, about 5 minutes per side. Transfer to a plate lined with paper towels and repeat with the remaining 4 crab cakes. Serve immediately.

QUICK RÉMOULADE

MAKES ABOUT 1½ CUPS

This simple sauce can be refrigerated for up to 3 days.

1	cup mayonnaise
1	tablespoon whole-grain mustard
¼	cup chopped dill pickles
1	scallion, sliced thin
1	tablespoon fresh lemon juice
¼	teaspoon cayenne pepper
	Salt and pepper

Stir together all of the ingredients, including salt and pepper to taste, in a small bowl. Refrigerate until ready to use.

SHOPPING WITH THE TEST KITCHEN

Buying Crabmeat: We engineered our recipe for Creole-Style Crab Cakes to work with several of the different kinds of crabmeat available at the supermarket, but we did find big differences in the quality of packed crabmeat and formed a few preferences.

Unless otherwise labeled, crabmeat starts with cooked Atlantic blue crabs. If money's no object, try lump crabmeat. Usually packed in plastic containers available in the refrigerator near the fish counter, this product features big, tender chunks of crabmeat. It has the best texture and freshest flavor.

Most lump crabmeat is pasteurized to extend its shelf life. If you find fresh crabmeat from just-cooked crabs (available locally when crabs are in season), it will taste even sweeter. Whether fresh or pasteurized, lump crabmeat is pricey, anywhere from $19.99 to $23.99 per pound.

Backfin crabmeat has a more shredded texture. Although we missed the large chunks found in lump crabmeat, the backfin tasted sweet and fresh and cost a little less than lump—roughly $10.99 to $16.99 per pound.

Pouched crabmeat is a relatively new option. Similar to tuna in a pouch, this shelf-stable product features pasteurized lump crabmeat at a lower cost—just $6.99 for 12 ounces. The quality was okay (our tasters found it a bit watery), but it was not as good as the refrigerated lump or backfin crabmeat.

There is one product you should avoid. Imitation crabmeat, made of pollock that has been dyed orange, does not taste anything like crab. In fact, it doesn't taste like anything, period. Don't be tempted by the seemingly low price. A 6-ounce can may cost just $5, but that works out to a price of about $14 per pound. In this case, imitation is not the sincerest form of flattery.

SHOPPING WITH THE TEST KITCHEN

Nonstick Skillets: We've always recommended buying inexpensive nonstick skillets, because with regular use the nonstick coating inevitably scratches, chips off, or becomes ineffective. Why spend big bucks on a pan that will last only a year or two? We rounded up eight models priced under $60 and pitted them against our gold standard, the $135 nonstick skillet from All-Clad, to see how they measured up. After running them through a battery of tests and abuse, we determined that the $135 All-Clad is still the best pan out there, but some of the cheaper pans performed nearly as well. Of the inexpensive pans,

our favorite is the WearEver Premium Hard Anodized 12-Inch Nonstick Skillet ($24.99). This light pan was a breeze to maneuver, sautéed at a rapid pace, and resisted our best efforts to damage its nonstick finish. Testers liked the comfortable handle, which stayed cool on the stovetop. Even better, you can buy four of the solid WearEver pans (and get change back) for the cost of the All-Clad.

Crab Boil

The scene at a crab boil always looks the same. Picnic tables are covered with layers of newspaper, towering stacks of napkins, and piles of mallets and other utensils for extracting meat from cooked crabs. A large tub of ice-chilled beer is somewhere nearby. Usually made for a crowd or party, a traditional crab boil is simply sausage, corn, potatoes, and crabs thrown together in a huge pot of spicy boiling broth set over an outdoor propane burner. When cooked through, the contents of the pot are strained and dumped over the newspaper-clad tables, and with the help of the mallets, the meal begins. We wanted to find a way to bring the party indoors without losing the authentic flavor, simple cooking method, and rustic charm of a true crab boil.

Although several types of crabs are edible, most boils call for blue crabs. Both male and female blue crabs are available, and although the males offer more meat, they are harder to find and more expensive. Many markets sell bushels of male and female crabs separately; buy male crabs if you can. Blue crabs also come in a variety of sizes, the price increasing along with the weight. Keep the crabs cool and accessible to circulating air, but contained, until you are ready to cook them. Although some recipes call for washing and scrubbing the crabs in cool water, we found this to be a nearly impossible as well as unnecessary task, as the crabs are "washed" when plunged into the boiling broth.

EATING WHOLE BLUE CRABS

1. Twist off the claws and legs and break them open with a mallet to expose the meat. Turn the crab upside down, insert a paring knife, and twist.

2. Remove the knife and pry the bottom shell away from the top shell. Discard the top shell.

3. Use your fingers to remove the feathery white gills on either side of the crab.

4. Use your hands to break the crab in half front to back. Break each piece in half again to expose the meat of the crab.

With the crabs confined to the refrigerator, we amassed the other ingredients and began to work on the method. The traditional boil includes sausage, potatoes, and corn, all of which are cooked in the same spicy broth as the crabs. Although these ingredients are usually cooked at once in the same pot, we couldn't find a pot large enough to fit them all. Because the crabs take up most of the room in a large stockpot, we quickly realized that they would have to be cooked separately from the other ingredients, but we still planned to cook the potatoes, corn, and sausage together in the pot at the same time.

We found that small red potatoes were flavored nicely by the sausage. We tested several varieties and preferred the toothsome, dense texture and sweet flavor of Red Bliss. Tasters liked the potatoes when they were cooked whole rather than cut into pieces, which became messy. The corn, however, was more appropriately sized when cut in half. Tying the potatoes and sausage loosely in a cheesecloth sack and adding the corn in the last 5 minutes of cooking, we found, made them extremely easy to remove from the pot, leaving the broth ready for the crabs. We found the crabs took anywhere from 7 to 15 minutes, depending on their size, to turn dark red and cook through.

With the method in place, we focused on the spices. We found several types of prepackaged crab boil mixtures, such as Old Bay and Zatarain's, along with many recipes for creating a mixture. Although the idea of creating our own spice mixture sounded appealing, the ingredient list quickly became very long and involved. More important, we liked the results (and ease) of Old Bay and Zatarain's just as well. Zatarain's comes in a "boil-in-bag" pouch, and we found its flavor milder than that of Old Bay. Tasters preferred the free-floating, fuller flavor of Old Bay as it clung to the potatoes and worked its way into the crevices of the corn and crabs. We found 8 quarts of water seasoned with ½ cup of Old Bay (along with a little extra cayenne pepper) made just the right amount of well-seasoned broth.

We tested adding onions and garlic to the pot and found the onions did very little, whereas the garlic added a nice flavor. Other recipes call for either lemon or cider vinegar, and we liked the stronger flavor of vinegar. But because the vinegar did not agree with the potatoes and corn, we found it best to add it to the boil along with the crabs.

For the first few tests, we brought the water to a boil with the seasoning and then added the sack of potatoes and sausage. With an eye toward efficiency, however, we tried bringing the cold water, potatoes, sausage, spices, and garlic to a boil at the same time. The result was fantastic, as the gently heated water evenly cooked the potatoes alongside the flavorful sausage. By the time the water hit a boil, the potatoes were almost done and the sausage was heated through, lending its smoky flavor to the broth along with the Old Bay.

Made in 45 minutes using only one pot, this recipe looks and tastes absolutely authentic when dumped out over a newspaper-covered kitchen table and served with melted butter, lemon wedges, and rolls of paper towels.

CRAB BOIL

SERVES 4

Make sure to buy crabs that are alive; don't cook any crabs that appear to be dead or whose eyes do not react to a gentle blow of breath. Handle the crabs with gloves or tongs, as their small, sharp claws are agile and can pinch. You will need a large pot (at least 12-quart capacity) for this recipe. Mallets, paring knives, meat pounders, hammers, and small frying pans are among the utensils that may be employed to help retrieve bits of crabmeat from the shell.

1	pound small red potatoes, preferably Red Bliss, about 1 inch in diameter
1	pound kielbasa sausage, cut into 1-inch pieces
½	cup Old Bay seasoning
1	head garlic, skins on, smashed with a mallet
1½	teaspoons cayenne pepper
⅓	cup salt
4	medium ears corn, husks and silk removed, cut in half
¼	cup cider vinegar
20	live blue crabs, preferably males (about 6 ounces each; if smaller, use 28 to 32 crabs)
½	pound salted butter, melted
	Lemon wedges

1. Loosely tie the potatoes and kielbasa in a large single layer of cheesecloth. Bring 8 quarts of water, the Old Bay, garlic, cayenne, salt, and the bag containing potatoes and kielbasa to a boil over high heat in a large stockpot. Cook until the potatoes are almost tender (a paring knife can be slipped into and out of the center of a potato with slight resistance), 10 to 15 minutes. Add the corn and cook until both the corn and potatoes are tender, about 5 minutes longer.

2. Remove the corn and the sack of potatoes and kielbasa with long tongs and transfer them to a large colander set in the sink to drain. Bring the spiced water back to a boil; add the vinegar and the crabs. Cook until the crabs are dark red, 7 to 15 minutes, depending on their size.

3. Meanwhile, remove the potatoes and sausage from the cheesecloth and place on a platter with the corn; cover to keep warm. When the crabs are fully cooked, carefully drain the entire pot into a colander set in the sink and allow to drain thoroughly. Spread several layers of newspaper over a large table and dump the crabs onto the paper. Serve immediately with the melted butter, lemon wedges, crab-cracking utensils (see note above), and a large empty bowl for the shells.

Dipping Sauces
for Seafood

These sauces work especially well with salmon cakes (page 382), trout or catfish fillets (pages 385 to 386), and crab cakes (page 397). You might also serve one of these sauces with steamed lobsters (page 402).

TARTAR SAUCE

MAKES GENEROUS ¾ CUP

This is the classic sauce for fried seafood.

- ¾ cup mayonnaise
- 1½ tablespoons minced cornichons (about 3 large), and 1 teaspoon cornichon juice
- 1 tablespoon minced scallion
- 1 tablespoon minced red onion
- 1 tablespoon capers, minced

Mix all of the ingredients in a small bowl. Cover and refrigerate until the flavors blend, at least 30 minutes. (The sauce can be refrigerated for several days.)

CREAMY LEMON-HERB SAUCE

MAKES GENEROUS ½ CUP

This sauce is flavorful, but it won't overpower delicate seafood.

- ½ cup mayonnaise
- 2½ tablespoons fresh lemon juice
- 1 tablespoon chopped fresh parsley
- 1 tablespoon minced fresh thyme
- 1 scallion, minced
- ½ teaspoon salt
-   Pepper

Mix all of the ingredients in a small bowl, including pepper to taste. Cover and refrigerate until the flavors blend, about 30 minutes. (The sauce can be refrigerated for several days.)

CREAMY CHIPOTLE CHILE SAUCE

MAKES ABOUT ½ CUP

This sauce is the richest and most complex of the three.

- ¼ cup mayonnaise
- ¼ cup sour cream
- 2 teaspoons minced canned chipotle chiles in adobo
- 1 garlic clove, minced
- 2 teaspoons finely chopped fresh cilantro
- 1 teaspoon fresh lime juice

Mix all of the ingredients in a small bowl. Cover and refrigerate until the flavors blend, about 30 minutes. (The sauce can be refrigerated for several days.)

Steamed Lobsters

As is the case with most seafood, we find that knowing how to shop for lobster is just as important as knowing how to cook it. Lobsters must be purchased alive. Choose lobsters that are active in the tank, avoiding listless specimens that may have been in the tank too long. Maine lobsters, with their large claws, are meatier and sweeter than clawless rock or spiny lobsters, and they are our first and only choice. Size is really a matter of preference and budget. We found it possible to cook large as well as small lobsters to perfection as long as we adjusted the cooking time.

During the initial phase of testing, we confirmed our preference for steamed lobster rather than boiled. Steamed lobster did not taste better than boiled, but the process was simpler and neater, and the finished product was less watery when cracked open on the plate.

Although we had little trouble perfecting our cooking method, we were bothered by the toughness of some of the lobster tails we were eating. No matter how we cooked them, most of the tails were at least slightly rubbery and chewy.

It turns out that the secret to tender lobster is not so much in the preparation and cooking as in the selection. Before working on this topic in the test kitchen, the terms hard-shell and soft-shell lobster meant nothing to us. Unlike crabs, lobsters are not clearly distinguished in this way at the retail level. Of course, we knew from past experience that some lobster claws rip open as easily as an aluminum flip-top can, whereas others won't crack until you take out your shop tools. We also noticed the small, limp claw meat of some lobsters and the full, packed meat of others. It turns out that these variations are caused by the particular stage of molting that the lobster was in at the time it was caught.

Most of the lobsters we eat during the summer and fall are in some phase of molting. During the late spring, as waters begin to warm, lobsters start to form new shell tissue underneath their old shells. As early as June off the shores of New Jersey and in July or August in colder Maine and Canadian waters, the lobsters shed their hard exterior shell. Because the most difficult task in molting is pulling the claw muscle through the old shell, the lobster dehydrates its claw (hence the smaller claw meat).

Once the lobster molts, it emerges with nothing but a wrinkled, soft covering, much like that on a soft-shell crab. Within 15 minutes, the lobster inflates itself with water, increasing its length by 15 percent and its weight by 50 percent. This extra water expands the wrinkled, soft covering, allowing the lobster plenty of room in which to grow long after the shell starts to harden. The newly molted lobster immediately eats its old shell, digesting the crucial shell-hardening calcium.

Understanding the molt phase clarifies the deficiencies of soft-shell summer lobster. It explains why it is so waterlogged, why its claw meat is so shriveled and scrawny, and why its tail meat is so underdeveloped and chewy. There is also far less meat in a 1-pound soft-shell lobster than in a hard-shell lobster that weighs the same.

During the fall, the lobster shell continues to harden, and the meat expands to fill the new shell. By spring, lobsters are at their peak, packed with meat and relatively inexpensive, since it is easier for fishermen to check their traps then than it is during the winter. As the tail grows, it becomes firmer and meatier and will cook up tender, not tough. Better texture and more meat are two excellent reasons to give lobsters a squeeze at the market and buy only those with hard shells. As a rule of thumb, hard-shell lobsters are reasonably priced from Mother's Day through the Fourth of July.

STEAMED LOBSTERS

SERVES 4

Hard-shell lobsters are much meatier than soft-shell lobsters, which have recently molted. Because hard-shell lobsters are packed with more meat than soft-shell lobsters, you may want to buy slightly larger lobsters if the shells appear to be soft. To determine whether a lobster has a hard or soft shell, squeeze the side of the lobster's body. A soft-shell lobster will yield to pressure, and a hard-shell lobster will feel hard, brittle, and tightly packed.

- 4 live lobsters
- 8 tablespoons unsalted butter, melted (optional)

  Lemon wedges

Bring about 1 inch of water to a boil over high heat in a large stockpot set up with a wire rack, pasta insert, or seaweed bed. Add the lobsters, cover, and return the water to a boil. Reduce the heat to medium-high and steam until the lobsters are done (see chart at right). Serve immediately with the melted butter (if using) and lemon wedges.

APPROXIMATE STEAMING TIMES AND MEAT YIELDS FOR LOBSTER

	LOBSTER SIZE	COOKING TIME (MINUTES)	MEAT YIELD (OUNCES)
SOFT-SHELL	1 pound	8–9	about 3
	1¼ pounds	11–12	3½–4
	1½ pounds	13–14	5½–6
	1¾–2 pounds	17–18	6¼–6½
HARD-SHELL	1 pound	10–11	4–4½
	1¼ pounds	13–14	5½–6
	1½ pounds	15–16	7½–8
	1¾–2 pounds	about 19	8½–9

Indoor Clambake

A clambake is a rite of summer along the East Coast. At this festive beach party, loads of shellfish and a variety of vegetables are steamed in a wide, sandy pit using seaweed and rocks warmed from a nearby campfire. This feast usually takes a day or more to prepare—digging the pit is no small chore—and hours to cook. Though some may mock the idea of a kitchen clambake, it is nonetheless a simple and efficient way (taking a mere half hour) to prepare a fantastic shellfish dinner—complete with corn, potatoes, and sausage—for a hungry crowd.

An indoor clambake is not a novel idea; we found dozens of recipes in our cookbook library. The methods used to put together an indoor clambake vary dramatically, but the ingredients, in keeping with tradition, are fairly consistent, including clams, mussels, lobsters, potatoes, corn, onions, and spicy sausage. Some recipes tell the cook to partially cook each ingredient separately and then finish things

together on the grill; others recommend specific systems for layering the ingredients in a stockpot. Some recipes use seaweed or corn husks for extra flavor, and others tout the importance of smoky bacon. The common goal of all these recipes, however, is to manage the process so that the various components are cooked perfectly and are ready to serve at the same time. Taking note of these different clambake styles, we began our testing.

It soon became apparent which methods were worthwhile and which simply made a mess. Partially cooking the ingredients separately before combining them was time-consuming and produced a clambake without that authentic clambake flavor. Layering the various ingredients in a stockpot, on the other hand, was both easy to do and produced tasty results. With the stockpot set over high heat, the components steamed and infused one another with their flavors. This method was not without problems, however; half the ingredients wound up submerged in shellfish-flavored water. Using this pot method as a point of departure, we began to tinker with the method and the ingredients.

Although all of the recipes we uncovered called for adding water to the pot to create steam for cooking, we found the shellfish released enough of their own liquid to make adequate steam. When placed over high heat, the shellfish took only a few minutes to release the moisture needed to steam the whole pot, with a cup or more left over to use as a sauce for the clams and mussels. We took advantage of those first few minutes when the pot was dry by lining it with sliced sausage, giving it a chance to sear before the steam was unleashed. We tested several kinds of sausage, and tasters preferred mild kielbasa. The light smoky flavor of this sausage works well with seafood, and the sausage is fairly juicy and fatty, making it perfectly suited to this cooking method.

With the sausage layered on the bottom, we played with the order in which to add the remaining ingredients. We found it best to lay the clams and mussels right on top of the sausage because they provided most of the necessary liquid for the steam and needed to be close to the heat source. Wrapping them loosely in a cheesecloth sack made them easy to remove when done. Although potatoes actually take the longest to cook, they were best laid on top of the clams and mussels, close to the heat source yet easily accessible to a prodding knife to test their doneness. We shortened their cooking time by cutting the potatoes into 1-inch pieces.

Corn, with a layer of husk left on, was placed on top of the potatoes. The husk protects the corn from any foam released by the lobsters, which we placed on top of the corn. We decided to omit the onions, which no one ate; the bacon, which smoked out the delicate flavor of the shellfish; and the seaweed, which was hard to find and unnecessary for flavor.

Layered in this fashion, the clambake took just 17 to 20 minutes to cook through completely over high heat. Surprisingly, the shellfish liquid is quite salty and naturally seasons all the ingredients. After taking a couple of minutes to remove the ingredients from the pot and arrange them attractively on a platter, we had a feast that had been made from start to finish in half an hour.

INDOOR CLAMBAKE

SERVES 4 TO 6

The recipe can be cut in half and layered in an 8-quart Dutch oven, but it should cook in the same amount of time. To remove the weedy beard from the crack between the two shells of a mussel, trap the beard between the side of a small knife and your thumb and give it a tug.

2   pounds littleneck or cherrystone clams, scrubbed

2   pounds mussels, shells scrubbed and beards removed (see note above)

1   pound kielbasa sausage, cut into ⅓-inch slices

1   pound small new or red potatoes, scrubbed and cut into 1-inch pieces

4   medium ears corn, silk and all but the last layer of husks removed

2   live lobsters (about 1½ pounds each)

8   tablespoons salted butter, melted

1. Place the clams and mussels on a large piece of cheesecloth and tie the ends together to secure; set aside. In a heavy-bottomed 12-quart stockpot, layer in the following order: the sliced kielbasa, the sack of clams and mussels, the potatoes, the corn, and the lobsters on top of one another. Cover with the lid and place over high heat. Cook until the potatoes are tender (a paring knife can be slipped into and out of the center of a potato with little resistance) and the lobsters are bright red, 17 to 20 minutes.

2. Remove the pot from the heat and remove the lid (watch out for scalding steam). Remove the lobsters and set aside until cool enough to handle. Remove the corn from the pot and peel off the husks; arrange the ears on a large platter. Using a slotted spoon, remove the potatoes and arrange them on the platter with the corn. Transfer the clams and mussels to a large bowl and cut open the cheesecloth with scissors. Using a slotted spoon, remove the kielbasa from the pot and arrange it on the platter with the potatoes and corn. Pour the remaining steaming liquid in the pot over the clams and mussels. With a kitchen towel in your hand, twist and remove the lobster tails, claws, and legs (if desired). Arrange the lobster parts on the platter. Serve immediately with the melted butter and an ample supply of napkins.

CHAPTER THIRTEEN

Slow-Cooker Favorites

SLOW-COOKER FAVORITES

Country-Style Pot Roast with Gravy

The idea of coming home on a weeknight to a hearty dinner of pot roast and gravy is very appealing. A slow cooker can make this possible; however, using a slow cooker for making pot roast isn't without its challenges. The meat tends to dry out, and the gravy—or what's left of it—can be bland. We wanted to develop a slow-cooker pot roast that was just as good as the old-fashioned version.

Most of the pot roast recipes we looked at suggested using cuts from the bottom round or top sirloin. Past experience in the test kitchen told us that these cuts would have too little fat and too little flavor, and retesting them only confirmed this point. For best results, we found that a boneless chuck roast is a much better choice. When slow-cooked, it becomes super-tender and tasty.

Most recipes call for a 3½- to 4-pound roast. After cooking close to 100 pounds of pot roast, we found that each hunk of beef lost an average of 2 pounds. If you start with a roast that's only 3½ pounds...well, you get the picture.

We had much better luck when we tried a large 5½- to 6-pound roast. The slow cooker was nearly filled to the brim (you must use a slow cooker with a capacity of at least 6 quarts; see page 416 for recommendations), but after a day of cooking there was something substantial left for dinner. At some markets you will have to special-order a roast this big. If that seems like too much bother, two small roasts (each weighing about 3 pounds) can be used. Either way, this much meat needs to cook for 6 to 7 hours on the high setting or 9 to 10 hours on the low setting to become tender. The latter regimen is perfect if you want to get dinner going in the morning.

Next we tackled the gravy. To minimize kitchen time, many slow-cooker recipes instruct you to add the ingredients to the pot uncooked. This sure is easy, but you end up with bland gravy. We decided to first brown the meat and vegetables in a skillet to develop some flavor. A slow cooker traps moisture and tends to dilute whatever you are cooking, so you need a strong start for a flavorful finish. To save time in the morning, we found that we could brown the meat and vegetables the night before and refrigerate them overnight.

Adding red wine, broth (not water), tomatoes, and herbs to the base we had created in the skillet gave us a flavorful gravy. But the consistency was too thin. We wanted a gravy that would coat the meat and fill the well in mashed potatoes.

To get that good gravy, when the meat was done, we strained the cooking liquid, discarded the vegetables, and thickened the juices with a mixture of flour and water. This method gave us the consistency we were looking for, but it had two drawbacks: the lumps had to be strained out (we hate lumpy gravy!), and the gravy had to cook over high heat for 30 minutes.

One test cook, bothered by the fact that we were throwing away all of the vegetables in the pot, suggested pureeing them along with the cooking juices. Sure enough, we found this to be both an economical and a quick way to add substance to the gravy—no starch, no fuss. And if you have children who won't eat their vegetables, this is a good way to sneak them in.

COUNTRY-STYLE POT ROAST WITH GRAVY

SERVES 8

Boneless chuck-eye roast is essential in this recipe; other cuts will cook up dry and tough. At most markets you will have to order a 5½- to 6-pound chuck-eye roast. Alternatively, use two 3-pound roasts, which are common in most markets.

1	large boneless beef chuck-eye roast (5½ to 6 pounds; see note above), tied
	Salt and pepper
4	teaspoons vegetable oil
3	onions, minced
1	celery rib, chopped
4	carrots, chopped
6	garlic cloves, minced
1	cup red wine
1	(28-ounce) can crushed tomatoes
2	cups low-sodium chicken broth
½	teaspoon red pepper flakes
3	bay leaves
1	teaspoon dried thyme
2	tablespoons chopped fresh parsley

1. Season the roast liberally with salt and pepper. Heat 2 teaspoons of the oil in a large skillet over medium-high heat until shimmering but not smoking. Brown the roast thoroughly on all sides, 8 to 10 minutes. Transfer the browned roast to a slow-cooker insert.

2. Reduce the heat to medium. Add the remaining 2 teaspoons oil to the now-empty skillet, along with the onions, celery, carrots, and garlic. Cook, stirring occasionally, until lightly browned, about 4 minutes. Transfer to the slow-cooker insert.

3. Increase the heat to high. Add the red wine to the again-empty skillet, scraping up any browned bits with a wooden spoon, and simmer for 5 minutes. Add the tomatoes and broth and bring to a boil. Add the red pepper flakes, bay leaves, and thyme and transfer to the slow-cooker insert.

4. Cover and cook on low until the meat is tender, 9 to 10 hours (or cook on high for 6 to 7 hours). Transfer the roast to a carving board; loosely tent with aluminum foil to keep warm. Discard the bay leaves. Allow the liquid in the pot to settle for about 5 minutes, then use a wide spoon to skim the fat off the surface. Puree the liquid and solids in batches in a blender or food processor. (Alternatively, use an immersion blender and process until smooth.) Stir in the parsley and season with salt and pepper to taste.

5. Remove the twine from the roast and cut into ½-inch slices. Transfer the meat to a warmed serving platter. Pour about 1 cup of the gravy over the meat. Serve, passing more gravy separately.

Variation
SOUTHWESTERN POT ROAST
SERVES 8
Corn tortillas are used to thicken the gravy for this pot roast. Vary the heat by adjusting the amount of cayenne pepper. Serve with rice or egg noodles. At most markets you will have to order a 5½- to 6-pound chuck-eye roast. Alternatively, use two 3-pound roasts, which are common in most markets.

1	large boneless beef chuck-eye roast (5½ to 6 pounds; see note above), tied
	Salt and pepper
4	teaspoons vegetable oil
2	onions, minced
1	red bell pepper, chopped
4	jalapeño chiles, seeded and minced
8	garlic cloves, minced
1	(28-ounce) can crushed tomatoes
2¾	cups low-sodium chicken broth
3	tablespoons chili powder
2	tablespoons ground cumin
1–2	teaspoons cayenne pepper (see note above)
1	teaspoon dried oregano
6	(6-inch) soft corn tortillas
2	tablespoons chopped fresh cilantro

1. Season the roast liberally with salt and pepper. Heat 2 teaspoons of the oil in a large skillet over medium-high heat until shimmering but not smoking. Brown the roast thoroughly on all sides, 8 to 10 minutes. Transfer the browned roast to a slow-cooker insert.

2. Reduce the heat to medium. Add the remaining 2 teaspoons oil to the now-empty skillet, along with the onions, bell pepper, chiles, and garlic. Cook, stirring occasionally, until the vegetables are lightly browned, about 4 minutes. Transfer the vegetables to the slow-cooker insert.

3. Increase the heat to high. Add the tomatoes and 2 cups of the broth to the again-empty skillet, scraping up any browned bits with a wooden spoon. Add the chili powder, cumin, cayenne, and oregano and bring to a boil. Transfer to the slow-cooker insert.

4. Tear the tortillas into small pieces and combine in a medium microwave-safe bowl with the remaining ¾ cup broth. Heat on high until softened, about 2 minutes. Puree in a food processor until smooth. Transfer to the slow-cooker insert.

5. Cover and cook on low until the meat is tender, 9 to 10 hours (or cook on high for 6 to 7 hours). Transfer the roast to a carving board; loosely tent with aluminum foil to keep warm. Allow the liquid in the pot to settle for about 5 minutes, then use a wide spoon to skim the fat off the surface. Puree the liquid and solids in batches in a blender or food processor. (Alternatively, use an immersion blender and process until smooth.) Stir in the cilantro and season with salt and pepper to taste.

6. Remove the twine from the roast and cut into ½-inch slices. Transfer the meat to a warmed serving platter. Pour about 1 cup of the gravy over the meat. Serve, passing the remaining gravy separately.

Pork Pot Roast

A slow-cooker pot roast made with a pork shoulder roast—either a Boston butt or a picnic shoulder—makes perfect sense; after all, pork shoulder's fat content and marbling are similar to beef chuck's, meaning it requires the same low-and-slow cooking to become tender. To test this theory, we prepared the test kitchen's beef pot roast recipe using both cuts from the pork shoulder. We browned the meat, sautéed the onions and garlic, added the braising liquid, and let the roasts simmer in the slow cooker until the meat was fall-apart tender.

The good news is that there was no difference between the Boston butt and the picnic shoulder. The bad news is that neither pot roast was very good. The pork roasts also released a lot of liquid, which made the sauce thin and watery. And the potent flavors in the sauce (red wine, beef broth, and canned tomatoes) overwhelmed the flavor of the pork.

We addressed the liquid problem first. Eliminating the broth altogether was a good first step, as the pork juices were plenty flavorful on their own. Using just ½ cup of red wine and draining the diced tomatoes also helped tighten things up, but the sauce was still a little too thin. Flour and cornstarch gave the sauce a pasty texture, but instant tapioca (a thickener the test kitchen likes for its neutral flavor and ease of use) produced just the right thick, glossy texture.

Draining the tomatoes and eliminating the broth had lightened the flavors of the sauce, but it was still a bit too strong. Switching from red to white wine was an improvement. Adding a splash of white wine vinegar at the end of cooking refreshed the wine flavor and added brightness and acidity. Thyme lent a soft herbal note.

Onions, garlic, and carrots were essential to the base flavor, and after trying plenty of other vegetables, tasters arrived at a surprise favorite: parsnips, which contributed a welcome sweetness and heady perfume to the dish. The carrots and parsnips, however, were turning to tasteless mush after hours of cooking. Carefully arranging the ingredients in the slow cooker was the solution—we poured the tomatoes and onion over the meat and then arranged the carrots and parsnips on top, out of the liquid, where they cooked perfectly.

PORK POT ROAST

SERVES 8

If you cannot find 2½- to 3-pound pork shoulder roasts, you can substitute one 6-pound pork shoulder roast. (We like to use two smaller roasts for this recipe, because the meat cooks more quickly and the small roasts are easier to manage in the slow cooker—and to find in the supermarket.) See page 411 for more information on preparing a larger roast for the slow cooker.

2	boneless pork shoulder roasts (2½ to 3 pounds each; see note above), **netting removed and tied according to the photos** Salt and pepper
2	tablespoons vegetable oil
2	onions, minced
6	garlic cloves, minced
1	tablespoon tomato paste
½	cup white wine
3	tablespoons Minute tapioca
1	(28-ounce) can diced tomatoes, drained
2	teaspoons minced fresh thyme
1	pound carrots, peeled, halved lengthwise, and cut into 2-inch pieces
1	pound parsnips, peeled, halved lengthwise, and cut into 2-inch pieces
2	teaspoons white wine vinegar

1. Pat the roasts dry with paper towels and season with salt and pepper. Heat 2 teaspoons of the oil in a large skillet over medium-high heat until just smoking. Brown the roasts all over, about 10 minutes. Transfer to a slow-cooker insert.

2. Add the onions and 2 teaspoons more oil to the now-empty skillet and cook until browned, about 5 minutes. Add the garlic and tomato paste and cook until fragrant, about 1 minute. Stir in the wine and simmer, scraping up any browned bits with a wooden spoon, until thickened, about 2 minutes. Stir in the tapioca, tomatoes, and thyme; transfer to the slow-cooker insert.

3. Toss the carrots, parsnips, ¼ teaspoon salt, ¼ teaspoon pepper, and the remaining 2 teaspoons oil in a bowl until the vegetables are well coated. Scatter the vegetable mixture over the pork. Cover and cook on low until the meat is tender, 9 to 10 hours (or cook on high for 4 to 5 hours).

4. Transfer the roasts to a cutting board, tent with aluminum foil, and let rest for 10 minutes. Remove the twine from the roasts and cut the meat into

PREPARING PORK ROASTS

1. Remove the netting from the pork shoulder roasts. Open each pork roast and trim any excess fat using a sharp chef's knife or paring knife.

2. To ensure even cooking, fold the smaller lobes under, then tie each roast with kitchen twine every 1½ inches around the width and once around the length.

½-inch slices; transfer to a serving platter. Using a slotted spoon, transfer the carrots and parsnips to the platter with the pork. Stir the vinegar into the sauce and season with salt and pepper to taste. Serve, passing the sauce at the table.

SHOPPING WITH THE TEST KITCHEN

Pork Roasts: After testing every pork roast we could find for our slow-cooker Pork Pot Roast, we found that well-marbled shoulder cuts such as picnic shoulder and Boston butt held up best to the moist heat and long cooking time. We had no preference between the two cuts, although we did prefer to use two smaller boneless roasts in this recipe, because they cooked faster than one large cut. Most grocery stores carry the 2- to 3-pound boneless pork shoulder roasts (usually wrapped in netting) that we preferred; if you can find only a 5- to 6-pound roast, you can cut away the netting, open the roast up, and cut it into two equal pieces.

Beer-Braised Short Ribs

Short ribs are just what their name says—short pieces cut from any part of the beef ribs. Because they are rich with fat and connective tissue, they are perfect for slow-cooking—a process that turns tough meat soft and also melts excess fat, which can be easily discarded. The problem is that most of us rarely have hours to tend a simmering pot. That's where we thought the slow cooker might come in.

For our first test we simply tossed the ribs into the slow cooker, added onions and beer for flavor, turned on the cooker, and waited. After 10 hours in the slow cooker, these ribs were pretty much a disaster. The sauce was bland and watery, an inch of fat floated on top, and the meat was gray.

Our next efforts were aimed at adding flavor to this dish. First we browned the short ribs in a skillet, and this helped to develop a beefy flavor (it also rendered quite a bit of fat). Next we tested combinations of beef and chicken broth with varying amounts of beer and were continually disappointed. The sauce had no personality and little beer flavor. But when we used only dark beer—and no broth— the sauce was nicely enriched with its hearty flavor. Wanting an even more complex flavor, we tried an unlikely ingredient that we'd seen in another recipe: prunes. They melted into the sauce—no one detected them in the finished dish (not even those who don't like prunes)—yet magically sweetened it, adding deep color and flavor.

The onions were of course also crucial to flavor, and we found that we had to use a hefty 3 pounds, browning them in the skillet after browning and removing the ribs. A little tomato paste and soy sauce further punched up the flavor and color of the sauce, and tapioca worked like a charm to thicken the liquid as it cooked. (Flour and cornstarch imparted raw, starchy flavors that no one liked.)

The only remaining problem was the fat. Even after meticulous skimming, each dinner plate ended up with a slick of orange grease that challenged even the strongest dishwashing liquid. There was just one way to solve this problem: make the ribs the night before we wanted to serve them, letting the slow cooker work through the night. The next morning, we refrigerated the ribs and sauce separately. Just before dinner, we scraped away and discarded the fat that had solidified on top of the sauce, so that the meat could be reheated in the defatted sauce— and enjoyed.

BEER-BRAISED SHORT RIBS

SERVES 4 TO 6

The only way to remove fat from the braising liquid is to prepare this recipe a day or two before you want to serve it. Luckily, the short ribs actually taste better if they are cooked in advance and then reheated in the defatted braising liquid. Many of the beers we tested in our short ribs recipe turned bitter after 10 hours in the slow cooker, but Newcastle Brown Ale had a good balance of sweet and bitter flavors and was the test kitchen's top choice. O'Doul's Amber Nonalcoholic Beer was also good.

5	pounds beef short ribs (6 to 8 English-style ribs), trimmed of excess fat
	Salt and pepper
2	tablespoons vegetable oil
2	tablespoons unsalted butter
4–5	large onions (about 3 pounds), halved and sliced thin
2	tablespoons tomato paste
2	(12-ounce) bottles dark beer (see note above)
2	tablespoons Minute tapioca
2	bay leaves
2	teaspoons minced fresh thyme
2	tablespoons soy sauce
12	pitted prunes
3	tablespoons Dijon mustard
2	tablespoons chopped fresh parsley

1. Season the ribs with salt and pepper. Heat the oil in a large skillet over medium-high heat until just smoking. Add half of the ribs, meaty side down, and cook until well browned, about 5 minutes. Turn each rib on one side and cook until well browned, about 1 minute. Repeat with the remaining sides. Transfer the ribs to a slow-cooker insert, arranging them meaty side down. Repeat with the remaining ribs.

2. Pour off all but 1 teaspoon of the fat from the skillet. Add the butter and reduce the heat to medium. When the butter has melted, add the onions and cook, stirring occasionally, until well browned, 25 to 30 minutes. Stir in the tomato paste and cook, coating the onions with tomato paste, until the paste begins to brown, about 5 minutes. Stir in the beer, bring to a simmer, and cook, scraping the browned bits from the pan bottom with a wooden spoon, until the foaming subsides, about 5 minutes. Remove the skillet from the heat and stir in the tapioca, bay leaves, 1 teaspoon of the thyme, the soy sauce, and prunes. Transfer to the slow-cooker insert.

3. Cover and cook on low until the ribs are fork-tender, 10 to 11 hours (or cook on high for 4 to 5 hours). Transfer the ribs to a baking dish and strain the liquid into a bowl. Cover the ribs and sauce and refrigerate for at least 8 hours, or up to 2 days.

4. When ready to serve, use a spoon to skim off the hardened fat from the liquid. Place the short ribs,

MAKING RIBS IN THE SLOW COOKER

1. Brown the meaty side of the ribs, then turn them on each side to finish browning (you can lean the ribs against each other if they won't stand on their own).

2. Place the browned ribs in the slow-cooker insert with the meaty side facing down and the bones facing up. This placement will ensure that the meat stays submerged throughout the long cooking time.

meaty side down, and liquid in a Dutch oven and reheat over medium heat until warmed through, about 20 minutes. Transfer the ribs to a serving platter. Whisk the mustard and remaining 1 teaspoon thyme into the sauce and season with salt and pepper to taste. Pour 1 cup of the sauce over the ribs. Sprinkle with the parsley and serve, passing the remaining sauce separately.

SHOPPING WITH THE TEST KITCHEN

Short Ribs: When it comes to choosing a cut of meat for our Beer-Braised Short Ribs, you have two options, both of which will deliver good results. English-style short ribs are cut from a single rib bone and feature a long flat bone with a rectangle of meat attached. Flanken-style ribs are cut across several bones and contain two or three small pieces of bone surrounded by pieces of meat. Because flanken-style ribs are more expensive and less widely available, we prefer English-style.

Brisket and Onions

Everyone knows brisket is tough and needs prolonged cooking to make it tender, which, of course, is just what the slow cooker does best. Or so we thought. We wanted to adapt a traditional braised brisket recipe with a potent onion and red wine sauce for our slow cooker. We browned the brisket, cooked the onions, and then added both to the slow cooker along with broth, red wine, tomato paste, and herbs. Nine hours later, we had a shrunken (but tender) brisket swimming in a vast sea of watery, greasy sauce.

What we came to realize is that brisket (unlike most cuts of meat) releases a lot of liquid as it cooks—up to 4 cups by our measurements. Given the copious brisket juices, it was a mistake to add much more liquid to the slow cooker. In an effort to trim the liquid, we replaced 1 cup of red wine with 2 tablespoons of red wine vinegar, a concentrated ingredient that added depth with a touch of acidity. Then we cut the amount of broth in half and used flour to thicken the sauce. But because each brisket we cooked lost varying amounts of liquid, the resulting sauces were either too thick or thin. In the end, we found the only way to achieve a consistent result was to reduce the sauce on the stovetop at the end of cooking. Finishing the sauce on the stovetop also allowed us to skim off excess fat.

With our sauce taken care of, we revisited the meat. Although many slow-cooker recipes advocate a dump-and-cook approach, in the test kitchen we've found that browning meat before it goes into the slow cooker is a crucial step. But given how much our brisket was shrinking, we had to start with a really big piece. Unfortunately, a 5-pound brisket doesn't fit neatly in any skillet in the test kitchen. Could we flavor the meat another way?

We thought of our other favorite brisket recipe—barbecued brisket. Rubbing the meat with spices is a key step in that recipe. Could we replace the barbecue spices with onion powder, garlic powder, paprika, cayenne pepper, and salt? Sure enough, this simple spice rub added a lot of flavor. Pricking the meat with a fork before applying the spices helped them to penetrate even more. In side-by-side tests, tasters said the spice rub added even more flavor than browning—and it was a whole lot easier.

Now that we weren't browning the brisket, we wondered if we could lose this step for the onions. No matter what we tried, the sauce tasted weak and watery unless we took 20 minutes to brown the onions and build a sauce. Logistically, it was easy to season the brisket and make the onion gravy the night before. With the two main components in the fridge, in the morning we could get everything (including some fresh herbs) into the slow cooker in the time it took to make two slices of toast.

BRISKET AND ONIONS

SERVES 8

If you don't want to spend the time in the morning preparing the onion gravy and spice rub for the brisket, do so the night before. Simply prepare the onion gravy through step 1 and refrigerate overnight. For the brisket, prepare the spice mixture, rub onto the meat, wrap tightly in plastic wrap, and refrigerate overnight. Then pick up from step 3 in the morning. The leaner flat-cut brisket is the better choice for this recipe. The thicker point cut is much fattier—a good thing on the grill, where the excess fat can drip away, but a disadvantage in a slow cooker, where the fat can make the sauce greasy. If you end up with an especially thick piece of brisket, extend the cooking time to 11 hours.

1	tablespoon vegetable oil
3	large onions (about 2 pounds), halved and cut into ½-inch slices
1	tablespoon light brown sugar
	Salt
1	tablespoon tomato paste
2	tablespoons all-purpose flour
3	garlic cloves, minced
1¾	cups low-sodium chicken broth
2	tablespoons plus 1 teaspoon red wine vinegar
1	tablespoon paprika
2	teaspoons onion powder
1	teaspoon garlic powder
⅛	teaspoon cayenne pepper
1	flat-cut beef brisket (about 5 pounds), trimmed of excess fat (see note above)
3	sprigs fresh thyme
3	bay leaves

1. Heat the oil in a large skillet over medium-high heat until shimmering. Cook the onions, brown sugar, and ¼ teaspoon salt until the onions are golden, 10 to 12 minutes. Stir in the tomato paste and the flour and cook until darkened, about 2 minutes. Add the garlic and cook until fragrant, about 30 seconds. Stir in the broth and cook until the sauce thickens, about 4 minutes. Off the heat, stir in 2 tablespoons of the vinegar and transfer the mixture to a bowl.

2. Combine 1 teaspoon salt, the paprika, onion powder, garlic powder, and cayenne in a bowl. Using a fork, prick the brisket all over. Rub the spice mixture over the brisket.

3. Add half of the onion mixture to the slow-cooker insert. Add the thyme and bay leaves and place the brisket, fat side up, on top. Spread the remaining onion mixture over the brisket. Cover and cook on low until the brisket is fork-tender, 9 to 10 hours (or cook on high for 5 to 6 hours). Turn the cooker off and allow the brisket to rest for 30 minutes in the sauce.

4. Transfer the brisket to a cutting board, cut across the grain into ½-inch slices, and transfer to a serving platter. Tent with aluminum foil. Pour the sauce into a large skillet, discard the herbs, and simmer over high heat until slightly thickened, 8 to 10 minutes. Skim the fat, add the remaining 1 teaspoon vinegar, then pour half of the sauce over the brisket. Serve with the remaining sauce on the side.

THE INCREDIBLE SHRINKING BRISKET

Don't be alarmed if the edges of the brisket sit above the liquid in the slow cooker. As the brisket cooks, it will shrink and the edges will become submerged in the liquid.

Liquid Dish Detergents: Liquid dish detergent is one of those household staples that most of us don't put a lot of thought into. After all, how different can dish detergents be? Curious about how newer, eco-friendly detergents stacked up against traditional brands, we rounded up seven detergents, systematically burned several classic hard-to-clean foods onto stainless-steel skillets, and then started scrubbing. At the end of the testing, every pan was clean, but a few detergents stood out above the others for their ability to clean the pans as much as 25 percent more quickly. Surprisingly, the most effective dish detergent was one of the "natural" ones. Method's Go Naked Ultra Concentrated Dish Detergent ($2.99) is our favorite. This eco-friendly detergent comes in a sleek bottle, but we were impressed by the contents—this detergent aced all of our scrubbing tests. Our favorite among the mass-market brands was Dawn Ultra Original Scent Concentrated Dishwashing Liquid ($2.69). This bright blue detergent scored well in each washing test and proved its worth.

Hearty Beef Stew

The typical slow-cooker recipe for beef stew has many drawbacks. Ingredients are usually just dumped into the pot and left to their own devices, which means no browning and little flavor. The meat and vegetables heat up, but the flavors never really marry, producing a dish that is watery and flavorless. Who would want to marry those vegetables anyway? They're usually cooked to the point of exhaustion. Potatoes take on an unappetizing brown color, and carrots and parsnips assume the texture of baby food.

We wanted a rich, substantially thick and beefy stew, with lots of root vegetables that would taste the way nature intended. We didn't mind a bit of kitchen prep before we headed off to work in the morning (or the night before), but we didn't want to have to fuss with dinner too much once we got home.

We started with generous pieces of beef chuck (a cut that is ideal for long, slow cooking) and browned them well for maximum flavor. With the browned meat off to the side, we browned onions and added tomato paste—a chef's secret for adding color and flavor to many soups, stews, and sauces.

The stew that resulted from these efforts was pretty good, but not good enough; the color was washed out, and it lacked truly meaty flavor. After several failed attempts, we hit upon an unusual solution: a splash of soy sauce. No one could identify this mystery ingredient, but everyone in the kitchen appreciated the rich brown color and intense savory flavor it gave the stew.

To thicken the stew, we tried flour, cornstarch, and even potato flakes, but we had the best results with another unlikely ingredient, Minute tapioca, which is most often used to thicken fruit pies. It withstood the test of time in the slow cooker and thickened the stew without giving it a starchy aftertaste.

The last problem to solve was that of the drab and mushy vegetables. At first we tried roasting them separately and adding them to the pot just before serving. The roasted vegetables tasted great, but an hour of chopping and roasting vegetables pushed the family meal closer to bedtime than dinnertime. Stealing a trick often used in grilling, we wrapped the vegetables in a "hobo pack" made of aluminum foil, then placed the pack on top of the beef in the slow cooker. It may have looked like a flying saucer, but when we unfolded the foil the aroma of sweet, earthy vegetables filled the kitchen. Frozen peas turned gray in the pack, so we added them to the stew itself at the last minute.

Finally, it was time to taste our stew. The meat was fork-tender, the broth rich and just thick enough to coat a spoon, and the vegetables were perfectly cooked. Tasters agreed that this version was just as good as traditional.

MAKING THE VEGETABLE PACKET

To make the pack, place the vegetables on one side of a large piece of heavy-duty aluminum foil. Fold the foil over, shaping it into a packet that will fit into your slow-cooker insert, then crimp to seal the edges.

HEARTY BEEF STEW

SERVES 6 TO 8

If you're going to be away from your slow cooker for more than 10 hours, cutting the vegetables into larger, 1½- to 2-inch pieces will help them retain their texture.

1	boneless beef chuck-eye roast (about 5 pounds), trimmed and cut into 1½-inch cubes
	Salt and pepper
3	tablespoons vegetable oil
4	onions, minced
1	(6-ounce) can tomato paste
2	cups low-sodium chicken or beef broth
3	tablespoons soy sauce
1	pound carrots, peeled and cut into 1-inch pieces (see note above)
1	pound parsnips, peeled and cut into 1-inch pieces (see note above)
1	pound red potatoes, cut into 1-inch pieces (see note above)
1½	teaspoons minced fresh thyme
2	bay leaves
2	tablespoons Minute tapioca
2	cups frozen peas, thawed

1. Dry the beef with paper towels, then season with salt and pepper. Heat 1 tablespoon of the oil in a large nonstick skillet over medium-high heat until just smoking. Add half of the beef and brown on all sides, about 8 minutes. Transfer to a slow-cooker insert and repeat with the remaining beef (you shouldn't need more oil).

2. Add 1 tablespoon more oil, the onions, and ¼ teaspoon salt to the now-empty skillet and cook until golden brown, about 6 minutes. Add the tomato paste and cook, stirring to coat the onions well, about 2 minutes. Add the broth and soy sauce, bring to a simmer, and transfer to the slow-cooker insert.

3. Toss the carrots, parsnips, potatoes, ½ teaspoon of the thyme, and the remaining 1 tablespoon oil in a bowl. Season with salt and pepper to taste. Wrap the vegetables in a foil packet that will fit in the slow-cooker insert. Add the bay leaves and tapioca to the slow-cooker insert and stir; set the vegetable packet on top of the beef.

4. Cover and cook on low for 10 to 11 hours (or cook on high for 6 to 7 hours). Transfer the vegetable packet to a plate. Discard the bay leaves. Carefully open the packet (watch out for steam) and stir the vegetables and juices into the stew. Add the remaining 1 teaspoon thyme and peas and let stand until heated through. Season with salt and pepper to taste and serve.

SHOPPING WITH THE TEST KITCHEN

Slow Cookers: Part of the appeal of a slow cooker has always been price. But as slow cookers have gained popularity in recent years, manufacturers have added new features—and larger price tags. Does more money buy a better slow cooker? To find out, we rounded up seven models. All the slow cookers we tested did a good job on the cooking tests, but more important were the features we deemed essential: timers that automatically shift to a "keep warm" setting at the end of cooking, a clear lid, an "on" indicator light, and handles on the insert. Our favorite is the All-Clad Stainless Steel Slow Cooker with Ceramic Insert ($149.95). This cooker aced all of the tests, and it has every feature we want, including insert handles and a clear lid.

Italian Sunday Gravy

The hearty Italian American tomato sauce, often referred to as Italian Sunday gravy, calls for simmering meatballs, pork chops, and *braciole* (stuffed and rolled flank steak) in a vat of simmering tomato sauce. As the meats slowly simmer over several hours, they lend the sauce an incomparable richness. Since this dish is all about long, slow cooking, we wondered if we could use a slow cooker to streamline its preparation.

Stovetop recipes call for a large stockpot, so the quantity and variety of meat don't really matter. In our 6-quart slow cooker, however, we had to be more selective. The meatballs disintegrated when we added them at the outset and although braciole tasted great, it was too unwieldy for a slow cooker, so we omitted both.

But without the meatballs and braciole, our sauce lacked depth. To replace their beefy flavor, we tried other cuts of beef that work well in long-cooked recipes. Tasters preferred flank steak to brisket and chuck roast (both of which made the sauce too greasy). Moving on to the pork, regular chops were tough and chewy, and baby back ribs didn't add enough flavor. But country-style spareribs provided flavorful meat that fell off the bone after 8 hours in the slow cooker. In fact, both the steak and the spareribs were tender enough to shred and stir back into the sauce. Sweet and hot Italian sausages, sliced in half, added kick to the sauce while staying juicy.

For the tomatoes, testing revealed that a combination of drained diced tomatoes, canned tomato sauce, and tomato paste had the best balance of flavor and texture. As for other flavors, we found that cooking onions, lots of garlic (a whopping 12 cloves), wine, and oregano in the sausage drippings at the outset built a rich flavor base that carried through to the end of cooking. And to brighten the finished sauce, we added fresh basil.

ITALIAN SUNDAY GRAVY

SERVES 8 TO 10

Most sausage has enough seasoning to make extra salt unnecessary. This hearty sauce makes a meal when paired with 2 pounds of rigatoni, ziti, or penne.

1	tablespoon vegetable oil
1	pound sweet Italian sausage
1	pound hot Italian sausage
2	onions, chopped medium
12	garlic cloves, minced
2	teaspoons dried oregano
1	(6-ounce) can tomato paste
½	cup dry red wine
1	(28-ounce) can diced tomatoes, drained
1	(28-ounce) can tomato sauce
2	pounds bone-in country-style spareribs, trimmed of excess fat
1½	pounds flank steak
3	tablespoons chopped fresh basil
	Pepper

1. Heat the oil in a Dutch oven over medium-high heat until just smoking. Add the sweet sausage and cook until well browned and the fat begins to render, about 8 minutes. Using a slotted spoon, transfer the sausage to a paper towel–lined plate to drain, then place in a slow-cooker insert. Repeat with the hot sausage.

2. Cook the onions in the sausage fat over medium heat until well browned, about 6 minutes. Stir in the garlic and oregano and cook until fragrant, about 1 minute. Add the tomato paste and cook until the paste begins to brown, about 5 minutes. Stir in the wine and simmer, scraping the browned bits from the pan bottom with a wooden spoon, until the wine is reduced, about 3 minutes. Transfer to the slow-cooker insert and stir in the diced tomatoes and tomato sauce.

3. Submerge the spareribs and flank steak in the sauce in the slow-cooker insert. Cover and cook on low until the meat is tender, 8 to 10 hours (or cook on high for 4 to 5 hours).

4. About 30 minutes before serving, transfer the sausages, ribs, and flank steak to a baking sheet and set aside until cool enough to handle. Shred the ribs and flank steak into small pieces, discarding the excess fat and bones; cut the sausages in half crosswise. Use a wide spoon to skim the fat off the surface of the gravy, then stir the sausages and shredded meat back into the sauce. Stir in the basil and season with pepper to taste. Serve. (Any leftover gravy can be stored in an airtight container in the refrigerator for up to 3 days.)

Chili con Carne

One of our favorite chilis features big chunks of tender beef in a thick, fiery red sauce. In Texas this chili is called a "bowl of red." We wondered if we could adapt this Lone Star classic to the slow cooker.

Your typical Texas chili-head believes there is one and only one true recipe for chili, and that is one in which large pieces of cubed beef are browned and then simmered with dried chiles in broth or water. Many authentic chili recipes demand a mix of dried chiles—which must be toasted, seeded, and ground—in place of all-purpose supermarket chili powder. Tomatoes and onions are a matter of local preference, although the former are not accepted in true Texas chili circles. And beans are strictly for amateurs. Let's get this straight: this dish is about meat.

In the test kitchen we've found that ready-cut stew meat usually makes dry, dull chili. These scraps often come from pretty lean parts of the cow, and for chili you want something with some fat and flavor. A chuck-eye roast is our top choice for chili, and it takes just 10 minutes to cut up the meat.

For most slow-cooker chili recipes you just dump the meat and other ingredients into the pot, throw

---

THE AMERICAN TABLE
CHILI CON CARNE

Nobody knows exactly when chili con carne was invented, but by the mid-1800s it was a staple in Texas. The rest of the country discovered this iconic dish in 1893 at the Chicago World's Fair. Called the World's Columbian Exposition (in honor of the four hundredth anniversary of Columbus discovering the New World), the fair drew more than 25 million visitors. The Texas exhibit contained an authentic San Antonio chili stand selling bowls of its signature dish. The chili was a huge hit, and soon enterprising restaurateurs were opening chili joints in every major American city.

Chili wasn't the only culinary icon to get its start at the fair. Juicy Fruit gum, Cracker Jack, Shredded Wheat cereal, and the hamburger were introduced to America at the 1893 fair. And the architecture at the fairgrounds was impressive enough to have served as the inspiration for two of America's better-known fantasy lands: Disneyland (Walt Disney's father was a builder on the project) and Oz, whose creator, L. Frank Baum, visited the fair on several occasions before writing *The Wonderful Wizard of Oz* in 1900.

SECRETS TO THICK CHILI IN A SLOW COOKER

1. How the meat is cut changes the texture of the chili. Cut one roast into ¾-inch pieces that will break down during cooking and thicken the chili. Cut the other roast into 1¼-inch pieces to give the chili its chunky heft.

2. Because food must cook with the lid on in a slow cooker, watery sauces are a recurring problem. We thicken the chili with toasted corn tortillas, pureed in a blender with chicken broth for best flavor.

on the lid, and hope for the best. You would never make Texas chili this way on the stovetop; the beef is always browned. Just to make sure this extra step was worth the mess and time, we made two batches of chili—one with raw beef, the other with beef browned in a hot skillet filmed with oil. There was no comparison. The chili made with browned beef tasted much, much beefier. It was also less watery.

With our beef browned and waiting in the slow cooker, we sautéed onions and jalapeño chiles. Instead of taking the trouble to toast and grind dried chiles, we were hoping to use commercial chili powder and cumin, but they tasted bland. Cooking these spices with the onions and some fresh chiles brought out their flavor. It was like wiping away the fog from a windshield. Canned chipotle chiles (dried, smoked jalapeños) added more complexity, and tasters preferred chili made with—that's right—tomatoes. We often find that herbs are best added when a slow-cooker recipe is basically done. Texas chili was no exception. When we added oregano at the outset, its flavor disappeared.

At this point we were more than happy with the taste of the chili, but the sauce was still on the thin side. Pureed corn tortillas turned out to be part of the solution, but we still needed help. We got that help quite by accident one morning when we were rushed for time and used unevenly cut pieces of beef, some large and some quite small. By the end of the day, the smaller chunks had cooked to the point of falling apart, while the larger chunks held their own. Now we had a meaty chili with a varied texture and a sauce that had just the right beefy thickness.

Beans helped to extend the pot and their starch helped balance the heat. We found that it's best to stir in the beans during the last minutes of cooking so they'll retain their shape and texture.

CHILI CON CARNE

SERVES 10 TO 12 WITHOUT BEANS,
12 OR MORE WITH BEANS

Chuck-eye roasts are fatty, so don't be surprised if you trim off a pound or more from each one. You should have 5 to 6 pounds of trimmed meat when you start the recipe. Eight jalapeños can be substituted for the chipotles. This chili is authentically spicy; for milder chili, reduce the chipotles and jalapeños by half.

6	(6-inch) soft corn tortillas
3	cups low-sodium chicken broth
1	(28-ounce) can diced tomatoes
5	canned chipotle chiles in adobo (see note above)
1½	tablespoons dark brown sugar
2	boneless beef chuck-eye roasts (3½ to 4 pounds each), trimmed and cut as shown in the photo Salt and pepper
5	tablespoons vegetable oil
¼	cup plus 2 tablespoons water
3	onions, chopped medium
4	jalapeño chiles, stemmed and minced (see note above)

6   tablespoons chili powder

2   tablespoons ground cumin

8   garlic cloves, minced

3   (15.5-ounce) cans pinto or kidney beans
    (optional), drained and rinsed

1   teaspoon dried oregano

1. Heat a large skillet over medium-high heat. Add 3 of the tortillas, overlapping them as necessary, and cook until blistered on both sides, about 2 minutes per side. Transfer to a plate and repeat with the remaining 3 tortillas. Tear the tortillas into 2-inch pieces and combine with 2 cups of the chicken broth in a microwave-safe bowl. Heat in the microwave on high until the tortillas are saturated, 2 to 3 minutes. Puree the mixture in a blender or food processor until smooth, then transfer to a slow-cooker insert. Add the tomatoes and chipotles to the blender or food processor and blend until smooth. Transfer to the slow-cooker insert along with the remaining 1 cup chicken broth and the brown sugar.

2. Dry the beef thoroughly with paper towels, then season with salt and pepper. Heat 2 teaspoons of the oil in a large skillet over medium-high heat until just smoking. Brown one-third of the beef thoroughly on all sides, 8 to 10 minutes. Transfer the browned beef to the slow-cooker insert, return the skillet to medium-high heat, and repeat with 2 more teaspoons oil and another third of the beef. Transfer to the slow-cooker insert and repeat with 2 more teaspoons oil and the remaining beef. Transfer to the slow-cooker insert. Add ¼ cup of the water to the skillet, scrape up any browned bits with a wooden spoon, and return the skillet to medium-high heat. Cook until almost all the water has evaporated, about 3 minutes. Transfer the skillet contents to the slow-cooker insert, and wipe the skillet dry with paper towels.

3. Heat the remaining 3 tablespoons oil over medium heat until shimmering. Add the onions,

jalapeños, and ¼ teaspoon salt and cook until the onions are softened, about 5 minutes. Stir in the chili powder and cumin and cook, stirring occasionally, until the spices are deeply fragrant, about 2 minutes. Add the garlic and cook until fragrant, about 30 seconds longer. Transfer the vegetables to the slow-cooker insert. Add the remaining 2 tablespoons water to the skillet, scrape up any spices, and transfer the contents to the slow-cooker insert. Stir the ingredients to combine thoroughly.

4. Cover and cook on low until the meat is tender, 9 to 10 hours (or cook on high for 6 to 7 hours). Stir in the beans (if using) and cook for 15 minutes. Stir in the oregano and adjust the seasoning with additional salt and pepper if desired. (Leftovers can be refrigerated for several days or frozen for several months.)

Weeknight Chili

The gentle, protected heat of a slow cooker is perfect for the lengthy simmering that turns ground beef, tomatoes, and spices into chili. But this convenience comes at a price. Slow cookers are notorious for dulling even the most assertive flavors. When we dumped the ingredients for our favorite chili recipe into a slow cooker, we found out just how bad this problem can get. After 6 hours our "chili" was a greasy, soupy mixture devoid of any spice flavor.

A handful of slow-cooker chili recipes suggested partially cooking ingredients on the stovetop—before adding them to the slow cooker—to develop flavor. Gently sautéing onion and red pepper (preferred over green pepper, celery, and carrot for their mild sweetness) did just that. The potent combination of chili powder, cumin, coriander, oregano, cayenne pepper, and red pepper flakes, chosen for their traditional chili flavors, tasted stale and gritty when added to the slow cooker straight from the jar. We got better results when we added the spices to

the onions and peppers as they sautéed, but sometimes the spices scorched. Since spices can go from
fragrant to burned in seconds, we found it easier to
toast the spices alone (so we could catch them at the
right moment) and then remove them from the pot
before cooking the onions and peppers.

Although tasters agreed that chili should be all
about the beef, several requested a supplemental
smoky flavor. Kielbasa tasted odd in chili, but bacon
was a welcome addition. Some tasters were wary of
the added grease, but quickly browning the bacon
on the stovetop and draining it solved this problem—
and increased the meaty flavor of the finished chili.

Slow cookers are great for tenderizing tough
cubes of meat, but ground beef is another story.
Prolonged cooking can make it tough and stringy.
We discovered that the degree to which we browned
the beef before adding it to the slow cooker made a
big difference. When fully browned on the stovetop,
the beef emerged tough after 6 hours in the slow
cooker; when left slightly pink, it emerged toothsome and tender.

We had one more issue to resolve: our chili was
a bit greasy. We had been using 80-percent lean
ground beef and wondered if a leaner choice would
help. Sure enough, the 85-percent lean meat was
just as tender and less greasy. Straining the beef
and vegetable mixture before adding it to the slow
cooker eliminated any remaining grease.

WEEKNIGHT CHILI

SERVES 10 TO 12

*Serve this all-American classic with sour cream and
shredded cheese to cool the burn. For less heat, reduce
the cayenne pepper to ¼ teaspoon or omit it altogether. The ground beef will become dry if the chili is
cooked for more than 8 hours.*

¼   cup chili powder
1   tablespoon ground cumin
2   teaspoons ground coriander
1   teaspoon dried oregano
½   teaspoon cayenne pepper (see note above)
½   teaspoon red pepper flakes
8   slices bacon, chopped fine
2   onions, chopped medium
1   red bell pepper, chopped medium
6   garlic cloves, minced
2   pounds 85-percent lean ground beef
    Salt and pepper
1   (28-ounce) can tomato puree
1   (28-ounce) can diced tomatoes
2   (15.5-ounce) cans dark red kidney beans,
    drained and rinsed

1. Toast the chili powder, cumin, coriander, oregano, cayenne, and red pepper flakes in a large Dutch
oven over medium heat until fragrant, about 2 minutes. Transfer the toasted spices to a bowl. Add the
bacon to the Dutch oven and cook over medium
heat until crisp, 8 to 10 minutes. Transfer the bacon
to a paper towel–lined plate and pour off all but
1 teaspoon of the fat. Return the pot to medium
heat, add the onions and bell pepper, and cook until
softened, about 5 minutes. Stir in the garlic and
cook until fragrant, about 30 seconds.

2. Add the beef, 2 teaspoons salt, and 1 teaspoon
pepper. Increase the heat to medium-high and cook,
using a wooden spoon to break up the beef into ½-
inch pieces, until just slightly pink, about 5 minutes.
Drain the beef and vegetables in a colander.

3. Add the tomato puree, diced tomatoes, and
toasted spices to the now-empty pot and bring to
a simmer over medium-high heat, scraping up any
browned bits from the bottom of the pot with a
wooden spoon. Return the drained beef and vegetable mixture and the bacon to the pot, stir to combine, and bring to a simmer. Transfer the contents
to a slow-cooker insert.

4. Cover and cook on low until the beef is tender, 6 to 8 hours (or cook on high for 3 to 4 hours), stirring in the beans during the last hour of cooking. Adjust the seasonings as desired and serve. (Any leftovers can be refrigerated for several days or frozen for several months.)

Black Bean Chili

Packed with bold ingredients like garlic, chiles, tomatoes, ham hocks, and plenty of chili powder, Latin-inspired black bean chili should explode on the palate. Slow-cooker recipes vary in their choice of dried versus canned beans, but all the recipes we tried had three things in common: a muddy gray color, improperly cooked (either too hard or too soft) beans, and a distinct lack of flavor. Was a slow-cooker black bean chili with creamy, tender beans, a fresh appearance, and big flavor even possible?

We knew that if we were going to build assertive flavor, we'd have to get the cooking going before the ingredients hit the slow cooker. We began by sautéing chopped onion, bell pepper, garlic, and jalapeños in a Dutch oven to build a savory, spicy base for the chili. Starting this sauté with bacon fat, rather than the usual oil, helped amplify the meaty richness of the chili. The test kitchen likes to sauté spices to intensify their flavor, so when the vegetables were tender we added ¼ cup of chili powder, plus cumin and oregano, and let the spices bloom in the hot pan. Tasters preferred the brighter flavor and chunky texture of canned diced tomatoes to sauce or puree.

Ham hocks traditionally add flavor to the broth and a few shreds of meat to the chili, but tasters wanted enough meat to chew on. After testing several kinds of pork, we opted for the salty richness a small smoked ham lent to the chili as it cooked; removing the ham at the end of cooking and chopping it provided plenty of meat.

Canned beans were much too soft and yielded a mushy chili, but dried beans added to the cooker at the onset were still too hard by the time the chili was done. Soaking the beans overnight helped them cook faster, but we wanted a quicker way. We tried a test-kitchen shortcut of boiling the beans for 5 minutes and then letting them sit off heat for an hour. This helped jump-start the cooking, but we discovered an even simpler solution—simmering the beans right in the Dutch oven with the sautéed vegetables for 15 minutes before transferring the contents to the slow cooker. A full 10 cups of liquid was essential to evenly cook the 1½ pounds of beans we were using, and tasters preferred the clean flavor of a combination of water and chicken broth.

To thicken this brothy chili (slow cookers don't allow for much evaporation), we tried mashing some of the cooked beans right in the slow cooker; this was messy and gave the chili a muddy look again. Remembering the mushy canned beans from our initial testing, we mashed the contents of one can and stirred them into the finished chili to thicken it. For a fresher, more appealing texture and appearance, we found it better to also add the tomatoes and half the sautéed vegetables at the very end of cooking. This black bean chili was worth the wait.

BLACK BEAN CHILI

SERVES 6 TO 8

The black beans, unlike navy beans (see page 424), do not need to be soaked—boiling them for 15 minutes before they're added to the slow cooker is all it takes to soften them. Small boneless hams are available in the meat case at most supermarkets. The aluminum foil in step 2 helps keep all the beans under the surface of the liquid, where they cook evenly. We like to serve this chili with sour cream, shredded Monterey Jack cheese, and fresh cilantro.

- 8 slices bacon, chopped
- 2 onions, minced
- 2 red bell peppers, seeded and chopped

2	jalapeño chiles, seeded and minced
¼	cup chili powder
2	tablespoons ground cumin
2	tablespoons dried oregano
5	garlic cloves, minced
6	cups water
4	cups low-sodium chicken broth
	Salt
1½	pounds dried black beans, rinsed and picked over
1	boneless smoked ham (1 to 1½ pounds; see note above)
1	(28-ounce) can diced tomatoes
1	(15.5-ounce) can black beans, drained and rinsed
3	tablespoons fresh lime juice

1. Cook the bacon in a Dutch oven over medium heat until crisp, about 8 minutes. Transfer the bacon to a paper towel–lined plate. Cook the onions, bell peppers, and jalapeños in the bacon fat until softened, about 8 minutes. Transfer half of the sautéed vegetables to a medium bowl, cover with plastic wrap, and reserve in the refrigerator. Add the chili powder, cumin, and oregano to the pot with the remaining vegetables and cook until deeply fragrant, about 2 minutes. Add the garlic and cook until fragrant, about 30 seconds. Stir in the water, broth, 2 teaspoons salt, the dried beans, ham, and cooked bacon. Bring to a boil and let simmer for 15 minutes.

2. Transfer the bean mixture to a slow-cooker insert and arrange a piece of aluminum foil on the surface of the liquid. Cover and cook on low until the beans are tender, 7 to 9 hours (or cook on high for 4 to 6 hours).

3. Remove the lid and discard the foil. Add the tomatoes to the slow-cooker insert, stir, cover, and cook on high until the tomatoes soften, about 20 minutes. Meanwhile, transfer the canned beans

to a bowl and mash with a potato masher until a rough paste forms. Once the tomatoes are softened, remove the ham from the slow-cooker insert, transfer to a cutting board, and chop into bite-sized pieces. Stir the mashed beans, chopped ham, lime juice, and refrigerated vegetables into the slow-cooker insert. Cook, covered, until heated through, about 5 minutes. Season with salt to taste. Serve.

Boston Baked Beans

Boston baked beans, redolent with salt pork, onion, brown sugar, and molasses, require hours on the stovetop, with occasional stirring. We thought it would be nice to develop a slow-cooker version so that we could have beans without standing at the stove.

At the start, we were worried that a "dump and forget" strategy using a slow cooker might not yield the rich, creamy baked beans we were after, but we forged ahead anyway. Our concerns were well founded. The beans turned out pale and watery, and even after cooking for 12 hours, they sounded like hail when they hit our dinner plates. After more tests we hit on two partial solutions. First, these beans would need an overnight soak. Second, they would need an additional 15-minute parboil; this seemed to soften the beans to the point where the slow cooker could take over and finish the job.

SPEEDING UP SLOW COOKER BEANS

Slow cookers are notorious for failing to soften baked beans. Placing a layer of aluminum foil directly on the beans helps to keep the heat in the beans—rather than at the surface.

To our surprise, even after taking both steps, undercooked beans were still a problem. We did some research and found that baking soda is often added to beans to soften the skins. When we added the soda to the slow cooker, the beans turned mushy. The better solution was to parboil the beans with a little baking soda, then throw out the cooking water before adding the beans to the slow cooker.

The sauce proved trickier. When we bake beans in the oven, we take the lid off the pot during the final hours of cooking, which allows the sauce to thicken. But take the lid off a slow cooker and you lose all of the heat. We started with 8 cups of water (the amount specified in many recipes) but clearly needed less, because with the slow cooker evaporation was not an issue. A mere 2 cups was the right amount for 1 pound of beans!

Following traditional recipes, we browned the salt pork (to render some fat) and the onion (to maximize the flavor). If we skipped this step, the beans were greasy and lacking in flavor.

To brighten the flavor, we added a bit more molasses just before serving. Mustard and vinegar perked things up, too; they are always best added at the end of cooking because their acidity can toughen the beans.

Finally, we had Boston baked beans that were rich, creamy, and every bit as good as those served for Saturday-night suppers across New England—all without stirring a pot all day.

BOSTON BAKED BEANS

SERVES 4 TO 6

Dried navy beans, unlike dried black beans (see page 422), do require soaking. Don't use dark or black-strap molasses, which will become bitter-tasting in the slow cooker.

1   **pound dried navy beans, picked over and soaked in cold water for 8 to 12 hours**
½   **teaspoon baking soda**
2   **bay leaves**
4   **ounces salt pork, rind removed**
1   **onion, minced**

THE AMERICAN TABLE
THE GREAT BOSTON MOLASSES FLOOD

On January 15, 1919, around lunchtime, Beantown suffered an experience that would stick in Boston's collective memory for years to come. A giant holding tank containing more than 2 million gallons of molasses exploded and sent a near tidal wave of the stuff up to 15 feet high through the streets of the city's North End. Twenty-one people were killed as the molasses demolished everything in its path.

Given the relative obscurity of molasses in today's economy, it's hard to imagine a tank filled with 2 million gallons of it. But a century ago, molasses remained an important commodity. From colonial times onward, it was distilled into rum, enjoyed by the colonists, and exported to Europe. But molasses, a by-product of the cane-sugar-refining process imported from the Caribbean and West Indies, could also be used to make industrial-grade alcohol. This was in turn used to manufacture gunpowder and other munitions, both in great demand during World War I. But with the end of the war in late 1918, the demand for industrial alcohol fell, and the coming of Prohibition signaled the end of the legal manufacture of drinking alcohol. In fact, the day after the great molasses flood, the state of Nebraska ratified the Eighteenth Amendment to the Constitution, and Prohibition became the law of the land. Molasses never regained its importance in the New England economy.

¼ cup plus 2 tablespoons mild molasses
(see note above)

¼ cup packed dark brown sugar

2 cups boiling water

1 tablespoon Dijon mustard

2 teaspoons cider vinegar

Salt and pepper

1. Drain the beans and transfer to a large Dutch oven. Add 8 cups water, the baking soda, and bay leaves. Bring to a boil over medium-high heat, then boil for 15 minutes, using a wide spoon to skim off any foam that rises to the top. Drain the beans and transfer to a slow-cooker insert; discard the bay leaves.

2. Meanwhile, score the fatty side of the salt pork and cut into 2 pieces. Place the pork, scored sides down, in a medium nonstick skillet over medium heat and cook until the fat is rendered, 8 to 10 minutes. Turn the salt pork over, add the onion, and cook until lightly browned, about 5 minutes. Transfer the pork and onion to the slow-cooker insert. Add ¼ cup of the molasses, the brown sugar, and boiling water to the slow-cooker insert and stir.

3. Arrange a piece of aluminum foil on the surface of the liquid, then cover the slow-cooker insert with the lid. Cook on low until the beans are tender and creamy, 10 to 12 hours (or cook on high for 5 to 6 hours).

4. Turn off the slow cooker and remove the lid and foil. Stir in the remaining 2 tablespoons molasses, the mustard, and vinegar and season with salt and pepper to taste. Cover and let the beans sit until the sauce has slightly thickened, 15 to 20 minutes. Serve.

Barbecued Shredded Beef Sandwiches

Barbecued shredded beef sounds like an ideal recipe for the slow cooker, as both outdoor barbecue and slow cookers use slow-and-low heat to tenderize tough cuts of meat. But most of the slow-cooker recipes we found had us simply dumping a few bottles of barbecue sauce over a piece of brisket, turning on the slow cooker, and calling it a day. Eight hours later, the beef was dry, stringy, and chewy. Even worse, the meat tasted more like sour pot roast than barbecue, as the moist heat of the slow cooker washed away the flavor of the sauce.

With smoky, moist, and tender beef cloaked in a tangy sauce as our goal, we started with the meat. Our testing proved brisket to be unreliable—too often it was tough and impossible to shred, even after hours of cooking. Flank steak, round steak, and chuck-eye roast worked better; tasters preferred the chuck for its big, beefy flavor and silky, pull-apart texture.

Although bottled barbecue sauce can be pretty good, we knew we could do better. To create a smoky flavor base, we rendered bacon and cooked

PREPARING CHUCK FOR SLOW-COOKER

1. Select a well-marbled roast and carefully trim and discard any exterior fat

2. Slicing from the top of the meat, cut the roast in half (as shown) and then cut each piece in half again.

onion, chili powder, and paprika in the drippings. Ketchup, brown sugar, and mustard are a must for any barbecue sauce, but tasters wanted deeper, more complex flavor. Neither beef nor chicken broth added the necessary richness, but a surprise ingredient—coffee—gave the sauce a depth that tasters appreciated (and couldn't identify).

We poured this sauce over the beef, and after 10 hours of cooking we had tender meat swimming in a watery sauce; as it cooked, the chuck exuded juice into the sauce, dulling its flavor and thinning its texture. Using only half the sauce for cooking and reserving half for dressing the cooked meat worked well, especially when we reduced the cooking liquid before adding it back to the beef. Splashes of cider vinegar and hot sauce brightened things up, and a teaspoon of liquid smoke gave the dish a nice smoky flavor.

After pulling the tender meat into shreds, tossing it with the sauce, and piling it high on a bun, we knew we'd hit the mark. We'd finally made slow-cooker barbecued beef that looked and tasted like it had come off the grill.

BARBECUED SHREDDED BEEF SANDWICHES

SERVES 10

Don't shred the meat too finely in step 3; it will break up more as it is combined with the sauce.

1	boneless beef chuck-eye roast (about 5 pounds), trimmed and cut into 4 pieces, according to the photo on page 425
4	slices bacon, minced
1	onion, minced
2	tablespoons chili powder
1	tablespoon paprika
1½	cups brewed coffee
1½	cups ketchup
¼	cup packed dark brown sugar
2	tablespoons brown mustard
1	tablespoon hot sauce
1	tablespoon cider vinegar
1	teaspoon liquid smoke
	Salt and pepper
10	sandwich rolls, split

1. Place the beef in a slow-cooker insert. Cook the bacon in a large skillet over medium-high heat until crisp, about 5 minutes. Using a slotted spoon, transfer the bacon to the slow-cooker insert. Pour off all but 2 tablespoons of the fat from the pan and cook the onion in the remaining fat until softened, about 5 minutes. Add the chili powder and paprika and cook until fragrant, about 30 seconds. Stir in the coffee, ketchup, sugar, and 1 tablespoon of the mustard and simmer until reduced slightly, about 10 minutes. Add half of the sauce to the slow-cooker insert and refrigerate the remaining half. Cover the slow cooker and cook on low until the meat is tender, 9 to 10 hours (or cook on high for 5 to 6 hours).

2. Using a slotted spoon, transfer the meat to a large bowl and cover with aluminum foil. Transfer the cooking liquid to a large skillet, skim off the fat, and simmer over medium-high heat until reduced to 1 cup, about 10 minutes. Off the heat, stir in the reserved sauce, the remaining 1 tablespoon mustard, the hot sauce, vinegar, and liquid smoke.

3. Pull the meat into large chunks, discarding any excess fat and gristle. Toss the meat with 1½ cups of the sauce and let sit, covered, until the meat has absorbed most of the sauce, about 10 minutes. Season with salt and pepper to taste. Serve on the rolls, passing the remaining sauce at the table.

North Carolina Pulled Pork

Authentic North Carolina pulled pork begins with a dry spice rub that coats the meat. The spice-rubbed meat is then smoked over hickory or mesquite, low and slow, for hours (tended all the while by a devoted pit master). When cool enough to handle, the meat is "pulled," or "picked," into tender, bite-sized shreds and served with a vinegar-based sauce. This fairly thin sauce is nothing like the gooey molasses-based barbecue sauces most of us know and love.

Could we get all of this from a slow cooker? We had our doubts but were willing to give it a shot. Although the slow cooker abides by the same low-and-slow mantra as the barbecue, the cooking mediums (dry and smoky versus wet and watery) couldn't be more different. Our first test, which produced pork that tasted more boiled than barbecued, had us worried. The meat also had an odd pickled taste that we found distressing.

In most slow-cooker recipes for pulled pork the meat is simply simmered in bottled barbecue sauce. We decided to try a more traditional route. First, we rubbed dry spices (a mix of paprika, chili powder, cumin, salt, and pepper) into our favorite cut, a Boston butt. This gave the meat more flavor, but not enough. Next time we decided to cut open the roast, spread the spices all over, and then close up the roast. This was much better; the flavor of the spices penetrated deep into the meat. Letting the rubbed roast "cure" overnight in the refrigerator also intensified the flavor.

We decided early on that barbecue sauce, whether homemade or bottled, was the wrong cooking medium for the pork. The vinegar in these sauces was making the meat taste pickled. Given the 10-hour cooking time, this shouldn't have been much of a surprise. In a slow cooker some sort of cooking liquid is a must, but what should we use in place of the sauce? Chicken broth added a neutral, meaty flavor. Just 2 cups did the job, in part because the pork gave up so much moisture as it cooked. By the time the meat was tender, we had 6 cups of super-flavorful liquid. Unfortunately, the meat itself was a bit bland. What the slow cooker had stolen from the pork in 10 hours, we had to put back.

We skimmed the fat from the liquid and reduced it to 1 cup while the pork was cooling. To transform the liquid into the characteristic vinegar-based barbecue sauce, we added cider vinegar, brown sugar, and some ketchup. We now had 3 cups of rich, tangy, pork-flavored sauce. After shredding the pork, we poured 1½ cups of the sauce onto the pork and watched as the meat drank it up like a thirsty pit master. The elusive barbecued pork flavor was back where it belonged, but something was still missing: the smoke flavor that makes pulled pork so appealing.

We tried adding liquid smoke to the cooking liquid, with disastrous results. The smell was reminiscent of a campfire drenched by a summer rainstorm. Next we tried throwing bacon into the slow cooker as the pork cooked, but it brought little flavor to the party. Ham steak tasted fine, but it cost almost as much as the pork butt and was quickly ruled out. We finally hit on terrific smoky flavor when we tried smoked ham hocks. It may sound like a strange addition to a pulled pork recipe, but the hocks became meltingly tender (we shredded them with the pork) and added an authentic smoke flavor. Although super-concentrated liquid smoke didn't work in the cooking liquid, it worked well in the finished sauce. (It seems that you shouldn't cook liquid smoke for 10 hours!) Piled high on a soft white bun, this pulled pork had an authentic outdoor flavor.

NORTH CAROLINA PULLED PORK

SERVES 8 TO 10

Ham or pork hocks are available smoked and cured or just smoked. Although either will work in this recipe, smoked and cured hocks (which are deep red) will provide the best flavor. We prefer to use Boston butt for this recipe, but a picnic roast can be used instead. You will need a 6-quart slow cooker for this recipe. Don't be tempted to speed up the process by turning the cooker to the high setting—the pork will have a decidedly boiled texture. Serve the pork piled high on white bread or hamburger buns, with plenty of coleslaw and pickle chips on top. To warm up leftovers, add 1 tablespoon water for every cup of pork and heat in a large skillet over medium-low heat until warmed through.

SPICE RUB

4	tablespoons paprika
3	tablespoons dark brown sugar
2	tablespoons chili powder
1	tablespoon ground cumin
1	tablespoon pepper
2	teaspoons salt

PORK

3	smoked ham hocks (see note above)
1	boneless pork butt (Boston butt, 5 to 6 pounds; see note above)
2	cups low-sodium chicken broth

SAUCE

1	cup cider vinegar
¾	cup ketchup
3	tablespoons dark brown sugar
1½	teaspoons liquid smoke
	Salt and pepper
	Hot sauce for serving

SEASONING THE PORK

1. Using a sharp knife, slice lengthwise down the center of the roast and pull the two sides apart.

2. Cut a horizontal slit into each lobe of meat so that the roast will sit flat on the cutting board.

3. Apply the spice rub with your hands, massaging the spices deep into the meat.

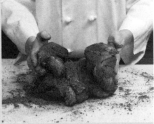

4. Loosely reshape the meat back to its original shape so it will fit in the slow-cooker insert.

1. FOR THE SPICE RUB: Combine all of the ingredients in a small bowl.

2. FOR THE PORK: Place the ham hocks in the bottom of a slow-cooker insert. Following the photos, separate the pork into two pieces and then cut each piece open to lie flat. Thoroughly coat the meat with the spice rub. Loosely reshape the meat back to its original size and place on top of the ham hocks, tucking the meat down into the slow-cooker insert as far as possible. Cover the insert with plastic wrap and refrigerate overnight.

3. The next morning, discard the plastic wrap and set the insert into the slow-cooker base. Pour the chicken broth over the pork, cover, and cook on low until the pork is very tender, 8 to 10 hours.

4. Using 2 large spoons, carefully transfer the pork butt and ham hocks to a rimmed baking sheet. Using two forks, separate the pork butt into two large chunks. Set aside to cool slightly. When cool enough to handle, shred the pork butt and ham hocks, discarding the excess fat from both as well as the small bones from the ham hocks.

5. FOR THE SAUCE: While the pork is cooling, pour the cooking liquid through a strainer into a medium saucepan. (You should have 5 to 6 cups.) Using a large spoon, skim the excess fat from the surface. Bring to a boil over medium-high heat and cook until the liquid is reduced to 1 cup, 30 to 40 minutes. Whisk in the vinegar, ketchup, and brown sugar, and simmer for 1 minute. Off the heat, stir in the liquid smoke. (You will have about 3 cups of sauce.)

6. Pour 1½ cups of the sauce over the meat, toss to combine, and let stand until the meat has absorbed most of the sauce, 10 to 15 minutes. Season with salt and pepper to taste. Serve, passing the remaining sauce and hot sauce separately.

Smothered Pork Chops

The best smothered pork chops are fall-off-the-bone tender, covered with caramelized onions, and enriched with a deeply flavored onion gravy. We wondered if we could slow this recipe down to an 8-hour braise in the slow cooker, starting it in the morning and having it ready by dinnertime that evening. More important, would it still be as good as the original?

The test kitchen's favorite skillet recipe uses relatively thin ¾-inch rib chops, so that's where we started. It took exactly 8 hours to disprove the notion that you can't overcook anything in a slow cooker. The chops were dry and stringy, and the onions were surprisingly undercooked and swollen. To round out the failure, the sauce was watery and bland. Center-cut loin chops of similar size fared no better. It seemed that thin was not in, and we had to move to thicker chops. We were certain that huge 2-inch-thick chops, special-ordered from the butcher, were going to be the answer. We just had to determine which was better, rib or center-cut chops. To our dismay, both of these cuts also overcooked in 8 hours, even on the low setting.

We weren't willing to cut back on cooking time, so we had to find another solution to overcooked chops. A test-kitchen colleague suggested blade chops, which are cut from the shoulder end of the loin and contain a lot of fat and connective tissue. The fat melted into the meat, keeping it moist and tender, and the connective tissue all but disappeared over the course of 8 hours. Best of all, there was no need to special-order extra-thick chops, since readily available ¾-inch blade chops worked perfectly.

Unfortunately, the same couldn't be said for the gravy and onions. It was becoming clear that the "dump and cook" method of loading the slow cooker with raw ingredients wasn't going to produce enough flavor. By first browning the chops on the stovetop in bacon fat, we not only added color and richness to the chops but also created a savory foundation for our sauce. When the chops were nicely seared, we removed them and cooked the onions—with garlic and thyme—in the empty pan. Tasters wanted more sweetness, and a little brown sugar added to the mix gave them just that (and helped to speed up the browning of the onions).

With the chops and the flavor of the onions and gravy set, our last challenge was to get the texture of the onions and gravy right—the sauce was still too watery. More onions thickened it, but they also threw off the flavor. Fortunately, our solution was sitting on the counter right next to the slow cooker: the blender. We removed the cooked onions from the sauce and pureed them with a cup of cooking liquid, then reduced that sauce in a saucepan (adding cornstarch to help it thicken) before pouring it back over the chops. We now had a thick, rich, emulsified gravy that truly smothered each chop.

We finished the sauce with a splash of cider vinegar to brighten things up, then garnished the chops with the bacon we'd cooked earlier as well as some chopped parsley. These were pork chops we'd look forward to coming home to.

SMOTHERED PORK CHOPS

SERVES 6

These pork chops are so tender that you'll need to remove them from the slow cooker with a spoon.

4	slices bacon, chopped fine
	Vegetable oil (if necessary)
6	bone-in blade-cut pork chops, about ¾ inch thick
	Salt and pepper
3	onions, halved and cut into ½-inch slices
1	teaspoon plus 1 tablespoon light brown sugar
¼	cup plus 2 tablespoons water
3	garlic cloves, minced
2	teaspoons minced fresh thyme
3	cups low-sodium chicken broth
1	tablespoon soy sauce
2	bay leaves
1	tablespoon cornstarch
1	tablespoon cider vinegar
1	tablespoon chopped fresh parsley

1. Fry the bacon in a large skillet over medium heat until lightly browned, about 8 minutes. Using a slotted spoon, transfer the bacon to a paper towel–lined plate, leaving the fat in the pan (you should have 2 tablespoons fat; if not, supplement with oil). Refrigerate the bacon.

2. Heat the fat over high heat until smoking. Meanwhile, pat the pork chops dry with paper towels and season with salt and pepper. Cook 3 of the chops until golden brown on both sides, about 3 minutes per side. Transfer the chops to a slow-cooker insert. Repeat with the remaining 3 chops and transfer to the slow-cooker insert.

3. Pour off all but 1 teaspoon of the fat from the skillet; add the onions, 1 teaspoon of the brown sugar, ¼ teaspoon salt, and ¼ cup water to the skillet. Using a wooden spoon, scrape the browned bits from the pan bottom and cook over medium-high heat until the onions are soft, about 6 minutes. Stir in the garlic and thyme and cook until fragrant, about 30 seconds longer. Pour the onion mixture over the chops in the slow-cooker insert. Add the broth, soy sauce, and remaining 1 tablespoon brown sugar to the skillet, bring to a boil, and add the bay leaves. Pour the mixture over the onions in the slow-cooker insert.

4. Cover and cook on low until the pork is very tender, about 8 hours (or cook on high for 4 hours).

5. When ready to serve, reheat the bacon in a large saucepan until crisp and transfer to a small bowl. Carefully transfer the chops to a serving platter with a large spoon and tent with aluminum foil. Discard the bay leaves and pour the liquid through a mesh strainer into the now-empty saucepan. Transfer the solids to a blender with 1 cup of the liquid and blend until smooth. Stir back into the remaining liquid in the saucepan. Mix the cornstarch and the remaining 2 tablespoons water together in a small bowl and stir into the sauce. Cook over medium heat until thickened, about 8 minutes. Add the vinegar, season with salt and pepper to taste, pour over the chops, and sprinkle with the bacon and parsley. Serve.

Country Captain Chicken

We've seen many slow-cooker recipes for chicken, but we've had our doubts about them; cooking chicken for hours on end usually produces stringy, bland results. But we decided to forge ahead and try a favorite chicken dish in the slow cooker. We thought the fragrant stew known as country captain, rich with mango, raisins, tomatoes, and curry, would have flavors bold enough to withstand hours in a slow cooker.

Our first thought was to dismiss the host of "dump and cook" country captain recipes typical of slow-cooker manuals. From past experience we knew that browning the chicken and vegetables would be essential to building flavor.

Our next task was to decide between white and dark meat. Tasters rejected all the stews made with breast meat (dry as dust no matter what we tried), but the thighs were very moist and meaty. Thighs are sold in two forms: boneless and skinless, and bone-in, skin-on. Without skin to protect the meat during browning, the boneless, skinless thighs turned tough and stringy. The stews made with bone-in, skin-on thighs had moist, tender meat and a richer overall flavor. To avoid a mouthful of rubbery chicken skin, we removed it after browning without sacrificing any flavor.

Unlike tough cuts of meat, which typically need as much as 12 hours to become tender, chicken will overcook—even in a slow cooker. Many recipes called for 8 hours of cooking on the low setting, but this left us with chicken so soft it literally fell off the bone. We found that 6 hours was a much better option, making this recipe more suitable to a day when you're around the house as opposed to a workday.

Although the chicken tasted great, the long, slow cooking was taking a toll on the seasonings; the curry flavor had faded, and not a hint of sweetness remained in the raisins and mango. Bumping up the curry to a whopping 2 tablespoons was an easy fix, but we had to be really creative about the fruit. Simmering it for 6 hours left it bloated and bland. We could have added the fruit near the end of the cooking time, but we didn't want to fuss with the slow cooker as the chicken cooked. On a whim, we swapped the mango and raisins for a jar of mango chutney, which added just the right amount of sweet-tart flavor.

With a bowl of steamed rice and the full array of country captain garnishes (nuts, coconut, fruit) before us, tasters lined up to enjoy a slow-cooked feast.

COUNTRY CAPTAIN CHICKEN

SERVES 6 TO 8

Basic curry powder turns bitter after 6 hours in a slow cooker, so stick with Madras curry powder. By tradition, this dish can be garnished with any or all of the following: sliced toasted almonds, shredded coconut, diced Granny Smith apples, and diced banana. Steamed long-grain rice is a must. Unlike beef, which can be browned and chilled the night before it goes into the slow cooker, once the chicken is browned it should be cooked right away.

8	bone-in, skin-on chicken thighs (about 4 pounds), excess fat trimmed
	Salt and pepper
1	tablespoon vegetable oil
2	onions, chopped coarse
1	green bell pepper, seeded and chopped coarse
1	cup low-sodium chicken broth
1	(14.5-ounce) can diced tomatoes
5	tablespoons tomato paste
1	(9-ounce) jar mango chutney, such as Major Grey's
4	garlic cloves, minced
2	tablespoons Madras curry powder (see note above)
1½	teaspoons paprika
1	teaspoon dried thyme
¼	teaspoon cayenne pepper

1. Season the chicken with salt and pepper. Heat the oil in a large skillet over medium-high heat until shimmering. Add the chicken and brown on both sides, about 10 minutes. Slightly cool the chicken on a plate, remove and discard the skin, and transfer the chicken to a slow-cooker insert.

2. Discard all but 1 tablespoon of the fat from the skillet and return the pan to medium-high heat. Add the onions, bell pepper, and ½ teaspoon salt and cook until the vegetables soften, about 5 minutes. Add the broth, tomatoes, and tomato paste and, using a wooden spoon, scrape up the browned bits from the pan bottom. Simmer until thick and smooth, about 2 minutes. Off the heat, stir in the chutney, garlic, curry powder, paprika, thyme, and cayenne. Pour the mixture into the slow-cooker insert, submerging the chicken in the sauce.

3. Cover and cook on low until the chicken is tender, about 6 hours. Turn off the slow cooker, remove the lid, and gently stir the sauce to recombine. Replace the lid and let stand for about 15 minutes to thicken the sauce before serving.

SHOPPING WITH THE TEST KITCHEN

Madras Curry Powder: Sweeter and hotter than regular curry powder, whose flavor fades and turns bitter after hours of cooking, Madras curry powder can stay the distance in the slow cooker when you're making Country Captain Chicken. But that doesn't mean you have to travel along the old spice route to find it. Madras curry powder is widely available in supermarkets. In the test kitchen we like Sun Brand Madras Curry Powder, which has a more complex flavor than the other brands we tried.

CHAPTER FOURTEEN

Cookies and Bars Galore

COOKIES AND BARS GALORE

Snickerdoodles

With their crinkly tops and liberal dusting of cinnamon sugar, chewy snickerdoodles are a favorite in New England. The name is a corruption of a German word that translates as "crinkly noodles."

Traditionally, a snickerdoodle has a subtle tang or sour undertone that contrasts with the cinnamon-sugar coating. Most recipes rely on baking soda and cream of tartar as the leavening agents for two reasons. First, the cream of tartar provides the characteristic tang. Second, the cream of tartar and baking soda cause the cookie to rise very quickly and then collapse somewhat. The result is the characteristic crinkly top.

We tested both baking powder and the baking soda and cream of tartar combination. As we expected, the latter is essential to this cookie. To make the cookies especially tangy, we found it helpful not to add vanilla. The vanilla can take away from the sourness, which is fairly subtle.

We noticed that most of the recipes we tested resulted in cookies that were not nearly chewy enough. We found that increasing the amount of sugar helped, but we wondered why some traditional snickerdoodle recipes contained vegetable shortening. Although we generally don't recommend using shortening in cookies (it does not taste as good as butter), we thought it might be worth trying in this case. Unlike butter, which contains about 18 percent water, shortening is 100 percent fat. The water in butter evaporates in the oven and helps the cookies to spread. Since shortening does not contain water, in theory it should help reduce spread in the oven and keep cookies thick and chewy.

Our tests revealed that this bit of common culinary wisdom is in fact true. When we used 1 part shortening to 1 part butter, the butter flavor still dominated but we got the chewy texture that makes these cookies so irresistible.

SNICKERDOODLES

MAKES ABOUT 24 COOKIES

Cream of tartar is essential to the flavor of these cookies, and it works in combination with the baking soda to give the cookies lift; do not substitute baking powder. For best results, bake only one sheet of cookies at a time.

1¾	cups sugar
1	tablespoon ground cinnamon
2½	cups all-purpose flour
2	teaspoons cream of tartar
1	teaspoon baking soda
½	teaspoon salt
8	tablespoons (1 stick) unsalted butter, softened
½	cup vegetable shortening
2	large eggs

1. Adjust an oven rack to the middle position and heat the oven to 375 degrees. Line 2 large baking sheets with parchment paper. Combine ¼ cup of the sugar and the cinnamon in a shallow dish for rolling. In a medium bowl, whisk the flour, cream of tartar, baking soda, and salt together.

2. In a large bowl, beat the butter, shortening, and remaining 1½ cups sugar together with an electric mixer on medium speed until light and fluffy, 3 to 6 minutes. Beat in the eggs, 1 at a time, until incorporated, about 30 seconds, scraping down the bowl and beaters as needed.

3. Reduce the mixer speed to low and slowly add the flour mixture, mixing until combined, about 30 seconds. Give the dough a few final stirs with a rubber spatula to make sure it is combined.

4. Working with 2 tablespoons of dough at a time, roll the dough into balls with wet hands, then roll in the cinnamon sugar to coat. Lay the balls on the prepared baking sheets, spaced about 2 inches apart.

5. Bake the cookies, one sheet at a time, until the edges are set and just beginning to brown but the centers are still soft and puffy, 10 to 12 minutes, rotating the baking sheet halfway through baking. (The cookies will look raw between the cracks and seem underdone.)

6. Let the cookies cool on the baking sheet for 10 minutes, then serve warm or transfer to a wire rack and let cool completely.

SHOPPING WITH THE TEST KITCHEN

Baking Sheets: Most baking sheets (also called cookie sheets) have the same basic design. They are pieces of metal that are usually slightly longer than they are wide. (A standard size is 16 inches long and 14 inches across.) Some are dark; some are light. Some have rims on all four sides. Others have rims on one or two sides but elsewhere have flat edges. We tested eleven sheets in a variety of materials and came to some interesting conclusions.

First of all, shiny, light-colored baking sheets do a better job of evenly browning the bottoms of cookies than dark baking sheets do. Most of the dark sheets are nonstick, and we found that these pans tend to overbrown cookies. It also turns out that a nonstick surface (whether light or dark) is highly water-repellent and speeds evaporation by driving moisture away, which can make cookies too dry. Shiny, silver-colored sheets heat much more evenly; if sticking is a concern, there is always parchment paper, which also helps prevent the bottoms of the cookies from overbrowning. After we baked more than 2,900 cookies, the Lincoln Foodservice Half-Size Heavy-Duty Sheet Pan ($15.40) and the Norpro Heavy Gauge Aluminum Jelly Roll Pan ($17.99) came out on top. Each turned out perfect cookies every time.

Thin and Crispy Oatmeal Cookies

Some people like a big, hearty, and chewy oatmeal cookie, with raisins and nuts in every bite. A lesser known, but just as beloved, version of oatmeal cookies is thin, crisp, and delicate. This style allows the simple flavor of buttery oats to really stand out. We wanted to develop just such an oatmeal cookie that combined the refinement of a lace cookie with the ease of a drop cookie.

We began our testing with the choice of fat. Because we wanted rich, buttery flavor, we rejected the idea of shortening from the get-go (even though it typically provides a crisper texture) and settled on butter.

As for sugar, most recipes use a combination of brown and granulated sugars. Brown sugar lends rich flavor and moisture, and granulated provides crispness and encourages browning.

To contribute better structure and richer flavor to the cookies, an egg or two is beaten in next. One egg held the cookies together nicely, but two gave them a cakey texture. Along with the one egg, we added a teaspoon of vanilla to round out the flavor. Now that the wet ingredients were all set, we were ready to tackle the dry stuff.

A fairly standard amount of 1½ cups of flour gave the cookies a thicker texture. We slowly cut down the amount until we ended up with 1 cup of flour. Though these cookies emerged from the oven with enough structure and were crisper than their predecessors, they still weren't on the mark. Because they didn't spread enough, they lacked the thinness we were looking for, and the dry edges and slightly chewy centers were obviously wrong. We tried reducing the amount of oats as well, but that still didn't solve the problem.

Could the leavener be the issue? The basic principles of leavener are as follows: use too little and there won't be enough bubbles to help the dough rise; use too much, and you end up with excess carbon dioxide, which causes the bubbles to get too big. These big bubbles eventually combine with one another, rise to the top of the dough, and burst, resulting in a flat product. But since what we wanted was a thin, flat cookie, perhaps we could make this "mistake" work to our advantage. After testing varying amounts and combinations of baking powder and baking soda, we found that ¾ teaspoon of baking powder coupled with ½ teaspoon of baking soda gave us exactly what we wanted. This time, the cookies puffed up in the oven, collapsed, and spread out, becoming a much thinner version of their former selves.

One last issue remained; to guard against the tough, dry cookies that can result from overbaking, most recipes for thick and chewy cookies say to remove them from the oven when they still look slightly raw. Suspecting this was a precaution we didn't need to heed, we tried baking the cookies all the way through until they were fully set and evenly browned. Since the cookies were now thin, they didn't become tough. Instead, they were crisp throughout. Baking the cookies one sheet at a time ensured that they cooked evenly. And rather than transferring them warm from the baking sheet to a cooling rack, we accidentally discovered that the cookies got crisper when left to cool completely on the baking sheet—less work, with even better results! We'd finally achieved our goal: a thin, delicate oatmeal cookie with buttery flavor and just the right amount of crunch.

THIN AND CRISPY OATMEAL COOKIES
MAKES ABOUT 24 COOKIES

To ensure that the cookies bake evenly and are crisp throughout, bake them one sheet at a time. Place them on the baking sheet in three rows, with three cookies in the outer rows and two cookies in the center row. If you reuse a baking sheet, allow the cookies on it to cool for at least 15 minutes before transferring them to a wire rack, then reline the sheet with fresh parchment paper before baking more cookies. We developed this recipe using Quaker Old Fashioned Rolled Oats. Other brands of old-fashioned oats can be substituted but may cause the cookies to spread more. Do not use instant or quick-cooking oats.

1	cup all-purpose flour
¾	teaspoon baking powder
½	teaspoon baking soda
½	teaspoon salt
14	tablespoons (1 ¾ sticks) unsalted butter, softened
1	cup granulated sugar
¼	cup packed light brown sugar
1	large egg
1	teaspoon vanilla extract
2½	cups old-fashioned rolled oats (see note above)

1. Adjust an oven rack to the middle position and heat the oven to 350 degrees. Line 3 large baking sheets with parchment paper. Whisk together the flour, baking powder, baking soda, and salt in a medium bowl.

2. In a large bowl, beat the butter and sugars together with an electric mixer on medium-low speed until just combined, about 20 seconds. Increase the mixer speed to medium and continue to beat until light and fluffy, about 1 minute longer. Scrape down the bowl and beaters with a rubber spatula. Add the egg and vanilla and beat on medium-low until fully incorporated, about 30 seconds. Scrape down the bowl and beaters again. Reduce the mixer speed to low and slowly add the flour mixture, mixing until just incorporated and smooth, 10 seconds. With the mixer still on low, gradually add the oats and mix until well incorporated, 20 seconds. Give the dough a final stir with a rubber spatula to ensure that no flour pockets remain and the ingredients are evenly distributed.

3. Working with 2 tablespoons of dough at a time, roll the dough into balls and lay them on the prepared baking sheets, spaced about 2½ inches apart, 8 dough balls per sheet (see note above). Using your fingertips, gently press each dough ball to ¾-inch thickness.

4. Bake the cookies, one sheet at a time, until the cookies are a deep golden brown, the edges are crisp, and the centers yield to a slight pressure when pressed, 13 to 16 minutes, rotating the baking sheet halfway through baking. Let the cookies cool on the baking sheet for 10 minutes, then serve warm or transfer to a wire rack and let cool completely.

Variation
SALTY THIN AND CRISPY OATMEAL COOKIES

We prefer the texture and flavor of a coarse-grained sea salt, such as Maldon or fleur de sel, but kosher salt can be used. If using kosher salt, reduce the amount sprinkled over the cookies to ¼ teaspoon.

Reduce the amount of salt in the dough to ¼ teaspoon. Lightly sprinkle ½ teaspoon coarse sea salt evenly over the flattened dough balls before baking.

Peanut Blossom Cookies

When Freda Smith entered her peanut blossoms in the 1957 Pillsbury Bake-Off, little did she know that she had created a cookie sensation that would endure for nearly five decades. This Gibsonburg, Ohio, native may not have won the $25,000 first prize (although as a runner-up her winnings included a General Electric stove), but her peanut blossoms—chocolate-kissed peanut butter cookies—quickly eclipsed that year's winner, a recipe for walnut-flavored butter cookies called accordion treats.

Since Freda's recipe is where it all began, we used it as a starting point to create our own version. Although her recipe produced a good cookie, tasters

wanted more peanut flavor. Freda's recipe calls for creamy peanut butter. Cookies made with chunky peanut butter received praise for their strong peanut flavor, but tasters disliked their craggy texture and appearance. We decided to stick with creamy peanut butter and try replacing some of the flour with ground peanuts. Sure enough, finely ground peanuts added a deep peanut flavor to the cookies without compromising their texture.

The cookies were almost perfect, but we were frustrated by one thing: the Hershey's Chocolate Kiss. Every recipe that we found called for the Kisses to be pressed into the cookies immediately after baking. But we found that the residual heat in the cookies softened the Kisses so much that they took at least 4 hours to firm up again. If we took a bite any sooner, chocolate would squirt out of the cookie.

After a bit of tinkering, we found an unlikely solution to the problem of gushing Kisses. Strangely enough, placing the chocolates on the cookies during the last 2 minutes of baking helped them to firm up more quickly. Why? It turns out that a little direct heat stabilizes and sets the exterior of the chocolate; the Kisses handled this way were firm enough to eat after just 2 hours on a cooling rack.

PEANUT BLOSSOM COOKIES

MAKES ABOUT 4 DOZEN COOKIES

Any Hershey's Chocolate Kiss works in this recipe; you will need one 1-pound bag of Kisses. For best results, bake only one sheet of cookies at a time. Note that although the cookies will be cool enough to eat after about 30 minutes, the Kisses will take 2 hours to set completely.

1⅓	cups all-purpose flour
½	cup salted dry-roasted peanuts
¼	teaspoon baking soda
¼	teaspoon baking powder
¼	teaspoon salt
8	tablespoons (1 stick) unsalted butter, softened
⅓	cup packed dark brown sugar
⅓	cup granulated sugar
½	cup creamy peanut butter
1	large egg
1	teaspoon vanilla extract
48	Hershey's Chocolate Kisses, unwrapped (see note above)

1. Adjust an oven rack to the middle position and heat the oven to 350 degrees. Line 2 large baking sheets with parchment paper. Process ⅔ cup of the flour and the peanuts in a food processor to a coarse meal, about 15 seconds. Transfer the mixture to a medium bowl and stir in the remaining ⅔ cup flour, the baking soda, baking powder, and salt.

2. In a large bowl, beat the butter and sugars together with an electric mixer on medium-high speed until light and fluffy, 3 to 6 minutes. Beat in the peanut butter, egg, and vanilla until combined, about 30 seconds, scraping down the bowl and beaters as necessary.

3. Reduce the mixer speed to low and slowly add the flour mixture, mixing until combined, about

30 seconds. Cover the bowl and refrigerate until the dough is stiff, about 30 minutes.

4. Working with 1½ teaspoons of dough at a time, roll the dough into balls and lay them on the prepared baking sheets, spaced about 1½ inches apart.

5. Bake the cookies, one sheet at a time, until just set and beginning to crack, 9 to 11 minutes, rotating the baking sheet halfway through baking. Working quickly, remove the baking sheet from the oven and firmly press one Kiss into the center of each cookie. Continue to bake the cookies until lightly golden, about 2 minutes longer.

6. Let the cookies cool on the baking sheet for 10 minutes, then transfer to a wire rack and let cool completely before serving.

Chewy Chocolate Chip Cookies

An attractive variation on the traditional chocolate chip cookie on which some bake shops and cookie stores have recently made their reputations—not to mention a lot of money—is the oversized cookie. Unlike cookies made at home, these cookies are thick and chewy right from the edge to the center. Although we knew at the outset that molding the dough rather than dropping it into uneven blobs would be essential to achieving an even thickness, we didn't realize how much of a challenge making a truly chewy cookie would be.

We added more flour, which helped the cookies hold their shape and remain thick but also made the texture cakey and dry rather than chewy. When we tried liquid sweeteners, such as molasses and corn syrup, the dough spread too much in the oven, and the cookies baked up thin.

At this point in our testing, we decided to experiment with the butter. Some chewy cookies start with melted rather than creamed butter. In its solid state, butter is an emulsion of butter and water. When butter is melted, the fat and water molecules separate. When melted butter is added to a dough, the proteins in the flour immediately grab the freed water molecules to form elastic strands of gluten. The gluten is what makes a cookie chewy.

Our first attempt with melted butter was disappointing. The dough was very soft from all the liquid, and the cookies baked up greasy. Because the dough was having a hard time absorbing the liquid fat, we reduced the amount of butter from 16 tablespoons to 12. We also reduced the number of eggs from two to one to stiffen the dough.

The cookies were chewy at this point, but they became somewhat tough as they cooled, and after a few hours they were hard. Fat acts as a tenderizer, and by reducing the amount of butter in the recipe, we had limited its ability to keep the cookies soft. The only other source of fat is the egg. Since our dough was already soft enough and probably could not stand the addition of too much more liquid, we decided to add another yolk (which contains all the fat) and leave out the white. This dough was still stiff enough to shape; when baked, the cookies were thick and chewy, and they remained that way when they cooled. Finally, we had the perfect recipe.

THICK AND CHEWY CHOCOLATE CHIP COOKIES

MAKES ABOUT 24 COOKIES

For best results, bake only one sheet of cookies at a time. These cookies are best served warm from the oven but will retain their chewy texture when cooled. If you want to keep cookies for several days, we suggest storing them in an airtight container at room temperature. You can restore that just-baked freshness to the cookies by re-crisping them in a 425-degree oven for 4 to 5 minutes. Let the cookies cool on the baking sheet for a couple of minutes before removing them and serve them while they're warm.

2	cups plus 2 tablespoons all-purpose flour
½	teaspoon baking soda
½	teaspoon salt
12	tablespoons (1½ sticks) unsalted butter, melted and cooled
1	cup packed light brown sugar
½	cup granulated sugar
1	large egg plus 1 large egg yolk
2	teaspoons vanilla extract
1½	cups semisweet chocolate chips

1. Adjust an oven rack to the lower-middle position and heat the oven to 325 degrees. Line 2 large baking sheets with parchment paper. Whisk the flour, baking soda, and salt together in a medium bowl.

2. In a large bowl, beat the melted butter and sugars together with an electric mixer on medium speed until smooth, 1 to 2 minutes. Beat in the egg, egg yolk, and vanilla until combined, about 30 seconds, scraping down the bowl and beaters as needed.

3. Reduce the mixer speed to low and slowly add the flour mixture, mixing until combined, about 30 seconds. Mix in the chocolate chips until incorporated.

4. Working with 2 tablespoons of dough at a time, roll the dough into balls and lay them on the prepared baking sheets, spaced about 2 inches apart. Bake the cookies, one sheet at a time, until the edges are set and beginning to brown but the centers are still soft and puffy, 15 to 20 minutes, rotating the baking sheet halfway through baking.

5. Let the cookies cool on the baking sheet for 10 minutes, then serve warm or transfer to a wire rack and let cool completely.

Hand-Held Mixers: Hand-held mixers are compact, portable, and relatively inexpensive. And even if you own a standing mixer, there are some jobs, like whipping cream or beating eggs, for which it's just easier to grab a hand-held mixer.

Over the years, however, we've been disappointed by many hand-held mixers; they can be little more than glorified whisks. And who hasn't encountered the disconcerting smoky odor of a hand-held mixer's motor as the beaters slog their way through particularly stiff dough? So we headed into the kitchen with eight leading models to see if we could separate the wimps from the workhorses. Many models had their shortcomings, including lack of power and excessive splattering. The overall winner was the KitchenAid 7-Speed Mixer (Model KHM7T, $79.99) for its compact size, ease of operation, and ability to plow through stiff doughs like a champ. The only thing this mixer can't do is knead bread dough. But the cookies, cakes, and frostings you make with it will be identical to those made in a standing mixer that costs four times as much.

Slice-and-Bake Cookies

Having slice-and-bake cookie dough in the refrigerator or freezer is great, because you can bake cookies whenever the mood strikes. But because these simple cookies have so few basic ingredients (just butter, sugar, salt, egg, vanilla, and flour), imperfections are impossible to hide. The cookies can be crisp but dry and bland or they are rich but soft and misshapen. We set out to create a recipe that would result in a cookie that was both crisp and rich with butter and vanilla flavor.

Classic slice-and-bake cookie recipes start with creaming butter and sugar with an electric mixer until light and fluffy. Egg, vanilla, and flour are added to form a soft dough, which is rolled into a log, refrigerated, and kept ready to slice and bake. Easy enough, but we weren't sure how to get more flavor into the cookies without changing their texture and character. We added as much butter as we could without making the cookies lose their crispy edges. Most recipes use a whole egg, but we found that using only the yolk made the cookies richer and firmer. We doubled the amount of vanilla, but the flavor still lacked something. Then we found that replacing some of the granulated sugar with light brown sugar gave the cookies the richness and complexity we were after.

Next, we focused on texture. The traditional creaming method is to use an electric mixer to beat air into the butter and sugar. This is great if you want a light, delicate texture, but we were trying to create a dense shortbread texture. Mixing the stiff dough by hand was effective, but it took a lot of work. A better option was the food processor, which combined the ingredients in seconds without whipping in much air. Along with their rich, buttery vanilla flavor, our cookies finally had the shortbread-like texture we wanted—and they were ready to bake whenever the craving hit.

SLICE-AND-BAKE COOKIES

MAKES ABOUT 3 DOZEN COOKIES

Be sure that the cookie dough is well chilled and firm so that it can be uniformly sliced.

- ⅓   cup granulated sugar
- 2   tablespoons light brown sugar
- ½   teaspoon salt
- 12   tablespoons (1½ sticks) unsalted butter, cut into pieces and softened
- 2   teaspoons vanilla extract
- 1   large egg yolk
- 1½   cups all-purpose flour

1. Process the sugars and salt in a food processor until no lumps of brown sugar remain, about 30 seconds. Add the butter, vanilla, and egg yolk and process until smooth and creamy, about 20 seconds. Scrape down the sides of the work bowl, add the flour, and pulse until a dough forms.

2. Turn out the dough onto a lightly floured work surface and roll into a 10-inch log. Wrap tightly with plastic wrap and refrigerate until firm, at least 2 hours or up to 3 days. (The dough can be wrapped in aluminum foil and frozen for up to 1 month. There's no need to defrost the dough—simply slice and bake, increasing the baking time by a couple of minutes.)

3. Adjust the oven racks to the upper-middle and lower-middle positions and heat the oven to 350 degrees. Line 2 baking sheets with parchment paper. Slice the chilled dough into ¼-inch rounds and place 1 inch apart on the prepared baking sheets. Bake until the edges are just golden, about 15 minutes, switching and rotating the sheets halfway through baking. Let the cookies cool for 10 minutes on the baking sheets, then transfer to a wire rack and cool completely before serving.

Variations
COCONUT-LIME COOKIES
In step 1, add 2 cups sweetened shredded coconut and 2 teaspoons grated fresh lime zest to the food processor along with the sugars and salt.

WALNUT–BROWN SUGAR COOKIES
In step 1, add 2 more tablespoons brown sugar and 1 cup chopped walnuts to the food processor along with the sugars and salt.

ORANGE–POPPY SEED COOKIES
In step 1, add ¼ cup poppy seeds and 1 tablespoon grated fresh orange zest to the food processor along with the sugars and salt.

New York Black and White Cookies

A treat found in nearly every New York City deli, the black and white cookie is made from butter, sugar, eggs, milk, flour, and a touch of lemon and painted with side-by-side coats of chocolate and vanilla icing. We set out to develop a cakey, tender cookie with a low, even rise and smooth, flavorful chocolate and vanilla icings.

Our testing began with a range of black and white cookie recipes. We knew we did not want the dense richness of a butter cookie or the sweet crunch of a sugar cookie, so the recipes that fell into these categories were summarily rejected. We focused our testing instead on a widely circulated recipe claiming to be the authentic black and white cookie recipe.

Neither crisp like sugar cookies nor rich like shortbread, these cookies did approximate the distinctive cake-like texture of a black and white cookie. But they needed a lot of work. Doughy and thick, the cookies had a texture that lay somewhere between a scone and an eggy cake. The cookies had thin edges but mottled and bumpy centers, not the smooth-surfaced, perfectly round cookies we had imagined. Although it fell short, we sensed that this recipe had the very rough-hewn makings of an ideal New York black and white cookie.

We followed the traditional creaming method, using 2 sticks of butter and 1¾ cups sugar. Then we turned to the eggs and flour. We knew we wanted to reduce both. The original recipe called for 2½ cups of all-purpose flour and 2½ cups of cake flour. We tried reducing the total amount of flour to 4 cups, 2 cups of each type. The reduction of flour improved the texture of the cookies dramatically, but we still found them on the tough side. We then experimented with different combinations of all-purpose and cake flour and finally settled on using only cake flour, which has less protein than all-purpose flour and yields a more delicate crumb. The resulting cookies had a tender, cake-like texture and very fine crumb.

As for the eggs, we tried using two eggs and two egg yolks, three whole eggs, and four yolks, among other variations, and found that two large whole eggs worked perfectly in combination with the flour. One cup of milk added to the batter in stages, alternating with the flour, was just right. In addressing the leavener, we discovered that just ½ teaspoon of baking powder gave our cookies a thin, even rise. They were almost perfect.

To give the cookies their traditional subtle lemon flavor, we found that ½ teaspoon of lemon extract did the job. Although 1 tablespoon of lemon juice is an acceptable substitute if lemon extract is unavailable, tasters preferred the cookies made with lemon extract. They also preferred vanilla extract; 1 teaspoon gave the subtle, higher lemon notes some depth and rounded out the flavor.

Black and white cookies derive their name from their characteristic icing: half of the cookie is covered in chocolate icing and the other half in vanilla. We came up with numerous versions of the icing recipe, all calling for confectioners' sugar, some with milk or cream, some with water, boiling water, or corn syrup. In most recipes some of the vanilla icing is combined with melted chocolate; others used melted chocolate and cream alone for the chocolate icing. We wanted an icing that would be easy to spread and would coat the cookie in a smooth, even layer. We also wanted the icing to have a bit of a shine and to harden so that our fingers wouldn't be covered in frosting. We wanted our vanilla icing to have a subtle vanilla flavor and our chocolate icing to taste of chocolate, not of brown-colored confectioners' sugar. After numerous tests, we discovered that confectioners' sugar in combination with corn syrup had the best

TWO WAYS TO MELT CHOCOLATE

Stovetop: Place the chopped chocolate in a heatproof bowl set over a pot of barely simmering water, but be sure the bowl is not touching the water or the chocolate could scorch.

Microwave: Microwave chopped chocolate at 50 percent power for 2 minutes. Stir the chocolate and continue heating until melted, stirring once every additional minute.

consistency and appearance. Unsweetened chocolate gave the icing a richer, darker color than bittersweet, semisweet, or milk chocolate.

BLACK AND WHITE COOKIES

MAKES ABOUT 24 LARGE COOKIES

Don't substitute "lemon flavor" or lemon oil for the lemon extract. In a pinch, however, you can substitute 1 tablespoon fresh lemon juice. If the chocolate icing cools so that it is no longer spreadable, microwave it for 30 seconds to resoften.

COOKIES

4	cups cake flour
½	teaspoon baking powder
½	teaspoon salt
16	tablespoons (2 sticks) unsalted butter, softened
1¾	cups granulated sugar
2	large eggs
1	teaspoon vanilla extract
½	teaspoon lemon extract (see note above)
1	cup whole milk

ICING BLACK AND WHITE COOKIES

1. Ice half of each cookie with chocolate icing. Tilt the cookie and run the spatula around the edge to scrape off the excess icing.

2. Once the chocolate icing is set, ice the other half of each cookie with vanilla icing. Tilt the cookie and run the spatula around the edge to scrape off the excess icing.

ICINGS

¼	**cup light corn syrup**
⅓	**cup plus 2–4 teaspoons water**
5	**cups confectioners' sugar**
1	**teaspoon vanilla extract**
2	**ounces unsweetened chocolate, melted (see page 443)**

1. FOR THE COOKIES: Adjust the oven racks to the upper-middle and lower-middle positions and heat the oven to 350 degrees. Line 2 large baking sheets with parchment paper. Whisk the flour, baking powder, and salt together in a medium bowl.

2. In a large bowl, beat the butter and sugar together with an electric mixer on medium speed until light and fluffy, 3 to 6 minutes. Beat in the eggs, vanilla, and lemon extract until combined, about 30 seconds, scraping down the bowl and beaters as needed.

3. Reduce the mixer speed to low and beat in one-third of the flour mixture, followed by half of the milk. Repeat with half of the remaining flour mixture and the remaining milk. Beat in the remaining flour mixture until combined.

4. Scoop ¼-cup mounds of batter onto the prepared baking sheets, spaced about 2 inches apart. Use the back of a spoon or a finger dipped in water to smooth the tops of the cookies. Bake the cookies until the edges are just beginning to turn light golden brown, about 15 minutes, switching and rotating the baking sheets halfway through baking.

5. Let the cookies cool on the baking sheets for 10 minutes, then transfer to a wire rack. Repeat with the remaining dough, using cooled, freshly lined baking sheets.

6. FOR THE ICINGS: Bring the corn syrup and ⅓ cup water to a boil in a medium saucepan over medium-high heat. Remove the pan from the heat and whisk in the confectioners' sugar and vanilla until smooth. Measure half of the icing into a bowl and whisk in the melted chocolate and the remaining 2 to 4 teaspoons water as needed until the mixture is smooth and spreadable.

7. Place 2 large wire racks over parchment paper for easy cleanup. Following the photos, spread about 2 tablespoons of the chocolate icing over half of each cookie with a small spatula, then let sit on the wire rack until the icing has just set, about 15 minutes. Spread the vanilla icing over the other half of each cookie and let sit until the icings have hardened, about 1 hour, before serving.

Whoopie Pies

Some of us in the test kitchen admit to a not-so-secret addiction to convenience snack cakes. From Devil Dogs to Oatmeal Cream Pies, if it's packaged in cellophane, we'll eat it. Whoopie pies—two chocolate cookie–like cakes stuffed to the gills with a fluffy marshmallow filling—are right up our alley. Where did these treats come from? Why the funny name? And, most important, how could we make this treat at home?

It turns out that Maine and Pennsylvania—the Pennsylvania Dutch of Lancaster County, to be specific—both claim whoopie pies as their own. After weeks of reading through old newspapers and talking to librarians and bakery owners, here's what we learned.

Maine's earliest claim dates back to 1925, when Labadie's Bakery in Lewiston first sold whoopie pies to the public. As we continued our research, we ran across an advertisement for a whoopie pie wrapper contest in the *Portland* (ME) *Press Herald*: "Collect the most wrappers and a brand new 1950 Plymouth Sedan could be yours!" In small letters underneath we saw the words "Berwick Cake Co.—Boston." Some research showed that the Berwick Cake Company began manufacturing Whoopie! Pies (the exclamation point was part of the name) in 1927. These sources claim that whoopie pies were named after the musical *Whoopie* (from which came the well-known song "Makin' Whoopie"); *Whoopie* had its debut in Boston in 1927. In addition, Marshmallow Fluff, a key ingredient in many whoopie pie recipes, was invented in nearby Lynn seven years earlier.

What about Pennsylvania's claim on whoopie pies? We found an article in a copy of the *Gettysburg Times* from 1982 that spoke of a chocolate cake sandwich with a fluffy cream center. These sandwiches were called "gobs" and were sold by the Dutch Maid Bakery of Geistown, Pennsylvania. The name was different, but the description (and a huge picture) showed that these were no doubt whoopie pies by another name. In 1980 Dutch Maid Bakery purchased the rights to the gob from the Harris-Boyer Baking Company, which had started manufacturing gobs in 1927.

We weren't able to resolve the conflicting claims about the origins of the whoopie pie (although we're pretty confident that they date back to the 1920s), but we figured we could bake some up ourselves. Whoopie pie recipes haven't changed much over the years. Original recipes used a devil's food cake base, with "soda" and "soured milk" to lift the cakes. In today's vernacular, baking soda and buttermilk work well in their place. The original cakes contained lard, but many recipes have switched to shortening or vegetable oil, both of which extend the cakes' shelf life. Although it's considered heresy in the whoopie world, we used butter instead of shortening. Moist and tender, these cakes were snatched up as fast as we could bake them, so we had no concern about shelf life.

MAKING WHOOPIE PIES

1. Scoop generous mounds of batter onto each prepared baking sheet.

2. Spoon the filling evenly on the bottoms of the cakes. Then press the bottoms of the remaining cakes over the filling to make sandwiches.

Originally, the filling was a whipped frosting made of sugar and lard, but recipes soon switched to marshmallow creme, which was easily purchased under the name of Marshmallow Fluff. Instead of mixing the marshmallow with lard or vegetable shortening, we turned once more to butter. We slathered this fluffy filling between two chocolate cookie-cakes and our whoopie pies were done. And as soon as we put them on a plate, they were history, too.

WHOOPIE PIES

MAKES 6 PIES

Marshmallow creme with a thicker consistency (like Marshmallow Fluff) yields the best results in this recipe. If the filling is too soft to work with, chill it briefly; alternatively, if the filling seems stiff, 15 seconds in the microwave will do the trick.

CAKES

2	cups all-purpose flour
½	cup Dutch-processed cocoa powder
1	teaspoon baking soda
½	teaspoon salt
8	tablespoons (1 stick) unsalted butter, softened
1	cup packed light brown sugar
1	large egg, room temperature
1	teaspoon vanilla extract
1	cup buttermilk

FILLING

12	tablespoons (1½ sticks) unsalted butter, softened
1¼	cups confectioners' sugar
1½	teaspoons vanilla extract
⅛	teaspoon salt
2½	cups marshmallow creme (see note above)

1. FOR THE CAKES: Adjust the oven racks to the upper-middle and lower-middle positions and heat the oven to 350 degrees. Line 2 large baking sheets with parchment paper. Whisk the flour, cocoa powder, baking soda, and salt together in a medium bowl.

2. In a large bowl, beat the butter and brown sugar together with an electric mixer on medium speed until light and fluffy, 3 to 6 minutes. Beat in the egg and vanilla until combined, about 30 seconds, scraping down the bowl and beaters as necessary.

3. Reduce the mixer speed to low and slowly beat in half of the flour mixture, followed by half of the buttermilk. Repeat with half of the remaining flour mixture and the remaining buttermilk. Add the remaining flour mixture until combined.

4. Scoop six generous ¼-cup mounds of batter onto each baking sheet, spaced about 2 inches apart. Bake the cakes until they spring back when pressed, 15 to 18 minutes, switching and rotating the baking sheets halfway through baking. Let the cakes cool completely on the baking sheets, about 1 hour.

5. FOR THE FILLING: Beat the butter and confectioners' sugar together in a medium bowl with an electric mixer on medium speed until light and fluffy, about 2 minutes. Beat in the vanilla and salt. Beat in the marshmallow creme until incorporated, about 2 minutes.

6. To serve, spread ⅓ cup of the filling evenly over the bottom of a cake, then make a sandwich by pressing the bottom of another cake onto the filling; repeat with the remaining cakes and filling.

Joe Froggers

We like to think that we know our way around the cookie jar, but that doesn't mean we can't still be taken by surprise. Recently, in a Massachusetts bakery, we ran across a "new" cookie that actually dates back to the late 1700s. These cookies were as big as saucers and as flat as a pancake. Their texture was incredibly moist from molasses, and they tasted strongly of clove and rum and were just a little salty. Called Joe froggers, these cookies hail from Marblehead, Massachusetts. We set out to develop our own version.

We got several recipes from Web sites, cookbooks, and magazines, but they baked up hard, with no warm and salty rum flavor. We then e-mailed the Marblehead Museum and Historical Society, and they recommended that we consult *The Spirit of '76 Lives Here*, by Virginia Gamage and Priscilla Lord (Chilton Book Company, 1972). The authors tell the story of Joseph Brown, a freed slave and Revolutionary War veteran who lived in Marblehead more than two hundred years ago.

Brown (known as "Old Black Joe") and his wife, Lucretia (affectionately known as Auntie Cresse), opened Black Joe's Tavern in a part of Marblehead called Gingerbread Hill. Besides serving drinks (mostly rum), Joe and Auntie Cresse baked cookies: large, moist molasses and rum cookies made salty by the addition of Marblehead seawater. These cookies were popular sustenance on long fishing voyages, as they contained no dairy to spoil, and the combination of rum, molasses, and seawater kept them chewy for weeks.

According to Samuel Roads Jr.'s *History and Traditions of Marblehead*, published in 1880, the funny name for these cookies referred to the lily pads (similar in size and shape to the cookies) and large croaking frogs that would fill the pond behind Black Joe's Tavern. Thus the cookies became known as Joe froggers.

At Marblehead's Abbot Public Library, the librarians produced recipes from local news journals and town cookbooks, such as the one published by the Marblehead, Massachusetts, Baptist Women's Fellowship (1965). In these recipes molasses is first stirred together with baking soda. The reaction between the two makes the mixture bubble and froth, leaving the soda with little leavening power. That, combined with the absence of egg, explains why the cookies are so flat. (The soda also contributes a deep, dark color.)

To achieve the rum flavor we desired, we doubled the amount of rum and halved the amount of water. We weren't going to use seawater (although we did test it), but dissolving 1½ teaspoons of salt into the rum and water worked fine. Some recipes called for shortening (Auntie Cresse most likely used lard), but butter tasted better.

Our version of this old-fashioned American cookie won't stay fresh for weeks at sea like the original, but it is so salty, spicy, sweet, and chewy we're not sure that matters.

JOE FROGGERS

MAKES 24 COOKIES

Place only 6 cookies on each baking sheet—they will spread. If you don't own a 3½-inch cookie cutter, use a drinking glass. Use regular (not dark or robust) molasses. Make sure to chill the dough for a full 8 hours or it will be too difficult to roll out.

⅓	cup dark rum (such as Myers's)
1	tablespoon water
1½	teaspoons salt
3	cups all-purpose flour
¾	teaspoon ground ginger
½	teaspoon ground allspice
¼	teaspoon ground nutmeg
⅛	teaspoon ground cloves
1	cup molasses (see note above)
1	teaspoon baking soda
8	tablespoons (1 stick) unsalted butter, softened
1	cup sugar

1. Stir together the rum, water, and salt in a small bowl until the salt dissolves. Whisk the flour, ginger, allspice, nutmeg, and cloves together in a medium bowl. Stir the molasses and baking soda together in a large measuring cup (the mixture will begin to bubble) and let sit until doubled in volume, about 15 minutes.

2. In a large bowl, beat the butter and sugar together with an electric mixer on medium-high speed until light and fluffy, 3 to 6 minutes. Reduce the speed to medium-low and gradually beat in the rum mixture. Add one-third of the flour mixture, beating on medium-low until just incorporated, followed by half of the molasses mixture, scraping down the sides of the bowl and beaters as needed. Add half of the remaining flour mixture, followed by the remaining molasses mixture, and finally the remaining flour mixture. Using a rubber spatula, give the dough a final stir (the dough will be extremely sticky). Cover the bowl with plastic wrap and refrigerate until the dough is stiff, at least 8 hours or up to 3 days.

3. Adjust the oven racks to the upper-middle and lower-middle positions and heat the oven to 375 degrees. Line 2 baking sheets with parchment paper. Working with half of the dough at a time on a heavily floured work surface, roll out to ¼-inch thickness. Using a 3½-inch cookie cutter, cut out 12 cookies. Transfer 6 cookies to each baking sheet, spaced about 1½ inches apart. Bake until the cookies are set and just beginning to crack, about 8 minutes, switching and rotating the baking sheets halfway through baking. Cool the cookies on the sheets for 10 minutes, then transfer to a wire rack to cool completely before serving. Repeat with the remaining dough, using cooled, freshly lined baking sheets.

Sand Tarts

Thin, crisp, buttery, and dusted with a "sandy" coating of cinnamon sugar, sand tarts were once one of America's favorite cookies. We found recipes in *The Presbyterian Cookbook* and *Buckeye Cookery*, both from the 1870s, and in *Fannie Farmer Original Boston Cooking-School Cook Book*, from 1896. It is believed that these cookies were brought to American shores by German immigrants in the nineteenth century, and they became especially popular in Maryland, Pennsylvania, and Ohio.

Twentieth-century recipes aim for flat, crisp cookies dusted with cinnamon sugar and decorated with a ring of sliced almonds (which makes the cookies look a bit like sand dollars). Almost every recipe we uncovered gave similar instructions: cream copious amounts of butter and sugar; add two whole eggs and flour; refrigerate the dough to make it more workable; then roll it thin, stamp out the cookies, adorn them with cinnamon sugar and almonds, and bake until crisp. But when we prepared these recipes, we began to see why this cookie has fallen out of favor. Even when chilled overnight, the rich, sticky dough was almost impossible to roll out to the desired thickness without tearing.

Considering other shaping options, we tried a trick the test kitchen often employs for sugar cookies—rolling the dough into balls, rolling the balls in a potent cinnamon-sugar mixture, and then

---

THE AMERICAN TABLE
JOE FROGGERS

Joe froggers cookies date back more than two hundred years to Black Joe's Tavern, located in Marblehead, Massachusetts, a seaside town about twenty-five miles north of Boston. The original recipe for these spicy cookies called for local seawater, which gave the cookies their distinctly salty flavor.

flattening them with the bottom of a measuring cup before baking. This was easy and worked great, provided we flattened the cookies in two steps, with more cinnamon sugar added between pressings to minimize sticking and add even more flavor.

But the cookies were still doming, and we wanted them to be flat and crisp. Eliminating one of the egg whites reduced the doming slightly, but not enough. Turning to our mixing method, we realized we were beating a lot of air into the dough as we creamed the butter and sugar—air that was giving the cookies extra height. Switching from an electric mixer to a food processor helped minimize air in the dough, but our real breakthrough happened when we switched the order in which we added ingredients to the processor. Cutting the butter into the sugar and flour (a technique known as reverse creaming) incorporated almost no air and finally produced the flat, crisp cookies we were after. In the end, a modern appliance helped make this recipe relevant for a new generation of American bakers.

SAND TARTS

MAKES ABOUT 3 DOZEN COOKIES

We prefer the look of sliced natural almonds for this recipe, but blanched slices will work fine.

2	cups all-purpose flour
1¾	cups sugar
¾	teaspoon salt
16	tablespoons (2 sticks) unsalted butter, softened
1	large egg plus 1 large egg yolk
1½	teaspoons ground cinnamon
¼	cup sliced almonds (see note above)

1. Adjust the oven racks to the upper-middle and lower-middle positions and heat the oven to 350 degrees. Line 2 baking sheets with parchment paper. Process the flour, 1½ cups of the sugar, and the salt in a food processor until combined. Add the butter,

SHAPING A SAND TART

1. Use your hands to roll the dough into 1½-inch balls, then roll each ball in cinnamon sugar and place them 3 inches apart on the baking sheets.

2. Press each dough ball into a 2-inch disk with the bottom of a measuring cup or a flat-bottomed glass.

3. After sprinkling each 2-inch disk with more cinnamon sugar, use a measuring cup to further flatten each disk into a 2½-inch round.

4. Lightly press 5 almond slices into each round of dough in a circular pattern.

1 tablespoon at a time, and pulse until just incorporated. Add the egg and yolk and pulse until a soft dough forms.

2. Wrap the dough in plastic wrap and flatten into a 1-inch-thick disk. Transfer to the freezer until firm, about 15 minutes. Combine the cinnamon and remaining ¼ cup sugar in a small bowl. Break the disk of chilled dough into two pieces and return one piece to the freezer. Working with 1½ tablespoons of chilled dough at a time, roll the dough into 1½-inch balls with floured hands, then roll the balls in the cinnamon-sugar mixture to coat. Lay the balls on the prepared baking sheets, spaced about 3 inches apart. Press the balls into 2-inch disks, sprinkle with more cinnamon sugar, flatten into 2½-inch disks, and garnish with the almonds.

3. Bake the cookies until the edges are lightly browned, 10 to 12 minutes, switching and rotating the sheets halfway through baking. Let cool for 5 minutes on the baking sheets, then transfer the cookies to a wire rack and cool completely before serving. Repeat with the remaining dough using cooled, freshly lined baking sheets.

Hermits

The hermit is a cookie certainly worthy of its eccentric name. Depending on whom you ask, it can be soft and cakey or dry and biscuit-like; packed with dried fruit and nuts or free of both; and heavily seasoned with warm spices like ginger, cloves, and nutmeg or flavored only with molasses.

After a taste test that included cookies we baked in-house and commercially produced hermits from local and national bakeries, tasters agreed that an ideal hermit should have a texture in between a cake and a brownie—that is, it should be soft, moist, and dense. We decided that hermits should be studded with raisins and taste predominantly of molasses, but with warm spices lingering in the background.

From the outset we knew that attaining the right texture would be tricky. Most hermit recipes we tried relied on two eggs as well as some baking soda for their rise. The result is a puffy cookie that is dry and too cakey for our taste. Leaving out one of the eggs made them too dense, but we realized we were on the right track. In the next batch we omitted the white of one of the eggs, and the resulting cookies were everything we wanted—soft and rich but

with a slightly cakey crumb. The cakey crumb is the secret to their longevity; we enjoyed these cookies up to a week after baking them. And, as the story of how they got their name suggests, the flavors were better after a couple of days of storage.

For both sweetening and flavor, hermits depend on molasses. Most tasters favored mild, although some liked the stronger-flavored dark molasses. Molasses alone was not enough to fully sweeten the cookies, so we included light brown sugar.

A healthy amount of raisins also helped sweeten the cookies and rounded out the flavors. Raisins also lent the cookies a pleasing toothsome quality that contrasted nicely with the crisp crust and soft crumb.

As for spices, cinnamon, cloves, allspice, and ginger were essential and an unlikely spice, pepper, contributed a kick that heightens the piquancy of the other spices. These soft, homey cookies are the perfect accompaniment to a cup of tea or glass of milk.

HERMITS

MAKES ABOUT 16 COOKIES

The dusting of confectioners' sugar is optional, but it does improve the cookies' appearance.

2	cups all-purpose flour
½	teaspoon baking soda
½	teaspoon ground cinnamon
½	teaspoon ground cloves
¼	teaspoon ground allspice
¼	teaspoon ground ginger
⅛	teaspoon pepper
½	teaspoon salt
8	tablespoons (1 stick) unsalted butter, melted and cooled
½	cup packed light brown sugar
2	large eggs, 1 whole and 1 separated, white lightly beaten
½	cup light or dark molasses
1½	cups raisins
2	tablespoons confectioners' sugar (optional; see note above)

1. Whisk the flour, baking soda, spices, and salt together in a medium bowl; set aside.

2. Whisk the melted butter and brown sugar together in another medium bowl until just combined. Add the whole egg, egg yolk, and molasses and whisk thoroughly. Using a rubber spatula, fold the flour mixture into the molasses mixture until combined. Stir in the raisins. Cover the bowl with plastic wrap and refrigerate for at least 1 hour.

3. Adjust an oven rack to the middle position and heat the oven to 350 degrees. Line a baking sheet with parchment paper.

4. Following photo 1, use your hands to form the dough into two logs on the prepared baking sheet. Brush the logs with the beaten egg white.

SHAPING HERMITS

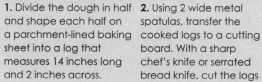

1. Divide the dough in half and shape each half on a parchment-lined baking sheet into a log that measures 14 inches long and 2 inches across.

2. Using 2 wide metal spatulas, transfer the cooked logs to a cutting board. With a sharp chef's knife or serrated bread knife, cut the logs crosswise into cookies about 2 inches thick.

5. Bake until the tops of the logs have browned and spring back when touched, 20 to 25 minutes, rotating the baking sheet front to back halfway through the baking time. Set the sheet on a wire rack and cool for 15 minutes. Using 2 wide metal spatulas, transfer the logs to a cutting board, and slice following photo 2. When the cookies have completely cooled, dust them with confectioners' sugar (if using) before serving.

Washboards

A good tea cookie is not too sweet, not too greasy, and not too filling. Washboards fit the bill. The name refers to the fork-indented ridges on top of each cookie that give it the appearance of an old-fashioned washboard. These cookies are crisp and not too sweet, with the distinct flavor and aroma of coconut.

Turning to the Internet, we punched in "washboard cookies" and found some promising recipes. When we baked these cookies, however, they were distinctly different from the ones just described. These rich cookies were decidedly moist and chewy—not a bad thing as cookies go, but much too sweet and greasy for the garden club set. As for the coconut, these recipes used so little that if we hadn't made the cookies ourselves, we never would have guessed that coconut was involved.

Our luck improved when we turned to our collection of old and out-of-print cookbooks. Many dating back to the early 1900s made mention of crisp coconut cookies, but we first saw the name "washboards" in mid-century cookbooks, such as *Betty Crocker's Picture Cookbook* (1950). That book described washboards as "coconut-taffy bars." We whipped up a batch, and here indeed were cookies that actually tasted of coconut and were snappy-thin and crisp, just as a tea cookie should be. The word "bars" seemed to refer to the cookies' rectangular shape (they were not at all like "bars" of the brownie and blondie variety).

Step by step, we played with the recipe to get closer to our own ideal. Away went the saccharine taste of granulated sugar and in went light brown sugar, which gave the cookie a toastier flavor and enhanced the coconut. Knowing when enough brown sugar was enough was important—a good tea cookie should not give one a toothache. We reduced the amount of butter to keep the cookie lean, and we loved the flavor of nutmeg that we found in one recipe. When it came to the coconut, we added just enough to make it the star of the show without turning the cookie into a macaroon. Absolutely delicious.

Antique recipes had us painstakingly shaping each washboard by hand. After we had shaped more than a hundred this way, the task began to lose its charm. In search of an easier method, we took a cue from refrigerator cookies and rolled the dough into a log. We bashed the top and sides, making a rough rectangular box, then cut very thin slices of cookie dough and spaced the slices on baking sheets. Talk about easy!

Other parts of the process, we decided, were best left untouched. We're sure there's an electric supermatic cookie-ridge-digger out there somewhere, but if Grandma Mavis used a fork to make the washboards' ridges, then a fork is good enough for us.

Into the oven they went, and out of the oven they came: beautiful, toasty little coconut cookies—just perfect with a cup of tea.

MAKING WASHBOARDS

1. Using floured hands, shape the cookie dough into a 15-inch-long log.

2. Flatten the top and sides of the log so that it is 1 inch tall and 3 inches wide. Wrap the dough in plastic wrap and chill about 45 minutes.

3. Cut the chilled log crosswise into ¼-inch slices and transfer them to parchment-lined baking sheets, arranging them 1 inch apart.

4. Use the floured tines of a fork to gently press crosswise indentations into the dough slices.

WASHBOARDS

MAKES ABOUT 3 DOZEN COOKIES

The dough can be made ahead of time. Simply shape the dough into a rectangular log, wrap the log in plastic wrap, and refrigerate for up to 2 days or freeze for up to 1 month. If frozen, defrost the dough for 20 minutes before slicing.

2	cups all-purpose flour
½	teaspoon baking powder
¼	teaspoon baking soda
¼	teaspoon salt
¼	teaspoon ground nutmeg
1	large egg
2	tablespoons whole milk
8	tablespoons (1 stick) unsalted butter, softened
1	cup packed light brown sugar
1	cup sweetened shredded coconut

1. Whisk together the flour, baking powder, baking soda, salt, and nutmeg in a medium bowl. Whisk together the egg and milk in a small bowl. Place the butter and brown sugar in a large bowl and beat with an electric mixer on medium-high speed until light and fluffy, about 3 minutes. Add the egg mixture and beat on medium-high, scraping down the sides of the bowl and beaters until well combined, about 30 seconds. Add the flour mixture and coconut, and mix on low speed until just incorporated, 15 to 30 seconds.

2. Following the photos, turn the dough out onto a lightly floured surface and, using floured hands, shape the dough into a 15-inch-long log. Flatten the top and sides of the log so that it measures 1 inch high and 3 inches wide. Wrap tightly with plastic wrap and refrigerate until firm, about 45 minutes.

3. Adjust the oven racks to the upper-middle and lower-middle positions and heat the oven to 350 degrees. Line 2 baking sheets with parchment paper. Remove the chilled dough from the refrigerator and unwrap it. Cut the dough into ¼-inch slices and arrange the slices 1 inch apart on the prepared baking sheets. Dip a dinner fork in flour, then make crosswise indentations in the dough slices. Bake until the cookies are toasty brown, 15 to 18 minutes, rotating and switching the baking sheets halfway through baking. Let the cookies cool on the baking sheets for 10 minutes, then transfer to wire racks to cool completely before serving.

Christmas Cookies

The holidays aren't complete without a plate of freshly baked cookies—either for snacking or for gift-giving. Each year readers of *Cook's Country* magazine submit their family favorites to the test kitchen—and we bake our way through hundreds of their recipes. Of the many inspired creations we found, here are our favorites.

CHOCOLATE-TOFFEE BUTTER COOKIES

MAKES ABOUT 5 DOZEN COOKIES

Two kinds of Heath Toffee Bits are sold at the supermarket. Make sure to buy the ones without chocolate.

2⅓	cups all-purpose flour
½	teaspoon baking powder
½	teaspoon salt
16	tablespoons (2 sticks) unsalted butter, softened
1	cup packed light brown sugar
1	large egg
1	teaspoon vanilla extract
1	cup Heath Toffee Bits (without chocolate; see note above)
1½	cups semisweet chocolate chips
1	tablespoon vegetable oil
⅔	cup pecans, toasted and chopped fine

1. Whisk the flour, baking powder, and salt together in a bowl. With an electric mixer, beat the butter and brown sugar together on medium speed until fluffy, about 3 minutes. Add the egg and vanilla and beat until combined, about 30 seconds. Reduce the mixer speed to low, add the flour mixture in two batches, and mix until incorporated. Stir in the toffee bits. Divide the dough in half and roll each piece into a log about 9 inches long and 1½ inches in diameter. Flatten the logs until 2½ inches wide. Wrap in plastic wrap and refrigerate until firm, about 1½ hours.

2. Adjust the oven racks to the upper-middle and lower-middle positions and heat the oven to 350 degrees. Line 2 baking sheets with parchment paper.

3. Using a chef's knife, cut the dough into ¼-inch slices; transfer to the baking sheets, spaced 1 inch apart. Bake until just browned around the edges, 10 to 12 minutes, switching and rotating the baking sheets halfway through baking. Cool the cookies completely on the baking sheets. Repeat with the remaining dough, using cooled, freshly lined baking sheets.

4. Transfer the cooled cookies to a wire rack set on a baking sheet. Melt the chocolate chips and mix with the oil in a bowl until smooth. Dip part of each cookie into the melted chocolate or drizzle the chocolate over the cookies with a spoon. Sprinkle the pecans over the cookies. Don't touch until the chocolate sets, about 1 hour.

MOLASSES-SPICE LEMON SANDWICH COOKIES

MAKES ABOUT 3 DOZEN COOKIES

The bright lemon filling is a terrific match to the warm spices in these cookies.

2	cups all-purpose flour
2	teaspoons baking soda
1	teaspoon ground cinnamon
1	teaspoon ground ginger
	Salt
¼	teaspoon ground cloves
2	cups granulated sugar
¼	cup dark molasses
1	large egg
12	tablespoons (1½ sticks) unsalted butter, melted and cooled, plus 3 tablespoons unsalted butter, softened
3	tablespoons fresh lemon juice
2	cups confectioners' sugar

1. Whisk the flour, baking soda, cinnamon, ginger, ¾ teaspoon salt, and cloves together in a medium bowl. In a separate bowl, stir 1½ cups of the granulated sugar, the molasses, egg, and melted butter together until combined. Add the flour mixture to the butter mixture in three batches, stirring after each addition. Cover the bowl with plastic wrap and refrigerate until the dough is firm, about 1 hour.

2. Adjust the oven racks to the upper-middle and lower-middle positions and heat the oven to 375 degrees. Line 2 baking sheets with parchment paper.

3. Place the remaining ½ cup granulated sugar in a small bowl. Shape the dough into ¾-inch balls. Roll the balls in the granulated sugar, then transfer to the prepared baking sheets, spaced 2 inches apart. Bake until the tops are just beginning to crack, 8 to 10 minutes, switching and rotating the sheets halfway through baking. Let the cookies cool on the baking sheets for 3 minutes, then transfer to a wire rack to cool completely. Repeat with the remaining dough, using cooled, freshly lined baking sheets.

4. Whisk the softened butter, lemon juice, and a pinch of salt together in a medium bowl. Whisk in the confectioners' sugar until smooth. Turn half of the cooled cookies over (bottom side up) and spread each with 1 teaspoon lemon filling. Sandwich with another cookie.

NO-BAKE CRUNCHY SPICED RUM BALLS

MAKES ABOUT 18 COOKIES

The unique flavor of spiced rum is perfect in these cookies, but regular rum will work, too.

½	cup raisins, chopped fine
¼	cup spiced rum (such as Captain Morgan's; see note above)
1	cup confectioners' sugar
2	tablespoons Dutch-processed cocoa powder
1	teaspoon cinnamon
¼	teaspoon nutmeg
¼	teaspoon salt
¼	cup granulated sugar
¾	cup cornflakes
12	vanilla wafers
¾	cup whole almonds, toasted (see page 198)
½	cup sweetened shredded coconut
2	tablespoons light corn syrup

1. Soak the raisins in the rum in a small bowl until plumped, about 10 minutes. Whisk together the confectioners' sugar, cocoa powder, cinnamon, nutmeg, and salt in a large bowl until combined. Place the granulated sugar in a shallow dish.

2. Process the cornflakes, vanilla wafers, almonds, and coconut in a food processor to fine crumbs and add to the confectioners' sugar mixture. Mix in the corn syrup, plumped raisins, and rum until the mixture looks wet. Shape the mixture into 1-inch balls, roll in the granulated sugar, transfer to a large plate, and refrigerate until firm, about 1 hour. (The rum balls can be refrigerated in an airtight container for up to 1 week.)

POOR MAN'S TOFFEE

MAKES ABOUT 15 PIECES

Saltines seem like an unlikely ingredient for toffee, but they work remarkably well.

TOFFEE

24	saltine crackers
1	cup sugar
½	cup light corn syrup
1½	cups salted roasted peanuts
1	tablespoon unsalted butter
1	teaspoon vanilla extract
1	teaspoon baking powder

TOPPING

½	cup semisweet chocolate chips
4	tablespoons unsalted butter
1	tablespoon light corn syrup

1. FOR THE TOFFEE: Adjust an oven rack to the middle position and heat the oven to 250 degrees. Line the bottom of a 13 by 9-inch baking dish with waxed paper and spray the paper with vegetable oil spray. Arrange the crackers in a single layer, salt side down, on the waxed paper.

2. Combine the sugar, corn syrup, and peanuts in a medium microwave-safe bowl. Microwave on high power until the sugar melts, about 2 minutes. Stir and microwave until the mixture begins to boil, about 2 more minutes. Stir in the butter and vanilla until the butter melts. Microwave until the liquid begins to brown, about 2 minutes. Stir in the baking powder.

3. Working quickly, pour the sugar mixture over the saltines and spread evenly (if the mixture hardens too quickly to spread, place the baking dish in the oven for 5 minutes). Refrigerate until firm, about 1 hour. Invert the brittle onto a cutting board, peel away the waxed paper, and, using your hands, break into large pieces. Return the pieces, toffee side up, to the baking dish.

4. FOR THE TOPPING: Melt the chocolate chips and butter in a saucepan over low heat until smooth, about 5 minutes. Stir in the corn syrup and, using a spoon, drizzle the mixture over the brittle. Let harden for 1 hour. (The brittle can be stored in an airtight container at room temperature for up to 4 days.)

COCONUT SNOWDROPS

MAKES ABOUT 4 DOZEN COOKIES

These buttery cookies will spread and fall during baking if the dough gets too warm. For the best texture, chill the dough well before forming the cookies and roll only half the dough at a time, keeping the other half in the refrigerator.

COOKIES

16	tablespoons (2 sticks) unsalted butter, softened
1	cup granulated sugar
¼	cup packed light brown sugar
1	large egg plus 1 large egg yolk
1	teaspoon vanilla extract
1	teaspoon coconut extract
2	cups all-purpose flour
2	cups sweetened shredded coconut
½	cup finely chopped blanched almonds

FILLING

½	cup semisweet chocolate chips
2	tablespoons unsalted butter

1. FOR THE COOKIES: In a large bowl, beat the butter and sugars with an electric mixer on medium-high speed until fluffy, about 2 minutes. Beat in the egg, egg yolk, and extracts until incorporated, about 1 minute. Reduce the speed to low and add the flour, coconut, and almonds. Mix until a dough forms, about 1 minute. Cover the bowl with plastic

wrap and refrigerate until the dough is firm, at least 1 hour or up to 3 days.

2. Adjust the oven racks to the upper-middle and lower-middle positions and heat the oven to 350 degrees. Line 2 baking sheets with parchment paper. Roll the dough into ¾-inch balls and place 1 inch apart on the prepared baking sheets. Bake until the edges are just golden, 12 to 14 minutes, switching and rotating the sheets halfway through baking. Let the cookies cool on the baking sheets for 10 minutes, then transfer to a wire rack to cool completely. Repeat with the remaining dough, using cooled, freshly lined baking sheets.

3. FOR THE FILLING: Melt the chocolate chips and butter in a saucepan over low heat until smooth, about 5 minutes. Spread some of the chocolate mixture on the bottom of 1 cookie, then press the bottom of a second cookie onto the chocolate to form a sandwich. Repeat with the remaining cookies and chocolate mixture.

Lunchbox Brownies

Here in the test kitchen, we're pretty serious about brownies and usually stick with tradition—we'd thought nuts were as much adornment as brownies need. But we began to reconsider our thinking as perhaps too stick-in-the-mud. And once we started tossing around ideas about how to make brownies more fun, we knew we were on to something.

To make things simple, we decided to use the same basic brownie as the base for all of our recipes. We knew we needed fairly sturdy brownies (you can't frost crumbly brownies), but they had to taste great on their own for those of us who prefer brownies in their most pure state. The test kitchen had already developed one such brownie, so it was time to let loose with brownie add-ons.

A few test cooks suggested frosted brownies and no one argued. First, we focused on developing a thick, creamy chocolate frosting. We figured this variation would be easy to develop. Unfortunately, melted chocolate alone wouldn't set up correctly. After experimenting with various additions (including cream and butter), we found that a little vegetable oil helped to create a shiny glaze that firmed up quickly.

We assumed that a white chocolate frosting could be made the same way as regular chocolate frosting, but time after time the white chocolate frosting cracked as it cooled. White chocolate is pretty fickle. Some brands contain cocoa butter, but others do not. We thought that white chocolate chips, which are made with emulsifiers and other stabilizers, might work better. Sure enough, these chips melted perfectly on their own, without any other ingredients. A dusting of crushed peppermint candies gave these brownies a festive appearance—perfect for the holidays.

Cream cheese brownies are a favorite and tasters clamored for that variation next. We found that plain sweetened cream cheese was too stiff to swirl into the brownie batter, but after a few tests, we found that one egg yolk lightened the cheese just enough to easily swirl into the batter. The yolk also contributed rich flavor to the cheese filling, and vanilla extract further improved matters.

We next focused on the favorite flavor combination of chocolate and peanut butter. Would we have to add other ingredients (butter, cream cheese, or sugar) to the peanut butter, or could we just dollop some over the brownie batter and then swirl it in? As long as we used a sweetened peanut butter (rather than an old-fashioned variety with oil on top), the peanut butter was fine on its own.

German chocolate cake was the inspiration for brownies topped with melted butterscotch chips and toasted sweetened coconut. This variation couldn't have been easier.

At this point we thought we were done having fun. But then we spied some mini-marshmallows in the pantry, and our thoughts turned to campfire meals and s'mores. Could we use brownies in place of the chocolate bar? We baked a simple graham cracker crust and then poured the brownie batter on top. Once the brownies were done, we arranged mini-marshmallows in the pan and set the oven to broil. Tasters lined up once the brownies had cooled—and after one bite our normally adult colleagues were transformed into ravenous kids fighting for seconds.

LUNCHBOX BROWNIES

MAKES 16 BROWNIES

This is a classic brownie no one can resist. Be sure to use unsweetened chocolate; do not substitute semisweet or bittersweet chocolate.

8	tablespoons (1 stick) unsalted butter
3	ounces unsweetened chocolate, chopped coarse (see note above)
⅔	cup all-purpose flour
½	teaspoon baking powder
¼	teaspoon salt
1	cup sugar
2	large eggs
1	teaspoon vanilla extract
½	cup pecans or walnuts, toasted (see page 198) and chopped (optional)

KNOWING WHEN BROWNIES ARE DONE

A toothpick placed in the center of a perfectly baked batch of brownies should have a few moist crumbs clinging to it. If it comes away clean, the brownies are overbaked.

1. Adjust an oven rack to the middle position and heat the oven to 350 degrees. Line an 8-inch square baking pan with an aluminum foil sling and grease the foil. Microwave the butter and chocolate together, stirring often, until melted, 1 to 3 minutes. Let the mixture cool slightly.

2. In a medium bowl, whisk together the flour, baking powder, and salt. In a large bowl, whisk together the sugar, eggs, and vanilla. Whisk in the melted chocolate mixture until combined. Stir in the flour mixture until just incorporated.

3. Scrape the batter into the prepared pan, smooth the top, and sprinkle with the toasted nuts (if using). Bake the brownies until a toothpick inserted into the center comes out with just a few moist crumbs attached, 22 to 27 minutes, rotating the pan halfway through baking.

4. Let the brownies cool completely in the pan, set on a wire rack, about 2 hours. Remove the brownies from the pan using the foil, cut into 16 squares, and serve.

Variations
CHOCOLATE FROSTED BROWNIES

After the brownies have cooled for 1 hour, melt ⅔ cup semisweet chocolate chips and 1 tablespoon vegetable oil together in the microwave, stirring often, 1 to 3 minutes. Cool the mixture until barely warm, about 5 minutes, then spread evenly over the brownies with a spatula. Continue to let the brownies cool until the topping sets, 1 to 2 hours.

WHITE CHOCOLATE AND PEPPERMINT FROSTED BROWNIES

Pulse ⅓ cup peppermint candies in a food processor until finely chopped. When the brownies come out of the oven, sprinkle 1 cup white chocolate chips evenly over the brownies and let sit until the chips are softened but not melted, about 5 minutes. Smooth the softened chips into an even layer, then sprinkle with the peppermint candies. Continue to let the brownies cool until the topping sets, 1 to 2 hours.

CREAM CHEESE SWIRL BROWNIES

Whisk 8 ounces softened cream cheese, ¼ cup sugar, 1 egg yolk, and ½ teaspoon vanilla extract together until combined. Drop small dollops of the cream cheese mixture over the brownie batter in the baking pan, then run a butter knife through the batter to create swirls. Bake as directed.

PEANUT BUTTER SWIRL BROWNIES

You can use either crunchy or smooth peanut butter here; note that room-temperature peanut butter is much easier to work with and regular peanut butter will taste better than natural peanut butter, which is less sweet.

Drop ⅓ cup peanut butter in small dollops over the brownie batter in the baking pan, then run a

---

MAKING A FOIL SLING

1. Lay two large sheets of foil in the pan, perpendicular to each other, leaving the extra foil hanging over the edges of the pan. Push the foil into the corners and up the sides of the pan. Grease the foil, if directed in the recipe.

2. After the brownies (or other baked goods) have baked and cooled, use the foil sling to transfer them to a cutting board before cutting or slicing. The foil should easily peel away.

butter knife through the batter to create swirls. Bake as directed.

GERMAN CHOCOLATE BROWNIES

When the brownies come out of the oven, sprinkle 1 cup butterscotch chips evenly over the brownies and let sit until the chips are softened but not melted, about 5 minutes. Smooth the softened chips into an even layer, then sprinkle with ½ cup toasted sweetened shredded coconut (see page 461). Continue to let the brownies cool until the topping sets, 1 to 2 hours.

S'MORES BROWNIES

You will need 6 whole graham crackers to yield ¾ cup crumbs when finely ground in a food processor. Prepare the brownie batter while the crust bakes. This recipe will not work in an oven with a separate broiler compartment.

1. Preheat the oven and prepare the pan according to step 1. With your fingers, combine ¾ cup graham cracker crumbs, 1 tablespoon sugar, and 4 tablespoons melted butter in a bowl until evenly moistened. Firmly pat the crumbs into the prepared pan and bake until firm and lightly browned, 8 to 10 minutes. Scrape the brownie batter over the crust and gently push the batter into the corners to cover the crust. Bake as directed. Remove the pan from the oven and turn the oven to broil.

2. Sprinkle the brownies evenly with 2 cups mini-marshmallows. Return the pan with the brownies to the oven and broil until the marshmallows are lightly browned, 1 to 3 minutes. (Watch the oven constantly. The marshmallows will melt slightly but should hold their shape.) Immediately remove the pan from the oven. Cool the brownies to room temperature, about 2 hours. When cutting the brownies, coat the knife with vegetable oil spray to prevent the marshmallows from sticking to the knife.

Mississippi Mud Brownies

Mississippi mud might not sound like something you'd like to eat, but Mississippi mud brownies definitely are. These moist, fudgy brownies are related to Mississippi mud pie and Mississippi mud cake—desserts that can be defined in countless ways but share one trait: dense gooeyness that approximates the texture of the silt that settles in the Mississippi River delta. The brownie variation is topped with mini-marshmallows when the base is set but still quite moist, briefly returned to the oven, and then covered with chocolate frosting when the confection has cooled.

We prepared brownies using several existing recipes, but they were more like candy than brownies—and their chocolate flavor was lost under the marshmallows and cloying frosting (which is generally spread much too thick). All these great ingredients were not living up to their potential.

We started with the most promising brownie recipe from our initial testing, which had a decent fudgy texture, thanks to plenty of butter and sugar, but little chocolate flavor. Most mud brownie recipes call for unsweetened chocolate, and adding more helped, but the flavor was still a little flat. We tried introducing chocolate in a couple of other forms: syrup and cocoa powder. The chocolate syrup did add flavor, but it made the brownies too sticky and messy. Cocoa powder lent deeper chocolate flavor and had no adverse effect on the brownies' texture. Rather than using mini-marshmallows, we found that a thin layer of marshmallow creme evenly coated the brownies and kept the sugar quotient in check. Tasters agreed.

Tasters thought the thick blanket of chocolate frosting was overkill. A colleague suggested that since the brownie layer was so chocolaty, the frosting could now be minimized to just a melted drizzle.

MAKING MISSISSIPPI MUD BROWNIES

1. Use a spatula to spread the marshmallow creme evenly over the hot brownies.

2. Drizzle the melted chocolate from a spoon to create a decorative pattern.

We melted a few chocolate chips and added a little oil to keep the chocolate flowing from the spoon we waved back and forth over the brownies. With just a small quantity of chocolate, we were able to create a polished finish to these brownies, which were now decadent but not over the top.

MISSISSIPPI MUD BROWNIES

MAKES 24 BROWNIES

Be careful not to overbake these brownies; they should be moist and fudgy.

BROWNIES

6	ounces unsweetened chocolate, chopped
16	tablespoons (2 sticks) unsalted butter
1½	cups all-purpose flour
⅓	cup Dutch-processed cocoa powder
½	teaspoon salt
3	cups sugar
5	large eggs
¾	cup chopped pecans

TOPPING

¾	cup marshmallow creme
¼	cup semisweet chocolate chips
2	teaspoons vegetable oil

1. FOR THE BROWNIES: Adjust an oven rack to the middle position and heat the oven to 325 degrees. Line a 13 by 9-inch baking pan with an aluminum foil sling and grease the foil (see page 458).

2. Melt the chocolate and butter in a large heatproof bowl set over a medium saucepan filled with ½ inch of barely simmering water (don't let the bowl touch the water), stirring occasionally, until smooth, 5 to 7 minutes; cool slightly. Combine the flour, cocoa, and salt in another bowl. Whisk the sugar and eggs together in a third bowl, then whisk in the melted chocolate mixture. Stir the flour mixture into the chocolate mixture until no streaks of flour remain. Fold in the pecans and scrape the batter evenly into the prepared pan. Bake until a toothpick inserted into the center comes out with a few wet crumbs attached, about 35 minutes. Transfer the pan to a wire rack.

3. FOR THE TOPPING: Spoon the marshmallow creme over the hot brownies and let sit until softened, about 1 minute. Meanwhile, microwave the chocolate chips and oil in a small bowl until smooth, 30 to 60 seconds. Spread the marshmallow creme evenly over the brownies and then drizzle with the melted chocolate. Let the brownies cool completely in the pan, about 2 hours. Remove the brownies from the pan using the foil (see page 458), cut into 24 squares, and serve.

Seven-Layer Bars

With layers of chocolate chips, coconut, and nuts piled high over a buttery graham cracker crust, seven-layer bars sound appealing. There's no batter or dough to make—just layer pantry staples into a baking dish and wait for the oven to transform a jumble of ingredients into a chewy, crispy, sweet bar cookie. But after testing the original recipe (first published on a can of Eagle brand sweetened condensed milk), we weren't very impressed. Yes, the recipe was easy, but the crust was bland and soggy, the coconut and nuts tasted raw, and the bars were dry. We decided to give this 1950s classic a makeover.

We started with the crust. Prebaking produced the crisp texture we were looking for. We experimented with ingredients to boost flavor in the crust and finally hit upon the solution: toffee bits. Their buttery, salty flavor gave the crust real personality.

To improve their flavor and texture, we pretoasted the coconut and nuts. Rice Krispies (not part of the original recipe) lent welcome crunch and lightness. To emphasize the chocolate flavor, we added a layer of milk chocolate, melted right over the hot crust, in addition to the usual chocolate chips.

For us in the test kitchen, the best part of this recipe is the rich butterscotch flavor and chewy texture added by the sweetened condensed milk. To remedy the sandy, dry texture of the original recipe, why not use more than one can? We found that two full cans created a rich, moist, candy-like bar cookie with plenty of chew and great caramel flavor.

SEVEN-LAYER BARS

MAKES 24 BARS

There are two kinds of Heath Toffee Bits sold at the supermarket; be sure to buy the ones with chocolate. Don't substitute store-bought graham cracker crumbs here because they will taste too sandy in the bars.

- 1 **cup chocolate-covered Heath Toffee Bits (see note above)**
- 12 **whole graham crackers, broken into 1-inch pieces (see note above)**
- 8 **tablespoons (1 stick) unsalted butter, melted and cooled**
- 8 **ounces milk chocolate, chopped fine**
- 1 **cup Rice Krispies cereal**
- 1 **cup pecans, toasted (see page 198) and chopped coarse**
- 1 **cup semisweet chocolate chips**
- 1 **cup sweetened shredded coconut, toasted**
- 2 **(14-ounce) cans sweetened condensed milk**
- 1 **tablespoon vanilla extract**

1. Adjust an oven rack to the middle position and heat the oven to 350 degrees. Line a 13 by 9-inch baking pan with an aluminum foil sling and grease the foil (see page 458).

2. Process the toffee bits to a fine powder in a food processor, about 10 seconds. Add the graham

TOASTING COCONUT

The best way to toast coconut is to spread it on a rimmed baking sheet and toast it in a 350-degree oven, stirring often, until lightly golden, 7 to 10 minutes. As the toasted coconut cools, it will turn crisp.

MAKING AN EVEN CRUST

Sprinkle the crumb mixture over the pan bottom and press down firmly, using the flat bottom of a measuring cup to form an even layer.

cracker pieces and continue to process the mixture to fine crumbs, about 30 seconds. Drizzle the melted butter over the crumbs and pulse to incorporate. Sprinkle the crumbs into the prepared pan and press into an even layer with the bottom of a measuring cup. Bake the crust until fragrant and beginning to brown, about 10 minutes.

3. Remove the crust from the oven, sprinkle with the milk chocolate, and let sit until the chocolate is softened but not melted, about 5 minutes. Smooth the softened chocolate into an even layer.

4. Layer the Rice Krispies, pecans, chocolate chips, then coconut into the pan, in that order, pressing on each layer to adhere. Whisk the condensed milk and vanilla together and pour the mixture evenly over the top. Bake the bars until golden brown, 25 to 30 minutes, rotating the pan halfway through baking.

5. Let the bars cool completely in the pan, set on a wire rack, about 2 hours. Remove the bars from the pan using the foil (see page 458), cut into 24 squares, and serve.

Oatmeal Butterscotch Bars

"Oatmeal scotchies," sweet oat bars studded with sweet, orange-hued butterscotch chips, are a fond childhood favorite for many of us in the test kitchen. The simplest recipes consist of oatmeal cookie dough with a bag of butterscotch morsels stirred in. But when we tasted bars made from a recipe on a bag of Toll House butterscotch chips—the recipe most of our mothers probably used—we found they were awfully sweet, and all the tasters felt that the chips gave the bars an "unnatural taste." Instead of melting into the dough like chocolate chips, these chips turned hard and waxy. The "cakey and crumbly" texture of the bars was okay, but we wanted a chewier, moister version.

We hit the grocery store in search of better-tasting butterscotch products. We tried jarred butterscotch sauce, but it was too mild and the bars turned tough and taffy-like. Crushed butterscotch candies were even more artificial-tasting than the chips. Having nowhere else to turn, we grudgingly reconsidered the butterscotch chips.

Reducing the amount of sugar solved the sweetness issue, and melting the chips eliminated their textural shortcoming. We found that melting the butter rather than creaming it gave the bars the chewy texture we wanted. Only one problem remained: several tasters still complained about the "artificial" flavor of the chips.

Toasting the oatmeal didn't make much of a difference, but browning the butter (rather than just melting it) improved the bars tremendously, deepening their flavor and masking the unnatural taste of the chips. Substituting assertive dark brown sugar for light brown sugar created even more depth of flavor—and "scotchies" far better than the recipe on the bag.

OATMEAL BUTTERSCOTCH BARS

MAKES 24 BARS

For chewier bars, substitute old-fashioned rolled oats.

BARS

1¼	cups all-purpose flour
2	cups quick-cooking oats (see note above)
½	teaspoon baking soda
½	teaspoon salt
¾	cup butterscotch chips
16	tablespoons (2 sticks) unsalted butter
1	cup packed dark brown sugar
1	large egg
2	teaspoons vanilla extract

GLAZE

¼	cup butterscotch chips
2	tablespoons dark brown sugar
1	tablespoon water
⅛	teaspoon salt

1. FOR THE BARS: Adjust an oven rack to the lower-middle position and heat the oven to 350 degrees. Line a 13 by 9-inch baking pan with an aluminum foil sling and grease the foil (see page 458). Whisk the flour, oats, baking soda, and salt together in a medium bowl.

2. Place the butterscotch chips in a large bowl. Melt the butter in a small saucepan over medium-low heat and continue to cook until golden brown in color, about 12 minutes. Pour the hot butter over the butterscotch chips and whisk until melted and smooth. Whisk in the brown sugar until dissolved. Whisk in the egg and vanilla until combined. Stir in the flour mixture, in two additions, until just incorporated.

3. Scrape the batter into the prepared pan and smooth the top. Bake the bars until a toothpick inserted into the center comes out with just a few moist crumbs attached, 16 to 20 minutes, rotating the pan halfway through baking.

4. FOR THE GLAZE: While the bars bake, place the butterscotch chips in a medium bowl. Bring the brown sugar, water, and salt to a simmer in a small saucepan over medium-high heat. Pour the hot sugar mixture over the butterscotch chips and whisk until melted and smooth.

5. Drizzle the glaze over the warm bars. Let the bars cool completely in the pan, set on a wire rack, about 2 hours. Remove the bars from the pan using the foil (see page 458), cut into 24 squares, and serve.

Lemon Squares

With their thin smear of timidly flavored filling, most lemon squares seem designed to please people who like the shortbread crust more than the lemon filling. But we like our lemon squares to have a thick, creamy topping with a bold—though not mouth-puckering—lemon flavor.

Most recipes instruct you to mix lemon juice, sugar, and eggs, pour this mixture over a prebaked crust, and then continue baking until the filling has set. Unfortunately, we found that these easy recipes produce a lemon layer that's thin and rubbery. A better option is to cook the filling ingredients into a thick curd. Once poured onto the crust and popped into the oven, the curd bakes up creamy and rich.

A combination of yolks and whole eggs is necessary to give the curd its structure and creaminess, whole eggs providing the former and yolks the latter. For a curd that was solid enough to hold its shape but was plenty creamy as well, the winning

MAKING LEMON SQUARES

1. The lemon curd is done when dragging a finger through the curd on the back of a spoon leaves an empty trail behind.

2. Press the curd through a fine-mesh strainer to remove the lemon zest.

combination was two whole eggs and seven egg yolks. For even more creaminess, we finished the curd with 4 tablespoons of butter and 3 tablespoons of heavy cream.

For serious lemon flavor, we learned that it's essential to use both juice and zest. Many recipes rely on juice alone, but its flavor fades in the oven. The zest has the stronger, brighter lemon flavor. Tasters weren't wild about the stringy bits of zest in their lemon squares, though, and we easily eliminated them by straining the cooked curd.

The shortbread crust is nothing more than flour, confectioners' sugar, and butter. To support a thick layer of lemon curd, the crust has to be sturdier than most. A few extra tablespoons of butter ensured a firm crust that didn't crumble under the thick lemon topping. Our lemon squares are not the lightest you'll ever find, but each creamy bite is packed with bright, bold lemon flavor.

LEMON SQUARES

MAKES 16 SQUARES

It is important that both the filling and the crust be warm when assembling the bars in step 4; this ensures that the lemon curd filling will cook through evenly. Be sure to zest the lemons before juicing them.

CRUST

1¼	cups all-purpose flour
½	cup confectioners' sugar
½	teaspoon salt
8	tablespoons (1 stick) unsalted butter, cut into 8 pieces and softened

FILLING

2	large eggs plus 7 large egg yolks
1	cup plus 2 tablespoons granulated sugar
¼	cup grated fresh lemon zest (4 lemons)
⅔	cup fresh lemon juice (4 lemons)
	Pinch salt
4	tablespoons unsalted butter, cut into 4 pieces
3	tablespoons heavy cream
	Confectioners' sugar for dusting

1. Adjust an oven rack to the middle position and heat the oven to 350 degrees. Line an 8-inch square baking pan with an aluminum foil sling and grease the foil (see page 458).

2. FOR THE CRUST: Process the flour, confectioners' sugar, and salt together in a food processor to combine, about 3 pulses. Sprinkle the butter over the top and pulse until the mixture is pale yellow and has the texture of coarse sand, about 8 pulses. (If you don't have a food processor, grate the cold butter on the large holes of a box grater and toss into the flour, sugar, and salt mixture. Using a fork, press the butter into the mixture until it is the texture of coarse meal.) Sprinkle the mixture into the prepared pan and press into an even layer with the bottom of a measuring cup (see page 462). Bake the crust until fragrant and beginning to brown, about 20 minutes.

3. FOR THE FILLING: While the crust bakes, whisk the eggs and egg yolks together in a medium saucepan. Whisk in the granulated sugar until combined, then whisk in the lemon zest, lemon juice, and salt. Add the butter and cook over medium heat, stirring constantly, until the mixture thickens slightly and registers 170 degrees on an instant-read thermometer, about 5 minutes. Strain the mixture immediately into a bowl and stir in the cream.

4. Pour the filling over the warm crust. Bake the squares until the filling is shiny and opaque and the center jiggles slightly when shaken, 10 to 15 minutes, rotating the pan halfway through baking.

5. Let the bars cool completely in the pan, set on a wire rack, about 2 hours. Remove the bars from the pan using the foil (see page 458), cut into 16 squares, and dust with confectioners' sugar before serving.

Peach Squares

A peach square should be packed with peach flavor and be sturdy enough that it can be eaten out of hand—just like the perfect summer peach. But judging from the half-dozen recipes we made at the outset of our research, both of those qualities are pretty rare in most peach squares. Some squares collapsed in our hands as we took a bite, and others were devoid of peach flavor. We had our work cut out for us.

The biggest discovery we made in our testing was frozen peaches. Not only were they more convenient than fresh (no peeling, pitting, and chopping), but their quality was more consistent. Chopping

the peaches in the food processor before cooking them down in a skillet with peach jam gave us a rich, deeply flavored filling, and because excess liquid evaporated during cooking, the filling also had just the right texture: not wet but jammy, with bits of peach to bite into. We found that both lemon zest and lemon juice brightened the filling's fruit flavor.

With our filling down, we turned to the crust. Almonds are a natural flavor pairing with peaches, so we developed a simple almond streusel to work as both crust and topping. Tasters found a crust made with brown sugar to be richer-flavored than one made with granulated sugar and a better match to our peach filling. We incorporated some almonds into the crust and reserved some for sprinkling over the top of the bars. Once the bars were cooled, we cut into them, and tasters gave a thumbs up to these summery bars that, with the help of frozen peaches, we could enjoy year-round.

ALL-SEASON PEACH SQUARES
MAKES 24 SQUARES
Lay the thawed peaches on a kitchen towel to rid them of excess moisture before using.

CRUST
- 1½ cups all-purpose flour
- 1¾ cups sliced almonds
- ⅓ cup granulated sugar
- ⅓ cup plus 1 tablespoon packed light brown sugar
- Salt
- 12 tablespoons (1½ sticks) unsalted butter, cut into 12 pieces and softened

FILLING
- 1½ pounds (6 cups) frozen peaches, thawed and drained (see note above)
- ½ cup peach jam
- ½ teaspoon grated fresh lemon zest
- 1 teaspoon fresh lemon juice

1. Adjust an oven rack to the middle position and heat the oven to 375 degrees. Line a 13 by 9-inch baking pan with an aluminum foil sling and grease the foil (see page 458).

2. FOR THE CRUST: Process the flour, 1¼ cups of the almonds, the granulated sugar, ⅓ cup of the brown sugar, and ½ teaspoon salt together in a food processor until combined, about 5 seconds. Add the butter and pulse the mixture until it resembles coarse meal with a few pea-sized pieces of butter, about 20 pulses.

3. Reserve ½ cup of the flour mixture for the topping. Sprinkle the remaining flour mixture into the prepared pan and press into an even layer with the bottom of a measuring cup (see page 462). Bake the crust until fragrant and golden brown, about 15 minutes.

4. While the crust bakes, mix the remaining 1 tablespoon brown sugar and the reserved flour mixture together in a small bowl and pinch the mixture between your fingers into hazelnut-sized clumps of streusel.

5. FOR THE FILLING: Pulse the peaches and jam together in a food processor until the peaches are roughly ¼-inch chunks, 5 to 7 pulses. Cook the peach mixture in a large nonstick skillet over high heat until it is thickened and jam-like, about 10 minutes. Off the heat, stir in the lemon zest, lemon juice, and a pinch of salt.

6. Spread the cooked peach mixture evenly over the hot crust, then sprinkle with the streusel topping and remaining ½ cup almonds. Bake until the almonds are golden brown, about 20 minutes, rotating the pan halfway through baking.

7. Let the bars cool completely in the pan, set on a wire rack, about 2 hours. Remove the bars from the pan using the foil (see page 458), cut into 24 squares, and serve.

Variations
ALL-SEASON APRICOT SQUARES
Substitute 1 pound dried apricots for the frozen peaches and apricot jam for the peach jam. Add 1 cup water to the food processor with the apricots in step 5.

ALL-SEASON CHERRY SQUARES
Substitute frozen pitted cherries for the frozen peaches and cherry jam for the peach jam. Omit the lemon zest, reduce the lemon juice to ½ teaspoon, and add ¼ teaspoon vanilla extract in step 5.

Key Lime Bars

Key lime pie is a brilliant pairing of rich and refreshing, sweet and tart, all in a buttery, crisp crumb crust. But what this classic dessert offers in elegance and simplicity it lacks in portability. We wanted a Key lime bar—all the appealing qualities of Key lime pie but without the need for a fork. Turning a round pie into square bar cookies shouldn't be too hard, right?

To get our footing, we started out with two recipes: one for Key lime bars made with cream cheese (typical of many recipes), the other for Key lime pie. The bars with cream cheese were heavy and dense, like lime cheesecake—not quite what we had in mind. As for the pie, we transformed it into bars by baking it in a square baking dish. Naturally, the pie version set the flavor standard, but for a bar cookie, the filling was too soft and supple, the crust too thick, dry, and crumbly. Clearly, some fine-tuning would be required to get this transformation to come out right.

First things first: the crust. A graham cracker crust is traditional for a Key lime pie, so it was the obvious choice. But we were not enamored of the graham cracker crust. Its flavor was too assertive (especially given the amount we needed to make a bar we could hold in our hands), and it didn't really complement the filling. We swapped in animal cracker crumbs, the test kitchen's crust of choice for coconut cream pie. Their more neutral flavor placed the lime flavor squarely in the limelight. Whereas a pie crust can be tender and delicate, the crust for the bars needed sturdiness; this meant increasing the amount of butter, but not so much that the crust would become greasy. Brown sugar outdid granulated because it gave the crust a slightly richer, rounder flavor.

With the crust firmly in place, we focused on the filling. Key lime pie filling is an easy mixture of sweetened condensed milk, lime juice, lime zest, and, more often than not, eggs. We already knew that the test kitchen's Key lime pie filling didn't have a texture firm enough for bar cookies, but we were determined to make it work with some minor retooling. Leaving the condensed milk and lime juice in place, we tried everything that we thought might set the texture. Nothing worked. Then we recalled the cheesecake lime bars that we'd made at the outset. After incorporating various amounts of cream cheese into the filling, we found that only 2 ounces made a just firm enough, sliceable bar.

Last, we addressed the issue of a topping for our bars. Some bar recipes include some sort of streusel or crunchy topping. A streusel didn't make sense, but we took a cue from the tropics and experimented with a toasted-coconut topping, which added a subtle textural contrast and more depth of flavor. The test kitchen was split over whether this topping was an improvement, so we left it optional. Finally, we had distilled the essence of a billowy slice of Key lime pie into a tidy, portable bar.

KEY LIME BARS

MAKES 16 BARS

You can use either Key limes or regular limes here; Key limes have a delicate flavor whereas regular limes have a stronger, more tart flavor. In order to yield ½ cup of juice, you'll need about 20 Key limes or 4 regular limes; do not substitute bottled lime juice. Be sure to zest the limes before juicing them.

CRUST

5	ounces (2½ cups) animal crackers
3	tablespoons light brown sugar
	Pinch salt
4	tablespoons unsalted butter, melted and cooled

FILLING

2	ounces cream cheese, softened
1	tablespoon grated fresh lime zest
	Pinch salt
1	(14-ounce) can sweetened condensed milk
1	large egg yolk
½	cup fresh lime juice (see note above)
¾	cup sweetened shredded coconut, toasted (see page 461; optional)

1. Adjust an oven rack to the middle position and heat the oven to 325 degrees. Line an 8-inch square baking pan with an aluminum foil sling and grease the foil (see page 458).

2. FOR THE CRUST: Process the animal crackers, sugar, and salt together in a food processor to fine crumbs, about 15 seconds. Drizzle the melted butter over the crumbs and pulse to incorporate, about 10 pulses. Sprinkle the mixture into the prepared pan and press into an even layer with the bottom of a measuring cup (see page 462). Bake the crust until fragrant and deep golden brown, 18 to 20 minutes.

3. FOR THE FILLING: Stir the cream cheese, lime zest, and salt together in a medium bowl until combined. Whisk in the sweetened condensed milk until smooth. Whisk in the egg yolk and lime juice until combined.

4. Pour the filling evenly over the crust. Bake the bars until set and the edges begin to pull away slightly from the sides of the pan, 15 to 20 minutes, rotating the pan halfway through baking.

5. Let the bars cool completely in the pan, set on a wire rack, about 2 hours, then cover with aluminum foil and refrigerate until thoroughly chilled, at least 2 hours. Remove the bars from the pan using the foil (see page 458), cut into 16 squares, sprinkle with the toasted coconut (if using), and serve.

Variation
TRIPLE-CITRUS BARS
Be sure to zest all of the citrus before juicing.

Reduce the amount of lime zest to 1½ teaspoons and combine with 1½ teaspoons each grated fresh lemon zest and grated fresh orange zest. Reduce the amount of lime juice to 6 tablespoons and combine with 1 tablespoon fresh lemon juice and 1 tablespoon fresh orange juice.

SHOPPING WITH THE TEST KITCHEN

Baking Pans: The 13 x 9-inch Pyrex (tempered glass) baking dish does a great job of turning out casseroles, stratas, and lasagnas. But Pyrex baking dishes are slightly curved, with somewhat rounded edges. The shape of the edges isn't an issue for these dishes, but for cakes, brownies, and bars, where we want clean, neat edges, we prefer pans with straight edges—and those pans are metal. We tested a variety of metal pans by baking up batch after batch of blondies and found that blondies baked in pans with darker-colored surfaces browned very well. When we baked the same recipe in a light-colored metal pan, the browning was spotty. Baker's Secret 13 x 9-inch Nonstick Cake Pan finished ahead of all the metal pans tested. It browned evenly and cleaned up easily—and at just $3.99 it's a great bargain, too.

CHAPTER FIFTEEN

Blue Ribbon Cakes

BLUE RIBBON CAKES

Wacky Cake

During the First World War, butter, sugar, milk, and eggs were often in short supply, leading American women to devise a variety of "make-do" cakes. During World War II, American women revived and improved upon the make-do cake recipes their mothers had used a generation earlier. Several sources suggested that wacky cake was invented during the 1940s, but we couldn't understand how it earned its name until we read a recipe in *The Time Reader's Book of Recipes*, a collection of reader recipes compiled by the editors of *Time* magazine in 1949.

Mrs. Donald Adam of Detroit, Michigan, submitted this strange recipe, which called for mixing the dry ingredients—flour, cocoa powder, sugar, salt, and baking soda—right in the baking pan. If that wasn't strange enough, three holes—two small and one large—were made in the dry mix. Into the large hole went melted vegetable shortening, and vanilla and vinegar were placed in the smaller holes. Cold water was poured over everything, then the whole mess was stirred and popped into the oven.

Back in the test kitchen, we followed the instructions, and right before our eyes the batter began to bubble and rise—even before it hit the oven. It was the easiest cake we'd ever made. And it was surprisingly good.

How does this strange recipe work? Without eggs, this cake depends on the last-minute reaction of vinegar and baking soda to lift the thick batter. The three holes ensure that the dry ingredients remain dry until the last possible second. Mixing in the pan might seem like a gimmick, but when we combined the ingredients in a bowl and scraped the batter into a pan, the cake did not rise as well. The lift provided by the baking soda and vinegar reaction is fleeting, and the recipe's odd mixing method ensures that the batter gets into the oven quickly.

The 1949 recipe we had found needed little improvement. To simplify things, we replaced the melted shortening with vegetable oil, and to boost the chocolate flavor we added another tablespoon of cocoa. The cake was a bit sweet, so we trimmed a little sugar, and because several tasters complained about a slight "soapy" flavor, we decreased the amount of baking soda.

On a whim, we decided to try this cake with more "modern" ingredients. We replaced the oil with melted butter and used milk instead of water. This cake was less chocolaty and more crumbly; we honestly felt that the original was better. Hard times gave rise to a not-so-wacky recipe that still deserves a place in the American kitchen.

WACKY CAKE

SERVES 6 TO 8

This easy chocolate cake can be served as is or with a dollop of whipped cream.

1½	cups all-purpose flour
¾	cup granulated sugar
¼	cup natural cocoa powder
¾	teaspoon baking soda
½	teaspoon salt
5	tablespoons vegetable oil
1	tablespoon white vinegar
1	teaspoon vanilla extract
1	cup water
	Confectioners' sugar for dusting

1. Adjust an oven rack to the middle position and heat the oven to 350 degrees. Grease an 8-inch square baking pan.

2. Whisk together the flour, granulated sugar, cocoa powder, baking soda, and salt in the prepared pan. Make one large and two small craters in the dry ingredients. Add the oil to the large crater and the vinegar and vanilla separately to the small craters. Pour the water into the pan and mix until just a few streaks of flour remain. Immediately put the pan in the oven.

1. Make one large and two small craters in the dry mix. Pour the oil into the large crater, and the vinegar and vanilla into the smaller craters. Pour the water over everything.

2. Using a wooden spoon or spatula, mix the batter, taking care not to over-mix; the batter should still contain a few streaks of flour.

3. Bake until a toothpick inserted in the center of the cake comes out with a few moist crumbs attached, about 30 minutes, rotating the pan halfway through baking. Cool in the pan, set on a wire rack, then dust with confectioners' sugar before serving.

SHOPPING WITH THE TEST KITCHEN

Milk Chocolate: Milk chocolate must contain at least 10 percent chocolate liquor (a mix of chocolate solids and cocoa butter) and 12 percent milk solids, with sweeteners and flavorings making up the balance. The result is a mellow, smooth, milky flavor. Yet because of its relatively weak chocolate flavor (milk chocolate is usually more than 50 percent sugar), we don't use it in very many recipes. We reserve milk chocolate for frostings and for eating out of hand. We pitted ten brands of milk chocolate against one another, and although none were losers, we were still able to pick a clear favorite. Tasters preferred Dove Milk Chocolate for its flavor and declared it a good all-around milk chocolate.

Hot Fudge Pudding Cake

Most recipes for hot fudge pudding cake read like recipes for disaster. You mix flour, sugar, cocoa powder, baking powder, milk, and oil by hand—much like a brownie batter. Once the batter is scraped into the pan, the fun starts. A mixture of cocoa powder and sugar is sprinkled over the top, and then boiling water is poured into the pan. The "batter" goes into the oven—no stirring allowed—looking like a mess.

But as the batter bakes, the water, cocoa, and sugar bubble and brew and—as if by magic—form a chocolate sauce while the cake rises to the top. The result is a chewy, brownie-like cake saturated with pockets of pudding-style chocolate sauce. It's scooped out of the pan (not sliced like a regular cake) and usually gilded with a dollop of whipped cream or a scoop of ice cream that melts into the hot pudding.

Although this might sound like chocolate heaven (chocolate cake and chocolate sauce!), this recipe isn't without problems. What looks deceptively rich and fudgy often has little chocolate flavor, and the cake layer can be hit-or-miss—it can easily get too dry or too wet in the center. Our goal was to develop a hot fudge pudding cake with the texture and flavor of a brownie and plenty of spoon-clinging pudding sauce dotted throughout.

For fuller, rounder chocolate flavor, we switched from the natural cocoa powder used in most old-fashioned recipes to Dutch-processed cocoa, the European-style cocoa now available in American supermarkets. We also doubled the amount of cocoa in the batter. A big handful of semisweet chocolate chips added another layer of chocolate flavor and ensured plenty of gooey pockets in the baked cake. Trading flavorless vegetable oil for melted butter was another big improvement. For a more brownie-like texture, we added an egg yolk.

We found that the success of the sauce depends on using the right proportions of boiling water, sugar, and cocoa. Too much water (a common problem in the recipes we tested), and the sauce turned out thin and watery. We found that 1 cup of boiling water poured over ½ cup of sugar and ¼ cup of cocoa created a thick sauce with solid chocolate flavor. This dessert now sported big chocolate flavor to match its gooey, fudgy appearance.

HOT FUDGE PUDDING CAKE

SERVES 6 TO 8

Do not overbake this cake or the pudding sauce will burn in the pan and the cake will be dry, not fudgy. If you're having a dinner party, try our variation on page 474 where the cakes are baked in individual ramekins.

1	cup sugar
½	cup Dutch-processed cocoa powder
1	cup all-purpose flour
2	teaspoons baking powder
¼	teaspoon salt
½	cup whole milk
4	tablespoons unsalted butter, melted
1	large egg yolk
2	teaspoons vanilla extract
½	cup semisweet chocolate chips
1	cup boiling water
	Vanilla ice cream or whipped cream for serving

1. Adjust an oven rack to the middle position and heat the oven to 350 degrees. Grease an 8-inch square cake pan. Whisk ½ cup of the sugar with ¼ cup of the cocoa in a small bowl.

2. Whisk together the flour, remaining ½ cup sugar, remaining ¼ cup cocoa, baking powder, and salt in

a large bowl. Whisk the milk, butter, egg yolk, and vanilla together in a medium bowl until smooth. Stir the milk mixture into the flour mixture until just combined. Fold in the chocolate chips (the batter will be stiff).

3. Using a rubber spatula, scrape the batter into the prepared pan and spread into the corners. Sprinkle the reserved cocoa mixture evenly over the top. Gently pour the boiling water over the cocoa mixture. Do not stir.

4. Bake until the top of the cake looks cracked, the sauce is bubbling, and a toothpick inserted into a cakey area comes out with moist crumbs attached, about 25 minutes, rotating the pan halfway through baking. Cool in the pan, set on a wire rack, for at least 10 minutes. To serve, scoop the warm cake into individual serving bowls and top with vanilla ice cream or whipped cream.

CHECKING PUDDING CAKE FOR DONENESS

1. When the pudding cake is crackled like a brownie and the sauce is bubbling up from the bottom, it's time to start testing for doneness. For the most accurate test, insert a toothpick close to the edge, where the cake is firmest.

2. The toothpick should have large, moist crumbs—but no gooey batter—attached. Check at least two spots to be certain that what's sticking to the toothpick isn't just a melted chocolate chip.

INDIVIDUAL HOT FUDGE PUDDING CAKES

Put a fancy spin on this homey recipe by baking up individual pudding cakes.

Grease 8 (6-ounce) ovenproof ramekins or coffee cups. Fill each with 2 tablespoons of the batter. Top each with 1½ tablespoons of the cocoa mixture, followed by 2 tablespoons of the boiling water. Arrange the cups on a rimmed baking sheet and bake until the tops are just cracked, 20 to 25 minutes, rotating the pan halfway through baking.

Texas Sheet Cake

Texas sheet cake—the official state cake of Texas—is a huge, pecan-topped chocolate cake with three distinct layers of chocolaty goodness. A diverse range of textures is created when a sweet chocolate icing is poured over a cake that's still hot out of the oven; when the cake cools, you're left with an icing layer, a fudgy layer where the icing and hot cake have mixed together, and a bottom layer of moist cake. The cake is easy to make (no mixer is required) and great to take to potlucks and barbecues because, as its name implies, it's baked in a sheet pan and serves a crowd. But the cakes we baked from recipes we found all had one big problem: they didn't pack much chocolate wallop.

Most Texas sheet cake recipes start with blooming cocoa powder in water with margarine, oil, butter, vegetable shortening, or a combination thereof. The cocoa mixture is then combined with flour, sugar, baking soda, eggs, dairy (milk, buttermilk, or sour cream), and vanilla in a single bowl. We baked up cakes with different combinations of margarine, oil, butter, and shortening, and tasters agreed that margarine imparted an unpleasant artificial flavor. The cake made with all butter tasted great, but the texture was too light and cakey. The cake made with a combination of butter (for flavor) and vegetable oil (to keep the cake moist) was the best overall, producing a cake with a dense, brownie-like texture.

All of the recipes we found had a skimpy ¼ cup of cocoa, which accounted for the measly chocolate flavor. Doubling the amount of cocoa certainly helped, but adding 8 ounces of melted semisweet chocolate gave us the strong chocolate flavor tasters were craving. The semisweet chocolate also contributed moisture and fat to the batter, which made for a fudgier cake. As for the dairy, tasters preferred rich, tangy sour cream over buttermilk or milk.

Standard recipes for the icing call for a stick of butter, milk, another ¼ cup of cocoa, and 4 cups of confectioners' sugar. Tasters deemed this formula too sweet, so we took the amount of sugar down to 3 cups and doubled the amount of cocoa (as we had done in the cake) to ½ cup. To give the icing more body, we replaced the milk with heavy cream, and we added a tablespoon of corn syrup to give the frosting a lustrous finish.

Since the cake was already pretty moist, we were curious as to whether the icing absolutely had to be poured over the cake while it was hot. We baked two sheet cakes, icing one directly out of the oven

ICING THE CAKE

The key to perfectly moist, fudgy Texas sheet cake is to let the warm icing soak into the hot cake. As soon as the cake comes out of the oven, pour the warm icing over the cake and use a spatula to spread the icing to the edges.

and icing the other after it had cooled. The results were clear—the cake iced while hot had that characteristic moist, gooey, fudgy layer under the frosting, but the other cake was an ordinary frosted cake. This sheet cake may come from Texas, but we think the rest of the country deserves to share its big chocolate flavor.

TEXAS SHEET CAKE

SERVES 20 TO 24

You'll need an 18 by 13-inch rimmed baking sheet for this popular potluck cake. To ensure that the frosting will sink into the cake, making a fudgy layer, be sure to pour the icing over the cake while the cake is still hot.

CAKE

2	cups all-purpose flour
2	cups granulated sugar
½	teaspoon baking soda
½	teaspoon salt
¼	cup sour cream, room temperature
2	large eggs plus 2 large egg yolks, room temperature
2	teaspoons vanilla extract
8	ounces semisweet chocolate, chopped
¾	cup vegetable oil
¾	cup water
½	cup Dutch-processed cocoa powder
4	tablespoons unsalted butter

ICING

8	tablespoons (1 stick) unsalted butter
½	cup heavy cream
½	cup Dutch-processed cocoa powder
1	tablespoon light corn syrup
3	cups confectioners' sugar
1	tablespoon vanilla extract
1	cup pecans, toasted (see page 198) and chopped

1. FOR THE CAKE: Adjust an oven rack to the middle position and heat the oven to 350 degrees. Grease an 18 by 13-inch rimmed baking sheet. Whisk the flour, granulated sugar, baking soda, and salt together in a medium bowl. In another medium bowl, whisk the sour cream, eggs, egg yolks, and vanilla together.

2. Melt the chocolate, oil, water, cocoa, and butter together in a large saucepan over medium heat, stirring occasionally, until smooth, about 5 minutes. Remove the saucepan from the heat and slowly whisk in the flour mixture until just incorporated. Whisk in the egg mixture until combined.

3. Give the batter a final stir with a rubber spatula to make sure it is thoroughly combined. Scrape the batter into the prepared baking sheet, smooth the top, and gently tap the sheet on the work surface to settle the batter. Bake the cake until a toothpick inserted in the center comes out with a few moist crumbs attached, 18 to 20 minutes, rotating the pan halfway through baking.

4. FOR THE ICING: During the cake's last few minutes of baking, cook the butter, cream, cocoa, and corn syrup together in a saucepan over medium heat, stirring occasionally, until smooth. Off the heat, whisk in the confectioners' sugar and vanilla until combined.

5. Spread the warm icing evenly over the hot cake and sprinkle with the pecans. Let the cake cool in the pan to room temperature, about 1 hour, then refrigerate until the icing is set, about 1 hour longer, before serving.

Chocolate Blackout Cake

Mention Ebinger's to most Brooklynites over the age of forty and you'll see a sparkle of nostalgia in their eyes. Bring up chocolate blackout cake and you might actually see a tear or two. When the Brooklyn-based chain of bakeries closed its doors, the borough went into mourning. On that fateful day, August 27, 1972, the *New York Times* ran a story titled "Tears Replace the Coffee Cakes." Of all the lost Ebinger's recipes, none has received more attention in the last thirty-plus years than its chocolate blackout cake.

A forerunner of "death by chocolate" confections, chocolate blackout cake is decidedly decadent, marrying fudgy, dark chocolate layers with a rich, creamy chocolate pudding that acts as both filling and frosting. But what really sets this cake apart is yet another dimension of chocolate flavor—its signature shaggy coating of chocolate cake crumbs.

Blackout cake got its name from the blackout drills performed by the Civilian Defense Corps during World War II. When the navy sent its ships to sea from the Brooklyn Navy Yard, the streets of the borough were "blacked out" to avoid silhouetting the battleships against the cityscapes of Brooklyn and Manhattan. The cake was so named because of its darkly chocolate—practically black—appearance.

Ebinger's original recipe was never published, leaving cookbook authors and Brooklyn grandmothers to rely on their taste buds to reproduce "authentic" versions. We compiled a folder of promising recipes, but the only things they had in common were long ingredient lists and complicated cooking techniques. We wanted a great-tasting cake, but it also had to be simple and easy to make.

We started with the cake layers. For big chocolate flavor, most recipes rely on regular cocoa powder, but we found it too astringent. The less acidic Dutch-processed cocoa was better, but we wanted even more chocolate flavor. We tried adding melted chocolate, but the cake became dense and gummy.

We had better luck when we used a few test-kitchen tricks to bring out the subtleties of the cocoa. The tang of buttermilk carried the chocolate flavor; other dairy products seemed to mute it. Adding brewed coffee to the batter enhanced the nuances of the cocoa, as did a combination of brown and granulated sugar. But still we pined for more depth. Borrowing a spice-blooming technique from the savory kitchen, we added the cocoa powder to the butter that we were already melting for the cake. As the pungent aroma of cocoa filled the kitchen, we knew that we would be rewarded for our gamble. The cake made with toasted cocoa was dark and rich, with a distinct chocolate flavor.

To keep things simple, we decided to mix the

THE AMERICAN TABLE
A LOST ICON

Ebinger's Baking Company opened in 1898 on Flatbush Avenue in Brooklyn and grew into a chain of more than sixty stores before going bankrupt in 1972. Started by Arthur Ebinger, a baker who emigrated from Germany with a vast collection of recipes, the business grew to include his wife and their three sons. During its heyday, Ebinger's was a point of bragging rights for Brooklynites, as celebrities and the well-to-do from Manhattan never went to Brooklyn without taking home a cake or one of Ebinger's other specialties, which included challah, rye bread, pumpkin pie, Othellos (filled mini sponge cakes covered in chocolate), and crumb buns.

1. Using your hands, crumble one cake layer into medium-sized crumbs.

2. Sprinkle the cake crumbs all over the top of the cake, then use your hands to gently press the crumbs onto the sides.

cake batter right in the saucepan with the butter and cocoa. Although unconventional, this streamlined method yielded a perfect cake and saved time.

The traditional pudding component of the cake should be velvety, with a chocolate tang, yet rich enough to cling to the sides of the cake like a frosting. Some recipes achieve this with a mixture of cocoa, chocolate, cornstarch, and water. Given the already pronounced chocolate flavor in the cake, tasters preferred a sweeter, more dairy-rich chocolate flavor in the pudding. A combination of half-and-half and milk gave the pudding a satiny quality, and unsweetened chocolate produced the most depth of flavor.

Once the two cake layers and the pudding had cooled, it was time to assemble this skyscraper. We divided the cakes along their equators, planning to use three of the four resulting rounds as layers and the fourth for the crumbled cake topping. We spread a generous amount of pudding between the layers and coated the exterior of the cake with the rest. To finish it off, we crumbled the reserved cake layer, sprinkled it over the top of the cake, and pressed the crumbs into the sides. After just one bite, we realized why Brooklynites still talk about this cake more than thirty-five years after the closing of Ebinger's.

CHOCOLATE BLACKOUT CAKE

SERVES 8 TO 10

Be sure to give the pudding and the cake enough time to cool or you'll end up with runny pudding and gummy cake.

PUDDING

- 1 ¼ cups granulated sugar
- ¼ cup cornstarch
- ½ teaspoon salt
- 2 cups half-and-half
- 1 cup whole milk
- 6 ounces unsweetened chocolate, chopped
- 2 teaspoons vanilla extract

CAKE

- ¾ cup Dutch-processed cocoa powder, plus extra for dusting pans
- 1 ½ cups all-purpose flour
- 2 teaspoons baking powder
- ½ teaspoon baking soda
- ½ teaspoon salt
- 8 tablespoons (1 stick) unsalted butter
- 1 cup strong brewed coffee, room temperature
- 1 cup buttermilk, room temperature
- 1 cup packed light brown sugar
- 1 cup granulated sugar
- 2 large eggs, room temperature
- 1 teaspoon vanilla extract

1. FOR THE PUDDING: Whisk the granulated sugar, cornstarch, and salt together in a medium saucepan and slowly whisk in the half-and-half and milk. Bring the mixture to a simmer over medium heat, whisking constantly, until the mixture thickens, 2 to 3 minutes. Stir in the chocolate and cook, stirring constantly, until melted and smooth, about 1 minute. Off the heat, stir in the vanilla. Transfer the pudding to a large bowl and press plastic wrap directly onto the surface. Refrigerate the pudding until cold, about 4 hours.

2. FOR THE CAKE: Adjust an oven rack to the middle position and heat the oven to 325 degrees. Grease two 8-inch cake pans, then dust with cocoa powder and line the bottoms with parchment paper. In a medium bowl, whisk the flour, baking powder, baking soda, and salt together.

3. Melt the butter in a large saucepan over medium heat. Stir in ¾ cup of the cocoa and cook until fragrant, about 1 minute. Off the heat, whisk in the coffee, buttermilk, and sugars until dissolved. Whisk in the eggs and vanilla, then slowly whisk in the flour mixture until no streaks remain. (The batter will be very loose.)

4. Give the batter a final stir with a rubber spatula to make sure it is thoroughly combined. Scrape the batter into the prepared pans, smooth the tops, and gently tap the pans on the work surface to settle the batter. Bake the cakes until a toothpick inserted in the center comes out with a few crumbs attached, 30 to 35 minutes, rotating the pans halfway through baking.

5. Let the cakes cool in the pans for 10 minutes. Run a small knife around the edge of the cakes, then flip them out onto a wire rack. Peel off the parchment paper, flip the cakes right side up, and let cool completely before filling and frosting, about 2 hours.

6. Line the edges of a cake platter with strips of parchment paper to keep the platter clean while you assemble the cake. Slice each cake into two even layers using a long serrated knife. Crumble one of the cake layers into medium-sized crumbs following the photo on page 477.

7. Place one of the cake layers on the platter. Spread 1 cup of the pudding over the cake right to the edges. Top with a second cake layer and spread with another 1 cup of the pudding. Place the remaining cake layer on top and press lightly to adhere. Frost the cake with the remaining pudding. Sprinkle the cake crumbs evenly over the top and press them onto the sides of cake following the photo on page 477. Remove the parchment strips from the platter before serving.

Tunnel of Fudge Cake

In 1966, Ella Helfrich of Houston, Texas, won second place—and $5,000—in the annual Pillsbury Bake-Off for her tunnel of fudge cake recipe. Ella's glazed, nutty, and brownie-like cake was baked in a Bundt pan, but its most distinguishing feature was the ring (or "tunnel") of creamy fudge that formed inside the cake as it baked. Intrigued, we aimed to develop our own version.

To start, we dusted off the old Pillsbury recipe, which specifies creaming three sticks of butter with 1½ cups of granulated sugar, then mixing in eggs, flour, and nuts along with a secret ingredient: a package of powdered Pillsbury Two Layer Double-Dutch Fudge Buttercream Frosting mix. This mix was the key to the cake, as it contained large amounts of cocoa powder and confectioners' sugar, which separated out during baking—this cake was always slightly underbaked—and came together to help form the fudgy center. Pillsbury no longer sells this frosting mix, but the company does offer an updated recipe on its Web site.

We had high hopes as we pulled the cake made from the new Pillsbury recipe out of the oven. Sadly, it was lacking in chocolate flavor, and even worse, it had no fudgy center. Other modern recipes attempt to replace the frosting mix with ingredients like instant chocolate pudding and homemade chocolate ganache, but they hardened into a ring in the middle of the batter. Some recipes include chunks of chocolate inserted in the batter, but these cakes baked up with a liquid interior that gushed when the cake was sliced. A proper tunnel of fudge cake has a creamy, frosting-like filling that holds its shape when the cake is cut. We decided to see if we could fix the updated Pillsbury recipe.

To add more chocolate flavor, we switched from natural cocoa powder (which can be sour) to less acidic Dutch-processed cocoa. Adding melted chocolate to the batter made the cake more moist and contributed big chocolate punch. As for the tunnel, we knew that slightly underbaking the cake was a big part of it, but the interior of our cake was still too dry.

To add moisture (and flavor), we swapped out almost half of the granulated sugar for brown sugar. But the big key was adjusting the amounts of two base ingredients: flour and butter. Cutting back on the flour made the cake much more moist, and using less butter helped the cakey exterior set more quickly. Finally, after two dozen failed cakes, the "tunnel" was back—and better than ever.

TUNNEL OF FUDGE CAKE

SERVES 12

It's no use to use a cake tester, toothpick, or skewer when testing this cake for doneness because the fudgy interior will look just like undercooked cake batter; when the cake is done, the sides will begin to pull away from the pan and the top will feel springy when pressed with a finger.

CAKE

½	cup boiling water
2	ounces bittersweet chocolate, chopped
2	cups all-purpose flour
2	cups pecans or walnuts, chopped fine
2	cups confectioners' sugar
¾	cup Dutch-processed cocoa powder, plus extra for dusting pan
1	teaspoon salt
20	tablespoons (2½ sticks) unsalted butter, softened
1	cup granulated sugar
¾	cup packed light brown sugar
1	tablespoon vanilla extract
5	large eggs, room temperature

GLAZE

4	ounces bittersweet chocolate, melted
⅓	cup heavy cream, hot
2	tablespoons light corn syrup
¼	teaspoon vanilla extract
	Pinch salt

1. FOR THE CAKE: Adjust an oven rack to the lower-middle position and heat the oven to 350 degrees. Prepare a 12-cup nonstick Bundt pan following the photo on page 480.

2. Whisk the boiling water and chocolate together in a small bowl until melted and smooth; let the mixture cool slightly. In a medium bowl, whisk the flour, nuts, confectioners' sugar, cocoa, and salt together.

3. In a large bowl, beat the butter, sugars, and vanilla together with an electric mixer on medium speed until light and fluffy, 3 to 6 minutes. Beat in the eggs, one at a time, until combined, about 1 minute. Beat in the chocolate mixture until combined, about 30 seconds. Reduce the mixer speed to low and slowly beat in the flour mixture until just incorporated, about 30 seconds.

4. Scrape the batter into the prepared pan and smooth the top. Wipe any drops of batter off the sides of the pan and gently tap the pan on the work surface to settle the batter. Bake the cake until the edges begin to pull away from the sides of the pan and the top feels springy when pressed with a finger, about 45 minutes.

5. FOR THE GLAZE: Meanwhile, whisk all of the glaze ingredients together in a medium bowl until smooth and let sit until thickened, about 25 minutes.

6. Let the cake cool in the pan for 10 minutes, then flip it out onto a wire rack. Let the cake cool completely, about 2 hours. Drizzle the chocolate glaze over the top and sides of the cake. Let the glaze set, about 25 minutes, before serving.

PREPARING A BUNDT CAKE PAN

To ensure a clean release, make a simple paste from 1 tablespoon melted butter and 1 tablespoon flour (or cocoa powder for chocolate cakes) and apply it to the pan with a pastry brush.

Red Velvet Cake

Red velvet cake is a velvety tender, brilliant red cake, swathed in sweet but tangy cream cheese frosting. This cake is as delicious as it is eye-catching. We set out to create our own version.

Some research revealed that red cakes have been around for years. A faint red color is the by-product of a chemical reaction between vinegar and/or buttermilk and cocoa powder. Red cakes—with names like Red Devil Cake and Oxblood Cake—date back to the late nineteenth century. Over time, the naturally occurring faint red color was augmented first by beets (a common ingredient during the sugar rations of World War II) and then by red food coloring (the standard choice in most recipes published since the 1950s).

The exact origins of red velvet cake are muddled. Most sources mention the Waldorf-Astoria Hotel and the 1950s, but this history is most definitely false—the recipe did not start there. During the 1960s the recipe appeared in countless newspapers, which sourced this cake in the Deep South, the Pacific Northwest, and even Canada. The best-known version of the recipe appeared in James Beard's 1972 classic *American Cookery*.

Although we weren't able to figure out the precise origins of this cake, we had accumulated enough research to start baking. We tried a few recipes with beets, but no one liked their vegetal flavor. After several tests, we realized food coloring was a must and there was no use trying to skimp on it; any less than 2 tablespoons yielded a cake that was more pink than red. Despite the addition of cocoa, red velvet is not a chocolate cake—the cocoa is there for color. Some recipes include as little as 1 tablespoon of cocoa. We found that 2 tablespoons produced the best color and gave the cake a pleasant (but mild) cocoa flavor.

Now the cake was definitely red, but it was also speckled with brown at the edges. We were mixing the cocoa powder with the dry ingredients, yet it didn't seem to be evenly distributed in the cake. A few recipes suggested combining the cocoa powder with the red food coloring to make a paste before adding it to the batter, a step that had seemed fussy. It turns out that it was necessary; mixing the paste made the cakes uniformly red, even at the edges.

Now that we had the red part down, we turned to the velvet. After fiddling with the basic formula, we realized that a super-acidic batter (with both buttermilk and vinegar) was needed to react with the baking soda and create a fine, tender crumb. Thoroughly creaming the butter also helped create a velvety texture. To top it off, tasters loved the contrast in color and flavor that a sweet, tangy, white cream cheese frosting gave the cake. We now had a cake that lived up to both the "red" and the "velvet" in its name—and it tasted great, too.

RED VELVET LAYER CAKE

SERVES 8 TO 10

For the cake to have the proper rise and color, you must use natural cocoa powder; do not substitute Dutch-processed cocoa.

2	tablespoons natural cocoa powder (see note above), plus extra for dusting pans
2¼	cups all-purpose flour
1½	teaspoons baking soda
	Pinch salt
1	cup buttermilk, room temperature
2	large eggs, room temperature
1	tablespoon white vinegar
1	teaspoon vanilla extract
2	tablespoons red food coloring
12	tablespoons (1½ sticks) unsalted butter, softened
1½	cups sugar
1	recipe Cream Cheese Frosting (page 504)

THE AMERICAN TABLE
RED VELVET CAKE
- -

Red velvet cake fell out of fashion in the 1970s amid health scares relating to red dye no. 2 (a similar fate befell red M&Ms, even though the candies never contained the dye in question). Once consumers were convinced that other red dyes were safe, red candies made it back into the M&Ms assortment (in 1987) and red velvet cakes started a comeback in bakeries.

1. Adjust an oven rack to the middle position and heat the oven to 350 degrees. Grease two 9-inch cake pans, then dust with cocoa powder and line the bottoms with parchment paper.

2. Whisk the flour, baking soda, and salt together in a medium bowl. In another medium bowl, whisk the buttermilk, eggs, vinegar, and vanilla together. In a small bowl, mix 2 tablespoons of the cocoa and the red food coloring together to a smooth paste.

3. In a large bowl, beat the butter and sugar together with an electric mixer on medium-high speed until light and fluffy, 3 to 6 minutes. Reduce the mixer speed to low and beat in one-third of the flour mixture, followed by half of the buttermilk mixture. Repeat with half of the remaining flour mixture and the remaining buttermilk mixture. Beat in the remaining flour mixture until just combined. Beat in the cocoa mixture until the batter is uniform.

4. Give the batter a final stir with a rubber spatula to make sure it is thoroughly combined. Scrape the batter into the prepared pans, smooth the tops, and gently tap the pans on the work surface to settle the batter. Bake the cakes until a toothpick inserted in the center comes out with a few crumbs attached, about 25 minutes, rotating the pans halfway through baking.

5. Let the cakes cool in the pans for 10 minutes. Run a small knife around the edge of the cakes, then flip them out onto a wire rack. Peel off the parchment paper, flip the cakes right side up, and let cool completely before frosting, about 2 hours.

6. Line the edges of a cake platter with strips of parchment paper to keep the platter clean while you assemble the cake. Place one of the cake layers on the platter. Spread 1 cup of the frosting over the top, right to the edge of the cake. Place the other cake layer on top and press gently to adhere. Frost the cake with the remaining frosting and remove the parchment strips from the platter before serving.

SHOPPING WITH THE TEST KITCHEN

Round Cake Pans: Does the type of cake pan you use make a difference? Yes, and we've baked our fair share of pale cakes or, even worse, ones that have refused to turn out of the pans regardless of how diligently we greased them. We baked three of our basic cakes in seventeen different pans, which ranged widely in price and construction, testing each one for quick release, even browning, and overall appearance. For the neatest and most attractive appearance, we prefer cakes baked in pans with straight sides. Of the seventeen brands we tested, we liked the Chicago Metallic Professional Nonstick Cake Pans ($14.95) the best. In addition to promoting the best browning, the nonstick surface ensured the quickest and best release every time.

Boston Cream Cupcakes

Boston cream pie is composed of two layers of sponge cake, a custard filling, and a rich chocolate glaze. This popular dessert (which, of course, is not a pie but a cake) was invented in 1855 at Boston's Parker House Hotel and is the official dessert of Massachusetts. Tradition is all well and good, but we wondered if this old-fashioned cake could use a modern makeover—and thus we set our sights on transforming this venerable cake into a cupcake.

We found more recipes for the cupcake version of this dessert than you might expect; unfortunately, most of them called for just three ingredients: a box of cake mix, a packet of pudding, and a can of frosting. What we had in mind was something with more homemade flavor, so we turned instead to recipes for the original dessert, which is made with sponge cake. But these recipes weren't quite right either; tasters disliked sponge cupcakes, finding their light, airy texture too insubstantial in small form.

Then we thought of cream-filled cupcakes—especially the popular Hostess cupcakes many kids favor. Soft and moist, those cupcakes have a very fine texture and are incredibly tender. We started with a basic yellow cake, which was a bit too coarse-textured. We then switched from the traditional creaming method (which calls for beating the butter and sugar first) to the reverse creaming method, which calls for cutting the butter into the dry ingredients, as is done with biscuit dough. These cupcakes were soft, moist, and tender. The reason? The traditional creaming method, which relies on aerating the butter with the sugar, creates large air pockets that result in a coarser crumb. In the reverse creaming method, the butter coats the flour before the batter is aerated, keeping the cake tender and fine-crumbed.

Coming up with recipes for the filling and the glaze was easy compared with the work we did on the cupcakes. We wanted a rich, creamy custard that was stiff enough to hold its shape inside the cupcake but still gooey enough to ooze slightly when we bit into it. Heavy cream (rather than milk or half-and-half), three egg yolks, and a good amount of cornstarch gave our pastry cream the perfect consistency. For the glaze, tasters preferred the strong flavor of bittersweet chocolate to semisweet or milk chocolate, and they loved the sheen that corn syrup provided.

Now that we had assembled all of the components, the real challenge began. How were we to get the pastry cream inside the cupcake? Again looking to Hostess for guidance, we found it in the form of a small hole in the bottom of the cupcake, where the filling was piped in. We didn't have a multimillion-dollar cream injector, but we did have a pastry bag, so we filled it with pastry cream, stuck the tip into the cupcake, and squeezed. It seemed as if we had put a good bit of pastry cream inside, but when tasters took a bite they scowled and demanded more filling. It was clear that some of the cake would have to go to make room for more pastry cream.

Though surgery was unavoidable, we were loath to hack up our cupcakes too much. One option was to simply cut off the top, scoop out a bit of the cake, fill the hole, and then replace the top, but the scar was obvious, even when the chocolate glaze was added, and the top tended to slide when tasters took a bite. We had more success by removing a cone-shaped section of cake (see the photos on page 484). Once the glaze was applied, the incision became invisible.

These pretty little cupcakes are not the quickest dessert (nothing beats the convenience of opening a package of Hostess cupcakes), but they taste so good that the adults in your house will be fighting the kids for seconds.

BOSTON CREAM CUPCAKES

MAKES 12 CUPCAKES

It's important to bake these cupcakes in a greased and floured muffin tin rather than paper cupcake liners, so the chocolate glaze can run down the sides of the cupcakes.

PASTRY CREAM

1⅓	cups heavy cream
3	large egg yolks
⅓	cup sugar
	Pinch salt
4	teaspoons cornstarch
2	tablespoons unsalted butter, cut into 2 pieces
1½	teaspoons vanilla extract

CUPCAKES

1¾	cups all-purpose flour
1	cup sugar
1½	teaspoons baking powder
¾	teaspoon salt
12	tablespoons (1½ sticks) unsalted butter, cut into 12 pieces and softened
3	large eggs, room temperature
¾	cup whole milk, room temperature
1½	teaspoons vanilla extract

GLAZE

8	ounces bittersweet chocolate, chopped
⅔	cup heavy cream
¼	cup light corn syrup
½	teaspoon vanilla extract

1. FOR THE PASTRY CREAM: Bring the cream to a simmer in a medium saucepan over medium heat. Meanwhile, whisk the egg yolks, sugar, and salt together in a medium bowl, then whisk in the cornstarch until pale yellow and thick, about 30 seconds.

2. Slowly whisk the hot cream into the egg mixture to temper, then return the mixture to the saucepan and cook over medium heat, whisking constantly, until thick and glossy, about 1½ minutes. Off the heat, whisk in the butter and vanilla. Transfer the mixture to a small bowl, press plastic wrap directly onto the surface, and refrigerate until chilled and set, about 2 hours.

3. FOR THE CUPCAKES: Adjust an oven rack to the middle position and heat the oven to 350 degrees. Grease and flour a 12-cup muffin tin.

4. Whisk the flour, sugar, baking powder, and salt together in a large bowl. Using an electric mixer on medium-low speed, beat the butter into the flour mixture, 1 piece at a time, about 30 seconds. Continue to beat the mixture until it resembles moist crumbs, 1 to 3 minutes. Beat in the eggs, one at a time, until combined, about 30 seconds. Beat in the milk and vanilla, then increase the mixer speed to medium and beat the batter until smooth, light, and fluffy, 1 to 3 minutes.

5. Using a greased ⅓-cup measure, portion the batter into each muffin cup. Bake the cupcakes until a toothpick inserted in the center comes out with a few moist crumbs attached, 18 to 20 minutes, rotating the tin halfway through baking. Let the cupcakes cool in the tin for 10 minutes, then transfer them to a wire rack to cool completely.

6. FOR THE GLAZE: Microwave all of the glaze ingredients together, whisking often, until melted and smooth, 1 to 2 minutes. Let the glaze cool, uncovered, until it is thickened but still pourable, about 20 minutes.

7. Following the photos, cut around the inside edge of the top of each cupcake, removing a cone-shaped piece of cake, and fill with 2 tablespoons of the pastry cream. Trim and replace the cupcake top and set each cupcake on a wire rack over a parchment-lined baking sheet (for easy cleanup). Spoon the glaze over the cupcakes, letting it run down the sides. Refrigerate the cupcakes until the glaze has set, about 10 minutes, before serving.

FILLING BOSTON CREAM CUPCAKES

1. Insert the tip of a small knife at a 45-degree angle about ¼ inch from the edge of the cupcake and cut all the way around, removing a cone of cake.

2. Cut off (and discard) the pointed end of each cone, so that the remaining cake disk measures about ¼ inch thick.

3. Using a small spoon, fill each cupcake with 2 tablespoons of the pastry cream and then cover each with a cupcake top. Press lightly on top of the cupcake to adhere.

4. Spoon 2 tablespoons of the glaze over each filled cupcake, allowing it to drip down the sides.

Black-Bottom Cupcakes

Cousins to black-bottom pie, black-bottom cupcakes are moist, fudgy, nearly black cupcakes containing a creamy center of tangy cheesecake studded with mini chocolate chips. What's not to love? Determined to make our own version, we gathered a stack of printed recipes and headed into the test kitchen with high hopes.

Our confidence quickly faltered as soon as we lined up our cupcakes for tasters. Most of them were greasy, slumped, and devoid of rich chocolate flavor. As for the cheesecake centers, they baked up dry, chalky, or completely separated from the cake in sunken craters. We were looking for a cake that had big chocolate flavor and was sturdy enough to support the cheesecake filling.

The cake portion of black-bottom cupcakes traditionally gets its dark color and chocolate flavor from cocoa. Tasters much preferred the rounded flavor of Dutch-processed cocoa to natural cocoa. Adding a little sour cream to the batter accentuated the chocolate and added richness. Although the cake was now tasting good, we were frustrated that the cheesecake center was still pulling away. It turns out the problem was with the cake, not the filling.

Black-bottom cupcakes are usually made with oil, which contributes to the soft, fudgy texture. But oil also makes the cake leaden and greasy—so greasy that the filling can't adhere to it. However, when we used butter (creaming it with the sugar) instead of oil, the aerated batter baked up too tender to support the filling. As a last resort, we tried melting the butter. The batter looked dense and sticky (just like the batter made with oil), but as the cupcakes cooled we saw a big difference. The butter had resolidified and the cake was no longer greasy. Best of all, it was sturdy enough to support the cheesecake filling.

But we still weren't happy with the filling's flavor.

Most recipes consist of cream cheese, sugar, and a whole egg, but the yolk lent an unappealing yellow hue and mealy texture when baked. Using two whites added moisture and helped the filling look better, but it also dulled the tang of the cream cheese. Since we were already using sour cream in the cake batter, we added some to the cheesecake filling, and it restored a needed tang. The inclusion of mini chocolate chips made the filling complete and reinforced the chocolate flavor of the fudgy cupcakes.

BLACK-BOTTOM CUPCAKES

MAKES 12 CUPCAKES

Do not substitute regular chocolate chips for the miniature chips; regular chips are much heavier and will sink to the bottom of the cupcakes.

FILLING

1	(8-ounce) package cream cheese, softened
¼	cup sugar
⅛	teaspoon salt
1	large egg white
1	tablespoon sour cream
¼	cup semisweet mini chocolate chips (see note above)

CUPCAKES

¾	cup all-purpose flour
⅔	cup sugar
¼	cup Dutch-processed cocoa powder
½	teaspoon baking soda
¼	teaspoon salt
¾	cup water, room temperature
6	tablespoons sour cream, room temperature
4	tablespoons unsalted butter, melted and cooled
½	teaspoon vanilla extract

1. Adjust an oven rack to the lower-middle position and heat the oven to 400 degrees. Line a 12-cup muffin tin with cupcake liners.

2. FOR THE FILLING: In a medium bowl, beat the cream cheese, sugar, and salt together with an electric mixer on medium speed until smooth, about 30 seconds. Beat in the egg white and sour cream until combined, about 30 seconds. Stir in the chocolate chips.

3. FOR THE CUPCAKES: Whisk the flour, sugar, cocoa, baking soda, and salt together in a large bowl. Whisk in the water, sour cream, melted butter, and vanilla until just incorporated.

4. Using a greased ⅓-cup measure, portion the batter into each muffin cup. Spoon a rounded tablespoon of the cream cheese mixture onto the center of each cupcake.

5. Bake the cupcakes until the tops just begin to crack, 18 to 22 minutes, rotating the tin halfway through baking. Let the cupcakes cool in the tin for 10 minutes, then transfer them to a wire rack to cool completely before serving.

Lemon Buttermilk Sheet Cake

When cookouts demand an easy bake-and-take dessert, nothing smacks of summer more than lemon sheet cake. A single bite should offer a punch of bright and sweet lemon flavor—like a gulp of great lemonade. But most recipes we tried missed the mark. The lemon flavor was either too fleeting or overpowering.

Before we addressed flavor issues, we needed a solid foundation. We started by preparing batches of the test kitchen's white and yellow sheet cakes (white cakes use only egg whites, whereas yellow cakes employ whole eggs), replacing a few tablespoons

MAKING LEMON SUGAR

1. Beating the sugar with the lemon zest releases the flavorful oils in the zest.

2. The lemon sugar provides a foundation of lemon flavor to the cake. Sprinkle extra lemon sugar over the glazed cake for added flavor and crunch.

of the milk in each recipe with lemon juice. Tasters much preferred the denser yellow cake, as the richness of the whole eggs balanced the acidity of the lemon. This recipe uses cake flour for a fine, velvety crumb and utilizes the traditional creaming method (beating butter and sugar before adding the wet and dry ingredients) to develop structure and height in the cake.

Tasters liked the flavor of this cake, but we weren't pleased with the domed top and sloping sides. Adding the lemon juice had changed the chemistry of the recipe. Replacing some of the baking powder with baking soda helped, as did reducing the baking temperature from 350 to 325 degrees—the slower baking meant that the edges and interior of the cake set at the same time, resulting in a perfectly flat top.

We had already started down the path to bright, clean lemon flavor—swapping out some of the milk for freshly squeezed lemon juice. But we could only go up to ¼ cup before the cake started tasting medicinal. We added the grated zest from three lemons to round out the lemon flavor and used a test-kitchen trick of beating the zest with sugar to create a homemade lemon sugar that lent a wallop of lemony richness to the cake. Replacing the remaining milk with buttermilk (and once again adjusting the ratio of baking powder to baking soda) added extra tang that reinforced the lemon flavor.

Tasters passed over both buttercream and cream cheese frostings in favor of a simple glaze made with confectioners' sugar, buttermilk, and lemon juice. A sprinkle of some reserved lemon sugar added crunch and a final flourish of lemon flavor and color.

LEMON BUTTERMILK SHEET CAKE

SERVES 15 TO 18

If you do not have cake flour on hand, there is an alternative. For every cup of cake flour, substitute ⅞ cup of all-purpose flour and 2 tablespoons of cornstarch. For this recipe you would use 2 cups plus 3 tablespoons of all-purpose flour and 5 tablespoons of cornstarch. We recommend using an offset spatula to evenly glaze the warm cake.

CAKE
- 2½ cups cake flour (see note above)
- 1 teaspoon baking powder
- ½ teaspoon baking soda
- ½ teaspoon salt
- ¾ cup buttermilk, room temperature
- ¼ cup fresh lemon juice and 3 tablespoons grated fresh lemon zest (3 lemons)
- 1 teaspoon vanilla extract
- 1¾ cups granulated sugar
- 12 tablespoons (1½ sticks) unsalted butter, softened
- 3 large eggs plus 1 large egg yolk, room temperature

GLAZE
- 3 cups confectioners' sugar
- 3 tablespoons fresh lemon juice
- 2 tablespoons buttermilk

1. FOR THE CAKE: Adjust an oven rack to the middle position and heat the oven to 325 degrees. Grease and flour a 13 by 9-inch baking pan. Combine the flour, baking powder, baking soda, and salt in a medium bowl. Combine the buttermilk, lemon juice, and vanilla in a liquid measuring cup.

2. In a large bowl, beat together the granulated sugar and lemon zest with an electric mixer on medium speed, until moist and fragrant, about 1 minute. Transfer ¼ cup of the sugar mixture to a small bowl, cover, and reserve. Add the butter to the remaining sugar mixture and beat until light and fluffy, about 2 minutes. Beat in the eggs, one at a time, and the yolk until combined. Reduce the mixer speed to low. Mix in one-third of the flour mixture, followed by half of the buttermilk mixture. Repeat with half of the remaining flour mixture and the remaining buttermilk mixture. Add the remaining flour mixture and mix until smooth, about 30 seconds. Give the batter a final stir with a rubber spatula to make sure it is thoroughly combined.

3. Scrape the batter into the prepared pan, smooth the top, and gently tap the pan on the work surface to settle the batter. Bake until the cake is golden brown and a toothpick inserted into the center comes out clean, 28 to 34 minutes, rotating the pan halfway through baking. Transfer the pan to a wire rack and let the cake cool for 10 minutes.

4. FOR THE GLAZE: Meanwhile, whisk the glaze ingredients together until smooth. Gently spread the glaze over the warm cake and sprinkle evenly with the reserved sugar mixture. Cool completely, at least 2 hours. Serve.

Orange Bundt Cake

An orange Bundt cake should be moist, rich, and tender. Although the correct texture is relatively easy to achieve, developing assertive orange flavor is more of a challenge. All citrus dulls when baked, but whereas a lemon is tart and bright—thanks to its high acidity—the mild flavor of an orange is especially fleeting. We armed ourselves with crates of Florida's finest and headed to the test kitchen to create an orange Bundt cake that tasted like it was straight from the grove.

Since most lemon cakes are flavored with lemon zest, we used a favorite lemon Bundt cake recipe, swapping the lemon zest for orange zest. The recipe called for a mere teaspoon of zest, but tasters demanded 2 tablespoons, which yielded the most orange flavor without tasting medicinal.

The zest did produce a fair amount of orange flavor, but it was one-dimensional and flat. We wondered if any other orange ingredients might help. We baked cakes with powdered Tang, orange juice concentrate, orange extract, and orange oil. The cakes made with Tang and juice concentrate were sickeningly sweet, with weak orange flavor, and the cakes made with extract and oil tasted like furniture polish. We returned our attention to fresh oranges—but this time to their juice.

Bundt cake recipes typically call for about a cup of dairy, usually milk or buttermilk. We wondered if we could replace the dairy with fresh orange juice. We made a cake with each of the three liquids. It was clear that the juice lent a mellow orange background flavor to the more astringent and perfumed zest, whereas the cakes made with milk and buttermilk seemed bland.

For more orange flavor, we made a thin confectioners' sugar glaze that was easily absorbed into the hot cake, then added more confectioners' sugar to the mixture to thicken it for an eye-catching glaze.

We had been using a mixture of orange juice, lemon juice (for brightness), and confectioners' sugar in the glaze, but replacing the orange juice with undiluted orange juice concentrate provided an extra punch of flavor.

A dusting of granulated sugar flavored with orange zest lent a final burst of flavor and delicate crunch to our cake. With three layers of orange flavor—zest, fresh juice, and concentrate—our cake now tasted as bright as the Florida sun.

ORANGE BUNDT CAKE

SERVES 12

When grating orange zest, remove just the outer orange part of the peel—the inner white part is very bitter.

CAKE

4	large eggs, room temperature
2	tablespoons grated fresh orange zest and ¾ cup fresh orange juice (2 to 3 oranges)
1	teaspoon vanilla extract
2½	cups all-purpose flour
2	cups granulated sugar
1	teaspoon baking powder
½	teaspoon baking soda
1	teaspoon salt
18	tablespoons (2¼ sticks) unsalted butter, cut into 18 pieces and softened

GLAZE AND ORANGE SUGAR

2	cups confectioners' sugar
½	cup frozen orange juice concentrate, thawed
4	teaspoons fresh lemon juice
	Pinch salt
1½	teaspoons grated fresh orange zest
3	tablespoons granulated sugar

1. Brushing the just-baked cake with a thin glaze produces a moist and flavorful crust.

2. When the cake is partially cooled, slowly pour the thicker second glaze over the cake. Then sprinkle the orange sugar over the glazed cake.

1. FOR THE CAKE: Adjust an oven rack to the middle position and heat the oven to 350 degrees. Prepare a 12-cup nonstick Bundt pan following the photo on page 480. Whisk the eggs, orange zest, orange juice, and vanilla together in a medium bowl.

2. With an electric mixer on the lowest setting, combine the flour, granulated sugar, baking powder, baking soda, and salt in a large bowl. Add the butter, 1 tablespoon at a time, and beat at medium-low speed until the mixture is crumbly with pea-sized pieces, about 30 seconds after the last tablespoon of butter is added. Add the egg mixture in a steady stream. Scrape down the sides of the bowl, increase the speed to medium-high, and beat until the batter is light and fluffy, about 2 minutes. Give the batter a final stir with a rubber spatula to make sure it is thoroughly combined. (It's fine if the batter looks slightly broken.)

3. Scrape the batter into the prepared pan and smooth the top. Wipe any drops of batter off the sides of the pan and gently tap the pan on the work surface to settle the batter. Bake until a toothpick inserted into the middle of the cake comes out clean, 45 to 55 minutes, rotating the pan halfway through baking.

4. FOR THE GLAZE AND ORANGE SUGAR: While the cake bakes, whisk together 1½ cups of the confectioners' sugar, the orange juice concentrate, lemon juice, and salt in a small bowl until smooth. Cool the cake in the pan on a wire rack for 20 minutes, then turn it out onto a wire rack placed over a rimmed baking sheet. Brush the still-warm cake with ¼ cup of the glaze and let stand until just warm, about 1 hour. Whisk the remaining ½ cup confectioners' sugar into the remaining glaze and pour evenly over the top of the cake. Using a fork, mix the orange zest and granulated sugar together in a small bowl and sprinkle over the glaze. Cool the cake completely, about 2 hours. (The cake can be stored, tightly wrapped, at room temperature for up to 3 days.) Serve.

Cold-Oven Pound Cake

What is cold-oven pound cake? It is a pound cake that is baked in an oven that has not been preheated; thus the oven is stone-cold when the cake is first placed inside. Our hunt for the origin of this curious recipe took us back over a hundred years. At the turn of the twentieth century, gas lighting was being phased out in favor of newer electric technology. Looking to replace lost revenue, gas companies set their sights on the oven business. One of their marketing gimmicks was to push easy and "thrifty" recipes, like cold-oven pound cake, that didn't require preheating the oven. This cake became popular throughout the South and was later reported to be Elvis Presley's favorite pound cake. It is described as rising tall without the aid of chemical leaveners like baking powder or baking soda. The cake is also purported to have a light, tender crumb with a surprisingly crisp crust. We were intrigued and set out to develop our own version.

We gathered several existing recipes and headed to the kitchen. Although most of the cakes lacked the lift and tenderness that we'd read about, one contemporary recipe showed promise; it did, however, contain a nontraditional ingredient: baking powder. The addition of just ½ teaspoon of this leavener (less than half the amount used for standard pound cake) produced a consistently lofty, even rise. We were able to get away with using so little because baking powder is double-acting (it produces carbon dioxide bubbles—and thus rise—when mixed with liquid and then again in the heat of the oven); putting the cake into a cold oven meant that the gluten did not set up as quickly, allowing the carbon dioxide more time to produce greater rise.

Though grand in stature, the cake was still too dense. To create a lighter crumb, we exchanged the heavy cream from the working recipe for leaner whole milk. This helped a little, but swapping out all-purpose flour for cake flour yielded an even finer, more delicate crumb. Baking the cake on the lower-middle rack of an oven turned to 325 degrees ensured an evenly cooked cake with a crisp, golden crust.

COLD-OVEN POUND CAKE

SERVES 12

This cake is made in a tube pan. It must be started in a cold oven; the recipe will not work in a preheated oven.

3	cups cake flour
½	teaspoon baking powder
1	teaspoon salt
1	cup whole milk, room temperature
2	teaspoons vanilla extract
20	tablespoons (2½ sticks) unsalted butter, softened
2½	cups sugar
6	large eggs, room temperature

1. Grease and flour a 16-cup tube pan. Whisk the flour, baking powder, and salt together in a medium bowl. In a small bowl, whisk the milk and vanilla together.

2. In a large bowl, beat the butter and sugar together with an electric mixer on medium speed until light and fluffy, 3 to 6 minutes. Beat in the eggs, one at a time, until combined, about 1 minute.

3. Reduce the mixer speed to low and beat in one-third of the flour mixture, followed by half of the milk mixture. Repeat with half of the remaining flour mixture and the remaining milk mixture. Beat in the remaining flour mixture until just incorporated.

4. Scrape the batter into the prepared pan and smooth the top. Wipe any drops of batter off the sides of the pan and gently tap the pan on the work surface to settle the batter. Adjust an oven rack to the lower-middle position and place the cake on the rack. Set the oven to 325 degrees and turn it on; bake the cake, without opening the oven door, until a toothpick inserted in the center comes out with a few moist crumbs attached, 70 to 80 minutes.

5. Let the cake cool in the pan for 10 minutes. Run a small knife around the edge of the cake to loosen it, then flip it out onto a wire rack. Turn the cake right side up and let it cool completely, about 2 hours, before serving.

Classic Lemon Pound Cake

Pound cake has been around for a long time (it was popular in colonial America), but that doesn't mean that most recipes for it are reliable. It often turns out heavy, leaden, and dry, when it should be rich, buttery, and moist.

The easily memorized ingredient list (1 pound each of butter, sugar, eggs, and flour) and instructions (beat softened butter and sugar until fluffy, add eggs, and finish with flour) probably explain its longevity. Since pound cake predates the widespread availability of chemical leaveners by about 150 years, traditional recipes don't contain baking powder. As a result, the only air in the batter comes from creaming the butter and sugar. If the butter is too warm or too cold (and there's little margin for error), the cake turns out not airy and tender but dense and tough.

Several years ago the test kitchen developed a recipe that skirted this problem by using melted butter and the whirring action of the food processor to ensure its even incorporation. But not everyone has a big food processor. Could we devise a less radical solution to make this recipe more reliable—one that would employ an electric mixer and the classic mixing method?

To lighten the load, many modern recipes include baking powder. Some of the recipes we tested went overboard, and the texture of the resulting cakes was like that of a fluffy layer cake. In the end, we found that a half-teaspoon of baking powder was enough to lighten the texture. The crumb was still fine and compact, but it wasn't quite so leaden.

We realized we needed to try something a bit bolder, and we wondered if a dairy ingredient (usually not part of the pound cake formula) would help. Milk turned the cake springy and layer-cake-like, and cream cheese imparted an odd flavor that reminded tasters of a breakfast Danish. Sour cream, however, transformed the cake, making the crumb tender and moist. Creaming the butter and sugar was still an important step, but the recipe was no longer so fickle.

It was time to introduce lemon into the equation. Lemon juice was losing most of its punch in the oven, so we determined that a mix of juice and zest was a must. Beating the zest with the sugar helped to release its flavorful oils. But even hefty amounts of juice and zest got us only so far. Some recipes resort to lemon extract, but this gave the cake an artificial flavor. Lemon syrup (nothing more than lemon juice simmered with sugar), brushed over the cake once it emerged from the oven, was a better option. We added another blast of lemon by replacing the usual milk in the white glaze spread over the cooled cake with lemon juice.

CLASSIC LEMON POUND CAKE

SERVES 8

The test kitchen found this cake to be more moist the day after it was baked. In fact, when tightly wrapped, the cake will stay fresh for up to 5 days.

CAKE

1¾	cups all-purpose flour
½	teaspoon baking powder
½	teaspoon salt
¼	cup sour cream
1½	tablespoons fresh lemon juice
1½	tablespoons grated fresh lemon zest
1	cup plus 2 tablespoons granulated sugar
16	tablespoons (2 sticks) unsalted butter, softened
5	large eggs, room temperature, beaten

SYRUP

¼	cup granulated sugar
¼	cup fresh lemon juice (3 lemons)

GLAZE

½	cup confectioners' sugar, sifted
1	tablespoon fresh lemon juice

1. FOR THE CAKE: Adjust an oven rack to the middle position and heat the oven to 325 degrees. Grease and flour a 9 by 5-inch loaf pan. Sift the flour, baking powder, and salt into a bowl. Stir the sour cream and lemon juice together in a second bowl.

2. Using your fingers, toss the lemon zest and granulated sugar together in a large bowl until the clumps are gone. Add the butter and beat with an electric mixer at medium-high speed until light and fluffy, 3 to 6 minutes. Scrape down the sides of the bowl. Add the beaten eggs in three additions, mixing until smooth and scraping down the bowl after each addition (the mixture will begin to look curdled). With the mixer on low, add one-third of the flour mixture, followed by half of the sour cream mixture. Repeat with half of the remaining flour mixture and the remaining sour cream mixture. Beat in the remaining flour mixture until combined. Scrape down the bowl, then mix on low speed until smooth, about 30 seconds. Give the batter a final stir with a rubber spatula to make sure it is thoroughly combined.

3. Scrape the batter into the prepared pan, smooth the top, and gently tap the pan on the work surface to settle the batter. Bake until golden brown and a toothpick inserted in the center comes out with a few crumbs attached, 55 to 70 minutes.

4. FOR THE SYRUP: While the cake bakes, stir the granulated sugar and lemon juice together in a saucepan over medium-high heat until the sugar dissolves. Simmer for 2 minutes, remove from the heat, and set aside.

5. Cool the cake in the pan on a wire rack for 10 minutes, then turn it out onto the rack. Brush the top and sides of the still-warm cake with the syrup and cool completely, about 2 hours.

6. FOR THE GLAZE: Whisk together the confectioners' sugar and lemon juice in a bowl until smooth. Spread the glaze over the cake, allowing some to drip down the sides. Let the glaze set for at least 15 minutes before serving.

Tennessee Stack Cake

This eight-layer cake, an Appalachian specialty, is known by various names, including Apple Stack Cake, Pioneer Stack Cake, and Washday Stack Cake. The last name refers to how the cookie-like layers were often baked on washday and then layered with an apple filling and left to sit for a day or two before being served. As the cake sits, the cookie-like layers soak up moisture from the apple filling and soften, becoming tender and cake-like in the process. We'd never seen a cake quite like this before and were eager to start research on developing our own version.

Starting with the filling, we found that recipes most often relied on applesauce or apple butter. We prepared recipes using each. The applesauce tasted fine, but it was too fluid and turned the cake mushy, rather than just softening it. Apple butter was best—fluid, but not too much so. Next we tried apple butter made with fresh apples and apple butter made with dried apples (dried apples were a common mountain staple). The flavor of the butter made with dried apples was intense and a winner with tasters. We pitted jarred apple butter, hoping to take advantage of its convenience, against our own homemade

version, but everyone preferred the homemade butter spiced with cinnamon, cloves, and allspice.

With our filling set, we turned to the cake layers. The cake batter is more akin to cookie batter—stiff enough to roll out. But the mixing method is very much like that of a cake: butter and sugar are creamed together, and then the dry ingredients (flour, baking powder, baking soda) are incorporated in stages, alternating with the wet ingredients (buttermilk, eggs, and vanilla). Once the dough comes together, it's divided into portions and rolled out. We found that using a cake pan as a template ensures that the layers line up perfectly.

It didn't take us long to determine the proportions of the ingredients, but we did wrestle with spicing our cake layers. Traditionally, the layers are flavored with ginger, or sometimes cinnamon, but we decided to leave the spices out and simply let the spiced apple butter infuse the cake with its warm flavor.

Once the layers cooled, we spread them with the apple butter, stacked them, and then set the cake aside in the refrigerator to set up. We hoped we didn't have to wait 2 days to enjoy the cake (as is tradition), but we did have to wait 24 hours—any sooner and the cake layers weren't sufficiently softened.

MAKING TENNESSEE STACK CAKE

1. After dividing the dough into eighths, roll out 1 piece of the dough into a 10-inch circle.

2. Using a 9-inch cake pan as a template, cut out a neat circle from the dough.

3. Gently slide the dough round onto a removable tart pan bottom and transfer to one of the baking sheets.

4. Place one layer on a serving plate and spread with ¾ cup filling. Repeat, leaving the final layer plain.

TENNESSEE STACK CAKE

SERVES 10 TO 12

This cake takes a while to create, but each step is simple and the dough rounds that form each layer are sturdy and easy to handle. Be sure to let the cake set at least 24 hours, as the moisture from the filling transforms the texture of the cookie-like layers into a tender apple-flavored cake.

FILLING

3	(6-ounce) bags dried apples
1	cup packed light brown sugar
1½	teaspoons ground cinnamon
½	teaspoon ground cloves
½	teaspoon ground allspice

LAYERS

6	cups all-purpose flour
1	tablespoon baking powder
1	teaspoon baking soda
¼	teaspoon salt
½	cup buttermilk
2	large eggs
1	teaspoon vanilla extract
16	tablespoons (2 sticks) unsalted butter, softened
2	cups granulated sugar
	Confectioners' sugar for dusting

1. FOR THE FILLING: Bring the apples and water to cover to a boil in a large saucepan. Reduce the heat and simmer until the apples are completely softened, about 10 minutes. Drain the apples and let cool until just warm, about 15 minutes. Puree the apples in a food processor until smooth. Transfer to a bowl and stir in the brown sugar, cinnamon, cloves, and allspice. (The filling can be refrigerated for up to 2 days.)

2. FOR THE LAYERS: Adjust the oven racks to the upper-middle and lower-middle positions and heat the oven to 350 degrees. Grease two baking sheets. Whisk the flour, baking powder, baking soda, and salt together in a medium bowl. Whisk together the buttermilk, eggs, and vanilla in a large measuring cup.

3. In a large bowl, beat the butter and granulated sugar together with an electric mixer at medium-high speed until light and fluffy, 3 to 6 minutes. Beat in half of the flour mixture, followed by half of the buttermilk mixture. Repeat with the remaining flour mixture and the remaining buttermilk mixture, beating until combined. (The dough will be thick.)

4. Divide the dough into 8 equal portions. Following the photos on page 493, work with 2 portions at a time on a lightly floured surface, rolling each out into a 10-inch circle about ⅛ inch thick. Using a 9-inch cake pan as a template, trim away the excess dough to form two perfectly round 9-inch disks. Transfer the disks to the prepared baking sheets and bake until golden brown, 10 to 12 minutes, switching and rotating the baking sheets halfway through baking. Transfer the disks to wire racks and cool completely, at least 1 hour. Repeat with the remaining dough. (The layers can be wrapped tightly in plastic wrap and stored at room temperature for up to 2 days.)

5. TO ASSEMBLE THE CAKE: Place 1 layer on a serving plate and spread with ¾ cup of the filling. Repeat six times. Top with the final layer, wrap tightly in plastic wrap, and refrigerate until the layers soften, at least 24 hours or up to 2 days. Dust with confectioners' sugar and serve.

TENNESSEE STACK CAKE (page 494)

TOP: **BOSTON CREAM CUPCAKES** (page 483), **SAND TARTS** (page 449)
BOTTOM: **HOT FUDGE PUDDING CAKE** (page 473), **SEVEN-LAYER BARS** (page 461)

WHOOPIE PIES (page 446)

TOP: **TRES LECHES CAKE** (page 515), **NEW ORLEANS BOURBON BREAD PUDDING** (page 567)
BOTTOM: **RUSTIC PEACH CAKE** (page 511), **MIXED-BERRY STREUSEL PIE** (page 547)

MISSISSIPPI MUD BROWNIES (page 460)

TOP: **CHOCOLATE BLACKOUT CAKE** (page 477), **STRAWBERRY POKE CAKE** (page 514)
BOTTOM: **ICEBOX OREO CHEESECAKE** (page 520), **APPLE SLAB PIE** (page 529)

ICEBOX KEY LIME PIE (page 549)

CLASSIC LEMON POUND CAKE (page 492)

Old-Fashioned Spice Cake

Spice cake should be moist and substantial, with spices that are warm and bold without being overpowering. And a great spice cake isn't complete without a thick layer of rich, tangy cream cheese frosting. Looking to develop our ideal spice cake, we decided to do a little research in our library, where we found as many variations on the spice cake theme as there are cooks to make them. We found Bundt cakes with raisins and nuts; squat, square versions that resembled gingerbread or carrot cake; cakes calling for everything from apples and stewed figs to chocolate chips and pumpkin puree. Some had spice overload, tasting gritty and dusty. Others were so lacking in spice flavor that it seemed as if a cinnamon stick had only been waved in their general direction. In fact, other than a mixture of warm spices, there were few common denominators linking any of these desserts. And, unfortunately, not one had the old-fashioned simplicity of the frosted spice cake we sought. We would have to begin from scratch.

We started with a favorite recipe for yellow cake.

But simply adding spices to this recipe didn't work. The cake crumbled under the heavy frosting, and the spice flavor was overwhelming. To add volume and heft, we replaced the cake flour used in that recipe with all-purpose flour. The switch made for a slightly tougher, drier cake. Adding more yolks to the batter increased the cake's tenderness; so did switching from milk to buttermilk, which also enriched the cake's flavor. Doubling the amount of dairy from ½ cup to 1 cup was enough to fix the dryness issue.

We wanted our cake to be spicy and looked to techniques the test kitchen has used to get the most out of the spices. We knew from preparing curries and chili that heating spices (either through dry-toasting them or blooming them in hot oil) intensifies their aroma. This is because heat drives moisture out of the spice, carrying the aromatic oils along with it. Both techniques created a fuller-flavored cake, but dry-toasting the spices was not as successful as blooming them in oil. Toasting allows more of the piquant aromas to escape into the air; because the aromatic oils are soluble in cooking oil, blooming the spices was a more effective way of making sure the oils made it into the cake.

KEYS TO SPICE FLAVOR

1. Browning the butter imparts a faint nuttiness that deepens the cake's spice flavor.

2. Blooming the spices in the browned butter brings out their volatile oils, boosting their impact.

3. Molasses adds a bittersweet note that underscores the warm flavor of the spices.

4. Finely grated ginger adds a fresh, zesty quality to the cake that dried ginger can't provide.

Up to this point, we had been using ground cinnamon, cloves, cardamom, allspice, and nutmeg. The mixture contributed a respectable spiciness to the cake, but we wanted more complexity. We found that a tablespoon of grated fresh ginger added noticeable zing. For yet another flavor dimension, we replaced the oil we had been using to bloom the spices with browned butter, which imparted a faint nuttiness and filled out the overall taste of the cake. As a finishing touch, we incorporated a couple of tablespoons of molasses into the batter—just enough to balance the spices with a slight bittersweet nuance without turning the cake into gingerbread.

Once we spread the cake with our cream cheese frosting, tasters gave their thumbs up, but a few of us thought that there seemed to be some discord between the frosting and the cake. One test cook suggested adding some of the spices from the cake to the frosting. While optional, this step gave the frosting a subtle yet perceptible flavor that made it work beautifully with the cake.

OLD-FASHIONED SPICE CAKE WITH CREAM CHEESE FROSTING

SERVES 15 TO 18

Fresh ginger, as opposed to dried ground ginger, gives this cake a brighter flavor. You can serve the cake right out of the pan, in which case you'll need only 3 cups of frosting for the top of the cake.

CAKE

- 1 tablespoon ground cinnamon
- ¾ teaspoon ground cardamom
- ½ teaspoon ground allspice
- ½ teaspoon ground cloves
- ¼ teaspoon ground nutmeg
- 16 tablespoons (2 sticks) unsalted butter, cut into 16 pieces and softened
- 2¼ cups all-purpose flour
- ½ teaspoon baking powder
- ½ teaspoon baking soda
- ½ teaspoon salt
- 2 large eggs plus 3 large egg yolks, room temperature
- 1 teaspoon vanilla extract
- 1¾ cups granulated sugar
- 2 tablespoons light or mild molasses
- 1 tablespoon grated fresh ginger
- 1 cup buttermilk, room temperature

CREAM CHEESE FROSTING

- 2 (8-ounce) packages cream cheese, softened
- 10 tablespoons (1¼ sticks) unsalted butter, cut into chunks and softened
- 2 tablespoons sour cream
- 1½ teaspoons vanilla extract
- ¼ teaspoon salt
- 2 cups confectioners' sugar

1. FOR THE CAKE: Adjust an oven rack to the middle position and heat the oven to 350 degrees. Grease a 13 by 9-inch baking pan, then line the bottom with parchment paper.

2. Combine the cinnamon, cardamom, allspice, cloves, and nutmeg in a small bowl; reserve ½ teaspoon of the spice mixture for the frosting, if desired. Melt 4 tablespoons of the butter in a small skillet over medium heat and continue to cook, swirling the pan constantly, until the butter is light brown, 3 to 6 minutes. Stir in the spice mixture and cook until fragrant, about 15 seconds. Set the mixture aside to cool slightly.

3. In a medium bowl, whisk the flour, baking powder, baking soda, and salt together. In a small bowl, whisk the eggs, egg yolks, and vanilla together.

4. In a large bowl, beat together the remaining 12 tablespoons butter, the granulated sugar, and molasses with an electric mixer on medium-high speed until light and fluffy, 3 to 6 minutes. Beat in the ginger, cooled butter-spice mixture, and half of the egg mixture until combined, about 30 seconds. Beat in the remaining egg mixture until combined, about 30 seconds.

5. Reduce the mixer speed to low and beat in one-third of the flour mixture, followed by half of the buttermilk. Repeat with half of the remaining flour mixture and the remaining buttermilk. Beat in the remaining flour mixture until just combined.

6. Give the batter a final stir with a rubber spatula to make sure it is thoroughly combined. Scrape the batter into the prepared pan, smooth the top, and gently tap the pan on the work surface to settle the batter. Bake the cake until a toothpick inserted in the center comes out with a few moist crumbs attached, 30 to 35 minutes, rotating the pan halfway through baking.

7. FOR THE FROSTING: Meanwhile, beat the cream cheese, butter, sour cream, vanilla, reserved spices (if using), and salt together in a large bowl with an electric mixer on medium-high speed until smooth, 2 to 4 minutes. Reduce the mixer speed to medium-low, slowly add the confectioners' sugar, and beat until smooth, 4 to 6 minutes. Increase the mixer speed to medium-high and beat until the frosting is light and fluffy, 4 to 6 minutes.

8. Let the cake cool completely in the pan, about 2 hours. Run a small knife around the edge of the cake and flip the cake out onto a wire rack. Peel off the parchment paper, then flip the cake right side up onto a serving platter. Spread the frosting evenly over the top and sides of the cake and serve.

SHOPPING WITH THE TEST KITCHEN

Inexpensive Standing Mixers: If you plan on baking with any frequency, a standing mixer is an invaluable piece of equipment because it makes mixing easy and kneading a breeze. Unfortunately, not all brands of standing mixers are created equal. In the process of testing the top-selling standing mixers here in the test kitchen, we found that some models are simply too difficult and frustrating to work with to make them worthwhile purchases. Our favorite standing mixer is the Cuisinart 5.5-Quart Stand Mixer ($349), but the average home cook doesn't need this much power. If you're looking for a good standing mixer but need less muscle and want to spend far less money, we recommend the KitchenAid Classic Plus Stand Mixer ($199), which features a 4.5-quart bowl, enameled metal dough hook and paddle, and metal whisk. While not as powerful as more expensive models, it aced our tests and testers praised its intuitive controls and solid feel.

Tropical Carrot Cake

Existing somewhere between health food and decadent dessert, carrot cake was the cake to make during the 1960s. And it wasn't long before cooks came up with variations like chocolate, banana, and our favorite, tropical carrot cake. Building on the warm flavors of traditional carrot cake, the tropical version adds coconut, pineapple, dried fruit (papaya, mango, or raisins), and macadamia nuts.

But when making several of these cakes, we found quite a few problems. The most obvious was the flavor—or lack thereof. Tasters were hard-pressed to identify anything tropical. The texture was even worse; a regular carrot cake can be made soggy by the carrots and oil, but tropical carrot cake compounds the problem by including juicy pineapple. And the dried fruit and nuts made the cake too heavy, like bad fruitcake. Tasters told us they wanted coconut and pineapple to be the predominant flavors, so the nuts and dried fruit were out. We set out to make a light, moist cake with big hits of coconut and pineapple.

Starting with the coconut, we wanted to intensify its profile in the cake while eliminating its stringy texture. Toasting the coconut improved the flavor incrementally, but it made the stringy bits even tougher. Thinking about how some recipes use flavored sugars (vanilla sugar being the most common), we wondered what would happen if we ground the coconut and sugar into a powder in the food processor. This worked great; the stringy texture was gone, and the grinding extracted maximum coconut flavor.

Moving on to the pineapple, we tried building flavor by substituting pureed canned pineapple for some of the oil in the recipe. Unfortunately, it added weak flavor and was too wet (even when drained before pureeing). Frozen pineapple chunks worked much better, adding fresher flavor—although not quite enough of it—and a drier texture.

Since we were looking for concentrated pineapple flavor, it made sense to try frozen pineapple juice concentrate; we mixed the concentrate with the pureed frozen pineapple and cooked it down with a little cornstarch to evaporate excess moisture. We added this homemade pudding to the cake batter in place of much of the oil; we knew we were on to something when, after the cake had been in the oven for 20 minutes, the test kitchen was filled with the aromas of coconut and pineapple. Tasters lined up to try this fluffy cake, and then they came back for seconds.

A plain cream cheese frosting was good, but we wanted to add another layer of tropical flavors. Since we had some extra pudding mixture, we tried incorporating it into the cream cheese frosting; it worked like a charm. To put this dessert over the top, we toasted coconut and pressed it into the sides and on top of the cake. Tasters approved our carrot cake with a light, full-flavored tropical accent.

TROPICAL CARROT CAKE

SERVES 8 TO 10

You'll need one 14-ounce bag of sweetened shredded coconut for both the cake and the frosting.

PUDDING

1	pound frozen pineapple chunks, thawed
½	cup frozen pineapple juice concentrate, thawed
6	tablespoons cornstarch

CAKE

2½	cups all-purpose flour
1	tablespoon baking powder
4	teaspoons pumpkin pie spice
¾	teaspoon ground ginger
½	teaspoon salt
¾	pound carrots (about 5 medium), peeled and cut into 1-inch chunks
1	cup sweetened shredded coconut (see note above)
1¼	cups granulated sugar
½	cup packed light brown sugar
4	large eggs
1½	cups vegetable oil

FROSTING

12	tablespoons (1½ sticks) unsalted butter, softened
3	cups confectioners' sugar
2	(8-ounce) packages cream cheese, cut into 8 pieces and softened
	Pinch salt
3	cups sweetened shredded coconut, toasted (see page 461)

1. FOR THE PUDDING: Process the pineapple chunks and concentrate in a food processor until smooth. Transfer to a medium saucepan and whisk in the cornstarch until smooth. Bring to a simmer over medium heat and cook, stirring constantly,

until thickened, about 2 minutes. Transfer to a bowl and refrigerate until cold, at least 1½ hours.

2. FOR THE CAKE: Adjust an oven rack to the middle position and heat the oven to 350 degrees. Spray two 9-inch cake pans with vegetable oil spray. Line the pans with parchment paper and spray the parchment with vegetable oil spray. Whisk the flour, baking powder, pumpkin pie spice, ginger, and salt together in a large bowl.

3. Process the carrots in a food processor until finely ground. Transfer to a large bowl and wipe the processor bowl dry. Process the coconut with the granulated sugar until the coconut is finely chopped. Add the brown sugar and eggs and blend until the mixture is smooth, about 1 minute. With the machine running, slowly pour in the oil and process until combined.

4. Transfer the mixture to the bowl with the carrots. Add the flour mixture and ¾ cup of the pudding mixture and stir until no streaks of flour remain. Scrape into the prepared pans, smooth the tops, and gently tap the pans on the counter to settle the batter. Bake the cakes until a toothpick inserted into the center of the cake comes out clean, 30 to 35 minutes, rotating the pans halfway through baking. Cool the cakes in the pans for 10 minutes, then turn them out onto a wire rack, peel off the parchment paper, and let cool completely, about 2 hours.

5. FOR THE FROSTING: In a large bowl, beat the butter and confectioners' sugar together with an electric mixer at medium-high speed until fluffy, about 2 minutes. Add the cream cheese, one piece at a time, and beat until incorporated. Beat in the remaining pineapple pudding and salt. (The mixture will appear slightly grainy.) Refrigerate until ready to use.

6. When the cakes are cooled, spread 2 cups of the frosting on one cake. Top with the second cake and spread the top and sides with the remaining frosting. Refrigerate for 15 minutes. Sprinkle the toasted coconut on the top, press into the sides of the cake, and serve.

Pumpkin Cake with Cream Cheese Frosting

Pumpkin cake, made with canned pumpkin, should be moist and velvety, with just the right balance of pumpkin and spice, but too often the result is damp cake with a harsh burn of spice.

Canned pumpkin pie filling proved to be too watery and spicy. Instead we reached for the other canned pumpkin product at the supermarket, 100 percent packed pumpkin puree, which contains just pumpkin and no spices. The cake made with the puree actually tasted pumpkin-y. Using the puree also meant we could control the amount of spice; we used 2 teaspoons of cinnamon and ¼ teaspoon each of ground ginger and allspice to add a subtle spiciness to the cake.

The texture of our cake was still too wet. Our working recipe used 1½ cups of oil; we tried reducing the amount. Anything less than a cup resulted in dry cakes with no structure, but the lone cup of oil was still producing cakes that were too heavy and wet. We finally found the solution in one recipe that instructed us to beat the oil, eggs, and sugar together until they were creamy and emulsified (which took just a few minutes). Because the oil was suspended in the other ingredients, it didn't have a chance to saturate the cake, which was now soft, moist, and velvety. Finished with tangy cream cheese frosting, this full-flavored pumpkin cake was finally complete.

PUMPKIN CAKE WITH CREAM CHEESE FROSTING

SERVES 15 TO 18

You can serve the cake right out of the pan, in which case you'll need only 3 cups of frosting for the top of the cake.

2	cups all-purpose flour
2	teaspoons ground cinnamon
2	teaspoons baking powder
1	teaspoon baking soda
1	teaspoon salt
¼	teaspoon ground allspice
¼	teaspoon ground ginger
1⅔	cups sugar
1	cup vegetable oil
4	large eggs, room temperature
1	(15-ounce) can plain pumpkin puree
1	recipe Cream Cheese Frosting (page 504)

1. Adjust an oven rack to the middle position and heat the oven to 350 degrees. Grease a 13 by 9-inch baking pan, then line the bottom with parchment paper. Whisk the flour, cinnamon, baking powder, baking soda, salt, allspice, and ginger together in a medium bowl.

2. In a large bowl, beat the sugar, oil, and eggs together with an electric mixer on medium-high speed until thick and fluffy, about 5 minutes. Reduce the mixer speed to low and beat in the pumpkin puree until combined, about 1 minute. Slowly beat in the flour mixture until just incorporated, about 30 seconds.

3. Give the batter a final stir with a rubber spatula to make sure it is thoroughly combined. Scrape the batter into the prepared pan, smooth the top, and gently tap the pan on the work surface to settle the batter. Bake the cake until a toothpick inserted in the center comes out with a few moist crumbs

attached, 30 to 35 minutes, rotating the pan halfway through baking.

4. Let the cake cool completely in the pan, about 2 hours. Run a small knife around the edge of the cake and flip the cake out onto a wire rack. Peel off the parchment paper, then flip the cake right side up onto a serving platter. Spread the frosting evenly over the top and sides of the cake and serve.

Blue Ribbon Apple Cake

Most apple cakes are nothing more than spice cakes with a few pieces of cubed raw apples tossed in. We'd rather have a slice of spice cake with a fresh apple on the side! We wanted a cake with big apple flavor, so we got busy in the test kitchen.

Apple cake recipes call for all sorts of different batters, from a simple American yellow cake to a rich French butter cake, but our favorite was a sour cream cake batter, which produced a fine, tender crumb. This rich cake paired nicely with the apples. The batter is unusual in that room-temperature butter is beaten into the dry ingredients.

The apples, however, were a big problem. When they were left raw, the cake was so bad that we ended up tossing it into the trash. The apples obviously needed some precooking, so we decided to try a quick sauté with sugar in a skillet first. We discovered that the apples must be cooked to the point at which the juices reduce and thicken. Otherwise, the cake ends up sitting in a puddle, hardly the effect we were looking for. But we still weren't getting enough caramel flavor. The best—and easiest—solution was to use light brown sugar.

Now we had good apple flavor, but we were bothered by the final look of this dessert. We had been treating it like an old-fashioned upside-down cake: once the apples were caramelized, we added the batter to the skillet and then put the whole thing in the oven. This made for a messy cake (it often fell apart during unmolding), so we decided to transfer the cooked apple mixture to a 9-inch cake pan before adding the batter. Now we had a much prettier, more compact cake, and it wasn't much more work.

We also discovered that the cake should be inverted onto a platter about 10 minutes after it comes out of the oven. This allows enough time for the cake to set slightly but not enough for the caramel to harden. Once the cake was inverted, we found it best to let it sit a bit—gravity helps the cake and apples release without too much banging. At last, we had an apple cake in which the apple was truly the star.

BLUE RIBBON APPLE CAKE

SERVES 8

We like to use Granny Smith apples here because they hold their shape nicely and have a tart flavor. Cortland apples, although they are less tart, can be substituted. Serve with vanilla ice cream or whipped cream.

APPLES

4	tablespoons unsalted butter
½	cup packed light brown sugar
1½	pounds Granny Smith apples (3 to 4 apples; see note above), peeled, cored, and cut into ½-inch slices
⅛	teaspoon salt

CAKE

½	cup sour cream, room temperature
1	large egg plus 1 large egg yolk, room temperature
½	teaspoon vanilla extract
1¼	cups all-purpose flour
¾	cup granulated sugar
½	teaspoon baking powder
¼	teaspoon baking soda
¼	teaspoon salt
8	tablespoons (1 stick) unsalted butter, cut into 8 pieces and softened

1. Adjust an oven rack to the middle position and heat the oven to 350 degrees. Grease and flour a 9-inch cake pan.

2. FOR THE APPLES: Melt the butter in a large heavy-bottomed skillet over medium-high heat. Stir in the brown sugar and cook, swirling the pan occasionally, until the sugar looks dark brown (like dark brown sugar), about 2 minutes. Stir in the apples and salt and cook, stirring often, until the apples have softened slightly and the juices are thickened and syrupy, 5 to 7 minutes. Scrape the apple mixture into the prepared cake pan and lightly press into an even layer.

3. FOR THE CAKE: Whisk the sour cream, egg, egg yolk, and vanilla together in a small bowl. In a large bowl, whisk the flour, granulated sugar, baking powder, baking soda, and salt together. Using an electric mixer on medium-low speed, beat the butter into the flour mixture, one piece at a time, about 30 seconds. Continue to beat the mixture until it resembles moist crumbs, 1 to 3 minutes.

4. Slowly beat in the sour cream mixture until combined, about 30 seconds. Increase the mixer speed to medium and beat the batter until smooth and fluffy, about 1 minute.

5. Spoon the batter over the apples and gently spread it into an even layer. Gently tap the pan on the work surface to settle the batter. Bake the cake until a toothpick inserted in the center comes out with a few moist crumbs attached, 35 to 40 minutes, rotating the pan halfway through baking.

6. Let the cake cool slightly in the pan, about 10 minutes. Place a serving platter over the top of the cake pan, invert the cake, and let sit until the cake releases itself from the pan (do not shake or tap the pan), about 1 minute. Gently remove the cake pan and serve the cake warm or at room temperature.

Rustic Peach Cake

The most popular recipes for peach cake are rustic, single-layer yellow cakes studded with chunks of fresh peaches. We gathered a dozen recipes, bought a bushel of peaches, and got baking to see if we could develop the ultimate version.

These recipes had big problems. Some cakes were made mushy and wet by an excess of peach juice, and others featured chunks of bloated peaches that had sunk to the bottom of the pan. Since peaches inside the cake were causing so many problems, we decided to start with one recipe we'd tried in which peaches were put on top of the cake. The top portion of this cake (where the fruit met the cake) was soggy, but we could fix that problem later.

PREVENTING SOGGY CAKE

1. Chopped dried peaches or apricots soak up the excess peach juice from the fresh peaches, eliminating a soggy cake top.

2. Arrange the peaches in a circular pattern around the edge of the cake, reserving 3 slices to fill in the center.

Tasters liked the fruit on top of this cake, but they didn't love the cake itself, so we shifted to using the test kitchen's recipe for yellow cake, planning to make the necessary adjustments to make it work with fresh peaches. Our first move was to replace the cake flour in the yellow cake with all-purpose flour to create a sturdier crumb that could better support the fruit on top. Instead of the ¼ cup of milk in our recipe we used a few tablespoons of sour cream for a denser, heartier texture. And because the peaches were so sweet, we cut back the amount of sugar from ¾ cup to ½ cup, using a mixture of granulated and light brown sugars for more flavor. Now that we had a rich but sturdy cake base, we could concentrate on fine-tuning the texture of the peaches. To reduce the amount of moisture they were shedding, we tried precooking the peaches, but that muted their fresh flavor. Some recipes call for sugaring the peaches and letting them exude liquid before adding them to the cake, but the peaches continued to weep moisture into the cake no matter how long we let them sit. Tossing the peaches with thickeners like flour, cornstarch, and tapioca only made the peaches gluey.

Since we needed something dry to absorb excess moisture from the peaches, we wondered if dried peaches might work. We chopped a handful of dried peaches and scattered them on top of the cake batter before layering on the sliced fresh peaches. The dried peaches softened beautifully in the oven as they soaked up the flavorful juices from the fresh fruit, resulting in a moist—but not soggy—cake bursting with two layers of peach flavor. As dried peaches aren't always available, we tried using dried apricots and had the same great flavor and results.

RUSTIC PEACH CAKE

SERVES 8

Since overly ripe peaches will make the cake soggy, look for barely ripe peaches that give slightly to the touch. Serve this cake with lightly sweetened whipped cream or a scoop of vanilla ice cream.

PEACHES
¼	cup granulated sugar
¼	teaspoon ground cinnamon
2	medium peaches (see note above), peeled, pitted, and each cut into 8 wedges

CAKE
1	cup all-purpose flour
1	teaspoon baking powder
¼	teaspoon salt
¼	cup granulated sugar
¼	cup packed light brown sugar
8	tablespoons (1 stick) unsalted butter, softened
2	large eggs
2	tablespoons sour cream
1	teaspoon vanilla extract
⅓	cup dried peaches or apricots, chopped fine

1. FOR THE PEACHES: Adjust an oven rack to the middle position and heat the oven to 350 degrees. Grease a 9-inch springform pan. Combine the granulated sugar and cinnamon in a medium bowl; reserve 2 tablespoons of the sugar mixture. Add the peaches to the bowl with the remaining sugar mixture and toss to coat.

2. FOR THE CAKE: Whisk the flour, baking powder, and salt together in a bowl. In a large bowl, beat the sugars and butter together with an electric mixer on medium-high speed until light and fluffy, 3 to 6 minutes. Beat in the eggs, sour cream, and vanilla until incorporated. Reduce the mixer speed

to medium-low. Slowly add the flour mixture and mix until just combined, about 30 seconds. Scrape the batter into the prepared pan. Scatter the dried peaches or apricots over the batter, then arrange the sugared peaches in a circular pattern over the top, reserving 3 slices to fill the middle. Sprinkle the reserved sugar mixture over the peaches.

3. Bake until the cake is golden brown and a toothpick inserted in the center comes out clean, 35 to 45 minutes. Cool at least 1 hour on a wire rack. Serve.

SHOPPING WITH THE TEST KITCHEN

Serrated Vegetable Peelers: Our preferred method for peeling peaches is to use a serrated vegetable peeler. The serrated blade easily removes the peels from soft fruit and vegetables like peaches, plums, and tomatoes. Our favorite serrated peeler, the Messermeister Serrated Swivel Peeler, is available at most kitchen supply stores for about $6. The traditional method of blanching the peaches in hot water and shocking them in an ice bath does work to loosen their skins, but it's a lot more work than using the peeler.

Cranberry Upside-Down Cake

You'd be hard-pressed to find someone who isn't familiar with pineapple upside-down cake, but its cranberry counterpart is far less famous. And that's a shame. This ruby-crowned cake is a visual stunner, and the delicate balance of sweet-tart cranberry topping and tender butter cake makes it every bit as appealing as the pineapple version. But the fruit topping is often thin and runny or, worse, a supersticky candied mess that won't leave the pan at all.

As for the cake itself, though a sturdy texture is a must to support the fruit, most recipes overcompensate and the cakes bake up dry and dense.

We baked a lineup of cakes that ranged from fluffy to leaden in texture, with one coarse-crumbed cake standing out as the tasters' favorite. This cake featured ground almonds, which lent a moist richness and hearty texture to the crumb. The cake was a little heavy, so rather than beating whole eggs into the batter, we added the yolks and then whipped the egg whites separately. Folding the fluffy beaten whites into the finished batter produced a beautiful cake—light and tender but still sturdy enough to support the heavy fruit topping.

Recipes that called for lining the cake pan with berries tossed with sugar produced watery, runny toppings. Precooking the cranberries and sugar on the stovetop to evaporate some of the fruit's moisture proved to be a better option. To make the topping more cohesive, we strained out the berries after 4 minutes and continued to reduce the juices to a thick syrup.

The topping now had the right consistency, but it was a little too tart. Increasing the amount of sugar made the topping taste like candy, and after trying sweeteners like honey, maple syrup, and corn syrup, tasters settled on raspberry jam, which perfectly rounded out the tartness of the cranberries and enhanced the fruit flavor of the topping. We now had a cranberry upside-down cake that wowed both the eyes and the palate.

CRANBERRY UPSIDE-DOWN CAKE

SERVES 8

To prevent this cake from sticking, do not let it cool in the pan for more than 10 minutes before turning it out.

TOPPING

6	tablespoons unsalted butter
3	cups fresh or defrosted frozen cranberries
¾	cup sugar
2	tablespoons seedless raspberry jam
½	teaspoon vanilla extract

CAKE

¼	cup blanched slivered almonds
1	cup all-purpose flour
1	teaspoon baking powder
¼	teaspoon salt
½	cup whole milk
½	teaspoon vanilla extract
½	teaspoon almond extract
6	tablespoons unsalted butter, softened
¾	cup sugar
3	large eggs, separated

1. FOR THE TOPPING: Adjust an oven rack to the middle position and heat the oven to 350 degrees. Grease and flour a 9-inch cake pan, line the bottom with parchment paper, and spray with vegetable oil spray. Melt the butter in a large nonstick skillet over medium heat. Add the cranberries, sugar, and jam and cook until the cranberries are just softened, about 4 minutes. Strain the cranberry mixture over a bowl, reserving the juices.

2. Add the strained juices to the empty skillet and simmer over medium heat until syrupy and reduced to 1 cup, about 4 minutes. Off the heat, stir in the vanilla. Arrange the strained berries in a single layer in the prepared pan. Pour the juice mixture over the berries and refrigerate for 30 minutes.

3. FOR THE CAKE: Process the almonds and ¼ cup of the flour in a food processor until finely ground. Add the remaining ¾ cup flour, the baking powder, and salt and pulse to combine. Whisk the milk and extracts together in a measuring cup. In a large bowl, beat together the butter and sugar with an electric mixer on medium speed until light and fluffy, 3 to 6 minutes. Beat in the egg yolks, one at a time, until combined. Reduce the mixer speed to low and add one-third of the flour mixture, followed by half of the milk mixture. Repeat with half of the remaining flour mixture and the remaining milk mixture. Beat in the remaining flour mixture.

4. Using a clean bowl and beaters, beat the egg whites on medium-high speed until they hold soft peaks, about 2 minutes. Whisk one-third of the whites into the batter, then fold in the remaining whites. Pour the batter over the chilled cranberry mixture and bake until a toothpick inserted in the center comes out clean, 35 to 40 minutes, rotating the pan halfway through baking. Cool on a wire rack for 10 minutes, then run a small knife around the edge of the cake and invert onto a serving plate. Serve.

Strawberry Poke Cake

Strawberry poke cake, a tender white cake streaked with strawberry gelatin, was invented by Kraft Kitchens in 1969 as a vehicle to increase strawberry Jell-O sales. Most corporate recipes are quickly forgotten, but strawberry poke cake became extremely popular, thanks to its festive look and ease of assembly. The original recipe has only three ingredients: strawberry Jell-O, white cake mix, and whipped cream. Strawberries, cake, and cream sounded pretty good to us.

But when we made this cake, our optimism quickly faded. The boxed-mix cake was so tender and fine that the hot gelatin made it soggy, especially around the edges, where the domed shape of the cake had channeled most of the liquid. And the strawberry gelatin was bright in color but dim in flavor. We headed into the test kitchen to see if we could make a sturdier cake with fresh strawberry flavor.

We eschewed a boxed cake in favor of the test kitchen's recipe for white cake; it worked perfectly, giving us a sturdy crumb and little doming, which

meant the gelatin mixture didn't pool around the edges of the pan.

Using strawberry gelatin as the streaking agent gave the cake beautiful red stripes. We now needed some berry flavor. Strawberry soda and syrup both tasted artificial, and strawberry jams and jellies looked and tasted washed-out. Pureed fresh strawberries produced inconsistent results, as sometimes the berries were soft and sweet and other times they were hard and sour. We turned to frozen strawberries, which are reliably sweet. Blending and straining the frozen berries gave us the best flavor, but the texture was too thick.

A colleague suggested cooking the frozen strawberries with orange juice and sugar. This released strawberry juice, which, when strained out of the solids and mixed with the strawberry gelatin, was thin enough to pour and potent with rich strawberry flavor. Our cake now tasted as good as it looked.

We made a homemade "jam" from the leftover berry solids and spread the mixture on top of the cake for an extra layer of flavor. When it was topped with sweetened whipped cream and served cold, we could finally see—and taste—why strawberry poke cake has remained so popular.

MAKING STRAWBERRY POKE CAKE

1. Using a wooden skewer, poke about 50 deep holes all over the top of the cake, being careful not to poke all the way through to the bottom.

2. Slowly pour the cooled gelatin mixture evenly over the entire surface of the cake. Cover and refrigerate until the gelatin is set, about 3 hours.

STRAWBERRY POKE CAKE

SERVES 15 TO 18

The top of the cake will look very dark and slightly overbaked—this helps keeps the cake from becoming too soggy after the gelatin is poured over the top. This cake is sliced and served right out of the cake pan, so it is not necessary to line the pan with parchment paper.

CAKE

2¼	cups all-purpose flour
4	teaspoons baking powder
1	teaspoon salt
1	cup whole milk, room temperature
2	teaspoons vanilla extract
6	large egg whites, room temperature
12	tablespoons (1½ sticks) unsalted butter, softened
1¾	cups sugar

SYRUP AND TOPPING

4	cups frozen sliced strawberries
6	tablespoons sugar
½	cup water
2	tablespoons orange juice
2	tablespoons strawberry-flavored gelatin
2	cups heavy cream, chilled

1. FOR THE CAKE: Adjust an oven rack to the middle position and heat the oven to 350 degrees. Grease and flour a 13 by 9-inch baking pan. Whisk the flour, baking powder, and salt together in a medium bowl. In another medium bowl, whisk the milk, vanilla, and egg whites together.

2. In a large bowl, beat the butter and sugar together with an electric mixer on medium-high speed until light and fluffy, 3 to 6 minutes. Reduce the mixer speed to low and beat in one-third of the flour mixture, followed by half of the milk mixture. Repeat with half of the remaining flour mixture and the remaining milk mixture. Beat in the remaining flour mixture until just incorporated.

3. Give the batter a final stir with a rubber spatula to make sure it is thoroughly combined. Scrape the batter into the prepared pan, smooth the top, and gently tap the pan on the work surface to settle the batter. Bake the cake until a toothpick inserted in the center comes out clean and the top is very brown, about 35 minutes, rotating the pan halfway through baking. Let the cake cool completely in the pan, about 2 hours.

4. FOR THE SYRUP AND TOPPING: Combine 3 cups of the strawberries, 2 tablespoons of the sugar, the water, and orange juice in a medium saucepan, cover, and cook over medium-low heat until the strawberries are softened, about 10 minutes. Strain the mixture into a medium bowl, reserving the strained solids. Whisk the gelatin into the liquid and let cool to room temperature, about 20 minutes.

5. Use a wooden skewer to poke 50 large holes in the cooled cake. Don't poke the cake through to the bottom but do twist the skewer when poking to enlarge the holes. Pour the cooled gelatin mixture evenly over the top of the cake, making sure to cover the holes. Cover the cake with plastic wrap and refrigerate until the gelatin is set, about 3 hours.

6. Pulse the reserved strained strawberries, 2 more tablespoons sugar, and the remaining 1 cup frozen strawberries together in a food processor until the mixture resembles strawberry jam, 5 to 7 pulses. Spread the mixture evenly over the cake.

7. Before serving, whip the cream and remaining 2 tablespoons sugar together with an electric mixer on medium-high speed to soft peaks and spread evenly over the cake. (The cake can be covered in plastic wrap and refrigerated for up to 3 days.)

Tres Leches Cake

Tres leches cake is a sponge cake soaked with a mixture of "three milks" (heavy cream, evaporated milk, and sweetened condensed milk), then topped with whipped cream. This tender, creamy cake is especially popular in south Texas, where the Mexican American community has been making it for generations. We aimed to develop a tres leches cake that was moist (but not mushy) and not overly sweet. We gathered together several recipes found in our cookbook library and got to work.

Most of the cakes we sampled in our testing failed in one or both of those regards. Some recipes produced decent tres leches cakes, but nothing remarkable. One test cook recalled enjoying a tres leches cake spread with a caramel topping called dulce de leche. This flavor addition sounded intriguing, so we regrouped to develop a caramel-accented tres leches cake that was truly moist without being soggy.

Although some make tres leches cake into a layered affair, we preferred the convenience of baking, soaking, and serving the cake all in one 13 by 9-inch baking pan. Many sources suggested that the crumb of a sponge cake did the best job of absorbing the milk mixture, so we started with the test kitchen's sponge cake recipe, which gets its lift from beaten egg whites. It emerged from the oven puffed and golden but sank in the center when we poured on the milk mixture. In search of a sturdier sponge cake, we tried several other recipes, with no success. A colleague finally suggested a "hot milk" sponge, made by heating milk and butter and then pouring the mixture into whipped whole eggs (which are sturdier than just whites). This cake baked up tall and sturdy enough to handle the milk mixture.

Most recipes use one can each of evaporated and sweetened condensed milk (12 and 14 ounces, respectively) and an equal amount of cream. Cutting back the amount of cream to just 1 cup produced a thicker mixture that didn't oversaturate the cake. Many of the recipes we reviewed in our research warned us that the specifics of adding the milk mixture were critical, and they were right. After many tests, we found that pouring room-temperature milk over warm cake worked best.

We next focused on the dulce de leche aspect of our cake. This type of caramel is traditionally made by boiling an unopened can of sweetened condensed milk for about an hour; since we were already using sweetened condensed milk, we wondered if we could cook it down a little to get the dulce de leche flavor inside our cake. Since boiling the can seemed too dangerous, we poured the milk into a bowl and microwaved it until it became slightly thickened and straw-colored. We mixed this with the other milks and poured it over the cake.

With a hint of rich caramel in each custard-laden bite, this was the tres leches cake we had been looking for: one that could pass muster among Texans.

TRES LECHES CAKE

SERVES 15 TO 18

If using a standing mixer to beat the eggs in step 3, be sure to use the whisk attachment. The cake becomes more moist and dense as it sits.

MILK MIXTURE

1	(14-ounce) can sweetened condensed milk
1	(12-ounce) can evaporated milk
1	cup heavy cream
1	teaspoon vanilla extract

CAKE

2	cups all-purpose flour
2	teaspoons baking powder
1	teaspoon salt
½	teaspoon ground cinnamon
1	cup whole milk

8 tablespoons (1 stick) unsalted butter,
   cut into chunks and softened
2 teaspoons vanilla extract
4 large eggs, room temperature
2 cups sugar

FROSTING
1 cup heavy cream
3 tablespoons corn syrup
1 teaspoon vanilla extract

1. FOR THE MILK MIXTURE: Pour the condensed milk into a microwave-safe bowl and cover tightly with plastic wrap. Microwave on medium-low power, stirring often and replacing the plastic wrap several times, until slightly darkened and thickened, 9 to 15 minutes. Gradually whisk in the evaporated milk, cream, and vanilla. Set the mixture aside to cool to room temperature, about 30 minutes.

2. FOR THE CAKE: Adjust an oven rack to the middle position and heat the oven to 325 degrees. Grease and flour a 13 by 9-inch baking pan. Whisk the flour, baking powder, salt, and cinnamon together in a medium bowl. Heat the milk, butter, and vanilla together in a small saucepan over low heat until the butter is melted.

3. In a large bowl, whip the eggs with an electric mixer on medium-high speed and gradually add the sugar, about 1 minute. Continue to whip the mixture until very thick and voluminous, 4 to 8 minutes.

4. Reduce the mixer speed to low and add the melted butter mixture until combined, about 30 seconds. Add the flour mixture, in 2 additions, until incorporated, about 30 seconds. Increase the mixer speed to medium and whip the batter until fully combined and smooth, about 30 seconds.

5. Scrape the batter into the prepared pan, smooth the top, and gently tap the pan on the work surface to settle the batter. Bake the cake until a toothpick inserted in the center comes out with a few crumbs attached, 30 to 35 minutes, rotating the pan halfway through baking. Let the cake cool in the pan for 10 minutes.

6. Using a skewer, poke about 50 holes in the warm cake—you do not need to poke all the way through. Slowly pour the cooled milk mixture over the cake. Let the cake cool for about 15 minutes, then refrigerate it until the milk mixture is completely absorbed and the cake has cooled completely, about 3 hours.

7. FOR THE FROSTING: Let the cake sit at room temperature for 30 minutes. Beat the heavy cream, corn syrup, and vanilla together in a medium bowl with an electric mixer on medium speed to soft peaks, 1 to 2 minutes. Spread the frosting evenly over the top of the cake and serve. (The cake can be covered in plastic wrap and refrigerated for up to 3 days.)

New York Cheesecake

At the core, New York cheesecake is cool, thick, smooth, satiny, and creamy; radiating outward, the texture goes gradually from velvety to suede-like, until finally becoming cake-like and fine-pored at the edges. The flavor is simple and pure and minimalist, sweet and tangy, and rich. We headed into the test kitchen to develop a cheesecake that would truly wow New Yorkers.

We decided to start with the crust and work our way up. A graham cracker crust made with a cup of crumbs, some sugar, and melted butter, pressed into the bottom of the springform pan and prebaked until it was fragrant and brown around the edges, was ideal at a thickness of about ⅜ inch. If served within a day of baking, it retained its crispness. If the cheesecake was held for a couple of days, the crust softened, but tasters didn't seem to mind.

A great New York cheesecake should be of great stature. One made with 2 pounds (four bars) of cream cheese was not tall enough. We threw in another half-pound; the springform pan reached maximum capacity, but the cheesecake stood tall and looked right. The amount of sugar was quickly settled upon—1½ cups. The cheesecake struck a perfect balance of sweet and tangy.

Cheesecakes always require a dairy supplement to the cream cheese, usually either heavy cream or sour cream, or sometimes both. Additional dairy loosens up the texture of the cream cheese, giving the cake a smoother, more luxurious feel. Sour cream, with a tartness of its own, supplemented the tangy quality of the cream cheese. Tasters preferred just ⅓ cup. It was enough to offer a touch of tartness and help give the cheesecake a smoother, creamier texture without advertising its presence.

Eggs help bind the cheesecake and give it structure. They also help create a smooth, creamy texture. We tried as few as four and as many as six whole eggs; these cheesecakes had textures that were called "light" and "fluffy." Recipes for New York cheesecake seem to agree that a few yolks in addition to whole eggs help to get the velvety, lush texture of a proper New York cheesecake. Our testing bore this out, and ultimately we concluded that a generous number of eggs—six whole and two yolks—yield a cheesecake of unparalleled texture: dense but not heavy, firm but not rigid, and perfectly rich.

Perfecting the flavor of the cheesecake was easy. A couple of teaspoons of lemon juice helped to perk up the flavors, and just a bit of salt (cream cheese already contains a good dose of sodium) and a couple of teaspoons of vanilla extract rounded out the flavors. Everyone in the test kitchen appreciated this minimalist cheesecake.

There are many ways to bake a cheesecake: in a moderate oven, in a low oven, in a water bath, and in accordance with the New York method—500 degrees for about 10 minutes, then 200 degrees for about an hour—which appears to be a standard technique. We tried them all, but the New York method was the only one that yielded the nut-brown surface that is a distinguishing mark of an exemplary New York cheesecake. The New York baking method was not without flaws, however. After an hour at 200 degrees, the very center of the cheesecake—even after chilling—was loose and slurpy, a result of underbaking. Some recipes stipulate leaving the cheesecake in the still-warm, turned-off, propped-open oven for about 30 minutes to finish "baking." Handled this way, the cheesecake was marginally better but still insufficiently baked.

We tried extending the hour-long baking time to get the center of the cheesecake to set up to the right consistency. We took it 15 and 30 minutes past an hour. The cheesecake baked for 1½ hours to an internal temperature of about 150 degrees was whisked out of the oven. Chilled, it was cheesecake perfection. It sliced into a neat slab with a cleanly set center texture—not a wet, sloppy one. Each slice kept its shape, and each bite felt satiny on the tongue. At last, we had produced a New York classic that could hold its own in the Big Apple.

NEW YORK CHEESECAKE

SERVES 12

You will need 1 tablespoon of melted butter for brushing the pan in step 4. For neat, professional-looking pieces of cake, wipe the knife clean between slices. Serve as is or with Strawberry, Blueberry, or Peach Topping (pages 518 and 519).

CRUST

  8   **whole graham crackers, broken into 1-inch pieces**

  6   **tablespoons unsalted butter, melted and cooled, plus extra for brushing (see note above)**

  3   **tablespoons sugar**

FILLING

   5   **(8-ounce) packages cream cheese, cut into chunks and softened**

1½   **cups sugar**

⅛   **teaspoon salt**

⅓   **cup sour cream**

   2   **teaspoons fresh lemon juice**

   2   **teaspoons vanilla extract**

   6   **large eggs plus 2 large egg yolks**

1. FOR THE CRUST: Adjust an oven rack to the middle position and heat the oven to 325 degrees. Process the graham cracker pieces in a food processor to fine, even crumbs, about 30 seconds. Sprinkle the melted butter and sugar over the crumbs and pulse to incorporate. Sprinkle the mixture into a 9-inch springform pan. Press the crumbs firmly into an even layer using the bottom of a measuring cup (see page 462). Bake the crust until fragrant and beginning to brown, 10 to 15 minutes. Let the crust cool to room temperature, about 30 minutes.

2. FOR THE FILLING: Meanwhile, increase the oven temperature to 500 degrees. Beat the cream cheese in a large bowl with an electric mixer on medium-low speed until smooth, 1 to 3 minutes. Scrape down the bowl and beaters as needed.

3. Beat in ¾ cup of the sugar and the salt until incorporated, 1 to 3 minutes. Beat in the remaining ¾ cup sugar until incorporated, 1 to 3 minutes. Beat in the sour cream, lemon juice, and vanilla until incorporated, 1 to 3 minutes. Beat in the eggs, 2 at a time, and the egg yolks until combined, 1 to 3 minutes.

4. Being careful not to disturb the baked crust, brush the inside of the prepared springform pan with melted butter. Set the pan on a rimmed baking sheet. Carefully pour the filling into the pan. Bake the cheesecake for 10 minutes.

5. Without opening the oven door, reduce the oven temperature to 200 degrees and continue to bake the cheesecake until an instant-read thermometer inserted in the center of the cake registers 150 degrees, about 1½ hours, rotating the pan halfway through baking.

6. Transfer the cake to a wire rack and run a knife around the edge of the cake. Let the cheesecake cool until just barely warm, 2½ to 3 hours, running a knife around the edge of the cake every hour or so. Wrap the pan tightly in plastic wrap and refrigerate until cold, about 3 hours.

7. To unmold the cheesecake, wrap a hot, damp kitchen towel around the cake pan and let sit for 1 minute. Remove the sides of the pan and carefully slide the cake onto a cake platter. Let the cheesecake sit at room temperature for 30 minutes before serving. (The cheesecake can be wrapped in plastic wrap and refrigerated for up to 3 days.)

STRAWBERRY TOPPING

MAKES ABOUT 3 CUPS

This topping is the perfect accompaniment to cheesecake, pancakes, or ice cream. It is best used the day it is made. We don't recommend using frozen strawberries in this recipe.

   4   **cups (20 ounces) fresh strawberries, hulled and sliced thin**

¼   **cup sugar**

        Pinch salt

½   **cup strawberry jam**

   1   **tablespoon fresh lemon juice**

1. Toss the strawberries, sugar, and salt together in a large bowl and let sit, stirring occasionally, until the strawberries have released their juice and the sugar has dissolved, about 30 minutes.

2. Process the jam in a food processor (or blender) until smooth, about 8 seconds. Simmer the jam in a small saucepan over medium heat until no longer foamy, about 3 minutes. Stir the warm jam mixture and the lemon juice into the strawberries. Let the topping cool to room temperature before serving, about 1 hour. Serve at room temperature or chilled.

Variations
BLUEBERRY TOPPING

We don't recommend using frozen blueberries in this topping.

Substitute 3 cups fresh blueberries for the strawberries and blueberry jam for the strawberry jam. Gently mash the blueberries to help release their juice before letting them sit in step 1.

PEACH TOPPING

One pound of frozen peaches, thawed, can be substituted here; you may need to slice these peaches thinner after thawing.

Substitute 4 peaches, peeled (see page 511), pitted, and sliced very thin, for the strawberries and peach jam for the strawberry jam.

SHOPPING WITH THE TEST KITCHEN

Springform Pans: A springform pan is an essential piece of equipment for a variety of cakes, such as New York Cheesecake, that would otherwise be impossible to remove from a standard cake pan. In addition to a smooth-working buckle, we found the most crucial feature on a reliable springform pan to be its ability to resist leakage—either batter out or water in (for those cakes that are baked in a water bath). Of the six pans we tested, we favored the Frieling Handle-It Glass Bottom 9-inch Springform Pan ($31.95), for its sturdy, rimless glass bottom (which allows you to monitor the browning progress of a crust) and its convenient handles.

Icebox Oreo Cheesecake

The idea of a no-bake Oreo cheesecake is especially appealing in the summer months, because there's no hot oven and no messy water bath (which many baked cheesecakes require). The method for this cake is simple: thicken heavy cream with gelatin, mix it with sweetened cream cheese and ground Oreos, pour the mixture into a crust, and chill until set. These gelatin-based cheesecakes are easy to prepare, but their texture is never quite as creamy as an egg-thickened baked cheesecake's. We set out to make an icebox Oreo cheesecake that would rival the best baked cheesecake for flavor and texture.

Our quest for great icebox Oreo cheesecake began with preparing several existing recipes for this popular dessert. We were disheartened to find that all of these cheesecakes were either too springy from gelatin overload, or so runny that they wouldn't slice properly. And if the Oreos weren't dispersed as an unappealing gray powder, they remained distractingly chunky.

For big Oreo flavor, we started by grinding some cookies and mixing them with melted butter to make an easy press-in crust for our springform pan. We thought we could finesse the amount of gelatin in standard recipes to get the creamy-textured filling we were after, but we were wrong. After countless tests, tasters determined that cakes made with gelatin were never going to have the dense, velvety texture that comes from the eggs in baked versions. Was there a way to incorporate eggs into icebox cheesecake?

Thinking an eggy pudding might work, we cooked a mixture of egg yolks, milk, and cornstarch, combined it with sweetened cream cheese, poured the filling over the Oreo crust, and put the cake in the refrigerator. This cheesecake tasted pretty good and held together well, but the cornstarch had given it a slippery, glossy texture. Replacing the cornstarch with flour gave the cake stability without the slippery texture.

But it still didn't exhibit the creamy density of baked cheesecake. We tried adding sour cream and ricotta cheese, but neither was dense enough to help create that compact, baked texture. A colleague suggested that melted white chocolate might help make the cheesecake denser while adding a pleasant sweetness. We gave it a shot by stirring some melted and cooled white chocolate into the pudding before combining it with the cream cheese. When set, the white chocolate firmed up the filling, and the resulting texture (and flavor) was very close to that of baked cheesecake.

We were almost there, but tasters were clamoring for more Oreo flavor. Working to avoid the ugly gray cheesecake of our earlier tests, we broke a dozen cookies into large pieces and added them to the cheesecake in distinct layers. With the flavorful crust, the clean look of the layered filling, and the smooth, velvety texture created by the pudding and white chocolate, we had an icebox Oreo cheesecake that rivaled the best baked versions.

ICEBOX OREO CHEESECAKE

SERVES 12

Though not technically white chocolate, 2 cups of white chips can be substituted for the 8 ounces of white chocolate.

CRUST

- 30 Oreo cookies, broken into rough pieces
- 7 tablespoons unsalted butter, softened

FILLING

- 1 cup whole milk
- 4 large egg yolks
- ¼ cup all-purpose flour
- 8 ounces white chocolate, chopped (see note above)
- 4 (8-ounce) packages cream cheese, cut into chunks and softened
- ⅓ cup confectioners' sugar
- 2 teaspoons vanilla extract
- ⅛ teaspoon salt
- 12 Oreo cookies, broken into rough pieces

1. FOR THE CRUST: Process the cookies and butter in a food processor until finely ground. Sprinkle the mixture into a 9-inch springform pan and press evenly onto the bottom and sides of the pan. Refrigerate until set, at least 1 hour and up to 2 days.

2. FOR THE FILLING: Heat ¾ cup of the milk in a medium saucepan over medium heat until simmering. Meanwhile, whisk together the egg yolks, flour, and remaining ¼ cup milk in a large bowl until smooth. Slowly whisk the hot milk into the yolk mixture. Return the mixture to the saucepan and cook over medium heat, whisking constantly, until very thick and glossy, 1 to 2 minutes. Off the heat, whisk in the white chocolate until melted. Transfer the custard to a bowl, press plastic wrap directly onto the surface, and refrigerate until cold and set, at least 1 hour and up to 2 days.

3. Using an electric mixer on medium-high speed, beat together the cream cheese, sugar, vanilla, and salt until light and fluffy, about 2 minutes. Reduce the mixer speed to medium-low and mix in the custard until just combined, about 30 seconds. Pour one-quarter of the cream cheese mixture evenly into the prepared pan and sprinkle one-third of the cookie pieces over the surface. Repeat the process twice, then top with the remaining filling. Refrigerate until set, at least 6 hours. To unmold the cheesecake, wrap a hot, damp kitchen towel around the cake pan and let sit for 1 minute. Remove the sides of the pan and carefully slide the cake onto a cake platter. Serve. (The cheesecake can be wrapped in plastic wrap and refrigerated for up to 3 days.)

CHAPTER SIXTEEN

Homespun Pies and Fruit Desserts

HOMESPUN PIES AND FRUIT DESSERTS

American Pie Dough

Simple as it can be, pie crust—essentially a combination of flour, water, and fat—raises numerous questions: What are the ideal proportions of the main ingredients? What else should be added for character? What methods should be used to combine these ingredients?

The most controversial ingredient in pie crust is fat. We've found that all-butter crusts taste good, but they are not as flaky and fine-textured as those made with some shortening, which are our favorites for their combination of great flavor and flaky texture.

We next experimented with the relative proportions of fat and flour and finally settled on a ratio of 2 parts flour to 1 part fat, which produces crusts that are easy to work with and, when baked, more tender and flavorful than any other.

We also tackled the proportions of salt and sugar. After testing amounts ranging from ¼ teaspoon to as much as 2 tablespoons of each, we settled on 1 teaspoon of salt and 2 tablespoons of sugar for a double-crust pie, amounts that enhance the flavor of the dough without shouting out their presence.

We experimented with a variety of liquid ingredients, such as buttermilk, milk, and cider vinegar, a common ingredient in many pastry recipes. No liquid additions improved our basic recipe, so we recommend that you stick with ice water.

Pie dough can be made by hand, but we've found that a food processor is faster and easier and does the best job of cutting the fat into the flour. Proper mixing is important. If you undermix, the crust will shrink when baked and become hard and crackly. If you overprocess, you'll get a crumbly, rather than flaky, dough. The shortening should be pulsed with the flour until the mixture is sandy; butter is then pulsed in until the mixture looks like coarse crumbs.

Once the flour and fat have been combined, the dough can be transferred to a bowl, and the ice water can be added and mixed in. We recommend a rubber spatula and a folding motion to mix in the water. Use the flat side of the spatula to press the mixture until the dough sticks together. Incorporating the water in this manner allows for the least amount of water to be used (less water means a more tender dough) and reduces the likelihood of overworking the dough. Still, we've also learned that it doesn't pay to be too stingy with the water. If there isn't enough, the dough will be crumbly.

Finally, we found that pie dough need not be difficult to roll out if you remember two basic guidelines: make sure the dough is well chilled before rolling, and add a minimum of flour to the work surface.

ROLLING AND FITTING PIE DOUGH

1. Roll the dough outward from its center into a 12-inch circle. After every few rolls, give the dough a quarter turn to help keep the circle nice and round.

2. Toss additional flour underneath the dough as needed to keep the dough from sticking to the work surface.

3. Loosely roll the dough around the rolling pin, then gently unroll it over the pie plate.

4. Lift the dough and gently press it into the pie plate, letting the excess hang over the edge.

Flour added during rolling will be absorbed by the dough, and too much flour will cause the dough to toughen. If the dough seems too soft to roll, it's best to refrigerate it rather than add more flour.

DOUBLE-CRUST PIE DOUGH

MAKES ENOUGH FOR ONE 9-INCH PIE

See the photos on page 523 for tips on rolling out pie dough. The dough, wrapped tightly in plastic wrap, can be refrigerated for up to 2 days or frozen for up to 1 month. If frozen, let the dough thaw completely before rolling out.

- 2½ **cups all-purpose flour**
- 2 **tablespoons sugar**
- 1 **teaspoon salt**
- ½ **cup vegetable shortening, cut into ½-inch pieces and chilled**
- 12 **tablespoons (1½ sticks) unsalted butter, cut into ¼-inch pieces and chilled**
- 6–8 **tablespoons ice water**

1. Process the flour, sugar, and salt together in a food processor until combined. Scatter the shortening over the top and process until the mixture resembles coarse sand, about 10 seconds. Scatter the butter pieces over the top and cut the butter into the flour until the mixture is pale yellow and resembles coarse crumbs, with butter bits no larger than small peas, about ten 1-second pulses. Transfer the mixture to a medium bowl.

2. Sprinkle 6 tablespoons of the ice water over the mixture. With a rubber spatula, use a folding motion to mix. Press down on the dough with the flat side of the spatula until the dough sticks together, adding up to 2 tablespoons more ice water if the dough will not come together. Divide the dough into 2 balls and flatten each into a 4-inch disk. Wrap each in plastic wrap and refrigerate for at least 1 hour, or up to 2 days, before rolling.

Variation
SINGLE-CRUST PIE DOUGH

MAKES ENOUGH FOR ONE 9-INCH PIE

- 1¼ **cups all-purpose flour**
- 1 **tablespoon sugar**
- ½ **teaspoon salt**
- 3 **tablespoons vegetable shortening, cut into ½-inch pieces and chilled**
- 5 **tablespoons unsalted butter, cut into ¼-inch pieces and chilled**
- 4–6 **tablespoons ice water**

1. Process the flour, sugar, and salt together in a food processor until combined. Scatter the shortening over the top and process until the mixture resembles coarse sand, about 10 seconds. Scatter the butter pieces over the top and cut the butter into the flour until the mixture is pale yellow and resembles coarse crumbs, about ten 1-second pulses. Transfer the mixture to a medium bowl.

2. Sprinkle 4 tablespoons of the ice water over the mixture. With a rubber spatula, use a folding motion to mix. Press down on the dough with the flat side of the spatula until the dough sticks together, adding

CRIMPING A SINGLE-CRUST PIE

For a fluted edge: Use the index finger of one hand and the thumb and index finger of the other to create fluted ridges.

For a ridged edge: Press the tines of a fork into the dough to flatten it against the rim of the pie plate.

up to 2 tablespoons more ice water if the dough will not come together.

3. Turn the dough onto a sheet of plastic wrap and flatten into a 4-inch disk. Wrap the dough tightly in the plastic wrap and refrigerate for about 1 hour. Before rolling out the dough, let it sit on the work surface to soften slightly, about 10 minutes.

4. Following the photos on page 523, roll the dough into a 12-inch circle and fit it into a pie plate. Trim, fold, and crimp the edge of the dough. Wrap the dough-lined pie plate loosely in plastic wrap and place in the freezer until the dough is fully chilled and firm, about 30 minutes, before using.

No-Fear Pie Dough

Let's face it: mixing, rolling, and fitting pie dough can be frustrating for many of us. Some of us turn to store-bought pie dough, but what about those times when only a homemade crust will do? Pat-in-the-pan crusts (where the dough is shaped right in the pan) are an option, but we've never met one that baked up flaky and full of buttery flavor. Thus, we made it our goal to develop a pat-in-the-pan crust whose flavor and texture rivaled those of traditional pie crust.

But after making more than twenty pat-in-the-pan crusts, we were discouraged. Without exception, our tests yielded dough that was either too sticky or too stiff to press into a pie plate thinly and evenly, and none baked up flaky enough to replace the store-bought standby. You can imagine our surprise when our twenty-third test—a crust made with cream cheese—fooled several pie snobs in the kitchen.

Why was cream cheese so successful? It turns out that acidity promotes tenderness. But not any old acidic ingredient will work. Vinegar made a sour crust, and sour cream and buttermilk made the dough too sticky. Dense cream cheese made the dough easier to manipulate. We found this dough could handle a whopping 12 tablespoons of fat, almost twice as much as a standard pie dough, and it didn't require ice water. This dough also relies on an unusual mixing method. Softened butter and cream cheese are beaten together and then mixed with flour, sugar, and salt. The fat in the cream cheese coats the particles of flour and prevents toughness, a problem in many crusts. At last, we'd developed an easy pie crust that baked up flaky and tasted great.

EASIEST EVER PRESS-IN SINGLE-CRUST PIE DOUGH

MAKES ENOUGH FOR ONE 9-INCH PIE

The cream cheese makes this dough easy to manipulate and press into the pan—no rolling required! Make sure you press the dough evenly into a glass pie plate; if you hold the dough-lined plate up to the light, you will be able to clearly see any thick or thin spots. The unbaked crust can be wrapped tightly in plastic wrap and frozen for up to 2 months.

1¼	cups all-purpose flour
2	tablespoons sugar
¼	teaspoon salt
8	tablespoons (1 stick) unsalted butter, softened
2	ounces cream cheese, softened

1. Grease a 9-inch pie plate. Whisk the flour, sugar, and salt together in a medium bowl.

2. In a large bowl, beat the butter and cream cheese together with an electric mixer on medium-high speed until completely combined, about 2 minutes. Reduce the mixer speed to medium-low and beat in the flour mixture until it resembles coarse crumbs, about 20 seconds. Increase the mixer speed to medium-high and beat until the dough begins to form large clumps, about 30 seconds.

3. Transfer 3 tablespoons of the dough to a small bowl. Turn the remaining dough clumps out onto a lightly floured work surface, gather into a ball, and flatten into a 6-inch disk. Transfer the disk to the prepared pie plate.

4. Following the photos, press the dough evenly over the bottom of the pie plate using the heel of your hand. With your fingertips, continue to work the dough over the bottom of the plate and up the sides until evenly distributed.

5. On a lightly floured work surface, roll the reserved 3 tablespoons of dough into three 8-inch-long ropes. Arrange the ropes around the top of the pie plate, leaving small gaps between them. Squeeze the ropes into the crust to make a uniform edge. Crimp the edge of the dough. Cover loosely with plastic wrap and place in the freezer until the dough is fully chilled and firm, about 30 minutes, before using.

MAKING PRESS-IN PIE DOUGH

1. Press the dough evenly over the bottom of the pie plate. With your fingertips, continue to work the dough evenly over the bottom and up the sides of the pie plate until evenly distributed.

2. Roll the reserved dough into three 8-inch ropes. Arrange the ropes around the perimeter of the pie plate, leaving small (about 1-inch) gaps between them. Squeeze the ropes into the crust to make a uniform edge.

Deep-Dish Apple Pie

Deep-dish pies were traditionally baked crustless in casserole dishes, the generous filling blanketed with a layer of thick, flaky pastry. Today it is more common to find double-crust deep-dish apple pies, in which the apples are nestled between two layers of pastry. Unfortunately, these pies often bear little resemblance to their name, instead looking suspiciously like your standard apple pie. But we didn't want a thin slice of plain old apple pie; we wanted a towering wedge of tender, juicy apples, fully framed by a buttery, flaky crust.

After foraging for recipes that met our specifications for deep-dish—a minimum of 5 pounds of apples as opposed to the meager 2 pounds in a standard pie—we realized why most recipe writers stick with pies of modest size: your standard apple pie may have a juicy filling, but most deep-dish pies are downright flooded, with the apples swimming in an ocean of liquid. As a result, the bottom crust becomes a pale, soggy mess. In addition, the crowd of apples tends to cook unevenly, with mushy, applesauce-y edges surrounding a crunchy, underdone center. Less serious—but no less annoying—is the gaping hole left between the apples (which shrink considerably) and the arching top crust.

After a week of rescue efforts, we had made little progress. Our failed attempts included slicing the apples into thick chunks to prevent overcooked edges, cutting large vents in the crust to promote steam release, and baking the pies at different temperatures. Chunky apples were unevenly cooked and both larger vents and varied oven temperatures proved, well, fruitless. No matter what we tried, we were confronted with the same two problems: soupy filling and soggy crust. To sop up the copious amount of liquid exuded by 5 pounds of apples, we added a thickening agent. But so much thickener was required to dam the flood that it muddied the bright flavor of the apples.

Desperate times call for desperate measures. During our research, we had come across recipes that called for cooking the apples before assembling them in the pie, the idea being both to extract juice and cook the apples more evenly. Although this logic seemed counterintuitive (how could cooking the apples twice cause them to become anything but insipid and mushy?), we went ahead with the experiment. We dumped a mound of apples (a combination of tart and sweet for balanced flavor) into a Dutch oven and covered it to promote even cooking. After cooling and draining the apples (so the butter in the crust would not melt immediately), we baked the pie, which was free of excess juice and resulted in a nicely browned bottom crust. The apples were miraculously tender. And because the apples were shrinking before going into the pie rather than after, we had inadvertently solved the problem of the maddening gap! The top crust now remained united with the rest of the pie, and slicing was a breeze. At long last, we had the perfect slice sitting up nice and tall on the plate.

BLUE RIBBON APPLE PIE

SERVES 8

A combination of sweet and tart apples works best in this pie. For sweet apples, we recommend Golden Delicious, Braeburn, and Jonagold. And for tart apples, we prefer Granny Smith, Empire, and Cortland.

1	recipe Double-Crust Pie Dough (page 524)
2½	pounds firm tart apples (5 to 7 apples; see note above), peeled, cored, and cut into ¼-inch slices
2½	pounds firm sweet apples (5 to 7 apples; see note above), peeled, cored, and cut into ¼-inch slices
½	cup plus 1 tablespoon granulated sugar
¼	cup packed light brown sugar
½	teaspoon grated fresh lemon zest and 2 teaspoons fresh lemon juice

CORING AND SLICING APPLES

1. Cut the sides of the apple squarely away from the core.

2. Cut each piece of apple into ¼-inch slices.

¼	teaspoon salt
⅛	teaspoon ground cinnamon
1	large egg white, lightly beaten

1. Following the photos on page 523, roll one disk of dough into a 12-inch circle on a lightly floured work surface, then fit it into a 9-inch pie plate, letting the excess dough hang over the edge; cover with plastic wrap and refrigerate for 30 minutes. Roll the other disk of dough into a 12-inch circle on a lightly floured work surface, then transfer to a parchment-lined baking sheet; cover with plastic wrap and refrigerate for 30 minutes.

2. Toss the apples, ½ cup of the granulated sugar, the brown sugar, lemon zest, salt, and cinnamon together in a large bowl. Transfer the apples to a Dutch oven, cover, and cook over medium heat, stirring frequently, until the apples are tender when poked with a fork but still hold their shape, 15 to 20 minutes. Transfer the apples and their juice to a rimmed baking sheet and let cool to room temperature, about 30 minutes.

3. Adjust an oven rack to the lowest position, place a rimmed baking sheet on the rack, and heat the oven to 425 degrees. Drain the cooled apples thoroughly in a

MAKING A DOUBLE-CRUST PIE

1. After rolling out the top crust, loosely roll it around the rolling pin, then gently unroll it over the filling.

2. Using scissors, trim all but ½ inch of the dough overhanging the edge of the pie plate.

3. Press the top and bottom crusts together, then tuck the edges under.

4. Crimp the dough evenly around the edge of the pie, using your fingers, and cut vents in the crust.

colander set over a bowl, reserving ¼ cup of the juice. Stir the lemon juice into the reserved apple juice.

4. Spread the apples in the dough-lined pie plate, mounding them slightly in the middle, and drizzle with the lemon juice mixture. Following the photos, loosely roll the second piece of dough around the rolling pin and gently unroll it over the pie. Trim, fold, and crimp the edges, and cut 4 vent holes in the top. Brush the crust with the egg white and sprinkle with the remaining 1 tablespoon granulated sugar.

5. Place the pie on the heated baking sheet and bake until the crust is golden, about 25 minutes. Reduce the oven temperature to 375 degrees, rotate the

baking sheet, and continue to bake until the juices are bubbling and the crust is deep golden brown, 25 to 30 minutes longer. Let the pie cool on a wire rack until the filling has set, about 2 hours; serve slightly warm or at room temperature.

Variations
CRANBERRY-APPLE PIE

We use all sweet apples here because the cranberries are quite tart.

Omit the tart apples and increase the amount of sweet apples to 3½ pounds. Cook 2 cups frozen or fresh cranberries, ¼ cup fresh orange juice, ½ cup granulated sugar, ¼ teaspoon cinnamon, and ¼ teaspoon salt in a medium saucepan over medium-high heat, stirring often, until the berries have broken down and the juice has a jam-like consistency, 10 to 12 minutes. Off the heat, stir in ¼ cup water and cool to room temperature. Spread the cooled cranberry mixture over the bottom of the dough-lined pie plate before adding the cooked apples.

CARAMEL-APPLE PIE

We like to use either Kraft Caramels or Brach's Milk Maid Caramels for this recipe, but any brand of soft caramels (not hard caramel candies) will do.

Sprinkle 30 soft caramels, halved, into the pie with the apples before baking.

Apple Slab Pie

Traditional apple pie and apple slab pie are both two-crusted affairs filled with spiced apples—but that's where the similarities end. Unlike a traditional pie, slab pie is made in a baking sheet and can feed twenty people. It is short in stature, its filling is thickened to ensure neat slicing, and it's topped with a sugary glaze. We were excited to give this pie a try.

It was best to start with sturdier store-bought pie dough rounds. By gluing two of them together with water and then rolling out the double dough into a large rectangle, we were able to get the crust into the pan without a tear. Now that we had the shaping down, we needed to find a way to improve the bland flavor of the store-bought dough. Using an old test-kitchen trick, we tried rolling the dough in crushed animal crackers for a welcome sweet and buttery flavor. Brushing the rolled dough with melted butter added even more richness.

In the test kitchen we like to use two kinds of apples in pies: a tart variety that will hold its shape and a sweet, soft variety that will cook down to create a saucy filling with balanced flavor. Using firm, tart Granny Smiths and sweet, softer Golden Delicious, we needed eight of each to adequately fill our pie. We added cinnamon, sugar, lemon juice, and a little flour (to help thicken the filling) to the sliced apples, filled and covered the pie, and baked it. The flavor was great, but the filling was too soupy to cut into neat squares. We tried adding more flour, but the result was too pasty. Cornstarch made the filling slimy, but tapioca thickened the filling without making it starchy.

But even with this thickened filling, the bottom crust was getting soggy. We'd been making the filling right before assembling the pie, but for one test we got pulled away from the kitchen and left a batch of apples sitting for about 30 minutes. We noticed a pool of juice in the bottom of the bowl, so we drained away the juice and baked the pie as usual. This time the filling was much firmer, and the crust wasn't soggy at all.

As for the glaze, the traditional combination of confectioners' sugar and milk tasted a little flat. Remembering the pool of apple juice that had drained from the filling, we reduced it in a saucepan to concentrate its flavor, then mixed the reduced juice with confectioners' sugar and lemon juice. Spread over the cooled top crust, this glaze offered just the right finish for our crisp and buttery giant of a pie.

APPLE SLAB PIE

SERVES 18 TO 20

We prefer the convenience of store-bought pie crust in this recipe, but if desired, 2 recipes of Double-Crust Pie Dough (page 524) can be substituted. You will need an 18 by 13-inch rimmed baking sheet for this recipe; we prefer to use a nonstick baking sheet, but a greased conventional baking sheet will work. For sweet apples, we recommend Golden Delicious, Braeburn, and Jonagold. And for tart apples, we prefer Granny Smith, Empire, and Cortland.

FILLING AND CRUST

3½	pounds firm tart apples (7 to 10 apples; see note above), peeled, cored, and cut into ¼-inch slices
3½	pounds firm sweet apples (7 to 10 apples; see note above), peeled, cored, and cut into ¼-inch slices
1½	cups granulated sugar
1½	cups (4 ounces) animal crackers
2	(15-ounce) boxes Pillsbury Just Unroll! Pie Crust (see note above)
4	tablespoons unsalted butter, melted and cooled
6	tablespoons cornstarch
3	tablespoons fresh lemon juice
2	teaspoons ground cinnamon
½	teaspoon salt

GLAZE

2	tablespoons fresh lemon juice
1	tablespoon unsalted butter, softened
1¼	cups confectioners' sugar

1. FOR THE FILLING AND CRUST: Adjust an oven rack to the lower-middle position and heat the oven to 350 degrees. Toss the apples with 1 cup of the granulated sugar in a large bowl and let sit, tossing occasionally, until the apples release their juice, about 30 minutes.

MAKING APPLE SLAB PIE

1. Use water to "glue" together 2 store-bought pie crusts.

2. Add flavor to the crust by rolling it out in a mixture of crushed cookie crumbs and sugar.

3. Brush the dough with melted butter for extra richness.

4. Top the filled pie with a second "double" crust. Use a fork to tightly seal the edges of the crust.

2. Meanwhile, pulse the animal crackers and remaining ½ cup granulated sugar together in a food processor to coarse crumbs, about 15 pulses. Sprinkle ⅓ cup of the crumbs onto a work surface and lay 2 of the pie dough rounds on top of the crumbs. Overlap the rounds by half and brush water between them to help seal them together. Following the photos, sprinkle ⅓ cup more crumbs over the top and roll the pieces of dough together into a 19 by 14-inch rectangle.

3. Loosely roll the large rectangle of dough around the rolling pin, then gently unroll it over an 18 by 13-inch nonstick rimmed baking sheet. Gently fit the dough into the baking sheet, brush with the melted butter, then cover with plastic wrap and refrigerate until needed.

4. Drain the apples thoroughly in a colander set over a bowl, reserving ¾ cup of the juice for the glaze. In a large bowl, toss the drained apples, cornstarch, lemon juice, cinnamon, and salt together until well combined. Spread the apples evenly in the dough-lined baking sheet, pressing on them lightly to flatten. Cover with plastic wrap and refrigerate until needed.

5. Following the photos and the directions in step 2, roll the remaining 2 dough rounds together with the remaining ⅔ cup crumbs to a 19 by 14-inch rectangle. Loosely roll the large rectangle of dough around the rolling pin and gently unroll it over the pie. Trim, fold, and crimp the edges using the tines of a fork.

6. Poke vent holes in the top crust at 2-inch intervals using a fork. Bake the pie until the juices are bubbling and the crust is golden brown, about 1 hour. Let the pie cool slightly on a wire rack, about 30 minutes.

7. FOR THE GLAZE: While the pie is cooling, simmer the ¾ cup reserved apple juice in a small saucepan over medium heat until it is syrupy and measures ¼ cup, about 6 minutes. Stir in the lemon juice and butter and let the mixture cool to room temperature. Whisk in the confectioners' sugar and brush the glaze evenly over the warm pie. Let the pie cool on a wire rack until the filling has set, about 2 hours; serve slightly warm or at room temperature, cut into squares.

Store-Bought Pie Crusts: A flaky, buttery home-made pie crust is the ultimate crown for our pies, but it's also a fair amount of work. How much would we sacrifice by using a store-bought crust instead? To find out, we tried several types and brands—both dry mixes (just add water) and ready-made crusts, either frozen or refrigerated. The dry mixes didn't save much work, and homemade pastry has infinitely better flavor and texture. Frozen crusts were the ultimate time-savers, but they were impossibly difficult to remove from their packaging, and they baked up pasty and bland. The one refrigerated contender, Pillsbury Just Unroll! Pie Crust ($2.79 for two 9-inch crusts), wasn't bad. Though the flavor was somewhat bland, it wasn't offensive, and the crust baked up to an impressive flakiness.

Blueberry Pie

There's nothing like blueberry pie to shake the confidence of even the most experienced baker. Unlike apple pie, which requires little (if any) starch to thicken the fruit, the filling in blueberry pie needs special attention because the berries are so juicy. We started our search for a juicy yet sliceable pie by filling our dough-lined pie dish with a fairly standard mixture of 6 cups of fresh blueberries, ¾ cup of sugar, and tapioca. The 6 tablespoons recommended on the back of the tapioca box produced a stiff, congealed mass, so we slowly cut back the amount. At 4 tablespoons, the filling was still too congealed for tasters' liking, but this amount proved to be the tipping point; any less and the pie needed to be served with a spoon.

The problem, of course, was the juiciness of the berries. After some experimentation, we found that cooking just half of the berries was enough to adequately reduce the liquid. We then folded the remaining raw berries into the mixture, creating a satisfying combination of intensely flavored cooked fruit and bright-tasting fresh fruit that allowed us to cut down the amount of tapioca to 3 tablespoons. Encouraged by this success, we wondered if we could decrease the amount of tapioca even further.

As we watched the blueberries for our pie bubble away in the pot, we thought about blueberry jam. Well-made jam boasts a soft, even consistency that is neither gelatinous nor slippery. The secret to this great texture is pectin, a carbohydrate found in fruit. Blueberries are low in natural pectin, so commercial pectin in the form of a liquid or powder is usually added when making blueberry jam. The only downside to commercial pectin is that it needs the presence of a certain proportion of sugar and acid in order to work. This would mean increasing the amount of sugar. No-sugar-needed pectin was an option, but this additive contains lots of natural acid, which compensates for the lack of extra sugar—and its sourness made our tasters wince. A colleague then offered a suggestion: since apples contain a lot of natural pectin, could an apple be added to the blueberries to help set the filling?

We folded one peeled and grated Granny Smith apple into a new batch of fresh and cooked berries that we had mixed with 2 tablespoons of tapioca. We baked the pie and waited. When we finally tried a slice, we knew we'd hit on a great solution. Combined with a modest amount of tapioca, the apple provided enough thickening power to set the pie beautifully, plus it enhanced the flavor of the berries without anyone guessing our secret ingredient. Just as important, it left no evidence of its own texture.

Tweaking the crust was the last step. We found that baking the pie on a heated baking sheet on the bottom rack of the oven produced a crisp, golden bottom crust that didn't get soggy. As for the top crust, berry pies are often made with a decorative lattice topping that allows the steam from the berries to gently escape. But after making more than fifty lattice tops, we were determined to find a faster, easier approach. We decided to try making a crust we had seen in our research that had vents in the form of simple round cutouts. After rolling out the dough, we used a small biscuit cutter to cut out circles, then transferred the dough onto the pie. This method saved time and made an attractive, unusual-looking top crust that properly vented the steam from the berry filling as it baked. At long last, we had a blueberry pie with perfectly thickened filling that was bursting with bright berry flavor.

BLUEBERRY PIE

SERVES 8

This recipe was developed using fresh blueberries, but unthawed frozen blueberries (our favorite brands are Wyman's and Cascadian Farm) will work as well. In step 2, cook half the frozen berries over medium-high heat, without mashing, until reduced to 1¼ cups, 12 to 15 minutes. Grind the tapioca to a powder in a spice grinder or mini food processor. If using pearl tapioca, reduce the amount to 5 teaspoons.

  1   recipe Double-Crust Pie Dough (page 524)

  6   cups fresh blueberries (see note above)

  1   Granny Smith apple, peeled and grated on large holes of box grater

  2   teaspoons grated fresh lemon zest and 2 teaspoons fresh lemon juice

 ¾   cup sugar

  2   tablespoons Minute tapioca, ground (see note above)

      Pinch salt

  2   tablespoons unsalted butter, cut into ¼-inch pieces

  1   large egg, lightly beaten with 1 teaspoon water

1. Following the photos on page 523, roll 1 disk of dough into a 12-inch circle on a lightly floured work surface, then fit it into a 9-inch pie plate, letting the excess dough hang over the edge; cover with plastic wrap and refrigerate for 30 minutes. Roll the other disk of dough into a 12-inch circle on a lightly floured work surface, then transfer to a parchment-lined baking sheet; cover with plastic wrap and refrigerate for 30 minutes.

2. Adjust an oven rack to the lowest position, place a rimmed baking sheet on the oven rack, and heat the oven to 400 degrees. Place 3 cups of the berries in a medium saucepan and set over medium heat. Using a potato masher, mash the berries several times to release their juices. Continue to cook, stirring frequently and mashing occasionally, until about half of the berries have broken down and the mixture is thickened and reduced to 1½ cups, about 8 minutes. Let cool slightly.

3. Place the grated apple in a clean kitchen towel and wring dry. Transfer the apple to a large bowl. Add the cooked berries, remaining 3 cups uncooked berries, lemon zest, lemon juice, sugar, tapioca, and salt; toss to combine. Transfer the mixture to the dough-lined pie plate and scatter the butter pieces over the filling.

MAKING A CUT-OUT CRUST

1. Use a 1¼-inch biscuit cutter (or spice jar lid) to cut holes in the dough.

2. The cut-out crust vents the steam from the berry filling and is an easy alternative to a fussy lattice.

4. Using a 1¼-inch round biscuit cutter, cut a round from the center of the second round of dough. Cut another 6 rounds from the dough, 1½ inches from the edge of the center hole and equally spaced around it. Following the photos on page 528, roll the dough loosely around the rolling pin and gently unroll it over the pie, leaving at least a ½-inch overhang on each side. Trim, fold, and crimp the edges. Brush the top and edges of the pie with the egg mixture. If the dough is very soft, chill in the freezer for 10 minutes.

5. Place the pie on the heated baking sheet and bake for 30 minutes. Reduce the oven temperature to 350 degrees and continue to bake until the juices bubble and the crust is a deep golden brown, 30 to 40 minutes longer. Let the pie cool on a wire rack until the filling has set, about 4 hours; serve slightly warm or at room temperature.

Strawberry-Rhubarb Pie

If you visit any New England farm stand in the late spring, you're likely to see a table groaning under the weight of strawberry-rhubarb pies for sale. With a crusty golden brown top stained pink by rivulets of escaping juice, the pies are irresistible—a welcome harbinger of warm weather. But those homespun looks can be deceiving; too often, that crispy crust covers a soupy, bland filling, more fruit soup than fruit pie. Or the crust may mask the other extreme: a filling so loaded with thickener that it's gummy. So what's the secret to a juicy, but not watery, full-flavored strawberry-rhubarb pie?

Both strawberries and rhubarb have a high moisture content, especially when it's been a wet spring. And if you've ever cooked rhubarb, you know how quickly rhubarb transforms from firm stalk to soupy sauce—mere moments. Now imagine all that liquid contained within a pie. Where is it all supposed to go? Our goal, then, was to reduce the pie's moisture content and use as little thickener as possible for the freshest, brightest-tasting pie.

There are two approaches to eradicating excess moisture from fruit pies: cooking the fruit prior to assembling the pie, and preparing the pie in such a way that excess moisture can escape, as with an open-faced or lattice-topped pie. Strawberry-rhubarb pie is almost always covered (rhubarb can take on a muddy brown color once cooked), and we weren't out to buck tradition, so we opted to try precooking the fruit. Slowly stewing the rhubarb until it was completely broken down before mixing it with the strawberries yielded a flat-tasting filling, as the rhubarb was overcooked and had lost its characteristic brightness. But on a promising note, the filling was much drier. Borrowing from a savory rhubarb recipe we had found, we sautéed chopped rhubarb in a smoking-hot skillet until the juices were exuded but the pieces of rhubarb were still on the firm side. Once the rhubarb had cooled, we tossed it with the strawberries and assembled the pie. The baked pie tasted bright and clean and was much less soupy than before. Clearly we were on the right track.

But the moisture was only partially tamed; we still needed to pick a thickener. For many of our fruit pie recipes, we favor instant or Minute tapioca, but tasters disliked it in this case: the combination of tapioca and rhubarb yielded an unpleasant viscous texture. Even when we reduced the amount of tapioca to a bare minimum, tasters found fault with the filling's texture. Revisiting the other starches, tasters most preferred cornstarch. A scant 2 tablespoons proved perfect.

Since the filling was still on the moist side, we opted to add a few more vents to the top crust. We made a total of eight slits radiating outward from the center, four more than we usually add to covered pies. The difference was slight but noticeable: the pie's interior was definitely drier. So with a few tweaks, we finally had a gorgeous (and not soupy) strawberry-rhubarb pie well worth the effort.

STRAWBERRY-RHUBARB PIE

SERVES 8

To accommodate the extra-juicy filling in this double-crust pie, it's necessary to cut 8 vent holes, rather than the standard 4.

1	recipe Double-Crust Pie Dough (page 524)
1½	pounds rhubarb (3 to 4 large ribs), leaves discarded, peeled, stalks cut into 1-inch pieces
4	cups strawberries, hulled and quartered
1–1¼	cups plus 1 tablespoon sugar
2	tablespoons cornstarch
1	teaspoon grated fresh orange zest (optional)
½	teaspoon vanilla extract
	Pinch salt
1	egg white, lightly beaten

1. Following the photos on page 523, roll 1 disk of dough into a 12-inch circle on a lightly floured work surface, then fit it into a 9-inch pie plate, letting the excess dough hang over the edge; cover with plastic wrap and refrigerate for 30 minutes. Roll the other disk of dough into a 12-inch circle on a lightly floured work surface, then transfer to a parchment-lined baking sheet; cover with plastic wrap and refrigerate for 30 minutes.

2. Toss the rhubarb, strawberries, and 1 cup of the sugar together in a large bowl and let sit, tossing occasionally, until the fruit releases its juice, about 1 hour. Adjust an oven rack to the lowest position, place a foil–lined rimmed baking sheet on the rack, and heat the oven to 425 degrees.

3. Drain the fruit thoroughly in a colander set over a bowl, reserving ¼ cup of the juice. In a large bowl, toss the drained fruit, ¼ cup reserved juice, cornstarch, orange zest (if using), vanilla, and salt together until well combined. (If the fruit tastes tart, add up to ¼ cup more sugar.)

4. Spread the fruit in the dough-lined pie plate, mounding it slightly in the middle. Following the photos on page 528, loosely roll the second piece of dough around the rolling pin and gently unroll it over the pie. Trim, fold, and crimp the edges, and cut 8 vent holes in the top. Brush the crust with the egg white and sprinkle with the remaining 1 tablespoon sugar.

5. Place the pie on the heated baking sheet and bake until the top crust is golden, about 25 minutes. Reduce the oven temperature to 375 degrees, rotate the baking sheet, and continue to bake until the juices are bubbling and the crust is deep golden brown, 25 to 35 minutes longer. Let the pie cool on a wire rack until the filling has set, about 2 hours; serve slightly warm or at room temperature.

Shaker Lemon Pie

Shakers were renowned for their ingenuity, attention to detail, and thrift. These qualities, famously evident in the austerity and simple grace of their architecture, furniture, and handcrafts, also influenced their food. Shaker lemon pie is a fine example. Instead of using only the juice and/or zest of lemons, the Shakers used the entire fruit. To make the bitter pith and rind palatable, they sliced whole lemons thinly and macerated the slices with sugar to mellow them. The sugared lemons were then combined with eggs and baked into a double-crust pie. As if by magic, the spartan ingredients were transformed into a brightly flavored pie filling. This we had to try.

SHAKER COOKING

The Shakers' food was never ornate and was always healthful and hearty enough to support their industrious, hardworking lifestyle. Shakers scrubbed—rather than peeled—their vegetables (and, in the case of Shaker lemon pie, their citrus fruit) to minimize waste. They were also pioneers in using exact measurements in cooking at a time when many recipes called for a "dash," "glob," or "handful" of something.

Nearly every recipe we found gave the same directions: macerate 3 thinly sliced lemons with 1¾ cups of sugar, add 4 beaten eggs, pour the filling into an unbaked crust, top it with a second crust, and bake the pie until golden. The only difference in the recipes was the macerating time; some called for only 2 hours, whereas others demanded a full 24. A pie using the former timing was bitter and medicinal, as the sugar didn't have adequate time to draw the bitterness out of the lemon's pith. The 24-hour maceration produced a lemon pie with bright, sweet lemon flavor—but we were determined to find a faster way.

One modern recipe suggested quickly boiling the whole lemons before slicing them. Since the bitter pith wasn't exposed to the boiling water, this did nothing to temper its harsh flavor, but the idea inspired us to try boiling the sliced lemons. After quickly boiling the slices, we drained them, stirred in the sugar and the eggs, and poured the filling straight into the pie shell. Some bitterness remained, but there was marked improvement. Increasing the cooking time to several minutes took away all bitterness but also diluted the fresh lemon flavor. The solution was to squeeze the sliced lemons and

reserve the brightly flavored juice before simmering the slices; we then added the juice back in with the sugar and eggs. We finally had bright—not bitter—lemon flavor without any macerating time.

We were almost ready to finalize the recipe, but we couldn't help noticing that each time we made the pie the texture of the filling was slightly different. Since the pie spent a generous 40 minutes in the oven, the heat-sensitive eggs were occasionally curdling. Recipes for similar egg-rich custard pies avoid this problem by including a thickener to stabilize the eggs. Flour made the filling unappealingly pasty, but a tablespoon of cornstarch ensured a smooth filling every time.

This was a pie worthy of the highest praise, with bold lemon flavor, silky texture, and an efficiently Shaker-like preparation time of just about an hour.

SHAKER LEMON PIE

SERVES 8

You will need 6 tablespoons of lemon juice for this recipe. Have an extra lemon on hand in case the 3 sliced lemons do not yield enough juice.

1	recipe Double-Crust Pie Dough (page 524)
3	large lemons, sliced thin and seeded (see note above)
1¾	cups sugar
⅛	teaspoon salt
1	tablespoon cornstarch
4	large eggs
2	teaspoons heavy cream

1. Adjust an oven rack to the lowest position, place a rimmed baking sheet on the rack, and heat the oven to 425 degrees. Following the photos on page 523, roll 1 disk of dough into a 12-inch circle on a lightly floured work surface, then fit it into a 9-inch pie plate, letting the excess dough hang over the edge; cover with plastic wrap and refrigerate for 30 minutes. Roll the other disk of dough into a 12-inch circle on a lightly floured work surface, then transfer

BUILDING BOLD LEMON FLAVOR

1. Squeeze the seeded lemon slices and reserve the juice for the filling.

2. Simmer the slices to mellow the bitterness of the pith and then add them to the filling with the uncooked juice.

to a parchment-lined baking sheet; cover with plastic wrap and refrigerate for 30 minutes.

2. Squeeze the lemon slices in a fine-mesh strainer set over a bowl; reserve the juice (you should have 6 tablespoons). Bring the drained slices and 2 cups water to a boil in a saucepan, then reduce the heat to medium-low and simmer until the slices are softened, about 5 minutes. Drain well and discard the liquid. Combine the softened lemon slices, sugar, salt, and 4 tablespoons of the reserved lemon juice in a bowl; stir until the sugar dissolves.

3. Whisk the cornstarch and remaining 2 tablespoons lemon juice in a large bowl. Whisk the eggs into the cornstarch mixture, then slowly stir in the lemon slice mixture until combined. Pour into the chilled pie shell. Following the photos on page 528, loosely roll the second piece of dough around the rolling pin and gently unroll it over the pie. Trim, fold, and crimp the edges, and cut 4 vent holes in the top. Brush the crust with the cream.

4. Place the pie on the heated baking sheet and bake until light golden, about 20 minutes, then decrease

the oven temperature to 375 degrees, rotate the pie, and continue to bake until golden brown, 20 to 25 minutes longer. Let the pie cool on a wire rack, about 2 hours. Serve at room temperature.

TEST KITCHEN SHORTCUT

Slicing Lemons: We found that using a knife to evenly cut the lemons into paper-thin slices was a difficult and time-consuming task. We had better results with a mandoline (or V-slicer), which produced perfectly thin slices in no time at all. If you don't have a mandoline, freeze your lemons. Popping the lemons into the freezer for about 30 minutes firms them up for better hand-slicing, which is best accomplished with a serrated knife.

Mile-High Lemon Meringue Pie

Making a modest meringue is tricky enough. Double the amount of topping for a mile-high meringue and you've got double the problems. Weeping (the leaching of liquid from the meringue) was a sad reality in every recipe we tried.

We found that cream of tartar helped make the meringue more stable. But even with cream of tartar, our meringue wept. Undercooking is the main problem. For regular lemon meringue pies, the test kitchen has solved this problem by spreading the meringue over a piping-hot filling and baking the pie in a hot oven. The hot filling cooks the bottom half of the meringue, while the heat from the oven takes care of the top half.

But when we used this normally reliable method with twice as much meringue, the topping disintegrated into a puddle as we sliced the first piece of pie. What went wrong? We realized that this method works only with a modest amount of meringue. The center of our super-sized meringue wasn't cooking through. Baking the pie longer was not an option—the top of the meringue burned.

We then recalled Italian meringue, which is made by pouring boiling-hot sugar syrup into the egg whites as they are whipped. The hot syrup cooks the whites and helps transform them into a soft, smooth meringue that is stable enough to resist weeping. Best of all, this meringue is extra-fluffy and billowy. We needed eight egg whites to achieve mile-high results with a regular meringue, but four egg whites yielded plenty of Italian meringue. Doubling the amount of meringue without doubling the number of egg whites is a neat trick.

There's only one problem with an Italian meringue. Professional bakers use a candy thermometer to heat the sugar syrup to the correct temperature (between 238 and 245 degrees), but many home cooks don't have this tool. Could we make an Italian meringue without a thermometer? After much trial and error, we found that boiling the sugar syrup for exactly 4 minutes worked perfectly every time.

Since we no longer needed a hot filling to cook the meringue, we thought we might be able to let the filling set up in the shell in the fridge. Two hours later (this can even be done the day before), our filling emerged firm yet still silky. Tasters wanted the filling to be extra-lemony and very rich to balance all the meringue. It took a full cup of lemon juice, 2 tablespoons of zest, and 8 yolks—more than we had seen in any other recipe—to please everyone.

With lots of lemon, miles of meringue, and absolutely no weeping, this pie can be counted on to deliver smiles all around the table every time you make it.

MILE-HIGH LEMON MERINGUE PIE

SERVES 8

You can use Easiest Ever Press-In Single-Crust Pie Dough (page 525) or Single-Crust Pie Dough (page 524) for this pie. If using a hand-held mixer, you will need a very large, deep bowl and should move the beaters vigorously in step 4 to avoid underbeating the egg whites. This pie is best on the day it's made.

- 1 **recipe single-crust pie dough, fitted into a 9-inch pie plate and chilled (see note above)**

FILLING
- 1¼ **cups sugar**
- 1 **cup fresh lemon juice and 2 tablespoons grated fresh lemon zest (about 6 lemons)**
- ½ **cup water**
- ¼ **cup cornstarch**
- ¼ **teaspoon salt**
- 8 **large egg yolks (reserve 4 large egg whites for the meringue)**
- 3 **tablespoons unsalted butter, softened**

MERINGUE
- ½ **cup water**
- 1 **cup sugar**
- 4 **large egg whites (reserved from the filling)**
  Pinch salt
- ½ **teaspoon cream of tartar**
- ½ **teaspoon vanilla extract**

APPLYING THE MERINGUE

1. Spread the meringue onto the edge of the crust to prevent it from shrinking.

2. Use the spatula to make dramatic peaks and swirls all over the meringue.

MAKING MERINGUE

1. After the sugar syrup comes to a full boil, cook it for exactly 4 minutes.

2. Beat the egg whites with the salt and cream of tartar until they hold soft peaks.

3. With the mixer still running, carefully pour the hot sugar syrup directly into the beaten egg whites.

4. Continue beating until the meringue has cooled to room temperature and is thick and fluffy.

1. Adjust an oven rack to the middle position and heat the oven to 375 degrees. Line the chilled crust with a double layer of aluminum foil and fill with pie weights. Bake until the pie dough looks dry and is light in color, 25 to 30 minutes. Remove the weights and foil and continue to bake the crust until deep golden brown, 10 to 12 minutes longer. Let the crust cool on a wire rack to room temperature.

2. FOR THE FILLING: Whisk the sugar, lemon juice, water, cornstarch, and salt together in a large saucepan until the cornstarch is dissolved. Bring to a simmer over medium heat, whisking occasionally,

until the mixture becomes translucent and begins to thicken, about 5 minutes. Whisk in the egg yolks until combined. Stir in the lemon zest and butter. Bring to a simmer and stir constantly until the mixture is thick enough to coat the back of a spoon, about 2 minutes. Strain through a fine-mesh strainer into the pie shell and scrape the filling off the underside of the strainer. Place plastic wrap directly on the surface of the filling and refrigerate until set and well chilled, at least 2 hours and up to 1 day.

3. FOR THE MERINGUE: Adjust an oven rack to the middle position and heat the oven to 400 degrees. Combine the water and sugar in a small saucepan. Bring to a vigorous boil over medium-high heat. Once the syrup comes to a rolling boil, cook for 4 minutes (the mixture will become slightly thickened and syrupy). Remove from the heat and set aside while beating the whites.

4. With an electric mixer on medium-low speed, beat the whites in a large bowl until frothy, about 1 minute. Add the salt and cream of tartar and beat, gradually increasing the speed to medium-high, until the whites hold soft peaks, about 2 minutes. With the mixer running, slowly pour the hot syrup into the whites (avoid pouring the syrup onto the beaters or it will splash). Add the vanilla and beat until the meringue has cooled and becomes very thick and shiny, 5 to 9 minutes.

5. Following the photos on page 537, use a rubber spatula to mound the meringue over the filling, making sure the meringue touches the edge of the crust. Use the spatula to create peaks all over the meringue. Bake until the peaks turn golden brown, about 6 minutes. Let the pie cool on a wire rack until the filling has set, about 2 hours. Serve at room temperature.

Pumpkin-Praline Pie

What's not to like about a pie that combines the familiar spiced custard of a pumpkin pie with the praline-like chew of a pecan pie? Most recipes start with pumpkin pie as the base and include a layer of pecan praline—in the crust, in the filling, or as a topping. We tried all three arrangements and arrived at a few conclusions. First, tasters preferred their praline crunchy, and that meant keeping it on top. Second, they preferred a lot of topping, and that meant the pumpkin custard base would have to be pretty sturdy. Third, some of the pies were so sweet they made tasters' teeth ache, so we would use sweeteners judiciously.

To fortify the pumpkin base, we added three eggs (one more than usual) to a can of plain pumpkin puree. Tasters preferred the richness of evaporated milk to either heavy cream or milk and the caramel flavor of dark brown sugar to granulated sugar.

The filling tasted good, but it was too loose to support the praline, and we didn't care for the stringy pumpkin fibers. Getting rid of the stringiness was as easy as a whirl in the food processor, and cooking the pureed filling on the stovetop evaporated the excess moisture. (This last step had the added benefit of reducing the baking time by 30 minutes.)

The pie was now ready for the praline topping. Some recipes have the cook make authentic praline candy by boiling sugar, water, and pecans. This candy was good for snacking but much too complicated—and too sweet—for our pie. Other recipes included "shortcut" candy—pecans boiled in copious amounts of corn syrup. Sticky and insipid, this topping tasted nothing like rich praline.

We found a few recipes that didn't get into boiling sugar at all. Instead, they called for tossing chopped pecans with granulated sugar and a smidgen of corn syrup—just enough to make the topping clump like streusel; this uncooked mixture was scattered on top of the still-hot, baked

pumpkin pie. Intrigued by the apparent ease of this method, we topped our pumpkin pie with the crumbly nut mixture and popped it back into the oven. Ten minutes later the kitchen was filled with the smells of toasty sugar and pecans, and the topping bubbled enticingly around the edges.

The topping was now nearly perfect. All we wanted was a little more praline flavor, and we got it by replacing the granulated sugar with dark brown (just as we'd done with the pumpkin filling). We reserved 2 teaspoons of granulated sugar for sprinkling on the top, as it helped to crisp the praline.

The last obstacle concerned timing: exactly when should we add the topping? If added too early—a few minutes before the center was set (as other

MAKING PUMPKIN-PRALINE PIE

1. Puree the pumpkin (with the brown sugar and spices) to break up any fibers.

2. Cook the pumpkin mixture to get rid of excess moisture.

3. Pour the hot filling into a hot pie crust to minimize baking time and promote even cooking.

4. Bake until the filling cracks on top, then add the praline topping and finish baking.

recipes suggested)—the topping caused the filling to buckle under its weight. We turned to a visual cue that is the bane of many pumpkin pie bakers: the notorious cracking on top of the pie. As the pie just began to crack, it was perfectly set and ready to receive the topping, which covered any trace of the cracks. This worked like a charm every single time, and we now had a pie that would satisfy everyone.

PUMPKIN-PRALINE PIE

SERVES 8

You can use Easiest Ever Press-In Single-Crust Pie Dough (page 525) or Single-Crust Pie Dough (page 524) for this pie. Be sure to use pumpkin puree, not pumpkin pie filling, in this recipe.

1	recipe single-crust pie dough, fitted into a 9-inch pie plate and chilled (see note above)

FILLING

1	(15-ounce) can plain pumpkin puree (see note above)
¾	cup packed dark brown sugar
2	teaspoons ground cinnamon
1	teaspoon ground ginger
½	teaspoon ground allspice
	Pinch ground cloves
½	teaspoon salt
1	cup evaporated milk
3	large eggs
2	teaspoons vanilla extract

TOPPING

1	cup pecans, chopped fine
½	cup packed dark brown sugar
	Pinch salt
2	teaspoons dark corn syrup
1	teaspoon vanilla extract
2	teaspoons granulated sugar

1. Adjust an oven rack to the middle position and heat the oven to 375 degrees. Line the chilled crust with a double layer of aluminum foil and fill with pie weights. Bake until the pie dough looks dry and is light in color, 25 to 30 minutes. Remove the weights and foil and continue to bake the crust until golden brown, 5 to 10 minutes longer. Remove the pie shell from the oven, set aside, and reduce the oven temperature to 350 degrees. (The crust must still be warm when the filling is added.)

2. FOR THE FILLING: Puree the pumpkin, brown sugar, spices, and salt together in a food processor until smooth, about 1 minute. Cook the mixture in a large saucepan over medium-high heat until sputtering and thickened, about 4 minutes, and remove from the heat.

3. Whisk the evaporated milk into the pumpkin mixture, then whisk in the eggs and vanilla. Pour the filling into the warm pie shell and bake until the filling is puffed and cracked around the edges and the center barely jiggles when the pie is shaken, about 35 minutes.

4. FOR THE TOPPING: While the pie is baking, toss the pecans, brown sugar, and salt in a bowl. Add the corn syrup and vanilla, using your fingers to ensure that the ingredients are well blended.

5. Scatter the topping evenly over the puffed filling and sprinkle with the granulated sugar. Bake until the pecans are fragrant and the topping is bubbling around the edges, about 10 minutes. Let the pie cool on a wire rack until the filling has set, about 2 hours; serve slightly warm or at room temperature.

Sweet Potato Pie

There are two kinds of Southern cooking: lady food and down-home food. Sweet potato pie is from the latter category, since historically sweet potatoes were cheap and available and the recipes for this dessert were short on eggs, milk, and white sugar. Instead of scarce white sugar, country cooks relied more heavily on the natural sweetness and texture of the sweet potatoes themselves, combined with sorghum syrup or molasses. The question for the test kitchen was how to create a distinctive sweet potato pie, a recipe that honored the texture and flavor of sweet potatoes while being sufficiently recognizable as a dessert. Neither a custardy, pumpkin-style pie nor mashed-potatoes-in-a-crust would do.

A review of more than thirty recipes led us to five distinctive approaches to this dish. In some recipes the eggs were separated and the whites whipped; some recipes included evaporated or condensed milk; others used a combination of white and sweet potatoes; and most of them used a profusion of spices. To our surprise, all of them had abandoned molasses or sorghum for either granulated or brown sugar.

Although the classic pumpkin pie style was good, tasters were drawn to more authentic recipes, especially one published in *Dori Sanders' Country Cooking* (Algonquin Books of Chapel Hill, 1995), which had more sweet potato flavor. One problem with all such recipes, however, was their mashed-potatoes-in-a-crust quality. We wanted a recipe that would work as a dessert, not a savory side dish.

The first step was to determine the best method of preparing the sweet potatoes. We quickly ruled out both sliced potatoes (shingled in the pie under a custard) and food processor–whipped potatoes in favor of coarsely mashing them with a potato masher. Unlike in savory mashed potatoes, everybody loved a few lumps in the filling to offset the sweetness. We decided on microwaving as the easiest method of precooking the sweet potatoes.

Next, sweetened condensed milk and half-and-half were tossed aside in favor of regular milk. Blending two extra yolks into three whole eggs properly moistened the filling, and a bit of bourbon helped to accentuate the flavor. We were off to a good start.

A major problem with modern sweet potato pies is that they call for the usual pumpkin pie spices, which overwhelm the taste of the sweet potatoes. The solution was to use only a modest amount of nutmeg. Granulated sugar was fine, but since older recipes often call for molasses (or sorghum syrup, cane syrup, dark corn syrup, and even maple syrup), we decided to test it. The results were mixed, so we settled on 1 tablespoon of molasses as optional. This boosts flavor without overpowering the pie with the distinctive malt taste of molasses. (Even 2 tablespoons of molasses were too many.)

At this point we had a pie that tasters liked a lot, with real sweet potato flavor and enough custardy richness to place it firmly in the dessert category. But something was still lacking. The pie tasted a bit vegetal; it needed more oomph. We'd seen some recipes in which brown sugar was sprinkled over the bottom crust before the filling was poured in. We gave it a shot and were pleasantly surprised with the results. The pie now had an intense, thick, pure-sweet-potato filling, perfectly complemented by a layer of melted brown sugar just beneath. Its unique nature is reflected in the color of the filling, which is a fantastic orange rather than the dull brown that results from the use of too much molasses and too many spices. This is a sweet potato pie that any Southern cook would be proud of.

SWEET POTATO PIE

SERVES 8

You can use Easiest Ever Press-In Single-Crust Pie Dough (page 525) or Single-Crust Pie Dough (page 524) for this pie. The crust must still be warm when the filling is added.

1 recipe single-crust pie dough, fitted into a 9-inch pie plate and chilled (see note above)

FILLING

2 pounds sweet potatoes (about 3 potatoes)
2 tablespoons unsalted butter, softened
3 large eggs plus 2 large egg yolks
1 cup granulated sugar
½ teaspoon ground nutmeg
¼ teaspoon salt
2 tablespoons bourbon
1 tablespoon light molasses (optional)
1 teaspoon vanilla extract
⅔ cup whole milk
¼ cup packed dark brown sugar

1. Adjust an oven rack to the middle position and heat the oven to 375 degrees. Line the chilled crust with a double layer of aluminum foil and fill with pie weights. Bake until the pie dough looks dry and is light in color, 25 to 30 minutes. Remove the weights and foil and continue to bake the crust until golden brown, 5 to 10 minutes longer. Remove the pie shell from the oven and set aside. (The crust must still be warm when the filling is added.)

2. FOR THE FILLING: While the crust bakes, prick the sweet potatoes several times with a fork and arrange over several layers of paper towels in the microwave. Microwave at high power for 5 minutes. Turn each potato over and continue to microwave until tender but not mushy, about 5 minutes longer. Let the potatoes cool slightly.

3. Working with 1 potato at a time, slice it in half and scrape the cooked flesh into a large bowl using a soup spoon (you should have about 2 cups). Discard the skins. Mash the butter into the potatoes until just a few small potato lumps remain.

4. In a medium bowl, whisk the eggs, egg yolks, granulated sugar, nutmeg, and salt together. Stir in the bourbon, molasses (if using), and vanilla, then whisk in the milk. Gradually stir the egg mixture into the mashed sweet potatoes until smooth and combined.

5. Sprinkle the brown sugar evenly over the bottom of the warm pie crust, then spread the sweet potato mixture evenly over the top. Bake the pie until the filling is set around the edges but the center jiggles slightly when shaken, about 45 minutes. Let the pie cool on a wire rack until the filling has set, about 2 hours; serve slightly warm or at room temperature.

Raspberry Chiffon Pie

At its best, raspberry chiffon is light, billowy, and creamy. Rarely, however, is it intensely flavored. That's because the filling doesn't contain much fruit—it's mostly whipped egg whites and/or heavy cream, sugar, and gelatin (which allows the filling to set, without baking, in the refrigerator). Chiffon pies that rely on potent ingredients, such as lemon or coconut, can be flavorful, but after eating a half dozen of our raspberry chiffon pies, tasters were not very excited. The pink pies were pretty, but they tasted more like sweet foam than fruit.

Our first thought was to add more raspberries. From these tests we learned that in the best recipes the berries and sugar were cooked into a puree, which was strained to remove the seeds. Why not just add more of this puree? The solution was not so simple. Tasters preferred fillings made with gelatin-stabilized whipped cream to those made with gelatin-stabilized egg whites (the latter were billowy but not really creamy and smooth). Unfortunately, the cream filling could only "hold" so much fruit puree before it would collapse and refuse to set.

How could we help stiffen the chiffon filling? More gelatin helped (3 tablespoons was ideal), but there was a limit—we didn't want a bouncy Jell-O pie. A little cream cheese thickened the whipped cream and added more richness. In the end, these measures allowed us to add ⅓ cup of raspberry puree to the filling. A good start, but tasters wanted more fruit flavor.

Replacing the usual plain gelatin with raspberry-flavored gelatin bumped up the fruit flavor and gave the filling a vibrant color, but we were now officially out of ideas. Our filling had better flavor than the fillings most recipes produced, but it wasn't what we would call intense. Then inspiration struck.

Many diners serve no-bake berry pies. The filling is basically sweetened fruit thickened with pectin (the stuff used to turn fruit into jam). We wondered if we could use this kind of filling in a thin base layer for our chiffon pie.

This idea worked perfectly. We cooked frozen berries (one-quarter the price of fresh berries) until they started to break down and then added the pectin, followed by the sugar. The mixture thickened beautifully and the flavor was intense. We set aside some of this smooth puree to flavor the chiffon filling and poured the rest (with fresh fruit added for texture and flavor) into a prebaked pie shell. After about 10 minutes on the counter, this jam-like mixture set into a thin, dark red layer of pure raspberry flavor.

Next we prepared the chiffon filling (with the reserved berry mixture), spooned it over the fruit layer, and let the gelatin work its magic in the refrigerator. Three hours later, we had a perfectly set, sliceable pie with great color and intense raspberry flavor. With a crown of lightly sweetened whipped cream, our pie finally tasted as good as it looked.

RASPBERRY CHIFFON PIE

SERVES 8

You can use Easiest Ever Press-In Single-Crust Pie Dough (page 525) or Single-Crust Pie Dough (page 524) for this pie. The most common brand of pectin we found at the market is Sure-Jell, but any brand will work. The raspberry-flavored gelatin is important for the color and flavor of the chiffon layer; do not substitute unflavored gelatin.

1   recipe single-crust pie dough, fitted into a 9-inch pie plate and chilled (see note above)

FRUIT

2   cups (10 ounces) frozen raspberries
3   tablespoons pectin (see note above)
1½ cups sugar
    Pinch salt
1   cup fresh raspberries

CHIFFON

3   tablespoons raspberry-flavored gelatin (see note above)
3   tablespoons boiling water
3   ounces cream cheese, softened
1   cup heavy cream, chilled

TOPPING

1¼ cups heavy cream, chilled
2   tablespoons sugar

1. Adjust an oven rack to the middle position and heat the oven to 375 degrees. Line the chilled crust with a double layer of aluminum foil and fill with pie weights. Bake until the pie dough looks dry and is light in color, 25 to 30 minutes. Remove the weights and foil and continue to bake the crust until deep golden brown, 10 to 12 minutes longer. Let the crust cool to room temperature.

2. FOR THE FRUIT: Cook the frozen raspberries in a medium saucepan over medium-high heat, stirring occasionally, until the berries begin to release their juice, about 3 minutes. Stir in the pectin and bring to a boil, stirring constantly. Stir in the sugar and salt and continue to boil, stirring constantly, until slightly thickened, about 2 minutes. Strain the mixture through a fine-mesh strainer into a medium bowl, pressing on the solids to extract as much puree as possible; discard the solids.

3. Transfer ⅓ cup of the raspberry puree to a small bowl and cool to room temperature. Gently fold the fresh raspberries into the remaining puree, then spread the mixture in the baked and cooled pie crust.

4. FOR THE CHIFFON: Dissolve the gelatin in the boiling water in a large bowl. Add the cream cheese and reserved ⅓ cup raspberry puree and beat with an electric mixer on high speed until smooth, about 2 minutes. Add the cream and beat on medium-low until incorporated, about 30 seconds. Increase the mixer speed to high and beat until very thick, 1 to 2 minutes. Spread the chiffon evenly in the pie crust on top of the fruit. Cover the pie loosely with plastic wrap and refrigerate until the filling is chilled and set, about 3 hours.

5. FOR THE TOPPING: Before serving, whip the cream and sugar together with an electric mixer on medium-low speed until frothy, about 1 minute. Increase the mixer speed to high and continue to whip until the cream forms soft peaks, 1 to 3 minutes. Spread the whipped cream over the chiffon.

Variation
STRAWBERRY CHIFFON PIE
Substitute frozen strawberries for the frozen raspberries, fresh strawberries, hulled and quartered, for the fresh raspberries, and strawberry-flavored gelatin for the raspberry-flavored gelatin.

Black-Bottom Pie

Black-bottom pie is a chocolate cream pie—chocolate custard and sweetened whipped cream—with two added bonuses: an airy rum chiffon layer between the chocolate and whipped cream layers and a chocolate cookie crust. Recipes for this pie first appeared in the early twentieth century, but its popularity didn't take off until the late 1930s, when restaurant reviewer Duncan Hines wrote about experiencing the pie's "unbelievably light texture" at the Dolores Restaurant and Drive-In in Oklahoma City, Oklahoma.

But after preparing a handful of recipes, we realized why black-bottom pie is so rarely made. Between making the cookie crumb crust, chocolate custard, rum layer (which must be stabilized with gelatin, chilled over an ice bath to set, and lightened with beaten raw egg whites to create a chiffon texture), and whipped cream, we dirtied three saucepans, seven bowls, and four whisks during 3 hours in the kitchen. But we had to admit, the contrast in texture and flavor between the chocolate custard, fluffy rum chiffon, and whipped cream was worth the mess.

SECRETS TO BLACK-BOTTOM PIE FILLING

1. For a stable, silky filling, beat the egg white mixture over a pot of barely simmering water to soft peaks, about 2 minutes.

2. Off the heat, beat the mixture until it becomes very thick and glossy and cools to room temperature, about 3 minutes.

We started our kitchen work at the bottom, with the crust. Although the pie was originally made with a gingersnap crust, by the 1940s, recipes began to shift to pastry or chocolate cookie crusts. We compared all three, and tasters agreed that the chocolate crust provided superior flavor—and actually lived up to the name "black-bottom." We crushed chocolate cookies, bound them with melted butter, pressed the mixture into a pie plate, and then baked the crust for 10 minutes to assure a crisp foundation for our pie.

A few recipes saved time by using one large batch of custard as a base for both the chocolate and rum layers. This sounded promising, so we made a basic custard with sugar, half-and-half, egg yolks, and cornstarch. We removed half of the custard and stirred in chopped chocolate until it was melted, and then we poured this portion into the crust to chill and set.

For the rum chiffon layer, our plan was to flavor the remaining custard with rum, stabilize it with a little gelatin, and then add whipped raw egg whites for the signature light and airy texture. We were disappointed to find that the whipped whites weren't quite sturdy enough to support the sweetened whipped cream on top. One way to make egg whites sturdier is to cook them, so we tried making a 7-minute frosting (made by beating egg whites, sugar, water, and cream of tartar over a

double boiler) and adding it to the rum-enhanced custard. This worked like a charm, producing a voluminous, sturdy, and flavorful chiffon that was well worth the effort. With a piping of whipped cream on top, it was easy to see why Duncan Hines was so impressed with black-bottom pie all those years ago.

BLACK-BOTTOM PIE

SERVES 8

Nabisco Famous Chocolate Wafers are the test kitchen's favorite brand for making the crust. This recipe makes a generous amount of filling; to prevent the filling from overflowing the pie crust, add the final ½ cup of the rum layer after the filling has set for 20 minutes.

CRUST

32	chocolate cookies (see note above), broken into rough pieces (about 2½ cups)
4	tablespoons unsalted butter, melted

PIE

⅔	cup plus 2 tablespoons sugar
4	teaspoons cornstarch
2	cups half-and-half
4	large egg yolks plus 1 large egg white
6	ounces semisweet chocolate, chopped fine
3	tablespoons golden or light rum
2	tablespoons water
1	teaspoon unflavored gelatin
¼	teaspoon cream of tartar
1½	cups heavy cream, chilled

1. FOR THE CRUST: Adjust an oven rack to the middle position and heat the oven to 350 degrees. Process the cookie pieces in a food processor to fine crumbs. Add the butter and pulse until combined. Press the crumbs into the bottom and sides of a 9-inch pie plate and refrigerate until firm, about 20 minutes. Bake until set, about 10 minutes. Cool completely.

2. FOR THE PIE: Whisk ⅓ cup of the sugar, the cornstarch, half-and-half, and egg yolks in a saucepan. Cook over medium heat, stirring constantly, until the mixture comes to a boil, about 8 minutes.

3. Divide the hot custard evenly between 2 bowls. Whisk the chocolate into one bowl until smooth, then pour into the cooled pie crust; refrigerate. Whisk together the rum, 1 tablespoon of the water, and the gelatin in a third bowl and let sit for 5 minutes; stir into the bowl with the plain custard and refrigerate, stirring occasionally, until the mixture is wobbly but not set, about 20 minutes.

4. Combine ⅓ cup more of the sugar, the egg white, the remaining 1 tablespoon water, and the cream of tartar in a large heatproof bowl set over a medium saucepan filled with ½ inch of barely simmering water (don't let the bowl touch the water). With an electric mixer on medium-high speed, beat the egg white mixture to soft peaks, about 2 minutes; remove the bowl from the heat and beat the egg white mixture until very thick and glossy and cooled to room temperature, about 3 minutes.

5. Whisk the cooled egg white mixture into the chilled rum custard until smooth. Pour all but ½ cup of the rum custard into the chocolate custard–filled pie crust. Refrigerate for 20 minutes, then top with the remaining rum custard. Refrigerate until completely set, 3 hours or up to 24 hours. Before serving, whip the cream and remaining 2 tablespoons sugar together with an electric mixer on medium-low speed until frothy, about 1 minute. Increase the mixer speed to high and continue to whip until the cream forms soft peaks, 1 to 3 minutes. Spread the whipped cream over the top of the pie and serve.

Mixed-Berry Streusel Pie

Fresh berries guarantee a pie with great flavor, but their juices can make for a sodden crust and streusel. We wanted to create a pie with intense berry flavor that would slice neatly and have a crisp crust and crunchy streusel topping. Most important, we wanted it to be as easy as possible.

To keep things simple, we started with the test kitchen's Easiest Ever Press-In Single-Crust Pie Dough (page 525), which relies on cream cheese to make the dough easy to handle. The texture was ideal, but we were disappointed that tasters said they wanted a more flavorful crust to accent the sweet berry filling. We tried our recipe for a graham cracker crust, which tasted great but was too sandy and loose to handle the moist berry filling. Thinking that flour and finely ground cracker crumbs aren't totally dissimilar, we made a hybrid dough by replacing some of the flour in our Easiest Ever recipe with graham cracker crumbs. This dough had the best of both worlds: rich graham flavor and sufficient sturdiness.

MAKING A SLICEABLE PIE

1. When the berry mixture is thick enough, it will be bubbling and a spatula will leave a trail when dragged through the mixture.

2. To further tighten the filling, toss the cooked berry mixture with the remaining fresh berries and tapioca.

A little lemon zest added brightness to our mixed-berry filling, but it was still too watery to slice neatly. Cooking the berries before adding them to the pie thickened the filling nicely, but it compromised their fresh flavor. Cooking just a portion of the berries gave us a thicker filling with nice depth of flavor, but we still couldn't coax tidy slices from the pie. We needed to thicken the berry juices.

In search of a neutral-tasting thickener that wouldn't make the filling too rubbery or stodgy, we did a side-by-side test of pectin, flour, cornstarch, and tapioca. Tasters preferred the pie made with tapioca for its ability to thicken the filling without calling attention to itself. We could now cut perfect slices from the pie, so all that was left was the crowning streusel.

The raw pie dough already contained the butter and flour-crumb mixture that forms the base of streusel. We made a batch of our pie dough as usual and reserved enough to pat in the pan for our crust. We then fortified the remaining dough mixture with oats for texture and brown sugar for sweetness, filled the pie, and sprinkled the streusel on top. It baked up sweet, crunchy, and buttery. Finally, all the elements were in place for a perfect slice of pie.

MIXED-BERRY STREUSEL PIE

SERVES 8

Any combination of strawberries, blackberries, blueberries, and raspberries will work here, but we recommend using no more than 2 cups of strawberries, which tend to be watery. If your berries aren't sweet enough, you can add an extra ¼ cup of sugar to the filling in step 3.

CRUST AND STREUSEL

1½ cups all-purpose flour
  9 whole graham crackers,
      broken into rough pieces
  ½ teaspoon salt
 12 tablespoons (1½ sticks) unsalted butter,
      cut into ½-inch pieces and softened
  2 ounces cream cheese,
      cut into ½-inch pieces
  1 teaspoon vanilla extract
  ½ cup old-fashioned oats
  ½ cup packed light brown sugar

FILLING

  6 cups mixed fresh berries (see note above)
  ¾ cup granulated sugar
  ½ teaspoon grated fresh lemon zest
  3 tablespoons Minute tapioca

1. FOR THE CRUST AND STREUSEL: Grease a 9-inch pie plate. Process the flour, graham cracker pieces, and salt in a food processor until finely ground. Add the butter, cream cheese, and vanilla and pulse until a dough forms. Remove 2 cups of the dough from the food processor (leave the remaining dough in the work bowl of the food processor) and turn out onto a lightly floured work surface. Flatten the dough into a 6-inch disk and transfer to the prepared pie plate. Following the photo on page 526 press the dough evenly into the pie plate. Flute the edges following the photo on page 524. Cover the dough with plastic wrap and refrigerate until firm, at least 1 hour or up to 24 hours.

2. Add the oats and brown sugar to the food processor with the remaining dough and pulse until the mixture resembles coarse meal. Transfer to a bowl and use your fingers to pinch the topping into peanut-sized clumps; cover and refrigerate the streusel.

3. FOR THE FILLING: Adjust an oven rack to the lowest position and heat the oven to 350 degrees. Cook 2 cups of the berries in a saucepan over medium-high heat until juicy, about 3 minutes. Stir in the sugar and lemon zest and simmer until thickened, about 5 minutes. Let cool for 5 minutes, then gently toss the cooked berry mixture, remaining 4 cups berries, and tapioca in a large bowl until combined.

4. Transfer the berry mixture to the chilled crust. Scatter the streusel evenly over the pie. Bake the pie on a rimmed baking sheet until the fruit is bubbling around the edges and the streusel is browned and crisp, 45 to 55 minutes. Let the pie cool on a wire rack for 30 minutes, then refrigerate until set, at least 2 hours or up to 24 hours. Serve.

Icebox Key Lime Pie

Key lime pie was invented in the Florida Keys more than one hundred years ago. The original recipe was considered an icebox pie because the filling of sweetened condensed milk, egg yolks, and lime juice wasn't cooked. Everything was simply stirred together and poured into a prebaked graham cracker crust. The pie was then refrigerated for several hours, where the lime's acid "cooked" the milk and yolks, creating a custardy filling bursting with lime flavor.

Due to concerns about eating raw eggs, today's Key lime pies fall into two distinct camps: uncooked pies in which the eggs are replaced with whipped cream or gelatin, and those whose egg-based filling is cooked on the stovetop. We tried a handful of uncooked pies and were consistently disappointed. Their texture was never custardy; the pies were either too fluffy from whipped cream or too rubbery from gelatin. We set our goal high: to create a Key lime pie as easy and custardy as the original without having to cook the filling.

We started with the lime juice. Most recipes don't use enough, and the resulting pie is too timid. We found that we needed a full cup of fresh lime juice (bottled lime juice tasted artificial) to produce a pie with bracing lime flavor. Lime zest added another layer of flavor, and processing the zest with a little sugar offset its sourness and eliminated the annoying chewy bits.

To the juice and zest we added a can of sweetened condensed milk. We now needed something other than egg yolks to thicken this soupy mixture. Potato starch, non-fat dry milk, Egg Beaters, and store-bought lime curd failed miserably, producing weepy pies we could have drunk with a straw. Cream cheese had the opposite problem; it made the filling too dense—more cheesecake than custard pie. Then we tried instant pudding mix—not the cook-and-serve kind, but the stuff you just mix with milk, chill, and serve. Although we weren't crazy about the flavor (tasters rejected lemon and lime varieties, but vanilla was deemed acceptable), the texture was almost custard-like. The filling was still a little too thin, but it gave us a glimmer of hope.

Going back to the drawing board, we decided to try the instant vanilla pudding mix in combination with small amounts of gelatin and cream cheese—two ingredients that showed promise but had each caused textural problems when used as the

---

THE AMERICAN TABLE
KEY LIME PIE

Before Gail Borden invented sweetened condensed milk in 1856, drinking milk was a health risk, as there was no pasteurization or refrigeration for fresh milk. The shelf stability and safety of sweetened condensed milk made it especially popular in areas like the Florida Keys, where the hot climate promoted rapid spoilage of anything perishable.

Like many of our iconic foods, no one knows for sure when or by whom the first Key lime pie was made, but with canned milk in every pantry by the 1870s and an abundance of tiny Key limes throughout the area, it was only a matter of time. Most food historians trace the history of this pie back to the 1890s, but there are those—especially in the Keys—who claim the recipe is decades older.

sole thickener. After several days of trial and error, we finally hit on the right ratios to thicken our pie filling into custardy perfection. A block of cream cheese, ⅓ cup of instant vanilla pudding mix, and a stingy 1¼ teaspoons of gelatin did the trick. After squeezing and scraping 250 limes into twenty-nine pies, we'd discovered the secrets to a custardy no-cook, no-egg Key lime pie.

ICEBOX KEY LIME PIE

SERVES 8

Feel free to use Key limes if desired; note that you'll need about 40 Key limes to yield 1 cup of juice. Do not, however, use bottled Key lime juice or the pie will have a serious lack of flavor. Serve with whipped cream, if desired.

CRUST

8	whole graham crackers, broken into 1-inch pieces
5	tablespoons unsalted butter, melted and cooled
3	tablespoons sugar

FILLING

¼	cup sugar
1	tablespoon grated fresh lime zest and 1 cup fresh lime juice (8 to 10 limes; see note above)
1	(8-ounce) package cream cheese, softened
1	(14-ounce) can sweetened condensed milk
⅓	cup instant vanilla pudding mix
1¼	teaspoons unflavored gelatin
1	teaspoon vanilla extract

1. FOR THE CRUST: Adjust an oven rack to the middle position and heat the oven to 325 degrees. Process the graham cracker pieces in a food processor to fine, even crumbs, about 30 seconds. Sprinkle the melted butter and sugar over the crumbs and pulse until combined.

2. Sprinkle the mixture into a 9-inch pie plate and wipe out the work bowl. Following the photo on page 545, use the bottom of a measuring cup to press the crumbs into an even layer on the bottom and sides of the pie plate. Bake until the crust is fragrant and beginning to brown, 13 to 18 minutes.

3. FOR THE FILLING: Process the sugar and lime zest together in a food processor until the sugar turns bright green, about 30 seconds. Add the cream cheese and continue to process until combined, about 30 seconds. Add the condensed milk and pudding mix and continue to process until smooth, about 30 seconds. Scrape down the sides of the work bowl.

4. Stir the gelatin and 2 tablespoons of the lime juice together in a small bowl and microwave until warm (but not bubbling), about 15 seconds. Stir to dissolve the gelatin.

5. With the food processor running, pour the warm gelatin mixture, remaining lime juice, and vanilla through the feed tube and continue to process until thoroughly combined, about 30 seconds. Pour the lime filling into the baked and cooled pie crust. Refrigerate the pie, uncovered, until chilled and set, about 6 hours. Serve chilled or at room temperature.

Grasshopper Pie

At once creamy and fluffy, grasshopper pie boasts great mint and chocolate flavor. But many modern recipes switch the cool, silky filling for mint chocolate chip ice cream. We were determined to revisit the classic version of this recipe.

The pie takes its name from a cocktail, the grasshopper, which was invented at Tujague's Restaurant in New Orleans near the end of Prohibition. This bright green drink is a mix of heavy cream, white crème de cacao (a clear version of the dark chocolate cordial), and green crème de menthe (a mint cordial) that is shaken with ice and strained into a cocktail glass. Grasshopper pie was born during the 1950s, when chiffon pies were the rage. These fluffy pies start with a flavored gelatin base into which whipped egg whites and/or whipped cream are folded.

We found a classic Knox Gelatine recipe reprinted in Jean Anderson's *The American Century Cookbook* (1997). The gelatin was softened and dissolved in water, then mixed with green crème de menthe and white crème de cacao. After it firmed up a bit, in went stiffly beaten egg whites and whipped cream. It was light and fluffy and darn good, but not perfect. The whipped egg whites made this pie a little less creamy than we had hoped.

We finally found a near-perfect recipe in *Gourmet's Menu Cookbook* (1963). It, too, started with gelatin, this time softened in heavy cream instead of water. After the liqueurs were added and the mixture set up, only whipped cream was folded in—no egg whites. Soft and super-minty, it was the closest thing yet to the grasshopper pie of our dreams.

Because we still wanted the pie to be a bit creamier and also taller, we increased the amount of whipped cream. Where we made our big breakthrough, however, was the crust. We kept the melted butter, but rather than using the traditional ground chocolate wafers, we tried Mint 'n Creme Oreo cookies—Oreos flavored with mint. They worked

like a charm, and now both the filling and the crust were flavored with both chocolate and mint. A new cookie made this old recipe even better than we had thought possible.

GRASSHOPPER PIE

SERVES 8

The festive green color of this pie filling depends on the color of the liqueurs; be sure to buy green crème de menthe (not clear) and white crème de cacao (not dark). Once chilled and set, the pie can be covered loosely with plastic wrap and refrigerated for up to 24 hours before serving. Garnish the pie with chocolate shavings, if desired.

CRUST

16	Double Delight Mint 'n Creme Oreo cookies, broken into rough pieces
4	tablespoons unsalted butter, melted and cooled

FILLING

2	cups heavy cream, chilled
½	cup sugar
2¼	teaspoons unflavored gelatin
	Pinch salt
3	large egg yolks
¼	cup green crème de menthe (see note above)
¼	cup white crème de cacao (see note above)

Chocolate for shavings (optional)

1. FOR THE CRUST: Adjust an oven rack to the middle position and heat the oven to 350 degrees. Process the cookies in a food processor until coarsely ground, about fifteen 1-second pulses, then continue to process to fine, even crumbs, about 15 seconds longer. Sprinkle the melted butter over the crumbs and pulse to incorporate.

MAKING CHOCOLATE SHAVINGS

For pretty chocolate shavings, simply use a vegetable peeler and peel them off a large block of chocolate. (Large blocks of chocolate make nicer shavings than thin bars of chocolate.)

2. Sprinkle the mixture into a 9-inch pie plate. Use the bottom of a measuring cup to press the crumbs into an even layer on the bottom and sides of the pie plate (see page 545). Bake until the crust is fragrant and looks set, 10 to 15 minutes. Let cool completely on a wire rack.

3. FOR THE FILLING: Combine ½ cup of the cream, the sugar, gelatin, and salt in a medium saucepan and let sit until the gelatin softens, about 5 minutes. In a medium bowl, whisk the egg yolks together.

4. Cook the cream mixture over medium heat until the gelatin dissolves and the mixture is hot (but not boiling), about 2 minutes. Slowly whisk the hot gelatin mixture into the egg yolks to temper. Pour the mixture back into the saucepan and continue to cook over medium heat, stirring constantly, until slightly thickened, about 2 minutes.

5. Off the heat, stir in the crème de menthe and crème de cacao. Pour the mixture into a clean bowl and refrigerate, stirring occasionally, until very thick but not set, 20 to 25 minutes.

6. Whip the remaining 1½ cups cream in a large bowl with an electric mixer on low speed until frothy, about 1 minute. Increase the mixer speed to high and continue to whip until the cream forms soft peaks, 1 to 3 minutes.

7. Thoroughly whisk 1 cup of the whipped cream into the gelatin mixture to lighten it. Using a rubber spatula, fold the lightened gelatin mixture into the remaining whipped cream until no streaks remain. Spread the mixture in the baked and cooled pie crust and smooth the top. Refrigerate the pie, uncovered, until the filling is chilled and set, about 6 hours. Serve chilled or at room temperature.

Easy Apple Turnovers

Hot turnovers, fresh from the oven, are a great treat, but preparing turnovers from scratch—starting with a homemade pastry dough—can be labor-intensive. Frozen puff pastry from the supermarket makes turnovers easy to prepare, but it doesn't ensure success. The recipes we tested yielded mushy, messy, and mediocre turnovers. We had our work cut out for us.

Most recipes called for either sliced or shredded apples, but we found both to be unappealing. Slices were undercooked (unless paper-thin, a real kitchen headache), and shredded apples looked like little worms. Searching for a happy medium, we pulsed the apples and sugar in the food processor until the apples were roughly chopped. The random chunkiness of the processed apples was great for texture, but now they gave off too much liquid and waterlogged the pastry.

We tried straining the apple mixture, but this left the filling too dry and grainy. What we needed was a binder to create a cohesive filling. Cooking some of the apples would do the trick, but we didn't want to complicate a simple recipe. Could we get away with a shortcut—store-bought applesauce—to produce that "cooked apple" texture? Sure enough, the applesauce combined with the strained apple mixture made for just the right consistency and boosted the apple flavor. With a little lemon juice and a pinch of salt, our filling was just right.

Over the years, we've learned that puff pastry works well as long as you play by its rules. For the perfect puff, the pastry must be cold and the oven hot. After assembling the turnovers, we placed them in the freezer for 15 minutes just to firm them up. When cooked in a 400-degree oven, the pastry layers puffed perfectly—well, almost.

Most of the turnovers split at the seams while they baked. What we needed was some sort of "glue" to brush over the edges of the pastry before sealing. After glancing over at the draining apple mixture, we realized that we could use the juice from the apples; we'd been planning to throw it out anyway! The sticky, sugary juice made a great sealant. Getting a little apple-crazy, we brushed more of the apple juice over the tops of the turnovers. This helped them to brown, and a sprinkle of cinnamon sugar made them look as good as they tasted.

EASY APPLE TURNOVERS

MAKES 8 TURNOVERS

If you don't have a food processor, grate the peeled and cored apples on the coarse side of a box grater before mixing them with the lemon juice, sugar, and salt. This recipe is easily cut in half. You can fill, fold, and freeze the unbaked turnovers up to 1 month in advance. Freeze them on a baking sheet, then transfer to a zipper-lock plastic freezer bag. Before baking, allow the turnovers to sit at room temperature for 20 minutes, then proceed with the recipe as directed in step 4.

¾	cup sugar
1	teaspoon ground cinnamon
2	Granny Smith apples, peeled, cored, and chopped coarse
1	tablespoon fresh lemon juice
⅛	teaspoon salt
½	cup applesauce
2	(9 by 9½-inch) sheets frozen puff pastry, thawed overnight in refrigerator

1. Adjust the oven racks to the upper-middle and lower-middle positions and heat the oven to 400 degrees. Combine ¼ cup of the sugar and the cinnamon in a small bowl. Set aside.

2. Pulse the apples, remaining ½ cup sugar, lemon juice, and salt in a food processor until the apples are chopped into pieces no larger than ½ inch. Allow to sit for 5 minutes, then drain in a fine-mesh strainer set over a bowl. Reserve the juices. Transfer the apple mixture to a medium bowl and stir in the applesauce.

MAKING PERFECT TURNOVERS

1. Place 2 tablespoons of the apple mixture in the center of each 5-inch square of pastry. Brush the edges of the pastry with the reserved apple juice.

2. Bring one corner of the pastry over to meet the opposite corner to form a triangle. Use a fork to crimp the edges and seal the turnovers.

3. Unfold 1 sheet puff pastry onto a lightly floured work surface and roll into a 10-inch square. Following the photos, cut the pastry into four 5-inch squares and fill each square with 2 tablespoons of the apple mixture. Brush the edges with some of the reserved apple juice, then fold and crimp. Place the turnovers on a plate and freeze until firm, about 15 minutes. Repeat with the remaining sheet puff pastry and filling.

4. Line 2 rimmed baking sheets with parchment paper. With the turnovers still on the plate, brush the tops with some of the reserved apple juice and sprinkle with the cinnamon sugar. Place 4 turnovers on each baking sheet and bake until well browned, 20 to 26 minutes, switching and rotating the sheets halfway through the baking time. Transfer the turnovers to a wire rack and let cool slightly. Serve the turnovers warm or at room temperature.

Variation

SUGAR AND SPICE APPLE TURNOVERS
Reduce the amount of cinnamon to ½ teaspoon and add ½ teaspoon ground ginger, ¼ teaspoon ground nutmeg, and a pinch ground cloves to the cinnamon sugar.

Brown Sugar Berry Shortcakes

Homemade light and flaky baking-powder biscuits (although perfect for slathering with butter) don't stand a chance against juicy berries in berry shortcake. We set out to develop an honest-to-goodness shortcake—a biscuit with enough structure and flavor to hold its own against the berries and whipped cream topping.

Shortcakes are basically biscuit dough enriched with sugar and fat, usually in the form of eggs or something richer than the usual milk or buttermilk. This fat adds heft and structure, creating a slightly more cakey texture that's perfect for soaking up the juices from the berries.

Starting with a basic baking-powder biscuit recipe, we enriched the dough with an egg and half-and-half (milk was too thin, cream too heavy). This provided the density and crumb that we were after, but the flavor was muted. A fellow test cook suggested we try sour cream in place of the half-and-half, and this gave the shortcakes just the savory, tangy kick we were looking for. Replacing the usual granulated sugar with brown sugar added a welcome caramel note.

Although these shortcakes now tasted much better, they were squat and gummy on the inside; once we added the sour cream, they lost their tender, pillowy texture. We tried adding more baking powder to improve the rise, but this just gave the shortcakes a chemical flavor. Getting frustrated, we were about to remove the sour cream from the recipe when we realized that we were still treating these shortcakes like biscuits. Up to this point, we had been carefully rolling out the dough and using a biscuit cutter to punch out the rounds. But this dough, enriched with egg and sour cream, was more similar to a muffin or cake than a biscuit. What if we skipped the rolling and cutting?

We turned the oven down to a more cake-friendly 375 degrees (biscuits are usually baked at 425 or 450 degrees) and used an ice cream scoop to portion the dough directly from the mixing bowl onto a parchment-lined baking sheet. The large, domed scoops solved our squat shortcake problem, and the oven's moderate heat gave the shortcakes plenty of time to cook through, creating a craggy, rustic exterior and a moist, fluffy interior. For one last touch, we tried brushing the unbaked domes of dough with melted butter and sprinkling them with granulated sugar. The crunchy, crystallized topping added another layer of texture.

As for the berries, we mashed some with brown sugar (preferred over granulated sugar for its more complex flavor) to release their juices but kept most of them whole because we liked their tartness and texture. To tie everything together, we dolloped our berry shortcakes with a tangy whipped topping made from heavy cream, brown sugar (again, everyone liked its caramel flavor), and sour cream. This sweet-tart, old-fashioned dessert is a perfect way to enjoy summer berries.

BROWN SUGAR BERRY SHORTCAKES
SERVES 6
Depending on the sweetness of the berries, you may have to use more or less brown sugar. If you don't have a large ice cream scoop, divide the dough into 6 equal portions and use your hands to form shortcakes in a rough semispherical shape. If you don't have a food processor, you can prepare the shortcakes by hand: Freeze the stick of butter until hard and then grate it into the dry ingredients using the large holes of a box grater. Toss gently to distribute the butter evenly and proceed with the recipe. To make sure that they maintain their integrity while they macerate, we mash only one-third of the berries. In addition, we prepare each berry according to its size and structure—raspberries, blueberries, and currants can remain whole, but strawberries should be hulled, halved, and sliced; blackberries should be halved.

FRUIT

6	cups mixed fresh berries (see note above)
4–6	tablespoons light brown sugar (see note above)

SHORTCAKES

2	cups all-purpose flour
3	tablespoons light brown sugar
1	tablespoon baking powder
½	teaspoon salt
8	tablespoons (1 stick) unsalted butter, cut into ½-inch pieces and chilled, plus 2 tablespoons unsalted butter, melted (for brushing on shortcakes)
1	large egg
½	cup sour cream
2	tablespoons granulated sugar

TOPPING

1	cup heavy cream
¼	cup sour cream
¼	cup packed light brown sugar

1. FOR THE FRUIT: Crush 2 cups of the berries and the brown sugar in a large bowl with a potato masher. Fold in the remaining 4 cups berries and let sit at room temperature until the sugar has dissolved and the berries are juicy, about 30 minutes.

2. FOR THE SHORTCAKES: Adjust an oven rack to the upper-middle position and heat the oven to 375 degrees. Line a rimmed baking sheet with parchment paper. Pulse the flour, brown sugar, baking powder, and salt together in a food processor until no lumps of sugar remain. Scatter the chilled butter pieces over the top and pulse until the mixture resembles coarse meal, about 7 pulses. Transfer to a large bowl.

3. Whisk the egg and sour cream together in a small bowl. Stir into the flour mixture with a rubber spatula until large clumps form. Using your hands, knead lightly until the dough comes together and no dry flecks of flour remain.

4. Using a large (#10) ice cream scoop, scoop 6 dough rounds onto the baking sheet. Brush the tops with the melted butter and sprinkle with the granulated sugar. Bake until golden brown, 25 to 30 minutes, rotating the baking sheet halfway through the baking time. Cool the shortcakes on the baking sheet for 10 minutes. (The cooled shortcakes can be wrapped tightly in plastic wrap and kept at room temperature for up to 24 hours.)

5. FOR THE TOPPING: With an electric mixer on medium speed, beat together the heavy cream, sour cream, and brown sugar to stiff peaks. Split each shortcake in half using a serrated knife and place the bottoms on individual plates. Spoon a portion of the fruit over the bottoms, top with some of the whipped cream, and cap with the shortcake tops. Serve.

Cranberry-Apple Crisp

A bowl of warm cranberry-apple crisp with a scoop of vanilla ice cream is a great fall dessert. We thought we'd achieve success by simply adding cranberries to our favorite apple crisp recipe, but we soon had doubts. Our crisp had no balance of flavors; one bite tasted super-tart and overloaded with cranberries, and the next tasted of apples, with no cranberry flavor at all. To make matters worse, the soggy topping was a long way from crisp.

We had our work cut out for us. To start, we ran across a crisp recipe that called for canned cranberry sauce. The idea of using canned cranberries when our supermarket was overflowing with bags of fresh berries seemed ridiculous, but what if we made our own cranberry sauce with fresh cranberries? That way we could get even cranberry distribution (a sauce would be easy to stir into the apples) and sweeten the cranberries before they met the apples.

We cooked fresh cranberries with sugar and a little water until they burst and thickened into a homemade sauce. We then added the mixture to diced Granny Smith apples (the test kitchen's favorite for baking) and topped the fruit with the classic combination of butter, flour, sugar, cinnamon, and oats.

After an hour and a half in the oven, when the fruit juices started to bubble up, we thought we had a winner. The scarlet filling looked like it was packed with cranberry flavor, but it actually tasted pretty dull and the consistency was soupy.

A colleague suggested that dried cranberries might be the answer to deeper cranberry flavor. Adding a cup of dried berries gave our crisp a one-two punch of concentrated cranberry flavor and added a welcome textural hit that tasters loved. And as the dried berries rehydrated, they absorbed some of the excess juices, making for a drier topping. Adding some tapioca to the filling (better than either flour or cornstarch) also helped to thicken the fruit juices.

Now that we had the berries sorted out, we took another look at the apples. We liked the way Granny Smiths held their shape in the oven, but they were awfully tart. To get a better balance of flavors, we tried combining the Grannies with sweeter apples like Gala, Golden Delicious, Red Delicious, and Braeburn. The Braeburns were tasters' favorite, followed by Golden Delicious.

The crisp was taking nearly 90 minutes to bake. Any less time and the apples were too firm, but in 90 minutes the topping turned almost as hard as a stale granola bar. Since we were already dirtying a pot to make the cranberry sauce, we thought we'd use the same pot to jump-start the apples on the stovetop. Just 5 minutes of stovetop cooking was all it took to reduce the baking time from 90 to 30 minutes. The apples now cooked evenly in the baking dish, and

the topping was no longer a dark, hard shell.

After peeling our way through bushels of apples (more than 150 pounds!) and puckering up to pounds of cranberries, we had finally found the path to perfect cranberry-apple crisp.

CRANBERRY-APPLE CRISP

SERVES 8 TO 10

If you can't find Braeburn apples, Golden Delicious will work. Serve with vanilla ice cream or whipped cream.

TOPPING

¾	cup all-purpose flour
½	cup packed light brown sugar
½	cup granulated sugar
1	teaspoon ground cinnamon
12	tablespoons (1½ sticks) unsalted butter, cut into ½-inch pieces and chilled
¾	cup old-fashioned oats

FILLING

1	pound fresh or frozen cranberries (about 4 cups)
1¼	cups granulated sugar
¼	cup water
2½	pounds Granny Smith apples (5 to 7 apples), peeled, cored, and cut into ½-inch pieces
2½	pounds Braeburn apples (5 to 7 apples; see note above), peeled, cored, and cut into ½-inch pieces
1	cup dried sweetened cranberries
3	tablespoons Minute tapioca

1. FOR THE TOPPING: Adjust an oven rack to the middle position and heat the oven to 400 degrees. Pulse the flour, sugars, cinnamon, and butter in a food processor until the mixture has the texture of coarse crumbs (some pea-sized pieces of butter will remain), about twelve 1-second pulses. Transfer to a medium bowl, stir in the oats, and use your fingers to pinch the topping into peanut-sized clumps. Refrigerate while preparing the filling.

2. FOR THE FILLING: Bring the fresh or frozen cranberries, ¾ cup of the sugar, and water to a simmer in a Dutch oven over medium-high heat and cook until the cranberries are completely softened and the mixture is jam-like, about 10 minutes. Scrape the mixture into a bowl. Add the apples, remaining ½ cup sugar, and dried cranberries to the Dutch oven and cook over medium-high heat until the apples begin to release their juices, about 5 minutes.

3. Off the heat, stir the cranberry mixture and tapioca into the apple mixture. Pour into a 13 by 9-inch baking dish set on a rimmed baking sheet and smooth the surface evenly with a spatula.

4. Following the photo, scatter the topping evenly over the filling and bake until the juices are bubbling and the topping is a deep golden brown, about 30 minutes. (If the topping is browning too quickly, loosely cover with a piece of aluminum foil.) Transfer to a wire rack to cool. Serve warm.

MAKING CRANBERRY-APPLE CRISP

1. Cook the cranberries, sugar, and water until the mixture is thick and jammy. Transfer to a bowl and cook the apples to release their juices.

2. Mound the topping in the center of the dish, then use your fingers to rake the topping out toward the edges of the dish.

Blueberry Crumble

Just because this dish is simple—sweetened blueberries baked under a crunchy streusel topping—doesn't mean it's foolproof. Many blueberry crumbles have soupy fillings, because the thick layer of streusel on top of the fruit prevents the excess moisture in the berries from evaporating. This filling soaks into the topping, leaving both components compromised. We wanted to make a crumble that featured a thick, fresh-tasting blueberry filling topped with a contrasting layer of crunchy streusel.

Most crumble recipes typically use a streusel topping of flour, butter, sugar, and oats over a simple filling of blueberries, sugar, and spices. We weren't impressed by any of the blueberry crumble recipes we tested, so we decided to build our own from scratch.

Five cups of fresh blueberries was an ample amount for our 8 by 8-inch baking dish. We baked batches of untopped filling (we'd get to the streusel later) to test granulated sugar against light brown and dark brown sugars, and the results were unanimous: the brown sugars competed with the fresh berry flavor.

We had two choices to firm up the filling: precooking the berries or adding a thickener. Simmering the mixture on the stovetop thickened the filling, but it also reduced the blueberries to mush and cooked out their fresh flavor. Moving on to the thickeners, we tried tossing the sugared berries with flour, tapioca, and cornstarch. The flour worked but made the filling pasty. Tapioca needed at least 40 minutes in the oven to thicken, which was too much cooking time for the berries. A mere 4 teaspoons of cornstarch was enough to quickly tighten up the filling without muting the flavor of the berries.

Next, we made our own streusel by combining flour, butter, sugar, and oats in the food processor. Although tasters liked our simple berry filling, they wanted more flavor in the streusel, so we replaced the granulated sugar with light brown sugar and added a touch of cinnamon for spice.

Our tasty new topping still sank into the filling and became quite soggy. We wondered if the size of the crumbles was the problem. Rather than processing the mixture until it was fine, we pulsed the cold butter into the dry streusel ingredients just until they clumped together. Better, but not perfect. To get even bigger crumbles, we pulsed the mixture into rough dime-sized pieces and used our fingers to incorporate the last dry bits. This streusel baked up crisp and crunchy, and we finally had a foolproof blueberry crumble.

BLUEBERRY CRUMBLE

SERVES 6

Avoid instant or quick oats here—they will make the crumble mushy. In step 2, do not press the crumble into the berry mixture or it may sink and become soggy. Frozen berries do not work in this recipe. Serve with vanilla ice cream or lightly sweetened whipped cream.

- ½   cup granulated sugar
- 4   teaspoons cornstarch
- ¼   teaspoon salt
- 5   cups fresh blueberries (see note above)
- ⅔   cup all-purpose flour
- ½   cup old-fashioned oats (see note above)
- ⅓   cup packed light brown sugar
- ½   teaspoon ground cinnamon
- 6   tablespoons unsalted butter, cut into 6 pieces and chilled

1. Adjust an oven rack to the lower-middle position and heat the oven to 375 degrees. Combine the granulated sugar, cornstarch, and ⅛ teaspoon of the salt in a large bowl. Add the berries to the bowl and toss to coat. Transfer to an 8 by 8-inch baking dish.

2. Process the flour, oats, brown sugar, cinnamon, and remaining ⅛ teaspoon salt in a food processor until combined. Add the butter and pulse until dime-sized clumps form. Transfer the crumble to a bowl and pinch together any powdery parts. (If you don't have a food processor, mix the flour, oats, brown sugar, cinnamon, and ⅛ teaspoon salt in a large bowl. Add the chilled butter to the bowl, and use a pastry blender or two knives to cut the butter into the dry ingredients until dime-sized clumps form. Pinch together any powdery parts.) Sprinkle the crumble evenly over the berries.

3. Bake until the filling is bubbling around the edges and the topping is golden brown, about 30 minutes. Cool on a wire rack for at least 30 minutes. Serve. (Once fully cooled, Blueberry Crumble can be wrapped with plastic wrap and refrigerated for up to 1 day. Bring to room temperature before serving.)

Skillet Peach Cobbler

Anyone who has bitten into a ripe peach knows just how juicy peaches can be. Unfortunately, so does anyone who's ever made a peach cobbler, where the filling becomes watery and the topping soggy. We wanted tender peaches and a crisp, buttery biscuit topping.

Most recipes attempt to solve the soupy peach problem by loading them up with starchy thickeners, but when we tried this the fruit turned glucy and gummy. Another technique is to draw moisture out of the sliced peaches by sprinkling them with sugar and letting them drain in a colander. Although this prevented a watery filling, we couldn't help but think that a lot of flavor was draining away with all that peach juice.

Searching for a way to thicken our peach filling without running off any of its flavorful juice, we turned to our skillet. We first sautéed the peaches in butter and sugar to release their juices and then cooked them down until all their liquid had evaporated. The resulting peaches were buttery sweet, with a concentrated taste, but their texture was mushy. We decided to withhold some of the peaches from the sautéing process and add them to the skillet just before baking. Prepared in this manner, the filling had a deep, concentrated flavor (from the sautéed peaches) and a tender, but not at all mushy, texture (from the second addition of peaches). To finish, a splash of lemon juice brought out the sweet-tart taste of the fruit, and a dusting of cornstarch brought the filling together.

As for the topping, tasters liked the flavor of buttermilk biscuits, but their texture was too delicate. Buttermilk biscuits get their light and flaky texture from having cold butter cut into the dry ingredients. Using melted butter made our biscuits sturdier, and they held up much better on top of the fruit. With a final sprinkling of cinnamon sugar, we finally had a reliable recipe for peach cobbler.

SKILLET PEACH COBBLER

SERVES 6 TO 8

We suggest using a serrated vegetable peeler to remove the skin from the peaches. Four pounds of frozen sliced peaches can be substituted for fresh; there is no need to defrost them. Start step 2 when the peaches are almost done cooking.

FILLING

4	tablespoons unsalted butter
5	pounds peaches, peeled, pitted, and cut into ½-inch wedges (see note above)
6	tablespoons sugar
⅛	teaspoon salt
1	tablespoon fresh lemon juice
1½	teaspoons cornstarch

TOPPING

1½	cups all-purpose flour
6	tablespoons sugar
1½	teaspoons baking powder
¼	teaspoon baking soda
¼	teaspoon salt
¾	cup buttermilk
4	tablespoons unsalted butter, melted and cooled
1	teaspoon ground cinnamon

1. FOR THE FILLING: Adjust an oven rack to the middle position and heat the oven to 425 degrees. Melt the butter in a large oven-safe nonstick skillet over medium-high heat. Add two-thirds of the peaches, the sugar, and salt and cook, covered, until the peaches release their juices, about 5 minutes. Remove the lid and simmer until all the liquid has evaporated and the peaches begin to caramelize, 15 to 20 minutes. Add the remaining peaches and cook until heated through, about 5 minutes. Whisk the lemon juice and cornstarch together in a small bowl, then stir into the peach mixture. Cover the skillet and set aside off the heat.

2. FOR THE TOPPING: Meanwhile, whisk together the flour, 5 tablespoons of the sugar, the baking powder, baking soda, and salt in a medium bowl. Stir in the buttermilk and melted butter until a dough forms. Turn the dough out onto a lightly floured work surface and knead briefly until smooth, about 30 seconds.

3. Combine the remaining 1 tablespoon sugar and the cinnamon. Break the dough into rough 1-inch pieces and space them about ½ inch apart on top of the hot peach mixture. Sprinkle with the cinnamon sugar and bake until the topping is golden brown and the filling is thickened, 18 to 22 minutes. Let cool on a wire rack for 10 minutes. Serve. (Although best eaten the day it is made to maintain the texture of the topping, leftovers may be refrigerated for up to 1 day. Individual portions may be removed from the skillet and reheated in the microwave.)

CHAPTER SEVENTEEN

Spoon Desserts

SPOON DESSERTS

All-American Pudding

Grade-school cafeterias regularly serve up dishes of pudding (vanilla, chocolate, butterscotch, you name it) that are sweet and satisfying—but only to children. Kids love pudding in any form, even the boxed kind; but to adults this type can taste gluey, artificial, and one-dimensional. We knew that pudding made from scratch would be altogether different. We wanted a perfectly fresh and creamy pudding with a deep, rich flavor that would satisfy children and adults alike—and we wanted it in all our favorite flavors.

From early tests we learned that to achieve a lush texture, it is important to monitor the strength of the heat beneath the saucepan and to use a reasonably slow hand to stir (not whisk or beat) the pudding mixture as it approaches the thickening point, then continue to stir slowly as it cooks for about 2 minutes. Vigorous beating can break down the starch granules built up during the thickening process. We also found that it helped to strain the finished pudding through a fine-mesh strainer to ensure a suave, smooth texture.

With these points in mind, we began to test individual ingredients. We made puddings with all milk, milk and heavy cream, all heavy cream, and half-and-half. What did we find? Half-and-half gave us a pudding with a rich, balanced flavor and creamy texture. Whole milk tasted too lean and cream tasted far too rich.

As for eggs, use only egg yolks. Pudding made with whole eggs has a stiff, rubbery texture. Thicken the pudding with cornstarch. We found that some pudding recipes rely on flour for thickening, but flour tended to give the pudding a starchy flavor, and it marred the pudding's smooth texture. We found, too, that a tablespoon of butter stirred into the pudding off the heat gives the pudding an attractive glossy sheen.

With our basics down, it was on to flavoring our pudding. Vanilla pudding is as easy as adding vanilla extract, which perfectly sets off the creamy, eggy flavor of the custard. Butterscotch pudding gets its deep caramel flavor from a duo of dark brown sugar (its intense flavor was preferred over light brown sugar) and jarred caramel or butterscotch sauce. And for chocolate pudding with deep chocolate flavor, we settled on a combination of cocoa powder and melted semisweet chocolate (bittersweet works well, too). With little more effort than making pudding from a box, you can make old-fashioned pudding with flavor that everyone will love.

VANILLA PUDDING

SERVES 4 TO 6

For a smooth texture, it is important to pass the pudding through a fine-mesh strainer in order to remove any bits of cooked egg. We like serving pudding with dollops of fresh whipped cream.

¾	cup sugar
2	tablespoons cornstarch
⅛	teaspoon salt
3½	cups half-and-half
3	large egg yolks
1	tablespoon unsalted butter
1	tablespoon vanilla extract

1. Combine the sugar, cornstarch, and salt in a medium saucepan. Slowly whisk in the half-and-half and then the egg yolks.

2. Bring the mixture to a simmer over medium-high heat, whisking gently but constantly and scraping the bottom and sides of the pot. Reduce the heat to medium and cook, stirring constantly, until the pudding is thick and coats the back of a spoon, 1 to 2 minutes.

3. Strain the pudding through a fine-mesh strainer into a bowl, scraping the inside of the strainer with a rubber spatula to pass the pudding through. Stir the butter and vanilla into the pudding until the butter is melted. Press plastic wrap directly onto the surface to prevent a skin from forming and refrigerate until set, about 3 hours, before serving.

Variations
BUTTERSCOTCH PUDDING

Increase the cornstarch to 3 tablespoons. Substitute ½ cup packed dark brown sugar for the granulated sugar. Reduce the vanilla extract to 2 teaspoons. Stir ½ cup store-bought butterscotch or caramel sauce into the pudding with the butter and vanilla.

DOUBLE-CHOCOLATE PUDDING

Reduce the cornstarch to 4 teaspoons. Add 2 tablespoons Dutch-processed cocoa powder with the cornstarch in step 1. Add 6 ounces melted semisweet or bittersweet chocolate to the mixture following the egg yolks in step 1, and reduce the vanilla to 2 teaspoons. (The chocolate may form clumps, but they will smooth out during cooking.)

Banana Pudding

Banana pudding is a classic Southern recipe that combines homemade vanilla pudding with vanilla wafers, sliced bananas, and, often, a meringue topping. Disappointing versions of this dessert couple pudding that is too sweet, bland, or starchy with cookies that are dissolved and pasty. We wanted a creamy, fresh pudding with lightly softened cookies and pure banana flavor.

We started by pulling a number of banana pudding recipes from our library, including the recipe from the back of the vanilla wafers box. The first conclusion tasters came to was that they weren't especially fond of meringue-topped puddings. Although

beautiful, puddings topped with meringue struck our tasters as odd—they all preferred a whipped cream topping. So we set out to develop a recipe for individual puddings topped with whipped cream.

Banana pudding typically relies on a vanilla custard or pudding as its base, so we dug out our recipe for vanilla pudding, which gets its creamy texture and rich flavor from egg yolks and half-and-half. We wondered if this dessert should have a richer pudding base, so we prepared a second recipe and switched out the half-and-half for heavy cream. After just a few bites of this richer pudding, tasters put their spoons down. Clearly, our vanilla pudding was plenty rich enough and required no embellishments.

With our pudding set, we turned our attention to the bananas. Only bananas that were just ripe (not speckled with brown spots) did the pudding justice—overripe bananas were too mushy and got lost in the silky pudding. Tasters also rejected banana chunks, preferring thinner, more refined slices.

The last step was to figure out how to deal with the cookies. Vanilla wafers are the cookie of choice for this dessert, but we ran across a recipe in which gingersnaps were substituted and gave it a try. A minority of tasters enjoyed the contrast of spicy ginger with the mellow flavors of banana and vanilla, but most thought that the combination strayed too far from the customary flavors. We decided to stick with vanilla wafers, but we had to determine if they should be left whole or crushed.

Tradition fell by the wayside when tasters preferred crushed vanilla wafers layered in the pudding over whole cookies. Crushed cookies had more visual appeal (they made a more distinctive layer in a parfait glass, which is our favorite way to serve the pudding), and tasters didn't like having to "cut" whole cookies with a spoon. To add some crunch, we garnished the finished puddings with a whole cookie.

BANANA PUDDING

SERVES 6

The flavor of homemade vanilla pudding really shines here, but if you are pressed for time, any type of vanilla pudding will work. We like the way these parfaits look when assembled in individual parfait glasses, but the recipe can also be layered in a small trifle bowl or doubled to fit in a larger trifle bowl.

PUDDING

1	recipe Vanilla Pudding (page 561)
3	large bananas, peeled and cut into ¼-inch slices
30	vanilla wafers, coarsely broken, plus 6 whole wafers for garnishing

WHIPPED CREAM

¾	cup heavy cream, chilled
2	teaspoons sugar
¾	teaspoon vanilla extract

1. FOR THE PUDDING: Spoon ¼ cup of the pudding into each of six 8-ounce parfait or wine glasses. Top each with several banana slices, then sprinkle with a thin layer of wafer pieces. Repeat this layering once more.

2. Spread the remaining pudding evenly over the tops of the parfaits. Press plastic wrap directly onto the surface of the parfaits to prevent a skin from forming. Refrigerate until well chilled, about 2 hours.

3. FOR THE WHIPPED CREAM: Whip the cream, sugar, and vanilla with an electric mixer on low speed until frothy and the sugar has dissolved, about 1 minute. Increase the mixer speed to high and continue to whip until doubled in volume and soft peaks have formed, 1 to 3 minutes. Dollop each parfait with ¼ cup of the whipped cream and garnish with a whole vanilla wafer.

Rice Pudding

At its best, rice pudding is simple and lightly sweet, and it tastes of its primary component: rice. At its worst, the rice flavor is lost to cloying sweetness, condensed dairy, and a pasty, leaden consistency.

Right from the start we agreed on the qualities of the ideal candidate: intact, tender grains bound loosely in a subtly sweet, milky sauce. We were looking for a straightforward stovetop rice pudding, in which the texture and the flavor of the primary ingredient would stand out.

We decided to explore the cooking medium and method first. For our first experiment, we prepared eight existing recipes for rice pudding, each using a different combination of water, milk, and cream and each with varying ratios of rice to liquid. The tasting revealed that cooking the rice in milk or cream obscured the rice flavor, whereas cooking the rice in water emphasized it. The most appealing balance of rice flavor and satisfying yet not too rich consistency was achieved when we cooked 1 cup of rice in 2 cups of water until it was absorbed and then added 4 cups of whole milk to make the pudding. Whole milk imparted just the right degree of richness; in our test with cream, the pudding was so rich, tasters couldn't abide more than a few bites.

We also tried a couple of variations in the cooking method, such as covering the pot or not, and using a double boiler. The double boiler lengthened the cooking time by 25 minutes and turned out a pudding that was gummy and too sweet. By far the best results came from cooking the rice and water in a covered pot, then simmering the cooked rice and dairy mixture uncovered. This technique gave us just what we wanted: distinct, tender grains of rice in a smooth sauce. We found we could cut 10 minutes off the total cooking time by simmering the rice in the water and milk from the start, but this approach sacrificed the texture of the grains and resulted in a pudding that our tasters described as overly dense and sweet.

Now it was time to try different kinds of rice. We tested the readily available varieties: supermarket brands of long-grain white, Arborio (a super-starchy Italian short-grain white used to make risotto), and basmati (an aromatic long-grain white).

Arborio made a stiff, gritty pudding. The flavor of the basmati rice was too perfume-y, overwhelming the milk. Long-grain rice cooked up moist and sticky and proved ideal for our rice pudding, which had a creamy texture and tasted distinctly of rice and milk.

STOVETOP RICE PUDDING

SERVES 6

Any brand of long-grain rice will work in this recipe; just stay away from aromatic rice like basmati or jasmine. Low-fat milk can be substituted for whole milk. The pudding can be covered tightly with plastic wrap and refrigerated for up to 2 days. It can be served either cold or hot, by reheating in the microwave on high power for 1 to 2 minutes.

2	cups water
1	cup long-grain rice (see note above)
¼	teaspoon salt
4	cups whole milk (see note above)
⅔	cup sugar
1¼	teaspoons vanilla extract

1. Bring the water to a boil in a large saucepan. Stir in the rice and salt. Cover, turn the heat to low, and simmer, stirring occasionally, until the water is almost fully absorbed, 15 to 20 minutes.

2. Microwave the milk until steaming, 1 to 2 minutes. Stir the hot milk and sugar into the rice and bring to a slow simmer. Cook, uncovered and stirring often, until the mixture is thick and a spoon is just able to stand up in the pudding, about 45 minutes.

3. Off the heat, stir in the vanilla. Let the mixture cool slightly before serving or refrigerate until chilled, about 2 hours, and serve cold.

Variations

STOVETOP RICE PUDDING WITH CINNAMON AND DRIED FRUIT

Stir ½ cup dried fruit (such as raisins, cranberries, cherries, or chopped prunes or apricots) and 1 teaspoon cinnamon into the pudding with the vanilla in step 3.

STOVETOP RICE PUDDING WITH CARDAMOM AND PISTACHIOS

Stir ½ teaspoon ground cardamom into the pudding with the vanilla, and sprinkle with ⅓ cup toasted chopped pistachios just before serving.

STOVETOP RICE PUDDING WITH ORANGE AND TOASTED ALMONDS

Stir 2 teaspoons grated fresh orange zest into the pudding with the vanilla, and sprinkle with ⅓ cup toasted slivered almonds just before serving.

Indian Pudding

Indian pudding, a cornmeal-thickened custard assertively flavored with molasses, is the sort of dessert that could only have originated in New England, where molasses was once as common a seasoning as salt. What may sound like an odd dessert is actually quite delicious. Long baking at low heat makes for a silky-textured yet hearty pudding, deeply flavored with bittersweet molasses and warm spices.

But outside of a few restaurants in the Boston area known for traditional New England cookery, Indian pudding is hard to find these days. Admittedly, it is labor-intensive and time-consuming, requiring attentive stirring while it cooks on the stovetop and then lengthy baking time. Determined to make a pudding that would be worth all of this effort, we set to work to create a dessert that would taste great and cook faster than most.

After making and tasting many batches of Indian pudding, we decided that the major problems associated with it were poor flavor, a curdled or "broken" texture after baking, and an extremely long cooking time—most recipes requiring upward of 3 hours in the oven. We decided to tackle each of these issues separately.

The flavor of good Indian pudding has a complexity that belies its brief ingredient list. The molasses, in conjunction with the spices, imparts a mysterious depth to the pudding. The trick is balancing the flavors; too many recipes we tried produced a pudding that was either overwhelmingly molasses-flavored or too heavily spiced and reminiscent of pumpkin pie. We made batch after batch with varying amounts of molasses and spices until we hit on the ideal amount of each—balanced enough that each component in the pudding could still be tasted. We also limited the spices to cinnamon and ginger because most tasters felt that additional spices, like nutmeg and mace, just muddied the pudding's flavor. To round out the flavors and add more sweetness (using only molasses for sweetening overwhelmed the spices), we added maple syrup, which is a little untraditional, but it greatly improved the pudding.

Most Indian pudding recipes call for fine-ground cornmeal, but we discovered that coarser stone-ground meal made for a more richly flavored pudding. Fine-textured, commercially produced cornmeal is usually so overprocessed that it has lost most of its flavor, whereas coarser stone-ground meal retains its sweet, characteristic corn flavor. Although not quite toothsome, the pudding had an appealing texture when made with stone-ground meal.

We quickly discovered that Indian pudding "breaks" or curdles for one of two reasons: too much fat in the mix or too high a baking temperature. The fat issue was easy enough to overcome by excluding butter and adding a little cornstarch to stabilize the milk fat. Because the pudding is so heavily seasoned, tasters did not miss the fat. And a dollop of whipped cream or scoop of ice cream on top of the pudding adequately replaced any missing fat. As for the baking temperature, we found that anything over 275 degrees was too hot and that a water bath was essential to prevent curdling. A pudding baked at 300 degrees without a water bath cooked incompletely and had the texture of cottage cheese. The water bath insulates the pudding from overheating and ensures that it cooks evenly. Unfortunately, the low temperature necessitated a longer cooking time than we hoped—a full 2 hours. But this is still a good hour shorter than most recipes required.

INDIAN PUDDING
SERVES 6
The pudding may also be flavored with a couple of teaspoons of rum and served with whipped cream or vanilla ice cream.

4	cups plus 2 tablespoons whole milk
½	cup mild molasses
¼	cup maple syrup
1	teaspoon vanilla extract
½	teaspoon ground cinnamon
½	teaspoon ground ginger
½	teaspoon salt
¾	cup yellow cornmeal, preferably stone-ground
2	large eggs, lightly beaten
1	teaspoon cornstarch

1. Adjust an oven rack to the lower-middle position and heat the oven to 275 degrees. Lightly grease a 2-quart casserole dish or 9-inch soufflé dish. Cover the bottom of a roasting pan with a dish towel. Bring a kettle of water to a boil.

2. Bring 4 cups of the milk, the molasses, maple syrup, vanilla, cinnamon, ginger, and salt to a simmer in a medium saucepan over medium heat. Slowly whisk in the cornmeal. Reduce the heat to low and cook, stirring frequently, until the mixture has thickened and the whisk leaves trails when the mixture is stirred, about 15 minutes.

3. In a bowl, whisk the eggs, cornstarch, and remaining 2 tablespoons milk together until smooth, then slowly whisk into the cornmeal mixture. Increase the heat to medium-high and cook, stirring constantly, until large bubbles rise to the surface, 1 to 2 minutes.

4. Pour the cornmeal mixture into the prepared dish, wrap tightly in aluminum foil, and set inside the roasting pan. Place the roasting pan in the oven and carefully pour boiling water into the pan until it reaches halfway up the sides of the dish. Bake until the pudding is no longer runny and has gently set, about 2 hours.

5. Remove the baking dish from the water bath and let cool on a wire rack for 20 minutes before serving.

New Orleans Bourbon Bread Pudding

The best bourbon bread pudding is a rich, scoopable custard that envelops the bread with a perfect balance of sweet spiciness and musky bourbon flavor. The history behind New Orleans's most famous dessert is as eclectic as the city itself. The basic custard and bread combination is of English origin. The bread—which in New Orleans is almost always a baguette—is from France. The addition of raisins to the custard can be credited to German settlers,

---

THE AMERICAN TABLE
THE HISTORY OF BOURBON

How did Kentucky bourbon (the name given to whiskey distilled from at least 51 percent corn) end up playing such an important role in New Orleans's signature dessert? Right after the Revolutionary War, settlers in what eventually became Kentucky planted significant amounts of corn. Because there weren't many passable roads on which to transport this much grain back over the mountains to populated areas along the East Coast, many farmers distilled their crop to make whiskey. Bottles were packed in crates (stamped with the words Old Bourbon, after the region of Kentucky where this liquor was produced) and shipped down the Ohio and Mississippi rivers to New Orleans and, eventually, the rest of the world.

---

and it was the Irish who infused the cream base with various liquors. The bourbon, of course, originally came from Kentucky traders.

We decided to stick to a custard-based recipe with raisins because it seemed both traditional and easy; unfortunately, the bread puddings we made in our initial test of five published recipes were awful. We, along with tasters, encountered a wide range of problems, from harsh bourbon flavor to curdled eggs to rock-hard raisins to slimy bread swimming in a river of custard. These bread puddings were nothing like our New Orleans ideal.

In some recipes the bread is cubed and staled overnight, but these bread puddings looked more like the cobblestone streets in the French Quarter than something we'd like to eat for dessert. We wanted a more rustic look and had much better results tearing the baguette into ragged pieces. Toasting the torn pieces to a deep golden brown enriched their flavor and gave the bread a crispness that helped to prevent the finished dish from turning soggy.

The ratio of eggs to dairy (1 egg to ½ cup dairy) in the custard is time-tested, and we found that a mixture of 3 parts cream to 1 part milk was rich but not over the top. Tasters preferred the caramel flavor of brown sugar (rather than the usual white sugar) to sweeten the custard. Now it was time to tackle the most problematic aspect of this dish: the curdling custard.

Setting the baking dish with the pudding in a roasting pan filled with hot water (called a water bath) was one way to moderate the oven heat and keep the eggs from curdling, but this method is awfully cumbersome. We found that replacing the traditional whole eggs with just egg yolks helped stave off curdling. (We later found out that's because the whites set faster than the yolks.) Also helpful in curdle-proofing the pudding was lowering the oven temperature (to 300 degrees) and covering the baking dish with aluminum foil.

But with its foil cover, our pudding never formed much of a toasted top. Taking inspiration from pie recipes in which cinnamon and sugar are sprinkled on top of the pie to form a crunchy topping, we adapted this idea for our bread pudding. Once the custard had set up in the oven, we removed the foil, added cinnamon, sugar, and some butter, and let the pudding bake for another 30 minutes. The topping caramelized and formed a golden crust.

There's no doubt that bourbon bread pudding is an adult dessert. It should have enough robust bourbon flavor to warm you up, but not so much that it knocks you down. One-half cup to plump the raisins (which solved the rock-hard raisin problem from earlier tests) and another ¼ cup in the custard gave our bread pudding just enough bourbon punch. And for a real taste of New Orleans, we drizzle servings of the pudding with a warm bourbon-based cream sauce.

NEW ORLEANS BOURBON BREAD PUDDING

SERVES 8 TO 10

A French baguette from a bakery rather than the supermarket makes this pudding even better.

PUDDING

6	tablespoons unsalted butter, cubed and chilled, plus more for greasing the pan
1	(18- to 20-inch) French baguette, torn into 1-inch pieces (about 10 cups)
1	cup golden raisins
¾	cup bourbon
3	cups heavy cream
1½	cups packed light brown sugar
1	cup whole milk
8	large egg yolks
1	tablespoon vanilla extract
1½	teaspoons ground cinnamon
¼	teaspoon ground nutmeg
¼	teaspoon salt
3	tablespoons granulated sugar

SAUCE

1½	teaspoons cornstarch
¼	cup bourbon
¾	cup heavy cream
2	tablespoons granulated sugar
2	teaspoons unsalted butter, cut into small pieces
	Pinch salt

1. FOR THE PUDDING: Adjust an oven rack to the middle position and heat the oven to 450 degrees. Butter a 13 by 9-inch baking pan. Arrange the bread in a single layer on a baking sheet and bake until golden and crisp, about 12 minutes, flipping the bread and rotating the baking sheet halfway through baking. Let the bread cool. Reduce the oven temperature to 300 degrees.

SECRETS TO NEW ORLEANS BOURBON BREAD PUDDING

1. Toasting the torn French baguette enhances its flavor and texture.

2. Soaking the bread for 30 minutes in the custard softens the bread without turning it soggy.

3. Covering the bread pudding with aluminum foil allows the custard to set without drying out.

4. Sprinkling the half-baked pudding with a sugary topping adds a crisp crust.

2. Meanwhile, heat the raisins with ½ cup of the bourbon in a small saucepan over medium-high heat until the bourbon begins to simmer, 2 to 3 minutes. Strain the mixture over a bowl, reserving the bourbon and raisins separately.

3. Whisk the cream, brown sugar, milk, egg yolks, vanilla, 1 teaspoon of the cinnamon, nutmeg, and salt together in a large bowl. Whisk in the remaining ¼ cup bourbon and the bourbon used to plump the raisins. Toss in the toasted bread until evenly coated. Let the mixture sit until the bread begins to absorb the custard, about 30 minutes, tossing occasionally. (If the majority of the bread is still hard when squeezed, soak for another 15 to 20 minutes.)

4. Pour half of the bread mixture into the prepared baking pan and sprinkle with half of the reserved raisins. Pour the remaining half of the bread mixture into the pan and sprinkle with the remaining half of the raisins. Cover with aluminum foil and bake for 45 minutes.

5. Meanwhile, mix the granulated sugar and the remaining ½ teaspoon cinnamon in a small bowl. Using your fingers, cut the 6 tablespoons butter into the sugar mixture until the mixture is the size of small peas. Remove the foil from the pudding, sprinkle with the butter mixture, and bake the pudding, uncovered, until the custard is just set, 20 to 25 minutes. Increase the oven temperature to 450 degrees and bake until the top of the pudding forms a golden crust, about 2 minutes. Transfer the pudding to a wire rack and cool for at least 30 minutes or up to 2 hours.w

6. FOR THE SAUCE: Meanwhile, whisk the cornstarch and 2 tablespoons of the bourbon together in a small bowl. Heat the cream and granulated sugar in a small saucepan over medium heat until the sugar dissolves. Whisk in the cornstarch mixture and bring to a boil. Reduce the heat to low and cook until the sauce thickens, 3 to 5 minutes. Off the heat, stir in the remaining 2 tablespoons bourbon, butter, and salt. Drizzle the warm sauce over the bread pudding before serving.

Caramel Bread Pudding

The test kitchen's recipe for basic bread pudding starts with soaking stale or oven-dried bread in a rich custard of egg yolks, heavy cream, milk, and sugar before baking the pudding at a low temperature. This rustic dessert emerges from the oven with a soft, creamy interior and a slightly crunchy crust. We hoped that we could introduce caramel flavor by simply adding store-bought caramel sauce to the egg custard, but that made the custard too heavy. Worse, the custard was so sweet that the caramel flavor was barely detectable. We wanted the whole package—silky interior, crispy top, and deep caramel flavor throughout—and we had a long way to go to get there.

We started with the bread. Tasters thought French bread was too chewy for this pudding, and challah and brioche were too rich. White sandwich bread (dried in the oven so it absorbed more custard) was preferred for its light texture and mild flavor. As for the custard, taking the sugar out of the recipe and relying on the caramel sauce to sweeten the pudding was a step in the right direction, but the egg yolks were muting the flavor of the caramel sauce. We switched to whole eggs, which lightened the custard enough to allow more of the caramel flavor to come through. At the same time, we also decided to streamline things and replace the heavy cream and milk with half-and-half.

We were making progress, but the flavor of the jarred caramel sauce was still too weak. For our next test, we made a traditional, from-scratch caramel by carefully boiling sugar and water to 350 degrees (measured on a candy/deep-fry thermometer) and

adding cream; although better, the caramel flavor was too subtle and the overall dish was too sweet. Because brown sugar is more flavorful than white, our next test was to make a quick caramel (technically more of a butterscotch sauce) with brown sugar, butter, cream, and corn syrup, and it worked much better: the caramel flavor was more prominent in the pudding, and the method was much less fussy than making a true caramel sauce.

We were almost there, but tasters wanted still more caramel pop. Topping the baked pudding with extra caramel was a nice touch, but starting with an additional layer of caramel sauce under the bread pudding as it baked elevated the caramel flavor to new heights. Finally tasters were treated to a caramel bread pudding that truly lived up to its name.

CARAMEL BREAD PUDDING

SERVES 8 TO 10

Firm-textured breads such as Arnold Country Classic White or Pepperidge Farm Farmhouse Hearty White work best here.

15	slices hearty white sandwich bread, cut into 1-inch pieces (about 16 cups; see note above)
12	tablespoons (1½ sticks) unsalted butter
2	cups packed light brown sugar
1	cup heavy cream
¼	cup light corn syrup
5	teaspoons vanilla extract
3	cups half-and-half
5	large eggs
¼	teaspoon salt

1. Adjust the oven racks to the upper-middle and lower-middle positions and heat the oven to 450 degrees. Arrange the bread in a single layer on 2 baking sheets. Bake until golden and crisp, flipping the bread and switching and rotating the sheets halfway through baking, about 12 minutes. Let cool. Reduce the oven temperature to 325 degrees.

2. Grease a 13 by 9-inch baking pan. Melt the butter and brown sugar in a large saucepan over medium-high heat, stirring often, until bubbling and straw-colored, about 4 minutes. Off the heat, whisk in the cream, corn syrup, and 2 teaspoons of the vanilla. Pour 1 cup of the caramel over the bottom of the prepared pan; set aside. Reserve an additional 1 cup of the caramel for serving, then whisk the half-and-half into the remaining caramel.

3. Whisk the eggs and salt together in a large bowl. Whisk in the half-and-half mixture, a little at a time, until incorporated, then stir in the remaining 3 teaspoons vanilla. Fold in the toasted bread and let sit, stirring occasionally, until the bread is saturated, about 20 minutes. (If the majority of the bread is still hard when squeezed, soak for another 15 to 20 minutes.)

4. Transfer the bread mixture to the caramel-coated pan and bake on the lower-middle rack until the top is crisp and the custard is just set, about 45 minutes. Let cool for 30 minutes. Drizzle with ½ cup of the reserved caramel sauce and serve, passing the remaining ½ cup sauce at the table.

Trifle

Trifle, that familiar tower of cake, cream, custard, and fruit, is quite the looker on the holiday buffet table (or any other occasion requiring a dessert to feed a crowd), but beneath that fragile facade there is often little more than soggy cake, grainy custard, and fruit strewn about helter-skelter. So when we read about a different sort of trifle called Tipsy Squire, we were intrigued. The cake was described as soft but sturdy; and the custard light and fluffy. The trifle also boasted plenty of sweet sherry. Even better, save for the top, this was a trifle without any forlorn pieces of fruit, just a layer of jam sandwiched inside the pieces of cake. We needed to develop our own version.

We began our research by scouring cookbooks from Great Britain, home of the trifle. Books from the nineteenth century were packed with concoctions from the straightforward Tipsy Cake (a sherry-soaked sponge cake filled with cream) to the more whimsical Tipsy Hedgehog (a booze-laden sponge cake covered with cream and studded with sliced almond "spikes"). Next we turned to American cookbooks. Miss Drucy Harris offered her rendition of Tipsy Charlotte in the *Dayton, Ohio, Presbyterian Cookbook* (1873). She made it by stuffing a large, hollowed-out sponge cake with sherry and vanilla cream. Tipsy Pudding—sherry-spiked custard poured over sponge cake—appeared in a number of American cookbooks, including *Fannie Farmer's Boston Cooking-School Cook Book* (1896).

But we finally found a recipe for Tipsy Squire (the name referring to the effect this dessert might have on a teetotaling man of importance) in a classic American cookbook by Mrs. S. R. Dull called

Southern Cooking (first published in 1928, this popular book was updated and released again in 1941 and 1968). This Southern specialty was well known in Georgia, and it was definitely a trifle. It carried all of the tipsy traits: lots of sherry, layers of custard, and sponge cake. The dessert made from this recipe tasted good, but it was still soggy—until we incorporated a technique from the other tipsy recipes we found in nineteenth-century cookbooks: stale sponge cake. This recipe, prepared with stale cake, produced a tidy trifle with distinct components; the modern trifles made with fresh cake all turned into a gloppy mess.

Stale sponge cake may have been commonplace a century ago (there were plenty of leftovers), but today few home cooks make sponge cake (never mind having any leftover pieces). Luckily, most good bakeries offer high-quality sponge cake. After some serious cake staling, which requires an overnight sit (unwrapped) on the countertop or 3 hours in a 200-degree oven, it was time to build the tipsy.

No matter how soaked with sherry (very soaked) or buried beneath layers of custard (deeply), the cake retained some of its texture, and the custard was fresh and fluffy. A winner on all fronts, this trifle is a beauty inside and out.

TIPSY SQUIRE

SERVES 10 TO 12

The beauty of this trifle is that most of the components can (if not should) be made in advance. Once assembled, Tipsy Squire actually improves after an overnight stay in the fridge. You'll need a 3-quart trifle dish to make this impressive dessert. Bake shops sell sponge cake in various sizes; just trim larger cakes to suit this recipe. To stale cake rounds, leave them uncovered on the counter overnight or place them on a wire rack over a baking sheet in a 200-degree oven for 3 hours.

CUSTARD

2	cups heavy cream
½	cup sugar
	Pinch salt
5	large egg yolks
3	tablespoons cornstarch
4	tablespoons cold unsalted butter, cut into 4 pieces
1½	teaspoons vanilla extract

TRIFLE

2	(8-inch) round stale sponge cakes (each about 1½ inches thick), homemade or store-bought (see note above)
1½	cups cream sherry
1	cup seedless raspberry jam
2	cups heavy cream
40	small almond macaroons or amaretti cookies, homemade or store-bought
1	cup fresh raspberries

1. FOR THE CUSTARD: Heat the cream, 6 tablespoons of the sugar, and salt in a heavy saucepan over medium heat until simmering, stirring occasionally to dissolve the sugar. Meanwhile, whisk the egg yolks in a medium bowl until thoroughly combined. Whisk in the remaining 2 tablespoons sugar until the sugar begins to dissolve. Whisk in the cornstarch until the mixture is pale yellow and thick, about 30 seconds.

ASSEMBLING TIPSY SQUIRE

1. For the jam sandwiches, make 5 long slices into the filled cake rounds, then make five more slices crosswise.

2. Arrange one layer of soaked macaroons in the bottom of a trifle bowl.

3. Using the back of a serving spoon, spread 2 cups of the custard mixture over the macaroons in an even layer.

4. Place the jam sandwiches around the perimeter of the dish. Fill in the center with more sandwiches. Then spread with 2 more cups custard. Repeat layers once more.

2. When the cream mixture reaches a full simmer, gradually whisk half into the yolk mixture to temper. Return the mixture to the saucepan, scraping the bowl with a rubber spatula; return to a simmer over medium heat, whisking constantly, until 3 or 4 bubbles burst on the surface and the mixture is thickened, about 1 minute. Strain the pudding through a fine-mesh strainer into a bowl, scraping the inside of the strainer with a rubber spatula to pass the pudding through. Whisk in the butter and vanilla. Transfer the mixture to a bowl, press plastic wrap directly onto the surface to prevent a skin from forming, and refrigerate until set, at least 3 hours or up to 2 days.

3. FOR THE TRIFLE: Slice each cake round in half horizontally. Brush each cut side of one cake with ¼ cup of the sherry, then spread with ¼ cup of the jam. Stack 2 cut sides together (resulting in a jam sandwich). Repeat with the second cake to make a second jam sandwich. Cut each cake into 5 long slices, then cut 5 more slices crosswise. (Reserve the smaller jam cakes for nibbling; you will need 30 to 40 of the larger jam cakes for step 5.)

4. Beat the cream and ¼ cup more sherry with an electric mixer at medium-high speed to soft peaks. Reduce the mixer speed to low, gradually add the custard, and mix well, about 1 minute. Toss the macaroons or amaretti with the remaining ¼ cup sherry in a large bowl.

5. Arrange 12 to 14 (depending on size) cookies in a single layer to cover the bottom of a 3-quart trifle bowl. Spoon 2 cups of the custard mixture evenly over the cookies. Arrange 15 to 20 jam cakes in a single layer on the custard. Top with 2 cups more custard mixture. Repeat the layering of the cookies, custard mixture, jam cakes, and custard mixture once more. Arrange the remaining 12 to 16 macaroons or amaretti in a circle midway between the rim of the bowl and the center of the trifle, so that they stick up slightly like a crown. Cover tightly with plastic wrap and refrigerate for at least 12 hours or up to 2 days. When ready to serve, pile the raspberries inside the circle of cookies.

INDEX

NOTE: *Italicized* page references indicate recipe photographs.

Country-Style Pot Roast with Gravy, 407–8
Cowboy Beans, 124–26
Crab(meat)
    blue, how to eat, 399
    Boil, 398–400
    buying, 397–98
    Cakes, Creole-Style, *363*, 396–97
    Imperial, 394–96
    -Stuffed Sole, 390
Cranberry(ies)
    -Apple Crisp, 554–56
    -Apple Pie, 528
    Gingerbread with Dried Fruit, 198
    -Orange Nut Bread, 188–89
    Upside-Down Cake, 511–13
Cream Cheese
    Apple Pie French Toast, 163
    Apricot-Almond French Toast, 163
    Black-Bottom Cupcakes, 485–86
    Blueberry Cobbler French Toast, 162
    Chocolate Chip French Toast, 163
    Frosting, 504–5
    Icebox Oreo Cheesecake, *500*, 519–20
    New York Cheesecake, 516–19
    spreads for bread, 188
    Stuffed French Toast, 161–62
    Swirl Brownies, 458
Creamed Corn, 100–101
Creamed Corn with Bacon and Blue Cheese, 101–2
Creamy Broccoli and Cheddar Soup, 70–71
Creamy Buttermilk Coleslaw, 47
Creamy Chipotle Chile Sauce, 401
Creamy French Dressing, 32
Creamy Lemon-Herb Sauce, 401
Creamy Mashed Sweet Potatoes, 107–8
Creamy Peas with Ham and Onion, 105–6
Creole Baked Stuffed Shrimp with Sausage, 391
Creole Fried Chicken, 293–95
Creole-Style Crab Cakes, *363*, 396–97
Creole-Style Shrimp and Sausage Gumbo, 74–76
Crisp, Cranberry-Apple, 554–56
Crispy Baked Potato Fans, 115–17
Crispy Garlic Chicken Cutlets, 278–79
Crispy Iowa Skinnies, 142–43
Crispy Roast Chicken and Potatoes, 298–99, *366*
Crumble, Blueberry, 556–57
Crunchy Potato Wedges, *91*, 117–18
    From-the-Freezer, 119
    Italian-Style, 119
Cucumber(s)
    Avocado, and Jicama, Chopped Salad with, 37
    Chopped Salad, 36–37
    24-Hour Picnic Salad, 45–46
Cupcakes, Black-Bottom, 485–86
Cupcakes, Boston Cream, 482–84, *496*
Curry
    Country Captain Chicken, *364*, 431–32
    Curried Spiced Nuts, 3
    powder, Madras, taste tests on, 432

D

Denver Omelet, Family-Sized, 165–67
Desserts
    Blueberry Crumble, 556–57
    Brown Sugar Berry Shortcakes, 553–54
    Cranberry-Apple Crisp, 554–56
    Easy Apple Turnovers, 551–52
    Skillet Peach Cobbler, 557–58
    Sugar and Spice Apple Turnovers, 552
    Tipsy Squire, 570–72
    see also Bars; Brownies; Cakes; Cookies; Pies; Puddings
Dilly Peas and Carrots, 106
Dips and spreads
    Chunky Guacamole, 9–10
    Clam Dip with Bacon and Scallions, 9
    Classic Cheddar Cheese Ball, 5–6
    cream cheese, for breads, 188
    Creamy Chipotle Chile Sauce, 401
    Creamy Lemon-Herb Sauce, 401
    Green Goddess Dip, 8–9
    Hot Spinach and Artichoke Dip, 11–12
    Mexicali Cheese Ball, 7
    One-Minute Salsa, 10–11
    Port Wine–Blue Cheese Ball, 6–7
    Santa Maria Salsa, 326
    Tartar Sauce, 401
    Ultimate Seven-Layer Dip, 12–13, *88*
    Ultimate Smoky Seven-Layer Dip, 13
    Zesty Smoked Salmon Cheese Ball, 6, *88*
Dirty Rice, 127–28
Dish detergents, liquid, ratings of, 415
Double-Chocolate Pudding, 562
Double-Crust Pie Dough, 523–24
Doughnuts
    Banana Drop, 204
    Buttermilk, Cinnamon-Sugar, 206
    Buttermilk, Old-Fashioned, 204–6
    Buttermilk, Powdered Sugar, 206
    Orange Drop, 203–4
    Spice Drop, 204
Dumplings, Easier Chicken and, 304–5
Dutch ovens, inexpensive, ratings of, 64

E

Easier Chicken and Dumplings, 304–5
Easiest Ever Press-In Single-Crust Pie Dough, 525–26
Easy Apple Turnovers, 551–52
Easy Cheddar Biscuits, 219
Easy Fried Eggs, 164
Easy Meat Lasagna, 251–52
Easy Parmesan-Garlic Biscuits, 219
Easy Split-Pea Soup with Ham, 71
Eggplant
    Parmesan, 256–58
    and Zucchini, Roasted, Lasagna, 254

A NOTE ON CONVERSIONS

Some say cooking is both a science and an art. We would say that geography has a hand in it, too. Flour milled in the United Kingdom and elsewhere will feel and taste different from flour milled in the United States. So we cannot promise that the loaf of bread you bake in Canada or England will taste the same as a loaf baked in the States, but we can offer guidelines for converting weights and measures. We also recommend that you rely on instincts when making our recipes. Refer to the visual cues provided. If the bread dough hasn't "come together in a ball," as described, you may need to add more flour—even if the recipe doesn't tell you so. You be the judge. For more information on conversions

and ingredient equivalents, visit our Web site at www.cookscountry.com and type "conversion chart" in the search box.

The recipes in this book were developed using standard U.S. measures following U.S. government guidelines. The charts below offer equivalents for U.S., metric, and Imperial (U.K.) measures. All conversions are approximate and have been rounded up or down to the nearest whole number. For example:

1 teaspoon = 4.9292 milliliters, rounded up to 5 milliliters

1 ounce = 28.3495 grams, rounded down to 28 grams

VOLUME CONVERSIONS

U.S.	METRIC
1 teaspoon	5 milliliters
2 teaspoons	10 milliliters
1 tablespoon	15 milliliters
2 tablespoons	30 milliliters
¼ cup	59 milliliters
⅓ cup	79 milliliters
½ cup	118 milliliters
¾ cup	177 milliliters
1 cup	237 milliliters
1¼ cups	296 milliliters
1½ cups	355 milliliters
2 cups	473 milliliters
2½ cups	592 milliliters
3 cups	710 milliliters
4 cups (1 quart)	0.946 liter
1.06 quarts	1 liter
4 quarts (1 gallon)	3.8 liters

WEIGHT CONVERSIONS

OUNCES	GRAMS
½	14
¾	21
1	28
1½	43
2	57
2½	71
3	85
3½	99
4	113
4½	128
5	142
6	170
7	198
8	227
9	255
10	283
12	340

CONVERSIONS FOR INGREDIENTS COMMONLY USED IN BAKING

Baking is an exacting science. Because measuring by weight is far more accurate than measuring by volume, and thus more likely to achieve reliable results, in our recipes we provide ounce measures in addition to cup measures for many ingredients. Refer to the chart below to convert these measures into grams.

INGREDIENT	OUNCES	GRAMS
1 cup all-purpose flour*	5	142
1 cup whole wheat flour	5½	156
1 cup granulated (white) sugar	7	198
1 cup packed brown sugar (light or dark)	7	198
1 cup confectioners' sugar	4	113
1 cup cocoa powder	3	85
4 tablespoons butter† (½ stick, or ¼ cup)	2	57
8 tablespoons butter† (1 stick, or ½ cup)	4	113
16 tablespoons butter† (2 sticks, or 1 cup)	8	227

* U.S. all-purpose flour, the most frequently used flour in this book, does not contain leaveners, as some European flours do. These leavened flours are called self-rising or self-raising. If you are using self-rising flour, take this into consideration before adding leavening to a recipe.

†In the United States, butter is sold both salted and unsalted. We generally recommend unsalted butter. If you are using salted butter, take this into consideration before adding salt to a recipe.

OVEN TEMPERATURES

FAHRENHEIT	CELSIUS	GAS MARK (IMPERIAL)
225	105	¼
250	120	½
275	130	1
300	150	2
325	165	3
350	180	4
375	190	5
400	200	6
425	220	7
450	230	8
475	245	9

CONVERTING TEMPERATURES FROM AN INSTANT-READ THERMOMETER

We include doneness temperatures in many of our recipes, such as those for poultry, meat, and bread. We recommend an instant-read thermometer for the job. Refer to the above table to convert Fahrenheit degrees to Celsius. Or, for temperatures not represented in the chart, use this simple formula: Subtract 32 degrees from the Fahrenheit reading, then divide the result by 1.8 to find the Celsius reading.

EXAMPLE: "Roast until the juices run clear when the chicken is cut with a paring knife or the thickest part of the breast registers 160 degrees on an instant-read thermometer."

TO CONVERT: 160°F − 32 = 128°
128° ÷ 1.8 = 71°C (rounded down from 71.11)

SALVATION

SALVATION

PETER F. HAMILTON

DEL REY

NEW YORK

Published in the United States by Del Rey, an imprint of Random House, a division of Penguin Random House LLC, New York.

Del Rey and the House colophon are registered trademarks of Penguin Random House LLC.

Published in the United Kingdom by Pan, an imprint of Pan Macmillan, London.

LIBRARY OF CONGRESS CATALOGING-IN-PUBLICATION DATA
Names: Hamilton, Peter F., author.
Title: Salvation / Peter F. Hamilton.
Description: New York : Del Rey, [2018]
Identifiers: LCCN 2018009573 | ISBN 9780399178764
(hardcover : acid-free paper) | ISBN 9780399178771 (Ebook)
Subjects: | BISAC: FICTION / Science Fiction / Space Opera. |
FICTION / Action & Adventure. | GSAFD: Science fiction.
Classification: LCC PR6058.A5536 S25 2018 | DDC 823/.914—dc23
LC record available at https://lccn.loc.gov/2018009573

Printed in the United States of America on acid-free paper

randomhousebooks.com

2   4   6   8   9   7   5   3   1

First U.S. Edition

Book design by Jo Anne Metsch

Music as background for reading *Salvation* has been created by film and TV composer Steve Buick. His long, evocative musical piece works as the perfect atmospheric accompaniment to any part of the book. Search "Peter F. Hamilton's Salvation: Atmospheres and Soundscapes" on Amazon, iTunes, or Google Play. You can find out more at stevebuick.com.

SALVATION

EARTH CALLING

Drifting through interstellar space, three light-years out from the star 31 Aquilae, the Neána abode cluster picked up a series of short, faint electromagnetic pulses that lasted intermittently for eighteen years. The early signatures were familiar to the Neána, and faintly worrying: nuclear fission detonations, followed seven years later by fusion explosions. The technological progress of whoever was detonating them was exceptionally swift by the usual metric of emerging civilizations.

Metaviral spawn chewed into the cometry chunks that anchored the vast cluster, spinning out a string of flimsy receiver webs twenty kilometers across. They aligned themselves on the G-class star fifty light-years away, where the savage weapons were being deployed.

Sure enough, a torrent of weak electromagnetic signals was pouring out from the star's third planet. A sentient species was entering into its early scientific industrial state.

The Neána were concerned that so many nuclear weapons were being used. Clearly, the new species was disturbingly aggressive. Some of the cluster's minds welcomed that.

Analysis of the radio signals, now becoming analogue audiovisual broadcasts, revealed a bipedal race organized along geo-tribal lines, and constantly in conflict. Their specific biochemical composition was one that, from the Neána perspective, gave them sadly short lives. That was posited as the probable reason behind their faster than usual technological progression.

That there would be an expedition was never in doubt; the Neána saw that as their duty no matter what kind of life evolved on distant worlds. The only question now concerned the level of assistance to be offered. Those who welcomed the new species' aggressive qualities wanted to make the full spectrum of Neána technology available. They almost prevailed.

The spherical insertion ship that left the cluster—it didn't know if it was one of many being dispatched, or alone—measured a hundred meters in diameter, a mass comprised of active molecule blocks. It spent three months accelerating up to thirty percent of light speed along a course to Altair—a trip that took just over a hundred years. During the lonely voyage the ship's controlling sentience continued to monitor the electromagnetic signals coming from the young civilization that was its ultimate goal. It built up an impressive knowledge base of human biology, as well as a comprehensive understanding of their constantly evolving tribal political and economic structures.

When the ship reached Altair, it performed a complex flyby maneuver, which aligned it perfectly on Sol. After that, the physical section of the sentience's memory that contained all the astrogation data of the flight from the cluster to Altair was jettisoned and the constituent blocks deactivated. Its weakened atomic structure broke apart into an expanding cloud of dust, which was quickly dispersed by Altair's solar wind. Now, if it was ever intercepted, the insertion ship could never betray the position of the Neána abode cluster—for it no longer knew where it was.

The last fifty years of the voyage were spent formatting an emplacement strategy. By now, human ingenuity had produced starships that were flying past the insertion ship in the other direction, in quest of new worlds out among the stars. The information blasting out from Earth and the solar system's asteroid habitats had become increasingly sophisticated, yet, conversely, there was a lot less of it. Radio signals had been in decline since the internet had begun to carry the bulk of human data traffic. For the final twenty years of the insertion ship's approach it received little apart from entertainment broadcasts, and even those were shrinking year by year. But it had enough.

It flew in south of the ecliptic, shedding cold mass in irregular bursts like a black comet—a deceleration maneuver that took three years. This was always the riskiest part of the voyage. The humans' solar system was scattered with a great many astronomical sensors scanning the universe for cosmological abnormalities. By the time it passed the Kuiper belt, the insertion ship was down to twenty-five meters in diameter. It emitted no magnetic or gravitational fields. The outer shell was fully radiation absorbent, so there was no albedo, making it invisible to any telescopes. Thermal emission was zero.

No one perceived its arrival.

Inside, four biologics began to grow within molecular initiators, attaining physical patterns the ship's sentience had designed, based on the information it had acquired during the long voyage.

They were human in size and shape; skeletons and organs carried the mimicry down to a biochemical level. Their DNA was equally authentic. You would have to go a lot deeper into the cells to find any abnormality; only a detailed audit of the organelles would reveal alien molecular structures.

It was the minds of the biologics that gave the insertion ship the greatest difficulty. Human mental processes were complex verging on paradoxical. Worse, it suspected the performances in all the fictional dramas it received were overemphasizing emotional responses. So it constructed a stable primary architecture of thought routines, while including a fast learning and adaptive integration procedure.

As it closed to within a million kilometers of Earth, the insertion ship discarded the last of its reaction mass as it performed a final deceleration maneuver. Now it was basically just falling toward the southernmost tip of South America. Tiny course correction ejecta refined the descent vector, steering it at Tierra del Fuego, which was still thirty minutes from greeting the dawn. Even if it was detected now, it would simply appear to be a small chunk of natural space debris.

It hit the upper atmosphere and began to peel apart into four pear-shaped segments. The remaining matter broke away in fizzing sparks that produced a short-lived but beautiful starburst display streaking through the mesosphere. Below it, sheltered under their blanket of thick winter cloud, the residents of Ushuaia, the southernmost city on Earth, remained oblivious of their interstellar visitor.

Each segment carried on down, aerobraking with increasing severity as the atmosphere thickened around them. They slowed to subsonic velocity three kilometers above the surface, plunging through the clouds, still unobserved by anyone on the planet.

The segments were aimed at a small inlet a few kilometers west of the city, where, even in AD 2162, the rugged land lay unclaimed by developers. Two hundred meters from the shore, four tall splash plumes shot up into the air like thick geysers, crowning and splattering down on the slushy ice that bobbed along the waters of the Beagle Channel.

The Neána metahumans floated to the surface. All that now remained of the insertion ship landing segments was a thick layer of active molecule blocks covering their skin like a pelt of translucent gel, insulating them from the dangerously cold water. They began to swim ashore.

The beach was a narrow strip of gray stones cluttered with dead branches. A dense woodland occupied the slope above it. The aliens scrambled a short way up the incline as the pale dawn light began to seep through the murky clouds. Their protective layer liquidized, draining down into the stones where it would be flushed away by the next high tide. For the first time, they drew air down into their lungs.

"Oh, that is cold!" one exclaimed.

"Good classification," another agreed through chattering teeth. "I'll go with it."

They looked at one another in the gray light. Two were crying from the emotional impact of arrival, one was smiling in wonder, while the fourth appeared singularly unimpressed by the bleak landscape. Each carried a small pack of outdoor clothing copied from a winter wear ad broadcast eighteen months earlier. They hurried to put it on.

When they were fully dressed, they set off along an ancient track up through the trees until they came to the remnants of National Route Three, which led to Ushuaia.

THE ASSESSMENT TEAM

FERITON KAYNE, NEW YORK, JUNE 23, 2204

I was never really that impressed with New York. The natives always banged on about how it was the city that never sleeps, how it had elevated itself to the center of the human universe. Self-justifying their choice of living in cramped, overpriced apartments—even today, when they could live anywhere on the planet and commute in through a dozen different Connexion hubs. They claimed it still had the buzz, the vibe, the kick. Bohemians came to dose up on *the experience, maaan* that helped them create their art, while corporate drones sweated through their junior management years to prove *commitment*. But for service staff proximity was simply convenient, while the truly poor couldn't afford to leave. And yes: Guilty, I lived in SoHo. Not that I'm junior management. Right there on my desk the nameplate says: Feriton Kayne, Deputy Director, Connexion Exosolar Security Division. And if you can work out what I actually do from that, you're smarter than most.

My office was on the seventy-seventh floor of the Connexion Corp tower. Ainsley Zangari wanted his global headquarters in Manhattan, and did he ever want everyone to know about it. There are few other people alive who could get a site on West 59th Street just along from Columbus Circle. He had to keep the façade of the old hotel as the base of his 120-story glass-and-carbon monstrosity— why I don't know; it had no architectural value as far as I can make out, but City Hall listed it as a landmark structure. So there you have it. Not even Ainsley Zangari, the richest man there's ever been, can argue City Hall out of *heritage*.

I'm not complaining. My office gives me the greatest conceivable view out over the city and Central Park—one that the mere super-rich along Park Avenue can't afford. I've actually had to position my desk so I work with my back to the floor-to-ceiling window. I'd be too distracted otherwise. Mind, it is a swivel chair.

That cloudless June afternoon I was standing looking out at the view, mesmerized as always; the vista resembled one of those seventeenth-century oil paintings where everything glows with heavenly radiance.

Kandara Martinez was shown in by a receptionist. The corporate mercenary wore a plain black singlet under a jacket from some midrange fashion house. The way she carried herself made it look like a military uniform. That part of her life just never left her, I guess.

Sandjay, my altme, splashed the data at me, which the tarsus lenses I wore over my eyeballs presented as a grid of green-and-purple text. The file didn't tell me much I didn't already know. She had enrolled in Mexico City's Heroico Colegio Militar when she was nineteen. After graduation she saw several active deployments in the Urban Rapid Suppression Force. Then her parents were killed by a drone bomb some bunch of anti-imperialist anarchist whack-jobs launched at the sneering symbol of their evil foreign economic oppressors—or, in English, the Italian remote drone systems factory where her father worked. After that her escalating kill rate in action started to "concern" her superiors. She received an honorable discharge in 2187. Freelance corporate security ever since—the real dark jobs.

In the flesh she was 170 centimeters tall, with chestnut hair, cut short, and gray eyes. I wasn't sure if they were real or gened-up; they didn't quite seem to belong with the rest of her Mexican ancestry. There'd certainly been some bodywork. She kept herself trim—in her line of work that was survival 101—but that couldn't account for the thickness of her limbs; her legs and arms were heavily muscled. Gened-up or Kcells; the file didn't say. Ms. Martinez left a very small dataprint on solnet.

"Thank you for accepting the contract," I said. "I'm a lot happier knowing you're coming with us." Which was only partially true. Her presence made me uncomfortable, but then I know whom she's eliminated during her career.

"I was curious," she said, "because we all know Connexion has so few people in its own security division."

"Yeah, about that. We might need something that goes beyond our guys' pay grade."

"Sounds interesting, Feriton."

"My boss wants protection, serious protection. We're dealing with the unknown here. This expedition . . . it's different. The artifact we've found is alien."

"So you said. Is it Olyix?"

"I don't see how it could be."

A small smile lifted her lips. "Not going to hide from you, I'm very interested. And flattered. Why me?"

"Reputation," I lied. "You're the best."

"Bullshit."

"Seriously. We have to keep this small; the three other people coming with us represent some serious political interests. So I wanted someone with a genuine track record."

"You're worried that rivals will find out about where we're headed? What sort of artifact have you found?"

"Can't tell you that until we're en route."

"Are you retro engineering its tech? Is that why you're worried about rivals?"

"This isn't about new technology and market impact. We have a bigger problem than that."

"Oh?" She lifted her eyebrow in query.

"You'll get a full briefing when we're underway. Everybody does."

"Okay, that's a reasonable containment strategy. But I do need to know: Is it hostile?"

"No. Or at least, not yet. Which is where you come in. We need to pack a large punch in a small place. Just in case."

"Even more flattered."

"One last thing, which is why you and I are having this meeting before I introduce you to the rest of the team."

"This doesn't sound good."

"There are some first-contact protocols involved, severe ones. Alpha Defense insisted. We're going to be very isolated for the duration of this mission—something none of us are familiar with. Today, no matter what disaster hits you, everybody can shout for help wherever they are. Everyone functions under the assumption an emergency team is two minutes away. It's all we know. I consider that to be a weakness, especially in this situation. If things go wrong—badly wrong—that's when the Alpha Defense first-contact protocol applies."

She caught on fast. I could see the slight change in body posture, humor retreating, muscles tightening.

"If they're hostile, they can't know about us," she said.

"No prisoners. No data downloads."

"Really?" Her humor swept back in. "You're worried about an alien invasion? That's very quaint. What does Ainsley Zangari think they're going to plunder, our gold and our women?"

"We don't know what they are, so until we do . . ."

"The Olyix turned out okay. And they had a shitload of antimatter on board the *Salvation of Life*. There isn't another conventional power source powerful enough to accelerate a vessel that size up to a decent fraction of light speed."

"We were fortunate with them," I said carefully. "Their religion gives them a whole different set of priorities to us. All they want to do is travel across space in their arkship to the end of time, where they believe their God will be waiting for them. They don't want to expand into new star systems and bioform planets to live on; it's a whole different imperative to ours. I guess we didn't really understand what *alien* meant until they arrived in the Sol system. But, Kandara, do you really want to gamble our species' survival on every race being as benign as the Olyix? It's been sixty years since they arrived, and we've both benefited from trade. Great, but we have a duty to consider that at some time we're going to encounter a species that isn't so benign."

"Interstellar war is a fantasy. It makes no sense. Economically, for resources, for territory . . . it's all crap. Hong Kong doesn't even make drama games about it anymore."

"Nonetheless, we must respect the possibility, however remote. My department has developed scenarios we don't ever reveal to the public," I confided. "Some of them are . . . disturbing."

"I bet they are. But at the end, it's all human paranoia."

"Maybe. However, the non-exposure protocol must be enacted if the contact species turns out to be hostile. Will you accept that responsibility? I need to know I can rely on you if I'm incapacitated."

"Incapacitated!" She took a moment, breathing in deeply as she finally realized what I was asking.

Getting her assigned to the mission on that basis—that thanks to her quirks she was genuinely dedicated and fearless enough to initiate the self-destruct sequence—had been an easy sell to Yuri. He had never questioned my choice.

"All right," she said. "If it comes to that, I'm prepared to press the big red button."

"Thank you. Oh, and the other three, they might not appreciate—"

"Yeah. We'll keep that part to ourselves."

"Good. Let's go meet them, then."

Exosolar Security occupied seven adjacent floors. The departmental conference room was on the seventy-sixth floor. I took Kandara down the big spiral stairwell in the middle of the tower.

Naturally, the conference room occupied a corner of the tower, giving it two glass walls. The oval teak table stretching along the middle of the floor probably cost more than my salary. It had fifteen chairs spaced around it. More chairs lined the non-glass walls for flunkies to sit in. Pure psychology, emphasizing the importance of those invited to sit at the table with the grown-ups.

There were seven people waiting, and none of them using a wall chair. As far as I was concerned, only three of them were relevant, the representatives of true power: Yuri Alster, Callum Hepburn, and Alik Monday.

Yuri was sitting at the far end, with his executive assistant and tech advisor Loi next to him. He's one of the real old-timers, born back in St. Petersburg in 2030; all broody and sullen like only Russians who emigrate from the Motherland can be. Couple that with his age, and I doubt his mouth was even capable of smiling anymore. He'd got his first telomere extension therapy about a century ago, and then progressed to gene-up to keep himself alive. If you called that living; most people call all the myriad extension therapies *the undying,* stretching out their existence at any price. I've seen people who never got rich until their eighties then go for treatments. It's not pretty.

All those treatments and procedures had left Yuri's appearance suspended in his late fifties, with his round face slightly bloated and his thin sandy hair shading lighter as it was infiltrated by gray strands that'd resisted the gene-up. Hooded gray-green eyes completed the image of a man who was suspicious about the whole universe.

But for Yuri an eternal fifty wasn't so bad. As well as his deferred face there had to be replacement organs, too. For a start, no original liver could survive immersion in that much vodka. His replacement parts would all be high-end bioprinted clone cells. He was too xeno-phobic (and maybe snobbish) to use Kcells. The alien biotechnology was the main trade item between the Olyix and humans; cells with a biochemistry compatible with a human body, which could be assem-bled into organs and muscles at a significantly lower cost than gene-up treatments and printed stem cells. They had a reputation (unfounded, in my opinion) of being slightly inferior to human med-ical technology. But by making advanced medical treatment available to millions of people who had been too poor to receive it before, it had become the biggest boon to social improvement since Connex-ion Corp started providing universal egalitarian transport through its portal hub network.

I nodded respectfully at him. After all, he was my boss and the author of this whole expedition. Me, I'd seen it for the terrific oppor-tunity it was.

As usual, Loi was wearing an absurdly expensive suit, as if he'd strayed in from Wall Street. Not too far from the truth, given he's Ainsley's great-grandson (one of many). Twenty-eight years old, and always keen to tell you about his shiny new quantum physics degree from Harvard—earned, not bought, as he'll explain. Right now he was desperately validating himself by working his way up through Connexion Corp the way everyone does. Because everyone age twenty-eight pulls an assistant's job with a department head as soon as they join. Just a regular guy, all smiles, after-work drinks with col-leagues, and bitching about The Boss.

Interestingly, Callum Hepburn had chosen to sit next to Yuri. He'd arrived twenty minutes ago from the Delta Pavonis system, where the Utopial culture was based. These days he was one of their senior troubleshooters, possessing a craggy face that gene-up had failed to soften with age. His thick crop of hair was the bold silver-white that all redheads turn, rather than the insipid gray that lies in wait for most humans.

I could sense a great deal of unhappiness behind those blue-gray eyes of his. From my briefing with Ainsley I gathered Callum hadn't exactly volunteered for the expedition. Allegedly, the Utopials with their perfect democracy can't be ordered to do anything, no matter what level of citizenship you've attained (and he's grade two). So that must be one hell of a favor domino Ainsley Zangari had knocked into Emilja Jurich—given Emilja was the closest thing the Utopials had to a leader, and therefore the only one who could pressure Callum into coming back to Earth.

And I don't suppose having Yuri along on the expedition was helping his temperament. The two of them haven't talked since Callum left Connexion in what I can only describe as intriguing circumstances a century ago, after he officially died.

Actually, it was 112 years ago. Whatever. That's an impressive amount of time to hold a grudge. But then he's Scottish, and in my experience they're just as stubborn and dour as Russians. It says something about the artifact we'd found that those two were prepared to put personal issues aside and cooperate—however nominally. Having them together in the bus was really going to make this a full-out fun-time trip.

Callum had brought two assistants with him from Delta Pavonis. Eldlund was obviously from Akitha—the Utopial's main world, orbiting Delta Pavonis. Like all people born into the Utopial movement today, sie was omnia: genetically modified to be both male and female, spending hir adult life in a thousand-day cycle between genders. That baseline genome alteration to every person born into the Utopial culture—enabling and enhancing their core philosophy of equality at a fundamental level—had been hugely controversial when it first began, back in 2119, condemned as extremist by some religions and old-school moralists. There had been plenty of discrimination and even violence against the omnias to begin with, by the usual suspects—the ignorant and prejudiced and fearful. But, as always, what was once exceptional decayed to mundane over time. Today, Eldlund could probably walk down most streets on Earth without any trouble. Sie would be noticed, mind you, but that was down to hir height; all the omnias were tall. And Eldlund was an easy fifteen centimeters higher than anyone else in the room, and also marathon-runner thin with it. Normally I'd call that willowy, but there was nothing fragile-looking about hir—although sie had a very pretty face with sharp cheekbones highlighted by an artfully trimmed beard.

And I could tell just how much confrontational attitude was coiled up in that rigid pose. Utopials from Akitha are always the most evangelical about their way of life; I hoped that wasn't going to be a problem. Sandjay's data splash listed hir as a Turing specialist.

Callum's other companion was Jessika Mye, the greatest political flip-flopper of us all. A Hong Kong native who at twenty went all radical and aligned herself with the Utopial ethic so she could train as an exobiologist on Akitha, only to flip back politically, enabling her to earn those dirty capitalist big bucks available in the Universal culture. I knew she was seventy-four; my altme was spraying the data up as my glance swept across her. She didn't look it. Interesting fact: She worked for Connexion security back in the day, which is where she got the money for telomere therapy in her early thirties. Then, after one volatile case, she upped and moved back to Akitha where her experience dropped her right into their Olyix Alien Observation Bureau. Five years ago she was promoted to Callum's senior assistant—an appointment that clearly gave her plenty of time off to work out in the gym. If I was the cynical sort, I'd say Callum appreciated that.

And finally we had Alik Monday. Access "corrupt" in the dictionary, and it'll likely give you his name. A genuine made-in-America bastard. Occupation: FBI Senior Special Detective, operating out of DC. Believe it or not, when I tried a data mine, his age was classified. He's a walking, talking federal secret, all personal data restricted. Connexion's Security G8Turing could have hacked his profile easily enough, but cracking an FBI core would be a huge deal, and not just for the feds. I'd have pattern sniffers all over my ass, and Yuri would be asking questions I could do without. I needed him to keep thinking this was his mission. Some things you just have to let go.

Anyway, I guessed Alik at about 110; he wasn't so much an undying as a reanimated corpse. Easy tells. That plastic smooth skin comes from so many therapies you'd have to use electric shocks to get his facial muscles to express an emotion. I suspected the color was gened-up, too. Most African Americans are a light brown, but Alik was black like he'd been sunbathing on the equator for a decade; you can't get any darker. Full bodywork, too. Take his shirt off, and you'll see the physique of a twenty-year-old Olympian, with every replacement muscle designed and bioprinted in a top San Francisco clinic. I'd give good odds there are some aggressive peripherals lurking in among all those perfect tendons and muscle bands, too.

But . . . all that time and money, wasted. Anyone looking at him knew he was old, and terribly calculating.

He was connected to the globalPACs operating out of DC, the rich old men who really run Earth, who make sure Universalism, the established democratic capitalist society, stays in place and doesn't get seduced away from its oh-so-holy guiding principles by shiny new concepts like Utopialism. Just like everyone, the PACs wanted to get a jump on the implications from the artifact. And Alik was their eyes on the prize, with a loyalty that only serious quantities of dollars can buy.

I sat with my back to Central Park and smiled graciously. "Thank you all for coming, and the people you represent for agreeing to this."

Alik frowned at me. "You're in charge? I thought I was requested because Alpha Defense was running this."

"Technically they are," I said. "We're running this investigation under their authority. But it is Mr. Alster's expedition. I'm basically just admin."

"Keep 'em in their place, huh, Yuri?" Alik grinned.

Yuri's impassive gaze looked down on Alik from some immeasurable height. "Every time."

I caught Alik mouthing "Smartass."

"What's the schedule?" Callum asked.

"We'll go from here directly to Nkya in the Beta Eridani system. Our transport is ready. Journey time from the base camp to the artifact should take about forty-eight hours, maybe a bit longer."

"Fuck's sake," Alik grunted. "Why so long?"

"Quarantine," Yuri said tersely. "We need to keep it completely isolated. Physically and digitally. So there's no portal opening to it; we're going the old-fashioned way, by ground vehicle."

"Digitally isolated?" Alik's stiff face registered nothing. It didn't have to; his tone revealed all. "Please tell me you have access to solnet onsite?"

"No access," Yuri said. "It's the Alpha Defense contact protocol. We can't take the risk. I'm sure DC appreciates that."

Callum smirked.

"There's a science team already onsite," I told them, and gestured at the three assistants. "And we welcome the additions you're bringing."

"The additions," Jessika said. "Makes us sound like a band." She and Eldlund shared a smile. Loi ignored them, staring directly at me.

"You'll be given total access to the science team's data," I continued. "And if there are any further aspects of the artifact you want to examine, we'll prioritize them for you. In effect, you'll be determining the direction of the investigation."

"How long will we be there for?" Callum asked. I could still hear an Aberdeen burr in his voice, even though the file said he hadn't been back there for over a century.

"Our investigation has two priorities," Yuri pronounced. "First priority is to assess the artifact's threat potential. Is it hostile, and if so, to what extent? Secondly, based on that, we're required to formulate a response recommendation. So that's going to take as long as it takes. Good enough?"

Alik wasn't happy, but he nodded.

"If there's nothing else?" I queried. Nobody seemed to have a question. "Excellent. Please follow me."

The seventy-sixth floor had a portal door direct to Connexion's Exosolar division in Houston. Alik Monday was 188 centimeters high, so he walked straight through after me, but Eldlund had to duck slightly. Connexion Corp portal doors are a standard two-meters-fifteen-centimeters high. Maybe sie didn't really need to duck, but no denying it, sie was tall.

We came out into a circular hub, with fourteen other portal doors around the edge. Bright morning sunlight shone in through the glass cupola above. Air-conditioning thrummed loudly as it battled Texas heat and humidity. Our trollez were all waiting for us in a cluster at the center of the hub: meter-high pearl-white cylinders with very flexible wheels, carrying all our personal luggage. Sandjay pinged mine, and it locked on. Of course, Loi had two trollez. All those designer shirts need careful packing.

I walked clockwise around the wall, trying not to peer through the portal doors. Some led into neat department lobbies while a couple opened directly into big assembly halls that looked empty.

The door to Connexion's Exoscience and Exploration Department was the fifth one along. I stopped in front of it and waited until all the trollez had caught up with us before going through.

Given that interstellar travel is *the* most glamorous activity the human race has ever undertaken, the building housing E & E is surprisingly ordinary. Concrete, carbon, and glass, just like the thousand other corporate blocks scattered across Houston's technology zone. The entrance lobby had four portal doors opening into it, all of them with a picket of security barriers—slim silver bars spaced close enough to prevent physical access. That was the visible obstacle. There were other, more discreet, and lethal, security measures (the company got quite jumpy after the *incident* 112 years ago that caused Callum to switch from being a good and loyal Connexion Corp employee to a full-on Utopial). The G8Turing that managed building security interrogated Sandjay and scanned us all. Then the bars slid down into the floor.

Geovanni, the Beta Eridani mission director, was waiting for us just beyond. He bobbed about uneasily as so many alpha visitors stepped into his domain. He introduced himself, shook hands tentatively, and finally said: "This way, please."

He led us down a long corridor, with pictures of various star fields and cheerless exoplanet landscapes on the walls. Our trollez trundled along quietly behind us. The few Connexion personnel we passed gave us curious glances; most of them recognized Yuri. Amazing how many people suddenly look guilty when they're face-to-face with that level of authority.

"What's the planet like?" Kandara asked.

"Nkya? Fairly typical, if you can say that about exoplanets," Geovanni said. "Let's see: ten thousand three hundred kilometers in diameter, which gives us a gravity of point nine Earth. Thirty-seven-hour days; so not good for our diurnal rhythms. Atmospheric pressure is two thousand pascals, which makes it two percent Earth sea level pressure; that's made up mainly of CO-two, with traces of argon, nitrogen, and sulfur dioxide. It's orbiting five and a half AUs out from Beta Eridani, so cold, cold, cold. Minimal tectonic activity, meaning no volcanoes. No moons, either. Nobody's going to be terraforming this baby."

"So no indigenous life?"

Geovanni turned around and grinned at her. "Not a chance."

"Does Beta Eridani have any other planets, save Nkya?"

"Three. Two small solids, both in close orbits to Beta Eridani, as hot as Mercury and tidal-locked so you could melt bricks on their light side. One gas-mini, fifteen AUs out; makes Nkya look tropical."

At the end of the corridor, a pair of solid doors swung open for us, taking us through into a nondescript anteroom. Then Geovanni practically rushed through an identical set of doors on the opposite wall. The Nkya egress chamber looked remarkably like an industrial warehouse. Smooth polished concrete floor, high blue-gray composite panel walls, black composite roof obscured by bright lighting strips hanging down over the aisles. Metal racks ran almost the length of the chamber, three times Eldlund's height, stacked with white plastic pods and bulky metal cases. Commercial cargo trollez rolled along, either collecting supplies from a couple of portal doors that led away to distribution centers and slotting them in the correct place on the racks or picking equipment from the racks and taking it down to the portal at the far end.

One wall was inset with long windows that looked into a series of labs where samples were analyzed. Technical personnel wandered around their benches loaded with expensive analysis equipment, dressed in double-sealed white environment suits, peering through bubble helmets.

"Sure there's no indigenous life there?" Kandara asked, staring into the labs. "Looks to me like you're taking contamination protocols very seriously."

"Standard procedure," Geovanni replied. "It takes seven to twelve years to receive preliminary Sol Senate Exolife Agency clearance, confirming there's no autochthonous microbiology. Personally I think that ought to be increased to fifty years, with a quadrupled sample range, before you can formally announce an all clear with any form of authority. But that's just me. Over the years we've found some interesting microbes on some otherwise inhospitable planets."

Kandara stared around as if she was trying to memorize the facility. "Any chance you missed something on Nkya?"

"No. Beta Eridani was a classic by-the-book arrival procedure. *Kavli* spent a couple of months decelerating down from point-eight-C. She arrived in-system this February. We sent a squadron of astronomy satellites through her portal. So far all standard and good; my people know what they're doing." He waved a hand at the semicircular room at the end of the labs, nearest the portal to Nkya. It was a control center, with two lines of big, high-resolution holographic windows all along the curving wall. Several desks had smaller screen stacks, with senior researchers and their gaggle of graduate astronomers drooling over images of strange, dark planetary crescents, orbital paths, fluctuating data tables, star maps, and rainbow graphics that to me resembled bad abstract art. "We picked up the signal straight away. Hard not to. It was multispectral, low power but constant."

"Signal?" Alik barked in surprise. "Nobody said this was an active artifact. What the fuck are you sending us to?"

Geovanni gave Yuri a quick, resentful glance. "I don't know. I don't have clearance."

"Go on, please," I told him. "What happened after you detected the signal?"

"It was just a beacon signal, coming from the fourth planet: Nkya. So we followed protocol and informed Alpha Defense. A robot lander was flown down from orbit, keeping a minimum designated quarantine distance from the source. Once the lander put a portal on the surface, we started sending equipment through." He pointed at the big circular portal at the end of the egress chamber. "I've never set up a base camp so fast. Just about the first thing we sent through was a twelve-person science ranger vehicle. Connexion security drove it and two Alpha Defense officers out to the artifact and came straight back. That was ten days ago. Next thing I know, Alpha Defense has ruled the whole expedition ultra-classified, and I get orders to send a secondary base through. That's a joke, because it's actually better than base camp; it even includes its own hospital, for crap's sake. Some trucks hauled it out to the artifact, and an engineering crew set it up. They only got back yesterday. The preliminary science team left seven days ago, with another convoy of trucks packed with research equipment. Now you guys are here, and I've been ordered to give you total priority."

"Sorry about that," Loi said.

"Why?" I asked him. "Everyone is doing their job."

The kid blushed, but had the smarts enough to shut up.

Geovanni took us right up to the five-meter-diameter portal. They don't come much bigger; it was circular with an elevated metal ramp bridging the rim at the bottom so the cargo trollez could drive over unimpeded. Bundles of thick cables and hoses snaked through to Nkya underneath the ramp. Three sentinel pillars stood on either side, blank ash-gray surfaces concealing the formidable weaponry they contained. God help any alien that tried to come through without Ainsley's approval.

Not that it would ever come to that. The G8Turings would cut power to the portal in a millisecond if any bug-eyed, tentacled monster even approached the other side.

I stared through the broad circle. It opened directly into a thirty-meter-wide geodesic dome, also stuffed full of supply racks. Two multi-sensor globes on chest-high posts were positioned on either side, letting the G8Turing scan anything that approached.

"This is it," Geovanni said proudly, sweeping an arm toward the portal. "This is what we do. Welcome to another world."

"Thanks." I went up the ramp's shallow slope after him. I couldn't help a little flash of unease as I drew level with the portal's rim. The Nkya base camp was less than a meter away from me now—*a single step*, as Connexion's famous first ad said. A step that would span eighty-nine light-years.

Using ordinary Connexion Corp portal doors to walk between the company's Earth-spanning network of hubs never bothered me. The greatest distance one of those doors covered was trans-oceanic, maybe six thousand kilometers. But . . . eighty-nine light-years? You couldn't not be aware of the time and effort it'd taken to cover that awesome gulf.

Long before Kellan Rindstrom demonstrated quantum spatial entanglement at CERN back in 2062, human dreamers had been coming up with semi-realistic plans for starships. There were proposals to mine Jupiter's atmosphere for helium-3 that could power a town-sized pulse-fusion ship that would scout nearby stars. Country-sized sails a molecule thick that would ride the solar wind out to the constellations. Skyscraper-sized laser cannon that would accelerate smaller lightsails. Antimatter rockets. The Alcubierre drive. Quantum vacuum plasma thrusters . . .

Kellan Rindstrom's discovery consigned them all to the history folder marked: "quirky inventions that never made it past the concept study." When you can connect two separate physical locations via a quantum entanglement portal, so many problems cease to exist.

Even so, starships require a phenomenal amount of thrust to accelerate up to a decent percentage of light speed, and Connexion Corp's modern designs achieve in excess of eighty percent. Before Rindstrom, that would have required carrying vast amounts of energy and reaction mass on board. Now, all you do is drop a perfectly spherical portal into the sun. Meta-hot plasma slams into that hole at near-relativistic speed. At the same time, the portal's exit is fixed at the apex of a magnetic cone, which channels the plasma into a rocket exhaust. There is no limit on how much plasma from the sun you can send through, and the starship masses very little—just the portal and its nozzle, guidance units, and a smaller portal communication link to mission control. It can accelerate *fast*.

When it reaches a star, it decelerates into orbit, delivering a portal link back to Earth's solar system. That means you can start sending through entire preassembled asteroid industrial complexes straight away. Within a day you're ready to start crunching minerals and begin manufacture. The pioneer crews build habitats that house the workforce, which builds the next generation of starships, which fly off to new stars. It's almost an exponential process. And in their wake, the newly discovered exoplanets are ripe for terraforming.

Connexion Corp has been one of the major players when it comes to sending starships out from Earth, building and flying them for more than a hundred years. Every new Universal settled star system is another huge income source for the company. Beta Eridani is the farthest star humans have reached. Eighty-nine light-years from Earth.

One step.

I felt the slight drop in gravity as soon as I was through the portal. Not quite enough to mess with my balance, but I took the down ramp carefully just in case.

The dome was a smaller version of the egress chamber back on Earth, piled high with pods and equipment cases. A quarter of it was given over to life support equipment: big spherical tanks, air filters, pumps, ducts, quantum batteries, thermal exchanges; everything to keep humans alive in a hostile environment. If the main portal and the redundant emergency portals were closed for whatever reason, those chunks of machinery could sustain the base personnel for years if necessary.

Sandjay coupled to the base camp's network and splashed local schematics across my tarsus lenses. Connexion Corp's foothold on Nkya was laid out in a simple triangular array, with passageways leading out radially from the main dome to a trio of slightly smaller domes.

"Ordinarily, this would be full of geologists and exobiologists," Geovanni said as he headed for one of the three big airlocks at the edge of the dome. "But right now we're keeping base staff to an absolute minimum. We've taken local samples, but further field trips are on hold. The only people here today are engineering support and your security teams."

He took us through the airlock, which was large enough to hold all of us and our trollez while it cycled. The passageway on the other side was a plain metal tube with light strips and cable conduits running overhead. Even with all the insulation layers built into base camp's structures, the surface had a faint mist of condensation— proof of just how cold Nkya was.

The air in the garage dome held a throat-tickling sulfur tang. It was cool, too. But I didn't pay that much attention; I was too busy staring at the waiting machine. The Trail Ranger occupied the floor like a possessive dragon come to cozy down in its lair. Like everybody in this day and age, I'm completely unfamiliar with ground vehicles. This brute was wildly impressive. It came in three sections. A cab and engineering section were at the front, with a smooth fluorescent-green egg-shaped body. Lights resembling insect eyes clustered around the blunt nose, just below a curving windscreen; smaller sensor wands protruded like thick black stubble hairs on the underside. The heat radiators were four slim mirror-silver strips running perpendicular down both sides, as if the designers had added missile fins just for the hell of it.

Behind the cab, linked by an articulated pressure coupling, were the two cylindrical passenger sections. They were made of the same smooth metalloceramic, with slit windows on both sides.

Each section rode on six fat tires, individually powered by an electric axle motor. The damn things were as high as I was, with tread patterns deep enough that I could put my hand in them.

Everybody was smiling in appreciation; even Alik managed to twitch his lips with interest. I joined them. I wanted to drive the beast; it was an impulse I guessed most of the team were experiencing. No such luck. Geovanni introduced us to Sutton Castro and Bee Jain, the Trail Ranger drivers.

The interior convinced me Yuri had ordered the Trail Ranger printed specifically for us. I don't believe Connexion's exoscience staff would generally be bused about a new planet in such comfort. The rear section contained sleeping pods with a locker for everyone's trollez. Forward of those, I peeped into one of the four small washroom cubicles, finding a miracle of convertible units and compact storage cabinets to cater for every need from a toilet to a shower. There was also a tiny galley with packets of gourmet meals that a servez was still loading into the fridges.

Our lounge dominated the middle section, fitted with luxurious reclining chairs. Everyone settled down in there as the drivers went forward to the cab. A couple of stewards came in and asked us if we wanted any food or drink. It was all slightly surreal. I've seen old videos that included plane flights and traveling on the Orient Express. For a moment I could believe the portal to Nkya had actually transported us into the twentieth century. This was traveling in history.

I have to admit, there was a degree of elegance to it. If it wasn't so ridiculously time consuming, I could probably get used to it.

"We're sealing up in two minutes," Sutton Castro announced over the PA.

Sandjay splashed the garage airlock schematic, showing me both doors closing and undergoing pre-start pressure tests. I didn't ask for it, but Sandjay was an adaptive altme, about as smart as an old G6Turing, so it can pretty much anticipate what I want and need to know. The biometrics my medical peripheries were reading would've revealed rising heart rate, a small adrenaline flush, and raised skin temperature. All its core algorithms would interpret that as one thing: *anxiety rising*. So Sandjay did what it could to reassure me, and showed me lots of systems working smoothly.

The garage dome pumped its atmosphere away. "Access the vehicle net," I whispered soundlessly. The peripheral fibers riding alongside my vocal cord nerves picked up the impulses, and Sandjay coupled to the Trail Ranger's net. "Give me an external camera feed."

I closed my eyes and watched the image splash. In front of the Trail Ranger, the big garage door was opening, slowly hinging up.

It was dark outside. Gray sky lidded a rust-brown rock plain. A fine dust suspended in the super-thin atmosphere gave everything a hazy quality. Yet I could see tiny zephyrs twirling along across the metamorphic mesa, sucking up spirals of sand. Spectacularly sharp mountains shredded the eastern horizon. The sight was entrancing. Virgin land, desolate and alien.

The Trail Ranger rolled forward. I could feel the movement, the slight rise and fall of the suspension pistons as if we were a yacht sailing over mildly choppy waters. Then the tires were biting into the loose regolith, churning up big fantails.

I opened my eyes, and Sandjay canceled the camera feed. Yuri, Callum, and Alik were all doing the same thing as I was, watching the images coming from the Trail Ranger's net, while Kandara and the three aides had chosen to stand, pressed up against the long windows, seeing the landscape for real. I guess that's a comment on age.

It wasn't long before the base camp domes were white splinters on the horizon. The Trail Ranger was purring along at fifty kilometers an hour, with the occasional lurch as we rolled over a ridge. Sutton and Bee were following a line of marker posts that the original science rover had dropped every four kilometers to mark the route, their scarlet strobes flashing bright against the sullen rock.

The stewards came around again, taking drink orders. I asked for a hot chocolate. Most of the others had something alcoholic.

"Right," Alik said. "We're out of range from base camp, and I can't access solnet. What the fuck is out there?"

I glanced at Yuri, who nodded. "I can give you the initial team's report," I said, ordering Sandjay to release the files for them.

Everyone sat down, closing their eyes to survey the data.

"A spaceship?" Callum blurted in astonishment. "You're taking the piss."

"I wish we were," Yuri said. "It's a spaceship, all right."

"How long has it been here?" Alik asked.

"Preliminary estimate: thirty-two years."

"And it's intact?"

"Reasonably. It didn't crash, though there is some hard-landing damage."

"I'm surprised by the size," Eldlund said. "I'd expect a starship to be bigger."

"The drive—if that's what it is—doesn't use reaction mass. We believe it has exotic matter components."

"A wormhole generator?" Callum asked sharply.

"Currently unknown. Hopefully, the science team will have some results for us when we arrive. They've had a week's lead on us."

"And there's no sign of whoever built it?" Kandara said thoughtfully.

Yuri and I exchanged a glance.

"No," I said. "However, some of the . . . cargo is intact. Well, preserved, anyway."

"Cargo?" She frowned. "What's the file number?"

"There's no file on the cargo," Yuri said. "Alpha Defense ruled that we absolutely cannot afford a security breach on that one."

"Something worse than an alien starship?" Callum said. "This should be good."

"So . . . ?" Kandara narrowed her eyes.

I took a breath. "There are several biomechanical units on board which can only be classed as hibernation chambers, or modules that . . . ah fuck it, you'll see. Whatever: They contained humans."

"You are shitting me," Alik growled.

"Again, no," Yuri said. "Somebody took humans from Earth thirty-two years ago and flew them out here. The implications are not good."

I smiled at Kandara. "Still think we're paranoid?"

She glared back at me.

"How many humans?" Eldlund asked; sie sounded badly shaken.

"Seventeen," I told hir.

"Are they alive?" Jessika asked quickly.

"The hibernation chamber machinery appears to be functional," I said diplomatically. "Half of the science team we sent out are medical personnel. We'll be given a more definitive answer when we arrive."

"Fuck me," Alik said, and took a big drink of bourbon from his cut-crystal tumbler. "We're eighty-nine light-years from Earth, and they flew here thirty years ago? Is the ship FTL capable?"

"Unknown. But possible."

I watched them, Callum, Yuri, Kandara, and Alik, as they stared around at one another, trying to read their expressions, to see any forgeries amid the shock and surprise. They gave nothing away. And I still didn't know which one of them was the alien.

JULOSS

YEAR 583 AA (AFTER ARRIVAL)

"They've gone," Dellian declared with a mixture of excitement and resentment as he raced out of the changing pavilion and onto the short grass of the games fields. His head was tipped back to gaze up at the bright blue sky. For all of his twelve years, there had been a great many sharp points of silver light orbiting far above Juloss, like stars that could be seen in daytime. Now several of those familiar specks (the larger ones) had vanished, leaving the remaining skyforts to their lonely vigil, constantly alert for any sign of the enemy's warships approaching their home world.

"Yeah, the last traveler generation ships portaled out last night," Yirella said wistfully as she tied back some of her hair.

Dellian was fond of Yirella. She was nothing like as solemn as the other girls in the Immerle clan, who were uniformly quiet and smiled so very little. And unlike her, none of them ever joined the boys in the pitches and arenas as they played their team competitions. But

Yirella had never been content to take her place in the arena's command pens, observing and advising.

As he stared up into the empty sky, he could feel the sweat starting to bead on his skin. Immerle's estate was in the planet's semi-tropical zone, and this close to the coast the air was permanently hot and humid. With his red hair and pale skin, Dellian always used to slather himself in sunblock for the five afternoons a week when the kids played games on the estate's sports fields. But since he and his year-mates reached their tenth birthday, they'd moved on to more combative games in the orbital arena.

"I wonder where they've gone?" he asked.

Yirella pushed her shaggy ebony hair aside and smiled down at him. Dellian liked that smile; her rich black skin always made a flash of white teeth seem quite dazzling—especially when it was directed at him.

"We'll never know now," she said. "That's the point of dispersal, Del. The enemy will find Juloss eventually, and when they do they'll burn its continents down to the magma. But when that day comes, the generation ships will be hundreds of light-years away. Safe."

Dellian answered with a grin of his own, acting as if it didn't matter to him, and looked around at his muncs to check they were paying attention. All the clan's children were assigned a group of six homunculi on their third birthday to act as permanent companions and playmates. It was Alexandre who had told the breathless and excited children that the stocky human-shaped creatures were "homunculi"—a word that Dellian and his clanmates shortened to muncs within a minute, and it had stuck ever since.

The muncs were genderless, 140 centimeters tall, with thick arms and legs that were slightly bowed, alluding to a terrestrial ape heritage somewhere in their DNA. Their skin had a glossy gray and chestnut pelt, with thicker, darker fur on their scalps. They were also extremely affectionate and always eager to please. Their creators hadn't given them many words, but they had instilled a strong sense of loyalty and empathy.

Around his ninth birthday Dellian had finally grown taller than his cohort. It had been a thrilling moment when he realized he'd gained that advantage, after which their play tumbling took on a different aspect, becoming more serious somehow as they all squirmed around on the dormitory floor laughing and shouting. He still adored them—a feeling now mingling with pride as they read his intent, providing an instinct-driven extension of his body during games. The years spent with him during childhood allowed them to learn his moods and identify his body language perfectly, which would pay dividends later in his life when he began his military service. The best integration in his yeargroup, Alexandre had acknowledged approvingly. And Alexandre's approval meant a great deal to him.

Dellian and Yirella shuddered in unison as they heard the distinctive drawn-out ululation of a lokak's menacing hunting cry coming from beyond the estate's perimeter fence. Thankfully, they rarely saw the agile, serpentine beasts slipping through the snarled-up forest outside. The animals had learned not to stray too close to the estate; but the fence and the sentry remotes that patrolled in endless circles were a constant reminder of how hostile Juloss could be to anyone who let their guard down.

The arena's portal was on the edge of the sports field, sheltering under a small Hellenic roof. Dellian shook off his chill as he walked through. He and Yirella stepped directly into the arena, a simple cylinder with a diameter of a hundred meters, and seventy wide, with every surface padded. He breathed in happily, feeling his heartbeat rise. This was what he lived for, to show off his prowess in the tournaments and matches, for with that came the prospect of beating the opposing team, of *winning*. And nothing on Juloss was more important than winning.

The arena was in neutral mode, which was spinning about its axis to produce a twenty percent Coriolis gravity around the curving floor. Dellian always wished there was a window—the arena was attached to a skyfort's assembly grid, orbiting 150,000 kilometers above Juloss, and the view would have been fabulous.

Instead he did what he always did when he came in, and studied the arena's interior to see if the stewards had made any changes. Floating above him were thirty bright hazard-orange hurdles: polyhedrons of various sizes, also padded.

"They've bigged them up, look," Dellian said enthusiastically, as he took in the hurdles, committing the positioning to memory. Alexandre had promised the senior yeargroup they would receive their databuds in another couple of months, uniting them directly with personal processors and memory cores that would handle all the mundane mental chores Dellian had to labor away at right now. He considered it monumentally unfair that all the clan's adults had them.

"You mean they have enlarged the hurdles," Yirella said primly.

"Saints, you've gone and joined the grammar police," he moaned. At the same time he saw how intently she was studying the new layout and smiled to himself. They started to walk along the floor, necks craning up, his cohort studying the hurdle layout as attentively as he was.

The rest of Dellian's yearmates started to show up. He saw the boys grinning at the larger hurdles suspended above them, relishing the extra bounce the wider pentagonal and hexagonal surfaces would give them—if they landed true, of course.

"Saints, we'll reach the axis like lightning," Janc said.

"Going to ace this," Uret agreed.

"Is it going to be a capture the flag, do you think?" Orellt asked.

"I want to play straight takedown," Rello said wistfully. "Just hit them and knock them out of the arena."

"Inter-clan matches are flag captures," Tilliana said loftily. "They allow a greater range of strategy options and cooperative maneuvers. That's what we train for, after all."

Dellian and Falar exchanged a martyred grin behind Tilliana's back; the girl was always dismissive of any enthusiasm the boys showed to expand the tournament. Even so, she and her pair of muncs were reviewing the new arrangement keenly.

"Where are they?" Xante exclaimed impatiently.

They didn't have long to wait. The visiting team from the Ansaru clan, whose estate was on the other side of the eastern mountains, came jogging into the arena in a single regimented line, their munc cohorts forming columns on either side. Dellian scowled at that; the Ansaru boys had discipline. With his own yearmates spread halfway around the curving floor, joking around, their cohorts scattered and jostling spiritedly, it already put the Ansaru team ahead on style. *We should organize like that.*

Alexandre and the Ansaru referee came in, talking together cheerfully. Dellian was grateful he had Alexandre as his year mentor; some of the other adults who looked after the clan children didn't have hir empathy. He could still remember the day, six years ago, when he and his yearmates had it gently explained to them that they weren't omnia like the adults, that their gender was binary, fixed—like people on Earth millennia ago.

"Why?" they'd all asked.

"Because you need to be what you are," Alexandre had explained kindly. "It is you who will be going out to face the enemy in combat, and what you are will give you the greatest advantage in battle."

Dellian still didn't quite believe that. After all, Alexandre, like most of the adults, was nearly two meters tall. Surely soldiers needed that size and strength, and sie'd also told the boys they were unlikely to reach that height.

"But you will be strong," sie'd promised. Only that was a poor consolation for Dellian.

He always felt mildly guilty whenever he studied their mentor too closely nowadays, drawing comparisons in his head. Despite hir considerable height, Dellian could never consider hir as strong as a body that size could (or should) be. Of course age played a part in that.

Out in the middle of the zone floor, Alexandre remained reasonably robust looking; though Dellian did wonder if the black V-neck referee's shirt sie wore revealed maybe too much cleavage for someone with so many years behind hir. (Dorm rumor put hir at 180.) But Alexandre's cinnamon-shaded skin was practically wrinkle-free, contrasting nicely with hir thick honey-blond hair, which was always cut in a severe bob ending level with hir chin. Wide gray eyes could express a great deal of sympathy, yet as Dellian had found on the many occasions his misbehavior had been discovered, they could also be stern. And this year Alexandre had decided to grow a thin beard. "Because it's stylish," sie told the kids, slightly defensively, when they asked and snickered. Dellian still wasn't sure about that.

Alexandre caught his eye and gestured: *Get into position.*

The teams started to line up along the center of the floor, spacing themselves evenly, each taking a half, with the referees between them. Dellian and his cohort claimed his customary place in the middle of the Immerle team's semicircle. Yirella was at his side, her two muncs flanking her. Girls only had two muncs each—why would they need more? Dellian craned his neck, giving the visiting team a fast appraisal, seeing which player's cohort seemed tightest and most responsive.

"Their number eight," Yirella said. "I remember him from last year. He's good. Watch him."

"Yeah," Dellian muttered absently. He remembered number eight as well—remembered spinning tackles that sent him cartwheeling away from the hurdles, cursing as his opponent streaked away with the flagball.

Number eight was a thickset boy with brown hair oiled back over his skull. From a quarter of the way around the arena floor he gave Dellian a fast, dismissive look, calculated to insult; his munc cohort copied it perfectly.

Dellian's fists closed in reflex.

"Mistake," Yirella chided. "He's goading you."

A quick flush rose to Dellian's cheeks. She was right, and he knew it. Too late to try to return an insult; number eight was no longer looking in his direction.

The Ansaru team's three girls took their places in the command pens around the rim, walking across the floor with a grace Dellian envied; his own gait resembled a boulder leading an avalanche—no style, but it did get him places. However, he enjoyed their obvious disapproval as they registered Yirella remaining in the arena, wearing her protective bodysuit and an easy forty-five centimeters higher than the tallest boy. Teams were restricted to thirteen members, including tacticians, but there was nothing in the rules about one of the tacticians actually taking part. Yirella had won that argument a long time ago.

With a theatrical flourish, Alexandre and the Ansaru referee produced two flagballs each, holding them up high; the Immerle pair started flashing with a red light, while Ansaru's were yellow.

Both teams grinned as they saw them.

"Two," Dellian breathed in delight. *Now that's more like it.* Until now, they'd always played one flagball. This was going to be a real test of skill and teamwork. He and the rest of the team put on their helmets, giving one another slightly nervous looks.

This was both the pain and the joy of being the first generation of binary humans to be birthed on Juloss. There wasn't an older year to pass down the wisdom, like warning them the arena game rules would change. Dellian and his yearmates were always dropping hints to the younger years about how to handle themselves in games and tournaments. But they were the pioneers; everything they underwent in the estate's training program was fresh and new. Sometimes it felt like an unfair burden—not that he'd ever admit that to Alexandre.

"A point will only be given when both flagballs are put through the goal," Alexandre announced. "Winner is first to fifteen points."

"Janc and Uret, play defense on one flagball," Ellici's voice announced in Dellian's helmet comset. "Rello, you take the second."

"Gotcha," Rello announced greedily.

"Hable and Colian, go midblock on Rello's flagball," Tilliana said. "Let's lure them in. Only intercept when they're on final snatch flight."

Dellian breathed out in relief. He'd been fearful the girls would assign him defense—*again*. He knew he was so much better at intercept.

"Ready one," Alexandre said loudly.

Everyone tensed up. Dellian's munc cohort clustered around him, holding hands to form a ring.

"Ready two?" the Ansaru referee asked.

Ansaru's boys yelled: "Yeah!" Dellian and his team let loose their signature call—a hooted warble they'd developed over the last couple of years, which to their ears sounded magnificently savage.

Alexandre smiled tolerantly. The light strips ribbing the arena walls turned gold. Dellian felt the gravity start to reduce further as the arena's spin slowed. All the boys swayed about like seaweed in a current. As always, falling gravity made him feel bizarrely light-headed. The referees both threw the flagballs upward. All four of the flashing globes soared up toward the axis.

Gravity reached about five percent. Alexandre blew the whistle.

Dellian's muncs crouched down fast, thrusting their clenched hands into the center of the ring they were forming. Dellian hopped onto the platform of stumpy hands, squatting down. The cohort read his every muscle movement perfectly; he jumped as if he was trying to power himself all the way to the planet below. The muncs flung their arms up in perfect synchronization, slim flower petals bursting open.

He rocketed upward, body turning a half somersault, as he headed for the first polyhedron—and a hexagonal surface that was angled *just so*. Drawing his knees up almost to his chin. And hit-kick. The power bounce. Soaring toward the polyhedron two up. The air around him full of flying boys. Tracking them and the flagballs, trying to project where they were all going. Then the muncs were rising, from above an impossibly hefty bird flock startled into the air.

Dellian saw which of the Ansaru boys was going defensive on one of their flagballs. "Intercepting a D," he yelled.

As he thumped down onto the next polyhedron, he altered his angle and bounced on a good interception course.

"Mallot, take Dellian's D-2," Tilliana called. "Yi, snatch it."

The Ansaru defender saw him coming and curled up. Dellian rotated around his center of gravity, drawing his legs up, ready for the kick.

They collided hard. The defender tried to grab Dellian's feet (technically illegal; you could only bump opponents, not grapple), but Dellian used only one foot, which gave him an unexpected slant. The defender's hands swung through empty air. He made good contact on the boy's hip, sending him spinning away to thud into a polyhedron, which whirled him off along a horizontal trajectory.

Yirella zipped past him as Mallot struck the second defender. She bounced accurately off a polyhedron and streaked straight toward the yellow flagball. Dellian's cohort caught up with him and formed up in a globe cage of tense limbs with him in the center. Together they bounced off a hurdle, four munc legs kicking to give extra velocity. He rose toward Yirella, providing cover.

The arena light strips flashed violet for three seconds. Dellian grunted in dismay. The cohort bundle read his micro-flexing and twisted, legs rigid, arms extended so they spun slowly—ready.

The gyroscopic shells that contained the arena shifted around and spun faster. The centrifugal gravity direction altered sharply. The hurdles suddenly appeared to be moving through the air, like solid clouds in a storm front. A couple of cohort bundles were swatted, flailing away chaotically. Tilliana and Ellici were both yelling instructions, redirecting the team. Dellian saw a hurdle approaching fast, and his cohort bundle shifted their dynamic slightly. Hit and bounce-kicked in roughly the right direction. Not that he'd ever been at sea, but Dellian thought the arena's irregular shifts must be like being in a ship as it was tossed about by a hurricane.

Yirella had stayed on course. She grabbed the Ansaru flagball and shot through the axis. Her muncs clung to her hips, producing an X shape. They twisted gymnastically, flipping her as they went through the axis—and even Dellian was impressed by the smoothness of the maneuver. Yirella bounced off a hurdle to dive headfirst toward the floor, which now had an apparent tilt of forty-five degrees.

"Yi, incoming three o'clock Z," Ellici called. "Now! Nownow!"

Dellian bit back his own comments; the girls always got overexcited in the games, he felt. They were supposed to be the calm, analytical ones. He saw the Ansaru defender (number eight shirt) at the center of a cohort star formation, pinwheeling toward Yirella.

"Got him," he yelled. A hurdle on his right. His awareness and posture had two munc arms shooting out, slapping, which gave the whole bundle a fast roll—putting them on course for the next hurdle. Bounce—and he crashed into number eight's bundle a couple of seconds before he took Yirella out. The impact was strong enough to break the bundles, and muncs and boys twirled apart like explosion debris riding a blast wave.

Yirella made one more bounce and landed hard on the angled floor, rolling gracefully to absorb the impact. She raced to the Immerle goal hoop and dropped the ball into it.

Dellian smacked painfully into a hurdle and flailed about, trying to stabilize himself. Two of his muncs scrambled over a hurdle and jumped toward him. Light strips started flashing violet.

"Oh, Saints," he groaned as the arena shifted again. A hurdle came sweeping through the air at him. A munc caught his ankle. They spun end over end, and he just had time to crouch and bounce.

"Zero on Rello," Tilliana commanded. "Quick quick!"

Dellian searched around frantically. He saw Rello cartwheeling next to their flashing flagball. Three Ansaru bundles were heading for him. Instinctively Dellian bounced another hurdle and flew, arms outstretched in summoning. In five seconds his cohort had coalesced around him again, and together they flashed across the arena to help Rello.

The Ansaru team managed to capture an Immerle flagball and dunk it into their goal hoop, then fifty seconds later Xante snatched the second Ansaru flagball. The arena stabilized, and both teams bounced gently down to the floor.

"Two minutes," Alexandre announced.

Dellian and the rest of the team went into a delighted huddle. Getting the first point was always a good sign, and it demoralized the opposing team. Tilliana and Ellici started telling them everything they'd done wrong. They barely had time to snatch a gulp of juice before the referees called them back to play.

The four flagballs went zipping high into the arena. Alexandre's whistle blew.

Immerle was up 11–7, and playing the next point, when things changed. The arena was producing centrifugal gravity at right angles to the axis—which Dellian always hated—when the hurdles themselves started tumbling.

"What the Saints?" Xante exclaimed in panic as he bounced off a moving surface in a completely unexpected direction.

Dellian just laughed in delight. The lights flashed violet, and the arena shifted again; it had been barely thirty seconds since the last shift.

"Concentrate, for Saints' sake!" Tilliana yelled furiously, as a flailing Janc missed the Ansaru flagball he'd been aiming to snatch. He careered into a hurdle, whose rotation flung him away toward the arena's center point.

Dellian glided toward a hurdle, manipulating his limbs carefully. His cohort bundle flexed responsively, and he could tell which surface they were going to land on, how it would be angled. He altered fractionally, and munc legs bent accordingly. The bounce propelled him straight up toward the Ansaru flagball. Four munc hands reached out as if they were lifting a trophy in victory.

Yirella sailed across his trajectory and snatched the flagball, curling around to land square on a hurdle.

"Too slow," she chided, laughing—and bounced.

Admiration for her agility mingled with the annoyance of being beaten to the flagball, Dellian studied the tumbling hurdle he was now heading for and judged the rotation almost right. He bounced to follow Yirella down, ready to provide support against any Ansaru intercept.

Two Ansaru players tried. But the moving hurdles were an unex-

pected complication for them, too. Both missed, swishing ineffectu-
ally behind Yirella as she flew true toward the goal hoop below.

Violet light flashed again.

"Oh, *come on*," Dellian groaned. If the arena kept this up, it would
take them hours to get the final points. And he was already tired.

He could see from the course Yirella was on that she only had one
more hurdle bounce planned out, which would put her directly on
the floor. Then he caught sight of Ansaru's number eight going for a
last-minute intercept. The boy was good, he admitted grudgingly as
he watched his munc bundle smack into a hurdle and break apart in
a complex slingshot-spin that transferred a lot of kinetic energy to
him. Number eight soared out of his collapsing cohort, alone and at
a speed that startled Dellian.

Things came together in his mind as he examined number eight's
trajectory: that the boy would have to slow down, because to strike
anything at that speed would hurt, maybe even break some bones. He
couldn't slow because there was no hurdle close by to bounce off and
transfer momentum. The way he flew, with arms thrust out above his
head, and hands clenched into fists, that was deliberate, calculated to
injure Yirella. Then there was the sullen resentment number eight
had shown throughout the game when Yirella scored a point, and
she'd got six of Immerle's total. That was back with a vengeance.

It's not the flagball he's going for, Dellian knew. His arms jerked
around, hands in a grasping motion. The muncs reacted instantly,
elongating the bundle shape. One of the muncs hit the side of a hurdle, managing to grab an edge for a brief moment. It was enough. The
hurdle's rotational velocity was transferred through the cohort, and
they slung Dellian away.

Now he was the one going far too fast.

"What—?" Tilliana gasped. "No! Yi, Yi, look out!"

Dellian's elbow punched into number eight's side, and the two of
them rebounded, veering sharply away from Yirella. The force of the
impact dazed him as something like fire engulfed his arm. Some-

where close by he heard his target cry out in pain and fury. They were both twirling around each other like twin stars bound in a single orbit. The arena's lights strobed scarlet as a siren went off.

Dellian hit a surface hard enough to knock the breath out of him. It must have been the wall, because he was immediately slithering down to thud onto the floor. Number eight landed on top of him.

A fist struck Dellian's leg. He shoved back. Both of them were yelling wordlessly. Hands scrabbled at each other. Then Dellian made a fist and drove it into number eight's stomach. The boy let out a howl of anger and pain, and immediately head-butted Dellian. Their helmets made it pretty ineffectual, but the adrenaline was pumping now. Dellian tried to chop his opponent's neck.

"Stop it!" Tilliana and Ellici were both shrieking in his ears.

Then both cohorts of muncs arrived and jumped on the wrestling boys. Yirella was shouting. Small fingers clawed at the boys; high-pitched squeals of distress rose. Little pointed teeth snapped viciously. Dellian hit out twice more as they writhed around, only to receive a punch that dislodged his helmet, squashing it into his nose. Blood started to flow out of a nostril. No pain, just rage. He brought a knee up with all his force, feeling it sink deep into his enemy's abdomen.

That was when Alexandre and the other referee arrived. Hands closed around the snarling, kicking boys, prying them apart. The scrum of muncs was going berserk, both cohorts tearing into each other. It took another couple of minutes for them to break apart and cluster anxiously around their beloved masters. By then Dellian was sitting heavily on the arena floor as it spun up to full gravity, gripping his nose to try to stanch the unsettling quantity of blood pouring out. Number eight was curled up, hugging his stomach, his dark complexion now sickly pale as he drew juddering breaths. The two teams had grouped together on opposite sides of the antagonists, staring belligerently at each other. Even the girls had joined them.

"I think the match is now officially over," Alexandre said firmly. "Boys, back to the pavilion, please."

The Ansaru referee was also ordering hir boys out of the arena. Alexandre consulted with hir for a moment, the two of them nodding together and keeping their voices low as adults always did when a serious infraction had been committed. "And no team tea," they both announced.

Dellian walked slowly through the portal, emerging blinking into the bright afternoon sunlight searing over the estate's pitches. Boys from the younger yeargroups were playing football, oblivious to the drama that had just transpired in the arena. The normality of the scene somehow made Dellian feel sheepish.

The Ansaru referee was walking with hir team, keeping them in line as they marched off toward the guest team's changing pavilion. Several of the boys glowered at Dellian. He stiffened, wondering how far he should take it . . .

An arm came down on his shoulder. "To Zagreus with them," Orellt said. He raised his voice: "We won! Twelve to seven."

The Ansaru team switched their glares to Orellt.

"Enough," Alexandre snapped behind them.

Orellt grinned unrepentantly. "Saints, but you got him good," he confided to Dellian.

Dellian managed a weak grin of his own. "I did, didn't I?"

"No, you didn't," Ellici said.

Both boys looked around and up at the girl looming over them, their expressions locked into guilt. "You put no thought into it," she continued. "That's tactically stupid. You should have planned how to strike. People can be incapacitated with a single blow. All you had to decide on was the severity of the damage you wanted to inflict."

"I didn't have time, it was too fast," Dellian protested. "He deliberately tried to hurt Yirella."

"It was nice that you thought to protect her, I suppose, but the Saints know the way you did it was stupid," Ellici said. "Next time either shout her a warning or be more forceful when you attack."

"More forceful," Orellt said softly in wonder as Ellici dropped back to talk to Tilliana.

"Not a bad idea," Dellian admitted.

"I think you were forceful enough with him. Alexandre is going to chuck you into the world's deepest hole. And then Principal Jenner will fill it in—probably with poop."

"Maybe." Dellian shrugged. He looked around at his cohort. They all had bruises and scratches, and two were limping. "I'm proud of you guys."

The muncs nuzzled up against him, each wanting the reassurance of touch. He stroked the glossy fur on their heads, smiling fondly. Dellian glanced around for Yirella, the one person who hadn't thanked him or even said anything. She was walking behind Tilliana and Ellici, her face devoid of expression.

As if nothing's happened, he thought, *or too much.*

In the home team changing pavilion, the boys took their muncs away to clean up first. Sports clothes were thrown into the laundry hopper, then the cohorts showered, soaping then sluicing their pelts before standing on the air-dryer where they larked about under the warm jets. Finally they put on their everyday tunics—simple sleeveless one-pieces that went over the head. Dellian had chosen a fabric of orange-and-green stripes for his cohort, which stood out from the blander choices of his yearmates.

Once the muncs were done, he showered himself. Standing under the hot water, he suddenly felt profoundly tired. His nose was swelling badly now, and it was aching. His arm felt horribly stiff and a little numb. Bruises were making themselves known. The brief fight replayed in his mind, and, strangely, he began to appreciate Ellici's comments. It was all dumb instinct, no thought, no strategy. Hit and be hit. "Stupid," he told himself.

Uranti, the munc-tech, was waiting in hir clinic. Arena matches always produced a variety of injuries and bruises among the cohorts that sie patched up. This time Uranti's head shook in bemusement as Dellian brought his cohort in.

"My my, what have we got here?" sie said with acid sarcasm. "Am I tending your cohort or you?"

Dellian stared at the floor. Uranti was female cycling, which Dellian always found more intimidating than when sie was in a male
cycle. He didn't know why; he just did. When the grown-ups were
female it somehow managed to make any guilt bite deeper. With a
groan he remembered Principal Jenner was also in hir female cycle
now.

The clan's dormitory domes were all clustered together in the middle
of the Immerle estate—grand white marble buildings with tall arches
around the base, and inset with slender, dark windows. After he finished in the clinic, Dellian started off toward them through the lush
gardens, but when he was still a hundred meters away, he caught
sight of the figures racing around the thick base columns, heard the
chatter and laughter of his clanmates—all so perfectly normal. He
promptly turned off the path and wandered through the tall old trees
(great for climbing), winding up in one of the sunken lawns, surrounded by high hedges of pink sweet-scented flowers. There was a
stone-lined pond in the center, with two fountains playing in the
middle. He sat on the edge and watched the long gold-and-white koi
carp slide about below the surface, hiding from the curious muncs
under big lily pads.

Right now he just didn't feel like company. He knew his yearmates
would be gathering in the lounge, gossiping about the match. By now
the news of the fight in the arena would have spread to every yeargroup. The clan would be talking about it for days; all the younger
kids would ask him a thousand questions.

But I did the right thing, he told himself. *He was going to hurt
Yirella.*

It wasn't long before he heard someone coming down the stone
steps behind him. His muncs all turned around, but he kept staring
at the fish; he was pretty sure who it was. All the clan kids reckoned
the adults who looked after them could mainline the genten that
managed the estate; it was how they kept track of where everyone

was the whole time. Because sure as Zagreus this wasn't a random encounter.

"Something on your mind?" Alexandre asked.

Dellian suppressed a grin at being right. "I'm sorry."

"Why?"

"Huh?" Dellian twisted around to find a surprisingly lively smile on hir lips. "But . . . we were fighting."

"Ah, but why were you fighting?"

"If he'd hit Yirella at that speed he would have hurt her. It was deliberate, I was sure of it."

"Okay, that's good enough for me."

"Really?"

Alexandre's arm swept around. "Why do we have a fence around the estate?"

"To keep the beasts out," Dellian replied automatically.

"Right. If you haven't learned just how unsafe Juloss is by now, you never will. The enemy is out there, Dellian; they search for humans constantly. And because we have to be silent, we never know how successful they are. We live in a dangerous galaxy, and it may be that Juloss is home to the last free humans. You have to look out for each other to survive. That's the real lesson you're learning here. And you practiced it today. I'm pleased about that."

"So . . . does that mean I'm not in detention?"

"Very calculating, Dellian. No, you're not in detention. But you don't get a reward, either. Not yet."

"Yet?"

Hir smile grew wider. "We'll leave that for when you get to the real battle games in your senior years. For now, you need to learn about strategy and teamwork, which is what the arena tournaments are all about. So let's concentrate on getting that right first, shall we?"

"Okay!" He grinned, and his cohort began reflecting his relief, smiling and flapping their hands in contentment. "Good good," they cooed.

"Now get yourself back to the dormitory. You need to eat something before afternoon class. And the longer you put off talking to your clanmates, the longer they will want to talk."

The afternoon class for Dellian's year was held in the Five Saints Hall, which sat at the western end of the estate, a good five-minute walk from the dormitory domes. He always enjoyed the stories they heard in the Five Saints Hall, because they were always about the Five Saints, who one day would defeat the enemy.

"How's the nose?" Janc asked as they sauntered along the palm-lined path. The fronds were just stirring above their heads, a sign of the evening breeze starting its daily journey along the massive valley from the sea.

Dellian just managed not to touch it in reflex. "Okay, I guess."

"Saints, I still can't believe you didn't get detention!"

"Yeah, me too." He saw the three girls up ahead, keeping together like they always did. "Catch you later."

The girls turned as one when he called out. Tilliana and Ellici gave Yirella knowing looks. For a moment Dellian thought she might not stop, or worse, the others would wait with her. Thankfully, they walked on.

"Sorry," he said as he caught up.

"For what?"

He looked up into her heart-shaped face, troubled that she was treating him like this. They normally got on so well. Girls were all destined to be smart—a lot smarter than boys, Alexandre had explained; it was how their genes were sequenced. But he just knew Yirella was going to be the smartest of them all. Having her as a special friend was something he didn't want to lose. "Are you angry with me?"

She sighed. "No. I know why you did it, and I am grateful. Really. It's just . . . it was very violent. Saints, Dellian, you were both going so fast when you hit! Then there was fighting. Your nose was bleeding. I didn't . . . It was awful."

"Ellici said I should be more forceful next time."

"Ellici is right. You can debilitate with a single strike, you know. Then it would all be settled quickly."

An image of the boy's expression inside his helmet at the moment of impact flashed through Dellian's mind. "I know. Maybe I should learn how."

"In three years, we'll get combat tutorials for the battle games."

"I bet you could hack the data now."

Her lips twitched. "Of course I could."

"Seems funny to be talking about it. Hurting people."

"It's a dangerous universe out there." She indicated the four-meter-high fence they were approaching. There was only silence outside in the valley's tangled vegetation, which somehow managed to be even more threatening than when the creatures were on the prowl.

"So everyone tells us." He stared through the fence. Twenty-five kilometers away, across the flat expanse of the valley floor, the crystal and silver towers of Afrata rose up amid the lower slopes of the mountains. Even now the old city was impressive, which Dellian found quite sad. No humans had lived in it for forty years. It seemed that every day the verdant vines and creepers had twined their way several more meters up the skyscrapers. The streets had long since been engulfed by wild greenery. And all those fancy apartments were now home to the various predatory animals of Juloss that stalked each other along Afrata's broken boulevards.

"Doesn't make it right," Dellian said. "Saints, I know we're all okay and safe living here in the estate. It's just . . . I want to be out there!"

"We'll get there," she said sympathetically. "One day."

"Ugh, you sound like Principal Jenner. Everything good's going to happen *tomorrow*."

She smiled. "It is."

"I want to walk outside the fence. I want to climb one of those towers. I want to go to the beach and swim in the sea. I want to be on board one of the warships they're building up there, and fight the enemy."

"We're going to do all those things. You. Me. All of us. The clans are what's left, we're the pinnacle of Juloss, the best and greatest of all."

Dellian sighed. "I thought the Five Saints were the greatest?"

"Their sacrifice was the greatest. We have to live up to that."

"I'm never going to make it."

Yirella laughed. "You will. Out of all of us, you will. Me? I just dream the Sanctuary star is real."

"You think it is? Marok is always saying that Sanctuary is just a legend, a fable that the generation ships carry with them between worlds."

"All myths start from a truth," she said. "There must be so many humans spread across the galaxy now; it isn't hard to think they found one star that's safe from the enemy."

"If it is real, we'll find it together," he promised solemnly.

"Thanks, Del. Now come on, I want to hear what Marok has to tell us about the Saints."

Five Saints Hall was the most ornate building in the estate—a long entrance hall with glossy black-and-gold walls leading to five big chambers. Hot sunlight was diffused to a pervasive glow as it shone through the gold-tinted crystal roof.

The fifteen boys and three girls of Dellian's yeargroup filed into chamber three. It contained plump sprawling chairs of faux-leather that they could flop into, the cushions undulating to take the weight like sluggish liquid. Up above them, the crystal roof was etched with monochrome images of the Saints themselves, while softboards around the walls had dozens of pictures pinned to them, drawn by the younger clan kids, the phosphorescent parchments glowing gently. This wasn't a classroom in the usual sense. They didn't make notes, there would never be an exam. The tutors wanted them re-laxed, eager to take in the stories of the Five Saints. This was to be something they wanted to know, to learn.

Marok, the estate's Sol historian, came in and smiled. Sie was in female cycle, so sie'd grown hir chestnut hair down to hir waist. Hir face was composed of long, thin bones, giving hir a very attractive if somewhat delicate appearance. Dellian always thought if he'd been lucky enough to have a parental group like the people who'd left on the generation ships had, he'd want Marok to be part of it.

"Settle down," sie told the kids. "So then, has everyone recovered from the arena?"

There was some giggling and plenty of glances thrown in Dellian's direction. He bore it stoically.

"I ask because violence isn't something we've really talked about concerning the Saints," sie continued. "Up until now we've only dealt in generalities. Today, I'm going to start filling in formative events. To put the Five Saints in context, and appreciate what they did, we need to examine their activities in greater detail. Just what motivated them? How did they come together? Did they really get on so perfectly as the tales you've heard said? And most importantly, what was going on around them? All these things need to be looked at properly."

Xante stuck his hand up. "Weren't they friends, then?"

"Not necessarily, no. Certainly not at the start. Remember how Callum and Yuri had parted a hundred years earlier? It wasn't on the best of terms, was it? So who can tell me the two reasons they were brought back together?"

"Politics and treachery," everyone chorused.

"Well done." Sie smiled softly. "And where did that happen?"

"New York!"

"Quite right. Now, New York in 2204 was a very different city from anything you know, even from Afrata. And Nkya was even stranger . . ."

THE ASSESSMENT TEAM

When the Trail Ranger was an hour out from Nkya's base camp, the stewards started serving dinner. The gourmet food packets were microwaved, but they still tasted pretty good to me. I chose seared scallops on mint-pea risotto for a starter, followed by minute steak and fries with red wine sauce. The wine was a three-year-old Chablis. Not bad. I finished with lemon crème brûlée drizzled in raspberry sauce. I ate mostly in silence; everyone else was running through the files, consuming every piece of data we had on the derelict ship. It wasn't enough to draw any definitive conclusions. I know. I'd been trying to work out what had happened for ten days.

"Have you identified any of the humans on board?" Callum finally asked as he finished off his salted almond truffle tart.

"No," Yuri told him tersely. "We can't do that."

"Can't, or won't? An identity check is one of the easiest search requests to load into solnet. Nobody can hide in our society, right, Alik?"

The FBI agent gave him a soft smile. "It's difficult," he conceded. "Government keeps an eye on people."

"For their own good," Callum sneered.

"How many terrorist attacks have there been in the last fifty years? The last seventy-five, even?"

"Not many," Callum agreed grudgingly.

"Your infamous preemptive rendition," Eldlund said sharply. "Arrest people because a G8Turing thinks they might do something based on behavior and interests. What sort of justice is that?"

Alik shrugged. "What can I say? Pattern recognition works. And FYI, every National Security removal warrant has to be signed off by three independent judges. Nobody gets exiled without a fair hearing."

"That must make your citizens feel so much safer. What is it every authoritarian government says? If you've done nothing wrong, you have nothing to fear."

"Hey, you want them to be free to immigrate to Akitha or one of the Delta Pavonis habitats, pal?"

"That's not a justification, that's a threat."

Alik's stiff mouth managed to crank out a self-righteous smile, and he poured himself a shot from the vintage bourbon bottle he'd brought in his luggage.

"Why haven't you tried to identify them?" Callum asked. His gaze had never left Yuri.

"The same reason there is no solnet out here, and that Alpha Defense insisted we keep a very secure separation distance between portal and ship. Security."

"Man! You're still fucking doing it, aren't you? Still claiming everything you do is the *right way*, the only way. Anyone who says or thinks different isn't just wrong, they're evil with it."

"Because this happens to *be* the right way. Try thinking about this—because that's what you're actually supposed to be here for, to produce an impartial informed opinion. Though fuck knows why Emilja and Jaru sent you."

"Because I'm actually capable of having a rational thought, not just paranoid ones."

"You'll give it away," Kandara said in a weary voice. She'd taken her jacket off, exposing heavily muscled arms as she sat in the recliner, picking at the vegetarian meal on her fold-out tray.

Yuri and Callum both turned to stare at her.

"What?" Callum asked.

"Sorry, but Yuri is quite right," she said. "The aliens, whoever they are, are going to know who those people in their ship are. So if we start loading their image or DNA sequence into solnet, they'll know we found the ship. And as keeping this discovery secret is our one advantage . . ." She shrugged.

"Thank you." Yuri grinned. "What she said. Which is what I was trying to explain."

Callum growled and held up his empty tumbler. A steward came over to pour him a shot of malt whiskey.

Alik sat back, swirling his bourbon around the glass. He looked at Yuri, then Callum, came to a decision. "Okay, I gotta ask. What did happen with you two? Even the Bureau doesn't have files on it, but I heard rumors. And now here you are, both of you trying to make nice—and screwing that up."

"This is bigger than us," Yuri said sourly—a tone that would have made anyone else stop like they'd run smack into a stone cliff.

"Showing some humanity now, are we?" Callum said.

"Fuck you," Yuri spat back.

Jessika, Loi, and Eldlund watched the scene intrigued, and maybe a little nervous. Understandable; you don't often see two powers of this magnitude go head-to-head.

"You're a corporate robot," Callum said. "You were back then, and nothing's changed. You're not just employed by Connexion, you're its high priest, leading the worship."

"You're alive, aren't you?"

"Am I supposed to be grateful?"

"It wouldn't hurt!"

"Really?" Callum sneered. "You want me to tell them? Let them judge? Because it's not just my story, is it?"

"Go ahead," Yuri said belligerently. He reached for the bottle of iced vodka.

Callum looked around the rest of us in turn. Uncertain.

"Do it," Kandara said with a small smile, daring him.

"It was a long time ago."

"Ha!" Yuri snorted. He downed his vodka shot in one. "Was it a dark and stormy night, too?"

"You didn't know where it started. That was a huge part of the problem. And you didn't know because you don't fucking care about people!"

"Fuck you! I cared—about her. Not you. Nobody cared about you. Asshole."

"The real beginning was in the Caribbean," Callum said, his expression softening at whatever ancient memory he was reliving. "That's where Savi and I got married."

"Illegally," Yuri countered. "If you'd told us like you were supposed to, it would never have happened."

"It wasn't illegal. For all its size, Connexion is a company, not a government, and we didn't need your fucking permission! Just because Ainsley paid our salary doesn't mean he owned us. So screw your fucked-up corporate policy! And it did happen."

"We have those policies for a reason. If you'd told us you were in a relationship, if you'd been honest, everything would have been different. You created the problem. Don't try and make me out as the bad guy."

I couldn't have planned it better. I wanted their stories, especially Yuri's. It had taken me a while to convince him he should come along on the mission in person, rather than just rely on my reports.

And now here they were, angry but uncensored, with something to prove. All they could use against each other now was the truth, because it was truth that could inflict damage more accurately than any smart missile strike, and their animosity hadn't even begun to heal over, not after 112 years. It always amazes me how long humans can hold on to grudges.

I glanced around as unobtrusively as I could, saw Kandara and Alik holding back smiles, enjoying the show they'd provoked. Yuri and Callum reheated their old war, ready to say anything, spill any secret.

"So it wasn't a dark and stormy night," Callum began. "Quite the opposite."

CALLUM AND YURI

The beach was perfect. That was a major part of Barbuda's appeal. The tiny Caribbean island had a single Connexion portal door, which led to its larger and more prosperous neighbor, Antigua. In 2092, a solitary portal serving an entire population made it almost unique on Earth, where quantum spatial entanglement had brought everywhere "one step away"—as Connexion's tag line ran.

The resorts spaced along Barbuda's southern coastline depended on that exclusivity. The prices they charged for a week of privacy and seclusion were phenomenal. Callum Hepburn considered it entirely worthwhile. The Diana Klub just north of Coco Point was a sprawl of thirty boutique cabins set a few meters back from the top of the pristine white sands. By day it was gorgeous, a tropical sun searing down out of a cloudless azure sky to enhance the verdancy of the palm trees that ran along the top of the beach, turning the white sand into a dazzling slope that by midday was too hot for bare feet to walk on, while the turquoise water with its languid waves was clear enough to reveal the colorful shoals of fish that flittered playfully through the shallows.

At midnight it was equally lovely. The silver light of the crescent moon poised above the horizon bathed the warm sands in a spectral radiance, while deepening the lapping water to a dark and mysterious expanse. Atop the beach, the crowded border of trees cast a ragged ebony silhouette along the base of a starry sky.

Two figures in white terry cloth robes held hands and giggled as they scampered along the path from the cabins and down onto the sands.

Callum let out a gasp as his feet touched the hot surface.

"What's the matter?" Savi asked in concern.

"Hotter than I was expecting," Callum admitted.

"This?" Her feet slid through the sand then flicked some up. "This is nothing. You're a wimp."

"I'm from Aberdeen," he protested. "You put your bare foot on the beach there, and it'll freeze to the pebbles. That's just in summer."

"Wimp!" She let go and ran on. "Wimp wimp."

Laughing, he sprinted after her. He caught her and swung her around with a loud, happy howl.

"Shush! Callum. They'll hear."

He glanced back at the tall trees with their long palms swaying in the gentle night breeze. The shadows amid the smooth trunks were an impenetrable black, deeper than the gulf between stars. Anything could be hiding in there; he'd never know. "Who'll hear?"

"Them," she said with a snicker. "Our fellow vacationers. The staff. All the Peeping Toms."

He put his arms around her, pulling them together, and kissed her. "Would that be naughty for you?" he asked, nuzzling her throat. "Being watched?"

"No."

But there was that familiar edge to her voice that made him smirk. Savi had no inhibitions when it came to exploring her sexuality. "No need to worry about them telling anybody," he said. "They'd die of envy before we finished."

Savi licked her lips. "Promises, promises," she murmured hotly. "Now take your robe off."

"Yes, wife."

She smiled broadly. "You're the one that wanted to have sex on the beach. So, get on with it, husband."

Callum shrugged out of his robe and spread it out on the sand, the very same sand they'd stood on that afternoon, him in a t-shirt and swim trunks (plus trainers with soles thick enough to stop his feet catching fire); her in a white bikini and a scarlet sarong. The ceremony had lasted barely five minutes. Only four other people were there: the padre from the local town, who performed the ceremony, the resort's assistant manager, and two of their fellow guests, somewhat bemused to be serving as witnesses.

Savi giggled again, eyeing the tree line defiantly. "Lie down," she told him. "I get to go on top."

Callum heard the rising excitement in her voice and did as he was told. Savi stood above him, her feet planted outside his hips. She made a show of slowly undoing her belt, then let the robe fall open.

He gazed up in wonder at his wife, her lithe body gleaming in the pastel moonlight. *My wife!* "You're a goddess," he said hoarsely.

She slipped the robe from her shoulders and tossed her long, ebony hair. "Which one?" she taunted.

"Parvati, the goddess of love and feminine energy."

"Clever boy." She grinned down hungrily.

Thank you, internet, I will never curse you again, Callum promised.

"Did you know she bestows a woman's skill and power to the whole universe?" Savi murmured as she sank to her knees.

Callum whimpered helplessly.

"And prowess." Her eyes flashed wickedly.

In the sky above Savi's head, a shooting star scorched a silent, scintillating tail across the heavens. Callum made a wish.

It was granted.

Callum woke to find strong morning sunlight filtering through the cabin bedroom's wooden shutters. The air-conditioning was humming softly, but the temperature in the bedroom was already warmer than midsummer in Scotland. He turned his head to see Savi lying naked on the mattress beside him.

"Morning, husband," she said drowsily.

He gently brushed thick strands of tangled black hair from her face. All he could do was smile at how lovely she was.

"What?" she asked.

"I thought I'd had the best dream of my life," he said softly. "Turns out it's actually a memory."

"Oh, Cal!" She reached for him, and they began kissing ardently.

"I'm a married man," he said, and there was no way to keep the incredulity out of his voice. "I can't believe you said yes!"

"I can't believe you asked!"

"I was always going to ask."

"Were you?"

"Yeah. From the moment I saw you. But I knew I'd have to wait. You know—actually say hello first, maybe find out your name."

"Silly man."

"I thought I'd blown it yesterday."

She stroked his cheek. "You didn't."

"We're married!" Callum started laughing.

"Yes. Now we just have to work out how to tell everyone."

"Oh. Crap. Yeah." He frowned; just the thought of it was a real passion killer.

Savi gave him an interested look. "You're not worried about that, are you?"

"No. No, it's fine."

"You're scared of telling my father," she decided shrewdly.

"Am not."

"You are! Fine husband you make; you're supposed to fight demons and dragons for me."

"I'm not scared of your father. Your mother, on the other hand . . ."

"Mummy likes you."

"She's very good at hiding it."

"You know what they say: If you want to know what the girl's going to grow into, look at the mother."

Callum had a brief, if frightening, memory flash of his own father, standing in Pittodrie Stadium, cheering on The Dons, a beer can in each hand. "I would be delighted if you turned out like your mother."

Savi's mouth parted to a wide O, which she covered with her hand as she laughed. "Oh, no, I married a horrific liar!"

"Well, you have to admit, they are a bit conservative. And I am white."

She ran her hand through his short ginger hair. "White and red. Proper Scottish. I could get snow-blind staring at your skin."

"Hey, you said my freckles are cute."

"Freckles are cute on a ten-year-old, Cal; when you're thirty-one they're just funny."

"Oh, thanks." Callum kissed her. *Best way to shut that conversation down.* "Anyway," he said, shrugging, "it's not family we really have to worry about."

"Ah, our bloody Connexion Corp lords and masters. I hate them!"

"Company policy. Human Resources gets right tight-assed about personal relationships. They're paranoid about sexual harassment lawsuits."

"I never had to harass you for sex."

"True."

"Actually," she said, "it's not HR that's the problem."

"What?"

"Anyone employed by the security division has to have their friends vetted."

"Vetted? You mean, they get to say who you can date? That's outrageous! They can't do that."

She grimaced. "Ah. You see, in fact, there's this clause in my contract about who I can associate with outside work. It's very clear."

"Wait . . . you didn't sign it, did you?"

"It's the security division, Cal; it's the way it is. If you work in security you have to know who you're seeing. *Exactly* who. If another company is trying to launch an infiltration mission, we can't afford to be vulnerable."

"Bloody hell, that's depressing."

"I know. But realistic. The world is a bad place filled with bad people."

"Okay, so . . . what was my report like?"

"Ah." She flinched. "I haven't actually told them."

"This doesn't sound good."

"I . . . It's . . . Cal, that day when we met, it was so much fun, remember? I thought it was . . . you know."

"What?"

She sucked her lower lip in faux remorse. "I thought you were just going to be a one-night stand."

"Shit!" He slumped back and stared up at the ceiling, feeling quite petulant. "It wasn't actually one night," he said, acting the martyr.

"Oh, the male ego! Yes, all right: a one-weekend stand. And when it turned out you wanted more than that, I was so happy. But, the point is, I didn't report it at first because I thought I wouldn't see you again, and you were Connexion, too. So it wasn't a huge security risk, and a girl doesn't want a big file of these things following her around. We still get judged, you know. It's unfair. Men don't."

"I get it," he said.

"So then, when we started seeing each other properly, I was in an awkward position."

"Is this going to cost you your job?" he asked, suddenly anxious.

"No. Look, it's still only been six weeks. Yuri will understand if the notification goes in a little late. He's an okay guy."

"Yuri?"

"Yuri Alster. My boss."

"All right. So we both come clean together, then, as soon as we get back. Good plan, actually. You go 'fess up to Yuri, and I'll notify Brixton HR. We'll say it was a spontaneous thing. Right; this is it, okay? We met here on Barbuda, we fell in love, we got married. It's not really a lie. If people are going to be that reckless about love, it's going to be on an island like this one."

Savi grimaced again. "Um, we might just have to wait."

"What? Why?"

"It's my current assignment."

"What about it? Actually, what is it, this assignment?"

"Hey, no fair. You promised you would not ask about my undercover assignments."

"Sorry."

"There will always be aspects of what I do that I can't tell you. You know that, don't you?"

"Yeah, yeah, I get it."

"You have no idea how hard it is for an Indian girl to make a decent career for herself in this business. I worked bloody hard to get into covert ops, and I love what I do. I can't risk crashing it now."

It's exciting, too, which is what you really like, he thought, but he wasn't going to say that to her face. "Sorry, sorry. You know I just get concerned for you."

"I know. It's very sweet. But your work is physically dangerous, too; one slipup, and you've got a disaster area on your hands. And I know how dedicated you are. So just think how you'd feel if I asked you not to take the worst assignment."

"Emergency detoxification isn't quite as extreme as the media plays it up to be. And I'm not asking you to give security up. I was just showing an interest in my wife's work, like a good husband."

"Nice try," she mocked.

"Er, it's not really unsafe, is it?"

"You judge: There's this evil billionaire with a fiendish plan for world domination—no: solar system domination. My assignment is to use all my feminine assets to seduce him and steal the plans from his bedroom safe."

Callum grinned lecherously. "That should work, 'cause those are amazing assets."

She laughed and kissed him again. "Actually, this one is really boring. I go around university campuses pretending to be a student and showing up at anti-corporate rallies and meetings—with particular attention to anti-Connexion gatherings—seeing who's there, who's the angriest of them all, who's the silent smoldering type, who's all talk . . . We're monitoring potential future troublemakers."

"That sounds quite sinister, the company keeping profiles on a bunch of twenty-year-olds. Is it legal?"

"They're kids, Cal. Ninety-nine percent are just rebelling against their parents now they've finally left home. But they're susceptible to radicalization. Somebody's got to stop them being exploited by the real zealot shits; the university deans don't do a damn thing."

"Also true."

"It's important work. Work I'm proud of. Urban violence is in decline for the first time in decades, Cal."

"I wasn't arguing. So how exactly does this prevent you from telling Yuri about me?"

"I'm in the middle of an assignment. It was a miracle I managed to swing this four-day break. If I tell him about us on Tuesday when we get back, he'll lift me from the job until you've been vetted. And if I'm away for too long, it might make the group I've been hanging out with suspicious. The whole assignment collapses."

He frowned in confusion. "It can't take more than a couple of hours for them to read through my file, surely?"

"That's not how you vet someone, Cal. Internal Assessment will put a couple of case officers on reviewing you, and now that we're married you'll have to come in for an interview. If you're clean, it'll only take a week; but if there are any question marks, you're looking at months for verification."

"Bloody hell! If I'm that questionable, how come they let me do what I'm doing? Look at how potentially dangerous my job can be; I could cause Connexion more grief than any street mob. Just one hesitation or wrong action, and tons of toxic crap leaks out, into the water, across a city . . ."

"You're not getting it. Intelligence gathering is about acquiring information and analyzing it. What we do is try to find the people who are looking to subvert you. Yes, if you'd been turned you probably could cause two or even three bad toxic spills before Security realized you'd become a militant. Our job is to halt that subversion before it happens."

"Are you telling me if one of my cleanup operations does go pear-shaped, Security will come looking for links with fanatics?"

"Depends on how big the damage is, but basically: yes. And if there are suspicious patterns in behavior or your data footprint, our division's G5Turings will find them."

"Shit on a stick! I didn't know that. It's not even a whisper in the department."

"Which, as you've now got an undercover security agent lying about her relationship with you, is going to be really bad if they do stick a pattern analysis on you. So we're both on the line here. Don't screw up your next job."

"Hell! I'll do my best."

Savi kissed him, resting her face against his. "I love you, husband."

"Not as much as I love you, wife. So how long before we can shock everyone with the announcement?"

"Couple of weeks. No more, I promise."

"You're not going to be away all that time, are you?" he asked in dismay.

"I'll try and finish as quickly as I can. But be prepared, contact's going to be difficult while I'm active."

"Come on, you can sneak a minute to call me. Just an email will do. Let me know you're okay."

"If I can, I will, but I can't risk blowing my cover, Cal."

He found that frustrating, as if she wasn't willing to make the effort. Which wasn't fair. Like she said, to get where she was at just twenty-six must have been tough. That resolve of hers, pursuing what she wanted without hesitation every time, was intoxicatingly attractive.

"I understand," he told her.

"Thank you." Savi rolled onto her back and stretched sensuously. "This is the first day of our honeymoon now, isn't it?"

"Yes."

"That means I'm entitled to sex with my husband all day long."

"It certainly does."

"So what are you waiting for?"

The alarm woke Cal, a vile, insistent buzz coming from the antique digital clock with numbers that glowed scarlet in the gloomy bedroom. He reached for it. But of course it sat on a neat stack of plastic storage boxes half a meter from where his fingers stretched to. "Bastard!" He had to scramble to the edge of the mattress and swing his legs out from under the heavy duvet before he could reach the cube of black plastic.

In the silence that followed he shook his head, trying to wake up properly. An ex had set up the beyond-reach trick. Savi had thought it was a great idea, so he'd claimed it was all his own. Wives—so touchy about old girlfriends.

He looked around at the empty bed and sighed. Five days without her now. There'd been no call, not even an email. *How is some bunch of dickhead students going to notice anything wrong with a two-minute call? Do they all live together in a cult compound or something?* That wasn't a thought he wanted to explore.

The alarm started off again. He'd only hit the snooze button before. Cursing, he switched it off properly and headed for the shower.

His flat was on the top floor of a grand old Georgian terrace house in Moray Place, one of the best addresses in Edinburgh, so the estate agent swore: a small, beautiful park of ancient trees, circled by the New Town stone architecture the city was renowned for. That was why the flat was only four rooms, and even on his salary paying the rent was a stretch. But as a bachelor pad it was a classic.

Maybe too much of a classic, he thought as he went back into the bedroom with a towel wrapped around his waist and his hair still damp. He'd spent serious money on the king-size bed. But that was where the extravagance had to end. His clothes were all supposed to be put away in the three towers of plastic boxes along one wall, but mostly they were dumped on the washing pile in the corner. The Barbuda break had messed up his laundry service routine. It also seemed to have messed up his shopping program.

"House," he yelled.

The wallscreen lit up with the G3Turing's house utilities menu—two years since he'd installed it, and he still hadn't gotten around to customizing the cheap, obsolete unit. "Good morning, Callum," it said in a sharp female voice. He hadn't changed that from the factory setting, either.

"Why are we out of shampoo? I had to use the shower glass cleaner on my hair. It smells weird."

"Your household items replacement order has been placed on hold."

"What? Why?"

"You are now over your preapproved monthly credit limit by three and a half thousand pounds. The credit company has suspended all future account payments until this is resolved."

"Shit! How did that happen?"

"The last large payment was to the Drexon International Leisure Group for five thousand eight hundred and ninety pounds, which put you over the specified limit. Your credit company suspended the account at midnight and is now charging you double interest on the excess amount."

"Bloody hell." He hadn't realized Barbuda had been quite that expensive. *Worth it, though. She married me!* He gave the empty mattress a forlorn look. *Five days, and it's already unbearable without her.*

He started going through what was supposed to be the underwear box. There was only one clean pair of boxer shorts left. "House, why didn't you warn me I was maxed out?"

"You have told me to be silent six times in the last four days when I asked your permission to review your current financial status."

"Oh, yeah, right. You should have told me it was about the current account."

"I did. The credit company has issued five statutory warnings."

"Okay. Uh, next time just throw the debt figure up on all the wallscreens in red. I'll catch it properly, then."

"Very well."

Callum could have sworn the G3Turing's voice sounded disapproving.

He found a fresh shirt and started putting it on. "Is there any breakfast in the kitchen?"

"There is some printed bacon available. Eight containers of natural food currently need to be removed from the fridge for recycling. All have passed their use-by date. A new food and beer delivery is pending resumption of credit."

"Yes, mother," he grumbled under his breath. "So resume it."

"You will first have to agree to a new overpayment charge with the credit company."

"Right. Look, just sort the thing out, okay? I get paid in a couple of days anyway."

"Your next salary payment is in six days."

"Whatever. Get my credit flowing again."

"The new extension terms they are offering are not favorable."

"Hey, stop being such a bloody lawyer! You're supposed to be adaptive software, right? Well, pay attention and learn. I don't like being distracted with this kind of crap while I'm working. This is why I buy programs like you, so, just . . . make my life easier, okay?"

"Very well, Callum."

He held back on a bad-tempered reply. That easier life could have been real if he'd bought a fifth-generation Turing. They were so much smarter; one of them would have picked up on all his nuances and understood what he wanted, sparing him this grief of having to spell everything out. But a G5 was beyond his current budget.

Next time I get promoted . . .

Callum pulled on his trousers. There were no clean socks. "Fuck's sake!" He tugged a reasonable-ish pair out of the washing pile. His trainers still had beach sand in them; he grinned fondly at that as he strapped them up. Next to the alarm clock was the tube with his e-contacts, and next to that was a pair of basic screen glasses. He chose the glasses. Somehow this morning he was in no mood to faff about with contact lenses. *Damn, I miss her.*

Finally he put his smartCuff on, a simple band three centimeters wide that could have passed as black glass if it hadn't been so flexible. Once he'd slipped it over his knuckles it shrank to a perfect fit around his wrist. It ran a biometric to check his identity and immediately linked to his dermal grains through mInet. A neat column of sapphire data slid down the left-hand side of his screen lens.

He didn't bother reading it. Just having it there, up and active, was reassuring. The mInet made him part of the world again.

"Hey there, Apollo, are we running smooth?"

"Good morning, Cal," the mInet's electronic identity replied through the audio grain embedded in his ear. Everybody gave their mInet a tag; and Callum had been obsessed with the Apollo moonshot when he was in his teens, to the extent of building flying models of Saturn V's.

"You've got full mInet connectivity with your peripherals," Apollo said. "Your blood sugar levels aren't good."

"Yeah, it's morning, pal. Keep a watch on House; I want to know when my credit's back up."

"You're already solvent again."

He would have said thank you to House, but some deep Luddite part of his mind refused to recognize the G3Turing as a genuine personality.

Like all meat these days, the bacon was printed, with a use-by date eighteen months away. He dropped a couple of rashers in the frying pan. He didn't need to check the bread's use-by; it was moldy, so no bacon sandwich. There was one egg left, a natural one. He couldn't scramble it because the buttermilk was ripe enough to make his eyes water when he sniffed it; and as his grandmother had drilled into him, that was the only true way to make scrambled eggs. Black coffee, then. He shoved a capsule into the outsize chrome-plated Italian barista machine and waited while it ran through its usual tune of choking steam noises.

"Stream the overnights for me," he asked Apollo as he cracked the egg on the side of the frying pan. By some miracle the yolk didn't break.

The kitchen wallscreen produced a grid of news streams determined by adaptive preference filters. He sipped the coffee with growing satisfaction as five of the ten news channels focused on disasters across Europe. He scanned them quickly to see if any of them threatened to contaminate the surrounding area; those he might well wind up dealing with during his shift. The major one that had developed while he slept was a blaze in a Frankfurt theatre. Seven fire tenders were dealing with it, sending long white arcs of foam playing over the inferno. "No," Callum said. Apollo tracked his gaze slipping to the second grid and pulled that one to the front. A landslide in Italy brought on by excessive rains, three houses in a mountain village washed away. He glanced at the next grid. A sinking yacht in the sea off the coast of Malta, surrounded by Coast Guard ships and news drones. "Sorry, my friend, can't help you." He flipped the bacon. Fourth, a radioactive waste disposal facility just outside Gylgen, Sweden, which had undergone an evacuation during the night. Unconfirmed reports that the waste storage containers had cracked. "Crap."

A live feed gave him a company spokesman standing outside the gates, assuring reporters that evacuation was "just a precaution," and there was absolutely no spillage.

Callum stared at the uneasy spokesman, not believing a word of his clichés. "Call Moshi," he said.

His deputy's comms icon came up in the screen lens. "Are you monitoring the Gylgen facility?"

"Way ahead of you, boss," Moshi Lyane replied cheerfully. "The G5Turing caught it within a minute. There's been a lot of executive chatter with the Environment Enforcement Agency."

"Spillage?"

"Satellite's not showing anything. Yet. But the containers are below ground level. If there's a leak, it's not vapor."

"What does Dok say?

"She's talking to Boynak executives. And we're on an open channel to the EEA in case they order intervention."

Callum's screen lens showed him the Boynak file: the owner of the Gylgen plant, in turn owned by a tangle of interlocked holding companies, registered in a scattering of independent asteroids. He grunted in contempt. "Fucking typical."

"Boss?"

"Can their in-house team handle it?"

"Best guess: no. They're shouting 'nobody panic' quite loud. And we're not seeing any cleanup equipment on its way through the hubs."

"All right, I'll be with you in ten."

"I welcome that."

Callum grinned, then looked down at the frying pan. The rashers were overcooked, and the yoke had turned solid. "Aww, bastard."

The huge old trees in Moray Place were all budding early thanks to the unseasonable winds that had been blowing in from the southwest for most of February. With the low morning sun striking them, it looked like an emerald frost had materialized overnight to coat the circular park. What had been the cobbled road surrounding the verdant urban isle was now broken up by two lines of raised circular troughs with cherry trees planted in the center of each one. Callum smiled up at the cherry blossom glowing a luminous pink in the bright sunlight. Savi had enjoyed the blossoms on her last visit.

He walked around the troughs, keeping a wary eye out for cyclists. Ever since Connexion had started establishing its hubs across the globe, civic authorities had been pedestrianizing cities and towns, starting with the centers and gradually expanding out as the hub network coverage increased. There was still room for taxez, delivery bugez, and emergency vehicles to maneuver along Moray Place and the neighboring streets, but even the taxez were few and far between these days. The only time Callum really saw them was during one of Edinburgh's not infrequent rainstorms. Cyclists, though—cyclists were very intense about their right of way, which seemed to include every flat surface in existence.

Callum turned down Forres Street. "Any emails from Savi last night?" He didn't know why he asked. The inbox was on his screen lens and had nearly two dozen emails pending, most of them work related, with one from his mother.

"No," Apollo replied.

"What about everything you sent to the junk archive? She might be using a one-time address. Check them for a personal message."

"There are none."

"Calls? Ordinary phone calls or a sightyou?"

"No."

"Calls made but no answervoice recorded?"

"No."

"Has she made any social posts?"

"Not since she posted her Barbuda videos the night before you left. Her parents and sister have both left messages on her MyLife site in the last thirty hours, asking her to call them."

"How about . . . have I been tracker pinged?"

"None since you lost your smartCuff last November. You left it at Fitz's apartment after his party."

"Yeah, yeah. Can you ping Savi's mInet?"

"Yes."

"Do it."

"Her mInet is not responding."

"Ping it again."

"No response."

"Fuck." *She's super smart, so why isn't she doing something to let me know she's all right? Anything?*

Like every city, Edinburgh's Connexion hubs were arranged in a spider web pattern. On a map, it registered as concentric loops intersected at right angles by radial spurs. Commuters could walk in both directions around the loops, clockwise or counterclockwise, and inbound or outbound along the radial spurs. A simple mInet app called Hubnav told everyone the quickest route to their destination. Callum never bothered with it in the morning; his route to work was so familiar it had become simple muscle memory.

He walked into the metrohub on the junction with Young Street. It was a loop hub, with five pay barriers across the entrance leading to a drab gray-and-green tiled lobby. Apollo gave the barrier his Connexion code, and he went straight through. As in every hub lobby, portal doors faced each other on opposite sides. Standing between them was like staring at the infinity image when you stand between two mirrors, except it wasn't himself he could see in all the identical lobbies stretching out ahead. Looking through the portal doors, he could see his fellow commuters walk between a few lobbies then turn off.

He automatically turned right to go through the clockwise circuit portal door that led to the Thistle Street hub, which in turn opened into the St. Andrew's Square hub, which was an intersection hub, so turn right and through the inbound portal door of the radial spur directly to the Waverley hub.

Waverley was the center of Connexion's Edinburgh metro net-work, standing on the site of the old train station. The twelve radial spurs that led into it emerged onto the floor of a plain circular build-ing with a glass dome roof overlooked by the severe old castle perched on its stone cliff high above. At the center of the hub were two wide portal doors for the National City network—one in, one out. Even this early in the morning, it was busy. Callum took the portal door out.

The British National City hub was the Waverley hub built on an industrial scale, constructed twenty-five years ago on a cheap derelict industrial zone in Leicester; because its physical location was irrele-vant, the accountants just wanted the lowest local tax rate on offer in the country. It was an annular concourse a hundred meters wide with high, polished black granite walls and a black-and-white marbled floor. Huge lighting galleries hung from an arched ceiling, bringing an intense noonday glare to the dense throng of twenty-four/seven commuters.

It was built to operate a hundred and thirty portal doors: sixty-five on the inner wall, all exiting their respective cities to deposit people into the concourse; and a matching sixty-five on the outer wall, the outbounds, each one with its city name glowing in bright turquoise neon above. There were no neat channels along the concourse desig-nated for people to walk between them, no convenient moving floor strips, no smiling staff to help. The concourse was a purely Darwin-ian melee. Travelers used their Hubnav app to find where their city door was, then they just put their heads down and went for it, result-ing in a permanent rush hour of intolerance and midlevel aggression, of people running urgently only to clash with the slow movers, peo-ple cursing each other, parents checking children were keeping up, luggage and shopping bugez being booted as they strove to follow their owners, all of them kicking up a noise to rival a football sta-dium crowd.

Callum slipped through them all as if he were Teflon coated. The door to London was six to the left of the Edinburgh exit. He made it in forty seconds. Through that and he was in the Trafalgar Square hub, with its twenty-five radial doors to take you out across the huge capital city, plus one door in a recess, guarded by a security barrier. It opened for Callum, allowing him directly into Connexion Corp's internal hub network.

Three portals later he was in Emergency Detoxification, a big, purpose-built facility in Brixton where for once no expense had been spared to give it eight specialist handling garages full of support machinery, wrapped around a core of offices and maintenance depots.

ED operated seven active response crews, ensuring two would always be on standby at all times to cover most of Europe. The division's mission was to prevent any emerging contamination situation from getting anywhere close to the point where leakage occurred. That meant getting the first-response teams in fast and early, and dealing with the problem directly with the resources only a company like Connexion could deliver. That required a full backup for the on-site teams, from full technical support in the Brixton office to fast civil evacuation procedures and emergency medical crews that could be brought in from right across the globe in worst-case scenarios.

Everything depended on the first-response teams managing things professionally and disposing of the problem in minimal time (and at a minimal cost). The practical, political, and financial expectations focused on the team leader were huge.

Callum's first-response crew used an office that had a window wall overlooking the facility's Monitoring and Coordination Center, whose architects had clearly modeled it on Connexion's starflight mission control. Callum greeted his crew and stood beside the tall glass, watching the activity in the M & C Center. He could see the long lines of consoles below and noted a full support crew was already in place, bolstering the normal monitoring staff. A sure sign of a building situation. They were studying fast-changing data displays under the supervision of five separate operations directors. The wall they faced was covered in a dozen screens. Most of the secondary screens showed the same news streams of minor disasters he'd seen in the flat. One of the two main screens was showing the cleanup at an aging chemical plant on the banks of the Wista just outside Gdańsk. The ED crews had been working that one since before his Barbuda trip. The land around the plant had been used as a chemical drum burial ground for decades, and none of the contents or locations had been logged. The Environmental Enforcement Agency only discovered the site when the drums started leaking into the Wista. ED was having to excavate the whole area down to fifty meters to clear it.

The second big screen relayed the gates of the Gylgen disposal plant, with snow falling as if to soften the problem. There wasn't much activity going on outside the long, dark buildings behind the double chain-link fence. That was when Callum knew for sure Brixton would be sending a crew in.

He watched Dokal Torres, their corporate liaison counselor, standing beside Fitz Adamova—in Callum's opinion the best of ED's operations directors. The two were having a very intense conversation.

"That looks serious," he decided.

"There's money in play on this," Moshi Lyane said cheerfully. "Corporate always gets serious when money's in the room." At twenty-eight, Moshi was keen to prove himself; he had a puppyish eagerness combined with fierce intelligence. Callum was convinced that back in the rocket age, his deputy would have been a right-stuff astronaut for NASA. But now Connexion had changed the world, so Moshi was at the new cutting edge of risk-taking, and helping to make the world a better place at the same time. It was like an addiction; all the crew had it. "Update?" he asked.

"We're going to get the call," Moshi said. "Boynak still haven't moved anything through their hubs that can help."

"Nothing?" Callum asked in surprise. "Are we even sure there's an emergency?"

"They might not be moving equipment," Alana Keates said, "but Dok just confirmed four of their top engineers arrived onsite an hour ago." She glanced through the window at the counselor.

"Evaluating," Callum said. "That must be it."

"Dok thinks so," Alana agreed. "By the way, what happened to your hair?"

"My hair is fine." Callum ran his hand over his hair. It seemed a bit stiffer than usual, and he could still smell the glass cleaner. "Okay. Do we have plans of the plant?"

"Way ahead of you," Raina Jacek said. She was the crew's data expert, and privately Callum would trade any two of the others for her. She knew her way around network systems better than anyone with a standard degree out of university. Most of her teens had been spent as a hacktivist, mainly for political and environmental causes. She'd been arrested several times, and even served three months in a Norwegian junior offenders' camp. Normally that would red-flag her as far as Connexion was concerned, but her file said she had switched sides after rehabilitation.

One night at a party when they were both mildly stoned, Raina had told Callum that she had actually had a near-death experience after her friends were sold a bad batch of crystal Nsim. Her boyfriend had died, but the paramedics were good enough to revive her. It had made her realize just how dark the underworld could go. So it wasn't a switch of allegiance, exactly, but Emergency Detoxification was making a visible difference, even if she didn't like the profit motive . . .

They sat around the office table, and Raina threw schematics of the Gylgen plant on the wallscreen.

"Standard disposal setup," said Henry Orme, their radioactive materials expert. "Boynak have a contract with a whole bunch of European companies to get rid of their radioactive waste."

"What sort of waste are we taking about?" Callum asked.

"Standard items: medical tracers, research lab material. Nothing too bad, until you start to lump it all together."

"Which is what they do?" Colin Walters said knowingly.

"Yep. There's a portal between the Gylgen plant and one of the ventchambers on our Haumea asteroid station. Boynak gathers the waste into batches at the Gylgen plant, and sends it through to Haumea, which vents it away into deep space along with all the other crud Earth's desperate to dispose of. Forty AUs being what everyone agrees is a safe distance. It's a simple and easy system."

"What could possibly go wrong?" Raina said happily.

Callum ignored the snark. "Show me."

Colin used a pointer to highlight a section of the plans. The center of the main building had five large cylinders, four meters in diameter and fifteen long, arranged in a vertical cluster. Each of them funneled down to a meter-wide pipe at the bottom, and they all connected to the one-meter portal below via a series of valves. "These tanks are pressure chambers," Colin said. "You collect the waste from clients in small sealed canisters and drop them into the tank through an airlock at the top. When the tank is full, you pressurize it to five atmospheres." His pointer dot reached the bottom of a tank. "Then you open the valve. Gravity and pressure send the waste straight down to the portal, along with the vacuum suck from Haumea. Whoosh, out it all goes."

Callum nodded. He'd seen variants on the system dozens of times. It was deliberately simple, keeping the process safe and reliable. Tens of thousands of tons of toxic waste were sent harmlessly into space from Haumea every year; it was all the asteroid did.

"Unfortunately, it's not going whoosh in this case," Dokal Torres said. The counsel was walking in from the M & C Center. Unlike the rest of the crew, she was wearing a light gray suit with a dark claret blouse—that way she stood apart and emphasized how far up the management chain she'd risen. For all her insistence on following protocol and routine, Callum liked her. She was smart enough to know when to give him the leeway to deal with problems. It was a good professional relationship. On rare occasions she'd even been known to join the rest of the crew for a beer after work.

"What's happening?" Moshi asked.

"Blockage at the base of the tank. It's been pressurized, and Boynak is worried about some of the seals holding for a prolonged period. We're creeping outside the design specs."

Callum tried to keep the excitement from his voice. "Do we go in?"

Dokal took a breath. "Yes."

The crew whooped and gave each other high-fives.

"Boynak and their insurers have authorized a full breach and vent. Whatever it takes."

"What's the blockage?" Callum asked.

"The valve won't open," Dokal said.

"Uh huh." Callum nodded shortly, instinct warning him something was wrong; the way she gave a lawyer's answer only confirmed it. "We can tack a blister to the base of the tank, and blow through the wall."

"Your call," she said.

"Okay." He clapped his hands. "Let's get moving. Moshi, Alana, Colin with me. Load our bugez with a couple of blisters and a pack of fifty-centimeter shaped charges. Raina, you're in the facility's control room—I want to know the real state of that cylinder and its seals. I'm also going to need every spec on the tank, especially what it's made of."

"On it, boss," she said happily.

"Henry, take Haumea station. Thread us."

"Oh, come on . . ." Henry complained.

"You're at Haumea," Callum said in a level tone. Henry's partner was seven and a half months pregnant. It made Callum feel strangely protective, especially as a newlywed himself. Having Henry away from the dangerous material at Gylgen made him feel a lot better.

Henry held up his hands. "You're the boss."

"I want to be through the hubs in ten minutes. And it's max hazmats, people; this is radiation we're dealing with."

The crew hurried out. Just as he reached the door to the handling garage, Dokal said: "A word, Cal."

Instinct made his skin crawl, but he just said, "Sure," like it was routine, some stupid paperwork to clear first.

"What's with the hair this morning?" she asked as they hurried up the stairs.

"It's . . . nothing."

She raised an eyebrow but didn't push it.

Dokal's office was on the ED core's second floor, which gave her a rare outside window. The white blinds were shut, preventing anyone from seeing out—or more relevantly, Callum thought, in. Two people were waiting for them. He recognized one: Poi Li, Connexion's security director, who had been with Ainsley Zangari since the very beginning. Company rumor had it she supplied him with pirated firewalls the day he rented his first office in Manhattan, because he didn't have the money to buy legit copies. Just the sight of the old woman made him feel guilty. She couldn't be here about Savi. *Could she?*

Poi Li gave him a quick appraisal. "You look worried, Mr. Hepburn," her deceptively light voice challenged.

Bastard! "My expenses are all legitimate." He made it light, office banter.

The second visitor stood up.

"This is Major David Johnston," Dokal said. "From the Ministry of Defense. Nuclear division."

The major was a heavy man in his early fifties, moving with some difficulty and wincing every time he bent his knees. Callum imagined him being injured during some kind of dark ops mission. A thin monk's band of white hair circled his scalp, and he wore wire-rimmed screen glasses, which gave him the air of a classics professor. His presence worried Callum a great deal more than Poi Li ever could. "Really?"

"Pleased to meet you, Callum. Counselor Torres here has been singing your praises."

Callum gave Dokal an ironic glance. "Nice to know."

"We have a delicate problem," the major said. "And by 'we,' I mean the British government. So we're asking for your help and discretion."

"Which Connexion guarantees," Poi Li said. "Correct, Callum?"

He spread his arms wide, trying not to let the dismay show. "Sure. So what's the problem?"

"The '68 Global Disarmament Treaty," Major Johnston said. "Terrific breakthrough event for global politics. Lots of voter happiness all 'round."

"I've heard of it," Callum said cautiously, not that he could remember details; politics and history weren't exactly his strongest subjects.

"It was inevitable, given the development of atomic bonding generators. Every major city in the world has an air shield now. Missiles and drones can't get through, and if you bond enough air together, it can withstand a nuclear blast. Whole national arsenals were rendered obsolete overnight—well, five years plus. That just leaves us with low-level threats now: terrorists building their own nukes, rogue nations, extreme political groups, etc., etc. Everyone realized the only way to prevent that menace being realized is to get rid of the world's stockpile of weapons-grade fissionable material."

"After the '68 treaty, everybody abandoned their warheads and their material stockpile," Dokal said. "It's one of the reasons Haumea was so profitable for Connexion right from the start; everyone made a show of shoving their nasties through."

Callum watched her closely. He really didn't like where this was heading now. And the vivisectionist gaze that Poi Li was using to study him didn't help.

"So we did," said Major Johnston. "Everybody minimized. The UK was left with five functioning warheads for deterrence purposes alone, and no ability to build more. However, I'm afraid we had a . . . uh, inventory issue."

"Oh, fuck," Callum groaned.

"The trouble is, back in the twentieth century and a fair bit of the twenty-first, the government was somewhat paranoid. They didn't declare the true amount of plutonium we had created."

"Jesus fucking wept! Are you telling me there's plutonium in that malfunctioning tank?"

"We were trying to dispose of it quietly," Major Johnston said. "To avoid an incident with the Transnational Inspectorate."

"You didn't tell them?" Callum said, aghast. "You didn't tell Boynak what you were sending through their disposal system?"

"Our senior management was aware," Poi Li said.

Callum turned to her, frowning. "*Our* management?"

"Connexion has a share in Boynak. However, the Gylgen facility staff were not informed. There was no need."

"So we're helping the British government to dump their illegal plutonium?"

"The plutonium was a mistake made by a previous generation," Major Johnston said emphatically. "We were trying to do the honorable thing and correct it."

"Is that what you call it?"

"Actually, yes."

"We need you, as crew chief, to be aware of what you're actually facing in Gylgen," Dokal said.

"Big thanks, pal." Callum rubbed his forehead with the tips of his fingers, trying to think. "I don't get this. Is the malfunction a terrorist group sabotage?"

"I don't believe so," Major Johnston said. "We have sent several batches through previously without any problem. Our canisters of plutonium are listed as medical waste from various London hospitals. The plutonium itself is broken down into small pellets, each of which is encased in a ceramic to prevent it oxidizing, then sealed in a standard canister. What I believe may have happened is plain bad luck. One canister dropped from the top of the tank landed badly. The ceramic might have cracked, or even shattered."

"You didn't test the ceramic for impact," Callum said in realization.

"It's a quiet project," Poi Li said. "Failure to fall test that particular ceramic was an oversight."

Callum closed his eyes, trying to remember his physics. "If you expose plutonium to moist air, it oxidizes and hydrides, then expands by . . ."

"Up to seventy percent," Johnston completed. "The canister itself may have ruptured from that expansion pressure. It is only a standard commercial plastic, printed in the Gylgen plant and shipped out to customers."

"Never designed to contain accidental plutonium expansion," Callum said wearily. "I'm guessing the residue trickled to the bottom of the tank and blocked the valve. Unlikely, but . . ."

"Our scenario is worse than that."

"Oh, bloody hell!"

"The powder which plutonium oxidization and hydration produces has been known to flake off and ignite spontaneously."

"*Ignite?*"

"Yes. If there was a fire resulting from that initial fracture, it would probably breach further canisters. And each one would multiply the problem."

"How many plutonium canisters are in this tank?"

"Twenty-five. That's a kilogram of plutonium in total."

"Fuck me! Well, let's hope I can vent the whole mess before that fire starts."

"Cal," Dokal said quietly. "The Gylgen facility engineers didn't pressurize the tank."

"But you said . . . Oh."

"Yeah, there was a fire inside the tank," Major Johnston said. "That's what caused the pressure increase. There's only a limited amount of oxygen in there, so that'll be consumed by now. But we suspect that while it was burning, it turned a lot of the other canisters molten, releasing more plutonium along with all the other residue. That is probably what's broken the valve. There are no sensors left inside; the fire took them out. We don't know what state the waste is currently in. The canister plastic may be liquid, or it may have recongealed. If you blow a hole in the bottom of the tank, the waste might not vent."

"We can't take the risk the fire will restart, Cal," Dokal said. "Some of those canisters contained radioactive water. If we get any more oxidization on the plutonium, it could combust and rupture. Time is becoming critical. You've got to send the whole tank through."

"It's fifteen meters long, and weighs sixty tons!"

"But it's only four meters wide. Whatever you need, Cal. There is no budget here today. You can thread up to six meters, our largest portal. I checked, and we have a pair available."

"All right, I accept the risk," Callum said calmly. "But my crew needs to be told."

"Not Raina Jacek," Poi Li said immediately. "Not with her political background."

He almost argued. Almost. But a very bad part of his brain was thinking about being vetted by security. The problem simply wouldn't exist if he had Poi Li's trust on this one.

"Okay, Raina will be in the Gylgen control room. I'm talking about Alana, Colin, and Moshi; they're the ones who'll be physically tackling the tank with me."

"They can be told," Poi Li agreed.

"Let's go, then."

When Callum got to handling garage five, the crew was almost ready to go. Moshi, Colin, and Alana were in their green-and-yellow hazmat suits, running tests on the life support packs. Raina was sitting on a bench, with a thick hi-rez wraparound screen band on her face, muttering away to her mInet, hands raised midair as she deftly moved virtual icons around. Henry was with two support staff, already wearing his thermal regulator suit, which resembled a body stocking knitted out of slim tubes. The staff walked him over to the Govnex Mark VI space suit, a rigid torso with a hinged backpack that was already open for him. He had to wiggle through the small rectangular opening. Legs went in first, then he had to bend almost double, shoving his arms into the sleeves as he pushed his head through the neck ring. Callum winced in sympathy as he started to pull on his hazmat suit.

"We're going for full disposal," he told them. "I want to drop the whole tank out through Haumea."

"What? Why?"

"You're kidding, chief."

"That's crazy!"

"It's not crazy," Callum said levelly. "Something in those containers has leaked and blocked the valve. We don't know what, and we don't know how much. I cannot risk a partial clearance; that'd leave us a worse problem than we have now. So the whole thing goes, quick and clean. Dok has already cleared it with corporate."

Raina had pulled her wraparound down to give him a skeptical stare. The others were all exchanging glances.

"It's four meters in diameter, chief," Colin protested.

Callum's lips twitched a grin. "So we thread up to six. There's a portal pair waiting for us on Haumea."

"You're shitting us!" Henry exclaimed in delight. "Nobody gets to use a six-meter portal."

"We do."

"Okay, then." Alana pursed her lips in approval. "Now you're talking!"

"So. Henry, we'll be taking two portals. One to depressurize the tank—that'll buy us some time—the second to thread up ready for complete disposal. That's going to take some serious cutting. Moshi, electron beams for all of us. Colin, we're going to need at least two cases of shaped charges. Raina, how's your timing? We're going to need some serious precision on this."

"I'm insulted you asked." But she was smiling. Like the rest of them, she had her eyes on the big prize. This operation was going to look great on their CVs, and the bragging rights they'd have over the other crews was incalculable. There was also the prospect of a bonus, always index-linked to the scale of the hazard you averted.

They used Connexion's internal European hub network to get them to Stockholm, then there was a private portal to the Boynak offices, which put the Gylgen facility one step away. As soon as they got there, Raina went straight for the operations control room. A technician in a hazmat suit led Callum and his crew to the disposal building.

It was a standard industrial structure of metal girders covered in composite panels. Inside was a three-dimensional lattice of pipes and loader rails interlaced with stairs and suspended walkways. At the far end was the reception bay, with cargo portals linked to various collection stations across the continent. Right at the center, suspended over a deep pit, were the five tanks.

Callum took one look at the imposing matrix of metal—a brutal edifice made worse by the red emergency lights flashing across it. The sirens had been switched off hours ago. Apollo threw up a swathe of schematics, identifying components. "Leave the bugez," he said. "They'll take too long to scale this. We'll carry the cases from here."

They didn't say anything, just did as they were told and plucked their equipment cases from the bugez. Callum guessed they were still in shock. He'd explained about the plutonium on the way over, cutting Raina out of the comms circuit.

It was two flights of stairs up to the walkway that led to the top of the tanks. He was sweating by the time he got up there. The cases were heavy, and he had an electron cutter slung over his back.

Loader rails ran parallel to the walkway, silent and still since the pressure warning started. He glanced at the blue plastic canisters frozen in position, stretching all the way back to the loading bay. Each one had a prominent radiation warning emblem. Ordinarily that might bother him; today he just didn't care. *Like they're going to make a difference if we screw up.*

Dokal had shown him the confidential file Johnston had provided. It had estimates of the potential damage should the tank rupture. Likely quantity of plutonium particles to spew out, wind patterns, ground dispersal . . . Emergency evacuation procedures to enact for anyone within two hundred kilometers, contamination effects on local wildlife and vegetation. Cost of a clear-up—shocking in both financial and environmental terms.

"Mini Chernobyl," she had said grimly.

Apollo had shown him that file. It banished his usual level of confidence, which he fought hard to hide from his crew.

They arrived at the cluster of tanks. Each one had a couple of air-locks on top, the size of oil drums, with a feeder mechanism above them to channel the canisters off the loader rails.

"Alana, clear the insulation off the top of our tank, enough for a blister. Moshi, get me a temperature reading, then prep a puncture charge. Colin, the blister, please. And guys—"

They turned to look at him, caught by the unaccustomed gravity in his voice.

"Calm and careful, okay? We cannot afford screwups."

"You got it, chief."

While the others got organized, he took a minute to study the tank and the lattice of steel girders that held it in place, working out where the supports would have to be cut. The schematic his mInet threw up across the hazmat helmet visor confirmed the load points. *Twenty of the bastards.*

Alana used a power plane to slice the insulation foam off the tank, cutting a circle more than a meter across.

"Thirty-eight Celsius," Moshi said. "That's well inside tolerance."

"Good," Callum said. "Let's keep it that way. Place the charge."

Colin put the puncture charge in the middle of the area—a black plastic circle like a fat coin, three centimeters across.

Callum opened the first of his cases. The portal it contained was a disk thirty centimeters in diameter. On one side it was a hole that opened into a metallic chamber in Haumea station, while the other side was a twenty-centimeter strata of molecular circuitry, stabilizing the entanglement. When Callum looked through, the portal was facing a wide airlock hatch, with amber caution lights strobing around it. As always, he had to resist sticking his hand through and wiggling it around.

"Henry? How are we doing?"

"I'm in the ventchamber. Portal is locked in position. Ready to open outer door." Henry's space-suited hand came into view through the portal, giving a thumbs-up.

"Stand by."

Colin held up the blister—a hemisphere of incredibly tough metalloceramic, with a meld-bonding rim. Callum twisted the portal disk into its locking slots in the apex of the blister, and they both lowered it onto the patch Alana had prepared.

"Seal it," Callum said. "Henry, open the ventchamber hatch, please."

"Confirmed, chief. Opening now."

Callum watched the data Apollo was throwing onto his visor display, seeing the pressure inside the blister wind down to zero. "Fitz, status, please."

"Haumea systems all stable," the operations director said. "Portal power supply confirmed and buffered. You're go, Cal."

"Raina, update?"

"Blister seal melded to the tank. It's secure, Cal. Good to go."

"Thank you. Moshi, blow the puncture charge."

There was a dull *crump* from the blister. Callum heard a loud whistling sound. Apollo showed him the pressure in the blister rising sharply.

"It's venting, chief," Henry reported. "Good plume. Mostly gas. Some particles."

It took three minutes for the tank to empty. Callum, Moshi, Alana, and Colin all kept watch on the casing, but although it trembled as the gas was expelled, nothing else happened; the whistling noise reduced to nothing after a couple of minutes. "Right, then. Let's get it prepped for dumping," Callum said. "Henry, I'm looking to start threading up in about an hour."

"I'll be ready at this end, chief."

Moshi had the job of blowing the horizontal support struts that fastened the tank to the surrounding lattice. He clambered along the metal girders, fixing a double charge to each strut. Alana and Colin used their electron beam cutters and severed the disposal pipe at the bottom of the tank below the jammed valve, then went on to slice out a two-meter section. When they were finished, there was a clear space below the valve.

While his crew was working on readying the tank, Callum started clearing an area to work in, level with the gap Alana and Colin were preparing. He cut into the girders, creating a cave to bring the portals through unencumbered. It was tough work, sending long lengths of metal tumbling down into the pit below, where they bounced and spun off the thick pipes leading in from the other tanks, clattering away to the very bottom of the pit. Several struck the side of the portal chamber five meters below him.

To hold the six-meter portal, they'd brought three support rails with them—telescoping composite tubes that Callum and Alana set up underneath the tank's severed pipe. Bonding pads at each end secured them to the remaining steel girders.

The whole procedure took nearly seventy minutes. Callum was sweating profusely when they finished, and Raina confirmed the rails had bonded correctly to the molecules of the lattice girders. Standing on the precarious walkway, he opened the second case, which contained another thirty-centimeter portal, and placed it base down on the mesh.

"Henry, we're ready. Start threading."

As soon as the tank's gas evacuation was complete, Henry had cycled out of the ventchamber airlock and headed back to the ED ready-one compartment. Haumea station's broad passageways were simple metal tubes with nearly a meter of insulation foam sprayed on the outside to help combat the cold imbued by the asteroid's lonely trans-Neptune orbit. The station didn't warrant the investment of its own manufacturing module; all its sections and components were shipped out directly from Earth. They were laid out across Haumea's ice-crusted rock surface in a series of basic geodesic spheres with radial spokes leading out to cylindrical ventchambers of varying size. There were more than eighty ventchambers already, most of them with their outer doors permanently open, allowing plumes of misty vapor to fountain up out of their portals as toxic chemicals or radioactive

gases were shunted far away from Earth. The remainder would intermittently produce bursts of canisters, which streaked out across interplanetary space like a blast of giant shotgun pellets. New spheres
and ventchambers were still being added as Earth methodically disposed of its historical pollution.

Technicians were already assembling the threader when Henry arrived in ED ready-one. The inside of the dome was the same triple-
level layout as a free-fall space station; with Haumea's minimal gravity
it made maneuvering large machinery a lot easier. The central deck
was the assembly area for threaders. Henry smiled inside his helmet
as he saw the six-meter one being prepared; the big machines always
delighted him.

The core of this one was the pair of six-meter portals, currently
pressed together so tightly they formed a single disk of molecular
circuitry a meter and a half thick. Nine robot arms were carefully
integrating an elegant egg-shaped frame of brushed aluminum ovals
around them, containing a multitude of mechanical components and
actuators, wound with power cables and data fibers.

Henry clicked his space suit boots into the floor grid, holding
himself in place while the technicians glided around the growing
threader like curious fish investigating a shining reef. He watched the
process advance while the voices of the crew back in Gylgen babbled
away in his ears.

Once the first part of the threader was complete, a similar, smaller
version was attached to its front end, then finally an even smaller edition was attached to the end of that. The three together resembled a
bizarre Russian doll mechanism caught in mid-separation.

"Henry, we're ready for you," the lead technician said.

Henry picked up the second of the two suitcases he'd brought
with him from Brixton. He kicked off the floor and floated easily
through the air to the threader. To stop he grabbed one of the ceiling
handholds, and maneuvered himself back to vertical relative to the
decking. Working in zero gee, constantly having to manipulate your
whole body mass with a single arm, built muscle bulk like no gym

exercise ever could. All space workers developed upper bodies like pro swimmers. And because portal doors meant everyone went back home to Earth at the end of shift, nobody suffered the kind of calcium loss and muscle wastage early astronauts were plagued with on long-duration flights.

He opened the suitcase and took out the circular thirty-centimeter portal. It locked into place on the front of the threader. "Integration complete," he reported.

"Reading it," Fitz said. "Running threader procedure checks. You are go to egress the ventlock."

The magnetic monorail grip on the bottom of the threader powered up, propelling it along one of several rails on the deck. Henry waited until it went past, then grasped one of the curving aluminum ribs at the back and let it tow him along. The rail led down a passageway to the largest ventchamber on Haumea.

As soon as it was inside the cylindrical metal cave, the inner door slid shut and sealed with a fast succession of metallic *clunk*s. The threader extended ten legs, which engaged with loading pins on the chamber floor.

"In position," Henry said. He looked up, checking the outer door above the threader. A ring of amber caution lights was flashing around the heavy-duty hydraulic actuators.

"Callum's almost ready," Fitz told him. "Stand by."

Henry drifted over to the airlock at the side of the big egress door he'd just come through and opened it in readiness. Once everything was in place, he was going to have to leave the ventchamber fast. His mInet was throwing up several data columns on the space suit visor, showing him the threader status.

He'd been listening to his friends back in Gylgen for several minutes before Callum said: "Henry, we're ready. Start threading."

Henry gave the instruction to his mInet. The smallest of the threader's three mechanisms started up. At its center was a paired portal, like a particularly thick dark-gray paving slab, twenty-five centimeters wide and one point five meters long.

"Initiating spatial entanglement on unit alpha," Fitz said, as the data on his displays showed him the system's progress. "Okay . . . we have zero gap. Power stable to both sides. Uncoupling now."

The actuators inside the threader mechanism split the slab apart into identical rectangles whose quantum spatial entanglement transformed them into linked doors. No matter how great the physical distance between the twinned segments, the entanglement provided an open gap that was no length at all: the portal.

Henry grinned in delight as the threader supports holding the portal pair lifted the two identical rectangles away from each other. Actuators moved with the fluidity of metal muscles, sliding one of the twins—short edge first—through the waiting thirty-centimeter portal, its edges just clearing to emerge directly into the Gylgen facility.

"Got it," Callum said.

In front of Henry, the threader mechanism rotated the remaining portal slab by ninety degrees, so its longer opening was ready to receive the shorter side of the next stage.

"Initiating spatial entanglement on unit beta," Fritz said.

Unit two was another rectangular portal, larger this time, one and a half meters by six and a half. The support arms pulled its twin segments apart and immediately slipped the short end of the upper segment into the waiting unit alpha portal, with a clearance of less than a centimeter. Inside the threader, the remaining unit beta portal was rotated to present its wider side to unit gamma, the six-meter portal.

"Here we go," Henry muttered. "Unit gamma ready for you, chief."

Callum caught the unit alpha slab as it threaded through from Haumea and placed it on the floor in the section he'd marked out. Unit beta quickly emerged out of it, and the legs on its back deployed, lifting it up, and flipping the open side ninety degrees so it finished up horizontal. He checked it was aligned with the rails bridging the gulf under the tank. Apollo adjusted its height until Callum was satisfied. Alana fixed its legs to the walkway's grid.

"Let's have it," he told Henry.

The six-meter portal came through, sliding out across the rails. Callum glanced into the opening, seeing the ventchamber's outer door dead ahead. He watched the data column showing him the state of the rails and their bonding points. Everything was well inside tolerance. "Looks good from here. Let's go."

Along with Moshi, Alana, and Colin, he clambered back up the metal stairs to the top of the lattice. Moshi had prepared straps and harnesses for all of them, fastened to the thickest girders. Callum eyed the top of the tank as he clipped himself in.

"Everyone secure?"

"Good to go, chief."

"Raina, I need you to keep watch on the building sensors."

"I'm on it, chief."

"Henry, open the ventchamber door," Callum said. "Moshi, get ready."

It began with a faint hissing sound. A breeze started up, plucking at the thick fabric of his hazmat suit. The hissing deepened, quickening his heartbeat. Peripheral vision showed things moving on the walkways that crisscrossed the lattice: old abandoned plastic cups, paper, scraps of wiring, plastic slivers, all wiggling and rolling along.

"Door at fifty percent," Henry reported.

The hissing had become a storm-roar now. Its force was buffeting him with a lot more force that he'd anticipated. Instinct made him check the harness clasps. Colin and Alana were already on their knees, gripping the walkway rail for extra security.

"Seventy-five percent," Henry said.

Callum could hear the whole building protesting now. Metal was creaking overhead. When he glanced up, he could see the lights swinging wildly. Above them, the ceiling panels were buckling, starting to peel from the frame.

"Hundred percent!"

The snarl of air venting into interplanetary space became a hurricane howl. Vapor was streaking across the lattice at incredible speed. Two roof panels ripped free and slammed down onto the tank, vibrating furiously as they were sucked away down the sides.

"Blow it," Callum shouted.

The charges on the tank support struts detonated simultaneously. He couldn't even hear them above the gale that was clawing at him. Snowflakes transformed to dangerous ice bullets, strafing down from widening cracks in the roof. The top of the tank vanished, dropping so fast he barely caught the motion. More lethal panels were scything through the air, following it into the cyclone funnel that had formed in the gulf its departure had created.

"It's clear," Raina yelled across their comms.

"Close it, Henry!" Callum shouted.

The gale took an age to subside as the ventchamber's outer door labored against the incredible pressure. Twice as long as it took to form, Callum was sure.

Silence, when it came, was like a physical force slapping him. Callum took a shaky breath and stood up, tensed against the eerily still air. "Everyone okay?"

They called it in, voices unsteady with relief. Callum slowly unclipped the harness. Snow was falling through wide fractures in the broken roof. The inside of the building resembled a bomb site. He checked his radiation sensor, which showed him background levels only.

"Bloody hell, we did it!" he said. Then he started laughing at the surprise in his own voice.

The alarm clock's buzzing woke Callum. Someone had turned the volume up to stadium-rock level and added earthquake-shake to it. Callum moaned weakly and opened his eyes—actions that were hideously painful. His hand groped around for the alarm clock. Somewhere in his aching brain he cursed the smartarse out-of-reach trick.

That was when he realized he wasn't even in the bedroom, let alone his bed. He was sprawled on the settee in the living room with a cricked neck and one arm wedged under his torso. And the alarm was still buzzing away. His vision was blurry, but he could see through the open door into the bedroom where the red glowing digits taunted him.

"House," he croaked.

"Good morning, Callum."

"Switch the alarm off."

"That is not possible. Your alarm clock has no interface. It is very old. I believe it was manufactured in the 1990s."

"Bastard." He staggered upright, groaning at the wave of pain the motion caused at the very center of his brain. The living room lurched nauseatingly around him. Somehow he managed to coordinate his limbs and tottered into the bedroom. He didn't bother with the snooze or cancel buttons on the clock, just switched the fucker off at the mains.

Relief lasted about five seconds. "Oh, shit," he gasped, and sprinted for the bathroom.

He didn't know what he'd had to eat last night, but he certainly managed to throw up most of it into the toilet bowl. He pressed the flush, then slumped on the floor with his back to the washbasin, breathing heavily as his body abruptly turned to ice and his clearly lethal bastard of a headache hammered at the inside of his skull in an attempt to break free.

They'd spent another hour at the Gylgen disposal facility yesterday after dumping the tank, first helping the staff check to make sure no waste canisters had split or leaked during the chaos; then threading the portal doors back to Haumea station. Media drones had caught the roof buckling and the snowy air screaming into fissures as the panels were sucked down into the massive emergency vent. Everyone assumed the tanks had imploded. It took Connexion's PR team a while to calm fears and reassure everyone that ED had worked their usual miracle, preventing radiation leakage from contaminating the surrounding area. Under Dokal's forceful guidance, the PR team underplayed the potential damage level, emphasizing the debris would have only been mildly radioactive medical waste.

The news streams ignored that modesty and started playing old Chernobyl videos. By that time, Callum and the crew were all back in Brixton, kicking back in their office, cheering and jeering at the deluge of alarmist reports. *If only you knew,* he thought smugly. After that, they all went out for a quiet celebratory drink.

The shower helped a little. But he took four ibuprofen as soon as he got out, washed down with half a carton of fresh orange juice he found in the fridge. A fully stocked fridge. "Oh, thank Christ for that." He slapped bacon rashers into the pan. Plenty of bread today, so two bacon sandwiches. Two mugs of extra strong coffee to go with them.

He found some clean clothes, shoved the entire dirty laundry pile into the housekeeping service's bags—they could sort everything out, and screw the extra cost—and left them outside his door for pickup.

Then he sat back down at the breakfast bar and took a couple of paracetamol, because a paramedic ex had told him it was okay to mix them with ibuprofen. He wasn't quite up to the walk to the Young Street hub yet. He couldn't be bothered to watch the overnight news streams. If there was anything bad, ED would have called him in.

He slipped on his screen sunglasses. "Hey, Apollo, any calls or emails from Savi?"

"No."

"Ping her mInet for me, pal."

"No response."

"Bastard."

Callum didn't get it. *Six bloody days and not a single minute away from dumb student radical eyes?* Maybe it'd all been some kind of con? She'd married him for his money, and the whole Diana Klub staff was in on it. They jacked a couple of romance-bewitched tourists every month, laughing as they cashed in his . . . His what? All he had were good prospects. *Can't take that to the bank.*

He shook his head wearily. "Grow up, you moron," he grunted angrily.

It was clear what his brain was doing—trying to deny the obvious conclusion. *Something's happened. Something bad.*

"Apollo?"

"Yes, Cal."

"Set up a new news filter. Find any female students fitting Savi's description, but not her name, reported missing from campus in the last six days."

"Which campus, Cal?"

He shrugged. "All of them."

"On the planet?"

I'm paranoid. But am I paranoid enough? "Yes," he sighed. "Everything on Earth."

"That might take a while. May I purchase additional processor time?"

"Do it."

When he walked into the crew's office, he might have laughed at the state of Alana and Colin—except he didn't exactly occupy the moral high ground. Besides, he suspected he looked even worse than they did. Their sunglasses weren't as dark as his. Raina looked as lively and peppy as she always did. And he was sure he had a memory of her matching his vodka shots. There was even a vague recollection of a cocktail glass alight with blue flame.

Raina gave him a weary, sympathetic smile. "How's it going, chief?"

"Still alive. Why aren't you hungover?"

"Younger, smarter, know where to score better drugs."

"Bastard," he grumbled.

Moshi was at the small kitchen bar in the corner, washing down pills with a big mug of tea. He hadn't shaved, and Callum was pretty sure he was wearing the same shirt as yesterday. "Morning," Moshi said, and slumped back into one of the settees before closing his eyes.

For Henry it was just another morning, and all was well with the world. But then Henry had been a responsible adult last night and gone home before midnight to be with his expectant partner.

Callum looked through the glass wall into the M & C Center. Fitz grinned and gave him a mocking two-finger salute. Callum responded with one finger.

"Okay." Callum tried to focus on the news streams running across the wallscreens. One of the central pair was still showing the Gylgen facility; there'd been a heavy snowfall overnight, covering some of the more blatant damage to the building. "What have we got?"

"Why do we care?" Moshi asked, his eyes still closed.

"Nothing even close to interesting," Raina said. "Especially no plutonium scares today."

Callum gave her an irritated glance. He knew she'd find out eventually. But she needed to be smarter about it, particularly inside their own office. *Does Security bug us?*

Dokal walked in and took a disapproving look around the human wreckage. "Jesus Christ, guys. You're supposed to be professionals. Couldn't you even wait till the weekend?"

"We'll probably have saved the world twice more by then," Moshi said.

"Not in this state you won't. Are you actually active-ready?"

"Alternatively," Raina said, "well done for yesterday, everyone; Connexion is delighted, so I come bringing news of your enormous thank-you bonus."

"There are two other crews on shift," Callum said. "If we get called after them, we'll be ready."

Dokal gathered herself up for a rebuke, then relented. "Actually, Corporate's appreciation will manifest in your next salary payment."

There was some feeble cheering from around the office. Only Henry looked genuinely grateful. But then he'd recently been telling Callum horrific stories of how much new baby gear cost.

"Cal, a word."

"Yes, ma'am." He followed her out of the office.

Dokal gave him a closer inspection. "Damn. The state of you."

"Hey, it's a mild hangover, okay? I'm entitled."

"Yes, but you're not as young as you were."

"Bloody hell, don't you start."

"At least your hair is normal today." She gave his clothes a final inspection and sighed in disappointment. "Come on, someone wants to meet you."

"Who?" Callum asked.

"You'll see. But let me tell you, your upcoming bonus is going to reflect the company's sincere appreciation for how you handled yesterday. There were some very senior people watching the feeds from the M and C."

"You didn't tell me."

"Would it have helped improve your operation?"

"No," he admitted.

Four portal doors in Connexion's internal hub network, and Cal found himself stepping out into a huge construction site. He knew it was London's Greenwich Peninsula before Apollo threw the Hubnav data onto his screen glasses. The old arena dome had been demolished two years ago, to colossal news stream coverage. Now he was standing about ten meters below ground level, in a circular pit with metal restraining walls and a floor of frosty mud. Big construction vehicles rumbled around him, some of them manually operated, the drivers sitting in high cabs, using small joysticks to control their machinery. In the cold morning light, it was a slice of a post-apocalypse world ruled by steampunk dinosaurs.

"He's over here," Dokal said, and set off across the mud.

Callum followed, realizing that this was probably the first time he'd seen her out of heels. She led him over to a group of suits who looked even more out of place in the pit than he did. Then he caught sight of who was standing in the center of them.

"You might have warned me," he grumbled.

"What? The man who saves the world before lunch every day, scared?"

"Fuck you."

"Remember, don't smile too wide for the photographer, you'll look insincere. But do smile. Oh, and be respectful."

"I'm always—"

The Pretorian guard of lawyers, accountants, architects, and PAs parted. Ainsley Baldunio Zangari looked around in interest. The side of his mouth lifted in wry acknowledgment. "Callum!" His voice was like a shout as he put his hand out in greeting.

Just like the news streams.

"Good to meet you, son," Ainsley said, shaking hands effusively. "People, this is Callum, who saved our collective asses yesterday."

The entourage finally mustered smiles of approval.

"Let's him and me get a picture here, for history's sake."

The entourage spread out as if they'd been threatened with a cattle prod. Callum saw one of them, in a slightly cheaper suit than the rest, stand directly in front of him, adjusting his screen glasses. To one side, Dokal mouthed "smile" with a furious expression.

Callum slowly produced a lopsided grin, and said: "Honor to meet you, sir."

"Good man." Ainsley's smile got even wider, and his other hand clamped down on Callum's shoulder.

Callum felt ridiculous. Ainsley was sixty-one, with thick silver-fox hair and a large frame that wasn't entirely apparent beneath a suit that was superbly cut to de-emphasize his bulk. Cal couldn't tell if it was fat or muscle; could have gone either way. And here he was in what media trolls would caption as a wrestling lock—or worse—with his boss, the richest man there'd ever been.

"Give us a moment," Ainsley said. The entourage melted away faster than an ice cube dropped on lava. "Good job yesterday, Callum. I appreciate it."

His hand and shoulder were released. "Just doing my job, sir."

"Shit." The jovial patriarch persona vanished. "You ain't a kiss-ass, are you, son?"

Callum took a moment and glanced at the nearest group of the entourage, which included Dokal, all clustered together and carefully not looking in his direction. "No. I live for this shit. I fucking saved Sweden from a nuclear catastrophe—well, me and my crew. You don't know what that is. But it's my life, and it's the best."

Ainsley grinned. "And you, son, have no idea how envious I am. These dicks that can only say yes." His hand waved around the pit. "This is my life. Don't worry, I'm not going to come ride along with you. Insurance, for one thing, and the board would go apeshit."

"Each to his own."

"Yeah, but seriously: Thanks for yesterday. Fucking Brits, can you believe that? Don't they get plutonium is a century past its sell-by date?"

"They were trying to get rid of it."

"Ha! Fucking Johnston; you shake hands with him, son, you count your fingers afterwards. Nations are dissolving; Connexion's made sure of that. Everyone's a neighbor now. It's not a race to kill each other anymore. We're off to the stars instead. How about that? You going to emigrate when the starships reach a proto-Earth exoworld?"

"Dunno. Depends how long it takes to terraform one."

"Yeah. I just got back from Australia yesterday, you know. Icefall was impressive, even by my standards."

Callum hoped he wasn't looking too blank and stupid right now. He vaguely recalled seeing something about Icefall on a pub's news stream late last night as a fickle media finally moved on from Gylgen.

Apollo threw up details—a Connexion media briefing. It was one of Ainsley's pet projects, irrigating the central Australian desert. "I heard it started well," Callum said uncertainly.

"Certainly did, apart from some dickhead protestors trying to spoil progress like they always do."

"Right."

"The beauty of it is: We can spin Icefall as a grand humanitarian project, but actually it's planetary engineering one-oh-one. That's why I'm really backing it. Get some experience in. This way we'll be ready to make the truly big decisions when the time comes. And it will."

"I guess it's reassuring to know someone's planning for the genuine long-term."

"That's why I'll never make it as a politician; I want to actually achieve something in life."

Callum put his hands on his hips and regarded the cluster of hulking machinery that was seeding piles deep into the pit floor. "I'd call this achievement."

"Bullshit, son. This is just a building. Egyptians and Incas were building big shit three thousand years ago. Sure, it's gonna be impressive—Connexion's European grand hub and headquarters, never going to be anything else. But it's already three years behind schedule, and we ain't properly started. Fucking bureaucrats here . . . Jeez, I thought they were bad in the US. You been to New York, son? The tower I'm putting up next to Central Park is going to be a real statement, like this one. But at the end of the day: just a pile of concrete and glass."

"Are you going to put Emergency Detox in here?"

"Fuck knows. I leave the small shit to assholes in the office ten floors under mine. Let them worry about it. I'm the concepts and deals guy."

Callum laughed. "Now I'm starting to envy you."

"Yeah, it's a long way from New Jersey to here. Not that I was ever New Jersey trash. Did you know that?"

"Your father was a hedge fund manager."

"And I followed him to Wall Street and made the right investment, huh?"

"No, your Harvard degree was in machine intelligence. You liquidated your inheritance to set up Connexion."

Ainsley nodded in satisfaction, as if Callum had just passed a test. "Not just a college jock on a rodeo ride at my expense."

"Sir?"

"You're smart, son, and I don't mean your degree. How many of your crew know about the big boss without their mInet throwing it up?"

"Some."

"But you did, and that counts. We're expanding, Callum, the human race. And Connexion is going to make it possible. The asteroid habitats were just the start. How did you feel when *Orion* reached the Centauri system?"

"Happy and disappointed; I was hoping for a decent exoplanet in orbit."

"Likewise, son. Zagreus was well named; that is one crappy little loser of an exoplanet. But we didn't let that stop us, no, not this time. We went into that goddamned useless star system hard and built us another wave of starships. That's what our society is these days. We've got the balls to look outward and dream like JFK again. Fuck, that makes me proud to be human. One of those new starships will find us somewhere worth terraforming, and if it doesn't, then the following wave will, or the twentieth wave. It doesn't matter. We are going to build new worlds out there, son, and Connexion is going to take you out to the stars—you and a billion others desperate for a fresh start on a new planet. Twenty years' time, you'll be standing on this very same spot, and you'll be able to walk into our interstellar hub and step onto one of a dozen planets that we've tamed. Connexion is going to be huge. It's going to span the whole fucking galaxy one day."

"It's pretty big now, sir."

"Sure. But this one solar system is just the start. And if the company is going to grow the way I know it can, I'm going to need me some real smart, tough bastards to wrestle it into shape for me. What do you say to that?"

It was probably the hangover damping his emotions down, but Callum was pleased with himself for not overreacting. He just kept his cool and said: "You offering me a job, Mr. Zangari?"

Ainsley chortled. "Oh, I like you, son, sure enough. But no. No fancy job offer. Not today. What I'm saying is enjoy your macho time in ED these next few years, and watch out for the next generation who'll rise up like fucking crocodiles to snap at your heels. Then when the time comes you're tired of the sound of those teeth getting closer and you apply to go on senior management courses or maybe do an MBA, you'll find Connexion is supportive. You're what I'm looking for, son. Don't get head swell, now; I talk to a hundred like you a week. But you got yourself noticed and approved yesterday. No small thing in an organization this size."

"Duly noted, sir, and thank you."

Ainsley put his hand out again. "Okay. Now I need people to say yes to me again."

Callum's smile stayed in place as he walked back through all four portal doors to the ED office where the crew was waiting.

"Ainsley fucking Zangari?" Alana yelled. "Himself?"

"Yeah."

"What did you say? Wait! What did he say?" Moshi demanded.

"He said: well done. Said to thank you guys, too. Christ knows why."

"What's he like?" Raina asked.

"Same as on the news streams. Loud."

"Holy shit. Did he know our names, too?"

"I don't know. Probably. You'll be in the report file—under mine."

"Fuck off!"

Callum laughed and went to make himself some tea. The pills had squashed his hangover now, and he'd had too much coffee already. His crew chatted away happily behind him. *The richest man who'd ever been, their boss, knew they existed and was pleased with their work. So how big is the bonus, do you think?*

He sank back into a settee facing the glass wall into the M & C, giving the news streams a proper look this time and getting Apollo to summarize potential problems. It seemed the world of toxicity troubles wasn't too dangerous today.

When he thought back to the meeting, it still seemed slightly surreal. *I could have mentioned Savi, told Ainsley we'd got married. He would have congratulated me. That way there'd have been no way Security could have kicked up about it, not with him approving. Except . . .*

he'd see me as a troublemaker. Probably blow my chances of getting fast-tracked to the top.

Why doesn't she just fucking call?

Dokal sat down beside him. "Congratulations."

"Cheers."

"I mean it. Ainsley does that to about three people a year."

"Huh? He said he sees a hundred a week just like me."

"Who'd have thought it?" She smiled softly. "Someone like that not telling the whole truth."

"Wow!"

"Well, don't forget us when you're lording it over Connexion's whole northern hemisphere operations in twenty years' time."

Callum turned to look at her, wondering just how far her corporate loyalty went. They'd always got on well, but . . . she was ambitious. And now she knew he was a favorite, she might be agreeable to some mutual backscratching. *I only need some advice.* "We're at Donnington this weekend. Come along if you've got a spare hour. Be good to see you there again."

Her smile was endearing; he didn't get to see it very often. "Thanks, Cal. Is Savi going? I liked her."

"Hands off, she's my girlfriend."

"Well, try and use your brain for once. She's a keeper."

He knew he was blushing, and he didn't care. "Yeah, I figured that."

Callum made it past the Craner Curves and throttled back into Old Hairpin. He leaned into it, and the Ducati 999 followed the track like it was a rail. *You beautiful machine, you.* Through Starkey's Bridge, and he opened the throttle again. The twin-cylinder engine roared like a small rocket. The instrument panel blurred as the bike accelerated hard. He wasn't wearing screen lenses. This was all about authenticity. He didn't need precise readings; he *felt* the bike.

Slowing to take the bastard sharp McLeans turn, he was slicing close to the patch of crumbling tarmac and slowed another fraction, weaving wide. A Kawasaki ZX-17B shot past him, followed by an Aprilia RSV4 1000. "Shit!" he screamed into his helmet mic. He throttled up hard—too much for the turn and had to brake, losing even more ground.

"Shit! Shit! Shit!"

"What's up, Cal?" Alana asked in his headphones.

"Overtaken," he called out in frustration.

He gunned the throttle again and charged at Coppice for the turn into the long Dunlop Straight. Open the Ducati full and revel in the sheer power as the landscape stretched out into streaks of color on both sides. Focus spot was the track and the screaming bikes ahead. But they were throttled up full, and just as fast. He wasn't going to catch them.

Four laps left. He did okay, didn't slip any farther down the field. But his edge was gone, and he knew it.

Nine days now, and nothing. Something's happened to her. This is serious. How bad is student radicalism these days? How violent do they get?

A checkered flag was waving on the gantry overhead. Ninth place; there were only fifteen bikes in the race. He took the slow lap around to the exit and drove through the paddock. The support vehicles parked in long lines down the tarmac lanes were even more antique than the Ducati. Spectators enjoyed them almost as much as they did the bikes. People were wandering along, wrapped against the cold February air, gawping at the old camper buses and engineering caravans, parents pointing out shapes and company badges to semi-interested children.

Callum's team had an old Mercedes Sprinter van converted to a mobile workshop for the Ducati. It was parked down at the far end of the paddock, opposite the Redgate turn. Colin and Henry had set up an awning beside it, covering their collapsible chairs. A barbeque stood just outside, where Henry was turning the sausages.

Callum tried not to grin at Henry's expectant father routine. After all, it was an excited Henry who had originally found the bike on a specialist auction site eighteen months ago, just as Callum was appointed crew leader. They'd formed a syndicate, all of them chipping in for the privilege of riding the superb old machine at rallies and club meetings. Between them they could afford it. But as they'd soon found out, it wasn't the initial cost that was the problem, but the maintenance. And as for the price of specially synthesized petrol . . .

Callum parked the Ducati and took his helmet off.

"So was that a good result?" Dokal asked with apparent innocence. She was sitting under the awning next to her girlfriend, Emillie, both of them with a can of beer.

"We need to have a handicap scheme for these club meetings," Callum said gruffly. "Some of those bikes are more powerful than the Ducati. They're a lot younger, too."

"That's the spirit, chief," Raina said. She came out of the back of the Sprinter, zipping up her leathers. "I'm going to have a couple of practice laps before my race, okay?"

"All yours." Callum dismounted, trying not to make old-man grunts as his legs protested. "Watch out for the tarmac at McLeans and Redgate. There's a patch starting on Craner, too."

"Thanks." She swung her leg over the saddle and started the engine.

"Should you be racing on broken tarmac?" Emillie asked in a light French accent.

Callum shifted his gaze from a fabulous scarlet-and-black Yamaha YZF-10R on the other side of the paddock lane. "Huh? Oh, the track owners do their best. There's only so much they can charge to hire Donnington for a day. We're just enthusiasts, that's all. It took three clubs combined to fund today."

"Owners have a legal responsibility. They can get into all kinds of trouble with negligence; all the way up to corporate manslaughter."

"Drivers sign a waiver before we go out."

"I'm not sure that's good enough."

"Excuse my friend," Dokal said. "You can take the girl out of the risk assessment department . . ."

"Just saying," Emillie replied with a pout.

"Test of skill," Callum told her. "I'm going to get these leathers off. Henry, how are we doing?"

"Fifteen minutes, and we're eating."

"Roger that. Where's Katya?"

"Too tired," Henry said. "But she sent her salmon quiche." He pointed at the foil-wrapped flan on the camping table.

"Now you're talking." Callum went into the dark Sprinter and struggled out of his leathers, trying not to jab elbows into the racks of tools along one side.

"Not like you," Dokal said. "Ninth place?"

He glanced over at her as she stood in the van's open doorway. "I wasn't concentrating," he admitted.

"I can see that. Have you and Savi broken up?"

"No." Callum shook his head. "Quite the opposite." He started to explain.

Dokal's hand covered her wide-open mouth. "Married?" she squeaked when he'd finished. "Seriously?"

"Deadly so."

"That's wonderful." She came over and gave him a hug, smiling widely. "You old romantic. How long have you been going out? Two months?"

"When you know, you know."

"Callum Hepburn, a married man. Who'd have thought it?"

"Thanks."

"Are you going to have a proper reception? Oh, please say yes. I love weddings! Her parents are quite old-style, aren't they? What did they say?"

"There's a few . . . formal issues we have to settle first. I wanted to talk them over with you."

"Of course."

"Human Resources, for a start."

She closed her eyes for a long moment, dropping right back into her corporate lawyer mode. "They'll grumble, but don't worry about them. They only have that notification procedure in case an injured party goes all hypersensitive and fires off a workplace sexual harassment suit. You two didn't, quite the opposite: happy ever after ending."

"Yeah." He scratched the back of his neck, pulling an awkward face. "But she's in Security. They take it all a lot more seriously."

Dokal grinned evilly. "My, oh my. You should have been vetted. What will they find?"

"I'm not bothered about being vetted. It's the not telling them earlier when we should have bit that's the problem. I don't want a black mark on her file."

"That's easy. Companies aren't allowed to do that anymore."

"What?"

"It's discriminatory. As an employee, you have the right to see your full file, including disciplinary entries—which you can challenge in tribunal if you think said remarks are having an undue negative impact on your career prospects. If the tribunal agrees they're disproportionate, they can be wiped. And they can't be handed on to a subsequent employer, either."

"Really?"

"Yes. That's why HR chiefs are always networking so hard with recruitment agency account managers. And why corporate treads but softly on their entertainment expenses. A lot of shit lists get passed over in bars."

"Bloody hell! I didn't know that."

"You have a long way to go before you're ready to sit behind a desk, don't you?"

"So it would seem."

"I know some people in HR who deal with Security personnel issues. I can have a quiet word. Best to get this kind of bollocks smoothed out before it even happens."

"Would you?"

She smiled. "You have to pick up my bar tab."

"Deal. And thanks."

"I'm just looking after number one. Ainsley thinks the sun shines out of your arse, remember?" She winked. "Leave it with me."

Savi walked through the international hub and straight into Rome's Municipio III metro network. Five hubs later and she was out on Via Monte Massico, a sloping road in the Tufell area, lined by high trees that partially obscured the five-story apartment blocks on both sides. Sunlight was only just beginning to filter through the boughs that interlaced above the pavement, forming a verdant tunnel.

She loved Rome, but at this time of year and this early in the morning, it was almost as damp and cold as Edinburgh. The only difference was that the trees here were all evergreens, though even those in the sheltered yard at the front of her apartment block seemed lackluster right now, waiting for the warmer spring air to pep them up.

Her apartment was on the second floor, so she ignored the creaky old lift and climbed the stairs, her bugez lumbering along after her. She'd chosen the one-bedroom place for its compact size. Nice for one person to live in by herself, especially after twenty-three years crammed into a comfortable Mumbai house with a large family. Here there was quiet and solitude. Family was welcome to visit, but wouldn't be able to stay.

The house G4Turing had used its flock of drudgez to vacuum the carpets and clean the surfaces while she was away on her Caribbean break, even polishing the centerpiece rosewood table properly. When she got to the galley kitchen, the fridge was properly stocked. She took out the pot of organic yogurt and fresh milk, then measured out a cafetière with natural ground beans from the delicatessen two streets away.

After a quick shower to wash away the last of Barbuda's insidious sand, she put on a robe and went back into the tiny kitchen. The yogurt had lost its chill, the way she liked it, and the coffee had brewed properly. She sprinkled granola into a bowl and poured the yogurt on top.

After four days of indulgent, large, and highly Westernized breakfasts delivered to the Diana Klub villa's balcony, it was quite a relief to come home to this. The memory made her hold up her hand and admire the single gold ring she was now wearing.

I'm married!

While she ate breakfast, she told Nelson, her mInet, to run the Icefall news streams. Preparations were well underway for the first fall day. Connexion's giant airships were buzzing along a kilometer above Australia's Gibson Desert in a careful holding pattern. Meanwhile, farther south, in Antarctic waters, the harvester boats were circling Iceberg V-71, which had broken off the Ross Ice Shelf three months ago. It was a colossus, with a surface area of 2,850 kilometers, making it larger than Luxembourg. Nelson refined the filter for any mention of opposition groups, political or active. There were a few global and Australia-based ecological groups posting about the sacrilege on social media, but not much of that was relayed by the mainstream. The Walungurru People's Review was more strident, but it wasn't saying anything new.

As always, the prospect of jobs and fresh money pouring into the outback *now* was winning the day. Deserts didn't have many committed friends in 2092.

Savi checked the time and went back into the bedroom. The bugez was standing obediently at the foot of the bed. She opened the luggage panniers and carefully placed all her dirty linen into the laundry basket ready for the concierge service to collect. Her lips twitched— *not that I wore much.*

She gazed at the gold ring again and very reluctantly took it off. It went in her jewelry box in the bedside cabinet. Cal had promised an engagement ring as soon as her assignment finished. "I know we did it backward, but you still deserve the set."

I miss him already. It shouldn't have happened, but I'm so glad it did. Maybe it is true: Opposites attract. Except we're not really that different.

He's smart, and funny, which is more than most men. And considerate, and oversensitive in that way Western men can be. She sighed. *And behaves like a sixteen-year-old half the time. Which is quite fun.*

Her gaze was drawn to the bed. Cal had stayed over several times, which left her with some memories—

Stop it!

She dressed in neutral clothes, blue denim jeans and a thick purple roll-top sweater; flat-soled pumps and a simple leather bag. Her long hair was plaited with practiced efficiency. To finish, she slipped into a pair of wire-rimmed screen glasses. She inspected herself in the mirror and nodded in satisfaction. Nothing special, nothing that would draw attention in a crowd. One of hundreds of thousands of identical young women thronging through Rome's metrohubs, on their way to their corporate offices to fend off another day's overfamiliarity from male managers.

Outside, the sun was making progress up the sky. Sharp, bright beams were slicing through the canopy of leaves as she walked back to the hub on the junction with Via Monte Eporneo. Five hubs took her to the center, where she switched to the national network. The Naples hub had a portal door into Connexion's internal network. Eight hubs later she emerged onto the ground floor of a skyscraper in Sydney's central business district.

The glass walls of the big lobby looked out onto a nighttime city, with pedestrian roads long since cleared of clubbers. Even with the air-conditioning thrumming away, she could feel the heat radiating in from the concrete pavement outside. A night watchman glanced up from his desk and gave her a quick wave.

She got into the lift and sensors performed a deep scan. Only then did the lift take her up to the fifteenth floor: the Security offices.

Here, Australia's time zone didn't apply. The fifteenth floor was wrapped in one-way glass that didn't allow anyone to look in, day or night, so nobody could see a department that kept the same operational level twenty-four/seven. Its layout of corridors and offices was similar to any of the commercial departments in the building; but instead of the usual conference rooms, there were armories and special equipment centers. Right at the center, through another two sets of safe checks, was the active ops center.

Australia's head of station's office was next to it. The door slid open to allow Savi in.

Yuri Alster looked up from the semicircle of screens on his desk. "You're late," he said.

"No, I'm not." Savi didn't much like Yuri. Thankfully, that wasn't a requirement of the job, but she certainly respected his toughness. His infiltration operations brought impressive results. She'd been on two of them so far and seen firsthand how his field agents were deployed to maximum effect. It didn't matter what a new operative's file said, or how well they'd done in training and simulations. Yuri was only interested how they performed in the field. If anyone showed emotional weakness, they were out, and he made sure your first mission would slam you straight up against cutting moral dilemmas.

For her first operation, he'd given Savi a case involving two brothers who were trying to sting a Connexion manager to pay for their mother's medical treatment. The woman had a brain tumor that needed some very expensive drugs. Savi always suspected he'd known her own mother had been treated for cancer, even though it wasn't in her file. She hadn't wavered. The brothers had got seven years for attempted extortion. Their mother had died eight months later.

"I hope you enjoyed yourself," he said. "We have the plastic explosive ready for you. Technical support tweaked the formula, so it's only ten percent as powerful as the real stuff. Even so, be careful around it."

"That's good. Should prevent too much damage. Thank tech support for me."

"You got a cover story?"

"Yes, sir." She half expected him to ask for it. But this wasn't high school, and she wasn't sitting an exam. A cover story was required, so a cover story for her short absence had been fabricated to tie in with her fake identity. It hadn't taken her long.

"All right." He tilted back in his chair. Savi just knew she was being judged. He treated everyone like that—with suspicion. Rumor around the department said he was ex–Russian Federal Security. He'd been in the border security department of the Russian National Portal Transport Company when it merged with Connexion; plenty of his colleagues had been made redundant, but he'd made it through the reorganization and come out in a strong position. Connexion Security approved of his methodology and the efficient way he ran his intelligence gathering agents, infiltrating them into anti-Connexion groups. "When are you going back in?" he asked her.

"Right away. Akkar wanted the charges by tomorrow, so I'm guessing their attack will be timed for first fall. Maximize the publicity."

"Okay. So you know, Ainsley himself will be at Kintore, too, for the starting ceremony."

"Shit."

"Which means Poi Li will be there." His finger pointed at the wall between him and the active ops center. "Making very sure no one gets near Ainsley, especially anyone hauling plastic explosives around. So this needs to go right, or we'll both be hunting new jobs."

"Got it."

"If the charges are for a suicide vest, we need to know right away."

"I don't think that's what Akkar is planning. But I'll update you via micropulse. Tech support seeded Kintore with relays, so I can shout from anywhere in the town. Akkar's group don't have the tech to spot that."

"Let's hope."

"I know them. They're dedicated politicals and greens, several hotheads busting for a fight, even some good technos and hacktivists, but they're not at this level."

"Yes, I read your report."

Of course you did, she thought. In a way, it was reassuring. She was almost tempted to blurt out that she was married—*just get it over with.* But she couldn't risk him pulling her off the case until Cal was vetted. Procedure was Yuri's bible.

"Sir." She got up to leave.

"What did you do?"

"Excuse me?"

"Your long weekend off. What did you do?"

"I went to the Caribbean. With a girlfriend; she thinks I'm a company economics analyst. We stayed at a spa; had a lot of treatments and drank cocktails in the beach bar. It was relaxing. Just what I needed."

"Uh huh." He returned to the semicircle of screens. "Well, make sure you don't smell nice when you get back to Kintore. Poverty-line cause-committed politics students don't go on middle-class spa breaks. Remember, it's the simplest things that can derail an op."

"Yes, sir. Thank you." Savi couldn't even summon up a mental sneer. He was quite right.

She went down to the prep facility. In the changing room she deactivated Nelson and put her gold smartCuff (a present from her father when she got the Connexion job) on her locker's top shelf, along with her screen glasses. Poor Cal would go slowly crazy when she didn't call, but she'd make it up to him. Next she stripped down to nothing, hanging up her jeans and sweater; pumps went on the bottom of the locker. She shut the door, keying it to her fingerprint, and leaving Savi Chaudhri hanging in limbo alongside her clothes.

Time for Osha Kulkarni, disaffected politics student, to return to the cause and fight capitalist imperialism with the only tools the corporate fat cats ever took seriously. Osha's clothes were in the next locker exactly where she'd left them, unwashed. Heavily used olive-green jeans, a sleeveless brown t-shirt. Trainers with soles almost worn through. Kangaroo-skin outback hat—though no corks dangling around the rim; she drew the line at that cliché. Cheap screen sunglasses with audio facility. A decades-old watch that seemed to be running a three-year-old mInet program tagged Misra, which bloated the strap's ancient processor. Finally, a backpack that'd been bleached several shades lighter by the sunlight of three continents.

Sometimes she worried Osha fit the angry young woman profile a little too well.

Tech support after the changing room, and there was Tarli waiting for her, yawning heavily. He held up a pair of resealable plastic food boxes.

"Your explosives. Please be careful with this stuff."

Smiling, she took the boxes from him and started putting them in her backpack, under her spare clothes. "I thought it was only TNT that blows up when you drop it."

"I'm sure it is. But just don't make any sudden moves while you're next to me."

"You take such good care of me, Tarli."

"I do, don't I? Okay, let's run your super spy kit."

She held her arm out. Tarli swept a scanner over her hand, his eyes dream-staring as he watched the data thrown up in his contact screen lenses.

"All right, your tracker grain is good. We can trigger a ping any-time if we need to. We'll always be able to find you, Savi. So you're safe."

"Fine. And Osha's mInet?"

"Old, crappy, and slow if anyone takes a keen interest. But level two is running in parallel underneath. You can use it to compose a message and squirt it out in a micropulse. Your *antique* watch is the primary. But if they're properly paranoid, you'll be told not to wear it on the mission, so the tracker grain will take over. Give active ops a test call, please."

"Misra?" she asked, subvocalizing for her audio grain. "Give ops a location ping."

"Confirmed," Misra replied.

"Got you, Savi," the level voice of active ops replied. "Full reception."

She nodded at Tarli, trying to reign in her nerves. "Thank you." It was always bad just before she hit the street, heart pumping away, anxiety making her jumpy. Once she was out there and the assignment was underway, she'd smooth out fine.

"Hey, I'm going to be in the active ops center myself when this one hits the fan," Tarli said. "Don't worry, I've got your back."

"Good to know."

"Come on, I'll walk you through to Brisbane."

They went through four hubs to a Connexion subsidiary building in Brisbane. Outside, the sun was starting to rise. The Brisbane Security office was a locked room that had a single portal inside.

"Good luck," Tarli said. "You're on truck eight-five-one. Pete's driving it."

"Got it."

"Go get 'em."

The portal came out in a toilet cubicle. She unbolted the door and looked around. It was inside a metal cargo container, one of six identical cubicles. Nobody about. When she closed it, the bolt slid back, locking it. There was an "Out of Order" sign pinned to the door.

She went outside into a swirl of warm dusty air. The old portable toilet container had been dropped next to a high chain fence that enclosed an area almost eight kilometers across: the North Brisbane Commercial and Government Services Transport Hub (C & GST). She thought it looked like a protective pen for endangered vehicles. There was hardly any greenery, just an expanse of tracks worn into rust-red earth that had spent a decade being compacted beneath big pounding tires until it reached the consistency of concrete. Various civil engineering companies had their own compounds staked out in the area, where big earthmovers and civil construction machinery were parked. Container stacks were laid out in grids like small towns, with G4Turing-managed gantries lifting them on and off flatbed trucks.

Right in the middle of the transport hub was a broad ring of tarmac, as if a land reclamation team had forgotten to break up a chunk of old highway. Around the outside of the ring, its off-ramps were just tongues of concrete leading to the tangle of dirt tracks snaking across the C & GST. The inner rim, however, hosted a circle of six-meter portals laid out like some modern homage to Neolithic standing stones. Even this early in the morning, trucks were rumbling around the tarmac, their powerful electric motors whining loudly in the still dawn air as they drove in and out of the portals. Only a few had human drivers in their cabs; the rest were truckez.

Savi left the toilet container behind, walking across the hard, rutted ground to the nearest container zone. She saw only a couple of other people wandering about, both in hi-viz jackets stained with the ruddy dust. If they saw her they didn't pay any attention.

Misra threw a nav guide across her screen sunglasses, and she wound up at the end of a container row where a truck was parked on the loading pad. It had "851" painted on the side of its cab. Someone (presumably Pete) sat inside, not looking down at her. She stood in the shade of the containers as the gantry slid along the row and carefully lowered a battered blue container onto the truck. Once the gantry moved away, Savi clambered up the couplings and found herself a ledge in the broad gap between cab and trailer. She jammed her feet against some cable, bracing herself, when the axle motors began buzzing, and 851 moved off.

They drove along one of the tracks, heading for the big loop of tarmac. She breathed in the grubby air, relishing the role she was now immersing herself in.

If Callum could see me now.

He'd be having kittens, she knew. Maybe one day she'd tell him. When they were home and cozy. In twenty years' time. After he'd had a lot of beer.

She daydreamed about what they were going to do next. No way did she want to leave fabulous Rome, certainly not for freezing Edinburgh. The Scottish capital was pretty enough, but even in summer it was bloody cold. And she certainly wasn't going to move into Cal's slob-out bachelor pad. He was going to need some serious house training once they got a place together.

Savi nearly asked Misra for the *agenzie immobiliari* who'd found

the Tufell flat for her, before she realized Misra wasn't the mInet storing that file, and Osha certainly wouldn't have had any reason to access it. The mistake chilled her mood. Yuri was right; it was the
simple things that betrayed you.

Truckez adjusted their speed, allowing 851 to slot into the stream
of traffic going around the tarmac ring. A minute later they drove
through the portal to Kintore. The town was half a continent away
from Brisbane, so it was still the middle of the night there. Darkness
closed around her, and the temperature took a big leap upward. Even
growing up in India didn't acclimatize Savi for the scorching desert
air. It was the lack of humidity, she'd realized the first time she came
to Kintore. Desert air was dead air.

Originally Kintore was a remote Northern Territory town, founded
in the early 1980s by the Pintupi people, who resented the white
Western culture that was slowly constricting them. After that it kept
going in its quiet way for a century until the newly formed Water
Desert consortium signed its deal with the investment-hungry Australian government.

Once again the Pintupi suffered a massively disruptive invasion.
For the last five years Kintore had expanded exponentially as Connexion set up the C & GST portal linking it to Brisbane, turning the
town's abandoned airstrip into a huge cargo and civil engineering
facility. Along with the heavy-duty earthmoving equipment pouring
through the C & GST portal, truckez brought prefab cabins for the
hardy site workers who didn't commute in every day from the coastal
areas. Bars and clubs and stores followed the money trail, along with
other services—some legitimate, some otherwise, all bringing in
their own prefabs. With such a population bump, the government
started to expand its own infrastructure. And if Icefall was successful
in transforming the desert, Kintore would double in size again within
two years.

Truck 851 slowed down near the edge of the old airfield, and Savi
jumped down. The walk into town wasn't far, for which she was
grateful. Kintore even had a tiny portal network of its own, but she

didn't want to use it. Everyone knew Connexion had sensors around each of its hubs, scanning for illegal substances such as drugs and weapons. The plastic explosives would have brought a whole platoon of urban suppression forces down on her, probably with drone support. Most of Kintore's illegal drugs were brought in through the C & GST route by truck drivers. If she'd come through any other way, Akkar would have been suspicious.

She reached her digs—a new boardinghouse of silvered composite panels that'd been dropped down on the west side of town, identical to every other building on the street. There were still several hours until dawn, so she flopped down on her bed and turned the air-con up. Five minutes later she was asleep.

Breakfast was a croissant in the Granite Shelf, one of the new cafés on what was now a long Main Street. A limp oblong of pastry that'd been microwaved for too long. The little cube of butter that came with it was as cold as ice. But the orange juice wasn't too bad. The waitress put it down with a semi-apologetic expression and hurried off to take an order from a group of digger drivers who'd just come off shift.

Savi gazed out of the window. The desert soil surrounding Kintore was rust-red, broken only by wispy tufts of petrified grass, bleached to a cream-white by the relentless sun. Today, like every day for the last two years, the air was stained with dust. Somewhere out across the desert, massive irrigation canals were being dug. Hundreds of kilometers long, they were destined to channel water across the parched lands, allowing the desert to bloom again. If Icefall worked, it would ultimately become an oasis more than a thousand kilometers across. Theoretically that would create its own new microclimate, changing wind patterns and luring in rain clouds from the coast.

But in the meantime, the powerful diggers working twenty-four/seven were kicking up dust that lingered for days in the tranquil air. A lot of people had taken to wearing plastic surgical masks when they were outside. What with the empty canals, the locals had started to call the whole enterprise Barsoom. The Mars reference wasn't pleasantly ironic.

After she finished eating, Savi put on her own mask and tramped down Main Street for a kilometer before turning off onto Rosewalk. Akkar had a tiny store repairing air-conditioning units—possibly the greatest boom business in Kintore. The dust was forever clogging motors and filters across town, giving Akkar as much work as he chose to accept.

She knocked on the bugez garage door at the back, giving the camera on the frame above a mildly pissed look. It opened, and she walked through into the gloomy composite cave. First glance revealed a typical printer store operation with metal shelving holding cartons of liquid crudes, plastics, and metals, ready to feed the printers. One cabinet down the far end held vials of the more expensive crudes, those used to produce electronics or pharma. Medium-size printers were lined up along the back wall, their central glass hatches making them look for all the world like a line of washing machines. Eye-twisting violet light shone out through the glass as they chittered away, building up components molecule by molecule in their extrusion cores. A couple of long benches held broken down air conditioners and impressive racks of electronics.

Akkar was sitting in a battered office chair, using a small vacuum nozzle to clear a filter grid. He was a tall North African in his late thirties, with a shaved scalp and plenty of tattoos chasing up his neck from a muscular torso that was always wearing vintage t-shirts with the logos of long-departed gamer companies. The tails of those tattoos snaked out of his sleeves to coil around his arms. When he spoke, light would sparkle on the rubies embedded in his teeth. He was one of the few people who could make Savi nervous just by him looking at her. Like Yuri, he was perpetually judging everyone.

"Welcome back," he said. "I heard you got in early this morning."

Savi glanced at the two other people in the garage. Dimon was a lot larger and even more menacing than Akkar, filling the role of lieutenant and enforcer. He never spoke much, and when he did it was in a whisper that emphasized his words more than any shout. Unlike most of Kintore's residents, he always wore a smart suit, which made him look like an ex–sports star.

Julisa sat in a chair next to Akkar, a twenty-two-year-old from Cairns, whose family used to run a crocodile farm just outside the town. Its bankruptcy and subsequent sale by the banks to developers hungry for such a prime chunk of land kicked her environmentalism into something approaching religious devotion, drawing her deeper into the movement until she reached the status of Akkar's cyber queen. She was painfully thin, surviving off caffeine and nose candy, as far as Savi could tell. Bleached blond hair was cut to an all-over centimeter bristle, giving her the face of an angry, strung-out pixie.

"I didn't tell anyone that," Savi said. She was impressed as always by Akkar's intel. Given he refused to use the internet or any kind of mobile network to communicate with his radical friends, he had to have a pack of real people watching Kintore's barren streets. *At four o'clock in the morning?*

"I know." He smiled. Violet printer light twinkled off his teeth jewels. "Did you get it?"

Savi nodded, giving herself a long moment of satisfaction, showing them how pleased she was with herself, how committed. "Sure." She unslung her backpack, and brought out the two plastic food boxes. "Don't drop it," she warned as Julisa picked one up eagerly.

"You have interesting friends," Dimon said.

"Who said they were friends?" she shot back.

Akkar held up a hand. "You've done well, Osha. Thank you for bringing us this."

"Does this get me in on the action?" she asked.

"Do you want to get into the action?"

"I want to do something, make people take notice of what's really going on here. Posting rants on MyLife don't do shit."

He glanced over at Julisa, who had carefully opened one of the food boxes. She stuck a small sensor on it, and glanced at the readout on a screen.

"Real," she said.

"Okay," Akkar said slowly. "Three days' time."

"First fall," she said approvingly.

"Yes."

"What do you want me to do?"

"Turn up here at eight. We'll give you something to do."

"Okay."

"Aren't you curious?"

She returned his gaze steadily. "Yes, but I get how security works. If you don't know, you can't tell."

"Smart girl. But I'll be asking you to plant some of this fine explosive you've brought us. Do you have a problem with that?"

"Just tell me, will I have to put it near people?"

"No. People are not the target. Life is sacred."

"Okay." She slung her backpack on again. "Be seeing you."

Savi walked home slowly and used Misra to message active ops.

I've been told the operation will happen on first fall. 90% certain that's for real. They're being cautious. I will be taking part. Details as soon as I find out what they're doing.

Misra sent it in a microsecond pulse while she was still on Main Street. Savi wouldn't have put it past Julisa to put e-surveillance around her digs.

An answering pulse came thirty seconds later.

Stay safe.
  Yuri.

The gigantic earthmoving equipment digging canals across the desert stopped work at midnight before first fall day. Desert Water's PR agency hoped that would at least reduce the quantity of infernal red dust in the air by the time the great event began midmorning, allowing cameras a decent view. All the big vehicles began driving across the desert for Kintore's airstrip field, where the contractors had scheduled them for maintenance.

A lot of people started arriving through Kintore's portals as dawn began to break, coming in not just from Australia's cities but from across the globe. Icefall promised to be quite a spectacle.

From Kintore, they went through a newly installed portal to a viewing area that had been prepared ninety kilometers from the town. Long tents serving iced drinks and snacks had been set up, along with air-conditioned medical marquees ready for the inevitable heatstrokes. One of the dry canals ran close by, its three-hundred-meter width giving everyone a sense of the project's scale.

A temporary VIP stadium had been built inside a high security fence, its overhanging roof protecting the dignitaries from the severe sunlight, but nothing could be done to keep the desert heat at bay. The forecast had it rising to thirty-three degrees Celsius by mid-morning.

Savi had never seen so many people in the desert town before. A month ago, Cal had taken her to a football match in Manchester. The crowds of boisterous supporters pouring into the stadium gates had been easier to push through than this. Everyone was heading along Main Street to the portal that would take them to the viewing area.

She made it to Akkar's store and went into the bugez garage. There were a dozen people inside, most of whom she recognized from the anti-Icefall meetings that Akkar had used to recruit them. These were his senior cell leaders, each of them in charge of around fifteen activists as far as she'd been able to determine. *So, over 150 mobilized for today, then.*

Julisa saw her and came over. "You ready for this?"

"Sure."

She was led to the back of the garage, where two young men were waiting beside the silent printers. They were introduced as Ketchell and Larik. "We're relying on you three," Julisa said in a low voice. "You've got the second most critical role today."

Which Savi didn't believe for a second. She knew she still wasn't fully trusted, that it would take several events like today to prove herself to them. *Events that are never going to happen, thanks to what I'm doing now.*

The lanky girl handed Savi a leather shoulder bag. The men were given small backpacks.

"Your target is the substation at the end of Fountain Street," Julisa went on. "That's where the whole town's electricity comes in via portal from the national grid. It's a huge amount of power; the damn thing supplies every piece of equipment Water Desert uses. So, this is how it happens. There's a three-meter-high fence around the transformers and switching gear, which is topped by razor wire. There's one super secure gate, which they've rigged with all sorts of scans and codes. We're not going in or over. You're going to blow a hole in the fence. The charge in your bag is armed by a dual-action switch. Look."

Savi peered into the bag, seeing the neat cube of plastic explosive with a small rectangle of electronics on the end. The only feature was a red hexagonal switch that seemed disproportionally large.

"Turn clockwise one eighty, and press," Julisa said. "Okay? Simple; twist and press."

"Got it."

"Once it's armed it cannot be disarmed. I've set the timer to detonate at exactly ten fifty-seven local time. So at about ten fifty-five you stroll past the fence, arm the charge, and drop the bag beside a post. Then you get away fast."

"Okay."

"Once the fence is breached, Ketchell and Larik, you're in there right away. Your targets are the two main transformers. Here." She showed them a crude map of the substation, with the transformers marked. "It's easy enough. Arm your backpacks. Drop your backpacks. They will detonate at eleven oh-three. Now they're bigger charges than Osha's, but we've built in enough time for you to get in and out. Any questions?"

"That's it?" Savi asked.

"That's it. Look, this is all about distraction. The ice starts to fall at ten thirty. We've got a lot of supporters crowded into the viewing area. They'll start a protest demonstration at ten forty-five outside the VIP enclosure. Smoke bombs, netruptors, throw some stones at security—fuck knows there's enough rocks lying around. That's where Water Desert will be looking to protect their precious guests— all the celebrities, corporate fat cats, and public pig parasites. So you get in and cut the power to the whole fucking town."

"What good is that going to do?"

"You don't need to know."

"Like bollocks! I never asked for details, but we're taking a huge risk here. For what? Cutting power to everyone's air conditioner for a few hours?"

"Problem?" Akkar asked. He was standing right behind her. She hadn't noticed him approaching.

"No," she said. "I'm happy to help. I asked for this gig, remember. I just need some assurance this isn't a token statement."

"It's not," Akkar said softly. "Trust me, Osha. Today is unique, and not because of Icefall. Today Water Desert has put a lot of its most expensive eggs in one basket. And thanks to Julisa's skills, we're going to crack them open. You will provide us with that window of opportunity."

Savi gave him a hard glance. "Okay," she said. "That sounds more like it."

"Good luck," he said. "All of you. We'll meet back here in thirty-six hours."

As she left the garage, she saw Dimon handing out home-printed semiautomatic rifles to three other men. He saw her watching, and Savi gave him an approving nod. Dimon grinned in return.

Outside, Savi, Ketchell, and Larik set off across town, avoiding Main Street and the crush of eager Icefall spectators.

"I've got my team waiting for instructions," Larik said. "How do you think we should deploy them?"

"Deploy them?" Savi said. "We don't. You heard Julisa; this is the three of us."

"Yeah, we have the primary task, sure," Larik said. "But what happens if there's a security patrol heading our way five minutes before we blast the fence? We need coverage. So whoever you think you are, you shut the fuck up and leave me to get on with my fucking job—of which you know fuck all. Clear?"

"The hell with you, dickbrain," Savi pressed back on a smile, enjoying the way she'd been designated a necessary pain. He didn't realize it, but he now included her as part of the team. The only thing he'd suspect now was that she'd screw up. Posting lookouts might be a problem, though.

She composed a message for Misra to send.

Large group activity starting. Distraction protest planned for observation zone 10.45. I am on team assigned to blow the substation on Fountain Street. Explosives pre-set for 10.57 to take out fence. Transformers targeted for 11.03. Location of main target unknown. I've seen home-printed semiautomatics handed out to group members.

Good work, *came the answering micropulse*. Do you know nature of main target?

Savi thought back, Exact target unknown, but it's a software attack, assembled by Julisa. The power cut will allow them access. Akkar said Water Desert has all its eggs in one basket. May be up to forty people involved.

Thanks. Analyzing now. Watching you. Tarli.

Savi kept her gaze level as they tramped through Kintore's back-streets. But it was so tempting to look up at the sky and wave at whatever satellite or drone active ops was using to observe her.

They met up with several of Larik's team as they made their indirect way to the substation. Larik and Ketchell studied a street map of Kintore on their screen sunglasses and assigned people to various road junctions around Fountain Street. Savi immediately sent their locations to active ops.

By twenty past ten, Kintore itself was practically deserted. Everyone who'd arrived to witness first fall was out at the observation zone, along with every local who was off duty. A news stream playing across Savi's screen sunglasses showed her the guests, including Ainsley Zangari himself, taking their place on the VIP stand.

Down in the Antarctic, the five Connexion harvester boats closed on V-71. Ex-navy frigates, their prows had undergone a drastic profile alteration during the refit. Instead of a sleek wedge shape, they were now bulging hemispheres ten meters wide, presenting the open maw of a portal to the frozen sea, like the mouth of a giant whale. Below the hull, two extra sets of newly installed propellers turned slowly, their huge electric motors powered from the global power grid via portal. They weren't designed to give the harvesters extra speed. Rather, their phenomenal torque allowed them to push the vessel forward relentlessly.

At just after ten thirty, the first harvester reached the sheer cliff of blue ice, its captain curving around so the portal rim grazed the surface at a thin angle, but then immediately sliced deeper inward. The propellers spun up, maintaining the ship's speed and momentum as fractured ice began to fall into the portal. For a brief moment, desert sunlight shone out of the gaping hemisphere, then the front of the harvester was almost completely buried in the cliff. Yet it continued to churn along parallel to the ice, gouging out a nine-meter-wide gash. Behind it, the second harvester struck the cliff at a similar angle, its portal biting deep.

In the desert observation zone, people squinted up into the glaring sapphire sky. The long, dark ovals of the airships maintained their positions a kilometer above the desert's desiccated white grass and Mars-red soil, five klicks from the front of the VIP stadium. It was close enough to see everything.

Gasps came from the crowd as a slim stream of glittering white splinters began to fall from the belly of an airship. It quickly grew wider, so that by the time the first few boulders of Antarctic ice smashed onto the desert, the flow was nine meters wide as it emerged from the portal slung below the airship. By that time, the second cascade of ice had begun from the neighboring airship.

Cheering and enthusiastic applause filled the dry air. By ten forty, all five airships had solid white cataracts pouring out, catching the sunlight in a dazzling refraction blaze as they tumbled downward. On the ground below, the five ice cones began to grow upward and outward with remarkable speed, their surface a constant avalanche of shattered ice. Subzero vapor churned up out of them, flowing with the viscosity of oil. The wave front of fog obscured the land, billowing upward to thin out and disperse as the heat of the sun finally began to impact.

The entranced crowd waited for the final aspect of the promised miracle: to be enveloped by freezing mist in the middle of a desert. As the brilliant cloud rolled toward them, angry shouts began to rise above the background buzz of chanting and laughter. Placards were raised. Fireworks rockets zoomed unnervingly low over heads. Smoke bombs were thrown. Cheers turned to screams. Lines of riot-shield-equipped police and corporate security officers snaked through the throng. Stones began to rise in short arcs. The screams grew louder. Images playing across the big screens that had been set up across the zone to show everyone dramatic close-up shots of the harvesters and airships broke up into a mash of static.

The crowd surged in random directions as people struggled to get away from the protestors. Police strove to get past them. Just as the chaos on the ground reached its peak, a colossal wall of fog rolled across the observation zone, blotting out the sun in a blast of cold so profound it seemed to suck oxygen from the very air. Then the panic frenzy really struck.

· · ·

Whoever named it Fountain Street clearly had a very misplaced sense of irony. Savi looked along the depressing track, with drab single-story prefab cabins on both sides, that led away from the intersection ahead of her. The compacted soil here probably hadn't seen any free-flowing water this side of Earth's last ice age. A double irony, she thought, considering what was visiting the desert today.

It was definitely the poorer side of town, home to the laborers who sweated through the endless, changeless desert days performing Water Desert's dirty, low-paid jobs. Their kids were left behind to find what fun they could amid the tired silvered boxes where they lived. One gang was playing basketball in an open area that passed for a park, trying to slam-dunk their ball into hoops on poles that were now leaning badly.

Savi had her white paper mask on again, like Ketchell and Larik, who walked along with her. Nobody could see their faces. But that didn't matter; all the kids and the few adults sitting outside their homes knew they didn't belong. Not that they cared.

What do you want me to do? *Savi asked active ops.* When are you going to intercept?

We are working on isolating the main target group. Continue with your mission.

Confirmed, *she sent back.*

Her apprehension was growing, and with it the thrill. What she was doing was going to take a lot of these people out of circulation. It was all that mattered to her. Talish would be proud. It was eight years now since her little cousin had been caught in the crossfire between the police and a radical group called Path of Light, as the militants stormed a government building in Noida. He had his cyber legs now, and an artificial kidney, but for three months the whole family had been immersed in an agony of waiting and praying around his hospital bed. Now Savi was playing her part in making sure no other innocents got hurt by psychotic ideologues who believed they had an absolute right to use force to achieve their goal.

> Arrest team moving into your area, *active ops sent*.
>   They're going to have to hurry. Only six minutes left.
>   These are our own real special forces. You're getting the red carpet treatment. Told you I've got your back.

She smiled beneath her mask.

They reached the end of Fountain Street. The substation was twenty meters ahead of them, a small square compound with a high gray metal fence around it, the base clotted with fast food wrappers and loose clumps of desert grass. She could hear the hum of the transformers as they fed power across the town and out to the airfield, keeping the air-con going and the civil engineering machines moving. Kintore's consumption was phenomenal.

It was twenty-three years since the China National Sunpower Corporation had dropped the first solarwell into the sun, a simple spherical portal that plasma poured into, whose twin was sitting at the bottom of a giant MHD chamber on a trans-Neptune asteroid. The solar plasma flared out of the chamber like rocket exhaust, its powerful magnetic field generating a phenomenal current in the chamber's induction coils. In one masterful stroke of ingenuity, the Chinese had solved Earth's energy drought. Now the entire planet's power came from a multitude of solarwells, producing vast amounts of cheap energy at zero environmental cost.

Ten fifty-two. Five minutes left to go, and they started loitering around the last houses. Three other roads ended in the same area. There was nothing on the other side of the substation other than the desert. Kids laughed and shouted behind them.

Savi turned to Ketchell. "Have your people seen anything?" As he swung around she caught a glimpse of the shoulder holster he was wearing under his white cotton jacket, weighed down by a large automatic pistol. *Oh, shit.*

"No. We're clear. Let's do this."

Some of the group with me are armed. Warn the arrest team.

Will do.

They began sauntering along the stony road. Savi put her hand into the bag and found the hexagonal switch. There was only a moment's hesitation before she turned it. *I hope to hell Julisa built this right.* She pressed down, hearing the button click.

Ketchell and Larik both glanced at her when she exhaled loudly. "It's armed," she said.

Ten fifty-three.

They reached the fence. Savi kept walking but unslung the bag. She dropped it at the base of a post.

Without saying anything, the three of them picked up their pace. Thirty seconds later they reached the top of Rennison Road. They crouched down behind a flimsy fence marking out a prefab's yard. Savi worried the thin composite might fragment in the blast, producing a blizzard of shrapnel. "Did anyone see us?" she asked urgently.

"All quiet," Larik said. He started putting in a pair of foam earplugs.

"Damn," Savi grunted. "You got any spare?"

He gave her another of his contemptuous glances and handed her a couple. She squeezed the first plug and started to worm it in. Something moved across the stony ground behind her. She stared in disbelief. A football was rolling out of Fountain Street heading straight for the substation. "No," she whispered.

Ketchell looked at her; then he saw the ball and his eyes widened in shock. "Shit."

The ball was only a few meters from the fence, and a boy was trotting along behind it; he was maybe eight or nine years old.

"No." Savi stood up. "No, get back."

"Stay down," Ketchell growled at her.

"Get away," Savi yelled. "Away!"

The boy looked around, seeing a woman wearing a white plastic mask waving frantically. He cocked his head and carried on following his ball.

"Fuck!" Savi screeched. All she saw now was Talish, lying in his hospital bed, with so many tubes and organ support machines inserted into his flesh he'd ceased to become purely human. She started running.

"No!" Larik bellowed behind her.

The boy had almost reached the ball, which was rolling to a halt a couple of meters from the fence, level with the abandoned shoulder bag. He turned again, his expression growing uncertain as Savi sprinted hard toward him. "Get away, get away," she yelled frantically.

He didn't know what to do. He took an uncertain step back, away from the wild eyes of the crazy woman. Then he realized she wasn't going to stop, that she was going to run right into him. He turned and started to run.

She flung her arms around him, picking him up despite his frightened wail and thrashing limbs. She kept running, desperate to build distance between her and the bag.

Savi saw a flash, then nothing—

The waiting room for the surgical wards was neutral in every respect. Pale gray carpet, white walls, with twin floor-to-ceiling windows looking out over nighttime Brisbane. Two rows of back-to-back settees were lined up down the center, their cushions thick and comfortable enough for worried families to spend the night curled up on them. High quality vending machines and a big wallscreen silently running news streams completed the décor.

Yuri Alster had been waiting in it for more than an hour, but refused to sit. It meant his deputy, Kohei Yamada, couldn't sit, either, which clearly pissed him off no end. They were the only two in the waiting room.

Finally, long after midnight, the Reardon family came out of Ward Two. Ben Reardon was a short, bulky man in his early forties, with a bald head and a face that looked like it had been squashed flat. He seemed angry, which Yuri suspected was a permanent expression.

Ben was employed running the machines that dug out the Icefall canals—tough work that he was well suited to. Dani, the current girlfriend, was barely twenty. A cliché relationship, Yuri decided, endorsed by her short denim skirt, showing off heavily tanned thighs, and a cheap green sport shirt that had the Alcides café logo on both sleeves.

They walked down the corridor on either side of nine-year-old Toby Reardon's wheelchair, as the boy was pushed along by a ward nurse. Ben scowled as Yuri stood in front of them.

"What do you want?" he asked, exhaustion and fear giving him a raspy voice.

"Just a couple of questions for Toby," Yuri said as pleasantly as he could. He winked at the boy, whose cheeks and right arm were covered in patches of medskin. There was a cast holding one leg rigid, too.

"No way," Ben snapped. "We've answered every question a dozen times."

"I'm not police," Yuri said. "I'm from Connexion Security."

"Clear off, mate. Come back in a week. My boy got blown up. You understand that? He's nine years old, and the bastards blew him up!"

"I know. And Connexion's medical plan covers your family, even for this. That's worth a minute, surely?"

Ben took a step forward, his fists bunching. "Are you threatening me?"

"I'm asking you to do the right thing."

"I don't mind, Dad," Toby said.

"We're going home!"

"A few questions and you won't see me again, okay? I can arrange for an extra week's paid leave, which you can spend here in the city, or maybe in a Gold Coast resort—next to the sea. Be nice, that. Big change from Kintore. You can be with Toby while he recovers. That's something we all want, isn't it?"

Ben hesitated, clearly hating himself for being tempted.

"It'd be good," Dani said tentatively.

Ben ignored her. "How about it, big fella?" he asked Toby. "Only if you're up to it."

"Game on, Dad."

Ben glared at Yuri. "Be quick."

"Sure." Yuri knelt down so his face was level with Toby's. "Did the doctors fix you up okay?"

"Yeah. I guess."

"So, you were playing football, right?"

"Yeah, with some of me mates. It's my ball, see. Dad gave it to me. I think it's gone now. I didn't see it after."

"I'll get you another one," Ben said.

"Was all this happening at the end of Fountain Road?"

"Yeah."

"And what happened?"

"Jaze kicked it. Hard, like. I went to bring it back."

"From the electric station?"

"Yeah, it didn't go in or nothing. Honest. Dad's told me it's dangerous in there."

"Your dad's quite right. So you got the ball?"

"No. This woman was shouting, stuff like 'no' and 'go away.' She ran at me."

Yuri held up a small tablet, which was showing Savi's picture. "Is this her?"

"Yeah." Toby nodded solemnly. "That's her."

"She ran at you—then what?"

"Picked me up. She was really strong. Then it happened, the bomb. It went off."

Yuri could see the moisture glinting in the boy's eyes; he was starting to withdraw. It was too vivid, too terrifying. "Now this is important, Toby. I need to know about what happened after. What happened to the woman?"

"They took her," Toby said simply. "She was hurt bad. There was . . . was blood. It was all over her."

"The police took her?"

Toby nodded, silent as he relived the memory.

"What did they take her away in?"

"Big car. Bigger than a normal police car. Same color, though. They carried her into the back, along with the other bloke."

"Another man? Was he injured, too?"

"I guess."

"Did they say anything to you?"

"Just that I'd be okay. He said they'd called the paramedics."

"The policeman that talked to you, what did he look like?"

"I don't know."

"Okay. Was he black, white, Indian, Chinese? Short guy, tall guy?"

"I don't know. He never took his mask off."

"What sort of mask, Toby?"

"They were all in armor. It was black. You know the dull kind of black."

"I do, Toby. Thank you." Yuri stood up.

"You finished?" Ben asked.

"Sure. Hey, Toby, you did okay. You're lucky to have a dad like this." He watched as the Reardons went into the lift.

"Threw them into the back of a car?" Kohei said skeptically.

"Savi told us she was with Ketchell and Larik. But there were more activists scouting 'round for them."

"So it was likely Ketchell or Larik who was caught in the blast with her. Everyone else would have got lost fast."

"They were both badly injured. Let's start with admissions to hospital emergency departments." Yuri let out a reluctant breath. "And morgues."

Yuri's office had full access to all the information from more than a dozen primary medical networks across Australia. Their reports covering the last week were open, swamping a pair of his desk screens.

The Security Department G5Turing was even running a real-time scan through hospital emergency department files for a Jane Doe matching Savi's description. So far it had turned up precisely zero. Savi had effectively vanished from the digital world the moment the bomb went off.

He was more concerned by Connexion Security's own logs. Kintore's files of first fall day had been deleted from the Sydney office's servers, transferred to New York under Poi Li's authority. Yuri's repeated requests to review the drone videos of Fountain Street had been blocked. There was going to have to be a showdown with Poi Li, and soon. Savi had taken the worst of the blast, protecting Toby Reardon. She needed treatment—if she wasn't already dead.

And the Sydney department was running another eight current operations, which all required his complete attention, all as important as the infiltration of Akkar's group. Those agents were depending on him as well. He dropped his head into his hands and massaged his temples. The text of the screens was out of focus no matter how many times he blinked.

The three empty coffee mugs lined up underneath the desk screens made him sigh. According to Boris, his mInet, he'd been in the office for eighteen hours straight. Yuri *did not* lose his own operatives. It weighed heavily on him. His people had to trust him, they had to know he had them covered. Everyone in Connexion regarded him as a real hard-ass, which he strove to be, but with asking people to undertake dangerous missions came responsibility. And Yuri took that very seriously indeed.

There was a swift rap of knuckles on his door, and Kohei Yamada came right in without waiting. "Sorry, chief, we have an incident outside. It's odd."

Yuri frowned and glanced over at the window, slightly surprised to see bright morning sunlight pouring down the skyscraper canyon of Sydney's central business district. "What's happening?" Boris hadn't alerted him to any crowds gathering on the street below.

"Callum Hepburn is in reception. He's refusing to leave until he sees you."

"Why do I know that name? Is he one of our targets?"

Kohei grinned. "No, chief." His mInet threw Callum's picture on the wallscreen.

Yuri peered at a young red-haired man with a mildly bewildered smile on his face as he shook hands with Ainsley Zangari himself. Boris backed it up with a biography file. "Riiight . . . he cleared up Gylgen. I remember." Connexion's Emergency Detoxification team had been headlining the news streams after the potential disaster at Gylgen had been averted . . . until Icefall took over media interest. "What's he doing here?"

"No idea. But he's started shouting quite loudly at our people when they asked him to leave—most impolite." Kohei pointed at the screen. "Given who he knows, I thought it best we shouldn't just sling him out on the street. He's angry about something."

"But—"

"Publicity, chief. We don't want it."

"Fuck it. Bring him up here."

"Yes, sir."

"And Kohei, I want two uniformed staff outside my door."

"Way ahead of you, chief."

Yuri spent the intervening minutes reviewing Callum Hepburn's file. It was ordinary enough, except for one entry concerning Gylgen, which was classified higher than Yuri's rating could access. He raised an eyebrow at that.

Callum stomped into the office. On his pale skin, the red flush of anger was very pronounced.

"Mr. Hepburn, please, have a seat—"

Callum marched over to the desk and put his hands down on it hard so his face was thrust over the screens, glaring down at Yuri. "Where is she?"

Yuri glanced over at Kohei, who was standing in the doorway, curious and amused. "I don't respond well to people shouting at me, Hepburn. So you need to back off, calm down, and tell me what this is about."

Callum paused for a moment, then took his hands off the desk, straightening up. "Savi Chaudhri. She's missing. Where is she?"

Training allowed Yuri to keep his face expressionless, but only just.

"I'm sorry. I've never heard of that person."

"Bollocks. She's one of your covert agents. She went undercover for you. She didn't come back."

"What makes you say that?"

Callum breathed in deeply, his nostrils flaring. "She's my fiancée. She went undercover after our holiday. It was supposed to be for five days. It's double that now. No way does anyone stay out of contact for that long."

"Your fiancée?"

"Yes. And yes, I know she's supposed to inform you lot so I can be vetted. But it was a whirlwind thing. So . . . what's happened and where is she? Just tell me she's safe, and I'll piss off and leave you alone."

Yuri could read the anxiety burning away behind the man's anger. "Okay, it's like this. If one of our agents is undercover, they have specific contact protocols. That includes several emergency methods of alerting us if they get into difficulty. If we had received one of those alerts, then we would extract them at once." He spread his hands: the reasonable man. "It's been quiet around here."

"Like bollocks it has. There was a riot out at Kintore when the Icefall started. Were her students there? It's the kind of stupid stunt those morons live for."

Once again, Yuri was startled by how close the man was to the truth. He was furious with Savi for compromising herself so badly— and for what? An impetuous fling? When he tracked her down, her career with Security was over. "What students?"

"She was . . . monitoring student groups for you, playing spot the radical. Are they the ones who protested Icefall?"

"No. No student groups Security watches were there. And you have my word on that."

"So where is she?"

"Look, I appreciate your concern. This is your fiancée, you've every right to be worried. But all of my personnel are accounted for. So I'm sure she'll be calling you as soon as she surfaces."

Callum stood still for a long moment, processing what he'd heard. "All right, then." He nodded as if he was generously letting Yuri off a felony charge. "I'll give it a couple of days."

Yuri watched him walk out of the office. "You're welcome," he told the empty doorway.

Kohei came in. "Did I hear that right? They're engaged?"

"So it would seem. And someone like Hepburn isn't going to lie about that. He's a fool; he sees the world in black and white."

"What do we do?"

"Only one option left now."

Yuri knew he should wait until he'd had a sleep, at the very least. His rumpled shirt, stubble, tired eyes, all spoke of someone not making the best decisions. But this couldn't wait any longer.

Poi Li's Manhattan office was in one of Connexion's downtown buildings, a temporary location until the new American headquarters was built overlooking Central Park. Like Yuri, she didn't put a lot of weight on expensive fittings as symbols of status.

Somehow he wasn't surprised that she was in there, working away in the middle of the East Coast's night. Very few senior management worked their physical office time zone's standard hours.

"You look like crap," she said as he came in.

"Thanks."

"Tea?"

"No. I've had enough caffeine today."

"I recommend chamomile. Very gentle."

He shook his head, trying to ignore the irritation. "We have a problem."

"You and I would be out of a job if there were no problems in the world."

"Very Zen. It's Savi Chaudhri."

"Your infiltration agent?"

"Yes. You've got her, haven't you?"

"No. Why do you say that?"

"I went back over our detention records," Yuri said. "I was surprised."

"In what way?"

"Akkar's idea was a good one. Using the power drop-out while the super truckez were recharging would've created a reboot window for Julisa's rogue control program. They would've taken over the ancient G3Turing drivers and had themselves the world's greatest demolition battle, smashing those brutes into each other and every other piece of equipment out there. Some of those things weigh over fifty tons. Everything would've been wrecked."

"I know," Poi Li said. "I was in active ops when Tarli worked out their methodology."

"Yes. And that was when we all realized how many activists they would be sending to the old airfield. That's also when you stood down the original arrest squads and the Arizona Search and Engage team was brought in. Your decision, your authorization."

"You originally tasked the Australian internal suppression force with the arrests. I judged they weren't large enough, nor capable, for a hundred and twenty odd fanatics. Quite rightly, as it turns out. S and E handled containment and detention very well."

"They were a bit too efficient; they scooped up Savi as well. They didn't know she was our asset. I'd like her back, please."

"We don't have her."

"Have you even checked?"

"As a matter of fact, yes. Arizona S and E were given the code for her tracker. We don't have her."

Yuri sat back in the chair and gave her a careful look. "Is this a dark rendition operation? Is that it? Have we got them stashed away at some Guantanamo in North Korea, or something?"

"That would only multiply our problem, wouldn't it? You can't hide that many people and not have anyone ask where they are. We'd have to let them go or bring them to trial eventually."

"I personally interviewed the only witness for the substation explosion. He told me the Arizona paramilitaries you sent threw her into the back of their vehicle. You have her."

"A nine-year-old boy suffering an explosion trauma is not the most reliable witness."

"You *know* I saw Toby Reardon? You're keeping tabs on me?"

"There was only one survivor of the Fountain Street attack according to our files. Are they incorrect?"

"No," Yuri said, hating the way he was being put on the defensive. "Look, I get that screwups happen, especially on a day as intense and confusing as last week's. Just let me access the Arizona S and E records. I'd like to see who they processed."

"You don't have clearance for Arizona S and E documentation. They're an internal outfit we deploy during extreme security events."

"I'm a divisional commander, for fuck's sake!"

"And that level does not give you clearance to go digging through Arizona S and E files. I'm sorry."

"Oh, come on, Poi, you've got to give me something. Let me walk down to the holding cells and quietly take her out of there. She's Security, one of us. She's not going running to some piece of shit libertarian civil rights lawyer."

"Can't be done."

"You do it, then."

"Again, we do not have her."

"She's dead, isn't she? That's what's being covered up here."

"I'll pretend you didn't say that."

"It's not going to go away, you know."

"The file is closed, Yuri. Drop this. That's a direct order."

"It's not me that's your problem," he said softly. "Have you heard of Callum Hepburn?"

"How is he the problem?"

"Wait—do you know him?"

"I know of him. I can't tell you why. But I can assure you he is a solid Connexion employee."

"Not for much longer. He's going to be trouble."

"Really? Has he joined a radical group?"

"Turns out he's Chaudhri's fiancé."

Poi Li sat up, all humor leaving her compact frame. "He's what?"

"All I know is they went on some kind of screw-fest holiday together in the Caribbean. And a nice diamond ring was the result. They didn't bother telling the department."

"This is unfortunate," she said. "He carries media weight right now."

"Exactly. So let me have Savi. I'll reunite the star-crossed lover idiots and everything goes away."

"I do not have her."

"Why are you doing this?" His voice was raised, which was never a good idea with Poi Li. But somehow, Yuri no longer cared.

"Yuri. Please. We genuinely don't have her. You have my word on that. I did check. And please don't call me a liar to my face. That would be bad for both of us. This is closed. Accept it and move on."

Yuri took a moment, but in the end he just nodded and said: "Okay." He simply couldn't afford to challenge Poi Li. Not directly.

"How did it go?" Kohei asked when Yuri got back to his Sydney office.

Yuri slumped into the chair behind his desk. Boris switched all the darkened screens back on, which showed the same mass of data as before—and still told him nothing.

"Question for you," he said to his deputy. "You're a criminal, in the middle of a serious criminal act, and someone assaults you. Who do you complain to? And what do you say? 'While I was trying to sabotage a hundred million wattdollars' worth of equipment, someone beat the crap out of me, then threatened me so badly I'm terrified for my life.'"

"You cut a deal," Kohei said immediately. "You get into the witness protection program in exchange for testifying."

"Nice theory. In practice, witness protection is for organized crime informants who can bring down whole cartels. Somehow I doubt some radical hothead smashing up our equipment is going to be given that same deal."

"You mean Akkar's eco-radicals who tried to bust up our super trucks?"

"I do indeed. They were rounded up by a Connexion Security subdivision called Arizona S and E. It's a paramilitary group we use for crowd control in bad urban disturbances."

"Do they have the authority to operate in Australia?"

"Yes. They've got an office registered here in the building, actually, and a private police license issued by the government. That allows them to detain persons found committing a criminal act. They then hand them over to the local justice department along with evidence of the alleged felony."

"Neat," Kohei said approvingly. "And if the suspects are held incommunicado?"

"Then who's going to notice them missing?" Yuri concluded. He massaged his temples again, which made no difference to the fatigue draining the energy from his muscles and thoughts. "There were over a hundred and twenty of them."

"Including Savi?"

"Given the way I was warned off, yes. But . . . a hundred and twenty people, maybe more. One of them has to have a family or friends kicking up a fuss. Poi can't vanish them with impunity. Can she?"

"Were there actually any witnesses?" Kohei asked. "It all happened out at the old airfield. That's ours."

"And New York has all the logs."

"Shit, Poi Li's thorough."

"Akkar's people will be well chosen activists, totally dedicated. The last thing they'll do before going on a raid like this is tell anyone. So it's going to be days before anyone even asks where they are. Weeks before there's any concern raised. And even if you can get some friendly official to start investigating on your behalf, there's no evidence linking them. No one apart from us knows the size of the group. As self-generating cover-ups go, it's impressive."

"You can't rendition that many people in this day and age," Kohei said. "The holding location would leak. Some smartass would fly a drone over it."

"I can't believe Poi Li would cut us out without reason," Yuri replied. "We know Arizona S and E picked Savi up right after the explosion. And Poi Li swears the Arizona guys haven't screwed up. She claims she checked personally."

"So she's running scared of the media getting hold of this? Christ, chief, what do they do to these people? Are we working for psychopaths?"

"I don't know—and that's bad whatever way you look at it. If Savi died because they didn't give her medical treatment quickly enough, why not just give us her body back? Why leave it like this? It doesn't make any sense!"

"So do we pack it in?"

"Savi is one of mine." Yuri closed his eyes, fighting the fatigue that was stopping him thinking straight. "I'm going home to catch some sleep. I need a clear head to figure out what to do next."

Callum stepped out of the Kintore portal hub onto Main Street. It was midafternoon, and the town had been roasting under the desert sun for more than ten hours. He wasn't prepared for the heat, nor the dry, scratchy dust he inhaled with every breath. Sweat emerged from every pore, and he was only wearing shorts and a purple t-shirt—along with factor fifty sunblock. He fumbled in his shoulder bag for his new surgical-style mask and slipped it on.

Apollo threw a navmap up on his screen sunglasses, and he began to walk down the street, following the direction graphics. There were very few of the dust-tarnished buildings with a second story. Why would you bother? Single-story prefabs were cheaper and land more so; if you wanted a big house here, you just spread outward. Or at least land had been cheap until a week ago, when the ice started to fall across the desert.

Now when he looked to the west, he could see a thick, oddly stable bank of cloud rising from the strata of ice that lay over the red sand. The chunks already covered an area more than two kilometers across, and that was with only five of the big airships on station. Another three were scheduled to join the squadron before the end of the month, with a further fifteen planned within a year. Melt water was now trickling along the waiting canals, soaking into the arid sand, but creeping a little farther every day. While in the air above, the freezing vapor was creating a microclimate alteration to the desert's ancient, lethargic wind patterns. Regular breezes had started to blow down Kintore's streets as the cold-sink drew in air from the coast to the north. For now all they brought was more dust, but within six months, Water Desert's climatologists were predicting, clouds would be lured inward across the continent, accelerating change. Within a couple of years, Kintore would become the newest, most exciting oasis on the planet. Money would flow in with the new rains, and speculators were already buying up plots along the canals.

But for now, Kintore retained its frontier atmosphere—a convenient home for its tough workforce, and scattered with the commercial establishments that supplied them with whatever they needed. Callum eyed the neon and hologram signs above the plethora of small thriving enterprises. He stopped outside the Granite Shelf, seeing just another prefab with long windows and three big air-con cabinets barnacled to the wall at one end. The glowing blue sign was younger than the prefab that it crowned.

Raina had found it for him, of course. After Yuri Alster had stonewalled him, he'd confided in his crew that he'd actually gone and made a commitment to a woman. That she was Security. Undercover. That she was missing, and he suspected the company was busy pulling together some kind of whitewash.

"Fucking typical," Raina had grunted.

They were all on board, all wanting to help. "Whatever it takes, chief. Whatever you need."

He'd nearly got emotional at that. But so far it was only Raina's expertise he'd needed.

Savi's mInet, Nelson, might have been taken offline, but that didn't leave her totally isolated, Raina explained. If she was undercover, she was going to be using a different mInet identity. They didn't have its universal address code; however, Savi's dermal grains would be networked with it. They all had a unique interface code, which would be incorporated into the mInet metadata. It took Raina less than an hour to track down the codes, extracting the data from the Mumbai clinic that had implanted them five years ago. It was the kind of webhead skill that both impressed and troubled Callum, that so much of a life could be accessed so easily.

If Savi had used a mInet connection to call anyone or access the internet, it would be logged in the local server, Raina told him. All she needed was a probable location; then she could hack into the servers. A search engine would be able to find the data.

Callum's only suggestion for a location was Kintore. It made sense to him when he confronted her boss, Yuri. Icefall had been the center of the biggest anti-Connexion protests for more than a year—just the kind of thing student wannabe radicals would join (or be manipulated into joining). Which was what Savi was investigating.

Perhaps Parvati had chosen to smile on his quest. Whatever. He'd been right about Kintore. It'd taken Raina just ninety-seven minutes to track down Savi's grains; they were interfaced with a mInet tagged

Misra, which had authorized payment for meals at the Granite Shelf. The last had been a croissant and green tea the morning Icefall started, a few hours before the protests. After that, there was nothing.

Callum walked into the café and sat down. He asked the waitress for orange juice and a croissant. When she brought it, he showed her the picture of Savi and asked if she recognized her.

No.

There were three other waitresses on that shift. He asked each of them. Two said no, one hesitated and said maybe. The Granite Shelf was a busy place, she said, we get a couple of hundred people every day. Your girl, she might have been in a few times, not dressed as smart as the photo, but it was a while ago now.

The rush of relief was so strong Callum had to go and sit down for a while. Apollo called Raina for him.

"One of the waitresses thinks she recognizes her," he said.

"So she should," Raina replied. "I've hacked the café's main server. It's got the internal surveillance video files. I accessed them at the time she made her last payment. Downloading it to you now."

Callum watched the image playing on his screen sunglasses, not knowing the Savi he was seeing, the shabby clothes, sun hat, and backpack. *She's good at undercover,* he thought admiringly. The clothes and hairstyle dropped her age back several years. Typical student type, maybe on a gap year.

When she walked out of the Granite Shelf that morning, she turned left and walked along Main Street.

"I'll see if I can get some more video files," Raina said. "But a lot of the surveillance cameras in Kintore are cloud stored, especially the civic ones covering the streets. Hacking them is going to be a little more difficult."

"Do what you can," he told her.

He left the Granite Shelf and turned left, just like Savi. The next café along was Alcides, serving Portuguese food. He sat at a table and showed Savi's picture to the waiter. A clothes printing store next.

Then a food printer. Bugez mart. A bar. Didn't bother with the finance house. Another café.

The sky was shading down to a rosy dusk when he left the café. Streetlights were coming on, blue-green cones of light revealed in the dusty air. More people were walking about now, not that the temperature had dropped. He could feel the ground radiating its daytime heat at him.

"I think I've got her turning into Rosewalk," Raina said. "That's about a klick from where you are. It's not the best image."

"You're doing better than me," he said. "The food store owner says she may have been a customer. Couldn't say when."

"There's not much camera coverage down Rosewalk. It's more residential down there."

"I'll take a look." Apollo threw up the navmap, and he started walking.

Three men came out of a bar just ahead of him. He moved to avoid them.

"Internet connection is dropping out," Apollo said.

"What?"

"Network signal lost. Unable to reconnect. My reception is being subject to access overload."

"How's that—"

The three men from the pub shifted to stand directly in front of him.

"Oh, shit," Callum grunted. He spun around fast. Two men right behind him, one dressed in a smart suit holding up a taser baton, and grinning in anticipation.

"Wanna make a break for it?" the suited man taunted.

Callum had only ever been in a couple of bar fights, and that'd been with people his own age at university—boozy shoving matches with added swearing. The bouncers had stepped in fast and closed it down. These five men looked like they could chop those bouncers apart as a warm-up routine.

"I've not got much cash on me," Callum said, wishing his voice wasn't shaking so much. *This is Main Street. Why isn't anyone calling the cops?*

"Down here, pal," one of the group from the pub said.

Callum saw the narrow street he was indicating and started to panic. "Look, I've got a smartCuff. I can wipe the universal code and the trackme app. It's top of the range, worth plenty."

"If only we wanted you for your money."

"Or your body," another sneered.

"Move."

It was his last chance to attempt a run. He was too frightened of the pounding they'd probably give him. Being put into hospital wasn't going to help Savi. But then, being forced into a dark alley wasn't exactly promising . . .

A hand shoved him between his shoulder blades. He tensed. If he ran to the right he'd be going directly down Main Street. *They won't chase me there . . . will they?*

The taser baton poked him in the back of his knee. It must have been a reduced charge. He yelped at the fast burst of pain, but didn't quite fall as his leg jerked about.

"Don't run," the voice warned.

Humiliated and fearful, he went with them.

Raina will know the link was deliberately broken. She'll hack the cameras and see them taking me. She'll call the police or our local Security officers. She'll help. She'll get me out of this. Come on, Raina. Come on!

They turned down another street, then made regular turns after that. Apollo's navmap tracked every turn, plotting their route. He could trace each footstep he was being forced to make.

Fat lot of fucking use that is.

After seven minutes, thirty-eight seconds, they finished up at a roller door in a sleep-pod hotel that was being refurbished. It slid up, and he was shoved into the dark cavern beyond. The door rattled as it rolled down again. Then the lights came on.

It was a storeroom, with empty metal racks on the walls and plenty of dust on the rough concrete floor. The air was hot and stale.

Right in the middle was a sturdy wooden chair with four handcuffs, two hanging off the arms, two on the front legs.

Callum took one look at it and—

The taser baton hit him, full power this time. The only muscles he could make work were in his throat, so he screamed as he tumbled over. The baton struck again, and the universe dissolved into terrible pain. His body jerked about and he howled, all sense leaving him.

His limbs were on fire, which slowly subsided, leaving him with painful cramps. Vision returned—or at least he could see light streaks amid the darkness. He tried to blink into focus. The shaking was bad. And he couldn't move his hands.

He was cuffed into the chair, wrists and ankles.

"Oh, shit. Shit shit."

His screen sunglasses had either fallen off or been taken. Whatever. He didn't have them anymore. When he looked at his wrist, he saw the smartCuff had been removed.

"Apollo?" he whispered.

A hand smacked him on the side of the head. Hard. "Don't do that again. Your mInet is dead. You are alone."

The red stars slowly faded. There was a man standing in front of him. Tall, African, with a bald head beaded by sweat and tattoos running sinuously along his arms. He wore a black t-shirt with a picture of a crystal prism splitting a rainbow.

Callum's chuckle was almost hysterical. "I have that album, too."

"What?"

"Pink Floyd, *Dark Side of the Moon*. Classic, but not as good as *Wish You Were Here*."

"Smartarse," the man grunted. His hand lashed out again, striking the other side of Callum's head.

Pain spiked through his ear, and there was a taste of blood in his mouth. "Fucking hell, what is this?"

"Where are they? Where have you taken them?"

"What? Who?"

"My people."

"What the fuck?" Callum eyed the hand as it rose threateningly again. "Which people? Wait, who do you think I am?"

"I know exactly who you are, Callum Hepburn." The African held up a piece of paper, printed with the publicity shot of him with Ainsley at the Greenwich Peninsular site. "Connexion's newest golden boy. Saved Northern Europe from a radiation plume. The world is so grateful."

"Why am I here? And who the fuck are you?"

The man raised his hand again, and Callum flinched.

"Where are they?"

"Who?" Callum bellowed back, more frightened than ever now, not just for himself but mainly for Savi. If these were the student radicals she'd been shadowing . . .

"You are either a fool or a very good actor."

"I'm not fucking acting. I don't know who you are or who you're talking about!"

The man walked around the chair. Callum tried to turn and watch him, worried that he'd be hit from behind. But he reemerged on the other side, carrying a tall glass of water.

"Tell me what you want to know," Callum said desperately. "Exactly what. If I know, I'll tell you. Fuck's sake." He had to tip his head back then; the man was standing directly in front of the chair.

"My name is Akkar, but I think you know that already, company boy."

"No. I don't fucking care, either."

Slowly Akkar tipped the glass, pouring the water down over Callum's crotch.

"What?" Callum stared down at his soaking shorts, then back up at his captor. "What the fuck?"

"To encourage the telling of truth," Akkar said. "Took us years and years of research, but we've found water improves conductivity to skin." He smiled mockingly. "Who knew?"

The suited man came around the chair to stand grinning down at Callum. He held up the taser baton.

Akkar's smile turned mirthless. "Dimon, how big a charge does it take to fry a man's balls?"

Dimon patted the taser baton. "Don't worry, boss, we have more than enough."

"No!" Callum yelled. "Fucking no! I'll tell you what you want to know, but I don't know what it is. Tell me! Fucking explain! What is going on?"

"First fall," Akkar said. "My people went into Water Desert's maintenance compound. Is that clear enough for you?"

"I know there was a riot out at the observation area that day," Callum said desperately. "Is this the same thing?"

"No, it is not the same thing, Callum Hepburn. One hundred and twenty-seven activists went into that compound. They were going to strike the greatest possible blow against the corporate criminals who are here to rape the desert. A blow that took me over a year to plan." His hand shot out, gripping Callum's chin. "One hundred and twenty-seven, company boy. None of them came home. Where are they?"

"I don't know," Callum said. "I wasn't here. I work in fucking Emergency Detox, for Christ's sake! I don't give a flying shit about your stupid fucking desert. Nobody does, only freaks like you."

"First they came for the rocks in space and took them away from us saying they now owned them," Akkar said in a low, dangerous tone. "And we did nothing, because they were just rocks. Then they came for the desert . . . You understand? You know how it goes? But this time, company boy, this time we will not let them ruin what nature has given to every human, the beautiful land which belongs to all of us. There are many with my belief, and our numbers grow, accepting the truth of our cause."

Callum gave his captor the most contemptuous look he could manage. "I've only seen six of you. That's not an oppressed minority with a cause, that's a mental health issue."

The baton jabbed down into Callum's shorts. He screamed, then realized there was no electric shock.

Both men were laughing at him.

"Fuck you!" he shouted. "I hope Connexion fucking drowns you in melting ice. I want the last thing you see to be green plants conquering every fucking useless rock in your worthless hell. I hope the water rots your corpse and turns you into fertilizer to help more plants. That's the only way dumbass shits like you will ever help any ecology."

"I think he means it."

"I think you're right."

Callum glared up at them. "You're fucking morons! A hundred and twenty-seven people don't just disappear. That's . . . That's . . . crazy. You're being fucked up the arse by your own cracked conspiracy theories."

"You're quite right, Callum Hepburn. People don't just disappear. It is madness." Akkar produced the picture of Savi, and thrust it into Callum's face. "So where is she?"

"I . . . I . . ." Callum knew guilt would be lighting him up like a solar flare. "She's not—"

"Not what?"

"Not one of you." He knew he was blowing it, and he didn't care. They knew Savi, and she'd vanished along with their fellow maniacs. Callum couldn't imagine a worse possible lead, but at least it was real. He was one step closer to her.

"Who is she?" Akkar asked in a deadly whisper.

"She's my fucking *wife,* you piece of shit! And if you've touched one hair on her head, I will fucking kill you!"

Akkar snatched the taser baton from Dimon and jabbed it into Callum's chest. The pain was abysmal. Callum writhed helplessly, unable to think, transformed to nothing but a lump of screeching agonized flesh.

Dimon pulled Akkar's hand, moving the baton away. "This is not you, my friend. We need him talking, not screaming."

Akkar nodded reluctantly, but beneath his anger he was giving Callum a puzzled look. "Speak to me. Your wife?"

Callum coughed pitifully, his body still shaking. "Yes, she's my wife. What do you think I'm doing coming here to shit-city central asking where she is? I want her back."

Akkar and Dimon exchanged a glance again, which Callum guessed was bad.

"What's her name?"

"Savi Hepburn." He knew he shouldn't tell them, but it was just a name. And appearing to help, to cooperate, might kick something loose. Where she was . . .

"A Connexion undercover agent," Akkar said in quiet fury. "She led us into a trap. Your bitch did this to us!"

Callum glared at him. "Yeah, so? She outsmarted you. It couldn't have been difficult. Where did you see her last?"

Akkar glared at him. "She betrayed us. I should make her watch while I cut your throat in front of her."

"You've got to find her first. When did you see her last? Come on! When?"

"I ask the questions, company boy."

"Yes, you do. So try asking this. How do you—you who's hiding in a crappy prefab cesspit in Kintore—how do you get into Connexion to find your precious people? How do you recruit someone on the inside? Someone they'll never suspect? Someone who's a lot more desperate than you are to find out what the fuck happened? Got any ideas on that, pal, huh? Got a name, maybe?"

Akkar gave an incredulous snort. "You want to work with us?"

"I would sooner chew my fucking leg off. But what choice have either of us got?"

"No way," Dimon growled.

"Really? Go on, then," Callum challenged recklessly. "Explain your alternative. Savi is with Security. She was watching you, recording you, gathering every detail of your pathetic little eco-cause lives. Connexion Security knows it all. A multi-trillion-dollar company with a security division budget bigger than the sodding CIA. The only thing—*only* thing—that they don't know about is your current location. But you can't get out of Kintore now, can you? Not through a portal, and drones or satellites will spot any vehicle driving away. You're in a jail just as secure as your missing comrades. Nicer food, maybe, and invisible walls. But this is where you'll stay for the rest of your life. Which, with drone surveillance and G5Turings searching the internet, probably isn't going to be more than another week. So go on, tell me your super smart master plan to bust out and save everyone, wherever they are. Got an address on that, have you?"

"How can Osha be missing as well?" Akkar asked.

"Who?"

"Your wife; that was the name we knew her by. If she's Connexion Security, why is she missing?"

"I don't know. I can't even get the bastards to admit she was working for them." He jerked his wrists against the cuffs. "Unlock me. Come on. We need to work out what to do next."

"A hundred and twenty-seven people vanished, Callum. Including one of their own, if we believe you. The only thing we're going to find now is their grave."

"No," Callum shouted. He tugged hard, as if that alone would break the handcuffs. "She's alive. I know you're paranoid enough to believe Connexion can murder that many people; it's all part of your sad little echo chamber conspiracy bollocks. But they don't. And I've met Ainsley. He's a ruthlessly clever businessman, sure, but he's not fucking Hitler."

"There won't be a grave to uncover," Dimon said. "Haumea station gets rid of all Connexion's problems, all the evidence."

"Buzzt! Wrong! Have you ever been to Haumea station? I have. I go every week. I know every ventchamber. I've watched our grandparents' toxic crap sail off into space. There aren't any corpses going through."

"If not Haumea, then another invisible asteroid out beyond Neptune. It's a big company, as you said. With infinite resources."

"She's alive!" Callum cried. "Now fucking let me go. I'm going to find her, with or without you. Do you want to know where your friends went or not? Because I'm your only chance to find out."

After a long moment, Akkar nodded. Dimon sighed in disapproval, but bent down and unlocked Callum's handcuffs.

"Okay, company boy," Akkar said. "What do we do now?"

Callum rubbed at the red marks on his wrists. "Secret rendition,
that's what's happened here, right? They're all sitting in some deep
hole somewhere: disused mine, hollowed out volcano, North Korea.
We're agreed on that, yes?"

"Yes."

"Then there's only one thing we can do now. They vanished down
the rabbit hole. We have to dive in after them."

The sun had set two hours before, leaving the Sydney skyline ablaze
in neon and office lights. As always, Yuri hadn't noticed.

"We've got movement, chief," Kohei Yamada said breathlessly.

Yuri looked up from the screens on his desk to see his deputy
leaning on the doorframe grinning excitedly.

"Movement?"

"Dimon just broke surface. Active ops is tracking him."

"Now?"

"Yeah. We're live!"

"Shit."

The two of them hurried along the corridor to the active ops center.
Omri Toth was duty operations manager. He gave Yuri a thumbs-up.
"Facial recognition got him outside the Kintore hub five minutes ago."

"Where did he go?" Yuri asked.

"He didn't."

"Show me."

Omri gestured at Tarli, who was on one of the desks. Yuri peered
at the main screen at the front of the room. It had a camera view of
the Kintore hub: a hexagonal green-and-white tiled lobby with four
portal doors, two for the town's tiny loop, the other pair leading to
the Northern Territory central hub.

"Seven minutes ago," Tarli said.

Yuri watched Dimon linger just outside the entrance barriers, looking around slowly. The big man spent a couple of minutes observing pedestrians come and go, then left.

"Current location, hanging 'round outside twenty meters away," Omri said in a bemused tone.

The screen switched to one of the hub building's external cameras. Sure enough, Dimon was standing farther down Main Street.

"Kohei, get me the duty captain at the Northern Territory central hub," Yuri said. "And put our armed response team on active alert."

"Yes, chief!"

"And no national police. Let's keep this in-house."

He watched Dimon, who was still standing on Main Street. The man was wearing one of his charcoal gray suits, which must have been disturbingly hot in Kintore's evening heat.

"Is his mInet using the internet?" Yuri asked.

"Difficult," Tarli said. "I'll put our G5Turing into the local servers, see if we can identify his digital signature."

Boris threw a communication icon across Yuri's screen lenses.

"Captain Dalager, the Northern Territory hub network security chief."

"Okay, captain," Yuri said. "We have some activity at the Kintore hub. A suspect on our critical wanted list may try to get through central hub. I need you to start shutting it down."

"Sir?"

"You heard me. Let everyone currently in the hub go through, but close the barriers and every portal door to new traffic apart from Kintore. My authority."

"That's going to cause chaos!"

"I don't care. Once the hub is empty, deploy the tactical response team to pick him up. I want him to walk straight into this eyes open."

"Yes, sir."

Omri was chuckling. "Oh, man, regional control is going to dump on you from a great height. You shut central, and you're closing down the whole Northern Australian Territory."

"The Hubnav app will throw everyone a route through the secondary networks; that's why we have multiple overlaps. It'll take people thirty seconds longer."

"As long as I don't get hauled in to corporate to explain this."

"You won't be. Now, get all our Kintore spy drones into the air. Do not lose Dimon. I don't care about stealth. This needs to be wrapped."

"Already launched."

"Tarli," Yuri said quietly. "Open a secondary cache, and copy all this operation's files into it. My access only, not New York."

"Got it, chief."

"Boris, notify Poi Li we have a situation developing—"

"It's him," Tarli exclaimed.

"Who?" Yuri stared at the screen.

"Akkar. That uniform isn't fooling anyone."

Yuri felt his excitement building as he saw the tall eco-warrior walking along Main Street toward Dimon. "He wouldn't dare," he breathed. Akkar was wearing the brown-and-green jacket of StepSmart couriers, along with matching shorts. The company's standard-issue canvas satchel was slung over his shoulder. His cap had a long peak which he'd pulled down until it almost touched his broad wraparound sunglasses. That, along with several days' stubble, was possibly enough to confuse a low-level facial recognition program, but not anyone in active ops.

"Ten dollars he's going to try," Kohei said.

"Bloody hell," Omri said. "Dimon was scouting it out for him in person. These blokes never use the internet for anything. They're religiously old-school."

"Keep on them," Yuri yelled. "Kohei, with me. Dalager, empty the hub, now! Our suspect is coming through."

He ran out of active ops. There was a portal door twenty meters away. Boris threw a route to the Northern Territory central hub on his screen lenses. The portal door led into Connexion's internal network. Left turn, through two more doors, right turn at the ten-portal junction hub. Three straight—

Poi Li's icon sprang up. "What's happening?" she demanded.

"Akkar's surfaced. We're about to take him down."

"All right, I've got the feed. I see him. What's in his courier bag?"

"We don't know. The portal sensors will pick up anything danger-ous."

"I don't want him in a central hub."

"If I send the tactical team through to Kintore now, he'll run."

"They can catch him," she said.

"There isn't time. Let him through, and he's contained on our ter-ritory."

"I need a decision," Omri said. "Akkar is ten meters from the Kin-tore hub."

"If the bag's a bomb, if he's going to suicide, we can't let him do it on Kintore's Main Street," Yuri yelled. "Too many people."

"Central hub is almost empty of pedestrians," Dalager confirmed. "Team assuming interception positions."

"Very well," Poi Li said. "Let him through."

"Dimon is walking away," Omri said.

"Keep the drones on him," Yuri said.

"Yes," Poi Li said. "And route their feed to me. I'm sending a team through the C and GST portal; they'll intercept before he can vanish on us again."

Yuri almost smiled at the déjà vu moment. It was exactly like first fall, when Poi Li had jumped in, putting her own people into the operation—but now she didn't have exclusivity on the operation's data. "Tell them to be careful," he said. "Akkar is the brains, but Dimon is the muscle. He'll likely be armed."

"I can access a file, thank you, Yuri," Poi Li said.

Yuri sprinted through the last portal. He was in a windowless cor-ridor. At the far end a locked double door closed off the hub. Boris sent it his access code, and the bolts clicked open.

"He's in the Kintore hub," Omri said. "Using a cash code. Through the barriers now."

"Scanners picked up some kind of flask in the bag," Tarli shouted.

"Is it a weapon?"

"The flask's metal. Can't scan the interior. No residual molecular traces. He's going through to central—"

"Dalager, intercept!" Yuri said. He burst through the double doors, with Kohei right behind him. They shot out onto the central hub floor, quarter of the way around the big circle from the Kintore portal. Shouts rang out, echoing along the eerily empty space.

"Down!"

"On your knees!"

"Hands where we can see them!"

"Down, down!"

"Do not move!"

Up ahead, Yuri saw the Kintore portal door. Akkar was in front of it. On his knees, his hands raised. Five figures in light armor were closing on him, their carbines raised, ruby target lasers slicing the air to form a neat grouping of dots over Akkar's heart.

Yuri skidded to a halt behind them. "What's in the bag, Akkar?"

Akkar smiled grimly. "Open it and find out."

"Put it down slowly," the tactical team's leader instructed. "There is too much firepower in here to risk making people nervous."

Akkar lifted the StepSmart satchel from his shoulder, holding it by its strap, a grin spreading across his face. Yuri didn't like that grin at all, but they had every angle covered. *Unless he's going to suicide. But he's not the type, according to Savi.*

"You mean this bag?"

"It's over, Akkar," Yuri said. "Put it down."

Akkar stared at him for a long moment, then the defiance collapsed, and he put the bag on the shiny tile floor and raised his hands.

Moments later the tactical response team had his wrists zip-locked and hauled him away. Yuri and Kohei stared at the satchel nervously.

"Bomb squad on the way," Omri said. "Ninety seconds."

"I don't feel the need to stand this close," Kohei said. "We can't contribute at this point."

"Yeah," Yuri growled. They both walked back, around the curve of the concourse.

The three members of the bomb squad jogged out of the same double door Yuri had just used, their bulky protective armor parodying a sumo suit. A safetez followed them, its tracks a blur. The spider-leg array of manipulator arms locked around its stubby central cylinder.

"Omri," Yuri asked. "How are we doing with Dimon?"

Boris immediately threw a drone camera image across the screen lens. It was the green-and-black monotone of light amplification circuitry, looking down on a street in Kintore's industrial zone. Dimon was running into a big warehouse with a Warbi Crude Metal Corp sign on the gable end.

"Bugger!" Tarli exclaimed.

"What is it?" Yuri asked as the drone's camera image flickered.

"He's got electronic countermeasures operating down there. It's nearly military grade. I can't send the drones in any closer, or we'll lose them."

"Use the drones to surround the warehouse. Make sure he doesn't leave."

"That's kinda rule one-oh-one, chief, you know?"

Yuri nearly smiled at the man's hurt tone.

"My team will be there in two minutes," Poi Li said. "They've cleared Kintore C and GST."

Yuri's heart rate was calming. By unspoken agreement, he and Kohei walked a little farther around the central hub.

"Well, look at that," Kohei said wryly as the drones showed them two big four-by-four vehicles pulling up outside the Warbi Crude Metal Corp warehouse, one at each end. "Like police responder cars, but bigger."

Yuri watched impassively as seven or eight men deployed from each four-by-four, all wearing dark head-to-toe armor. "Packing them in," he murmured.

Boris gave him a private channel to Poi Li. "I want to interrogate Akkar myself."

"He will be questioned by professionals," she replied.

"At least let me sit in."

"Yuri, we have this. You run an excellent department. Believe me, I am aware of that. Just trust our procedures. They exist for a reason, understood?"

"Yes, ma'am," he said resentfully.

Five minutes later the bomb squad chief announced: "Clear and safe."

Yuri and Kohei walked back to the StepSmart satchel, which was now being held aloft by one of the safetez's arms. The squad chief had his helmet visor hinged up. He was holding the flask and several sheets of paper.

"Two kilos of plastique," the chief said cheerfully, shaking the flask. "And plans."

"Plans of what?" Yuri asked.

The squad chief thrust the sheets toward Yuri. "Connexion's Sydney headquarters. Looks like he was coming to pay you blokes a visit."

"Holy shit," Kohei grunted.

Yuri watched the chief seal up the plans and flask in evidence bags and record their barcode.

"We have Dimon," Poi Li announced. "Well done, everyone. Yuri, looks like you can close down the Akkar file now."

The screens on Yuri's desk were showing three pictures: Savi, Akkar, and Dimon. He sat there motionless in his black leather executive office chair, staring at them.

Kohei walked in, carrying two empty shot glasses and smiling brightly. "Chief! If you fancy sharing some of that godawful vodka of yours, I thought we might toast our success. And the team's heading out to a club. Everyone invited."

Yuri looked up. Kohei's smile faded.

"Too easy," Yuri declared.

"Which part, the bit where we nearly got blown up? Come on, chief. We won."

"Savi didn't."

"Chief, Poi Li will fire your arse."

"Why would Akkar walk into one of our hubs? He knew our facial recognition systems would send up red rockets."

"He was disguised."

"Yes. Superficially. And this is a man who is so paranoid about our digital security systems he doesn't allow any internet-connected technology within a hundred meters of himself. So what does he do? Sends his lieutenant—in his customary suit—to scout the hub out. It was a shout. He wanted us to know he was coming."

"That's ridiculous. If he knew there was a chance we'd grab him, he wouldn't be carrying a satchel full of explosives."

"Right, and not forgetting a map with a big red cross on it, because what does that make him?"

"I don't get it."

Yuri grinned without humor. "Guilty. Without question, without the slightest ambiguity. He was going to blow up Connexion's headquarters. Us! He was coming for us. Guilty."

"I'm not arguing."

"And what do we do with guilty psycho eco-terrorists?"

"Rendition, by the looks of it."

"Yeah. He's gone to join his friends. That's what this was all about. He was never going to blow anything up."

"Okay, so he's joined them. Or he's dead, if it turns out we really are on the side of the fascist psychos."

"But how did he know they're all missing?"

"There's been nothing about his people raiding the Kintore maintenance depot in the news streams, no Connexion managers bragging about arrests, no prosecutors grandstanding that charges are pending. He had to know we've disappeared them."

"True. But you'd have to know, really fucking *know*, if you're going to pull a stunt like this. Akkar isn't stupid. He's not going to gamble his life on some piece of hyped-up underground propaganda. He must have been completely certain."

"How? Nobody knows."

"We know—because of her." Yuri stared at the picture of Savi. And in his mind the puzzle silently resolved itself, every factor slipping neatly together.

Boris obediently changed the picture of Savi at his command.

"And so does he," Yuri said, pointing at Callum Hepburn. "He knows his fiancée is missing. What happens when you put those two facts together? A member of Connexion's undercover security team and the company's fanatical opponents both vanishing in the same incident. You'd know there is a huge dark operation in play."

"But how would Akkar ever know Savi is one of ours?"

"Boris," Yuri said calmly. "Access Callum Hepburn's Connexion travel account."

"Online," Boris replied.

"How many times has Hepburn visited Kintore?"

"Five times in the last three days."

"Oh, shit," Kohei whispered.

"And when was the last time he arrived in Kintore?" Yuri asked.

"Seven hours ago."

"Has he left yet?"

"No."

"Why here?" Kohei asked as they approached the Warbi Crude Metal Corp warehouse.

"The other piece of this that makes absolutely no sense," Yuri said. "Dimon knew we'd identified him. Why run here?"

"It's where they've been hiding out."

"Most likely, but he led the drones here. And he'd got it screened with electronic warfare protection. Nobody could see what was going on inside. All communications were down."

"That didn't stop the Arizona S and E team."

"Didn't it?" Yuri had been reviewing the copied drone files as they walked through Kintore. The video images showed him sixteen armored figures entering the warehouse. Then the minutes ticked away, with the drones carefully holding station above the warehouse, until the electronic jamming was switched off. The drones' secondary data table reported all sixteen of the team linking to Connexion Security with secure encryption, sending in personal video feeds and basic telemetry.

"Confirm target detention," the Arizona S & E team reported. "No casualties."

They emerged triumphant. Two of them were escorting Dimon. Three more were carrying the modules of electronic countermeasure systems. The remaining eleven completed a sweep of the warehouse, confirming there were no further hostiles.

Dimon was put into one of the big four-by-fours, and the team departed.

"I bet those vehicles are fitted out with a portal door in the back," Kohei said. "That way, you can send prisoners directly to North Korea, or wherever they're being stashed. Be useful if there's more trouble than you're expecting, too. Just bump the S and E team numbers up directly from their barracks."

"I think you're right," Yuri said.

They reached the warehouse door. The Arizona team had broken it down when they went in after Dimon, then resecured it with a padlock and chain when they left. Yuri produced a power knife from his pocket and sliced through a link in the chain. He and Kohei took out their pistols and slipped inside.

There were no windows. Apart from maintenance crew inspections, people didn't work in the warehouse. It was all automated by an old G2Turing. Floor-to-ceiling shelving racks ran the length of the building, holding big drums of liquid metal crude of every type. They were held ready for the large-scale printers out at the airfield maintenance depot, which could fabricate any of the moving components in the civil engineering machines that were abraded by the desert's infernal dust. A meter-diameter portal door was installed at one end of the building, with a conveyor belt leading through it back to Warbi Crude Metal Corp's main refinery in Japan. A couple of forklift truckez slid silently along the long aisles, placing newly arrived drums on the shelves, their bright amber safety strobes the only light in the warehouse.

Yuri glanced around the eerie building where strobes sent sharp-edged shadows leaping across every surface. His screen contact lenses were trying to compensate for the darkness with an amplified image, but the strobes were disrupting the program. "Boris, can you interface with the warehouse Turing, get some lights on in here?"

"The warehouse light circuits have been physically disabled," his mInet reported. "The fault has been logged with the company maintenance office, and a repair crew is scheduled to arrive in ten hours' time."

"Damn," Yuri grunted—though it did confirm his suspicions.

They started edging forward, pistols held ready. Illumination lights mounted on the barrels sent out powerful but slim beams of white light.

"Why this place?" Kohei asked. "These racks channel you. There's nowhere to hide."

"Yeah, but Dimon rigged it with a jammer. He knew this was going to be his last stand."

"What are you thinking, chief?"

"I'm thinking he deliberately lured our people here."

"But we got him."

Yuri glanced around at the drums towering over him. "The Arizona S and E team were out of contact with each other. All they had were helmet-mounted infrared beams and light amplification goggles."

"He could see them coming?"

"Not just him." Yuri looked up and down the aisle, then lowered his pistol. "Hey!" he shouted. "Anyone here? We're from Connexion Security. Can you hear us?"

Kohei was giving him a puzzled look. "Who are you expecting, some more of Akkar's group?"

"No." Yuri shook his head. "Hey, are you in here? If you can't shout, make some kind of noise."

"What—"

Yuri put a finger to his lips. "Shush. Listen."

It was faint, but definite—a soft thudding sound.

"What is that?" Kohei murmured.

"Okay," Yuri called. "We hear you. Keep making the noise. We'll find you."

They carried on down the aisle, then went back up the next one. The noise was originating somewhere just along the third aisle. Both of them knelt down, shining their pistol beams through the slim gaps between the drums of crude.

"There's space behind here," Kohei exclaimed. "Something's moving in there. I can't see what."

They had to shift three barrels aside before there was a space wide enough for Yuri to crawl through. The back of the rack was covered in a thin metal mesh that had been fixed to the struts with gaffer tape. *Faraday cage,* Yuri realized with reluctant admiration. *It'll block any grain signals, but passively; doesn't show up on a sensor scan.* His power knife sliced through it, and he peered into the narrow gulf between the racks. A man in a t-shirt and shorts was lying on the concrete, looking like he'd been cocooned in gaffer tape. As well as tape binding his limbs, a big strip was across his mouth. More tape secured his shoulders to the rack's struts. The only part of his body he could move were his legs; he'd been pounding his ankles on the concrete.

Yuri wormed his way in. "This is going to hurt," he warned, and pulled the tape from the man's mouth in a fast jerk.

"Motherfucker!"

"Who are you?" Yuri asked.

"Phil. Phil Murray."

"You're from the team we sent in after Dimon, aren't you?"

"Yeah," Phil said furiously. "Arizona S and E squad seven. Our comms were out. Bastards must've jumped me. I think I got tasered. What's happened?"

"Where's your armor?"

"I don't know. I woke up like this. Fuck, I've been here for hours, man. It's . . . not good. Get me out of here."

Yuri checked his screen lens display. There was no signal. "One minute." He pushed his way back out through the rack.

"Hey, don't fucking leave me! Get your ass back in here."

The internet icon came back on as soon as Yuri was back in the aisle. He gave his knife to Kohei. "Cut him loose."

"You got it, chief."

"Boris, call Poi Li, emergency priority."

"Confirmed."

"What is it?" Poi Li asked straight away.

"They stung us."

"What?"

"Callum Hepburn and Akkar. We didn't catch Akkar and Dimon, they caught us. The warehouse was a trap. They snatched Phil Murray when the Arizona team's comms were down. We've just found him, without his armor. I'm guessing Callum is wearing it, escorting Dimon to whatever rendition site you bury our opponents away in."

"Holy fuck!"

It was the only time Yuri had ever heard his ice queen boss swear, which he found strangely satisfying. "You going to tell me what the hell is going on now?"

Wherever the facility was, it looked like it was deep underground. The corridor's walls, floor, and ceiling were all concrete, with ribs of more concrete reinforcing it every ten meters. Utilitarian ducts ran along the ceiling, carrying thick bundles of cable. Air grilles gusted dry, stale air down constantly.

Akkar and Dimon had been dressed in quilted black-and-green jumpsuits and calf-high boots, their wrists cuffed in high-security steel restraints. They were marched along past identical metal doors. Six Arizona S & E guards wearing full body armor with helmets and carrying snub-nosed carbines were escorting them.

The group stopped outside a blank door no different from any of the others. It slid open, and the guards nudged them in.

The room awaiting them was about twenty meters long and seven wide. There was a broad window in one wall, revealing a small control room with three consoles, all occupied by technicians. A thick conveyor belt ran down the center of the room, leading directly to a portal door set against the wall at the far end. It was dark, with small purple scintillations erupting across the surface, indicating it was active but not open. Four yellow plastic cylinders, one and a half meters high, sat on the conveyor belt.

In the control room, the lead technician peered through the glass. "Stand by," he said, his voice booming out of the speakers. "Get the flotation jackets on them."

"The what?" Akkar said in alarm.

Two carbines swung around to point directly at his chest. One of the escorts picked up a pair of orange flotation jackets that were lying on the end of the conveyor belt.

"Opening the portal," the technician announced.

"I can't swim," Akkar said.

"You go through with or without the jacket," a guard said. "Your choice, but you are going through. We've done this a hundred times already."

The scintillations in the portal door faded away. The darkness became a misty gray, revealing nothing. Air from the room started to flow through it. The ceiling grilles hissed loudly as more air was pumped in to compensate.

One of the guards walked over to the portal door and peered through.

"Careful, Phil," another said. "Not so close. Ain't no way back."

"Lowering the exit," the technician said.

"What is this?" Akkar demanded, his voice rising as his cuffs were unlocked. "Where are you sending us?"

"Shut up, and put the fucking life jacket on, tough guy."

"Watch the belt," the technician said. "I'm starting it up. The survival pods will go through first."

The metal door opened. Poi Li stepped into the room, five armed security personnel fanning out around her, pistols held ready. "This operation is canceled," she snapped. "Close the portal. Do it."

All three technicians in the control room stared at her in surprise. The conveyor belt started to move, carrying the four cylinders along.

"Escort guards, stand down," she ordered. "Remove your helmets. Now. You, by the portal, step away."

The guard who'd been staring into the emptiness beyond the portal door stood perfectly still in front of it.

"Take your helmet off," Poi Li ordered.

His hand went up slowly, gripped the helmet rim, and lifted it off. Callum smiled at Poi Li, then flipped backward through the portal.

"No!" Poi Li yelled.

The gray mist on the other side of the portal door swallowed him immediately, leaving no trace.

The call came in to Brixton seventy minutes after Moshi Lyane started his shift. "We need an on-the-ground assessment at the Berat plant," Fitz said. "The fire's starting to spread."

"Where the hell is Callum?" Dokal asked. "He should have been here an hour ago."

The crew exchanged glances across the office. They didn't say anything.

"We can handle this," Moshi said. "It's just an assessment."

Dokal glanced through the glass into the Monitoring and Coordination Center. Fitz was standing up at his console, hands on hips, giving her an impatient stare.

"Corporate has authorized our presence," she said. "All right. Moshi, take it."

He grinned reassuringly. "We're on it."

"Somebody tell me where Berat is," Colin complained.

Raina slapped him on the shoulder as they headed for the door. "Albania."

"Want to know where that is?" Henry asked.

He was shown two vigorous fingers.

They quickly dressed in their hazmat suits and strode through Connexion's portal door network. Plans of the old chemical plant were thrown up across Moshi's screen lenses. They showed him the fire approaching a cluster of storage tanks. Lists of the compounds they used to hold appeared.

"They'll be trouble to vent," Alana said. "It's just residuals, sticking to the casing."

"Let's find out," Moshi said, and stepped through the last portal. "Going in now, Fitz."

He found himself in a long courtyard formed by high, dilapidated buildings that had been abandoned years before. The portal door was surrounded by ten paramilitaries wearing full body armor. Each of them was leveling a carbine on the crew as they stepped out. Moshi's mInet reported a loss of connection with the Brixton Monitoring and Coordination Center. "Oh, crap."

Colin, Alana, Henry, and Raina pressed together around him.

Behind the ring of paramilitaries, a big gray four-by-four was parked in the shade. Yuri Alster stood beside it. "You can all take your helmets off," he said. "There is no fire."

Moshi pushed his visor up. "What's going on?"

Yuri walked right up to him. "Please don't be insulting. You know why you're here."

"Fuck you," Raina snarled.

"Ms. Jacek," Yuri said. "Fashionable rebel to the end."

She spat on the ground.

"You were all in Kintore six hours ago," Yuri continued levelly. "You'll be glad to know your plan worked. Callum is with his fiancée."

"Wife," Moshi said.

"Excuse me?"

"Savi is his wife."

"Ah, that explains a lot. Well, it doesn't matter now. I know you all helped him. Your travel logs showed us you were all in Kintore ten hours ago."

"Proves nothing," Alana said.

"We're not in court," Yuri said. "And, sadly, you're already dead in this terrible fire." His hand waved expansively at the empty, sun-soaked courtyard.

"Bastard!" Raina screamed. "I'm not some eco-warrior that you can disappear. I have friends, family."

"Yeah, it was all very fucking tragic," Yuri said. "The fire at the chemical plant reached some chemical drums that exploded. You were all killed. The coffins will be sealed, to spare your families."

"You can't do this."

"It's already done. It happened the moment you chose to help Hepburn."

"What are you going to do to us? Just execute us in cold blood? We didn't do anything wrong! You took his wife from him."

"Nobody is being executed."

"What then?"

"You will be joining Callum and Savi." Yuri turned to the para-militaries. "Take them away."

Yuri had been awake so long he'd lost track of time zones. So he wasn't surprised that dawn light was shining through the windows of Poi Li's New York office. He didn't even wait to be invited to sit, just slumped into a chair in front of her desk.

"It's over then?" she said.

"Yeah. Your Arizona team took them out of Albania. The deaths have been announced. We included Callum."

"Well done. That was a good catch, Yuri. Connexion appreciates it."

"So will I get to shake hands with Ainsley?"

"Gunning for my job?" she asked archly.

"No."

"Yes, you are. No need to be coy. We're both realists. You'll get here eventually. This operation showed me you have what it takes."

"Okay. But I will need to know Arizona S and E isn't Connexion's secret death squad."

"It's not. I would never agree to run such a thing for Ainsley Zangari and his associates."

"Associates? You mean it's not just Connexion doing this?"

"There is a covenant between several of the globalPACs," Poi said. "Ainsley is allied with some of them, naturally. They carry huge influence; some would say they are Earth's true supra-government. And I am a realist. I looked around at the world we live in and agreed with their proposal."

"Which is?"

"Society has been under siege from malicious elements for too long now. Law and order must be paramount for any civilization worthy of the name to flourish, especially now we are all neighbors, *one step away* from each other. Those who do not accept due process, who refuse to acknowledge the democratic mandate, are a cancer on society. And it is a terrible irony that our very liberalism allows such danger to flourish. There has to be a time when we say: no more. And thanks to Connexion, that time has now come. As Edmund Burke said—"

" 'The only thing necessary for the triumph of evil is for good men to do nothing,' " Yuri quoted.

"Indeed," Poi Li acknowledged. "The globalPACs knew they had to do something if our children were ever to live in a society free from the fear of maniacs blowing things up and killing people in the name of their cause. For there are so many causes. But we cannot descend to their level, where violence and death are the solution to anything that denies them their goal. We do not kill or maim, or even imprison; that is what sets us apart from them. This new transgalactic society we are about to embark on affords us the opportunity to deal with such unreasoning fanatics humanely. We will simply part company with their kind and allow them to live their lives by their own ideals."

"So what happens to them?"

"Exile."

Callum fell. He knew that was going to happen as soon as he lurched through the portal door. What he wasn't expecting was to keep on falling.

Whatever gloomy mist he was falling through seemed to be sucking the air from his lungs. When he did manage to inhale, it was as if he was gulping down frigid Arctic vapor.

Is that it? A polar gulag?

He landed in water, creating a huge plume that closed over his head as he plummeted down. He was expecting it to be cold, but it was so hot it was almost scalding. The shock of its heat knifing into his flesh made him yell—big mistake. His mouth and nose filled with disgustingly briny water as his arms and legs flailed around. There was no light, so he couldn't tell which way was up.

Don't panic. Panic will kill you.

He felt around for the torch clipped to his belt. In seconds his lungs had gone from freezing to burning as his body demanded he draw a breath. Water was slowly creeping farther along his nostrils.

The torch came on. And he could see through the murky water, which was now stinging his eyes. Bubbles swirled around him, and finally he could see which way they were going. Up.

He kicked urgently. Arms scrabbled in a pathetic stroke. The bulk of his saturated clothes and everything he was carrying combined to weigh him down. Progress was achingly slow. The pain in his lungs was growing intolerable. Instinct was trying to prise his mouth open so he could suck down blessed air.

He kicked harder, arms pumping.

His head broke through a thin surface layer of yellow scum, and he sucked down a fraught breath. Immediately he was coughing and spluttering. The air was dangerously thin, yet heavy with brimstone. He concentrated on staying afloat, getting his breathing under control.

After a few breaths, he realized the heat was going to prove lethal in a very short time. Already his skin was on fire. Apollo was throwing up all sorts of medical warning symbols on his screen lenses. Movement was difficult.

He shone the torch around, trying to see anything solid he could swim toward.

"Hey there!" a call came.

"Here! Here!" Callum cried out.

"This way, man."

A powerful beam of white light swept over the filthy layer of froth. Callum shone his own torch in the direction from which it originated. The beam found him, dazzling.

"We see you," the voice yelled. "Make your way toward us. Fast as you can. This water's gonna screw you up."

Every movement was difficult now. The heat was stabbing through his flesh to grip his bones, slowly paralyzing him. He felt like he was being boiled alive, but he kept sweeping his arms around, wiggling his feet rather than kicking strongly. Long flecks of foam streaked across his face. The torch beam moved off to shine just in front of him, presenting a moving target.

"Come on, you can do it," the voice urged. "Just a few meters more."

He wondered why, if he was this close to the shore, his feet hadn't touched anything solid yet.

"There you go. We got you."

The beam wavered. In the shadows behind it, shapes were moving.

"Catch this."

A rope dropped out of the dark air to land in the frothy surface. He stretched out a hand, unsure if his burning fingers could even manage to grip it.

"Wind it around your arm."

He did his best, but even his arm had become sluggish. Suddenly he was moving fast as the rope pulled him along. Then hands were gripping him, hauling him over a rock shelf that sparkled with a dusting of hoarfrost. He was dragged out of the water, trailing ripples of rank sludge behind him. Strands of mist threaded through the still air all around.

"Congratulations. You made it. Welcome to hell."

Callum swayed about on all fours, dripping steaming water and blobs of scum onto the rock. The intense heat permeating him made every movement painful, yet each breath of frigid air was a torment. He was desperate to get out of his broiling guard's uniform. Torchlight fell on him and held steady.

"Hey, what the fuck?" his male savior exclaimed.

"What is it?" a second voice asked. Female.

"That's a guard's uniform. The bastard's Connexion Security."

"What?"

"No," Callum said, or tried to. The glacial air just came out of his mouth as a loud wheeze.

A hand gripped the hair on the back of his head, forcing him to look up. "You a guard, dickhead? You fall through by mistake, huh?"

"No."

"I'm going to make you wish this was hell!"

The kick caught Callum in the side of his torso, shunting him across the rock. He flopped onto his back. The torch beam was still on him, blotting out the people behind. He could hear a footfall. Then another kick slammed into his ribs. Pain stars flashed across his vision. He wanted to scream in fury but didn't have the strength or breath.

"Throw him back in," the female voice demanded.

"Yeah—eventually."

Callum reached down to his belt, hoping his memory was good, that his hand was in the right place. Fingers protested every nerve impulse but slowly closed around the device's grip.

"Gonna make you bleed," the man growled. "Gonna make you scream. You'll beg me to kill you before I'm done slicing you. I know how to make that happen. Oh, man, do I ever." There was a flash in the gloom as the torchlight shone off a blade.

It gave Callum a target. He fired the pistol.

There was a furious screech that twisted off into agonized grunting. The man dropped to the ground. Callum could hear limbs thrashing about as the dart pumped electricity into his erstwhile tormenter.

"Shit!" the woman shouted.

Callum shifted around on the ground. The torch was a huge clue where she was. It was a massive effort to make his fingers respond, but he managed to fire again. Missed. The torch beam swung around, which gave him an indication of which hand she was holding it in, where her body must be. Then it was wobbling from side to side as she started running.

He fired again. She wailed as the dart struck, then fell. The torch tumbled away and rolled across the rock, ending up pointing out across the simmering water.

Callum rolled onto his back and squeezed his eyes shut for a long moment. "Holy fuck."

The heat was abating—fractionally. He knew he had to get out of his sodden clothes. The armored jacket was easy to shrug out of. Vapor billowed off his shirt and trousers, fluorescing a vivid white in the torchlight. He stripped them off quickly but left the slim backpack in place. The sight of his skin, now a nasty shade of salmon-pink, made him grimace. But the cold was cutting into him now, almost as bad as the heat from a minute ago. He could feel himself starting to go numb.

"Where the fuck is this place?" he muttered as he bent over the man he'd darted. His victim was in his late thirties with a thick beard, wearing a heavy quilted coat and equally thick trousers, similar to the ones they'd put on Akkar and Dimon.

Callum claimed the coat for himself but let the man keep his sweater. Next prize were the boots and trousers.

Once he was dressed properly, he made himself sit for a few minutes, spending the time sorting through the equipment that was attached to Phil Murray's stolen uniform. His abused skin was one giant itch, and he could feel his blood singing around his body as the adrenaline high gradually dissipated. As his heart calmed, he began to take in what had happened. The air was subzero and so thin he was clearly at considerable altitude, yet the lake he'd fallen into had to be a geothermal vent. *Iceland?* But his smartCuff couldn't get a lock on any navigation satellites, which was troubling.

He stood up and walked over to retrieve the big torch. When he shone it on the woman, he saw an elderly lady with ebony skin and a mass of frizzy gray hair flaring out from under a dark wool hat. Her quilted coat was similar to the man's, as were her trousers and boots.

He swung the torch beam back to the man. He'd left him his sweater, but his bare legs were turning blue, and frost was forming on them. "Ah, bollocks."

Callum turned in a slow circle, scanning the beam about. If the reception party was on some kind of watch to help the people Connexion dropped into the water, then they'd be ready with dry clothes. Sure enough, three of the yellow plastic drums were standing ten meters from the shore. He went over to them and rummaged through the blankets and coats he found inside. There was also a flask of tea, which tasted bitter—as if he cared.

One of the pouches on the stolen uniform contained zip-lock strips. Callum spent a couple of minutes binding the man and woman together and wrapping blankets around the man's bare legs so he didn't get frostbite or hypothermia.

Then he pulled up the coat's hood and settled down to wait.

The woman recovered consciousness first. She groaned a lot, and winced, and tried to move.

"Crap," she grunted when she found how securely she was fastened to her companion.

"Hello," Callum said.

She scowled at him. "You shot me, you piece of shit!"

"Just before you two started to cut chunks off me. Yeah, I'm mean that way. And the name's Callum."

"Start running, Connexion fascist. If you thought Donbul was pissed at you before, wait until he wakes up. The hunt will be fun."

"I'm not Connexion . . . Well, I do work for them, but not in security."

"Liar."

He shrugged and sipped some more of the odd tea. Sure enough, the woman managed to stay silent for about a minute.

"What are you doing?" she asked, genuinely bewildered.

"Waiting for my friends. Connexion is going to go apeshit that they helped me, so they should be shipping them out here in a day or so. By the way, where is here? I thought Iceland at first, but I'm not so sure now. Antarctic?"

"Like you don't know."

"'Fraid not."

She sniffed in contempt and turned her head away. When she looked back, he saw real anger in her expression. "We'll kill you!"

He grinned, specifically to annoy her. "No, you won't."

"What friends?"

"Who am I talking to?"

"I'm not telling you my name."

"But if you're going to torture me to death anyway, what difference will it make?"

She stared at him for a moment. "Foluwakemi."

"Where are you from, Foluwakemi? Nigeria, probably, right?"

"And you know this how, spy? I'm in your files, aren't I?"

"Ah, a promotion: dumb guard to spy in five fast minutes. How flattering. No, I'm not a spy. My mInet suggested Nigeria." He held up his arm so she could see the jet-black smartCuff.

"My God, you have working electronics?"

"Yep."

"Then you are a spy."

"Crap, but you're paranoid." He waved his hand at the surrounding darkness. "Mind, I suppose you have that right. Dumped here, wherever here is. Incidentally, my mInet can't lock on to any satnav signals. So that makes this place *extremely* remote. I'm guessing the Antarctic's Ellsworth Mountains. Quite high up them, too, with air this thin."

Her grin made him uneasy; it betrayed the fact she thought she still had some advantage. "Wrong. Who are you?"

"I told you: Callum."

Donbul groaned. His head came up, and his gaze fixed on Callum.

"Untie me," he demanded.

"So you can start stabbing me?" Callum said archly. "I don't think so."

"You are going to hurt so bad."

"Real tough guy, huh? You need to dial it down there, pal."

"You think you can outrun us?"

"Do I look like I'm trying to run somewhere?"

That brought a puzzled frown. "What the fuck is this? Who are you?"

Callum sighed. "Callum. I'm a team chief in Connexion's Emergency Detoxification division."

"All I see is a dead man walking."

"You need to be nicer to me," Callum said. "Really."

"Go fuck yourself, dead man."

"Why? You know someone else who's going to get you out of here?"

That made them both gawp. Callum grinned. "Oh, do I have your attention now?"

"Nobody can get us out of here," Foluwakemi said.

"We'll see."

"Why are you here?"

"I've come to find my wife. I think Connexion renditioned her."

"Why would they do that?"

"She was caught up in the protest against the Australian desert being seeded with ice. Did those people get sent here?"

"Yes." Foluwakemi nodded. "Over a hundred of them."

"Christ almighty! How many people are here?"

"There are thousands of us."

"Thousands?"

"Yes."

"But . . . Is this a camp?"

"No, there's nobody here but us. Connexion dumped us here to fend for ourselves."

Callum gave an involuntary shiver. "Pretty tough, huh?"

"Worse than you think. The crop seeds they provided aren't much good. The biologists among us think there's too much iron in the soil."

"Crops? In Antarctica? There's no such thing."

Foluwakemi gave him a pitying smile. "Look up, detoxification man."

Callum did as he was told. He hadn't noticed dawn arriving above the glare of the torch. That was reasonable enough, as it hadn't come to the horizon. Instead, directly overhead, a wide strip of the sky was tinged with an insipid gray light. He frowned at the anomaly, scanning around in a full circle. As the light grew, he realized he was in the bottom of a canyon, but the poor light was making it difficult to judge the scale of the rock walls on either side. That and his mind was refusing to accept what he saw. He was constantly trying to adjust the perspective.

His jaw slowly hinged open as reality soaked his brain in parallel to the weak sunlight. The sheer cliffs were at least seven kilometers high, probably more, with a floor maybe five kilometers across. He'd been to the Grand Canyon a few years ago, done the whole tourist routine—some rafting, climbed an easy face of rock. This was an order of magnitude larger, which was ridiculous.

"Where the hell are we?" he blurted.

"You just called it, asshole," Donbul mocked. "Hell. Otherwise known as Zagreus."

"No," Callum said. "No, no. That's not possible." He didn't have to consult Apollo's files for that; Zagreus was an exoplanet slightly larger than Earth, but with an atmosphere as thin as Mars and no surface water. It orbited three AUs out from Alpha Centauri A. When the *Orion* starship decelerated into the Centauri system, there had been quite a clamor to begin terraforming it. But it was so much cheaper to build a second wave of starships and send them farther out to stars with more suitable exoplanets.

"Still think you can get us out of here?" Foluwakemi sneered.

Yuri looked around the domestic disaster zone that was Callum's flat and wrinkled his nose, partly from the sight, but there was also a weird smell coming from the galley kitchen.

"Don't we pay him enough for a housekeeping service?" Kohei asked.

Yuri grunted. "Apparently not."

Two technical officers came in and went over to the small white block in the corner of the room, which was the G3Turing house manager.

"I want a complete memory download," Yuri told them. "Unlocked files available to my desk in two hours."

"Yes, sir."

He walked across the living area, frowning in disapproval at the large number of empty pizza boxes scattered around. "Plenty of people were here," he said. "He knew he was planning a one-way trip, so what's the point of clearing up?"

"You think they planned it here?" Kohei said.

"Probably. It doesn't matter now."

"So why are we here?"

Yuri pulled a face, unable to fully explain his sense that somehow they'd lost, that Callum was laughing at them. After so many years in the job you got a feel for things, for people in all their crazy glory. His old training back in Russia concentrated on individuals, where everyone was considered suspect, untruthful, corrupt. Now his corporate staff were all strictly procedure-focused, utilizing data trawls and analysis matrices. If they wanted someone, they didn't go out of the office and hunt them, they just waited until facial recognition algorithms pulled them out of a public street camera. There were no real chases, only drones auto-tracking their targets. It was one of the reasons he enjoyed running the undercover ops division; intelligence gathering was as close as he got to old-school these days. Until Callum Hepburn had come along.

Callum didn't fit any profile they were used to. He wasn't motivated by greed or ideology or religion; wasn't mentally ill or drug addled. Didn't want to rule the world. Callum was a man in love, and desperate. Best of all, he was smart and tough, unafraid to take chances.

"Do you not think something's wrong with all this?" Yuri asked.

Kohei let out a small groan. "We got them all. What could be wrong?"

"Yes. We were always going to get them."

"Not necessarily. It was only because you're smart enough to work out what was going down that we found Phil Murray."

"They stuck tape across his mouth. He'd have chewed through eventually."

"In a disused warehouse."

"Due a maintenance visit for the lights. And anyway, when Callum took a dive through the portal into exile, we'd have known Murray had been substituted."

"They're gone, chief. You need to close the file."

Yuri stared at a large framed picture on the wall with an August 2091 date along the base. It was Callum and his team gathered around their Ducati 999, all of them with their arms around one another's shoulders, smiling exuberantly. A tight crew.

"Would you do that for me?" Yuri asked his deputy.

"Chief?"

"If my fiancée had been renditioned, and I was planning to go after her, would you help me, knowing that help would be discovered, and the outcome would mean exile? Permanent exile in the most remote hellhole Connexion could find?"

"Well . . . I don't know."

"No, don't flatter me; you wouldn't do it." Yuri's forefinger tapped the picture. "Henry Orme's partner is about to give birth, for God's sake! Callum didn't even let him go to the Gylgen plant; he sent him to supervise the Haumea end of the operation where he'd be safe. And the rest, they all care about one another. They're friends, they face danger together on a weekly basis, they party together, they share the bike. But this . . ." He stared at the sunlit happy faces, trying to absorb the camaraderie. "To willingly go into an unknown exile together. To make that sacrifice, give up your whole life. Unanimously. I don't believe it."

"But . . . they did do it. They knew we'd send them after Callum, it's the only way we could be sure this whole rendition thing didn't leak to the media."

Yuri moved his finger over to Callum's head. "Yes. Why, though?"

"They owe him, maybe?"

"No, not owe. Trust. They *trust* him. Every time they face a disaster, they trust him with their life. He plans every operation. We think they take risks, but actually they don't. Callum's too clever for that. He's got backups and fresh angles and cutoffs all worked out in his head long before they actually take that one step into a danger zone. And that's what we're dealing with here."

"Sorry," Kohei said. "I just don't see it."

Yuri smiled at the picture. "That's it! We're not seeing it."

"Chief?"

His knuckles rapped the frame. "What's missing? They're all there. Callum, Moshi, Henry, Alana, Raina. The whole team."

"Yes? So?"

"So who took the picture?"

It took half an hour, and a lot of shouted insults, but by then Donbul was simply going through the motions. Callum could see doubts troubling the man, that just because he'd come through wearing a guard's uniform, that didn't actually make him a guard. That and hope. *A way out.*

Callum strapped the guard uniform belt around his coat, checked the weapons, and cut the pair of them loose. He stood back, one hand very close to the pistol holster. "Just so we understand each other, I don't trust you. So keep your distance and no fast moves. I've sacrificed everything to come here. Shooting you won't even register."

Foluwakemi stretched and rubbed her wrists. Donbul simply glared at him and went over to the drums to find himself new trousers and boots.

Now that the daylight had strengthened, Callum could see the lake was actually a rough circle a couple of hundred meters in diameter. Sitting on the rock shelf just out of the water was a raft made entirely of the yellow drums lashed together.

"It's a volcanic caldera," Foluwakemi said, watching him. "There's a group of them in this section of the canyon. Without them, we'd be dead. They supply all our heat and water."

Callum glanced up at the phenomenal walls of rock. "And the air? Do they vent that as well?"

"Only sulfur gas. We're seven kilometers below the planet's average ground level. That's why we have air. It's a tiny pocket, the last on Zagreus. It must have had a full terrestrial atmosphere at one time, maybe a million years ago. But now it's as thin as Mars, that's why no one bothered to try and terraform it. You'd have to import a whole new atmosphere. Too expensive, especially when exoworld astronomy has found so many worlds with a nitrogen-based atmosphere close by."

"How long's the canyon?"

"Three hundred kilometers, we think. A few of us remember the *Orion* survey images and news reports. But less than twenty percent is habitable, and this is the only cluster of geothermal vents."

Callum squinted up into the sky. It had brightened to an astonishingly deep sapphire blue. "Where's the portal?"

"It's on some kind of drone blimp, we think," Donbul said. "They lower it when they're sending a batch of people through—which only happens at night, so we can't ever see it. That way we can't jump on board and go back through the portal. The rest of the time it stays up there somewhere, all nice and safe from us badboys."

"Makes sense," Callum muttered. "So it won't come down again until tonight?"

"Never has," Foluwakemi said. "But then we've never had anyone like you come through before, either."

"It'll take security a while to work out what's happened. As soon as they do, they'll round my crew up and send them through along with Dimon and Akkar."

"Akkar?" she asked sharply, and crossed herself. "They caught Akkar? Well, shit."

"They didn't catch him. He went visible so I could position myself for this. Very visible, actually."

"You are joking, detoxification man."

"No joke."

"Akkar's coming?"

"Yes. And when he does, we're all out of here. Everyone goes home."

"I'll take you to the longhouses," Foluwakemi said. "You can see if your wife is there."

"Thank you."

"If she's not . . ."

Callum grinned weakly. "Don't worry, I'll still get you all out."

It wasn't far to the collection of buildings that the exiles had built for themselves. Callum ordered Apollo to record everything his screen lenses were capturing. They would all be relying on the images for leverage when he got back to Earth. He didn't know what to look for at first, so it took him a while to recognize what he was walking toward. In his mind he'd pictured a medieval-style village of circular huts with thatched roofs. Stupid, because Zagreus didn't have any vegetation; there were no trees for wood or palms. Instead the outcasts had built themselves stone walls three meters high, forming long rectangles. They were roofed with sheets of transparent polythene.

"It comes in big rolls," Foluwakemi explained. "They send it inside the survival barrels, like everything else. It's thin, but really tough, thankfully."

"What else do they give you?"

"Clothes." She patted her coat. "Seeds, eggs, some tools, a few utensils, basic medicine. Food, of course—to start with. You get enough to last a few months, by which time you should be growing your own." She shrugged. "At least, that's the theory some desk expert worked out. In practice, it's bloody hard. Poor nutrition causes a lot of health problems. And this air's none too good for us, either. Then there are . . . disputes."

There were plenty of people milling around outside. Five new longhouses were under construction. Callum stared at the wheelbarrows that stones were being carried about in, marveling at the ingenuity. Each was made of a barrel cut lengthwise, with a barrel rim as its wheel, strips of barrel forming the handles.

"They're damn useful," Foluwakemi admitted reluctantly as she caught him watching.

She went over to one of the crews building a wall. Callum's hand stayed very close to his pistol as she talked to them. A group started to gather, inspecting him from a distance, their voices a low grumble on the verge of menacing. It was the weapons on his belt that made him stand out, he knew; everyone here would be up-close familiar with the types and who carried that particular combination. He kept his nerve and stared back levelly, as if they were of no consequence.

Then, as he dreaded would happen, someone was striding across the ground toward him, a big man with a dark beard that hung a good twenty centimeters down the front of his coat. He was carrying an axe, its handle made from thick strips of yellow barrel plastic, bound to a stone blade. His supporters in the watcher group started to flow after him.

Foluwakemi turned around. "Oh, shit," she grunted.

"You," the big man shouted. "Shithead. Who the fuck are you?"

Callum knew that being reasonable was never going to be an option. He drew the short carbine, switched it to single shot, and fired just in front of the man's feet—not bothering to take good aim, just showing how nonchalant he was, how he was The Man now. The noise of the shot was astonishingly loud in the thin air. Everyone recoiled.

"I've got about seventy rounds," Callum said clearly, "so I can probably kill about fifty of you before you reach me. Alternatively"—he raised the carbine and flicked on the laser targeting beam, slapping the red dot squarely on the man's face—"I can take you all back to Earth. Your call."

The man kept jerking his head about, trying to dodge the beam. Callum kept it aligned pretty well given the circumstances.

"Listen to him, Nafor," Foluwakemi said. "He came through alone. They didn't drop any survival barrels with him. That's never happened before. He wasn't renditioned. He came here because he wanted to; he's searching for someone."

"No way," Nafor barked. He must have realized how much face he was losing in front of his followers.

"There's a portal door in my backpack," Callum said, raising his voice so everyone could hear.

That drew a universal gasp of surprise.

"Oh, yeah," Callum said contentedly. "You heard that right." He stopped and made an effort to dial down the arrogance. "I'm the only one who has the access code, so listen good. We are waiting until Connexion exiles my friends here; then—and only then—will I start the thread-up procedure. After that, if you want to come through after me, you're welcome." He saw Nafor draw a breath, his mouth opening to speak.

"No!" Callum bellowed. He raised the target dot slightly and fired another shot into the air. "No discussion! No arguing! That's the way it happens. Now either accept that, or fuck off."

Very carefully Nafor raised his arms. "You got it, buddy. Anyone who can get me out of here is my friend for life."

Callum scowled, covering up just how shit-scared he actually was.

Foluwakemi cleared her throat.

"What?" Callum snapped.

"I think I know which longhouse your wife's in. If you can calm down and not shoot me, I'll take you there."

She led him along the tracks between the longhouses, most of which seemed to have gullies of steaming water running alongside them. The gullies branched frequently, taking the water through low arches into individual longhouses. They'd only just started off when he realized that Nafor was following him, along with everybody else, all of them keeping a respectful distance. "I am not the messiah," he grumbled under his breath.

Foluwakemi opened a door (made from sections of yellow barrel), and they walked into a longhouse. The air inside was thick with strong scents, and hot. The humidity was almost tropical. Hot water flowed down a shallow stone channel running the length of the building.

Callum checked that Apollo was still recording everything he was seeing. Sandy soil was banked up between the water and the walls, with densely planted crops growing out of it. The majority of vegetation was maize, but he recognized tomato plants and avocados, eggplants, breadfruit, dwarf bananas, as well as several varieties he couldn't place. None of them looked particularly vigorous, as if they were suffering from a universal blight. When he looked up, he saw the polythene was coated in condensation that dribbled steadily toward the walls.

"How long is a day here?" he asked, looking at the sickly leaves.

"Nineteen hours thirty-two minutes," Foluwakemi said. "It messes with us and the plants, along with the minerals we can't filter out of the water. Nafor putting his Stone-Age axe through your skull can lower your life expectancy, as well."

"Is he in charge?"

"He'll tell you he is. This month, anyway. Someone as big and stupid will go for him soon, if we're still here. It's the worst kind of primitive. Frankly, I'm surprised we've lasted this long. Each new group that arrives brings their own set of opinions—with a capital O."

Pens of close-spaced yellow plastic poles marked the end of the vegetation. Scrawny chickens pecked at the rough ground inside; Callum held his breath against the smell. Beyond the pens was a curtain of polythene. Foluwakemi pushed it aside.

Inside was a sickbay with a row of ten cots, all of them occupied. The smell of vomit and feces and diseased breath was a miasma worse than anything the chickens produced. Callum nearly gagged as he scanned along the figures wrapped in blankets. Apollo sent out a ping for her grains, but there was no answer.

There. Halfway along the row. Thick, filthy, black hair hung limply over the side of a cot. He let out a sob and sank to his knees beside her.

Savi's face was wrapped in crude gauze bandages, heavily stained with old blood and yellow suppurations. More bandages covered her arms. A leg was splinted. Her breathing was shallow.

The sight of her in this state was terrifying. "Wife?" he whispered.

She inhaled, coughing. "Cal?"

"Yes." He smiled through his tears. "Yes, it's me."

Her head turned, and through the apertures in the bandage mask he saw her eyes open. One of them was a milky white orb. "How can you be here?" she asked.

"Better or worse, remember? I said I will follow you to the ends of the Earth—and beyond. I would never break that promise. Not to you."

Kohei stood inside the Brixton facility's Monitoring and Coordination Center, staring around at the wallscreens with their high-resolution images of potential ecological doom. He'd never really paid attention to the ancient industrial sites that human companies had abandoned all across the planet. Threats of midlevel disaster were a constant background buzz in his life, like taxes and online crime; you just lived with it. But now he was actually watching an unending parade of dilapidated tanks and pipes and storage bunkers flowing across the screens, with associated symbology highlighting impending problems.

"How much crap is out there?" he asked in dismay.

Fitz Adamova gave him a knowing grin. "Haumea station dumps about a quarter million tons a week. That's mostly low-level contaminants and their secure containers." He pointed to an Iraqi nuclear store. "And then there's the containment vessels themselves, along with the buildings and local soil. It adds up, volume-wise."

"Jesus, why do we do it?"

"War and profit, mainly."

Kohei shook his head, focusing on the job. "Okay, I need you to run an equipment audit."

Fitz's eyebrows shot up. "You are kidding? Our teams burn through equipment faster than a solar flare. We're lucky if we get half of it back from an operation."

"I'm not particularly bothered about the engineering junk. I want to know if all your portal doors are accounted for."

"Well, that's easy enough: yes."

"No," Kohei said firmly. "It's not easy. We suspect someone with inside access has manipulated your network. I need you to check. Go down to the storage bays and physically confirm they're all there if you have to."

Fitz blew out his cheeks. "Seriously?"

"Yes. And I need to know quickly. This has priority over everything. We believe someone is currently using one of this department's portal doors, and they really shouldn't be."

"Okay. Well, actually, that can be checked quite simply." He went over to his station, looking back at Kohei with a quizzical expression. "You sure it's in use?"

"Reasonably sure, yes."

Fitz started calling up data on his screens. "Do you know how portal doors are powered?"

"Not got a clue," Kohei said, amused by the way technical types always tried to establish some level of superiority over everyone else. *My knowledge is bigger than yours.*

"Portals."

"What?"

"Portals power portals." Fitz smiled and tapped a ridiculously complex graphic on his central screen. "The solarwells send electricity back to Earth's central grid via portal, and Connexion is the single biggest market for that power. Portals use up a hell of a lot of energy to maintain their entanglement. The greater the distance they bridge, the more power they consume. It's not governed by an inverse square law, thankfully, but this department consumes a pretty hefty number of megawatt hours."

"Okay, I get it. You can monitor that power consumption."

"Yes. Every Connexion portal door has a one-centimeter portal built in, which supplies it with power direct from the central grid. And we . . . Oh, wait, that's wrong." He leaned forward, studying the screen.

"What is?"

"Our power usage monitor is offline, but its display function has frozen in a loop. How the hell did that happen?"

"Can you restore it?"

"Sure. Hang on." Fitz typed quickly, muttering at his mInet. The graphics on the screen changed. Several red icons appeared. "Holy shit," he exclaimed. "What is doing that? Not even our six-meter portals eat this much power."

Callum sat beside Savi's cot all day long. She slid in and out of consciousness in front of him. Some of the times when she woke, she seemed puzzled by his presence.

The doctor, a middle-aged South African man, ran through her injuries for him. Her clothes had protected most of her skin from the direct blast, he said, but her head and arms and hands had been exposed, and she was close to the bag when it detonated. Callum guessed her grains had been ruined by the explosion, or ripped away when the blast wave tore her flesh off; which was why Connexion Security didn't know who she was when they dropped her through the portal. The surface wounds and burns were slowly turning septic, which if unchecked was going to produce severe blood poisoning. Connexion didn't send metabiotics to Zagreus to counter that. And even if she somehow got through that, she would need modern medskin applied under controlled conditions to restore her natural skin. Her eye was damaged beyond repair, although the doctor thought the optic nerve was still intact, so an artificial retina implant might return her vision. His biggest worry was head trauma. Her responses were deteriorating at a rate the other injuries didn't quite account for.

"Just a few hours more," Callum told her in one of her better lucid periods. "I have to wait for my crew. They exposed themselves to get me here." Though he was beginning to wonder if he dared wait that long. The sight of her, so weak and damaged, was agony. Delaying her admission to hospital was a violation of every feeling he had for her. Time itself became intolerable.

All day long he heard the voices outside, growing in volume. Not with anger, just the sheer number of people who were gathering outside the longhouse. Foluwakemi kept coming in to give him updates. Every human on Zagreus had arrived for the vigil. So far they were being patient, but expectation was growing. With that, tempers were shortening.

"Could you just come out and talk to them?" she pleaded.

"They wait," he said forcefully, gripping Savi's hand tighter so she moaned. "If Savi can do it, they bloody well can. When my friends arrive, then this is over. You have my word."

An hour before sunset, when the sheltered canyon was already reduced to a gloomy half-light, more than two hundred people marched down to the arrival lake. Foluwakemi said they were making very sure there were no screwups when Connexion dropped his friends in the geothermal vent.

Solar-charged lamps were switched on around the sickbay as darkness finally fell, making it appear even more macabre. Callum didn't know when he'd eaten last. Sleep was also a distant recollection, something he used to do in his previous existence. Apollo had to keep sending alert signals to his auditory grains as well as purple flashes to his screen lenses as he kept drifting off.

His time display told him it was two and a half hours after sunset when the cheering started outside. He frowned, puzzled by the sound. Then Foluwakemi rushed in. "They're here," she shouted excitedly. Moisture was glinting in her eyes. "You're telling the truth, aren't you, detoxification man? You can take us home now?"

"I can take you home," he promised. Somehow his voice had become hoarse.

Then they were there: Moshi, Alana, Colin, Raina, and Henry. All wearing thick Zagreus-survival coats, their skin flushed from immersion in the scalding water. Smiling, calling out wild greetings. Akkar and Dimon followed them in, looking dazed.

Callum was pulled to his feet and hugged exuberantly.

"We did it, we fucking did it," Raina was shouting.

"This really is Zagreus, isn't it?" Moshi said, an astounded smile on his face. "We've gone interstellar?"

"Oh, yeah."

"I had money on it being the Antarctic."

Nafor appeared, and the reunion damped down fast.

"It is time," he declared, his gaze never leaving Callum.

"We'll set up outside," Callum told him.

Colin and Dimon carried Savi out on her cot, using it like a stretcher. An area was cleared at the end of the stone longhouse, with one of the hot streams bubbling away along the side. People formed a broad circle around them; more perched on the walls of the longhouse. More than two hundred torch beams shone down.

Callum took off his coat and unfastened his backpack. He pulled the half-meter portal out, and a massive cry went up behind the multifaceted wall of beams.

Alana held it steady on the ground, while Moshi stood in front, ready.

Callum studied the status display on his screen lens. The amount of power the portal was pulling out of the grid to maintain entanglement with its twin back on Earth was spiking close to its internal circuitry safety limits. But it was functional. They had a link. "Activate it," Callum instructed Apollo.

Yuri walked along the tarmac lane that ran the length of the Donnington paddock. He was intrigued by all the old vehicles parked there, surrounded by their enthusiastic crews as they prepped the sleek bikes for racing. The noise of the engines was primal, bringing fond smiles to the older faces among the crowds who ambled along, admiring the mechanical history on show.

He gazed at each of the big vans and trucks carefully, making sure his screen glasses got a clear view. Boris ran pattern recognition, throwing up the model and manufacturer of each one.

The white Mercedes Sprinter van stood out anyway. A small canvas marquee had been erected at the rear end, its side panels zipped up. There was a Ducati bike standing beside it, but no crew or riders, as if the whole area had been abandoned. No genuine race team would leave their precious machine untended.

Sloppy, he thought. *It's always the little things.*

He went into the marquee and banged hard on the rear doors of the van. There was no response.

"Oh, come on," he said in a voice tired with the chase. "It's not as if I brought a tactical team. I'm by myself."

There was a *clunk* as the van's handle turned. Then the rear door swung open.

"Yuri," Dokal Torres said nervously. "What can I do for you?"

"You can stop being a lawyer for today."

"Really? Have you stopped being a security chief?"

"Let's just say I'm on my lunch break. Can I come in?"

She let out a heavy sigh. "Sure. It's a bit cramped."

"I'll live." He clambered into the Sprinter; Dokal checked the marquee was zipped up tight and shut the door behind him.

The threader mechanism almost filled the inside of the van.

"I genuinely wasn't expecting *you*," he admitted.

Her lips squeezed into a small moue. "I think that was the point."

"Callum's good. I should have him on my staff."

"So what now?"

He regarded the intricate mechanics of the threader with interest. "I've never been this close to one of these before, and I've been with the company a long time. I think I'd like to see one in operation. So we'll just wait, if that's okay with you?"

"Why?" she asked.

"Professional pride. Savi is one of my agents. I never leave one of mine behind."

"What does Poi Li think about that?"

"I expect we'll find out soon enough. When will they use it?"

"I don't know. Callum was going to wait until the crew arrived at wherever it is they're renditioned to."

"Ah. Well, they were scheduled to go through ten minutes ago. Apparently, it has to be night at the other end."

They waited in awkward silence for another fifty minutes, then Dokal jumped. "Bloody hell. The core portal is activating. He did it!" She hurriedly opened both of the van's rear doors. Yuri watched the half-meter portal in the middle of the threader turn a midnight black, then its surface twisted inward, falling away to leave a gap. Air started to gush through. "Threading now," she told him.

The rectangular solid-state slab in the first section of the threader split neatly along its narrow length, producing a set of entangled portals. Actuators separated the twinned segments and pushed one through the core portal Callum had opened. A different set of actuators flipped its remaining twin vertical. The airflow through it increased noticeably, making the marquee sides flap about excitedly.

"Help me," Dokal said, and jumped out of the van.

Yuri joined her as the threader's largest portal, a meter-wide circle, divided. One went through to Zagreus. Yuri helped Dokal as the threader turned its twin vertical. Air charged through the opening so fast Yuri had to brace himself to avoid being pulled in. He caught a glimpse of dull, rocky ground surrounded by a weird curving wall of torches. There was a lot of elated cheering going on.

A surprisingly strong impulse gripped him. *If I slip through, I'll be standing on an exoplanet. It's centimeters away, that's all. An alien star!* It was difficult to resist. Then the chance vanished.

Callum was crawling through on all fours. He flinched badly when he saw Yuri, and glanced at Dokal, who shrugged.

"Get on with it," Yuri said impassively.

Callum turned around and started pulling at something heavy on the other side. Yuri's jaw tightened as he saw the state Savi was in.

"Contact the emergency services," Yuri told Boris as his lost agent was manhandled through the portal. "I need a paramedic team here immediately."

Moshi followed Savi, then Raina, who gave Yuri a savage scowl when she saw him standing above her.

"Call Kohei," Yuri told Boris.

Henry came through the circular portal. Then it was Alana blocking the blaze of torchlight. Colin made up the rear.

Yuri squatted down and looked through at Zagreus. Akkar was on his hands and knees, centimeters from the portal.

"Kohei, kill the power," Yuri ordered. "Now."

Akkar screamed in fury, flinging himself forward, his hand reaching toward Earth.

The spatial entanglement between Earth and Zagreus ended. Akkar's fist landed on the paddock tarmac, splattering blood as it rolled to a halt.

"You bastard!" Raina shouted, staring at the severed hand in revulsion.

"Why?" Yuri asked levelly. "Did you want two thousand terrorists living here again, and madder than ever before? Maybe some of them could move into the flat next to yours; I read in your file it's available to rent. This you would welcome?"

"I promised them," Callum said, aghast. "I gave them my word they could come back."

"I didn't," Yuri said.

"They'll kill us if you send us back," Alana said in a shaky voice.

"So you need to behave then, don't you? Because Poi Li is pissed with you at a level even I find scary."

"You can't do this," Callum said; he was still on his knees, holding Savi's hand. He looked up at Yuri, beseeching. "They're people. You can't treat them like this; it's inhuman!"

"No," Yuri said, suddenly angry. "What they do—what they have done—goes way beyond simple criminal acts. They seek to destroy anything they dislike, no matter that it is enacted legally, or how many people are dependent on it. They smash and ruin others' endeavors freely, and feel nothing. That is what cannot stand, not anymore. For once I agree with Ainsley and his ultra-rich political collaborators. Your friend Akkar and his allies *have* been judged, and found guilty. Tough, that judgment didn't come after million-wattdollar-fee lawyers defended them in public courts, followed by ten years of taxpayer-funded appeals; tough, that we don't spend hundreds of thousands a year keeping them in prison. But judged they have been, and far more leniently than they judge you or I. And even now, we give them a second chance."

Raina's hand shot out, pointing at the inert threader. "That planet is not a second chance. That is a death sentence."

"Because of what they are," Yuri sneered. "They have been given an entire world of their own. We provide the means to survive, even to thrive if they learn the basic lessons of society and cooperate rather than fight each other like savages. So I'm really, really sorry if Zagreus isn't a five-star hotel with room service, but we can't afford the luxury of tolerating them anymore. This *is* the humane solution."

"Zagreus has one canyon where humans can breathe, a toxic shit-hole that's poisoning them," she shouted. "That's not a world, it's a freak site. Even if you send us back, we've got the recording of their conditions to blow this whole obscenity out of the water. It's already downloaded into a cache vault. Right, Callum?"

"That's your threat?" Yuri said contemptuously. "Okay, send it. Go right ahead. Send it to every news service in the solar system, every political commentator, every justice department. What do you think is going to happen?"

She glared at him, her facial muscles flexing.

"There'll be referendums in the democracies demanding we bring them back?" he asked in a pitying tone. "Is that it? There'll be international campaigns, million-person protest marches? Is that what you're counting on? That. Will. Not. Happen. What court are you going to take this to? You think it's just one country that exiles these people? One company? One continent? Some of those psychotic bastards are actually lucky they get sent there. Ten years ago, their own government would have simply executed them."

"That's not an excuse," she cried. "Escaping state-sponsored murder doesn't make this right."

"By your standards. Sadly, the rest of us can't afford them. Not anymore."

Raina looked down at Callum. "Chief? We have to go public. Please."

"This is only the beginning," Yuri said to Callum. "You're smart enough to get that, right? That one settlement is an experiment, to see if the most belligerent, dumb, ideological assholes the human race has ever misbegotten can survive on an alien world. And— hallelujah—it worked. They'll go public with it eventually, the unknown, unaccountable people who made this happen, whether you force them to or not. And when they do, that's when the real political pressure will kick in. A planet of no return, a wonderfully safe four light-years away, where every vicious criminal can be sent, and has to work all day long to grow their own food. We wipe our hands of them forever: public conscience clean, crime rates down. How do you think that vote will go, huh?"

"You bastard," Raina said.

"Why aren't we already on our way back there?" Callum asked. "What's actually happening here?"

"Ms. Keates was right. For all of you, Zagreus is now a death sentence. They're not going to wait and listen while you explain nicely that I'm the bad guy. They'll rip you to pieces the instant you drop through—probably eat you, too, given some of the ones we exiled there. I've seen the files."

"So what's the deal?"

"Very simple. You're all through as far as Connexion is concerned— besides which, you're officially dead, anyway. So you shut the fuck up and go away to live your lives wherever you want. I'm *authorized* to say that if you leave us alone, we leave you alone. Our screwup got Savi dumped on Zagreus; the explosion must have wrecked her grains so we couldn't track her digitally. But that's it. I got you this one concession, authorized by Ainsley Zangari himself, because of who the two of you are. And now you're right out of credit. This is a onetime, take-it-or-leave-it offer."

"Hey," a shout came from outside the marquee. "Paramedics here. We got an emergency call."

Yuri cocked his head to one side, regarding Callum carefully. "So?"

Callum gave his wife a desperate, loving look. "Take it," he said wretchedly.

"Shit!" Raina kicked the dead portal door.

"In here," Moshi shouted. He unzipped the marquee's side panel. "She needs help—badly."

Three paramedics ran in.

JULOSS

YEAR 587 AA

Dellian lay back on the warm sands, tired but happy with it, as he waited for the flyer to land. Even after ten days, he was still impressed by the beach—the whole island, actually. The resort was one of the very few that hadn't been allowed to decay naturally after most of the humans living on Juloss had flown off into the galaxy. Its management genten had been left with full control of all its original service and maintenance remotes, to preserve the water bungalows and communal buildings at the same high standard as it had for the previous two centuries.

That standard was one Dellian had swiftly come to appreciate after sixteen years spent in the confines of the Immerle estate and its communal dormitory. If nothing else, he could actually have solitude if he wished. Everyone in his yeargroup had been assigned their own water bungalow—a neat little construction of curving glass walls framed by ancient hardwood beams, topped off with a thatched roof.

They stood several meters out from the shore, resting on living coral pillars. The glass floor gave him a fantastic view of the superbly clear water a meter below and the amazing variety of colorful fish that came sporting through the shallows.

Of course, that solitude had been the last thing on anyone's mind, especially at night. Principal Jenner had announced the ten-day break as a surprise reward for passing their senior year assessments. No adults or muncs would be with them. For the first time in their lives they would be alone, without any external authority to impose order, devoid of responsibility except to themselves.

"So just relax and enjoy yourselves," sie said. "And keep it together. This is as much a test of maturity as anything else. We trust you. Don't let us or yourselves down."

The island had a broad circular lagoon on one side, where the water was barely two meters deep and as warm as a bath. Perfect for learning how to windsurf. The other side was the wide sun-saturated beach open to the ocean, with long jetties where the resort's boats and powerskis waited for anyone who fancied faster, more adventurous, activities. Food was available all day long in the open-walled central pavilion, cooked to perfection by the genten's remotes.

Dellian had swum, powerskied, learned the rudiments of windsurfing, canoed, played tennis and beach volleyball, lazed around drinking by the pool, or sat in the open-air amphitheater watching old dramas. Then as night fell all the boys would pair up, or form larger groups, and head back to the water bungalows for hours of energetic sex. The sea air and the freedom had reacted with their hormonal bodies to fire their libido up to a relentless height. In those ten days Dellian had been to bed with more than half of the boys, including Xante, of course. Xante, who had everyone queuing up to find out how big his cock really was, and who fucked like an angel.

Some of the boys had even been bedded by Tilliana and Ellici. And that had been a major disappointment for Dellian—which for some reason he couldn't let go of. He'd been extremely eager to find out what sex with a girl was like, but Yirella hadn't shared his enthusiasm. He told himself he could wait until she was ready for that level of intimacy, that their friendship was more important to him. Even so, lost in ecstatic congress with his friends every night, it was her face he'd pictured over theirs.

As he waited on the beach, the skin on his bare torso started to tingle in the sunlight. Every morning he'd put on the highest-rated sunblock, which the bungalow's dispenser assured would last all day, only for him to have to apply it again at midday—or, more often, for someone else to slather it licentiously all over his skin for him. He sat up and started pulling on his t-shirt. As he did, Yirella came off the wooden walkway that led to a cluster of the water bungalows. Dellian waved hopefully. She smiled and walked over.

Now that she and the other girls had molted, Dellian considered her bare skull to be quite erotic. He'd been fantasizing about rubbing sunscreen on for her; after all, who didn't like a scalp massage?

"The genten said our ride would be here in ten minutes," he said in greeting.

"And you don't think that's odd?"

Dellian frowned, not quite sure what she was talking about. "Odd how?"

She knelt on the sand beside him, looking down quizzically at his thickset form. Dellian had grown a lot over the last three years, but while he'd increased in shoulder-breadth and weight, mainly due to muscle mass, Yirella had continued her upward climb, leaving her and the other two girls increasingly spindly compared to the boys. When they stood up together now, his eyes were level with her boobs, which he considered a size match about as perfect as you could get.

"Why not just portal back to the estate?" she asked distantly.

"Uh . . . because there is no portal, would be my best guess," he retorted.

"But why is there no portal, Del?"

He frowned, wondering, as always, how her brain functioned. Her head was in direct proportion to the rest of her, which he reckoned made her skull a good twenty percent larger than his—or any boy's.

The geneticists who'd designed the clan's binary children had given her a cute flat nose, wide enough to hold additional blood vessels that fed into a carotid rete at the base of her cranium, a configuration of arteries and veins that basically served as nature's heat exchanger. Yirella and the girls needed it to help cool their larger brains, along with the absence of hair, which would've otherwise acted as insulation over their skulls, preventing the heat from escaping.

All that extra gray matter generated more and smarter thoughts than Dellian could ever manage, just as the geneticists intended. But it meant keeping up with her and the other girls was hard sometimes. "Because now everyone's gone, most of the portals have shut down, especially to somewhere as remote as this." He gave her an expectant look, pleased that he'd come up with a logical and rational answer.

"The resort is maintained to give people a holiday. Therefore, regular transport is an obvious requirement. So why shut it down?"

"I liked the sense of isolation we had here. It made me feel . . . I don't know, different, like seeing what being an adult is going to be like."

She grinned. "Me too. It felt like we were being trusted for the first time ever. That was nice."

His eyes tracked along her amazingly long legs, wondering how they'd feel straddling his hips. Perfection, he decided. "Could've been better," he said wistfully.

Yirella laughed and flicked some sand at him. "Oh, Del, you're not still cross that we didn't have sex, are you?"

"Saints, no. I wasn't cross. I was disappointed, that's all."

"It's just, I don't think this was the right place and time for you and me, that's all. The island was purely about everyone partying and having lots of fun sex. We deserve it after all those battle games we've been playing for the last couple of years; they've been tough. Now we're all as relaxed and happy as we've ever been."

"Yes, but . . . No, sorry, I still don't get it."

She gave him a genuinely caring smile. "Look, we both know we are going to have sex, and it'll be great sex, too. But we have feelings for each other, strong feelings—you know this. So being together could mean a lot more for us. I don't want to risk that by making it the same as a simple holiday fuck. That's why."

"Okay." Dellian's throat had suddenly become very dry. *We are going to have sex.* She actually said that. *Great sex!* He was frantic to ask: *Saints, tell me when?* "Shame you didn't have any ordinary holiday fun sex."

Her smile quickly turned wicked. "Oh, don't worry about me. I had plenty of sex. I mean, have you seen how long Xante's cock is?"

Hearing that was the same as being taken out early in one of the combat tactics games Dellian had spent so much of the senior year playing. It didn't physically hurt, but it was hugely upsetting. "I'm glad," he lied.

The flyer appeared—a matte-gray cylinder with rear stub wings, skimming in over the water. It slowed as it approached the beach, and trim landing legs unfolded from its fuselage.

Yirella shook her head at the machine as it touched down. "Doesn't make sense," she complained.

He laughed. "You really do want to solve every problem in the universe, don't you?"

"Give me time, and I will." Her dazzling smile returned, making Dellian's world a better place again.

They got to their feet together. Then Yirella bent fast and kissed him. "You're special to me," she said seriously. "You're not like the other boys. I don't want our friendship to end."

"It won't," he promised solemnly.

As he joined the queue for the flyer, he glanced around the other boys, seeing blissful expressions and hearing all the cheerful chatter. He tried his best to keep sullen resentment off his face when he saw Xante, whose arms were around Ellici's waist and Janc's shoulders, the three of them laughing away merrily.

Compared to the sun shining down on the island, it was so dark inside the fuselage, Dellian's eyes took a moment to adjust. He found a seat midway along and settled into it. Yirella sat next to him.

He let his head rest deep in the cushioning and half closed his eyes. "Advanced development year," he said, as if surprised by what awaited them when they got back to the clan estate. "I didn't think it would ever come."

"What do you think they'll do to us?" she mused.

"Alexandre said not to worry. The implants will help us boost up; we'll be able to merge with any weapons tech the design teams can produce. The surgery's routine; it doesn't hurt or anything."

"I can't see that I'll be any use fighting the enemy," she said. "You and the other boys, yes; you're all tough. But I'm not."

"You'll command," he said. "You have the tactics and the smarts. All we'll ever do is what you say."

"Suppose I get it wrong?"

"You won't. I trust you."

"Oh, great Saints." She shuddered. "I don't need that."

The flyer lifted from the beach and headed back out across the sea.

"Flight duration is one hundred and seven minutes," the genten pilot announced. "Immerle estate has been notified of your arrival time. Your year mentor, Alexandre, says sie hopes you all had a good time, and is looking forward to seeing you all again."

The statement was greeted with boos and cheers in equal measure. Dellian stared out of the window as they went supersonic. The sea was strangely uniform as it slid past twenty kilometers underneath them. He picked out several island groups but couldn't work out their size. Then they were over land again.

Old cities and settlements were easy to see, gray wounds in the verdant blanket of vegetation. Two or three times he saw columns of smoke winding up from bush fires. His view began to shift as the flyer banked slightly.

"Why are we changing course?" Yirella asked.

"Are we?"

"Yes!" She was looking around, as if seeking confirmation. "Pilot, what is happening?"

The boys in nearby seats glanced curiously at her.

"Stand by for systems confirmation," the genten said.

"What?"

Dellian pressed his face to the window. The land below was becoming rumpled as they started to pass over some low foothills. The green was diminishing, draining away to more rugged browns and ochres, beset with tiny dark specks.

"Systems undergoing irregularities," the genten said. "Please remain seated. Safety restraints will activate in ten seconds. Do not be alarmed, this is a precautionary measure only."

"Oh, precious Saints," Dellian moaned. The flyer's nose-down angle was getting steeper. He couldn't be sure, but he thought their speed was increasing. They certainly seemed to be losing altitude.

He held still as the cushions started to swell, extending a series of rib-like restraints around his torso and limbs.

"What is the nature of the problem?" Yirella demanded.

"Propulsion irregularities. Enabling compensation."

"Del, my databud can't reach the net."

"What?" he grunted.

"I'm cut off. Are you online?"

"Connection check," he ordered his databud.

"Global communication net offline," its voice whispered into his ear.

"Saints! No, it's down," he told her.

"Pilot, why are we offline?" she asked, her voice rising.

"Attempting to reestablish connection with global communication net."

"What do you mean 'attempting'?"

"Temporary connection loss."

"How can that happen? The network is orbital. Everywhere is in range."

"Attempting to reconnect. Operating on reserve power."

"Oh, great Saints!"

"What's our altitude?" Dellian asked.

"Fourteen kilometers. Descending."

"Saints! Are we going to crash?"

"Negative. Reserve power sufficient to enact zero velocity touch-down."

He was proud of himself for not panicking. In fact he was proud of all his clanmates for remaining equally cool, even though it was obvious they were all scared shitless.

The flyer's descent angle slowly became more pronounced as it dropped into a terrifying dive. The foothills expanded fast. Dellian tried to memorize what he was seeing. *Understand your terrain*—one of the golden commandments of tactical training.

The genten leveled them out. Then deceleration kicked in. G-force shoved Dellian down hard into his seat. His vision began to tunnel out, swirls of red closing like a misty iris. He managed to catch sight of ground that was becoming very rocky and steep.

"Touchdown in four, three, two—"

The impact immediately reversed the flyer's acceleration impetus, flinging Dellian and the others about wildly, shaking them. Deafening tearing sounds filled the cabin as the fuselage skidded along. He saw a wingtip spinning chaotically through the air, overtaking them. Then the whole cabin buckled. A split opened up in the front of the fuselage. Dust blasted in. Everyone screamed. There was a final *crunch,* and all movement ended abruptly.

Dellian fought to get his breathing back under control. His heart was thudding as if he'd just finished a marathon. Dust filled his mouth and nostrils, bringing a strange sulfurous smell. The cabin was lying at a perturbing angle, with the floor tilted a good twenty degrees, and nose down. A jagged sheet of sunlight shone through the forward split, fluorescing the ochre sand that saturated the air.

"Are you okay?" he asked Yirella urgently.

"Yes. I think so."

"Everyone okay? Any injuries?"

Rello and Tilliana had been sitting close to the split. They were badly shaken. The dust blast had left their exposed skin burned and abraded. Tilliana's face was bloody; Ellici was already at her side, worrying about the damage to her eye.

"The clan medics can fix that easily," Xante assured her.

"What clan medics?" Ellici snapped back.

"Let's get outside," Dellian told them, keeping his voice level.

Everyone was keen about that; the flyer now represented chaos and danger. But the doorway didn't open, not even when Janc slapped the emergency release button repeatedly. So they eased themselves out through the gash and stood on the sandy ground.

Dellian looked around. There were hills in every direction, with larger slopes blocking the eastern skyline. Soil was thin and dry, supporting a few straggly bushes with shriveled leaves. Odd black sleeper trees poked up at random. Boulders were scattered everywhere, most balancing precariously given the angle of the slope. It was colder than it ought to be with such a bright sun and no clouds.

"Now what?" Xante said.

"Rescue will be here soon," Orellt said positively.

"No, actually," Yirella said, wiggling through the fuselage gap. "There's no power in the flyer, and I can't get the genten to respond. It's dead along with the rest of the systems."

"The emergency beacon will be broadcasting our position," Ellici exclaimed.

Yirella shrugged. "Maybe. Let's hope so."

"It's self-contained!"

"And the flyer is failure proof. But here we are."

"What do we do?" Xante asked.

"Just stay calm and stay put," Dellian said. "Is anyone connected to the global net?"

The question was greeted with sour and nervous expressions as they all consulted their databuds. Nobody had any connection.

Dellian couldn't think how that was possible. But he knew he mustn't allow them to get spooked by the situation. "The second the flyer doesn't show up, they'll be searching for us," he told them confidently.

"We drifted a long way off course," Janc said anxiously.

"Every skyfort will be scanning for us," Dellian replied, trying to quash his own concern. "It won't take long."

"We need to gather branches and bushes," Yirella said. "Build a fire."

"A fire?" Orellt said skeptically. "What use is that?"

"First, it's a strong infrared signature, especially at night."

"Night? It's only just past midday. We're not going to be here that long."

"You hope. Face it, nobody's searched for a crashed flyer in our lifetime. We need to be ready for any eventuality. That includes protection."

"Protection from what?"

"Yirella's right," Dellian said. "We have no idea what beasts live in these mountains."

"After sunset, our best tactic is to retreat back into the fuselage and have a fire burning in front of the gap," she said.

"Oh, for Saints' sake," Orellt protested. "We're not going to be here at sunset! The rescue crews will arrive in an hour."

"I don't mind you betting your life on that wish," she retorted. "But my life isn't yours to risk. We need a fire."

"We do," Ellici agreed. "This is an exceptional situation. We have to adapt to it."

"There must be an axe in the emergency kit," Dellian said quickly; he could see Orellt gathering himself to argue. "Janc, Uret, Xante, you're with me. We'll fell some of those sleeper trees. The rest of you, start gathering the bigger bushes. I'm going to check and see what else we've been left with, especially water."

They started moving—reluctantly; nobody wanted to consider they would be here for any length of time—but they did it.

Dellian found two emergency cases in the rear of the fuselage. One was a medical kit, which he handed to Ellici to treat Tilliana's eye. The second contained basic survival equipment. It was mainly thermal blankets and ropes, a couple of knives, torches, and ten flasks each filled with a liter of distilled water, along with a hand-pumped filter. He was disappointed that was the total, but the case did have a small axe.

"Not much water," he said quietly to Yirella as he walked away from the flyer.

"No rainfall here, check the ground," she replied, equally subdued. "And the flyer is totally dead. I don't see how that could happen; everything is supposed to have multiple redundancy."

He glanced up at the empty cobalt sky. Far overhead, the bright specks of the skyforts shone with reassuring familiarity. Even Cathar, the system's gas giant, was a sharp spark just above the horizon. "Do you think . . ."

"The enemy? No. If Juloss was under attack, we'd see the skyfort weapons firing. They'd be as bright as the sun—at least. It's not that. We're living in the last days of this world's human civilization; things are bound to go wrong. I just never thought it would be this bad. I guess we've lived very sheltered lives."

Dellian scanned around to assess the sleeper trees. There weren't many on the bleak hillside, but at least they stood out.

"I don't want anyone to go more than a couple of hundred meters," he told his friends as they walked toward the closest tree. "Once we chop them down, we've got to break them apart to drag them back."

The sleeper trees were never more than four meters high, rising up to form twisted hemispheres of densely tangled twigs that bulged up out of five radial boughs. Dellian remembered from interminable boring botany lessons that they were desert plants native to a planet hundreds of light-years distant, with huge tuber roots that could hold precious water for years if necessary, while the branches and thick finger-leaves slumbered through the long, hot days of baking sunlight between the rains. Given the scarcity of water they received, their trunks were surprisingly hard. It took the boys a good thirty minutes to chop through, and they had to take turns. It was tough work in the cool, thin air.

They'd just felled the first one when they heard it—a high-pitched braying sound coming from farther up the mountain.

"What amid the Saints was that?" Janc asked nervously, scouring the ragged slope above them.

An answering cry came from the west.

"You mean *them*?" a badly perturbed Xante said. "Saints, how many are there?"

Dellian silently noted how easily Xante was spooked. A petty satisfaction, but the Saints would understand and forgive.

"A whole planet's worth," Uret replied grimly. "This is why the estate is fenced in."

"They sound like morox. I thought they only came out at night?"

"We're too exposed here," Dellian said. "Let's get this tree back to the flyer. Come on, we can do it if we all drag it together."

They each took hold of the trunk and started pulling. Around them, they could see the other clan boys towing bushes through the boulders.

"We need a weapons inventory," Yirella said when everyone had gathered next to the fuselage.

"Axe," Dellian said, holding it up.

"Two knives," Falar announced. "They're not the best for throwing."

"Bind them to the ends of poles," Ellici said. "That'll give you the advantage of reach if those beasts come close."

"Where the Saints are the rescue crews?" Janc shouted.

Dellian lined an accusing finger on him. "Stop that. Panic just makes things worse. Help get the fire ready."

"Wasn't panicking," Janc grumbled, his gaze downcast.

The boys set about preparing the fire, building a core of the driest bush twigs, then fencing it in with some of the smaller branches of the sleeper tree to work as kindling. The rest was broken apart and piled up ready to throw on once the flames were established.

Rello and Tilliana were helped back into the fuselage, where Ellici and Orellt did what they could with the small medical kit.

Dellian watched Yirella scramble onto the top of the largest boulder and slowly scan around. Once he'd finished chopping one of the sleeper tree boughs, he handed the axe to Hable and went to join her. "Keeping watch?" he asked.

"Yes. I can't see anything moving."

"The morox won't come close until dark, and even then the fire will keep them at bay."

"We've heard several now."

"Yes. Don't worry, they'll never get into the fuselage. Even I have trouble squeezing through that gap."

"What do they eat?"

"Well, not our clanmates tonight, that's for sure." He smiled, hoping it would help ease her.

"I don't mean tonight. I mean every other night."

"They're predators. So whatever they can catch. Rabbits, wild dogs, birds . . . I dunno. Whatever else lives up here?"

"Exactly. That's my point."

"What is?"

"We've heard probably four already, right? Yet do you see anything else living up here? The bushes are all dead, and there's no grass. What do their prey live on?"

"Well . . ." Dellian scratched his head, swiveling around to search the forlorn hillside.

"This entire hill can't support one morox, let alone four."

"They're passing through? Could be a seasonal thing, heading for a fresh hunting ground."

"Seasonal?" she scoffed. "This is the tropics."

"All right! I don't know. Happy?"

"Very much not." She gave him a nervous smile. "I wasn't getting at you. I just find all of this weird. The odds of each event that's hit us today are pretty near improbable, but together they're impossible."

"What are you saying?"

"I'm not sure, but this really doesn't feel good."

"Yeah, I figured that for myself. Come on, let's get back to the flyer." He held out his hand. After a moment, she took it, and together they slipped down the boulder.

"No water, either," she said. "That may be worse for us than moroxes."

"Let's get through the night before we start worrying about that. Besides, if the water situation doesn't improve, we can drain the sleeper tree roots. I'm sure I saw that being done in a text or a video or something."

"No, that's a myth. The tubers are all too deep. You'd expend too much energy digging down to them."

"There's no water up here."

"I know. It means that we have to leave first thing tomorrow and get to the bottom of the hill. There should be water there, even if we have to dig for it."

"Okay. For a bad minute there I thought you were going to rig up something that'd filter our own pee."

"That's not a bad idea, actually. Usually in this kind of climate, survivalists evaporate it and catch the condensed vapor. But maybe there's no need. The filter pump should be able to handle urine. We should all pee into a container, and save it in case."

Dellian groaned in dismay.

"It's not funny, Dellian. Dehydration is dangerous."

"All right. But I can't see anyone doing *that*."

"They will if you and I carry on doing what we have been doing."

"What's that?"

"Combined authority."

"Huh?"

"My knowledge and your leadership. Together it makes the rest do what we want."

He opened his mouth to protest, then realized what she had said was right.

"What?" she asked with a sly grin. "You hadn't noticed?"

"Uh, no, actually."

"Classically, a good leader has the ability to issue orders that people don't argue with. I don't quite know what category a good-leader-who-doesn't-notice-he's-giving-orders falls into, but it certainly seems to be successful."

"I'm not the only leader. Janc and Orellt, they're good captains, too."

Yirella lowered her voice as they approached the flyer. "In the tactical games, you've been team captain for thirty-two percent of this year's total. Janc was second with sixteen. You're the clear leader in our year, Dellian. So be a proper Saint, and don't let us down. We're going to need your skills to get through this disaster."

"Great Saints," he muttered.

He made a show of examining the filter from the survival case and asking for Ellici's opinion. She agreed with Yirella that it would filter urine.

"Just in case, then," Dellian said, and peed into a collapsible plastic carton, much to everyone's amusement. He played along with the joshing, then passed the carton to Janc, fixing him a level stare. Janc took a moment, then undid his fly.

They lit the fire as the sun fell below the horizon. The general mood was subdued. In their hearts, everyone had expected rescue within the first couple of hours.

"We have to keep the fire burning as long as possible," Yirella said. "That'll give the skyforts their best chance to spot the thermal signature."

"Three of us on one-hour duty outside to keep feeding the fire," Dellian said quickly. "Each with a weapon, that way we can watch each other's backs. No one else is to leave the flyer. I'll take the first watch with the axe. Falar, Orellt, fancy taking it with me?"

Both boys nodded without noticeable reluctance. The mountain air was a lot colder now that the sun had gone. Even with the modest fire burning three meters from the fuselage, the boys wrapped thermal blankets around their shoulders.

The moroxes began calling to one another. Dellian was convinced there were now at least six of them out there in the darkness beyond the firelight. *Yirella's right. What do they eat?*

Dellian flung some more logs on the fire. Sparks skittered up into the night, swirling like orange galaxies. Boulders glimmered yellow, transforming to dusty moons in a frozen orbit around them. The moroxes were closer now, the cries lower, more intense. Something moved in the gloom between boulders, a deeper shadow eclipsing empty air.

"Come back in," Yirella said from the fuselage split. "Pile some more logs on, and get safe."

Dellian was inclined to agree. Looking at Falar and Orellt, he couldn't see any argument. He bent over to pick up a couple of logs.

"Look out," Falar yelled.

The morox came hurtling out of the dark, skipping onto a boulder and leaping. The beast had pale gray skin like wet leather, mottled with green webs. The forelegs had huge paws, with seven knife-like talons fully extended. Its head was slim and streamlined, almost aquatic somehow, with wide white eyes and fangs longer than a human hand.

Some deep xenophobic instinct told Dellian this rapacious creature had never been born on Earth, adding to his fright. It was the fear of the *other*. He dropped to one knee, swiveling as he did so to bring the axe around in a powerful arc. On either side of him, Falar and Orellt were assuming a lunge pose, their knife poles stabbing forward. The three of them acted in unison as they'd done so many times in battle games, coordinating as fluidly as any munc cohort.

Too late, the morox tried to turn from the trio of deadly blades. Dellian's axe caught its flank, ripping open a huge cut. Dark purple blood squirted out. The morox howled and landed badly, legs scrabbling for purchase.

"Fall back," Dellian shouted. "Falar in first." He could see another two black spectral shapes circling the fire's radiance, biding their time.

"I'm in," Falar called. Then: "Danger left!"

Dellian and Orellt faced the new morox as it sprinted toward them. This time Orellt dropped to his knees. Dellian instinctively knew what he was doing—thrusting the knife blade ahead and low, forcing the morox to leap. Orellt began his swipe. Sure enough, the creature saw the blade solid and unmoving at its own head height, and sprang—

The axe hit it directly on the side of its short neck, penetrating so deep Dellian could barely wrench it out. Only the inertia of the creature's falling corpse helped free it.

Orellt was squirming backward through the gap. Dellian took two fast paces and saw the next morox appear on the top of the fuselage. No time. He flung the axe, sending it spinning through the air as the morox leaped at him. It hit the side of the beast's forelimb and bounced away, clattering off the rocks. And Orellt was standing in the gap, the knife pole ready to throw like a spear.

The creature smashed into Dellian, its forelimbs lashing out. He felt talon tips slash down his left arm, then it juddered, a knife pole sticking out of the back of its neck. Its weight was on top of him, carrying him to the ground. The fall dazed him, and all he knew was the mass of the dead carcass pressed unmoving against him, pinning him down. Then boys were yelling all around. Hands dragged the dead creature off him. He glimpsed Orellt and Falar back in the open, their knife poles jabbing into the darkness. Hable retrieved the axe. Xante, Janc, and Colian were holding burning branches, scything them about furiously. Uret picked him up and manhandled him through the gap, where Yirella half carried, half dragged him to a seat. She and Ellici were immediately busy with antiseptic sprays and long strips of a-skin while behind them the boys performed an orderly withdrawal back into the flyer's cabin.

"You'll be fine," Yirella was saying loudly as torch beams wobbled about, shining on his arm. There was plenty of blood. "The cuts aren't deep at all."

Orellt's face loomed up in front of him, grinning wildly. "We got another one! And we reset the fire. It'll burn for another hour at least."

"Terrific," Dellian gasped, and winced as Ellici applied a strip of a-skin to his bicep. It stung as it adhered.

"Drink this," Yirella ordered, shoving a flask at him. "You need fluid."

"It's not piss, is it?"

"No." She grinned. "I'm saving that for breakfast."

The surviving moroxes howled to each other for the rest of the night. One even ventured up toward the gap in the fuselage again, only to have Xante and Colian ward it off with the knife poles.

Dellian dozed for most of the time, falling into a deeper sleep sometime well past midnight, only to be dragged from slumber by a fresh morox howl. He saw Colian in the gap, holding a knife pole ready, but not jabbing or shouting for help.

The next thing he knew it was dawn, and the cabin was full of his yawning friends. A wan gray light was shining in through the small windows, and the smell of smoke was heavy in the air.

"Decision time," Yirella said as she inspected the strips of a-skin on his arm. "We can't hang around here if we're going to make it to the foot of the mountain before nightfall. We either set off now, or we don't do it at all. If the satellites didn't see the fire last night, then they never will. And if we leave it another day, we'll be a lot weaker."

"And an easier target for the moroxes," Dellian said. "We won't have the fuselage to shelter us, either."

Her face crumpled into a puzzled frown. "That's another thing wrong. They should never have ventured so close to the fire."

"But they did," Xante said. "Wishing they did what they're supposed to isn't going to help us."

Yirella gave him a long, disappointed look and shrugged.

For a moment, he thought she was going to say something else. "So what do you think we should do?" she asked.

"You tell me," Dellian said urgently. "I'll back you up."

"I don't know. In situations like this, you're normally supposed to stay at the crash site and wait for the rescue teams. But this isn't normal, is it?"

"Let's take a look outside," Dellian said reluctantly.

The fire had died down to a mound of embers that was barely warmer than the sand. Thick rose-gold sunlight was pouring over the tops of the hills, casting long, sharp shadows from the boulders.

Dellian carried the axe, scanning around cautiously. "I can't hear the moroxes."

"It's daytime," Xante said. "They'll be back in their lair."

Dellian saw Yirella shaking her head, but she didn't say anything. He looked at the three dead moroxes. The first one, which he'd caught with the axe, had crawled fifty meters away before collapsing from blood loss. The other two were closer.

"We could eat them," Ellici said.

"Can we?" Dellian asked. "They're alien. Doesn't that make them enati- . . . enty- . . . enamo—"

"Enantimorphic? No. We can eat them if we have to. Their biochemistry is different, but not by much. Their flesh contains nutrients we can use. I'm not so sure about the taste, though."

"We'll hold off for now," Dellian said with as much authority as he could summon. "First we need to build a bigger fire. Maybe burn a whole tree and then add more. Yeah." He nodded, staring at the biggest sleeper tree, standing a hundred meters away. "We'll light that one, and chop down others, add them to it. We can do it, all of us. A fire that's going to overload the skyfort sensors, it's so big."

He had them. He knew that. They were all gathering courage and hope from his determination. Even Yirella agreed.

"No walk down the hill then," she mumbled as he divided them up into three teams, each with a weapon.

"It makes no sense, exposing ourselves to more unknowns. The clan know we've been alone overnight now. Alexandre will bring back the Saints themselves to help find us. Sie will. We all know that."

"I suppose so." She stared at the closest morox corpse. "I need to know something," she said, and picked up a rock half the size of her own head.

"What?" he asked, then recoiled as she brought the sharp edge of the rock smashing down on the morox's head. Two more blows and she'd cracked the skull open. She shoved the edge of the rock through the fissure and began to prise it farther apart.

"Yirella!"

He had to fight back nausea as she began examining segments of the gore that was its brain.

"Why didn't it get eaten?" she asked.

"Huh?"

"They were so ravenously hungry they ignored a fire to try and kill us. Yet here they have three fresh corpses of their own kind, and they ignored them to carry on attacking us."

"Do they eat their own?" he asked, trying not to look at the way her carrion-slicked fingers were probing the brain tissue so enthusiastically. Yet there was something horribly fascinating about the scene.

"I don't know. I don't suppose we should judge them like they're terrestrial animals. Although you'd think basic instincts would be almost identical."

"I guess," he said. "So what are you hoping to find?"

"Don't know till I find it," she answered grimly.

"Okay." He knew that tone; she wasn't going to be stopped by anything he could say.

Cheering broke out around the sleeper tree. His clanmates had piled scrub bushes up around the trunk, which were now burning hot and fierce, their smokeless flames shooting vertically into the tree's boughs above, which were starting to smolder.

Dellian was glad of the excuse to look away from Yirella's gory task.

Despite the fresh air gusting across the slope, he was feeling sluggish. Lack of sleep and his throbbing arm seemed to be making his body intolerably heavy. Which was strange, given he was very aware of his empty stomach. With growing dismay, he knew it wouldn't be long before they'd have to start using the hand pump filter . . .

Falar and Uret were taking it in turns to attack another sleeper tree with the axe, the thuds reverberating through the crisp air. More boys were dragging bushes back to the rapidly expanding blaze. Dellian looked up at the invitingly empty sky with its flotilla of artificial stars. "Why can't the skyforts see us?" he murmured.

"Why fill Juloss with alien predators?" Yirella said. She'd risen to her feet, wiping jelly-strings of clotted morox blood from her hands. "I mean, seriously! Sure, keep some in orbital xenohabitats, and store their genetic molecule for study. But release them into the wild? That makes no sense at all. Our ancestors put in a century's effort just terraforming this world up to habitable status so a whole civilization of humans could flourish and expand. Now we can't even set foot outside our clan compound, it's so dangerous."

"Dangerous to the enemy, too."

"Like they're ever going to set foot here. The only landing they'll ever perform is with a dozen apocalypse-event asteroids."

"So what, then?"

"So I don't know!" she shouted bitterly.

Dellian was surprised. It hurt him to see her like this, so wound up and frustrated. Close to tears, too, if he was any judge. Yirella was always the cool, rational one. But then this situation was extreme. Without thinking, he put his arms around her. Her whole body was held as rigid as steel. "I remember someone telling me there are always answers; you just have to know where to find them."

She nodded, slowly and very reluctantly. "I know."

"Did you find anything in the morox's brain?"

"No."

"What were you looking for?"

"Not sure. Something that would make it act the way it did."

"They all behaved the same."

"I know. And that worries me. I'm scared, Dellian."

"Me too," he said softly. "But we'll get through this." He kept hold of one of her hands as he turned to face the sleeper tree, which was now a giant column of flame, burning with the aggression of rocket exhaust. The boys who'd lit it were having to stand well back, the heat was so strong. "The skyfort sensors will think we're zapping them with a laser when they pass over, the infrared emission is so strong."

"Yes." Yirella bent down and kissed him again. "You know what I'm thinking?"

"What?"

"This place is our Zagreus. So you know what that makes us?"

"Up shit creek without a paddle?"

"No! You and me. Look at us. You with your red hair, you're Saint Callum."

"And you're my Savi." He laughed. "Yes!"

"They escaped, didn't they? They got back home."

Dellian heard the urgency in her voice, the desperation. "Yes. They did. They even lived happy ever after for a couple of decades on Nebesa."

"If they can do it, so can we."

"Callum was always my favorite Saint," he confessed.

"Really. Yuri's mine."

"How come? I'd have you rooting for Kandara."

"Oh, no. She used violence to solve everything. Not as bad as Alik, though. But Yuri used to think through his problems. Remember the missing boyfriend story? He investigated properly and made decisions based on facts, and he never stopped until he finished the case. That's what I aspire to."

"He could be pretty ruthless, too. A lot of people died when he was hunting for Horatio."

"That wasn't his fault—well, apart from the matcher. And people like that deserved to be sent to Zagreus."

"Yeah—" He frowned at the latest outbreak of shouting, glancing around to see the boys yelling his name and pointing wildly. Xante had brought up the knife pole he was carrying, pointing it toward Dellian and Yirella. But the expression on his face . . . Dellian slowly turned around, fear turning his skin to ice.

Standing on top of the flyer's fuselage was a cougar. It shook its head, staring down at them. A small growl emerged from the back of its throat. The forelegs bent, taking it down into a pre-pounce crouch.

"Move back toward the flames," Dellian said, barely moving his lips, shifting slightly so his body was between the cougar and Yirella.

"Del—"

"Now!" He began his own slow backward creep, pushing her along, eyes frantically scanning the ground for a loose stone like the one Yirella had used, anything he could strike the lethal beast with. He knew it was hopeless, but he wasn't going down without a fight.

The cougar leaped, powerful muscles flinging it vigorously through the air toward them. Then it exploded. One instant a perfectly evolved killing machine . . . the next a cloud of flame and tatters of meat. Stinking steam belched out. The charred mess splattered down two meters from a paralyzed Dellian.

He dropped to his knees and vomited hard. Yirella was screaming. Clanmates ran toward them en masse, yelling and shouting.

A shadow fell across all of them. A shivering Dellian raised his head, watching in total incomprehension as the big flyer descended silently out of the clean morning sky.

THE ASSESSMENT TEAM

FERITON KAYNE, NKYA, JUNE 24, 2204

I was fascinated by the way Yuri and Callum resurrected their ancient conflict, shouting over each other, bickering with barrages of obscenities about trivial points and who was responsible for what, with neither giving ground. When the whole uncensored account was finally aired, I'd learned very little that I hadn't already accessed in Connexion's secure files.

From my tactical standpoint, Callum had always been a good suspect for an alien agent. I'd wondered about the whole "died in an Albanian chemical plant explosion" 2092 death certificate, along with the rest of his Emergency Detoxification crew. The Berat "disaster" was on the British government's official births and deaths registry for all of them. Then he and Savi officially popped up again in 2108, in the Delta Pavonis system, with their kids in tow, as if nothing untoward had happened and his death had been an unfortunate bureaucratic misunderstanding. He was listed as being a senior technical manager for the Nebesa habitat construction project.

That discontinuity was precisely the kind of record-keeping mistake I was looking for. Undercover agents assuming the identity of the recently deceased had been standard practice within the intelligence community dating all the way back to the twentieth century. And Callum is well placed. Ainsley recognized his drive and ability a century ago; since then he'd worked his way up the Utopial ladder to personal technology advisor to Emilja Jurich herself, one of the original Utopial movement founders. It put him in a perfect position to feed their senior council's growing xenophobia toward the Olyix, had he been an alien agent.

The hostile policies of the human elite toward the Olyix have been growing steadily, ever since the *Salvation of Life* arrived at Sol in 2144—fifty-two years after Callum's supposed death. Suspicion of an alien species is part of the human condition, and relatively understandable. What cannot be explained by logic is the rising paranoia people like Emilja Jurich and Ainsley Zangari have exhibited over the last couple of decades. Somebody, somewhere, *has* to be feeding that paranoia with a whole load of damaging bullshit.

The conclusion we came to is that a very different alien species— an ancient enemy of the Olyix? No one knows for sure—arrived undetected at Sol (time uncertain), and has been busy insinuating their way into positions of influence. And my real task in the Connexion Exosolar Security Division is to expose their possible agents.

And now, with his "death" explained and even confirmed by my boss, Yuri, it's likely not Callum. Obviously, no Earth company or Sol system habitat would employ him after 2092. But the emergent Utopials with their ideological goal of a pure and decent post-scarcity society, with a correspondingly technology-heavy infrastructure, were an ideal choice. Delta Pavonis welcomed everyone who rejected the Universal culture that dominated Earth and their terraformed planets. Which, actually, made the Utopial society his only choice.

"Did Savi recover?" Loi asked. He was sitting at a table with Jessika and Eldlund, where the three of them had remained silent the whole time.

Callum stirred from his sojourn into the bitter past, and it took his heavy gray-green eyes a moment to focus on his old adversary's assistant. "Yes, thank you. Savi recovered. We were together for over a quarter of a century, even had a couple of children. So yes, it was worth it."

Yuri merely grunted and downed another shot of arctic-cold Tovaritch vodka. The stewards had been providing him with a steady supply of the tiny frosted glasses all evening. I was beginning to think my boss had a special peripheral to filter out alcohol toxicity. He certainly didn't betray any signs of being drunk, apart from his ever-shortening temper.

Alik seemed to have the same resilience—or peripheral. He was sitting back in his chair, on his third glass of bourbon. His eyes were almost closed, but that didn't fool me; he'd been deeply absorbed by the confrontation.

Kandara, by contrast, was sitting straight-backed, fearsomely attentive from start to finish. "I had no idea Zagreus was a dark rendition site to begin with," she said.

"History," Yuri grunted. "The Conestoga asteroid went public with the penal colony's existence three years later. Exactly as the project's instigators always intended. And as a registered independent government, Conestoga couldn't be penalized in any international court the way corporations could."

"Government, my arse!" Callum said gruffly. "Conestoga was a chunk of valueless rock a hundred meters in diameter, in a trans-Jupiter orbit, with an automated industrial base that had a dormitory module bumped on. Total population: fifty." I watched him eyeing the three assistants in the lounge, anxious for them to understand, to take his side. "Every one of them was a corporate lawyer."

"Conestoga offered other Sol governments an exile destination for undesirables," Yuri said. "Everyone agreed on an improved standard for the survival packages, and *bam*, the queue of convicts was suddenly six months long. It's a tough life on Zagreus, but it works. The surveillance satellites show an expanding civilization. They're even venturing beyond the canyon now, building pressurized domes out on the surface. We tamed the bastards."

"Hoo-bloody-rah," Callum said. "Do the satellites tell you how many people died in the process?"

"If it bothers you, offer them a new terraformed world. Or maybe open up one of your precious Utopial planets to the poor misunderstood princesses. No? There's a surprise."

Callum stood up. "Zagreus is not the way we should judge civilized progress. It's a bloody disgraceful throwback. Education and a dignified standard of living is the true solution to elevate the poor and disenfranchised. Utopial society produces so few of what you class as exile-level criminals we don't even exile them. They are removed from the general population, given a comfortable residence, and supported. That is our society's triumph." His glance swept around the Trail Ranger. "I don't know what time zone you're all from, but I'm off to bed."

Yuri waited until he'd disappeared into the rear compartment. "Our judges don't have to hand out so many exile sentences because the threat of Zagreus keeps people in line. Actually!"

Loi nodded, making sure his boss saw his approval.

"No, actually, it's despicable," Eldlund said, and sie stalked off back into the rear compartment. I wondered how sie was going to fit into a sleeping pod. They were all standard size, so . . . Slight oversight on our part there. Maybe sie'd stick hir legs out into the aisle for the night, and no doubt complain about bias and anti-omnia discrimination tomorrow.

"I think that's it for me, too," Kandara said.

"Not a bad idea," Yuri conceded.

The others all made their way back to the sleeping pods. Sandjay connected me to the drivers. Bee Jain assured me we were making good time, and the Trail Ranger was running smoothly toward the alien ship. With that, I went to bed.

. . .

Loi, Eldlund, and Jessika were all awake and sharing a table for breakfast when I got up. At least they seemed to be bridging the deep ideological chasm between Yuri and Callum, but that's youth for you.

Alik came in, his hair still damp from the shower. He sat down opposite me. "No gym," he complained.

"Yeah. Really sorry about that."

He laughed and ordered coffee and toast from the steward. "Quite a showdown your boss had last night. I felt like I had a front-row seat into some real history."

"I knew the basic facts, but, yeah, some of the details they spilled were something else."

"Surprised they're both on this trip."

"It's important."

"Sure, I get that. But do they maybe have a little extra data to go on?"

I raised an eyebrow, scanning that handsome face with its immobile flesh. Alik Monday would make the perfect poker player; he lacked the ability to produce a single tell. The voice, though—that could convey a lot of emotion. I'm guessing he must practice that. "Connexion didn't play favorites here, Alik," I chided. "The Utopials were extremely keen for representation on the assessment team."

"And Callum is their prime troubleshooter."

"He's a grade-two citizen."

"If you think he's here to produce a technical assessment, you're fooling yourself. He might have been technical back in the day, but he's got his young acolytes for that now." His hand waved discreetly at Eldlund and Jessika.

"What are you saying?"

"He reports directly to the Utopial Senior Council, and maybe not even that. I expect it's going to be Jaru and Emilja themselves who'll have first access to his opinion. And that opinion will be entirely political."

"I concur," I told him. "As does Ainsley. That's one of the reasons he had me include representatives for all the truly important interested parties."

"Really?" It came out a challenge—old interrogation technique. *Back up what you just said.*

"There's an interesting parallel in history," I explained.

"Go on."

"When the original Space Age was underway back in the 1950s and '60s, part of the ideological struggle was the hypothesis surrounding first contact. The Soviet Union postulated that any civilization advanced enough to travel between the stars would logically be socialist, and would therefore choose to deal only with Moscow. The battle for ideological supremacy would be over, the world would undergo conversion to enlightenment, and the age of capitalism would be at an end."

"Aliens are all communists? Bunch of bull. The Olyix are savvy traders."

"Maybe. But today, instead of the Soviet Union, we have the Utopial culture." I glanced over at Eldlund and Jessika, still chatting happily with Loi. "Who will explain, at great and boring length, how their post-scarcity equality is not socialism, but a technology-driven evolution of egalitarian humanist society."

"Jeez, you mean Callum's here to confirm starfaring aliens will all be—"

"Good little Utopials? Yes. Beware, my son, the end days of capitalism are nigh."

"He'll swing contact their way?"

"Utopial society is very benign and nurturing. The thinking goes that aliens will instinctively favor that."

"Benign, my ass. Tranquil verging on stagnant, more like."

"Indeed."

"Oh, come on, you work for Connexion, for fuck's sake. The Universal market economy worlds and habitats are goddamn dynamic. The Olyix don't do much business with Utopials."

"The Olyix are a single arkship colony who care only about continuing their voyage to the end of the universe, where they will meet their God at the End of Time. Anything else is secondary to that doctrine, so by necessity they adapt to local conditions. In the Sol system, trade with Earth and the habitats is the method by which they can acquire the energy to build up their supply of antimatter and continue that voyage. Therefore, they trade. The argument being, had they arrived at Delta Pavonis instead, they would now be following Utopial doctrine in their contact with Akitha."

"Doesn't that kind of blow the shit out of the pan-galactic Utopial theory, that every species will embrace post-scarcity benevolence?"

"In the case of the Olyix, yes. Which is why Callum is hoping for a more favorable outcome this time."

"So what's the deal with Yuri, then?"

I leaned in a little closer, lowering my voice. "I didn't say this, but Yuri is a xenophobic son of a bitch. He's got a real bug up his ass about the Olyix."

"Why?"

"He doesn't like Kcells, apparently."

"That's crazy. They've turned out to be a medical miracle. Goddamn cheap one, too. Everybody wins."

I shrugged. "It's just the way he is." I smiled and sat back to watch if that particular seed of doubt would grow into anything I could use on my mission.

Outside the Trail Rover, Nkya's landscape was turning darker. The long screes of sandy regolith we traversed were now as black as volcanic dust. And maybe that's what the stuff actually was; I'm no geologist.

Callum appeared midmorning and gave the coffee machine a thorough workout. He and Yuri gave each other a curt nod. Their war wasn't yet over and probably never would be, but the truce was holding.

Alik went and sat next to Yuri. For a moment they both looked out of the window as we passed the scarlet strobe of a beacon post. The intrusive light caught their faces, shading them both a strange bloodred, its time-lapse flashes pulling the shadows out of hooded eyes like dramatic tears.

"So if after considered analysis we declare the alien ship hostile, what happens?" Alik asked. "Are we carrying a nuclear capability?"

"Our security drones can handle a high level of aggression," Yuri told him. "If the spaceship becomes actively belligerent, they will contain it while we retreat."

"Retreat in what?"

Yuri frowned, as if he'd misheard. "In this, of course."

"Jeez, you call this a getaway car?"

"The alien ship is isolated. It doesn't pose a threat to anything except the immediate vicinity. If that happens, we can return in a more forceful mode."

"Unless it wipes us out. Then the guys sent to find us get taken out, and the guys who get sent in after that . . . What's the cutoff? Team twenty?"

"There is no link with solnet. However, the satellites are keeping watch. If the mission's G8Turing spots any trouble, then the appropriate protocols will be followed."

"Great," Alik grunted. "And we're still racing away at walking pace."

"You were aware of the risk before we started."

"Risk, yeah. Your paranoia, not so much."

"We have to guarantee the safety of our entire species. That is no small obligation."

"Come on. If you can travel between stars, you aren't doing it for the glory of the empire. There's no such thing."

"Our own history and rationale cannot be used as a template for analyzing the motives of an extraterrestrial species," Yuri said levelly. "The alien ship was probably on some kind of scout mission—an exploration and assessment maybe, the equivalent of this very assessment mission. Whatever the exact classification, they *stole* humans to examine them. Already that puts them into an antagonistic classification."

"Do we know they were stolen?" Alik challenged. "Hell, they could have been fleeing some catastrophe or war, and the aliens were doing these people a favor. We're eighty-nine light-years from Earth, right? So if this ship was flying below light speed, it could have left Earth at anytime in the last five hundred years. There was some pretty bad shit going on then; not our finest era."

"Fleeing what?"

"Second World War, for starters. Think on it. You're stuck in the blitz in London, and some strange dude offers you a way out. The chance for you and a few others to start a new life on a new world. The only price is that you can't ever come back. You know you'd take that offer. We've got close to twenty terraformed planets now, every one of which cost us the biggest financial and political effort our species has ever known. If we'd spent half that much fixing Earth, we'd have us a genuine paradise. But no, getting a second chance is the greatest human dream and delusion we have. It even outranks religion."

"Benign aliens intervening to save us?" Yuri sneered. "What's that, second on the wish list?"

Alik spread his hands wide. "Then why are humans on board?"

"We don't have nearly enough information yet to confirm the intent."

"Hell, man, I know that. I'm offering up possibilities, that's all. Thinking wide. That's why we're all here, aren't we? Everything is up for consideration."

"So which do you think it is?" Kandara challenged. "You put up a good case for them being benign. Are they saving worthy people from Earth's brutality, or are they hostile imperialists, capturing specimens for the all-time rectal probing record in their laboratory?"

Alik gave her a quick salute. "I'm prepared for it to be the hostile, but intellectually I'm kinda thinking it's unlikely."

"Why?" Yuri said, his voice sharpening.

"Every reason given. You don't cross interstellar space for conquest. You do it for politics and wanderlust, like we have; and you do it for science, like we also have. But most interesting motive of all: as art. Because you can."

"You are a fool if you think that. You are assigning human behavioral traits to aliens—the worst form of anthropomorphism and intellectual dishonesty. They have taken these people, most likely against their will. Whoever they are, they're not our friends."

"You've prejudged, then?"

"My judgment comes from the—admittedly small—amount of information we've uncovered so far. It is what we don't know that bothers me even more. The potential for conflict here is enormous. Aliens can affect us in the most subtle ways. Our encounters with them show that we are always changed."

"Them?" Eldlund queried. "How many do you think we've encountered? As far as I'm aware, this is only the second."

"It is," Yuri said. "But look at what the Olyix have done to us."

"They brought knowledge."

"No, they didn't; a few clever chunks of biotechnology, that's all. Not real knowledge, no revelations. They're the greatest example of passive-aggressive we've ever known. But what else do you expect from a bunch of religious fanatics?"

I'd heard this speech many times. It was one of the reasons I'd urged my boss to come on the expedition in person. My hope was that he'd open up to his peers in a way he never would to me and provide some kind of insight into his xenophobia. As Callum was to Emilja, so Yuri was to Ainsley—and a more paranoid sonofabitch you cannot find.

Kandara regarded Yuri with some surprise. "I don't see the aggressive side of them. They seem more full-on passive to me."

"That's all part of the act. They adapt to circumstances. I don't blame them; it's an excellent survival trait, which is exactly what you need if you're on a voyage to the end of time. Even the Olyix don't know what they're going to encounter next, so they have to be ready for anything."

"Are you saying we're not seeing the real them?"

"No, quite the opposite. They see us, and adapt themselves to the systems we live by. That is the real them, even though for us it's looking into a mirror."

"You, the Sol system, turned them into traders," Callum said.

"Of course we did," Yuri said. "They came, they looked around, they saw what they had to do to get the energy they needed to rebuild their antimatter fuel supply—and they did it. No hesitation, no regrets. And to hell with the consequences."

"And there are consequences to them trading Kcells with us?" Eldlund asked in surprise. "I don't see how. Kcell treatments have saved the lives of millions of people in the Universal star systems. People who are too poor to afford stem cell printing and cloned organs. That's the only outrage here."

"I'm not saying Kcells have been bad for us," Yuri said. "But the nature of the Olyix, this adaptability, is detrimental when they encounter a species with politics as complex as ours. They lack discrimination. Because they are driven so relentlessly to achieve their own goal, it doesn't matter to them how they achieve it. They need our money to buy our electricity, so they will adopt our own methodology to obtain it. Any methodology we have, they see an opportunity. Anything else is probably a sin to them."

"You object to them because they've become capitalists?" Eldlund exclaimed.

"No," Callum taunted. "It's because they're better capitalists."

"You don't get it," Yuri said calmly. "They don't have our moral filter. It doesn't matter to them what they do to get money, nor the consequences. And there is an awful lot of money involved with supplying the *Salvation of Life* with energy. That's why we have to watch them very closely."

"Money is always going to distort everything," Alik said. "Nothing new in that. Greed is a constant. That just makes them more human, you ask me."

"You're wrong," Yuri said flatly. "You, with your job, should know the levels to which people will sink when there's real money involved. And because we race to the bottom, so do the Olyix. We are the architects of their current behavior. And I've seen the consequences firsthand. They're not good."

I watched with immense interest as Alik finally made his facial muscles contract, an expression approximating skepticism. "Such as?"

YURI'S RACE AGAINST TIME

LONDON, AD 2167

The summer of 2167 was exceptionally warm, even by Europe's new standards. In Yuri's London office, the whining air-con was making no difference to the wretched late-August temperature. By quarter past ten on Thursday morning he wanted to open the window—not that he could; his office was on the sixty-third floor. Connexion's extraordinary European central office rose out of the Greenwich Peninsular, a neo-Gothic helix-twist skyscraper of glass and black stone that topped out at ninety stories, like the watchtower of some fallen pagan archangel charged with guarding the city against invaders sailing up the Thames. From his office Yuri had a perfectly framed view of the huge old Dartford Bridge curving up out of the distant horizon. But that same panorama was one that poured sunlight through the glass all morning long.

Earth had been using solarwells to supply its power since 2069, with the last coal and gas power stations shutting down in 2082.

That had given the biosphere eighty-five years to reabsorb the excess carbon monoxide and dioxide produced in the twentieth and twenty-first centuries. Climatologists kept saying that was long enough for the atmosphere to stabilize at pre–Industrial Revolution levels, the idealized norm. Unfortunately, their elegant computer predictions never matched reality, and they all agreed 2167 was a fluke spike on the obstinately shallow cooling curve. One which the neogreen movement, whose ideology trumped science, was quick to blame on unusual solar activity, created by solarwells abusing the corona.

Yuri didn't care why it was ridiculously hot; he just wanted the god-awful heat wave to end.

"Executive priority call," Boris announced. "Poi Li for you."

"Crap." Yuri resisted the impulse to pull up his tie and fasten his top button. He couldn't think of any event that would warrant a personal call from Poi Li. She'd retired nineteen years ago, then immediately become an independent security advisor to the board—much to her successor's dismay. "Give her access."

"Yuri," Poi Li said.

"Poi, been a while."

"Anything of interest to report?"

"Not really. Any interesting reason you're calling this office?" He'd been appointed head of Connexion's small but elite Olyix Monitoring Office two years ago. At the time, Yuri hadn't been sure whether or not it was a promotion from director of the Sol Habitat Security Office, which he'd held before, but it had been created by Ainsley himself ten years after the Olyix arkship *Salvation of Life* had decelerated into the solar system in 2144 and had provided Yuri with almost unlimited authority. Despite his being completely office-bound, it was interesting work, plotting the political and financial influence of the Olyix across Earth and the habitats. It also gave him personal access to some very influential people. He'd come to regard it as an essential rung on his way up to Connexion's Security Chief, proving he had the executive skills to match his operational ability.

"There is a matter which we would like you to investigate personally," Poi Li said.

"We?"

"Ainsley and me."

Reflex made Yuri sit up fast. "I see."

"It is somewhat urgent."

He took the security department's portal door into the company's
general London network; from there he could walk straight into the
London metrohub inner loop. He took a radial out to the Sloane
Square hub. A short walk down King's Road, where there were a lot
of silver-blue two-person cabez breezing about, and he was at the address Poi Li had sent, an elegant brick Regency-style building that
contained phenomenally expensive pied-à-terres for the wealthy,
overlooking a small square with tall plane trees. He counted five security guards positioned around the square, dressed like normal people, hanging casually, and wondered how many more he was missing.

Boris gave his code to the entrance, which scanned him. The
glossy black door—which looked like wood but wasn't—opened
smoothly. Two guards in expensive suits were standing in the hallway. They gestured him in.

Yuri just had to admire the ancient lift with its iron grid doors and
manual brass operating handle. He was the sole occupant as it rattled
and groaned its way up to the fourth floor.

Poi Li was waiting on the landing for him. She looked the same as
she had when he first started working for Connexion almost a century earlier, but somehow more delicate now. The telomere treatments seemed to be gnawing away at her core, leaving only the shell
of a woman.

"Thank you for coming," she said and led him into the penthouse
apartment.

The décor was classical: marble floors and high ceilings, gold-plated chandeliers illuminating old master oil paintings and baroque modern canvases with equal intensity. The furniture style was unremittingly Louis XVI, heavy handcrafted pieces that looked hugely uncomfortable to sit on.

Ainsley Zangari was waiting in the lounge. Yuri was impressed. At 136, the richest man there'd ever been had clearly spent something like a medium-size country's arms budget on genetic therapy; his anti-aging treatments went far beyond the simple telomere extensions Yuri had spent decades of his generous bonuses on. Anyone who didn't know him would think he was a normal forty-year-old who ate sensibly and exercised properly. Even his hair had turned from silver back to a youthful brown, as if follicle hues were merely seasonal, and now spring had come once more.

"Yuri, good to see you." A handshake, with a strong grip, underscoring easy vigor.

"Sir. Poi said this was urgent."

"Yes, let me introduce you. This is Gwendoline." Ainsley gestured at a teenage girl sitting awkwardly on one of the antique settees.

"Pleased to meet you," Yuri said automatically. Boris was running facial recognition on her, but there was nothing in Connexion's database. That didn't bode well. Connexion had files on everyone remotely important. He told Boris to find out who owned the penthouse. Answer: a firm registered on Archimedes, a post-Jupiter-orbit habitat whose major industry was serving as a zero-tax enclave.

"Sorry to be so much trouble," Gwendoline said. Her voice was high and hesitant. Yuri stopped analyzing her and actually looked. She was pretty, of course, but not just in that way all teenage girls were. Gwendoline was groomed to perfection. Casually, of course, but not cheaply. Personal stylists and the right schooling had created an effortless ingénue elegance. He decided she was maybe seventeen or eighteen, with a thin face and strong jaw, giving her glass-cutter cheeks. A button nose was heavily freckled, and her long strawberry-blond hair possessed a healthy gloss that rivaled the gold ornaments glittering around the lounge. Her dress was also deceptively simple:

white and scarlet cotton with a square-cut neck and a hemline high above the knee. Yuri just knew it wasn't printed in any fabricator; this was Rome or Paris couture with an eye-watering price tag. Gwendoline was a true golden-child heartbreaker. So then: spoiled brat or wallet-busting mistress.

"I'm sure you won't be," Yuri said with as much sincerity as he could assemble.

"Gwendoline is my granddaughter," Ainsley said, letting the pride seep into his tone.

Yuri was suddenly much more alert. That fact wasn't listed in any Connexion security network, which was extremely odd. Ainsley already had nine marriages under his belt, producing thirty-two acknowledged children, most of whom worked in Connexion management. In turn they had numerous grandchildren and great-grandchildren, forming a large dynasty covering the full spectrum from dedicated workaholics to high-maintenance airhead princesses, every one of whom was guarded with a vigilance that was once the province of Earth's nuclear codes.

"I know," Ainsley said contritely. "You can't find a record of her. But her grandmother, Nataskia, and I only had a brief fling; Evette was the result. Nataskia didn't want Evette involved with Connexion, or the rest of the family. I couldn't blame her for that—fuck knows we're not exactly a convention of saints and introverts—so I respected her wishes. There was a discreet trust fund set up, which was increased when Gwendoline came along. The three of them have lived outside of media attention and corporate politics and done well for themselves. I kept minimal contact, which hurt, but I sucked it up, and everyone was happy ever after."

"I see," Yuri said diplomatically. "So what's happened?"

"Horatio Seymore," Gwendoline said, tears welling up.

"Who is he?"

"My boyfriend. He's vanished." It was a classic summer romance, she explained. Her first true love. She'd just started an internship with a London finance software firm—obtained entirely on her own merit, Ainsley chipped in proudly. Horatio was a waiter in one of the HazBeanz franchises in the City, frequented by her office. He was nineteen, and Bristol University had offered him a place studying social sciences, which was why he was signed up as a trainee barista for the summer, to earn some money toward the fees. He wanted a career working with underprivileged children in the ribbon towns, helping them get their lives in order.

Yuri did his best not to groan and roll his eyes. Classic wasn't the word, he thought; it was Lady Chatterley rewritten for the twenty-second century. She was comfortably off, leading a sheltered socialite life amid her own class, while he was poor and modest, dedicating his life to a worthy cause. The attraction was enacted at an atomic level. When Gwendoline's altme sent Boris a file loaded with images, Yuri found it hard to decide which of the two kids was the prettiest. Even given the summer's anomalous heat, there were an excessive number of pictures of Horatio with his shirt off—playing football with pals, at the beach, lazing in the park. As well as being adorably noble, given the whole social worker gig, he was quite a sports hunk, with Caribbean heritage giving his nicely muscled body a dark-honey sheen and dusting his brown eyes with a vivacious sparkle. His heavily curled hair was long and unkempt, adding to his desirability.

"Okay," Yuri said slowly when the story of the world's newest, greatest-ever love affair had been recited. "So when you say 'vanished,' what exactly makes you think that?" He could well imagine how besotted and loyally devoted the lovely Gwendoline was to her new beau, but boys Horatio's age . . . The lad would be a magnet for babes and cougars alike; he could quite easily be staying in some lingerie model's luxurious bedroom, fucking himself senseless night and day. *Lucky little bastard.* Yuri tried to focus on the girl again.

"I spent Tuesday night in his flat with him," Gwendoline said. "I left early Wednesday morning to come back here and get changed for work. We had tickets to see SungSolar play at the J-Mac club that night. He never showed up."

"So that's a day and a half?"

"I know what you're thinking," she said with sulky resentment, "but we liveline each other all day long. I visit his HazBeanz once or twice a day. After I left here on Wednesday morning, his altme was offline. He didn't respond to any type of call, not even a straight phone ping. He wasn't in HazBeanz when I went to check at lunch, and the manageress said he never came in that morning. My altme ran a check through London's ER registries, and he wasn't admitted to hospital. When he didn't show for the concert, I even called his parents. They didn't know where he was, and now they're worried. I went back to his flat but he never came home last night."

"You stayed there all night?" Yuri queried. "By yourself?"

"Yes. I accessed the London police network this morning, but their Turing said I can't file a missing person report until Horatio's been gone for forty-eight hours." She hung her head, long hair falling like a ragged curtain across her face. "I know you must think I'm really stupid for calling you, grandfather, but I didn't know what else to do. Horatio wouldn't just vanish without telling me, I know he wouldn't. We know everything about each other. We never kept secrets."

"Does he know who you are?" Yuri asked.

"He knows mummy and grandma are well off, but that's all."

"So he doesn't know you're actually a Zangari, that you are Ainsley's granddaughter?"

"No," she said in a tiny voice. "Please, I just want to know he's okay."

Ainsley patted her shoulder. "It's all right, sweetheart, you did the right thing letting me know. We'll find him for you. Can you give us a moment, please?"

Gwendoline nodded meekly and left the lounge.

"I ran a check through the London police network," Poi Li said. "Horatio wasn't involved in any incident yesterday morning, and there's no arrest record. The police don't have him in custody."

Yuri pulled a face. "He's young. That opens up a few options, especially if he's not the entirely faithful type."

"Ha!" Ainsley grunted. "If you were a horny nineteen-year-old and you had Gwendoline in your bed every night, would you go wolf-ing around the block?"

"It's been known," Yuri replied, as tactfully as he could.

"This whole thing: it's unusual," Ainsley said. "I don't fucking like unusual, not when there's family involved. Especially exposed fam-ily."

"We need to bring the women in," Poi Li said. "Give them proper security."

"Yeah," Ainsley agreed. "Shit, Nataskia will bust my balls. This is everything she didn't want. And fuck knows how Neva will react."

"Who's Neva?" Yuri asked.

"My second-to-last ex. I was married to her when Nataskia had Evette. She doesn't know about that."

"Oh." Yuri's gaze locked on Poi Li as he tried to remain expres-sionless.

"So what do you think?" Ainsley asked.

"Okay," Yuri said, and took a breath. "We have a few scenarios to consider here. Horatio has run off with another girl or boy, and he's too guilty right now to call Gwendoline and tell her it's over. Second: He's had an accident, and the hospital hasn't identified him—unlikely in this day and age, but possible. Third: He's dead. We'll need to check the morgues, but again he should have been identified already. Last option, and the most likely: He's in trouble with people you really should not be in trouble with."

"It's not blackmail?" Ainsley asked; he sounded surprised.

"I'm going to take Gwendoline at her word when she said that she never told him she's related to you. If this is blackmail, that would mean someone found out."

"How?" Ainsley snapped.

"Some junior in the legal division got the wrong file by mistake; same thing but with an employee in the finance company handling the trust fund; her mother or grandmother let something slip by accident." He paused, extrapolating the possibilities. "But if a professional gang did find out, they'd snatch her, not him. Unless . . ."

"What?"

Yuri glanced at the door Gwendoline had closed behind her. "She's scamming you."

"No fucking way!"

"Sir, she has no real bond with you, and she's excluded from the dynasty with all the wealth, privilege, and prestige that brings."

"Okay, I've only seen her a few times in her life, I admit that, but she knows there's a place for her in Connexion anytime she wants. She chose to be independent, she worked hard at her exams—and got herself good grades, too. And she's only seventeen, for Christ's sake! Girls like that, brought up the way she's been, they don't come up with criminal master plans. If she wants money, she can have it. I'm not broke. She just has to ask."

"All right, acknowledged. So that scenario would be doubtful."

"We need to find out what's happened to Horatio," Poi Li said. "But without any fuss. Which is where you come in. This has to be kept quiet."

"Poi Li recommended you," Ainsley said. "She said you were the one we needed for a job like this. I know this is a big ask, but fuck it, this is my family!"

"It's a logical ask," Yuri said, trying to make it sound businesslike— although inside he was flying. *A personal favor for Ainsley fucking Zangari? This is my cast-iron route to head of security.* "My office already has executive authority, and uses it. I can request any file or operation we need without anyone wondering why."

"Thanks," Ainsley said. "I appreciate that, Yuri, I mean it."

Yuri held up a hand. "This is not a one-person investigation, sir. I understand and appreciate the need for discretion, but I'll be bringing in some of my team to assist. Not many, but people I trust."

"Of course."

"If this is ordinary bad, I need to get started right now."

"What's ordinary bad?" Ainsley asked.

"He's got a dependency problem, or he's placed some bets offline—neither of which he'll tell Gwendoline about, for all their lovey-dovey honesty with each other. If he owes money to those kind of people, then right now he's in some blacked-out room having the shit kicked out of him. The danger there is that once they break him—and they will—he'll call Gwendoline, begging for money. So first priority, we install a link diversion on her altme. If he calls, that gets routed straight to me."

"Whatever you need, whatever it costs. Just get it done."

"Yes, sir."

Yuri called Jessika Mye while he was still in the rickety old lift on his way back down to the entrance hall. She'd joined the Monitoring Office as one of its first recruits, at age thirty-four—a Hong Kong native who'd immigrated to Akitha, where she'd got her exobiology master's degree. When he asked her why she'd come back to Earth, she'd told him that Akitha was too quiet for her, and she wanted the money to buy full telomere treatments. Yuri could sort of appreciate that; the Utopial principle strove for egalitarianism, but not even their society could afford to provide telomere treatments for the entire population from such an early age. Akitha democratically decided that, for a thirty-four-year-old, it was vanity, not necessity. Jessika was attractive and clearly motivated to remain so. Yuri quite liked that determination, to be able to reject past choices with confidence if they didn't meet her own demanding standard, so he gave her the job there and then.

"What's up, chief?" she asked.

"We have a new investigation. I can't even give you a priority rating, it's so high."

"Sounds cool. What is it?"

"Missing person."

"Seriously?"

Yuri smiled at the doubt in her tone. The lift reached the ground floor, and he tugged the cage door open. "Oh, yes."

"Why the hell are we doing a missing persons?"

"Because it's important. And that's why I want you. I'm sending the address over now. Be there in five minutes."

Yuri walked straight back to the Sloane Square hub and went out along a radial to loop, then around that to the Hackney hub at the end of Graham Road. As he went, Boris started loading instructions into the Olyix Monitoring Office G7Turing. He wanted a record of Horatio Seymore's travels through the Connexion network for the last four days. Bank search for financial status. Facial recognition search through Hackney's public surveillance cameras, going back three days. A request routed through the Connexion Metropolitan Police liaison office for gang activity in Hackney.

Those would do for a start.

Eleanor Road, on the edge of London Fields, was half old brick terrace houses with tall slate roofs that had all undergone conversions to add a loft room for the budget middle classes still inhabiting London's suburbs. The remainder of the buildings were newer, purpose-built tenements, narrow and tall to fit in as many one-bedroom flats as possible, with the rent and management optimized for a fast turnover of young low-wage workers with service jobs in the city. Exactly like Horatio.

Jessika's heels clattered on the pavement behind Yuri as he approached the front of Horatio's building.

"Good timing." He smirked as she caught up with him. She was wearing a smart cherry-pink office suit and white blouse, with slim five-centimeter heels; her face flushed even through her perfect makeup. Her normally immaculate jet-black hair was ruffled from hurrying along the street.

"And you blend in so flawlessly."

"Hey!" she protested. "I'm strictly an office meetings and cocktails kind of girl."

"Right." He told Boris to let them in; Gwendoline had given him the code.

The hallway and stairs were bare concrete, shaped by onetime printed molds and formed by civic construction bots—cheap and coldly utilitarian. Horatio's flat was two rooms: a slim shower and toilet suite; and the living room equipped with a tiny galley kitchen, a built-in wardrobe, and a sofa sleeper. With two stools standing beside the kitchen bar, there wasn't even room for a chair.

"Depressing," Jessika said as she glanced around.

"No sign of a struggle," Yuri said. "So he wasn't taken from here."

"Outside then."

"Boris, what have you got for me on Wednesday morning?"

"Connexion has no record of Horatio Seymore using the hub network since twenty-one-seventeen hours on Tuesday night, when he left the Hackney hub on Graham Road. That is a global negative, not just London."

"Did I ask for a global search?"

"No, but the G7Turing deduced it was relevant."

"Crap. If it gets any smarter, we'll be out of a job. Okay, what about Gwendoline?"

"Her record is complete and current. She entered the Hackney hub at six fifty-eight on Wednesday morning and went straight to Sloane Square. After a day at work in the City, using her usual hubs, she returned to Hackney on Wednesday evening at nine forty-nine. She left this morning at seven fifty."

"Right, get me a visual record of Eleanor Road on Wednesday, starting at six thirty that morning. Let's see where Horatio went."

"Confirmed," Boris said.

Jessika opened the wardrobe door. "Not much in here," she said, eyeing the clothes.

"He doesn't have any money."

"Then why are we interested?"

Yuri gave her an apologetic shrug. "Super classified: He's the boyfriend of one of Ainsley's granddaughters."

"Ah."

"There is no visual record of Horatio leaving his home address on Wednesday morning," Boris reported.

Yuri and Jessika exchanged a glance. He went over to the window at the rear of the flat, which gave him a view of the tiny gardens backing onto the houses of Horton Road, which ran parallel to Eleanor Road. The window was locked from the inside. "Okay, check Horton Road for me. If he jumped out here, he had to go through a house. Maybe he knows his neighbors well enough."

Jessika frowned and went back into the narrow shower room, checking the frosted glass cubicle. "Well, he's not here."

"You're looking in the shower cubicle?" he asked skeptically.

"Check out an old movie called *Psycho*."

"No visual confirmation of him on Horton Road on Wednesday or today," Boris said.

"What is this, the case of the vanishing magician?" Jessika asked.

"No," Yuri said, not liking where his thoughts were going. "Boris, run a visual recognition for Gwendoline on Eleanor Road Wednesday morning."

"There is none."

"How can that be?" Jessika grunted.

"Confirm she entered Hackney hub at six fifty-eight on Wednesday, please?"

"Our files have visual confirmation of that."

"Right, use public surveillance files. Backtrack her from entering the hub."

"There is a discrepancy. The visual record can track her back to the point where she emerged from the end of Eleanor Road onto Wilton Way."

"So the records for Eleanor Road are corrupted?"

"The Turing is running a diagnostic."

"What are you thinking?" Jessika asked.

"This snatch was well planned and executed," Yuri said. "We're dealing with some serious professionals here. So given Horatio was

one very fit, good-looking adolescent, I'd say we need to think absolute worst case."

"Shit. You're talking a body snatch? For . . . ? What? Ransom?"

"A dark market brain transplant. What we've seen so far certainly
seems to fit the idea."

She closed her eyes and shuddered. "Thanks. I wanted to go on
believing that is urban myth. You got any evidence other than you
watch too many Hong Kong drama games?"

"A myth has to start somewhere," he said. "And it did only start
after the Olyix arrived."

"The Olyix are behind it?" she asked incredulously. "That's crazy."

"Not behind it, no; but their Kcells make it possible." Yuri flinched
from her skeptical stare. "Supposedly." He sighed, wishing it to be
untrue. But the possibility of dark market brain transplants had become an insidious rumor, whispered between law enforcement agencies for several years now. The perfect explanation that case officers
offered up to their directors whenever a major-league criminal suspect eluded them: They were walking around in a whole new body.

Hong Kong drama game production houses loved the concept and
pushed it eagerly into their mainstream crime series. The alien science of Kcells made it sound deliciously plausible.

Until the Olyix arrived, cloning organs or using stem cell replacement tissue was expensive. But the Olyix were eager to trade, enabling them to buy the energy they needed so their arkship *Salvation
of Life* could continue its pilgrimage voyage to the end of the universe. Their advanced biotechnology produced the polyfunction
Kcell, which could be assembled in a number of ways from veins to
skin, bones to muscle, and even some organs. Like the flesh they replaced, they drew energy from blood, living in perfect symbiosis with
the human body, and they were also cheap.

The versatility of Kcells was the root of the whole brain transplant
story. Kcells, so the theory went, could be used to form a neural
bridge between brain and spine—an ability still far beyond human
medical science. And as it involved Kcells, Yuri's office had a dedi-

cated team to investigate and analyze possible cases to see if there was any truth in the claims. So far their conclusion was: We don't know.

"Let's just see where this leads," Yuri temporized. The idea that this might be the case that proved the dark market for brain transplants existed was thrilling. "Boris, how are we doing with those surveillance files?"

"The memory files for the public surveillance camera on Eleanor Road were altered," Boris said. "The hours between six and nine were replaced by a synthesized image."

"This is not an amateur operation," Yuri said. "Not if they can do that. So we're now time critical." He closed his eyes and told Boris to spray a map of the area across his tarsus lenses. "We know the Wilton Way camera files are good. Boris, get the G7Turing to run a search on all the surrounding roads, extending out for a kilometer. Tie it in with the local traffic net records. I want to know every vehicle that drove down Eleanor Road between six and nine on Wednesday morning. No, make that five and nine."

"How long do you think we've got?" Jessika asked.

"They've had Horatio at least twenty-four hours, so not much longer."

"There were two vehicles using Eleanor Road during the time frame you designated," Boris told him. "A civic contractor cleaning truckez, with six ancillary brush wagons, and a builder's merchant van."

"What was the builder's merchant?"

"Tarazzi Metropolitan Supplies. They are based in Croydon."

"Get into their network, find the delivery address."

"There is no delivery address. Error. That van is not licensed to them."

"Well, who is it licensed to?"

"Tarazzi Metropolitan Supplies ADL. That is a company registered on the New Hamburg asteroid. The company was formed on Tuesday, twelve o'clock GMT, and dissolved at five o'clock GMT this morning."

"Smart," Yuri conceded. "Any ownership records?"

"There was one share issued, registered to Horton Accounting. That is also a New Hamburg company, a Turing virtual that is now inactive."

"Horton?" Yuri glanced out of the window again at the backs of the neat row of houses that made up Horton Road. "Someone's having us on. Okay, what time was the van here?"

"It turned in to Eleanor Road at six twenty-two. It left, traveling along Wilton Way, at six forty-eight."

"Where did it go?"

"At six fifty-seven it entered the Hackney Commercial and Government Services Transport Hub on Amhurst Road."

"Track it. I want to know the destination. Jessika, we've got to split up. Call a cabez, follow the fake Tarazzi van to its destination, then find out what happened next. I'm going to assign you a tactical team; they'll follow you. Use them for any face-to-face situation. You're investigation only, understand? I don't want you physically exposed to any member of this dark market operation. They haven't eluded the authorities for years by being the forgiving type."

"Okay." She gave him a small, wild smile. "What are you going to do?"

"Come at it from a different angle. The more routes into this dark market we can open up, the better chance we have of getting Horatio back."

A cabez was pulling up outside the building by the time they walked out of the front door. Yuri watched Jessika climb in, then hurried back to the Hackney hub.

Seven minutes later he was coming out of the hub at the eastern end of Royal Victoria Docks, buffeted by the humid air gusting off the Thames. If he looked south across the river, the Connexion tower dominated the skyline. Around him, the buildings were a strange mixture of old industrial and new residential; at one time they'd all been hotels and restaurants to serve the vast exhibition center that stretched out alongside the docks. But with the advent of Connexion making every location on Earth *one step away,* such overnight business hotels had become obsolescent. They'd subsequently been refurbished as apartments, though some had remained derelict for decades.

Boris hacked the lobby lock of what had once been the classiest hotel on the block. Yuri walked across the high-ceilinged chamber and past the lifts to the stairwell. The office G7Turing was infiltrating the building's security network—which was top-of-the-range, but hardly a match for a G7. He didn't want to be trapped in a lift, with the doors opening at someone else's convenience.

The third-floor corridor ran the length of the building but only had a half dozen doors. Two men stood at the end, giving him a hard stare as he walked down the length of it toward them. Yuri ignored them and halted a couple of meters from the double doors they were guarding. He tipped his head to one side in his best condescending manner and looked at where he guessed the camera was hidden.

"Open it," he said in a tired voice.

"Don't—" one of the guards began.

"Not you," Yuri said, sounding even more tired.

The door buzzed and slid open. Yuri tipped the guards a silent salute and walked in. The inside had been the hotel penthouse suite a century ago and remained an opulent apartment overlooking the docks.

Karno Larsen looked like he'd been in residence for most of those hundred years. He was a huge man, whose sixtieth decade had been stretched out for a punishingly long time by telomere treatments, making him seem more like a mannequin than a flesh-and-blood person. He wore a burgundy silk gown embroidered with mythical creatures that barely covered his dome-like stomach. Thick bare legs waddled him forward from the outsize chair he'd been sitting in.

One of the high walls was covered in screens, all of them playing cult shows from fifty years ago. Karno prided himself on his encyclopedic knowledge of historic trash culture. Glass-fronted cabinets displayed a huge range of incredibly detailed miniatures and limited edition merchandise from the last 150 years. It all looked like cheap tat to Yuri, though he knew it was actually priceless.

"Yuri, my friend, what a surprise. I never thought you would visit me here. Welcome, welcome."

"Really?" Yuri asked. The screens were all playing crap now, but he guessed that a minute earlier they'd been displaying a tangle of finance data. As underground accountants went, Karno Larsen was the preferred go-to for the top men of London's underworld.

Karno performed a humbled shrug. "A short warning would be appreciated next time."

"Actual human guards. I'm impressed."

"One has to cultivate an air of civility. Their peripherals alone cost more than they do."

"I'm sure."

"So why are you here, Yuri? You're not good for business, you know."

"I need a name, and I don't have time for bullshit."

"In some ways, that is almost flattering."

"Who's the best matcher in East London?"

Karno's face locked into a rictus smile. "Matcher?"

"Don't," Yuri said.

"Yuri, please, I have a reputation to consider."

"The only reputation I know is of the person who sets up one-time virtual companies to use the Commercial and Government Services hubs. We talked about that misbehavior before, Karno, and we agreed you have to be useful to me in order to carry on existing. I need the name, and I need it now. I'm asking politely."

"Yuri, please, I don't move in such circles. I facilitate finance, you know this."

"Play close attention, Karno, because either I leave with what I want or you get renditioned to a world that makes Zagreus look like a fucking holiday resort."

"Jesus, Yuri, there's no need for this!" Karno's agitation was making his flab wobble obscenely. "We are friends."

"*Name!*"

"Conrad McGlasson."

"And where do I find him?"

There was no physical address, only an access code. The G7Turing was running tracers before Yuri reached the lobby.

He called Jessika as he went through the doors back out into the unrestrained heat of the street. "How's it going?"

"I'm on Althaea; some town called Bronkal. The Tarazzi van drove into the dredger docks. There's no traffic network, so I haven't got a final destination yet."

Yuri didn't have to get Boris to gather data on Althaea. It was a gas-giant moon in the Pollux system, which after fifty years of aggressive terraforming was just about capable of supporting terrestrial life. The flip point had almost been reached, when the biosphere became stable without any more intervention. "Okay. Call in our local office."

"Already have. And the tactical team is with me."

"Good. Those frontier towns can be rough in places."

"No kidding."

"I've got a possible lead here. If it checks out, I should be with you in half an hour."

"Can't wait."

Boris sprayed up a file of Conrad McGlasson's hub travel record. He traveled around London a lot, Yuri noted, which fitted the whole matcher profile. The G7Turing pulled up a lot of ancillary data: the flats he used, financial data, which was nowhere near complete; that could only mean Conrad had dark accounts.

"What was his last hub use?" Yuri asked.

"He left the QE-Two South Road hub seventeen minutes ago."

"Okay, he's probably on the bridge; there's a lot of footfall there. Cancel his hub access. I want to keep him there."

"Done."

"Send three hawkeye drone squadrons through to find him. And dispatch a tactical team to both ends of the bridge. They're to remain on standby until I call for them, zero public exposure."

"Confirmed."

Yuri walked out of the QEII South Road hub two minutes later and looked up the imposing concrete road ramp that rose up to the Dartford Bridge. As part of London's old M25 orbital motorway, the huge old suspension bridge that crossed the Thames used to carry 130,000 vehicles a day over the muddy tidal estuary. Now it was simply a monument to the obsolete past. He couldn't imagine what it had looked like while it was in use.

Since the last cars and lorries had driven away into history, new money and real estate opportunities had allowed the bridge to reinvent itself. Big tubs had been fixed to the carriageways and planted with trees, turning the whole edifice into a flying greenway. Lightweight buildings had colonized the edges of the bridge, glass walls giving bar, club, and restaurant customers an unrivaled view along the river, both into the city and out across the surrounding countryside. Smaller pop-up specialist fabricator stores shared the ancient tarmac with the verdant trees, completing the transformation to a funky concrete rainbow of small-trader commerce.

Yuri began the long walk up the ramp, sticking to the shade offered by the tree canopy. Here above the river, the humidity was reaching a dismal crescendo. He slung his lightweight suit jacket over his shoulder and wished he had some kind of hat. Unseen above him, the hawkeye drones spread out and started searching for Conrad McGlasson.

They found him sitting at an outdoor table halfway along the southern side. A beer glass was on the table in front of him as he watched the people thronging along the central greenway. Yuri approached at an unhurried pace, keeping his eyes on the target. "Boris, shut down the local internet nodes in a hundred-meter radius around him."

"Confirmed."

The man was in his forties, with short-cut hair as black as his skin. Shorts and an old orange t-shirt gave him an unremarkable air. The only unusual thing was his lack of sunglasses; everyone else on the bridge that day was wearing them like it was a compulsory dress code. Conrad's eyes were too precious for that. He scanned the people wandering past, studying them.

Conrad saw Yuri while he was still twenty meters away and immediately tensed up.

He's good, Yuri admitted to himself.

Conrad hunted around for other potential hostiles. When he didn't find any, he returned his gaze to Yuri.

"I'm not going to chase you," Yuri said as he arrived at the table.

"Nice to know," Conrad replied, trying to keep it cool. Small beads of sweat on his high forehead were giving away his inner anxiety.

Yuri pulled out a chair and sat down. "My teams will do that. They're all young and fit, and eager to show me how efficient they are. They're armed, too. Ever been hit with a taser dart? Ours are very good, because we can't be bothered restricting them to the legal maximum charge. Oh, and I've revoked your Connexion account. You'd have to run the whole way home. I imagine that would be quite exhausting in this heat. The teams will probably start a book on how far you'd get. I'd say about a hundred and fifty meters. What do you reckon?"

"What do you want?"

"I want you to tell me about me."

"Excuse me?"

"You're a matcher. You find specific people, ones who fit a profile. Any profile you're given. So show me how good you are."

"This is bollocks. You've got nothing on me."

"I have your name, and I was told you're the best."

"No proof, pal."

"Don't need it. You find people—people who are vulnerable without realizing it. I know how it works; my office has to deal with plenty of cases."

"Your office?"

"Yeah. All those starry-eyed graduate kids who've just grabbed themselves a shit job at the very bottom of a big company and think they're going to make it to CEO one day. You see their weakness, you *know* them. It's a special and rare talent you have there, Conrad. You read something in them that tells you they'll be tempted if they're offered some mild narcotics in the right circumstances, by their new best friend. You see one, out here on the bridge, or in a pub, and you sell his name to groups who specialize in trading information. And in a month's time that kid'll have a serious addiction, his credit will be deep negative, he'll do anything to get his next squirt, including handing over access to the company system. Or a girl, pretty but shy, one who can be corrupted easily. And the next thing she knows she's met a great guy, with a great smile, who's showing her a life she only fantasized about, one that pulls her in deeper and deeper. Bingo! Then after a time he's not just her boyfriend, he's her pimp. Another kid ruined. Are you getting the picture here, *pal*? Do you see I know you? Gotta admire the irony."

"You know nothing, you piece of shit! You're blind."

"This isn't personal, so don't make that mistake. You need to do better, a lot better. Am I right? Now tell me about me."

Conrad McGlasson glared at him. "You're not police."

"That was a fifty-fifty guess. Even I could get that one. Come on, live a little, Conrad. Impress me."

"Russian; the accent's still there. Received plenty of telomere treatments, and good ones. You're over a hundred, but hide it well. You work at that—body posture and clothes. The clothes are important; they indicate status. You don't cling to the old comforts; you make yourself stay fashionable. You have arrogance and surety, and you found me easily, so there's plenty of money behind you. It's corporate, not private wealth. You've done your time in the ranks, but you're now too important to be a tactical team leader, which means that if you're taking point, I'm valuable. I know that because people around us are getting antsy now that their internet feed's mysteriously dropped out. You did that to stop me alerting anyone you've found me. That takes clout, digital and political. You're a senior officer in Connexion Security." He picked up his beer and raised it in salute.

"Not bad," Yuri admitted. "A proper little Sherlock Holmes."

"So why am I valuable? What are you doing here?"

Yuri took out a card and told Boris to spray a picture of Horatio on it. When he put it on the table next to the beer, Conrad gave it a cursory glance.

"Did you match him?" Yuri asked.

"No."

"Okay, I'll accept that for now. But it's a small market; there can't be many of you."

"Is that a question?"

"No. Actually, I'm quite impressed. A Turing above G-five can do a similar job as you, but it requires access to a thousand databases. But you, you just look. I find that fascinating." His finger tapped the picture on the card. "What do you see?"

"Him? A nobody, which is something of a paradox considering how desperate you are to find him."

"Not really. He genuinely is a nobody. Your problem is that he met someone who is most definitely not a nobody. So tell me, what do you see, what do you *match*, when you have a contract?"

"This is hypothetical, right?"

"I don't give a shit about you. Your value is measured solely in the information you provide me today. There is no deal on the table here. So? What do you look for?"

Conrad's hands came up to massage his temple. "All right, it goes like this. You have a client, someone who wants information on a company, maybe for a share short, some corporate shit, and—"

"No."

"What?"

"I don't want a company scam. I'm a serial killer, a rich fuck who's more twisted than any politician. The cops are closing in, and I need to escape."

"What?"

"I need a new body. One I can transplant my brain into."

"Oh, no. No no no! Do not do this. You have no idea who you're fucking with."

Yuri leaned in closer, his skin warming with excitement. Conrad's reaction was the first indication that brain transplants might really be happening.

Conrad, of course, saw his reaction, and winced. "Walk away, pal. Tell your boss or whoever it is pulling your strings that you got it wrong. These people you're asking about, they won't respect who you are. You'll wind up with someone like Cancer on your arse, or worse."

"I didn't think there was anyone worse than her." Yuri knew all about Cancer—so called because she always got her victim in the end; a black ops specialist for the extremely wealthy, but illegitimate, playa. She'd never taken a contract that hadn't been fulfilled, and never a contract from anyone remotely legitimate—presumably to make sure it wasn't an entrapment sting. She was feared and respected by everyone in the trade, and the dream arrest of every law enforcement official in the Sol system.

"Don't do this," Conrad pleaded.

"If it helps, think of me as Cancer's opposite. You are my target. When you give me what I want, then—and only then—will this be over."

"It's a death sentence for both of us, you understand?"

"Completely. But just so you understand, if these people are not scared of me, then they're exceptionally stupid."

"Fuck you! Look, this deal, what you're asking for, it's rarer than unicorn shit, okay?"

"What? Snatches for a brain transplant?"

Conrad winced, glancing around nervously. "Stop saying that. I don't know what the client wants these people for, okay? It's weird, but it pays well."

"What people?"

"Low visibility people; that's what they ask for. People so insignificant no one will ever notice when they go missing. There's not as many as you'd think, actually."

"So you don't know for sure they're being snatched for a brain transplant?"

"Listen, pal, we don't exactly have contracts, you know."

"Okay, so why get so twitchy whenever I mention brain transplants? What do you know? Are they real?" Yuri had to work hard at keeping the enthusiasm out of his voice.

"I just think it through, you know," Conrad said edgily. "Working out the options. You gotta watch out for yourself in this trade, make sure nothing comes back to bite you. So when I look hard at some of the aspects I have to take into account, that kinda narrows the options, see?"

"All right, how does this work? Exactly? Tell me—all of it."

"Okay, it plays like this: You've committed a serious crime, something the authorities are never going to quit on—like you said, a serial killer or pedophile, totally bad shit. The only way out for you is a fresh body for your brain, just like on the drama games. That way, not even a DNA sample can show who you really are, because cops only ever sample the body, saliva, or blood, semen a lot of the time—but never the brain. So the deal goes down, and I get the word, a request to match, along with the condition that they have to be low visibility. Now what else, apart from a brain transplant, could it be?"

"Right. What else do they want, apart from low visibility?"

"My client gives me a picture. It's not an actual image, a photo file, or anything like that. This picture, it's a description, a data sketch. Height and weight combination, skin color, hair color, eye color. That's the basic parameter."

"I don't get it. Why would a criminal want to look the same? Why not go for someone who looks different?"

"Rejection. Come on; that part's obvious! This is the mother of all transplants, so I figure you have to have the greatest match possible. Physical traits are a good baseline. I see someone who matches the picture, and I start to assess them. Are they basically healthy, are they overweight? Stuff like that. It's amazing what you get to recognize. Some people are walking beacons for what's happened to them. Accidents make them flinch at the smallest things. Careful around food, they've got allergies. It's all there in the posture, you know? Once I have a potential, then secondary factors kick in, which are even more important. The biggest is: Is anyone going to care if they vanish? That rules out the rich, and most of the middle class. So I look for what they wear, where they live, what sort of places they visit, the kind of people they're hanging out with. All these are big indicators of who a person is. So I work it down to maybe ten possibles and get physically close enough to snatch their altme code when they go online—which everybody is, all the time. Once I have that, an e-head friend grabs their digital profile for a real exam. Eighty percent of the time I'm right and they're nonentities. Dig a little deeper, and they have awkward links—a good job, a big set of friends, things that make vanishing them different. So after you've run those filters, you're left with maybe three or four. Then you step it up a level and go for their medical records. That's when we find out blood type and any congenital conditions. There's normally a genome sequence as well, which gets reviewed by specialist algorithms for biochemical compatibility. If they're optimum, I'll pass the file on to my client, and I'm out with a nice fat bonus."

"Your client always asks for medical data?"

"Yes, of course. That's something else that's telling me what's actually going down. I mean, what else could they need that for, right? And I'll tell you something: Crime isn't race specific. All these requests have been really varied."

"*All,* the requests? I thought you said this kind of snatch was rare."

Conrad flinched. "It is. Compared with the other matches I make."

"So these rare cases—your victim is taken away and killed?"

"The body's still walking around."

"You know what you are?"

"Yeah yeah: inhuman, a psycho. Call me a bastard to my face, please. This is a tough life, pal. We all do what we have to."

"No, none of that. I'm beyond insults in your case. You've just described yourself. Who would ever notice or care if you disappeared?"

"Fuck you!"

"Okay, we're almost finished. Who is your client? Who puts in the order for a match?"

"You're kidding, right?"

"Does my face match someone who's kidding right now? Give me the name."

"I can't do that."

"Can and will. Don't make me ask again." Yuri watched with cold amusement as the warring emotions played across Conrad's face. Fear dominated.

"If I do this—"

"When," Yuri said.

"I'm protected, right?"

"Oh, yeah. Just like doctor-patient confidentiality; I signed the oath and everything. Give me the fucking name, dickhead."

Boris sprayed the incoming file across his tarsus lenses: Baptiste Devroy.

Yuri got up and walked away without another word, heading for the nearest hub out of the six on the bridge.

"Do you want Conrad's Connexion account reactivated?" Boris asked.

"Yes. Let him into the hub network again, but have the tactical team intercept him. He is to be dropped on Zagreus today."

"Confirmed."

"Then get me a complete profile on Baptiste Devroy, and run a cross-reference with Althaea; I want to know why the fake Tarazzi van went there. When you get that, send the file straight to Jessika; she can start checking it out. Oh, and put another tactical team on standby for me, a dark one. As soon as we have a location on Devroy, they're to bring him in to the Glastonbury safe house. I'll talk to him there."

"Processing now."

Yuri ducked into the nearest hub and walked around the loop until he came to a major junction. It had a private access to Connexion's internal network. From there it was five portals until he was walking out of the company's Geneva headquarters. The heat wave seemed to be Europe-wide; it was just as hot and humid walking Geneva's streets as it was in London. It took him three minutes to get to the Olyix European Trade and Exchange embassy on the Quai du Mont Blanc. Baptiste Devroy's file splashed up on his lens within the first twenty seconds. He was rumored to run a crew for the Woodwarde Macros, a south London gang that was rumored to deal in biosynth narcotics. Also rumored to have killed a rival gang soldier two years ago.

"Too many rumors," Yuri told Boris. "Do we have anything concrete?"

"His criminal activities are coming from the London Metropolitan Police gang intelligence task force files," Boris replied. "Legally, they cannot confirm his activities without proof. The information they've gathered on him has come from informers, and is not admissible in court."

"Fucking lawyers," Yuri muttered under his breath. "Do you have a location on him?"

"He has a flat in Dulwich Village. According to his Connexion account, he exited the hub on his road at twenty-three forty-seven hours last night. He has not used the account again so far today, which implies he's either at home in the flat or within walking distance. The tactical team are en route to Dulwich. Their G7Turing is reviewing local civic surveillance, and they will ping his altme before entering the flat to confirm his location before they intercept."

"Okay, keep me updated."

The Olyix European Trade and Exchange embassy was a modern nine-story structure of glass and concrete, facing the Jet d'Eau out in the lake. As well as two armed Swiss diplomatic police outside the doorway, there were twin security pillars who scanned Yuri as he walked past them. The police waved him in.

Stéphane Marsan was waiting for him inside—an elegantly suited Frenchman who served as a technology liaison officer for the aliens.

"Thank you for arranging this at such short notice," Yuri said as they went through the decontamination suite.

"Happy to oblige," Stéphane said, pressing his antique black glasses back onto his nose. "The Olyix are sensitive to any abuse of their technology."

Decontamination wasn't as intense as Yuri was expecting. A room with big glass doors at both ends was filled with a mist that he had to stand in for two minutes, eliminating the microbes clinging to his clothes—the kind that saturated the city air. Light heavy with UV shone down on him.

On the other side, the temperature was several degrees colder than outside. The embassy had its own life-support mechanism; no alien air was released into Geneva's atmosphere, and vice versa.

A lift took them up to the fifth floor. When the doors opened, dry, spicy air wafted in. Yuri peered around curiously. The fifth floor was different from the rest of the building, which mainly housed human-style offices. In front of him was a wide open space, with a hologram ceiling of an alien sky. Two huge gas giants hung above him, one with a vivid emerald cloudscape, the other more like Saturn but without the rings. Both had a plethora of moons, every one of them different, from planetoids locked under ice oceans to smog-smothered continents studded with sulfur volcanoes, from barren mono-deserts to jungle hellholes.

"Is that . . . ?" Yuri began.

"Their original home world?" Stéphane finished for him. "Non. It's an enhanced Jim Burns picture; they bought the rights to the original. Something about it appealed to them."

Yuri shook his head. Just when you thought you had a handle on the Olyix, the universe twisted ninety degrees and took it away from you again.

There were several of the aliens lumbering about the room. The main bulk of an Olyix was a fat disk two meters in diameter, with a semi-translucent skin that revealed a great many purple organ shapes lurking inside. The thin curving fissures between them were filled with thick fluid, which pulsed slowly around the body, and always made Yuri slightly queasy. Five stumpy legs emerged from the underside, with the forward limb nearly twice as thick as the other four. Clearly visible within each leg were helixes of muscle bending and flexing around a dark central rod of gristle. The wide hooves lacked the elegance of the legs with their sophisticated flexibility, which for some reason always made Yuri think of a donkey clopping along.

He watched carefully as one approached—and yes, each footfall was cumbersome, thudding down loudly on the marble floor. That was to be expected; not one of the weird creatures weighed less than 150 kilograms. There was a broad oval head above the body, and a fat ring-neck provided it with limited mobility. The nose extended to the circumference of the body, with a bulging gold-tinted compound apposition eye on the upper surface. At the front of the body's midsection was a flaccid skirt of clear tissue hanging down, which put Yuri unnervingly in mind of a loincloth of jellyfish. The lucid substance formed a shape mimicking a human hand and extended it toward Yuri on the end of a stubby tentacle.

Yuri clenched his jaw against the revulsion he knew he was about to experience and put out his hand. The Olyix flesh flowed around his palm, feeling like oiled velvet that had just come out of a fridge. He smiled as he shook hands. Someone had explained the whole human etiquette routine to the Olyix when their arkship arrived in the Sol system, and the aliens had swiftly incorporated the correct formal procedures into their dealings with people ever since. Privately, Yuri wished a prankster had got there first and shown them *Star Trek*'s Vulcan salute instead.

Boris reported a link being opened. "Pleased to meet you, Director Alster," the Olyix's vocalizer unit said in a husky female voice. Another attempt at endearment. If you were male they used a female voice, and vice versa. Yuri wondered why nobody had ever bothered explaining political correctness to them. *Pick a gender and stick with it, guys.* The aliens themselves were indefinable by human standards in both biology and gender. Every Olyix defined itself by its mind, which was always distributed between its quint: five bodies linked via a form of quantum entanglement between the neural structure of its separate brains.

"That's just Yuri, please," he said, withdrawing his hand as soon as politeness allowed.

"Of course. My quint designation is Hai. I personally am Hai-3."

"Thank you for agreeing to see me, Hai-3." Yuri resisted the impulse to look around the room and guess which, if any, of the other Olyix bodies were also Hai. An Olyix quint always kept at least a couple of itself on board the *Salvation of Life,* their arkship.

"I am happy to assist. Your message indicated you proceed with some urgency."

Yuri glanced at Stéphane. "That is correct."

"You need me gone?" Stéphane asked.

"This could be quite sensitive."

"Officer Marsan has our full confidence," Hai-3 said.

"Okay. I'm tracking a missing human, who may be a case of an illegal brain transplant. So I need to know if such a thing is theoretically possible, and the critical component behind the theory seems to be Kcells, which would be used to reconnect the nervous system. Is it possible to use them like that?"

A slow ripple made its way along Hai-3's loose flesh, tracking left to right. "This is most unfortunate," it said. "We have heard rumors of our Kcells being misused in this fashion."

"That's all we have as well, rumors and conspiracy theories. Which is why I'm here. I need to know once and for all if it is real."

"Have you any proof of this allegation?" Stéphane asked flatly.

"Nobody is making allegations," Yuri countered quickly. "Nor leveling charges of illegality. Right now, I have a kid I need to find—and fast. So I need to eliminate as many possibilities as I can, so I'm not wasting time. That's all."

"Once we heard claims of this abuse, our growthmasters looked into the process," Hai-3 said. "From a theoretical viewpoint only. We wished to see if it was indeed possible."

"Of course. And is it?"

"Without actually using a test subject, we cannot give a definitive answer."

"Best guess will do for me."

"Our simulation indicated it would ultimately be possible to transplant a human brain from one body to another, given the correct circumstances."

"What are those circumstances?"

"That the host and donor bodies would have to share a very similar biochemistry, extending far beyond simple blood type matching. The most ideal match would be between humans in the same family."

Yuri couldn't quite avoid the shudder of revulsion that brought on. He did manage to avoid a small prayer of thanks to the dear Virgin Mary that he'd never had children. He hadn't been inside a church for more than a century, but thanks to his mother, the Russian Orthodox Church had been an ever-present influence in his early childhood. "I see. But if a family member wasn't available?"

"It would still be possible, though the number of candidates would be small. You would have to be very lucky to find one."

"Or know a man that can," Yuri murmured. "Okay. So I've done my research and have a suitable donor body. What do I need from you?"

"Such a procedure would require a great deal more than Kcells profiled to conduct nerve impulses between human neuron junctions."

"What else do you need?"

"Nerve repair in humans is now relatively successful, if expensive.

The use of stem cells to regenerate damaged nerves is approaching an eighty percent success rate. However, reconnecting severed nerves is extremely difficult. And for a brain transplant, every nerve in the spinal cord would first have to be severed. Before you did that, you would need a micron-level scanner sophisticated enough to identify and tag the individual nerve pathways. It would first be used on the spinal cord of the person whose brain was to be transplanted, then on the victim, in order to know how to match them up."

"Yeah." Yuri closed his eyes, trying to visualize the problem. "I get that. You'd need to join the right pathways up; otherwise you'd think you were moving a leg when you're actually bending your arm."

"A crude analogy, but essentially correct," Hai-3 said. "However, it is not just the nerves that control muscle movement that would be required. You would also have to successfully reconnect the body's entire sensorium, or you would be completely numb and unable to control the muscles that you did command to move. Apparently our human partners have taken to calling it zombie syndrome."

"Sounds about right," Yuri conceded.

"I am not aware of any scanner that sophisticated being built," Hai-3 said. "Furthermore, as well as this hypothetical scanner, you would require a nanosurgical device to physically connect the severed nerves to both ends of the Kcell bridge. We have been examining this procedure with our human corporate partners."

"You've experimented on humans?" Yuri did his best to ignore Stéphane's sigh of exasperation.

"Certainly not," Hai-3 said. "We have formed development and sales partnerships with several human biogenetic companies; they provide us with their requirements, and we try to profile our Kcells accordingly. There have been attempts to use a Kcell nerve fiber to bridge a missing nerve section in pigs. Some were successful. Some not. Progress is slow, but is being made. I would caution you, the largest number of nerves in a bundle that were reconnected by company research teams was eleven. There are several million nerves at the top of the human spinal cord, so the problem is orders of magnitude more complex than anything currently achieved. If a scanner and surgical device could be built, the procedure would have to be controlled by a G7Turing. Given the number of nerves involved, the subject would probably have to be placed in a coma, and the operation would be conducted over a period of months. I am not certain how much human money would be involved in funding such an enterprise."

"Right," Yuri said. "So basically, what you're telling me is that brain transplants don't exist?"

"Currently, yes, although it may become possible in the future. Another factor in this equation is the Kcell nerves themselves. As I told you, several million individual fibers would be required for such an operation. In the last seven years, we have provided our research partners with a total of two and a half thousand."

Yuri felt strangely disappointed by Hai-3's reassurance. At the same time, it did make him wonder exactly what had happened to Horatio. "That's good to know, thank you."

"That such a criminal concept has taken root in human culture is most distressing to us," Hai-3 said. "This is not why we made our biotechnology available to you. We only wanted to help you before we fly onward to the God at the End of Time. Death is not something biological entities should suffer anymore. I hope you can explain that to people in your media companies who have influence—perhaps upon the successful conclusion of your case?"

"Of course. I'm sorry about the way people have twisted the possibilities of Kcell application. Unfortunately, there are those among us, thankfully a small minority, who live by a different set of rules, which makes such unpleasant stories believable."

"The Olyix understand. You are new to sentience. Your behavior is still affected by your animal origin. You seek to advance yourselves at the expense of others."

"As I said: a minority."

"We were like you once. Our biotechnology allowed us to modify ourselves, to cast aside such animal-derived impulses. We gave ourselves a higher purpose."

Yuri maintained a polite expression. He knew what was coming, and out of the corner of his eye he caught Stéphane grinning knowingly. The Olyix were unremittingly evangelical. Hai-3's cooperation came with a price: He had to endure the sermon. "Sadly for now," he said, "we are stuck with our more humble bodies and all their flaws."

"Indeed," Hai-3 said. "But consider that if you joined with us, crimes like the one you face today would be a thing of the past."

"What you ask is interesting, but as a species I don't think we're ready for a voyage to the end of time. We're not mature enough to face a deity—yours or anyone else's."

"You can be. That is what we hope to offer you before our arkship flies onward once more. We continue to learn how to adapt our Kcells to function in your bodies. Our growthmasters believe we can one day model clusters to duplicate your neural structure. When that happens, you can become immortal like us."

"The singularity download. Yes. I think our society has a long way to go before we accept that. If the body is not original, we would not be us."

"The body, any body—ours, yours—is merely a vessel for the mind. The mind is evolution's pinnacle. Sentience is extraordinarily rare in this universe. It must be cherished and protected at all costs."

"Good to know we agree on that."

"Would you consider coming with us, Yuri Alster?"

"I don't know. Anything is possible, I suppose," he replied diplomatically.

"I will pray for you, Yuri Alster," Hai-3 said. "And I urge you to consider what we can offer. Sentient species are the children of this universe, the reason it exists. It is our destiny to travel to the conclusion and join together in bliss and fulfillment with the final God."

"I see." He almost said it, almost asked: *What about steady state theory?* Human cosmologists were now almost convinced that the universe was eternal—that the idea of a trillion-year cyclic state, of Big Bang origins and Big Crunch collapses, was no longer valid. *So why do the Olyix think it's going to end?* But he had a job to do. "You have given me a lot to consider. For that I thank you."

Another ripple wound its way around Hai-3's midsection. "You are most welcome. And I consider it an act of friendship on my part to extend our help to you with this unpleasant case you are working on. To devote yourself to the recovery of others less fortunate is an honorable calling."

Yuri hoped the Olyix couldn't pick up on the flash of guilt he felt. "I do what I can." *And what Ainsley Zangari wants.*

"Your dedication is to be commended. I will pray for your success in recovering the unfortunate man who has been abducted."

Yuri gave the alien a level stare. "You are most kind. Your help eliminating one line of inquiry has been very beneficial for me. Thank you." He steeled himself and shook hands with Hai-3 again. This time he didn't flinch; anger allowed him to keep a tight rein on his reactions.

"Baptiste Devroy was not in his flat," Boris informed Yuri as soon as he was back out on Geneva's streets.

"Shit. Where is he?"

"He deactivated his altme and left the flat at ten fifty-seven this morning. Civic surveillance shows him getting into a cabez, which was requested by Dawn Mongomerie, his current girlfriend. The tactical team are backtracking it."

"Ten fifty-seven," Yuri mused. "Interesting coincidence; that's about when we started looking for Horatio. Where was I then?"

"At Horatio's flat on Eleanor Road."

"Fuck it, they were watching to see if anyone noticed he'd gone! And then Jessika and I turned up, Connexion security officers. They must have started shitting themselves." He called Jessika. "I hope you've made progress. They know we're coming."

"How the hell do they know that?" she demanded.

"Best guess, they were watching Horatio's flat. Baptiste Devroy is running; the tactical team is on his arse, but there's no guarantee when they'll catch up with him."

"Well, you're in luck. I've got a promising lead here."

"Good. I'll be with you in ten minutes." He called Poi Li as he entered the Connexion hub.

"What's happening?" she asked. "I see the tactical team missed Baptiste Devroy."

"Whoever snatched Horatio knows we're searching for him, which is bad. I'm concerned they'll cut and run."

"Then you have to find him fast."

"No shit!"

"Is he on Althaea?"

"I really hope so, because that's my only lead left."

"All right, do whatever you have to."

"There's a tactical team already there, supporting Jessika. It may get noisy."

"Althaea's barely been awarded its settlement certificate. It's a world without value. Nobody cares what happens there."

"You'll cover for me?"

"With our history, I'm insulted you asked."

Yuri grinned. "One more thing."

"What are you, a Columbo wannabe?"

"A what?"

"Old fictional detective. Ask your friend Karno Larsen."

"Whatever. I need to run something by you, and tell me if I'm being paranoid."

"Now you're talking."

"You're a major criminal gang, or one of Ainsley's rivals."

"Connexion doesn't have rivals."

"Envious small-timers. You know: the Brazilian SolarWell consortium. Someone who has the resources and patience to run a long con. Humor me here, please."

"Have I ever not?"

"Then this is how you operate. You find out Gwendoline is Ainsley's granddaughter and do your research. You create a flawless legend: Horatio and his whole family. Hell, maybe a dozen Horatios, to bump your chances. Then you drop him into place—a place where you know Gwendoline will meet him. And of course she falls for him big time, because they've matched him perfectly. He spends the next two years romancing her, and they marry. He tells her how she maybe should take a job with Connexion after all. She does, and works her way up the family ladder, which is a much shorter route to the executive level than anyone without Zangari blood. Zambam-thank-you-ma'am. It's taken fifteen years, but you now have access to the highest level of Connexion—finance, strategy—and the power to influence same. That's got to be a worthwhile investment for people like that."

"All right, I'm playing. So why pull him away?"

He flinched. "I'm not sure yet."

"Because he's a tart with a heart, and really, *really* fell for her?"

Yuri hadn't known that venomous level of sarcasm could carry across a solnet link. "No. I've come across something seriously wrong about this; I need to tell you about it in person."

"Yuri, a G7Turing would have trouble hacking this encryption."

"So color me paranoid."

There was only a short pause, but with Poi Li that was significant. "Okay."

"And in the meantime, run a full check on Horatio. Not just a G7Turing data mine; if he was put into place, his controllers will know we'd do that at some point. Go deeper. Maybe send someone you trust to physically interview his parents, get DNA samples and check them against residuals in his flat, talk to his school friends, his teachers, see if they have any memories of him as a boy. If he was planted, his controllers won't be able to cover everything. I want to know if he's real, Poi."

"All right, Yuri. Leave it with me."

"Thank you. I'm stepping into the Althaea hub now. I'll call you as soon as I have something."

The frontier town of Bronkal only warranted twenty-five Connexion hubs and a single commercial transport hub. It was a small town on the edge of the Estroth plains, a flatland plateau that extended for nearly two thousand kilometers before dropping sharply into the sea. It was that unbroken level ground that swung the decision to terraform in Althaea's favor.

Pollux, as a K0 orange-giant star, wasn't the obvious choice for a human world. But it did have a gas-supergiant planet, Thestias, which in turn had forty-eight moons. Four of the larger ones, Althaea, Pleuron, Iphicles, and Leda, were caught in a rosette orbit in the Lagrange-2 point, forever drifting around each other in Thestias's umbra. In most cases, being caged within a supergiant planet's shade would be a gloomy existence, but not when Thestias orbited a mere 1.6 AUs out from an orange giant. The reduced sunlight striking Althaea's surface was as intense as midday on Earth's tropics. Conjunctions with its L-2 co-moons provided a regular variable day-night cycle as it passed between their shadows.

It was midday between Pleuron-conjunction and Leda-conjunction (eighteen hours of light) when Yuri stepped out of the hub on Esola Street in the middle of town. He exhaled sharply. Compared to this humidity, London had been practically arctic. The monotonous carbon and glass buildings stretched out along the street with geometrical precision. Palm trees provided some shade along the cracked concrete pavements, but not much; they were swaying about from the surprisingly fast gusts of wind sweeping along the street. Few people were walking in the sweltering daylight, and even fewer cycled; the road itself was mainly occupied with single-occupant cabez and larger taxez humming along the shimmering asphalt, along with commercial vehicles rumbling between them. It was like a scene from the mid-twenty-first century, Yuri thought.

Boris connected to the local net, and twenty seconds later a three-wheeled cabez pulled up in the broad strip of empty concrete to one side of the hub. Yuri climbed in and sat down on the narrow seat, thankful for the AC vents blasting cool air into the tiny transparent bubble. He always agreed with the saying that you wore a cabez rather than rode one.

It drove forward, taking him quickly through the town's depressing grid of near-identical buildings, their panel walls mass-fabricated in an industrial estate on the outskirts. There was nothing else to see on the ground, no vista of the vast marshlands stretching out beyond the town's docks. That didn't bother him; on Althaea, the view was all about the sky.

Pleuron's orbit had already dropped it below Althaea's horizon, while Leda was now rising to the zenith—an airless cratered world with its vast silver-gray mares laced with glowing lava streams. Massive tectonic activity was constantly rearranging its geography, rendering mapping an irrelevance. And beyond that, dominating the apex of the bright azure sky, was the awesome globe of Thestias itself: a circle of darkness crowned by a blazing halo of golden light created by its perpetual eclipse of Pollux. The glowing edges illuminated fast-moving white and carmine clouds, their swirling kinesis producing the bizarre optical illusion that they were somehow spilling over the edge of a hole in space to flow down into its black heart. An optical illusion that made it seem as if Althaea was also falling toward the gas supergiant's eternal nightside. Locals called it the Eye of God.

Yuri shivered, shaking off the giddiness the sight conjured up. The cabez took him to a commercial block on Nightingale Avenue. He walked into the reception, and Boris directed him along one wing to the office suite Jessika had rented forty minutes earlier. The rooms backed onto a small warehouse where the tactical team had parked their farm truck. The team's captain, Lucius Sóćko, had brought a thirty-centimeter portal inside a briefcase, which they'd threaded up in the warehouse. The rest of his team was coming through the two-meter portal door, along with equipment and specialist mission support operators.

Lucius was in the main office standing behind Jessika, who had taken her pink jacket off to sit at a desk with several new electronic modules. Yuri hadn't encountered the captain before, but the file Boris was spraying across his tarsus lenses spoke of good work. You didn't get to his level in Connexion Security without being competent. One thing the file hadn't prepared him for was seeing Lucius's arm around Jessika's shoulders.

"What have you got for me?" Yuri asked.

Jessika looked around, smiling as Lucius quickly stood up straight. "I still haven't managed to trace the Tarazzi van in the docks," she said. "However, we have no record of it driving away again through the commercial transport hub after it delivered Horatio. It's probably still there."

"They will have reregistered it," Yuri said bluntly. "Probably within ten minutes of it arriving."

"There have only been seven similar vans departing Bronkal since then," she countered. "All of them legitimate."

"These guys are professional," Yuri said uncertainly.

"I think we have two options," Lucius said. "One: The gang has enough money to scrap the van straight away—break it up, take it to a vapor recycler plant, drive it out of town and dump it in the swamps, whatever. In which case we've lost it permanently."

"Or?" Yuri queried.

"They're not going to be snatching people every day. The van will be parked up in a shed somewhere, waiting until they get another job. Then it'll be reregistered and given a bodywork makeover."

"Good call," Yuri said.

"The dock area's a whole industrial district supporting the bioreactor site, as well as the barge maintenance companies," Jessika said.

"Plenty of big buildings. I want to send in a microdrone flock, scan the whole place for the van. Lucius has already brought them through the portal."

Yuri nodded. "Do it."

"Who are these people?" Lucius asked. "Any idea?"

"I don't know," Yuri told them. "I originally thought it might be a dark market brain transplant, but I've been disabused of that notion. Which leaves us with an old-fashioned kidnap and ransom."

"That's bullshit," Jessika said. "Ainsley isn't going to pay squat for the poor kid."

Yuri shrugged. "Whoever Devroy works for, they're professional."

"Are you sure he's working for someone?"

"No, but that's irrelevant at this point. We have to find Horatio, and fast."

"I'll launch the drones," Lucius said. "My people are ready to go."

"Do that," Yuri said. "But I have one other lead. The G7Turing found Baptiste Devroy has a cousin right here, in Bronkal. Joaquin Beron; he runs some kind of atmospheric sensor company, a one-man shop, has supply and maintenance contracts with the government climate monitoring board."

"That can't be a coincidence," Jessika said with a knowing grin.

"I wouldn't like to work out the odds."

"You got an address?"

"Yes. Fedress Meadows, block seventeen."

She paused, reading the information Boris had sent her. "An industrial park. Plenty of opportunity to fabricate items and reroute shipping consignments."

"You have a suspicious mind. I approve."

Ideally they would have infiltrated slowly, sent some drones to Fedress Meadows. The drones would be followed by tactical team members arriving at neighboring commercial modules. Then Lucius would have led a three-man detainment group in. Joaquin would have been contained and taken back to the Nightingale Avenue office. If he'd proved reluctant to cooperate immediately, the portal back to security's more secluded facilities was the first option.

Yuri didn't have time for that. Every minute was putting Horatio deeper into danger.

Boris confirmed that Joaquin Beron's altme was connected to block seventeen's solnet node, and Yuri made the decision to go in hard and fast. The department's G7Turing shut down Fedress Meadows's network. A flock of twenty-five microdrones deployed from Nightingale Avenue, their sensors probing the area in advance of Yuri's arrival. Five big gray four-by-four utility vehicles drove in a convoy to Fedress Meadows, which turned out to be a bleak collection of multi-role cubes able to accommodate a variety of small and medium businesses. Yuri stared at the square gray-and-black walls, inset with silvered glass, the skimped landscaping around them. The industrial park could have been on any of the non-Utopial terraformed worlds, or even the poorer areas of Earth itself. The age of cheap and easy fabrication seemed to have taken away any chance for architectural individuality. Places like Fedress weren't somewhere entrepreneurs went to begin their mega-corporate dream. They were the Darwinist incentive that bestowed determined people with the will to improve their enterprise and get the hell out.

Yuri asked Boris for a secure link to Poi Li as they drove manually along the roads at high speed, causing automated vehicles to brake and swerve sharply. "How's the review of Horatio going?"

"So far he's so perfect and sweet, he's like a puppy in human form. I might vomit," she replied. "I've got some people en route to his parents. Hopefully, they'll crack any legend. Because I can't believe anyone this noble still exists."

"Ever considered we might be getting too old and cynical for this job?"

"Speak for yourself. However, I am growing concerned that I don't understand the motive here."

"Money," Yuri said immediately. "It's always money in the end. I'm thinking it's a kidnapping; there's nothing else left it could be. Someone found out who Gwendoline is."

"We haven't had a ransom demand."

"There won't be one. Not now they know I'm on to them. I'm just praying they haven't already tossed Horatio into the swamp."

"Damn, that would devastate Gwendoline. Ainsley won't like it, either."

"Then Ainsley should keep it in his trousers."

"I'll pass that on."

Yuri couldn't help the small grin that played over his lips. "Look, I've got two possible ways of finding the kid. I'll work them to the end, you know that."

"I do. Ever considered you missed your vocation? I can recommend to Ainsley you take charge of instructing freshmeat at our training center."

"My reply contains some phrase about chewing my leg off."

"How long until you talk to Joaquin Beron?"

"Couple of minutes."

"Loop me in, please."

"You got it."

The vehicles encircled block seventeen, driving over the surrounding gardens, tires tearing up the lush grass. Seventeen was one of the smaller blocks, the dark external paneling fading to mud-brown in the relentless assault by Althaea's raw climate.

Lucius led five paramilitaries through the front door, while Yuri and Jessika waited in the vehicle. More paramilitaries deployed around the block. Yuri could see people in the neighboring blocks pressed up against the glass, watching in amazement. The light outside was dimming as thick black clouds rolled in; big drops of rain began to splatter against the windscreen.

"We got him," Lucius announced. "The location is secure."

Jessika pulled her pink jacket over her head as they scurried from the vehicle to the entrance. The rain was becoming a monsoon deluge, hitting Yuri from every direction as the wind whipped it around, plastering his hair against his scalp.

"So you and Lucius?" he said. "I didn't know. How long's that been going on?"

Raindrops slithered down the puzzled expression on her face. "What?"

"He seems like a good guy."

"Wow, my opinion of your detective superpower just took a massive dive."

"I know what I saw . . ."

"No, you don't."

"You need to inform HR."

"*What?*"

"I knew a guy, back in the day; basically a good guy, but a dick with it. He and one of my operatives hooked up. They didn't follow company procedure. It didn't end well."

"Good pep talk there, boss, thanks."

"Just saying."

She shook her head in bemused dismay as they slipped into the block.

"Give Poi Li a visual," Yuri told Boris. The altme would relay the feed from his tarsus lenses.

Joaquin Beron was a small man, a good head shorter than Yuri. His dark hair was styled in braids tight against his skull to try to negate a receding hairline. Tattoos glowed softly on his neck, snaking down below the collar of his green overalls. Yuri got Boris to run a scan on the patterns, but they weren't listed as any gang type.

Joaquin Beron was in the workshop at the rear of the building, sitting on a chair. The tactical team had followed Yuri's directions perfectly. His ankles had been zip-locked to the chair legs, hands fastened behind his back. Two of the paramilitaries stood on either side, large carbines held ready—not threateningly, but with easy confidence.

Jessika was shaking the water from her jacket as they walked across the concrete floor, surrounded by big fabricator units that were humming away efficiently.

"Seems like a legitimate setup," Lucius said. "I can pull some specialists in to go through his network if you want?"

"No need," Yuri said.

"You guys," Joaquin challenged, his voice high with bravado. "You are in shit so deep! I got rights, you know. My lawyer's going to bust your balls for this!"

Yuri smiled down at him. "For what?"

"You even got a warrant?"

"Why would I have a warrant? I don't work for a government."

"Huh? Then who the fuck are you?"

"My name is Yuri, and I'm conducting a small experiment."

Joaquin turned a troubled gaze at the statue-like paramilitaries. "What fucking experiment?"

"To see how smart you are, Joaquin."

"What the hell is this?"

"I'm going to talk now. I want you to listen. Understand?"

"Go fuck your whore mother up the ass, you piece of corporate shit!"

Yuri pointed to the paramilitary on Joaquin's left. "Do you have a knife?"

"Yes, sir."

"Take it out and stab Joaquin here, just above his knee. Don't puncture a major blood vessel. I don't want him bleeding out before he's told us what we want to know."

"What the actual *fuck*?"

"Yes, sir." The paramilitary drew a Bowie knife from his belt scabbard.

"Don't you fucking dare!"

"Why, what's going to stop him?" Yuri asked pleasantly.

"No way. Don't. Okay, I'm listening, all right? I'll listen to you. Just don't—"

Yuri held up a finger to the paramilitary. "That's good, Joaquin. Now it's important that you realize I'm prepared to cripple you just to get you to shut up before we even start the real session. So I'm thinking if you annoy me, I'm going to start walking around to see what kind of power tools I can pick up. You'll have plenty, I'm sure; you'll need them for your business. Big ones, small ones, very sharp ones, badly blunt ones . . . Am I right? Now try and imagine how I can use them. And on what bits of you."

Joaquin pushed himself back into the chair, panic making his breathing heavy.

"Now where were we? Oh, yes, I was going to say something. Think of this as your starter question for ten points—or in your case, you-get-to-keep-the-toes-on-your-left-foot points. Baptiste Devroy. Who is he?"

"I can speak now?"

"You may speak now. But let's keep it short and focused, shall we?"

"He's my cousin. I don't ever see him, honestly."

"But you're in contact, aren't you?"

"Some. Maybe a little. Yeah."

"Not anymore you won't be. As of an hour ago, cousin Baptiste will never be talking to you ever again—nor anyone else."

"Christ, what did you do?"

"I did nothing. Our London division dealt with him."

"London division . . . Who are you people?"

"People who only a terminally stupid asshole would piss off."

"Shit on a stick!"

"You're talking too much, Joaquin."

"Sorry. I'm sorry."

"Of course you are. So now you have to decide how far you're going to go to protect your cousin and his friends against how much of yourself are you prepared to lose. Got that?"

"Yes."

"So. Cousin Baptiste, he sent someone here yesterday, didn't he?"

Joaquin nodded urgently.

"Okay, good boy. So: two questions left. One: Why?"

"I don't know, please, I swear on my own fucking mother, I don't know where they go."

Yuri stiffened. "They?"

"Yeah. Baptiste, he does this, like, every couple of months. People he's taken get driven here to Bronkal; then they shoot them full of heavy-duty chemicals which put them in this really deep sleep, like a coma. After that they get shipped out again."

"Why?" Even knowing every second was critical now, Yuri couldn't help the question. "What for? What are they doing to them?"

"I don't know what the fuck happens to them, man! I'm not crazy stupid enough to ask. I figure it's got to be some weird rich dude who's off-the-scale perverted. I mean, what kind of normal person wants a bunch of unconscious people?"

"That's a very good question, Joaquin."

"I don't know. Really! Please, I don't. All I do is take care of the vehicles. I arrange new registrations for the vans. That's it!"

"I'll accept that for now. Second question. Baptiste snatched a friend of mine yesterday, a decent boy called Horatio Seymore."

Joaquin started rocking from side to side. "No, no, no. They'll kill me. Please!"

"We know Horatio arrived here in Bronkal—" Yuri clicked his fingers and turned to Jessika. "When?"

"The van came through the commercial transport hub thirty-one hours ago," she supplied.

"Thank you. Thirty-one hours ago. The van then drove to the docks. Where in the docks?"

"Please," Joaquin whimpered.

"Ah, you were making such good progress, too." Yuri held out his hand, and the paramilitary gave him the Bowie knife.

"Shit. All right. Christ!" Joaquin eyed the blade frantically. "It's the bioreactor complex." His shoulders slumped in defeat. "Okay? That's it. Please, just let me go."

Yuri slammed the knife down. Joaquin screamed. He looked down in terror to see the blade sticking into the chair, a centimeter from his crotch.

"Oops, missed," Yuri said. "Let me have another go, see if my aim improves, because that reactor complex is huge, and you fucking know that."

"Building seven! They've got them in building seven!"

The docks were the reason Bronkal existed. They sat on the edge of Althaea's lungs—the expansive sprawl of the plateau that was now a marshland that extended all the way to the cliffs. It was riddled with canals that had a flotilla of dredgers keeping them open, allowing the barges access to the entire area. Every day they would moor at the bioreactor next to the docks and load up with freshly grown algaox. Then they'd chug off down the canals, their powerful pumps squirting out long arcs of blue-green sludge to coat the saturated land. For thirty-eight years the genetically engineered algae had been photosynthesizing the oxygen which made Althaea's atmosphere breathable for humans. The barges were scheduled to keep going for another fifteen years at least, until the Sol Senate's climate monitoring board awarded Althaea its final clearance certificate.

A good seventy percent of Bronkal's working population was employed by the reactor complex or the docks, which is why eight of the town's twenty-five hubs were sited in the district. Yuri ordered them to be closed down, along with the commercial transport hub, which was also adjacent to the docks.

As soon as Joaquin had given them the location, Lucius and the paramilitaries got back into their vehicles and drove through the deluge of warm rain to the docks. Yuri had to grip the sides of his chair, the vehicles slid and skidded so much on the wet asphalt. He simply wasn't used to ground transport, and the motion was making him feel queasy.

"The rain is hindering our drones," Lucius complained. "Especially the microdrone flocks."

"But on the bright side, it's covering our approach, too," Jessika said.

"We need to be certain," Lucius said. "If Joaquin gave us the wrong information—"

"He didn't," Yuri said, recalling just how hard Joaquin had pleaded to be believed at the end.

"Okay," the tactical squad captain agreed. "We'll go with it."

Jessika peered out through the windscreen as the wipers flashed back and forth. "Must be getting closer," she said. "I can see the hangars."

Yuri looked out over the inundated road. Squatting on the horizon were four massive airship hangars. As well as maintaining the algaox barges, Bronkal's docks supported the airships that circled for months at a time over the ocean beyond the plateau's cliffs. They all had ten-meter portal doors fixed underneath their hulls, which were twinned to portals carried by ice harvesters pushing inexorably across the frozen ocean of Reynolds. At forty-three AUs out, Reynolds was the most distant planet orbiting Pollux—a planet with a Mercury-sized rock core coated in a hundred-kilometer mantle of ice. All of Althaea's water had come from there, arriving in colossal streams of ice shards that poured out of the airships to splash down and melt into the new seas. He stared at the big gray buildings in bemusement, remembering the first time Connexion had trialed icefalls in the Australian outback—now a lush savannah.

"Wonder what Akkar would make of this," he murmured.

"What?" Jessika asked.

"Nothing." They were speeding through the outside rank of dock buildings now. Yuri checked the map Boris was spraying over his tarsus lenses. The bioreactor complex and the airship hangars were positioned at opposite ends of the docks. A small purple star was shining in one of the reactor complex buildings—number seven, an old three-level warehouse and office block, which was registered to an independent maintenance company. Drones were orbiting it, keeping a safe half-kilometer distance. Through the heavy rain, their visual image was very low resolution. Normally they would release a flock of microdrones—biomechanical flies that would swarm through the target area, sending back detailed information via secure comlaser. But Lucius hadn't launched them; this rain would knock them out of the air.

"They'll know something's wrong," Jessika said. "Our Turing's taken solnet offline across the complex."

"She's right," Lucius said. "We can't do a stealth insertion. This is entry by the front door, all alarms screaming."

"Very likely," Yuri said grimly. "So I'll need some body armor."

Lucius handed a bag over without comment. It contained a bulky jacket and thick overtrousers along with a lightweight helmet. "You as well," Lucius said, holding another bag out to Jessika.

"I'm not going in there," she said indignantly.

"Of course not; you don't have any combat training, for one. But if we do wind up in a firefight, I'd like you to have some protection. We don't know what sort of weapons Baptiste's people are carrying."

Jessika glanced suspiciously at Yuri, who was doing his best not to smirk. The bodywork of the vehicle they were riding in was practically nothing but kinetic armor.

"Thank you, Lucius," she said dispassionately. "That's very considerate."

The tactical squad deployed in the same fashion as they had at Fedress Meadows, their vehicles encircling the building and coming to a halt. This time, when the paramilitaries climbed out, they were accompanied by a group of combat support drones: thick, dark disks with squat muzzles protruding from their rim, flying nimbly above the squad.

Yuri followed Lucius outside. Warm rain hit him full on, immediately soaking around the edge of his armor jacket. A thick unbroken layer of black clouds had closed off the sky, obscuring Thestias and its halo of golden sunlight.

"I guess God isn't going to be watching over us," Yuri muttered. He pulled down the enhanced vision visor. The squad's tactical grid sprayed across it, highlighting the locations of individual team members in green. The interior of the building was laid out for him, with the ground floor divided into three large spaces and the upper two floors split into a maze of rooms.

"Are you in the network?" he asked Boris as they walked behind eight paramilitaries who closed on the front door.

"The G7Turing has acquired limited access." A smattering of purple stars appeared, most of them on the first floor. "These are the heavy processing cores." Yellow circles materialized. "And these are the main power drains."

"Three overlaps," Yuri said. "Okay, Lucius, those three are our primary targets. Take them first, lock them down. You are authorized to use appropriate force."

"You heard the man," Lucius said. He snapped out orders to individual four-man squads and assigned each a target.

The combat drones shot forward. A camera on one showed Yuri somebody racing away from the entrance lobby, sprinting deeper into the building.

"Take the doors out," Lucius ordered.

A drone fired its scattergun at the glass doors, sending crystalline splinters slamming into the lobby. Twelve drones swooped in, followed by the paramilitaries.

"Yuri," Poi Li said quietly. "Stay safe."

"Working on that."

Yuri had decided on checking the biggest power drain point first. Whatever creepy procedure Baptiste was performing on his snatched victims, it would need power. He pulled out his semiautomatic pistol and headed up the stairs behind Lucius. His visor was showing him an array of images as the rest of the team smashed their way into the building. Drones zoomed along corridors, scanning for gang members.

He'd almost reached the second-floor landing when the shooting started. Gang members armed with machine pistols came crashing out of rooms, raking the corridors with full-magazine discharges, then snapping in reloads to carry on the carnage. Whatever weapons they'd fabricated had an astonishing fire rate, shredding walls, floors, and ceilings in chaotic shrapnel clouds. Drones returned fire, sending out a barrage of thunderburst grenades. They exploded in incandescent blooms, the blast waves shattering windows and tearing doors off their hinges. The drones advanced, electromagnetic rifles slamming super-velocity rounds toward any hostile their sensors detected. Gang members reeled back, diving for cover. Paramilitaries crept after them, directing the drones' fire, sometimes opening fire themselves.

Yuri hit the ground as soon as the shooting started. Just in time. Half the wall behind him disintegrated into a swirling cloud of fragments and dust as a gang member strafed it. His two escort drones zipped forward, blasting away in retaliation.

"Holy shit," he screeched. His head came up. Lucius was on the ground in front of him, also scanning around urgently.

"Looks like they saw us coming," Lucius shouted.

"No fucking kidding!"

The first clash ended as gang members either died or retreated deeper into the building. Yuri scrambled up and hurried along the smoldering wreckage of the main corridor. "How many gang members are there?"

"Four fatalities," Boris said. "Estimated seven hostiles remain active on this level."

Yuri reached the room that was drawing all the power. Its door was gone, wrenched off to leave a slim, jagged rim still attached to the hinges. Four drones sailed through the hole ahead of him. Someone opened fire on them. The response was swift. He heard the definitive sound of super-velocity rounds punching through furniture. A man started screaming—a long, terrified wail of pain.

"Hold fire and isolate the hostile," he ordered the drones. The visor graphics showed them surging deeper into the room. One of the paramilitaries went in just ahead of him. "Careful, sir, there's a floor breach."

"Got it," Yuri said. It took him a moment to make sense of the chaos laid out before him. So much of the room had been damaged by grenades and bullets. There were five hospital-style gurnez lined up along one side, most of them lying on their side. Medical equipment towers were shredded, pulsing out fluids from their torn casings. Two of the gurnez had unconscious bodies lying on them, which made Yuri's heart lurch in panic until he realized they were both female. One had taken a bullet to the thigh and was bleeding profusely.

"Shit!" He stared around, searching for a first aid kit. He couldn't see one.

Another firefight erupted somewhere down the other end of the building. He flinched, ducking down as bullets came slamming through the thin composite walls. "Jessika?"

"Hell, boss, are you okay?"

"Yeah. I need a combat medic case. Fast!"

"Are you hit?"

"Not me. Found our first victims."

"On my way."

"No. Stay in the vehicle. I'm sending someone to collect." He turned to the paramilitary who'd accompanied him. "Go!"

As the paramilitary left, Yuri snatched up a sheet from one of the fallen gurnez and jammed it against the woman's bullet wound, tying it on hard with a length of tube from the wrecked medical tower. Then he went over to where a pair of drones was hovering over the wounded gang member. Two laser target dots illuminated his forehead. The man had taken three hits, two in the arm, one in the chest. He was already ashen, gulping down breath. Blood was pooling on the floor. "Help," he beseeched.

"Sure thing," Yuri knelt down and pushed his visor up. "One of my people is bringing a medic kit. You'll be fine."

"Yeah?"

"Sure. I've seen worse."

"Man, it hurts!"

"I need to know, where are the other people that were brought here?"

"Please. I'm sorry. I just drive the vans, you know?"

"Sure." Yuri held up the card with Horatio's picture. "Did you see this kid? Is he still here?"

The man had trouble focusing. "Jeez, it hurts bad. Deep, you know, deep inside. Is that the bullet?"

"Keep it together. The paramedics are almost here. Before they give you a shot for the pain, tell me: the kid?"

Yuri heard more gunfire hammering in the big warehouse directly underneath. Then a series of grenades went off. The whole room shuddered for several seconds.

"Did you see him?" Yuri persisted.

"Yes. He was here. Overnight."

"Where is he now?"

"They took him downstairs."

"Downstairs where?"

"Ready—"

"Ready for what?"

The man's limbs started to shake.

"Ready for what?" Yuri shouted.

"Go." He held an arm up, fingers grasping for Yuri, as if that contact would somehow help. "Ready to go."

Yuri stood up, ignoring the clawing hand. "Our prime target may still be in the building. Ground floor. Proceed with extreme caution." He snapped the visor down again and studied the tactical display before striding out of the room and hurrying down the stairs. One of his drones flew point, the other took up position behind.

There was a doorway behind the lobby's reception desk. The door itself had been torn off, revealing a black gulf. The point drone flew through first. Yuri followed it into a long, windowless locker room with smashed light panels on the ceiling. His visor enhancements kicked in, converting the darkness into a clinical blue-and-white monochrome image. The drone navigated its way past buckled lockers that leaned against each other like a domino knock-down row that hadn't quite worked. It slipped through another open doorway into the first of the ground-floor warehouses. Yuri came out into a huge space, broken up by floor-to-ceiling cargo racks that were mostly vacant. Grenade blasts had pummeled hundreds of empty plastic crates out of their stacks, scattering them across the floor. Ancient heavy-lift trollez were parked around the five loading bay doors, the warehouse's vast interior making them look like abandoned toys. Two of the tactical team's drones had been brought down, their blackened armor fuselage casings badly crumpled. Yuri didn't like to think what weapon had done that. There were gunshots coming from the far end of the warehouse, obscured from Yuri's view as he crouched down and ran for cover behind a solid-looking workbench.

One of his drones slid along behind a rack, its sensors scanning around. He saw three gurnez behind a cargo rack down in the second loading bay. Two of them had toppled over, and one was upside down. All three had bodies strapped on. The drone's camera zoomed in. The upside-down gurnez had a big pool of blood spreading out from it.

"Holy fuck," Yuri exclaimed. One of the other slumbering bodies was Horatio.

"Jessika, Lucius, I've found him!"

A huge explosion detonated on the second floor. The entire warehouse ceiling undulated like an agitated storm cloud, and cracks began to appear, ripping along its length. Debris showered down. The gang members at the far end began shooting wildly.

"Shit," Yuri shouted. "Lay down suppression fire," he ordered the drones. They fired a fast barrage of grenades.

Explosions filled the big space with incandescent light as Yuri powered forward. Twice he fell as pressure waves slammed into him, sending him skidding along the filthy floor. Above him the drones opened up with their electromagnetic guns, firing clean through the metal racks.

"Lucius, some backup!" he yelled as he scrambled to his feet for the second time. A bullet caught his chest armor, spinning him and sending him crashing down again. The drones identified the source and sent more super-velocity rounds ripping down the warehouse.

Pain was a hot ball in Yuri's chest. Grimacing against it, he scrambled up into a crouch position and carried on toward Horatio's gurnez. His own semiautomatic was lost somewhere behind him. Flames were roaring up the wall at the far end, ignited by the hellish burn of the grenades. The drones hovered above him, constantly scanning for hostile activity.

"Lucius? We've got to get him out of here."

"Lucius has dropped out of contact," Boris said.

"What? Is he hit?"

"Unknown. His altme is no longer transmitting."

Yuri flinched. Connexion tactical team members were equipped with multiple access links, both implanted and on their armor, a hard lesson the department had learned after they lost track of Savi Hepburn. Today, it was practically impossible to take one of their personnel offline. Yuri didn't want to imagine the level of violence that weapons would have to inflict on Lucius to make that happen— nothing survivable.

He tried to focus on the tactical display. Five of their paramilitaries' icons were amber and red now, showing they were injured and pulling back. There was no sign of Lucius's icon. "Fuck!"

He arrived at the gurnez and practically collapsed over it. Horatio's unconscious face was caked in dust, but it was definitely him. Yuri felt unreasonably angry at how peaceful the boy looked. He worked the buckle on the strap. Another firefight broke out somewhere in the building.

"How much fucking ammunition have these bastards got?" he bellowed furiously. "Okay, everybody get out now! We have what we came for. And I could do with some help down here."

A low, torturous rumble came from somewhere overhead. Yuri flinched, glancing up. The ruined ceiling was bulging down, the cracks multiplying. Rubble began spilling through the gaps, hurling thick gray dust clouds ahead of it. They churned in a mad tango with the black smoke gushing out of the inferno.

"Oh, shit." He started to wonder just how good the body armor truly was. The tiny piece of rationality left in his mind was hunting down escape routes. They were all a long way off.

The loading bay door burst apart, and one of the tactical team's four-by-fours came screeching through the rent. Wheels locked on full turn, and its back end swung around, tires howling as they left a U of scorched skid marks on the concrete floor. The front door opened. Jessika was gripping the manual steering wheel with manic strength. "You called for backup?"

A line of bullets stitched deep craters in the windscreen. The drones hurled grenades and super-velocity bullets in reprisal. Above everyone, the ceiling cracks multiplied like black lightning bolts.

Yuri snatched up Horatio's limp form and lunged into the four-by-four. Jessika was already accelerating away before the door closed.

"Out out out!" he screamed. The tactical display showed him the paramilitaries moving fast.

Then they were outside, bucking across the wide parking lot, rain pounding the bodywork. A slender contrail streaked through the monsoon, moving so fast Yuri was still staring at it in bewilderment as it passed barely five meters above the four-by-four.

The hellbuster missile slammed into the collapsing building and detonated, obliterating it in a sun-bright plasma cloud. The blast wave punched the four-by-four with extreme force, sending it tumbling across the asphalt, every impact a hammer blow—

Yuri recovered consciousness amid a cluster of slowly deflating airbags that had completely filled the four-by-four's interior. A lot of the flaccid white fabric in front of him was smeared with blood. The roof was below him, and the windows were all a mosaic of cracks, though amazingly they'd retained their integrity.

Horatio Seymore was sprawled on the roof beside him. Yuri watched for a few moments, checking that the boy was still breathing. Then he heard Jessika groaning. When he looked around, he saw she was hanging upside down in the front seat safety harness, blood dribbling out of her nose to run down her forehead.

"How are you doing?" he asked.

"Just peachy, thanks." She dabbed at her nose and winced. "What *the fuck* just happened?"

"I have no idea."

JULOSS

Muncs didn't normally have names. It wasn't an infraction, but the clan's grown-ups had always discouraged it; the cohort should be uniform, they explained, no favorites. Language was also considered a communication impediment. Muncs should know their master's wishes without having to be designated and instructed; instinctive identification of any requirement or deployment was so much quicker. That also meant the boys had to learn how to communicate those commands at a subliminal level. The process was symbiotic.

Yirella had been five or six when she started mentally assigning her two muncs as Uno and Dos. They'd been studying old Earth languages at the time, and she'd liked the softness of classical Spanish. By the time she was seven, Uno had become Uma, because even Yirella rather enjoyed the idea of having a goddess as a companion, while Dos had become Doony—for no reason whatsoever except it sounded kind of fun. When she reached eight the names had become an ingrained facet of their association, and even Alexandre had given up asking her not to use them.

Now as Yirella leaned on the wall, staring through the big window into the treatment room, Uma and Doony had their arms wrapped around her legs in a loving hug. Her hands stroked their skulls, providing reassurance that she was all right and still cared for them despite leaving them behind for eleven days. When the rescue flyer had landed back at the Immerle estate, everyone's cohorts had come charging out of the dormitory to greet them. They ran into a wave of emotion—the relief and stress her yearmates were radiating in the wake of their ordeal. The poor muncs, expecting a happy reunion, had reacted badly, demanding affection, embracing their masters and mistresses in unbreakable hugs. It had taken a long time to calm things down. Uranti, the munc-tech, was called to deal with Dellian's semi-hysterical cohort, to allow the doctors to treat their injured master without having to constantly bat them away.

Yirella had watched the spray shot that was quickly administered to each of the creatures with interest. She was sure it wasn't a sedative, as they didn't become drowsy. Instead the drug seemed to banish their emotions. Then she realized Alexandre was studying her. For once in her life she didn't bow her head or look away; she returned hir gaze levelly.

"Did we pass?" she asked belligerently.

Surprisingly, Alexandre looked immensely sad and turned away. Yirella had followed the medical party as Dellian was carried into the treatment center. Now that the casualty team had finished with him, he was lying on a wide clinic bed, his wounds covered with long strips of surgical-grade a-skin, with various tubes emerging from blue blisters stuck to his arms. His munc cohort was snuggled up around him, drawing warmth and comfort from the touch—a scene reminiscent of puppies nestling around their mother. After spending her time on the resort island successfully playing the unattainable ice queen, she rather envied them and let out a sigh of regret.

Uma and Doony immediately tightened their hold on her legs,

sensing her affection was being directed elsewhere. They only came up to her hips now, so they couldn't see through the window. She stroked them again, down the nape of the neck, the way they enjoyed most, and cooed reassurance at them, body posture reinforcing the feeling, *I'm fine, and I'm relieved for my friend, too. Everything is going to be good.*

The chief doctor emerged from the treatment room and came over to her. "You can go in now, if you'd like," sie said. "You'll need to be quick. The sedatives are already making him drowsy."

"Thank you." For a moment Yirella hesitated, then she shook her head at her own reluctance. After everything they'd been through, having to find courage to face Dellian now seemed ridiculous.

She flicked a finger up, indicating that Uma and Doony should wait outside. They pouted and hung their heads, but didn't protest as she went in.

Dellian peered up at her and smiled in recognition amid his chemical-induced serenity. "Hey, you."

"Hey yourself. How are you?

"Doing okay, I think."

"Your poor arm."

" 'Sokay."

"I hope the a-skin brings your freckles back. I always liked them."

"We're alone in a bedroom together . . ."

She twitched a smile. "So we are. Savi and Callum, together again."

"You kissed me."

"What?"

"Back there, when we were stranded all alone on the tippity-ippity top of the mountain. You kissed me."

She took his hand and brushed the knuckles to her mouth. "I did, didn't I?"

"Do I get another?"

"Maybe. If you're good and do as the doctors tell you."

"How's that going?"

"The moroxes didn't cut you too deep." She arched her eyebrow. "How lucky was that? Unbelievable, in fact. I guessed right."

"So am I boosting?"

"What?"

"This is my boost, right? I'm being implanted with all my super wooper fighting gadgets?"

"Wow, what are they giving you? I could do with some myself. We don't start boosting until next week. That's to give us time to recover from our test."

He let out a long sigh, his head sinking deeper into the pillow as his muscles relaxed. "Are you testing me?"

"No. We never left, you know. Never got signed out of our training. The resort island, the fun we all had there, it was just the halftime break in another combat tactics game. That's all. It's never going to end, Dellian, not ever. Not for us."

"All righty," he mumbled as his eyes closed.

She gazed down fondly at the sleeping boy and kissed his forehead. "Get well. I need you."

Principal Jenner's office was at the top of the tallest building in the clan estate. Nothing as majestic as the skyscrapers in Afrata over the other side of the valley, but the view through the curving transparent walls was nonetheless impressive. The sight of the valley stretching away into hazy distance even roused Yirella from her mood as she stepped out of the portal door.

Alexandre was waiting for her and gave her a gentle embrace as soon as she entered. That was when she realized she was now a few centimeters taller than hir.

"How are you, my dear?" Alexandre asked, gesturing her to a couch.

"Absolutely fine," Yirella replied stiffly. She gazed at Jenner, sitting behind hir desk. The principal was male cycling, dressed in a suit of some shiny ebony fabric with a slim white collar and scarlet piping, which made hir look more imposing than any head of a simple educational establishment should be.

"But then I was never in any real danger, was I?"

Jenner and Alexandre exchanged a glance.

"No," Alexandre admitted with deep reluctance. "If you'll indulge me: When did you work it out?"

"Why? So you can avoid making the same mistake with the next yeargroup?"

"That's not quite as detrimental as you seem to think," Jenner said. "We are all of us learning here. We simply wish to know if we should adapt our procedures and tell the girls in advance."

"But not the boys?"

"No."

"Why not?"

"They are the point troops. You know this. They have to learn how to act together in a unit."

"I think even the boys have got that by now," Yirella growled. "Eighteen years of indoctrination tends to make that very clear."

"We are not indoctrinating you," Jenner said immediately. "This is a training facility, that's all."

"Training us to fight for you."

"Humans are a hunted species, Yirella. Sometime, somewhere in this galaxy, we have to stop running and fight back. You have known that it is your destiny, to confront the enemy, from the very beginning. We never withheld that from you. Everything which has followed, everything we have taught you and trained you to do, is designed to give you the greatest chance of success."

She arched her eyebrow. "Including the cougar?"

"No," Alexandre said ruefully. "The cougar was a mistake. We didn't know one was in the area."

"But the moroxes, they're not real, are they? They're just genten remotes."

"They used to be real," Alexandre said. "Thousands of years ago in a star system light-years away. A traveler generation starship found a planet with indigenous biological life not dissimilar to terrestrial evolution, which is always a rare and wonderful surprise. They stopped and studied the xenobiology for a century before moving on. We replicated the basic morox form in molecular initiators. It provided you with a believable threat."

"It nearly ripped Dellian's arm off!"

"No, it never did that. They were deep scratches, that's all. Plenty of blood, but no real damage."

"You scared the living crap out of us to give us *motivation*? You bastards!"

Alexandre sat next to her and reached out to put hir arm around her shoulders. She shook hir off angrily. "Don't. Not you. You were supposed to be the one we trusted, our almost-parent. You betrayed us." She wiped her eyes, struggling to hold tears in.

"I would die before I would betray you," Alexandre said. "I might not be your biological parent, but my love for you is just as strong."

Yirella shook her head. "No parent would do this. Doesn't matter what kind."

"All of us who volunteered to stay behind while our families left for the safety of the generation ships did so willingly, knowing the suffering—*this* suffering—that we would face raising you," Jenner said quietly. "We made that sacrifice freely because we not only love you, but we believe in you. You are destined to be our salvation."

"We're not your salvation. We're your slave soldiers," Yirella spat. "Why did you even birth us? Why not just use genten remotes?"

"Because of you, Yirella," Alexandre said softly. "You are the reason."

"What do you mean?"

"A genten is smart, fast, but ultimately has limits—in imagination, in intuition. You don't. You are human."

"That's . . . stupid. I'm not as clever as a genten. It doesn't matter how physically large my brain is. I could never match one of them."

"Not in absolute processing power, no. But like all technology,

Turings have plateaued. There is no 'next level' for them, no eleventh generation."

"I'm not a next level of evolution," she cried. "I'm the opposite. I'm a throwback, a binary human. You wanted us—the boys—for our aggression, for the primitives we are."

"Yes, we wanted boys for their aggression. Us omnias don't possess their level of testosterone bellicosity—not permanently, because we cycle. But a constant male gender . . . that gives them the greatest advantage a human can have in a combat situation. We have to win, Yirella. The enemy will never stop; we know this. They haven't stopped for thousands of years. We cannot send less than our best against them."

"Then what do you need me for? I'm not the best of anything."

"Deep down I think you understand perfectly well why. I know acknowledging what you are is difficult, and for that I am so very sorry. But you are what you are, Yirella: smart. Do you really think a genten would have worked out what was happening at the crash? A genten is not suspicious. Simply asking questions is not the same as possessing curiosity. Curiosity is a human trait, derived from emotion. A genten can analyze its situation and environment, but to believe what it experiences is fraudulent without prior knowledge—no. That was you. You worked it out, and not just because you were clever, but because you had feelings. To make the decisions you will be making . . . That is another flaw a genten cannot compensate for. You see, once you are out among the stars, face-to-face with the enemy, you will confront the final question—the very human question of trust. If you were to order Dellian and his yearmates into action, they would trust you because they know you would never, ever let them down; that whatever attack plan you come up with, it is the very best a plan can be. A genten's plan of action might be equally good—possibly better—but there will always exist a tiny fissure of uncertainty in those required to carry it out. In those circumstances, hesitance can mean death. Trust is at the core of human nature, one of our greatest curses—and blessings."

"You think you're the pinnacle of sophistication and human culture, but you're not. You are monsters," she said coldly. "You bred us poor, backward animals for one purpose. We have no choice; you have taken it away from us. Our life is preordained, controlled by you. We are nothing. You have denied us a soul."

"You are the salvation of the human race. That is not nothing."

"I don't want that!" she yelled. "I want a life! My life. I want to live in a culture where people respect each other, where we have the liberty to follow whatever goals we can find for ourselves. I want to be free!"

"We all do," Jenner said sharply. "But we had that freedom taken from us when the enemy found us. Now, all that is left is for humanity to run. To fly between the stars and find a refuge world for a few hundred years where we can breathe for a brief sweet time before running again. I too want to live a life without fear. I want a home to go to. But there is none in this damned galaxy, not for humans. None of us have a choice anymore. So now we will join the Five Saints, and fight back. We have to. My part in this campaign is trivial. It is so small that it will never be known. But you, you and the boys—you will gather together with others like you, and you will win. You will liberate this galaxy. And humans will have a home again."

Three days after they were rescued from the crash, the clan's senior year finally moved out of their dormitory dome in the middle of the main campus complex. Genten construction remotes had built them a crescent of neat little bungalows in a fresh section of the clan compound. They all had the same basic layout of five rooms and a cohort den under a curving roof, with broad glass doors opening onto a terrace shaded by palms and vines. In the center of the crescent was a communal hall, with indoor and outdoor swimming pools and gyms and a dining room if they still wanted to eat as a group, as well as lecture theatres and design studios and all-body combat simulation eggs. There were also portals to various sites for combat exercises with live weapons and out to a skyfort for more zero-gee training.

After breakfast on the exodus day, muncs and remote wagonettes carried everyone's belongings out of the senior dorm and across the compound to their new homes. Behind them, the new senior year swooped in on the vacated dormitories and started heated squabbles over who got which bed.

Dellian had been tempted to leave everything behind. After all, the only things in the boxes on the wagonette were relics of childhood. He considered that over now, obliterated by the resort island and subsequent ordeal on the wilderness mountain. But there were blankets the muncs were fond of, and books and old drawings that still managed to tug at a few sentimental strings deep inside. So he brought it all, telling himself he'd chuck most of it into his new home's disposal chute. Somehow, he suspected the long line of his fellow yearmates had come to the same conclusion.

The door opened for him, and he stepped over the threshold. *Everything's so blank*, he thought in dismay. The walls were tastefully colored, of course, in grays and reds and golds. The wooden floors in each room were dark polished hardwood, with simple furniture. Blank. Waiting for him to change it, to mold it into his own.

He didn't have any idea what he wanted. Just . . . not this.

His arms were by his side. He lifted them slightly and wiggled his fingers. The muncs bounced about happily at the freedom he'd just bestowed and rushed around the bungalow to explore. There was an outbreak of happy squeaks and groans as they discovered their den, with its shelf beds, next to his bedroom. They liked that.

Dellian stared down at the boxes they'd abandoned and the remote wagonette waiting patiently for his instruction, and scratched his head in perplexity. *Now what?*

"Hello?"

He turned to see Yirella framed by the open door, her head only just below the lintel. "Hey, you. Come in. Welcome to my home. Saints, that is so weird saying that!"

"I know." She walked in, looking around, her expression of dismay as deep as his. "Nice," she teased. "What are you going to do with it?"

"I have absolutely no idea."

"I can pull up some old files on décor if you'd like. Our ancestors seemed to have a much greater imagination than us, especially when it came to artistic flare. It may give you some ideas."

"Sounds good. Have you done that already? Looked, I mean?"

"Yeah. These homes all have a good fabricator. They can produce just about any effect you want, and the remotes will fit them for you. I've already been trying some stuff out."

Dellian realized he hadn't seen her in the line of yearmates walking into the crescent. "How long have you been here?"

"A couple of days. My bungalow is next door."

"Really? That's great!"

"It wasn't chance."

"Yeah? Who made that happen?"

"I did."

"How did you manage that?"

"We're the brains of the outfit, us girls, remember?"

"I thought this is an equal society?"

"No, Dellian, it isn't. It is very far from that."

His good humor faded at how serious she'd suddenly become. "Sorry."

"Don't be. We didn't choose any of this. It's not our fault."

"Are you okay?"

"Sure. How about you? What did the doctor say?"

"Oh, that? The a-skin has peeled off. So I'm fine."

"Dellian, you got attacked by a beast. That's not fine."

He grinned. "But I fought it and killed it. We won. That's what matters."

"I suppose so. Yes." She came over to stand in front of him, and for the first time Dellian felt strangely resentful she was so tall. He didn't want to have to tilt his head back just so he could look at her wide, enchanting face.

Her hand reached out and stroked his sleeve where the morox claws had sliced his arm. "Take your shirt off," she said quietly. "I want to see."

Dellian undid the buttons and slipped out of the shirt. He had no idea why, but standing in front of her bare-chested, he felt strangely vulnerable. His cohort were peering around their den door. He turned his hand, palm outward, banishing them.

Yirella's fingertip stroked down the streaks of pale skin where the medical skin had been. "No freckles," she said sadly.

"They'll come back." He paused, uncertain. "Did you say . . . ?"

"Yes. I like your freckles."

"I wasn't sure if that was real," he said. "Those sedatives they gave me when we got back were quite something."

"That was real," she said. "The second most real thing about it."

"Second? What was the first?"

She smiled and tipped her head forward so their noses touched. Her wild hair tickled his cheeks. "The cougar."

"Oh. Right. Saints, that thing frightened me!"

"You put yourself in front of me," she said huskily. "To protect me."

Fingers stroked his chest muscles. Dellian couldn't believe how such a delicate touch could light lines of fire across his skin. "I had to," he confessed. "I couldn't let it hurt you. Not you."

"That's the second time you've done that."

The side of his mouth lifted in a fond smile. "The arena match against the Ansaru team. Yeah! I remember. We were, what? Thirteen?"

"Twelve."

"Saints, we're old now, aren't we?"

Yirella kissed him. "Which room is your bedroom?"

"About time" was the most common remark among their yearmates.

They didn't quite move in with each other, not like Orellt and

Mallot, and a few of the other boys who were finally pairing up. But they certainly spent each night together. Some meals were taken in the dining room with their friends—after spending their entire lifetime in the company of everyone, no one wanted to be isolated. But they did take breakfast and sometimes dinner with each other in the solitude of a bungalow.

Combat training was kept to a minimum while the booster program was implemented. No one was surprised when Janc volunteered to be first.

"I hate it," Yirella exclaimed on their third night. They'd finished dinner and moved outside to sit on the terrace while the sun dropped out of the sky. The bungalow was playing some music recorded on Earth thousands of years ago. Yirella liked having music available. Back in the dorm it hadn't been particularly popular—at least not the quieter, more melodic tracks she always chose.

"Hate what?" Dellian asked in surprise.

"Boosting. They're changing us. We have no control."

"We do. Alexandre said; we don't have to do this." He poured the last of the beer into their glasses.

"And if we don't? If we don't go out there and fight, what do we do? Stay on Juloss? Because there's so much opportunity available here, isn't there?"

"Not everyone is going to be part of the war effort."

"Yeah, I can join the remotes scrubbing the decks on board our battleship."

He reached out and gripped her hand. "I hate it when you're this unhappy."

"This is not me being miserable. This is me being angry."

"Okay. Angry is scary."

She grinned weakly and took another sip of the beer. "I just hate that we can't control our lives, not really. I know we don't have to go to war, but, come on, what is there for us here? Everyone on Juloss is going to leave when the youngest yeargroup finishes their training and gets boosted. I don't know about you, but I can't see myself staying behind and waiting for the enemy to arrive. And they always do, you know. They go through any star system we settle like a plague, destroying everything."

"I know." He stared out at the dark trees at the end of the garden, where colorful birds were settling for the night. "So you will come with us? The boys need you. *I* need you."

"Of course I'm coming with you. I'm no martyr, waiting out in the jungle by myself for the enemy to finally find Juloss—if they ever do. And I will not let you down. Remember? But we're not a yeargroup anymore, are we? Not just a team playing tournaments against the other clans. You and the boys are becoming a proper military squad."

"For now. After the war, we can live how we want."

"If we win."

Dellian gave her a shocked look, but she seemed very earnest. "We'll win. We have the Saints on our side."

For a moment it looked like she might argue. But in the end she raised her glass to him. "That we do."

The next morning they went to the medical facility to visit Janc. His cohort were in a special den, with a long window allowing them to look in at their master, helping to keep them calm. But they weren't allowed into the recovery and activation room.

When Dellian and Yirella walked in, Janc was lying in the middle of a wide bed with his limbs covered in thick sleeves of green a-skin, and a broad strip across the top of his skull, running over the crown to the nape of his neck like a particularly flat Mohawk. The rubbery membranes sprouted a multitude of fiber optics that were plugged into the clinic's genten, which monitored and modified the boost implants.

Rello was sitting on the side of the bed, holding Janc's hand, the two of them grinning as if they'd just gotten away with some inane mischief.

"Well, you look okay," Dellian said cheerfully.

"Feeling good," Janc said. "I'm thinking the happy juice glands might be kicking in already."

Yirella knew that wouldn't be happening, but kept quiet.

"Timing is everything," Rello said. "We were just talking about that, how fine the control is going to be, if you can trigger a gland discharge when you're fucking. Double it up."

"Going to be doing plenty of experimenting there," Dellian agreed. "Oh, yeah."

Yirella sighed. "Don't you boys ever think of anything else?"

"No!" the three of them replied.

"I'm not sure any of the glands are amphetamine-based. They won't act as a serotonergic agonist."

"You had to say that," Rello complained.

"Whatever the crap it means." Janc laughed.

Yirella couldn't help her own smile. "What else did they give you?"

"Apart from the glands? The main arterial valves are in."

"Always going to be useful when you get a limb ripped off," Dellian said with mock enthusiasm.

Yirella knew his humor was slightly forced. Undergoing boosting had finally made it physical and actual. They really were going to be embarking on a battleship and portaling off into the galaxy. There weren't even statistics about how many of them would survive, if any.

"If there's any limb ripping going on, it'll be me doing it," Janc said. "They put the first batch of nerve induction sheaths in, too. For the larger muscles."

"So six more batches," Rello said, "and you'll be fully emittive."

Janc held a hand up to his face, flexing his fingers one at a time as if testing them. "Yeah. I didn't realize just how many subliminal gestures we make to the little guys. It's just natural now, you know?"

Yirella glanced over at the window where Janc's munc cohort were looking in on them. "After all this time, they're a part of us now, like mobile extra limbs. And you're going to need them," she said solemnly.

"When do they start modifying your cohort?" Dellian asked eagerly.

"Tomorrow," Janc said.

"Aren't you sad about that?" Yirella asked.

The boys looked at her with such incomprehension she thought she could actually hear the gulf splitting open between them. It was over, she realized; they weren't her family of brothers anymore. Difference now outweighed love. It was all she could do not to burst into tears in front of them.

"No," Janc said, careful not to sound indignant. "This way they'll still be relevant to me. More than relevant: necessary. Relationships change. We're growing up, Yirella. I don't need a bunch of cuddly pets anymore." He grinned up at Rello, who squeezed his hand fondly.

"Growing up," she said distantly. "Yes, we are."

Dellian put his arm around her, knowing something was badly wrong. "Nobody's changing that much," he assured her.

The munc center always used to be a reassuring place for Yirella. If Uma or Doony ever got knocked about, she would come to Uranti, knowing scratches and bruises would be tended to and soothed. If they'd stupidly eaten something bad, they'd get medicine and treatment in a ward. This time when she walked into the broad entrance hall that ran clean through the diameter of the dome, the old sensation of comfort was nowhere to be had. The hygienic white tile floor and light gray walls were too functional for her now, too symbolic of the true nature of muncs: artificial, doomed . . .

Uranti was in a treatment room at the back of the clinic, tending to a munc belonging to a boy in the clan's fifth yeargroup. Sie smiled and waved Yirella to a seat as sie finished wrapping a cut in black a-skin. Boy and munc held hands delightedly as they were dismissed, with Uranti's dire warnings not to exert themselves for twenty-four hours following them out.

"The arena?" Yirella asked.

Uranti stripped the sanitary gloves from hir hands. "Field hockey. I have no idea which genius thought it would be a good idea to give muncs hockey sticks that they can wave around on a crowded field." Sie sighed, shaking hir head. "This whole bonding procedure is one giant malleable experiment." Sie looked around. "Where are yours?"

"Back at the house."

"Really? Don't they mind being apart from you?"

"I guess. A little. I don't have the kind of bond the boys have with their cohorts. I suppose I'm more reserved. It's rubbed off on Uma and Doony."

Uranti gave her a soft smile. "And yet, no one else in your year-group has given their muncs an actual name."

"We're not allowed to."

"Dear me, is that a touch of rebellion I hear in your voice?"

"I was just being practical—and polite. Which seems a bit point-less now."

"How so?"

"The modification; it's the kind of phrase an old-Earth politician would use—given what you're going to do to our poor muncs."

"I see. Is that why you're here?"

"Yes."

"What do you want to know?"

"I want to see them."

"Them?"

"The combat cores you *modify* them into. I've seen the images, and I've studied the blueprints. But it's not *them*."

"I understand. The map is not the territory."

Yirella frowned for a moment. "Something like that. Yes."

Uranti led her back into the main corridor and into a hexagonal hub chamber. The portal sie chose emerged into a section of the building Yirella had never been in before. She was in an observation gallery that ran along a clean assembly facility 150 meters long, with seamless pearl-white walls, floor, and ceiling; smaller glass-walled rooms lined the sides. In her t-shirt and shorts, with sandals on her feet, Yirella felt totally out of place. The few people she could see walking amid the industrial-size fabricators were all wearing hospital-style gowns.

"Those are Neána-style molecular initiators," Uranti said, a degree of pride in hir voice as sie indicated the row of large cubes on the floor below. "We think, anyway. The insertion metahumans were never quite sure they mastered all the principles. Our own biogenetic science plateaued a long way short of this technology's ability."

"They made the muncs," Yirella said tonelessly.

"Yes. The muncs are biologics. But I'm proud to say, a completely human design. We never had access to the creation programs the Neána insertion ship possessed."

"And the combat cores, what are they?"

"A fusion of biologics and human weapons. This way."

They walked along the gallery until they were overlooking the construction bays. A cohort of combat cores lay in their cradles, with genten remote arms moving around them, integrating the final layer of components. The living machines were matte-gray cylinders three meters long and two wide, with a wasp-waist constriction a third of the way along; both ends curved to form sharp cones. Their skin had rings of silver studs and sockets, ready to linc with external armaments and sensors. Even additional propulsion systems could be linced if they were operating in space or within a gas giant's atmosphere.

"Aren't they amazing?" Uranti said, hir eyes fixed on one with complete admiration. "The center section has a life support nucleus that will house the munc brain after it's removed from the body. Drive units are exotic matter gravitonic manipulation. It's all powered by triplicated aneutronic fusion chambers. Quantum entanglement keeps them connected to their master."

"From the muscle sheaths," Yirella said.

"Yes. The muncs can read every single body language posture the boys produce. They understand and respond to it all, big or small, refining the simple verbal orders. It's the closest we'll ever come to telepathy. In combat situations, that will be a monumental advantage. No time wasted shouting orders or interpreting what to do. The combat cohort instinctively knows what their master wants, and deploys accordingly. You've all spent sixteen years refining that empathic bond. The fight response will be instantaneous. And you and the other girls will direct it; you'll be the lords of strategy."

"You must be so proud," Yirella said savagely.

Uranti gave her a long, questing look. "Yes. I am."

"I wonder if the muncs are?"

"You're anthropomorphizing, Yirella. That's a mistake. The muncs are just biologics, that's all. They're alien machines."

"That's bollocks. They're alive. Their neurology is modeled on a human brain. They have memory and emotional responses. Just because their cellular biochemistry is slightly different, that doesn't make them a machine. They're sentient. That's why they willingly undergo . . . this." Her arm jabbed out, taking in the combat cores. "They want it because the boys want it."

"Of course they do. It's why we're all here. This is our purpose."

"To wage war isn't a purpose, it's a threat reflex. We should be trying to think our way out of this mess."

"We've tried. We cannot flee out of their reach, for the enemy is more widespread than us. The Saints themselves know there is no Sanctuary star to be had, so the legend that a generation ship in our past vowed to look for one is nothing more than that: legend. We cannot call out to the Neána for help, even if they still exist, because to do so would betray our position to the enemy. We are alone, and their hunt is inexorable. Our only hope is to spread our generation ships wide and one day to turn and fight. Look it up; the files are open to you now. All the files. Principal Jenner authorized it. We don't even know how many humans have died or been taken trying to achieve that noble goal. All we have left now is our crusade to defend the human race. To destroy an enemy so relentless that this whole galaxy is unsafe."

"You can't be certain we'll win."

"Of course we can't. But we are striving to create the greatest army our science and technology can produce. This is my project. We've worked hard to achieve this level of success. If we fail, it will not be from weakness."

"Congratulations. And when does my boost begin?"

"Whenever you're ready."

"You're very confident about our empathy with the muncs, aren't you?"

"Yes. However, your muncs' neurology is slightly different from those in the boys' cohorts. They'll be your filters."

"Yes, but only when you've ripped their brains out and wired them up to gentens as peripherals."

"I don't have to."

"What?"

"The physical aspect . . . It's not strictly necessary. It's what they've learned that is important. The thought routines they're using today are the priceless result of sixteen years of your bonding. Think of it. When you finally go up against the enemy, you'll be receiving hundreds of signals from the squads at the moment of greatest conflict. Even your mind can't absorb that much information, no matter how good the direct neural connection boost we give you. You have to filter and prioritize. That's where the munc routines come in, providing a preliminary analysis and grading requests for your attention. The genten will use that interpretive ability to generate the right assessment for you."

"If the gentens are that good, then you don't need us."

"You know why we need you. Principal Jenner explained that. There has to be a human in the loop—not just for trust, but for intuition, too. We were all so proud of you at the crash site, the way you questioned your situation. None of us were expecting that."

"Bravo me."

"Look, if you are genuinely too fond of Uma and Doony to see this happen, I can download their thought routines and run them in a simulated munc neurology within the genten. Their brains have the facility for that built in." Sie smiled, searching for approval. "Would you like that?"

Yirella's shoulders slumped. "You really have thought of every-thing."

"I try. But I know I'm not as good as you."

"All right. I'll let you know."

Yirella woke up as the dawn chorus of birds began to seep across the estate. She lay in bed for a while, allowing her eyes to adjust to the weak pastel light that seeped through the reed blinds she'd chosen for her bedroom windows. Dellian was lying on the mattress beside her, sprawled on his chest, still sleeping. She looked at his pale body, seeming so childishly small on her long mattress, trying to hold her emotions back. Today was the day he was going to the medical facility for his first boost.

It was the day she was going to lose him. She knew he would still adore her, and she him, but what he was would be changed. No more of a change than every other day they devoted to training, to explor-ing a new tactical game, or spent in class learning about another weapon. Every day changed them; she acknowledged that readily enough. But this was a physical change underscoring his outlook. Today he would be claimed by inevitability.

He was definitely going to join the war. It was what he'd always wanted, the noblest cause a human could undertake in these strange times. His life was to be dedicated to salvation for all of them. He dreamed of it. He lived for it. And she would never try to stop him.

But that didn't make his choice any less painful for her.

Last night she'd clung to him with a passion that had surprised him as much as he'd been physically delighted. He'd asked if anything was wrong. And as they strained against each other on the bed, she'd clutched him tighter. "There could never be anything wrong with this," she'd promised him lustfully.

She'd been as energetic and enthusiastic as he'd ever known. Fulfilling every sexual craving wasn't just for his benefit. Her final time with her original beautiful Dellian deserved such an intimate celebration, locking the perfect memory for an age to come when she'd need it most. Then, after even his stamina had been exhausted, she'd cried silently while he slept.

This morning, she determined, there would be no tears. That was her change. Her choice.

Once upon a time, her favorite Saint had been Yuri Alster because of his logic and perseverance. Now, though, her allegiance had shifted to Alik Monday, in appreciation for showing her how ruthless you sometimes had to be, how self-belief kept you strong.

Yirella rose silently, making sure she didn't disturb him. She put on a simple robe and slipped into the den next door, where Uma and Doony were awake. She smiled at them, impressed that Uranti was right. They'd woken with her, even though there was a wall separating them. Maybe the empathy bond wasn't telepathy, but it certainly had a kind of magical quality excluded from the rest of her life.

Her soft motions, the way she held herself, prevented them from making a big burst of noise and movement that was their usual greeting. Smiling in welcome—false, so false, yet it fooled them—she stroked their soft pelts in reassurance. They regarded her expectantly, and she tilted her head in a playful gesture. The three of them slipped out of the bungalow and into the warm early-morning air.

The lake was half a kilometer from the snug crescent of bungalows, surrounded by tall, lush trees. Swans sailed calmly on the still waters, twisting their heads to give her curious looks as she appeared through the undergrowth.

Without hesitating, she waded straight into the water, shivering slightly at its cool embrace. She held Uma and Doony's hands, urging them in with her. Her posture was so perfect, so easy, that they walked along beside her eagerly, keen to share whatever adventure she was embarking on.

Feet pressed into the mud and the water rose to her waist. The little forest was serene and lovely. A nice sight for your last.

Her arms curled around the muncs' shoulders. "My choice," she told them guilelessly, so they would know this was the right thing, that this was what she wanted. Her knees bent until they too were sinking into the thick mud. Uma and Doony knelt obediently by her side. Her head was well above the surface, but the water closed over their scalps.

Uma struggled a little, as she suspected it might. Doony was completely passive as Yirella held them both under the water. She kept her face completely composed as her little companions died in her tight embrace. There were no tears.

And that was the most frightening aspect of the whole scene for Alexandre and the others who eventually came crashing through the trees, far, far too late.

THE ASSESSMENT TEAM

FERITON KAYNE, NKYA, JUNE 25, 2204

By the time Yuri finished telling us about finding Horatio, we still had another five hours on the Trail Ranger before we reached the crash site. Outside the long window, I could see Nkya's landscape changing again as we descended onto the dusty plain carpeted with red-gray regolith. The beacon posts stretching away to the sharp horizon were almost twice as high as the oddly smooth rocks littering the ground. Ahead of us, the wheel tracks of the earlier caravans cut across the pristine ground, their dark, laser-straight lines a monstrous act of graffiti against a geology untouched since dinosaurs walked the Earth.

"So what did happen on Althaea?" Alik asked.

"We're still not sure," Jessika said. "I spent a year on the post-mission analysis. A hellbuster was a good choice. Most of building seven was vaporized, so there was very little physical evidence for our forensic labs to analyze. My findings were inconclusive."

She was being modest; I'd checked her report myself. There were some interesting facts to be had amid all those secure files. Ainsley Zangari had certainly thought so. For a start, it's how Yuri claimed the prize: head of Connexion Security. The boss rewards loyalty.

"But the kid came out of it okay, right?" Kandara asked.

I thought she sounded rather amused, as if Yuri had recounted some traditional fairy tale.

"Yes, my father made a full recovery," Loi said. "Thank you for asking."

Like everyone else in the Trail Ranger, apart from Yuri, I turned to look at Loi in surprise. I only knew he was one of the third generation of Ainsley Zangari's offspring, but I hadn't actually bothered going deep enough into his file to check parentage. I admit the coincidence was slightly unnerving.

"You?" Jessika asked. Her face was lit up with a smile of pure fascination. "You're Gwendoline and Horatio's son?"

"Yeah."

"That is one hell of an impressive how-my-parents-met story," Eldlund said in admiration.

Loi took a while finishing his espresso. "Depends on your viewpoint. But, yeah, I guess."

"Nice happy ever after," Alik mocked. "But I'm biting." He leveled a finger at Jessika. "What were your findings? Bad enough to make you switch allegiance back again?"

She gave a reluctant nod, almost as if she was embarrassed. "That kind of criminality, snatching helpless low-visibility people for profit, simply doesn't happen in the Utopial society. And I really am an office girl at heart. So I went back, looking for the quiet life. How dumb is that?"

Yuri let out a dismissive grunt but didn't actually challenge her. "That whole case certainly justified Ainsley's suspicion about the Olyix," he said.

"How?" Alik said. "They helped you."

"That they did. They gave me all the information I asked for about

using Kcells for a brain transplant, and how the whole concept remains pure science fiction. All very diplomatic and cooperative. But
Hai-3 also said: man."

"I don't get it," Eldlund said.

"The exact words it said to me were: I will pray for your success
in recovering the unfortunate man who has been abducted."

"You didn't say who you were looking for," Alik said, clicking his
fingers. "Male, female, or omnia."

"Right," Yuri confirmed. "Ainsley never quite believed the Olyix
being so saintly. And this proves it. They've taken on the aspects of
our greed and run with it to an extreme, because they see that as a
normal human trait. Unchecked, it's a bad attitude. And it is unchecked, because they don't really understand us, they just mimic us.
No moral filter, remember? They just don't have it. That's why we
keep a very special watch on them now."

He glanced at me, and I nodded confirmation for everyone to see.
But I understood now where his prejudice came from; it was quite
reasonable given the circumstances. Yuri wasn't an agent for alien
disinformation; Hai-3 had been stupid. Its mistake there in the embassy had strengthened Yuri's paranoia, and in turn he'd gone on and
convinced Ainsley Zangari to suspect the Olyix of limitless intrigue
in the pursuit of money. Subsequently, every crime committed in the
Sol system, from jaywalking to political manipulation, Ainsley
blamed on the Olyix.

Okay, so eliminating Yuri as a suspect was a step forward, but
I still didn't understand where the whole Kcell-enabled brain transplant myth originally came from. Because that is now embedded
so deeply in popular culture, it's never going away. I'd been hoping
for a clue in Yuri's tale, but he was clearly as puzzled by that as I
was.

"You think the Olyix fired the hellbuster missile at you?" Alik
asked.

"Not directly," Jessika said. "That was Cancer."

Alik's reaction was interesting. He sat bolt upright. "You're shitting me!"

"No."

"Je-zus. Can you back that up?"

"Not in a court of law. But our G7Turings went through a lot of data. We composed a digital simulation of Bronkal for the three days prior to Yuri and I arriving, and extending two days after. She turned up with two associates when we were in the middle of interviewing Joaquin Beron. We backtracked her through the hubs to Tokyo. Before that, we have no idea. The Japanese criminal intelligence agency was unaware she was in their country."

"And the hellbuster missile? Don't tell me she came through your hubs carrying it?"

"No," Yuri said. "We have deep sensors on every trans-stellar hub. You can't carry weapons between star systems."

"Because you don't need to," Jessika said. "We had a little more luck with the hellbuster. It was a custom fabrication in Yarra, Althaea's capital. Someone called Korrie Chau brought it in through the Bronkal commercial transport hub in a taxez about four minutes before Yuri shut the hub down. The taxez was registered as a public vehicle, but that was a false flag; it belonged to him. He used to move a lot of illegal fabrications around in it."

"You did some good work there, tracing him," Alik said.

"We lost seven of the tactical team members in that explosion," Yuri said in a dangerously level voice. "And Christ knows what Baptiste's people did to poor old Lucius as well. Ainsley made sure we had whatever resources we needed afterwards."

"The hellbuster part wasn't difficult," Jessika said. "We found Korrie Chau and his taxez ten hours later, in a parking lot less than two kilometers from the docks. Cancer had slit his throat."

"Yeah, she doesn't leave loose ends," Alik said.

"Forensics tore Chau's place apart. We shipped entire rooms back to our crime labs for analysis. Forensic accounting tracked his payments, but they were all from one-shot finance houses based on independent asteroid settlements. Most of them don't even have a human population; they're just a bunch of G5 and G6 Turing rock squatters."

"So you don't know who paid him?"

"No."

"But you think it's the Olyix?"

"Not directly, but their actions, their acceptance of what they see as our normality, were ultimately what started this," Yuri said. "I told you, there are consequences to what they have been doing. We know Baptiste Devroy went on the run as soon as Jessika and I turned up at Horatio's flat. So he'd obviously got some kind of monitor there. And Hai-3 knew who I was trying to find when I showed up at their Geneva embassy. Whatever people are getting snatched for, the Olyix are at least aware of it."

"Why, though?" Kandara asked. "What's their motive?"

"Our working theory is illegal medical research," Yuri said. "Twenty-one percent of the total medical expenditure in the Sol system involves Kcell replacement treatments. That is serious money, because, let's face it, we are a species of hypochondriacs."

"But the research and development of new applications is slow," I explained. "Human regulatory agencies have pretty strict restrictions and protocols. The simple and easy Kcell applications, like a new heart, were first to gain approval, and still form the bulk of their sales. But the more complex organs and glands take time. The Olyix's human research partners have to proceed cautiously, and they're the ones making the investment. We think they might be aiming to shortcut that process. And if they propose an underground deal, the Olyix will adopt that mind-set. After all, it's human."

"Shit!" Kandara looked shocked. "Are you saying they're experimenting on live humans?"

"Not the Olyix themselves," I said. "It'll be the companies doing the Kcell functionality research, who've set up some dark labs to accelerate the work. They only get a small percentage of Kcell sales, but everything is relative. And new Kcell medical treatments hitting the market bring in more legitimate money. Which is the Olyix goal. They're complicit; they have to be. As Yuri says, the amount of money involved is phenomenal. Buying enough energy to recharge an arkship for interstellar flight doesn't come cheap."

"Are they still doing it? Kandara asked. "Are people still going missing?"

Yuri's laugh was more a groan of despair. "People are always going missing. Most cases are suspicious. We simply don't know if this kind of illegal experimentation is still going on." He shrugged. "There have been some good Kcell transplant products released over the last thirty-seven years; the spleen, lymph nodes, stomach lining tissue; not to mention the cosmetics."

"The Universal authorities must have some idea if people are being snatched," Eldlund said. "How many people go missing each year in suspicious circumstances?"

"Across fifteen solar systems and a thousand habitats? Who knows?" Yuri said. "On Earth alone, the figure is tens of millions a year. Most of them are what the agencies class as ordinary missing persons—people who are depressed or want out of their relationships or families, or petty criminals or people with debts, or they're girls and boys who've been groomed and get trafficked. Some turn up again, but plenty don't. There is just no way of knowing which of them are snatched by bastards like Baptiste."

"That many?" an aghast Eldlund exclaimed. "It can't be."

"It is," I told hir. "It always has been. The percentage is slightly down from twenty-first-century levels because our economy is so much better now, which reduces the level of disaffection in society. But the numbers are still staggering. Worse, they are too great even for our networks and G7Turings to cope with. People are always claiming we live in overpoliced states where authoritarian governments oversee every aspect of life. In truth, governments—Universal ones, anyway—really don't care about individuals."

"Until you don't pay your taxes," Callum muttered.

"Touché," I conceded.

"The Utopial governments take more care about citizen welfare," Jessika said. "It's fundamental to our constitution."

"Bravo you," Kandara said. "But you still have your dropouts."

"The percentage is minimal."

"We're here to assess an alien spaceship," I reminded them. "Not have a political pissing contest."

Alik snorted. "So whomever Baptiste was snatching people for hired Cancer to destroy all the evidence?" he asked.

"That's the conclusion we came to," Jessika said. "A medical research company, with money, zero ethics, and underground contacts."

Down the other end of the cabin, Eldlund put down hir cup. "This Cancer assassin, or dark mercenary, whatever she is—did you ever find her? Are you still looking?"

"We're always looking for her," Yuri said. "Just like everyone else."

"The bitch is good," Alik grunted. "Even the Bureau can't find her."

"You know her, then," Callum said shrewdly to Alik.

"She cropped up in one of my cases, yeah."

"Did you catch her?"

I watched Alik's rigid muscles creak into a scowl. "No. But it was an odd case."

"Odd how?" Callum asked.

"It wasn't strictly a Bureau matter. I was called in as a favor— friend of a friend kind of deal, someone who knows people connected to a globalPAC."

THE CASE OF ALIK'S FAVOR

AMERICA, AD 2172

January fourteenth, quarter to midnight, and the snow was blasting across New York City like the devil had left his gates open when he hit the town to party. And, Alik decided, the dark prince had partied hard indeed. He was staring down at the corpse when one of the crime scene cops pulled the coroner's sheet back. That spoiled his interrupted dinner and didn't leave him too keen on breakfast now, either.

The girl was a genuine blonde, he could tell. The roots always gave it away. And whatever psycho had scalped her had left some roots. At least her head was still on her neck, because there wasn't much left of her limbs. Alik studied the wall behind her, which was now a sick mural of thick blood splatter with gobs of flesh embedded in the blast craters. While the victim was standing, someone had used a bulled-up shotgun to take her down. His educated guess was that they blew her arms off first, then followed up with her lower legs. The scalping was last. She might have been alive for it, but blood loss and shock would have rendered her unconscious by that time. Thankfully.

"Je-zus fuck." Alik turned back to Detective Salovitz.

The cop's face was the color of a dead fish, but Alik preferred that to looking at the murdered blonde.

"I warned you," Salovitz said. "The others aren't much better."

"She's the only one in here, right?" Alik had arrived thirty minutes after the NYPD had crashed into the apartment, following all sorts of alarms—neighboring apartments and home security sensors screaming out that gunfire had been detected. He didn't care about that; he'd been asked to check out a specific digital problem originating in the apartment. However, the multiple homicides gave him a legitimate reason to observe and assist the NYPD. His cover, not that anyone would have the balls to query it, was to provide cross-jurisdictional authority, which was highly credible given the nature of the homeowner's apartment.

"Yeah," Salovitz agreed. "The rest are all over the place."

Alik took a proper look around the room. It was a big space, with a classy art-deco layout; walking into it was a time-step back into the 1920s. The ostentatious genuine period furniture was all arranged to make you look in one direction. That was understandable; he was on the seventeenth floor of a typical Central Park West block. One wall was floor-to-ceiling glass, providing a billionaire's view out across the park, all snug under its thick, fluffy snow blanket. He went over to check it out. The glass was programmable, allowing it to flow open onto the narrow balcony outside.

When he looked through, he could see footprints in the snow. "Come take a look at this," he called to Salovitz.

Salovitz pressed his face against the glass, leaving faint mist streamers on the cold surface below his nostrils. "So?"

"Footprints. Three, maybe four, sets."

"Yeah. Nobody went over, if that's what you're thinking. We'd have found the body on the street when we came in."

Alik bit back on a sigh. He liked Salovitz, he really did. The detective had seen enough of life's dark side to know how things worked, the dirty political wiring underneath the city that powered things along so smoothly. Every time Alik turned up on a case, no matter how cruddy the given reason, Salovitz knew not to question it. But there were times when Alik thought Salovitz must have gotten his badge on the back of some positive discrimination bullshit for terminal dumbasses. "Look again. Tell me which way those footprints are heading."

Salovitz glanced back out again. Then, "Holy crap!"

The footprints, which Alik had shown him, started at the stone balustrade and came toward the glass. One-way traffic.

"They came in from next door," Alik said. "Pulled some pretty fine techno-acrobat shit to zipwire across from the neighboring balcony."

"Okay," Salovitz said. "I'll get the precinct's G7Turing to run checks on next door, ownership and access."

"Good. Have forensics prioritize the balcony. Those prints are filling with snow, and Christ knows how it screws residual traces."

"Sure."

He went out to find his partner, Detective Bietzk. Alik turned to Nikolai Kristjánsson, a member of the forensics team, who was busy directing a line of microdrones that resembled snails. A dozen of them were sliding slowly over the carpet around the corpse, their molecular sensors mapping the particles they encountered.

Alik told his altme, Shango, to open a secure link to Kristjánsson. "Have you analyzed the bust yet?"

The way Kristjánsson's gaze slid away from him reminded Alik of ancient high school jock/nerd confrontations—all very secret agent tradecraft, which Kristjánsson probably got off on. "Not yet. They've got me scooping residuals to see who was here."

"I'm no expert, but maybe someone with a fuck-off shotgun? Get that equipment back to your lab and give me a report."

"It's not easy—"

"Do it." Even from an angle, Alik could see Kristjánsson scowl. His official job was with the mayor's Manhattan Forensic Agency, but friends of Alik's Washington friends also had him on a retainer, which was why he'd been assigned to the case. Those same people had made it very clear to Alik that the attempted digital mischief was of immense importance. To them, the murders were an irrelevance. Glancing down at the blonde again, as the sheet was drawn back over her, Alik wasn't so sure.

The apartment was a portalhome, owned by Kravis Lorenzo, a named partner in Anaka, Devial, Mortalo & Lorenzo (that original Lorenzo was Kravis's father), a very high-end New York legal firm. So high-end it was cleared for ultra-one Pentagon contracts, which was what drew Washington's attention. Earlier that night someone had tried using the portalhome's secure link to the legal firm's office to try to bust extremely secure Defense Department files.

Alik went out of the park view room through an ordinary door into the hubhall. It was a long oak-paneled cloister with nine portals, which were actually inside the Central Park West block apartment. Some of the doors simply led into old rooms like the kitchen, games nest, and utilities where the servicez are stored, as well as the New York entrance. The rest of the Lorenzo family house was widespread—on a whole solar system scale.

Another pair of forensic agents were working the hubhall with a squadron of sensor-heavy drones, along with three ordinary cops. Salovitz was talking to his partner, Detective Bietzk. He turned back to Alik. "Okay, the precinct G7Turing went into City Hall records. The neighbor is Chen-tao Borrego. We called him, and he's away in a Saskatchewan clinic undergoing telomere treatment. Been there ten days, due to remain for another two weeks. We're getting confirmation from the clinic, but it seems legit."

"So his place is unoccupied?" Alik asked.

"Yeah. A team's going in now."

"Okay. What's next?"

The detective pointed at one of the portals. "The Moon."

Alik always found it weird stepping directly into a lower gravity field. His body tensed up the way it did when he screwed up a pass at some babe at the end of a too-long night spent partying. It was the wrong thing to do. That involuntary reflex pushed his toes down hard on the black parquet floor, and forward momentum left him gliding farther into the room.

Lorenzo's lunar room was a fifteen-meter dome in the Alphonsus Crater. Off to one side of him was a large, luxurious Jacuzzi, its bubbles fizzing away with low-gravity leisure. Various ficus plants were growing in Greek-style clay pots, their glossy leaves strangely bloated yet also elongated.

Alik looked up, and there was Earth's crescent directly overhead, shining with blue-white splendor. It was utterly captivating. Crazy, too, that it was 384,000 kilometers or one footstep away. He always thought some little part of the human brain rebelled against quantum spatial entanglement. People needed to have distance in their lives; 200,000 years of evolutionary instinct couldn't be junked overnight.

When he finally lowered his gaze, he saw dozens of identical domes scattered across the crater floor, just far enough apart so the interiors couldn't be made out without magnification lenses. Half the resort facilities on the Moon were supposedly used for sex. Once Connexion started opening up the solar system, people soon found out that the so-called wonders of zero-gee sex, which overromantic futurology writers used to rave about, was a myth. They didn't call the aircraft that early astronauts used for free-fall training flights the Vomit Comet for nothing. Low gee, however—that was a different matter.

Lorenzo had certainly installed some very wide couches in his dome. One of them had red laser warning tape around it, glowing bright red. The cop who'd pulled the lunar duty gave Alik a respectful nod and said: "Stay at least two meters from the body, sir. The hazard disposal team is due in twenty minutes."

First guess on the corpse gave Alik an Italian American, or at least some kind of Mediterranean family heritage. His face was perfectly intact, as were his legs and hips. The chest was fuzzed by what appeared to be a thin gray mist. Underneath that, his torso was just a pile of so much red pulp. The blood pool on and around the couch was impressively big and congealing nicely. His arms were interesting; the buzz shot had taken them clean off his torso at the shoulder. One was on the couch, holding a custom-made stub-barrel auto-pump-action shotgun—which, judging from the eight-centimeter barrel diameter, Alik took to be the one used to take out the woman in the Central Park West room. A reasonable assumption, because this victim's second arm was lying on the floor, a scalp still gripped in its fingers, the blond hair sponging up blood.

"Buzz gun," Alik said. The gun itself was nothing special, just an electromagnetic barrel to ensure the projectile accelerated smoothly. But the buzz rounds it fired were mildly unstable. They were made from incredibly tightly wound coils of monomolecule filament, which expanded outward on impact, so the target got to experience what it was like being sliced apart by ten thousand razor blades all traveling in different directions.

That indistinct fog lingering on the victim's chest was the cloud of filament. Alik knew that if he'd stuck his hand in it, his flesh would have been diced like gourmet burger meat. He couldn't help glancing around nervously. If there were any breakaway strands drifting through the air—not unknown—inhaling one meant a slow, excruciating, and unstoppable death.

He let Shango capture the image through his tarsus lenses and stepped away quickly. Then he gave the dome a proper look as Shango pulled the dome's specs and splashed them for him. The transparent dome itself was made from multiple layers. The two inner shells were artificial sapphire, followed by a meter of carbon-rich glass to absorb radiation, another sapphire layer, then a smaller radiation barrier, two layers of photon filters to make sure raw sunlight was kept at bay during the unremitting two-week-long lunar day, and a thermal layer to keep the heat in during the equally long night. Finally there was the outer abrasion layer of sapphire that takes all the hits from sand-grain-sized micrometeorites. If anything bigger came along—say pebble-sized—the inner layers would soak up the kinetic energy. They'd been known to leave a nasty streak that would need repairing, but anyone inside the dome could carry on sitting in the Jacuzzi in perfect safety. In fact, he'd seen statistics that put standing on one of Earth's tropical beaches during the day more likely to kill you: sun-stroke, long-term melanomas, tsunami, satellite falling on your head . . .

"Only one buzz shot fired," Salovitz said. "So the killer was either remarkably cool, or very proficient. Our victim managed to get off two shots."

Alik looked where the corpse was facing. There were two yellow tags glowing on the sapphire shell, which showed a broad spider web of impact cracks. "Je-zus, not even these bulled-up shotguns can puncture the dome?"

"No, the developers like to make sure their clients are safe."

Alik focused on the victim again. "Anyone with a buzz gun tends to know what they're doing," he said thoughtfully. "So Mr. Shotgun here takes down the New York Broad, gets nasty on her head, then runs in here—"

"Chased by Buzz Gun Man," Salovitz concluded. "That's how we read it."

"Okay, what's next?"

"Next is where it gets interesting."

Next was Mars, the western edge of the Olympus Mons caldera, roughly twenty-two kilometers above the lowland plains, where geology had spent the last hundred million years quietly rusting the world to its barren death. The room was one of hundreds in a fifty-story structure of identical rooms. Its glass wall was facing north. To the west was the endless gentle slope of the solar system's largest volcano, spread out to the crystal-sharp horizon like an infinity plateau. You couldn't actually see the Martian plains; they were too far away behind the flat, pale sky. But Alik knew the kind of status-whores who owned a room here didn't care squat about that. They simply wanted The Summit.

Not that the rest of the view was too shabby. Two hundred meters away, the massive cliffs of the caldera wall gave a heroically vertiginous view out across the crater base—though that view was now partially blocked by the wide splash of solidified metal foam that had been sprayed over the big hole in the diamond molecule reinforced glass. Two mechez, like a mechanical spider-octopus hybrid, clung to the surface, their nozzles alert for any further outbreak of cracks.

Most of the furniture was missing, sucked through the rent before it was sealed. A tide line of mashed-up debris lay along the base of the window.

Keeping a wary eye on the foam metal, Alik edged up to the window and looked down. Fifty meters below, the ancient God of War's ginger sands showed a smear-plume of fragments that had once been Lorenzo's elegant antique Chinese ornaments. And a body.

Alik shuddered as best as his stiff flesh would allow as his mind ran through the sequence of what had happened. It was all so different from a faller on Earth. If you dropped a body off a fifty-meter-high balcony in standard gravity, all the coroner crew would be left with was mopping up the splat puddle. Impact would shatter every bone and split the skin open, leaving a gush of gore and shit to soak the sidewalk. On Mars, with its one-third Earth-standard gravity, the impact was different. The fall probably didn't kill whoever had gone through the window. On a pain level, the landing would have been like taking a Saturday night mob beating, but he would still have been alive. In agony. And up on the summit, atmospheric pressure was seventy pascals, which to a human body was indistinguishable from zero. That had pulled the air right out of his lungs, leaving the exposed capillaries to rupture. The blood that vomited out in a boiling pink spume would also be sucked away, to spray in a slow-motion arc across the ground in front of his face before freezing in the minus fifty-five degrees centigrade climate, along with the rest of the victim's body.

That is truly a bitch of a way to die, Alik thought. Whoever blew a hole in the window clearly had no love for the victim he could see on the ground below him.

He had to give NYPD credit; there were already space-suited figures down there, recording the scene. They had a trollez with them. He just hoped they didn't drop the corpse when they were loading it on. It would shatter like a drunk's beer glass.

"It's never the fall that kills you," Alik murmured.

"It's always the landing," Salovitz finished.

Alik touched an uneasy finger on the foam metal, praying it wouldn't give. "So what the fuck punched through this? Another buzz shot?"

"Armor-piercing round. Probably two or three. This diamond-reinforced glass is a tough mother. You got the dough to buy a room like this for your portalhome, and you get ball-backed guarantees that nothing can go wrong. Forensics picked up the chemical residue. Faint, because most of it got sucked out along with our guy down there, but the trace is positive."

"And it is a guy?"

"Yeah. These two combatants exchanged a few shots in another room first, then ran in here. The one with the armor-piercing rounds must have hung back in the doorway and just aimed at the window. He didn't need accuracy."

"Which room was he in?"

"The dining room. It's on Ganymede."

The Ganymede room was a similar setup to the lunar one: a fifteen-meter dome, fully radiation proof, with a sunken stone table in the middle, and twenty black leather chairs around it, their backs reclined so you could always see the king of the gods a million kilometers above you.

Alik stood above the edge of the table pit and stared at Jupiter. It didn't dominate the sky, it *was* the sky. There were other moons and stars out there; they just didn't register in the same way.

He instinctively kissed a knuckle, which immediately made him angry with himself. *You can take the boy out of Paris, Kentucky, without breaking sweat, but try taking the Southern Baptist out of the boy.*

Salovitz was pointing at the lambent yellow tags sticking to the chairs and table. "Ordinary nine-millimeter rounds. The pattern indicates our guy on Mars was in the doorway, shooting in." He turned and pointed to the red marker glowing low on the dome wall. It was sitting on an oval of foamed metal. The explosive-tipped round hadn't penetrated all the layers that made up this dome, but the emergency systems clearly weren't taking any chances. Three mechez were there on the side of the dome, ready in case the cracks started to multiply.

"The guy in here must have gotten cautious after that first shot. He didn't fire any more," Salovitz said.

"So cold Martian guy gets scared when the armor-piercing round gets fired in here," Alik said, working the events through. "And ducks into Mars."

"Pretty much."

"Dumb thing to do. Are there internal security sensors?"

"No. People like the Lorenzos don't like the idea of anyone being able to see what goes on inside their house. Someone hacks in, NYPD gets a warrant—all sorts of ways their privacy winds up as i-fodder. The block's entrance down on Central Park West has more security than the pants on a goomah. Then there's equally heavy security on the front door into the hubhall. It's tough for anyone who ain't on the list to get in. But once you're inside, you're totally private."

"Okay." He shifted his feet; the blob of foam metal was making him antsy. "Next?"

The master bedroom was in San Francisco, somewhere on Presidio Heights, looking down on the Golden Gate Bridge in the far distance. San Francisco was three hours behind New York, so the streetlights of that fine town were blazing bright into the night while the citizens headed for the Marina and Mission districts to start their revels. Looking at the bed, Alik started to appreciate Kravis and Rose Lorenzo's privacy dogma. It was a broad circle with a black leather base, the gelfoam mattress covered in a sheet of royal-purple silk. The four posts were also leather clad, with several insect-eye cameras clustered around them like crystal tumors erupting through the padding. The ceiling above had a circular screen practically the same size as the mattress—that is, before a shotgun blast had reduced it to a rosette of glass daggers and a snow of shattered crystal across the sheets—and the wall behind the headboard (also black leather) sported a broad screen.

Both the duty cops had opened the nightstand drawers to smirk at the pharmacological and electrical aids the Lorenzos took to their marital bed. When Alik and Salovitz came in, they quickly stood upright and studiously ignored the kinky treasure.

Salovitz gestured, and the coroner's sheet was pulled back. Body number four was another male, African, who had been hacked to death; the coup de grâce was a horizontal blow to the mouth, leaving the jaw hanging by a thin strip of skin. Judging from the size and depth of the wounds, Alik reckoned it was done by an axe rather than a machete, like a Viking on the rampage. There was another of the big shotguns beside him, identical to the one on the Moon.

"So Hacked Off here was in the same crew as Mr. Shotgun," Alik said. "And the boss is badging his guys with these bulled-up shotguns. Anyone like that operating out of New York?" Even as he asked, Shango was searching the FBI database for gangs who had adopted the model. Plenty of crews used them, but it wasn't standard issue, more a symbol that you were no longer a foot soldier. The higher up the shitheap you crawled, the bigger your gun.

"No," Salovitz said.

"But you've got to have a decent fabricator to produce one of these," Alik continued. "For a start, the barrel will need forty-one, fifty ordnance steel at least."

"I know where you're going," Salovitz said. "And you can stop right there. New York doesn't have fabrication substance permits outside of hazardous or toxic compounds."

Alik exhaled a martyred sigh. "The Twenty-Eighth?"

"Yeah. It's coming, and we're ready for it like the progressives we truly are."

Like every FBI agent, Alik hated the Twenty-Eighth Amendment: the right for all US citizens to fabricate for themselves whatever they wish unless it endangers the life or liberty of others, or they seek to use it to overthrow the government. It hadn't been fully ratified, but that was just a matter of time now. In his opinion, the AFA (American Fabrication Alliance) made the NRA look like a bunch of pussies when it came to strong-arming Washington. The outcome of Twenty-Eight was that any upright citizen could buy and use weapons-grade material as long as they did not utilize said material to fabricate a weapon. So Alliance members were free to sell whatever raw materials in whatever quantities they wanted. Individual states were already starting to incorporate Twenty-Eight into their legislation in anticipation. The result being in New York, you don't need a permit for pretty much anything outside of uranium or nerve gas. Which made life an order of magnitude tougher for law enforcement. In Alik's opinion, Twenty-Eight was storing up serious trouble for the near future, and all because midlevel politicians were money junkies in it for every wattdollar they could be bribed with.

He regarded the shotgun blast in the ceiling. The impact looked like it was a vertical shot, fired from the bed when Hacked Off was on his back, under attack from Viking Berserker. A last, desperate act, or maybe reflex? That suggested they were creeping around the bedroom, Viking Berserker stalking Hacked Off, while the others were duking it out in the rest of the portalhome.

Alik pulled the sheet back over what was left of Hacked Off's face. "So this killer got out?"

"Of the bedroom? Sure."

"How many rooms left?"

"We're over halfway."

"Fucking wonderful."

Beijing was the kids' bedrooms. He hesitated in front of the portal door. Kravis and Rose Lorenzo had two kids: Bailey, age nine, and Suki, age twelve. After everything else, Alik wasn't entirely sure he could face dead children.

"It's clean," Salovitz said, guessing the source of the hesitation.

The view through the Beijing window was tremendously imposing. Skyscrapers—every shape, every style, every direction as far as the eye could see. And all of them illuminated—some artistically, some nothing more than 150-story neon and laser ads. Even with four of Trappist 1's exoplanets terraformed by the Chinese state, and immigration at damburst levels, Beijing's population still topped twenty-five million.

Beijing wasn't quite what Alik would give children as their waking view every morning. But as his sister always told him on his infrequent visits to his young nephew, he was a piss-poor uncle, so he reserved judgment.

"Beds are made," he said after looking in both rooms. The duvets were newly pressed and straight. "The kids weren't here."

"We're accessing Kravis and Rose's diaries," Salovitz said. "It's taking more time than it should. They're stored on an independent rock squatter G7Turing. It's not cooperating."

"Get on it," Alik ordered Shango.

The Antarctic room was the least impressive Alik saw that evening. It was full night outside, and snow was drifting slowly past the curving window. Two forensic officers were on their knees in front of the glass. Sensor drones were infesting the floor like termites spilling from a kicked-over nest.

"What have you got?" he asked the lead tech.

"There's water here, sir," she said.

"Water?"

Her gloved finger tapped the glass. "This was opened. The room's climate control logged a sudden fall in temperature fifty-three minutes ago."

"So did someone come in, or go out?"

She gestured to the clutter of red tags on the floor. "Blood drops. Preliminary match with the victim in the San Francisco room."

"Good work," Alik said approvingly. "Our Viking Berserker would have been covered in the victim's blood. So he left San Francisco and escaped through here, dripping a trail as he went."

"Escaped?" Salovitz protested. "There's nowhere to go out there. It's the fucking Antarctic."

"You think he slung another body out there?"

"Why hide a dead body? Nobody cared about us finding the others."

"Okay, good point. And a blood trail isn't proof Viking Berserker actually went outside, just that he was in here."

"Chasing someone else?"

Alik contemplated the bleak nighttime snowscape outside. "A survivor? Maybe even the Lorenzos making a break for it?"

"Out *there*?" Salovitz sneered.

"Bigger survival chance than Mars, or Ganymede. All they have to do is make it to the next portalhome room. There's got to be some close by; developers build them in batches."

"Shit. Okay."

"Your people have coats, don't they?" Alik challenged. "Send them outside. We have to know who went out."

"We've got coats for New York, not the fucking Antarctic!"

"Okay." He turned to the lead tech. "Send a bunch of drones out. See what they can find. There have to be other portalhome rooms around here."

She gave the ice vista a dubious look. "Conditions aren't good, sir."

"Like I give a shit! I want some kind of camera looking around, even if you have to carry it yourself. I'm going to get some decent cold-weather gear priority-delivered from my office. When it arrives, we can follow up. Meantime, let's take a look at the last body."

Paris, dawn over the Seine, Notre Dame silhouetted on the cool rose-gold horizon. Very romantic, just right for a guest bedroom. Too bad the man on the floor at the end of the bed no longer appreciated the sight. The shotgun blast had taken most of his head off, sending brain and skull fragments slopping over the thick cream carpet like a rivulet of cold lava.

"So either Mr. Shotgun or Hacked Off did this," Alik said.

"Yeah."

"And this is the last body?"

"That we've found. I ain't promising you anything under oath."

"Which means we're missing whoever was using the axe and the buzz gun." Alik took a breath, trying to think. "One person, or two?"

"Once forensic has finished mapping DNA residuals, we'll have a better picture."

"Right. Let's see the last couple of rooms."

Alik had been expecting another gas-giant moon, or maybe a comet station, something exotic. Instead the portal door opened into a cabin on the *Jörmungand Celeste*. The huge ocean liner was the most famous on Earth—not hard considering it was about the only one left. All it did was sail around the oceans on the most leisurely course possible without ever making landfall, but taking in the coastlines of every continent.

He went outside to stand on the private deck belonging to the Lorenzo cabin and instantly regretted it as he was ambushed by tropical humidity. "Sonofabitch." The ocean was a deep gray-blue nearly twelve meters below, with vivacious whitecaps cresting the larger waves. Alik was dressed for New York winter in a nice real wool suit. The Bureau still hadn't let go of J. Edgar's dress code, and he stuck with it because of the peripherals that could be discreetly incorporated into the suit fabric. But a cooling circuit wasn't one of them. Every centimeter of his skin was immediately layered in sweat. "Where the hell are we?" he asked Shango.

"Approaching Cape Town from the east," it said. "The coast will be visible tonight, local time."

Salovitz was fanning his face with his hand, looking at the swell with disapproval. Neither of them could feel any motion; the *Jörmungand Celeste* was way too big for the waves to affect it.

"If you were going to dump a body, this is the room I'd use, not the Antarctic," Salovitz said.

"Good point. What's left?"

The tropical island. Alik rolled his eyes as another gust of heat and humidity sluiced over him. He took his suit jacket off as soon as they went through the portal door. It was against Bureau protocol; as well as peripherals, the fabric was lined with a decent armor weave. It made him a sitting duck to a sniper, but he decided to risk it.

The island was where the Maldives used to be—a beautiful coral archipelago in the Indian Ocean whose only industry was tourism. They were beautiful because they were so low-lying, a few meters at best, giving them broad, pristine beaches and secluded lagoons. That didn't go well for the indigenous population in the late twenty-first century when the ocean level started rising. The rest of the world built sea defenses and tidal barriers to protect their crumbling shorelines and inundated coastal cities. The Maldives didn't have that kind of money, not even with the microfacture revolution brought about by home fabricators and printers, which liberated so many from absolute poverty.

The archipelago claimed the crown of Atlantis and slowly sank beneath the waves. A true tragedy for a UN World Heritage Site.

Then along came astute developers in massive airships with portals fixed underneath. Torrents of desert sand poured down out of the sky, mixed with genetically modified coral seeds. New islands rose up and stabilized.

It was a bitch of a lawsuit. The ex-Maldives population claimed the artificial islands were squatting on their ancestral seabed and should be given to them. But the World Court declared against them—a decision helped by the Chinese, who had long experience with enforcing ownership claims over artificial island territories.

The contemporary islands weren't as big as the old originals. The new owners divided them up like the slices of an exceptionally rich cake, with wooden shacks on stilts at the back of the beaches.

Stylish mock-antique patio doors slid open in front of Alik, letting him out onto a raised veranda where steps sank into the oven-hot sands. Thirty meters farther on, the clear wavelets of the Indian Ocean lapped against the exquisite coral reefs that were still expanding out into the deeper waters.

"Beats the Hamptons," he muttered in reluctant approval as he walked across the nautical-themed designer-minimalist lounge. A forensic tech was working on the patio door.

"It was forced," the tech told Salovitz. "Alarms disabled, and the lock physically cut out."

"From the outside?" Alik guessed.

"Yes, sir."

"Any blood in here?" Salovitz asked.

"The preliminary scan didn't show any."

"One team comes in via crazy gymnastics seventeen stories up in a nighttime snowfall, the other saunters across a beach," Alik said. "No prizes here for which team has the brains."

He and Salovitz walked down the steps to the beach, where he reluctantly put his jacket back on, which earned several curious looks. But he figured that if this was a route in, the team might have a hot backup waiting to provide cover. So if they'd been waiting with growing anxiety for their buddies to return, and the first out of the boutique shack is a bunch of cops heading toward them . . .

Three of New York's finest were making their way back across the beach. They'd all taken their winter jackets off, and sweat was soaking their thick shirts.

"Found the way the intruder team got onto the island," the sergeant told Salovitz. "The shack two down. Its patio door was open. We went in. There's a body in the hubhall."

"Where is the hubhall?" Alik asked.

The sergeant pushed his cap back and gave him a rueful look. "My altme said Berlin."

"Aw, crap," Salovitz groaned, raising his eyes to the bright, cloudless sky. "This just keeps getting better. I fucking hate portalhomes."

"I'll put an official call through the Bureau to the Berlin police," Alik reassured him. "I know a guy in the city. They can run forensics at their end, and I'll send you the results."

"Okay," Salovitz said. "Set up a cordon around the shack, and don't go inside again."

"You got it, Detective," the sergeant said.

The forensic tech in the Antarctic room called over the police scene link. "We found something, Detective. Another portalhouse room, close to the Lorenzo property, with a broken window. I tried sending a drone through, but something killed it."

Alik and Salovitz looked at each other and headed back up the beach fast. As they went inside the shack, Shango checked with Alik's office. The Antarctic gear courier was en route, estimated three minutes from Central Park West.

"Run," Alik ordered them.

The tech in the Antarctic room was standing beside the window; her eyes closed as she controlled the drones through her altme. Snow was melting on the floor around her feet.

"Speak to me," Salovitz said.

"I sent five drones out," she said. "Their flight's not good in the snow, and the visual imagery is poor. I'm relying a lot on the millimeter wave radar. But they found another portalhome room a hundred and fifty meters away. The window is programmable glass, but it's not open; there's just a hole in it, roughly a meter across. I've tried sending two drones through now, but each one died. It's like an explosion. They fall apart, but there's no heat or energy flash."

"Buzz shot," Alik said. "The hole could be tangled with filament."

"What use is making a hole in the glass you can't get through?" Salovitz asked.

"If you take a buzz gun on a job, you wear the right protective armor," Alik told him. "Those filaments aren't the most reliable when it comes to traveling in the right direction after expansion."

"So they could have gotten through the hole?"

"Most likely."

The courier arrived with their Antarctic gear—five suits with "FBI" printed in bold yellow across the back. They were one-piece units, with boots and a hood that had a sealable visor, fully heated. Practically space suits. Alik and Salovitz started putting them on, as did the forensic tech and two cops.

"Try and avoid shooting your pistols," Alik told them. "The cold will affect them."

They gave him uncertain glances but agreed they'd hold off unless they were taking fire.

Alik took an electron pistol out of his underarm holster and clipped it onto the Antarctic suit's belt. The cold would make it brittle, but he thought the components would still work. Probably.

Shango confirmed the suit's integrity and ordered the glass to open. Snow swirled in.

Alik's feet sank a good ten centimeters into the loose snow as he started to tramp across to the next portalhome. He kept the drone sensor imagery on sharp resolution across his tarsus lenses, merging the bright scarlet grid of the millimeter radar with his own eyesight. The lens had a low-light amplification program that kicked in as soon as he got outside. He'd never liked the sparkly-green shading the two-tone image always produced. It wasn't much use in the Antarctic, either; a snowfield at night had as much contrast as a franchise coffee shop.

At least the suit worked okay, keeping him decently warm.

They all lined up facing the room. Most of the structure was covered in a layer of snow, making it look like a futurist's igloo, with the curving glass panorama window a jarring black bulge along the front. The three remaining disc-shaped drones hovered outside, constantly swooping about like alcoholic sparrows as they tried to hold position in the sharp squalls of freezing air.

Alik studied the hole carefully, but not even his tarsus lens enhancements could see if there was a hash of filaments clinging to it.

"If someone in a protective suit went through, wouldn't it clear the filaments away?" Salovitz asked.

"The bulk of them, yeah," Alik agreed. "But there will be plenty of strands left behind. You need a proper hazard disposal team to clear the area before it's rated human-safe again. The worse the environment you fire a buzz shot in, the bigger the dispersal problem. We just need to clear the hole enough to send one of those drones through."

"Your e-pistol?"

"Let's find out." He knelt down, knees compacting the snow, and angled the electron pistol up at the hole. That way, the beam would only strike the ceiling beyond. Shango selected a defocused beam on high power. He fired ten pulses.

Snowflakes inside the electron stream vaporized into steam puffs, shrouded in their own fizz of St. Elmo's fire. The hole itself scintillated with bright elongated sparks as the filaments broke down from the energy barrage.

"Send a drone through now," he said once the mini-fireworks had finished popping.

One of the drones flashed forward, passing unharmed through the hole. Its visual images improved immediately in the calmer air of the room. There were two bodies lying on the floor, a man and a woman in late middle age, both shot through the head. The sensors couldn't pick up any active power circuits, and that included the portal on the back wall.

"The escape route," Salovitz declared.

"Yeah. So now we just have to work out if Buzz Gun is also Viking Berserker, or if two of them go out afterwards. I also want to know where this room's hubhall is situated."

"The DNA profiles will be in within an hour. We can get a better timeline map from that."

"Okay, then, let's get back to the precinct."

. . .

New York's twentieth precinct house was situated on West 82nd Street, only two metrohubs from the apartment block on Central Park West. Even in the snow, it was less than three minutes to walk door to door.

Alik and Salovitz got in just before one in the morning. The precinct commander, Brandy "The Deacon" Duncan, was in her office on the second floor. She was courteous enough to Alik, but he knew he was about as welcome as a stripper in a cathedral.

Salovitz gave her a decent enough summary of the case. Seven bodies, the Lorenzo family's whereabouts unknown and not responding to any calls, their altmes off grid.

"Why would these crews target Lorenzo? What's he involved in?" the Deacon asked, staring at Alik. She was in her late fifties, streetwise, and with enough clout in City Hall to hang on to the twentieth for eight years now. Her face was etched with the entropy of a lifetime of prizefights on both sides of the desk—the ones that had got her where she was. Alik respected that; she was actually quite a good cop.

"I'm only here because of the jurisdiction thing," he said.

"Bullshit," she grunted. "Anaka, Devial, Mortalo and Lorenzo."

"What about it?"

"They have political contacts. Kiss a lot of important asses."

"I'm here to help. I can shortcut certain areas for you. I'm already helping with Berlin. If this is a snatch case, then time is critical here. Do you want the media to be showing the world a dead family on your watch?"

She looked at Salovitz. "Is it a kidnapping?"

"No way. Only one person got out of that goddamn abattoir: a genuine axe murderer."

Her umpire's gaze came back to Alik.

"Then where are they?" he asked. "We need to find out."

"I'll take your help," the Deacon said grudgingly. "But this is the twentieth precinct's case. Don't try claiming anything else, especially not to your media buddies."

"I have no buddies in the media, and I'm officially requesting that my name and involvement be kept off the record. If it is a kidnapping, we don't want to alert them to any Bureau involvement at this stage."

"Sure, I believe that. So if it's not a kidnapping, what else could it be?"

"There was an attempted bust into Lorenzo's secure company network," Salovitz said.

"What were they looking for?"

"I don't know yet; forensic has the systems in their digital lab. You know what it's like getting any sense out of those nerds."

"So one crew breaks in and starts a digital bust, then another crew shows up and the shit hits the fan," the Deacon said. "Any chance crew two were a black countermeasures crew contracted by Anaka, Devial, Mortalo and Lorenzo when they realized what was happening?"

"That's a stretch, chief," Salovitz said.

Her gaze flicked to Alik like a first-grade teacher's laser pointer highlighting the obvious. "But possible. Right, Agent Monday?"

"At this stage the Bureau is not ruling out anything. We want the surviving killer detained as swiftly as possible. However—"

"Here we go," the Deacon muttered with antipathy.

"If crew one was a digital bust operation, crew two got there remarkably quickly for countermeasures. Not impossible, but unusual. They also don't seem that professional. None of them were in the same clothes, and only two weapons were the same."

"So how do you read it?"

"The Lorenzos are away, for whatever reason. Somebody knew that, and two high-end burglary crews targeted the portalhome. There was a lot of wealth in there. Naturally one team came armed with an i-head; data is as valuable as jewelry, and more so if you have the right files."

"Coincidence? Seriously?"

"It doesn't read like one crew was there to defend the Lorenzos. If the family was out for one night only, then it's not quite coincidence that we have two teams showing up."

Alik could see how much she wanted to argue. Instead she had to reluctantly concede. "Okay. Priority one, find and secure the Lorenzo family. Call his colleagues and her friends; somebody has to know where they were going."

"Yes, chief," Salovitz said.

"And let me know if anyone slows you down." Again the laser pointer stab between Alik's eyes.

Salovitz grinned as they trooped downstairs to the first floor. "You're still alive. Impressive."

"Yeah," Alik grunted. "She's secretly got the hots for me; you can tell."

"You really think it's a coincidence?"

"It's a working theory that works. To get a handle on this, we need to know where the Lorenzos are. That's when we start to understand what the fuck actually happened."

"Yeah."

The office that the Deacon had assigned the case team was at the back of the building, with frosted glass windows, ten desks, and a hemispherical virtual stage at the far end, three meters in diameter.

Bietzk was already there when Alik arrived, along with a couple of sergeants he recognized from the portalhome. The precinct's senior forensic technician, Rowan El-Alosaimi, had claimed one desk, assembling data coming in from the sensors the Forensics Agency team had deployed.

Alik had barely got through the door when the stage lit up with a 3-D layout of the portalhome. They couldn't do it to scale; the rooms beyond the hubhall would have overlapped. The corpses started to materialize.

"Anything on the Lorenzos?" Salovitz asked.

"Not yet," Bietzk said. "I'm on to Connexion Security. They're going to send us their metrohub logs. Meanwhile, I'm running a continuing global ping on their altmes. No response yet. They're still off grid."

"We're getting the DNA results in," Rowan said. "There are some matches from the general medisure database and three already in the Justice Department POI list."

"Splash them," Alik told her.

Tags flipped up over the corpses. Shango interfaced with the stage, and his tarsus lenses magnified the data.

The scalped New York broad was Lisha Khan. According to Bureau records she was a midlevel soldier for a New York syndicate run by one Javid-Lee Boshburg, who'd carved himself a territory from South Brooklyn all the way down to Sheepshead Bay, thanks to an income from narcotics fabrication and distribution, along with a half dozen clubs and plenty of protection. He trafficked girls in from across North and South America, with Lisha Khan helping to keep them in order.

Mr. Shotgun on the Moon: Otto Samule. A lieutenant for Rayner Grogan, whose territory was a tumor bruising the citizens of western Queens, with ties to technology unions across the city, as well as standard-issue interests in clubs and land development enterprises. According to the NYPD gang task force, he also ran a couple of crash crews who went through high-end apartments like a locust swarm when the owner was out. Alik nodded in satisfaction at how that fitted with what they'd found in the Lorenzo portalhome.

That left—

The Cold Martian: Duane Nordon. Another known associate of Javid-Lee.

Hacked Off: Perigine Lexi. Senior lieutenant for Javid-Lee.

Paris Dawn: Koushick Flaviu, on Rayner Grogan's payroll, an inseparable buddy of Otto Samule; the two of them were known to work together most of the time.

"Now we're getting somewhere," Alik decided. "Grogan versus Boshburg."

Forensic files started to splash across his lenses. Koushick Flaviu and Otto Samule both had sand on their shoes, matching the Maldives island beach. Equally, Lisha Khan, Duane Nordon, and Perigine Lexi all had trace water on their soles indicating they had invaded the portalhome via the Central Park West balcony.

Salovitz stood with hands on hips, watching the data points rising across the stage as Rowan fed in more and more results. The deaths had all occurred within five minutes of each other, approximately eleven o'clock at night. "And at least one of the Rayner crew escaped," Salovitz beefed. He turned to Bietzk. "We need a full list of associates for both crews."

A secure file from Kristjánsson splashed across Alik's lens. He cleared it for the case office, and it splashed into the stage.

"Koushick was performing the secure network hack," Bietzk said, reading the new data. "His residuals were all over the node we pulled out of the Central Park West utility room."

Salovitz turned to Alik. "Do you think that's why Mr. Shotgun took his head off?"

"None of this was a warning, it was straight-out slaughter. They all knew there was no way out other than over the other team's bodies."

"Find out what kind of grudge match Javid-Lee and Rayner have going on," Salovitz told Bietzk. "If there's nothing on record, get the gang task force out of bed and see what whispers there are. I need some traction here."

Shango reported that the Lorenzo diaries had been accessed. "Got something for you," Alik said, and sent the files across the police case link. Both Kravis and Rose's diaries had the same entry for the previous day: Palm Beach with Niall and Belvina Kanoto, on their yacht.

Shango called Niall Kanoto.

It took a while to get a response. Niall's altme was set for zero-interruption, which Alik's Bureau authority overrode. He eventually answered, audio only.

"Yes?" It was a puzzled voice coming out of the office speakers.

"Niall Kanoto?"

"Who is this?"

"Special Agent Monday, FBI. Please access your altme call data certificate for authentication."

"Yeah, yeah, sure. You're FBI. What the hell do you want? Do you know what time it is?"

"I'm trying to locate Kravis Lorenzo and his family. Are they with you?"

"What is this? Is Krav in trouble?"

"Answer the question please, sir. Where is Kravis Lorenzo?"

"Back home, I guess."

"They were scheduled to visit you today."

"Sure, man. We were going to spend the weekend together, both families. But we had to cancel, you know?"

"I do not know, sir. Why was the visit canceled?"

"The goddamn yacht, *Sea Star III*. My marina service company called me this afternoon. They prep her for me every time before I take her out: food, power charge, general maintenance, that kind of shit. This time the engine diagnostics showed a fault. They had to take the old girl out of the water to fix her. So we canceled. It's a twenty-four-carat buttpain. Bel and Rose had been planning this for months; we were going to take *Sea Star* all the way down to the Keys."

"So you spoke to Kravis this afternoon?"

"Sure. He was disappointed. Our kids all get on, you know? It was a big family event."

"You spoke with him? It wasn't just an altme message?"

"Yeah. He was still in the office, at his desk."

"Did he say where he would go instead?"

"No. What is this? What's happened to Kravis?"

"We can't locate him. Did he indicate if he would go somewhere else for the weekend?"

"No. He was kind of pissed he'd have to spend the weekend at home, you know? Me too. Why, what's happened?"

"We don't know what's happened."

"Jesus, is he all right?"

Alik put that particular stupidity down to the time of night. "I need the name of your marina service company; please send it to my altme. And if any of the Lorenzo family contact you, you're to inform me at once. Understand?"

"Yeah. But come on, man, what's happened to them?"

"We don't know." Alik ended the call and told Shango to load an observation routine on Niall Kanoto's access codes, then put another on his immediate family as well. If Kravis did attempt to get in touch with his yachting buddy, the precinct G7Turing would know before him.

"Confirming this," Bietzk said. "Connexion logged the Lorenzo family entering the metrohub loop in the Village at nine seventeen in the evening and coming out at the Central Park West hub next to their block three minutes later. That's their last recorded usage."

A big wallscreen started showing the Central Park West metrohub's video surveillance log. Everyone in the case office watched as the Lorenzo family came out of the loop portal. The scene was exceptional in how ordinary it was. Alik could so easily believe it was some kind of ideal family ad. Mom: beautiful, young, smiling; dad: older and measured; the kids with smiles and laughter showing off great dentistry as they joked and teased each other.

Shango connected to the National Citizenship Records Agency and ran characteristics recognition. It was them.

Bietzk switched from the Central Park West hub to the street's civic surveillance video log. The Lorenzos left the metrohub behind and walked twenty-five meters down the sidewalk, until they turned in to the entrance of their apartment block. Metadata time stamp: nine twenty-one.

"Get the precinct Turing to run a sweep on that video file for the rest of the night," Salovitz said. "I want to know if they come out again after that. And who else went into the apartment block."

"Got it," Bietzk said.

While they were processing that, Alik called the Bureau office in Palm Beach, while Shango rode the precinct's G7Turing into the network of the marina service company Kanoto used. It pulled the file for *Sea Star III,* which to his inexpert eye looked like a slightly smaller version of the *Jörmungand Celeste.*

One of the service company's engineers had been on board that morning running a final seaworthiness inspection when the yacht's diagnostic had flagged up the engine problem, some kind of contaminant particles in the gear system. If the engine was switched on, there was a high risk the entire gearing mechanism would seize up. The service company logged a call to Niall Kanoto, informing him the whole thing had to be dismantled and cleaned.

The engineer was called Ali Renzi. An infiltration ping to his altme revealed his location in central Miami. Three agents from the Bureau's Miami Central office were dispatched to pick him up.

"The Central Park West civic surveillance log has been compromised," Bietzk said. "Someone's run a sophisticated non-space edit, cutting human-sized areas out and replacing them with looped background. I'm guessing that's the Rayner crew entering the apartment block."

"Can you track the infiltration?" Salovitz asked.

"Our department can't." Bietzk glanced at Alik. "I can contract a major digital audit outfit?"

"Do it," Salovitz said.

"What about the apartment block's internal security surveillance?" Alik asked.

"Deactivated. They infiltrated and shut it down without triggering any alarms. Whoever their i-head was, they knew what they were doing."

"All right," Alik said. "Let's take a step back here. They won't have come in through the nearest hub. That would give any investigation too much data. But . . . they weren't expecting this to be a major homicide investigation, either. So, have your Turing work all the surveillance around the apartment, see if you can backtrack the Rayner crew through their edits. Find out where they came from. Somewhere along the line they'll leave their image on a log."

Bietzk gave the agent a quick nod and started instructing his altme.

"Connexion hasn't logged the Lorenzos in any hub since they exited Central Park West," Salovitz said. "So where the fuck are they?"

Alik stared at the holographic display on the stage, mentally reviewing the number of ways out of that portalhome. "We're overthinking this," he decided. "Let's stop relying on Turings and forensics, and go back to basics."

"Like what?" Salovitz asked skeptically.

"We've been looking for a technical solution, and I'm not sure it's applicable. Think about this: Half a dozen fuckheads break into your apartment armed with some heavy-duty shit. You don't have time to get smart. You have to get yourself and your kids *out*, and fast. So, this apartment block is what? Twenty stories high? Three or four apartments on each floor? Have we physically searched the whole building?"

"Not yet," Salovitz admitted. "Just the seventeenth floor."

"You need to get it done."

"I'll call in some more people," he said reluctantly.

Alik claimed a desk and sat down. Coffee was brought in. Out of a vending machine, but he didn't complain out loud; he needed the cops on his side. Shango splashed a whole load of data on his lenses. He was examining family and known associates for each of the corpses.

And he was pretty certain he wouldn't be the only one looking at those lists. Word of the police arriving at the apartment would be spreading. The survivor who took the Antarctic plunge would have spoken to Rayner. Javid-Lee would be wanting to know why his people hadn't come back; probably sending someone to take a look along Central Park West, who would have seen the cops establishing a crime scene perimeter. He knew he didn't have much time. It wasn't as if the gangs still practiced *omertà*, but even the dumbest street soldier knew the one thing you didn't do was go shouting your mouth off to the cops—or worse, the feds.

But Alik was a firm believer in the truism that every chain was only as strong as its weakest link. He just had to make the right choice of link.

Twenty minutes later two agents from the FBI Miami office escorted Ali Renzi into the twentieth precinct. To keep the Deacon sweet, Alik suggested that Salovitz should lead the interview, leaving him and Bietzk to watch it on the stage, with a link open to the detective in case they wanted to put any extra questions to him.

The stage hologram was detailed, showing Renzi as a chill guy, an attitude fine-tuned to show everyone what an innocent he was, how this must be some big mistake. It was a dick move, Alik thought; the genuinely innocent get very nervous being waltzed into a precinct house at two o'clock in the morning.

Ali Renzi was still in his Miami clubbing clothes: a short-sleeved shirt with a weird fantasy alien lion embroidered on and tight black pants. A quick march through a New York January night had left him shivering as he stood under the interview room's air-con vent, trying to get warm.

Bietzk gave Shango access to the body scan. Renzi's heart rate was high, as was his blood toxicology. Neural activity showed his brain was cranked up. Alik suppressed a smile at the tell of nervous energy.

Salovitz walked in. "Sit, please."

Renzi gave the air-con grille a last look and reluctantly sat at the table opposite Salovitz.

"Would you like a lawyer present?" Salovitz asked. "If you don't have one, a public defender will be appointed. If you do not have insurance coverage, you will be liable for their costs."

"Am I under arrest? I didn't get read no rights."

"No, this isn't an arrest; for now you are a material witness."

"For what?"

"Tell me about the *Sea Star III*."

"That's a sweet yacht. I run service on it sometimes." He smiled broadly, putting on the Latino strut.

"Ali," Salovitz said the name like he was calling out a fifth grader.

"What?"

"Let me give you some free advice here. You don't have a criminal record, and I can see you're basically a decent guy, so don't get me pissed. Understand?"

"What's up, man? I service it. I told you."

"We track you down at two in the morning and bring you all the way up here, where I ask you about a yacht you serviced yesterday morning, and you tell me: sometimes? You need to start pumping up your IQ. Because serious doesn't even begin to cover this."

"Pump my what?"

"Get smart, Ali. What happened to the *Sea Star*?"

"The gearing, man. The diagnostics redlined. It was towed to dry dock. The company's working on it."

"Shit, you're just not listening, are you? Okay, then, this is how it's going to go now. You talking to me, telling me what I need to know; that results in the precinct giving you breakfast and letting you go. No charges, and our thanks for assisting us in a multiple homicide."

"Multip—*what?*"

"Shut the fuck up!" Salovitz's fist slammed down on the table. "I'm talking. Now if you don't cooperate, I will tie you in to this, and you'll be facing an accomplice charge—and probably conspiracy, too. For this crime—seven bodies that we've found so far—you'll be straight to Zagreus, and not the good end of the canyon."

"No fucking way, man! I didn't kill anybody."

"In law, complicity is the same as participating."

"I didn't do anything!"

"Good. So now I have a question for you, and you're gonna think hard about this, because I'm laying it out real simple. If I run a search through your accounts, which I haven't done yet because you're being a concerned, helpful citizen at this point, but *if* I run one, will I find an unexplained cash payment paid in recently? Take your time, and think. The rest of your life depends how you answer."

Renzi seemed to have gotten over his wintery cold. Sweat was breaking out across his forehead, and his skin was turning pale so fast Alik considered he could have had chameleon genes. "Yeah," Renzi said, not making eye contact with Salovitz. "Friend of a friend, he helped me out. These are bad times, you know. The economy."

Salovitz put his card down on the table like he was a Vegas pro about to scoop the cash. "Look at the faces, Ali. Are any of them the friend of a friend?"

Renzi glanced down. "Jesus!" He slapped a hand over his mouth as his cheeks bulged.

"Keep looking," Salovitz ordered.

The card was showing him all the bodies in situ. In the cases of Perigine Lexi and Koushick Flaviu, a mug shot from records was shown, to clarify their identity.

"That one," Renzi said, and turned away.

"Koushick Flaviu?"

"He said his name was Dylan."

"And what did you do for him?"

"Rigged the diagnostic. He wanted to be sure nobody was going anywhere on the *Sea Star* this weekend. Getting it out of the water was the easy answer."

"When did you meet him?"

"He turned up at my condo that morning. He knew who I was, what I did, everything. Man, you don't say no to people like that! And it didn't hurt nobody."

Salovitz's finger casually circled the card. "Nobody hurt, huh?"

"You know what I mean, man! I didn't do anything. This isn't down to me."

"Maybe. Now, what else did this guy who called himself Dylan say?"

"He didn't say anything, just to disable the yacht. I swear, man! I swear it; on my mother's grave."

"Did he say why he wanted it out of the water?"

"No. Nothing."

"So have you ever done favors like this for people before?"

"No, man, no way."

"You want to ask him anything?" Salovitz asked Alik through the precinct link.

"No. I'll have the Bureau run a full background review on him. If he's clean, you can bounce him out of here after breakfast."

While Salovitz was tidying up in the interview room, Alik put a call in to Tansan, his Capitol Hill contact. They'd met two decades ago and formed a mutually beneficial relationship. There were small discreet favors asked for, and since then Alik had enjoyed a smooth ride inside the Bureau, with clearance almost level with the director. And some of the things he knew, the director wouldn't have wanted anything to do with.

"It was a well-organized operation," Alik told Tansan. "To start with, at least. But I'm puzzled why a gang from South Brooklyn is trying to bust its way into Pentagon ultra files."

"You may have to go and ask them."

"That could get difficult. I suspect they'll be nervous right about now, what with their brothers in arms being butchered, and all."

"Do you need backup? I have some dark funds available if you need to hire the appropriate experts."

"I'm going to see where this investigation leads for a while. It's a very odd coincidence, both crews turning up at the same time. And if you do want to bust Pentagon ultra files, you don't hire a gang from South Brooklyn. I have to find out who escaped through Antarctica. They might have some answers."

"Very well. Keep me informed. I need to know who wanted those files, and why."

Alik ran through all the dead gang members again and decided the weakest link was likely to be Adrea Halfon, Perigine Lexi's squeeze. Some of the girls who attached themselves with connected guys could be tougher than their men. This one? Alik had a hunch she was one of the other kind: brittle and dependent. Perigine had lifted her out of the gutter. He was her world; without him she was nothing. If he and Salovitz could just get to her before Javid-Lee sent anyone around . . .

Alik and Salovitz walked along the south radial out of Manhattan, then took the 32nd loop to the Manhattan Beach Park hub. They almost called a two-seat cabez, but it had stopped snowing by then, so the pair of them walked west along Oriental Boulevard.

"So you think it was a kidnapping?" Salovitz asked. "Rayner went to a lot of effort to fuck up the Lorenzos' weekend. That crew wanted them at the portalhome."

"And Javid-Lee's crew thought they were going to be out on a yacht, so the portalhome would be empty. Which is why they both wound up in Central Park West together. But I don't think it was a kidnapping."

"What then?"

"Access to the Anaka, Devial, Mortalo and Lorenzo network requires some biometrics. Having Kravis present in the flesh would've been a big help to Koushick. His gear had biometric readers. Plus, if you're holding Kravis's family, that gives you plenty of leverage."

"So it was all about busting the files?"

"Could be, for the Rayner crew. But that still doesn't tell us where the Lorenzos are now."

They turned in to Dover Street just after three o'clock in the morning. Nothing else was moving, not even street cleanez. The snow was thick under Alik's feet, crunching down under his soles.

It was a decent neighborhood; the houses all had neat yards, several with boats parked outside. Perigine's was halfway along; the only one with its lights on.

Salovitz took the steps up onto the little porch and pressed the doorbell. The house network asked for identification, which their altmes supplied.

Adrea Halfon opened the door and peered out nervously. She'd been crying. "Yeah?" Her voice was soft, catching in her throat.

"NYPD, ma'am," Salovitz said. "May we come in?"

She didn't say anything, just backed in and left the door open. Alik and Salovitz followed her. They looked ahead, then looked at each other, careful to remain expressionless, then looked ahead again. Adrea's housecoat was a loose weave of black lace, lined with fluffy purple feathers—a Schrödinger masterpiece in being dressed and undressed at the same time. Perigine had found her in one of Javid-Lee's clubs, and she'd obviously thanked him for getting her out by keeping in the exact same shape that had captured him in the first place. Seeing Adrea in the flesh, Alik was certain he'd made the right choice; the smell of insecurity was as strong as her perfume.

"I have some bad news, ma'am," Salovitz said when they were in the living room. The place was as brash as Alik had expected. Somebody whose taste came straight out of Hong Kong virtuals had been given too much money and license to create their dream home. Everything clashed—colors, furniture, ornaments, pictures; he counted styles from at least four different eras.

Adrea nodded, a single sharp jerk of the head. She already knew. "What's that, officer?"

"Your partner, Perigine Lexi. I'm afraid our officers have found him dead. My sympathies."

She sank into a heavily cushioned couch and reached for the tumbler on the marble table beside it. A bottle of cheap bourbon was already open. "That's terrible," she said.

"The way he died, yeah," Alik agreed. "Terrible."

She shot him a fearful glance. "How . . . ?"

"He was in the wrong place in the wrong time with the wrong people. But you wouldn't know anything about that, right?"

"I don't know where he was tonight. He said he was meeting some friends in a bar."

"What does he do for a living?"

"He's a manager at Sidereal Urban Management."

Alik read the file Shango splashed for him. "City cleanup company, huh? Sidereal has the contract for Gravesend and Sheepshead Bay?"

"Yeah, that's the one." Her hand shook as she took another slug of bourbon.

"Strange, we found him in an uptown apartment. He was robbing the place."

"I don't know nothing about that."

"One of the people with him, we think it's Duane Nordon. Would you mind identifying him for me, please?" He held up his card.

"Sure." She glanced at the image of Duane's frozen bloodless face and screamed. Ran out of the room. Alik and Salovitz stared meaningfully at each other to the soundtrack of violent retching.

A couple of minutes later Adrea reappeared in the doorway, clutching her housecoat tightly closed; something it just wasn't built for. "You son of a bitch!"

"Yes, ma'am. There were two crews hit that apartment, and they ripped each other apart like sharks on acid. Your Perigine, he got lucky; a clean shot. Duane, not so much."

Her hand went to her mouth as the tears dripped down her cheeks.

"They took out two of the other crew," Alik continued relentlessly, "but one of them got away. Any idea who Rayner would use for a job like this?"

"I don't know anything."

"You think Javid-Lee is your friend? That he'll do right by you? Right now he's looking to cover his ass. So you tell me what you think is going to happen if we take you along to the twentieth precinct and hold you there for a couple of days. I can do that—you'll be a custodial witness, so there's no charge filed. That means you don't get Miranda rights, so no lawyer for twenty-four hours."

"I haven't done anything," she protested as she sank back into the couch.

"We might need to check that. But it doesn't matter, because Javid-Lee is going to want to know what you said for two days before we let his lawyer in to see you. He'll want to know pretty bad. And if you keep telling him *nothing*, is he going to believe you, do you think?"

She was really sobbing now, staring up at Alik with more hatred than a whole KKK chapter. "Bastard. I hope your balls get cancer and it creeps up your spine!"

"Sure thing, sweetheart. On the other hand, we came down here to inform you of Perigine's death, just like the city requires. We stayed a few minutes and left when it was obvious you weren't giving us squat. Do you think that would play better?"

"What do you want?"

"I want to know what the fuck is going on."

"Perigine didn't say much. I only heard about it after the fire."

"What fire?"

"The Blueshift Starlight Lounge. It's one of Javid-Lee's places."

"Where you worked?" Salovitz asked.

"I don't do that no more," she said petulantly. "And I never danced there; it's on the way down, you know? But I knew a couple of girls who wound up there."

"When was this fire?" I asked.

"A couple of days back. The fire started in the kitchen. Supposed to be an accident, but everyone knew that was bull. Peri said Javid-Lee knew it was Rayner that ordered it along with whacking Riek. That's when Javid told Peri to take care of the Farrons to equalize things with Rayner, you know? He can't afford to show any weakness, not after two strikes against him. You let that go, people think you're weak, and next thing you just vanish. He had to send a message, a loud one."

"Wait," Alik said. "Go back. Who the fuck is Riek?"

"He was small-time, right at the bottom of Javid-Lee's organization. But Peri said he did a shakedown for Javid-Lee a couple of days before. Next thing we know, he's being pulled out of the marina—same day as the Blueshift fire."

"What did Riek do? Who was the shakedown?"

"I don't know—just that it was one of Rayner's people. Whatever it was, it got Rayner pissed at Riek. That ain't exactly hard."

"And the Farrons? Who are they?"

"The people Peri was going to take care of to get Javid-Lee back level again."

"So Javid-Lee and Rayner are at war? How long's this been going on?"

She shrugged. "This week. Peri's been coming home late; he's been like in this real filthy temper the whole time. It's always respect with the boys. You gotta show respect. If you don't, if you step out of line, you get sent a message. That's how it's always been."

The Dover Street air was cold and rich with the sharp scent of the Atlantic that lurked a few hundred meters away. Alik inhaled deeply, hopeful it would be like some kind of cleansing agent. "These sons of bitches, they still live in the Middle Ages."

Salovitz chuckled. "You lowering yourself, coming down here from DC?"

"Nah," Alik admitted. "It's plenty more savage there. Maybe less blood, but twice as much pain."

"Amen to that, my friend. So what now?"

"This still isn't making a whole load of sense," Alik complained as they started walking back down the street. Shango splashed the NYPD report on Riek Patterson, who had been pulled out of the Caesar's Bay Marina two days ago. He couldn't swim. Well, Alik admitted, it would be difficult for anyone with fifty kilos of metal chain wrapped around their legs. On the same day, the district fire crew was called out to a kitchen fire in the Blueshift Starlight Lounge. "Okay," he said, lining it up in his head. "Whatever Riek did, Rayner was psycho enough about it to order two hits in retaliation. Javid-Lee counters by sending Perigine's crew to take out the Farrons, whoever the fuck they are. Then Perigine winds up in the Lorenzo portalhome, getting his ass blown off by Rayner's crew, who are also running a file bust there at the same time."

"Still think it's coincidence?"

"I have no idea what to think."

"Don't tell me. You need more information?"

"You think you don't?" Alik shot back. Then Shango splashed the weirdest file of the night. "Holy shit!"

"What?"

He shared the file. "Delphine Farron is the Lorenzos' housekeeper."

"Are you shitting me?" Salovitz barked.

"Access the fucking file."

"So who do you want to talk to next?"

"Wait one." Shango pinged Delphine Farron's code. No reply. Her altme was off grid. "Uh oh. Get a uniform squad 'round to their address, right now."

"Christ. I'm on it."

"Is that why Perigine was 'round at the Lorenzos' place?" Alik wondered out loud. "Hunting the Farron woman?" Then he read further down the file Shango had harvested on Delphine Farron. "Oh, this just keeps getting better. Look at this shit; Delphine is Rayner's second cousin."

"This can't be right," Salovitz said. "If Perigine had whacked the Farron woman in the portalhome, we'd have found her body."

"Not if they went for a walk in the Antarctic," I said. "We barely found the next portalhouse room."

"Perigine and his crew weren't wearing polar gear."

"Yeah," Alik admitted sourly. "Good point. Ask the precinct to get Connexion's log on Delphine Farron. I want to know where she is."

They reached the Manhattan Beach Park hub as Alik finished reviewing Riek Patterson's file. "Change of plan," he announced. "We're going to west Brooklyn."

"For what?"

"Pay our respects to the widow Patterson."

Geographically, Stillwell Avenue wasn't that far from Dover Street, but status-wise Alik was getting vertigo from the drop. They found the small projects where Riek Patterson rented a few rooms easily enough; nearly half of the building was derelict. The rest of the inhabitants vanished like rats into the cracks as soon as the two of them stepped over the threshold. Alik didn't think they'd be dumb enough to try to tangle with one of the city's finest and a fed, but you never knew what kind of weird neurochemical shit their twenty-year-old synthesizers squeezed out and how it affected them.

Colleana Patterson was awake. Ordinarily he'd take that as a sign of guilt—three thirty in the morning is when the baddest of them all come out to play—but the two-month-old cradled in her arm was evidence to the contrary. It looked like she'd been awake for half a year and crying for most of that. She was a complete physical and emotional wreck. The tiny apartment was a cluttered mess that smelled of stale food and toxic diapers.

"What now?" she wailed; she didn't even bother checking their credentials.

"Did you know Perigine Lexi and his crew were hit tonight?" Alik asked.

She collapsed back into her one big chair in the scabby living room, sobbing. That set the kid off, howling like a small banshee. Alik waited. Sure enough, a neighbor started banging on the wall.

"I need your help," he said when her misery reached a peak.

"I don't know anything! How many goddamn times do I have to tell you people?"

"I'm not NYPD, I'm FBI."

"You're all the same."

"Not quite. I have a lot more authority than Detective Salovitz here."

Salovitz cheerfully gave him the finger.

"I don't know anything," she repeated like it was her shiny new mantra, the one that would solve everything in life. Alik could tell she was on the verge of curling up into a fetal position tighter than junior could ever manage, one she might never uncurl from.

"I've been looking at Riek's file," he said. "He had some insurance. Not much, but it could make a big difference to you and the kid."

"They won't pay out, the company's legal department already said. Bastards. It wasn't an accident."

"It could be. I can speak to the coroner; they can officially record it as an accident. Like I said, I have authority."

She glanced up at Alik, her expression sullen and suspicious. "What do you want?"

"A name. We know Rayner's people took out Riek because of what he'd just done. It was a retaliation hit."

"Sure. Whatever."

"So tell me what it was he did for Javid-Lee? I know you know."

"Are you serious about the insurance company? You can really do that?"

"I can really do that. But you have to tell me everything."

"It was some bitch. That's why he took the job; not everyone would. But we needed the money. Javid-Lee rewards his people for loyalty, he's good that way."

"Sure he is. Who was the girl?"

"Samantha Lehito. Javid-Lee wanted a message delivered to her."

"What for? What had she done?"

"I don't know. Please, I really don't. Riek never asked. You don't. He was a solid soldier for Javid-Lee. He delivered the message like he'd been told. Put that skank in the hospital."

"She's alive, then?"

"I dunno. She was when he left her. Her altme was screaming for the paramedics."

"All right." Shango was already splashing Lehito's file across Alik's lens. She was in Jamaica Hospital on the Van Wyck Greenway, receiving credit-level-three treatment. That confirmed Rayner took care of his people—good politics on his part. But Alik was now very curious what Samantha Lehito had done that would make Javid-Lee send Riek to kick her ass.

"The insurance?" Colleana said desperately. "What about the insurance? I told you what you wanted to know."

The baby was grizzling again, picking up on mom's distress. Alik didn't give a rat's turd about her, but the kid deserved a chance; it was that damn Southern Baptist conscience of his, which never quit. "I've loaded it in the Bureau's network," he told her. "The coroner will pick it up in the morning."

She burst into tears again.

Alik scowled. He might be a guardian angel, but he didn't have to put up with that kind of shit.

"Nobody at the Farron address," Salovitz said as the pair of them walked through the practically deserted hubs.

"Yeah?"

"She has a kid, a boy, Alphonse. Our precinct officers asked around; neighbors say they were definitely at home earlier today, but haven't seen them for a while."

"Add them to the search list."

"Way ahead of you."

The staff at Jamaica Hospital were quite used to NYPD turning up in the bad hours. Salovitz talked to the receptionist, who directed them to the ninth floor. The strata of the hospital's fifty-year-old brutish carbon-and-glass structure reflected human status in a way the architect probably never intended. If he did, he had a bad sense of irony.

The Koholek Ward was decent enough, several social steps up from the five floors of MedicFare wards directly underneath it. But then again, it was quite a few floors down from the kind of treatment Alik would receive if he was ever, god forbid, admitted.

Samantha Lehito was in a bay off the main ward. There were two beds in there, but she was the only patient. A stack of equipment had been wheeled in, with plenty of tubes connecting it to Samantha. Her face and limbs were sheathed in a blue-tinged membrane that told

Alik Kcells were being used to replace chunks of flesh that were missing. In medical terms: superficial flesh. But Riek had really carved a
number on her face. Just looking at her, Alik was now regretting giving Colleana help with the insurance.

There was another woman dozing in a chair beside the bed, a
short woman in her midthirties, with black hair in a pixie cut, fram-
ing a face that was creased with worry. She stirred when Alik and
Salovitz came in, confusion rapidly becoming a disapproving frown.
Shango ran facial recognition: Karoline Kalin. There was a marriage
license for her and Samantha, issued four years ago, registered at City
Hall. Her employment record was patchy, but she was currently listed
as working in a local store called Karma Energy. Shango couldn't find
a connection between that and any of Rayner's enterprises.

"What do you want?" she asked in a voice just as weary as Colleana's.

Alik resisted a sigh. The reaction was so common he'd stopped
resenting it years ago. But it was a regular quirk of human nature that
anyone who'd been mugged or robbed welcomed the police like they
were a lottery win's delivery committee, while at any other time the
boys in blue were as wanted as an IRS audit.

"I want to talk to Samantha," Alik told her.

"She's tired. What he did to her . . ." Karoline reached out a hand
and caressed her face. "She's mending now. That takes so much
strength. You leave her be."

"You know Riek Patterson is dead?"

"Yeah. And I've got an alibi, too. I was in here, watching her. There
was even a cop on the ward. Good witness, huh?"

"I know you didn't touch Riek. That was Rayner, right?"

Karoline shrugged, running a hand back through her hair. "If you
say."

"Which means Javid-Lee is going to be looking for payback."

"No way. It's over now."

"Between Rayner and Javid-Lee? No. It is never going to be over
until one of them gets taken out of the picture."

"And who's going to do that? You? I don't think so. Not bastards like that. They don't get arrested, they don't stand trial, they don't do time, they don't need their gorgeous face rebuilt. That's what they have poor fucks like Sam for."

"True."

"You know it's painful, cosmetic application, having Kcells attach themselves to real flesh? The whole time they're doing it, adapting to the new host body, it hurts, even with the drugs. And it's going to take months to rebuild Sam's features so you can't tell what he did to her. Some people can't take that much pain. My Sam can; she's strong. And when she's done, when I get her home, she is out of this shit! Away from Rayner and all the other psychos."

"Nice story," Alik said. "Do you know how many times I've heard it before?"

"I'm not letting her go back. I won't."

"Good. Then let me help you. Tell me what she did. Why did Javid-Lee send Riek to do this to her? What was he warning Rayner to stay away from? Once I understand what's been happening, I can go to town on these guys. We've got seven bodies piled up tonight, and that's not including Riek. The Bureau won't ever quit on this case."

"Sam wouldn't tell you."

"Of course not, because they've sucked her into their world so far she'll never be able to leave. All your love and pleading, every argument you have, all those dreams about starting fresh someplace—all that's going to do is make her choose. You or them. Are you certain she'll choose you?" It was an effort to convince her, harder than polishing turds, but Alik thought he could see the doubt creeping into her expression.

"She's my fucking wife! She'll leave. For me."

"Make certain of that. Tell me what she did. I'll take it from there. Rayner and Javid-Lee will be gone."

"They never go. Only the names change. Some other sonofabitch will take over the territories."

"But there'll be a gap, a moment when no one is in charge. That's your moment, that's when you get her out."

"Sam wouldn't even want me talking to you like this," she said uncertainly.

"And that's the problem. This life she's in, it's a drug. She can't break it by herself. But you can."

Karoline let out a long sigh and gripped Samantha's limp hand. "Rayner wanted a message delivered. A clear one."

She didn't even have to say that; Alik understood the culture perfectly. Messages. Threats. It was all a variant of the old rackets when the shitty words were peeled away. What it boiled down to was the power the likes of Javid-Lee and Rayner could exert over others, enforced by either money or fear. Nobody ever backed down; they had too much dumb pride. To lose face among the gangs was to lose everything.

"What message?" Salovitz asked.

"To back off," she replied. "That's all. This woman, she'd got some kind of dispute going with one of Rayner's relatives. So Sam finds out when the woman visits her spa, a real fancy uptown one. She goes every couple of days, gets the whole treatment—hair, face, full-body skin cleanse. And she always has a massage, too, some fancy one, with warm stones or some shit. Thing is, even with an ordinary massage, you're mostly naked. Did you know just taking your clothes off makes people feel vulnerable, never mind lying there with someone standing over you, someone you suddenly find isn't who you thought they were?"

"Sam gave her the massage," Alik said.

"Goddamn right. But Sam never hurt her, never did anything like that fucking animal Riek. She just scared the crap out of her. Exactly what Rayner wanted."

Alik already knew the answer, but asked the question anyway. "This woman she warned, what was her name?"

"Rose Lorenzo."

. . .

Bietzk called just as Alik stepped out of the hospital. In front of him a long line of pine and oak trees stretched the whole length of the Van Wyck, a sweet stretch of parkland cutting through the slowly de-populating urban wilderness. The progressive idea behind convert-ing the old major routes through the city was to soften the environment, and through that make the lives of the citizens that bit more positive and pleasant. All very admirable and worthy.

He knew at its heart it was all bullshit. There had always been gangsters like Javid-Lee and Rayner right from when the city was founded, and there probably always would be. Poverty attracted a certain type—violent, without a conscience—and where there was poverty was its evil twin: exploitation. For all the money locked away in vaults uptown, the city retained a very old-style notion of equita-ble distribution. A bunch of long, skinny parks wouldn't change the attitude of any New Yorker; the eternal buildings and institutions kept them captive in the same old economic cycle as surely as any jail. The only way people growing up inside the projects and low-rent tenements could break their old ways was to leave and immerse themselves in something else, something new and different, such as an asteroid habitat or a terraformed world, Universal or Utopial. But Alik had seen the statistics, always slipped into the appendix of the innumerable reports on urban crime commissioned by state senators calling for "action." Depressingly few kids would leave the world they knew, no matter what opportunity was promised by slick gov-ernment policy advertising. It wasn't a surprise; nobody in a shiny clean habitat wanted a New York punk to screw up the perfect con-formity they'd woven to hold their neocorporate lives together. And ever since New Washington was successfully terraformed back in 2134, opening its endless verdant prairies to American settlers, New York's population hasn't reduced by more than ten percent. Most American cities were down fifteen to twenty percent from their peak twenty-first-century levels, as people, especially the wealthier young, flooded out for that mythical Fresh Start.

As Alik stood in the biting cold listening to Bietzk, his gaze tracked along the Van Wyck's trees with their mantle of thin, prickly ice, as if they'd grown thorns to protect themselves through the winter: a mirror of the citizens who walked among them, bristling with hostility and rooted in the structure of the past.

"You're not going to believe this," Bietzk said.

Alik and Salovitz exchanged a glance.

"Go on," he said.

"Connexion sent us the logs for Delphine Farron. She and her boy Alphonse walked out of Central Park West hub fifty-two minutes before the Lorenzo family came home. The civic surveillance video shows them walking into the apartment block."

"You've gotta be fucking kidding me," Salovitz exclaimed. "They were both at the portalhome? Where the fuck did they all go?"

"Bietzk," Alik said, "I need you to get on to the developer. Find out if they built a safe room into the portalhome."

"I'm on it."

"Come on," he said.

"Where are we going?" Salovitz asked.

"The Lorenzo place. Where else?"

There were still a few bored cops in the portalhome, waiting for their shift to end as they watched the forensic teams finishing up. Alik walked straight along the hubhall and into the cabin on the *Jörmungand Celeste*.

"You think there's a safe room here?" Salovitz asked.

"No." He took his jacket off, ready for the heat outside, as they went onto the private deck. Sure enough, the temperature and humidity had both risen in the couple of hours they'd been away. When Alik peered out over the rail, the water was slipping easily along the side of the hull. That was deceptive, he knew. There would be strong currents created by the sheer speed with which the big ship was moving through the ocean. The wake would be even worse: long cyclonic swirls that would show only as choppy ripples, unless you got caught in one. You'd have to be crazy to jump. Or desperate.

"What are you looking for?" Salovitz asked.

"Something missing. Which is always harder to find."

Both ends of the deck had big red-and-white cylinders fixed on the wall, containing life rafts. Alik flipped the clips on one and opened it, finding a fat package of orange fabric and five buoyancy jackets. The other one was empty.

"No fucking way," Salovitz exclaimed.

"They were desperate," Alik said slowly. "The kind of desperate that happens when two armed crews burst into your home."

"Holy shit."

"Find this ship's coordinates for eleven o'clock Eastern Standard Time last night," he told Shango, "then alert the South African Coast Guard. Ask them to get a boat out there, or a plane if they still use them."

They both went back to the twentieth precinct house to wait. Alik got a call from the Bureau while he and Salovitz sat in the case office drinking vending machine coffee. Agency forensics had made some progress on the portalhome with the Antarctic room. It belonged to the Mendozas, an elderly married couple in Manila, with zero links to any kind of crime. The person coming through had wiped and crashed the security system. But that was when luck had failed them for the first time. Alik and Salovitz watched the image from Manila's civic surveillance on the case office's stage.

A fair-haired woman emerged from the Mendozas' home on Makait Avenue, opposite the Ayala Park. A cabez pulled up, and she got into it. Less than thirty seconds later, the vehicle disappeared from Manila's transport logs. It wasn't the best image Alik had ever seen, but it clearly showed their suspect to be just over average height, and wiry with it—the kind of figure that only came from constant workouts. She wore a bulky parka-style coat to cover her armor—which must have helped in the Antarctic, but in Manila she would have swiftly roasted in that getup. The enhancement routines rectified her out-of-focus face, and the precinct's G7Turing ran facial recognition.

"Nothing," Salovitz exclaimed in disgust.

"Maybe," Alik said. "She's not part of Rayner's organization, that's for certain."

"You know her?"

"No," he lied. Admittedly it was only a partial lie, but he was pleased with himself for carrying it off through the deep unease that had just kicked his ass. No characteristics routine could ever grasp this particular suspect, because she changed her features after every job, which was easy now with the new Kcell cosmetics that had hit the market a few years back. Her height and build, however, remained constant to within five percent, as, bizarrely, did her hair color, which was always a sandy blond, no matter what style. Then there was the bloodbath in her wake. Not a visual characteristic, but the multiple murder was her signature sure as Ainsley Zangari had money. *Cancer,* Alik mouthed silently.

He left Salovitz to crank out the usual alerts and requests for cooperation to various global agencies, providing them with the new picture, and called Tansan.

"It's Cancer."

"Shit," Tansan snapped. "Are you sure?"

"The massacre at the portalhome is typical of her operation, and I've just seen surveillance of a woman who fits her profile. But she vanished in Manila hours ago."

"This is serious. Those files need to stay secure."

"I'm sure the people she's murdered will agree with you."

"I'm sorry about them, I really am. But the people I represent have other issues."

"And money."

"Money isn't actually part of it, this time. This is political."

"Yeah. I accessed Nikolai Kristjánsson's preliminary report. Those files she was trying to bust dealt with New York's shields."

"Which is why this is attracting so much attention here on the Hill."

"Nikolai said he didn't think they actually cracked the files."

"Not this time, but the fact someone was trying to bust them out is worrying. There's only one reason you want those files, and that's if you're planning to obliterate New York."

"I don't get it. There are enough freak-jobs in the solar system who can probably build their own nukes if they want to. But then you'd just bring the components in through hubs one chunk at a time and rebuild it on the ground. Shields are practically an anachronism."

"Not entirely," Tansan said. "Pulau Manipa."

Alik winced. Pulau Manipa used to be an Indonesian island. Then, in 2073, a reasonably sized chunk of space rock hit the atmosphere above it. Earth's atmosphere had provided a good level of natural protection against cosmic impacts since the end of the dinosaurs, with just a few little blips in its safety record, such as Tunguska in Siberia and Meteor Crater in Arizona. It even broke up the 2073 rock, which basically put Pulau Manipa directly under a cosmic shotgun blast rather than a single-shot impact. Astrophysicists and weapons techs were still arguing which kind of strike was worse: air burst or solid smackdown. Nobody on Pulau Manipa could be asked for their opinion. Between the multiple physical strikes, the overlapping blast waves, and the firestorms, none of them were left alive.

Up until that incident, countries had been fairly halfhearted about building shields. They were the tail end of big military spending, and nobody was enthusiastic. There were plenty of political and religious fanatics still waging insurgency campaigns against governments and society in general, but they were slowly and quietly being dumped on Zagreus. The era of national wars and standing armies with nuclear-tipped missiles was long over.

Shields were an artificially generated field that enhanced atomic bonds—a technology that emerged from molecular fabrication. Although air was a tenuous material even at sea level, if the bonds were enhanced within a thick enough section, it produced what was essentially a force field. Enhance a wall of air twenty meters thick, and it would be able to resist a hellbuster blast. But apply that same enforcement to a couple of kilometers of air, and you could set off a nuke outside a city, and all it would do is provide the residents with a grandiose light show.

Had there been a shield over Pulau Manipa, the rock wouldn't have made it through. So governments shifted shield construction contracts to civil authorities, and the old armaments companies got a last gulp of public Big Cash. Most large urban areas on the planet were equipped with fully operational nuke-proof shields. Of course, no wild-orbit asteroid would ever make it to within ten million kilometers of Earth now. The astro-engineering companies had so many people and so much ultra-sophisticated hardware up there that any approaching asteroid would be mined down to the last speck of gravel before it got inside lunar orbit. But no politician wanted to be responsible for a budget cut that would strip a layer of defense off their voters. City shields remained intact and alert. In the last ninety-nine years since Pulau Manipa, they'd mainly been used to ward off hurricanes.

"But rocks falling on our heads can't happen anymore," Alik insisted. "We're not fucking dumbasses like the dinosaurs; we're here to stay. It's Darwin."

"So why did Cancer try and bust the files out?"

Alik ran his hand back through his hair, but not even an imagination pumped by playing innumerable Hong Kong fantasy drama games could give him a viable suggestion on that. "We're going to get some answers on the multiple homicide soon; that'll point me in the right direction," he told Tansan. "But I might need some of those dark funds to finish the case."

. . .

It turned out the South African Coast Guard did still have some air-craft, a couple of squadrons of Boeing TV88s. They weren't drones, though they could deploy swarms of airborne and underwater drone clusters kitted out with all kinds of high-grade sensors. They even had actual humans in the cockpit telling the G6Turing pilot what to do. Two of them had zoomed out to the area where the *Jörmungand Celeste* had been at eleven o'clock New York time. They found the life raft easily enough, even though the beacon had been disabled. That told Alik just how scared the Lorenzo and Farron families were.

The TV88s had a portal door on board, so as soon as the families had been winched up, they were brought into the twentieth precinct—seventy minutes after the South African Coast Guard had officially been asked to help. Alik was impressed.

The two families arrived like refugees from some disaster area, hunched up, hair and clothes sodden with seawater, a silver blanket around their shoulders, clinging to water bottles and candy bars. It wasn't rescue workers triumphantly bringing the six of them in, but a trio of pissed-off cops.

Salovitz didn't put them into interrogation; he was saving that for the first wrong answer. They sat in a row of chairs at the back of the case office. For people who'd just had their lives threatened then spent hours in the same lifeboat in the middle of an ocean, they certainly didn't look like best buddies.

Delphine Farron had her arm around Alphonse's shoulders. The boy was only ten, but he'd already perfected a teenager's sulk. He scowled at Salovitz, pouting away like a runway model caught break-ing her diet.

The Lorenzos were only slightly more civilized. Alik tried not to stare too hard at Rose. She was a real trophy wife; Shango's splash told him she'd modeled for various brands a decade ago—couture and upmarket lingerie. Now she fitted into the perfect corporate spouse mold. Telomere treatments had preserved early-twenties looks, and surrogates had made sure her body wasn't punished by pregnancy, allowing her to play the chic, sultry babe to perfection. Even disheveled from the ocean ordeal, she stayed classy. He guessed she was also a tiger mom; her kids were kept by her side as they sat, her arms around them. Kravis Lorenzo was the other half of the stereotype package deal family: Ivy League, preened almost as much as Rose, sitting stiff-backed and defiant, maintaining the kind of pose that said "my criminal law colleague is on fast-access call."

"Quite a night," Salovitz said. "Five people dead."

Delphine Farron let out a short hiss of breath, but that was the only hint of emotion. Rose Lorenzo pulled her children in even tighter.

"So let's be quite clear," Salovitz continued. "Any smartass answers, any lies, and we take this way on down to the holding cells. City Social Division will claim the kids. And you know what they say. The difference between City Social and a rottweiler is that a rottweiler will eventually let go."

"You can't threaten us," Kravis Lorenzo blustered. "My God, man, what we've been through!"

"It's not just five, though, is it?" Alik said. "We can add Riek, whom they pulled out of the marina a couple of days ago. And Samantha—maybe not dead, but still in the hospital with a face cut up so bad a gorilla would puke at the sight of it."

"Who are these people?" Kravis asked.

"Wrong answer," Salovitz said. "Let's get you down to holding. We'll charge you and start the formal interviews." He stood up, beckoned—

"Wait!" Kravis said. "What do you want?"

"For you to cut the bullshit," Salovitz bounced back at him. "What in the fuck have you people gone and done? There's a gang war broken out in my precinct, and you're the heart of it. Why?"

"This is all wrong," Rose said. "We didn't want any of this to happen. That's the truth."

"What did Samantha warn you about?" Alik asked. "And before you claim memory loss, she's the one that gave you a massage with added extras. I've already talked to her tonight—in her hospital bed."

Rose gave Delphine an anxious glance. All the housekeeper did was stare at her toes.

"Waiting," Alik said.

"She assaulted my wife," Kravis said heatedly. "A sexual assault."

"Gonna count to three," Salovitz said. "And if I don't get an answer—"

"She told me to back off Delphine," Rose said wearily.

"I never asked her to do anything to you," Delphine said quickly. "I don't even know her."

"Back off why?" Salovitz asked.

"All I said was to return Bailey's game matrix, and I wouldn't enter a formal complaint with the housekeeping agency," Rose said.

"You're saying my boy stole from you?" Delphine said in outrage. "Lying bitch! Alphonse is a good boy, aren't you, honey?" She gave him a reassuring squeeze. The kid's head was bowed.

"He was with you the day it went missing," Rose countered. "Who else would take it? And you never asked permission to bring him into my home."

"It was the goddamn Christmas vacation! What am I supposed to do with him?"

"Ask his father to look after him?" Rose sneered. And Alik suddenly understood why Kravis married her, not just for plenty of hot sex with the finest piece of ass on the block. She belonged in his uptown world just as much as he did.

"Fucking bitch!" Delphine spat.

"Cool it, both of you," Salovitz said. "So"—he eyed Delphine— "Rose accuses your boy of stealing, and you go running to Rayner? That's the story here?"

"I didn't do that. What am I, stupid? It's only a goddamn matrix, a couple of hundred bucks. And that brat has dozens of them anyway. He probably just put it in the wrong case."

"You're blaming Bailey?" Rose shrieked.

"You called Al a thief!"

"Je-zus wept," Salovitz grunted.

"Alphonse," Alik said softly. The boy still didn't look up. "What did you tell your uncle Rayner?"

All that happened was the kid shook his head.

Delphine suddenly gave her son a suspicious look. "Hey! Did you go and see Rayner?"

"I don't know," Alphonse sobbed. "Maybe."

"You dumb—"

For a moment Alik thought Delphine was going to smack him in the head there and then.

"Did you take that matrix?" she challenged. "You answer me! You tell me the truth *right now*. Did you?"

The boy's shoulders were shaking now as tears dripped onto the floor. "I was going to give it back," he wailed. "I was. Next time we went back there, honest. It's Star Revenger Twelve, it's only just come out. I wanted to see what it was like. That's all."

The expression of satisfaction on Rose's face was so brutal Alik wanted to give her the smack Alphonse deserved.

"Your mom was all over you about the matrix," he said to Alphonse. "Right? So you asked Uncle Rayner, man to man, to get Rose to back off. That way you could sneak it back in."

"I guess," Alphonse mumbled.

"Did he laugh? Did he say yes? Did he say well done for taking it? 'I knew you were one of us, kid,' is that what he said?"

Alphonse's sobs got louder.

Alik turned to Kravis. "And you."

"What about me?"

"Why did Riek go and kick the shit out of Samantha, after she hijacked your wife's massage?"

"I don't know."

"Really? Because I have a list of your law firm's clients. My altme ran a cross-check. Longpark Developments mean anything to you?"

"No. I've had no dealings with it."

"Ha; lawyer's answer. It happens to be owned by Javid-Lee. In fact, that's one of fifteen perfectly legal companies owned by him that pay your firm retainers."

Kravis glared at Alik in stony silence.

"You went to him, didn't you—after the *massage*?" Alik carried on. "She's your wife, after all. You didn't want justice, not for what Samantha did. You wanted vengeance."

"You can't prove that."

"Don't be so sure. You went to him because you believed he was deniable. Wrong. Sure, he won't give you up; you're in too deep with him now. He fucking owns you, which I'll bet hasn't even registered yet. You made a deal with the devil, Kravis. He's got your soul by the balls now. But if we looked hard enough, if we leaned on the right people, the little people, there would be witnesses. I could send you down as an accessory to a multiple homicide. How long would you last on Zagreus, do you think, a nice well-bred guy like you? Those cannibal rumors, they had to start for some reason."

"Javid-Lee is a client," Kravis said in a shaky voice. "I discuss many legitimate business details with him. That's all I'm prepared to say."

"There's one thing I don't get," Alik said. "Delphine, why did you go to the Lorenzos' place last night?"

"Koushick called me," she said grudgingly. "I knew him back in the day. He said Javid-Lee was looking to hit back against Rayner for some kind of firebomb attack on one of his clubs, and that it was getting out of hand, which meant I could be a target. Said we should go quiet for a few days until it was all settled. I was scared; I know what Rayner's life is like. We're not tight, but to these people, we're all family, all the same. So I knew the Lorenzos were off for the weekend, away with their fancy friends on a boat. It was the last place anyone would look for us."

"Who was the woman?" I asked.

"What woman?"

"Javid-Lee sent two others with Perigine Lexi that night: Duane

Nordon and Lisha Khan. While Rayner used Koushick Flaviu and Otto Samule—the two that didn't make it—along with a third, a woman. She survived the bloodbath. Who was she?"

"I don't know. Really, I don't. I told you, I'm not involved in that part of the family life."

Alik glanced at Salovitz. "I'm out of questions."

"Six people dead," Salovitz said quietly. "Another in the hospital. You started a gang war that's still going on because a kid steals a fuck-ing virtual game. A *game*. Do you have any idea . . . Je-zus H. Christ!"

"I didn't know—" Kravis began.

"Shut the fuck up!" Salovitz bellowed. "You don't get to talk, not after what you've done!"

"What happens now?" Rose asked. Her kids were pushing up against her so hard it was like they were trying to bury their heads in her ribs.

"Darwin," Alik told them.

Salovitz gave him a filthy look.

"I don't understand what that means," Rose said.

"Survival used to be down to how fast and strong you were, how good a hunter," Alik told her. "That was back when we all lived in caves and got frightened by thunder. Today, it's all about being the smartest."

"Just tell us," Delphine said. "Please, tell us the smart thing to do."

"Option one, we charge you all with criminal conspiracy. Given what's happened tonight, that's an easy trip to Zagreus, certainly for you and Rose and Kravis. Your kids will be taken into City Service's care, or handed over to any remaining family."

"Or?" Kravis asked.

Alik almost grinned. He should have known. After all, Kravis was Wall Street; he could recognize a deal on the table from a block away.

"I make a report to my boss that you were all in the portalhome when two rival crews broke in, trying to burgle the place. You natu-rally fled and saved your families. All very dramatic, but you're not involved in any criminal act. But that would be a big favor I'd be doing you. And as we've all learned tonight, those kind of favors don't come cheap."

"You want money?" a puzzled Rose asked.

"No. I want the two of you to do me a favor in return. A simple personal call. That's all."

The Black Mariah went for Javid-Lee first. He was in the Costado restaurant on Broadway, sitting by himself, with three of his lieutenants at the bar where they could watch the patrons coming in, alert for anyone who might have been sent by Rayner; the war was still nuclear-hot. He was by himself because Kravis Lorenzo hadn't yet shown up.

Five guys in FBI jackets came in. The lieutenants sat up. Hands went to their holsters. They looked at the boss, not knowing what to do.

Javid-Lee gave a tiny shake of his head. The agents surrounded his table and activated a solnet restriction on his altme, leaving him dark. Lead agent Marley Gardner asked—politely but firmly—that he accompany them to the downtown federal building. Javid-Lee agreed. In the spirit of reciprocity, Gardner agreed he could call his lawyer after they reached the federal building, but before he was processed.

He was discreetly cuffed and led out to the Black Mariah. The NYPD and the Bureau still used them in preference to escorting suspects more than a couple of hubs through the public metrohub network; way too many tiresome attempts to run. Procedure was to send the Black Mariah through the Commercial and Government Services network, with the suspect safely contained. The nearest of those hubs was off the northeast corner of Central Park in Harlem. The Black Mariah drove in the opposite direction. Eight minutes later it drew up close to Gorgiano's Pizzeria.

Rayner was sitting in a booth by himself, with seven of his lieutenants divided between the bar and a nearby table, watching the pizzeria patrons coming in, alert for anyone who might have been sent by Javid-Lee. He was by himself because Delphine Farron hadn't yet shown up.

As before, the five guys in FBI jackets got out of the Black Mariah and walked confidently into the pizzeria. The lieutenants sat up. Hands went to their holsters. They looked at the boss, not knowing what to do.

Rayner held up a hand—a diminutive gesture preventing them from any unwise action. The agents surrounded Rayner's booth and activated a solnet restriction on his altme, leaving him dark. He invited lead agent Marley Gardner to join him, an invitation that was refused, and a counter-invitation was given that he accompany them to the federal building. Rayner agreed. In the spirit of reciprocity, Gardner agreed he could call his lawyer when they reached the federal building, but before he was processed.

He was discreetly cuffed and led out to the Black Mariah. The inside of the aging van was divided into six cages. Rayner stiffened when he saw the only other occupant sitting on a narrow bench, but he allowed himself to be placed into a separate cage opposite. Marley Gardner withdrew, and Alik stepped into the Black Mariah.

"What the fuck is this?" Javid-Lee asked when the back door slid shut and locked.

"Rendition," Alik said as the Black Mariah drove away.

"Fuck you, asshole!" Javid-Lee shouted. "You can't do that."

"Really? Who are you going to complain to? The Justice Department? Hey, maybe you could call the FBI, complain to my boss? Oh, wait, there is no solnet on Zagreus."

"I'm gonna make you watch your whore mother die slowly before I kill you! That's a promise."

"How are you going to do that from Zagreus?" Alik inquired lightly. "See, I was at the Lorenzo portalhome that night. I gotta tell you, that was impressive. That many people dead because of a motherfucking virtual game matrix? Shit, you two have taken dumbass feuds to a whole new level. So as a thank-you, my boss and I have decided not to waste taxpayer money on a trial."

"What do you want?" Rayner asked quietly.

"Nothing."

"Yes, you do. If this was a straight rendition, you wouldn't be in here with us."

"Darwin, huh?"

Rayner smiled magnanimously. "I'm on the wrong side of the bars here, pal. Whatever it takes."

"Cancer," Alik said.

"Aww, shit."

"Why did you choose her?"

"I didn't."

"I'm listening."

Rayner jabbed a finger at his rival. "This asshole doesn't know when he's lost."

"Fuck you!" Javid-Lee screamed.

"I sent Koushick to deliver a message so loud that someone even this dumb could recognize."

"You were going to whack the Lorenzos," Alik said in understanding.

"Fucking A I was; the whole fucking family. That way it's ended. Clean and over. No more loser paybacks."

"Like fuck it would have been," Javid-Lee snarled. "I can take you down anytime I want."

Rayner gestured around mockingly. "Sure you could."

"Get on with it," a weary Alik told Rayner.

"Okay, so Koushick and his crew are getting ready to take out the Lorenzos. Next thing I know, Cancer comes to *me*. I don't know how she knew; Koushick shouting his dumb mouth off around the clubs, most like."

"Then what?"

"Hey, I wasn't going to turn down that offer. Cancer! She would make fucking sure there wasn't a Lorenzo left alive in this universe. Koushick, he's good, okay. Loyal. But there were kids . . . That wouldn't mean shit to her. And she lived her rep, you know. The way she maneuvered people; getting the yacht trip canceled, putting the Lorenzos exactly where we wanted them to be. Shit, like Koushick could ever pull off a stunt like that!"

"Did she say why she took this contract?"

"Said it was a good fit, and we'd both come out ahead. Told me there was some files Kravis had at his firm that she'd like to bust. I figured what the hell, you know? She's Cancer, and she's working a job with me. Doesn't hurt to be tight with someone like that."

"Why did she want those files?"

"Seriously, man? You think I'd ask *her* a question like that? I just told Otto and Koushick she was going with them, and do what she said." He glowered at Javid-Lee, stabbing a finger through the bars. "And then that ratfuck ambushed them."

"We didn't know they were there," Javid-Lee yelled. "Your butt-ugly bitch cousin Delphine ran there after you warned her. Perigine was on his way to hit her kid. What? You think I was going to ignore you whacking Riek and firebombing my fucking club? You took it up to this level, you fuck, because you have no respect for me. So your ratfuck nephew—the little shit that started all this—his ass is mine, and you know that; you know that's the price you gotta pay. Only you're too chickenshit to stand up like a man. Your whole family hides and runs like pussies. That's what you are, gaping fucking pussies."

Rayner yelled wordlessly and spat at Javid-Lee through the mesh.

"Enough," Alik said. His finger lined up on Javid-Lee. "You were hunting Alphonse?"

"'Course we fucking were. Perigine's good. He tracked the kid and Delphine to the Lorenzo place, and that's when it all went to shit." Javid-Lee glared at Rayner. "Which is your fault because you're a fucking coward. Now look where you've put us."

"You?" Rayner smirked back. "Put *you*, pal! Me, I'm cooperating with the feds. I'm outta here."

"Fuck you!"

"Okay, then," Alik said. "I believe I got everything I need." Shango opened the back door for him.

"Hey," Rayner said. "Hey, wait! What about me?"

Alik paused. "You have my personal thanks for your cooperation."

"No! No, that's not the deal. You get your ass back in here and you unlock this motherfucking cage! You hear me?"

The door closed, and Alik stepped down onto the muddy ground of the Lewis County environmental processing site in upstate New York—a patch of rural ground covering six square kilometers, dominated by an impressive atmospheric cleansing plant. Five massive concrete hyperboloid air tunnels stood together in a line, each one sporting a necklace of molecular extractor filters. Three pulled carbon monoxide out of the air, while the remaining pair collected carbon dioxide. Both gases were stored in big high-pressure tanks, ready for disposal.

As reduction efforts went, the Lewis County site alone wouldn't have much effect on the global greenhouse gas legacy that was still uncomfortably high even after a hundred years of scrubbing the excess out of Earth's atmosphere. But there were more than five hundred similar plants dotted all over the planet, and between them they did make a difference. So much that in another hundred years the experts claimed the world would be down to pre-twentieth-century levels.

Alik could hear Javid-Lee and Rayner yelling obscenities at each other inside the Black Mariah. It was parked in line with six other equally ancient, identical vehicles.

Marley Gardner and his team were waiting in a four-by-four to one side. Alik climbed in.

"Nice job, thanks," he told them. Alik liked working with Marley on the occasions he needed to go off book. Marley ran an efficient team and knew never to ask questions. "Your money will be in the designated accounts by morning."

"Always a pleasure," Marley said. His altme instructed the four-by-four, and it started driving toward the hub portal.

Behind them, the line of Black Mariahs was facing a huge metal cylinder, fifty meters long, fifteen high. Alik watched in the mirror as the big circular door at the end slowly swung open. The first Black Mariah's autodrive carefully maneuvered it inside, followed by the second.

Direct disposal was a part of the Lewis County environmental processing site made possible by modern economics. With energy as the Sol system's currency, everything was costed in wattdollars; and with abundant super-cheap energy delivered from the solarwells, the value of most services and material was inexpensive.

A hundred years previously, people on Earth carefully recycled the last generation's garbage, breaking down matter into its component atoms, refining their castoffs and sludge into useful compounds, ready to supply manufacturing and microfacturing industries. But now, with so much raw asteroid matériel streaming in at minimal cost, that energy-intensive processing of recycling old things was no longer financially viable.

Those fiscal conditions meant that obsolete items—for example, the Bureau's fifteen-year-old Black Mariahs—were simply disposed of in the most economic fashion possible.

Just before the four-by-four carrying Alik went through the hub, the last Black Mariah drove into the giant cylindrical airlock and the door swung shut. The heavy-duty rim seal engaged. Carbon monoxide and carbon dioxide from the big extractor towers flooded in.

After all the nitrogen and oxygen had been expelled from the airlock, the door at the other end of the big metal cylinder opened, exposing the portal behind it, which twinned to Haumea station. The pressurized toxic gases acted like a shotgun cartridge, blasting the Black Mariahs out into trans-Neptune space.

JULOSS

YEAR 591 AA

The fifteen boys and five girls that made up the Immerle clan's current senior year were clumped together in a big old plaza, in the shade of a dilapidated seventy-story skyscraper. They had spent six days exploring the ancient abandoned city as part of their training, investigating and analyzing unfamiliar environments. The trip had been scheduled to end nineteen hours ago.

Their flyer hadn't arrived. Their personal databuds had been glitchy for the whole expedition and had now dropped out of the planetary network. They were isolated, hundreds of kilometers away from the clan estate. Their supplies were low. They had no weapons. They were completely alone.

The meeting was generating a lot of nervous chatter and some outbreaks of near-panicked shouting as they tried to work out what to do. Suggestions were dismissed or endorsed abruptly. A plan began to emerge; they were to set up camp in a more sheltered spot. Weapons were to be improvised, signal fires to be lit—

Dellian smiled at that, remembering his own insistence about signal fires on the arid hillside where his yeargroup had been marooned. From his vantage point, perched unseen a hundred meters up the side of a nearby skyscraper, he could make out the worry and uncertainty on several faces, while a few of the boys had started to assume a more determined posture.

Time to stir things up.

His biologic pterodactyl's talons let go, and he fell for thirty meters, building velocity. Then his wings opened wide, producing a leathery rushing sound. The avian beast had undergone a few artistic modifications from the original predator that had roamed Earth's skies millions of years ago, specialist designers accentuating a more dangerous aesthetic. Dellian thought they might have been a little too enthusiastic; the big creature was practically a dragon.

He leveled out and powered between the tall empty buildings. The positioning had been selected with a hunter's instinct, keeping the sun behind him, its glare making him invisible to his prey. Genuine birds took flight, squawking in alarm as the huge marauder raced past, a giant flock flowing in a colorful super-geometry murmuration in the clear air.

On the ancient plaza floor below, the clanmates looked up at the sudden airborne commotion, squinting against the sun. Shouts of alarm burst out. Dellian swooped lower, crying out in a long, aggressive ululation. The clanmates began to scatter, sprinting for cover. His huge shadow flashed over them. It was all he could do to prevent himself from turning the ominous cry to laughter.

He pitched left, rolling the big body, swooping around the corner of a pyramid-shaped building, seeing the reflection of his fearsome shape fluctuate as it slid across a thousand silvered windows. Then the plaza was behind him and he banked again, wings slowly pumping to gain altitude, terrorizing yet more birds as he rose up and up.

The original pterodactyl had been more glider than hawk, but now muscles had been enhanced to pump the big sail-like wings, adding range and speed to its already formidable abilities.

Finally he circled the Bedial tower on the southern edge of the city and slipped down to a sedate landing on its flat roof, dodging the slender air-con heat-pump panels.

Reluctantly he pulled in his wings with a haphazard shake. His databud gave him visuals from the city's sensors, showing him the dispersal pattern on the plaza floor. The boys hadn't kept together, splitting into three main groups, with a couple of stragglers. The girls had stayed together and remained with one of the boy groups. Tactically advantageous, but he felt it had been a random dispersal. Their combat game training hadn't kicked in yet.

"Great Saints, that was pitiful," Xante sent.

"Yeah. They haven't adapted to the situation; they're still in soft mode."

"We should change that."

Dellian had to smile at the eagerness in Xante's voice. "We will, but gradually. If we suddenly confront them with a tsunami of threats, they might start wondering how come none of the predators were around while they were carrying out their training mission."

"I guess. That's the kind of thing that clued Yirella in back when we were stranded, wasn't it?"

Dellian's humor deflated. "Yeah. Something like that."

"So what do we do?"

"Give them a couple of hours, see how they react now they know the area isn't as passive as they thought. Then buzz them again. Both of us."

"Okay."

Dellian released the big pterodactyl from his command bond, keeping his attention on the databud's display to make sure it settled quiescently. Subsentient biologics had been known to get *quirky* when released from human control.

He opened his eyes and stretched on the long couch. Phantom

sensations tingled along his limbs as the boost sheaths abandoned the biologic's wing nerves. After riding the pterodactyl's neurology for three hours, he felt faintly resentful his human body couldn't actually soar through the sky. His subconscious was busy convincing him he was made out of lead.

The training mission control room was a wide circle, with two tiered levels surrounding a central hologram stage. The couches were on the topmost level, where operatives commanded the various artificial creatures that would soon be stalking the poor innocent clanmates—a threat scenario designed to trigger the instinctive teamwork they'd trained for all their lives.

The graduation exercise had been refined considerably in the four years since Dellian had crash-landed after his island resort holiday. The introduction phase was more gradual to avoid suspicion; the period the exercise was conducted over had been lengthened, allowing a broad range of talents to be brought out and utilized. And the area itself was given a much greater level of scrutiny beforehand, eliminating unforeseen problems like cougars suddenly cropping up and wrecking everything.

Dellian sat up and looked over at the next couch where Xante was lying. His friend was still riding his own pterodactyl, eyes closed, limb muscles twitching at random. Most of the twenty couches were currently unoccupied. The threat action wasn't due to be ramped up until later that evening, when darkness closed over the deserted city.

On the tier below, the training masters were busy monitoring their pupils, listening and watching. Dellian's overflight had certainly stirred things up, bestowing a sense of urgency lacking until now. He watched the watchers for a while. Tilliana was a section leader now, although the majority of the instructors were the clan's tutors, evaluating their protégés, with Fareana, this yeargroup's mentor, directing the overall setup. Over the years since Dellian's graduation, the boys who'd been boosted were gradually taking over the animal rider duties. This was his third graduation exercise, allowing him to put his combat training to practical use.

It was strange. He felt like he was looking into the past, seeing Alexandre in Fareana's place, with himself and his yearmates performing on the visual stage, while the training masters made sarcastic and amusing comments among themselves at the antics of the hapless trainees. And now he was one of the puppeteers. It was a sensation he could feel his cohort picking up on and puzzling—mainly because he wasn't entirely sure of his own emotions at the development.

"Taking a break," Dellian told Fareana, and received a quick nod of permission. He left the control room and went through a portal out into Eastmal's riverside park.

The city was now the capital of Juloss, mainly by default; it was the only inhabited city left on the planet. Located 4,000 kilometers north of the Immerle estate, it had a temperate climate Dellian rather enjoyed after growing up exclusively in the tropics. Living there gave him a somewhat melancholy glimpse into what life on the world had been like before the traveler generation ships portaled out, taking everyone else with them. Not that he was resentful, he told himself every day he walked through the busy streets.

As he walked, he zipped up his jacket. Autumn was coming, sending gusts of cooler winds across the broad river. All around him, the park's terrestrial trees were wrapping themselves in the spectacularly rich red and gold tones that signaled winter's approach.

For a while he walked slowly along the stone promenade, relaxing into the park's slower pace of life. Below him, on the dark water, swans glided about with arrogant grace. Almost all of this year's cygnets had lost their gray plumage now, transforming to a pristine white, except for a couple of black swans he could see farther downstream. They were the only ones in sight. He grinned forlornly at them. The ratio was similar to the boy-girl quotient within the clans.

Up ahead, someone in a long blue wool coat was leaning on the rails, dropping bread to the big birds. If he had any, Dellian decided, he would have thrown it to the black swans first in sympathy. Then he realized it was actually Alexandre who was feeding the swans, and back in their hangar the cohort reacted with happiness. He knew it wasn't coincidence.

Since he'd moved to Eastmal, Dellian hadn't seen much of their former mentor. It wasn't deliberate; they'd all been so busy in preparation for their starflight. And partying, he admitted guiltily; that was a really good part of city life.

"You're looking very fine," Alexandre said as they hugged in greeting.

Dellian kept his welcoming smile in place as hir gray eyes gave him a level appraisal. Inside, he was mildly shaken by his mentor's appearance. Sie was male cycled, as sie had been for the last seven years now. It was an usually long time to remain as one gender and an uneasy indicator of age. Not only did gender cycles last longer as people grew older, the transition phase was also extended. It wasn't detrimental, simply a sign of an older body slowing down.

Alexandre had been there for him his whole life, and Dellian didn't like to acknowledge sie was getting older. But now he looked closely, hir dark-blond hair was thinner now and becoming lighter from the rise of gray strands. It wasn't something he wanted to consider, that one day Alexandre wouldn't be there to turn to. Death was something he'd only encountered on rare occasions, except poor Uma and Doony that one wretched morning . . .

"You too," he replied.

Alexandre's grin widened affectionately. "You were always a rotten liar. That's why you were always in detention."

"No more than anyone else!"

"I know. Your whole year—it's a miracle any of us came out of the estate alive."

"But here we are."

"Aye, here we are. So how's the graduation exercise going?"

"Pretty good. They've missed some caches that'll be useful, but I just gave them a scare that should send them back to reevaluate everything. If not, Xante and I are due back later. That should kick them into gear."

"Ah, the pterodactyls. I remember the arguments we had about introducing those. Some felt it was taking things a step too far."

"They're magnificent."

"Yes, you would think that." Alexandre's hand squeezed his shoulder fondly.

"This yeargroup seems a little more cautious than we were, or more controlled, maybe. Changing the training routines has helped."

"Somehow, I don't think they'll ever be a match for your year."

"You made us."

"Aye, that we did."

"It's funny to think there's only three more yeargroups left, then it's over. All of us will be real soldiers, and the fight begins."

"The search begins," sie corrected gently. "Who knows? You may never see the final conflict. It might even have happened already."

"No. We'll see action. I know it. I will meet the Five Saints, and I don't want to let them down."

"Ah, the optimism of youth. So how is Xante?"

"Fine, thanks."

"Have the two of you moved in together?"

"Not quite. It's good the way it is. We enjoy each other, we're very similar in some ways, and the differences can be fun, too. We're happy."

"If it's not broke, don't try and fix it?"

"Something like that." Dellian gave up. "How is she?"

"Doing rather well, actually. She's smart enough to know she needs to understand herself. It's an arduous process. She can be quite stubborn, but her progress is exceptional. I never expected anything else."

"So she's getting better?"

"Yirella was never ill, Dellian. Just different from what we expected."

"Different? She killed Uma and Doony!" Some nights he still woke in a sweat thinking about it. To do that to your own muncs . . .

"She liberated herself," Alexandre said. "The only way she could.

Our arrogance gave her no choice. What we did, the life we gave her, the training and environment of the clan, was simply wrong for her. We are at fault, not her, and we didn't recognize that until too late. Now we have to give her the space and ability to become what she wants to be."

"And what's that?"

"I don't know. I'd settle for her being happy."

"Isn't she?"

"I believe she's in a position where that might be possible now. There was so much she had to unlearn, so much to be forgiven. But there are aspects of her life she is comfortable with now."

It was almost too painful to ask, but he couldn't not— "Does she . . ."

"Ask about you?"

He nodded silently.

"Of course she does. You meant a lot to her."

Meant, he thought, not *mean.* "Can I see her?"

"Not yet. But soon, I hope. She still hasn't quite separated you from what we were molding you and your yearmates into. I don't want to introduce the possibility of further conflict until I'm sure she can distinguish between what you are and what you will achieve up there among the stars." Hir head tipped back, and sie stared calmly into the clear, cool sky. "You are a strong resonance in her life, Dellian. Perhaps the strongest."

"I want to help."

"I know. And she knows that, too. But let me ask you this, would you give up everything you have worked for to be with her?"

"I . . . What would we do? We can't stay here and live a planetside existence."

"It's not just the battleships that will portal away. There will be one last traveler generation ship, too, for all us old folks."

"You're not old."

Sie raised a chiding eyebrow. "What was it I said about your inability to lie convincingly?"

"I wouldn't want you to be in harm's way. You deserve to see a fresh planet, and have a peaceful life."

"And you deserve your chance."

"That's what you made us for."

"Now you sound like her."

"You think that's a bad thing?"

"No. I always said it would be a mistake to make you all arrogant; it leads to overconfidence. Better you have doubts. That way you will always question what you see."

"Like she did. I prefer a simpler life. Give me a gun and point me at the enemy."

"You can cut the humility routine, too. It doesn't work with me."

Dellian glanced down at the swans. Without tidbits of bread, they'd lost interest and were sliding away. "Will you tell her I asked about her? Tell her I'll wait until she's ready. That I still care. That I always will."

"Of course."

"Good."

They embraced again. Dellian broke away, smiling. "Now I have to go scare the living crap out of those kids again."

"That's my boy."

Alexandre had a wistful expression on hir face as sie watched Dellian walk away. After a minute sie turned hir gaze to the nearby clump of tall maples. The grass around them was smothered under a matting of fallen leaves. Yirella walked out from behind the widest trunk. She put her arms around Alexandre and bent down slightly so she could rest her head on hir shoulder.

"Thank you," she said.

Sie patted her back. "I'm still not convinced this was a good idea."

"I needed to know how he affects me. Seeing him in the flesh was a good indicator. I'm glad he's got Xante. He needs someone."

"I must be firmer with you. I'm too easily manipulated."

"It's called integrity, and caring. Without you I'd be sitting in a nice comfy room with lots of happy juice in my veins."

"So what's the result?"

"I looked at him and saw the false beauty of nostalgia for something that I've idealized. We were friends for eighteen years, then lovers, briefly; nothing will ever again be so important in my life. I've managed to self-edit the bad times."

"I was there for all those eighteen years. There weren't any bad times."

Yirella pulled some of her wild hair from her eyes where the breeze from the river kept blowing it. "That's very sweet."

"He really does care, you know."

"I heard."

"Good. I'm not sure if we shouldn't be filling him up with happy juice in the room next to you."

"I'm happy enough without the juice, and that's mostly down to you."

"I didn't want to raise any false hope."

"He does question things now, doesn't he? I think I may have infected him."

"That's not a bad thing. We don't want gentens. We want humans."

"You're projecting a future you cannot possibly know."

"And as he would say: That's why we made all you wonderful binaries."

She smiled sadly. "He is what he is. We all are. Humans adapt to the circumstances of their era. I think it's time I accepted that and grew up. This is not what I wanted for myself, but in a thousand years' time it could be. Imagine what we could accomplish as a species if we weren't under threat, if we weren't constantly running. We almost made it before. We were given a glimpse of how high we can climb if we didn't have to huddle in the darkness out of fear. That's probably why I always loved the Sanctuary star story, even though I knew in my heart it was probably just a lure. Every planet like Juloss has the potential to become more than a stopover, an island harbor in the long voyage; then just as the opportunity opens, we have to flee once more. Imagine what our knowledge and tools could birth if we were truly free, and had the luxury of time. I think I'd like to help bring that opportunity to the galaxy. I'm going to go out there and join the Saints in their battle."

"I'm very glad to hear that, my dear."

"I won't be any use in the fighting, but there are other ways I can contribute."

"There are," Alexandre said. "But they must be ones you devote yourself to spontaneously. Not out of guilt."

Yirella looked back down the promenade, hoping to catch one last glimpse of Dellian, but he'd stepped back through the portal. "This isn't guilt speaking. It's understanding. My graduation exercise is finally over."

"Did you pass?"

"Yes. I believe I did."

THE ASSESSMENT TEAM

"You killed them both?" Callum asked in shock. "You killed Javid-Lee and Rayner? Bloody hell, man, why?"

I have to admit, I was somewhat alarmed myself. Rendition I could understand, even almost approve of. But such readiness to kill another person was disturbing. I expected it from someone as damaged as Kandara, but I'd assumed Alik Monday was, frankly, more refined.

Alik shrugged, unruffled by the reaction. "Think of Rayner and Javid-Lee as contaminants that needed venting. It's an appropriate analogy for those sons of bitches. Ain't no need to thank me, I'm just a public servant doing my job."

"You executed them. No! It was murder; simple as that."

"What was I supposed to do?"

"Rendition," Callum said hotly.

"Oh, yeah," Yuri called out with vicious glee. "*Now* rendition is acceptable, is it?"

Callum glowered at him.

"Strange as it may seem, I don't have the authority to order a rendition directly," Alik explained. "I would have had to go through the National Security procedure, and we'd have needed three tame judges to sign off on it. Sure, I'd probably have got it for Rayner and Javid-Lee, but that would have involved a whole bunch of other people. The whole problem was a clusterfuck Washington wanted to disappear fast. We got the media to write it off as gang warfare. And the two asshole families involved got to keep their frightened mouths shut for life. Actually, it was the best solution. Go me."

"Bloody hell!" Callum dropped his head into his hands.

There was a long silence in the lounge as everyone tried to come to terms with what we'd just been told. I found it interesting to see how being judged riled Alik. He really was that arrogant. A lot of senior government officials come to have the attitude that nothing they do should ever be questioned or challenged. But it did explain a lot. He hadn't turned up on this case for any other reason than he'd been told to. It was politics, pure and simple. He was a Washington creature, receiving orders and reporting back to the executive and the dark globalPACs. What he reported no doubt contributed to policy, but he wasn't a policy maker. He wasn't the one I was looking for, but I would be very interested in talking to this Tansan character at some time in the near future.

"What about the New York shield?" Jessika asked. "Have there been more attempts to bust the files since Cancer tried?"

"Beyond my pay grade, my friend," Alik said, splaying his hands wide.

Like any of us believed that.

"But I did hear the whole national shield project had some pretty sharp security upgrades after that night," he conceded.

"Civic shields were taken back under military jurisdiction twenty-two years ago," Loi said. "In America, at least. So someone must have taken the attempt seriously."

"Over half of Earth's nations have placed their urban shields under military control in the last fifteen years," Kandara said. "Those that still have a military."

"Why did Cancer want the shield files?" Jessika asked.

"We don't know."

"Wrong question," Callum said. "What did Cancer's employers want with the files?"

"When I find out who they are, I'll be sure and let you know," Alik said.

"It'll be money," Eldlund said in a knowing tone. "It always is with Universal types."

I thought Callum looked irked with his assistant for the jibe, but my impression of Eldlund was of a devout Utopial—more so than most omnia who never left the comfort of the Delta Pavonis system. Sie simply couldn't resist the opportunity to establish cultural superiority. I'd guess that was why immigration to Akitha had leveled out in recent years. There's an old saying in the Sol system: Utopial culture would be a great place to live in, but the problem is that it's full of Utopials. And Eldlund was a perfect example of that unconscious patronizing privilege they all possessed.

"How can it be for money?" Yuri asked.

"Shields have protected cities from severe weather for decades," Eldlund said in a tone that told us sie clearly felt sie was explaining the utterly obvious. "People are complacent; they take that protection for granted. So if a shield fails during a storm, there'll be plenty of damage. That will have a big effect on spending patterns and insurance payments. If you knew in advance that was going to happen, you could make a killing in the markets."

"Wow," Loi said. "I hope you never become a criminal mastermind. You'd be terrifying."

Eldlund gave him a knowing grin. "If whoever wanted the files could afford Cancer, you know it has to be a big deal, right? That's got to be a Wall Street playa."

Yuri pursed his lips as if in approval. "Good point."

You had to be as familiar as I was with my boss to see just how much he was humoring the poor jerk. I'd seen those tactics played in a dozen meetings. It nearly always ended with someone getting fired, or worse.

"So what happened to Colleana's brat?" Kandara asked. "You?" Her index finger lined up on Eldlund.

"No!"

Loi laughed out loud; everyone else was grinning.

"Who gives a crap what happened to the kid?" Alik grumbled.

"You haven't been checking back on Colleana after you were so noble with her insurance?" Yuri joined in, parodying disappointment. "Shame on you."

"Do I look like a fucking fairy godmother?"

"Stranger things," Callum proclaimed.

"Fuck you all!"

"What about Cancer?" Loi asked. "Are you still looking for her?"

"Sure," Alik said. "The Manila police lost her cabez, of course; she scrambled the city's logs good and hard. Langley assigned a dark team, but even they couldn't catch the scent. The bitch vanished like she always does. We'll catch her one day. And when we do, I'll be having a long conversation with her before we dump her naked ass on Zagreus."

"No, you won't," Kandara said.

Alik bridled at what he took to be a challenge. "Yeah, how do you figure that?"

"Because she's dead."

"No fucking way. I'd have heard."

"You didn't hear."

Alik gave her a suspicious look. "How do you know this?"

"Because ten years ago, I watched her die."

THE DEATH OF CANCER

RIO, AD 2194

Early morning on Copacabana beach, before the gold-skinned body gods began strutting their glistening physiques for the tourists and lovelorn to envy, the horizontal rays of the sun were playing across the water to create a dazzling shimmer. Not even Kandara's category-four sunglasses seemed to offer much protection from the glare. She pounded barefoot along the sand, careful to keep out of the long tire furrows. Every day, the city's heavy-duty sand rake servez came out in the hour before dawn, restoring Copacabana to an implausible level of purity in readiness for the daily crowds. In doing so, the wheels often left sharp ruts behind, which could trip the unwary before fresh tides and ten thousand playful feet trampled them flat again.

Just before reaching the southern end she turned around and ran back. Zapata, her altme, monitored her heart rate and oxygen consumption, splashing the data across her tarsus lenses. She used it to keep her pace steady, the optimal cardio routine she'd followed faithfully since leaving Heroico Colegio Militar twenty-four years ago. Proper diet, some simple telomere treatments, disciplined exercise, and her body had retained the stamina and speed of that twenty-one-year-old cadet.

Eleven minutes later she was closing on the other end of the beach, and more people were venturing out onto the sands. Stalls along the promenade were opening, the time-honored volleyball nets going up. Kandara slowed and walked over the Avenida Atlantica, her soles slapping the old wave-pattern mosaic as she made her way across to her apartment.

The high-rise hotels bordering Copacabana for close on a century had suffered the same economic fate as all hotels post–quantum spatial entanglement and had long since been redeveloped into blocks of luxury apartments above the street-level clubs and restaurants. Kandara had bought her own relatively modest apartment seven years ago. It was only on the third floor of the twenty-story building, but it did have a balcony that looked out over the beach.

When she opened the front door, King Jaspar, her elegant Burmese cat, was in the hallway, protesting loudly, as usual. Before she got him, she'd never heard a cat as loud. Mr. Parker-Dawson, her neighbor, wasn't talking to her anymore because of the "infernal racket"; he'd also lodged several complaints with the residents' board.

"All right," she told King Jaspar. "Calm down, I'll get your breakfast."

In response he just mewled even louder.

"Shut up. It's coming."

Another penetrating cry.

"Shut it!" Her bare foot shoved at the cat's silky fur. Not too hard, but enough that he'd get the message. She received a sulky look for her troubles.

"You little—" A hiss of exasperation escaped from her lips, and she made an effort to calm down. *Mother Mary, it's just a goddamn cat.*

Get a grip. "Come on." She bent down fast and scooped him up. Her finger tickled him under his jaw as she carried him through into the kitchen's small utility room. There was contented purring as she filled his bowl one-handed. Then as she put him down, an extended claw snagged on her Lycra running top. "Hell!"

Kandara glared at the fraying strands he'd tugged from the tight black fabric, now more annoyed with herself for the anger. The whole incident was like a feedback loop. *Ridiculous!* "Give me a status update on my neurochemistry and skull peripherals," she told Zapata.

Standing in the middle of the long living room with its tall houseplants and Mexican rug wall hangings. Hands on hips. Impatient for the scan results. Sweat from the run glinting on legs and torso as the sun began to shine sharp gold rays through the big balcony windows.

"Neurochemistry stable," Zapata announced. "Gland functionality one hundred percent."

She snarled. It would have been easy to blame the little gland. It was a complex, delicate piece of medical bioware, secreting a carefully regulated dose of dopamine antagonist, helping keep the schizophrenia locked away in the darkness at the bottom of her thoughts like a slumbering beast. So she couldn't blame her frustration on that. Maybe it was the run, pumping her up. Or the lack of work— over two months now. And it was no good calling around to her contacts. Work came to her, not the other way around.

She walked down the short hallway and opened Gustavo's door. Gustavo had about the same status in the apartment as King Jaspar; he was certainly equally dependent—her houseguest, her charity case, her work in progress, her release. She'd found him in an alley behind a swish club seven weeks ago, beaten badly by a furious husband's security team. He was nineteen and male-model handsome, so he explained, which was why he'd come to Rio in the first place, loaded up with excitement and hope. Except the modeling work had never arrived, despite his being on the books of three local agencies. Instead the agency bookers suggested he escort aging fashionistas to parties, *to be seen, darling, so the right people know your name*—a flesh accessory with far less value than their glittering jewelry and this-week couture. The fashionistas, colder and more calculating than any street pimp, began to pass him around their wealthy clients. He partied with them, smiled at their nonsensical jokes, then fucked them for half the night like only a virile teenager could. And when that stamina began to falter from the excesses, he took the right drugs to carry on regardless.

Gustavo was sprawled on the bed, snoring softly. She'd gotten him on a program, and he was staying clean; he'd even snagged a couple of gigs modeling sports gear and once as an extra in a music viz-u. But as charity cases went, she knew exactly what she was doing, and altruism didn't much enter into it. He was convenient. Nothing more.

Her heel knocked the door shut. The noise woke him, and his head came up, showing him blinking sleep-confusion away. She grinned down at him as she tugged the spoiled Lycra top off over her head.

"Holy mother, what time is it?" he croaked.

"It's morning."

"You haven't slept again, have you?"

"A few hours."

"You need to sleep more."

She wiggled out of her shorts. "I can sleep when—"

"You're dead. Yes. You keep saying."

"That's right." Kandara tugged his sheet away and climbed onto the mattress beside him.

There was a moment when he might have resisted. But instead he gave a sigh that played at reluctance. That left him soon enough as her hands moved proficiently across his lean body, banishing the last fog of sleep. After all these weeks she knew exactly how to rouse him, how to keep him hard while she rode him greedily. The sexual gymnastics her gened-up muscles let her perform on his bed never strayed into true intimacy. They were fuck-buddies, not lovers. All she wanted was the physical.

The doctors had cautioned her about her anger management. The glands infiltrating her mesolimbic pathway were not a cure, they said with their wise nodding heads; the neurochemicals would only treat the symptoms. In doing so there might be side effects.

Now she couldn't even remember how she used to think before her parents had been slaughtered. Which behavior trait was new, artificial, psychological, bioneural, divine . . . Her trio of driving daemons had been brought under control: psychopathy, hypersexuality, insomnia. She ruled them with an iron fist now, used them as she needed to, gifting herself the perfect personality for her work. An avenging angel, cleansing the world of unchecked evil.

After she'd finished with him, she watched with mild fondness as he quickly fell asleep again before she slipped out to shower. Breakfast was a smoothie of her own concoction, a half dozen different berries and yogurt (natural organic; she didn't do printed food if she could avoid it) mixed in her blender. She drank it, sitting beside the open balcony door, wearing a robe, her hair wrapped in a towel.

Gustavo wandered in when she'd already drunk half of the smoothie. He was naked, a beauty that competed with the view of the beach for her attention. "Sheesh, don't you have any real food?" he moaned.

"Such as?"

"Orange juice? Toast?"

"I'm sure they're out there on the street stalls somewhere."

"Okay, okay. I get it."

"I can mix some honey with yogurt for you."

"Gee, thanks." He slumped on a stool at the kitchen's small bar.

She grinned as she busied herself with the array of expensive cookery gadgets she'd carefully acquired for her galley kitchen. All organic ingredients blended carefully, the deep-fill tray heating up to the perfect temperature.

"That's yogurt?" he asked, puzzled, as she poured the thick, creamy liquid out of the blender and into a measuring jug.

"I'm making you waffles. My thank-you treat for this morning."

His smile won out against the sun.

"You got anything on for the rest of today?" he asked as he wolfed down the third waffle.

"Meetings," she said. Which wasn't quite true; she'd booked a couple of hours on the shooting range to keep up her proficiency. Then she was due to meet a dark supplier to review some of the new lethal peripherals coming out of northern Russia. She probably wouldn't have any implanted, but it would be good to know their capabilities.

"Can I come? I won't get in the way or anything. I could be your assistant."

"I don't think so. Not today."

He gave her a sullen look. "Fine. Sure. I get it. You think I'm stupid."

"No," she said, proud she wasn't sighing in exasperation. After she'd moved him in, she'd told him she was a freelance design refiner for algae reactor initiators, used extensively during the early stage of terraforming. It was a good holding lie. But she hadn't expected this hiatus to last so long. "You just need some basic qualifications to work in my sector."

"Yeah, like I'm ever going to have that."

"You could have, if you go to university."

"Sure thing, mother."

She gave him a sly lecherous smile and stood up. The uncertain look in his eyes was arousing. Her hand closed on the jar of organic manuka honey. "Would your mother do this?" she murmured, and opened the front of her robe, ready to pour the luxurious golden goo over her chest.

"You have a call," Zapata informed her. The identity icon of her European agent splashed on her tarsus lenses made her stop.

"Go take a shower first," she told Gustavo. The dramatic return of the pout made her laugh outright. He stomped back to his bedroom.

"Accept," she told Zapata.

"Good morning to you, my greatest client," the agent said. "How are you today?"

"Restless," she admitted. "I thought you were dead, or in jail."

"Like you haven't got a dozen others the same as me tirelessly hunting the worthy jobs."

"Maybe. If I do, they're a lot more tireless."

"I'm hurt."

"I'm sympathetic. Come on, what have you got for me?"

"The biggest. The job of legend, the one that never happens. This is your pinnacle, my dear. You can retire after this and bore everyone in the bar all night long with tales of your imminent sainthood."

"Bullshit. You said that about Baja."

"This time, though. Oh, yes, this time."

"I need a better agent."

"No, you don't, because no other agent could bring you a contract with Akitha."

A small, cold shiver of excitement ran up Kandara's spine. "Double bullshit! That's Utopial central. They wouldn't touch me with a bargepole."

"Desperate times, my dear. Can I tell them you're interested?"

"Is this on the level?"

"I guarantee it. I had to meet their representative in the flesh. That I never do. But for you . . ."

"What's the job?"

"Oh, yeah, like they're going to tell me."

"Mother Mary. All right, when do they want me?"

"Now."

"Seriously?"

"No offense, but if they want *you*, it has got to be monumentally urgent."

"Give me an hour." She looked down at the jar of honey she was still holding. "Make it two."

It was King Jaspar who was the biggest problem. Kandara wasn't entirely surprised by that. Gustavo was simple. She fucked him until the honey was all used up, then told him he had to go. She did the decent thing and paid a fortnight's rent for an apartment in the respectable hilltop neighborhood of Santa Teresa.

Rage. Screaming. Threats. Pleading. But in the end he packed his bag and stormed out, yelling impressively obscene curses on both her ancestors and descendants.

Easy. Now try booking a pedigreed Burmese into a decent cattery in Rio with a half hour's notice. It cost her more than the Santa Teresa apartment. After that she paid a lawyer to find King Jaspar a suitable new owner if she wasn't back in a month. Rule 101: Always treat every mission as if it's going to be your last. And in this case, she wasn't under any illusion. If the Utopials were asking for her, it was going to be something very serious indeed.

The Rio metro network took her to the international hub, from which it was three hubs to Bangkok. That was where it started to get more interesting. She had to take a civic radial out to Prawet, where the Utopial embassy was situated. As she walked through the interminable portal doors with her bagez trundling along behind, Zapata checked her neurochemical balance, which was perfectly level. She breathed calmly into a Zen state. Ready.

A minute later she was walking up the embassy's broad steps with fountains playing on either side. A Utopial called Kruse was waiting for her at the top, just in front of the main arched entranceway. Sie looked about thirty, with a mane of chestnut hair in which rainbow jewels glowed discreetly. Hir fawn tweed suit was very formal, with a skirt that came down over hir knees. Kandara had to tip her head up when they shook hands; Kruse was an easy forty centimeters taller than she was. But the omnia's smile seemed genuine enough.

"Investigator Martinez, such a pleasure," sie said.

"Likewise, and it's just Kandara." Being called *Investigator* threw her slightly, but if that was the way they were going to deal with her, so be it.

"Of course. This way, please, Kandara."

Kruse showed her through a smaller door at the side of the main entrance. A short hall led to a single portal door. Kandara stepped through. She knew immediately they were on a space habitat; her inner ear could detect the subtle difference of rotation-induced gravity. Zapata confirmed the change, linking to the local net and questing its metadata.

"This is Zabok," it told her.

Kandara had been expecting that. Zabok was the first large self-sustaining habitat built by Emilja Jurich, one of the founders of the Utopial movement. It was still an important center for them in the Sol system. There were several portals facing the one she'd just come through.

The ever-formal Kruse gestured to one. "Please."

"Nebesa," Zapata informed her after she'd stepped through. Details splashed across her lens. The Nebesa habitat orbited 100,000 kilometers above Akitha, a terraformed planet, itself orbiting Delta Pavonis.

Her inner ear detected another change, a slowing of the balance instability. Understandable. Nebesa was considerably larger than Zabok, making its rotation ponderous by comparison.

They walked along a brightly lit passage that opened out on a broad paved square. Kandara looked up, smiling as she took in the habitat's interior. The massive cylinders always engendered sensations of awe and reverence. Most people considered terraforming to be the greatest technological wonder humans had achieved. Nature had taken a billion years to produce multicellular life on Earth; now the human race could duplicate that process on a barren planet in under a century. But Kandara considered that a cheat; simply spreading microbes and seeds across sterile rock plains was merely carrying nature's banner forward. The habitats, however . . . Ripping asteroids apart, forcing their raw metal and rock into cylinders the size of some of the old nations on Earth, bringing new air and water to the interior of these defiant islands in space—that was real engineering, combining all of scientific history's knowledge into a victory over the most hostile environment possible: the empty universe itself.

"Magnificent," Kandara said quietly, breathing down the humid air, cleaner than anything the South Atlantic winds swept across Copacabana.

"Thank you," Kruse said in genuine appreciation.

Nebesa's interior was sixty kilometers long and twelve in diameter. What looked like a splinter of captured sunlight burned sharp along the axis, bathing the interior in a tropical glare. That surface was a mixture of long lakes studded with islands, confined by land coated in a lush rain forest. There were even some mountains, with slender waterfalls tumbling down rocky slopes. Clouds beset with odd curlicues twisted slowly through the air.

They'd emerged at the foot of a gently curving endcap. The base of it formed a ziggurat ring of black-glass balconies, extending two hundred meters above the paving where they stood, a vertical city that made her mildly dizzy tracing its course all the way around the rim until she was looking at the tiny ebony band directly overhead.

"How many people live here?" she asked, trying to do the math without using Zapata. Even if everyone had an apartment ten times the size of hers, the population could be measured in millions.

"Just over a hundred thousand these days," Kruse said. "It was more than twice that when the terraforming was at its peak. But everyone wanted to move down to Akitha when it was cleared for habitation. Now it's just the senior grade industrial staff and administration personnel."

"Uh huh."

"You sound like you disapprove."

"I don't get the Utopial grading system, that's all. I thought the ethos was equality."

Kruse gave a quick smile. "Opportunity is equal. People are not. In our society, you can progress as far as your talent and enthusiasm can reach."

"The same as everywhere."

"Not quite. Here everyone receives a fair share of society's produce, no matter the level of practical contribution you make. If you choose to do absolutely nothing for your entire life, you will still be fed and clothed and housed, and given access to medical treatment or education without prejudice. But in reality, a life of total leisure, or sloth, is rarely chosen. It is human nature to want to perform some kind of activity. The difference is we do not require it to be what the old communist and capitalist theories interpret as economically viable. With the introduction of Turings and fabricators, the human race has advanced to a technology level that has given us a self-maintaining industrial base. It can provide consumerist products at practically zero cost. Nobody should be regarded as a parasite or sponger, as your media condemns and shames your underclass. Here, if you wish to devote your life to developing obscure philosophy, or an artistic endeavor that is outside the mainstream, that is to be welcomed and encouraged as much as someone who commits to designing new technology or researching pure science."

"Some are more equal than others?"

"That is how the rich Universal rulers like to spin the Utopial ethos, yes. It is rather childish, don't you think?" Hir hand gestured proudly at the glorious cylindrical panorama. "Could a flawed society produce and maintain this?"

"I guess not."

"One day, everybody will live like this. Free from constraints."

"Indeed." All Kandara could think of when she looked at the tall Utopial was the local priest who had governed so much of her childhood. The scriptures, his ethos, could never be wrong; he would have a patient smile as he explained away every question bold young minds could think of to challenge God's implacable word. "So what now?"

"There is someone who wishes to meet you before you can begin."

"Sounds interesting."

.   .   .

It was quite a hike, which Kandara hadn't been expecting. She followed Kruse into the trees. They'd only gone a few hundred meters before the overhead canopy merged to a single luxuriant emerald roof. Slim beams of light slithered through the long leaves to dapple the ground. Trunks grew closer together and the undergrowth shorter. Several times they crossed narrow, arched wooden bridges with streams gurgling away below. Birds squawked loudly in the high branches, unseen from the ground. It wasn't long before Kandara took her linen jacket off; the still air was so warm even her trademark black singlet seemed excessive

Finally they came to a small clearing with a stream running along one side. There was a tent in the middle, all billowing white cloth with scarlet edging and bronze guy ropes. The only thing missing to complete the look of medieval pageantry was a royal pendant fluttering from the apex. The whole structure was ludicrously incongruous in a space habitat orbiting an alien star.

Kandara gave Kruse a skeptical look. "Really?"

It was the first time Kruse's urbane expression faltered. Sie pulled the opening curtain aside. "Jaru is expecting you." Sie hesitated. "Please be aware of the importance so many Utopials assign to hir, though sie will of course dismiss any such devotion."

Once again Kandara felt a tingle of unease at Kruse's piety. "Of course." She walked into the tent.

It was noticeably cooler inside. The fabric seemed to glow with a rich luminosity lacking in the stark light outside. Somehow the interior didn't surprise Kandara. The cushions, small fountain, and a single stiff-backed wooden chair all sang: humble yet mystic guru.

Jaru Niyom sat in the chair, draped in sea-blue monk-style robes; gaining an immense dignity by looking as old as anyone Kandara had ever seen. *It has to be theatre,* she thought. But then sie had already been old when telomere treatments first became available. Old yet rich.

Jaru was the only child of a wealthy Thai family; hir father had made a fortune in property development as Thailand's prosperity grew. They had been estranged when the elder Niyom had died from a stress-induced coronary at sixty-one, never quite able to come to terms with his cherished offspring becoming kathoey. Most assumed the more gentle Jaru would let the company dwindle, but the family's entrepreneurial gene wasn't recessive. Hir inheritance came at the same time as Kellan Rindstrom demonstrated quantum spatial entanglement. With a flash of intuition sie would often demonstrate in later life, Jaru immediately saw a way of advancing hir company's fortunes, benefiting the environment, and providing cheaper housing which the world so desperately needed.

Thailand became the first country to construct ribbontowns. Jaru bought (at a bargain price) hundreds of kilometers of the nation's motorways and expressway networks, along with the entire 4,000 kilometers of the State Railway network—all of which were becoming redundant as Connexion continued its inexorable advance of portal hubs across the globe.

Jaru began building houses along the abandoned train tracks. Big vehicles ripped up the asphalt and concrete of the roads, exposing the raw earth ready for new foundations to be sunk. What sie had realized was that Ainsley Zangari's notorious slogan was correct—everything truly was *one step away*. In this new age of instantaneous transport, habitation didn't need a civic center anymore. All the facilities like schools, hospitals, and theatres could be accessed no matter where your home was physically located; you just needed a portal door nearby.

It was a model swiftly copied by the rest of the world. With governments desperate for the cash that selling obsolete roads and railways to developers would raise, and solving the global housing crisis at the same time, the resulting construction boom went on to save (or at least salvage) many economies suffering from the collapse of the traditional transport industries.

Multibillionairedom allowed Jaru to expand hir commercial interest out into the burgeoning space industries, constructing new habitats on Sol's asteroids. Then, in 2078, as a direct result of nine über-corporate habitats declaring themselves low-tax nations open for business, sie sponsored the First Progressive Conclave, where fifteen more idealistically minded space-based billionaires pledged to birth a true post-scarcity civilization for the human race. Each of them committed their habitat to an economy based on a Turing-managed self-replicating industrial base. It was the start of the whole Utopial movement.

Kandara didn't need any prompting to duck her head in a small bow of acknowledgment. "It's an honor to meet you."

"You are kind," Jaru said with a melodic voice. "Though I fear at my age I am no longer terribly spectacular."

"Age is wisdom."

Sie chuckled. "Age *can* be wisdom. It depends how you spend those years."

"True." Kandara was aware of Kruse coming into the tent behind her and bowing deeply.

"Are you acquiring wisdom, Kandara?" Jaru asked.

"My life has a purpose. You know that. It's why I am here."

"Of course. This is why I asked to meet you before we commit to this course of action."

"So you can judge me?"

"Yes."

"You are free to ask me whatever you wish. But please bear in mind my former clients have full confidentiality."

"I don't wish to know the darker commercial details of corporations. I am interested only in you."

"I'm not a serial killer who's found the perfect cover. Nor am I a sadist. If a client wanted someone to suffer before death, I would turn the job down. I execute people. It's that simple."

"What about those who can be redeemed?"

"If the person causing you trouble can be redeemed, you don't need me."

"So you judge us in turn, then?"

"Everybody judges everyone else. I don't deem myself infallible. I hope and believe I haven't made a mistake so far. Everyone I've been called upon to deal with has deserved what happened to them, in my view."

"Surely, we would be better served by you arresting these criminals and quietly renditioning them to Zagreus?"

"Again, if you can deal with them that way, you don't need me. I'm here for the ones who won't come meekly, or who are so far along their path that a fight to the death is what they want—consciously or otherwise."

"Is this a quest for revenge, then?"

"I don't want any more children to suffer as I did. If you want to call that revenge, feel free."

"You sleep at night, then?"

Kandara narrowed her eyes as she studied the ancient wrinkled face for any hint of guile, wondering if the Utopials had cracked her medical files. "My conscience is clear."

"I wish I could say the same."

"I can walk away if you'd like. No offense will be taken. No regrets."

"I believe we are past that point now," Jaru said sadly. "The senior council has made its decision based on the level of extremism we appear to be facing. I do not dispute this. If those who are harming us do not surrender to authority, then they must be dealt with. I simply wished to see what kind of person you were."

"I'm sorry to be the serpent in your Eden."

"I never deluded myself we could achieve a truly peaceful egalitarian society without suffering misfortunes along the way."

"I am a last resort. Most of my clients regret having to call me in, but they seldom have any choice."

"So it would seem. I cannot express how disappointed I am that people are so hostile to us."

"They fear you," Kandara said, "for you are change. And change frightens people, especially those with the most to lose as that change is enacted."

"You approve of us?" sie asked in charmed surprise.

"Yes. The economics you seek to replace are those which ultimately resulted in my parents' murder. How could I not approve?"

"Yet you have not come to live with us."

"My skill set has no place in your culture. When the human race comes to accept the Utopial ethos, embraces it even, then I will settle here with you—if you'll have me. Until then, I will always be needed."

"You may be in for a long wait. We are a small nation. The number seeking to join us is disappointingly few."

Kandara glanced wearily at Kruse, uncertain how the acolyte would respond to the immutable doctrine being questioned. "Do you mind if I tell you how I see it?"

"Acceptance of truth is fundamental to our ethos. To determine truth we must first listen to all opinion."

"Okay: You went too far too quickly."

"The Turings were nothing new, nor was the level of sophistication in the fabricators that manufacture our technology. The asteroids provide us with unlimited elements. Solarwells supply eternal energy. Synergy between such diverse developments was inevitable."

"Yes, but they were just the economic factors. You took it a stage further."

"Ah." Jaru smiled gently. "The omnia."

"Yes. You were asking too much of people. You offer converts to the Utopial ethos all the material goods they could want, practically for free, but first they have to accept the gender change."

"We prefer the term 'gender expansion.'"

"Whatever. The material benefits of post-scarcity shouldn't be wholly dependent on pimping the DNA of your children."

"But, dear child, the formation of Utopial society was never just about physical rewards. The Universal culture provides much to its citizens—to a great many of them, in fact. Today there are fewer living in relative poverty than ever before."

"So why insist on the omnia-only clause?"

"Because I seek more from people. I seek universal equality. And the most basic inequality is that caused by a binary gender. It fuels every disparity and bigotry present in the so-called Universal culture. It condemned our history on Earth to variants of the same mistakes because, before genetic modification, it could not be eradicated. I know this. In my youth I experienced it in ways you should be thankful you will never encounter. It is worse than any of the miseries brought about by the old foes of religion, capitalism, communism, and tribal nationalism. Those can all be cured in time with education and love, but genders would remain unless we took action." Hir hand was extended palm outward toward Kruse. "And now . . . even that problem has been solved. Quite beautifully, too."

Kruse beamed worshipfully. "Thank you."

"Nice theory," Kandara said. "But all you've done is set up an admittedly worthwhile society that exists in parallel to the majority society. You're not changing anything."

"The Universal factions are in constant conflict," Kruse said darkly. "They will fall as we will rise."

"Which is why I'm here," Kandara concluded. "Not falling the way you hoped, huh?"

"Their hostility is unremitting," Jaru acknowledged with a profound sigh. "And recently they have advanced that enmity to a level it is impossible to brush aside as petulance. They seek to inflict physical harm. Much as I would wish it, I am not Gandhi. My father's pragmatism remains strong in me."

"Tell me what you need," Kandara said.

"A group of Universal activists has been sabotaging our design bureaus. Some of the most promising research has been stolen and our results corrupted. They are damaging us, Kandara, quite badly— though that cannot be admitted in public. We don't know where they came from or who sent them. They elude us. Find them. Stop them."

Kandara nodded solemnly. "It's what I do."

"We've put a team together for you," Kruse said as they walked back through the trees.

"Oh, really? What kind of team? And who's we?"

"Our Home Security Bureau. We brought in a variety of experts and advisors. It is their task to track down the physical location where the attacks come from."

"Okay, that's good." Kandara had been expecting to use some of the specialists she was familiar with, but she was prepared to give Kruse's people a chance.

A portal door in the habitat's endcap took them down to a hub on Akitha. Seven hubs later, they reached the central metrohub of Naima, a city of some 700,000 inhabitants sprawling across the southern side of a large island. From there it was ten hubs around a metro loop to the street where Kruse had assembled the team.

Kandara stepped out of the hub and immediately dabbed at the sweat that was starting to bead on her brow. Naima was part of an archipelago in the equatorial zone, making it considerably hotter and more humid here than it had been back in Nebesa. They'd emerged into a white stone plaza that was several hundred meters above a calm indigo ocean. Naima occupied the rugged slope on all sides, comprised of modest stone-and-glass buildings that Kandara felt were a little too similar. It put her in mind of the Tuscan villages she'd visited in her childhood, when her parents had spent several weeks in Italy on management courses at their employer's head office. Pretty and peaceful, if bland.

They walked along the broad road with its central sentry line of tall palm trees, her bagez rattling over the authentically uneven cobbles behind her. A minute later they arrived at the villa. It squatted at the top of a small cliff, with a glass-walled living room presenting a magnificent view across the broad, curving bay below the city. In the distance, a clutter of small pillar-like rock islands stood proud from the sun-sparkled water. Beyond the open doors, a paved patio stretched out to an infinity pool. When Kandara walked over to it, she realized most of the pool must be supported on pillars; only the house itself was sitting on the terraced cliff.

"Okay, this will do," Kandara admitted.

"The team is in the kitchen," Kruse told her.

Naima might have been Italianate, but the kitchen clearly followed a more Nordic tradition—a minimalist spectacle of black-and-scarlet marble, with a dozen worktop recesses from which various culinary devices could slide out as required, looking more like sculptures than practical machinery. She tried not to show any envy, but it made her little kitchen seem quite tired in comparison.

Three people were sitting at the long crystal table in the middle of the pale-oak flooring, sipping wine from tall-stemmed glasses.

A rebuke was starting to form in Kandara's head. It was ridiculous; these people were acting like they were on some kind of delightful weekend break, not setting up a covert op that was likely to end with smoking ruins and dead bodies.

Two of them were clearly Utopial omnias—their height alone evidenced that—while the third was shorter and female. Kandara didn't think she was just female cycled, not that she could explain her conviction. Hopefully, it was solid detective's intuition.

The trio rose to greet her, smiling warmly.

"This is Tyle," Kruse said, introducing the tallest, who had sandy hair and a slim dark mustache with the tips precisely trimmed in neat curls. "Our network analyst."

"Excited to be working with you," Tyle said. Hir voice was high, and eager. Kandara thought sie was genuinely young, maybe in hir late twenties. But then hir sharp features were so disturbingly close to Gustavo's she felt she was being haunted.

"Oistad, a defensive program operator."

Sie was almost as tall as Kruse, but with thick honey-blond hair that came over hir shoulders in languid waves. The flowing blue summer dress sie wore left Kandara no doubt sie was in full female cycle. As always, age was difficult to pin down these days, but to Kandara the poised manner spoke of someone over half a century.

"And Jessika Mye, a strategic profiler."

Kandara shook hands cautiously. "What exactly is that?"

"It means I take a look at the crimes and how they were committed, the motivation behind them, and try to work out what's coming next." She shrugged. "I used to work for Connexion Security, so I have some experience."

"They brought you in, too?" Kandara asked in surprise.

"No, I was already here. I decided I prefer the Utopial life, after all. Long story, but I was Utopial before—lost faith, then regained it."

"Okay then." Kandara sat at the head of the table, pointedly refusing the glass of wine Tyle offered. "Not while I'm working."

Tyle pulled the glass back sheepishly.

"Brief me, please," Kandara told them.

Akitha's research institutes had been under attack for years, they said. Teams from Sol's dynamic and greedy companies got sent to Akitha, where they cracked files on anything that they believed was going to have commercial value. That data got fed into corporate design offices, improving consumer products that were the economic bedrock of Universal worlds.

"Blatant theft," Tyle said. "And it's crazy. We release all the data anyway. That's the Utopial way; we want everyone to benefit."

"Not quite so crazy," Jessika said. "It's a fairly basic market force. If you can get something into production before your rivals, you establish a good sales lead. Also, stealing is a lot cheaper than having a big expensive research team of your own."

"It is about the assignment of value," Kruse said disdainfully. "If something people want or need is limited, if it becomes rare, consequently it acquires value. That's the foundation of old-era economics. Giving a *thing* value is the end of equality and sharing. That is how so-called Universal culture maintains its status quo, by monetary force, controlled by the unelected elites. By taking our ideas from us and using them to enhance their wealth, they are inflicting a double violation upon us."

"Sure, I get that," Kandara said with careful neutrality. "But what we're dealing with here sounds like standard-issue industrial espionage. That's been around as long as industry itself."

"Data theft is just the first crack in the dam," Tyle said. "It has been an annoyance for decades, but what else can you expect from Universal-culture corporations, right? So we didn't put as much effort into preventing it as we should. There always has to be a balance between freedom and restriction; that is fundamental to any society. Without law there is anarchy. But too much law, applied rigorously, becomes oppression. Here on Akitha, of course, we favor as little restriction as possible—something that has been exploited ruthlessly by the corporations. Our mistake."

"Hindsight is always the clearest vision," Kandara told hir.

"It means our networks are not as secure as they should be, and they're susceptible to black routing. We're working to rectify that, of course, but fortifying an entire planetary network is no small task."

"And the activity of these Universal agents has changed," Kruse said. "They no longer simply steal our work for their own profit. More recently they have begun launching acts of sabotage."

"On what?" Kandara asked.

"Industrial facilities," Oistad said. "It's relatively subtle. Refineries lose efficiency; component failure in manufacturing facilities increases due to glitched management routines, decreasing productivity. The rate of these attacks has been gradually increasing. We're upgrading our electronic countermeasures, but we're behind on security development. Even our G8Turings have trouble defending themselves against the more sophisticated intrusion attempts."

"Your G8Turings are vulnerable?" Kandara asked in surprise. G8Turings had only been coming online in the last six months, almost in accordance with the Robson law of progression, which said the rate of development would double between each generation. Though they'd taken slightly longer than expected to develop, the G8Turings should have been utterly secure.

"They can't be cracked, obviously, but defense absorbs more of their processing capacity than I'd like. The G8Turings produced by commercial companies are more evolved in that regard."

"And this is why you brought me in?" Kandara asked skeptically. "A few items in short supply?"

"No," Jessika said firmly. "There's been a tipping point. Three weeks ago, the public biolife center here in Naima was subject to an intense digital assault. The entire production facility was taken off-line. Black routing opened a clean channel into the network. They penetrated the management routines so deeply, they even overrode safety limiters; the machines suffered actual physical damage from overloads. That all had to be repaired. And sleeper bugs were left behind. The entire network architecture has to be wiped and re-booted. And even that doesn't guarantee the bugs are eliminated; they're highly adaptive."

"What does the biolife center produce?" Kandara was very aware of the glances the team exchanged as soon as she came out with the question. For a moment she wondered if it was some kind of weapons research, a nice dirty little secret at the heart of Utopial society. *They have to have some kind of physical deterrent, surely? A way to defend themselves.*

"Naima produces ninety percent of the planet's telomere treatment vectors," Oistad said gloomily.

"We've had to implement rationing," Kruse said. "Treatment therapies have been delayed. We're now buying in vectors from Universal companies, but even they don't have enough. They use demand-match supply systems; nobody stockpiles anything these days, it's not *economically viable*. We were an unexpected new market."

"The big nine pharmas were delighted, of course," Jessika said. "But they're frustrated, too. By the time they expand their production facilities to meet our requirements, we'll have the Naima biolife facilities back up."

"So all that's happened is the price of the Universal vectors has risen, making the treatments more limited for everyone. Supply and demand." Kruse said it as if she was uttering a profane curse.

Kandara suspected that, in a way, sie was. "That's not good," she admitted.

"Thank you for your empathy," Kruse snapped.

"If you wanted a therapist, you came to the wrong person."

"They knew what they were doing," Jessika said. "They knew the effect damaging the telomere therapies would have. It's an attack on the fundamental principles of our society. In any decent civilization, healthcare is a right, not a privilege. Even their own, the Universals, suffered from this action."

"I see why you called me in," Kandara said. "Life expectancy is precious. Take a day away from everyone on a planet, and you've killed centuries of human life. It's subtle, but very real."

"I hoped you'd understand," Kruse said.

Jessika gave Kandara a sly conspiratorial smile, which quickly vanished. She drained her wineglass. "So. We've been trying to track down where the black routing originated from."

"And?" Kandara asked.

"We have absolutely no idea. Their routines are better than ours. They left nothing behind."

Kandara looked around the table, taking in for the first time just how glum some of them appeared. "So you're not going to find the source, are you? Not now?"

"If you can't backtrack the load point within a day, then no," Tyle said.

"What do you need to find it?" she asked. "Better routines? I know some experts we can bring in. Good ones."

"I'm not that bad. And I have been given the Bureau's G8Turing to work with."

"Then how do we catch them? Give me a best-case scenario."

"The dark routines are easiest to detect when they are being infiltrated into the target network. If we could just be monitoring that when it happened, we can backtrack effectively."

"So you have to upgrade security monitor routines."

"We are doing that, but there are hundreds of thousands of individual networks on Akitha. I told you, it will take time."

"All right," Kandara said. "Then we need to narrow it down. Jessika, you're supposed to be analyzing the strategic pattern. Is this one team or several?"

"We think there are up to fifteen industrial espionage groups currently operating here on Akitha, but most of them are only involved in theft. Judging by how infrequent these active sabotage attacks are, maybe one every six weeks, that suggests a lone team. They're being cautious and covering their tracks well."

"Okay. Do you keep track of all non-Utopial citizens in the Delta Pavonis system?"

"Certainly not," Kruse said.

"Really? Connexion Corp can find anyone using their hubs—any time, any place."

"Because Ainsley Zangari's company is an oppressive component of the Universal plutocracy. Our portal transport network is public; we don't spy on our citizens."

"Yeah, you've got civil liberties busting out of your pants. I get it. How about: Can the public network be used to watch for individual people in an emergency?"

"Theoretically, yes," Tyle said. Sie grinned at the annoyed glance Kruse directed at hir. "There's a sensor on every portal. Even we need basic police procedures."

"We'd need an order from the Superior Court," Kruse said.

"You haven't got one already?"

"We thought we could find these criminals through their digital signature."

"Right. So talk to whoever you have to, and get a warrant."

"A warrant for every non-Utopial in the Delta Pavonis system? I'm not sure we'd ever get that."

"A warrant for every region when this team finally tracks down a possible location," Kandara said. "That's the absolute minimum we need here. Without that, we're just wasting our time."

Kruse nodded. "I'll call my Bureau chief." Sie went out onto the patio, leaning on the railing to stare down at the ocean with its distant towering islands.

Kandara looked around at the others. "Seriously, you've got nothing after three weeks?"

"I know," Tyle said bitterly. "It's a shit result. We're not used to something of this magnitude."

"Not just that," Jessika said. "It's the nature of the people we're up against. They are very professional, and experienced. I keep telling the Bureau we should run an exchange program with equivalent Sol agencies; that way our operatives gain experience and understanding. But . . ."

"Too proud, huh?" Kandara guessed.

Everyone glanced out at the figure silhouetted at the end of the patio.

"Stubborn," Oistad said. "Self-righteous. Needlessly independent. It's a big thesaurus out there."

Kandara looked at each of them around the table. "Have you guys ever worked together before?"

"This collaboration is bright shiny new," Jessika said, and poured herself some more wine. "The Bureau brought us together because we're the top of our respective fields. So that's got to work well, right?"

"We do help each other," Oistad said.

"Some," Tyle said. He glanced out at Kruse. "We need direction."

"It's called leadership," Oistad said, flinching. "You don't get a lot of that here on consensus-world. I'm not criticizing. I love Akitha and what we've built here. The trouble is we have no familiarity in dealing with something at this level."

"Yeah, I see that," Kandara said. She stood up. "I need to think."

"You're not quitting, are you?" a worried Tyle asked.

"Don't worry; I don't give up on contracts I've agreed to. Professional pride. You're stuck with me."

Kandara's room had a set of wide glass doors opening onto the overhang patio. She unlocked the clothes section of her bagez and let a house servez put everything away in the closet, except her dolphin-skin swimsuit. Her mind was racing as she slipped it on, running through everything the so-called team had given her. It wasn't good.

She was used to working with top-grade corporate security or deniable spooks with bottomless accounts of dark money.

The infinity pool was barely long enough to take five strokes before she had to flip. Warmer, too, than the one in her Rio gym.

So many first-planet problems.

After twenty minutes she took a breather, clinging on to the drop-edge of the pool, so she could look down across Naima. The boulevard lights were coming on as the sun dipped below the horizon, creating a wan blue-green haze over the coastal town. Out on the sea, sailing boats were making their way back to the marinas. All very peaceful and bijou.

"This doesn't make any sense," she told Zapata.

"In what way?"

"Shutting down factories is an inconvenience, but it's not going to kill off Utopial society. In fact, all it's done is wake them up to how shitty their digital defenses are. In another six months Akitha will be immune to sabotage."

"Sabotage at this level. If digital attacks are thwarted, the perpetrator may step up a level to physical assaults."

"Sure. So if you're prepared to attack telomere vector production, why not go straight to inflicting physical damage? And while we're at it, who the hell genuinely wants to smash a whole planet full of people back into the Stone Age?"

"There are a great many zealots with extreme ideologies, even today."

"*Even today*. I hate that phrase. It assumes we're constantly improving."

"Is the human race not improving socially?"

"Don't see it myself. Like I told Jaru, this Utopial society of hirs isn't the answer. The way they've insisted any immigrants' second generation is always omnia is a dead end structure. All it's done is create a separate culture—which, incidentally, never stops whining on about its superiority. That always ends well."

"Then it is not unusual for such a culture to be subject to attack from ideological rivals."

She pulled a face. "I don't buy it. This is an odd assault. There's something else going on here."

"What?"

"Mother Mary!" she said out loud. "I don't know. I don't get hired to figure things out. My bit's the simple part at the end."

"Talking to yourself?"

Kandara looked around. Jessika was standing on the other side of the pool, a small smile on her lips as she held up a couple of wine-glasses.

"Sorry," Kandara grunted and climbed out of the pool. "I was try-ing to work something out. Don't know why I bother. Altmes aren't exactly G8Turings."

Jessika gave her one of the glasses. "Something wrong with this crime-fighting setup? I'm so disappointed you think that."

Kandara grinned. "It's fucking amateur hour. If this is how they tackle fanatics, the whole Utopial concept is doomed. You should pack your bow and arrows and head for the hills."

"Yeah, I've been biting my tongue since I got here."

"Didn't you tell Kruse we need professionals to work something like this?"

"Actually, Oistad and Tyle are good at what they do. And you and me, we are the professionals."

"Mother Mary help them." Kandara raised her glass in salute and sipped some of the wine; it was sweeter than she was expecting, and nicely chilled. Not bad.

Jessika glanced into the kitchen, where Kruse was now back at the table, in earnest conversation with the other two. "What we lack is leadership. Kruse and her Bureau were assuming that if you bring me and Tyle and Oistad together with a decent G8Turing, we'd have no trouble tracking down the perpetrators. Then all we have to do is stand back while you go in and eliminate them."

"Yeah. But there's something about this whole sabotage thing that bothers me."

"I know. They can't see it, but the cost-benefit ratio is all wrong."

"Excuse me?"

"People like Kruse, they genuinely don't get *old-economy* finance. Too enlightened. Here, if something needs to be done, it is done. Hey presto! With post-scarcity resources, no one thinks about the cost of anything, until you reach macro-projects like terraforming. But those are all political decisions reached democratically, and the manufacturing facilities are incorporated into what passes for this society's budget. If something is truly expensive in terms of resources, you don't borrow money to pay for it, you act rationally and spread the cost out, devoting what you can afford each decade. Timescale isn't so important now that we all live for a couple of centuries. It's all very nice and rational."

"Living within your means."

"Exactly. Which is why they don't see the problem. It costs commercial companies a lot to place an industrial espionage team here. Most of them pass themselves off as immigrants, converts to Utopials, looking for a better life and embracing the great new future culture. Immigrating here is easy enough; this is the second time I've done it. The only real requirement is that you agree to have baseline genome editing for any kids you have after you arrive."

"So that they're omnia. Yeah, ideologically that stinks."

"To you, yes. And it does kind of reinforce the difference between us and them."

"Actually, I liked Jaru's equality theory. Fuck knows I put up with enough shit from misogynistic pricks while I was in the military. I just think . . . there's got to be a different solution. Write me down as an old reactionary, I guess." Kandara grimaced at the slip and drank some more wine.

"So this is how a standard industrial espionage goes," Jessika said. "You're a professional gang tech that gets hired to steal data. You settle in your new town and go to barbeques with your neighbors, play sports in the local league—basically, blending in. But by night, you're a secret supervillain, you spend your time online black-routing malware to try and bust medical research files. You succeed, and your corporate employer earns a billion wattdollars from a revolutionary new headache vector. Like I said earlier, it's cheaper than paying a research team. Cost effective. But *this* . . . You get no benefit other than making your ideological enemy better prepared to resist further sabotage. Who can afford it?"

"There are a lot of zealots out there. Trust me, cost never deterred fanatics."

"Okay, so where did this sabotage team get their money from? Their digital ability is astonishing. Tyle is convinced their routines were formatted by a G8Turing, and there aren't many of them anywhere. So far only governments and the bigger companies have them."

"I don't know," Kandara said. "Maybe we are overlooking the obvious?"

"The Universal governments genuinely feel threatened by Utopials? It's a Cold War for our century?"

"Technically, that fits. But I'm thinking: just one team? Even if you're completely paranoid, that isn't how a government works. They have backups, fallbacks, hungry acolytes in training, whole departments given over to an ideological enemy's downfall."

"Okay: one rich bigoted billionaire, or a globalPAC. They don't care, and don't think logically. Or there's something else altogether going on."

"Urrgh." Kandara tensed up. "You know you're preaching to the converted, right? It's just that I can't figure out exactly what's wrong about this."

Jessika shot a glance at Kruse, who was staring glumly at the kitchen table. "Logically, given a poor cost-return, the sabotage is a diversion."

"For what?"

"Exactly the question we should be asking. When I raised it, I got shot down."

Kandara raised her gaze to whatever heavens occupied the sky above Akitha. "Oh, great. You want me to be your patsy."

"That's Trojan horse. But I think messenger is more accurate. Sie might listen to you. You are the expert, after all."

"I fucking hate office politics!"

"Me too." Jessika drained her glass and sauntered back into the villa. Kandara glared at her back, but she knew she was right.

"The attacks are a subterfuge?" Kruse said incredulously half an hour later when Kandara had changed back into her singlet and shorts and rejoined everyone in the kitchen.

"I don't know. But we have to cover all possibilities. Especially this one, as it might offer a route to tracking down the team launching these attacks. You cannot overlook this opportunity."

"But . . . what are we looking for?"

Kandara was pleased she managed to avoid looking at Jessika. "I'd suggest you review the networks that have suffered the attacks."

"We already have," Tyle said. "No other secure files were cracked."

"Even if you could guarantee that, which I don't believe you can, that's not what I want."

"So what are we looking for?"

"Some kind of pattern. Something common to every attack. Start by finding out what other science projects were using the same network."

Tyle gave Kruse a questioning look. "It wouldn't hurt. We haven't got anything else."

"All right," Kruse said. "Do it."

.   .   .

It must have been something about the bed, or maybe planet-lag time difference. Kandara slept for almost three whole hours, waking at four o'clock local time when the town was still buried beneath the clear night sky.

She lay flat on her back, eyes open but unable to see the ceiling behind the dense grids of fluorescent data that Zapata splashed across her tarsus lenses. The other four had spent most of the night reviewing the affected networks; there were hundreds of research and development projects sharing each one. The Bureau's G8Turing had sorted them into categories and attempted to match them, but there was no real pattern—not with the types of projects involved. Even the amount of resources they'd been allocated had no relation to where the attacks took place. She grinned at that grid column, suspecting Jessika had been the one insisting they provide a cost analysis. But in the end there was nothing. That was the problem with pattern analysis; you had to define the parameters correctly. *If it was easy, everyone would do it.*

So she began to feed in her own parameters, sending the columns twisting into new formations.

At five o'clock Kandara stalked down the villa's main corridor, banging on the bedroom doors. The team appeared grudgingly, rubbing sleep from their eyes, robes and PJs disarrayed as they ambled into the kitchen. They found Kandara operating the sleek coffee machine; she'd already filled a teapot with English Breakfast tea, allowing it to brew.

"What?" Kruse demanded.

"I've found the pattern," Kandara told hir.

"What is it?" Jessika asked sharply.

Kandara grinned. "Weapons."

"We don't have any weapons projects," Oistad protested.

"Which is why you didn't find the pattern."

Kruse sat at the big glass table and snagged a cup of coffee. "All right, show us how smart you are."

"I'm not smart. I got paranoid."

"Ah," Tyle exclaimed. "Developments that could potentially be adapted for weapons usage."

"Damn right."

"Which are . . . ?" Kruse asked.

Kandara raised a hand and started ticking off on her fingers. "The factory that produces pipe drilling remotes used by your water utility services, attacked nine weeks ago, that one shared a network with three teams researching lincbots. It's been a goal for decades, bots that can mechanically cling to each other to multiply their overall physical size and strength, and simultaneously network their processing power. We have lincbots, but the concept has plateaued; the network connectivity protocols are difficult to establish and glitchy even then. Your people are working on bots from ant-size up to big-dumb mechs. The ant-size are particularly interesting; when they linc up it's called the dry-fluid effect, where these things swarm in units of up to half a million. Picture a nest of army ants in perfect synchronization but with added intelligence—and purpose. I don't want to think of the damage they could inflict on a flesh body. While a clump of linced big-dumbs could take out entire city blocks."

"Okay, I'll give you that could have aggressive applications," Kruse said. "What else?"

"The molecular bond fabricators. That research had spin-off research on shields. Obvious." Kandara sipped her green tea, putting her thoughts in an order that would make the most compelling argument. "Then there was last month's attack on the assembly core that puts together relays for the planetary power grid. That network was hosting a university lab working on magnetic confinement systems—also for power applications, mainly MHD chambers, which the solar-wells use." She glanced around the blank expressions, enjoying the moment. "No? These ones are small-scale confinement chambers, with monopolar magnetic field generators—very powerful. Perfect for spaceships with plasma rockets—or maybe missiles."

"Oh, come on!" Oistad objected.

"Coherent X-ray beam emitter tubes, for micro-medical applications. Scale that up and you have gamma and X-ray beam weapons."

Tyle and Kruse exchanged a look.

"Damn," Jessika muttered.

"You said it," Kandara said. "The data attacks are irritants. This, on the other hand, takes everything to a whole different level."

"But why?" Kruse asked, genuinely puzzled.

"One aspect at a time," Kandara told hir. "Let's try and confirm there is a pattern first. Tyle, can you check those projects I've just mentioned, see if any of their files have been cracked or copied?"

"Sure."

"If you find anything, then we can start looking for motive."

Servez brought their breakfast on the patio as the sun rose, shining a sharp bronze glimmer across the bay below. Kandara had eggs benedict, with freshly squeezed orange juice, followed by croissants and wild blueberry jam. When she was working, she wasn't as strict with her health food regime, figuring you never knew if you'd need the calories for extra energy.

Jessika ate with her, while the others coordinated their review with the Bureau's G8Turing. "Nice job," she told Kandara.

"I'm familiar with the game."

"I wonder who we're up against."

"The obvious choice is a weapons company."

"Not so obvious. Why include the attacks? That's political, or maybe ideological. If you're stealing data you need to be stealthy."

"Misdirection?" Kandara mused.

"But they knew we'd react to this. We had no choice."

"Once we have more information, like who it is, the motivation should fall into place."

"But that's the thing. What motivations can there be? They damaged us, the whole of Akitha. Who does that?"

"Fanatics," Kandara replied automatically. "I'm no longer surprised by what they do, by the misery and suffering they inflict on others. Ideology is a sick-soul-meme; it gnaws basic decency away until you can self-justify the most extreme acts as worthwhile to further the cause. Any cause."

Jessika gave her a surprised look, a spoon of fruit salad poised in front of her mouth. "I didn't have you down as the philosophical type."

"I'm not philosophizing. I'm simply telling you what I've seen."

"Hell, I thought I'd seen bad stuff when I worked for Connexion Security."

Kandara gave her a sympathetic grin and reached for another croissant. That was when the villa doors opened and Kruse came out, followed by Tyle and Oistad.

"They cracked the files, didn't they?" Kandara said. She barely needed to ask.

"I had to go deep into the management routines," Tyle admitted. "And even then all we found were ghost traces. The routines they're deploying are extremely sophisticated, and incredibly hard to detect. The Bureau is worried. It's like nothing we've ever seen before."

"So it is a weapons company running an espionage team," Jessika said.

"I think it might be worse than that," Kruse said. "We've only had an hour, but I asked the research teams to check the files. Some of them appear to have been altered."

"Altered how?" Kandara asked.

"It's very subtle. The researchers are comparing the active files to deep cache copies. There are discrepancies. Not many, and not in all the files they've checked so far. But data has been tampered with." Sie looked worried. "Entire projects have been compromised."

"If hardware was built on the basis of those files, it wouldn't work," Oistad said. "The sabotage would have wrecked years of research and lost us all the industrial resources allocated to fabrication."

"Then it wasn't a distraction," Kandara said thoughtfully. "Not entirely. All of this is aimed at disabling your industrial base."

"It's going to paralyze us," Kruse said in a monotone. "We don't know how widespread this is. We can't start to build anything new until the development data has been reviewed. This is . . . a declaration of war!"

"Interesting analysis," Kandara said, "given that this seems to be concentrating on systems that have weapons applications."

"What are you saying?" Tyle asked.

"Your ability to build weapons that you can use to defend yourself against physical assault is being sabotaged."

"Nobody's going to invade us!" Oistad said. "That's insane."

"Pearl Harbor," Kandara muttered.

"No," Kruse declared firmly. "A couple of teams armed with the most advanced routines a G8Turing's written, and consumed by a hate agenda, that I can accept. But some kind of physical attack? From whom? Nations don't have standing armies anymore. You assemble ten thousand people, and start giving them military training, and everybody will know. There's another purpose behind this; there has to be."

"Glad to hear it," Kandara said. "So your intelligence service monitors everything on Zagreus, does it?"

Kruse shot her an exasperated look. "I'm not dealing in hypotheticals."

"Is that what I'm doing? We have reached over a hundred star systems. Twenty-three of them have planets that have been or are being terraformed. You have no idea what's going on in half of them. Did you know one criminal gang in Ukraine is claiming to have an independent portal door to Zagreus? If you're truly rich, and managed to hang on to your money, you can buy your way back after you're renditioned."

"Really?" a fascinated Tyle asked.

"Like I said: rumor. But I'm completely serious about not knowing what's going on in some of the star systems we're settling. And it doesn't have to be a human army. Soldier drones are cheap and easy to build."

"I appreciate your insights and feedback," Kruse said, "but actually this isn't helping."

"I understand your position. However, what we've found here provides us with the kind of projects that this enemy team is likely to strike next. Tyle can load hir monitors into the appropriate networks."

"Yes. We'll do that. I need to inform the Bureau." Sie managed a weak smile of gratitude and went back indoors.

"For a society that prides itself on individual freedom, sie certainly talks to hir boss a lot," Kandara observed.

The team was kept busy for the rest of the day, reviewing the initial discoveries and trying to identify more corrupted files. Most of the afternoon was spent trying to cross-index with current Universal visitors, and then recent immigrants. Finally the Bureau had them refining potential future targets.

It all allowed Kandara time to herself, which she spent jogging down to the beach and back up again before spending an hour in the villa's well-equipped gym. After that she ran test procedures on her weapons peripherals, using images splashed over her tarsus lenses for virtual target practice. She much preferred physical range practice, but doubted Naima had one. At least none they'd admit to. She supposed Kruse's mysterious Bureau possessed a training facility for agents.

By late afternoon, Kandara was considering another swim when Kruse came looking for her.

"You need to pack your bagez," sie said. "We're transferring up to Onysko."

"Where?" Even as she asked, Zapata was spraying information across her lens; it was the primary dormitory habitat for the Bremble asteroid. "Never mind. Why are we going there?"

"It's been identified as a high-probability target. The highest, actually."

Onysko wasn't quite as large as Nebesa, measuring only forty-eight kilometers long. This biosphere was temperate and edging into its chilly autumn season when the team walked out of the portal hub. Once they were out in the open, Kandara turned around to look up at the endcap. She'd been expecting a ring city around the base, the same as Nebesa. But here the flat circle was mostly a smooth gray faux-stone with several spectacular waterfalls curving sharply sideways from the Coriolis force. A few sections along the rim, like the one they'd emerged from, were urban zones, with their giveaway balcony stacks.

Zapata splashed up the habitat's population. "Seven thousand?" Kandara asked in surprise. "Are you sure?" She eyed the closest deciduous trees, which she guessed at a good fifty to sixty years old. The habitat really should have a larger population by now. Some of the larger habitats back in the Sol system were approaching populations of a quarter of a million.

"That is the information supplied by the Onysko G8Turing. It is current."

"Strange."

They were assigned quarters in the Gloweth residency, a ten-story ziggurat embedded in the endcap. Their apartment was on the third floor, larger than the Naima villa, but furnished in the same clinically minimalist style that had Kandara wondering if it was some kind of subtle Utopial conditioning therapy. It seemed to reinforce the feeling of middle-class conformity, which she already considered a little too prevalent in Delta Pavonis. It was as if everyone was reluctant about exposing a sign of individuality.

Tyle collected her for the meeting, the pair of them walking along a maze of corridors leading through the endcap. Jessika and Oistad were already waiting in the conference room when they arrived. Kandara's mouth lifted in a gentle smile as she appreciated where they were; one wall was a bulging window curving out from the habitat's external shell. She'd never seen anything like it; habitat shells were usually a solid hundred meters thick. Just thinking of the sleet of cosmic radiation striking the window made her nervous, as the transparent material didn't even look particularly thick. Despite that she sat at the rock slab table filling the middle of the room and stared unashamedly. The view made her wonder why she'd ever been impressed by the sight of Nebesa.

The window was facing the Bremble asteroid, which from Kandara's viewpoint proscribed a tight arc across the star field outside as Onysko rotated laboriously. She could see the town-sized sprawls of machinery hanging limpet-fashion to its dusty gray-brown surface, sharp light from Delta Pavonis sparking on crinkled gold-foil sheets to make it twinkle hypnotically.

Zapata splashed a visual overlay, tagging the image components with identifiers. Most of the machinery clumps were industrial stations, sending rootlike tendrils boring deep into the rock, extracting minerals for the refinery level to process before distributing them in turn to the construction units that formed the upper layer. Any elements that weren't available amid Bremble's complex weave of ore seams were fed in through portals linked to other asteroids and the moons of Lanivet, Delta Pavonis's solitary gas giant.

More than half of the stations were replicating themselves, Zapata said. A fascinated Kandara watched the glittering metallic encrustations that were slowly spreading over the oddly smooth regolith like mechanical bacteria. It would take years, but eventually the entire surface would be covered, converting the huge asteroid into a giant technological bauble.

Tags were flickering across the vast free-flying factory modules drifting around Bremble in a loose cloud, the majority constructing new habitats. The layout of the modules was predicated on the elegance of simplicity: a gantry ring eight kilometers in diameter, its plain geometric struts looking crude in comparison to the segments of enigmatically dark equipment they caged. They contained massive bonding field generators, a variant of those that produced city shields. With the refineries supplying a steady flow of vaporized material, the bonding fields squeezed the atoms back into a solid form again.

She stared in admiration at the energetic starlight glimmering across the smooth obsidian-like outer shells of the prodigious cylinders as they extruded out of the factory rings. As with Bremble's industrial stations, the process had an undeniable affinity with organic life.

And out beyond the collection of factory modules, recently completed habitats gleamed like first-magnitude stars, a swarm that was slowly dissipating across the Delta Pavonis system, traveling on decade-long trajectories that would bring them to their own asteroid, where the mining/refining/manufacturing process would begin afresh. It made her picture Bremble as a dandelion head, casting its expanding cloud of seed to propagate time and again across the hostility of interplanetary distances.

More organic equivalence.

"Real Utopial von Neumannism," Tyle said happily as sie sat next to her. Sie smiled contentedly at the vista. "Machines building machines, practically without any human intervention. Now that Onysko has G8Turings, they can manage so much more these days."

Kandara pursed her lips as she gave Bremble a more searching assessment. It was smaller than Vesta, which was Sol's leading space industry asteroid, but she thought the systems on show here were a lot more sophisticated. They weren't constrained by conventional economics anymore, she realized. "Is this exponential?"

"Not yet. Give it another twenty years. The industrial stations will have engulfed Bremble, at which point they won't bother replicating themselves. They'll just consume the remaining rock to build habitats. After another fifty years, there'll be nothing left, and they'll fly to new asteroids and begin again."

"That seems almost . . . dangerous."

"Not at all. It's a triumph. We really are aiming for a genuine post-scarcity economy," Oistad said earnestly. "The systems we're developing out here will finally make it possible. Right now, everything is macro, too interdependent. The industrial stations have a multitude of separate specialist fabricators, all of which knit together to make self-replication of the whole possible."

"Cells in an organism," she murmured.

"Right. Emilja wants to take us to the next, final stage and achieve an order of magnitude reduction in our current level of mechanical complexity. Ultimately down to a single unit that can replicate itself *ad infinitum,* then go on to produce specialist manufacturing systems like the ones out there building habitats. The G8Turings should finally make all that possible. Once they do, it's the point at which Universal culture economics collapse."

"And you smoothly replace it with an age of enlightenment?"

"Something like that," Tyle said sardonically.

"Which, if someone is wrecking your industrial production capacity and advanced research in an ideological crusade . . ."

"Exactly." Oistad gestured at the window. "What you see out there is the true beating heart of Utopialism."

Tyle chuckled. "Make sure Kruse doesn't hear you say that."

"Oh?" Kandara was interested. "Why's that?"

"There are two components to Utopial society being an unqualified success," Jessika explained. "We have the physical aspect. That's the technology being developed here which will make absolute post-scarcity possible by providing an overabundance of material items. And then there's the philosophy, which will allow people to live fruitful, meaningful lives within such a physically rich environment. It's something humans are unaccustomed to."

"I get that," Kandara said. "Why is Kruse upset by it?"

"Upset is the wrong word," Oistad said. "You see, Jaru promotes the philosophy aspect. It's hir belief that equality and human dignity are important above all else, even the material aspects of our culture."

"Reasonable," Kandara mused.

"Kruse is quite devout in her support of Jaru."

"Wait. There's a conflict inside the Utopial concept?"

"Conflict is a very strong word. There's a question of assigning priorities and resources. You see, Kruse and her fellow travelers think omnias are just the first stage of human transformation. That if we truly reach an overabundant supply state for our physical requirements, ordinary human personalities won't be able to cope, and we'll collapse into decadence within a couple of generations."

"The whole heaven-is-boring thesis," Kandara ventured.

"Yes. Which our more radical colleagues are saying can only be solved if you gene-up basic human neurology."

"Really? So if the people won't fit the new perfect society, alter the people? That sounds rather fascistic."

Oistad nodded wryly. "And yet, without Jaru's original notions of how to achieve equality, I wouldn't exist. And I am so very happy with what I am."

"So you're in favor of even more artificial evolution?"

Sie shrugged and glanced over at Tyle for support. "You have to solve the technological challenges first, and create the abundance problem for real, or the whole notion dissolves into debating how many angels can dance on a pinhead. And for all the progress the von Neumann teams have made here on Onysko, we haven't got that close to single-unit self-replication yet. Humans still have to problem-solve. Not going out there with a screwdriver,"—she pointed at the constellation of half-built habitats—"but developing and enhancing what we have already. Some of us are concerned the systems are starting to plateau, even with G8Turing involvement."

"All human technology is leveling out," Kandara said. "But we're a star-faring species now. It's to be expected."

"But we can go so much further. So many problems will simply vanish if we can build a proper von Neumann unit."

"It never starts with jackboots and black uniforms," Kandara said. "Just good intentions. But that's how it always ends."

"We're not going to impose our vision of how to live on others. That's not what we are at all."

Kandara grinned at how earnest sie sounded. Out of the corner of her eye, she caught Jessika squashing down her own amusement.

"What vision?" Kruse asked as sie walked into the conference room, followed by two other people.

"We're just talking philosophy," Kandara said. "As you do." Then she paid attention to the woman behind Kruse. It was difficult to actually see anything with Zapata suddenly splashing so much personal data across her vision. "Emilja Jurich," she blurted in surprise.

Emilja was looking good for someone 160 years old—certainly a lot better than Jaru, Kandara thought. Her hair was thick and dark, arranged in an elaborate nest around her head. Sharp cheekbones were prominent under the kind of healthy wrinkle-free skin that a twenty-five-year-old would take for granted. Light-gray eyes gave the room a swift scan, which left Kandara feeling judged, and not in a good way. The woman had an almost regal presence, allowing her to carry off her formal black-and-carmine high-collar dress of Indian silk with an easy grace.

Kandara took a malicious guess that the telomere treatments she received were probably from an exclusive Earth clinic rather than a standard Utopial medical facility. Then again, she was a grade one, entitled to the best Akitha could provide. In her case, that was fair enough.

Emilja Jurich's parents had emigrated from Croatia to London back in 2027. Their daughter dutifully studied 3-D printer programming at the London Metropolitan University and was working in the distribution division of a food printing company in 2063 when Connexion opened its first portal link between New York and Los Angeles. What she did next became a classic case study for business schools across the Sol system and beyond.

Connexion had of course produced a map app for its burgeoning hub network, but Emilja could see how basic that was—a situation that was only going to get worse for users as more portals were added. So she founded her Hubnav Company that December, and spent every spare hour developing a mInet app to guide people through

Connexion's rapidly expanding network. She started coding it when there were a grand total of 322 public quantum entanglement portal doors in the Sol system, with Connexion already announcing its ambitious plans for fifty thousand more across the continental United States. She coded it because, growing up in London, she'd always appreciated the elegant modesty of Harry Beck's classic London Underground map, drawn with the simple truth that it didn't matter where the stations were, nor the way the tunnels twisted between them, because Beck instinctively recognized that all you really needed to know was where the stations were in relation to each other. She coded it because she knew people were basically stupid and lazy, and their world was about to become more complicated by an order of magnitude.

As Emilja studied the burgeoning tangle of hubs, she saw a series of interconnecting spider webs spreading across the globe. If you wanted to travel from, say, Oakham, in the heart of England, to Atlanta, Georgia, it was a theoretically simple route. Go through the Oakham hub loop into the county hub network, which links to the national hub network, and takes you to London, where there's a link to the international hub network, which takes you to the America Arrivals Port in North Dakota (that state's senators were impressively fast at digging into the government Fair Deal quantum entanglement infrastructure pork barrel, helped by a Washington backroom pact with Texas senators who snagged the National Commercial Goods Import Station for Houston). From there you walk into the interstates hub to get to the Georgia hub network, and finally on to the Atlanta metro network where you step out into the welcome of that sunny city's warm, muggy air. A maximum of eight portals. Easy. Except with so many portals linking to other destinations, each central hub was a roundabout of hell, especially at local rush hours.

And Emilja was right. People were stupid. After decades of satnavs and autodrive cars, they just wanted to be held by the hand and guided, hassle-free. They wanted an app to tell them one central hub is jammed up with frustrated people, or a portal door is down for maintenance, so they could take a longer (but quicker) route through three alternative hubs. Where to go, which way to turn as soon as they emerge from a portal door, how many steps to the next, a green halo mInet graphic flashing around it just to be certain you've got the right one.

By 2078 there were twelve billion people living in the Sol system. Apart from toddlers, all of them had a copy of Emilja Jurich's Hubnav app, much to the fury of anti-monopoly legislators. By then, of course, the app provided its user with a rundown on their destination's weather, political status, canny bargains, top restaurants, cleanest beaches, hottest clubs, trendiest art, grooviest music events . . . The whole long, long list of profiled advertising, each one bringing in revenue. Emilja wasn't quite as rich as Ainsley Zangari, but her wealth was enough to found her own habitats, Dvor and Zabok, fueled by the age-old dream of a fresh start fully independent of Earth. She was also rich and philanthropic enough to attend the First Progressive Conclave.

Along with Jaru Niyom, she underwrote the Utopial movement.

Kandara guessed Emilja was the leader of the Utopial's technology development faction. She was the practical one, wrestling equipment into obedience, mirror-twinned to Jaru's philosophic dreams. "An honor to meet you," Kandara said.

Emilja gave her a sly grin of acknowledgment and sat at the head of the rock-slab table. The pale, redheaded man who'd accompanied her sat on her left.

"Callum Hepburn," Emilja said formally. "Our von Neumann project technology strategist."

"She means troubleshooter," Callum said amicably.

"Has there been any trouble?" Kandara asked.

"Not on the scale that hit Naima's telomere production," he said. "But there have been more glitches out on the Bremble stations than usual. Of course, defining 'usual' here is difficult in itself. All our industrial systems are under constant development as we evolve them up to the von Neumann mono-machine ideal. Some months everything goes smoothly; others we get overrun by problems. This current batch might be normal, or they might not. We'll need to give our files and routines a thorough audit."

"I'd like permission to install monitor routines in Onysko's networks, and on the Bremble industrial stations," Tyle said.

"If that's what you need," Emilja said. "Go ahead."

"What happens if you find evidence of tampering?" Callum asked.

"It depends on when it occurs. If it's historical, then we'll pass it on to you. Hopefully, you'll be able to assess and compensate for whatever damage there's been. And if it's current—" Tyle glanced over at Kandara. "We believe we can track the access point."

"And I'll deal with that for you," she said.

Callum gave her an uneasy look. "I think rendition to Zagreus would be more appropriate."

"We've had that discussion in senior council, Callum," Emilja said levelly. "As a result, Investigator Martinez has been hired. I believe she is even more necessary now that we know the full extent of the sabotage against us. If you're going to attack Utopial society, this is where to do it; the severity of the other attacks may be a diversion."

"It's your conscience at stake, not mine."

"Thank you," she said coldly. "Investigator?"

"Yes?"

"If it is possible to apprehend one or more of this team, I would like you to do so."

"I understand."

"But not at risk to yourself."

"I wouldn't expose myself to unnecessary risk; that has a habit of compromising my mission."

"Very well. But I am very curious about who is behind this. The level of planning and the commitment to damage our entire culture is one which I find profoundly disturbing. I fear it won't be resolved simply by you eliminating the current threat."

"I think you're right," Kandara said. "Do you have any idea who might have launched this?"

"I believe it highly unlikely to be a globalPAC or even a multistellar corporation. We've had our ideological disagreements with them; we still do. But this . . . No. They would understand that as soon as we uncovered their culpability, I would strike back."

"Also, generating physical conflict is not on the globalPAC agenda," Callum said. "Quite the opposite. Zagreus rendition was their idea in the first place." He grimaced. "I know that for a fact. They stamp down heavily against anyone who uses violence, especially political violence. And that's what this is."

"How long will it take to set up your routines?" Emilja asked Tyle.

"Hopefully within a day," sie replied. "There are a lot of networks, especially on Bremble. But the Bureau has allocated me additional G8Turings."

"Very well," Emilja said. "Keep me informed."

The team set up in an office on the ninth floor of the Gloweth residency, looking down the length of the habitat. Their desks had a full range of network access nodes and projectors, and there was a drink dispenser in the corner that produced a great hot chocolate. It still lacked the kind of professionalism Kandara was accustomed to, but she had to admit it was an improvement to sitting around a kitchen table. They'd also acquired additional support from Onysko's small police force—five officers specializing in network security.

Tyle supervised the review of Onysko's projects, examining networked files for the kind of discrepancies they'd found before. It took fifteen hours.

"I've got something," sie told Kandara. "There's a materials science team in one of the astro-engineering offices up here; they're running a development project for space suits. It researches active magnetic polymers that will deflect cosmic radiation—a layer of that in a space suit will weigh a great deal less than the carbon and metal layers we're using now."

"Okay, I can see that having some weapons capability," Kandara said.

"It looks like some of their key files were altered. We're running a comparison with deep cached copies to see how many, but it fits the profile."

"What about the access point?" Kandara asked.

Tyle's smile was confident. "I've been thinking about that. There have been so few traces, and the G8Turing up here isn't that slouchy. It was like the project networks were being accessed directly, physically—which is contrary to all the illegal file cracks I know; they're always remote. I-heads access from as far away as possible with multiple random routing, so it takes time to trace and intercept. But up here, remote access would be risky; the G8Turing can monitor all the links back to Akitha. There are five portal doors that carry all the habitat's digital traffic."

"They're doing this from inside the research lab?" Kandara said. "How did they get in there?"

"They didn't." Tyle's smile was growing broader. The others in the office had all stopped working to look at hir from inside the cages of glowing hologram icons. "We don't have a huge amount of security up here, but the critical areas are all covered with restricted systems the Bureau maintains. Someone cleared the standard coverage around the lab, but they didn't know about the additional Bureau systems." Sie pointed as a projection formed beside hir desk.

It was a standard digital services crypt, filled with row after row of equipment stacks—geometric galaxies of twinkling electronics encased in dark glass, altars devoid of worship. Except for the man walking along the narrow aisles, his stern features illuminated by diffuse blue lighting, a silver-white insulated coverall providing him with a little protection against the icy air.

Everyone watched him slide a glass panel open, exposing the tight-packed racks inside. He ran a hand down them, eyes shut as if he was communing with the systems. Kandara realized that in a way he was; his fingers must contain scanner peripherals, analyzing the racks. He stopped and slid one out, exposing the bundled optical cables along the side. What looked like a bar-code label was applied to the top of the electronics, then the rack was pushed back into place. He stood there for a minute, watching whatever graphics were being splashed across his tarsus lenses, before closing the glass cover.

Kandara pursed her lips. "Physical intrusion," she said, almost admiringly. "That's real old-school. You need a lot of balls to attempt that."

"We've all got 'em," Oistad said, grinning at Tyle, who groaned in dismay.

"Onysko's vulnerable to that kind of operation," Jessika said. "It was a smart move."

"They analyzed your systems and found the weak spot," Kandara said. "That's a professional team. I don't think they'll be the fanatics; all they're interested in is the money."

"Here you go," Jessika said. A projector above her desk was showing the man's face, this time with a lazy smile. "Baylis Arntsen, a botanist from the University of Phoenix, on a two-year research exchange scheme; his specialty is developing the synthetic biology of desert flora. We have two habitats under construction scheduled for arid-climate biospheres."

"Go back through all the restricted security files," Kruse demanded. "Find out what else he's done to our networks."

"The Bureau's G8Turings are running it now," Tyle said.

They had to wait another ten minutes before the next sensor recording materialized; another man in a different services crypt. Identified as Nagato Fasan, immigrated to Akitha seventeen months earlier, an enthusiastic convert to the Utopial ethos. Then a woman, Niomi Mårtensson. According to her file she had a physics doctorate from München University—knowledge she was applying to build synthesizers to create organosilicon life. She was on secondment from a North African open-source research institute.

Jessika took one look at her thin face and nerdy pale hair. "Son of a bitch!"

"What?" Kruse asked.

"That's Cancer!"

Kandara focused on Niomi Mårtensson's bland image, ignoring the way her skin temperature seemed to have suddenly dropped a couple of degrees. "Are you sure?"

"Goddamn right I am. I spent a year working on a case when I was with Connexion, trying to track her. She's changed her hair, and the eyes are a different color, but I know her."

"Everyone, stop right now," Kandara said abruptly. "Nobody is to ask any Turing for a check on Niomi Mårtensson. No file to be accessed, understand? Cancer will have loaded monitors into the network that'll spot any reference to her." She glanced around the office, half expecting to catch someone in the act of making a warning call.

"So what now?" Oistad asked cautiously.

Kandara turned to Kruse. "First, shut down all Onysko's portal doors."

"All?"

"Yes. Not just the pedestrian hubs back to Akitha and the other habitats; I want the cargo portals, too. Everything. We need to isolate her up here."

"I'll . . . ask."

"No. That's not good enough. Talk to someone—Jaru, or Emilja. Shit, both of them if you have to; whatever it takes, but get the authority without making a big deal of it. No committees, no standard procedures."

Kruse gave a determined nod. "Okay. I'll get it done."

Kandara turned to Tyle and Oistad. "When Onysko's isolated, and not before, we need to fix their locations."

"The Bureau Turings can run a visual search," Oistad said. "We'll have them straight away."

Kandara pulled a face as she studied the projections floating above

Tyle's desk. "As soon as the portals shut down, they'll know they've been blown and we're hunting them."

"I can find them fast," Oistad insisted. "Their altmes will be linked to the network. I can run an interface check; it'll register as a maintenance ping."

"We can go old-school, too," Jessika said. "Just call their colleagues, the ones they're supposed to be working with. Actually ask them to confirm who's in the room."

"Okay," Kandara said. "Go wide. All the methods of confirming their location, trigger them together."

Kruse took seven minutes to obtain the authority to divorce Onysko from the rest of the Delta Pavonis system, using an emergency bio-hazard quarantine procedure that Emilja provided authorization for. Kandara used the time to summon her bagez and suit up in the office washroom. Her armor was a skintight one-piece, with five individual protective layers; the innermost being thermal regulation, keeping her body temperature constant. Then a self-sealing pressure membrane for biological or toxic weapons, which also allowed her to function in a vacuum or underwater environment. Another thermal layer, this time to resist both high temperature or subzero exposure; on top of that was a radiation reflector, which could ward off energy beams and em pulses. And then the external layer—four centimeters of kinetic protection armor, which was flexible enough to give her full motion, but would harden when struck by bullets or shrapnel; it was also resistant to monomolecule filament. The helmet was a featureless shark-profile, equipped with active and passive sensors, interfaced with Zapata and providing enhanced vision through her tarsus lenses. Her slim segmented backpack provided life support, power for beam weapons, and projectile magazine storage, as well as a field medic kit. Microdrones clung to the base like a cluster of black beetles. Wrist bracelets contained gamma-laser emitters and mini-grenade launchers, while her left forearm had a vambrace mount for a small magrail rifle, with a projectile feed from her backpack.

She clumped back into the office, weighing in at more than eighty kilos.

"Holy shit," Jessika exclaimed. "You look like a seriously badass fallen angel. Does that thing pack a flaming sword, too?"

"Not today. But nice suggestion, thanks."

"I'm about to order the shutdown," Kruse said.

"Wait until I get down to the Gloweth hub," Kandara told hir. "Then I'll give you the go-ahead. When you have their locations, close Onysko's internal hubs, but leave me a route open to intercept whichever of them is nearest."

"I'm coming with you," Kruse said.

"No."

"But we have to deploy our local police. They'll physically cordon off the area you're operating in. I'm responsible for minimizing any damage and casualties."

"Fine. You can create a cordon to stop any of your citizens getting near, but make it very plain to the police that if Arntsen, Fasan, or Cancer exit the area, they are not to try and stop them. I will take them down."

"Agreed."

Kandara sighed, which went unheard inside her helmet. "The rest of you need to keep a tight watch on events. I'm going to need constant operational intel."

"You'll get it," Jessika said. "I know how to filter for this kind of procedure."

Kandara left the office and went down two levels to one of the Gloweth hubs.

"The police tactical team is ready for deployment," Kruse announced.

Kandara wondered if Cancer's monitors would be telling her the same thing. "Jessika, when we have locations, can you cut network access in each area, please?"

"Sure thing."

The hub was deserted. Kandara stood in the entrance, running a final check on her medical vitals. She took a breath. Switched her weapon systems to active. "Okay, Kruse: initiate."

Zapata's display showed her the portal doors powering down, reducing their twin links to a null-space entanglement. The three hub portals in front of her maintained their integrity. "Tyle?"

"Ping is active."

"Got them," Jessika cried.

Zapata splashed the results across her vision. Arntsen and Fasan were together inside a lab in the Eóin research block on Onysko's other endcap. Cancer was on Bremble, in a silicon refinery module.

A route to Eóin splashed across her tarsus lenses. She moved fast, running through the first portal door, turning sharp left in the next hub, another door. People milling around in confusion as portal doors started to shut down. One remained open. "Nice job," Kandara muttered as she sprinted through. Twist left again. Four fast steps. And she was out into Eóin's central oval atrium, lined with a broad ramp that spiraled up from the black-and-white marble floor, looping around eight stories of laboratories and offices.

"Eóin network suspended," Jessika reported. "All portal hubs closed."

"Can you seal the laboratory doors?" Kandara grunted as she hit the ramp and started sprinting. Arntsen and Fasan were in lab five on the second level.

"I think so."

She could see several people on the spiral, leaning over the white balustrade, frowning as they looked around to see what the problem with the hubs was. Several doors were opening, more people coming out. "Do it fast. There's too many people exposed here."

"The police are on their way," Kruse said. "They'll help clear the area."

"We're way past that point." Kandara said. Her sensors caught hir, with Zapata's feature recognition routines confirming. Kruse was walking out onto the black-and-white tiles of the floor below.

"What are you doing?" Kandara snapped furiously. Sie must have followed her from Gloweth.

"I'm responsible for this operation," Kruse replied levelly. "I'll supervise the police and start evacuating civilians."

"Fuck's sake! Just stay the hell back."

Two people on the ramp ahead of her turned to gaze in astonishment at the squat armor-clad figure pounding toward them. Surprise and fear rose on their faces in a near-comic slow motion. Then Kandara had barged past, with only one half circle of ramp left before she reached lab five.

Her helmet sensors picked up a drone descending fast down the center of the atrium. It was a standard bracelet shape, twenty centimeters wide, with internal contra-rotating fans. She instinctively knew it was *wrong*. "I thought you'd killed Eóin's network?"

"I have," Jessika said. "The only channel in is this secure comm."

"Then why is there a remote drone in here?"

"What drone?"

Kandara reached level two, the door to the lab seventeen meters ahead, and the drone was drawing level. Her right arm came up and target graphics closed on the little machine. A gamma beam sliced into it.

The explosion turned her armor layer completely rigid and slammed her against the wall. A big chunk of balustrade and ramp vanished in the blast, smoldering debris cascading down onto the tiles two floors below. People who'd been on the spiral ramp were struck by the brutal blast wave, bodies flung into the structure, limbs broken, flesh torn and burned. In the first few seconds' aftermath, the atrium was claimed by a vacuous silence. Then the screaming started.

"What the fuck was that?" Jessika yelled. "What's going on?"

"Weapons drone," Kandara grunted. Zapata splashed a fast suit status for her. External damage minimal, all systems functional. She pushed herself away from the wall and powered on toward lab five. Its metal door had buckled in the explosion. Kandara shot it with a mini-grenade.

Her armor stiffened up again as the grenade detonated, flinging shards of metal in all directions. She skirted the missing hunk of ramp carefully and launched three microdrones through the gaping hole into lab five.

Their images splashed across her tarsus lenses as they flew forward. The laboratory followed a standard layout: big bioreactor cabinets lined up along one wall; benches laden with glassware, tended by robot arms; workstations orbited by complex holographic data grids. A tall cylindrical fish tank stood in one corner. The mini-grenade had reduced the room to chaos: cabinets warped and cracked, glassware shattered into avalanches of shards saturated with sticky chemicals. Arntsen and Fasan were on their knees behind a bench, blood dripping from their eardrums, exposed skin cut by flying glass. Fasan was holding a small black tube that the drone's sensors revealed as a beam weapon, while Arntsen seemed to be dazed and disoriented.

The drones completed their scan of the lab. There was no one else inside.

Kandara flattened herself against the wall to one side of the ruined door and shoved her hand out across the gap. Three more mini-grenades were fired into lab five, programmed to detonate close to the back wall so the fugitives wouldn't be shielded by the bench.

The drone sensors showed her the overlapping explosions. She saw the fish tank finally disintegrate, sending water sloshing across the floor, with thrashing fish surfing the churning ripples. Several of them slithered to a halt around Arntsen, who was now facedown, his clothes badly ripped by the blasts. Several of his ribs were visible in the gashes where skin had been flayed and burned from his back.

Fasan, by some miracle, was still relatively undamaged. He was crawling toward the shattered window wall. Kandara selected a projectile for the magrail rifle and spun around the warped doorframe.

There were three benches between her and Fasan. Target graphics locked on to his head—a coordinate supplied by the microdrones. The rifle fired, punching the projectile through the benches as if they were holograms. His head exploded in a cloud of gore-vapor and bone shrapnel.

Kandara walked forward as slender white rods began to slide up out of the bruised flesh of Arntsen's forearms. "Shit!" She shot two mini-grenades at him. His body ruptured, spraying gobs of skin and organ across the laboratory.

Two of his projectile peripherals fired on her as they sailed through the air—one embedded in his wrist, another rooted in a long chunk of humerus bone that spun like a baton. Her armor's outer layer locked, deflecting the impacts. Even so, they were powerful enough to shove her back toward the broken door. Helmet sensors revealed his peripherals that had survived the grenades, splashing them like a cloud of gold embers across the lab. Kandara's arms moved as if she were karate-chopping an invisible foe, using her gamma lasers to kill the small devices before they could attack her.

Once they were reduced to smoking cinder points, she went over to Fasan's headless corpse and began a precision strike on his peripherals.

"Kandara, what's your status?" Jessika asked.

"Still active. You can restore Eóin's network now. Arntsen and Fasan have been eliminated. Tell whatever cleanup crew you send to be vigilant. I've disabled their peripherals, but they might have left other hostile systems behind."

"Understood. Kandara, we're worried about Kruse. Hir altme is offline."

Kandara walked out of the lab. "I'm not surprised. Sie was completely exposed to the drone explosion." She scanned around the ramp, her suit sensors picking up the moaning and cries of pain. "There are casualties. You can allow the paramedics in."

"Opening the hubs to Eóin now," Oistad said. "Can you get a visual on Kruse?

"I'm on my way down now. Do not open any portal doors to Bremble. It's imperative that Cancer remain isolated."

"We've got that. But what about Kruse?"

Kandara looked over the balustrade to see police in dark armor entering the atrium in a tactical formation. Debris from the shattered ramp was piled high on the prim black-and-white tiles, while the air remained hazed with dust.

"Kruse is dead. I can see hir. Sie was caught by the blast and the rubble. My sensors can't find a pulse."

"Holy fuck!" Jessika cried. "No!"

"Are you sure?" Tyle asked.

"Pretty much. Have you found out how the weapons drone was being controlled?"

"What?"

"The weapons drone in Eóin. You shut down the local network, yet it was being controlled. How?"

"Kruse is dead?"

Kandara cursed inside the privacy of her helmet as she arrived at the bottom of the ramp. This was what happened when the ops team weren't true professionals. "Yes," she ground out. "But the operation is still ongoing. Now where's my route to Bremble, and how does Cancer still have access to the network?"

The police watched warily as she hurried through them on her way back to the hub. In front of her, the first paramedics were arriving, each with a tight cluster of medical bagez rolling along at their heels.

"I have three possible routes to Bremble for you," Jessika said. "Coming through now."

Kandara studied the map that splashed across her lens. Three different portal doors, with one inside the silicon refinery's small pressurized control center and two outside the main section. "How good is that last known position?" According to the intel, Cancer was beside one of the material processing cores, almost at the center of the refinery.

"She was there as of three minutes ago," Jessika confirmed.

"Okay. I'm entering the hub now." Kandara didn't say what her exit point was going to be. Maybe basic training, maybe paranoia; but Cancer had compromised Onysko's data network. She might even be listening in to the secure channel.

"I think she's using the same black routing that they used to get into our networks originally," Oistad said. "The Bureau Turings are reviewing traffic packages for encrypted Trojans. I'll try to isolate them."

"Okay," Kandara said. "In the meantime, download me whatever real-time intel you can from inside the refinery. I also want you and the Turings to access every sensor in the area. If she goes external, I need to know."

"Understood," Tyle said.

Kandara went through the first hub door and turned right straight away. She could feel her heart rate increasing. So many law enforcement and security teams had confronted Cancer over the years, and there weren't many survivors. Every time, Cancer fought as if she was invincible, and with the ferocity of somebody who had nothing to lose.

Now she was going one-on-one, with no real backup. The only way to do that was fight fire with fire.

Four hubs—and twenty-three steps—brought Kandara to a long, tubular airlock designed for ten people. The hatch swung shut behind her, and she triggered the emergency vent. Air screamed around her, turning to white vapor; she could even hear it through the helmet insulation. The noise barely lasted a couple of seconds as the vanishing atmosphere buffeted her with the ferocity of mountaintop wind. Fifteen seconds later, she was in a hard vacuum. The circular hatch in front of her unlocked and swung open, revealing a star field above the crinkled gold surface of Bremble's huge industrial station.

"Low-gravity environment ahead," Zapata warned.

Kandara raised her left arm and fired a wide-pattern fusillade of smart sensor pellets at low velocity. The image they splashed across her lens showed the different industrial modules arranged like city blocks, with a grid of deep metallic canyons between them. The airlock was on top of a storage sector, with fifteen big spherical tanks bunched together, along with their piping and heating mechanisms. They were crowned by a broad circular platform, used as a landing and parking bay for small engineering pods. Five of the little craft were docked to it, their systems plugged into stumpy umbilical pillars.

"Jessika, disable those engineering pods."

"Way ahead of you. Three are locked down, and I have secure remote access to two of them if you need it."

"Thanks."

Half of the smart pellets had struck the refinery module walls, sticking to the flimsy foil surface. They scanned back across the gulf, seeking the signature of Niomi Mårtensson's space suit.

"Looks clean," Kandara said. "Moving out."

"Just—" Jessika hesitated.

"What?"

"Be careful," Tyle said.

"Always am." Kandara moved to the back of the airlock, then ran at the open hatch—and jumped. The airlock itself was still inside Onysko, while its hatch opened into a portal door that was on the top of the Bremble storage tanks. As soon as she crossed the threshold she was immediately subject to the asteroid's minute gravity field. She grinned savagely at the sensation of flying superhero-style above the platform and out across the gulf between the tanks and refinery. When she passed over the edge, tiny thrusters on her suit torso flipped her upright and pushed her course down slightly. She released two mini-grenades from her left bracelet.

The refinery module was built around a cluster of long, cylindrical material processor cores and their ancillary equipment, all encased in a thin shell of gold-skinned metallocarbon that was discolored from more than two decades of vacuum exposure. It was almost fifty meters tall, and seventy wide, sitting on top of a squat extractor rig the same size. Struts and odd mechanical protrusions stuck out into the dark canyons surrounding it, illuminated by tiny lights that drove down to a black vanishing point where the asteroid's surface was hiding.

The mini-grenades exploded in silence, violet light flaring in perfect intersecting hemispheres, consuming the fragile shell. A swarm of fizzing shards twirled out from the impact. Then the glare was fading, and Kandara's suit sensors revealed the irregular hole seared into the side. Her thrusters fired again, refining her trajectory, and she soared through the narrow gap, wincing as she went past the still-glowing jags.

There was no light inside other than the weak illumination seeping through the grenade rent. Her sensors switched to infrared, revealing a three-dimensional matrix of machinery and cables and pipes rendered in green and black. Directly in front of her was a narrow curving gridwork, approaching *fast*. She grabbed a crosspiece and jerked to a halt, straining her deltoid muscle. The refinery machines were producing a constant vibration, which she could feel through the gauntlet. High-voltage cables gleamed sunset orange as the sensors picked up their magnetic field.

"I'm in."

"We're getting sensor glitches on level seventeen," Jessika reported. "That's two below the control center she was in."

"Okay, going down."

Zapata splashed up a schematic of the refinery. Kandara started to haul herself along, using cables or support girders, whatever she could grab. Sometimes the equipment was packed so tight she could barely get through the gaps; then she'd be in empty spaces bigger than her apartment. Finally she found an accessway—a tube made from a composite grid allowing mechez and humans easy transit. There were dozens of the tubes winding their way around the interior of the refinery, as if some piece of rogue cybernetics had dug itself a warren. Looking at it all, she'd never felt more like a field mouse lost in a construction site.

"All the refinery's sensors just failed," Tyle said, a strong hint of panic in hir voice. "I'm working to restore them."

"She's still in here then," Kandara said, pulling herself along inside the accessway. The size of the refinery was going to give Cancer a huge advantage, she realized. Without sensors, they could spend a week moving around trying to find each other—and that was assuming Cancer would seek a confrontation. "She's going to want to escape," she said. "If she goes down into the extractor rig below, will she have a better route out?"

"Not particularly," Jessika said. "The extractor rig and refinery where you are have a physical gap between other modules. She'll have to cross that gap somehow."

"We've got active sensors on all sides of you," Oistad said. "If she makes a break for it, we'll know."

"And if she switches them off, as well?"

"I'm hardening the network," Tyle said. "But if she does disable some, at least that'll give us an indication of where she might be."

Three minutes later Kandara was at level seventeen. If it hadn't been for Zapata's guidance graphics, she wouldn't even have known which way was down, Bremble's gravity was so slight. She gripped one of the accessway's struts and held herself motionless. Her helmet sensors scanned around on their maximum magnification. Nothing.

"Do the G8Turing have control over the refinery's mechez?" she asked.

"No, I shut them out when I restricted the network. We'd have to open up a lot of bandwidth for that," Oistad said. "That'll give Cancer more channels to route a call out."

"Who's she going to call?" Kandara muttered. "All right, this is how we play it. Reopen the network as much as you need and move every mechez on the refinery inventory to level fifteen and level nineteen. I want every accessway physically blocked, so no one can get through those levels. Are there enough of them to do that?"

"Yes," Oistad said.

"Right. Once that's done, start moving them in to this level. Get the noose around her, and start contracting it."

While the team started organizing the remotes, Kandara snaked along the accessway. Every time she reached an intersection, she left a drone, then moved on. The one place she didn't venture into was the control center. She was worried Cancer might have booby-trapped it. In fact, she was surprised there were no smart mines concealed somewhere in the accessways.

Or perhaps there are, and I just haven't come into trigger range yet.

The thought made slithering along inside the dark, winding accessways a nervy experience. She didn't usually suffer from claustrophobia, but this was pushing her close.

"Kandara, we might have a problem," Jessika said.

She froze, surrounded by misty green thermal outlines, with the power cables forming an irregular glowing web around her—none of it real. The refinery's vibration was still present in the strut she was holding. No sign of a human heat signature. "What?"

"Something's blocking an extractor rig ice-feed chamber. Eight levels below you."

"You mean a feed inside the extractor rig?"

"Yes."

"I thought you said there's no way out down there?"

"Oh, shit. The feeds, they bring in ice."

"Ice?"

"Yes. The refinery process uses a lot of water."

"Where the hell does ice come fr— Oh, fuck! I said shut down all the portals."

"One of the harvesters on Verby is malfunctioning," Oistad said. "The ice feed has shut down. Sensors are offline. I can't see the damage."

"The *damage* is her, going through," Kandara realized. "Where the hell is Verby?"

"It's one of Lanivet's moons," Zapata informed her. "The surface is covered with extensive ice oceans. The water has a low mineral content, and is therefore an excellent resource for both industrial systems and habitat biospheres."

"Mother Mary. Jessika, give me a route down to the ice-feed chamber. Fast!"

"Coming through now."

Kandara started to haul herself along the accessway, following the glowing purple route line now splashed over her lens. "Is there anyone on Verby?"

"No, just the G7Turings controlling the ice harvest. The operation is completely automated."

"Good. You know the drill. Shut down every portal. Properly, this time."

"Kandara," Oistad said, "the ice feeds are essential to half of Bremble's industrial systems; and the habitats need water, too."

"How many people does she have to kill before you listen to me?" she shouted. "Shut the fucking ice feeds down!"

"Powering them down now," Jessika said. "Listen, that harvester she went through, it has three ice feeds into the extractor rig. I've stopped the other two."

Kandara smiled to herself. *Clever girl,* she thought. The locations of the other two feed chambers were suddenly splashed across her vision. She changed course and went for one Cancer hadn't used to reach Verby. Most likely the diabolical woman was waiting on the other side, or worse, a drone would be watching, and she'd blow the power while Kandara was halfway through.

Unless she's bluffing our bluff. She shook her head, angry with herself. *Too paranoid.*

The ice-feed chamber was a broad cylinder that sprouted five branches, which then went on to branch again deeper into the extractor rig, like some ancient tree that had long been entombed by machinery. As Kandara approached, an access hatch near the base slid aside. She eased herself in.

When Jessika shut down the ice flow, the extractor rig had continued to swallow the chunks of ice already inside the feed chamber. Now the cylinder which minutes ago had been packed with a constant stream of crushed ice was empty apart from a tenuous mist of twinkling particles. Kandara pushed off cautiously and sent several smart pellets on ahead. They revealed very little, just more curving metal walls, which was the mirror image of the extractor rig end; the harvester supplied the ice through more than a dozen smaller pipes. But her sensors couldn't detect any other sensors watching for her.

No more calculating risks. No more doubts.

Go!

She pushed off hard, zipping through the portal. Verby's one-fifth standard gravity abruptly tugged her down. She landed with a shoulder roll, springing up fast, which sent her rising off the floor. At the same time she held her left arm out and moved it in a smooth arc, firing armor-piercing rounds as she went. The munitions blasted through the feed chamber's walls on either side and above her, exploding inside the harvester. Her feet were pushed down by the rifle's impulse. She could feel the harvester juddering beneath her soles as it ground to a halt.

"Do you know how much those cost?" Tyle asked dryly.

"I thought you guys didn't lower yourself to talk money?"

"In terms of resources, and time to replace it."

"You wanted an accountant to do this job? Should've hired one." The ruined feed chamber began to split asunder; she stood directly under the slowly widening gap and jumped. In the low gravity, her gened-up muscles pushed her an easy five meters upward, landing precariously on a warped and splintered section of the upper bodywork toward the rear of the machine. "Now close down the last portals on Verby. Nothing apart from the data links, and if they're above ten centimeters in diameter, cut them too."

"Already done," Jessika said. "There's no way off that moon." She paused. "For either of you."

"You hear that?" Kandara asked, raising her voice despite how foolish that felt.

No answer. But then she hadn't expected one. She started to pick her way along the twisted bodywork as the broken harvester swayed about, settling ponderously.

It was a huge vehicle. The blade scoop at the front was thirty meters wide, cutting a five-meter-deep channel through the frozen ocean as it rolled forward. Power blades along the lower edge could chop through granite if they ever encountered any—not that this moon had any rock even approaching that level of toughness. The harvester fleet operated on the bottom of a pit the size of a small sea they'd gouged out over the last twenty years. In the distance, she could see vertical cliffs an easy three kilometers high.

When she looked up, Lanivet formed a vast crescent that filled a third of the sky. Its seething cloud bands were pale pink, streaked with white, with occasional slashes of cobalt blue squirting up from the unknown depths. A myriad of cyclones churned arrogantly through them, though nothing the world-swallowing size of Jupiter's Great Red Spot. The waning gas giant radiated a pastel light that shaded the sparkling ice a gentle damask.

Kandara clambered up the harvester's twisted metal and composite bodywork to the highest point and scanned around. "She's either got the greatest stealth technology ever built, or she's still here."

"Can you see any footprint tracks leading away?" Tyle asked. "There's no stealth that can cover that up."

She studied the surface a little more closely, moderately impressed with Tyle's suggestion. Five kilometers away another harvester was slowly braking, with high fantails of ice grains rising in sluggish arcs from either side of its scoop blade. The constant deluge from all the harvesters had coated the pit's surface of solid ice with several centimeters of ice granules, as neat and uniform as a Zen garden. "I can't see any tracks," she reported. "Jessika, can you get me any images of Cancer coming out to Bremble today? Specifically, what space suit she was wearing."

"I think I see where you're going with this. Hang on."

Kandara moved down the harvester several meters; being perched on top would make her a splendid target. *But I haven't been shot at. Why?*

The whole situation was making her jittery, gnawing at her resolution. Cancer wouldn't hold back. *Did I get her with those first shots into the harvester? Could I be that lucky?*

"Get me a schematic of the harvester," she told Zapata. "She's got to be inside somewhere."

The translucent image splashed across her tarsus lenses highlighted the harvester's internal walkways and small maintenance cubicles. Ninety percent of the interior was solid machinery. Of course, the explosive projectiles had opened up gashes big enough to shelter a human, but not many.

Kandara scattered a dozen microdrones and watched them scurry through the fissures. They'd be able to find her elusive target quickly enough.

"You were right," Jessika said. "I'm looking at video of her going out to Bremble this morning. She was in a standard-issue space suit."

"Did she bring it with her from Sol, or is it one of yours?"

"Ours."

"Ping the beacon."

Kandara held her breath, but the transponder didn't respond.

"Sorry," Jessika said. "She's wiped the standard routines."

Or one of my explosive rounds hit her. "Worth a try. But at least it's not armor."

"Kandara," Tyle said. "Are you shooting at the harvester again?"

"No. Why?"

"I'm reviewing the telemetry—what's left. Systems are going offline in the main power network. It looks like they're being physically damaged."

"Show me," Kandara instructed.

The schematic splashed up the harvester's power system. A tiny portal supplied power to the vehicle from Akitha's solarwell electrical grid, but there were several quantum batteries distributed through the big machine as backups, keeping essential equipment active in the case of a power failure. If the harvester cooled below thirty Celsius, it would be a lot tougher for the maintenance teams to restore.

She saw the failures were all in the same section, around a quantum battery that supplied power to the rear caterpillar tracks.

"What systems are being hit?" she asked as she sent three microdrones racing to the location. "Is there a pattern?"

Zapata mapped a route to the section. She'd need to go back into the harvester through a hatchway on the left-hand side. But—inside was the last place she wanted to be. "Find me a target line the magrail can shoot through," she told Zapata. From what she could see on the schematic, the section was almost completely surrounded by chunks of dense machinery.

"Er, Kandara," Tyle said. "It's the safety systems that are being taken out. Two more have just gone."

A microdrone crawled into the tiny cubicle that provided access to the quantum battery and its cabling. Kandara felt her breath catch. Cancer was there, using a tool to work inside a high-voltage cabinet. The woman turned in a smooth motion, lining her right hand up on the microdrone. The connection vanished, but not before its radiation sensor spiked.

Maser, Kandara realized. Cancer was using a peripheral to shoot through her suit. The narrow beam would wreck any active systems in the fabric it passed through, but wouldn't puncture it. Kandara opened her communications to an open broadcast.

"Cancer, there's no way out. You know that. Every portal is closed to you."

No answer.

"I'm authorized to offer you a deal. Tell us who hired you, and you'll be renditioned to Zagreus. Refuse, and you'll be terminated."

"She just took out another voltage regulator," Tyle said. "There's only two left to limit the quantum battery's output."

Kandara looked at her own feet. The crumbled bodywork she was standing on was composite—non-conducting. But the frame underneath was boron fiber–reinforced aluminum. *Is she trying to electrocute me? But she's inside; she'll receive a lot more of the charge.*

It didn't make much sense, but Kandara crouched down and jumped anyway. Her muscles were strong enough to propel her in a long arc, taking her over the side of the harvester. She landed hard in the mushy ice granules, but managed to keep upright as her boots slithered about. The ice came up over her ankles.

Mother Mary! "Tyle, if she rigs a full discharge, how far will the ice conduct the charge?" She looked back up at the broken harvester, ready to jump back. Her armor could ward off an electric shock ordinarily, but that quantum battery stored a lot of electricity.

"Not far. Remember the ground underneath is ice, too. It should just travel straight down. She'd be better off rigging . . . Oh, Kandara, if she shorts out that quantum battery, it'll explode—and trigger the others."

Kandara stared at the harvester in growing panic. "How big an explosion?"

"Uh—get away! Kandara, she's just taken out another voltage regulator. There's only one left. Run! Get out of there. Move!"

Kandara brought her arm up and started firing armor-piercing projectiles. The magrail rifle slammed them through dense machinery. An overlapping series of explosions sent dazzling yellow vapor streaming out through the tears in the bodywork. The whole mass of the harvester shifted slightly, the profile distorting.

She turned and jumped. Soaring above the lustrous ground took an age. She landed, wobbling; jumped again, a lower trajectory this time, carrying her farther.

"Last regulator!" Tyle exclaimed.

Landed—

The quantum battery exploded.

Kandara flung herself flat—a movement she never completed. Zapata instantly hardened her armor's outer layer, locking her limbs in mid-leap. Behind her, a flawless hemisphere of blue-white light erupted from the harvester. It flashed across her, physically nebulous but enriched with energy. Milliseconds behind the incandescent wave front came the shrapnel cloud.

Amid glitching electronics and mutilated lens displays, her outer armor rang like a bell from the impacts. She tumbled anarchically, punched by the disintegrating splinters. Beneath her the ice flash-evaporated from the energy deluge, forming a secondary blast wave. She hit the seething ground and plowed through the superheated slush.

Red danger graphics plagued her vision. She rolled along chaotically, banging elbows and legs as the solar-bright light dissipated. Finally the universe stabilized. Eclipsing the passive gas giant above, a scintillating debris cloud formed a spectacular short-lived galaxy of coral-pink embers that curved delicately back toward the ground.

Kandara groaned from the pain. Icons stabilized in her vision. Five red-hot fragments had pierced her hardened armor, stabbing through the suit layers underneath to sear into her flesh. No major blood vessels or organs punctured, Zapata reported. The suit's self-sealing layer was already closing, cutting off the flow of air and blood into space. Inside her backpack, the medical kit injected a coagulant agent, helping stanch the flow of blood from the wounds.

She winced as she attempted to sit up. The parts of her body spared lacerations seemed to be a single giant bruise. Where the harvester had been, a steam-cloaked crater had been blasted into the ice ocean, nearly twenty meters deep. A hazy aurora cavorted over it like a demonic will-o'-the-wisp. She watched in astonishment as effervescent geysers pirouetted around the jagged rim, their spume freezing before it even reached the ground. Within a few seconds the phenomena had abated, and the aurora's phosphorescence grounded out.

Larger chunks of wreckage started to tumble out of the clearing sky. They were scattered over kilometers, shining brightly in infrared, kicking up sprays of ice as they thudded down into the granules.

After a while, Zapata picked up a signal.

"Kandara? Are you receiving this? Can you hear me? Are you okay?"

"I'm here," she replied.

A burst of cheering came along the comms channel.

"A harvester is on its way," Tyle said. "I've diverted it to you. It's not fast, but we're dispatching a recovery team through an ice-feed portal. They'll be with you in ten minutes. Can you last that long? How bad are you hurt?"

"I can last ten minutes."

"What the fuck happened?" Jessika asked.

"You were right about shorting the quantum batteries. She didn't want to give us her employer, so she suicided."

"That's just twisted. You offered her a way out."

"I'm guessing she didn't like the odds. There are a lot of powerful people who'd like to act out some medieval-level vengeance on her. She'd probably never have made it to Zagreus, no matter how sincere Emilja was about the offer."

"So we still don't know who was paying her?"

"No. You'll have to wait until next time, and hope you make a better job of apprehending them than I did."

JULOSS

YEAR 593 AA

The passageway was circular, four meters in diameter, its cyan-shaded walls made from something resembling fluorescent cotton candy. Dellian floated down its empty center, his armor suit's thrusters firing almost constantly to keep his course steady. Four of his combat cohort clawed their way along in front. As they were in zero gee, they'd linced additional segments around their core to form a segmented oval shape wrapped in a shell of energy and kinetic armor, which bristled with tri-segment arms. Their gripper talons tore long rents in the corridor's glowing organic fibers. The remaining two from the cohort were tail-end-charlies, bringing up the rear, alert for any enemy soldiers creeping up.

What Dellian assumed to be nutrient fluid squirted out of each wound the cohort's talons inflicted, filling the passageway with clouds of shimmering drops—a glow that slowly faded as they merged into larger globules. He batted them away. Suit sensors ran compositional analysis. It wasn't a bioweapon.

"Another fifty meters, then take the third branch, coord, seven-B-nine," Tilliana told him.

"Got it."

"Any sign of hostiles yet?"

"No."

"There has to be something there to defend the asteroid."

"I'm looking." Which was almost true. He'd been relying on the cohort to scan the passageway. *That's complacent.* The cohort picked up on his mild anxiety, the way his eyes changed focus to watch the sensor data splash a little more attentively. The two following him immediately released a swarm of dronebugs. They slid through the thin nitrogen atmosphere, as agile as the terrestrial wasps they were modeled on, dodging the oscillating blobs of fluid, their sensors scanning the weird organic walls for any changes.

"Light level is decreasing behind," his suit announced. "Three percent down."

Dellian checked his squad display, seeing the platoon locations. They were sticking to formation, all of them snaking their way along the fluffy passageways that wound their erratic way through this section of the asteroid city. Their target was a large central chamber that earlier drone sweeps had discovered, containing a negative energy loop. Command had assigned the squad an infiltration mission to discover the nature of the loop and destroy it. Tilliana and Ellici had split them up, allowing a greater probability that one of them would make it through.

"Janc. Hey, Janc," Dellian called. "What's your light level? I've got a reduction here."

"I'll check."

Dellian was mildly pleased he'd been the one who found the drop. *More savvy than the others.* And now the fluffy glowing strands had lost five percent luminosity just behind the two tail-end cohorts.

Sensing his interest, they launched a batch of tik-drones. The size and shape of maggots, they landed on the passageway's soft walls. Tiny bodies, with fangs of artificial diamond dust, chewed down into the delicate material. New displays splashed over his vision, detailing the chemical composition of the alien organic. The cells were arranged in a very loose weave and threaded with a fiber conducting electrochemical impulses.

Nerves!

"Yeah, it's getting darker in here, too," Janc replied.

"For me, too," Uret announced.

Colian: "Same here."

"What's it doing?" Dellian wondered out loud. In response to his misgiving, the cohort stopped moving and began to scan around. Even on his ordinary visual splash, the light level was noticeably lower. Now down forty percent, his databud reported.

Dellian fired his suit jets, moving himself toward the cohort. All six of them started to close into a protective formation around him. Then the tik-drones began reporting that the structure of the alien cells was changing, the strands shrinking, growing denser. Through his helmet sensors, Dellian saw the darkening walls were starting to contract. Undulations began, moving slowly toward him. The appearance of a giant gullet swallowing was inescapable.

The cohort quickly surrounded Dellian, their limbs lincing to provide a solid cage with him at the center. Energy beams fired into the fuzzy mass of alien cells. The outermost layers were fried instantly, shriveling and steaming. But more of the stuff was advancing toward them like a sluggish tsunami, carrying a tide of dead cells and congealing liquid ahead of the still living tissue. Even the coherent X-ray beams could only penetrate the dead matter so far. The sticky fluid bleeding from the charred strands was absorbing the energy, forming a hot barrier ahead of the living surface. In less than a minute, the cavity was completely full, engulfing him and the cohort. Pressure began to increase rapidly, as did the temperature. It was proving impossible to dissipate the cohort's energy barrage.

Dellian clenched his hands, and the cohort switched off their beam weapons. Sensors located slim tendrils worming their way through the seething liquid toward the cohort. Power blades slashed at them, cutting through effortlessly. But the fluid was becoming more viscous, hampering movement. And still the tendrils kept coming, multiplying like a burgeoning root system.

The tactical feed connecting him to the rest of the squad cut out. *"Signal Lost"* splashed across his lens. "Shit." That shouldn't have happened; they were using entangled comms. He didn't waste time running diagnostics.

When he tried a swimming motion, the armor's actuators strained against the pressure to move his limbs. Low-level joint-seal warnings splashed up. He fired the suit thrusters, but all that did was send thin streams of phosphorescent bubbles out into the darkness.

The cohort immediately started to move, using their gravitonic drives to tow him along, heading toward the rock wall that lined the passageway. It was tough going. The new tendrils were insidious, coming at them almost like a solid wave. Dellian had given up trying to move his own limbs. Now he was starting to worry about the pressure seals; they'd never been designed for this kind of environment. Being immobilized was also starting to conjure up black phantoms in his mind. Bizarrely, for all the force being exerted on the armor, he was still in zero gee, which was somehow helping the sense of isolation.

Progress was slowing drastically as the tendrils grew thicker. The forward cohort started firing X-ray lasers to break them up; they'd become too thick for the power blades to cope with. Medical monitors showed Dellian's heart rate increasing. The claustrophobia was getting to him. His plan was to detonate grenades against the rock; that was where the thickest nutrient arteries were supplying the cells. If he could cut those, he might be able to disable more of the passageway and claw his way out of this clot.

One of the cohort stopped moving, every limb overwhelmed by the tendrils, and still they kept coming, wrapping it deeper and deeper in layers of alien cells. And tendrils were gaining on a second cohort.

Deep inside Dellian's neck one of his new glands discharged a mild tranquilizer into his bloodstream. It was odd. He knew he should be panicking, but he wasn't. Instead he ordered the cohort to fire a grenade. It barely moved ten centimeters from the launch tube nozzle. Tendrils began to coil around it.

Dellian triggered it. His armor was easily tough enough to withstand the blast, but the pressure waves shook him about violently. "Saints shitting," he groaned. Some of the suit seal warnings were now turning amber. His gland pulsed out another discharge. It didn't seem to make any difference. The explosion had died away, but his limbs were still shaking. Body temperature was up, except his skin now felt like ice.

"Calm!" he ordered himself. "For fuck's sake, keep calm!" His voice sounded thin and pathetic. *What would Yirella do?* A question that brought about a dangerously wild giggle. *Not get into this shit to start with.*

It was looking bad. The cohort had come to a halt; their gravitonic drives weren't strong enough to push any farther through the churning knot of tendrils.

Can't use grenades again.

Energy weapons are heating the fluid.

Power blades beaten.

Come on, think!

The suit sensors showed him tendrils starting to wrap around his legs. He'd be cocooned in minutes, probably less. He didn't have the power to tear the strands free.

Power!

He yelled out the old yeargroup games war cry. It was shockingly loud in the helmet, ratcheting up the claustrophobia another couple of degrees, and now there was the very real prospect of drowning in alien gunk if the seals were breached. It took him thirty seconds to issue instructions to the cohort, rerouting the electrical output of their aneutronic fusion chambers, taking safety systems offline, cranking the output to redline.

"Go," he commanded.

The combined power of the twenty-seven generators discharged through the cohort's shells. Everything went black. Dellian had no displays, no suit functions. He couldn't even sense the cohort, which spiked his fear.

Black panic really hit then. He began to struggle. The suit held him tight. He screamed.

"Hang on," Tilliana's smooth voice instructed through the unnerving darkness. "We're getting you out."

The high-pitched whine of actuators cut through Dellian's frenzy. He forced himself to stop thrashing about and drew some shaky breaths. A crack of bright light appeared right in front of him as the helmet hinged apart. *Faster! Great Saints, I want this to stop.* Then the spongy contact pads that made up the interior of the suit released their grip on his sweaty skin. The helmet finished opening, and he could see the simulation egg's upper segments rising away from his body on the end of metal tentacles. They withdrew into a service globe in the middle of the simulation chamber, leaving him drifting a few centimeters above the pedestal that formed the rear half of the egg. He reached up and peeled the medic patches from his neck and thighs, then pulled the waste tube cap from his dick.

The cohort returned to haunt the back of his mind, and they didn't seem upset at all. It had all been just another training session for them.

"You okay?" Tilliana asked.

"Sure. Fine." Right now Dellian didn't want to think about what had happened, how badly he'd reacted to the exercise. The stress had drained away, to be replaced by shabby embarrassment. He could barely bring himself to glance around the spherical chamber.

The other simulation eggs had opened, leaving his squad floating listlessly above the pedestals. Most of them didn't even have the energy to remove their patches and tubes.

That was bad, he thought—although a part of him was wondering if they didn't deserve it. The last eighteen months had seen them run through some of the toughest simulations the tech strategists could dream up—and they could dream nasty. Eighty-three percent success level, putting their squad well out in front of anyone else. This, though, this was on a whole other level of crap.

He could guess why it had been created. The senior staff had decided it wouldn't hurt for the squad to have their confidence beaten down once in a while. He could even agree with the theory. But the actual experience—fearing you were about to smother, totally alone, without even your cohort, buried alive in the center of malignant alien goop—it made him worry just how much it would affect them.

But he was squad leader, which made it his job to rally them. *I don't want to let them down.* He pushed off and glided through the air to Xante. "Well, fuck, huh?"

Xante gave him a weak smile. Even that clearly took a lot of effort.

"Hey," Dellian shouted, looking around. "Anyone make it out intact?"

Some shook their heads. Others couldn't even meet his gaze. The atmosphere in the chamber was worse than they'd known when they'd been stranded in the fake flyer accident all those years ago. The sim had taken them right back down to wrecked little kids again. And he resented that, feeling a spark of anger amid the gloom. "Tilliana," he called, "that was an eleven on my utter bastard meter. Uret, no sex for her tonight. That's an order, clear?"

Uret's lips lifted a fraction. "Clear."

A few halfhearted smiles appeared around the chamber.

The chamber door irised open five meters away from where Dellian was floating. Tilliana came sliding up through the gap, an arm reaching out to steady herself on Rello's egg pedestal.

Dellian had assumed she'd have a sly smile on her face, a few teasing phrases ready about how useless they all were. The banter would flow, camaraderie restored. Instead she looked troubled, which resurrected all his own doubts about what had just happened.

Ellici air-swam into the chamber, also looking upset. But with that came a degree of exasperation. She had always lacked Tilliana's patience.

"All right," Dellian said to the pair of them. "Tell us that wasn't a suicide mission."

"Of course not," Ellici said. "You barely got through fifteen percent of the asteroid."

"You?" Xante challenged dangerously. "What happened to *us*? To we? You're supposed to be our guardian angels. We're too dumb to figure out what's happening, remember? We *rely* on you."

"Ease off," Dellian said, making it as casual as he could.

"Fucking felt like a suicide job," Falar grunted. He was plucking medical patches from his neck, his mood dark.

"So how do we get through the asteroid?" Mallot asked.

"Come on," Tilliana said. "They don't give us cheat sheets. These sim missions are only going to get worse from now on. Better get used to it."

"Thanks," Xante said. "Demoralized—best way to go up against the enemy for real."

Dellian gave him a warning glance. "Enough. We're a team. We go through this together."

"I was about to warn you about the passageway organics," Tilliana said. "I was slow. Sorry."

"So you did have a way out?" Uret asked her gently.

"She still doesn't get any tonight," Rello chided.

At least that brought a few grins, Dellian thought.

"No," Tilliana said slowly. "But if the bioluminescence was dimming, it must mean the cells were diverting their nutrient energy for another function. And they were."

"Hindsight," Colian said regretfully. "Always the clearest."

"All right," Dellian said, making an effort to get them all back on track. "We'll have a full review tomorrow before we go back in. It's a wash for the rest of today. The Saints know we need a break after that. Maybe a drink."

They agreed, their mood lifting slightly. The last connection pads were pulled off bodies. The squad started to air-dive toward the entrance. Uret drifted alongside Tilliana and gave her a soft kiss as they slid past the rim, both of them laughing at the jeers they received.

Dellian was just about to leave when Xante clamped a hand around his ankle.

"We're not a team," he said.

"What do you mean?" Dellian asked. He certainly wasn't in the mood for this. He had a pleasant time all lined up, which he knew would ease him over his frustration. Then tomorrow they'd be back up here in the high-orbit station ready to kick the shit out of that bastard asteroid assault sim.

"Ellici and Tilliana are only two thirds of a team," Xante said.

"Great Saints, rest this! It's been years."

"And she's not coming back. I get it. But we need someone to replace her. Yirella wouldn't have let us get caught with our asses hanging out like this. Fucking Saints, I thought I was going to die back there!"

"It's a sim."

"Yeah, like you were all relaxed and calm. We were a fucking shambles in there, all of us."

"Overcommitted," Dellian muttered. "They warned us about that. The sims are so fucking real, you cooperate in suspending belief."

"Well, you'd better ask them for training to get over that, or therapy—or something." He shook his head. "I'm actually nervous about going back in there tomorrow. And that's ridiculous."

"I know."

After a shower and a change of clothes, Dellian took a portal over to Kabronski Station, orbiting 80,000 kilometers above Juloss. The heart of the old skyfort formation was a rectangular grid, twenty kilometers long, with weapon systems arranged in neat rows on the outer side, all powered up and vigilant for the enemy's arrival. In the middle of the side that faced Juloss, a gravity anchor pylon extended for fifty kilometers down toward the planet, keeping the whole structure aligned. The pylon ended at a small metal asteroid, where a two-kilometer toroid housed the military crew and construction managers for the battleships being fitted out in the attendant cluster of industrial stations that floated in the grid's shadow. There were also some other, more specialist, teams resident in the toroid.

Yirella was waiting for him in the garden section, a chunk of toroid three hundred meters long, with a geodesic roof of thick transparent hexagons. The vegetation was tropical and after two hundred years getting quite overgrown despite the best efforts of the horticultural remotes to trim and prune.

As always, she bent down and greeted him with a platonic kiss. After that unthinking greeting, she stopped and studied his face. "What happened?"

"Saints! That obvious?"

Her smile grew taunting. "Ah, the asteroid base with biowall tunnels."

"You know about it?"

"The sim team has been preparing that for weeks. They've been giggling like nine-year-olds telling fart jokes over how you'd all react."

"It wasn't funny, Yi."

"I know." She put her arm through his and walked with him down a path. "That contraction thing freaked me out."

"You've been in it?" he asked in astonishment, not knowing if he should be angry or impressed with her.

"Yeah. They needed volunteers for the test runs. I made a few suggestions to improve the effect. The threat of the suit seals failing and drowning you under pressure, that was me." She sounded proud.

"You helped make it worse?"

Now her grin was mischievous. "I know you boys best. The sim crew values my input."

"Bloody hell!"

"The enemy isn't going to go easy on us."

"I know, but . . . you!" He shook his head in mock bewilderment. "Such betrayal."

"Hey." She gave him an affectionate slap.

It was moments like that, the ease they had between them, that gave him hope for the future. Over the last year they'd regained so much of what they used to have. They met when their schedules matched, talked, sometimes viewed dramas together; several times they'd been to concerts. Not quite like the old times. They hadn't become lovers again. Yet. But the relationship, whatever it was, had been too much for Xante. "I can't compete with this," he'd told Dellian as he moved out of their quarters.

"With what?" a depressed Dellian had challenged.

Xante gave him a simple shrug. "Hope. That you'll get back together with her. That the pair of you will fly on to Sanctuary after the final battle, and live happily ever after. Crap like that, you're never here anymore."

"I am!"

"Not in your head, you're not. You spend all your head time thinking of her."

"I tried an electrical discharge," Dellian now explained to Yirella. "But I panicked and put too much power into it. Fried every chunk of technology in there."

"Okay, well, the idea was sound."

"Yeah? So—"

"No, I'm not giving you any clues."

Dellian managed a weak smile and put his arm around her. "But it is solvable? We can get to the negative energy loop chamber?"

"Probably." She laughed.

They wandered along to one of their favorite groves, where the trunks of the older trees grew upward in an identical shallow curvature as they followed the camber of the toroid's rotational gravity, as if they'd all bowed to the same wind. He always found walking underneath them to be slightly disconcerting. Orchids and trailing moss swamped the boughs above, with bright-plumed birds zipping about. On the edge of the grove was a small waterfall emptying into a pond filled with ancient gold and black koi fish. A marble table was perched beside it, inside the ribs of a radial pergola draped with sweet flowering jasmine.

When they sat down, remotes started to unpack their meal and lay it out for them. Dellian sipped some of the wine they poured and scanned the small slice of star field he could see through the shaggy vegetation. Juloss was always visible just above the lip of the geodesic, while the various free-flying subsidiary stations slipped in and out of view, tracing short arcs.

"Is that the *Morgan*?" he asked, as one of the battleship assembly stations appeared.

She barely glanced up from the plate of seared scallops the remote had put down in front of her. "No, the *McAuley*. You can't see the *Morgan* from here."

"It's nearly finished."

"I know."

He started eating his own scallops, wishing there were more than just three. Ship assignments had finally come through last week, and the *Morgan* was going to be carrying Dellian and his squad out into the galaxy. He was desperate to know if Yirella was going to be on board with them, but too terrified to ask. If she wasn't, then that was it; the end. Relativistic time dilation would ensure their parting would be final. Though perhaps one day in a few thousand years, one of them might read of the other in a history file, when the human race was finally reunited.

He opened his mouth to ask, but heard himself say: "How's the lure coming?"

Yirella's smile was bright and genuine. "Really good. The enemy won't be able to resist investigating this civilization when they start broadcasting radio signals. We're calling them the Vayan. They'll be quadruped, with a double-section body, like two doughnuts one on top of the other, with legs on the lower section, and arms and mouths on the second, then on the top they'll have a prehensile sensor neck. They can move in any direction without having to turn around."

Dellian frowned as he tried to picture that. "Really? I thought animals evolved to go in one direction. There's always a front and back."

"No," she said. "It's not an absolute. Wilant had an animal genus that possessed quintuple directionality."

"Where's Wilant?"

"It's a cryoplanet, over seven thousand light-years away. A traveler generation starship found it a long time ago. They stopped there for fifty years to study the indigenous species. There was some interesting biochemistry involved."

"A cryoplanet?"

"Yes."

"I thought everything moves slowly on a cryoplanet."

"Their metabolism energy levels are lower, so generally mobile life there isn't as fast as a standard world. But the species on Wilant had a chemical reserve, so they could move faster if they were threatened. Sort of like us with an adrenaline rush."

"Okay, and they had—what? Five heads?"

"No, they used sound waves to examine their environment. They could process the echo in every direction at once. They had a unique neurology to give them that ability."

"So these things were predators, like the morox?"

She shook her head in amusement and sipped some of the wine. "Not quite. More like starfish. They moved through seas of methane, clogged up with a lot of hydrocarbon slush—hence the sonar."

"You're kidding. You're dreaming up a sentient species based on blind starfish?"

"It's an extrapolation exercise. The Wilant neurology gives us a logical progression to make sentient Vayans appear realistic. We're already growing full-scale Vayan biologics in molecular initiators. They need refining, but they're valid. It's really interesting work, Dellian; very challenging. I love it."

He paused as remotes cleared the starter dishes away. "And that's what you do? Make the actual aliens?"

"The biochemistry is fascinating, but no. I'm on the worldbuilding team. We're fashioning their entire culture based on the physiology we created, along with their history, language, art. Deciding how territorial and aggressive they are, and why."

"And are they? Aggressive?"

"Oh, yes. Not quite as much as we were pre-spaceflight, but enough to give them a believably fast technological development. That way we can get the radio emissions up and broadcasting as soon as we find a suitable planet."

"The whole history of a species." He pursed his lips. "I'm impressed."

"Don't be—well, *do*. But our job is to design the parameters and plot the overall timeline. Even gentens lack imagination at that level, so it's still down to good old human creative brainpower. Once we've got that framework in place, the gentens will churn out the details, like names and places and micro-politics, scandal and gossip and celebrities. Crap like that."

He raised his wineglass to her. "So basically, you've become a goddess, creating a whole world."

She lifted her own glass and touched it to his. "Yep. So behave, or I'll start smiting you with thunderbolts."

"I believe you." Without any thought, he leaned over the table and kissed her. "Come with us on the *Morgan*. Please, Yirella. I can't bear the idea of doing this without you. No, forget *doing this*. I just don't want to be without you."

The expression she responded with frightened him. He'd seen it once before: that desperation and loneliness, the night before poor Uma and Doony.

Her arm stretched across the table toward him. He saw the fingers trembling and instinctively grasped her hand.

"Do you mean that?" she asked. "Really? After everything?"

"I mean it," he said. "I've never been more certain about anything."

"I'm not sure I deserve you."

"Wrong way round."

"I am coming with you, on the *Morgan*. I had them assign me there a month ago."

Dellian couldn't help it; he started laughing. "You are so much smarter than me, aren't you?"

"No. I just think things through quicker, that's all."

"If that's not a definition of smart, I don't know what is."

She came over and sat in his lap, grinning as she twined her arms around his neck. "I want to be honest with you."

"Same here."

"Dellian, I'm serious. We can't guarantee a long-term future; it's wrong to try and tell ourselves that can happen. You and I aren't traveler generation humans. We exist to fight a war—a fact that haunts me still, and probably always will. We may win, we may not, or we might die achieving victory. The only inevitable part of this is that the *Morgan* will fight. And the odds are not good."

"I know. But whatever time we have, we get to spend it together. That's all I need."

Her nose rubbed gently against his. "My Dellian. So noble."

Dellian pushed forward and kissed her. It was every bit as good as he remembered.

THE ASSESSMENT TEAM

hadn't known Jessika had been part of the team the Utopials had brought together to deal with Cancer. She was sitting down at the other end of the cabin, next to Loi. The pair of them had been sharing quite a bit of time since the Trail Ranger had left Nkya's base camp. And both of them had pasts I didn't know about. Not covered up, but it would clearly take a lot of digging to provide a full timeline for both of them.

Of course, you could say the same for Yuri, Callum, and Alik, too. More so, given how many layers of security their records were buried under. But they were my direct route into the real policy makers—the ones who mattered. The ones who logically could be the source of human paranoia toward the Olyix, and the phenomenal resources various human factions had wasted by spying on them. I had been convinced that one of them was working for an unseen malicious enemy who opposed every benefit the Olyix had brought to the Sol system. Kandara had been an outside chance, as well; it had been an odd decision for the Utopial senior council to bring her in to eliminate the sabotage. I thought it might be Callum, but now it seemed he didn't approve of her at all. Still, that much coincidence was unusual; perhaps God was trying to tell me something . . .

Alik nodded ruefully after Kandara finished telling her story. "So that's what happened to Cancer. I always wondered."

"Let me guess," Yuri said. "Your precious Bureau never found out who had employed Cancer to sabotage Bremble's industrial stations and Onysko's research teams."

"We looked," Callum said. "For years. But for all she was a complete bitch, Cancer was good. She left very little trace, digital or physical."

"Plenty took her place," Alik growled. "There's still a lot of dark ops teams duking it out with national agencies and corporate security. Her death didn't change anything."

"No big immediate change," I said. "But you'd never be able to crack New York's shield files these days. What about Bremble and Onysko?"

"Secure," Callum confirmed. "The incident with Cancer made us realize how exposed we were. We use G8Turings to manage and filter our critical networks now. The senior council made the Bureau swallow its pride and set up some exchanges with Sol agencies to share information on activists and fanatics. We developed our own safeguard routines."

"So everyone's a winner," Alik grumbled. "Except the people whose lives she ruined before you caught up with her."

"She won't ruin any more lives," Kandara said. "That's a good result to me."

"The people who hired her will just carry on," Alik said. "Killing her was just a glitch to their plans; it didn't solve anything."

Kandara gave him a frigid stare. "I didn't kill her. She committed suicide."

"You should have made a deal."

"I offered."

"Not very well, clearly. Genuine law enforcement is about balance. For all her reputation, Cancer was a small fish. Basically, your
mirror image."

"Go fuck yourself!"

The cabin became very still. A moment that stretched out—

"We're almost there," I said, as the images from the sensors on the
front of the Trail Ranger splashed across my tarsus lenses. The last
thing I wanted was a fight to break out, which would have soured the
atmosphere beyond repair. My suspects were still being open with
one another, and I needed that to continue. Somewhere in among all
the paranoia that dominated both sides of the Universal–Utopial divide had to be a clue to where it came from. They remained my best
hope of finding the origin, the alien.

Everybody perked up at hearing the trip was coming to an end
and started to access the Trail Ranger's sensors.

The crash site base had just appeared on the horizon—a cluster
of six silver-white geodesic domes, locked together with stubby
pressure tubes. Big as they were, they were dwarfed by the inflatable
hangar that had been thrown over the alien ship—a rectangle of
green-and-red silicone fabric large enough to cover a football field,
looking so tight against the structural containment webbing it might
burst at any second.

None of the domes had a garage; that would have been a waste of
expensive habitation space. Up in the cab, Sutton Castro and Bee Jain
carefully maneuvered the Trail Ranger to an airlock tube sticking out
from the side of a dome.

We all waited while the seal clanked and hissed. Then the "pressure normal" icon splashed up.

Lankin Wharrier, the base commander, was waiting for us on the
other side. One of Connexion's finest troubleshooters, he had an en-
gaging smile that backed up a dynamic air. When he spoke it was

with smooth authority, leaving no one in any doubt he was in charge here, no matter what title any of us had stuck on our desks back home.

"I guess you all want to go straight to see the ship?" he asked.

"Of course," Yuri said.

Lankin gestured down the tube. Like the first Eridanus base, this one gave the impression of being both a rugged pioneer outpost and incredibly expensive. The brief glimpses we got walking past labs and personnel quarters were of every facility and piece of equipment being top-of-the-range, but sitting in the starkest environment possible. I found that reassuring, after a fashion.

The clean chamber was divided into three sections, which was where corporate technobabble had claimed its fiefdom. We had the Alien Environment Suit (AES) egress room (changing room). Followed by the terra-bio sterilization section (eradicating terrestrial bugs from the surface of the AES before visiting the ship). And finally the xeno-bio decontamination suite, which resembled a bunch of cubicles in a country-club locker room, where you were showered and irradiated after leaving the ship, to make sure no alien pathogens got loose in the base.

My AES wasn't as bulky as some space suits I'd worn. For a start there was no need for a radiation layer, nor particle impact armor. The thermal moderator layer was also pretty thin. Basically it was like putting on an overall with an integrated helmet. When I'd slipped in through the long opening up the spine, Sandjay interfaced and the opening sealed up, followed by the collar at the base of the helmet tightening to form an airtight seal around my neck. It took another minute for the rest of the pale-blue fabric to contract around my skin, flushing excess air out. With the suit forming a thick second skin, my freedom of movement noticeably increased. The telemetry splash showed me everything was stable. If I read the display right, the power in the quantum batteries could keep the air recycler module operating for a month.

The helmets cut down on casual chatter, and the reflective coating hid faces from sight, but I could tell from body posture alone that everyone was keen to get going. They would have read the same thing in my stance.

We moved into the sterilization section, with three pressure doors closing behind us. Jets of gray-blue gas sprayed down from the ceiling to be sucked away by the grilles in the floor. The procedure took five minutes before Lankin Wharrier led us into the final airlock.

As soon as they arrived to set up camp, the engineering team and their remotes had scraped the regolith away from around the ship, exposing the bedrock underneath. With that clear, they'd fused the rim of the hangar directly onto the rock before inflating the envelope. A pure nitrogen atmosphere was pumped in, which had slowly been raised from ambient temperature up to ten degrees Celsius to assist the science teams.

We trooped down the ramp into a bright glare thrown by lights studding the hangar fabric. The ship they illuminated was a dark botanical red, like a once-vibrant flower losing its bloom. It measured about sixty meters long and thirty wide. At its highest it rose maybe twenty-five meters above the ground. But those were only the overall dimensions. The fuselage itself was probably fifteen percent smaller, a basic truncated cone shape with a flattened belly. The extra dimensions were made up from protrusions—call them small wings or fins—nearly three hundred of them sticking out from every part of the ship. Quite a few were bent or broken off, showing the kind of damage it'd suffered from its hard landing. From what I could see, it had struck the ground along its port side before coming to rest more or less flat on its belly.

A hatch was open near the front, where three of the stumpy fins had twisted out of alignment to clear a route to it. The hatch itself used electromechanical actuators, nothing too different from human technology.

"The ship's atmosphere had bled out," Lankin said, "so the techs just allowed it to fill with nitrogen; it's a good neutral, nonreactive gas. So far we haven't monitored any adverse reaction in the structure."

"Do you know what the original atmosphere was?" Loi asked.

"Preliminary examination of the life support indicates an oxygen nitrogen mix. The percentages seem to be different from Earth, but not much; slightly heavier on the oxygen percentage."

"What are all the wing-things?" Callum asked. "Are they functional?"

"They have a core of material similar to our active-molecular technology. As near as the physics team can figure it, they're negative energy conductors."

"Negative energy? You mean exotic matter? Wormholes?"

"Yes."

"So it is an FTL drive?" Eldlund said excitedly.

"Possibly."

"Possibly?"

"The fins are only conductors," Lankin said. "We think they were used to channel a flow of negative energy. So far we haven't found anything on board that can create negative energy."

"So how did it fly?"

"Best guess, it rode along a wormhole the way trains used to ride along railway tracks."

"But something went wrong," Yuri said suddenly. "It jumped the rails."

"Most likely. If it fell out of the wormhole somehow, and emerged back into space-time, it might not have been able to get back in. There are fusion chambers in the aft section, which would serve as rockets as well as generators."

"So . . . it dropped out of a wormhole tunnel into interstellar space, then flew here on a fusion drive?"

"That's pretty much the consensus here, yes."

"Holy shit!"

"And you said there are humans on board," Loi said. "Which means there's an alien wormhole terminus open in a human star system?"

"Yes," Lankin said. "That's about the size of it."

"The amount of energy required to create a wormhole is phenomenal," Loi continued, as if he was voicing thoughts as they formed. "Even the combined output of Sol's solarwells would probably fall short. It would take a type two civilization on the Kardashev scale to generate the power levels required."

"Again, yes."

"Oh, Je-zus wept," Alik hissed. "Are you telling me the conspiracy crazies were right all along? We're being fucking spied on by little green men? We have been since the 1950s? And they do shove things up our ass when they abduct us?"

"Oh, no," Lankin said in a darkly amused tone. "They do much worse than that."

"What the actual fuck—?"

"Let's go in, shall we?"

We followed him inside. The hatch opened into a simple airlock chamber. Engineers had removed the inner door, allowing a dozen power and data cables to snake through and work their way into the ship, branching at every junction.

Sandjay splashed up a schematic of the ship; ninety percent of it had been mapped. The missing sections were mainly big chunks of machinery, like the fusion tubes and various tanks. Corridors were wide tubes, illuminated with strings of lights threaded along them, stuck into place by dobs of takhesive. A human ship would have corridors running the length of the fuselage with branches at right angles. This ship had them in overlapping circles, some of which were inclined steeply, with the cylindrical chambers arranged in clusters.

Lankin took us to the central compartment, which ran the full height of the ship. It was divided into three levels by walkway grids, but without any handrails. All the bulkhead walls were made of a smooth, dull metal that looked like it had been extruded as a single unit, with no displays or control panels visible anywhere. The only breaks in its surface were small life-support grilles.

Several science techs were working inside, their instruments stuck to the bulkheads. Optical cables formed a messy spider's web, hanging between them and three G8Turings encased in their protective black metal cases, ribbed by cooling fins.

Lankin climbed a rope ladder up to the middle walkway.

"We're calling this the bridge," he said, "because this is what seemed to be in charge."

There was a two-meter-diameter sphere suspended in the center of the chamber by ten radial rods as wide as my hand. We crowded around it, feet close to the edge of the walkway. It was as blank as the rest of the structure, giving nothing away. Except now it had about twenty sensor pads stuck to it, and some big 3-D screens resting precariously on the rods. The image they were showing was like a deep scan of a big egg.

"Okay," Yuri said wearily. "What is it?"

"An organic neural processor unit," Lankin said. "Or to put it bluntly, the ship's brain. The onboard network isn't optical, or even digital. It's neurological." He patted the rods. "These are a combination of nerve conduits and nutrient feeds; think of them as the spine. The nerve fibers link every piece of machinery, and plenty of them are biomechanical."

"Is it still alive?" Kandara asked in alarm.

"No. However, two of the smaller fusion tubes are still functioning, so there is power. And as far as we can tell, the nutrient organ system that supports the brain was undamaged before it froze. We're theorizing the brain must have been alive to pilot the ship from when it fell out of the wormhole to Nkya, then died sometime after the landing. Cause of death unknown, but we're thinking one of the first systems that failed was the life-support heating."

"A brain this size couldn't work out how to fix a heating circuit?" Callum said skeptically. "Bollocks."

"It depends on what else was damaged by the landing. And this is where our alien's biology starts to get really interesting. We sampled the brain cells, of course. The genetic molecule has a similar functionality to Kcells."

"Shit, this is an *Olyix* ship?"

"I said similar. My team is telling me this is a lot more sophisticated than Olyix biogenetics. All the traits this alien molecule contains seem to be equally valid. There is no equivalent to the junk chromosome we have in human DNA, which effectively gives every cell the ability to become any type of cell required by the designer. It's like a super stem cell; any function can be switched on by the correct chemical activant code. As long as you have a valid pattern, you can build yourself whatever you want. In this case they chose to build a brain."

"Christ almighty!"

"It gets better. Some of the tanks on board are full of these cells in neutral mode. All dead now, of course."

"Enough," Alik snapped. "What about the fucking crew? Where are their bodies?"

"There aren't any," Lankin said. "None that we've found, anyway."

"Hell, man, that makes no sense," Callum said. "Okay, I get this isn't how we'd design a spaceship, for a start I have serious problems with the lack of redundancy. But if the brain didn't need a crew, why are there all these compartments?"

"Our working theory is that the brain simply builds itself whatever crew it needs out of the cells in the tanks, like biological Turing remotes. Our major onboard investigation is now focusing on the equipment that the tanks fed, which we're assuming is some kind of biomechanical womb. When the ship crashed here, something in that mechanism broke down. The brain couldn't build itself anything that could repair the other systems."

"No," Alik said bluntly. "That's wrong. You said the hatch was open when you got here, right?"

"Yes."

"That implies something left the ship after it arrived. The brain had no reason to open it otherwise. Some kind of mobile thinking alien was on board. Have you searched the surrounding area?"

"Right now there are over fifteen hundred drones outside, looking for any trace of activity that's taken place on the surface. So far they've covered just over a thousand square kilometers. There's nothing, not a dint that looks like a footprint—or hoofprint, claw mark, or tentacle squiggle—no line that could be some kind of wheel track, or a blast pit from a rocket exhaust. Nothing! If an alien left this ship, it flew off into the sky without touching the ground."

"If it'd been rescued, they wouldn't have left the distress beacon on," Callum said.

"We're dealing with alien psychology," Eldlund said. "You can't make assumptions like that."

"If they were rescued, why leave the cargo behind?" Lankin countered.

"Speaking of which," Yuri said, "I want to see them next."

"Of course."

The cargo section was the largest aft compartment, another cylinder, wider than the "bridge." This one was divided up into four levels. The walkways were a lot narrower to accommodate the hibernation pods. Several medical technicians were occupied examining the alien apparatus and the sensors that were probing their secrets.

"No atmosphere," Lankin said. "But the power has remained on for the hibernation systems."

"Lucky for them," Kandara said.

"Depends on your point of view," Lankin muttered.

The corridor had brought us out onto the compartment's second level. I glanced around at the hibernation pods, which were bulky sarcophagi with a smooth, curving, transparent front. They were all dark and cold, unoccupied.

"These look like something a human designed," Loi said.

"They're designed to accommodate humans," Lankin told him, "which is providing you with a visual bias. But I can assure you the components are of alien manufacture. Whoever made the ship produced them. You'll see why on the next level."

One by one we followed him up the rope ladder that had been rigged to connect the walkways.

"How did the hypothetical crew get up and down?" Eldlund muttered as he swung about.

"The compartments are all positioned at right angles to the assumed direction of flight," Lankin said. "So our conclusion was that there is no acceleration force while it flies along the inside of the wormhole, and that the docks at both ends are in free-fall."

I was last up the rope ladder. It was only when I was halfway up to the third level that I noticed everyone had fallen silent. When I stepped onto the walkway grid, the assessment team was bathed in the pale blue-white light shining out of the units. They were all staring in. And I could hear the awkward sounds of people trying to control their gag reflex.

The hibernation units did contain humans—just not complete ones. Their limbs had been removed, leaving the torsos and heads almost intact. They were held in place against the rear of the hibernation chamber by a blue-tinted membrane that looked as if it had been shrink-wrapped around them. It was translucent, revealing that the original skin had also been removed. The quadriplegic bodies were like medical anatomy models, with all their sinew, bones, blood vessels, and organs visible. The eye sockets were empty, and the ears had also been detached, along with any genitals. Four alien organics, resembling umbilical cords, were attached to the empty hip and shoulder sockets, their veins and arteries pulsing slowly as blood circulated in and out. They were connected to external organs that rested like flaccid cushions of flesh down the side of the hibernation unit.

"No fucking way," Alik announced.

I watched, mesmerized by the med-remotes that had invaded the sarcophagi through a tiny sterile airlock tube drilled into the glass casing. The insectile machines crawled across the taut restraining membrane, whisker-like feelers probing its structure down to the cellular level; larger clusters swarmed around the junctions between umbilicals and body, exploring the fusion.

Vital signs were displayed across screens rigged up on a temporary carbon-strut framework—a whole genre of symbology beyond my comprehension.

"Are these actual humans, or is this some kind of replica the ship's brain was building out of alien cells?" Yuri asked.

"They're human," Lankin said. "Or at least they used to be. The medical team has taken extensive samples. Their brains are completely intact, along with some of the original organs. However, the rest of their bodies have been replaced by Kcells. Basically, the torso organs have been reduced down to the brain's life support system, which is sustained by the nutrients supplied by the artificial organs in the hibernation chamber. They're powered by electricity, so as long as the fusion generators are working, these people stay alive."

"Are they conscious?" a horrified Loi asked.

"No. Brainwave activity is consistent with a coma in all of them. Blood chemistry analysis has revealed the presence of some sophisticated barbiturates, which we assume are sustaining the coma state."

Yuri was leaning so far forward, his helmet was practically touching the sarcophagi casing. "Why remove the limbs?"

"We can only assume they're not required. Certainly maintaining the muscle and bone structure would be a drain on the hibernation support organs. Incidentally, those exterior organs are made completely out of Kcells."

"It *is* an Olyix ship, then?"

"That's the only indicator we have of their involvement. We don't understand why the cells in the ship's tanks weren't used to fabricate the hibernation chamber mechanisms; they are considerably more sophisticated. Presumably because Kcells have been proven to work in combination with human biochemistry. Given this setup has successfully kept them alive for the thirty years since the ship crashed, it would be a valid explanation."

"They snatched seventeen humans," Callum said, "then did this to them to keep them alive. Why? I mean, what's the bloody point?"

"Is it reversible?" Eldlund asked. "Can they be given their bodies back?"

"We can clone every part of a human body, or print it with stem cells, or replicate it with Kcells," Jessika said. "The technologies are established. But actually doing a Frankenstein and stitching all those parts together is just about impossible. I'd say the only way to do it in this case would be to clone the original body, but somehow prevent the brain from developing. Which—" she sighed "—would take a lot of research. And even if you did succeed, you'd have the problem of transplanting the old brain into its new body."

"Ha!" Yuri grunted. "That again."

"I thought Hai-3 told you it was theoretically possible?" Eldlund challenged.

"Theoretically, yeah. But that's another huge research project. Even if Alpha Defense approved, it would take decades and billions of wattdollars to get them walking around in a decent body again."

Eldlund's hand gestured at the sarcophagi. "I imagine they would think it's worthwhile."

"But the risk . . ." Callum said.

"You want to know if it's acceptable? Ask one," Kandara said. "Put one of these poor bastards into a decent human-built life-support system, flush the barbiturate shit out of their brains, and they might wake up."

"And they might not," a shocked Eldlund replied.

"Then you learn enough about the failure to improve the technique for the next one," she said. "And keep going until we've perfected it. Because we all know we're going to have to try this at some point. We're not going to leave them like this."

"The psychological trauma alone would be massive," Loi said uneasily.

"Tough. For the record: If you ever find me like this, either wake me up or kill me. Don't leave me like this."

"I'm not—"

"There might be a way around this," Lankin interrupted. "The doctors are hopeful they can recover the Odd One."

"The Odd One?" Kandara queried. "What the hell is that?"

"Yeah, sorry. My team is a bit on the nerdish side, and they don't have a lot of imagination. They called him the Odd One because he's different from the rest."

"Different how?" I asked sharply.

"See for yourself," he said. "Next level up."

I went up the rope ladder after Alik. Three of the hibernation chambers contained the same kind of membrane-wrapped torsos we'd seen before. The fourth . . . he was intact. There was no restraining membrane. A single umbilical cord was fused to his navel, hanging down to a trio of external organs, larger than those in the other chambers. Shock froze me to the spot.

"That's not possible," an equally stunned Yuri said.

"What do you mean?" Callum asked.

"He can't be here. Not him!"

"Wait! You *know* him?"

"Yes. It's Lucius Soćko. He vanished when we rescued Horatio Seymore on Althaea."

They made the decision after dinner. Everyone who'd come on the Trail Ranger settled in the base's lounge to talk it over. Not that it was much of a democracy. Callum clearly had reservations, but in the end he conceded that attempting to revive Soćko was necessary. I didn't give an opinion; it would be out of character as the mission's humble administration guy. But Jessika approved, as I thought she would. Kandara didn't contribute much; she'd made her view clear back on the ship. Loi and Eldlund were a lot more cautious—we should investigate longer, bring in more equipment and specialists, make detailed risk assessments. Typical corporate culture kids. They had no concept of taking responsibility, because that meant consequences—

and Legal always hated consequences. Not that their views mattered. Ultimately it was down to Yuri, Callum, and Alik, and they were unanimous.

Lankin sat with us in the lounge as everyone talked it over, but didn't say anything. When he was given the verdict, he responded with a gruff: "Okay then," and left to organize the operation. It didn't take long; his people had been working balls-out to prepare for this ever since they put eyes on the Odd One.

It took them six hours. Remotes cut Soćko's hibernation chamber out of the ship's cargo compartment and carefully maneuvered it around the circular passages into the research base. The alien environment laboratory had been converted into an intensive care suite in anticipation.

A small observation room ran alongside, with a broad window looking in. We crowded around it to watch the hibernation chamber arrive. The trollez that delivered it was barely visible, the damn thing was surrounded by so many techs and doctors all in their protective blue suits.

"What's the atmosphere inside that thing?" Yuri asked.

"Earth standard gas mix," Lankin told him. "All the hibernation chambers are the same. No alien pathogens inside, either—that we've detected." His knuckles rapped on the window. "But we're not taking any chances. This lab is quadruple-walled, with positive pressure cavities on individual life support circuits. No bugs are going to get out of there and into my base."

The revival team slowly sliced around the edge of the hibernation chamber's transparent lid, allowing remote arms to lift it away. Out of the corner of my eye I saw Eldlund brace hirself, but Soćko's body remained inert.

The medics closed in. Monitor patches were bonded onto Soćko's skin, providing a more detailed picture of his vitals. Fleshmeld blisters were applied above his femoral and carotid arteries, ready to supply artificial blood or drugs if and when they were needed. He wasn't breathing. The blood generated in the external Kcell organs and fed through his umbilical was fully oxygenated. Artificial saliva was sprayed into his mouth, and they slid an intubation nozzle down his trachea—ready. With the prep done, they moved him out of the chamber and onto a bed.

A crash team stood by, watching and waiting as the extraction team clamped the umbilical cord—and cut it.

No warning went off. His heart kept on beating uninterrupted. Brainwave function remained flat.

The intubation nozzle started to pump oxygen-rich air into his lungs in a slow rhythm.

I watched his chest inflate, sink back down. Rise again. Soćko gave a slight shudder, then another, stronger shiver ran down his body. The revival team tensed up; crash-revival tools were held up ready. Soćko's shakes continued for a while longer before he went quiescent again.

"He's breathing naturally," the lead doctor announced. There was a note of surprise in her voice.

On the other side of the glass, the medical techs were high-fiving. Two of the doctors were preparing their surgical remotes to remove the stump of the umbilical from Soćko's navel.

"Now what?" Yuri asked.

"We wait," Lankin said. "Make sure he remains stable, and give his body a chance to filter out the barbiturates. If he wakes naturally, fair enough. If not, they'll try stimulants."

We all trooped back to the lounge, with its comfy chairs standing on the bare composite-panel floor. Loi and Eldlund went over to the freezer cabinets and started searching through the meal packs for breakfast. Alik got himself a Belgian hot chocolate from the dispenser and settled back in his chair.

"It can't be that easy," Kandara said when she sat next to me. "What about muscle atrophy? He's been lying there for thirty-two years, for fuck's sake!"

"Something took care of that," Loi said as he came over, carrying a plate of scrambled eggs, sausages, and hash browns straight from the microwave. "Something in the blood they haven't found yet. It all came from the Kcell organs, don't forget; we don't fully know what they're capable of."

"You're talking magic potions," Callum said dismissively. "Not real biochemistry. No chemical treatment will preserve an inactive body in healthy physical shape like that for thirty years."

"What then?"

Eldlund sat down beside him, blowing the steam from hir porridge. "Maybe Soćko is the success? The others are all being rebuilt by the alien cells, but he was just further along?"

"No," Yuri said. "The Kcell organs in his hibernation chamber were different. They supplied blood that's rich with oxygen and nutrients—a real hibernation as opposed to what's happened to the others."

I kept a very careful watch on the faces around me as I said: "He might not have been asleep the whole time."

Yuri gave me a look that invited me to continue. He was my boss, respecting my opinion. No change there. Callum was expectant, wanting to hear some options, clearly eager for answers. Alik continued to sit there, mug of hot chocolate in his hand, waiting like every good interrogator for the suspect to talk too much. Those lifeless face muscles of his were as still as a millpond.

"Exercise," Kandara said eagerly. She grinned at me. "That's what you mean, isn't it?"

I gave her an appreciative shrug. "The simplest solution always applies. And the only real way to maintain muscle tone is through exercise."

"So Soćko wakes up once a week," she said. "Or a month. Whatever. And spends a few days getting in some calisthenics sweat-time. Then goes back into hibernation. He's on a timer."

"Not a chance," Loi said.

Kandara shot him a challenging glance. "Why?"

"Where does he do his calisthenics? The ship has been in a vacuum for over thirty years. There's no space suit; he couldn't even step out of the hibernation chamber."

"So why is he in such good shape?"

"Genetic modification?" Loi said uncertainly.

"The medical team sequenced everyone's DNA," Lankin said. "Soćko doesn't have any modifications; we didn't even find vectors for telomere treatment in him."

"We'll find out soon enough if he wakes up," Alik said. "We just ask. Meantime, let's focus on what we do know. We came here to assess if this ship indicates a clear and present threat."

"It does," Yuri said. "Aliens with a significantly more advanced technology base have established a secret beachhead either in Sol or one of our settled systems. They snatch humans for unknown, but fucking dire, reasons."

"That's not necessarily a threat," Callum said.

"You're kidding, right?"

"Come on, man, face it: We're scary. We can cross interstellar space, and we're still aggressive, unreasonable, badly behaved, and own continents full of weapons. Hell, if I encountered us, I'd want to hold back and watch for a while."

Alik's hand shot out, pointing at random. "Did you even see what they did to those poor bastards? They *dissolved* them! They dumped humans into some kind of alien version of acid, or something, and dissolved them! What's left is being taken back home to be torture-experimented on. That is a fucking *threat*, you dumbass hippie! You got kids, right? Suppose you found one of them on board—no arms, no legs, their goddamned eyes ripped out. And that's just the start; fuck knows what else would've happened to them if this ship hadn't fallen out of the wormhole? That could be *you* and your family in there, asshole!"

For once Alik's neck and jaw muscles were flexing. Loi and Eldlund were regarding him in concern.

"Their ethics might not match ours," Callum said. "They are alien, after all. But they haven't been overtly aggressive. That has to mean something."

Alik snorted in contempt and turned to Yuri. "I need to talk to my people."

Yuri and I exchanged a slightly guilty look. "There are no direct comms with solnet," I said. "That was a major part of Alpha Defense's quarantine protocols."

"Oh, come on." Alik's voice dropped an octave to a bass purr, worldly-wise and oh-so-reasonable. "There's got to be some emergency line out, right?"

"No," I told him. "There really isn't."

"Jesus H. Christ. You are shitting me!"

"That's got to be the AI safeguard," Callum said. "Am I right?"

"Yeah," I conceded.

"The what?" Alik asked angrily.

"The ship we've found is from an alien race which, if not actively hostile, is certainly unsympathetic to humans," Yuri said. "Suppose that frozen brain-captain thing had been warm and running active routines, or it had an electronic AI like our Turings? If we had a link back to solnet, it could download itself into our networks; multiply itself a thousand times a second. The potential damage it could inflict is impossible to calculate."

"Je-zus," Alik wheezed. "That is one sonofabitch paranoia you've got going there."

"No," Yuri said levelly, "it's a very sensible precaution. Especially now I've seen what we're dealing with."

"But the aliens who built that ship are already in Sol, or one of our star systems," Alik countered. "They have been for decades, and they're smart enough to hide a fucking wormhole terminus from us. If they wanted to crash solnet, they'd have done it by now."

"We know that now," I said. "But we didn't when we set up the research base and started investigating. Deciding to allow a direct connection to solnet is one of the decisions you are here to assess. And we do still have the question of who or what opened the ship's airlock."

"Yeah, right," Alik said grudgingly.

"But I can offer you the Trail Ranger to drive you back to the portal."

Alik looked from me to Yuri. Clearly not a man used to being told *no*. "I'll give it a day," he said. "See if Soćko comes out of it. But after that, I have to file a report no matter what."

"I'll tell Sutton and Bee to have the Trail Ranger ready for you to go," I assured him.

"Which brings us back to what the bloody hell is going on," Callum said. "The aliens are watching us; they're taking us to experiment on. Why?"

"It's obviously an intelligence gathering mission," Kandara said. "They're learning our weaknesses. That can only have one outcome."

"No way," I said. "There's no such thing as interstellar war. There is no conceivable reason for it. Once a species gets off its birth world, it effectively has infinite resources. It wants for nothing. Total war is something that belongs to history for anyone who can reach orbit and beyond."

"They're alien," Jessika said. "Who knows what their motivations are? Like Callum said, we're probably quite frightening to a progressive, peaceful species."

"Taking people apart," Alik butted in loudly, the chocolate sloshing perilously close to the rim of his mug. "That ain't exactly what I'd call progressive, lady!"

"Hitler wasn't short of resources," Loi said. "Not to begin with. World War Two was an ideological war at heart, a crusade to impose Nazi imperialism on the rest of the world. Same goes for the Cold War which followed, with its capitalism versus communism."

Eldlund gave him a taunting smile. "Well, thank heavens those economic theories both lost."

Loi replied with a contemptuous finger.

"Do you believe the builders of this ship are the ones?" Callum asked. He was staring directly at Yuri.

"It's starting to look that way."

"The one what?" Jessika quizzed.

"We've all experienced it," Yuri said. "That's why we were chosen to interpret this. Though I have to admit, Soćko came as a big surprise to me. Didn't see that coming."

"Experience?" Alik clicked his fingers. "Ah, right: we've all had experiences which didn't quite add up, somehow."

"Yes," Yuri said, "and those personal cases of ours are the tip of the iceberg. We've been analyzing similar incidents for a while now, especially those with critical defense issues."

Kandara gave me a shrewd look. "I thought I was here for my professional expertise."

"That was a bonus," I told her. "You and Callum both encountered Cancer, who had been contracted on a sabotage mission that could have crippled the primary astromanufacturing capability at Delta Pavonis."

"What's the connection between that and this situation?"

"Defense," Yuri said flatly. "If Sol and the settled systems are attacked, Bremble would be essential to build—well, battleships, orbital fortress stations, everything we need to protect ourselves from an invasion."

"New York's shields," Alik said quietly. "She was going for those."

"And she was there on Bronkal, eliminating any evidence of Baptiste snatching low-visibility people—for no reason we could ever find," Yuri said. "Which is an even stronger association to what's going down here, now that we know Soćko was shipped directly from there to the ship."

"Nobody on Akitha could figure out the motivation for what Cancer was doing," Kandara said thoughtfully. "We all thought some kind of political fanatic was employing her to sabotage their industrial systems, but this . . . aliens scouting around the human race . . . I hate to say it, but this makes a kind of sense."

"Who the fuck are they," Alik snarled, "and how long have they been watching us?"

"Ask the Olyix," Loi said. "They're clearly complicit. Maybe it's them."

I let out a wearisome breath. "Not this again," I said in exasperation.

Callum gave me a sharp stare. "They lied to Yuri about Horatio Seymore. They knew he'd been snatched," he said. "They were involved. What more do you need?"

Which was an interesting outburst. Someone—some group—had to be pushing both Ainsley and the grade-one Utopials into believing the Olyix were chasing a hidden agenda, fueling the insecurities and paranoia of the old and powerful who inevitably see change as danger. And the only people with a reason to do that are the other aliens, trying to deflect attention from themselves. Aliens with influential agents in both Utopial and Universal ruling political classes.

"There was something odd about that," I agreed. "Maybe they employ corporate intelligence gathering companies to keep a closer look on things than we realized. I don't know. But face it, Ainsley Zangari's exposed granddaughter calling him in a panic is going to be noticed by *someone*. It may be Hai-3 was being a little too helpful and cooperative just to keep Zangari sweet. He is the richest, most powerful individual alive, and it would pay politically to keep him sympathetic. And I'm certain this ship we've found can't be theirs. The *Salvation of Life* is a slower-than-light arkship; the Olyix don't have wormholes. Loi, you said the power level a wormhole needs is beyond anything we produce in the Sol system."

"Yeah," he agreed almost grudgingly. "That's right."

"So it's not them," I said.

"You seem very certain," Kandara said.

I gave Yuri a quick glance. He nodded permission. It didn't go unnoticed. "It goes like this," I said. "Ainsley has been suspicious about the Olyix since before Horatio was snatched. He never quite believed their claim to be peaceful religious fanatics."

"Now that has truly got to be the universe's biggest oxymoron," Alik mocked

"Whatever they are, they're not actively hostile to humans," I said.

"You can't claim that," Eldlund said. "There's a lot of evidence piling up against them."

"Circumstantial," I replied. "Or maybe it's disinformation. Look, after Horatio, Ainsley decided to find out what was really going on. So we've been mounting a discreet surveillance on the *Salvation of Life* ever since."

"And?" Kandara prompted.

"They aren't being entirely honest with us; they are keeping secrets about themselves. But there's no conspiracy."

"You can't know that. Not for certain."

"I do."

"How?"

"Because five years back I took point on a covert mission that broke into the *Salvation of Life*."

FERITON KAYNE'S SPY MISSION

THE *SALVATION OF LIFE*, AD 2199

'd been living in Lancaster, Pennsylvania, for more than a year to physically inflate my cover story. Data-based legends are easy to install in solnet; these days you can basically be anyone you want to be, providing you have the money and expertise. Connexion Security had both in abundance. Even a G8Turing's search would only turn up the cover history I'd been given. But if the Vatican or the Grand Ayatollah actually sent someone to Lancaster, they'd be able to verify what a great citizen I was and how my attendance at local Quaker meetings was top rate. Not that anyone in the office expected any cardinals or imams to physically turn up and run a deep check. But given where I was heading, office policy was to make that cover story as real as possible. So if some dark-ops agent did come checking in person, they'd swiftly get wearied talking to neighbors and colleagues and friends who would all tell them what a great (if moderately dull) guy I was, complete with the personal anecdotes I'd generated by actually living there.

Ainsley Zangari was very clear about getting the mission absolutely right. Funding for his Olyix Monitoring Office was already over three quarters of a billion wattdollars a year. A portion of that money was spent on G8Turings that scoured solnet for evidence of operatives like Cancer corroding and corrupting corporations and institutions, with emphasis on the defense sector. Deals like that were absurdly easy to set up anonymously through solnet. So whenever we did come across an op that had defense connotations, it was virtually impossible to backtrack.

Outside of that, the Olyix Monitoring Office had two main divisions with dedicated tasks. The first ran an operation devoted to watching the Olyix embassies, which we did mainly by planting our own operatives inside among the human staff. To be honest, I don't think there was a single Olyix embassy employee who wasn't reporting back to some intelligence agency or other. Our knowledge of their official trade deals and financial status was absolute.

The second, and most involved, division was the one I wound up working for. We were trying to find out if the Olyix had opened any private portal doors between their arkship and Earth—something that would allow them to collaborate with their Kcell development partners without having to go through the official channels established by the Sol Senate—which would explain how they knew about Horatio's snatch. That was a tough one. It's not like the Olyix themselves could move around Earth unnoticed. They would have to use human agents to mount hostile operations.

But it didn't matter how many renditions we threatened and alt-legal interrogations we performed. There was no verifiable line of sight back to the Olyix. I never got that: people who would betray their own species. But I'd been in law enforcement and corporate security long enough to know that every bastard in that field simply took the money and skipped the questions. They wouldn't know and wouldn't want to know whom they were working for.

Our other problem was why the Olyix would bother. Their sole purpose for stopping in the Sol system was to buy energy to generate antimatter so they could continue their pilgrimage flight. The original theory was that they wanted to increase revenue for the Kcells by introducing new treatments and didn't care about their human partners performing illegal experiments to develop those treatments. But then we started to notice the buildup of hostile incidents in Sol's defense sector, like the attempt on the New York shield files. Nobody could figure out what was happening. Then after we heard what Cancer was doing at Delta Pavonis, Ainsley's paranoia skyrocketed up to whole new levels. The attack against Bremble made absolute sense if it was in preparation for an invasion.

My division was refocused on technology, physically locating quantum spatial entanglements between *Salvation of Life* and Earth. If we could find a portal that led back to Earth, or a habitat, we'd finally have solid proof the Olyix were hostile. But while it is possible to detect a portal's quantum signature, the equipment is short-range, large, and expensive. More than half of the Olyix Monitoring Office budget was spent on refining the sensor technology. First they had to perfect it. Then they had to make it small—really small. Finally, and with wonderful irony, they had to make it undetectable.

After that, smuggling it on board the *Salvation of Life* was almost easy. Which is where I came in.

The 2199 joint ecumenical delegation, of which I was a proud member, assembled in Vatican City. There were four such delegations every year. Somewhat inevitably, the Olyix were keen to welcome emissaries from human religions to the *Salvation of Life*. Equally understandably, our priests and rabbis and imams were eager to explore alien religion. Sorry, but the utterly devout Olyix were literally a heaven-sent opportunity in that respect.

There were seventeen of us smiling for the solnet news feeds in St. Peter's Square, with the basilica as our formidable backdrop. Most faiths were represented, so nobody was questioning a Quaker's inclusion. The robes some representatives wore were impressive; I thought they looked brand-new and obviously professionally tailored.

The most painful part of the mission was that long year in Lancaster learning about my new religion, which seemed to be about the most nonhierarchical, nonjudgmental faith anyone had ever formed. It took a great deal of self-discipline to focus on the tenets and (loose) structure, but I got there in the end. Anyone curious about Quaker history and practices would swiftly be bored into retreating as I recited it all to them.

Interestingly, it was Nahuel, the Buddhist monk, who was keenest to talk to me. He told me all about his acceptance and learning in the temple, in return listening politely to my cover story of how I came to my gentle faith. We chatted amicably as we walked through the Vatican's hub, into Rome's metro network. From the city's international hub it was just a few quick paces to the main Olyix transfer portal in Buenos Aires.

I stepped straight through into a rotational gravity effect. The toroid was small, and spinning faster than I was used to, as my inner ears were quick to let me know. I saw Nahuel pause, instinctively holding his arms out in a novice surfer's pose to regain his balance.

"Have you ever been in a space habitat before?" I asked.

He shook his head, which is always a mistake in fast-spin gravity; his lips puckered up as the combinations of deviant motion assailed his ear canals.

"It's okay," I assured him. "This is as bad as it'll get. The *Salvation* rotates very slowly; you won't feel the spin at all."

"Thank you," he said with an insincerity that his fellow monks would doubtless frown upon.

"Until then . . ." I proffered an anti-nausea tab.

"No. I wish my mind to remain clear."

"Of course."

Officially the station we were in was the Arkship Transfer Buffer Facility—a human-built space station that held position ten kilometers out from the forward end of the *Salvation of Life*. Everyone just called it the Lobby.

It was there because the Olyix had been very clear they didn't want a portal inside the arkship, especially not from Earth. They were concerned about a terrestrial plague devastating their biosphere. Fair enough; even we hadn't classified and analyzed all Earth's microbes and germs and viruses, let alone what they'd do if exposed to Olyix biology.

Negotiations via radio had started almost as soon as the *Salvation of Life* began decelerating into the Sol system back in 2144. First on the agenda after the Sol Senate's First Contact Committee started exchanging messages was: *You're not bringing that thing anywhere near Earth.* Simple reason: the forty-five-kilometer-long, multi-billion-ton arkship was powered by antimatter. The Olyix had enough of the stuff on board to accelerate it up to twenty percent of the speed of light. Which meant, should they prove hostile, the incoming aliens carried enough destructive energy to wipe out Earth and every asteroid habitat in the solar system, with plenty left over to wreck Mars and Venus for good measure (not that we'd ever bothered trying to terraform them). So the first agreement was that *Salvation* was to park in Earth's Lagrange-3 point, directly opposite Earth on the other side of the sun. Even that left some officials and old generals nervous.

Once *Salvation* reached that orbit, physical contact began. The Lobby was assembled in a couple of months—a kilometer-diameter toroid, rotating at the center of a hexagonal space dock, that serviced dozens of short-range cargo and passenger craft. All the little vehicles did all day every day was fly between the Lobby and *Salvation*'s zero-gee axis dock.

The ecumenical delegation was led into the decontamination suite—a fine name for what was basically a disinfectant shower. It lasted a compulsory eight minutes, ensuring every follicle and flesh fold on a human body was thoroughly saturated. I think prisoner hose-downs were more dignified. But it did give the contact staff time to irradiate our clothes and shoes and luggage.

We all reconvened in a small waiting room, trying not to show how disconcerting the cleansing experience had been. I wasn't sure my hair would ever recover from the chemical assault; it smelled like a bathroom air freshener.

"Do the Olyix undergo an equivalent process to travel to Earth?" Nahuel inquired. He was sitting in a plain plastic chair, holding his sandals up to give them a disapproving look. I'm pretty sure his robes were bleached a shade paler, too.

"I've no idea," I told him—not true, but I had to play the part of my new legend, and a Quaker accountant from Lancaster wouldn't know a whole lot about biological transference protection clauses in treaties the Sol Senate had negotiated. In fact, the Olyix do undergo a mild decontamination on their way to Earth, but then they never leave their embassies, which have a filtered atmosphere. However, when they come back, they're subjected to the same sanitization as humans before they can return to the *Salvation of Life*.

Our delegation took the elevator up to the toroid's axis, and free-fall. When we were halfway up, I offered Nahuel a tab again. This time he took it without a word.

A couple of stewards helped us along the zero-gee corridors in the center. The crossover chamber was a wide cylinder, with four hatch-ways on the toroid end and another four hatches at the dock end. Halfway between them was the seal, allowing the two halves of the cylinder to rotate without losing any air. Plenty of people were cross-ing between them, casually air-diving in and out of the hatches. It all seemed so crude to me, but then I'd grown up in a world that had come to live Connexion's slogan: Everywhere is one step away.

We pushed, wiggled, and knocked elbows along the corridor to airlock 17B, where our passenger ferry was docked. The cabin was a small cylinder, with thin padding on the walls, and twenty-four sim-ple metal seats in a couple of rows, with a lone seat at the front for our "pilot," who did nothing but monitor the G7Turing that actually flew us. Apparently that dates back to the days when autopilots were taking over more and more aircraft functions, but people still wanted a human in the control loop. Personally I'd trust the G7 over a human pilot any day.

I hauled myself along the cabin and claimed a seat beside one of the small windows. The dock grid stretched away out to the stars, its structure cluttered with tanks and cables that were covered in silver-white thermal blankets. Like everything in space, it was either sharply lit by sunlight or sheltering in the utter darkness of shadows. The contrast between sections was immediate and striking.

We left the dock with a soft motion and loud knocking sounds that reverberated down the cabin as the vessel's tiny rockets fired in short fast bursts. I saw the dock fall away behind us. The flight was due to take twelve minutes. At three minutes, the reaction control rockets began to fire again, rotating the craft.

The *Salvation of Life* slid into my line of sight. I'd seen enough images and diagrams of it, but even so, looking out at the real thing was a hell of a moment. I stared at it the same way jet pilots used to gaze at airships, with a twinge of envy and false nostalgia for a still-birthed alternate history where those giant, serene craft were kings of the world. To travel among the stars in an artificial planetoid would have been an awesome existence.

The Olyix had started with an asteroid drifting in some distant orbit around their home star. Humans, with their molecular bonding technology, would have simply mined the ores and minerals and used the refined mass to construct a habitat-sized arkship. But the Olyix used a cruder method, cutting away the rock's rumpled, crater-scarred outer layers until they were left with a smooth cylinder forty-five kilometers long and twelve in diameter. Further mining excavated the three main biochambers and a huge honeycomb of compartments that formed the engineering and propulsion section at the rear.

After so many millennia traveling between stars, the arkship's exterior was in remarkably good condition, shimmering like polished coal under the sun's unremitting glare. That unblemished sheen was all thanks to the impact defense screen, of course. When traveling across the interstellar gulf, the *Salvation of Life* generated a massive plasma cloud ahead of it to ablate and absorb any particles it ran into at twenty percent light speed. The arkship's forward section was studded with generators, fashioned like golden barnacles, to create the magnetic field that held the tenuous ionized gas in place.

Halfway through the passenger ferry's turn, we were sideways on to the arkship's counter-rotating axis dock, giving me a panoramic view. The dock was a disk, only slightly wider than the Lobby's toroid we'd left behind. But its apparent rotation was actually holding it motionless as the *Salvation* spun around its axis. Strangely, it looked like the most human part of the arkship, but then most engineering requirements have a common design solution no matter what kind of neurons create them. As well as possessing a number of airlocks, the dock was used to connect the power utilities. Free-flying human-built stations containing small portal doors, like geometric footballs a dozen meters across, hovered a few meters away from the dock. Their equators glowed with the intense turquoise shimmer of ion thrusters, holding them in position; while thick superconducting cables flexed in extreme slow motion across the gap between the two.

And they were the whole reason for the trade deals between the Olyix and the Sol Senate. Our solar system was just another stop on the Olyix's incredible journey to the end of the universe; they'd visited hundreds of stars already, and would visit thousands—millions—more in the future before finally coming face-to-face with their God at the End of Time. Each solar system they came across was a replenishment stop between flights, a time when they used (or traded) local resources to refurbish the *Salvation of Life* and generated enough new antimatter to accelerate them onward again.

Accelerating something that huge took energy. A lot of energy. All the various processes that human physicists had ever come up with to create antimatter were horrendously inefficient, converting maybe one or two percent of the energy input into actual antimatter. As the Olyix openly admitted, their procedures weren't a whole lot better.

Yet they needed enough antimatter to accelerate the *Salvation of Life* up to a fifth of the speed of light, then decelerate again as they approached the next star. The arrival of the Olyix was the greatest boon Sol's energy corporations had ever known. Every wattdollar the sale of alien Kcell technology brought in was spent buying electricity from human companies. A fifth of the solarwells dropped into the sun were currently being used to feed energy to the *Salvation of Life,* where deep inside its engineering section, alien machinery was churning out anti-hydrogen atoms one at a time.

The passenger ferry completed its flip, and we backed in toward the *Salvation*'s axis dock. Latching on was a series of metallic clunks. Then the airlock opened. As I was unbuckling my straps, dry, mildly spiced air drifted along the cabin, at a temperature several degrees lower than the cabin air. Not unpleasant, but definitely unusual.

The interior mechanics of the axis dock were similar to the Lobby's layout, but with living branches twined around conduits, sprouting waxy purple leaves. Small birds with ovoid bodies and five fin-like wings flitted along the wide corridors, effortlessly rolling around our delegation as we made our cumbersome way through the rotating seal. The reception chamber on the other side was a big hemisphere cut out of the rock, with a craggy surface carpeted in a dull topaz moss. There were ten wide elevator doors around the rim, made from what appeared to be a glossy honey-colored wood. An Olyix waited for us outside one of the doors, its feet sticking to the moss as if it were Velcro.

Sandjay, my altme, told me it was opening a general phone link. "Welcome," the Olyix said. "My designation is Eol, and this body is Eol-2. Please accompany me down to our first biochamber. I am sure you will prefer the increased gravity."

Most of us muttered a quick thank-you. There was an undignified surge to get into the elevator, which had curving walls of the same wood as the doors. It rattled and clanked its way downward, traveling a lot slower than any human elevator would. The biochambers were ovoids four kilometers in diameter, so the trip down seemed interminable—especially as Eol-2 insisted on trying to make small talk all the way. It didn't help that the spice scent grew more pungent as we descended.

When the doors finally opened, we were in a long rock tunnel, again covered in moss, and lit by bright green–tinged strips at waist

height. Gravity was about two-thirds Earth standard, for which Nahuel let out a sigh of relief.

The Olyix had made a considerable effort to make their human
visitors feel at home. Our quarters were on a terrace in the first biochamber; from the outside they looked like rather glamorous yurts.
Instead of using a heavy fabric over the frame, the Olyix employed
their ubiquitous wood in thin planks, laying them over a geodesic
frame like tiles on a roof. Furniture, too, was all solid chunks of
wood, its smooth contours making the pieces resemble a collection
of slightly surrealist sculptures. Orchid-like plants had coiled their
rubbery roots along the ceiling struts, dangling clusters of dark-
shaded alien flowers above my head. At least their perfume was
sweeter than the spice that hung thick in *Salvation*'s atmosphere.

Eol-2 did a perfect host imitation and left us to "settle in" before
the tour began. I unpacked my washbag and went into the curtained-
off bathroom section. A peripheral ran a fast scan for electronic surveillance, drawing a blank. I hadn't expected any. The Olyix favored
biotechnology solutions.

The yurt furniture might have been Olyix wood, but the shower,
bath, toilet, and basin were all imported from Earth, which was quite
a relief. I took my shirt off, washed my torso, and sprayed on a hefty
dose of cologne. Somehow I carelessly managed to miss myself quite
a lot with the spray. Then I killed time for a couple of minutes setting
up my toiletries and filled a couple of glasses with cold water. That
gave the chemicals in the cologne spray enough time to numb the
neural fibers in the flowering plants on the bathroom ceiling.

Previous agents had taken samples of the yurt environment for
study to prepare for my mission. Our labs had found fibers amid little
cuts in the plant roots and leaves that had conductive properties.
Without removing a whole plant and cutting it up under a micro-
scope, we couldn't say for sure what the fibers did and what kind of
receptors they were attached to, but visitors seemed to be under some
kind of general observation. Ainsley was pleased with that find; it

was another strand of proof that the Olyix weren't quite as trusting as they liked to project. Finding out whether that subterfuge came from a simple natural instinct to protect their biological heritage from human exploitation or they really were up to no good was the whole reason I was in the delegation.

With a degree of privacy assured, I squatted down and crapped out the biopackage I'd brought along. The human anal cavity has traditionally been a smuggler favorite for most of our existence on Earth. It made me really proud to carry that fine institution on into the starflight era. Yeah, right.

The biopackage resembled miniature frogspawn, which wasn't a bad analogy. I split it in two and dropped each half into the glasses I'd prepared. From my little medical kit, I took six indigestion tablets and put three in each glass. They foamed away on the surface, dissolving quickly.

You could have eaten the tablets—not that they would've done anything for your indigestion. However, they turned the water into a perfect nutrient solution; there was also a hormone released that would trigger the eggs into growth.

That phase would take six hours.

I shoved the glasses into the cupboard under the basin, then set the cologne bottle to release a spray every quarter of an hour to keep anesthetizing the plant fibers. Wearing a new shirt, and smelling like a Bel-Air gigolo, I went out to join the delegation for our tour.

All the *Salvation of Life*'s biochambers were ovoids measuring eight kilometers along their axis, with a four-kilometer diameter at their midpoint. The first one, where our quarters were, had a globe of light suspended in the exact center, shining a warm slightly orange-hued radiance out across the whole chamber. Human space habitats tended to have landscapes across the cylinder floor, leaving the endwalls clear. The Olyix biospheres were completely shrouded in vegetation.

Trees with fleshy, purple-tinged leaves never grew to the size you found in terrestrial forests, and there didn't seem to be much variety, either; to my mind they resembled giant bonsai—dumb comparison, but realistic enough. Their branches tangled together deftly, playing host to dozens of smaller plants, like the orchid-equivalents in my yurt, along with vines and ragged strings of trailing moss that hung in huge curtains. The loam was covered in the yellow moss-grass, riddled with patches in differing shades, making the ground look like an intricately stained mosaic rug. Little streams threaded their way through it all, bubbling down the slopes from the axis to empty into reed-packed ponds that were spread around the equator.

Humans would have deployed fleets of remotes to trim and maintain the plants. The Olyix with their biological oriented solutions allowed the plants to grow as their nature intended. According to Eol-2, the biochambers had reached equilibrium thousands of years ago. Supplied with light, warmth, and water, they would continue with minimal intervention indefinitely. Small birds resembling overgrown dragonflies buzzed about, while giant snail-equivalent creatures slid along the ground, eating every fallen leaf and leaving a film of rich mulch in their wake. Larger dead branches and trunks were swiftly reduced to powdery loam by a profusion of fungi.

Our delegation was impressed by the slower, more sedate life on show. I suppose it made sense, given how long the voyage was going to take.

Eol-2 took us into the second biochamber on a car that could have been modeled on pre–quantum spatial entanglement era human vehicles. It drove itself through a broad tunnel that had junctions every few hundred meters, with tunnels curving away out of sight. Despite a plethora of discreet recordings made continuously ever since the arkship had arrived, humans had never fully mapped out the maze of passages and caverns that riddled the *Salvation*'s interior.

The second biosphere was identical in shape to the first. The difference was in climate, which was more temperate, housing a different genera of plants, while the third was the warmest of the three, but dry, verging on a desert environment. Certainly the plants lacked the jumbled-up density found in the first two.

"Our three biochambers contain a vibrant range of our home world biota," Eol-2 explained to us as we walked about on the short reddish moss of the third biochamber, making polite sounds about yet another tiny dull flower sticking up out of tufts of drab gray-green leaves minutely different from the last. "Beyond here is the engineering section, which is not open to this delegation."

I looked around at my fellow delegates, seeing their poorly concealed expressions of relief. Everyone was profoundly bored; the last thing they wanted now was to walk along halls of incomprehensible machinery, listening to an unending monotonous commentary on power couplings and confinement chamber integrity.

I kept my own, darker, amusement in check. The engineering and propulsion section of *Salvation of Life* was actually a lot smaller than the Olyix claimed. Eol-2, like all the Olyix, had lied to us. *Salvation of Life* contained a fourth biochamber.

Back in 2189, Ainsley Zangari's Olyix Monitoring Office positioned five stealth satellites in a rosette formation two million kilometers out from the *Salvation of Life*. They contained small portal doors leading back to Teucer, an asteroid in Jupiter's Trailing Trojans. As far as the rest of the Sol system was concerned, Teucer was just another independent tax haven rock, but it actually contained a station that handled all our passive sensor flights. Day after day, pea-sized probes would be shot out of the satellite portals, flying along trajectories that would take them close to the *Salvation of Life*. Some would spin out thin strands of magnetically sensitive gossamer, mapping the arkship's flux fields. Others scanned for exotic neutrinos, analyzing the propulsion system, which remained highly radioactive from the antimatter reaction—itself a strong neutrino emitter. The majority were solid mass detectors with microtransmitters. They would glide along hyperaccurate trajectories, measuring the minuscule course variance as they tracked around *Salvation*, due to its correspondingly tiny gravity field, which varied according to density. That was what gave us our first clues that the Olyix weren't being entirely honest. The rear quarter had a density that couldn't be accounted for by the cavities that the Olyix said made up their engineering and propulsion section.

It wasn't as big as the trio of biochambers that humans were permitted to visit, but right behind biochamber three, the arid one, was a hollow space approximately five kilometers long. That, we concluded, had to be the heart of their clandestine activities. My goal.

The delegation reconvened under a broad, high pergola draped in violet-flowering vines, close to the equatorial ponds of the first biochamber. It was all very convivial, with a refreshment table and comfy chairs in a loose semicircle. Eol-2 rested its heavy body on a wide stool that curved around its lower abdomen.

"I hope you found the tour informative," it said over the general phone link.

We sipped our teas and coffees as we nodded reassurance. I'd grabbed an espresso, but somehow the taste was dulled by the ever-present smell of alien spice.

"You have three distinct biochambers," the cardinal said. "Are you divided along your original cultural lines?"

"I understand your interest in different cultural factions," Eol-2 said. "However, after a voyage so long, we are as one, a monoculture."

"So were there different cultures on your home world?"

I watched a small ripple progress around Eol-2's midsection flesh skirt. Xenopsychologists who'd spent a lifetime studying the Olyix assumed it was either irritation or amusement.

"We no longer know what we left behind," Eol-2 said. "For we look to the future, never the past. To us, it is obvious that a sentient species will eventually refine and resolve upon a single life philosophy as it matures. You are diverse because you are physically widespread and can indulge any number of experimental principles and ideas. As you are young, such exploration is good for you. However, despite this current period of extraordinary physical and political expansion you pursue, it is our belief that you will regather yourselves eventually, and live under a unified monoculture. The superior, most liberal, most welcoming, of your cultures will spread and adapt and eventually absorb to incorporate all others. Your merging legal systems and binding trans-government treaties are evidence of this, to us at least."

"You believe our religions will merge?" the cardinal asked, which brought a lot of smiles.

"The God at the End of Time will come to pass when all sentience, all thought, binds together within the great collapse of space-time. During the growth of entropy which is the past and future history of the universe, the God is many. Humans have already been blessed to witness fragments of the ultimate coalescence, which have formed the base of all your religious beliefs, interpreted in your many ways. We understand this, for we underwent it ourselves when we were first gifted with sentience. But there will only be one God in the end, which is when Its True Form will be revealed to all who have pilgrimaged successfully. If you are lucky, if you remain open to the Divine as you seem to be, you may hear a whisper of God's message again. Already you anticipate this, I believe. The Second Coming. End of Days. Revelation. Rapture. Reincarnation, to name but a few. So many of God's concepts are already bestowed upon your thoughts. They link many of your diverse cultures, and will flourish into a web upon which you can build your eventual unity."

Nahuel inclined his head toward me and muttered: "Is it politically incorrect to mention steady-state theory in front of an Olyix?"

I just managed to keep myself from laughing out loud.

"I have a question," the delegation's imam said, an old man with a full white beard and spotless black robes. To my mind, his stern voice indicated he wasn't going with the Olyix's liberal interpretation of how the Prophet's vision came to be. "You claim to be on pilgrimage to the end of time. If so, do you welcome humans who might wish to join with you?"

"Certainly," Eol-2 said quickly. "There are practical concerns, of course. We would have to adapt your biology to effectively provide you with immortality. Our Kcells are a good start on that endeavor, but considerable work remains to be done."

The imam gave Eol-2 a disbelieving stare. "You mean the Olyix are already immortal?"

"The bodies of a quint are the vessel of the mind, carrying it through time. We continue to reproduce physically, for all biological bodies decay over time, even ours. However, our identity remains steadfast."

"So there are no new Olyix?" Nahuel said.

"No. Physically and spiritually we have matured as far as possible. As you would put it, we have reached the end of our evolution. This is why we have embarked on our great journey; there is nothing else left for us in this universe."

"I find that hard to believe," the cardinal said. "God's universe is bountiful and limitless."

"We know all there is to know about this creation. Therefore, we await that which is to come after."

"After?"

"The God at the End of Time will look back upon the life of the universe, and use what It finds to create a new and better universe from the void into which all will collapse."

"That promise of immortality sounds suspiciously like a bribe to me," the imam said.

"It cannot be," Eol-2 replied. "Immortality, extending through this life and into the next, is something that only a mature mind can accept. If you are not worthy of it, you would never survive such an existence. And remember, there is no return from the path we would share. You would have to be very sure of yourself to accept such a daunting offer. We do not consider it a bribe. Abandoning all that you are—your belief, your life—is a decision you must come to by yourself."

"Then tell me why you are alone in the *Salvation of Life*?" the imam said. "You have been traveling for countless millennia; you have visited thousands of stars. Why has no one else joined you?"

"That is the saddest part of our journey, for we have discovered how terribly rare life is in this galaxy. And sentient life is the rarest of all. So many times we have listened to the faint radio cries of civilizations as they rise and fall. Very few ever succeed in reaching the stage you have achieved. Normally, all we find are empty ruins and creatures who have sunk back into the unthinking abyss as their star grows cold. This is why we love and cherish you so much. You are the most precious of all life; and to coexist in a galaxy so vast in space and time, to actually meet you and offer guidance, is truly a miracle. It will probably only happen a dozen times between now and the end of our flight."

"Statistics can be a real bitch, it would seem," the cardinal said in a level tone.

I caught the imam's lips twitching in surreptitious satisfaction.

"Do you have any records of these lost civilizations you encountered?" Nahuel asked. "I would be most fascinated to see them."

"I will inquire," Eol-2 said. "They would be small indeed, for we place no importance on such encounters. Our gaze is upon the future and the glory that awaits us there."

"What are your thoughts?" Nahuel asked me that evening as we ate supper. Thankfully, we'd been entrusted to manage that by ourselves. Eol-2 had shown us a communal area beside the yurts with freezers full of prepackaged human meals and a row of microwaves, along with a small selection of bottles. Before leaving us, Eol-2 imparted our schedule for tomorrow, which was mostly lectures going into greater detail of the pilgrimage and what their equivalent of philosophers thought they could contribute to the God's deliberations about

what universe to usher into existence next. There was also time reserved for us to advance our beliefs to the Olyix, but to me that looked
like a polite afterthought.

"I think we need an astrophysicist to start asking some difficult
questions about quantum cosmology," I told him.

"I believe those questions have been asked many times since contact. No substantiated astrophysical proof has ever been provided for
their assertion that the universe is cyclic in nature, and each iteration
can only exist for a finite time. In that respect, they exceed even our
most facile popularist politicians when it comes to delivering on a
promise."

"That's what I'm finding the most difficult about this," I admitted.
"They reached a technological level that allowed them to build the
Salvation of Life and heaven knows how many other arkships. They've
devoted their everlasting lives to voyaging to the end of the universe—
which, face it, is probably going to be physically impossible—yet
they can't provide quantifiable scientific proof that the universe follows the cyclic theory."

The cardinal turned to face me. "We have enough evidence in
cosmological background radiation to confirm the Big Bang, which
in itself argues against steady state."

"At least the Big Bang allows for a theoretical state that will lead to
an ultimate heat death," Nahuel said. "Not that the heat death of the
universe is the ideal sequence to birth this God at the End of Time.
I'm not even sure you can call heat death the end of time."

"An emergent god would have to reverse the maximum entropy
state," the cardinal mused. "That's not an act of creation. It's regener-
ating what already exists."

"We're getting lost in semantics," Nahuel countered.

"Forty-two."

"Excuse me?" I queried.

"Old joke," the cardinal admitted. "The number of angels that can
actually dance on a pinhead."

"See?" I told both of them. "This is why we need an astrophysicist."

"You are right, my friend," Nahuel said insistently. "Everything they do is based on the cyclic theory, but they have provided nothing to prove its eventuality. It could even be said they refuse to supply it. Yet, paradoxically, their belief is so strong, so intrinsic to what they are, that a proof must surely exist. Nobody would travel like this without proof."

"Ah." The cardinal held up a whiskey tumbler and smiled contentedly at us. "This is why we are here, is it not? We are the ones who understand: Above all, you have to have faith. Cheers." He downed the shot in one.

I got back to my yurt and sniffed cautiously. Sure enough, there was a melange of spice, flower perfume, and cologne. I went into the bathroom area and carefully opened the cupboard doors. The eggs had hatched, producing five hundred flies that were crawling sluggishly all over the shelf. Most of the nutrient in the glasses had been consumed.

I told Sandjay to switch on my emitter peripheral. The tiny lens embedded in my left eye began to shine ultraviolet light across the seething mass of insects. These flies had synthetic eight-letter DNA, which, as well as accelerating their pupae stage, gave them a neuro-processor instead of a natural brain. My ultraviolet pulse triggered a full boot-up, which took about a second. In response, they all activated their emitters. The cupboard was doused in ultraviolet light as the linc program connected them into a coherent swarm.

Data splashed down my tarsus lenses. Hatching rate had been over ninety percent successful. Malformation rate was under two percent. Linc connection was enacted. I had a viable swarm, each one endowed with a biosensor capable of detecting a quantum spatial entanglement, courtesy of their eight-letter DNA. Individually, the detector worked at extremely short range—just a couple of meters. Collectively, that sense was expanded by two orders of magnitude.

Now all I had to do was get the swarm to the general area where we suspected the portals were situated: biochamber four.

Sections of my bagez unclipped into a series of innocuous rods and rings. But clipped together in the right sequence they became basic tools—spanner, screwdriver, pliers . . . I took the panel off the side of the bath and set about opening the hatch cover underneath. Like the rest of the bathroom, it was human built, with locknuts on each corner that had stiffened over time. After plenty of sweaty effort I got them all off and levered the hatch up. No matter what angle I looked at it, that opening was not large. Getting through was going to be tight and most likely painful. But other agents had gotten through on scouting runs, so—

I stripped off and took my jogging kit out of my bagez. Like every good fitness fanatic I used several layers, from inner skintights to more baggy outers, finishing with a waterproof for any inclement weather. I was only interested in the skintights, which gripped as tight as any wet suit. The top even had a hood, which combined with my sunglasses, covered every square centimeter of skin. Sandjay interfaced with it, and the fabric surface turned a perfect black. As well as being visually nonreflective, it absorbed a vast section of the electromagnetic spectrum should you try probing it with radar or laser sweeps. And that was just its outer surface. Long ribbons of thermal battery were woven into the arms, legs, spine, neck, and skull, which used a web of heat-duct fibers to soak up all my body heat, making me thermally neutral. The ribbons could accumulate ten hours of heat before they needed to pump it out. A gill mask neutered my breath, siphoning out the heat and scrubbing telltale biochemical leaks. Wearing that stealth suit, I was like an empty human-shaped hole in the universe.

Sandjay linced to the fly swarm and sent them streaming down through the hatchway. I sucked in my gut and slipped through after them.

There was a cramped utility compartment running under all the yurts. It was filled with human-built sanitation equipment, which sterilized all the water and effluent from the baths, showers, and toilets above. Chemical and solid waste was separated out and stored in tanks that would ultimately be vented into space, while the clean water was released back into the *Salvation of Life*'s main environmental cycle. *That* was the outlet pipe I was looking for.

The compartment's floor was made from thick carbon slabs, as hard as granite. Agents we'd sent in before had cut the slab that the outlet pipe went through, slicing it into manageable rectangles with angled sides to hold them in place. Pulling them up was a bitch. They were as heavy as stone, and I was crouched over, which is a bad position to be lifting. Eventually I got them clear, and dropped down through the hole into a tunnel carved into the naked rock.

Pipes and cables ran along it, not all rigid and fastened into place like humans would lay them, but twining around like ivy clinging to the tunnel walls. They even looked like they were alive, or at least had been. I thought maybe a plant with hollow trunks, like terrestrial bamboo, that grew along the tunnel, then died and hardened, producing a natural tube. It made a kind of sense, given the way the Olyix liked to integrate their biological systems with mechanical ones.

Sandjay splashed an enhanced image across my tarsus lenses. The suit's thermal sensors showed me that several of the meandering tubes were warm, containing a heated fluid of some type, while the magnetic scan gave power cables a gold-sparkle glow. My inertial navigation took a location fix, and I set off down the tunnel.

Twenty percent of the fly swarm was behind me as I scrambled over the meandering tubes, covering my ass in case an Olyix came along on an inspection or maintenance job. The rest buzzed on ahead, scouting the way. Just as in the tunnel we'd driven through earlier, there were intersections and splits. Some went straight up; others branched down into the unknown depths. There were times when the tunnel sloped so much I had to get down on my hands and knees and crawl along to stop myself from slipping.

Inevitably, it wasn't a straight route toward the rear of the arkship. I had to check the inertial navigation every time the swarm found another junction, working out which was the way forward. Five times I miscalculated and had to turn back and try again as the tunnel I chose started to curve away. But then some tunnels were almost devoid of cables and tubes, allowing me to jog along for long stretches. Without those, I would never have made it back before morning.

After the inertial navigation confirmed I'd passed the end of the third biochamber, I started looking for a route into the fourth. There were plenty of junctions that had branched off into the bigger transport tunnels, with vehicles trundling along them. I began splitting the swarm at intersections, sending them out exploring farther ahead. Eventually, when I was four hundred meters short of where we'd worked out the fourth biochamber to be, I found a transport tunnel that seemed to be heading in the right direction.

The swarm flew on ahead, but there were no vehicles about. My problem now was the light. The transport tunnel was illuminated by long bright strips halfway up the walls. If the swarm saw anything coming, I'd have to sprint for a junction. There weren't many of them.

Four hundred meters. Most Olympic athletes could cover that distance in forty-five seconds. I was fit, and had some gene-up treatments, but not to that level. Besides, I was in a two-thirds gravity field—also not conducive to speed. Best estimate was over a minute.

The swarm snaked through the air in a long line before starting to spread out. There were three junctions between me and the start of the fourth biochamber. That gave me reasonable odds of reaching cover if anything appeared.

I drew down some deep breaths, then started running.

A minute seventeen, if you're that keen to know. I didn't go balls-out because I might need to keep moving when I reached it—or race back.

The fourth biochamber had a climate similar to the first. Its vegetation seemed more wild and ragged, as if they didn't maintain it to the same standard. There were no Olyix near the tunnel entrance.

I scooted into the cover of the shaggy trees and sent the swarm out in a circular formation, scanning for signs of life. A hundred-meter perception bubble revealed dozens of birds, hundreds of insects, but no large alien bodies moving around. My peripherals swept the electromagnetic spectrum, which was almost silent.

The trees threw heavy shade on the ground. It was useful cover. I stayed underneath the branches as the swarm reshaped into a row and began a circumferential sweep—the first of many. Sandjay was already plotting a methodical spiral course that would see them cover the entire interior. Looking up through the gaps in the leaves, I saw a distinct clearing along the equatorial line. The trees had given way to a perfectly circular patch of mustard-yellow moss. At the center was a five-sided pyramid structure, an easy hundred meters high but only twenty meters across the base. I'd never seen any kind of building in the other three biochambers. When I shifted position to get a better view, I caught sight of another clearing, also on the equator. I moved out into an open area between the trees. There were five identical clearings, each with a tall structure in the middle. I diverted the swarm to the nearest one so they could relay high-resolution scans back to me.

THE ASSESSMENT TEAM

"Okay, and?" Callum asked in fascination.

"Those structures in the center of each clearing were like slim Aztec temples, or very tall obelisks," I told my rapt audience. "Personally, I prefer the second option. They didn't seem to have any kind of entrance, at least not at ground level. And there weren't any openings higher up, either. But the clincher is the hieroglyphics. The exterior of each one was covered in them."

"Have you translated it?" Eldlund asked eagerly.

"No," I admitted, letting a hint of frustration show. "This isn't like a code, or an ancient human language. There is no possible Rosetta stone available to us here. The symbols are plain enough, just lines and shapes, but they are completely alien. There's simply no way of interpreting them. The only way we'll ever get to find out what they say is to ask the Olyix. And we can't really do that."

"I don't get it," Loi said in a petulant tone. "Why would they keep them secret?"

"The one thing the fly swarm did determine for me was the type of stone they were made out of," I said.

"What is it?"

"Sedimentary. It had a granular structure. There were no sharp edges left anywhere, and a lot of the symbols had worn down. Which is significant in that placid environment."

"So?" Kandara demanded.

"The *Salvation of Life* was an asteroid," Alik explained to her in a tediously patronizing tone. "You only find sedimentary rock on a planet. Which means those obelisks were brought on board from— what?" He lifted a quizzical eyebrow at me. "The Olyix home world?"

"That's our theory," I said. "The obelisks are incredibly ancient, which makes them the most sacred relics the Olyix possess. Obviously, they have a deeply religious significance. It may even be that those symbols contain their proof of the cyclic-state universe— which, given the level of their orthodoxy, can *never* be challenged, let alone by an upstart species like us."

"Hence the whole secrecy obsession," Kandara concluded, her head dipping in understanding.

Callum leaned forward in his chair, keen for details. "What about the fly swarm? Did they detect any quantum spatial entanglement?"

"No." I shrugged. "Obviously there's a great deal of volume inside the *Salvation of Life* we haven't explored, but the fourth biochamber is their biggest, darkest secret. And in strategic terms, it's irrelevant. They just don't want us disbelieving aliens contaminating it with our heresy."

I could tell from Callum's creased brow that he was about to fire off another query, which is when events became strange. I saw Alik starting to pour himself another bourbon from his precious vintage bottle. His focus shifted to me, his eyes widening, betraying surprise. Then his fingers began to open, allowing the bottle to fall. My attention flowed to Kandara in the chair next to him, who was grabbing a handful of roast pistachios from a dish. Her formidable muscles were stiffening in a classic threat response. I even saw her forearm flesh ripple as buried peripherals activated. Suspicion and alarm triggered a strong sense of threat within me, and I determined something very wrong was occurring behind my chair. My head started to turn as I heard Callum's panicked yell begin, and I caught a blur of motion. Jessika was standing behind me, face contorted with effort, her arms gripping a long red pole she was swinging toward me. Instinct forced my own arm up protectively even as I attempted to duck. It was no use at all; she was moving too fast. Then I saw the wickedly sharp head of the fire axe as it expanded into my vision, becoming my whole universe. I even briefly heard the cracking sound of my skull breaking as it struck. Then the blade penetrated my brain—

JULOSS

YEAR 593 AA

Before they left, before every item of human technology in the Juloss star system was reduced to its constituent atoms, they went back to Kabronski Station's garden for a final nostalgic look. Their marble table by the little waterfall was still there, the elegant koi sliding about in the water just as they always had.

"I feel like we should take them with us," Dellian said as he watched the fish glide across the pond and vanish under the sluggish waterfall, only to reappear again a few seconds later.

Yirella slipped her arm around his shoulders. "You can't think like that. Not anymore."

"I know."

Together they looked up through the vaulting geodesic glass roof. Juloss was a thick crescent below the station, its terminator line creeping across the Deng Ocean.

"It's beautiful," she said wistfully.

"We can come back. When it's over."

"That would be nice. I don't think there would be many of us, though."

"Really? I bet most of the squad would come. Hell, maybe most of the *Morgan*. Where else could we go? This is home."

She gave him a gentle kiss. "It's where we were born. It's where we trained. But home? I don't think we have one. Not yet. That's something we have to build for ourselves. Afterwards. Hey, who knows, perhaps the Sanctuary star legend will turn out to be real after all, and we can go and live there."

He gazed up at the blue-and-white crescent, his mind filling in the continental coastlines on the nightside. "You know, back on Earth they said whole continents were lit up by city lights at night, that they were like miniature galaxies. Can you imagine that? There were so many of us on one world."

"And look what happened to them. Human worlds can't afford that kind of population again. Not until we win the war. We have to have enough traveler generation ships to lift everyone off a settled planet in an emergency. Nobody must ever be left behind. Not again."

"But if we could've stayed here . . . what a world we would have built."

Yirella rested her cheek on the top of his head. "You really are an old romantic at heart, aren't you?"

"I just believe in us, that's all. I mean, look at it!" Dellian gestured extravagantly at the planet. "We did that! It was a lump of naked rock when our ancestors arrived. Fifty years to terraform it. Fifty years— that's how long it took us to give life to a whole planet! And it's brilliant."

"It's tragic."

"It'll still be here when this is all over. We were careful; no signal ever escaped. They don't know humans were here, and they never will, now."

"I hope you're right. All the worlds in this system have terrestrial life on them now—bacteria in the comets, lichen on the asteroids, weird frogs on Cathar's moons." She grinned at the memory.

"Damn right. Even if they pulverize Juloss, they can't eliminate us from this system now. Terrestrial DNA is here to stay. We mutate. We adapt. We evolve every time. In a billion years, this will still belong to our life. Because we rock." He tilted his head back to kiss her.

Beside them, the waterfall cascade slowly shrank away until only drips were falling from the stony lip. A loud chime sounded across the garden zone.

"Time to go," Yirella said softly.

They both looked up at Juloss again for a long moment, then made their way along the path to the exit.

The *Morgan* was made up of seven principal structures, all contained in spherical grids fifteen hundred meters in diameter, with silver thorn thermo-dumps rising up out of the strut junctions like metallic porcupine spikes to radiate excess heat out into space. The rear globe contained the gravitonic drive, capable of accelerating the battleship up to point nine light speed. Next came the main aneutronic fusion generators and their ancillaries, along with tanks of boron-11 and hydrogen fuel. Ahead of that, the third globe was basically a warehouse, containing asteroid mining equipment, along with refineries and one-stage von Neumann replicators. It was the same payload every human traveler generation ship carried, giving them the ability to start an entire high-level civilization in whatever star system they arrived at. As long as there was solid matter available—in the form of planets, asteroids, or comets—human society could build habitats and thrive. Globe four was the main life-support section, housing a pair of counter-rotating toroids that offered a pleasant park-like environment and comfortable apartments for the *Morgan*'s five-thousand-strong crew. Ahead of that was the weapons level, packed with a long and frighteningly impressive inventory of munitions that could devastate entire star systems, let alone enemy ships. Then came the hangar, with fifty genten-controlled attack cruisers capable of hundred-gee acceleration, along with fifteen troop carriers designed for both deep space and atmospheric flight. Finally, the forward globe housed the main portal shield which would open out like an umbrella around the warship to swallow any interstellar dust and gas the *Morgan* encountered at its incredible velocity, shunting it harmlessly away through twinned portals trailing a light-second behind the ship.

Dellian and Yirella were among the last to arrive on board, which won them a knowing wink from Janc and smiles from the rest of the squad. The *Morgan's* crew was assembled in the main auditorium. Dellian was still getting used to the relatively fast gravity spin of the toroid, so he had to hold the back of the seats as he made his way down the row to his squad. Captain Kenelm walked onto the stage just as Dellian sat down. Sie was tall, though not as tall as Yirella, wearing a smart gray-and-blue uniform that had a single star on its epaulet. Dellian gave the uniform a curious look as part of his brain categorized it as a sad and silly historical throwback. It wasn't that the crew hadn't worn their uniforms before, but seeing the captain standing there in the flesh ready to give hir departure speech was a hard reality strike. He'd been operating within a hierarchy for his whole life, but this—being on a warship about to launch into the galaxy—this made it suddenly very tangible. They were going out to fight, and there was a good chance they might actually die.

His hand fumbled for Yirella's. Even the melancholic humor she'd shown a few minutes ago in the garden had now vanished. He knew she was just as nervous as he was.

The screen at the rear of the stage came on with a live feed showing a battleship accelerating slowly away from its skyfort berth. Dellian's databud identified it as the *Asher*. Three advance seedships accompanied it.

"I wish Alexandre was here," Yirella whispered. "I miss hir."

"Me too. But sie did see you reunited with the rest of us before hir traveler generation ship left. I think that made hir happy at the end."

Yirella nodded, a glint of moisture in her eyes. "I wanted hir to come with us."

"Sie couldn't. Sie was too old. Sie knew that right from the start, when sie left her own family behind to raise us."

"I know. I'm being selfish."

He squeezed her hand. "Me too."

Up on the screen, the *Asher* and her escorts were closing on the clump of coiling fronds, barely a hundred meters across, that was an interstellar portal. The loops began to glow a dark blue. Then they were blossoming, expanding out as if a circle of the planet's midnight-blue sky was spilling across space. The cerulean haze faded to black, and the portal was indistinguishable from the rest of the star field above Juloss. The *Asher* slipped through the hole first, quickly followed by the seedships. As soon as they were all through, the portal closed up behind them, its constituent fronds shrinking back to a seething clutch of insubstantial energy folds.

The auditorium burst into a round of applause, but Dellian carried on watching the screen. He knew people on the *Asher*. Now they were gone, lost to him forever in both space and time. The other side of that portal had been traveling at point nine-eight light speed away from Juloss for more than five hundred years, ever since the traveler generation ship had arrived, one of thousands of identical portals that had been sent out along random courses, providing an escape route should the enemy detect that Juloss was home to a human civilization.

Now another portal was expanding, glowing a hellish orange against the stars as it opened to its twin deep in Cathar's atmosphere. The skyfort began to twist and buckle as it was captured by the pull of abnormally strong gravity. Chunks broke off, twirling away into the blaze, streaming ahead of the skyfort itself, which was now moving with increasing speed into the smoldering abyss.

There was no applause this time, just a wise, sober acknowledgment of the skyfort's fall into the heart of the gas giant, where the hypervelocity storms and terrible gravity gradient would pull the detritus down and down until it became nothing but a smear of heavy atoms slithering atop the planet's metallic hydrogen core. All of Juloss's orbital defenses were scheduled to follow it, then the portals themselves would surrender, and collapse. The Juloss system would be naked among the myriad stars once more, with teeming life and crumbling ruins the only legacy that humans had once visited.

"I would like us to take a moment," Captain Kenelm said in a level voice. "We should thank this star and its planets for being a peerless haven to so many of our ancestors. Humans have lived a good life here. And now it is our turn to honor and repay that gift. We venture out into the galaxy to join the very Saints themselves. Somewhere out there, they are waiting for us. When they call—and they will—we will join them, no matter how far away they are in time and in space. Know this, Saints; we will not let you down."

"We will not let you down," Dellian intoned, along with the rest of the audience. He'd said it a thousand times in his life, but this time it finally meant something. *We're on our way!*

Kenelm gestured with his palms, and everybody stood. "The *Morgan* is about to launch," sie said. Behind hir, the screen was showing a view from the front of the *Morgan*. Up ahead, a twisting gray knot was churning amid the stars.

"We thank you, Saint Yuri Alster, for your fortitude," Kenelm said respectfully.

"We thank you, Saint Yuri," the auditorium responded.

The portal turned blue and began to swell out, its physical components undulating in a fast rhythm.

"We thank you, Saint Callum Hepburn, for your compassion."

"We thank you, Saint Callum."

The *Morgan* started to accelerate smoothly as the hole across interstellar space stabilized.

"We thank you, Saint Kandara Martinez, for your strength."

"We thank you, Saint Kandara."

Beautiful new stars were glimmering through the darkness at the center of the portal.

"We thank you, Saint Alik Monday, for your resolution."

"We thank you, Saint Alik."

Dellian smiled and held his breath as they traveled more than five hundred light-years in a single heartbeat.

"And lastly, we thank Saint Jessika Mye, for traveling out of darkness to guide us."

"We thank you, Saint Jessika."

Unknown constellations shone bright around the *Morgan* and its accompanying seedships. Behind it, the portal closed. Then the entanglement ended, and the mechanism died.

Dellian stared at the wondrous sweep of fresh stars outside. "The Olyix are out there, somewhere." He said it loudly, as a raw challenge to the universe into which he was venturing. "Hiding like we used to. But we're not hiding anymore now. We're coming for *you*, fuckers!"

THE ASSESSMENT TEAM

NKYA, JUNE 26, 2204

Everyone in the lounge was perfectly still. Three targeting lasers produced small red dots on Jessika's forehead. The only sound was the steady *drip, drip, drip* of blood from Feriton's ruined skull.

Jessika kept hold of the fire axe handle, her gaze moving across the room, from Alik, to Kandara, to Callum, and finally to Yuri. In an astonishingly level voice she said: "Look at the brain."

"What the FUCK?" Callum bellowed.

Eldlund began a high keening sound of distress, slapping hir hand across hir mouth. Loi turned his head away and threw up.

"What?" Yuri demanded. "*What?*"

"I said, look at the brain."

"The . . ."

"Can I take my hands off the axe?"

"You move like a glacier is fast," Alik growled at her. "You let go, and put your arms high, then link your fingers over your head. Take one step back. Understand?"

"I understand. Letting go now." Very carefully, she released her grip on the handle. The axe sagged down as the blade pivoted around inside the skull, ripping more brain tissue. Feriton's body began to slouch forward, only just staying in the chair.

Kandara's face produced an expression of extreme distaste. "Mother Mary!"

Her arms in the air, fingers locked, Jessika took a step back. "Look at the brain."

Alik and Kandara glanced at each other.

"You cover her," Alik said.

Kandara nodded sharply, keeping her gaze on Jessika. "Got it." Her left arm was held perfectly level, a slit of flesh along the forearm open to expose a small silver cylinder that never wavered from its lock on Jessika's head. "Go see what the sweet fuck she's talking about."

The target laser shining from Alik's upper wrist switched off. He took a cautious step forward. Even his forehead crinkled up as he peered at the slumped figure. He held his breath and reluctantly pulled the axe free. It made a horrible squelching sound as the blade came out. Alik leaned forward a fraction. Everyone heard him suck down a breath. He gave Jessika a confused stare. "What the fuck?"

"What is it?" Yuri asked.

"I . . ." Alik flinched. "I don't know."

Yuri took an impatient step over and examined the massive wound in Feriton's skull. "Shit." He gave Jessika an astonished look.

"What the bloody hell's in there, man?" Callum demanded.

"It's an Olyix brain," Jessika told him.

"Bollocks!"

"See for yourself," she said. "That's not human gray matter. The Olyix scooped out Feriton's brain and replaced it with one from a quint. Does that procedure sound familiar?"

Yuri scowled at her.

Callum walked over, grimacing against the carnage, forcing himself to look into the gore. He knew what a human brain looked like, and whatever the mass of tissue was inside Feriton's skull, it wasn't human. The structure was all wrong, long strands arranged neatly rather than the usual jumble of lobes, and beneath the thick splatter of blood, the surface was fish-belly white.

"No fucking way!"

"It is a brain of a quint unit," Jessika said. "Which means the other four bodies in the union have seen and heard everything that Feriton heard and saw—including their damaged ship. They will also know every aspect of your Olyix Monitoring Office."

"Fucking hell!" Yuri grunted in dismay.

"What do you mean, *their* damaged ship?" Kandara asked.

"That ship outside? It's an Olyix midlevel transport. It was traveling back to their enclave when my colleague crashed it out of the wormhole."

"The Olyix have a wormhole?" Callum asked numbly. "But . . ." He turned to Yuri. "Did you know all this?"

Yuri shook his head, his gaze never leaving Jessika.

"That's how I knew Feriton was part of an Olyix quint," Jessika said. "The fourth chamber in the *Salvation of Life* is not full of precious artifacts. It contains a wormhole terminus, which leads back to the enclave. They all do."

"All?" Callum implored.

"The Olyix always arrive in vessels like the *Salvation of Life*. It is a subterfuge which allows them to observe the species they've discovered before they elevate them."

"Elevate?" Eldlund asked weakly.

"Take them on their pilgrimage to the God at the End of Time. And, trust me, joining them isn't voluntary. They seize every sentient race they find. They already have thousands imprisoned back in their enclave, maybe more."

"I don't believe a fucking word of this," Alik snapped. "I mean, just how the fuck could you know all this shit?"

Jessika's expression turned sorrowful. "Because I am Neána."

"What the fuck is *that*?"

"Alien, but not an Olyix. We're very different."

"Oh, Je-zus wept!"

"Do you recall the Fermi paradox?" Jessika asked. "Fermi asked: *Where are they?* You always assumed life in the galaxy is rare, that because of its size you would never coexist with another species. That is only partly true. When sentience arises, and begins to make itself known with radio emissions, the Olyix arrive—with their false friendship, and their religious greed. So, in truth, the answer to Fermi is: We have been hiding. And now you must join us, out in the silent darkness between the stars. That is where you will be safe."

"Your colleague is Soćko, right?" Yuri said.

"Yes. He allowed himself to be captured by Baptiste Devroy's people during the firefight on Althaea. We have been searching for an Olyix snatch operation since our arrival. Horatio Seymore was a stroke of good fortune. The Olyix proxies like Devroy would be instructed to snatch low-visibility humans, and that's what Horatio was—apart from Gwendoline. She was a rogue factor that would elude even the most talented matcher."

"Holy shit," an ashen Loi muttered, looking like he might be sick again.

"So Soćko is the one who crashed that ship out of the wormhole," Yuri said. "He flew it here. He switched on the beacon before he went back into hibernation."

"Correct. Our bodies have the ability to resist contamination by Olyix biotechnology. They would have been unable to elevate him, though that would not have been apparent to them at first. It gave him time to infiltrate their operation. I have been waiting for a disabled Olyix ship to be detected ever since the firefight at the warehouse."

"Sonofabitch," Alik spat. "Then the others in the ship, they've been . . . elevated?"

"The Olyix truly believe the God at the End of Time to be real. It will coalesce out of the thoughts of every species left as the universe collapses. Because life is so rare, and so many civilizations are destined to fall long before the end of time, the Olyix see it as their duty to carry every sentient species to the apex of evolution. But the God only needs your thoughts, your personality, not your body. The Olyix have been stealing humans right from the start to experiment on. We were the ones who started the rumor about Kcells making brain transplants possible, because we knew that's what they'd do—allowing a captured, cored-out body to move among you unseen. But their main focus, the reason they snatched so many people, was to research the best way to sustain a human brain on the pilgrimage. Their technology is far more advanced than they have revealed to you."

"That's insane!" Callum protested. "Even if the universe was cyclical, and due to collapse, that won't happen for billions of years. I don't care how bloody good your technology is; you can't keep a brain alive for that long."

"The Olyix's journey will not take them billions of years," Jessika said wearily. "Their enclave is an extremely sophisticated manipulation of space-time; minutes pass inside it, while the millennia flow by outside. It is what makes them so difficult to fight."

"Is that why you're here?" Kandara asked. "To get us to join you in some kind of galactic war? A counter-crusade?"

"No, you are on your own. I do not know where the Neána are, or even if they still exist. My people fled the Olyix eons ago; there is no knowing how far they have gone now. I know some part of them remains in this galaxy, for that is where I came from. But we were never given any knowledge of them, in case we were captured. My colleagues and I have discussed this many times. We assumed the logical thing for the Neána would be to leave this galaxy altogether. It may be that they just left automated stations behind, alert for new species so they can send guides like me."

Kandara looked over at Yuri. "Do you believe her?"

He glanced down at the pale alien flesh inside Feriton's skull. "I believe they caught Feriton when he was on his spy mission. That means Ainsley was right all along. I don't know what they'll do, if they'll elevate us like Jessika claims, or just nuke us back to the Stone Age. But I accept the Olyix are not our friends."

Kandara nodded. "I agree—until anything better comes along." Her targeting laser switched off, and she lowered her arm as the flesh resealed over the weapon. "I'm watching you," she told Jessika.

If it bothered Jessika, she didn't show it. "If any of you have received Kcell implants, I would advise you to have them surgically removed immediately," she said. "They can alter and multiply faster than any tumor; that's why they were given to you. And the *Salvation of Life* now has confirmation humans have been warned by the Neána. I'm sorry, but that isn't good. They will begin your elevation."

"Yeah? How?" Alik demanded. "I'd like to see them try. The *Salvation*'s a big-ass ship, for sure, but it's only one, all by itself. And Alpha Defense has a shitload of real evil weapons."

"I told you," Jessika said, "the *Salvation of Life* contains the entrance to a wormhole that leads back to the Olyix enclave. They will send an armada of their deliverance-class ships through to elevate you. In simple terms, that's a planetary invasion force."

"Je-zus fucking wept!" Alik snarled. He turned to confront Yuri. "We have to go. Now! We have to get back to the portal and warn Alpha Defense."

"We certainly do," Yuri said.

"How the fuck are you so calm about this?"

Smiling, Yuri took a dark ten-centimeter disk from his pocket and placed it on the floor. "Thread it," he said loudly.

Callum peered at the disk's eerily black surface and grinned. "I taught you well."

Yuri gave him the finger as a slim rectangular portal slid up from the disk.

"You son of a bitch," Alik grunted.

A wider rectangle was threading out. Callum and Loi deployed the short legs on its back, readying it to thread a full-size portal door. "Old times," Callum said.

"No," Jessika told him. "They are over. Forever."

"Ainsley and Emilja are going to love talking to you," he told her.

"Good. I have a lot to tell them."

JIO-FERITON QUINT

THE *SALVATION OF LIFE*, JUNE 26, 2204

The Olyix do not have pain. We eradicated it from our new bodies when we elevated to them at the beginning of our pilgrimage to the End of the Universe.

But our human body, Jio-Feriton, experienced a ferocious spike of pain impulses as the female alien's axe blade smashed into our skull. We were attuned to human thought routines, enabling our responses and reactions to emulate original Feriton Kayne without arousing suspicion.

The nerve signals from the blade cutting into our strange Jio-Feriton flesh and bone was interpreted correctly. It was *agony*.

Our remaining four Olyix bodies temporarily lost control of their limb function. We wanted to cry, but we had no tear ducts. We wanted to scream, but we had no vocal cords. We wanted—we *yearned*—for the pain to end. That was swiftly granted.

Our Jio-Feriton body died. Its mindfunction vanished from our entangled essence. We had experienced single mindfunction loss hundreds of times before as we replaced an old body within the quint, but never like this. The rest of our bodies were almost paralyzed from the shock. We have no coping mechanism for such an experience. We have no endorphin override. Feriton's legacy was an immediate craving for both these very human things.

Slowly, we regained equilibrium. Our thoughts first turned to replacing our Jio-Feriton body, to become full quint again. This was accompanied by *regret* at the loss we had just suffered. Regret is alien. Therefore we learned that absorbing alien thoughts to perform a subterfuge is dangerous; it detracts from our purity. We will not undertake such a task again.

We have no need to.

The *Salvation of Life's* onemind queried us, its serene essence curious at our eccentric outburst of chaotic thoughts. "Explain the occurrence," it asked.

"We are now four Jio. Our Jio-Feriton body was killed."

"How?"

"The suspect human, Jessika Mye, inserted an axe into Jio-Feriton's head, causing immediate fatal damage."

"Why?"

"We must have said something to betray Feriton was Olyix. We determine this would be our statement that the fourth chamber was a biochamber containing holy relics. If Jessika Mye knew this to be incorrect, she would know Feriton Kayne had been compromised. In order to know that, she would have to be Neána."

"They are here," the *Salvation of Life* said in disapproval. "Therefore Soćko is also Neána."

"Yes. He ruined the transport ship's onemind and crashed it out of the wormhole."

"The humans now know our purpose."

"They do."

"We cannot lose the humans to the sedition of the Neána. Humans are vibrant and beautiful. The God at the End of Time will love them. It will love us for carrying them with us."

"Yes," we agreed.

The *Salvation of Life*'s onemind opened itself to all its Olyix. "We will now begin the human elevation."

The end of *Salvation*
The story will continue in volume two
of the Salvation Sequence,
Salvation Lost.

CAST OF CHARACTERS

SOL SYSTEM AND HUMAN TERRAFORMED WORLDS

ALIK MONDAY...................... FBI, senior special detective
KANDARA MARTINEZ .... Dark-ops mercenary
EMILJA JURICH .... Utopial movement founder
JARU NIYOM .... Utopial movement founder
LOI...................... Yuri's assistant and technology advisor
ELDLUND .... Callum's advisor
AKKAR .... Ecowarrior
GWENDOLINE........ Ainsley's (unacknowledged) granddaughter
HORATIO SEYMORE .... Gwendoline's boyfriend
LUCIUS SOĆKO............... Connexion security squad captain
CANCER.............................. Dark-ops mercenary
SALOVITZ .... Detective, NYPD
KRAVIS LORENZO .... NY lawyer
ROSE LORENZO .... NY socialite
JAVID-LEE BOSHBURG........................... NY gang boss
RAYNER GROGAN .... NY gang boss
KRUSE..................... Akitha Home Security Bureau
TYLE .... Home Security Bureau
OISTAD............................ Home Security Bureau
NAHUEL........... Buddhist monk, 2199 ecumenical delegation

JULOSS

Immerle Estate Boys

DELLIAN

ORELLT

FALAR

JANC

URET

XANTE

RELLO

COLIAN

Immerle Estate Girls

YIRELLA

TILLIANA

ELLICI

Immerle Estate Adults

ALEXANDRE.. year tutor

JENNER .... principal

URANTI .... munc-tech

KENELM.............................. Captain of the *Morgan*

TIMELINE

1901 . . . Guglielmo Marconi transmits radio message across Atlantic Ocean.

1945 . . . First nuclear explosion (above ground).

1963 . . . Limited Test Ban Treaty signed, prohibiting atmospheric nuclear bomb tests.

2002 . . . Neána cluster, near 31 Aquilae, detects electromagnetic pulse(s) from atomic bomb explosions on Earth.

2005 . . . Neána launch sublight mission to Earth.

2041 . . . First commercial laser fusion plant opens in Texas.

2045 . . . First commercial food printers introduced.

2047 . . . The US Defense Advanced Research Project Agency reveals artificial atomic bonding generator—the so-called force field.

2049 . . . US Congress passes act to create Homeland Shield Department, charged with building force fields around every city.

2050 . . . China forms Red Army's City Protection Regiment, begins construction of Beijing shield.

2050 . . . Saudi kingdom installs mass food-print factories. Twenty percent of the kingdom's remaining crude oil allocated for food printing.

2050 . . . Russia starts National People's Defense Force; its shield generator project starts with Moscow.

2052 . . . European Federation creates UDA (Urban Defense Agency)—builds force fields over major European cities.

2062 . . . November: Kellan Rindstrom demonstrates quantum spatial entanglement (QSE) at CERN.

2063 . . . January: Ainsley Baldunio Zangari founds Connexion.

2063 . . . April: Connexion twins portal doors between Los Angeles and New York, charges ten dollars to go between cities.

2063 . . . Global stock market crash, car companies lose up to ninety percent of their share value. Shipping, rail, and airline stocks fall. Aerospace stocks rally as space entrepreneur companies announce ambitious asteroid development plans.

2063 . . . November: Space-X flies a QSE portal into LEO on a Falcon-10, providing open orbit access. Commencement of large-scale commercial space development.

2066 . . . Astro-X Corporation's mission to Vesta. Establishment of Vesta colony.

2066–2073 . . . Thirty-nine national and commercial colony/development missions to asteroids (the Second California Rush—so called because of the number of American tech company CEOs involved). Large number of World Court injunctions filed by developing nations and left-wing groups against exploitation of exo-resources by for-profit companies.

2066 . . . Connexion Corp merges with emergent European, Japanese, and Australian public transit portal companies to form conglomerate. Major cities now portal networked. Noncommercial vehicle use declining rapidly.

2067 . . . Globally, thirty cities now protected by shields, two hundred more under construction. Start of decline of conventional military forces. Phased air force and navy Reduction Treaty signed at UN by majority of governments. Armies reconfigured as counter-insurgency paramilitary regiments—numbers cut substantially.

2068 . . . Seven corporations established at Vesta. Astro-X completes its Libertyville habitat colony. Houses 3,000 people.

2069 . . . First solar powerwell portal dropped into sun by China National Sunpower Corporation. Five-kilometer-long magnetohydrodynamics chambers built at Vesta, positioned on large asteroids, outside Neptune orbit.

2070 . . . Armstrong resort dome assembled on Moon. Similar resorts under construction on Mars, Ganymede, and Titan.

2071 . . . All major cities on Earth linked by Connexion stations—except North Korea.

2071 . . . UN treaty forbidding nonequitable exo-resource exploitation. Any asteroid or planetary minerals mined for use by commercial companies must be equally distributed among all nations on Earth. US, China, and Russia refuse to sign. European Federation awards treaty Principal Acknowledgment status; starts to draw up its own nonexploitation regulations, where "excess profits" of asteroid development companies will be channelled into Federation foreign aid agencies.

Commercial asteroid development companies reregister in nonsignatory countries.

2075 . . . Seventeen self-sustaining habitats built in asteroid belt. Construction of Newholm starts at Vesta (by Libertyville)—fifty kilometers long, fifteen kilometers in diameter. Takes three years to form, two years to complete biosphere.

2075 . . . Fifty-five percent of Earth's energy now comes from solar powerwells. Decommissioning of nuclear power stations begins, radioactive material flung into trans-Neptune space via portals.

2076 . . . Increasing number of asteroid developments become self-sustaining and Earth-exclusionary. Start of habitat independence movement.

2077 . . . Interstellar-X launches first starship, *Orion*, propelled by QSE portal solar plasma rocket. Destination Alpha Centauri. Achieves .72 light speed.

2078 . . . March: Global tax agreement signed by all governments on Earth, abolishing tax havens.

2078 . . . August: Nine space habitats declare themselves low-tax societies.

2078 . . . November: First Progressive Conclave gathers at Nuzima habitat; fifteen billionaires sign Utopial pact to bring post-scarcity civilization to humanity. Each launches asteroid colony expansion, with an economy based on AI-managed self-replication industrial base.

2079 . . . China National Interstellar Administration launches starship *Yang Liwei*. Destination: Trappist 1. Achieves .82 light speed.

2081 . . . All Earth's energy supplied by solar powerwells. Connexion largest energy customer.

2082 . . . Major national currencies now backed by kilowatt hours. Global de facto currency is wattdollar.

2082 . . . Interstellar-X–led General Starflight Accord signed between all starfaring organizations (capable of building starships) and governments, ensuring open access to new stars and no duplicated star missions.

2082–2100 . . . Twenty-five portal-rocket starships launched from Sol to nearby stars.

2083 . . . *Orion* arrives at Alpha Centauri. Psychroplanet discovered 2.8 AU from star, named Zagreus. Too expensive/difficult to terraform. Eleven government missions transfer into Centauri system and establish asteroid manufacturing bases, along with eight independent asteroid companies. Construction of multiple portal starships at Centauri system begins.

2084–2085 . . . Twenty-three starships launched from Centauri.

2084 . . . Last car factory on Earth (in China) shuts down. Connexion hub network serves ninety-two percent of human population, including space habitats.

2085 . . . Utopials launch starship *Elysium*.

2086 . . . Alpha Centauri asteroid manufacturing stations abandoned. Small joint-venture solar rocket plasma monitoring station maintained in orbit around the star, providing drive plasma for the starships.

2096 . . . Chinese starship *Tranage* arrives Tau Ceti, exoplanet discovered.

2099 . . . Chinese begin terraforming of Tau Ceti exoplanet, named Mao.

2107 . . . US starship *Discovery* arrives Eta Cassiopeiae. Exoplanet discovered.

2110 . . . US begins terraforming Eta Cassiopeiae exoplanet, named New Washington.

2111 . . . European Federation agrees to terraform exoplanet at 82 Eridani, named Liberty.

2112 . . . *Elysium* arrives at Delta Pavonis. Terraform-potential planet discovered, named Akitha. Construction of habitat Nebesa and extensive orbital industrial facilities. Terraforming of Akitha begins.

2127 . . . The *Yang Liwei* arrives at Trappist 1. China begins terraforming two Trappist exoplanets T-1e and T-1f, Tianjin and Hangzhou.

2134 . . . New Washington terraforming stage two complete, open only to American settlers.

2144 . . . Olyix arkship *Salvation of Life* detected 0.1 light-year from Earth as its antimatter drive is switched on for deceleration. Communication opened. Four-year deceleration to Earth-Sun Lagrange-3 point opposite side of sun from Earth.

2150 . . . Earth population 23 billion; 7,462 space habitats completed, population 100 million.

2150 . . . Olyix begin to trade their biotech with humans in exchange for electricity to generate antimatter, allowing them to continue their voyage to the end of the universe.

2153 . . . Mao declared habitable. Farm settlers transfer from China, begin stage two planting—trees, grass, crops. Fish introduced into ocean.

2162 . . . Neána mission reaches Earth.

2200 . . . Eleven exoplanets now in stage two habitation. Large-scale migration from Earth. Twenty-seven further exoplanets undergoing stage one terraforming. No more being developed; fifty-three marked as having terraform potential. Portal starship missions ongoing, but reduced.

2204 . . . Portal starship *Kavli* arrives in Beta Eridani system, eighty-nine light-years from Earth. Detects beacon signal from alien spaceship.

ABOUT THE AUTHOR

PETER F. HAMILTON is the author of numerous novels, including *The Abyss Beyond Dreams*, *Great North Road*, *The Evolutionary Void*, *The Temporal Void*, *The Dreaming Void*, *Judas Unchained*, *Pandora's Star*, *Misspent Youth*, *Fallen Dragon*, and the acclaimed epic Night's Dawn trilogy (*The Reality Dysfunction*, *The Neutronium Alchemist*, and *The Naked God*). He lives with his family in England.

peterfhamilton.co.uk
Facebook.com/PeterFHamilton
Twitter: @PeterFHamilton1